The Handbook of

Cognitive

Neuropsychology

The Handbook of

Cognitive

Neuropsychology

What Deficits Reveal About the Human Mind

Edited by

Brenda Rapp
Johns Hopkins University

USA   Publishing Office: PSYCHOLOGY PRESS
                                 A member of the Taylor & Francis Group
                                 325 Chestnut Street
                                 Philadelphia, PA 19106
                                 Tel: (215) 625-8900
                                 Fax: (215) 625-2940

        Distribution Center: PSYCHOLOGY PRESS
                                 A member of the Taylor & Francis Group
                                 7625 Empire Drive
                                 Florence, KY 41042
                                 Tel: 1-800-624-7064
                                 Fax: 1-800-248-4724

UK   PSYCHOLOGY PRESS
                                 A member of the Taylor & Francis Group
                                 27 Church Road
                                 Hove
                                 E. Sussex, BN3 2FA
                                 Tel: +44 (0) 1273 207411
                                 Fax: +44 (0) 1273 205612

THE HANDBOOK OF COGNITIVE NEUROPSYCHOLOGY: What Deficits Reveal About the Human Mind

Printed by Edwards Brothers, Ann Arbor, MI, 2000.
Cover design by Ellen Seguin.
Cover art: Umberto Boccioni. *Composizione di una testa uomo*. (Dynamism of a Man's Head). 1914. Civica Museo d'Arte Contemporanea—Milano.

A CIP catalog record for this book is available from the British Library.
 ∞ The paper in this publication meets the requirements of the ANSI Standard Z39.48-1984 (Permanence of Paper).

Library of Congress Cataloging-in-Publication Data
The handbook of cognitive neuropsychology : what deficits reveal about the human mind / [edited by] Brenda Rapp.
     p. cm.
   Includes bibliographical references and index.
   ISBN 0-86377-592-6 (alk. paper) — ISBN 1-84169-044-9 (pbk.)
   1. Cognitive neuroscience—Handbooks, manuals, etc.   2. Neuropsychology—Handbooks, manuals, etc.   I. Rapp, Brenda.

QP360.5 .H357 2001
612.8′2—dc21

                                                              00-042545

ISBN 0-86377-592-6 (case)
   1-84169-044-9 (paper)

To the individuals described in this book,
whose cognitive deficits have taught us about the human mind,
and whose courage and generosity in the face of adversity
have taught us about the human spirit.

Contents

Part 1: Foundations

Part 2: Objects and Space

Part 3: Attention and Consciousness

Part 4: Words

Part 8: Actions and Plans

Part 9: Future Directions

About the Editor

Brenda Rapp is an Associate Professor of Cognitive Science at Johns Hopkins University. She also holds a joint appointment in the Department of Psychology and is an associate member of the Zanvyl Krieger Mind/Brain Institute of Johns Hopkins University. She earned a B.S. in Special Education from the University of Maryland and a Ph.D. in Psychology from Johns Hopkins University. Her research focuses on the mental representations and computations that are involved in comprehending and producing words. In this work she has examined questions regarding the relationship between orthography and phonology in reading and spelling, the nature of interactivity and componentiality in lexical processing, and the internal structure and content of orthographic representations. Other research interests include the areas of spatial representation and attention, where she has carried out work on questions regarding spatial frames of reference and cross-modality attention. Brenda Rapp's research is multi-disciplinary, making use of the methods of cognitive neuropsychology, neuroscience, cognitive psychology, and computer simulation.

Contributors

Mark Allen
Johns Hopkins University, USA

William Badecker
Johns Hopkins University, USA

Rita Sloan Berndt
University of Maryland School of Medicine, USA

Laurel J. Buxbaum
Moss Rehabilitation Research Institute, USA

Alfonso Caramazza
Harvard University, USA

Max Coltheart
Macquarie University, Australia

H. Branch Coslett
Temple University, USA

Edward H. F. De Haan
Utrecht University, The Netherlands

Chad S. Dodson
Harvard University, USA

Martha J. Farah
University of Pennsylvania, USA

Jocelyn R. Folk
Kent State University, USA

Emer M. E. Forde
Aston University, United Kingdom

Tamar H. Gollan
University of California San Diego, USA

Argye E. Hillis
Johns Hopkins University School of Medicine, USA

Glyn W. Humphreys
University of Birmingham, United Kingdom

Richard B. Ivry
University of California, Berkeley, USA

Judith F. Kroll
Pennsylvania State University, USA

Jennifer A. Mangels
Columbia University, USA

Randi Martin
Rice University, USA

Michael McCloskey
Johns Hopkins University, USA

Lyndsey Nickels
Macquarie University, Australia

Marie-Pascale Noël
Catholic University of Louvain, Belgium

Alan J. Parkin
University of Sussex, United Kingdom

Isabelle Peretz
University of Montreal, Canada

M. Jane Riddoch
University of Birmingham, United Kingdom

Ola A. Selnes
Johns Hopkins University School of Medicine, USA

Daniel L. Schacter
Harvard University, USA

Jennifer R. Shelton
Wayne State University, USA

Marie-Josèphe Tainturier
University of Wales, Bangor, United Kingdom

Carlo Umiltà
University of Padova, Italy

Preface

Can we perceive without awareness? Is understanding music like understanding spoken language? How do we keep track of time? Do our memories provide an accurate record of past events or do we invent our own histories? Can we appreciate the structure of a sentence without knowing its meaning, and vice versa? Do we recognize a favorite friend's face in the same way we recognize a favorite pair of sneakers or a written word? People have long been intrigued by these and many other questions regarding human cognition. These kinds of questions have been asked and investigated in different ways by philosophers, psychologists, neuroscientists, computer scientists, linguists, and others.

In attempting to develop answers to these questions one is struck by the fact that humans carry out, in an apparently seamless manner, highly complex activities such as producing and comprehending one or more languages, calculating sums and products, manipulating objects, coordinating the attentional demands of multiple tasks, and so forth. The ease and speed with which these activities are carried out often make it difficult to uncover the psychological and neural mechanisms that underlie these abilities. However, neurological damage can sometimes expose the inner workings of the cognitive mechanisms, rendering them more accessible to investigation. In this way, neurological damage opens a window onto cognition. *Cognitive Neuropsychology* looks through this window in order to further our understanding of normal cognitive processing and representation.

This volume provides a comprehensive review of the wide range of the cognitive domains that have been investigated using cognitive neuropsychological methods and evidence. Each chapter identifies the central cognitive issues in a particular domain and then focuses on how the study of deficits has contributed to our understanding of these issues. Relevant evidence from cognitive psychology, computational modeling, and neuroscience is also reviewed.

The primary goal of this volume is to bring together in one place the most significant contributions that the study of deficits has made to our understanding of normal cognition. The volume is comprehensive in that most major areas of cognition are covered. However, each chapter is not an encyclopedic review of all of the cognitive neuropsychological work that has been carried out in the domain. Instead, each chapter focuses on the most significant and revealing cognitive neuropsychological findings. Each chapter reviews these contributions, discusses the manner in which they have influenced theory development, and presents the current state of thinking about representation and processing within that domain. Although the evidence that is discussed comes primarily from the study of cognitive deficits, the reader should not expect a review of deficit types. For example, in discussing language comprehension and production, the focus is on showing how patterns of impaired and spared performance reveal the structure and organization of the intact language system rather than on defining and describing types of disorders such as anomia, Broca's aphasia, conduction aphasia, and so on.

This book should be useful to a number of different audiences. For cognitive psychologists and students of cognitive psychology whose work relies on evidence from cognitively intact subjects, this volume provides ready access to the major contributions of cognitive neuropsychology. Furthermore, the chapters on methods and history (as well as the glossary and brain diagrams) provide the necessary background for those unfamiliar with the assumptions and rationale of the cognitive neuropsychological approach. The volume reviews evidence that complements findings derived from the study of unimpaired subjects and, in this way, makes available a richer set of constraints on theory development.

For students and researchers working within cognitive neuropsychology, this volume provides a focused review and discussion of the cognitive questions that have been amenable to cognitive neuropsychological investigation. This provides the student with detailed illustrations of the reasoning and methods used to bring data from deficits to bear on questions of normal cognition. For researchers already working within the field, the chapters provide substantive reviews of cognitive domains that may be unfamiliar. Finally, each chapter identifies unresolved issues, providing indications of directions for future cognitive neuropsychological research.

The study of deficits sometimes provides unexpected and intriguing evidence that serves as a challenge to current theorizing. Other times the study of deficits is particularly useful because it allows us to address questions that have been difficult to investigate or resolve through the study of unimpaired subjects. In all cases, however, cognitive neuropsychological studies serve to remind us of the extraordinary complexity and beauty of human cognition and of the challenges faced in seeking to understand it.

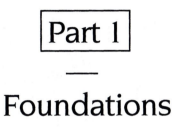

Foundations

The most beautiful thing we can experience
is the mysterious. It is the source of all true art
and science.

—*Albert Einstein*

1

Assumptions and Methods in Cognitive Neuropsychology

Max Coltheart

WHAT IS COGNITIVE NEUROPSYCHOLOGY?

Cognitive neuropsychology is a branch of cognitive psychology.

Cognitive psychology is that science which seeks to learn more about the nature of the mental processes responsible for our ability to perform such basic cognitive activities as understanding and producing language, recognizing objects and people, storing information in memory and subsequently being able to retrieve it, acting intelligently upon the physical world, and so on. Cognitive psychologists also interest themselves in higher-level cognitive processes such as reasoning and problem-solving, the formation of beliefs about the world and about other people and how we assess the plausibility of such beliefs once they have occurred to us, and the cognitive nature of social interaction.

The most common way of investigating cognition is to study people with normal cognitive abilities as they are performing some particular cognitive task; the cognitive psychologist develops a theory about the nature of the mental processes used for performing this task, makes deductions from this theory about what results should be observed in some experiment involving that kind of cognition, carries out such an experiment, and considers whether the data confirm or falsify the theory.

Another way of doing cognitive psychology is to collect data relevant to the theory from people who have disorders of cognition. Any such disorder might be *acquired* or it might be *developmental.* If someone in whom a particular cognitive function had been normal suffers damage to the brain which specifically impairs that form of cognition that person has an acquired disorder of cognition. In contrast, someone who has not been able to acquire the cognitive ability to a normal degree has a developmental disorder of cognition. These disorders of cognition are relevant to theories about normal cognition, because such theories make predictions not only about the results of experiments with cognitively intact people, but also about ways in which brain damage can impair cognition, and about ways in which the acquisition of a cognitive ability can go awry. Thus, data from people with acquired or developmental disorders of cognition can confirm or falsify theories about cognition; this way of doing cognitive psychology is cognitive neuropsychology.

For example, suppose one believed that our ability to recognize all kinds of visual stimuli—objects, faces, and the printed word—used a single common visual recognition system. This theory predicts that if in a particular person brain damage has impaired the ability to recog-

3

nize visually-presented objects, such a person will also have an impairment in the ability to recognize faces and an impairment in the ability to recognize visually-presented words. If experimental investigations of this person reveal that face recognition and visual word recognition are both intact, that falsifies the original theory about visual recognition. The same would be true if one found, in a person who had no history of brain damage, that as he grew up he had acquired the ability to recognize faces and printed words but was never able to acquire the ability to recognize visually-presented objects.

Cognitive neuropsychology is not a kind of neuropsychology (even though it is highly relevant to neuropsychology) because, to put the matter in a nutshell, cognitive neuropsychology is about the mind, while neuropsychology is about the brain. Consider the hypothetical patient described above, who after brain damage could no longer recognize objects but could still recognize faces and visually-presented words. Presumably that means that there must be a region of the brain that is needed if we are to recognize objects, but not needed for recognizing faces or printed words. One might use brain-imaging methods with this patient to try to discover where in the brain this object-recognition system is located. However, whether one succeeded or failed in the attempt to locate such a region in the patient's brain is simply irrelevant to the conclusion drawn about the cognitive organization of visual recognition on the basis of the patient's performance. The theory that objects, faces, and visually-presented words are all recognized by a single common visual recognition system is still falsified by the finding of a person in whom brain damage affected only object recognition, regardless of what can or can't be discovered from studying the damaged brain of such a person.

Cognitive neuropsychology is also not necessarily concerned with treatment or rehabilitation, even though it might be relevant, even highly relevant, to them. Suppose one became convinced that all of the kinds of acquired or developmental cognitive disorders studied by cognitive neuropsychologists were completely untreatable—convinced, that is, that a child with a particular developmental disorder will never be able to acquire that cognitive ability, no matter what treatment is used, and that a brain-damaged patient who has lost a particular cognitive ability will never be able to regain it, no matter what treatment is used. Even if all of this were true, that would have no implications at all for the practice of cognitive neuropsychology. Data from people with cognitive disorders could still be used to confirm or falsify theories about normal cognition. On the other hand, it might be true one day—though it isn't true at present—that our theories about how normal cognitive processes operate have become so detailed that they make predictions about whether particular treatment techniques will or won't be effective. If that day comes, then treatment studies will be relevant to theories about normal cognition, and cognitive neuropsychology will be directly concerned with issues involving treatment.

Of course, there is already a way in which treatment studies can yield cognitive-neuropsychological evidence, since sometimes theories make predictions about the outcomes of treatment studies. If whether or not function Y depends upon function X is a question of relevance to a theory, and if a patient has an impairment of function X, and if successful treatment of function X is achieved, then one should observe an improvement in function Y. Failure to observe this would count as evidence against the theory.

Finally, although cognitive neuropsychology is distinct from clinical neuropsychology, it is important for clinical neuropsychology in a number of ways. For example, highly sophisticated methods of cognitive assessment can be developed if one uses as a starting point a detailed theory of the relevant cognitive system. The PALPA (Psycholinguistic Assessments of Language Processing in Aphasia) battery for assessing disorders of language (Kay, Lesser, & Coltheart, 1992) and the BORB (Birmingham Object Recognition Battery) for assessing disorders of visual perception and visual recognition (Riddoch & Humphreys, 1993) are good examples of such theory-based assessment methods. Cognitive-neuropsychological assessment methods such as these allow the clinician to pinpoint precisely which aspects of cognition are still intact and which are impaired in particular patients, and this provides a specific focus for treatment and rehabilitation.

THE CASE OF AC

Investigations of the patient AC by Coltheart et al. (1998) provide a useful example that provides a more detailed illustration of just how cognitive neuropsychologists seek to learn more about the nature of normal cognition from investigations of people with impairments of cognition.

AC was a 67-year-old man at the time of these investigations, and had formerly been employed as a clerical worker with the public railway system in New South Wales, Australia. He had a history of cardiovascular and cerebrovascular disease, and a CT scan performed four days after he had suffered a stroke revealed a recent lesion in the territory of the left middle cerebral artery, plus a number of older small lesions in both cerebral hemispheres indicative of earlier more minor cerebrovascular incidents.

Assessment of AC's linguistic and other cognitive abilities revealed some impairments that were surprisingly severe given the relatively minor damage evident in the CT scan. For example, AC's reading ability was almost completely abolished; he could not even judge that *A* and *a* are two forms of the same letter while *A* and *e* are not, a very elementary reading task. This was not because of some impairment of vision, since he could judge that *A* and *A* are the same while *A* and *E* are not, and could copy such letters correctly, indicating that he could see perfectly well. And since he had been a clerk, it is not likely that his severely impaired ability to read would have been present prior to his stroke. AC's writing was also almost completely abolished; he could write almost nothing to dictation except his name and address, and when shown an uppercase letter and asked to write its lowercase form next to it, he could not do so. This was not a motor problem, because he was entirely capable of copying an uppercase letter in its uppercase form, as mentioned above.

AC's ability to generate spoken words, in conversation or when trying to name a picture, was also severely affected; he knew what he wanted to say, but could rarely find the actual word he wanted to produce. He was also very poor at copying pictures and at drawing to dictation.

Studying his reading, his writing, or his drawing could well have provided interesting new information about how these cognitive activities are normally carried out. However, a conversation with AC involving his knowledge about the properties of objects—in particular, animals—led to a series of studies of his knowledge of word meanings. This conversation was prompted by a paper with the title "The Oyster with Four Legs" (Sartori & Job, 1988) which had appeared just before we first met AC. The conversation went as follows:

MC: How many legs does an oyster have?
AC: A few.
MC: I see. What about an ant?
AC: Some.
MC: A caterpillar?
AC: No legs.
MC: What about a snake?
AC: None.
MC: And a seagull?
AC: Four legs.

This inability to provide the required information about animals was formally tested by choosing a set of 18 animals, 9 possessing legs and 9 not, and asking AC to respond "Yes" (i.e., it has legs) or "No" (it hasn't) when the names of these animals were spoken to him. Chance performance would be 9 out of 18; AC scored 10 out of 18.

Why did he have such difficulty performing this task? One possibility is a category-specific loss of semantic information where the affected category is animals: This was the case with the patient described by Sartori and Job (1988). That was easy to test: A set of 20 inanimate objects, 10 with legs (e.g., chair, table, sofa, etc.) and 10 without legs, was chosen. When asked to indicate whether or not these objects had legs, in response to the spoken names of the objects, AC again failed to perform better than chance, scoring 11 out of 20 correct. So the difficulty here was not with loss of semantic information specifically concerning animals.

Perhaps it had something to do with the word or the concept "leg"? No, because AC was also at chance when the task was to respond to the question "Does it have a tail?", scoring 12 out of 22 correct and on a subsequent occasion, 11 out of 22 correct with the same items.

Was it just knowledge of the *parts* of objects that AC had lost? No, because he was unable to make judgements based just on the overall shapes of objects ("Is it round or not?" yielded 15 out of 28 correct) or just on their color ("Is it colored or just black and white?" yielded 12 out of 20 correct).

Well, perhaps what he had lost was information about the *perceptual properties* of objects; so he was then tested for his knowledge of nonperceptual information about objects. Asked to classify animals as Australian or not, he did very well (18 out of 20 correct; so he knew that a kangaroo is Australian and an elephant is not, despite his inability to report how many legs each has). Asked to classify animals as dangerous or not, he also did very well (19 out of 20 correct), and he also succeeded with the question "Do people usually eat this animal?" (23 out of 24 correct) and "Does this animal live in water or not?" (18 out of 20 correct). These four tests all require access to nonperceptual knowledge about objects, and AC performed all four very well.

His failures on the legs, tails, shape, and color tests could be because he had lost all *perceptual* knowledge about objects; or was it just specifically *visual* knowledge which had gone? That was tested by asking for perceptual but nonvisual knowledge. On a test of auditory perceptual knowledge (i.e., "Does it make a sound?"), he scored 24 out of 26 correct; and on a test of olfactory perceptual knowledge (i.e., "Does it have a smell?"), he scored 19 out of 20 correct.

These results support the following conclusion: What happened to AC is that he lost all information about the visual properties of objects, while still retaining knowledge about their nonperceptual properties, and also knowledge about perceptual properties which are not visual.

What does this tell us about how knowledge of objects is represented mentally? If everything we know about objects is represented in a single object knowledge system, it is hard to see how one particular form of knowledge (e.g., visual knowledge) could be lost while other forms of knowledge are still essentially intact. We are therefore led to the view that there is a system of knowledge about what objects look like which is quite separate from other stores of knowledge about other kinds of properties of objects.

Now, it is possible that there are just two systems of object knowledge, one which tells us what objects look like and another which tells us everything else about them (i.e., whether an object has a smell, lives in Australia, makes a noise, lives in water, etc.). But it doesn't seem very plausible to argue that all the forms of perceptual information are stored together with nonperceptual information, except for visual information, which has its own proprietary store. What seems more plausible, given that we want to say that there's a system just for visual knowledge of objects, is that there is also a system just for auditory knowledge about objects, and another one just for olfactory knowledge about objects—indeed, a separate system of perceptual object knowledge for each of our senses, plus a system of nonperceptual object knowledge. If so, we should find patients who know that a radio has no legs and a table does, but can't tell you which of them makes a noise (these hypothetical patients have lost their system of auditory knowledge about objects but still have their system of visual knowledge), patients who know that gasoline isn't normally drunk and vodka is, but can't tell you which of these has a smell (loss of olfactory object knowledge), and so on.

A key point here is that, although we have been led to this theory about how object knowledge is stored by studies of someone with impaired object knowledge, the theory is a theory about how such knowledge is represented in the intact person—it is a theory about all of us, including about AC prior to his brain damage. That, of course, is the essence of cognitive neuropsychology: building a theory about normal cognition from a study of abnormal cognition.

Like any other methodology, cognitive neuropsychology makes certain assumptions—that is, there are certain things which need to be true, or at least approximately true, if studies of people with impaired cognition are to be informative about the nature of intact cognitive systems. Those assumptions are discussed below, but before they can be discussed, it is necessary first to say something about a concept that is central for those assumptions—the concept of *modularity*.

MODULARITY

Let's suppose the cognitive task we are interested in is the very general task of understanding visual stimuli, whether they be objects or faces or printed words. One hypothesis that might be offered here is that such understanding involves three processing stages: detection of visual features, followed by visual recognition, followed by access to stored meanings. That hypothesis is represented in diagrammatic form in Figure 1.1.

What's being proposed here is that there is one single system containing representations of each of the stimuli we have learned to recognize by sight, whether these be objects or faces or visually-presented words, and a separate single system containing information about the meanings associated with each of these stimuli. The representation of a particular stimulus in the visual recognition system would be linked to the feature detectors for just those visual features which that stimulus possesses, so that when just those features are present in the visual stimulus, the representation of that stimulus in the visual recognition system would be maximally activated. This would lead in turn to the activation of the meaning of that stimulus in the semantic system. The visual recognition system does not contain any information about meanings; its domain is visual structure, not semantics.

According to this theory, then, the system we use for understanding what we see has three components. Such components are typically depicted by cognitive neuropsychologists as boxes in box-and-arrow diagrams like that of Figure 1.1. We need some term to refer to these components, and a commonly used term is *module*. A theory like that represented in Figure 1.1 is referred to as a modular theory, since it claims that the system we use for understanding what we see is composed of three modules. So it is necessary to say something about what's meant by the term module.

The most useful discussion of what this term means is to be found in Fodor (1983), even though what Fodor said about modularity has been widely misunderstood. Fodor approached this issue by listing a number of properties which are *characteristic* of modules. These properties included the following:

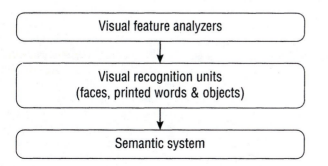

Figure 1.1. A schematic representation of a possible theory of object recognition.

- domain specific
- innately specified
- informationally encapsulated
- fast
- hardwired (neurally specific)
- autonomous
- not assembled

Misunderstandings of Fodor have mainly arisen via the belief that what he was offering was intended as a definition of modularity—that is, that he was proposing a list of properties all of which were necessary conditions for applying the term. But Fodor was very clear that this was not his intention: "I am not, in any strict sense, in the business of defining my terms. . . . So what I propose to do instead of defining 'modular' is to associate the notion of modularity with a pattern of answers to such questions as 1–5" (Fodor, 1983, p. 37; Here the five questions he was referring to were questions about possible features of modularity, questions such as "Is the system innately specified?" or "Is the system domain-specific?")

And again: "Given that a system has any of the properties in question, then the likelihood is considerable that it has all the rest. . . . However, I doubt that a claim that strong could be empirically sustained, since it is reasonably easy to think of psychological processes that are fast but not encapsulated, or involuntary but not innate, and so forth. The present contention, in any event, is relatively modest: it's that if a psychological system has most of the modularity properties, then it is very likely to have all of them" (Fodor, 1983, p. 137).

So, for example, Fodor would not *require* that a system be innate for it to be called a module; he is simply suggesting that most systems that deserve to be called modules turn out to be innate. But the system that skilled readers use for reading, whilst certainly not innate, is fast, neurally-specific, domain-specific, and autonomous (Fodor means "automatic" by this term), and so is modular to some interesting extent—compare: "One would thus expect—what anyhow seems to be desirable—that the notion of modularity ought to admit of degrees. The notion of modularity that I have in mind certainly does. When I speak of a cognitive system as modular, I shall therefore always mean 'to some interesting extent'" (Fodor, 1983, p. 37).

Elsewhere (Coltheart, 1999) I have suggested a concept of modularity that departs very slightly from Fodor's, but appears more useful, at least for cognitive psychologists and cognitive neuropsychologists, and which I am adopting throughout this chapter:

Fodor was not concerned with defining modularity, nor with specifying any properties that a cognitive system must necessarily possess for it to be considered modular. I am suggesting that one can be more ambitious than this, by defining 'module' as 'a cognitive system whose application is domain specific'; here domain-specificity is a necessary condition for the applicability of the term 'modular'. Now it is necessary to say something about what might be meant by 'domain-specific'. I mean that a cognitive system is domain-specific if it only responds to stimuli of a particular class: so that to say that there is a domain-specific face recognition module is to say that there is a cognitive system which responds when its input is a face, but does not respond when its input is, say, a written word, or a visually-presented object, or someone's voice. There's no circularity here, since the claim that there is a face recognition module does not derive merely from the existence of faces as a stimulus class that is conceptually distinguishable from other stimulus classes such as written words, objects or voices. The claim is derived from empirical observations, as follows. Suppose first that we were entertaining the idea that there was a single module for visual recognition which accepts as inputs faces, objects and printed words. Then we noticed that in the neuropsychological literature there were reports of patients with impaired visual word recognition but retained face recognition and of patients with impaired visual word recognition but retained visual object recognition. We also noticed reports of patients with impaired visual object recognition but retained face recognition [11] and patients with impaired visual object recognition but retained visual word recognition. Finally, we also noticed reports of patients with impaired face recognition but retained visual object recognition and of patients with impaired face recognition but retained visual object recognition. This collection of results refutes our original idea that there is a cognitive module whose domain is the recognition of all forms of visual stimuli. Instead, there are three separate modules: a face recognition module, a visual object recognition module, and a visual word recognition module [a claim that I believe is in fact correct]. The domain-specificities are obvious here: visual objects, faces, printed words." (Coltheart, 1999, pp. 118–119)

Note that this conception of domain specificity does not require that there be some kind of gatekeeper which decides which stimuli should be admitted to a module and which should not. The retina does not respond to auditory stimuli (its domain is light in a certain wavelength range) but no one would suppose that this is because there is some mechanism which actively blocks sound waves from reaching the retina. Sound waves pass through the whole head; but only some structures in the head are activated by these waves. In the same way, visual information from print would reach the face recognition module, but that module would not contain any structures that would be activated by this particular kind of visual information.

Here, then, a module is an information-processing mechanism which is domain-specific (i.e., which is responsible for processing just certain kinds of information for certain specific purposes). Modules can themselves be modular in organization; as we've seen from the example of AC discussed earlier, the semantics module itself is made up of a number of different modules.

So is Mike McCloskey's laser printer, discussed in Chapter 24. In that chapter McCloskey reports data from studies of that printer showing that an overload of memory affects the printing of graphics but not the simultaneous printing of text. From this dissociation he inferred with extreme caution that inside his laser printer " . . . text is somehow treated differently from graphics" (this volume, p. 594); a less cautious but perfectly reasonable inference is that the printer contains two distinct modules, one a memory for graphic information and the other a memory for text information. This proposal about the printer's functional architecture might be refuted by further investigations of the printer's behavior, but given the data reported in Chapter 24 the proposal is not only reasonable but plausible.

Here, "functional architecture" means a description of an information-processing system in terms of what its modules are and what the pathways of information flow between these modules are. Any information-processing system, be it a person or a printer, has a functional architecture—and also a hardware architecture, this being a neural architecture in the case of persons.

Having said what I mean by the terms "module" and "functional architecture," I can now return to the issue of the assumptions of cognitive neuropsychology.

THE ASSUMPTIONS OF COGNITIVE NEUROPSYCHOLOGY

Firstly, let's be clear what "assumption" means here. It does not mean "here are some things which cognitive neuropsychologists assert to be true of people." It means something quite different: "here are some things which need to be true of people, at least to a good approximation, for cognitive neuropsychology to be able to succeed in its aims." There are four major assumptions, as follows.

Assumption 1: Functional Modularity

Since a fundamental aim of cognitive neuropsychology is to discover functional architectures of cognitive systems, and since a functional architecture is a configuration of modules, cognitive neuropsychology will get nowhere except when cognitive systems actually are configurations of modules. Fodor (1983) is interesting again here. In that book he offers an account of the mind as consisting of two systems. There's the system of input modules and there's the central system. The input modules are responsible for encoding and recognizing perceptual inputs. The central system is responsible for such "higher-level" cognitive processes as the fixation of belief. The input-module system is, of course, modular, but the central system is nonmodular. What follows from that, according to Fodor, is that, because cognition which involves the central system is nonmodular, it is not amenable to scientific study: Indeed, he offered this as Fodor's First Law of the Nonexistence of Cognitive Science. If he is correct that some forms of cognition depend upon cognitive systems that are not functionally modular, then these forms of cognition cannot be successfully studied by cognitive neuropsychology. It remains to be seen whether this is the case.

Assumption 2: Anatomical Modularity

Even if cognitive systems are actually configurations of modules, it does not follow that any of these modules is realized in some specific and relatively small region of the brain. It could be that the neural tissue for each individual functional module is very widely spread throughout the brain. In other words, it is possible for there to be functional modularity but no anatomical modularity. If so, almost any form of brain damage must affect very many—even all—modules. In that case, cognitive neuropsychology would get nowhere because the functional modularity of cognition would not manifest itself in the performance of brain-damaged patients—for example, even if the face recognition system and the spoken-word recognition system were two quite distinct functional modules, one would never see a patient who could recognize faces but not spoken words, nor a patient who could recognize spoken words but not faces.

Assumption 3: Uniformity of Functional Architecture Across People

Even if cognitive systems are actually configurations of modules (i.e., there is functional modularity), and even if individual functional modules generally are realized in restricted brain regions (i.e., there is anatomical modularity), cognitive neuropsychology would still not get anywhere if different individuals had different functional architectures for the same cognitive domain. That's because it would not be possible to make inferences about the functional architecture of the cognitive systems of people in general from the data of a single patient, however well-justified the inference was from that patient's data to claims about that particular patient's functional architecture. Of course, this assumption is not peculiar to cognitive neuropsychology; it is widespread throughout the whole of cognitive psychology. Thus if this assumption is false, that's not just bad news for cognitive neuropsychology; it is bad news for all of cognitive psychology.

Assumption 4: Subtractivity

Cognitive neuropsychology treats the functional architecture of an impaired cognitive system as the functional architecture of the intact cognitive system with one or more of its components damaged or deleted. The assumption here is that brain damage can impair or delete existing boxes or arrows in the system, but cannot introduce new ones: that is, it can subtract from the system, but cannot add to it. If this were not so, studying impaired systems could not tell us about normal systems. This is not at all to say that brain-damaged patients do not adopt new strategies to cope with their impairments, strategies that intact individuals do not use. Such compensatory strategies could consist of using the normal functional architecture in an abnormal way. For example, in patients with pure alexia (letter-by-letter reading), a condition discussed in Chapter 10, visual word identification is typically achieved by spelling out the letters of a word one-by-one, and identifying the whole word after having spelled out all of its letters. That is not how intact readers recognize words. But intact readers have a letter-naming capability, and they are also capable of recognizing a word if it is spelled aloud to them. Hence the procedures for word recognition used by the pure-alexic patient have not been introduced to the language system by the brain damage; these procedures are present in the intact system, but are not normally used to assist visual word identification.

If one or more of these four assumptions is untrue, what are the implications for cognitive neuropsychology? The worst-case scenario is happy oblivion. The cognitive neuropsychologist's data appear to make sense, and interesting theories about functional architectures are suggested by them; little does the cognitive neuropsychologist know that this happy state of affairs has only arisen because a false assumption has been assumed to be true. Here, all is illusion, but there is no way for the cognitive neuropsychologist to know this. Yet, a little thought shows how unlikely this scenario is. Suppose for example that Assumptions 1, 2, and 4 are true but Assumption 3 is false. This will mean that patients A and B will, before their brain damage, have possessed functionally modular cognitive architectures which were also anatomically modular, and that their brain damage has subtracted from, but not added anything to, these architectures; but the architectures of each patient were, and so still are, very different. This will be immediately apparent: Patient A's data will strongly suggest a certain cognitive architecture, so will patient B's, but the two architectures thus suggested will be different ones. Thus, the cognitive neuropsychologist will not be happily oblivious here: It will be obvious that something is deeply wrong if different patients yield quite different ideas about what the functional architecture is.

What if Assumption 1 is false, or Assumption 2? In both cases, the consequence will be that we simply won't see patients with highly selective cognitive disorders, patients such as AC (whose semantic impairment was just for visual information). But we do—and there are many other examples of such highly selective cognitive disorders in other chapters of this book. If just Assumption 1 is false, then we won't see such cases because the cognitive system does not have the modular organization that would cause them. If just Assumption 2 is wrong, then we won't see such cases because the brain does not have the degree of anatomical modularity that would allow brain damage to produce such disorders.

Finally, Assumption 4: If the other assumptions were all correct but this one were false, that would soon be evident, because the functional architectures inferred from studies of brain-damaged patients could not be successfully applied to the explanation of results obtained by cognitive psychologists studying people without brain damage.

In sum, then, if any of these four assumptions were false, that would have soon become apparent, because cognitive-neuropsychological research would soon have run into severe difficulties; thus there is a kind of fail-safe mechanism here. From this follows an even more important point: If one considers that cognitive neuropsychological research over the past 30 years or so has yielded much coherent evidence about cognition that has led to proposals about cognitive architectures which are also useful in explaining data from studies of people with intact cognitive systems, that conclusion constitutes evidence that all four of these quite fundamental assumptions about mind and brain are in fact correct.

INFERENCE FROM DATA TO THEORY IN COGNITIVE NEUROPSYCHOLOGY

Cognitive neuropsychology seeks to interpret cognitive disorders as selective impairments of functional architectures. Suppose, for example, you have a particular theory about how visually-presented objects are recognized, and you express the functional architecture proposed by this theory in the form of a modular box-and-arrow diagram. Then, whenever you come across a patient with any kind if impairment of visual object recognition, you will try to determine which boxes and arrows of the diagram are still intact in the patient's visual recognition system and which have been damaged. If you can demonstrate that a certain pattern of damage to the functional architecture you've proposed would cause that damaged system to show just the same symptoms that the patient is showing, then you have achieved two things: you've obtained empirical support for the theory of visual object recognition, and you've gained an insight into exactly what is wrong with this patient that's much deeper than simply saying, "The patient has an impairment of visual object recognition." If on the other hand you can demonstrate that there is *no* pattern of damage to the boxes and arrows which would cause the system to behave like the patient, then you have also achieved something: you have shown that the theory is false. The data from the patient have refuted the theory.

It is important here to distinguish between three different kinds of data that brain-damaged patients may yield, these kinds being associations of deficits, dissociations of deficits, and double dissociations of deficits.

Associations, Dissociations, and Double Dissociations

With associations the patient is impaired on task X and also on task Y. For example, he or she is poor at understanding printed words and poor at understanding spoken words. Here the two impairments are said to be associated, because both are present in the same patient

With dissociations the patient is impaired on task X but responds normally on task Y. For example, he or she is poor at understanding printed words but normal at understanding spoken words. Here the two impairments are said to be dissociated, because one is present and the other is absent in the same patient

With double dissociations we typically need two patients: patient A who is impaired on task X but normal on task Y, and patient B who is normal on task X but impaired on task Y. Both patients show a dissociation; when the two dissociations occur in opposite directions, this is called a double dissociation.

One can still speak of dissociations between two tasks even if performance is impaired on both tasks. If a patient is impaired at both task A and task B, but is significantly more impaired on the second task than on the first, that can be treated as a dissociation; and if a second patient is observed who is also impaired at both task A and task B, but is significantly more impaired on the first task than on the second, that can be treated as a double dissociation. A more detailed and technical analysis of associations, dissociations, and double dissociations may be found in Chapter 10 of Shallice (1988).

It is possible to have double dissociations within a single patient. For example, Rapp, Benzing, and Caramazza (1995) described a patient who was worse with nouns than with verbs when producing them in speech, but worse with verbs than nouns when producing them in print.

How can we use data like these to learn more about cognition?

We might interpret the data as evidence that there is a single cognitive module responsible for word comprehension, and that module is damaged. If so, one would expect that both spoken words and printed words would suffer.

A problem here is that this interpretation could be correct, but an alternative is obvious: There are separate cognitive systems for the comprehension of speech and print, but these systems are so close together in the brain that it is unlikely, or even impossible, for only one to be damaged. Take, for example, Gerstmann's syndrome, which is diagnosed when four symptoms are present: acalculia, finger agnosia, right–left disorientation, and dysgraphia. It is conceivable that this association of four impairments occurs through damage to one single cognitive system that we use for finding square roots, finding our way around the environment, knowing which finger is the thumb, and writing; but this is hardly a plausible cognitive theory. A far more plausible interpretation for such a syndrome is that these tasks involve a variety of separate cognitive systems but since these systems are located so close together in the brain (in this case, in the left parietal cortex), any damage to the region on which one of the cognitive systems depends is highly likely to have also affected the regions upon which the other cognitive systems depend, thereby producing impairments in the other cognitive tasks.

Although this challenge to the use of association data in cognitive neuropsychology is a standard one, it is by no means so strong as to completely eliminate associations from consideration. Suppose, for example, one were studying a patient who had both impaired ability to read aloud and also impaired spelling ability. Detailed investigation of his reading showed that he could read aloud pronounceable nonwords such as *choe* or *plood* successfully, but he often made errors with real words which disobey standard spelling-to-sound rules, exception words such as *shoe* or *flood*; and his errors here were "regularization errors," such that he read these words according to the rules, pronouncing *shoe* to rhyme with *toe* and *flood* to rhyme with *mood*. This form of acquired dyslexia is known as surface dyslexia, and is frequently interpreted in relation to a dual-route theory of reading aloud.

In such a theory, one way to read aloud is by applying letter-to-sound rules to the printed letter string. This will succeed with nonwords (and also with regular words, which obey standard spelling-to-sound rules) but will fail with exception words, producing regularization errors for such words. The other way to read aloud is via a lexicon of known words: the letter string is recognized as an entry in an orthographic input lexicon and that allows retrieval of its pronunciation from a phonological output lexicon. This will succeed with all words, regular or exception, but will fail for all nonwords, since nonwords are not represented in the orthographic input lexicon (nor in the phonological output lexicon). Given this theory, if brain damage impairs the orthographic input lexicon but spares the nonlexical (rule-based) method of reading, the patient will be able to read nonwords successfully, but will make regularization errors with exception words—that is, will exhibit surface dyslexia.

Exactly the same kind of theory can be applied to the task of spelling. In a dual-route theory of spelling, there's a rule-based procedure (applying sound-to-spelling rules) which will succeed for nonwords and for words which obey such rules, but which will yield regularization errors in spelling words which don't obey such rules; so *flood* would be spelled *flud* and *shoe* as *shoo* by this procedure. And there's a second procedure for spelling: looking up the item to be spelled in an orthographic output lexicon. This will succeed with all words, regular or exception, but will fail for all nonwords, since nonwords are not represented in the orthographic output lexicon. Given this theory, if brain damage impairs the orthographic output lexicon but spares the nonlexical (rule-based) method of spelling, such a patient will be able to spell nonwords successfully, but will make regularization spelling errors with exception words—that is, will exhibit the form of acquired dyslexia known as surface dysgraphia.

What has all this got to do with associations? Well, suppose that we see a patient who exhibits both surface dyslexia (e.g., reads *flood* to rhyme with *mood*) and surface dysgraphia (e.g., spells *flood* as *flud*). It is very tempting to conclude that this shows that it is wrong to distinguish between an orthographic input lexicon and an orthographic output lexicon. One could interpret such a patient much more economically by supposing that there is only one orthographic lexicon, used both for reading and for spelling. A single lesion, just of this orthographic lexicon, would produce both surface dyslexia and surface dysgraphia. If instead one wished to distinguish between an orthographic input lexicon and an orthographic output lexicon, then one would have to propose that any patient like this has two separate lesions.

But a defender of the two-orthographic-lexicon theory could reply: Yes, many patients with surface dyslexia also show surface dysgraphia, but that's not because there is only one orthographic lexicon; instead, there are indeed separate input and output orthographic lexicons, but they are neuroanatomically close, and so when one is affected by brain damage the other is also very likely to be affected too. This association of deficits is not telling us anything about the functional architecture of the reading and spelling systems, the defender would say; it is just an accident of the way in which the components of this system are represented in the brain.

But now suppose that an investigator showed that the irregular words that a surface dyslexic and surface dysgraphic patient could not read were exactly those that he could not spell, and all of the irregular words he could read correctly he could also spell correctly. What are we to conclude from this? Either there are distinct orthographic input and output lexicons, and this item-specific correspondence between reading and spelling is just a huge coincidence; or, far more plausibly, the item-specific correspondence between reading and spelling here is telling us that there is just a single orthographic lexicon use both for reading and for writing. Some of the entries in this lexicon have been damaged; for all words which are irregular and whose entries have been damaged, both reading and spelling will have to be nonlexical, and therefore erroneous. This is an example of a point made in more detail in McCloskey's chapter, namely, that cognitive-neuropsychological data are not limited to gross level-of-performance measures such as percent correct. More sophisticated analyses such as the analysis of consistency of performance in the above example can overcome the limitations of inferences from associations of deficits.

Dissociation. Suppose we observe a patient who is poor at understanding printed words but good at understanding spoken words. What might we infer from this about the cognitive psychology of language? We might interpret the data as evidence that there are separate cognitive modules responsible for written word comprehension and for spoken word comprehension, and the first of these modules is damaged whilst the second one is still intact.

In this case the problem is that this interpretation could be correct, but an alternative is obvious: there might be just one cognitive module responsible for word comprehension, and comprehension of written words might be harder for it than comprehension of spoken words. So when it is partially damaged, printed words will suffer more than spoken words.

This challenge to the use of single dissociations in cognitive neuropsychology is referred to as the *resource artifact* objection by McCloskey (Chapter 24, this volume), and he points out that in many situations it is so implausible a challenge that it is not a serious problem for attempts to make inferences from single-dissociation data. One example he uses is the patient who can produce picture names in writing but not in speaking. To rebut the claim that this result implies that there are separate orthographic and phonological output lexicons, one would have to argue that spoken picture naming is somehow intrinsically harder than written picture naming. Such a claim would seem to have no justification at all.

Double dissociation, suppose we observe the following two patients: Patient A is impaired on comprehending printed words, but normal at comprehending spoken words; patient B is normal on comprehending printed words but impaired on comprehending spoken words.

What might we infer from this about the cognitive psychology of language? We might interpret the data as evidence that there are separate cognitive modules responsible for spoken word comprehension and written word comprehension. One patient has damage to the first module, the other to the second. That reasoning is not subject to the objections to associations and single dissociations; that's one reason for the popularity of the double dissociation method. For example, the claim that the dissociation found in patient A arose because there's just a single language comprehension system which finds printed-word comprehension harder than spoken-word comprehension is refuted by the data from patient B, for whom printed-word comprehension is easier than spoken-word comprehension

However, the inference that there are separate cognitive modules responsible for spoken word comprehension and written word comprehension is not the correct one to draw from the data of patient A and patient B, or at least it is too vaguely stated, because of the ambiguity of the term "separate." Suppose, as surely is the case, that spoken-word comprehension is achieved by a cognitive system which consists of a number of different components (modules); and suppose this is also true of written-word comprehension. If we say that there are separate cognitive modules responsible for spoken word comprehension and written word comprehension, "separate" might be taken to mean "completely distinct" (i.e., having no modules in common). It would not be reasonable to infer, from the double dissociation seen with patients A and B, that the spoken-word comprehension and written-word comprehension systems have no modules in common.

What is reasonable to infer is the conclusion that the two systems are not identical—and, in particular, that there is *at least one* module that is part of the spoken-word comprehension system but not part of the written-word comprehension system (this module is damaged in patient A but intact in patient B), and that there is *at least one* module that is part of the written-word comprehension system but not part of the spoken-word comprehension system (this module is damaged in patient B but intact in patient A).

TWO COMMON MISUNDERSTANDINGS ABOUT COGNITIVE NEUROPSYCHOLOGY AND DOUBLE DISSOCIATIONS

There are two misunderstandings that are sufficiently common that I once heard both made in conference talks at the same conference. Because they are so common, it is worth identifying them and explaining just why they are mistaken.

Speaker A at this conference argued that the use of double dissociation data to make inferences about the structure of cognitive systems is always based on a simple logical fallacy, known since Aristotle: the fallacy of affirmation of the consequent. The argument from double dissociation, he said, always runs thus:

1. If cognitive architecture A were true, then one would see double dissociation B;
2. Double dissociation B has been observed;
3. Therefore, it follows that cognitive architecture A must be true.

This is indeed fallacious. But it isn't the way cognitive neuropsychologists argue. Instead, they argue thus:

1. I have observed double dissociation B.
2. Let me think . . . what's a cognitive architecture which, when damaged in two different ways, would produce double dissociation B?
3. Well, here's one: cognitive architecture A.
4. So I hypothesize that the architecture of the cognitive system is architecture A.

Cognitive neuropsychologists never claim that certain data logically *require* a particular architecture, because, of course, it is never the case that data logically require a particular theory. A theory is a reasonable interpretation of data, not a logical consequence of data.

Speaker B at this meeting argued that inference based on double dissociation evidence is always fatally flawed because it is always the case that there might be some cognitive architecture different from the one proposed that is also compatible with the observed double dissociation data.

This is indeed true. But it isn't just true of the double dissociation approach. It is true of all the methods psychology uses when building theory from data. Indeed, it is true of all science, not just psychology. Consider, for example, Mendel's postulation of the gene to explain the data he had collected concerning the characteristics of successive generations of sweet peas. He didn't say, nor could he have, that this was the only possible explanation of his data.

Nor would Gell-Mann have said that the only possible explanation of the data he considered was the proposal that quarks exist. Observations from experimental physics indicated the existence of some 100 particles in the atom's nucleus. Gell-Mann proposed that all of those particles, including the neutron and proton, are composed of fundamental building blocks that he named "quarks." The quarks are permanently confined by forces coming from the exchange of "gluons." He and others later constructed the quantum field theory of quarks and gluons, called "quantum chromodynamics," which seems to account for all the nuclear particles and their strong interactions.

Mendel did not claim that the only logically possible explanation of the sweet-pea data was that genes exist; Gell-Mann did not claim that the only logically possible explanation of the particle-physics data was that quarks exist; and a cognitive neuropsychologist would not claim that the only logically possible explanation of a particular double dissociation is that a certain cognitive architecture exists.

Despite the errors made by the two above mentioned speakers, these kinds of objections do crop up quite a lot as a response to work based on double dissociation evidence. A cognitive neuropsychologist might describe data documenting a double dissociation, then describe a cognitive architecture which, when damaged in two different ways, would yield this double dissociation, and conclude by saying: "So I am proposing that this is the cognitive architecture of the system." To which someone replies, appearing to believe that a devastating criticism is being made: "That doesn't have to be the case. There could well be another quite different architecture that would also yield the same double dissociation."

There are two effective responses that the cognitive neuropsychologist can make here. The first is just to say "I agree." A puzzled silence will follow.

The second is to say "Tell me what this other architecture is." If the critic cannot do so, the criticism loses all force. If the critic can do so, then we have two different hypotheses about what the functional architecture is, both of which can explain the data; so then we need new empirical work which will allow us to decide which hypothesis is to be preferred—for example, new data which are compatible with one of the hypotheses and inconsistent with the other.

SYNDROMES, THE SINGLE-CASE-STUDY APPROACH, AND COGNITIVE NEUROPSYCHOLOGY

A syndrome is a collection of symptoms which often co-occur in the same individual. As mentioned above, the symptoms finger agnosia, dyscalculia, left–right disorientation, and impaired spelling with intact reading co-occur sufficiently often that this conjunction of symptoms has a name: Gerstmann's syndrome. One can ask: Why do these symptoms co-occur? One possible answer is that there is some cognitive module which plays a role in finger identification, calculation, left-right orientation, and spelling. Damage to that module would therefore result in all four symptoms; and in that case, studying patients with Gerstmann's syndrome would provide information about the functional architecture of some cognitive system. However, there are no currently-proposed theories of any cognitive processing system which contain a module that plays a part in the performance of all four of these tasks, and it is very hard to conceive of what such a theory (and module) would be like. Hence, we are led to seek another answer to the question of why these symptoms co-occur, an answer in terms of neural rather than functional architecture; namely, that these tasks depend on cognitive modules which are functionally distinct but realized adjacently in the brain (in the left parietal cortex, as it happens). In that case, studying Gerstmann's syndrome can tell us nothing about functional architectures of cognition.

Cognitive neuropsychologists believe that the kind of argument made in the previous paragraph regarding Gerstmann's syndrome applies in general to all syndromes. So they do not engage in the investigation of syndromes, and the reason they don't is because studying a syndrome will not yield information about functional architectures of cognition. Consider the syndrome known as Broca's aphasia, the typical symptoms of which are halting, effortful, nonfluent speech, impoverished grammatical structure in sentence production, especial difficulty with grammatical function words; and an especial difficulty with prefixes and suffixes. If all of these symptoms arose from a single impairment of the language-production system, we would need to propose a functional architecture for that system which contained one element (box or arrow) which, when impaired, would cause the system to show every one of these symptoms. This very idea was proposed by Kean (1977) and by Zurif and Caramazza (1976). Kean proposed that all of the symptoms of Broca's aphasia arise because of damage to a system needed for processing morphemes that do not carry stress. Zurif and Caramazza proposed that all of the symptoms of Broca's aphasia arise because of damage to a syntactic parsing module of the language system.

Subsequent studies, however, showed not only that neither of these theories of Broca's aphasia are correct, but also that no theory which offers an explanation for all of the symptoms of Broca's aphasia in terms of damage to a single component of the language-processing system could be correct. That is because, even though these symptoms commonly co-occur, they do not invariably co-occur; that is, they dissociate. Symptoms which dissociate cannot of course have a single common cause.

That is not to say that the study of syndromes has no part at all to play in cognitive neuropsychology. To see how this is so, consider the modern history of the cognitive-neuropsychological study of acquired dyslexia. This began 25 years ago with the seminal paper of Marshall and Newcombe (1973). In that paper the authors made two important contributions: They defined three syndromes of acquired dyslexia (surface dyslexia, deep dyslexia, and visual dyslexia), and in relation to a theory of normal skilled reading they interpreted each syndrome as arising from a particular pattern of preserved and impaired components of that theory. This revolutionized the study of acquired dyslexia. Detailed studies of many cases of deep dyslexia (for a review see Coltheart, Patterson, & Marshall, 1980) and of surface dyslexia (for a review see Patterson, Marshall, & Coltheart, 1985) followed; and other syndromes of acquired dyslexia were defined and investigated, such as phonological dyslexia (Beauvois & Derouesne, 1979) and letter-by-letter reading (Patterson & Kay, 1982).

But then what happened next in the cognitive-neuropsychological study of acquired dyslexia was that syndrome-oriented research was gradually abandoned. The motivation for abandoning the syndrome approach was as follows:

> The concept of the syndrome has been a useful one in developing work relating (acquired) dyslexic syndromes to theories about reading. However, its usefulness is likely to be short-lived. The reason is that, if a dyslexic syndrome is a specific pattern of preservations and impairments of reading abilities . . . and if a modular theory of reading is appropriate, it follows that there are many different possible dyslexic syndromes. Any unique pattern of impairments to the boxes and arrows of (the theory) will produce a unique syndrome; since (the theory) has enough boxes and arrows to produce a large number of different unique patterns of impairments, it generates a large number of different syndromes. (Coltheart, 1984a, p. 370)

Following this logic (and see also Marshall, 1984), Howard and Franklin (1988) pointed out that, since their theory of language-processing contained 27 components (boxes or arrows), the number of possible syndromes according to this theory is $2^{27}-1$, which is a large number (2,220,075). If there are several million possible syndromes, the concept of syndrome will not be a useful one. Reasons for abandoning the concept of the syndrome were further spelled out by Caramazza (1984), Coltheart (1987), and Ellis (1987).

But if so, how does one generalize the findings from one patient to findings from another, if the two patients are not being treated as representative examples of the same syndrome?

> The generalizations do not take the form of claiming that there exists a single syndrome which many patients exhibit. Instead these generalizations take the form of claiming that there exists a single theory of the relevant cognitive system which can offer interpretations of the various sets of symptoms exhibited by various different patients. (Coltheart, 1984b, p. 6)

Hence,

> Even if every (dyslexic) patient exhibited a unique reading disorder, it might still be possible to interpret every patient's behaviour in the context of a single theory for reading. The assumption that a single theory should be applicable to all patients allows each new patient to be an appropriate source of data for testing the theory; and this permits one to generalize from previous to future patients even if one has rejected the policy of thinking in terms of syndromes. (Coltheart, 1984a, p. 371)

The moral is: When one is dealing with a domain of cognition about which nothing cognitive-neuropsychological is currently known, it is likely to be profitable to begin by seeking to define syndromes within that domain, just as Marshall and Newcombe (1973) did for reading. This will be a useful initial ground-clearing exercise which will provide the cognitive neuropsychologist with ideas about what kinds of distinctions are of relevance to this domain (words vs. nonwords and regular words vs. irregular words, for example). Such ideas can be used to develop a modular model of the functional architecture of the system responsible for performance in this cognitive domain. That's the point at which the syndrome approach has outlived its usefulness. From that point on, the job is to use data from individual patients, not groups of patients, to test that model and any other models which are also formulated.

COMMON CONCERNS

In this section I will discuss four worries about cognitive neuropsychology that people often articulate.

"Aren't these kinds of cases very rare?"

Certainly. But why is this a problem? What seems to be behind this question is the suggestion that, because a particular pattern of cognitive impairment is very rarely seen in the neuropsychology clinic, it is somehow unrepresentative of the population in general—that is, conclusions about how cognitive processing systems are organized in all of us that are reached on the basis of rarely-seen patterns of impairment are unsafe. However, such conclusions are safe if we make the following assumption: that the architecture of cognition is constant across people. This is the assumption of uniformity of functional architectures which was discussed earlier, where it was pointed out that *all* of cognitive psychology, not just cognitive neuropsychology, relies upon this assumption.

Naturally there will be individual differences in the contents and perhaps even the efficiencies of particular cognitive modules; all that is being assumed is that normal individuals who have been exposed to the same environments will possess the same set of cognitive modules.

"The case you reported is not a pure case; he had more than one impairment of the cognitive system in which you are interested"

One criticism levelled at the work of Marshall and Newcombe (1973) was that their cases were not pure examples of the reading syndromes they were defining. Take, for example, the dual-route theory of reading discussed earlier in this chapter. As was pointed out earlier, a person with an impairment affecting just of the orthographic lexicon in such a theory would be normal at nonword reading while being poor at reading irregular words: that is surface dyslexia. But the first surface dyslexics described in the literature (by Marshall & Newcombe, 1973) also had some impairment of nonword reading, though this was far less marked than their impairment of exception word reading. There are two ways of responding to this.

The first approach is to take the impurity of these cases as evidence against the theory (since the theory predicts that pure cases should exist) and even as evidence against the usefulness of the syndrome approach.

The second approach is to take the view that a brain lesion will in most cases affect a number of different cognitive processing systems (those whose anatomical loci are close together) even when the systems themselves are functionally distinct. Hence it will be rare to find patients whose lesion affects the lexical reading route but completely spares the nonlexical reading route. But it should be possible to find such patients, given enough patients, and patience.

This second approach turned out to be the correct one. Eventually, surface dyslexic patients with very impaired irregular word reading but normal nonword reading were found (Bub, Cancelliere, & Kertesz, 1985; McCarthy & Warrington, 1986)—that is, pure cases of surface dyslexia.

"If every patient is unique, how can you replicate your results?"

Consider what replication means in cognitive psychology. Suppose a cognitive psychologist reports, say, that high-frequency words yield shorter latencies than low-frequency words in a reading-aloud experiment. Another cognitive psychologist, interested in this finding, wants to be sure that it is true in general, rather than being confined just to the subjects, or just to the stimuli, used by the first investigator. So the second investigator chooses comparable but new sets of high-frequency and low-frequency words, and a comparable but new set of subjects, and carries out a reading-aloud experiment with these.

Now suppose a cognitive neuropsychologist were to report a patient with a severe impairment of semantic knowledge who was nevertheless normal at picture and object naming. This is something that has never been reported, so that, if it ever is, it will certainly immediately attract the attention of other cognitive neuropsychologists. The reason for this is that all current theories about how pictures and objects are named propose that the *only* route from a picture or object to its name is via its semantic representation. If that is so, every patient with an impairment of the semantic system must also have an impairment of picture and object naming. So the discovery of a patient with a semantic impairment but no impairment in naming pictures or objects would refute all existing theories of how pictures are named.

Any scientist would want to replicate a finding which is inconsistent with all relevant existing theories. So it is essential to consider what might count as replication in this context. The analogue here to replication as it is done in cognitive psychology might be thought of as: choosing a new but comparable patient and a new but comparable set of pictures or objects, and carrying out a naming experiment with these. But what is meant here by "comparable patient"? Certainly not just another patient with a semantic impairment. If one such patient were chosen, and proved completely unable to name pictures or objects, this would not be taken as a failure to replicate the study with the first patient, because the conclusion drawn from that first study was *not* that all patients with semantic impairments will have intact picture and object naming. It was that *some* patients with semantic impairments can have intact picture and object naming.

In fact, replication in this sense may sometimes be impossible in cognitive neuropsychology. Let's imagine that the relevant cognitive system is such that there is a pathway from pictures and objects to their names which bypasses semantics (that's why it is possible to name pictures and objects normally even when the semantic system is impaired). The neural realizations in the brain of this pathway and of the semantic system might be such that it is almost impossible for damage to the semantic system to spare the picture/object-to-name pathway. It happened with the first patient referred to here but may never happen again, in which case the result is literally unreplicable, no matter how genuine.

The way out here is to appeal to the assumption of uniformity of functional architecture across people. If one accepts that it has been demonstrated that this first patient possess a pathway from pictures/objects to names that bypasses semantics, and if the uniformity assumption is made, then it follows that all people have such a pathway, even if no subsequent patient is ever seen who is normal at picture and object naming but has a semantic impairment. Anyone who wanted to challenge the view that there is a pathway from pictures/object to names that bypasses semantics in all people would therefore either have to abandon the uniformity assumption or seek to show that there was something unreliable about the study on which this claim was based.

And here there's a different type of replicability which is relevant—within-patient rather than across-patient replicability. If a cognitive neuropsychologist noticed that, in a set of words given to a patient to read, words of Romance origin were read much better than words of Germanic origin, where the words were not chosen with that variable in mind, it would be poor science to take this as evidence that the reading system's performance is etymologically sensitive. At a minimum, one would select two sets of words, one set for each type of origin, matched on all the variables that are known to affect reading by people with acquired dyslexia, and administer these to the patient. If the remarkable etymological effect still occurred, a prudent investigator would anticipate scepticism and seek to head it off in advance by further studies seeking to replicate the effect with different word sets. While it is certainly true that spectacular findings of this kind in cognitive neuropsychology may not always have been adequately supported in this way, there is nothing about the discipline of cognitive neuropsychology which prevents such within-patient replications from being carried out, and they often are.

"Aren't these kinds of theories too powerful? Aren't they able to explain anything?"

This objection rests upon an ambiguity of the concept of "explaining everything." A theory which can explain *all logically possible data* is too powerful, because there is no possible observation which could refute it. But a theory which can explain *all so-far-observed data* is not too powerful; on the contrary, it is exactly what we want. Cognitive neuropsychologists grow their box-and-arrow diagrams because each new box or arrow is compelled by some new datum; to put this another way, if any box or any arrow were removed, some piece of data would no longer have an explanation. Thus the boxes and arrows are not added by whim; they are demanded by data.

And, in any case, the kinds of theories current in cognitive neuropsychology cannot explain all logically possible data. For example, the dual-route theory of reading aloud discussed elsewhere in this chapter would be instantly refuted by the discovery of a patient who is more successful at reading nonwords than regular words, because there is simply no way of damaging any component or components of that theory which would result in an impaired system that read nonwords better than regular words. And as discussed above, the theory of picture and object naming according to which mediation via semantics is obligatory, a theory which is currently accepted by all, would be instantly refuted by the discovery of a patient with intact picture and object naming but with a semantic impairment.

SUMMARY

Modular theorizing is widespread in contemporary cognitive psychology. In very many cognitive domains, cognitive psychologists develop theories about the system via which the cognitive activity in question is performed by proposing a modularly-organized functional architecture for that system. Such cognitive psychologists generally assume not only modularity, but also architectural uniformity: that is, they assume that any such architecture is uniform across all the people they might study (apart from merely quantitative individual differences, such as differences in vocabulary size, or differences in capacity of working memory, for example).

Any theory of this kind can be effectively tested by carrying out studies of people with acquired or developmental disorders of the relevant domain of cognition (that is, can be effectively investigated by cognitive neuropsychology), provided that a third and a fourth assumption are made. It needs to be assumed that the functional modules are also anatomically modular (allowing them to be susceptible to dissociations after brain damage), and it needs to be assumed that brain damage or abnormal development cannot add new modules, or new pathways of communication between modules: Abnormality must only take the form of impairing or deleting modules or pathways of the normal system. Unless both assumptions were at least approximately correct, nothing coherent would have emerged from cognitive-neuropsychological research—which is by no means the case, as the other chapters in this volume so clearly demonstrate.

REFERENCES

Beauvois, M. F., & Derouesné, G. (1979). Phonological alexia: three dissociations. *Journal of Neurology, Neurosurgery, and Psychiatry, 42,* 115–124.

Bub, D., Cancelliere, A., & Kertesz, A. (1985). Whole word and analytic translation of spelling-to-sound in a non-semantic reader. In K. E. Patterson, M. Coltheart, & J. C. Marshall (Eds.), *Surface dyslexia: Neuropsychological and cognitive studies of phonological reading* (pp. 15-34), London: Lawrence Erlbaum.

Caramazza, A. (1984). The logic of neuropsychological research and the problem of patient classification in aphasia. *Brain & Language, 21,* 9–20.

Coltheart, M. (1984a). Theoretical analysis and practical assessment of reading disorders. In Cornoldi, C. (Ed.), *Aspects of Reading and Dyslexia*. Padua, Italy: Cleup.

Coltheart, M. (1984b). Acquired dyslexias and normal reading. In Malatesha, R. N., & Whitaker, H. A. (Eds.), *Dyslexia: A Global Issue*. The Hague: Martinus Nijhoff.

Coltheart, M. (1987). Functional architecture of the language-processing system. In Coltheart, M., Sartori, G., & Job, R. (Eds.), *The cognitive neuropsychology of language*. London: Lawrence Erlbaum.

Coltheart, M. (1999). Modularity and cognition. *Trends in Cognitive Sciences, 3,* 115–120.

Coltheart, M., Inglis, L., Cupples, L., Michie, P., Bates, A. & Budd, B. (1998). A semantic subsystem specific to the storage of information about visual attributes of animate and inanimate objects. *Neurocase, 4,* 353–370.

Coltheart, M., Patterson, K., & Marshall, J. C. (Eds.) (1980). *Deep dyslexia*. London: Routledge & Kegan Paul.

Ellis, A. W. (1987). Intimations of modularity, or, the modelarity of mind: Doing cognitive neuropsychology without syndromes. In Coltheart, M., Sartori, G. & Job, R. (Eds), *The cognitive neuropsychology of language*. London: Lawrence Erlbaum.

Fodor, J. A. (1983). *The modularity of mind*. Cambridge, MA: MIT Press.

Howard, D., & Franklin, S. (1988). *Missing the meaning? A cognitive neuropsychological study of the processing of words by an aphasic patient*. Cambridge, MA: MIT Press.

Kay, J., Lesser, R., & Coltheart, M. (1992). *PALPA: Psycholinguistic Assessments of Language Processing in Aphasia*. Hove, UK: Lawrence Erlbaum.

Kean, M-L. (1977). The linguistic interpretation of aphasic syndromes. *Cognition, 5,* 9–46.

Marshall, J. C. (1984). Towards a rational taxonomy of the acquired dyslexias. In Malatesha, R. N. & Whitaker, H. A. (Eds.), *Dyslexia: A Global Issue*. The Hague: Marinus Nijhoff.

Marshall, J. C., & Newcombe, F. (1973). Patterns of paralexia: A psycholinguistic approach. *Journal of Psycholinguistic Research, 2,* 175–199.

McCarthy, R., & Warrington, E. K. (1986). Phonological reading: Phenomena and paradoxes. *Cortex, 22,* 359–380.

Patterson, K. E., & Kay, J. (1982). Letter-by-letter reading: Psychological descriptions of a neurological syndrome. *Quarterly Journal of Experimental Psychology, 34A,* 411–441

Patterson, K. E., Marshall, J. C., & Coltheart, M. (Eds.) (1985). *Surface dyslexia: Cognitive and neuropsychological studies of phonological reading*. Hove, UK: Lawrence Erlbaum.

Rapp, B,, Benzing, L., & Caramazza, A. (1995). The modality-specific representation of grammatical category. Paper presented at the 36th Annual Meeting of the Psychonomic Society, Los Angeles, CA

Riddoch, M. J., & Humphreys, G. W. (1993). *BORB: Birmingham Object Recognition Battery*. Hove, UK: Psychology Press.

Sartori, G., & Job, R. (1988). The oyster with four legs: A neuropsychological study on the interaction of visual and semantic information. *Cognitive Neuropsychology, 5,* 105–132

Shallice, T. (1988). *From Neuropsychology to Mental Structure*. Cambridge, UK: Cambridge University Press

Zurif, E., & Caramazza, A. (1976). Psycholinguistic structures in aphasia: Studies in syntax and semantics. In T. Whitaker & H. A. Whitaker (Eds), *Studies in Neurolinguistics, Vol 2*. New York: Academic Press.

2

A Historical Overview
of Contributions
From the Study of Deficits

Ola A. Selnes

INTRODUCTION

The history of our attempts to understand how the brain gives rise to mental activity can be divided into three major periods. During classical antiquity, the emphasis was not on specific cognitive functions but rather on the question of the localization of the soul (Cassano, 1996). The medieval period saw the development of a three-part model of cognition and was dominated by the ventricular localization theory (Schiller, 1997). The modern era of cortical localization is often considered to have begun with the work of Paul Broca (1861, 1863), but there were of course many antecedents to his discovery.[1]

This chapter will provide a brief overview of trends in the evolution of our understanding of how brain injury has provided insights into the structure of mental activity. Progress in the field of neuroscience has been characterized by discovery and rediscovery, and established theories of cognitive functions have often survived much longer than would have been predicted based on clinico-pathological evidence.

An obvious first step in understanding the process of how brain activity gives rise to cognition was to determine that the brain was actually the source of all mental activity. The earliest known proponent of the brain as the source of sensation and cognition was the Greek physician Alcmaeon (ca. 450 B.C.). He may also have been one of the earliest to practice anatomical dissection as a method for understanding the workings of the brain. Many of Alcmaeon's contemporaries preferred to think of the heart as the principal seat of intellectual functions, and this cardiocentric view persisted until Aristotle's time. A curious vestige of this view of cognition can still be found in everyday language, as when we refer to rote memoriza-

---

[1]Many excellent resources are available for the reader who is interested in more details of the history of cognitive neurology and neuropsychology. The comprehensive and richly illustrated text by Stanley Finger, covering the origins of the neurosciences from the earliest written works to the 20th century, is perhaps the gold standard for the field (Finger, 1994). Other excellent introductions to the history of neuroscience include Charles Gross' recent text *Brain, Vision, and Memory* (1998), the text by Marshall and Magoun (1998), and the classic text by R. M. Young (1970). In addition to these comprehensive works, there are many excellent reviews covering specific cognitive domains, such as Whitaker's review of neurolingusitics from the Middle ages to the premodern era (Benton & Joynt, 1960). An excellent review of the history of spatial abilities and topographical disturbances has beeen provided by J. Barrash (1998) and Boller and Grafman (1983) have reviewed the history of calculations deficits.

tion as "learning something by heart." Alcmaeon was principally interested in the senses, in particular vision. His views on cognitive functions are not known in any detail (Gross, 1998).

By far, the most explicit early proponent of the brain as the source of intellectual functions was Hippocrates (ca. 425 B.C.), who practiced medicine on the island of Cos. Unlike Alcmaeon, the Hippocratic physicians did not perform autopsies, and their knowledge of the anatomy of the brain was therefore less advanced. In his well-known essay on the "Sacred Disease," in which he discussed the causes of epilepsy, Hippocrates argued that the cause of this disorder is to be found in the brain, and he rejected the notion that seizures are due to supernatural or divine causes. In addition to discussing the role of the brain in disease, he also specified some of the normal functions in which the brain is involved:

> It ought to be generally known that the source of our pleasure, merriment, laughter, and amusement, as of our grief, pain, anxiety, and tears, is none other than the brain. It is specially the organ which enables us to think, see and hear, and to distinguish the ugly and the beautiful, the bad and the good, pleasant and unpleasant...It is the brain too which is the seat of madness and delirium, of the fears and frights which assail us, often by night, but sometimes even by day; it is there where lies the cause of insomnia and sleep walking, of thoughts that will not come, forgotten duties, and eccentricities. (Gross, 1998, p. 13)

The above quote contains no reference to speech and language functions, and little is known about Hippocrates' thoughts about the role of the brain in language. The following quote suggests that he may have thought of speech disorders as resulting from non-specific disease or perceptual problems: "Indistinctness of speech is caused either by disease or by defective hearing, or because before a thought is expressed, other thoughts arise; before words are spoken, other words are formed" (Adams, 1939).

To further emphasize the preeminence of the brain in mental functions, Hippocrates explicitly mentioned that neither the diaphragm nor the heart plays any role in cognition. Nonetheless, Aristotle (384 B.C.) persisted in his belief that the heart, not the brain, was the "seat and source of sensation." Aristotle, however, may have thought of the brain and heart as one system, in which the brain is not without function, but simply not as important as the heart (Gross, 1998). One reason why Aristotle did not revise his views may be explained by his lack of access to human cases suitable for clinico-pathological correlation. Unlike his predecessors, Alcmaeon and Hippocrates, who were both practicing physicians, Aristotle limited his inquiries to animal dissections.

The next event of great significance in the evolution of our understanding of the brain was the formation of the Museum of Alexandria. This institution, which was state-supported, was a continuation of Aristotle's Lyceum and provided the first opportunity for systematic study of human anatomy based on open dissection. Curiously, after this period of immense progress in the understanding of the anatomical structure of the human brain, dissection of human cadavers for medical or scientific purposes disappeared until the thirteenth century. On the basis of their studies of dissections of the human brain, the anatomists Herophilus (ca. 270 B.C.) and Erasistratus (260 B.C.) provided the first detailed descriptions of the ventricular system of the brain, and thus laid the groundwork for one of the most prominent and enduring theories of brain functioning, the cell doctrine (Gross, 1998).

Neither Herophilus nor Erasistratus left much information about their views on how cognition related to the cerebral ventricles. Herophilus reportedly assigned a primary role to the fourth ventricle, but it is unclear whether this was in reference to mental abilities or more basic life-sustaining functions. Erasistratus provided detailed descriptions of the convolutions of the brain, and compared the number of gyri in the human brain to those of several animals. He concluded, not surprisingly, that the human brain contained more convolutions and correlated this with higher intellectual functions in man versus animals. One of the most prominent figures of ancient medicine, Galen of Pergamon (129–199 B.C.) subsequently denounced this idea, apparently based on his observations that the donkey brain contained as many, if not more, convolutions as the human brain! Galen's point of view proved so influential that a significant role for the cerebral cortex in mental abilities was not resurrected until the work of Thomas Willis in the seventeenth century.

While Herophilus had prepared the anatomical foundation for the ventricular theory, the localization of cognition to the intraventricular spaces was not immediately accepted. Galen took an intermediate position. Although he did subscribe to the idea that cognitive functions could be divided into the three basic components of (a) sensory functions, (b) reasoning, and (c) memory, he was not very specific about the precise localization of these functions. He apparently preferred to localize the soul itself, the ultimate origin of the intellectual faculties, to some unspecified portion of the brain parenchyma. The instruments of the soul, the so-called animal spirits (*spiritus animalis*; animal is derived from *anima*, the soul), mediated cognitive functions using the fluid-filled cerebral ventricles as the intermediary between the non-material soul and the physical brain parenchyma. He apparently believed that the individual components of cognition could be affected separately by disease, but he did not assign a specific intraventricular localization for any of them. However, from his clinical observation, he considered the posterior ventricle to be the most important one for life-sustaining functions (Rocca, 1997) He remained noncommittal as to specifics of the anatomical correlates of cognition, and ridiculed the notion that the number of cortical gyri was an index of intelligence. By comparison with later phrenological studies attributing functional significance to quantity of cerebral tissue, he was clearly ahead of his time in his opinion that it was the *quality*, not the *quantity*, of the cerebrospinal fluid (psychic pneuma) that determined an individual's intellectual functioning.

THE CELL DOCTRINE

The pre-eminent model of the cognitive functions of the brain during medieval times was the so-called cell doctrine. According to this theory, the basic faculties of the mind are located in the ventricles, each being allocated to a specific ventricle. The lateral ventricles were treated as one, and referred to as the first ventricle (or cell). The second, or middle cell, corresponded to our third ventricle and the third cell corresponded to our fourth ventricle. The first cell received input from all of the sensory organs, and was commonly labeled *sensus communis* ("common sense"). As an aside, in contemporary neuropsychology, "common sense" is typically thought of as a frontal lobe type function. It is a curious coincidence that in traditional depictions of the cell doctrine, *sensus communis* is shown as being in the frontal lobes of the brain. The sensory input to the first cell formed the basis for image formation (*imaginativa* and *phantasia*). The second cell was the seat of general intellectual abilities, including reasoning (*ratio*), judgment (*aestimativa*), and thought (*cogitativa*). The third cell was devoted to memory functions (*memoria, reminiscentia*).

The most basic outline of the cognitive components of the cell doctrine is generally traced back to the Syrian Bishop Nemesius (born 340 A.D.) and St. Augustine (354–430 A.D.) This schema of cortical representation of cognitive functions was to become the predominant view until the end of the Renaissance, when major advances in knowledge of brain anatomy also brought advances on the cognitive front.

How did this curious model of brain functioning come about? Although the intraventricular transport of the animal spirits through cerebrospinal fluid has been likened to engineering accomplishments analogous to viaducts and aqueducts, the localization of cognitive functions to the ventricles was clearly inspired by other factors. Cognitive functions were the product of the noncorporeal soul, which according to most Christian writers could not be localized. The faculties or functions of the mind, however, were thought to be localizable. The fluid-filled ventricles were apparently thought of as a more suitable intermediary between the body and the noncorporeal soul than the material and earthy brain parenchyma itself. There were some attempts at clinico-pathological correlation, but these were directed more towards the question of which cognitive functions were affected by damage to which ventricle. It did not speak to the issue of whether cognitive changes could result from injury restricted to brain parenchyma as opposed to the ventricles. Nemesius wrote:

> The most convincing proof is that derived from studying the activities of the various parts of the brain. If the front ventricles have suffered any kind of lesion, the senses are impaired but the faculty of intellect continues as before. It is when the middle of the brain is affected that the mind is deranged, but then the senses are left in possession of their natural functions . . . If it is the cerebellum that is damaged, only loss of memory follows, while sensation and thought take no harm. (Translation in Telfer, 1955, pp. 341–342)

Although the basic tripartite view of cognition was never challenged, the interpretation of each component was subject to considerable variability. The attractiveness of a three-part model may also have been related to the tripartite conception of the soul.

THE TRANSITION TO MODERN TIMES

The transition from a ventricular to a cortical-based theory of brain functioning was fueled by two important events. The first was the extraordinary advance in the anatomical knowledge of the brain initiated by the studies of comparative anatomy by Andreas Vesalius of Padua (1514–1564). Vesalius expressed strong arguments against the ventricles playing a special role in mental functions. Because many animals had ventricular systems very similar to those of humans, he considered this conclusive evidence that the ventricles did not house the human soul. Nonetheless, in accordance with Emily Dickinson's principle that "Truth must dazzle gradually, lest it blind," Vesalius continued to subscribe to the notion of animal spirits. Furthermore, based on comparative studies, he agreed with Galen that the cerebral convolutions were not correlated with intelligence. Vesalius nonetheless provided some of the most extraordinarily detailed depictions of the cerebral cortex in man.

The second impetus for bringing mental functions back from the ventricles into the brain substance proper came from the works of Thomas Willis (1621–1675). In his beautifully illustrated monograph on the brain, *Cerebri Anatomie* (1664), he spelled out a role for the cortex in higher cognitive functions such as memory (Figure 2.1). Unlike his predecessors, Willis used comparative anatomy to argue *for* a specific role of the cerebral cortex in intellectual abilities:

> Hence, these folds or convolutions are far more numerous and rarer in man than in any other animal because of the variety and number of acts of the higher faculties, but they are varied by a disordered and almost haphazard arrangement so that the operations of the animal function might be free, changeable, and not limited to one. (Gross, 1998, p. 45)

Although Willis explicitly rejected the idea of the ventricles playing a special role, he maintained a solid link with the past by still referring to the animal spirits. Not much is known, however, in terms of Willis' more specific views on localization of cognitive functions. He apparently subscribed to the traditional Aristotelean division of cognitive functions into sensation, cognition, and memory. Interestingly, he localized "imagination" to the corpus callosum, a term that he used to refer to the bulk of the white matter rather than the interhemispheric commissure. The following quote illustrates how certain aspects of his theory of cognitive functions are still firmly anchored in the basic principles of the medieval cell doctrine:

> But here (if I may digress a little) we should inquire in what part of the Head the Ideas of sounds are left: whether only in the Brain, which is the Chest of Memory acquired as it were artificial; or

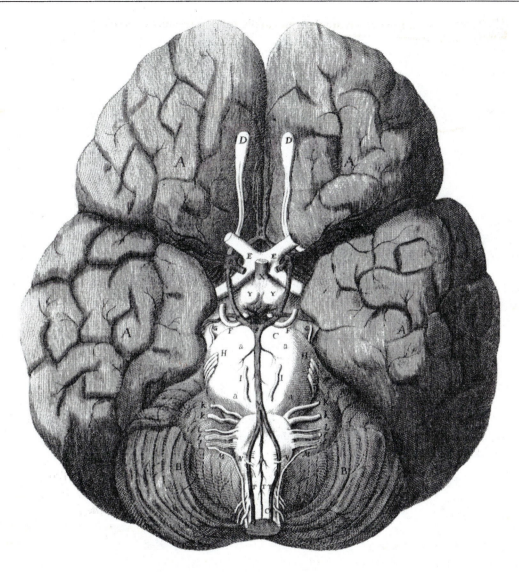

Figure 2.1. Illustration depicting the base of the brain from Willis' textbook. From *Cerebri Anatome* by T. Willis, T., 1664, p. 25. Copyright 1664 by Ja. Flesher. Reprinted with the permission of the Institute of the History of Medicine, The Johns Hopkins Hospital.

whether not also in the Cerebel, which is the place of natural memory? Truly we suppose, that sounds belong to both of these, as it were to distinct Store-houses. Every audible impulse being struck against the Ear, it is presently being carried by the passage of the auditory Process to the annulary protuberance; but from thence it is carried, as other sensible species, to the chambered bodies or the common Sensory; (which way it passes thither, shall be showed afterwards) this impression tending from thence farther, and also being delivered to the brain, stirs up the Imagination, and so leaves in its Cortex an image or private mark of it self for the Memory. Further also, as the auditory Process depends on the Cerebel, and receives from it the provision of the animal Spirits: so it is most likely, that by the recess of the same Spirits the Ideas of the Sounds are conveyed also to the Cerebel. (Willis, 1664, p. 118)

The terms hemispheres and lobes were also introduced by Willis. In addition, he described the fornix, and perhaps because of its thin, string-like appearance, assigns to it the unusual function of binding the brain together. Moreover, it also served the more important role of circulating the spirits from one end of the brain to the other. His writings also contain case histories of patients with right hemiparesis and aphasia, but not much is known in terms of his ideas of language functions were represented in the brain. Willis' (1664) proposed relocation of mental activities to the brain substance itself did not have an immediate impact, and it was not until the works of Franz Joseph Gall that serious attention was again focused on the cerebral cortex as the source of mental activities.

One cognitive domain that was conspicuously absent in the medieval cell doctrine was language. The reason for this omission is not entirely clear. Since there were no specific predictions for relating injury of the brain to speech and language symptoms, this may explain the paucity of reports devoted to clinico-pathological correlates of language disorders. As pointed out by Benton, a number of reports from the eighteenth century describe *symptoms* of speech and language impairment, but they are at best thought of as "allusions to different forms of aphasic disorder" rather than attempts to sort out the neuropathological correlates of speech and language syndromes. In keeping with the prevailing tripartite view of cognition, speech and language disorders were thought of as a subset of memory disorders. Thus, Johann Gesner (1738–1801) describes several cases of aphasia in a chapter entitled "Die Sprachamnesie" (amnesia for speech). The general interpretation of the underlying deficit in these cases of aphasia was that the association between ideas and their corresponding verbal labels or symbols had been forgotten or lost:

> Speaking and writing are functions of memory while reading and hearing are functions of ideation. . . . I look for the seat of amnesia for speech in the interior of the organs, less in their organization as determined by the senses, than in the physical relationships of their parts, and particularly in a sluggishness in these relationships which arises out of dryness or rigidity. (Benton, 1965, p. 58)

The reference to dryness and rigidity suggests that he subscribed to a fairly traditional ventricular localization theory. The quality of a person's memory was thought to depend on the proper balance of moisture and temperature of the third ventricle. The lack of the proper humoral balance was used to explain the loss of memory associated with old age: The very old were thought to be too dried out and too cold to be able to form "impressions" of memory (Theiss, 1997).

GALL AND FACULTY PSYCHOLOGY

Franz Joseph Gall (1758–1828) is generally credited with introducing the notion that different mental functions are located in different parts of the brain. As with most progress in the understanding of the brain's cognitive functions, Gall's theory combined some preexisting ideas with some new ones. The basic starting point of using features of the face or body to predict character and disposition was clearly inherited from physiognomy. The strikingly new idea, however, was the proposal that individual cognitive functions (or organs) were located in different parts of the brain. In addition, the degree of prominence or hypertrophy of a given region of the brain was indicative of how well developed its corresponding function was. This idea undoubtedly arose by analogy with other parts of the body, such as bones and muscles, where increased size was related to better function. Curiously, even in today's high tech conception of the brain, the notion that increased brain mass or other gross morphological features somehow reflects a functional "advantage" is alive and well (Foundas, Eure, Luevano, & Weinberger, 1998; Witelson, Kigar, & Harvey, 1999; Witelson, 1985). Gall further hypothesized that the external form of the brain reflected the underlying brain mass, thus giving rise to the palpable bumps that were used to "localize" functions.

While Gall's phrenological system represented a conceptual quantum leap by assigning individual cognitive functions to different regions of the cerebral cortex, it is noteworthy that he does not entirely sever the links with the old cell doctrine. For example, on most phrenological maps, certain sensory functions (e.g., form, size, weight, and color) are located in the general area of the *sensus communis* from the cell doctrine. Gall also incorporated faculties that clearly overlap with the reasoning and memory functions from the cell doctrine. What is new, however, is that Gall introduced some cognitive functions, such as language and calculations, which up until his time had not enjoyed a separate representation in the brain. Gall recognized two different aspects of language: memory for words (or, word-finding) and the faculty of spoken language, localized to distinct but adjacent regions of the orbital frontal lobes. Unfortunately, he also confounded the picture enormously by including a variety of ill-defined personality traits, such as firmness, amativeness (connubial love), adhesiveness (love of friends), combativeness (self-defense, love for discussion), destructiveness, secretiveness, and hope. Less than a handful of the proposed faculties were actually concerned with specific cognitive functions. It is thus paradoxical that although Gall made multiple contributions to advancing the knowledge of the anatomy of the brain, his concept of cognitive domains and their fractionation were in many ways inferior to the system already in place from antiquity. As noted by Brown and Chobor (1992), if Gall had limited his inquiry of the localization of mental faculties to language, and had not gone on to describe 25 other poorly specified functions, he may well have enjoyed a more respectable place in the history of cognition. As is well known, Gall's scientifically based cranioscopy eventually evolved into parlor games and quackery, and was gradually replaced by a system of cortical localization that was focused on broader cognitive domains rather than poorly defined personality traits. The British Phrenological Society, however, was not disbanded until 1967!

AN INTERLUDE IN VERMONT

The now famous case of Phineas Gage represents an interesting transition between the phrenological school and more modern localization of cognitive functions. The story of the 25-year-old construction foreman who miraculously survived a work-related accident in which his frontal lobes were penetrated by a 3-foot long, 13-pound iron rod, continues to attract scientific interest and attention (Damasio, Grabowski, Frank, Galaburda, & Damasio, 1994; Neylan, 1999) After the accident with the tamping iron in 1849, Gage eventually recovered his former physical strength, but his personality was markedly altered. Before the accident, he had been described as efficient and highly capable, but after the accident, he was characterized by his treating physician (Dr. Harlow) as unreliable, socially inappropriate, and disrespectful of the feelings of others. There was, however, a striking paucity of cognitive deficits. This was interpreted by some as evidence against the phrenological position. Since the tamping iron had clearly destroyed major portions of his frontal lobes, several of the phrenological faculties, such as language, musical talent, comparative sagacity, would have been expected to be impaired. The absence of specific deficits was thus thought to be consistent with the more prevalent view according to which all parts of the brain were equipotential. Henry J. Bigelow, who was Professor of surgery at Harvard University at the time, was initally so reluctant to accept the facts of this case that he paid for Gage and his physician to travel to Boston. Bigelow had spent some time in Paris, and had been influenced by the antilocalizationist views of one of his teachers, Professor Longet. In his presentation of the case to the Boston Society for Medical Improvement on December 11, 1848, Bigelow frequently emphasized the intactness of Gage's mental status. In a later publication, he stated "It is well known that a considerable portion of the brain has been in some cases abstracted without impairing its function. Atrophy of an entire cerebral hemisphere has also been recorded" (Barker, 1995), making reference to the fact that certain parts of the brain are known to be dispensable. Dr. Harlow, who had been exposed to phrenological teachings, was intrigued by the possibility of finding some tangible evidence of alterations in personality or cognition as a result of Gage's severe brain injury. The only example of a cognitive deficit mentioned in his initial report is that of "estimation" or calculations, a faculty that Gall had located in the frontal lobes (Harlow, 1848). The evidence for a deficit of numbers was based on relatively informal observation, however:

> He keeps the day of the week and time of day, in his mind. Says he knows more than half of those who inquire after him. Does not estimate size or money accurately, though he has memory as perfect as ever. He would not take $100 for a few pebbles which he took from an ancient river bed where he was at work. (p. 392)

In the absence of any evidence of language impairment, or deficits of musical abilities, Harlow thus chose to interpret Gage's cognitive impairment as a poor sense of comparison and numbers. He elaborated on his observations of the changes in Gage's personality and mental state in a second publication (Harlow, 1868) which did not attract much attention until about ten years later. At that time, the English neurophysiologist Dr. David Ferrier was alerted to the case, and incorporated Dr. Harlow's findings in his Goulstonian lectures to support his theory of cerebral localization. Ferrier proposed that the frontal lobes were involved in supervisory or executive functions, and used the reported alterations in Mr. Gage's personality to illustrate how injury to the frontal lobes can result in behavioral changes that are not evident from either sensory or motor examination. Ferrier was rather taken back by the conflicting interpretations of the medical facts of the case of Mr. Gage, and recommends therefore revisiting the original source of the data:

> In investigating the reports of diseases and injuries of the brain I am constantly being amazed at the inexactitude and distortion to which they are subjected by men who have some pet theory to support. The facts suffer so frightfully that I feel obliged always to go to the fountain-head—dirty and muddy though this frequently turns out. (Barker, 1995, p. 680)

An aspect of the story of Phineas Gage which is often omitted from contemporary descriptions is that he recovered sufficiently well to travel to Chile where he was gainfully employed for a number of years as a stage coach driver. Because of worsening health problems, he eventually returned to America, and died in San Francisco, presumably from complications of seizures, in 1860. Only one year after his death, a new chapter in the history of neuroscience would begin.

PAUL BROCA AND THE FACULTY OF LANGUAGE

It is now well known that although Broca presented the pivotal cases that eventually proved that nonfluent aphasia is associated with left anterior lesions, the groundwork for his discovery was already laid. In particular, the work of Jean-Baptiste Bouillaud (1796–1881) deserves special mention. Bouillaud's views of aphasia clearly bridge the gap between the traditional view of aphasia as an amnestic disorder and aphasia as a speech and language disorder (Bouillaud, 1825). He refers to the amnestic part as "internal speech" and the articulatory part as "external speech." Bouillaud also presented the first systematic clinico-pathological data supporting a relationship between aphasia and lesions involving the anterior parts of the brain. His ideas were thought to be influenced too much by the prevailing phrenological winds, and they were therefore not readily accepted by the scientific community. Bouillaud eventually changed his mind regarding phrenology, and described it as a pseudoscience. It is noteworthy, however, that he recognized that other scientific endeavors had also had their roots in pseudoscience:

That the science of Gall or, as you call it phrenology, . . . is . . . in some respects a pseudoscience . . . I will agree willingly. I add that here is a point of resemblance between it and the most true sciences of our day such as astronomy, physics, chemistry, experimental and rational physiology itself. Actually, what were these sciences at their birth and the beginning of their evolution? They were pseduosciences under the names of astrology, magic, alchemy . . . (Cole, & Cole, 1971, p. 122)

Bouillaud forced the issue of cortical localization of speech by offering a prize of 500 francs to anyone who could produce a patient with a significant lesion of the frontal lobes of the brain with no disturbance of speech. The prize was eventually claimed by the well-known surgeon Alfred Velpeau in May of 1865, for a patient who had a bilateral frontal lobe injury but no aphasia!(Schiller, 1992).

In the midst of the ongoing localization debate in Parisian scientific and medical circles, Paul Broca was focused on his interests in anthropology, and founded the Anthropological Society in May of 1859. He initially remained a neutral observer to the language localization debate, but his encounter with patient Leborgne (Tan) was to change that (Broca, 1861). Although it is not entirely clear why this case and Broca's subsequent case, Lelong, had such an immediate impact, they undoubtedly changed the course of neuroscience. Finger attributes the impact of Broca's first case to several factors, including the amount of detail in the description of the patient's speech deficit, the careful localization of the brain lesion, which did not correspond to the phrenological localization of speech, and the general respect for Broca as a scientist and physician (Finger, 1994).

From a contemporary clinico-pathological point of view, however, both of Broca's early cases were highly unsuitable for proving much of anything about brain–language relationships (Mohr, et al., 1999). Patient Tan suffered loss of speech at the age of 30, and the exact time course (sudden versus gradual onset) is not known. It is believed that he was admitted to Bicêtre about three months after the onset of his symptoms. About 10 years later, he began to develop a gradual hemiparesis of his right arm. This was followed by gradual weakness of his right leg, and eventually he became unable to walk. By the time Broca examined him, he had been bed-bound for a number of years and 21 years had passed since the onset of his symptoms. The mysterious etiology of patient Tan's neurological disorder notwithstanding, it is also paradoxical that his speech symptoms today would be considered more consistent with global than with Broca's aphasia (Selnes & Hillis, in press).

Broca's second case, Lelong, is referred to by MacDonald Critchley as a "crippled dement," and there is little doubt that patient Lelong, who was 84 years old, may have suffered from a degenerative condition (Critchley, 1960, p. 135). Thus, when considering the rather obvious limitations of Broca's first two cases, it is even further tribute to his scholarship that he turned them into the very foundation on which the theory of localized cortical functions was constructed.

In addition to Broca's attention to the actual evidence at hand, he also provided a very carefully worded opinion concerning the relationship between language and articulate language, and he defined very precisely what it was that he attempted to localize. In this respect, he expands on the groundwork laid by Bouillaud in his discussions of external versus internal speech. Broca devotes the first half of his paper on Tan to a theoretical discussion of speech and language.

There are, in fact several kinds of language. Every system of science which permits to express ideas in a manner more or less intelligible, more or less complete, more or less rapidly is a language in a more general sense of the word. Thus, the speech, mimetics, finger language, figurative writing, phonetic writing, etc. are so many kinds of languages. There is a general faculty of language which governs all these expressions of thought and which can be defined as the faculty to establish a constant relationship between an idea and a sign, whether this sign is a sound, gesture, a figure or some kind of trace. (von Bonin, 1960, p. 50)

Having provided this general definition of the faculty of language, Broca went on to argue that specific components of language, such as articulate speech, can be impaired by a cerebral lesion while the general faculty of language is left intact. He considered this "a sufficiently important symptom" that it deserves its own name, and he refered to it as "aphemia."

> What is missing in these patients is only the faculty to articulate word; they hear and understand all that is said to them, they have all their intelligence and they emit easily vocal sounds. . . . Their vocabulary, if one can use that word, is composed of a short series of syllables, sometimes a monosyllable which expresses everything or rather nothing, for this unique word is most often a stranger to all vocabularies. (von Bonin, 1960, p. 51)

It is clear that from this brief description, which is meant to be representative of aphasic speech characteristics in general, that Broca generalizes from his observation of a single patient: patient Tan. His emphasis on the preservation of comprehension is consistent with the general belief of the time that lack of comprehension was related to a defect of intelligence, not language *per se*. He concludes with the following succinct description to characterize patients with aphemia:

> What they [have] lost is therefore not the faculty of language, is not the memory of the words, nor is it the action of nerves and of muscles of phonation and articulation, but something else. It is a particular faculty considered by M. Bouillaud to be the faculty to coordinate the movements which belong to articulate language, or simpler, it is the faculty of articulate language; for without it, no articulation is possible. (von Bonin, 1960, p. 52)

Thus, Broca provides a description of a syndrome that corresponds largely to the contemporary terms aphemia or anarthria (Lebrun, 1982). Initially, he remained convinced that language functions were entirely normal in cases such as his own Tan. It was only in his later publications that Broca indicated that components of language, such as auditory comprehension, if carefully assessed, were also impaired. However, he did not anticipate Carl Wernicke's (1874) discovery that lesions of the posterior areas of the brain could result in relatively selective impairment of auditory comprehension.

Broca clearly had a sense of the importance of his discovery. In order not to alter the evidence, he chose not to slice the brain, and instead deposited the intact brains of Tan and Lelong in the Duputryen Museum. The brain of Tan temporarily disappeared, but was subsequently recovered. Although there has been some controversy concerning the catalog number, it is assumed that the correct brain is still available (Schiller, 1992). It has been CT-scanned, and the extent of the lesion confirmed (Signoret, Castaigne, Lhermitte, Abelanet, & Lavorel, 1984). In yet another attempt to re-examine the etiology of patient Tan's progressive neurological illness, the brain was recently (1999) also subjected to an MRI, but the results have not yet been published. The foot of the third frontal convolution was apparently first referred to as "Broca's area" by David Ferrier (Young, 1970, p. 243).

Although Broca's theory concerning the anatomical correlates of nonfluent aphasia was severely criticized by a number of subsequent investigators, most notably Pierre Marie, it has nonetheless stood the test of time. The basic tenet of a motor aphasia caused by a lesion limited to Broca's area became so entrenched in neurological thinking that numerous well-documented exceptions to this dictum were largely ignored. It demonstrates rather convincingly that a well-developed hypothesis or theoretical construct, in particular one with considerable face validity, can withstand the force of new clinico-pathological evidence. Thus, what lesions of the brain teach us about cognition is, and almost certainly will continue to be for some unforeseeable time, more influenced by prevailing theory than by the clinico-pathological evidence itself.

An example of how Broca's basic hypothesis persisted essentially unchanged until modern times is the following quote from Benson, summarizing results from a study originally published in 1967 (Benson, 1967). His conclusions were based on radioisotope scan findings from 100 patients classified as having fluent or nonfluent aphasia:

> The results were almost absolute. Patients classified as nonfluent had a locus of pathology anterior to Rolando's fissure (central sulcus) while those considered fluent had pathology posterior to this demarcation. This demonstration was neither radical nor unexpected; in fact, it agrees entirely with observations and predictions Wernicke published in 1874. Broca aphasia typically indicates structural damage in the posterior-inferior frontal lobe, Wernicke aphasia in the posterior-superior temporal region and conduction aphasia most often follows damage somewhere in the posterior perisylvian region, between the two areas. (Benson, 1979; Tross & Hirsch, 1988)

With the benefit of hindsight, when examining the actual data on which these conclusions were based, one may not be as convinced that these cases had lesions consistent with the "classical" theory of Broca's area. Benson's conclusions were based on the now out-dated technology of radioisotope scans, but this may not be the only explanation why his results did not result in a revision of classical theory of localization of aphasia syndromes. Rather, it may have been because the basic notion of a frontal lobe localization of nonfluent aphasia was close enough to being correct. Therefore, at the time of Benson's study there appeared to be no compelling reason to question the basic idea that a lesion of Broca's area is necessary and sufficient to produce the syndrome of Broca's aphasia. Nevertheless, if one inspects the actual figures accompanying Benson's paper, it appears that the actual data may well foreshadow the revision of the localization of Broca's aphasia offered by J. P. Mohr only 11 years later (Mohr, et al., 1999). In Figure 2.2, the center of the radioisotope identified lesions for patients with nonfluent aphasia

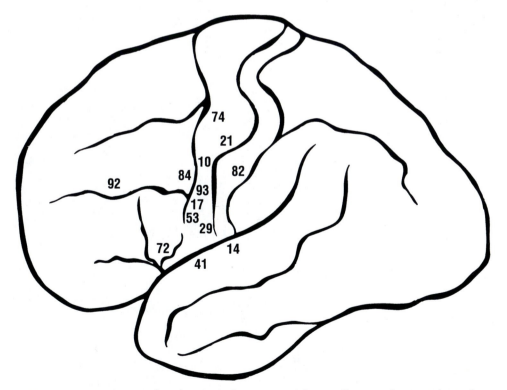

Figure 2.2. Brain scan localization of patients with non-fluent aphasia. Adapted from "Fluency in Aphasia," by D. F. Benson, 1967, *Cortex*, 3, pp. 373–394. Copyright 1967 by Oxford University Press. Reprinted with permission.

cluster at the motor strip, not in the pre-motor or Broca's area. Only three of the nonfluent patients had lesions anterior to the motor strip, and the same number of patients had lesions posterior to the central sulcus (Benson, 1967). Thus, this is another example of how classical theory often prevails, even in the presence of new findings that may not be entirely consistent with it.

What stimulated Mohr to re-examine the basic hypothesis of Broca's area aphasia? Although the availability of the new technique of computed tomography (CT) clearly played a role, Mohr also references a large number of cases documented by autopsy that were inconsistent with the idea that a lesion limited to the foot of the third frontal convolution results in the syndrome of Broca's aphasia. Mohr's findings from his own series of 22 cases with Broca's aphasia demonstrated that lesions limited to Broca's area itself did not result in persistent aphasia. Rather, the lesion associated with chronic, persistent Broca's aphasia extended beyond the boundaries of the third frontal convolution to include the fronto-parietal operculum and insula. Would Broca have been surprised by these findings? Perhaps not. In making reference to the beautiful drawings accompanying Foville's anatomical text (Figure 2.3)—he considered the following possibility in his 1863 paper: "Instead of being exclusively localized in the posterior portion of the third frontal convolution, might the seat of articulate speech not extend to the inferior parietal convolution, which is directly continuous with it" (Broca, 1863, p. 207).

CONDUCTION APHASIA

An even more striking example of how an attractive and intuitively plausible hypothesis may prevail even in the absence of substantive clinico-pathological data comes from the story of

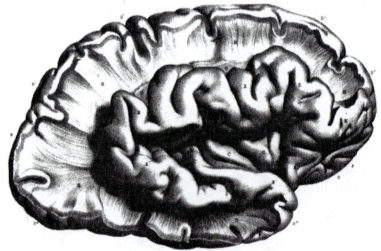

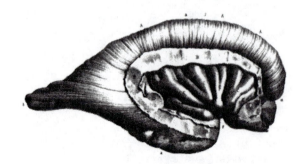

Figure 2.3. Illustration showing the region of the insula from Foville's textbook. From *Traite Complet de l'anatomie* by A. L. Foville, 1844, leaf II. Reprinted with the permission of the Institute of the History of Medicine, The Johns Hopkins Hospital.

conduction aphasia. The syndrome of conduction aphasia is currently defined as disproportionate impairment of repetition in the setting of fluent paraphasic speech and relatively normal comprehension. The underlying mechanism of this disorder is widely believed to be related to damage to pathways interconnecting Wernicke's and Broca's area, principally the arcuate fasciculus (Geschwind, 1965). Although there has never been compelling clinical or anatomical evidence in support of this model, the basic concept has nonetheless survived.

First introduced by Carl Wernicke, in his monograph on the symptom-complex of aphasia, the syndrome of conduction aphasia was conceptualized as resulting from an interruption of the white matter tracts that connect the language comprehension area in the superior temporal lobe with the speech production area of the frontal lobe (Wernicke, 1874). Thus barely 15 years after Broca had provided convincing evidence for a localized cortical representation of language, Wernicke introduced the brand new concept that not only is there more than one speech area, but that a unique language impairment can result from interrupting the white matter connections between these areas. Surprisingly, Wernicke did not include impaired repetition as part of the clinical characterization of conduction aphasia, but emphasized instead the paraphasic errors in speech and the intact auditory comprehension. Of the ten cases of aphasia described in his monograph, two were examples of conduction aphasia. Neither one of them came to autopsy, but Wernicke hypothesized that the white matter tract connecting the posterior and anterior speech centers ran through the insula.

Lichtheim is often credited with expanding the concept of conduction aphasia, in that he pointed out that the paraphasic errors that occur in spontaneous speech are also present when the patient attempts to repeat. As noted by De Bleser and colleagues, however, Lichtheim's description of conduction aphasia did not in fact include any reference to a specific deficit of repetition (De Bleser, Cubelli, & Luzzatti, 1993). An autopsy of Lichtheim's (1885) case of a laborer with conduction aphasia was thought to support the notion that the connection between the frontal and temporal lobe speech areas passed through the insular region.

The concept of conduction aphasia was also discussed by Sigmund Freud, in his largely overlooked monograph, On Aphasia, originally published in 1891 (Freud, 1953). During the first year after its publication, 142 copies were sold. Freud's interest in aphasia came largely from spending some time with Charcot in Paris in 1886 (Henderson, 1992). In his treatment of conduction aphasia, Freud introduced a brand new concept: the selective impairment of repetition of meaningful as opposed to nonmeaningful speech. He argued that, in the models of conduction aphasia proposed by Wernicke and Lichtheim, repetition of nonmeaningful speech should not be possible. Freud remained convinced, however, that such a selective impairment would not be observed:

> The faculty of repeating is never lost as long as speaking and understanding are intact. It is absent only if (1) there is no speech at all, or (2) hearing is impaired. (p. 11)

Freud then went on in that same paper to reject the idea that a lesion of pathway or connection by itself can cause aphasia:

> Our considerations have led us to attribute a certain clinical type of speech disorder to a change in the functional state of the speech apparatus rather than a localized interruption of a pathway." (p. 29)

In his revised edition of the *Symptom Complex of Aphasia* published in 1906, Wernicke incorporated the inability to repeat as part of the syndrome of conduction aphasia (Wernicke, 1874). He now also distinguished between repetition of meaningful speech and nonmeaningful speech, but surprisingly, he did not quote Freud:

> Further proof will be the ability to repeat meaningless words or word sequences, for example, those borrowed from a completely foreign language. If there were a case in which only this form of

repetition would be destroyed in the context of spared language comprehension and production and if paraphasia is associated with the retained ability to judge the misselections, I would believe that the requirements for a paradigm would be clinically satisfied. I must, however, emphasize that the anatomoclinical reports available (of exclusive or predominant insular lesion) are not appropriate to support the conduction aphasia I postulated. (De Bleser et al., 1993)

Wernicke abandoned the idea that the pathway between the posterior and anterior speech areas went through the insular region, and instead hypothesized that the lesion responsible for the syndrome of conduction aphasia would include the more posterior arcuate fasciculus. Although there was at best only circumstantial evidence to support this interpretation, there was nonetheless a certain inherent plausibility. Remarkably, the notion that a lesion of the arcuate fasciculus is responsible for the symptoms of conduction aphasia has survived until present times, and has become neurological dogma. It was revived by Konorksi in 1961 who presented a paper at the International Neurological Congress in Rome. This presentation sparked the interest of Norman Geschwind, who subsequently included conduction aphasia as one of many examples of so-called "disconnexion" syndromes (Geschwind, 1965).

In light of the paucity of systematic clinico-pathological evidence in support of the arcuate fasciculus hypothesis of repetition disorders, it is rather surprising how resistant this idea has been to revision. There are numerous cases of impaired repetition in which the arcuate fasciculus was not involved (Green & Howes, 1977), and conversely, there are cases of documented lesions of the arcuate fasciculus with no repetition impairment (Shuren et al., 1995; Pujol, Bello, Deus, Marti-Vilalta, & Capdevila, 1997). Cases of persistent conduction aphasia secondary to a lesion presumed to be limited to the arcuate fasciculus are rare, but have been reported (Tanabe et al., 1987; Arnett, Rao, Hussain, Swanson, & Hammeke, 1996). Nonetheless, there are no known cases of conduction aphasia in which autopsy-confirmed lesions are limited to the arcuate fasciculus. What is even more puzzling is how little work has been done to confirm the anatomical realities of the proposed connection between Wernicke's area and Broca's area. Recent studies by Petrides and colleagues suggests that it is only the posterior third of Wernicke's area that is connected via the arcuate fasciculus. The bulk or anterior two thirds of Wernicke's area is connected through the insula (Petrides & Pandya, 1988).

The history of conduction aphasia thus suggests that an attractive, or intuitively plausible theory will prevail even in presence of new evidence that is inconsistent with the theory. Studies like those of Pujol and colleagues also demonstrate a new era in clinico-pathological correlations. Until recently, typically only patients with symptoms of aphasia or other cognitive disorders were being investigated. Patients without symptoms do not routinely receive imaging studies, and it is therefore not known how often a small lesion of, for example, the insula may be unaccompanied by any obvious symptoms of aphasia or cognitive impairment. The widespread routine availability of MRI for conditions such as headaches, multiple sclerosis, connective tissue disorders, and others has made it possible to observe, for the first time, lesions unaccompanied by cognitive symptoms. The incidence of so-called silent infarcts depends on the study population, but has been reported to be as high as 28% in some populations (Price et al., 1997). These kinds of studies thus represent a potential source of valuable clinico-pathological information that until very recently has not been utilized.

The transition from classical localization theory to more contemporary views of cortical representation of higher cortical functions was a gradual one. The seeds of more current points of view had already been planted by Hughlings Jackson, who published his first paper on aphasia only 3 years after Broca's seminal observations. Jackson did not regard speech and language functions as being localized to specific areas of the brain, and cautioned against contemporary tendencies of defining function as the reciprocal of the impairment resulting from a lesion. Although there were some champions of Jackson's points of view, most of his contemporaries may not have fully understood his ideas (Critchley & Critchley, 1998). Some of the more notable proponents of the Jacksonian point of view included Freud, Marie, Head, and Goldstein (Wallesch & Bartels, 1996). Marie argued for a single type of aphasia, resulting from an underlying intellectual disturbance. In a similar vein, Goldstein argued for a loss of abstract attitude as the common denominator underlying all language and cognitive deficits.

Benton cites the publication of Weisenburg and McBride's 1935 book describing the performance of aphasic patients on tests on nonverbal intelligence as the transition to the "modern period" (Benton, 1981, p. 16) Coincidentally, this is also the year that Ward Halstead established the first laboratory of neuropsychology, dedicated to the systematic study of the behavioral and cognitive correlates of brain injury (Reitan, 1994). Weisenburgh and McBride compared the performance of a group of aphasic patients with that of patients with unilateral lesions but no aphasia, as well as a group of controls. They observed that although many of the aphasic patients were also impaired on tests of nonverbal cognition, others were not. They concluded, therefore, that aphasia by itself does not necessarily entail generalized nonverbal cognitive impairment, as had been argued by Marie and others (Marie, 1906). Research on recovery from aphasia continued to flourish after the second World War, and the comprehensive observations on recovery of aphasia after traumatic brain injury was published by the Russian neurologist and psychologist Luria in 1947 (Luria, 1947).

The birth of neurolinguistics is often traced back to the writings of Roman Jacobson, who published his monograph on child language and aphasia in 1941 (Benton, 1981). The work of Geschwind and his writings on disconnection syndromes in animals and man two decades later rekindled interest in the classical Wernicke-Lichtheim models of aphasia, and emphasized the concept of neural disconnection to explain conditions like apraxia, transcortical aphasia, and conduction aphasia (Geschwind, 1965). Neuropsychological studies during this period continued to be influenced by behavioral neurology and the quest for cognitive symptoms or syndromes of localizing significance. Despite the rather limited evidence in support of the localizing value of some of these syndromes, such as the famous Gerstman syndrome, they nonetheless remain firmly entrenched in neurological teaching (Benton, 1992).

The availability of computed tomography inspired large group studies of the lesion correlates of the classical aphasia syndromes (Tognola & Vignolo, 1980; Naeser & Palumbo, 1994). Because of the known heterogeneity of aphasia syndromes, and because only 30–40% of patients with aphasia could be classified, there was a gradual shift away from the focus on syndromes to the study of individual components of language. Rather than investigating the time course and patterns of recovery of patients meeting criteria for the syndrome of Wernicke's aphasia, recovery of more specific aspects of language, such as auditory comprehension, became the focus of investigation (Selnes, Niccum, Knopman, & Rubens, 1984). The influence of psycholinguistics on aphasia research became more apparent, and there were attempts to recast the traditional aphasia syndromes in terms of their principal grammatical or syntactic features. Thus, patients with Broca's aphasia were found to have deficits of sentence comprehension which mirrored their asyntactic output, and were therefore characterized as being "agrammatic" (Caramazza, Berndt, Basili, & Koller, 1981).

The 1970s and 1980s saw the growth of cognitive approaches to the study of brain functions. There was a move away from large scale group studies to more detailed investigations of individual patients. Rather than averaging results across 30 patients with left hemisphere lesions, for example, the results of multiple trials in an individual patient were analyzed to test predictions of a given model of the cognitive behavior under study (Caramazza, 1986). Thus, the traditional deficit measurement approach of clinical neuropsychology was supplemented by a new, cognitive approach. The tradition of clinical neuropsychology originating with Halstead and Reitan had started out as a method for differentiating "organic" from "psychiatric" deficits. With the development of modern imaging, this was no longer a useful question, and clinical neuropsychology focused instead on the characterization and objective measurement of various cognitive deficits. Although the goals of these evaluations were often pragmatic clinical issues such as prediction of recovery and planning for rehabilitation, there were at the same time explicit attempts to use these findings to test hypotheses concerned with normal brain-behavior relationships.

The origins of cognitive neuropsychology occurred in the context of more widespread interest in the field of general cognitive science. The journal *Cognitive Psychology* was started in 1970 and was followed by the *Cognitive Science* journal in 1977. In that same year, a meeting to discuss deep dyslexia was convened in Oxford, and this is often considered by many to be a convenient marker for the early beginnings of cognitive neuropsychology (E. Saffran, personal communication, 2000). The book *Deep Dyslexia* (Coltheart, Patterson, & Marshall, 1980) which resulted from this conference is considered by many to be the first major book that deals with the cognitive approach to neuropsychology. The journal *Cognitive Neuropsychology* was first published in 1984. Cognitive neuropsychologists, many of them with backgrounds in psycholinguistics and experimental psychology, began to use data from patients with acquired cognitive impairments in a radically different fashion (Coltheart, 1982; Saffran & Marin, 1977; Shallice & Coughlan, 1980; Warrington & Shallice, 1984). The purpose of the investigation was no longer to localize or quantify the nature of the deficit, but rather to treat the cognitive impairment as an experimental condition (induced by nature) suitable for probing specific hypotheses relevant to normal cognitive processing mechanisms. Thus, the exact nature, size, localization, or lateralization of the lesion was no longer the focus of the study. The question was not what part of the brain is responsible for the deficit or the function, but rather what can the nature of cognitive deficit reveal about issues like modularity and units of processing in the complex architecture of normal cognition. As a consequence, even data from patients with no focal lesion, such as for example. Alzheimer's disease, could be used to explore associations and dissociations of functions (Robinson, Rossor, & Cipolotti, 1999).

In tracing the roots of cognitive neuropsychology, Graves notes that there are clearly similarities between the early Wernicke-Lichtheim models (without the anatomical labels) and more current cognitive neuropsychology models, such as the model for recognition and production of spoken words proposed by Ellis and Young (Ellis & Young, 1988). Although the details of the models are obviously different, they are similar in that they both represent components of cognitive processes as interconnected modules. Although the nature of the interconnections are left unspecified in contemporary models, they are perhaps a reminder of the still powerful influences of previous concepts of disconnection in contemporary models of cognition (Graves, 1997).

Progress in science often depends on increasing accuracy of measurements or observations. In the case of brain-behavior correlations, there has been an expectation that increasingly greater detail and image quality of methods such as MRI and PET would eventually lead to more answers. Technological advances by themselves are, however, unlikely to provide major new insights into the neural architecture of human cognition. Nonetheless, newer techniques such as magnetic resonance spectroscopy (MRS) and functional magnetic resonance imaging (fMRI) can now begin to address the question of which brain regions are active participants in specific cognitive operations in neurologically intact individuals, and thus supplement the classical "deficit" measurement approach. Functional magnetic resonance imaging relies on the general principle that changes in neuronal activity is also associated with regional deoxyhemoglobin changes. However, the inter-relationships between mental activity, neuronal activity, and blood flow are complex, and these newer imaging techniques still face methodological challenges to establish the range of their validity in single subject clinical or research applications. The somewhat extravagant claims of some early fMRI findings have already prompted some investigators to emphasize the need for rigorous methodological scrutiny to prevent these imaging methods from becoming the phrenology of the twentieth century (Cohen, 1996; Nemeroff, Kilts, & Berns, 1999).

This brief historical overview has traced only a narrow path through the fascinating history of cognitive neuroscience. The last couple of decades has brought significant progress in understanding the neurological substrates of cognitive functions such as language, but contemporary textbooks nonetheless lag behind. The idea that language is subserved by two small areas of the left hemisphere, one in the frontal lobe and the other in the temporal lobe, interconnected by a fasciculus, is clearly no longer tenable (Damasio, 1997). Newer findings support the idea that multiple additional brain regions are active participants in language and other cognitive functions, without necessarily being "specialized" just for language processing. Areas such as the supplementary motor area, the insula, the basal temporal area, and others are part of the cortical networks important for language and other higher cognitive functions (Mesulam, 1990). As is often the case, contemporary views have been foreshadowed by earlier ideas. The following quote from de Watteville suggests that he may have envisioned, in 1885, a distributed network view of higher cognitive functions: "... we must not search for the physiological substratum of mental activity in this or that part of the brain but we have to regard it as the outcome of processes spread widely over the brain" (quoted in Freud, 1953, p. 17).

Acknowledgement:

The author thanks Drs. Pamela Tallay and Brenda Rapp who provided helpful comments and encouragement.

REFERENCE

Adams, F. (1939). *The genuine works of Hippocrates*. Baltimore: Williams & Wilkins.

Arnett, P. A., Rao, S. M., Hussain, M., Swanson, S. J., & Hammeke, T. A. (1996). Conduction aphasia in multiple sclerosis: A case report with MRI findings. *Neurology, 47*, 576-578.

Barker, F. G. (1995). Phineas among the phrenologists: The American crowbar case and nineteenth-century theories of cerebral localization. *Journal of Neurosurgery, 82*, 672-682.

Barrash, J. (1998). A historical review of topographical disorientation and its neuroanatomical correlates. *Journal of Clinical and Experimental Neuropsychology, 20*, 807-827.

Benson, D. F. (1967). Fluency in aphasia: Correlation with radioactive scan localization. *Cortex, 3*, 373-394.

Benson, D. F. (1979). *Aphasia, alexia, and agraphia*. New York: Churchill Livingstone.

Benton, A. (1981). Aphasia: Historical perspetives. In M. T. Sarno (Ed.), *Acquired aphasia* (pp. 1-25). New York: Academic Press.

Benton, A. L. (1965). J. A. P. Gesner on aphasia. *Medical History, 9*, 54-60.

Benton, A. L. (1992). Gerstmann's syndrome. *Archives of Neurology, 49*, 445-447.

Benton, A. L., & Joynt, R. J. (1960). Early descriptions of aphasia. *Archives of Neurology, 3*, 205-222.

Boller, F., & Grafman, J. (1983). Acalculia: Historical development and current significance. *Brain and Cognition, 2*, 205-223.

Bouillaud, J. B. (1825). Recherches cliniques propres à démontrer que la perte de la parole correspond à la lésion des lobules antérieurs du cerveaux (Clinical Research documenting that loss of speech is associated with a lesion of the anterior lobes of the brain), *Archives générales de Médecine, 8*, 25-45.

Broca, P. (1861). Remarques sur le siège de la faculté du langage articulé, suivies d'une observation d'aphémie (perte de la parole) (Remarks on the seat of the faculty of articulate language, followed by an observation of aphemia). *Bulletin de la Societe Anatomique, 6*, 330-357.

Broca, P. (1863). Localisation des fonctions cerebrales. Siège de la faculté du langage articulé (Localization of cerebral functions. Loss of articulate language). *Bulletins de la Societe d'Anthropologie de Paris, 4*, 200-208.

Brown, J. W., & Chobor, K. L. (1992). Phrenological studies of aphasia before Broca: Broca's aphasia or Gall's aphasia? *Brain and Language, 43*, 475-486.

Caramazza, A. (1986). On drawing inferences about the structure of normal cognitive systems from the analysis of patterns of impaired performance: The case for single-patient studies. *Brain and Language, 5*, 41-66.

Caramazza, A., Berndt, R. S., Basili, A. G., & Koller, J. J. (1981). Syntactic processing deficits in aphasia. *Cortex, 17*, 333-348.

Cassano, D. (1996). Neurology and the soul: From the origins until 1500. *Journal of the History of the Neurosciences, 5*, 152-161.

Cohen, M. (1996). Functional MRI: A phrenology for the 1990's? *Journal of Magnetic Resonance Imaging, 6*, 273-274.

Cole, M. F., & Cole, M. (1971). *Pierre Marie's Papers on Speech Disorders*. New York: Hafner.

Coltheart, M. (1982). The psycholinguistic analysis of acquired dyslexias: some illustrations. *Philosophical Transactions of the Royal Society of London, 298*, 151-164.

Coltheart, M., Patterson, K., & Marshall, J. (1980). *Deep Dyslexia*. London: Routledge.

Critchley, M. (1960). Broca's contribution to aphasia reviewed a century later. In H. Garland (Ed.), *Scientific aspects of neurology* (pp. 131-141). Edinburgh: E. S. Livingstone.

Critchley, M., & Critchley, E. A. (1998). *John Hughlings Jackson. Father of English Neurology.* New York: Oxford University Press.

Damasio, A. R. (1997). Brain and language: What a difference a decade makes [editorial]. *Current Opinion in Neurology, 10,* 177–178.

Damasio, H., Grabowski, T., Frank, R., Galaburda, A. M., & Damasio, A. R. (1994). The return of Phineas Gage: Clues about the brain from the skull of a famous patient. *Science, 264,* 1102-1105.

De Bleser, R., Cubelli, R., & Luzzatti, C. (1993). Conduction aphasia, misrepresentations, and word representations. *Brain Language, 45,* 475-494.

Ellis, A. W., & Young, A. W. (1988). What is cognitive neuropsychology? In A. W. Ellis & A. W. Young (Eds.), *Human cognitive neuropsychology.* Hove, UK: Lawrence Erlbaum.

Finger, S. (1994). *Origins of neuroscience.* New York: Oxford University Press.

Foundas, A. L., Eure, K. F., Luevano, L. F., & Weinberger, D. R. (1998). MRI asymmetries of Broca's area: The pars triangularis and pars opercularis. *Brain and Language, 64,* 282-296.

Foville, A. L. (1844). *Traite complet de l'anatomie, de la physiologie et de la pathologie du systeme nerveux cerebro-spinal, 1.ptie., Anatomie.* Paris: Fortin, Masson.

Freud, S. (1953). *On Aphasia: A critical study* (E. Stengel, Trans.). London: Imago.

Geschwind, N. (1965). Disconnexion syndromes in animals and man. *Brain, 88,* 237-294.

Graves, R. E. (1997). The legacy of the Wernicke-Lictheim model. *Journal of the History of the Neurosciences, 6,* 3-20.

Green, E., & Howes, D. H. (1977). The nature of conduction aphasia: A study of anatomic and clinical features and underlying mechanisms. In H. Whitaker & H. A. Whitaker (Eds.), *Studies in neurolinguistics* (pp. 123-156). New York: Academic Press.

Gross, C. G. (1998). *Brain, vision, memory. Tales in the history of neuroscience.* Cambridge, MA: MIT Press.

Harlow, J. M. (1848). Passage of an iron rod through the head. *Boston Medical and Surgical Journal, 39,* 389-393.

Harlow, J. M. (1868). Recovery after severe injury to the head. *Publication of the Massachusetts Medical Society, 2,* 327-346.

Henderson, V. W. (1992). Early concepts of conduction aphasia. In S. E. Kohn (Ed.), *Conduction aphasia.* Hillsdale, NJ: Lawrence Erlbaum.

Lebrun, Y. (1982). Aphasie de Broca et anarthria. *Acta Neurologica Belgica, 82,* 80-90.

Luria, A. R. (1947/1970). *Traumatic aphasia.* The Hague: Mouton de Gruyter.

Marie, P. (1906). Aphasia from 1861 to 1866: Essay of historical criticism on the genesis of the doctrine of aphasia. *Semaine Medicale, 26,* 565-571.

Marshall, L. H., & Magoun, H. W. (1998). *Discoveries in the human brain.* Totowa, NJ: Humana Press.

Mesulam, M. M. (1990). Large-scale neurocognitive networks and distributed processing for attention, language and memory. *Annals of Neurology, 28,* 597-613.

Mohr, J. P., Pessin, M. S., Finkelstein, S., Funkenstein, H. H. , Duncan, G. W., & Davis, K. R. (1999). Broca aphasia: Pathologic and clinical. *Neurology, 28,* 311-324.

Naeser, M. A., & Palumbo, C. L. (1994). Neuroimaging and language recovery in stroke. *Journal of Clinical Neurophysiology, 11,* 150–174.

Nemeroff, C. B., Kilts, C. D., & Berns, G. S. (1999). Functional brain imaging: twenty-first century phrenology or psychobiological advance for the millennium? [editorial]. *American Journal of Psychiatry, 156,* 671-673.

Neylan, T. C. (1999). Frontal lobe function: Mr. Phineas Gage's famous injury. *Journal of Neuropsychiatry and Clinical Neurosciences, 11,* 280-283.

Petrides, M., & Pandya, D. N. (1988). Association fiber pathways to the frontal cortex from the superior temporal region in the rhesus monkey. *The Journal of Comparative Neurology, 273,* 52-66.

Price, T. R., Manolio, T. A., Kronmal, R. A., Kittner, S. J., Yue, N. C., Robbins, J., Anton-Culver, H., & O'Leary, D. H. (1997). Silent brain infarction on magnetic resonance imaging and neurological abnormalities in community-dwelling older adults. The Cardiovascular Health Study. CHS Collaborative Research Group. *Stroke, 28,* 1158-1164.

Pujol, P., Bello, J., Deus, J., Marti-Vilalta, J. L., & Capdevila, A. (1997). Lesions in the left arcuate fasciculus region and depressive symptoms in multiple sclerosis. *Neurology, 49,* 1105-1110.

Reitan, R. M. (1994). Ward Halstead's contributions to neuropsychology and the Halstead-Reitan Neuropsychological Test Battery. *Journal of Clinical Psychology, 50,* 47-70.

Robinson, G., Rossor, M., & Cipolotti, L. (1999). Selective sparing of verb naming in a case of severe Alzheimer's disease. *Cortex, 35,* 443-450.

Rocca, J. (1997). Galen and the ventricular system. *Journal of the History of the Neurosciences, 6,* 227-239.

Saffran, E. M., & Marin, O. S. (1977). Reading without phonology: Evidence from aphasia. *Quarterly Journal of Experimental Psychology, 29,* 515-525.

Schiller, F. (1992). *Paul Broca.* New York: Oxford University Press.

Schiller, F. (1997). The cerebral ventricles: From soul to sink. *Archives of Neurology, 54,* 1158-1162.

Selnes, O. A., & Hillis, A. E. (in press). Patient Tan revisited: A case of atypical Global aphasia? *Journal of the History of the Neurosciences.*

Selnes, O. A., Niccum, N., Knopman, D. S., & Rubens, A. B. (1984). Recovery of single word comprehension: CT-scan correlates. *Brain and Language, 21,* 72-84.

Shallice, T. & Coughlan, A. K. (1980). Modality specific word comprehension deficits in deep dyslexia. *Journal of Neurology, Neurosurgergy, and Psychiatry, 43,* 866-872.

Shuren, J. E., Schefft, B. K., Yeh, H. S., Privitera, M. D., Cahill, W. T., & Houston, W. (1995). Repetition and the arcuate fasciculus. *Journal of Neurology, 242,* 596-598.

Signoret, J. L., Castaigne, P., Lhermitte, F., Abelanet, R., & Lavorel, P. (1984). Rediscovery of Leborgne's brain: Anatomical description with CT scan. *Brain and Language, 22,* 303-319.

Tanabe, H., Sawada, T., Inoue, N., Ogawa, M., Kuriyama, Y., & Shiraishi, J. (1987). Conduction aphasia and arcuate fasciculus. *Acta Neurologica Scandinavica, 76,* 422-427.

Telfer, W. (1955). *Cyril of Jerusalem and Nemesius of Emesa.* Philadelphia: The Westminster Press.

Theiss, P. (1997). Albert the Great's interpretation of neuropsychiatric symptoms in the context of scholastic psychology and physiology. *Journal of the History of the Neurosciences, 6,* 240-256.

Tognola, G., & Vignolo, L. A. (1980). Brain lesions associated with oral apraxia in stroke patients: A clinico-neuroradiological investigation with the CT scan. *Neuropsychologia, 18,* 257-272.

Tross, S., & Hirsch, D. A. (1988). Psychological distress and neuropsychological complications of HIV infection and AIDS. *American Psychologist, 43,* 929-934.

von Bonin, G. (1960). *Some papers on the cerebral cortex.* Springfield, IL: C. C. Thomas.

Wallesch, C.-W., & Bartels, C. (1996). Freud's impact on aphasiology—aphasiology's impact on Freud. *Journal of the History of the Neurosciences, 5,* 117-125.

Warrington, E. K., & Shallice, T. (1984). Category specific semantic impairments. *Brain, 107*(3), 829-854.

Wernicke, C. (1874). *Der aphasische Symptomencomplex: Eine Psychologische Studie auf anatomischer Basis* (The Symptom Complex of Aphasia: A Psychological Study on an Anatomical Basis). Breslau, Germany: Cohn & Weigert.

Willis, T. (1664). *Cerebri anatome: Cui accessit nervorum descriptio et usus* (Anatomy of the Braing and Descriptions and Functions of the Nerves) (S. Pordage, Trans.). London: Ja. Flesher.

Witelson, S. F. (1985). The brain connection: the corpus callosum is larger in left-handers. *Science, 229,* 665-668.

Witelson, S. F., Kigar, D. L., & Harvey, T. (1999). The exceptional brain of Albert Einstein [published erratum appears in Lancet 1999 Jul 17; 354(9174): 258]. *Lancet, 353,* 2149-2153.

Young, R. M. (1970). *Mind, brain and adaptation in the nineteenth century.* Oxford, UK: Clarendon Press.

Part 2

—

Objects and Space

—

The history of the living world can be summarized as
the elaboration of ever more perfect eyes within a cosmos
in which there is always something more to be seen.

—*Teilhard de Chardin*

3

Object Recognition

M. Jane Riddoch
Glyn W. Humphreys

INTRODUCTION

The ease with which we recognize objects in everyday life belies the underlying complexity of visual processing in the brain. However, insights into the intricacies of these processes can be drawn from the study of brain damaged subjects who have lost some of the abilities we take so much for granted. For instance, damage can result in selective impairments in the visual perception of form (Goodale, Milner, Jakobson, & Carey, 1991), color (Heywood, Cowey, & Newcombe, 1991), and motion (Zihl, Von Cramon, & Mai, 1983), suggesting that these properties are processed in separable neural pathways. We focus on selective impairments of visual form perception (or visual agnosia) in this chapter, though the other disorders are discussed. Since we have already published a number of reviews on agnosia (Humphreys & Riddoch, 1987a, 1993; Riddoch & Humphreys, 1988) we will not place so much emphasis on the different types of visual agnosia, but instead will focus our discussion on some of the current issues and controversies.

We start our review with an account of the transmission of visual information from the retina to the occipital cortex. Our discussion will focus particularly on the geniculo-striate pathway and the effects of lesions to this pathway at the level of the occipital lobes, which can lead to the disorder known as blindsight. Subsequently we discuss the deficits that can arise as a result of lesions to 'higher-level' visual areas, including those specialised for the processing of color and motion. We then address the issue of visual object recognition itself. In particular, we will discuss two different approaches to the understanding of perceptual deficits that result in agnosia: the hierarchical approach adopted by Humphreys and his colleagues (Humphreys & Riddoch, 1987a; Riddoch & Humphreys, 1988), and the hemisphere specialization approach suggested by Warrington and her co-workers (Davidoff & Warrington, 1999; Warrington, 1985; Warrington & Taylor, 1978). We also outline different forms of memorial deficit that lead to associative agnosia and will then spend some time discussing the fate of stored visual knowledge when perception is damaged. In a final section we will consider (a) the relations between the visual processing of objects, faces, and words, and (b) whether the processes involved in object recognition operate in a discrete or a more iterative manner, with 'higher-level' information sometimes influencing processing at lower levels. We suggest that the consequences of iterative processing are important for our understanding of vision.

45

VISUAL PROCESSING FROM THE RETINA TO THE OCCIPITAL CORTEX

The Retino-Striate Pathway

Detailed studies of visual processing in primates have revealed that there is substantial functional segregation in the visual pathways from the retina onwards (see Livingstone & Hubel, 1987; S. Zeki, 1990, 1993). Information about the visual world is transmitted from the retina for further processing via the optic nerve. While the majority of fibres from the optic nerve travel via the geniculo-striate pathway to the striate cortex (V1) in the occipital lobes, approximately 10% of the fibres terminate in the mid- and fore-brain (e.g., in the superior colliculus, see Weiskrantz, 1990). At the retinal level, there are two forms of ganglion cells (alpha and beta) which have distinctly different roles in visual processing. Fibres from these cells remain segregated in the optic nerve up to the visual cortex. Fibres from alpha cells project first to 'parvo cellular' cells of the lateral geniculate nucleus (LGN) and from there to 'blob' and 'interblob' regions in cortical area V1. Cortical area V2 receives inputs from the blobs and interblobs and in turn projects it outputs to cortical area V4. This 'P' channel provides color opponent information and has low luminance contrast gains. There are two separate inputs from the 'P' channel to the temporal lobes: the cells in the blob regions in V1 are wavelength but not orientation selective (responsible for the coding of color), while in the interblob regions the reverse is true (such cells are likely to be responsible for the coding of form). Fibres from beta cells in the retina project to 'magnocellular' cells in the LGN, the thick stripe regions in V1 and then to cortical areas V2, V3 and MT. This 'M' channel has characteristic features of high luminance contrast gain, orientation and direction selectivity, and sensitivity to binocular disparity. The 'M' channel is thought to convey motion, stereo depth, and coarse form information to the parietal lobes (Livingstone & Hubel, 1987). More recent work, however, suggests that the separation between these streams may be partial rather than all-or-none. For example, blob and interblob regions of the 'P' channel receive input from the magnocellular system (Nealey & Maunsell, 1994). At higher levels of cortex (e.g., within infero-temporal cortex) cells may also respond to specific conjunctions of visual attributes (e.g., color as well as form, see Tanaka, Saito, Fukada, & Moriya, 1991). Nevertheless, the distinction between input streams for different visual dimensions such as color, form, stereo depth, and motion provides a framework for understanding the functional isolation of the streams following brain damage.

The general distinction between the cortical pathways projecting to visual processing areas in the temporal and parietal lobes is also supported by lesion studies with primates. Selective lesions to the pathways generate contrasting behavioral deficits. For instance, Ungerleider and Mishkin (1982) have shown that monkeys with lesions to the parietal cortex show little or no deficit in object recognition, but are profoundly impaired in visuospatial tasks requiring memory for location. On the other hand, monkeys with lesions to the temporal cortex may be impaired at recognizing objects visually but have no deficits in remembering location information. Results such as these have led to the argument that the temporal lobes contain cells that code 'what' an object is while the parietal lobes contain cells that code 'where' it is (Ungerleider & Mishkin, 1982). Lesion studies in humans too support the distinction between the 'what' and 'where' pathways (see Humphreys & Riddoch, in press for a review), as do studies using functional brain imaging. For example, Haxby et al. (1993) compared the areas activated when subjects indicated which of two faces matched a third face with the areas activated, in an analogous location matching task with the same stimuli. They found that identity judgements were associated with activation in the occipito-temporal region, while location judgements were associated with activation in occipito-parietal regions. Our review is concerned with neuropsychological deficits of the 'what' system, including those affecting the coding of the basic dimensions of visual stimuli.

Visual Processing in Striate Cortex: The Issue of 'Blind Sight'

Early writers, such as William James, argued that the occipital lobes were essential to human vision, hence the ablation of these areas would cause total blindness (James, 1890). Studies with human subjects with lesions of the striate cortex have indeed shown total blindness when assessed by visual field perimetry using static stimuli; however, other forms of assessment have shown that the loss of vision need not be total. George Riddoch first observed that such patients could detect motion in the field of view, although they appeared blind to everything else (G. Riddoch, 1917). Riddoch argued that movement may be recognized as a special visual perception, separate and in addition to perceptions of light, form, and color. George Riddoch's findings (1917, 1935) can be appreciated in the light of what is now known about the functional segregation of the visual processing pathways in the brain (see above), but at the time his findings were disputed (Holmes, 1918; Teuber, Battersby, & Bender, 1960). More recently however, using similar techniques to those originally described by G. Riddoch, several investigators have demonstrated perception of movement in an otherwise blind field (Barbur, Ruddock, & Waterfield, 1980; Bridgeman & Staggs, 1982; Weiskrantz, 1990). Indeed, 'blindsight' can extend to include a number of residual visual abilities. For instance, such patients can move their eyes to the position at which a light is presented in the visual field (e.g., Barbur et al., 1980; Perenin & Jeanerrod, 1985; Pöppel, Held, & Frost, 1973), and, though early evidence for shape discrimination was absent (Barbur et al., 1980) or weak (Perenin, 1978; Weiskrantz, 1990), more recent studies suggest that there can be high level processing of shape in some cases (Marcel, 1998). Cowey and Stoerig (1992) further demonstrated effects of wave length discrimination in the 'blind' field. These forms of blindsight are typically revealed by having patients make forced-choice responses between stimuli, even though the patient can deny 'seeing' any stimulus at all. Interestingly, some patients can report experiencing 'something,' but this experience is usually non-visual (e.g., a patient has described 'feeling' a moving stimulus in the blind field), although it can be visual (e.g., feeling that quite a bright light had been turned on; see Cowey & Stoerig, 1992). To some extent, the disparity between the visual properties that can be discriminated in blindsight, and those that cannot, is consistent with the physiological distinction between a visual route into the cortex via area V1 and a subcortical visual route (through the superior colliculus), with final projections into extra-striate regions. The subcortical route can support basic coding of position, motion and simple aspects of form and even wavelength (Weiskrantz, 1990), though the evidence for higher-level processing of form (Marcel, 1998) is less easy to account for in these terms unless it represents compensatory developments in some patients. Whatever account is offered for the stimulus properties that can be processed in blindsight, the evidence suggests that activity in primary visual cortex V1 is integral to conscious visual perception. We will return to the issue of consciousness later, in the final section of the chapter.

ELEMENTARY VISUAL PROCESSING OF COLOR, MOTION, AND FORM

Selective Deficit in Motion Perception—Akinetopsia

Damage to extrastriate areas of cortex can lead to problems in deriving some of the basic dimensions of visual stimuli, such as their color or their form, although such patients can perceive other nonimpaired properties. The most detailed study of impaired motion perception has been conducted with patient LM. LM suffered a superior sagittal sinus thrombosis when aged 43 (originally reported by Zihl, Von Cramon, & Mai, 1983). A magnetic resonance scan (MRI) showed severe bilateral damage to the middle temporal gyrus and the adjacent part of the occipital gyri together with subcortical damage affecting lateral occipital and occipito-parietal white matter (Zihl, Von Cramon, Mai, & Schmid, 1991). LM was profoundly disabled in everyday life and found moving stimuli to be highly disturbing and unpleasant: moving objects appeared to jump from one position to the next, making busy streets or shops very frightening. As a result, she became wary of venturing from home, which led to an initial diagnosis of agoraphobia—an interpretation which could not account for some of her other difficulties, such as with understanding language (people's lips appeared to hop up and down), and meal preparation (she had difficulty in pouring and measuring out liquids because they appeared frozen like a glacier; see Heywood & Zihl, 1999). LM's visual recognition was intact: She had no visual-field defect, acuity was unimpaired, and she performed normally on tests of visual identification and recognition of objects, faces, and places. In contrast, formal tests of movement vision revealed a number of specific impairments, such as a reduced sensitivity to motion and a reduced appreciation of subjective velocity. Not all movement perception was lost, however, LM was able to discriminate the direction of motion of high contrast stimuli and she could also perceive some aspects of higher order motion normally. For instance, she could discriminate various forms of biological motion formed when lights were placed on the joints of actors who were filmed in a dark room (McLeod, Dittrich, Driver, Perrett, & Zihl, 1996). LM could tell whether the light dots were jumbled or consistent with walking figures, whether figures were walking or cycling, and the direction of motion. This dissociation, between impaired perception of some basic aspects of motion and an ability to perceive relatively complex patterns of biological motion, suggests that contrasting neural substrates may serve different forms of motion coding—in particular, there may be some neural areas specialized for processing biological motion, which are relatively preserved in LM. Converging physiological evidence for this proposal has been reported by Perrett and colleagues (Perrett, Harries, Benson, Chitty, & Mistlin, 1990), who have found cells in the superior temporal sulcus of primates that were specialized for processing biological motion.

LM's lesions were in the region of visual area V5 in both hemispheres. In the macaque monkey, cells in this area have been shown to be sensitive to motion, the majority of cells being directionally sensitive (S. M. Zeki, 1974). Furthermore, again in the macaque monkey, neurons in V5 have been shown to be selective for binocular disparity and direction and speed of motion but not for color (Maunsell & Van Essen, 1983a, 1983b). LM's behavioral deficits in perceiving basic aspects of motion information are consistent with these physiological data. In normal human observers, the functions of V5 have been studied using both functional brain imaging (fMRI and PET) and transcranial magnetic stimulation (TMS). TMS provides a means of disrupting activity in regions of the cortex with millisecond accuracy. Walsh, Ellison, Battelli, and Cowey (1998) stimulated V5 using TMS and found this disruption improved search for a non-motion target amongst moving distractors. This interesting result suggests that inhibition of selective neural areas may play a functional role in many tasks, especially when areas selectively process distracting information. Functional imaging studies also reveal modulation of motion processing areas (V5) by attention. For instance, Rees, Frith, and Lavie, (1997) measured activity in V5 generated by a moving background using fMRI. When the primary task required reading a word at fixation, there was less activity in V5 than when subjects simply had to detect whether or not a target word was in lower case. Hence these areas of cortex specialized for processing various visual attributes do not seem to operate in a purely bottom-up mode but they may also be influenced in a top-down fashion, by how much attention is paid to the dimension of interest. The notion that emerges here is of a dynamically modulated visual system, tuned to task demands as well as to specific visual properties of the world—an argument we return to in the final sections of the chapter. It can even be speculated that one reason for the functional specialization of vision is to facilitate dynamic modulation of processing of specified properties. We note too that a patient such as LM will not only be impaired at processing motion, but also in attending and ignoring motion information selectively. LM's deficit is striking, but relatively rare. It is possible that akinetopsia only results from bilateral lesions and that a single area V5 may be sufficient for motion perception in cases with unilateral lesions.

Loss of Color Perception (Achromatopsia)

The term achromatopsia is applied to the syndrome in which a patient loses the ability to see colors after cortical damage. The loss may be partial or complete, and it may or may not be accompanied by other visual defects. The patient often reports seeing the world in black and white and shades of grey (Humphreys & Riddoch, 1987b). The disorder is one of color perception and not just recognition (e.g., associating red with a mail box) or naming. Thus patients can perform poorly at perceptual ordering tasks (such as the Farnsworth Munsell 100-Hue Test), but they can arrange achromatic grey discs in terms of their lightness (Heywood, Wilson, & Cowey, 1987). Achromatopsia often occurs in association with prosopagnosia (failure to recognize familiar faces; Ratcliff & Newcombe, 1982; Riddoch & Humphreys, 1987a), but not always (Kölmel, 1988; Sachs, Wasserman, Zeki, & Siegel, 1988) and is associated with lesions in the region of the lingual and fusiform gyri. This region in humans is probably analogous to visual area V4 in the macaque, which has been shown to be specialized in the processing of color (S. Zeki, 1990; S. M. Zeki, 1973, 1978, 1980). This supposition has been strengthened with data from PET studies (Corbetta, Meizin, Dobmeyer, Shulman, & Petersen, 1991; Lueck et al., 1989; S. Zeki, 1993). When subjects view a multicolored abstract display (such as a 'Color Mondrian') there are regions of heightened activity in the lingual and fusiform gyri, relative to when the colors are replaced with grey shades matched in luminance (Lueck et al., 1989). Troscianko et al. (1996) reported forced-choice color-matching tasks in two achromatopsic patients. Despite failing to report conscious color perception, both patients matched isoluminant colors above chance (see also Heywood et al., 1991). Either static or dynamic (moving) luminance 'noise' was then added into the color stimuli. With one patient, performance was poor with static noise but improved with luminance noise. This is consistent with any residual color processing being based on the 'P'–pathway, which is sensitive to static but not motion cues. In contrast, the second patient showed the opposite pattern of performance, being more impaired with the dynamic than the static noise. Troscianko et al. (1996) suggest that another color-sensitive system may be involved in this case: possibly the 'M' channel, which is sensitive to red-green border information (Li, Martin, & Valberg, 1989) or to some further system that remains able to discriminate colors at isoluminance. In this second patient the dominant P-pathway for color processing seemed to be abolished.

Impaired Depth Perception

Impairments affecting all aspects of depth perception, including the use of monocular as well as binocular cues, have been reported in patients with bilateral occipital-parietal damage (Gloning, Gloning, & Hoff, 1968; Holmes & Horrax, 1919; Riddoch, 1935; Rizzo & Damasio, 1985; Valkenberg, 1908). Such patients describe the world as if it is two-dimensional; for instance, " . . . To the patient a chair is flat, though he knows from experience that his visual impressions are cheating him. . . . A stair is a flat inclined plane with no protruding steps, and yet he knows from the light and shade that he ought to see the steps . . . " (G. Riddoch, 1917, pp. 47–48). More specific impairments that affect stereo depth perception have been documented after unilateral lesions of the right versus the left hemisphere (Benton & Hécaen, 1970; Carmon & Bechtold, 1969; Hamsher, 1978), though problems of sampling bias here need to be taken into account (e.g., if patients with aphasia after left hemisphere lesions have been omitted; see Danta, Hilton, & O'Boyle, 1978). It is also unclear whether problems in global stereo depth perception are related to damage to the magnocellular stream in humans. For example, Ptito and colleagues (Ptito & Zatorre, 1988; Ptito, Zatorre, Larson, & Tosini, 1991) have documented deficits in global stereopsis after temporal lobectomies. The precise relations between disorders of depth perception and the 'M' and 'P' streams need to be evaluated.

Selective Deficits of Form Perception (Apperceptive Agnosia)

Perhaps equivalent to impairments affecting processing of basic visual dimensions of color, motion, and depth, are those affecting the basic processing of form. The neurologist Lissauer first distinguished visual recognition deficits consequent on damaged perceptual processes from those consequent on damaged access to stored memories giving these deficits the labels apperceptive and associative agnosia (Lissauer, 1890). Using this terminology, damage to the processes involved in extracting basic form information can be classed as a type of apperceptive (perceptual) agnosia.

Patients with impaired perception have been reported by Efron and Milner and his associates (Efron, 1968; Milner et al., 1991). Such patients are unable to identify or to copy line drawings of common objects or even simple geometric shapes; however, while figural properties such as size, orientation, and shape are lost, other abilities such as color, brightness, and movement discrimination may be preserved (Efron, 1968; Milner et al., 1991). In many instances, patients with these deficits have been exposed to carbon monoxide poisoning. Campion and his coworkers have argued that the visual recognition problem in patients with carbon monoxide poisoning is due to many small scotoma produced by the multiple lesions. This could have the effect of causing the patient to view the world through a peppery mask. However, on this account, we might expect that patients could adapt to the presence of such a mask; in addition, some form of integration of the information should operate across the mask when patients move. Against this, recognition is severely disrupted in free vision in everyday life. Others have argued that the problem with visual recognition results from impaired grouping processes (Humphreys, Riddoch, Donnelly, et al., 1992; Humphreys, Riddoch, Quinlan, Donnelly, & Price, 1992). Cells in early visual areas can respond differentially when local grouping cues, such as collinear line segments, are present (see Von der Heydt & Peterhans, 1989, for evidence from area V2). Damage to such areas may prevent patients from linking edge elements into coherent perceptual structures disrupting object recognition.

Data contrasting the effects of peppery masks versus disruption of grouping have recently been reported by Vecera and Gilds (1998) with normal subjects. Vecera and Gilds had subjects respond to a spatially cued target. There were two viewing conditions to the experiment: either a peppery mask was present, or stimuli were degraded to mimic impaired grouping. They examined effects of spatial cueing on targets that appeared in the same object as the cue (both appeared with a rectangular box) relative to targets that fell in a similar object, but on the opposite side of fixation. Previous work by Egly had shown an 'object' benefit, with there being faster RTs to targets that appear in the same object as the cue relative to targets that appeared in the noncued object (Egly, Driver, & Rafal, 1994). Vecera and Gilds (1998) degraded the boxes by either removing their mid-sections or removing the corners. Removal of the mid-sections leaves cues such as collinearity and closure present, while removal of the corners would makes it more difficult to group the parts into objects (see Biederman, 1987, for evidence in object recognition and Humphreys, Romani, Olson, Riddoch, & Duncan, 1994, for evidence with simultanagnosic patients). Vecera and Gilds found that removing the mid-sections left the object-cueing advantage intact, whilst the advantage was lost when corners were removed. In contrast, effects of object-cuing were additive with the effects of a peppered mask. Vecera and Gilds suggest that object coding is selectively impaired by disruption to grouping processes rather than degradation due to masking.

Interestingly, some patients with poor basic perception of form can use the same information to guide motor behavior. This was first reported by Milner and his colleagues (Milner et al., 1991). Patient DF suffered anoxia as a result of fumes leaking from a faulty gas water heater. Subsequently her visual object recognition was severely impaired, she could recognize few real objects and no line drawings. Her copying was poor, and she was at chance at making perceptual judgements even about the basic dimensions of form (see Milner et al., 1991).

Despite this, DF was able to reach appropriately to objects. Her grasp aperture and hand orientation were tuned to the size and orientation of stimuli and the kinematics of her movements were normal. Milner and Goodale (1995) propose that the dissociation between perceptual judgements and action in DF reflects the contrast between the ventral and dorsal streams of the visual cortex. They propose that DF's lesion affected the ventral rather than the dorsal visual system compromising perceptual judgements about even the basic dimensions of form. However, the dorsal visual stream remained intact. Milner and Goodale argue that the dorsal stream not only codes stimulus location (cf. Ungerleider & Mishkin, 1982), but also provides visual information for prehensile actions—such as reaching and grasping. Orientation and size information can be coded by the dorsal stream and used for action, even if coding of the same information in the ventral stream is impaired. On this view, the ventral stream (for object recognition) and the dorsal system (for location coding and action) are separated even from the early stages of cortical coding. Consequently, patients such as DF can have a deficit in early shape coding in the ventral system along with intact early shape coding in the dorsal system. An alternative possibility is that vision for action is not completely independent of vision for perceptual judgements and object recognition; rather that vision for action can bring into play feedback processes that do not operate in recognition. The dorsal system may mediate rapid feedback in visually-guided prehensile actions. According to this view, DF may be able to reach appropriately to objects by means of an intact feedback process (see Edwards & Humphreys, 1999, for evidence on visual feedback in the syndrome).

Interestingly, DF's ability to code orientation has been shown not only in action but also in perceptual judgement tasks where orientation information operates independently. The McCollough effect is a long-lasting instance of adaptation in which a negative color aftereffect is produced by a stimulus that has the same orientation as the adaptation pattern (McCollough, 1965). DF was unable to report the orientation of black and white test gratings which were either horizontally or vertically oriented. However, the orientation of these gratings affected the color aftereffect following adaptation to green and black horizontal gratings and red and black vertical gratings. For instance, if the adapting grating was green and horizontal, then a pink negative aftereffect was found on the subsequently viewed horizontal black and white grating. Thus, while she was unable to *explicitly* report the orientation of the test grating, the McCollough effect demonstrates that at some level in DF's visual system, orientation is being encoded (Humphrey, Goodale, & Gurnsey, 1991). This suggests either of two possibilities. One is that orientation is coded along with color within the color-sensitive part of the 'P' channel, so that DF manifests sensitivity to orientation when relying on that visual stream. She is impaired at using orientation only within the form-sensitive part of the 'P' channel. The second is that DF can use orientation information implicitly for perceptual judgements, but she does not have explicit access to that information unless it is used for action. In the final section of the chapter we return to consider differences between the implicit and explicit coding of visual information for recognition tasks.

VISUAL OBJECT RECOGNITION

As we have noted, the deficits in form perception can be classed as a type of apperceptive agnosia, using Lissauer's (1890) distinction between apperceptive and associative agnosias. In addition to disorders of basic form perception, though, case studies over recent years have demonstrated that a variety of other types of object recognition deficits can occur, and that finer grain distinctions are required between contrasting forms of both apperceptive and associative agnosia. Thus, rather than there being a dichotomy between frank deficits of perception or memory access (apperception and association), there are sets of impairments reflecting particular operations involved in recognition. (Arguments for the finer-grained distinctions are provided in: Farah, 1990; Humphreys & Riddoch, 1987a, 1987b; Humphreys, Riddoch, & Boucart,

1992a; Riddoch, 1999; Riddoch & Humphreys, 1988; Warrington, 1982, 1985.) Here we present two contrasting ways of conceptualizing the distinctions in terms of two underlying frameworks for understanding visual processing: a hierarchical account of visual perception and object recognition, and a hemisphere-specific account.

The Hierarchical Processing Account

One of the most influential views of visual perception over the past 20 years was that proposed by David Marr and his colleagues (Marr, 1982; Marr & Hildreth, 1980; Marr & Nishihara, 1978). Marr suggested that vision results from processing via a number of modular subsystems, which, when combined in a hierarchical fashion, give rise to object recognition. For example, he proposed that early visual processes act to code edges in a retinal coordinate subsystem (the raw primal sketch). Subsequently, these edges are grouped and linked with surface information, again represented according to viewpoint (the 2½-D sketch). Finally, a viewpoint-independent representation is constructed in which the parts of the object are coded in relation to the object's main axis (the 3-D modal representation). Since this general hierarchical framework was proposed, many queries have been raised—for example whether a surface based representation is coded en route to recognition (Biederman & Gerhardstein, 1993 vs. Edelman & Duvdevani-Bar, 1997), and whether the processes leading up to object recognition operate in a purely bottom-up manner (see Humphreys, Riddoch, & Price, 1997). For our present purposes what matters is not whether Marr was right in the precise details (although we will discuss evidence where neuropsychological results are relevant), but whether the general principles of this approach apply: (a) that vision involves a set of separate processes, and (b) these processes are arranged in a hierarchical fashion. We have argued (Humphreys & Riddoch, 1987a, 1993; Riddoch & Humphreys, 1988) that neuropsychological data can be accounted for in terms of these two general principles. The quasi-modular decomposition of visual processing not only applies to the basic dimensions of form, color, depth, and motion, but to object recognition itself. A framework derived on the basis of observations of performance of patients with impaired visual recognition is shown in Figure 3.1.

The Basic Coding of Color, Depth, and Motion

As shown in Figure 3.1, the initial processing of an object is along the basic dimensions of color, depth, and form. We have already covered issues relating to such processing in Section 3.

Edge Grouping by Collinearity

A first stage of visual processing involves organization of the input. Elements are grouped on the basis of their similarity to each other, allowing the derivation of edges. This grouping probably happens in early parts of the visual cortex, perhaps involving long range horizontal connections even within striate cortex (area V1; see Gilbert, 1992; Gilbert & Wiesel, 1989). Certainly within area V2 there is evidence of grouping by collinearity taking place (Von der Heydt, Peterhans, & Baumgartner, 1984). As we go on to discuss in the following section, there is also neuropsychological evidence that edge grouping by collinearity operates prior to the assignment of edges to shapes (Giersch, Humphreys, & Boucart, in press). This is consistent with edge grouping being a first stage in perceptual organization. It may well be that patients such as DF (see above) are impaired at this early stage since they are unable to perform simple shape matching tests. An example of this is the Efron (Efron, 1968) test. This involves discrimination between shapes varying in two dimensions which are matched for brightness, it is typically administered under conditions with no time limitations and with one or at the most two spatially separated shapes present, such a shape matching test is likely to be contingent on

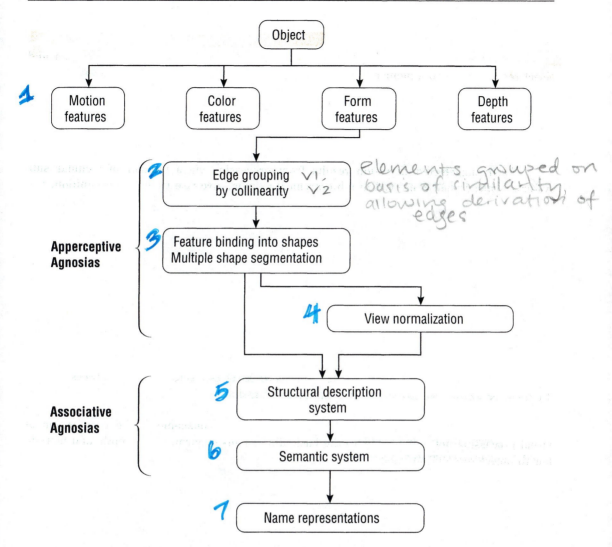

(Handwritten annotations in the figure: "V1, V2" beside "Edge grouping by collinearity"; "elements grouped on basis of similarity, allowing derivation of edges"; blue numbers 1–7 marking each stage.)

Figure 3.1. A hierarchical model of object recognition and naming, specifying different component processes which, when impaired, can produce varieties of apperceptive and associative agnosia.

coding the appropriate edges (perhaps in addition, requiring the assignment of edges to the shape). DF was also impaired at judgements about simple patterns grouped on the basis of properties such as proximity and collinearity (Milner et al., 1991).

Feature Binding into Shapes and Multiple Shape Segmentation

In other cases patients may be able to extract basic features and to perform some elementary feature-grouping, but they are still impaired at binding features into shapes. These problems are most clearly demonstrated under conditions in which multiple items are present in the field, when there may be competition in assigning elements between shapes. In a detailed study of one agnosic patient, HJA, we have shown the contrast between relatively good assignment of elements into shapes when only one item is present, and poor assignment elements to multiple shapes. HJA was profoundly agnosic and particularly impaired at recognizing line drawings.

Despite this, he performed well on the Efron shape matching task (Humphreys, Riddoch, Quinlan, et al., 1992). In contrast to this, HJA was impaired at search tasks that required that visual elements bind together in a spatially parallel manner across a field containing multiple stimuli. Targets were defined on the basis of a particular conjunction of form features (e.g., a horizontal and vertical line combining to form an inverted T), relative to homogeneous distractors containing the same features but in a different arrangement (e.g., upright Ts; see Figure 3.2).

(a) Feature search (target an oriented T)

Target present   Target absent

(b) Conjunction search (homogeneous distractors)
(target an inverted T)

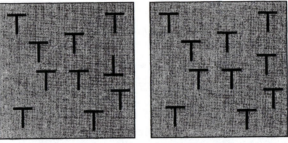

Target present   Target absent

(c) Conjunction search (heterogeneous distractors)
(target an inverted T)

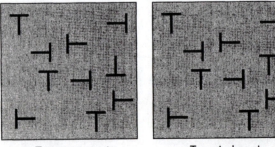

Target present   Target absent

Figure 3.2. Examples of some of the visual search displays used with HJA: (a) illustrates a feature search (the 'feature' being orientation), (b) a conjunction search with homogeneous distractors, and (c) a conjunction search with heterogeneous distractors.

Normal subjects can detect such targets efficiently by binding elements in targets and distractors in parallel and by then grouping and then rejecting distractors on the basis of their 'bound' feature conjunctions (Duncan & Humphreys, 1989; Humphreys, Quinlan, & Riddoch, 1989). HJA was unable to do this and was significantly impaired relative to age-matched controls (see Figure 3.3). Nevertheless, he could detect targets in parallel when they were differentiated by a salient feature from distractors (e.g., a T having a contrasting orientation to distractors), so he was capable of processing elements in parallel when binding elements together was not crucial. He could also conduct efficient serial search for form-conjunction targets amongst heterogeneous distractors (e.g., upright and 90° rotated Ts). For normal subjects segmentation of targets and distractors by similarity at the level of feature conjunctions is disrupted when heterogeneous stimuli are presented, and subjects then adopt a serial search strategy (see Figure 3.4). HJA's deficit is not apparent under these circumstances, although it appears when parallel binding of elements is necessary (see Figure 3.4).

The distinction between intact coding of basic features and impaired binding into shape has been illustrated in recent experiments with HJA that use simple shape matching tasks. Giersch, Humphreys, and Boucart (in press) presented line drawings of three geometric shapes that could be spatially separated, superimposed, or occluding (see Figure 3.5a, b, c respectively). In addition, sets of occluding silhouettes were also presented. Subsequently, the target array was exposed again along with a distractor array in which the positions of the shapes were rearranged. HJA performed relatively well on this task with separated shapes and with silhouettes, but he performed poorly with superimposed and occluding shapes. Interestingly, the deficit with occluding shapes was most pronounced when the length of the occluded edge was small—the condition when the missing fragment should be easiest to compute based on collinearity between the non-occluded edges (see Figure 3.5c). Other studies showed that HJA sometimes

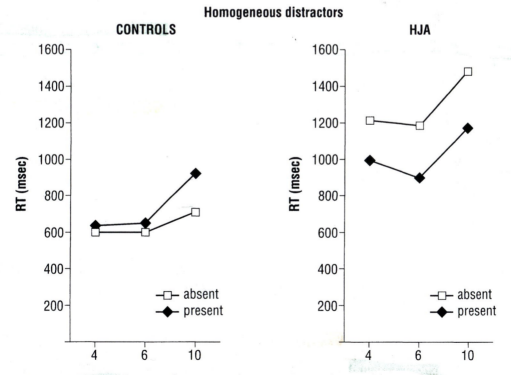

Figure 3.3. Data showing the contrast between HJA and controls in a conjunction search task with homogeneous distractors.

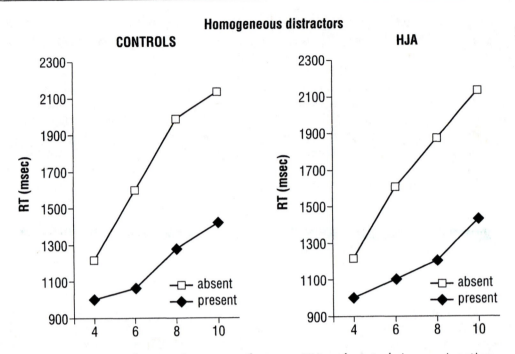

Figure 3.4.   Data showing the contrast between HJA and controls in a conjunction search task with heterogeneous distractors.

used the occluded edge to segment the occluder, and sometimes he assigned the edge to the shapes as if it were visible. These results suggest that HJA could compute the occluded edge (using collinearity), but he was then impaired at assigning it to the correct shape and in using it in the process of segmenting the multiple shapes apart. Feature coding, including edge grouping by collinearity, precedes feature binding into shapes and multiple shape segmentation. The fact that HJA performed reasonably well with silhouettes here is also illuminating. Normal subjects tended to find the silhouettes more difficult than line drawings, presumably because local details that facilitate segmentation of shapes is lacking, and hence performance relies on more global descriptions of the overall configuration. HJA seemed able to use these global descriptions reasonably well, given his relatively good matching of silhouettes. However, the local detail present (e.g., the occluded edges) disrupted his performance, due to his impaired binding and segmentation of the shapes.

The contrast between HJA's good performance with silhouettes and his poor performance with line drawings extended beyond simple shape matching tasks. Riddoch and Humphreys (1987a), for example, first reported this in an object decision task with HJA (see also Lawson & Humphreys, 1999, for further recent evidence). With complex stimuli, the problem with line drawings can be demonstrated with even single items. With limited presentation times, the problem was even greater, and it was also exacerbated by overlapping figures (Riddoch & Humphreys, 1987a). A similar pattern, with strong effects of figural overlap and better performance with silhouettes was found by Butter and Trobe (1994) with their agnosic patient. Patients described by de Renzi and Lucchelli (1994) and Kartsounis and Warrington (1991) have also shown poor performance with overlapping figures despite good discrimination of simple Efron shapes. In more complex line drawings, edges provide cues for segmentation of objects into parts, and they must also be bound correctly to yield appropriate object descriptions. Some agnosic patients find this binding difficult and are prone to segment even single line drawings. This can lead to a piecemeal approach to object identification in which objects are identified from their parts (see Goldstein & Gelb, 1918; Grossman, Galetta, & D'Esposito,

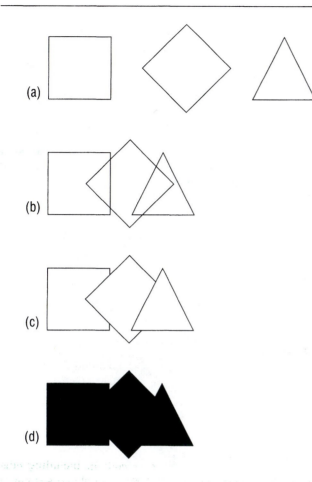

Figure 3.5. Examples of the stimuli used by Giersch, Humphreys, and Boucart (in press).

1997; Sirigu, Duhamel, & Poncet, 1991; Wapner, Judd, & Gardner, 1978, for other examples). Interestingly, despite placing a good deal of weight on the parts of objects for identification, such agnosic patients typically do not report the whole object as if it were just the part (e.g., describing a bicycle as a wheel). Thus, they appear to have some information about the whole. This proposal is supported by the silhouette advantage that can occur. In an additional experimental test of the proposal with HJA, Humphreys, Riddoch, and Quinlan (1985) examined responses to compound stimuli in which the whole is composed of separately identifiable local parts (e.g., a large letter made up of smaller letters; cf. Navon, 1977). They found that HJA responded normally to the global form but, unusually, he showed no effect of the global form on the identification of the local parts (see also Lamb, Robertson, & Knight, 1990, for a similar result with patients with unilateral lesions to the superior temporal gyrus).

Riddoch and Humphreys (1987a) used the term 'integrative agnosia' to describe patients such as HJA. They argued that the deficit was not in early feature extraction but in integrating together both local features and local and global aspects of form. According to Riddoch and Humphreys, shape integration is a second dissociable process in the hierarchy leading to object recognition.

View Normalization

Following shape integration and segmentation of figural shape from ground, theories differ in terms of whether object recognition proceeds directly or whether there is a form of 'normalization' to enable a viewpoint-invariant representation to be derived. Normalization here refers to

Normalization: objects can be seen as having the same shape despite differences in viewing conditions the fact that objects can be seen as having the same shape despite differences in viewing conditions. An upright chair, and same chair knocked over will be perceived as being the same object despite the different patterns of retinal stimulation. There are a number of different theories regarding view normalization, and detailed discussion of these is outside the scope of this chapter. Warrington and colleagues (e.g., Warrington & James, 1986; Warrington & Taylor, 1973, 1978) first described patients with damage to the right hemisphere who were poor at matching prototypical views of objects with 'unusual' views. Warrington and James (1986) suggested that patients had difficulty in extracting critical features that would enable objects to be matched across viewpoints. Humphreys and Riddoch (1984) reported a further double dissociation between patients who were either affected by alteration of critical features across the viewpoints or by changes in the principal axis of the object. They manipulated whether the 'unusual' view reduced the saliency of the critical features of object (the minimal feature condition) or whether it maintained these features but foreshortened the main axis of the object (the foreshortened condition; see Figure 3.6). They found one patient whose performance was impaired in the minimal feature condition but not the foreshortened condition, whereas other patients were disrupted in the foreshortened but not the minimal feature condition. Converging evidence that foreshortening the axis is important was provided by the further finding that depicting foreshortened objects against a background with strong linear perspective cues to depth improved the performance of this last group of patients. The depth cues aligned with the principal axis of the object. These results are consistent with proposals that recognition depends on the derivation of viewpoint invariant representations. For example, Marr (1982) suggested that recognition involved derivation of a 3-D model representation in which the parts of objects were described in relation to the principal axis. Humphreys and Riddoch's evidence indicates that some patients find it difficult to encode such representa-

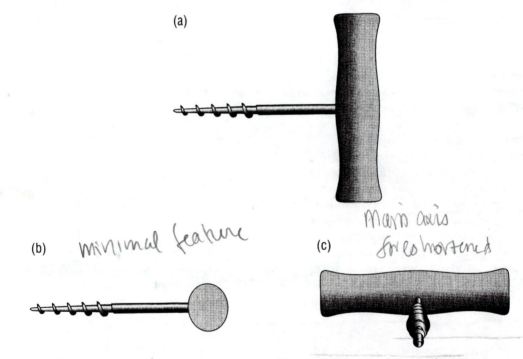

Figure 3.6. Examples of the stimuli used by Humphreys and Riddoch (1984) in their unusual view tests: (a) is a prototypical view of a corkscrew, (b) is a minimal feature view (the handle of the corkscrew is not so readily apparent), (c) is a foreshortened view (the main axis of the corkscrew has been reduced in length).

tions when the principal axis is obscured. However, it remains unclear whether this 'normaliza-tion' process is a necessary part of object recognition. It could be that problems with 'unusual views' reflect impaired procedures for coping with particular forms of object degradation, but these procedures are not needed when objects are not degraded. Indeed, many of the patients reported with deficits with 'unusual views' do not have problems in recognizing prototypical views of objects (see also Davidoff & De Bleser, 1994; Davidoff & Warrington, 1999). Thus, evidence from such patients does not impact on the issue of how objects in familiar viewpoints are recognized. We return to these issues in the next section when we discuss the hemisphere-specialization approach to object recognition.

Access to Stored Knowledge (Structural descriptions)

Neuropsychological evidence also indicates that the process of accessing stored knowledge for object recognition can be fractionated. This is shown most clearly by patterns of sparing and deficits on 'object-decision' tasks. In these tasks patients have to discriminate between depic-tions of real objects and depictions of non-objects. Non-objects can vary in their similarity to real objects, in some cases being equally perceptually good (e.g., where non-objects are con-structed by joining together parts of real objects, see Figure 7). With such non-objects, object decisions appear to rely on access to stored knowledge rather than being based on perceptual information alone. Several patients have been reported who can succeed on difficult object decision tasks but who still seem unable to recognize objects (Hillis & Caramazza, 1995; Riddoch & Humphreys, 1987b; Sheridan & Humphreys, 1993; Stewart, Parkin, & Hunkin, 1992). For instance, patient JB (Riddoch & Humphreys, 1987b) performed object decisions at a normal level but was impaired at judging from vision which two of three objects would be used together (e.g., hammer, nail, spanner). This problem with matching objects based on their functional associations was modality specific; when given the name of the objects JB carried out the same task with ease. Thus JB was impaired at accessing functional-associative knowl-edge from vision but could access forms of visual knowledge to perform the difficult object decision task. Riddoch and Humphreys (1987b) proposed that this reflected a distinction be-tween access to stored structural descriptions for objects and access to stored semantic infor-mation (specifying functional and associative knowledge). The former, but not the latter, was intact in JB. Note that access to both forms of knowledge conform to what Lissauer (1890) originally termed the association process. We suggest that this association process is com-posed of separable hierarchically arranged stages including access to stored structural descrip-tions followed by access to semantic knowledge (see Figure 3.1).

   Other patients have been shown to be impaired at performing object-decision tasks even though they succeed on tests stressing earlier perceptual processes (up to and including un-usual view matching; Forde, Francis, Riddoch, Rumiati, & Humphreys, 1997; Rumiati & Humphreys, 1998; Rumiati, Humphreys, Riddoch, & Bateman, 1994; Sartori & Job, 1988). These patients are typically poor at retrieving stored perceptual knowledge about objects from auditory questions which may be measured in tasks such as drawing from memory or imaging the shape and dimensions of stimuli (e.g., does an elephant have a long tail relative to its body?). This suggests that stored structural descriptions may be accessed not only in order to recognize objects visually but also in the retrieval of visual knowledge to non-visual input. This process of mapping from structural to semantic knowledge may be particularly problematic for stimuli belonging to classes that are both visually and semantically close. This appears to be the case for stimuli from living categories, relative to objects from non-living categories that are perceptually more heterogeneous (see Humphreys, Riddoch, & Quinlan, 1988, for evidence on perceptual similarity differences between object categories). For example, JB (Riddoch & Humphreys, 1987b) showed worse identification for living than non-living things. Humphreys et al. (1988) attributed this to the greater overlap between both structural and semantic

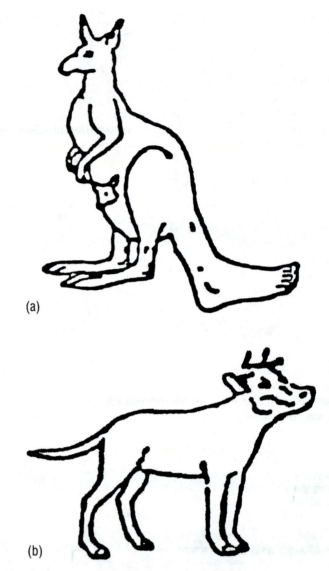

Figure 3.7. Examples of nonobjects: (a) illustrates a nonobject constructed from parts of objects from *different* categories, (b) illustrates a nonobject constructed from parts of objects from the *same* category.

(a)

(b)

representations for living things, which renders identification more difficult for a patient with a deficit mapping between the representations. A similar argument has been made by Arguin, Bub, and colleagues (Arguin, Bub, & Dudek, 1996; Dixon, Bub, & Arguin, 1997)). They examined the ability of an agnosic patient to learn relationships between visual shapes and names. The shapes could vary either along one or along two dimensions (e.g., elongation and bending, to describe a banana-like shape). The performance of the patient was disrupted when stimuli varied along two rather than one dimensions, and when the paired names came from a semantically close set. Semantic proximity had little effect when the stimuli varied along a single dimension, and the number of dimensions involved had little effect when the names referred to semantically dissimilar items. Arguin et al. (1996) argued that the patient could attend, and make discriminations along, a single visual dimension but failed to discriminate more complex visual information (varying along two rather than one dimension). This led to particular difficulties when the visual descriptions had to be related to close rather than more distant semantic representations. Outside the laboratory these difficulties may occur for visually complex and semantically similar living things. Other accounts of differences between the recognition of living and non-living things have been summarized recently by Humphreys and Forde (Forde & Humphreys, 1999; Humphreys & Forde, in press), and they are taken up in the chapter by Shelton and Caramazza (this volume).

6 Access to Stored Knowledge (Semantics) and Phonology

In addition to patients failing to recognize objects because of a difficulty in mapping from structural descriptions to semantics, recognition problems can be caused by a semantic deficit. In such patients naming and recognition problems may be expected even with verbal descriptions of the functional properties of objects, as well as when objects are presented visually. Nevertheless, access to stored structural descriptions, assessed via object decision tasks, can be intact (see Sheridan & Humphreys, 1993; Stewart et al., 1992).

The model outlined in Figure 3.1 has, as its final step, the process of name retrieval for objects. According to this model, name retrieval operates following access to semantic knowledge. This is not a commitment to the view that all one's semantic knowledge must be retrieved before name retrieval can occur, since each stage in the model may operate based on partial activation at earlier stages ('in cascade'; see Humphreys et al., 1988). Nevertheless, access to some forms of semantic information is deemed necessary. The evidence that object naming can proceed non-semantically is weak (Hodges & Greene, 1998, though see Brennen, Danielle, Fluchaire, & Pellat, 1996).

Optic Aphasia

For this model, the syndrome of optic aphasia is something of a puzzle. In optic aphasia patients may misname visually presented objects while (sometimes) being able to gesture how to use the object. Good gestures suggest that semantic access is achieved (see Lhermitte & Beauvois, 1973). Is there then a problem in accessing names from semantic information? The answer here is no, because the same patients can name objects to verbal definitions. The syndrome is problematic for accounts that assume that object naming is achieved via access to a semantic system that is common across modalities, given that visual access to semantics and semantically-based naming from verbal definitions both appear to be intact. Based on such *explanation* reasoning, some authors have argued that optic aphasia is consistent with modality specific *(1)* semantic systems. According to this view, the syndrome arises because access from visual semantics to name information is impaired. Naming to definition, on the other hand, is supported by an intact route from verbal semantics to names (Beauvois, 1982; Shallice, 1987). Another proposal accounts for optic aphasia in terms of hemispheric differences in access to *(2)* name information. Coslett and Saffron (1989b, 1992), for example, suggest that optic aphasic patients can access intact semantics in the right hemisphere but are impaired at accessing name information in the left hemisphere due to hemispheric disconnection. A problem for this account though, is in explaining why accurate gestures can arise in optic aphasia when there is a left hemisphere dominance for gesturing as well as naming (see De Renzi & Faglioni, 1999) for a recent review. In addition, when detailed tests of semantic access have been carried out in patients with optic aphasia, then deficits have been shown (De Renzi & Faglioni, 1999; Hillis & Caramazza, 1995; Riddoch & Humphreys, 1987b). We have already discussed the case of JB who was able to carry out object decisions but was impaired at making functional/associative judgements to visually presented objects. JB also showed a good ability to make gestures to visually presented objects, sometimes making responses that were not only object-specific but also hand-specific (e.g., using his left hand to gesture to a fork, and his right hand to gesture to a knife). Riddoch and Humphreys (1987b) argued that JB's gestures did not indicate access to semantics but rather a direct association between stored structural descriptions and learned actions. These object-action associations may extend beyond single object usage to include familiar action routines, where objects are used sequentially. Lauro-Grotto, Piccini, and Shallice (1997) reported a patient, RM, with dementia that involved loss of semantic (functional and associative) knowledge about objects. Despite this, RM was able to perform routine cooking tasks, with objects being used appropriately in the correct order.

In other instances, patients appear to make actions based on the parts of objects without even necessarily gaining access to stored knowledge of the whole objects. Sirigu, Duhamel, and Poncet (1991), for example, described an agnosic patient, FB, with bilateral temporal lobe lesions who was unable to match visually presented objects using functional or contextual information. Nevertheless, FB demonstrated the use of objects and described how this was done based on the parts present. The parts of objects may be said to 'afford' actions without the objects being recognized—either in terms of accessing stored perceptual or stored functional knowledge (cf. Gibson, 1979).

Hillis and Caramazza (1995) take a similar view to that of Riddoch and Humphreys (1987b) but suggest that partial semantic knowledge may also be used by patients to support gesturing, but that this is insufficient to generate correct naming. The framework offered in Figure 3.1 is consistent with these latter views of optic aphasia.

The Hemisphere Specialization Approach to Object Recognition and Naming

Warrington and colleagues (Rudge & Warrington, 1991; Warrington & James, 1986; Warrington & Taylor, 1973, 1978) have proposed that disorders of object recognition and naming can be understood in terms of hemispheric specialization for the processes of perceptual and semantic classification (see Figure 3,8). They propose that perceptual classification involves assigning objects with different image structures to a common higher-level perceptual category if they have the same underlying shape. This perceptual classification process is probed by the unusual-views matching task that we discussed in the last section. On this view, the process of view normalization (see Figure 3.1) is achieved by perceptual classification. An impaired ability to perform unusual view matches has been found in patients with posterior right hemisphere damage (though see Bulla Helwig, Ettlinger, Dommasch, Ebel, & Skreczeck, 1992; Mulder, Bouma, & Ansink, 1995, for counter evidence), and consequently Warrington and colleagues (Rudge & Warrington, 1991; Warrington & James, 1986; Warrington & Taylor, 1973) have argued that perceptual classification is achieved in the right hemisphere. The means by which perceptual classification is achieved remains unclear, however. Warrington and James (Warrington & James, 1986) suggested that classification was based on the extraction of critical features from objects (though see Humphreys & Riddoch, 1984, for evidence for axis-based coding). Whether access to stored knowledge is also involved, though, is unspecified. This account further proposes that following perceptual classification, information is fed forward to semantic categorization processes performed by the left hemisphere. Consequently patients with left hemisphere damage are impaired at making functional/associative judgements to objects though perceptual classification can be achieved (assessed by means of unusual view matches). Semantic categorization is a necessary precursor to object naming.

This hemispheric specialization account has many similarities to the hierarchical model outlined in Figure 3.1, with one difference being that the hemispheric account is less clear concerning the role of stored structural descriptions in the recognition process. For instance, Rudge and Warrington (1991) found that patients with impaired unusual view matching were not agnosic for prototypical views of objects. From this they argued that prototypical views may be recognized by the left hemisphere. For the hemisphere specialization account this would appear to involve mapping early representation of objects through to left-hemisphere semantic classification processes. How this can be achieved without access to stored structural knowledge is unclear. In addition, functional imaging studies of object recognition suggest that

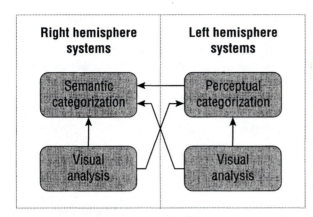

Figure 3.8. Illustrating the hemisphere specialization approach to object recognition and naming (adapted from "Selective impairment of memory and visual perception in splenial tumours," by P. Rudge & E. K. Warrington, 1991, *Brain*, 114, 349–360.

perceptual descriptions for objects are at least as strongly represented within the left as in the right hemisphere. For instance, when brain activations associated with objects or with structurally plausible non-objects are compared with visual noise of meaningless shape baselines, there is bilateral activity in posterior areas of the ventral cortex (lateral and middle occipital regions, fusiform gyrus and inferior, posterior temporal areas; see Kanwisher, Woods, Iacoboni, & Mazziotta, 1997; Martin, Wiggs, Ungeleider, & Haxby, 1996; C. J. Price, Moore, Humphreys, Frackowiak, & Friston, 1996; Schacter et al., 1995). Access to structural representations does not seem to be the sole province of the right hemisphere. In one functional imaging study that assessed the processing of objects in unusual views there was evidence for activation in the inferior parietal cortex but this was present in both hemispheres (Kosslyn et al., 1994). In addition there was evidence for dorsolateral frontal activity (again in both hemispheres) which Kosslyn et al. attribute to problem solving processes needed when objects are distorted from their familiar views. Such problem solving strategies are unlikely to be part of a perceptual classification system used in everyday object recognition.

In some cases recently described by Turnbull and colleagues (Turnbull, 1997; Turnbull, Breschin, & Della Sala, 1997; Turnbull, Laws, & McCarthy, 1995), damage to the right parietal lobe has been associated with a further problem—namely impaired judgements of whether objects are in an upright orientation or not. Typically such patients believe that objects rotated in the plane are upright, and in copying the objects such patients may depict rotated objects as upright. It may be that damage to the parietal lobes impairs the ability to encode object orientation, making performance reliant on a ventral visual system that is insensitive to orientation, perhaps because ventral representations are viewpoint invariant. Rotated versions of objects may be mapped onto these viewpoint invariant representations by having matching features. However, without parietal information specifying the retinal or environmental orientation of the object, patients may then be unable to judge whether or not the object is upright. Being sensitive to orientation, the parietal lobes may play a useful role in identifying objects when they are depicted from unusual viewpoints—in deriving a principle axis, in encoding features across the orientation change, or even in mental rotation conducted as an explicit problem-solving strategy. On this view, hemispheric differences in object processing may be less crucial than differences between ventral and dorsal visual areas.

The Role of Perception in Maintaining Visual Knowledge

Agnosic patients may have intact stored knowledge about the visual appearance and functions of objects, but may not be able to access this knowledge from vision. For instance, HJA, when originally tested, was able to draw items from memory and to provide detailed descriptions of the same items despite having a profound problem in perceptual processing (see section above;

Riddoch & Humphreys, 1987a). The fact that HJA was able to perform such tasks is germane to debates about the relationship between stored visual knowledge and visual imagery. There is some evidence for a shared substrate between perceptual and imagery processes from studies of functional brain activation and from studies of patients with cortical blindness. For instance, there have been a number of reports of activation of even the primary visual cortex during imagery tasks, measured by means of SPECT (Goldenberg et al., 1989), PET (Kosslyn et al., 1993), fMRI (Le Bihan, Turner, Zeffiro, Cuenod, & Bonnerot, 1993), and EEG (Farah, Peronnet, Gonon, & Giard, 1988). However, data obtained in other PET studies has shown activation in occipitoparieto and temporoparietal regions rather than early visual areas in visual imagery tasks (Decety, Kawashima, Gulyàs, & Roland, 1992; Roland & Gulyás, 1994). It has been argued that this may be due to differences in the visual imagery tasks (see Policardi et al., 1996).

If primary visual cortex is critical in visual imagery, then loss of it (as in cases of cortical blindness) should result in a similar loss or severe impairment to visual imagery. Support for this proposal comes from Policardi et al. (1996) who describe a patient, TC, who became cortically blind following a road traffic accident. Neuroimaging studies showed bilateral metabolic reduction in calcarine and associative occipital areas, and extending to mesial and temporal cortex. TC demonstrated a severe impairment of visual imagery which was tested extensively in a number of different ways (including measures of topographical imagery, symbol imagery, animal and object imagery, and color imagery). The impaired visual imagery did not result from a degradation of stored knowledge, as TC performed well on tests of stored associative/functional information.

However, while the case of TC can be used to support the contention that there is a common substrate for imagery and perception, other cases of cortical blindness do not fit this pattern. Chattergee and Southwood (1995) report intact visual imagery in a case of a patient with cortical blindness. The patient suffered a subarachnoid hemorrhage as a result of a right frontal arteriovenous malformation, which caused infarctions of the posterior cerebral arteries. Her imagery abilities were assessed in some detail and she was shown to perform at (or above) control levels in all tests bar one (a test of spatial imagery). A similar case of preserved visual imagery in a case of cortical blindness has been described by Goldenberg, Müllbacher, and Nowak (1995). The patient, HS, suffered a bilateral posterior cerebral infarction resulting in destruction of Brodmann's areas 18 and 19, and atrophy of areas 28, 35, 36, and 37. There was bilateral damage of area 17. HS was blind, although she denied this (this was also true of patient TC, above). Goldenberg et al. (1995) argued that TC had a lack of awareness because she confused her mental visual images with real percepts. Assessment of HS's imagery included tests of her ability to access knowledge of the shapes of letters and the shapes and colors of objects. In all instances, she performed well (see Goldenberg & Artner, 1991).

A number of patients have been reported with relatively preserved visual imagery following visual agnosia, and of these, four have been described in some depth (see Behrmann, Winocur, & Moscovitch, 1992; Behrmann, Moscovitch, & Winocur, 1994; Jankowiak, Kinsbourne, Shalev, & Bachman, 1992; Riddoch & Humphreys, 1987a; Servos & Goodale, 1995; Servos, Goodale, & Humphrey, 1993; Young, Humphreys, Riddoch, Hellawell, & de Haan, 1994). CK (Behrmann, Winocur, et al., 1992, 1994) was thought to have sustained bilateral thinning of the occipital lobes as a result of a head injury; MD (Jankowiak et al., 1992), DF, and HJA suffered bilateral occipito-temporal lesions.

The four patients showed different degrees of severity of visual agnosia, with MD (Jankowiak et al., 1992) showing the greatest sparing of visual recognition (91%, 75%, 62%, and 48% correct for naming visually presented real objects, for MD, DF, HJA, and CK, respectively). All four patients were also more impaired at naming line drawings than at naming real objects. When initially tested, all four patients were able to draw from memory objects that they were no longer able to recognize. However, in a long-term follow-up of HJA, Riddoch et al. (1999) found that there was a deterioration in performance over time (and relative to control performance) which was most pronounced for objects from categories with visually similar exemplars (natural kinds). This drop in drawing performance was mirrored by HJA's verbal definitions of objects. In the first years post lesion, HJA's verbal definitions contained many visual as well as nonvisual (functional and associative) details about objects. In the follow-up examination, the number of nonvisual properties had increased, while the number of visual properties had decreased. Since there was an increase in the number of nonvisual properties listed, there was no evidence for a general decline in his abilities; rather, there was a shift away from being able to recall the visual properties of objects. These findings are consistent with there being some interaction between visual perception and memory (and with the consequent expression of memory in imagery). In particular, perceptual processing of objects may lead to a consistent updating of visual memories over time, so that these memories remain tuned to the visual properties of objects in the world. Such consistent tuning of memorial processes to vision fits with connectionist accounts of cognition, in which recognition systems change adaptively to the inputs they receive over time (Ellis & Humphreys, 1999). When perceptual inputs are impaired, as in forms of agnosia, visual memorial processes may gradually show some decline, with there being less fine tuning of the system to the visual properties of objects. In cases where imagery appears to be preserved, either in agnosia or in patients with cortical blindness, testing needs to be conducted over a longer time period to evaluate the sustained effect of perceptual degradation on memory.

These results on the relation between perception and memory can be related to recent studies using PET studies on visual perceptual learning. An object in a degraded image which appears meaningless when seen for the first time can be easily recognized when an undegraded image of the object is presented first (when the recognition system is 'primed'). Dolan, Frith, and colleagues (Dolan et al., 1997; Frith & Dolan, 1997) have found that changes between the first (naive) and second (primed) state were associated with enhanced processing of inferior temporal regions involved in visual object processing (particularly the fusiform gyrus). Effects were differentially lateralized for objects and faces suggesting that item-specific learning takes place in these regions. The data match results on learning-related tuning of temporal lobe activity in the monkey (Sakai & Miyashita, 1994, 1995; Tovee, Rolls, & Ramachandran, 1996). In addition, Dolan and Frith (1997) reported enhanced activity in medial and lateral parietal cortex that was specific to perceptual learning (the change between the naive and primed state). They suggested that the parietal activity could reflect the involvement of imagery in reconstructing degraded stimuli and in binding the parts of these stimuli together. The critical lesions in forms of apperceptive (perceptual) agnosia involve the inferior occipito-temporal regions, consistent with the site of item-specific learning in PET studies. It is possible that this brain area is intimately involved in the updating of visual knowledge about specific objects in everyday life, a process that can be impaired after the occurance of brain lesions (see Riddoch et al., 1999).

OBJECTS, FACES, AND WORDS

The visual system is presented with many different perceptual forms—including faces and word as well as other object types. Are all visually presented forms processed in the same way, or is there specialization for different stimuli? It can be argued that some of the computational requirements of object recognition differ from those of, say, face and word recognition; hence different routines and neural structures may be involved. For instance, face recognition requires the identification of a specific exemplar within a visually homogenous category, while object recognition generally only requires categorization at a base level (Henke, Schweinberger, Grigo, Klos, & Sommer, 1998).

Have special processes evolved for object recognition? Some of the computational requirements for object recognition differ from those of, say, face and word recognition; hence different routines and neural structures may be involved. There are a number of pieces of evidence which point to face processing being 'special'. Face recognition has been shown to be selectively impaired relative to objects of equivalent difficulty (Farah, Tanaka, & Drain, 1995). Single unit recordings in the temporal cortex of the monkey show selective responses to faces (some responding differentially to particular characteristics (Desimone, 1991). Developmentally, face recognition appears to have an innate component (Johnson, Dziurawiec, Ellis, & Morton, 1991). Furthermore, unlike most other stimuli, faces are particularly hard to recognize when they have been inverted (Valentine, 1988). Farah and her colleagues have argued that faces are represented as parts and wholes to the same degree as other visual patterns, but, for faces, the whole level representation is particularly important (Farah, Wilson, Drain, & Tanaka, 1998). As concerns neuropsychological disorders, Farah (1990) has argued that there are particular relations between agnosia, prosopagnosia (deficits in recognizing faces), and alexia (difficulties in reading), that are informative about the nature of the visual information used to recognize the different classes of stimulus. In a review of historical cases, she noted that there were patients with 'pure' alexia and 'pure' prosopagnosia (i.e., without concomitant deficits with other classes of stimulus), and cases of mixed deficits where patients had agnosia and alexia, agnosia and prosopagnosia, and also all three deficits. However, there were no convincing cases with 'pure' agnosia (i.e., without problems in reading or face recognition) and no cases with a 'mixed' impairment including alexia and prosopagnosia without agnosia. From this she concluded that there were two underlying visual processes that could be affected and lead to recognition deficits in patients: one concerned with processing holistic[1] visual representations (needed for face recognition), and one was concerned with processing multiple parts in parallel (e.g., the letters in words). These two processes would each contribute to object recognition, to different degrees, depending on the properties of the object. She argued that lesions to the process dealing with holistic representations would disrupt face recognition and possibly also object recognition (if the lesions are more severe), while lesions to processes dealing with multiple parts would disrupt word recognition and again object recognition to some degree (for those objects dependent on these part-based processes, with joint impairments found with more severe damage). Pure object agnosia, on the other hand, should not occur because there is not a unique process used for object recognition. Similarly, it should not be possible to damage both face and word recognition without there also being some disruption to object recognition, which will depend on the same processes. However, recent neuropsychological data contradict the view that all visual recognition impairments can be accounted for in terms of disruption to either holistic or parts-based perceptual processes. For example, Rumiati, Humphreys, and colleagues (Humphreys & Rumiati, 1998; Rumiati et al., 1994) have reported two cases of 'pure' agnosia, where the patients seemed to have good face and word recognition (reading words at a normal rate rather than letter-by-letter), but impaired object recognition. Both patients suffered degenerative impairments and had some problems in retrieving semantic information about objects even from words, but the problems were more serious with objects. Both were impaired at object decision tasks and one made primarily visual errors. This pattern of impairment is consistent with the patients having damage to stored visual memories for objects, and both performed well on a range of perceptual tests (including unusual view matching). The pattern would not be expected if all recognition impairments were due to perceptual impairments affecting either holistic or parts-based representations. If such perceptual impairments were important here, patients should always have associated deficits with

---

[1] By 'holistic processing' we mean that the processing of individual features is significantly influenced by the configuration of the complete stimulus (e.g., a face). Thus, while subjects may be able to identify people even when only half the face is presented (the face split down the midline), they have extreme difficulty in identifying the component halves in chimeric faces (faces composed of halves of faces of two different individuals; Young, Hellawell, & Hay, 1987).

either faces or words in addition to any problems in object recognition. The second pattern of deficit that goes against a simple two-process account has also been documented recently by Buxbaum, Glosser, and Coslett (1999) and by De Renzi and Di Pellegrino (1998). These investigators have reported patients with alexia and prosopagnosia but with relatively preserved object recognition. The data suggest that memory representations for faces, objects, and words can differ, so that there can be selective degeneration of visual memories for objects rather than for words or faces (and perhaps also vice versa). These last results also emphasize that not all recognition deficits are perceptual in nature, and that some reflect memorial rather than perceptual impairments—as we have suggested by both hierarchical and hemispheric specialization accounts of recognition disorders. It may be the case that the dichotomy between holistic and parts-based descriptions accounts for many of the perceptual differences between face, object, and word recognition, but memorial differences need to be considered. In addition, we need to distinguish between parts-based descriptions that are coded independently for individual parts (e.g., the letters in words) and those that are grouped to form a larger perceptual unit (e.g., supraletter codes in words). We suggest that a full account of face, object, and word processing will need to accommodate effects of grouped features in recognition (see also De Haan, this volume).

INTERACTIVE EFFECTS IN OBJECT PROCESSING

The hierarchical and hemispheric specialization approaches to visual recognition have been discussed in terms of strict bottom-up activation processes. For instance, there is a stage of visual grouping prior to access to stored structural descriptions, and we have suggested that structural descriptions can be accessed prior to (and in the face of impairments to) semantic knowledge. However, other evidence indicates that visual processing may be more interactive, with later forms of information influencing earlier processes. For top-down effects to operate during on-line object recognition, partial activation would need to be transmitted between processing stages rather than each stage being discrete. Evidence for partial transmission of information can be drawn from a number of sources. One piece of evidence concerns the errors made by normal subjects in object naming. When forced to respond to a fast response deadline. Normal subjects make errors that are *both* visually and semantically close to target objects (Vitkovitch, Humphreys, & Lloyd-Jones, 1993). Naming to a deadline seems to comprise the process of name retrieval (Vitkovitch & Humphreys, 1991). If visual access to semantics is complete by the time name retrieval starts, then naming errors should only be semantic in nature. That errors are *both* visual and semantic suggests that visual access to semantics is not fully complete before name retrieval gets underway.

There are also data consistent with top-down feedback during early stages of visual coding. Peterson and colleagues (e.g., Peterson & Gibson, 1994) have had normal subjects make figure–ground judgements to stimuli with ambiguous figure–ground relationships. With such displays, judgements to perceptual figures are biased to familiar forms. Information about the familiarity of objects can be activated whilst figure–ground coding takes place. Top-down activation may further help explain some of the evidence on functional brain imaging which has shown selective activation of particular neural areas for particular objects (e.g., artifacts vs. natural kinds; see Martin et al., 1996; Moore & Price, 1997, 1999; Perani et al., 1995). The identification of particular object types may involve top-down activation of forms of knowledge that differentiate between members of the relevant object class. Hence, there is enhanced activation of perceptual information in the inferior occipito-temporal cortex for the regions identification of living things, since living things are typically defined in terms of their perceptual attributes (Farah & McClelland, 1991). There is activation of knowledge about action and movement in more middle temporal and inferior frontal regions for the identification of artifacts, since these objects are defined in terms of this information. Price, Moore, Humphreys,

Frackowiak, and Friston (1996) further showed that enhanced activation of posterior, inferior temporal regions was found when naming rather than recognition was stressed. This is consistent with top-down activation particularly coming into play when activation needs to be sufficiently precise to enable a unique name to be derived (see Humphreys et al., 1997, for this argument).

If object naming is indeed interactive (top-down as well as bottom-up), then this is likely to impact on the performance of patients. For instance, object naming may be selectively impaired by lesions affecting the ability to activate early forms of knowledge in a top-down fashion, although basic recognition may be achieved in a bottom-up manner. Data that fit with this have been reported by Forde et al. (1997) and Humphreys et al. (1997). They documented evidence on patients with unilateral (left) medial extrastriate lesions whose problem was much more pronounced in naming than in recognition. They suggested that the posterior lesion disrupted top-down reactivation of perceptual knowledge, required to name rather than to recognize (particularly) living things.

COVERT PROCESSING

At various junctures throughout this chapter we have discussed findings in which patients have shown an ability to process information when tested covertly but not when tested overtly. We refer to a covert procedure as requiring either: (a) the patient does not have to respond directly to the stimulus property of interest, but the effect of processing that property is shown through its effect on another stimulus; or (b) the patient is made to guess when they cannot discriminate the stimulus property directly. An example of (a) is the finding that the agnosic patient DF showed the McCollough aftereffect for color which was contingent on another property (orientation) that the patient could not discriminate in an explicit orientation discrimination task. An example of (b) is the above chance performance shown by patients with blindsight when asked to guess about the location of a stimulus that they are unaware of (see section on visual processing earlier in the chapter). In addition to the covert abilities we have mentioned, several others have been shown in patients with a variety of visual disorders. To cite but three: (a) achromatopsic patients can show above chance discrimination in same-different matching with isoluminant stimuli (Heywood et al., 1991; Troscianko et al., 1996); (b) prosopagnosic patients can shown better face-name learning for familiar but unrecognized faces than for unfamiliar faces (De Haan, Young, & Newcombe, 1987); and, (c) alexic patients can be above chance at discriminating the categories of words presented so briefly that the patients claim not to be able to read them (Coslett & Saffran, 1989a). McNeil and Warrington (1991) have gone so far as to argue that tests of covert recognition in prosopagnosic patients can provide a means to separate patients with a deficit in stored visual knowledge for faces and patients with a deficit after this stage. Tests of covert processing then provide at least an important source of convergent evidence for diagnosing the locus of functional deficit in a patient. They may even throw new light on the functional diagnosis.

Several different accounts of covert processing can be offered. One is that covert abilities reflect visual processing in visual pathways that do not lead to conscious awareness. This form of account can be offered to explain blindsight, where the residual abilities in blindsight patients can be related to processing in a residual collicular pathway (Cowey & Stoerig, 1992). Another account of covert processing is that it is produced by partial activation of visual processes to a subthreshold level. This can be sufficient to generate above-chance guessing and even to affect the processing of other stimuli, but not to produce overt discrimination (see Burton, Bruce, & Johnson, 1990; Farah, 1994, for simulations; also Farah, this volume). Another possibility is that covert processing is contingent on transitory activation that cannot be sustained long enough to generate overt behavior. Whatever the case, the evidence demonstrate that it is important to test for covert processing abilities in patients to help document the functional nature of the disorder.

SUMMARY

We have reviewed evidence that visual processing can break down in a variety of ways after brain damage. Damage to striate and extra-striate cortical areas can lead to selective disorders in coding basic properties of images, such as color, elementary form, depth, and motion. In instances of blindsight, there can be coding of these properties without any perceptual awareness on the part of the subject. In addition to these disorders of early vision, contrasting impairments can also arise in higher-level processes that lead to object recognition. Here we have distinguished disorders of: feature binding and shape segmentation, view-normalization, access to stored structural descriptions, access to semantic knowledge, and access to names. These different disorders can be conceptualized in several ways and we have discussed the hierarchical and hemispheric specialization views. We have also noted evidence indicating that failures in object recognition can coincide with patients being able to use the information for action both for prehensile reaching and grasping and also for learned actions in cases of optic aphasia. Finally, evidence on the relations between visual perception and imagery, and on top-down as well as bottom-up factors in vision, indicates that vision is interactive in at least two ways: (a) it is constantly updating our visual memories of the world, and (b) even in on-line naming tasks, top-down processes may play a role in differentiating objects with their categories. The evidence we have considered not only throws light on different neurological conditions, but also on the processes underlying normal visual recognition and naming.

Acknowledgements

We gratefully acknowledge the support of the MRC.

REFERENCES

Arguin, M., Bub, D. N., & Dudek, G. (1996). Shape integration for visual object recognition and its implication in category-specific visual agnosia. *Visual Cognition, 3*, 221–275.

Barbur, J. L., Ruddock, K. H., & Waterfield, V. A. (1980). Human visual responses in the absence of the geniculocalcarine projection. *Brain, 102*, 905–928.

Beauvois, M.-F. (1982). Optic aphasia: A process of interaction between vision and language. *Philosophical Transactions of the Royal Society, B289*, 35–47.

Behrmann, M., Moscovitch, M., & Winocur, G. (1994). Intact visual imagery and impaired visual perception in a patient with visual agnosia. *Journal of Experimental Psychology: Human Perception and Performance, 20*, 1068–1087.

Behrmann, M., Winocur, G., & Moscovitch, M. (1992). Dissociation between mental imagery and object recognition in a brain damaged patient. *Nature, 359*, 636–637.

Benton, A. L., & Hécaen, H. (1970). Stereoscopic vision in patients with unilateral cerebral disease. *Neurology, 4*, 344–358.

Biederman, I. (1987). Recognition by components: A theory of human image understanding. *Psychological Review, 94*, 115–145.

Biederman, I., & Gerhardstein, P. C. (1993). Recognising depth-rotated objects: Evidence and conditionsfor three-dimensional viewpoint invariance. *Journal of Experimental Psychology: Human Perception and Performance., 19*, 1162–1182.

Brennen, T., Danielle, D., Fluchaire, I., & Pellat, J. (1996). Naming faces and objects without comprehension. *Cognitive Neuropsychology, 15*, 93–110.

Bridgeman, B., & Staggs, D. (1982). Plasticity in human blindsight. *Vision Research, 22*, 1199–1203.

Bulla Helwig, M., Ettlinger, G., Dommasch, D., Ebel, E., & Skreczeck, W. (1992). Impaired visual perceptual categorisation in right brain-damaged patients. Failure to replicate. *Cortex, 28*, 261–272.

Burton, M., Bruce, V., & Johnson, R. (1990). Understanding face recognition with an interactive activation model. *British Journal of Psychology, 81*, 361–380.

Butter, C. M., & Trobe, J. D. (1994). Integrative agnosia following progressive multifocal leukoencephalopathy. *Cortex, 30*, 145–158.

Buxbaum, L. J., Grosser, G., & Coslett, H. B. (1999). Impaired face and word recognition with object agnosia. *Neuropsychologia, 37*, 41–50.

Carmon, A., & Bechtold, H. P. (1969). Dominance of the right cerebral hemisphere for stereopsis. *Neuropsychologia, 7*, 29–40.

Chattergee, A., & Southwood, M. H. (1995). Cortical blindness and visual imagery. *Neurology, 45*, 2189–2195.

Corbetta, M., Meizin, F. M., Dobmeyer, S., Shulman, G. L., & Petersen, S. E. (1991). Selective and divided attention during visual discrimination of shape, color and speed: Functional anatomy by positron emission tomography. *Journal of Cognitive Neuroscience, 11*, 2383–2402.

Coslett, H. M., & Saffran, E. M. (1989a). Evidence for preserved reading in 'pure alexia'. *Brain, 112*, 327–359.

Coslett, H. M., & Saffran, E. M. (1989b). Preserved object recognition and reading comprehension in optic aphasia. *Brain, 1989*, 1091–1110.

Coslett, H. M., & Saffran, E. M. (1992). Optic aphasia

and the right hemisphere: A replication and extension. *Brain and Language*, *43*, 148-161.

Cowey, A., & Stoerig, P. (1992). Reflections on blindsight. In A. D. Milner & M. D. Rugg (Eds.), *The neuropsychology of consciousness*. London: Academic Press.

Danta, G., Hilton, R. C., & O'Boyle, D. J. (1978). Hemispheric function and binocular depth perception. *Brain*, *101*, 569-590.

Davidoff, J., & De Bleser, R. (1994). A case study of photographic anomia: impaired picture naming with preserved object naming and reading. *Brain and Cognition*, *24*, 1-23.

Davidoff, J., & Warrington, E. K. (1999). The bare bones of object recognition: implications from a case of object recognition impairment. *Neuropsychologia*, *37*, 279-292.

De Haan, E. H. F., Young, A. W., & Newcombe, F. (1987). Face recognition without awareness. *Cognitive Neuropsychology*, *4*, 385-415.

Decety, J., Kawashima, R., Gulyàs, B., & Roland, P. E. (1992). Preparation for reaching: A PET study of the participating structures in the human brain. *NeuroReport*, *3*, 761-764.

De Renzi, E., & Faglioni, P. (1999). Apraxia. In G. Denes & L. Pizzamiglio (Eds.), *Handbook of Clinical and Experimental Neuropsychology*. Hove: Psychology Press.

De Renzi, E., & Lucchelli, F. (1994). Are semantic systems separately represented in the brain? The case of living category impairment. *Cortex*, *30*, 3-25.

De Renzi, E., & Di Pellegrino, G. (1998). Prosopagnosia and alexia without object agnosia. *Cortex*, *34*, 41-50.

Desimone, R. (1991). Face-selective cells in the temporal cortex of monkeys. *Journal of Cognitive Neuroscience*, *3*, 1-8.

Dixon, M., Bub, D. N., & Arguin, M. (1997). The interaction of object form and object meaning in the identification performance of a patient with a category-specific visual agnosia. *Cognitive Neuropsychology*, *14*, 1085-1130.

Dolan, R. J., Fink, G. R., Rolls, E., Booth, M., Holmes, A., Frackowiak, R. S. J., & Friston, K. J. (1997). How the brain learns to see faces and objects in an impoverished context. *Nature*, *389*, 596-599.

Duncan, J., & Humphreys, G. W. (1989). Visual search and visual similarity. *Psychological Review*, *96*, 433-458.

Edelman, S., & Duvdevani-Bar, S. (1997). A model of visual recognition and categorisation. *Philosophical Transactions of the Royal Society Series B*, *352*, 1203-1220.

Edwards, M. G., & Humphreys, G. W. (1999). Pointing and grasping in unilateral neglect: effect of on-line visual feedback in grasping. *Neuropsychologia*, *37*, 959-973.

Efron, R. (1968). What is perception? *Boston Studies in Philosophy of Science*, *4*, 137-173.

Egly, R., Driver, J., & Rafal, R. D. (1994). Shifting visual attention between objects and locations: Evidence from normal and parietal lesion subjects. *Journal of Experimental Psychology: General*, *123*, 161-171.

Ellis, R., & Humphreys, G. W. (1999). *Connectionist psychology*. London: Psychology Press.

Farah, M. J. (1990). *Visual agnosia*. Cambridge: MIT Press.

Farah, M. J. (1994). Neuropsychological inference with an interactive brain: A critique of the locality assumption. *Behavioural and Brain Sciences*, 43-61.

Farah, M. J., & McClelland, J. L. (1991). A computational model of semantic memory impairment: Modality specificity and emergent category specificity. *Journal of Experimental Psychology: General*, *120*, 339-357.

Farah, M. J., Peronnet, F., Gonon, M. A., & Giard, M. H. (1988). Electrophysiological evidence for a shared representational medium for visual images and percepts. *Journal of Experimental Psychology: General*, *117*, 248-257.

Farah, M. J., Tanaka, J. N., & Drain, M. (1995). What causes the face inversion effect? *Journal of Experimental Psychology: Human Perception and Performance*, *21*, 628-634.

Farah, M. J., & Wallace, M. (1991). Pure alexia as a visual impairment: A reconsideration. *Cognitive Neuropsychology*, *8*, 313-334.

Farah, M. J., Wilson, K. D., Drain, M., & Tanaka, J. N. (1998). What is "special" about face perception? *Psychological Review*, *105*, 482-498.

Forde, E., & Humphreys, G. W. (1999). Category-specific recognition impairments: A review of important case studies and influential theories. *Aphasiology*, *13*, 169-193.

Forde, E. M. E., Francis, D., Riddoch, M. J., Rumiati, R. I., & Humphreys, G. W. (1997). On the links between visual knowledge and naming: A single case study of a patient with a category-specific impairment for living things. *Cognitive Neuropsychology*, *14*, 403-458.

Frith, C., & Dolan, R. J. (1997). Brain mechanisms associated with top-down processes in perception. *Philosophical Transactions of the Royal Society*, *352*, 1221-1230.

Gilbert, C. D. (1992). Horizontal integration and cortical dynamics. *Neuron*, *9*, 1-13.

Gilbert, C. D., & Wiesel, T. N. (1989). Columnar specificity of intrinsic horizontal and corticocortical connections in cat visual cortex. *Journal of Neuroscience*, *9*, 2432-2442.

Giersch, A., Humphreys, G. W., & Boucart, M. (in press). The computation of occluded contours in visual agnosia: Evidence of early computation prior to shape binding and figure-ground coding. *Cognitive Neuropsychology*.

Gloning, I., Gloning, K., & Hoff, H. (1968). *Neuropsychological symptoms and syndromes in lesions of the occipital lobes and adjacent areas*. Paris: Gauthier-Villars.

Goldenberg, G., & Artner, C. (1991). Visual imagery and knowledge about the visual appearance of objects in patients with posterior cerebral artery lesions. *Brain and Cognition*, *15*, 160-186.

Goldenberg, G., Müllbacher, W., & Nowak, A. (1995). Imagery without perception - a case study of anosagnosia for cortical blindness. *Neuropsychologia*, *33*, 1373-1382.

Goldenberg, G., Podreka, I., Steiner, M., Willmes, K., Suess, E., & Deecke, L. (1989). Regional blood flow patterns in visual imagery. *Neuropsychologia*, *27*, 641-664.

Goldstein, K., & Gelb, A. (1918). Psychologische Analysen hirnpathologischer Falle auf Grund von Untersuchungen Hirnverletzer. *Zeitschrift fuer die gesamte Neurologie und Psychiatrie*, *41*, 1-142.

Goodale, M. A., Milner, A. D., Jakobson, L. S., & Carey, D. P. (1991). A neurological dissociation between perceiving objects and grasping them. *Nature*, *349*, 154-156.

Grossman, M., Galetta, S., & D'Esposito, M. (1997). Object recognition difficulty in visual apperceptive agnosia. *Brain and Cognition*, *33*, 306-342.

Haxby, J. V., Grady, C. L., Horwitz, B., Salerno, J., Ungeleider, L. G., Mishkin, M., & Shapiro, M. B. (1993). Dissociation of object and spatial visual processing pathways in human extrastriate cortex. In B. Gulyas, D. Ottoson, & P. E. Roland (Eds.), *Functional organisation of the human visual cortex*. Oxford: Pergamon Press.

Henke, K., Schweinberger, S. R., Grigo, A., Klos, T., & Sommer, W. (1998). Specificity of face recognition: Recognition of exemplars of non-face objects in prosopagnosia. *Cortex, 34*, 289-296.

Heywood, C., Cowey, A., & Newcombe, F. (1991). Chromatic discrimination in a cortically blind observor. *European Journal of Neuroscience, 3*, 802-812.

Heywood, C. A., Wilson, B., & Cowey, A. (1987). A case study of cortical color "blindness" with relatively intact achromatopic discrimination. *Journal of Neurology, Neurosurgery and Psychiatry, 50*, 22-29.

Heywood, C. A., & Zihl, J. (1999). Motion blindness. In G. W. Humphreys (Ed.), *Case studies in the neuropsychology of vision*. Hove: Psychology Press.

Hillis, A. E., & Caramazza, A. (1995). Cognitive and neural mechanisms underlying visual and semantic processing: Implications from "Optic Aphasia". *Journal of Cognitive Neuroscience, 7*, 457-478.

Hodges, J. R., & Greene, J. D. W. (1998). Knowing about people and naming them: Can Alzheimer's Disease patients do one without the other? *Quarterly Journal of Experimental Psychology, 51A*, 121-134.

Holmes, G. (1918). Disturbances of visual orientation. *British Journal of Opthalmology, 2*, 449-468 & 506-518.

Holmes, G., & Horrax, G. (1919). Disturbances of spatial orientation and visual attention with a loss of stereoscopic vision. *Archives of Neurology and Psychiatry, 1*, 385-407.

Humphrey, G. K., Goodale, M. A., & Gurnsey, R. (1991). Orientation discrimination in a visual form agnosic: Evidence from the McCullough effect. *Psychological Science, 2*, 331-335.

Humphreys, G. W., & Forde, E. M. E. (in press). Category-specific deficits: A review and presentation of the Hierarchical Interactive Theory (HIT). *Behavioural and Brain Sciences*.

Humphreys, G. W., Quinlan, P. T., & Riddoch, M. J. (1989). Grouping effects in visual search: Effects with single- and combined-feature targets. *Journal of Experimental Psychology: General, 118*, 258-279.

Humphreys, G. W., & Riddoch, M. J. (1984). Routes to object constancy: Implications from neurological impairments of object constancy. *Quarterly Journal of Experimental Psychology, 36A*, 385-415.

Humphreys, G. W., & Riddoch, M. J. (1987a). The fractionation of visual agnosia. In G. W. Humphreys & M. J. Riddoch (Eds.), *Visual object processing: A cognitive neuropsycholological approach*. London: Lawrence Erlbaum.

Humphreys, G. W., & Riddoch, M. J. (1987b). *To see but not to see: A case of visual agnosia*. London: Lawrence Erlbaum.

Humphreys, G. W., & Riddoch, M. J. (1993). Object agnosias. In C. Kennard (Ed.), *Bailllieres Clinical Neurology* (pp. 339-359). London: Bailliere Tindall.

Humphreys, G. W., Riddoch, M. J., & Boucart, M. (1992). The breakdown approach to visual perception: Neuropsychological studies of object recognition. In G. W. Humpreys (Ed.), *Understanding vision: An interdisciplinary perspective*. Oxford, UK: Oxford University Press.

Humphreys, G. W., Riddoch, M. J., Donnelly, N., Freeman, T., Boucart, M., & Müller, H. (1992). Intermediate visual processing and visual agnosia. In M. J. Farah & G. Ratcliff (Eds.), *The Neurophysiology of High Level Vision*. Hillsdale, N. J.: Lawrence Erlbaum Associates.

Humphreys, G. W., Riddoch, M. J., & Price, C. J. (1997). Top-down processes in object identification: Evidence from experimental psychology, neuropsychology and functional anatomy. *Philosophical Transactions of the Royal Society, B352*, 1275-1282.

Humphreys, G. W., Riddoch, M. J., & Quinlan, P. T. (1985). Interactive processes in perceptual organisation: Evidence from visual agnosia. In M. I. M.I. Posner & O. S. M. Marin (Eds.), *Attention and Performance XI*. Hillsdale, N.J.: Erlbaum.

Humphreys, G. W., Riddoch, M. J., & Quinlan, P. T. (1988). Cascade processes in picture identification. *Cognitive Neuropsychology, 5*, 67-103.

Humphreys, G. W., Riddoch, M. J., Quinlan, P. T., Donnelly, N., & Price, C. A. (1992). Parallel pattern processing and visual agnosia. *Canadian Journal of Psychology, 46*(3), 377-416.

Humphreys, G. W., Romani, C., Olson, A., Riddoch, M. J., & Duncan, J. (1994). Non-spatial extinction following lesions of the parietal lobe in humans. *Nature, 372*, 357-359.

Humphreys, G. W., & Rumiati, R. I. (1998). When joys come not in single spies but in battalions: Within-category and within-modality identification increases the accessibility of degraded store knowledge. *Neurocase, 4*, 111-126.

James, W. (1890). *The principles of psychology*. New York: Holt.

Jankowiak, J., Kinsbourne, M., Shalev, R. S., & Bachman, D. L. (1992). Preserved visual imagery and categorisation in a case of associative visual agnosia. *Journal of Cognitive Neuroscience, 4*, 119-131.

Johnson, J. C., Dziurawiec, S., Ellis, H. D., & Morton, J. (1991). Newborns' preferential tracking of face-like stimuli and its subsequent decline. *Cognition, 40*, 1-19.

Kanwisher, N., Woods, R. P., Iacoboni, M., & Mazziotta, J. C. (1997). A locus in human extrastriate cortex for visual shape analysis. *Journal of Cognitive Neuroscience, 9*, 133-142.

Kartsounis, L. D., & Warrington, E. K. (1991). Failure of object recognition due to a breakdown of figure-ground discrimination in a patient with normal acuity. *Neuropsychologia, 29*, 969-980.

Kölmel, H. W. (1988). Pure homonymous hemiachromatopsia: findings with neuro-opthalmologic examination and imaging techniques. *European Archives of Psychiatry and Neurological Sciences, 237*, 237-243.

Kosslyn, S. M., Alpert, N. M., Thompson, W. L., Chabris, C. F., Rauch, S. L., & Anderson, A. K. (1994). Identifying objects seen from different viewpoints: a PET investigation. *Brain, 117*, 1055-1071.

Kosslyn, S. M., Alpert, N. M., Thompson, W. L., Maljkovic, V., Weise, S. B., Chabris, C. F., Hamilton, S. E., Rauch, S. L., & Buonanno, F. S. (1993). Visual mental imagery activates topographically organised visual cortex: PET investigations. *Journal of Cognitive Neuroscience, 5*, 263-287.

Lamb, M. R., Robertson, L. C., & Knight, R. T. (1990). Component mechanisms underlying the processing of hierarchically organised patterns - inferences from patients with unilateral cortical lesions. *Journal of Experimental Psychology: Learning, Memory and Cognition., 16,* 471–483.

Lauro-Grotto, R., Piccini, C., et al. (1997). Modality-specific operations in semantic dementia. *Cortex, 33,* 593–622.

Lawson, R., & Humphreys, G. W. (1999). The effects of view in depth on the identification of line drawings and silhouettes of familiar objects: Normality and pathology. *Visual Cognition.*

Le Bihan, O., Turner, R., Zeffiro, T. A., Cuenod, C. A., & Bonnerot, V. (1993). Activation of human primary visual cortex during visual recall: A magnetic resonance imaging study. *Proceedings of the National Academy of Sciences, 90,* 11802–11805.

Lhermitte, F., & Beauvois, M. F. (1973). A visual-speech disconnection syndrome. Report of a case with optic aphasia. *Brain, 96,* 695–714.

Li, B. B., Martin, P. R., & Valberg, A. (1989). Nonlinear summation of M- and L-cone inputs to phasic retinal ganglion cells of the macaque. *Journal of Neuroscience, 9.*

Lissauer, H. (1890). Ein fall von seelenblindheit nebst einem beitrage zur theorie derselben. *Archiv für Psychiatrie und Nervenkrankheiten, 21,* 222–270.

Livingstone, M. S., & Hubel, D. H. (1987). Psychophysical evidence for separate channels for the perception of form, color, movement and depth. *Journal of Neuroscience, 7,* 3416–3468.

Lueck, C. J., Zeki, S., Friston, K. J., Deiber, M.-P., Cope, P., Cunningham, V. J., Lammertsma, A. A., Kennard, C., & Frackowiack, R. S. J. (1989). The color centre in the cerebral cortex of man. *Nature, 340,* 386–389.

Marcel, A. J. (1998). Blindsight and shape perception: deficit of visual consciousness or of visual function? *Brain, 121,* 1565–1588.

Marr, D. (1982). *Vision.* San Francisco: W.H. Freeman.

Marr, D., & Hildreth, E. C. (1980). Theory of edge detection. *Proceedings of the Royal Society of London., B275,* 187–217.

Marr, D., & Nishihara, H. K. (1978). Representation and recognition of the spatial organisation of three-dimensional shapes. *Proceedings of the Royal Society of London, B200,* 269–294.

Martin, A., Wiggs, C. L., Ungeleider, L. G., & Haxby, J. V. (1996). Neural correlates of category-specific knowledge. *Nature, 379,* 649–652.

Maunsell, J. H. R., & Van Essen, D. C. (1983a). Functional properties of neurones in the middle temporal visual area of the macaque monkey. II Binocular interactions and sensitivity to binocular disparity. *Journal of Neurophysiology, 49,* 1148–1167.

Maunsell, J. H. R., & Van Essen, D. C. (1983b). Functional properties of neurones in the middle temporal visual area of the macaque monkey. I Selectivity for stimulus direction, speed and orientation. *Journal of Neurophysiology, 49,* 1127–1147.

McCollough, C. (1965). Color adapation of edge-detectors in the human visual system. *Science, 149,* 1115–1116.

McLeod, P., Dittrich, W., Driver, J., Perrett, D., & Zihl, J. (1996). Preserved and impaired detection of structure from motion by a 'motion blind patient'. *Visual Cognition, 3,* 363.

McNeil, J. E., & Warrington, E. K. (1991). Prosopagnosia: A real classification. *Quarterly Journal of Experimental Psychology, 43A,* 267–287.

Milner, A. D., & Goodale, M. A. (1995). *The visual brain in action.* Oxford: Oxford University Press.

Milner, A. D., Perrett, D. I., Johnston, R. S., Benson, P. J., Jordan, T. R., Heeley, D. W., Bettucci, D., Mortara, F., Mutani, R., Terazzi, E., & Davidson, D. L. W. (1991). Perception and action in 'visual form agnosia'. *Brain, 114,* 405–428.

Moore, C., & Price, C. J. (1997). Category-specific object naming differences: A functional imaging study. *27th Annual Meeting of the Society of Neuroscience, 414,* 5.

Moore, C. J., & Price, C. J. (1999). A functional neuroimaging study of the variables that generate category-specific object processing differences. *Brain, 122,* 943–962

Mulder, J. L., Bouma, A., & Ansink, B. I. J. (1995). The role of visual discrimination disorders and neglect in perceptual categorisation deficits in right and left hemisphere damaged patients. *Cortex, 31,* 487–501.

Navon, D. (1977). Forest before trees: The precedence of global features in visual perception. *Cognitive Psychology, 9,* 353–383.

Nealey, T. A., & Maunsell, M. A. (1994). Magnocellualar and parvocellular contributions to the responses of neurons in macaque striate cortex. *Journal of Neuroscience, 14,* 2069–2079.

Perani, C. A., Cappa, S. F., Bettinardi, V., Bressi, S., Gorno-Tempini, M., Matarrese, M., & Fazio, F. (1995). Different neural systems for the recognition of animals and man-made tools. *Cognitive neuroscience and neuropsychology, 6,* 1637–1641.

Perenin, M. T. (1978). Visual function within the hemianopic fieldfollowing early hemidecortication in man. II. Pattern discrimination. *Neuropsychologia, 16,* 696-708.

Perenin, M. T., & Jeanerrod, M. (1985). Residual vision in cortically blind hemifields. *Neuropsychologia, 13,* 1–7.

Perrett, D. I., Harries, M., Benson, P., Chitty, A., & Mistlin, A. (1990). Retrieval of structure from rigid and biological motion: An analysis of the visual response of neurones in the macaque temporal cortex. In A. Blake & T. Troscianko (Eds.), *AI and the eye.* Chichester: John Wiley.

Peterson, M. A., & Gibson, B. S. (1994). Must figure-ground organisation precede object recognition? *Psychological Science, 5,* 253–259.

Policardi, E., Perani, D., Zago, S., Grassi, F., Fazio, F., & Làdavas, E. (1996). Failure to evoke visual images in a case of long-standing cortical blindness. *Neurocase, 2,* 381–394.

Pöppel, E., Held, R., & Frost, D. (1973). Residual visual functions after brain wounds involving the central visual pathways in man. *Naure, 243,* 295–296.

Price, C. J., Moore, C. J., Humphreys, G. W., Frackowiak, R. S. J., & Friston, K. J. (1996). The neural regions sustaining object recognition and naming. *Proceedings of the Royal Society, B263,* 1501–1507.

Ptito, A., & Zatorre, R. J. (1988). Impaired stereoscopic detection thresholds after left or right temporal lobectomy. *Neuropsychologia, 4,* 547–554.

Ptito, A., Zatorre, R. J., Larson, W. L., & Tosini, C. (1991). Steropsis after unilateral temporal lobectomy. *Brain, 114,* 1155–1158.

Ratcliff, G., & Newcombe, F. (1982). Object recognition: Some deductions from clinical evidence. In A. W. Ellis (Ed.), *Normality and Pathology in Cognitive Function* (pp. 147–171). London: Academic Press.

Rees, G., Frith, C. D., & Lavie, N. (1997). Modulating irrelevant motion perception by varying attentional load in an unrelated task. *Science, 278,* 1616–1619.

Riddoch, G. (1917). Dissociation of visual perception due to occipital injuries, with especial reference to the appreciation of movement. *Brain, 40*, 15–57.

Riddoch, G. (1935). Visual disorientation in homonymous half-fields. *Brain, 58*, 376–382.

Riddoch, M. J. (1999). Optic aphasia: A review of some classic cases. In G. W. Humphreys (Ed.), *Case Studies in the Neuropsychology of Vision*. Hove: Psychology Press.

Riddoch, M. J., & Humphreys, G. W. (1987a). A case of integrative agnosia. *Brain, 110*, 1431–1462.

Riddoch, M. J., & Humphreys, G. W. (1987b). Visual object processing in optic aphasia: A case of semantic access agnosia. *Cognitive Neuropsychology, 4*, 131–185.

Riddoch, M. J., & Humphreys, G. W. (1988). Visual agnosia: Anatomical and functional accounts. In C. Kennard & F. Clifford Rose (Eds.), *Physiological aspects of clinical neuro-ophthalmology*. London: Chapman Hall.

Riddoch, M. J., Humphreys, G. W., Gannon, T., Blott, W., & Jones, V. (1999). Memories are made of this: The effects of time on stored visual knowledge in a case of visual agnosia. *Brain, 122*, 537–559.

Rizzo, M., & Damasio, H. (1985). Impairment of stereopsis with focal brain lesions. *Annals of Neurology, 18*, 147.

Roland, P. E., & Gulyás, B. (1994). Visual imagery and visual representation. *Trends in the Neurosciences, 17*, 281–287.

Rudge, P., & Warrington, E. K. (1991). Selective impairment of memory and visual perception in splenial tumours. *Brain, 114*, 349–360.

Rumiati, R. I., Humphreys, G. W., Riddoch, M. J., & Bateman, A. (1994). Visual object agnosia without prosopagnosia or alexia: Evidence for hierarchical theories of object recognition. *Visual cognition, 1*, 181–225.

Sachs, O., Wasserman, R. L., Zeki, S., & Siegel, R. M. (1988). Sudden color blindness of cerebral origin. *Society for Neuroscience Abstracts, 14*, 1251.

Sakai, K., & Miyashita, Y. (1994). Neuronal tuning to learned complex forms in vision. *Neuroreport, 5*, 829–832.

Sakai, K., & Miyashita, Y. (1995). Neural oraganisation for long-term memory of paired associates. *Nature, 354*, 152–155.

Sartori, B., & Job, R. (1988). The oyster with four legs: A neuropsychological study on the interaction of visual and semantic information. *Cognitive Neuropsychology, 5*, 677–709.

Schacter, D. L., Reiman, E., Uecker, A., Polster, M. R., Yun, L. S., & Cooper, L. A. (1995). Brain regions associated with retrieval of structurally coherent visual information. *Nature, 376*, 587–590.

Servos, P., & Goodale, M. A. (1995). Preserved visual imagery in visual form agnosia. *Neuropsychologia, 33*, 1383–1394.

Servos, P., Goodale, M. A., & Humphrey, G. K. (1993). The drawing of objects by a visual form agnosic: Contribution of surface properties and memorial representations. *Neuropsychologia, 31*, 251–259.

Shallice, T. (1987). Impairments of semantic processing: Multiple dissociations. In M. Coltheart, G. Sartori, & R. Job (Eds.), *The cognitive neuropsychology of language*. London: Lawrence Erlbaum Associates.

Sheridan, J., & Humphreys, G. W. (1993). A verbal-semantic category-specific recognition impairment. *Cognitive Neuropsychology, 10*(2), 143–184.

Sirigu, A., Duhamel, J.-R., & Poncet, M. (1991). The role of sensorimotor experience in object recognition. *Brain, 114*, 2555–2573.

Stewart, F., Parkin, A. J., & Hunkin, H. N. (1992). Naming impairments following recovery from herpes simplex encephalitis. *Quarterly Journal of Experimental Psychology, 44A*(2), 261–284.

Tanaka, J., Saito, H. A., Fukada, Y., & Moriya, M. (1991). Coding visual images of objects in the infero-temporal cortex of the macaque monkey. *Journal of Neurophysiology, 66*, 170–189.

Teuber, H.-L., Battersby, W. S., & Bender, M. B. (1960). *Visual field defects after after penetrating missile wounds of the brain*. Cambridge: Havard University Press.

Tovee, M. J., Rolls, E. T., & Ramachandran, V. S. (1996). Visual learning in neurons of the primate temporal visual cortex. *Neuroreport, 7*, 2757–2760.

Troscianko, T., Davidoff, J., Humphreys, G. W., Landis, T., Fahle, M., Greelee, M., Brugger, P., & Phillips, W. (1996). Human color discrimination based on a nonparvocellular pathway. *Current Biology, 6*, 200–210.

Turnbull, O. H. (1997). A double dissociation between knowledge ofobject identity and object orientation. *Neuropsychologia, 35*, 567–570.

Turnbull, O. H., Breschin, N., & Della Sala, S. (1997). Agnosia for object orientation: Implication for theories of object recognition. *Neuropsychologia, 35*(2), 153–163.

Turnbull, O. H., Laws, K. R., & McCarthy, R. A. (1995). Object recognition without knowledge of object orientation. *Cortex, 31*, 387–395.

Ungerleider, L. G., & Mishkin, M. (1982). Two cortical visual systems. In J. Ingle, M. A. Goodale, & R. J. W. Mansfield (Eds.), *Analysis of Visual Behavior* (pp. 549–586). Cambridge, MA: MIT Press.

Valentine, T. (1988). Upside-down faces: A review of the effects of inversion on face recognition. *British Journal of Psychology, 79*, 471–491.

Valkenberg, C. T. (1908). Zur Kenntis der gestoerten Tiefenwahrnehmung. *Deutsche Zeitschrift fur Nervenheilkunde, 34*, 322–337.

Vecera, S. P., & Gilds, K. S. (1998). What processing is impaired in apperceptive agnosia? Evidence from normal subjects. *Journal of Cognitive Neuroscience, 10*, 568–580.

Vitkovitch, M., & Humphreys, G. W. (1991). Perseverant responding in speeded picture naming: Its in the links. *Journal of Experimental Psychology: Learning, Memory and Cognition, 17*, 664–680.

Vitkovitch, M., Humphreys, G. W., & Lloyd-Jones, T. J. (1993). On naming a giraffe a zebra: Picture naming errors across object categories. *Journal of Experimental Psychology: Learning, Memory and Cognition, 19*, 243–259.

Von der Heydt, R., & Peterhans, E. (1989). Mechanisms of contour perception in monkey visual cortex 1. Lines of pattern discontinuities. *Journal of Neuroscience, 9*, 1731–1748.

Von der Heydt, R., Peterhans, E., & Baumgartner, G. (1984). Illorsory contours and cortical neuron responses. *Science, 224*, 1260–1262.

Walsh, V., Ellison, A., Battelli, L., & Cowey, A. (1998). Task-specific impairments and enhancements induced by magnetic stimulation of human visual area V5. *Proceedings of the Royal Society London Series B, 265*, 537–543.

Wapner, W., Judd, T., & Gardner, H. (1978). Visual agnosia in an artist. *Cortex, 14*, 343–364.

Warrington, E. K. (1982). Neuropsychological studies of

object recognition. *Philosophical Transactions of the Royal Society of London, Series B., 298*, 15–33.

Warrington, E. K. (1985). Agnosia: The impairment of object recognition. In P. J. Vinken, G. W. Bruyn, & H. L. Klawans (Eds.), *Handbook of Clinical Neurology* (Vol. 45,). Amsterdam: Elsevier Science Publishers.

Warrington, E. K., & James, M. (1986). Visual object recognition in patients with right hemisphere lesions: Axes or features? *Perception, 15*, 355–356.

Warrington, E. K., & Taylor, A. (1973). The contribution of the right parietal lobe to object recognition. *Cortex, 9*, 152–164.

Warrington, E. K., & Taylor, A. (1978). Two categorical stages of object recognition. *Perception, 9*, 152–164.

Weiskrantz, L. (1990). *Blindsight: A case study and implications.* Oxford: Oxford University Press.

Young, A. W., Humphreys, G. W., Riddoch, M. J., Hellawell, D. J., & de Haan, E. H. F. (1994). Recognition impairments and face imagery. *Neuropsychologia, 32*, 693–702.

Zeki, S. (1990). A century of cerebral achromatopsia. *Brain, 113*, 1721–1777.

Zeki, S. (1993). *A vision of the brain.* Oxford: Blackwell Scientific Publications.

Zeki, S. M. (1973). Color coding in rhesus monkey prestriate cortex. *Brain Research, 53*, 422–427.

Zeki, S. M. (1974). Functional organisation of a visual area of the posterior bank of the superior temporal sulcus of the rhesus monkey.

Zeki, S. M. (1978). Functional specialisation in the visual cortex of the rhesus monkey. *Nature, 274*, 423–428.

Zeki, S. M. (1980). The representation of colors in the cerebral cortex. *Nature, 284*, 412–418.

Zihl, J., Von Cramon, D., & Mai, N. (1983). Selective disturbance of movement vision after bilateral brain damage. *Brain, 106*, 313–340.

Zihl, J., Von Cramon, D., Mai, N., & Schmid, C. (1991). Disturbance of movement vision after bilateral posterior brain damage. *Brain, 114*, 2235–2252.

4

Face Perception and Recognition

Edward H. F. De Haan

HISTORICAL BACKGROUND

The observation that the perception and recognition of faces can be impaired in neurological patients can be traced back to the ancient Greeks (Thucidydes II, 47–50). This Greek general who fought in the Pelopenesian Wars described in his second book the strange behavior of soldiers who survived the plague. He observed, among other impairments, severe memory problems and, in some, an inability to recognize friends. Neurological case studies published in the second half of the nineteenth century often mention problems in this domain in patients who have suffered neurological disease (e.g., Charcot, 1888; Wilbrand, 1892). Hoff and Potzl (1937) suggested that face recognition might be a separate function that can be impaired after brain injury. However, it was not until 1947 that the German neurologist Bodamer published a report on a number of patients who experienced a particularly selective difficulty in recognizing faces. Bodamer named the condition "prosopagnosia" with reference to the Greek prosopon (face) and a-gnosis (without knowledge). Having this condition was, obviously, an extremely unpleasant experience. When Bodamer asked his patient (case 1) to inspect his own face in the mirror: "He first explored the mirror as if it were a picture, corrected himself, stared in the mirror for a long time as if he had a completely unknown object in front of him and subsequently stated that he did see a face, including all the features which he described, he also knew it was his face. However, he did not recognize it as his own. It could just as well be someone else's or even a woman" (Bodamer, 1947, p. 15). As far as we know now, all prosopagnosic patients know when they are looking at a face, and they can identify and describe separate features such as the eyes and mouth (Blanc-Garin, 1984). Therefore, they clearly know that they are looking at a human face. However, the face has lost its value as a cue for identification of a person. In severe cases, even the faces of family members and close friends and sometimes the patient's own face seen in a mirror are unrecognized. The patient studied by MacRae and Trolle (1956) commented that on several occasions, while looking in the mirror, he had grimaced or stuck his tongue out, "just to make sure" (p. 96). Not even a vague feeling of familiarity, when the patient is looking at a known face, survives.

In general, faces are described as looking similar and having lost their individuality, such that "all are neutral, a dirty grey colour" (Pallis, 1955, p. 219), "they are all alike" (Bornstein & Kidron, 1959, p. 120). Another common comment from prosopagnosic patients is that faces are not perceived as an integrated whole. Pallis' (1955) patient commented: "I can see the eyes, nose and mouth quite clearly, but they just don't add up" (p. 219). A similar account is given by a case studied by Cole and Perez-Cruet (1964) who, "could not pull it all together" (p. 238). In this chapter, I will first argue that there are good reasons to postulate a dedicated face-processing system. Subsequently, the relevant neuropsychological data and normal studies will be discussed in order to develop a coherent account of the cortical mechanisms involved in the processing of facial information.

ARE FACES SPECIAL?

The first question that needs to be asked in a chapter on the cognitive neuropsychology of face processing is whether there is a need for such a separate chapter. Is there anything special about the stimulus category 'faces' or are they just like any other class of objects (Farah, 1996; Tovee, 1998)? A seminal chapter on this subject by Hay and Young (1982), in which one of the first models of face processing was postulated, commences with exactly this same question. The researchers distinguish two separate questions. The first question concerns the issue of whether or not the perceptual and cognitive processes used for recognizing faces are different in nature from those used for the processing of other visual stimuli. They refer to this as the question of *uniqueness*. The second question is whether the processes involved in the perception and analyses of facial information, irrespective of their nature, are organized into a separate system that deals only with faces. This is what they call the *specificity* question. It refers to the suggestion that there are isolable brain processes that are solely dedicated to the perception and recognition of faces. As Hay and Young point out, a face-processing system with unique properties would also be specific to faces but the reverse is not necessarily true. Finally, recent data indicates the possibility of there being a genetic basis. Thus, the question of whether faces are special can be addressed at the cognitive, the neural, and the genetic levels.

EVIDENCE FOR COGNITIVE DISTINCTIVENESS

Complexity

First, the ability to recognize faces is probably the most difficult visual recognition task that we are able to perform, despite the subjective ease with which we do it (Stevenage, 1995). In a lifetime, we learn thousands of faces, most of which we are able to recognize relatively unaffected by changes due to aging and variable additions such as spectacles and facial hair. Faces, however, only differ very slightly in visual appearance. This is a point well illustrated by the general experience that faces from another race than one's own are difficult to remember. Bothwell, Brigham, and Malpass (1989) carried out a meta-analysis on the data of eleven publications in which the recognition proficiency of Black and White people was assessed for Black and White faces. Overall, for both groups an approximately equal effect-size of 0.70 was observed in direction of an own-race bias. Thus, given the complexity of the task and the specific task demands involved, it is conceivable that a separate system has evolved.

Visual Illusions and Rotations

Second, visual illusions give us a rare insight into the functioning of the brain. The famous Kaniza triangle constitutes a good illustration of the point that there is a fair amount of top-down processing occurring during shape perception. There are at least two illusions that are restricted to faces. The famous Thompson illusion (Thompson, 1980) is shown in Figure 4.1a. At first glance there appears to be nothing wrong with the face on the right. However once we have viewed the face up-side-down and then turned over the page, it becomes apparent that the eyes and the mouth have been misoriented in the face. In the illusion investigated by Young,

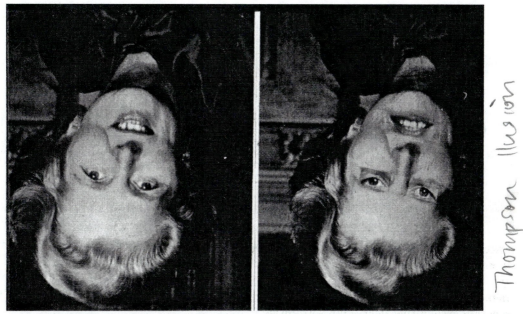

Figure 4.1a: The Margaret Thatcher illusion. When the faces are viewed upside-down, there is no perceived abnormality. However, when the page is turned and the faces are viewed the right way, the grotesqueness of the composite face is clear. From: Thompson, P. (1980). Margaret Thatcher—a new illusion. *Perception*, 9, 483–484. Reprinted with permission.

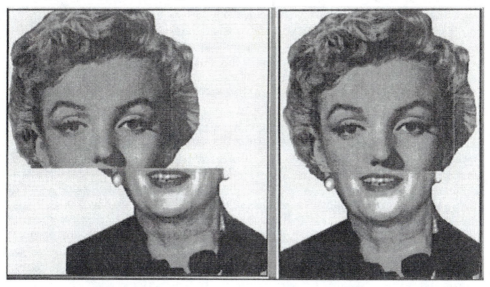

Figure 4.1b: A composite and non-composite of Margaret Thatcher and Marilyn Monroe. When upright, a new face seems to emerge from the composite such that the original identities become very hard to extract. However, the Gestalt formed in the upright composite appears to be removed when the image is inverted and in this situation the original identities can be extracted as easily from the composite as from the non-composite. From: T. Valentine (Ed.) (1995). *Cognitive and Computational aspects of face recognition: Explorations in face space.* London: Routledge. Adapted from an original figure by Young, A. W., et al. (1987). Reprinted with permission.

Hellawell, and Hay (1987) the top half of a famous face and the bottom half of another famous face have been put together to make a chimeric face. This new face looks like a vaguely familiar face despite the obvious horizontal line. Their research showed that the constituent parts are much easier to recognize when the top and the bottom halves are slightly offset compared to when they are fitted together to form a chimeric. The effect of the composite, however, disappears when the chimeric is presented upside-down. Whereas the upright composite appear to fuse into a whole face, the inverted chimeric is perceived as two separate halves of a face. A widely accepted but somewhat vague theoretical position holds that inverted presentation of faces (Yin, 1970) disturbs the 'wholistic' processing mode for faces (Lewis & Johnston, 1997). This would explain why faces are less easily perceived and recognized when they are presented upside-down compared to presentation in the normal orientation and why this is true to a much lesser degree with objects such as houses. It thus appears that upright chimerics are processed using a wholistic processing mode, while inverted ones are processed using a more configural mode. Obviously, one could argue that the necessary control is missing when the same photo-shop manipulations are carried out on objects other than faces. The problem is that a demonstration with one particular object will always be insufficient, since the observation that the effect does not occur with one particular object does not preclude the possibility that it does happen with another kind of object. Because there are no publications that claim to have created such illusions, for now it is assumed that the phenomenon is restricted to faces until demonstrations to the contrary are produced.

Single Cases

In cognitive neuropsychology (e.g., A. W. Shallice, 1988; Ellis & Young, 1988), patient data are often used to make inferences about cognitive structure without reference to the underlying neuro-anatomical substrate. A powerful methodology is based on dissociations between functions in patients or groups of patients. In the literature, several studies exist that describe pure deficits in the recognition of familiar faces such as the one by Tiberghien and Clerc (1986). This particular patient was unable to recognize any familiar faces but his ability to recognize common objects appeared completely spared. How selective are the recognition impairments of these prosopagnosic patients? The answer is that it varies, and more often than not these patients do experience subtle problems in object recognition. It should be noted that the task demands in face and object recognition are not comparable. Instead of recognizing a hammer as a tool, it would be a more comparable situation to recognize my neighbor's hammer amongst many other exemplars. However, there is evidence that general within-class discrimination problems do not always occur in prosopagnosic patients (e.g., Henke, Schweinberger, Grigo, Klos, & Sommer, 1998; Farah, Levinson, & Klein, 1995). De Renzi (1986a) described prosopagnosic patients who were able to perform visual recognition tasks that resemble face recognition in terms of task-demands. The recognition of one's own car in a parking lot, for example, requires the identification of a personally familiar item from an array with many visually similar items. One of those patients studied was able to recognize his own car in the parking lot, his own wallet from an array of similar wallets, and his own handwriting amidst that of others. Until recently, the controversy about a dedicated cognitive system for face recognition continued, as the other half of the necessary double dissociation (Teuber, 1968) was still lacking. Despite a number of clinical reports that described a statistical trend towards a relatively more severe problems in recognizing objects than faces (McCarthy & Warrington, 1986; Feinberg, Schindler, Ochoa, & Kwan, 1994), there was no convincing description of a clear object agnosic patient whose face recognition abilities were normal. In a series a well-designed experiments, Moscovitch, Winocur, and Behrman (1997) investigated a patient who performed normally on face recognition tasks while being severely impaired in the recognition of common objects. An elegant demonstration involved the use of the painting "Rudolfo" by Giuseppi Arcimboldo which shows a face made up from different vegetables. Although the patient CK had no problem recognizing the face, he was very poor at identifying the constituent vegetables.

Other indirect evidence comes from the clinical phenomenon of 'Metamorphopsia' where the patient sees faces—and only faces—in a distorted manner. Whiteley and Warrington (1977) describe a patient whose visual world appears unaffected by his brain damage apart from the fact that all faces look like fish heads. Despite this distortion, he is able to recognize most familiar faces without any problems. The fact that this phenomenon is restricted to faces supports the notion of a separate cognitive system that is dedicated to the perception of faces.

EVIDENCE RELATING TO NEURAL DISTINCTIVENESS

Single-Cell Recording

An important source of evidence for the position that faces are special comes from studies using single-cell recording of the macaque monkey brain. Several studies have now identified single neurons in the superior temporal sulcus (STS) that are selectively responsive to faces. Gross (1992), showed that these cells that are sensitive to face stimuli but do not respond to other complex visual patterns like leaves or even hands. This selectivity can be even more specific though. Perrett and his colleagues (Perret, Mistlin et al., 1988; Perret, Rolls, & Caan, 1982) have demonstrated that certain cells in the STS are selectively tuned to the face of one known individual, irrespective of the size or the orientation in which the face is presented. Figure 4.2 shows response frequency to the faces of two people who are known to the animal. The fact that such cells exist has been the subject of many long debates. Obviously, it is not necessary at all that such a cell signifies the 'recognition' of a face. In fact, it is very difficult to imagine what it would mean for a cell to recognize a face. There are several alternative interpretations but the consensus appears to be that such cells are probably part of larger cell-ensembles (cf. Hebb). For instance, a parallel distributed processing (PDP) account (e.g., McClelland & Rumelhart, 1988) would surmise that a large number of cells form a network and that information, like a representation of a face, can be stored by assigning specific weights to the nodes of the network. Weights could then be conceptualized as firing thresholds of the cells, and a specific cell within the network could just happen to have a very low firing threshold for this particular face. It is not, however, within this particular cell that the representation is stored but in the complete network. Many different face representations could be stored in such a network by varying the weights of the nodes. In this view, face selective cells suggest that there is a network that is specific for storing face information. The point here is that the observation that these cells exist suggests a high level of selectivity in information processing and this points again in the direction of a dedicated face-recognition system.

Lateralization

From numerous experiments with normal subjects using the visual half-field procedure and neuropsychological studies with patients with unilateral lesions it has become clear that the right hemisphere is dominant for face perception in general and recognition in particular (see, for instance: Young, Hay, & McWeeny, 1985; Rhodes, 1985). More recently, this hemispheric advantage was again demonstrated using modern EEG analysis techniques (Burgess & Gruzzelier, 1997). However, other studies have indicated this advantage is susceptible to variations in a number of task variables such as stimulus characteristics (Sergent, 1988) and instructions (Cormier & Jackson, 1995). This hemispheric advantage for face processing has often been interpreted in terms of a generalized hemispheric difference in processing mode (e.g., local vs. global, feature-based vs. sholistic, and even low vs. high spatial frequency-based; but see Newcombe De Haan, Ross, & Young, 1989). At present there is little evidence directly supporting a

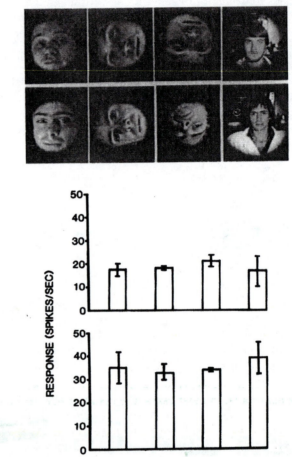

Figure 4.2: Sensitivity to face identity. Upper: Illustration of two faces under different viewing conditions. Lower: Illustrates the mean and standard error of responses of one cell to the different instances of the two faces. Reprinted with permission.

qualitatively different processing of facial information in the two hemispheres, although there is a large body of evidence pointing to 'overall' processing strategy differences.

An attempt to develop this idea further comes from Farah (1991), who suggested, on the basis of the available neuropsychological data, that there might be two recognition systems. The first one is geared towards the processing of detail, and disruption of this system would in the first instance cause dyslexia and in more severe cases also impair object recognition. The second system is more holistic in nature and would, when damaged, cause face-perception deficits. More extensive damage would also affect object recognition. This is not a new idea. In fact, the eminent neurologist Ritchie-Russell suggested in 1941 that one could conceptualize visual object agnosia as a breakdown of the ability to perceive 'gestalts,' with reference to the work of, for instance Kohler (1930). This proposal constitutes an elegant account of the available evidence. However, studies are emerging that describe clinical patterns that would not be expected on the basis of Farah's (1991) proposal. For instance, De Renzi & De Pellegrino (1998) reported on a patient with alexia and prosopagnosia but without object agnosia. This observation is for obvious reasons problematic for Farah's suggestion, as one would need to hypothesize a coincidence of two very selective deficits. However, even more problematic for this position are patients such as the one described by Humphreys and Rumiati (1998) who experienced a selective deficit in object recognition while reading and face recognition were spared. Farah herself now also appears to subscribe to the idea of a specialized face-recognition system and the idea that this system uses a wholistic processing mode in which part composition contributes little (Farah, Wilson, Drain, et al., 1995; Farah, Wilson, Maxwell, & Tanaka, 1998).

Aetiology and Anatomy

Face processing disorders have been described in a wide range of patient populations. Patients suffering from diffuse brain damage such as dementia (Hodges, Salmon, & Butters, 1993; Becker, Lopez, & Boller, 1995) or closed head injury (De Haan & Campbell, 1992) have been shown to suffer from severe deficits in face processing. De Renzi (1986b) and Evans, Heggs, Antour, and Hodges (1995) observed progressive visual recognition problems, notably for faces, as the prevailing clinical symptom in patients with a selective degenerative illness that specifically affects the posterior areas of the cortex. In addition, several studies have shown that autistic patients demonstrate problems in the perception and recognition of faces. Teunisse and De Gelder (1994) tested the ability of autistics to match facial features such as eyes, either presented within a face or in isolation. There was no difference between autistics and normal controls when the features were presented on their own but the autistic patients were impaired when the features were embedded within a face. This result indicates that autistics can still perceive faces and their features but that they are impaired in the configural processing specific to faces. A number of patients with visual recognition deficits, including prosopagnosia, have been described after carbon monoxide poisoning (e.g. Sparr, Jay, Dislane, & Venna, 1991). Face-processing disorders have also been described in patients with neurological illnesses resulting in more localized damage. For instance, Braun, Denault, Cohen, and Rouleau (1994) showed that both temporal and frontal lobectomy impairs the perception of faces and of facial expressions. In addition, the famous prosopagnosic case of HJA, described by Humphreys and Riddoch (1984, 1987), suffered a large posterior stroke.

Prosopagnosia is, in most cases, the result of bilateral posterior damage to the cortex (e.g., Meadows, 1974; Clarke, Lindeman, Maeder, Borruat, & Assal, 1997). The left and right occipitotemporal junctions have traditionally been identified as the substrate for face recognition. Most patients with prosopagnosia (and all patients who have come to postmortem investigation) had lesions in those areas (Cohn, Neumann, & Wood, 1977; Damasio, Damasio, & Van Hoesen, 1982). In humans the fusiform and lingual gyri are most often implicated. These observations are somewhat at odds with the primate single-cell recording studies of Perrett et al. (1988) and Rolls (1984) that localize the cells sensitive to face identity much more anteriorly in the upper bank of the superior temporal sulcus. Obviously, these differences could be explained as differences between species, nonetheless it might be prudent to keep this in mind when comparing the human and the primate data on face perception. In this context it is interesting to note that a recent study (O-Scalaidhe, Wilson, & Goldman-Rakic, 1997) found face-specific cells in the pre-frontal area of the macaque monkey.

A number of reports have more recently claimed that a unilateral right hemisphere lesion might be sufficient to cause prosopagnosia (Landis, Cummings, Christen, Bogen, & Imhof, 1986; De Renzi, Perani, Carlesimo, Silveri, & Fazio, 1994), but the status of these demonstrations remains somewhat unclear as long as they depend on neurosurgical reports and neuroimaging instead of postmortem findings. It is known from clinical practice that transient or partial prosopagnosia can occur after a unilateral lesion but that full-blown prosopagnosia appears to require bilateral damage.

Functional Imaging

The recent upsurge in functional neuro-imaging studies has largely served to confirm the existing evidence from neuropsychology. Magnetoencephalograph (MEG) has supported the notion of bilateral processing as well as the importance of the right inferior temporal lobe for familiar face recognition (Zouridakis, Simos, Brier, & Papanicolaou, 1998, Sams, Hietenen, Hari, Ilmoniemi, & Lounasmaa, 1997). Recent work using PET and *f*MRI scanning by Andreasen, O'Leary, Arndt, and Cizadlo (1996), Kanwisher, McDermott, and Chun (1997) and George et al. (1999) have identified a number of areas involved in the perception of familiar faces in the posterior, occipital-temporal areas of the brain, and again the fusiform gyrus—especially on the right side—appears to play a major role. Using *f*MRI, Kanwisher, Stanley, and Harris (1999) provided further evidence for a specific face-processing system demonstrating that the face area is not especially activated when the subjects are presented with pictures of animals. Perhaps the most interesting result to come out of neuro-imaging until now is the suggestion from the Washington group (e.g., Haxby et al., 1994; Clark et al., 1996) that the area involved in face processing is actually an area which overlaps with that involved in object recognition. This raises the possibility that this area processes visual primitives that happen to be important for face recognition. If these observations are replicated and extended they might well form the basis for a more tractable definition of holistic/configural processing.

EVIDENCE REGARDING A GENETIC BASIS

Normal Infants

A number of studies have shown that neonates, a few hours after birth, are able to discriminate between face-like patterns and patterns consisting of the same elements but organized in a random configuration. Even though the infant may not have developed adult levels of acuity or contrast sensitivity until the age of six months or so, such face-like patterns can specifically engage the child when the patterns are moved, as movement improves contrast sensitivity and acuity (Flin & Dziurawiec, 1989). Even more suggestive is the demonstration that newborn babies can distinguish their mothers from other women at just two days of age (Bushnell & Sai, 1987; Simion, Valenza, & Umilta, 1998). There is now very clear evidence that babies a couple of months old can recognize faces of familiar people, when their visual acuity is sufficient to perceive faces properly. The rapid development of this skill suggest that face recognition might be 'modular' in the strict sense that Fodor (1983) originally postulated, and that this ability might to some degree be built-in (Walton, Armstrong, & Bower, 1997). The early development of face recognition mirrors that of voice recognition. Soon after birth babies are able to distinguish their mother's voice from that of other women.

Developmental Prosopagnosia

The ability to recognize familiar faces can, thus, be characterized as 'modular' in terms of the ideas put forward by Fodor. It is a highly specialized function with a well-circumscribed neurological substrate that appears to be hard-wired at birth. Faculties are modular as a consequence of their importance to the individual, and therefore, are designed to mature and to develop in an efficient and relatively 'protected' way. This modular, hard-wired nature of face recognition suggests that the variability in capacity in the general population can be attributed largely to biological factors. A genetic basis for language processing is now generally accepted (see, for instance, Gopnik, 1997). Developmental face recognition problems have been described in a handful of case studies (Tranel & Damasio, 1989; Newcombe, Mehton, & De Haan, 1994; Ariel & Sadeh, 1996). By definition, the problem is present from early childhood. In addition, there should be no known neurological history that could explain the recognition problem. There is one case of developmental prosopagnosia that has been extensively followed (McConachie, 1976; De Haan & Campbell, 1992). This is an intelligent and verbal woman who experienced very severe difficulties in recognizing familiar faces. Reading and object recognition were preserved, but she encountered problems on most tasks that depend on the use of facial information, such as the visual analysis of expressions and the short-term memory of unfamiliar faces. Her problem is best described as an inability to form an adequate internal representation of faces. As a result, faces have never gained the significance for her that they have for most of us. Instead, she relies heavily on voices for the recognition of familiar people. In a recent study, Duchaine (2000) argues strongly against the suggestion that developmental prosopagnosia is caused by a generalized deficit in configural processing.

An interesting observation, mentioned in some case studies on developmental face-recognition deficit, concerns the anecdotal reference to other family members who are supposedly also poor at recognizing faces (De Haan & Campbell, 1992). A recent study (De Haan, 1999) concerns a family of two parents, three daughters and one son. Two of the daughters and the father were very poor at recognizing familiar faces. The other family members did not have any problems. Thus, the face recognition problems did not only occur in two family members of the same generation, but also in family members of different generations. These observations present clear evidence for a familial factor in the development of face recognition problems.

Conclusions

The available evidence supports the notion of a separate cognitive processing system for faces. There are experiments with normal subjects demonstrating qualitatively different processing of faces and objects, and patient studies that show very selective deficits of face processing and a convincing double dissociation between face and object recognition. Next, there is strong converging evidence for a separate system in the brain for recognizing familiar faces. In the subsequent paragraphs, it will be argued that there are good reasons to assume that this system fractionates further into a number of isolable subprocesses. What might be computationally distinctive about face processing? One possibility that has been put forward is the notion that faces are processed in a wholistic manner while objects are analyzed in a more feature-based processing mode (e.g., Farah, 1991). The problem with dichotomies like this is that the characterizations of the different processing modes often remain vague and subsequently are difficult to test experimentally. Therefore, it is imperative that future work be aimed at a more precise description of the cognitive representations that are used in face processing. The work by the Washington group (e.g., Ishai, Ungerleider, Martyin, Scouten, & Haxby, 1999) might form a good starting point. The suggestion is that there is a highly organized arrangement of form detectors that are more or less involved in different visual tasks ranging from object to face perception. In this sense, the face area is selective for face processing but just an area that happens to harbor a number of form detectors that are important for the perception of faces. Under this hypothesis, however, it is not clear how to explain the very selective deficits that can be observed in neuropsychological patients as the hypothesis would seem to predict graded rather categorical differences between face- and object-agnosic patients.

A NEUROCOGNITIVE THEORY OF FACE PROCESSING

Perceptual Processes

Several models have been postulated regarding the processes involved in face processing. Notable contributors to this endeavor were Hay and Young (1982), H. Ellis (1983), Rhodes (1985), and Damasio and colleagues (Damasio, Damasio, & Tranel, 1986; Damasio, Damasio, & Van Hoesen, 1982). The model shown in Figure 4.3a is the one put forward by Bruce and Young in 1986 and reflects the general line of thinking at the end of the 1980s and early 1990s. These component-based models were extended with neural network models (Figure 4.3b) such as the one by Burton, Bruce, & Johnston (1990), who use an interactive activation model to simulate

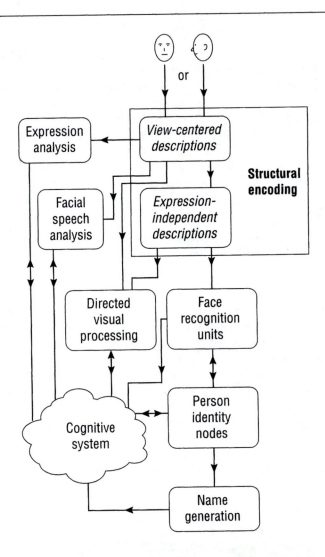

Figure 4.3a: Bruce and Young's (1986) model of face recognition. Adapted with permission from the British Journal of Developmental Psychology, © The British Psychological Society.

the effects observed in normal subjects and brain-lesioned patients. These PDP models mimic the component models to a large degree and the main point here is the fact that all of these models propose a number of separable subprocesses within the realm of face processing. In the remainder of this section, I will focus on the processes involved in the recognition of familiar faces.

One major challenge for the modular approach comes from those who claim that there are no grounds for postulating separate processing stages. As early as 1950, Bay (1950, 1953) suggested that a subtle sensory impairment ('Funktionswandel') or a certain constellation of sensory deficits can produce the clinical symptoms that look like higher-order recognition deficits (see Humphreys & Riddoch, 1985). This debate is fuelled by the fact that even the most 'pure' cases of prosopagnosia often show some mild problems on tasks of visual perception. In a seminal study, Ettlinger (1956) argued that sensory status alone could not explain the presence or absence of recognition disorders. The crux of his argument is that although patients with a recognition deficit may have sensory impairments, other patients who do not experience recognition problems can show equal or worse impairments on the sensory tests. Recent advances in neuropsychological and neurophysiological understanding of the visuo-sensory apparatus have put us in a good position to address this issue. De Haan, Heywood,

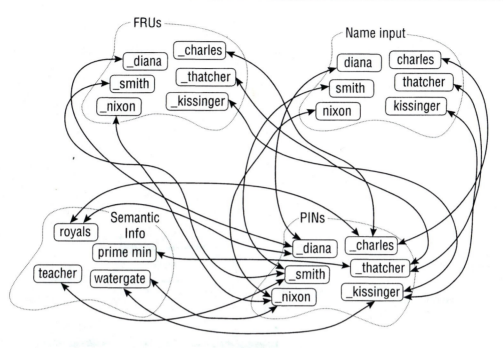

Figure 4.3b: Central architecture of Burton and co-workers' (1990) interactive activation model. Adapted with permission from the *British Journal of Developmental Psychology*, © The British Psychological Society.

Young, and Edelsteyn (1995) studied three densely prosopagnosic patients. The evaluation of primary visual proficiency was done with a screening battery comprised of tasks for shape, spatial location, color, luminance, movement, texture, and line orientation. In comparison with age-matched control subjects, the patients showed subtle impairments on several of the screening tasks. These problems are, however, insufficient to explain the pronounced recognition problems, as other patients with unilateral brain lesions who do not have recognition deficits are at least as impaired on these sensory tasks as the agnosics. The conclusion is, therefore, that the visuo-sensory impairments cannot explain the agnosic problem. However, others, like De Renzi, Faglioni, and Nicinelli (1991), maintain that there are both perceptual and mnestic forms of prosopagnosia.

There is good evidence for postulating sequential perceptual stages. First, the visuo-sensory information is used to produce an internal representation of a seen face that entails the richness of the particular view including the expression, perceived under specific conditions (such as lightning, etc.; e.g., Marr's 21/2-D sketch; Marr, 1982). Next, there is a need to create a more abstract representation of the perceived face that allows for the recognition of that face under different circumstances (Marr's 3-D representation; Marr, 1982). This idea is very similar to the proposals of, for instance, Humphreys and Riddoch (ibid), concerning object recognition and that what holds for objects is likely to be true for faces, which do not only change with viewpoint but also as a result of emotional and communicative expressions. For face recognition, the Benton Facial Recognition test (Benton & Van Allen, 1973) can be used to investigate whether a perceptual problem is at the 2½- or the 3-D level by comparing items involving identical photographs and items with photographs taken from different viewpoints. This 3-D representation is then matched against stored representations of faces that are familiar. A successful match is signalled to the cognitive system and the retrieval of person-related information, such as profession, is instigated. Complete recognition is achieved when the name of the person whose face is seen can be accessed.

Stored Representations or Face Recognition Units

How familiar faces are stored for future recognition remains largely a mystery. We know now from cognitive psychological studies that we are very poor at recognizing photographic negatives, faces from which texture cues are removed, and that we focus on the internal features of familiar faces, in contrast to unfamiliar faces, which we often recognize from external features such as hairline (De Haan & Hay, 1986). Caricatures enhance recognition and have been shown to help patients with familiar-face recognition problems. Again, the recent studies of Ishai et al. (1999) regarding the visual form detectors might, in the future, give us a better description of the nature of the internal representation(s) of perceived faces.

Several authors have commented on the use of mental imagery tests to evaluate the integrity of the stored representations. A number of patients have been described who are able to 'picture faces in their mind' that they cannot recognize overtly (Tiberghien & Clerc, 1986). Obviously, testing such a subjective ability as mental imagery is not easy, but a number of useful procedures have been developed. The method of 'odd-one-out,' in which the patient has to decide which one of three people looks most unlike the other two (e.g., the patient is given the names Charlie Chaplin, Adolf Hitler, and Bill Clinton) has been used successfully to demonstrate clinical dissociations between impaired recognition and spared mental imagery of familiar faces (Young, Humphreys, Riddoch, Hellawell, & De Haan, 1994; Bartolomeo et al., 1998).

It is useful to note at this point that prosopagnosia entails, in fact, two impairments: the inability to recognize familiar faces and the inability to learn new faces or relearn old ones (e.g., Hécaen, 1981; Damasio, Damasio, & van Hoesen, 1982). These problems have subsequently been described in isolation. Transient forms of prosopagnosia such as the one described by Landis, Cummings, Christen, Bogen, & Imhof (1986) can be interpreted as 'retrograde' prosopagnosia, while Damasio, Tranel, and Damasio (1990) describe a case of anterograde amnesia. This woman was no longer able to learn new faces but could recognize faces she had learned before the onset of her condition.

Biographical Information

ME was a right-handed female who, after a vasculitic disorder, suffered from a selective memory deficit. She performed normal to above normal on tasks for the perception of faces (e.g., Benton Facial Recognition test), and on tasks that required her to choose the familiar face from an array with unfamiliar faces. However, she was very poor at retrieving personal information about the people whose faces she had recognized. Often she would claim that a face looked familiar but that was all she could say about it. These findings provide a strong indication that her face-recognition system is unimpaired to the level of familiarity recognition. Table 4.1 summarizes ME's performance on a test where she was asked, for each of 60 photographs of faces (20 highly familiar, 20 familiar, 20 unfamiliar), to indicate how familiar the face appeared (on a 7-point scale ranging from unfamiliar to very familiar); to retrieve some biographical information that would indicate that the person had indeed been identified; and finally—when possible—to give the name. It is obvious that her familiarity ratings are in the normal range, while she is very poor at producing biographical information. When she is able to retrieve person related information she is, in most instances, also able to retrieve the correct name. The dissociation between intact face familiarity and degraded access to biographical information was further supported in a subsequent experiment where subjects were shown a series of familiar and unfamiliar faces and asked to indicate as quickly as possible on two response buttons whether the face looked familiar or not. Although ME could not identify most of the familiar faces used in this experiment, she was 100% accurate and even slightly faster than control subjects on this task (De Haan, Young, & Newcombe, 1991).

Table 4.1

Faces and Names Line-up Tasks. The rating score is the mean rating on a 7-point scale (1 = unknown; 7 = very familiar). The occupation and name scores are number correct out of 20 trials. The control data for the names line-up have been taken from Hanley, Young, and Pearson (1989).

| | Faces Line-Up | | | | |
	ME	Controls Mean SD		ME	Controls Mean SD
Ratings					
High familiarity	5.7	5.98	0.51	6.2	6.27 0.63
Low familiarity	3.3	4.18	1.02	5.6	5.92 0.92
Unfamiliar	1.5	1.36	0.45	1.6	1.10 0.10
Occupation					
High familiarity	7.0	18.86	1.15	8.0	19.66 0.84
Low familiarity	2.0	13.07	4.54	5.0	19.16 1.14
Name					
High familiarity	7.0	16.25	2.81		
Low familiarity	1.0	9.39	4.44		

Hécaen and Angelergues (1962) give a brief, anecdotal description of a patient with a similar face-recognition deficit. Van der Linden, Bredarf, and Schweich (1995) also report a single case of what appears to be a developmental problem in accessing autobiographical information from the face. The observation that a sense of familiarity can be achieved from a face while the identity of the person remains obscure has also been made in normal subjects. Young, Hay, and Ellis (1985) asked healthy people to keep a diary of every day face recognition mistakes, and they found this 'familiar only' experience to be a frequent occurrence. This finding has been replicated in a laboratory setting by Hanley, Smith, and Hatfield (1998).

Face Naming

Anomias, impairments in naming, constitute a well-described neuropsychological condition. Flude, Ellis, and Kay (1989) studied a patient with an impairment at the last stage of face recognition: retrieval of the name. Their patient, EST, showed a preserved ability to: (a) match unfamiliar faces on identity; (b) distinguish between familiar and unfamiliar faces and names; and (c) access semantic information from faces and written names of familiar people. However, EST was severely impaired in naming familiar faces. The finding of this selective functional deficit supports the idea that the mechanism dealing with name retrieval (which was severely impaired for EST) is separable from mechanisms responsible for the sense of familiarity and access to appropriate semantic information (which were both well preserved for EST). Flude et al.'s (1989) investigation of EST, then, demonstrates that name retrieval can be impaired when access to identity-specific semantic information is preserved. Hodges and Greene (1998) showed, in a recent investigation with Alzheimer's patients, that there were no patients who could name a face without producing any autobiographical information concerning that person. This again supports the proposal that name retrieval is a separate stage that takes place *after* accessing personal information.

FRACTIONATION OF FACE PERCEPTION

Faces form the source for a multitude of inferences. From a perceived face, we are able to determine gender, age, and whether we would buy a second-hand car from the person in question. We can assess the emotional state of the person (e.g., happy, sad) by analyzing the facial expression, and by observing the movements of the lips and tongue we gain additional information regarding the verbal message that the speaker is trying to convey. Finally, the face constitutes the principal cue for visual identification of people we know. On the basis of evidence from experimental psychology and neuropsychology, it has been proposed that the processes involved in these different abilities are to some extent independent from each other (See Figure 4.3). Thus, it is suggested that there is a further fractionation into separate processing units for analyzing different aspects of the information that can be read from a face. First the evidence will be reviewed regarding information that can be obtained from familiar as well as unfamiliar faces and subsequently the status of unfamiliar face recognition will be evaluated.

Expression Analysis

Evidence for a dissociation between the recognition of familiar faces and the processing of facial expressions was first reported by Bornstein (1963) and has been confirmed by Tranel, Damasio, and Damasio (1988). In both studies it was observed that some patients with severe impairments of facial identity recognition showed relatively intact ability to recognize facial expressions. Conversely, Kurucz, Feldmar, and Werner (1979) and Kurucz and Feldmar (1979) reported findings indicating that disoriented patients were impaired at recognizing facial expressions and at recognizing American presidents, but the identity and expression impairments did not correlate with each other. The conclusion is that some of those patients must have had intact familiar-face recognition while being poor at perceiving facial expressions. These patients would provide the double dissociation with the previously mentioned studies. More recent evidence for this dissociation comes from the study by Braun et al. (1994), who studied patients with temporal and frontal lobe damage.

There is also evidence for distinct processing pathways involved in the recognition of facial expressions and the matching of unfamiliar faces. For example, Bowers, Bauer, Coslett, and Heilman (1985) tested patients with left and right hemisphere damage and patients with no neurological disease. They were given a series of facial affect tests and tasks for unfamiliar face perception. The patients with right-hemisphere lesions were significantly impaired on both types of tasks but the impairments on the affect tests remained significant even when their face perception deficit was statistically partialed out. Other reports of dissociable impairments on facial expression recognition and unfamiliar face matching after brain injury have been made by Cicone, Wapner, and Gardner (1980), Pizzamiglio, Zoccolotti, Mammucari, and Cesaroni (1983), and Etcoff (1984). Regarding the analysis of facial expressions, there are exciting new data (e.g., Hamann et al., 1996). The right posterior hemisphere is obviously instrumental in the perceptual processing of the facial information, but the amygdala (bilaterally) has now been identified as a crucial structure for the experience of emotions, and most likely especially for fear and anger (Young, Hellawell, van de Wal, & Johnson, 1996; Broks et al., 1998; Adolphs, Tranel, Damasio, & Damasio, 1994; Adolphs, Tranel, Hamann, et al., 1999).

Lipreading

Campbell, Landis, and Regard (1986) describe two Swiss patients. One patient is able to recognize faces but can no longer lipread, and the other shows the opposite pattern. Lipreading is tested using a recognition task in which the patient is shown photographs of the face of an actor making a speech sound, for instance 'ee' or 'aa.' The other method uses what is known as the 'McGurk Illusion.' This involves the video tape recording of a face making a speech sound (e.g., 'da') and the simultaneous sound recording of a different speech sound (e.g., 'ta'). A normal observer confronted with such a stimulus would 'hear' a blend of these two speech sounds (e.g., 'ga'). Subjects who can no longer lipread will report the auditory stimulus and not the blend. Apart from this seminal paper there is little neuropsychological evidence for this dissociation, but there is now some evidence from cognitive psychology that familiar-face recognition and speech perception are perhaps not completely independent (Campbell & De Haan, 1998; Campbell, Brooks, De Haan, & Roberts, 1995). Lipreading proficiency appeared to be modulated by whether or not the face had been presented before to the subject on a previous occasion.

Unfamiliar Face Perception

The literature also supports Bruce and Young's (1986) proposal of distinct pathways for the processing of familiar and unfamiliar faces. This was first suggested by Warrington and James (1967). Benton and Van Allen (1972) reported a case of prosopagnosia in which performance on a task of matching unfamiliar faces was well within the normal range. Similar findings in prosopagnosic cases were made by Assal (1969), Rondot, Tzavaras, and Garcin (1967), Warrington and James (1967), and several subsequent authors. Conversely, patients with unfamiliar face-matching impairments often are not clinically prosopagnosic (Tzavaras, Hécaen, & Le Bras, 1970). Benton (1980) also emphasized the independence of familiar-face recognition and unfamiliar-face matching impairments.

Malone, Morris, Kay, and Levin (1982) reported direct observations of a double dissociation between the recognition of familiar faces and the matching of unfamiliar faces in two cases of prosopagnosia. Case 1 was initially unable to recognize familiar faces, and he was also impaired on the matching of unfamiliar face photographs. Later testing revealed that the familiar-face recognition impairment had improved significantly, while his unfamiliar face matching problem remained. Case 2 was unable six weeks after an initial testing to recognize both relatives and various familiar personalities by their faces alone. There was a significant improvement, however, in his initially impaired unfamiliar-face matching performance, which now fell within the normal range. The idea of independence of familiar-face recognition and unfamiliar-face perception in terms of gender decision is supported by priming studies with normal subjects (A. W. Ellis, Young, Flude, & Hay, 1987).

Knowledge without Awareness

Our introspection regarding the processes involved in face recognition is minimal. It appears that we have little insight into the underlying mechanisms. Furthermore, it is questionable to what degree face recognition is under voluntary control. At least it does not seem to be possible to instruct oneself not to recognize any faces for the next 10 minutes. These observations suggest that face recognition may be carried out by 'automatic' processes that may continue to function in the absence of conscious knowledge of their output (Young & De Haan, 1993).

Physiological Studies

Bauer published his seminal paper in 1984 that fueled the research on face recognition and awareness. He investigated a patient, LF, who had become prosopagnosic after a severe closed head injury. First, Bauer asked his patient to select the correct name from five alternatives to match a photograph of a familiar face. All five alternative names were of celebrities and therefore familiar to the patient (who had no problem recognizing names). As expected of a prosopagnosic patient, LF performed at chance level. However, skin conductance responses recorded during the experiment occurred significantly more often and with higher amplitude to the correct name than to the other four foils. Similarly, Tranel and Damasio (1985) recorded significantly increased autonomic responses when their prosopagnosic patients looked at slides of familiar faces embedded among those of unknown people. These observations have been corroborated using ERP measures. Renault, Signuret, DeBruille, Breton, and Bolgert, (1989) used an "odd-ball paradigm" in which the patient is looking at long series of faces. Most of these photographs are of completely unfamiliar people but once in a while the face of a very famous person is embedded in the series. Each time a famous face appears there is a clear increase in the amplitude of the P300 response. Finally, the recording of eye movements (Rizzo, Hurtig, & Damasio, 1987) has suggested spared processing of familiar faces in prosopagnosic patients. They demonstrated that the way in which normal people look at faces depends on whether they know the person or not. Unfamiliar faces are scanned in a rather global manner with about an equal amount of attention given to all aspects of the face. However, with familiar faces the emphasis is clearly to the internal part of the face (eyes-nose-mouth region). Although the prosopagnosic patient is unaware of the fact that he is looking at a familiar face, his scanning behavior is as if he is looking at a familiar face. These demonstrations of differential processing of familiar and unfamiliar faces despite the inability to recognize the familiar faces overtly thus appears robust. These data were first interpreted as indicating two separable recognition systems, one for overt and another for covert recognition (Bauer, 1984). The overt system would result in a conscious experience of recognition, while the covert system would feed into the limbic system and serve an alerting function.

Behavioral Evidence

However, there were also some indications that covert recognition might not be restricted to autonomic or physiological measures. Bruyer et al. (1983) had already described a patient who showed some degree of preserved knowledge of familiar faces of which he did not appear to be aware himself. These suggestions have been extensively followed up by our research group in a number of studies with the patient PH, who is completely unable to recognize familiar faces overtly. The extent of PH's recognition problems is well illustrated by his performance on a forced-choice task where he had to choose the familiar face from an array of two faces. This test procedure is sensitive to small degrees of residual processing as it is not influenced by possible language or memory dysfunction or subject to the common response bias of agnosic patients to respond 'don't know' in standard line-up confrontation tasks. PH performed this task at chance-level (correct on 51% of the trials) indicating that he has no access to familiarity information from faces.

Next, in seeking to demonstrate covert knowledge, we used experiments that have been shown to be sensitive to knowledge of face familiarity in healthy individuals but which do not require overt identification of the famous faces used as experimental stimuli. Such experiments used the procedures of matching, interference, associative priming, and paired associate learning. In the matching experiment, subjects are required to decide whether two simultaneously presented photographs of faces are taken from the same person or two different people. Two different views of the face are used to avoid the possibility of visual pattern rather than a matching strategy that involves the identity of the person shown in the two pictures. Studies with normal, uninjured subjects have shown that they are faster to match photographs of familiar than unfamiliar people. Thus, we are quicker to decide that two photographs are taken from the same people or not if we know the people. Note that this procedure does not call for conscious recognition of the face per se. PH showed exactly the same effect of faster matching of familiar faces as the control subjects, yet he was unable to identify any of the faces used (De Haan, Young, & Newcombe, 1987a).

The 'interference' experiment (see Figure 4.4) was also based on normal studies. Subjects were shown a series of photographs of faces, each with a printed name in a cartoon-like speech bubble. The printed name was that of the person in the photograph, a person in a related occupation (e.g., the name of George Bush with a photograph of Ronald Reagan), or is entirely unrelated (e.g., the name of Andre Agassi with a photograph of Ronald Reagan). Ostensibly,

Figure 4.4: Examples of stimuli from a condition of de Haan et al.'s (1987a, task 4) study in which there was significant interference of the distractor face on classification of the name as being that of a politician or non-politician. The non-politician Frank Bough's name is combined with the face of politician Neil Kinnock, and vice versa. As can be seen, the two faces are of similar appearances. Copyright 1987 by Lawrence Erlbaum Associates. Reprinted with permission.

the subject's task is to say as quickly as possible whether the printed *name* is that of a politician or not. Control subjects are, nevertheless, influenced by the accompanying face photograph to the extent that they take somewhat longer to respond correctly when the printed name is attached to an unrelated face. PH, who has no difficulty in judging correctly whether a printed name, presented on its own, is that of a politician or not, was nevertheless influenced when face photographs were simultaneously presented with printed names. He showed the same interference effect as normals: He was faster to respond correctly to the printed name when it was attached to the correct or a related face compared to when the face was *unrelated* (De Haan, Young, & Newcombe, 1987b).

Covert processing can also be demonstrated in "associative priming" experiments. Such experiments show the influence of previously presented stimuli on a subsequent response. In this particular case, the response explicitly required of subjects is to decide whether the targets (i.e., written names of familiar and unfamiliar people) were familiar or not. The responses of control subjects are influenced by the presentation of a "prime" stimulus (e.g., a face) shortly before the target appears. If there is a strong association between the prime stimulus (e.g., a photograph of Prince Charles) and the target (e.g. the name of Princess Diana), the subject responds faster than when the prime is either the face of an unfamiliar person or that of a familiar person who is not closely associated with the target (i.e., the face of Prince Charles followed by the name of George Bush).

The patient, PH, shows this type of priming effect from faces that he does not overtly recognize. Moreover, we were able to compare the size of the priming effect with that triggered by *name*-primes (which PH recognizes without difficulty). The effects are equivalent: Overt recognition of name-primes makes no additional contribution to the associative priming effect. This suggests that PH not only covertly recognizes faces, but that his recognition is 'normal' in the amount of associative priming that it produces (Young, Hellawell, & De Haan, 1988). It might, of course, be argued that these experimental effects were derived from weak degrees of overt face recognition that were enhanced by the particular manipulations. In our study, this objection was overridden by the demonstration that, even in forced-choice experiments where the patient had to guess which of two face photographs were familiar, no such weak traces of recognition emerged (Young & De Haan, 1988).

To warrant the conclusion that Bauer's original explanation of two face recognition systems had become less plausible, it was thought prudent to verify whether we had been talking about the same phenomenon as Bauer (1984). Therefore, De Haan, Bauer, and Greve (1992) investigated the possibility of covert face recognition using behavioral tasks in the patient LF who had been the subject in the original studies where Bauer used autonomic indices of recognition. Using a similar task as the priming experiment described above, we were able to demonstrate covert face recognition on a behavioral measure in this patient. The conclusion was reached that autonomic and behavioral manifestations of covert recognition presumably reflect the same underlying phenomenon. However, it was also stressed that this particular association did not preclude the possibility of a dissociation. In our 1992 model, we suggest that autonomic and behavioral indices reflect different outputs from one and the same face recognition system (see also Farah et al.,1995; Newcombe & Lie, 1995; Tranel, Damasio, & Damasio, 1995).

Another useful method to demonstrate covert recognition concerns an adaptation of an experiment carried out by Bruyer et al. (1983). This requires the patient to learn names to faces along the lines of the traditional paired associate learning experiments used in studies of memory. On half the trials, the name belonged to the person depicted on the photograph; on the other half, an untrue name was used (but also belonging to a familiar person). Covert face recognition is indicated when a patient is better at relearning the true than learning the untrue face–name pairings. One question that we addressed using the paired associate learning paradigm was whether PH continues to learn new faces despite the absence of awareness. One group of people he had never met before his accident was the staff at the research institute. To our surprise, but in accordance with the idea of a recognition system that continues to operate, he has learned to recognize us covertly. Thus, he finds it easier to learn my name to my face than my name to the face of Andy Young.

The most convincing demonstrations of covert recognition in PH (and other cases reported in the literature) appear to depend on experiments in which both the names and the faces of familiar people are employed. The effect of covert face recognition is apparent in responses to names in the interference, the priming, and the paired-associate learning paradigms. In addition, De Haan et al. (1991b) showed that PH showed some covert recognition effect on a binary-choice task where he had to chose the correct familiar name to match a photograph of a familiar face. This suggests that covert face-recognition effects are derived from the interconnections between the face and other person-identification systems, such as name recognition (see also Verstichel, 1997). Farah (1994) and Burton et al. (1990) have suggested that covert face recognition phenomena can be modelled using neural-network simulations. The idea is that in a 'degraded' network reduced or partial activation at the intermediate processing levels results in failure to reach threshold activation at the output level. There is, however, enough activation at the intermediate level to influence the weights of connected nodes and thereby influence the working of the network in such a way that resembles covert recognition. This is an elegant explanation of the data, and it is in accordance with the observation that in certain specific experimental conditions overt recognition can actually be provoked in patients with covert recognition (De Haan, Young, & Newcombe, 1991b). Despite the theoretical controversies, covert face recognition is now a well-established phenomenon, that has been observed in many different patient groups, such as Alzheimer's disease (Winograd, Goldstein, Monarch, Peluso, & Goldman, 1999). Also, studies with normal subjects in which familiar faces were presented subliminally have produced convincing evidence of covert recognition (H. D. Ellis, Young, & Koenken, 1991).

It should be noted that covert recognition effects are not invariably found in agnosias. Some prosopagnosic patients do not show any covert effects at all (Newcombe et al., 1989; Etcoff, Freeman, & Cave, 1991) and others have exhibited partial covert recognition effects. De Haan, Young, and Newcombe (1992) observed covert effects only for a subset of the people known to the patient, and Schweinberger, Klos, and Sommer (1995) found covert recognition on some but not other implicit tasks in one patient.

Face Anosognosia

In this context, it useful to mention that there is a converse to covert face recognition. Some patients do not appear to be aware of the fact that they have lost a specific cognitive function like face recognition. Young, De Haan, and Newcombe (1990) report the case of a woman who, after a severe right hemisphere stroke, was very poor at recognizing familiar faces. She was, however, completely unaware of this impairment. Neither the failures in everyday life nor the demonstrations in our laboratory over the years have managed to instill even a remote sense of her problem in recognizing familiar faces. This complete lack of insight for prosopagnosia was starkly contrasted by her good insight in the other cognitive and physical disabilities. These observations lead to the conclusion that SP suffered from a deficit-specific anosognosia. Like Bisiach, Vallar, Perani, Papagno, and Berti (1986), it is argued here that such deficit-specific anosognosia reflects the existence of the need to monitor our own performance. This monitoring might be especially important when it concerns cognitive abilities, such as face recognition, which are carried out automatically and do not rely on conscious control. The patients reported in the literature who suffer from 'false recognition of unfamiliar faces,' such as those who often feel that unfamiliar faces correspond to known individuals (Rapscak, Polster, Glisky, & Comer, 1996; Rapscak et al. 1998) would also fit in with the suggestion of a monitoring mechanism that can go astray.

CONCLUSIONS

We now have considered the main sources of information that have been used to develop functional models of face processing. First, there is evidence for a number of separable processing routes. There is evidence for dissociable face processing abilities, but nearly all are based on the double dissociation method, thus examining various permutations of two of the four face-processing pathways of interest here (facial expression, lipreading, familiar face recognition, and unfamiliar face matching). However, there are a couple of studies that have looked at three or more of the possible distinct processing pathways in one and the same study (e.g., Parry, Young, Saul, & Moss, 1991). Young et al. (1993) employed a stringent methodology to test the independence of processing for familiar face recognition, expression analysis, and unfamiliar face matching. A group of patients with unilateral, posterior brain lesions was tested with two separate tasks for each of the three face processing functions. A selective deficit was defined as a significant impairment on both tasks for that function while the other four tasks were performed within the normal range. On accuracy scores there were examples of, at least, one selective deficit for each of the three functions. The response latencies, however, indicated that unfamiliar-face perception and familiar-face recognition are perhaps not completely independent. These results provided clear evidence for separate processing of facial expressions but there appears to be a common factor in the processing of familiar and unfamiliar faces. It is interesting to note that recent *f*MRI studies (Andreasen et al., 1996) showed activity in the same brain regions for familiar and unfamiliar faces and, as indicated earlier, that Ishai et al. (1999) found evidence suggesting a system of form detectors or processors selective for specific visual primitives.

Neuropsychological research on face processing has produced a number of intriguing and often counter-intuitive results during the last two decades. If the fractionation of reading and object recognition remained controversial until quite recently, we have now seen the general acceptance of a specialized face processing system which itself fractionates further into a system responsible for familiar face recognition, expression analysis, face perception skills such as gender decision and age estimation, and perhaps lipreading. Within the processing route involved in familiar-face recognition, separate sequential processing stages have been identified for the processing of the incoming visual image, access to stored representations of faces, autobiographical information, and names. These processing stages are largely automatic and escape conscious introspection as demonstrated by the phenomenon of covert face recognition where these automatic processes continue to operate despite the fact that the output never reaches conscious awareness.

Recent studies have refined this general theoretical framework. There are now a number of studies that question too strict a fractionation of function. The dissociation between unfamiliar face perception and familiar face recognition (Young et al., 1993) and between familiar-face recognition and lipreading (Campbell & De Haan, 1998) does not appear absolute and data from functional imaging techniques have produced exciting new hypotheses suggesting that the apparent selectivity of face processing can actually be traced back to the functional organization of the fusiform gyrus where there may be a continuous representation of form information that has a highly consistent and orderly topographical arrangement. Additionally, it is promising that these ideas are obviously very well suited for modelling with network models.

Acknowledgements

I am greatly indebted to my research collaborators Freda Newcombe, Andy Young, and Russ Bauer.

REFERENCES

Adolphs, R., Tranel, D., Damasio, H., & Damasio, A. R. (1994). Impaired recognition of emotion in facial expressions following bilateral damage to the human amygdala. *Nature, 372,* 669–672.

Adolphs, R., Tranel, D., Hamann, S., Young, A. W., Calder, A. J., Phelps, E.A., Anderson,. R., Lee., G. P., & Damasio, A. R. (1999). Recognition of facial emotion in nine individuals with bilateral amygdala damage. *Neuropsychologia, 37,* 1111–1117.

Andreassen, N. C., O'Leary, D. S., Arndt, S., & Cizadlo, T. (1996). Neural substrates of facial recognition. *Journal of Neuropsychiatry and Clinical Neurosciences, 8,* 139–146.

Ariel, R., & Sadeh, M. (1996) Congenital visual agnosia and prosopagnosia in a child: A case report. *Cortex, 32,* 221-240.

Assal, G., Favre, C., & Anderes, J. P. (1984). Non-reconnaissance d'animaux familiers chez un paysan: Zooagnosie ou prosopagnosie pour les animaux (Inability to recognize familiar animals in a farmer: zoo-agnosia or prosapagnosia for animals). *Revue Neurologique, 140,* 580–584.

Bartolomeo, P., Bachoud-Levi, A-C., De Gelder, B., Debes, G., Dalla Barba, G., Brugieres, P., & DEgos, J-D. (1998). Multiple-domain dissections between impaired visual perception and preserved mental imagery in a patient with bilateral extrastriate lesions. *Neuropsychologia, 36,* 239-249.

Bauer, R. M. (1984). Autonomic recognition of names and faces in prosopagnosia: A neuropsychological application of the guilty knowledge test. *Neuropsychologia, 22,* 457–469.

Bay, E. (1950). Agnosie und Funktionswandel (Agnosia and "Funktionswandel"). *Monographien aus dem Gesamtgebiet der Neurologie und Psychiatrie, 73,* 1–94.

Bay, E. (1953). Disturbances of visual perception and their examination. *Brain, 76,* 515–551.

Becker, J. T., Lopez, O. L., &Boller, F. (1995). Understanding impaired analysis of faces by patients with probable Alzheimer's disease. *Cortex, 31,* 129-137.

Benton, A. L., & Van Allen, M. W. (1972) Prosopagnosia and facial discrimination. *Journal of the Neurological Sciences, 15,* 167–172.

Benton, A. L. (1980). The neuropsychology of facial recognition. *American Psychologist, 35,* 176–186.

Benton, A. L., & Van Allen, M. W. (1973). *Tests of visual function.* Iowa:

Bisiach, E., Vallar, G., Perani, D., Papagno, C., /7 Berti, A. (1986). Unawareness of disease following lesions of the right hemisphere: anosognosia for hemiplegia and anosognosia for hemianopia. *Neuropsychologia, 24,* 471–482.

Blanc-Garin, J. (1984). Perception des visages et reconnaissance de la physionomie dans l'agnosie des visages (Perception and recognition of faces in prospagnosia). *L'Année Psychologique, 84,* 573-598.

Bodamer, J. (1947). Die Prosop-Agnosie. *Archiv für Psychiatrie und Nervenkrankheiten, 179,* 6-53.

Bornstein, B. (1963). Prosopagnosia. In: L. Halpern (Ed.), *Problems of dynamic neurology* (pp. 283–318). Jerusalem: Hadassah Medical Organization.

Bornstein, B., & Kidron, D. P. (1959). Prosopagnosia. *Journal of Neurology, Neurosurgery and Psychiatry, 22,* 124–131.

Bothwell, R. K., Brigham, J. C., & Malpass, R. S. (1989) Cross-racial identification of faces. *Personality and Social Psychology Bulletin, 15,* 19-25.

Bowers, D., Bauer, R. M., Coslett, H. B., & Heilman, K. M. (1985). Processing of faces by patients with unilateral lesions 1. Dissociations between judgements of facial affect and facial identity. *Brain and Cognition, 4,* 258–272.

Braun, C. M.,J., Denault, C., Cohen, H., & Rouleau, I. (1994). Discrimination of facial identity and facial affect in temporal and frontal lobectomy patients. *Brain and Cognition, 24,* 198–212.

Broks, P., Young, A. W., Maratos, E. J., Coffey, P. J., Calder, A. J., Isaac, C., Mayes, A., Hodges, J. R., Montaldi, D., Cezayirli, E., Roberts, N., & Hadley, D. (1998). Face processing impairments after encephalitis: Amygdala damage and recognition of fear. *Neuropsychologia, 36,* 59–70.

Bruce, V., & Young, A. W. (1986). Understanding face recognition. *British Journal of Psychology, 77,* 305–327.

Bruyer, R., Laterre, C., Seron, X., Feyereisen, P., Strypstein, E., Pierrard, E., & Rectem, D. (1983). A case of prosopagnosia with some preserved covert remembrance of familiar faces. *Brain and Cognition, 2,* 257–284.

Burgess, A. P., & Gruzelier, J. H. (1997). Localization of Word and face recognition memory using topographical EEG. *Psychphysiology, 34,* 7–16.

Burton, A. M., Bruce, V., & Johnston, R. A. (1990). Understanding face recognition with an interactive activation model. *British Journal of Psychology, 81,* 361–380.

Bushnell, I. W. R., & Sai, F. (1987). Neonatal recognition of the mother's face. *University of Glasgow Psychological Report, No. 87/1.* Glasgow, Ireland: Glasgow University.

Campbell, R., & De Haan, E. H. F. (1998). Priming faces: Speechreading can prime face identification judgements but not vice-versa. *British Journal of Psychology, 89, 309–323.*

Campbell, R., Brooks, B., De Haan, E. H. F., & Roberts, A. (1995). Dissociated face processing skills: reaction time evidence on seen speech, expression and identity matching from photographs. *Quarterly Journal of Experimental Psychology, 49,* 295–314.

Campbell, R., Landis, T., & Regard, M. (1986). Face recognition and lipreading: A neurological dissociation. *Brain, 109,* 509–521.

Campion, J. (1987). Apperceptive agnosia: The specification and description of constructs. In G. W. Humphreys & M. J. Riddoch (Eds.), *Visual object processing: A cognitive neuropsychological approach* (pp. 197–232). London: Lawrence Erlbaum.

Charcot, J. M., & Bernard, D. (1983). Un cas de suppression brusque et isole de la vision mentale des signes et objects (former et couleurs) (A case of sudden and isolated deficit in the imagery of letters and objects [shapes and colors]). *Progres Medicine, 11,* 568–571.

Cicone, M., Wapner, W., & Gardner, H. (1980). Sensitivity to emotional expressions and situations in organic patients. *Cortex, 16,* 145–158.

Clark, V. P., Keil, K., Maisog, J. M., Courtney, S., Ungerleider, L G., & Haxby, J. V. (1996). Functional magnetic resonance imaging of human visual cortex during face matching: A comparison positron emission tomography. *Neuroimage, 4,* 1–15.

Clarke, S., Lindemann, A., Maeder, P. Borruat, F. X., & Assal, G. (1997). Face recognition and posterio-inferior hemispheric lesions. *Neuropsychologia, 35,* 1555–1563.

Cohn, R., Neumann, M. A., & Wood, D. H. (1977). Prosopagnosia: A clinicopathological study. *Annals of Neurology, 1,* 177–182.

Cole, M., & Perez-Cruet, J. (1964). Prosopagnosia. *Neuropsychologia, 2,* 237–246.

Cormier, P., & Jackson, T. (1995). Effects of instruction on a divided visual-field task of face processing. *Perceptual and Motor Skills, 80,* 923–930.

Damasio, A. R., Damasio, H., & Tranel, D. (1986). Prosopagnosia: Anatomic and physiological aspects. In H. D. Ellis, M. A. Jeeves, F. Newcombe, & A. Young (Eds.), *Aspects of face processing.* Dordrecht, The Netherlands: Martinus Nijhoff.

Damasio, A. R., Damasio, H., & Van Hoesen, G. W. (1982). Prosopagnosia: Anatomic basis and behavioral mechanisms. *Neurology, 32,* 331–341.

Damasio, A. R., Tranel, D., & Damasio, H. (1990). Face agnosia and neural substrates of memory. *Annual Review of Neuroscience, 13,* 89–109.

De Haan, E. H. F. (1999). A familial factor in the development of face recognition deficits. *Journal of Clinical and Experimental Neuropsychology, 21,* 312–315.

De Haan, E. H. F., Bauer, R. M., & Greve, K. W. (1992). Behavioural and Psychophysiological evidence for covert face recognition in a prosopagnosic patient. *Cortex, 28,* 77–95.

De Haan, E. H. F., & Campbell, R. (1992). A fifteen year follow-up of a case of developmental prosopagnosia. *Cortex, 27,* 489–509.

De Haan, E. H. F., & Hay, D. C. (1986). The effect of unilateral brain lesion on matching famous and unknown faces given either the internal or the external features: A study on patients with unilateral brain lesions. In H. D. Ellis, M. A. Jeeves, F. Newcombe, & A. W. Young (Eds.), *Aspects of face processing* (pp. 279–290). Dordrecht, The Netherlands: Martinus Nijhoff.

De Haan, E. H. F., Heywood, C. A., Young, A. W., & Edelsteyn, N. (1995). Ettlinger revisited: the relationship between agnosia and sensory status. *Journal of Neurology, Neurosurgery and Psychiatry, 58,* 350–356.

De Haan, E. H. F., & Newcombe, F. (1992). Neuropsychology of vision. *Current Opinion in Neurology and Neurosurgery, 5,* 65–70.

De Haan, E. H. F., Young, A. W., & Newcombe, F. (1987a). Face recognition without awareness. *Cognitive Neuropsychology, 4,* 385–415.

De Haan, E. H. F., Young, A. W., & Newcombe, F. (1987b). Faces interfere with name classification in a prosopagnosic patient. *Cortex, 23,* 309–316.

De Haan, E. H. F., Young, A. W., & Newcombe, F. (1991a) A dissociation between sense of familiarity and access to semantic information concerning familiar people. *European Journal of Cognitive 3,* 51-67.

De Haan, E. H. F., Young, A., & Newcombe, F. (1991b). Covert and overt recognition in prosopagnosia. *Brain, 114,* 2575–2591.

De Haan, E. H. F., Young, A. W., & Newcombe, F. (1992). Neuropsychological impairments of face recognition units. *Quarterly Journal of Experimental Psychology, 44A,* 141–175.

De Renzi, E. (1986a). Current issues in prosopagnosia. In H. D. Ellis, M. A. Jeeves, F. Newcombe, & A. Young (Eds.), *Aspects of face processing.* Dordrecht, The Netherlands: Martinus Nijhoff, 243–252.

De Renzi, E. (1986b). Slowly progressive visual agnosia or apraxia without dementia. *Cortex, 22,* 171–180.

De Renzi, E., & Di Pellegrino, G. (1998). Prosopagnosia and alexia without object agnosia. *Cortex,*

De Renzi, E., Perani, D., Carlesimo, G. A., Silveri, M. C., & Fazio, F. (1994). Prosopagnosia can be associated with damage confined to the right hemisphere—An MRI and PET study and a review of the literature. *Neuropsychologia, 32,* 893–902.

De Renzi, E., Faglioni, P., & Nichelli, P. (1991) Apperceptive and associative forms of prosopagnosia. *Cortex, 27,* 213–221.

Duchaine, B. C. (2000). Developmental prosopagnosia with normal configural processing. *Neuroreport, 11,* 79–83.

Ellis, A. W., & Young, A. W. (1988). *Human cognitive neuropsychology.* London: Lawrence Erlbaum.

Ellis, A. W., Young, A. W., Flude, B. M., & Hay, D. C. (1987). Repetition priming of face recognition. *Quarterly Journal of Experimental Psychology, 39A,* 193–210.

Ellis, H. (1983). The role of the right hemisphere in face perception. In A. W. Young (Ed.), *Functions of the right hemisphere.* London: Academic Press.

Ellis, H. D., Young, A. W., & Koenken, G. (1993) Covert face recognition without prosopagnosia. *Behavioural Neurology, 6,* 27–32.

Etcoff, N. L. (1984). Selective attention to facial identity and facial emotion. *Neuropsychologia, 22,* 281–295.

Etcoff, N. L., Freeman, R., & Cave, K. R. (1991) Can we lose memories of faces? Content specificity and awareness in a prosopagnosic. *Journal of Cognitive Neuroscience, 3,* 25–41.

Ettlinger G. (1956). Sensory deficits in visual agnosia. *Journal of Neurology, Neurosurgery and Psychiatry, 19,* 297–308.

Evans, J. J., Heggs, A. J., Antour, N., & Hodges, J. R. (1995). Progressive prosopagnosia associated with selective right temporal lobe atrophy. *Brain, 118,* 1–13.

Farah, M. (1991). Patterns of co-occurence among the associative agnosias: Implications for visual object representations. *Cognitive Neuropsychology, 8,* 1–19.

Farah, M. (1994). Neuropsychological interference with an interactive brain: A critique of the "locality" assumption. *Behavioral and Brain Sciences, 17,* 43–104.

Farah, M. (1996). Is face recognition 'special'? Evidence form neuropsychology. *Behavioural Brain Research, 17,* 43–104.

Farah, M., Levinson, K. L., & Klein, K. L. (1995). Face perception and within-category discrimination in prosopagnosia. *Neuropsychologia, 33,* 661–674.

Farah, M., O'Reilly, R. C., & Vecera, S. P. (1993) Dissociated overt and covert face recognition as an emergent property of a lesioned neural network. *Psychological Review, 100,* 571–588.

Farah, M., Wilson, K., Maxwell, D., & Tanaka, J. (1998). What is 'special;' about face recognition? *Psychological Review, 105,* 482–498.

Farah, M., Wilson, K. D., Drain, H. M., & Tanaka, J. R. (1995). The inverted face effect in prosopagnosia: Evidence for mandatory, face-specific perceptual mechanisms. *Vision Research,* 2089–2093.

Feinberg, T. E., Schindler, R. J., Ochoa, E., & Kwan, P. C. (1994). Associative visual agnosia and alexia without prosopagnosia. *Cortex, 30,* 395–412.

Feinberg, T. E., Schindler, R. J., Ochoa, E., & Kwan, P. C. (1994). Associative visual agnosia and alexia without prosopagnosia. *Cortex, 30,* 395–412.

Flin, R., & Dziurawiec, S. (1989). Developmental factors in face processing. In A. W.Young & H. D. Ellis (Eds.), *The handbook of research on face processing* (pp 335–378). Amsterdam: Elsevier.

Flude, B. M., Ellis, A. W., & Kay, J. (1989). Face processing and name retrieval in an anomic aphasic: Names are stored separately from semantic information about familiar people. *Brain and Cognition, 11,* 60–72.

Fodor, J. (1983). *The modularity of mind.* Cambridge, MA: MIT Press.

Freud, S. (1953). *On aphasia: A critical study.* London: International University Press, Imago.

George, N., Dolan, R. J., Fink, G. R., Bayliss, G. C., Russell, C., & Driver, J. (1999). Contrast polarity and face recognition in the human fusiform gyrus. *Nature Neuroscience, 2,* 574–580.

Gross, C. G. (1992). Representation of visual stimuli in inferior temporal cortex. In: V. Bruce, A. Cowey, A. W. Ellis, & D. I. Perrett (Eds.), *Processing the facial image.* Oxford, UK: Clarendon Press.

Gopnik, M. (1997). Language deficits and genetic factors. *Trends in Cognitive Science, 1,* 5–9.

Hamann, S. B., Stefanacci, L., Squire, L. R., Adolphs, R., Tranel, D., Damasio, H., & Damasio, A. R. (1996). Recognising facial emotion. *Nature, 379,* 497.

Hanley, J. R., Smith, S. T., & Hadfield, J. (1998). I recognise you but I can't place you: An investigation of familiar only experiences during tests of voice and face recognition. *Quarterly Journal of Experimental Psychology, Section A, 51*(1), 179-196.

Hanley, J. R., Young, A. W., & Pearson, N. A. (1989). Defective recognition of familiar people. *Cognition Neuropsychology, 6,* 179–210.

Haxby, J. V., Horwitz, B., Ungerleider, L. G., Maisog, J. M., Pietrini, P., & Grady, C. L. (1994). The functional organisation of human extrastriate cortex: A PET-rCBF study of selective attention to faces and locations. *Journal of Neuroscience, 14,* 6336–6353.

Hay, D. C., & Young A. W. (1982). The human face. In A. W. Ellis (Ed.), *Normality and pathology in cognitive functions* (pp. 173–202). New York: Academic Press.

Hécaen, H. (1981). The neuropsychology of face recognition. In G. Davies, H. Ellis, & J. Shepherd (Eds.), *Perceiving and remembering faces* (pp. 39–54). London: Academic Press.

Hécaen, H., & Angelergues, R. (1962). Agnosia for faces (prosopagnosia). *Archives of Neurology, 7,* 92–100.

Henke, K., Schweinberger, S. R., Grigo, A., Klos, T., & Sommer, W. (1998). Specificity of face recognition: recognition of exemplars of non-face objects in prosopagnosia. *Cortex, 34,* 289–296.

Hodges, J. R., & Greene, J. D. W. (1998). Knowing about people and naming them: Can Alzheimer's disease patients do one without the other? *Quarterly Journal of Experimental Psychology, (Section A), 51*(1), 121–134.

Hodges, J. R., Salmon, D. P., & Butters, N. (1993). Recognition and naming of famous faces in Alzheimer's disease: A cognitive analysis. *Neuropsychologia, 31,* 775–788.

Hoff, H., & Pötzl, O. (1937). Uber eine optisch-agnostische störung des "physiognomie-gedachtnisses" (On an optici-agnostic impairment of face memory). *Zeitschrift für die Gesamte Neurologie and Psychiatrie, 159,* 367–395.

Humphreys, G. W., & Riddoch, M. J. (1984). Routes to object constancy: Implications from neuropsychological impairments of object constancy. *Quarterly Journal of Experimental Psychology, 36A,* 385–415.

Humphreys, G. W., & Riddoch, M. J. (1987). *To see but not to see.* London: Lawrence Erlbaum.

Humphreys, G. W., & Rumiati, R. I. (1998). Agnosia without prosopagnosia or alexia: Evidence for stored visual memories specific to objects. *Cognitive Neuropsychology, 15,* 243–277

Ishai, A., Ungerleider, L. G., Martyin, A., Scouten, J. L., & Haxby, J. V. (1999). Distributed representation of objects in the human ventral visual pathway. *Proceedings of the National Academy of Science USA, 96,* 9379–9384.

Kanwisher, N., McDermott, & Chun, M. M. (1997) The fusiform face area: A module in human extrastriate cortex specialised for face perception. *Journal of Neuroscience, 17,* 4302–4311.

Kanwisher, N., Stanley, D., & Harris, A. (1999). The fusiform gyrus is selective for faces not animals. *Neuroreport, 10,* 183–187.

Kohler, W. (1920). *Gestalt Psychology.* New York: Liveright.

Kurucz, J., & Feldmar, G. (1979). Prosopo-affective agnosia as a symptom of cerebral organic disease. *Journal of the American Geriatrics Society, 27,* 225–230.

Kurucz, J., Feldmar, G., & Werner, W. (1979). Prosopo-affective agnosia associated with chronic organic brain syndrome. *Journal of the American Geriatrics Society, 27,* 91–95.

Landis, T., Cummings, J. L., Christen, L., Bogen, J. E., & Imhof, H-G. (1986). Are unilateral right posterior cerebral lesions sufficient to cause prosopagnosia? Clinical and radiological findings in 6 additional patients *Cortex, 22,* 243–252

Lewis, M. B., & Johnston, R. A. (1997). The Thatcher illusion as a test of configural disruption. *Perception, 26,* 225–227.

Lissauer, L. (1889). Ein Fall von Seelenblindheit nebst einem Beitrag zur theorie derselben (A case of mind blindness and a contribution towards a theoretical explanation). *Archiv für Psychiatrie und Nervenkrankheiten, 21,* 222–270.

Luckman, A. J., Allinson, N. M., Ellis, A. W., & Flude, B. M. (1995). Familiar face recognition: A comparative study of a connectionist model and human performance. *Neurocomputing, 7,* 3–27.

MacRae, D, & Trolle, E. (1956). The defect of function in visual agnosia. *Brain, 79,* 94–110.

Malone, D. R., Morris, H. H., Kay, M. C., & Levin, H. S. (1982). Prosopagnosia: A double dissociation between the recognition of familiar and unfamiliar faces. *Journal of Neurology, Neurosurgery and Psychiatry, 45,* 820–822.

Marr, D. (1982). *Vision.* San Fransisco: Freeman.

McCarthey, R. A., & Warrington, E. K. (1986). Visual associative agnosia: A clinico-anatomical study of a single case. *Journal of Neurology, Neurosurgery and Psychiatry, 49,* 1233–1240.

McClelland, J. L., & Rumelhart, D. E. (1988). *Explorations in parallel distributed processing.* Cambridge, MA: Bradford.

McConachie, H. R. (1976). Developmental Prosopagnosia. A single case report. *Cortex, 12,* 76–82.

McGlynn, S., & Schacter, D. L. (1989). Unawareness of deficits in neuropsychological syndromes. *Journal of Clinical and Experimental Neuropsychology, 11,* 143–205.

Meadows, J. C. (1974). The anatomic basis of prosopagnosia. *Journal of Neurology, Neurosurgery and Psychiatry, 37,* 509–516.

Mehta, Z., Newcombe, F., & De Haan, E. H. F. (1992). Selective loss in imagery in a case of visual agnosia. *Neuropsychologia, 30,* 645–655

Moscovitch, M., Winocur, G., & Behrman, M. (1997). What is special about face recognition? Nineteen experiments on a person with visual object agnosia and dyslexia but normal face recognition. *Journal of Cognitive Neuroscience, 9,* 555–604.

Newcombe, F., De Haan, E. H. F., Ross, J., & Young, A. W. (1989). Face processing, laterality, and contrast sensitivity. *Neuropsychologia, 27,* 523–538.

Newcombe, F., Young, A. W., & De Haan, E. H. F. (1989). Prosopagnosia and object agnosia without covert recognition. *Neuropsychologia, 27,* 179–191.

Newcombe, N., & Lie, E. (1995). Overt and covert recognition of faces in children and adults. *Psychological Science, 6,* 241–245.

Newcombe, F., Mehta, Z. M., & De Haan, E. H. F. (1994). Visual agnosia. In M. Farah & G. Ratcliff (Eds.), *The neuropsychology of higher vision: Collected tutorial essays* (pp. 103–113). New Jersey: Lawrence Erlbaum.

O-Scalaidhe, S. P., Wilson, F. A., & Goldman-Rakic, P. S. (1997). Areal segregation of face-processing neurons in prefrontal cortex. *Science, 278,* 1135–1138.

Pallis, C. A. (1955). Impaired identification of faces and places with agnosia for colours. *Journal of Neurology, Neurosurgery and Psychiatry, 18,* 218–224.

Parry, F. M., Young, A. W., Saul,, J. S., & Moss, A. (1991). Dissociable face processing impairments after brain injury. *Journal of Clinical and Experimental Neuropsychology, 13,* 545–558.

Perrett, D. I., Mistlin, A. J., & Chitty, A. J. (1987). Visual neurons responsive to faces. *Trends in neuroscience, 10,* 358–364.

Perrett, D. I., Mistlin, A. J., Chitty, A. J., Harries, M., Newcombe, F., & De Haan, E. H. F. (1988). Neural mechanisms of face perception and their pathology. In C. Kennard & D. Clifford-Rose (Eds.), *Physiological aspects of clinical neuro-ophthalmology* (pp. 137–154). London: Chapman and Hall.

Perrett, D. I., Rolls, E. T., & Caan, W. (1982). Visual neurons responsive to faces in the monkey temporal cortex. *Experimental Brain Research, 47,* 329–342.

Pizzamiglio, L., Zoccolotti, P., Mammucari, A., & Cesaroni, R. (1983). The independence of face identity and facial expression recognition mechanisms: Relationship to sex and cognition style. *Brain and Cognition, 2,* 176–188.

Rapcsak, S. V., Polster, M. R., Glisky, M. L., & Comer, J. F. (1996). False recognition of unfamiliar faces following right hemisphere damage: Neuropsychological and anatomical observations. *Cortex, 32,* 593–611

Rapcsak, S. Z., Kaszniak, A. W., Reminger, S. L., Glisky, M. L., Glisky, E. L., & Comer, J. F. (1998). Dissociation between verbal and autonomic measures of memory following frontal lobe damage. *Neurology, 50,* 1259–1261.

Renault, B., Signoret, J. L., DeBruille, B., Breton, F., & Bolgert, F. (1989). Brain potentials reveal covert facial recognition in prosopagnosia. *Neuropsychologia, 27,* 905–912.

Rhodes, G. (1985). Lateralized processes in face recognition. *British Journal of Psychology, 766,* 249–271.

Ritchie-Russell, W. (1941). Visual object agnosia with special reference to the gestalt theory. *Brain, 64,* 43–62.

Riddoch, M. J., & Humphreys, G. W. (1987). A case of integrative visual agnosia. *Brain, 110,* 1431–1462.

Rizzo, M., Hurtig, R., & Damasio, A. R. (1987). The role of scanpaths in facial recognition and learning. *Annals of Neurology, 22,* 41–45.

Rolls, E. T. (1984). Neurons in the cortex of the temporal lobe and the amygdala of the monkey selective for faces. *Human Neurobiology, 3,* 209–222.

Rondot, P., Tzavares, A., & Garcin, R. (1967). Sur un cas de prosopagnosie persistant depuis quinze ans (On a case of prospagnosia persistent for fifteen years). *Revue Neurologique, 117,* 424–428.

Sams, M., Hietanen, J. K., Hari, R., Ilmoniemi, R. J., & Lounasmaa, O. V. (1997). Face-specific responses from the human inferior occipito-temporal cortex. *Neuroscience, 77,* 49–55.

Schweinberger, S. R., Klos, T., & Sommer, W. (1995). Covert face recognition: A dissociable function? *Cortex, 31,* 517–529.

Sergent, J. (1988). Face perception and the right hemisphere. In L. Weiskrantz (Ed.), *Thought without language* (pp. 108–131). Oxford, UK: Clarendon Press.

Shallice, T. (1988). *From neuropsychology to mental structure.* Cambridge, UK: Cambridge University Press.

Simion, F., Valenza, E., & Umilta, C. (1998). Mechanisms underlying face preference art birth. In F. Simion & G. Butterworth (Eds.), *The development of sensory, motor, and cognitive capacities in early infancy.* East Sussex, UK: Psychology Press.

Sparr, S. A., Jay, M., Drislane, F. W., & Venna, N. (1991). A historic case of visual agnosia revisited after 40 years. *Brain, 114,* 789–800.

Stevenage, S. V. (1995). Expertise and the caricature effect. In T. Valentine (Ed.), *Cognitive and computational aspects of face recognition* (pp. 24–46). London: Routledge.

Teuber, H-L. (1968). Alteration of perception and memory in man. In L. Weiskrantz (Ed.), *Analysis of behaviour change.* New York: Harper & Row.

Teuber, H-L. (1955), Physiological psychology. *Annual Review of Psychology, 6,* 267–296.

Teunisse, J-P, & De Gelder, B. (1994)/ Do autistics have a generalised face processing deficit? *International Journal of Neuroscience, 77,* 1–10.

Tiberghien, G., & Clerc, I. (1986). The cognitive locus of prosopagnosia. In R. Bruyer (Ed.), *The Neuropsychology of face perception and facial expression* (pp. 39–62). Hillsdale, NJ: Lawrence Erlbaum.

Tovee, M. J. (1998). Face processing: Getting by with a little from its friends. *Current Biology, 8,* 317–320.

Tovee, M. J. (1998). Is face processing special. *Neuron, 21,* 1239–1242.

Tranel, D., & Damasio, A. R. (1985). Knowledge without awareness: an autonomic index of facial recognition by prosopagnosics. *Science, 228,* 1453–1454.

Tranel, D., & Damasio, A. R. (1987). Evidence for covert recognition of faces in a global amnesic. *Journal of Clinical and Experimental Neuropsychology, 9,* 15.

Tranel, D., & Damasio, A. R. (1989). Developmental prosopagnosia? A new form of learning and recognition defect. *Society for Neurosciences Abstracts, 15,* 303.

Tranel, D., Damasio, H., & Damasio, A. R. (1995). Double dissociations between overt and covert face recognition. *Journal of Cognitive Neuroscience, 7,* 425–432.

Tranel, D., Damasio, H., & Damasio, A. R. (1988). Intact recognition of facial expression, gender, and age in patients with impaired recognition of face identity. *Neurology, 38,* 690–696.

Tzavaras, A., Hécaen, H., & Le Bras, H. (1970). Le probleme de la spécificité du déficit de la reconnaissance du visage humain lors des lésions hémispheriques unilaterales (The problem of specificity of deficit of human face recognition after unilateral lesions). *Neuropsychologia, 8,* 403–416.

Van-der-Linden, M., Bredart, S., & Schweich, M. (1995). Developmental disturbance of access to biographical information and people's names: A single-case study. *Journal of the International Neuropsychological Society, 1,* 589–595

Verstichel, P. (1997). Reconnaisance implicite des visages par stimulation de l'imagerie mentale chez un patient prospagnosique (Implicit face recognition after mental imagery in a prosopagnosic patient). *Reveu de Psychologie, 7,* 71–94.

Walton, G. E., Armstrong, E. S., & Bower, T. G. R. (1997). Faces as forms in the world of the newborn. *Infant Behavior and Development, 20,* 537–543.

Warrington, E. K., & James, M. (1967). An experimental investigation of facial recognition in patients with unilateral cerebral lesions. *Cortex, 3,* 317–320.

Warrington, E. K., & James, M. (1986). Visual object recognition in patients with right hemisphere lesions: Axes or features? *Perception, 15,* 355-366.

Whiteley, A. M., & Warrington, E. K. (1977). Prosopagnosia: A clinical, psychological and anatomical study of three patients. *Journal of Neurology, Neurosurgery and Psychiatry, 40,* 395–403

Wilbrand, J. (1982). Ein fall von Seelenblindheit und Hemianopsie mit Sections-befund (A case of mind blindness and hemianopia including postmortem examination). *Deutsche Zeitschrift für Nervenheilkunde, 2,* 361–387.

Winograd, E., Goldstein, F. C., Monarch, E. S., Peluso, J. P., & Goldman, W. P. (1999). The mere exposure effect in patients with Alzheimer's disease. *Neuropsychology, 13,* 41–46.

Yin, R. K. (1970). Looking at upside-down faces. *Journal of Experimental Psychology, 81,* 141–145.

Young, A. W., Aggleton, J. P., Hellawell, D. J., Johnson, M., Broks, P., & Hanley, J. R. (1995). Face processing impairments after amygdalotomy. *Brain, 118,* 15–24.

Young, A. W., & De Haan, E. H. F (1988). Boundaries of covert recognition in prosopagnosia. *Cognitive Neuropsychology, 5,* 317–336.

Young, A. W., & De Haan, E. H. F. (1993) Impairments of visual awareness. In M. Davies & G. W. Humphreys (Eds.), *Consciousness* (pp. 58–73). Oxford, UK: Basil Blackwell.

Young, A. W, De Haan, E. H. F., & Newcombe, F. (1990). Unawareness of impaired face recognition. *Brain and Cognition, 14,* 1–18.

Young, A. W., Hay, D. C., & Ellis, A. W. (1985). The face that launched a thousand ships: Everday difficulties and errors in recognizing people. *British Journal of Psychology, 76,* 495–523.

Young, A. W., Hay, D. C., & McWeeny, K. H. (1985). Right cerebral hemisphere superiority for constructing facial representations. *Neuropsychologia, 23,* 195–202.

Young, A. W., Hellawell, D., & De Haan, E. H. F. (1988). Cross domain semantic priming in normal subjects and a prosopagnosic patient. *Quarterly Journal of Experimental Psychology, Section A, 40*(3)

Young, A. W., Hellawell, D. J. van de Wal, C., & Johnson, M. (1996). facial expression processing after amygdalotomy. *Neuropsychologia, 34,* 31–39.

Young, A. W., Hellawell. D., & Hay, D. C. (1987). Configural information in face perception. *Perception, 16,* 747-759.

Young, A. W., Humphreys, G. W., Riddoch, M. J., Hellawell, D. J., & De Haan, E. H. F. (1994). Recognition impairments and face imagery. *Neuropsychologia, 32,* 693–702.

Young, A. W., Newcombe, F., De Haan, E. H. F., Small, M., & Hay, D. C. (1993). Face perception after brain injury: Selective impairments affecting identity and expression. *Brain, 116,* 941–959.

Zouridakis, G., Simos, P. G., Breier, J., & Papanicolaou, A. C. (1998). Functional hemispheric asymmetry assessment in a visual language task using MEG. *Brain Tomography, 11,* 57–65.

5

Spatial Representation in Mind and Brain

Michael McCloskey

The ability to represent and manipulate spatial information is crucial for a wide range of perceptual, cognitive, and motor functions, including object recognition, reading, writing, attention, visually-guided reaching, and navigating through the environment. As a consequence, spatial processing has attracted considerable interest among cognitive psychologists, and is one of the most active areas of neurophysiological research. However, many of the most fascinating results have come from cognitive neuropsychological research on spatial deficits.

My aim in this chapter is not to review the extensive literature on spatial deficits, but rather to explore some fundamental issues about spatial representation through discussion of selected studies. I first consider a deceptively simple question: In what sense(s) are spatial representations spatial? Exploring this question proves surprisingly helpful in clarifying basic issues. I then examine a concept of central importance in research on spatial representation: that of a reference frame. Here again I attempt to clarify the issues and the implications of results.

WHAT IS SPATIAL ABOUT SPATIAL REPRESENTATIONS?

A pervasive assumption in research on spatial perception and cognition is that (at least some) spatial representations in the brain are spatial not merely in the sense of representing spatial information, but also in some other, more fundamental, sense. For example, the psychological, neuropsychological, and neuroscientific literatures are replete with terms like *depictive representation, quasi-pictorial representation, internal representational space, cortical map, cognitive map, visuo-spatial scratch pad, mental image, image scanning,* and *mental rotation.* Such terms seem to suggest that internal representations of spatial information are somehow similar to external spatial representations like pictures or maps. Except in the literature on mental imagery (see Kosslyn, 1995, for an overview), this notion has not received much scrutiny, and it remains unclear in what sense(s) internal representations of spatial information are spatial.

In the following discussion I use neuropsychological evidence from studies of unilateral spatial neglect as a springboard for exploring this issue. I first describe several neglect phenomena that have been taken as evidence for internal representations with interesting spatial properties. Using these phenomena as examples, I consider what spatial properties a representation might have, and what the significance of these properties might be.[1]

Examples

Figures Viewed through Slits

Bisiach, Luzzatti, and Perani (1979) tested 19 participants with right-hemisphere lesions and symptoms of left neglect. Pairs of cloudlike figures were presented (see Figure 5.1 panel A), and the participant judged whether the figures in each pair were the same or different. When the figures differed, the difference was sometimes on the left side (as in Figure 5.1 panel A), and sometimes on the right.

In the static condition each figure in a pair was displayed in its entirety for two seconds. In the dynamic condition each figure was presented as if it were moving behind a central vertical slit, with only a narrow slice visible at any given time (Figure 5.1 panel B). The figure made a single pass behind the slit, moving from left to right or right to left over a two-second period.

Left neglect was evident in the results from the static condition: The participants as a group showed normal performance in detecting differences on the right sides of figures, but were impaired in detecting left-side differences. Remarkably, the same pattern was observed in the dynamic condition. Even though all parts of a figure were presented in the same central vertical slit, the participants as a group were impaired in detecting differences on the left but not the right sides. (See Ogden, 1985, for a replication in which results from individual participants as well as group averages were reported.)

These findings suggest that even when figures were presented bit-by-bit in the central slit, participants constructed internal representations of whole figures. Furthermore, given that the participants' neglect affected spatially-defined parts of the figures (i.e., the left sides), it appears that the whole-figure representations were spatial not merely in the sense of representing spatial information about the shapes of the figures, but in some other way as well. In the terms of a metaphor frequently invoked in discussions of neglect (e.g., Bisiach & Luzzatti, 1978), we might say that the representations were spread across the left and right sides of an internal representational space, and that the participants neglected the left side of this internal space.

NV and the Piazza del Duomo

An elegant demonstration by Bisiach and Luzzatti (1978; see also Bisiach, Capitani, Luzzatti, & Perani, 1981) also points to representations that are spatial in some interesting sense. NV, a 72-year-old lawyer who had suffered a right temporo-parietal hemorrhage, was asked to describe a familiar place—the Piazza del Duomo in Milan—from two imagined perspectives. When told to imagine himself at one end of the square looking toward the cathedral at the other end, he described many landmarks that were on the right side of the square from the imagined viewpoint, but very few landmarks from the left side of the square (Figure 5.2). He was then told to imagine himself at the opposite end of the square, looking toward his initial vantage point (so that the side previously on his left was now on his right, and vice versa). From this perspective NV described many landmarks from the previously-neglected side of the square, and failed to mention any landmarks from the side he had originally described in detail.

---

[1]Unilateral spatial neglect is a label applied to individuals with brain damage who show impairment in processing information about the contralesional side of space. For example, a neglect patient with right-hemisphere damage may omit material from the left side when asked to copy a picture or draw an object from memory. Neglect has been observed following lesions to a variety of brain regions, but occurs most commonly as a consequence of parietal damage (e.g., Vallar, 1993).

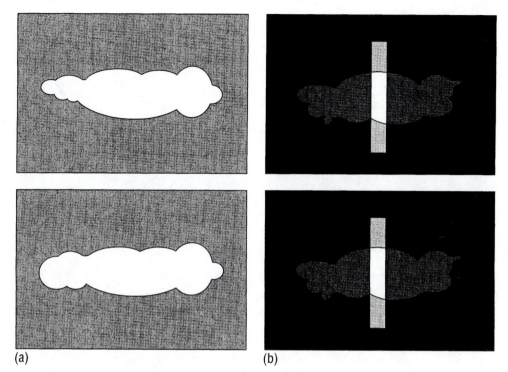

Figure 5.1: Panel A. Example of stimuli from the Bisiach et al. (1979) study. Adapted with permission of Oxford University Press. Panel B. Presentation of stimuli in the dynamic condition. The vertical slit was 1.5 cm wide, whereas the stimulus shapes had a width of 20 cm. After Bisiach (1996), Figure 1, p. 63. Adapted with permission of Blackwell Publishers.

Here again the metaphor of an internal representational space seems apt. NV, it appears, represented in some internal space the square as it would look from a specified vantage point, and was impaired in representing or processing information from the left side of the representational space. The temptation is strong to conceive of the internal space as a screen upon which spatial information is displayed, with neglect involving damage to, or impairment in attending to, one side of the screen.

NG and Single-Word Reading

Caramazza and Hillis (1990a, 1990b; see also Hillis & Caramazza, 1995) reported an extensive study of NG, a 79-year-old woman who had suffered a stroke affecting the left temporo-parietal region. NG showed signs of right-sided neglect in a variety of circumstances (e.g., failing to eat food on the right side of her plate, omitting the right sides when drawing objects from memory). In single-word reading NG evidenced right neglect dyslexia; that is, she made errors that almost always involved the right side of the word (e.g., *humid* ⟶ *human, journal* → *journey*). These errors suggested that NG's right-sided neglect affected her ability to represent, attend to, or otherwise process, the right sides of the word stimuli.[2]

---

[2]NG's errors did not usually involve simply omitting material from the right side of the word; for example, she did not read *humid* as *hum*. Her errors are perhaps best described by saying that when she misread a word, her response was almost always consistent with the left half of the stimulus word, but inconsistent with part or all of the right half. Apparently, NG's word recognition processes usually had information about the presence of letters on the right side of the word, but often did not have information about the identities of these letters (see also Ellis, Flude, & Young, 1987).

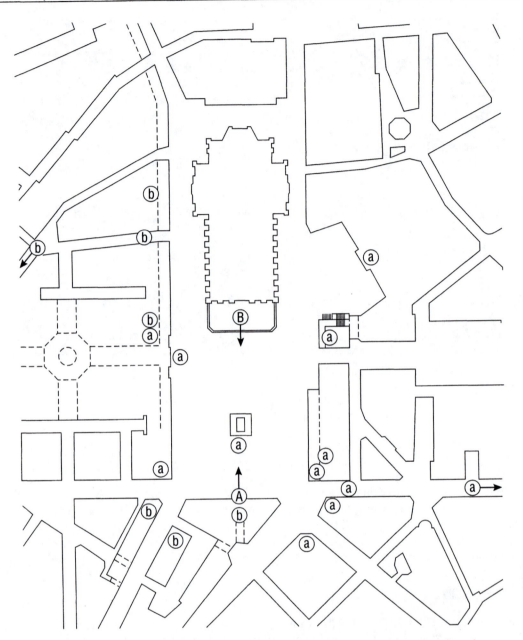

Figure 5.2: NV's performance in describing the Piazza del Duomo in Milan, from two imagined perspectives. NV imagined himself first at location 'A' and then at location 'B,' facing in each case in the direction indicated by the arrow. Landmarks described from perspective A are indicated by 'a,' and those described from perspective B by 'b.' After Bisiach and Luzzatti (1978), Figure 1, p. 130. Adapted with permission.

However, additional results made clear that NG's neglect errors in reading did not result from neglect for the right sides of *stimuli*. When words were presented with the letters arrayed vertically instead of horizontally (see Figure 5.3), NG's error rate remained the same, and her errors still involved the ends of words (e.g., *fraud* → *frame*), even though all of the letters in the vertical stimuli had the same central position on the left–right dimension.

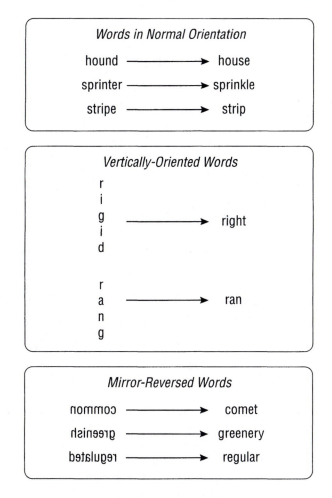

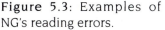

Figure 5.3: Examples of NG's reading errors.

Even more remarkable were NG's errors in reading mirror-reversed words (e.g., ꜱomꜱoɔ). In mirror-reversed stimuli the beginning of the word appears on the right, and the end of the word on the left; therefore, neglect affecting the right sides of stimuli should lead to errors on the beginnings of mirror-reversed words (e.g., ꜱomꜱoɔ → *lemon*). In fact, however, NG's errors for mirror-reversed stimuli—like her errors for normal and vertically-oriented stimuli—consistently involved the ends of the words (e.g., ꜱomꜱoɔ → *comet*; see Figure 5.3). Caramazza and Hillis (1990a, 1990b) interpreted these results by proposing that regardless of how a word is presented—normally, vertically, mirror-reversed—word recognition processes construct an internal spatial representation in which the letters are arrayed from left to right in their canonical positions, with initial letters on the left and final letters on the right. They argued that NG was impaired in processing the right side of these canonical representations, leading her to err on the ends of words regardless of how the stimuli were oriented.

Stimuli, Represented Scenes, and Representations

The results reported by Bisiach et al. (1979), Bisiach and Luzzatti (1978), and Caramazza and Hillis (1990a, 1990b) offer compelling glimpses of internal spatial representations, and the metaphor of an internal representational space seems to provide a useful way of thinking about these representations. How, though, should we interpret the notion of a representational space? What does it mean to suggest that participants in the Bisiach et al. (1979) study represented the shapes of whole figures in an internal space, and neglected the left side of this space? Also, how should we interpret assertions about the left or right sides of representations, such as the claim that NG neglected the right side of internal word representations?

Aspects of Representation

In addressing these questions it is useful to distinguish among (a) the stimulus, or other source of information, from which an internal representation is constructed; (b) the state of affairs specified (i.e., represented) by the representation; and (c) the representation itself. For example, in the dynamic condition of the Bisiach et al. (1979) study each stimulus was a continuous succession of slices presented over time in a central vertical strip. However, the internal representation constructed from the stimulus apparently specified the figure as it would have appeared if presented as a whole. In other words the representation apparently described a state of affairs—which I will call the *represented scene*—in which the figure was extended in space in front of the viewer, with the left part to the viewer's left, and the right part to the viewer's right. Finally, the representation itself was a set of brain states or events that stood for the represented scene.

In the Bisiach and Luzzatti (1978) study NV generated internal representations of the Piazza del Duomo not from stimuli presented during the study, but rather from knowledge acquired through prior experience. Instructed to imagine the Piazza from two different perspectives, he apparently constructed two different representations. For each representation the represented scene was a view of the Piazza as it would appear from the specified vantage point. Because the represented scenes were different in the two cases, the brain states or events constituting the representations themselves must also have been different.

In the Caramazza and Hillis (1990a, 1990b) study NG constructed internal representations from visual word stimuli in normal, vertical, or mirror-reversed orientation. From all three types of stimuli NG apparently generated representations specifying states of affairs (represented scenes) in which letters were arrayed in their canonical positions, with initial letters on the left and final letters on the right. Thus, for any given word (e.g., *house*) the represented scene—and probably the representation itself—was the same regardless of how the stimulus was oriented.

The distinctions among stimuli, represented scenes, and representations can be summarized succinctly: Representations are constructed on the basis of stimuli (or other sources of information), and stand for represented scenes. Two points of clarification may be in order. First, the represented scene can be thought of as the informational content of the representation. Distinguishing represented scenes from stimuli is necessary because the informational content of a representation may not correspond closely to the eliciting stimulus. This is most obvious in cases of misrepresentation (e.g., misrepresenting the lengths of lines when viewing the Müller-Lyer illusion), but is also true when processes constructing a representation substantially elaborate or abstract away from stimulus properties, as in the Bisiach et al. (1979) and Caramazza and Hillis (1990a, b) studies.

Second, in characterizing the representations themselves as brain states or events I do not intend to imply that representations must be described in neural terms; other vocabularies (e.g., that of symbols, or subsymbolic units) are more appropriate for many purposes. The distinction between represented scenes and representations is therefore not a distinction between cognitive and neural levels of description, but rather a distinction between what is represented (i.e., the informational content), and what is doing the representing.

Maintaining the Distinctions

There is nothing profound about these distinctions; nevertheless, they can be easy to lose sight of. As we have seen, for example, the findings from some studies of neglect cannot be described by saying that participants neglected the left or right side of the stimuli, and researchers attempting to characterize these findings have typically resorted to saying that neglect affected one side of an internal representation, or one side of an internal representational space.

However, interpretations couched in these terms blur the distinction between representations and what they represent. To say that NG neglected the right half of a canonical word representation (e.g., Caramazza & Hillis, 1990a, p. 425) is to conflate the representation (a set of states or events in the brain) with the state of affairs it represents (a sequence of letters in their canonical positions). The claim Caramazza and Hillis intended to make is best stated not by saying that NG neglected the right half of the representations, but rather by saying that she neglected the right half of the represented scenes.

Similar points apply to interpretations stated in terms of the internal representational space metaphor. Unless supplemented with more explicit statements, such interpretations are ambiguous: Is the intent to say something about representations, represented scenes, or perhaps both? For the Bisiach et al. (1979) and Bisiach and Luzzatti (1978) results a more straightforward characterization is that the participants neglected the left sides of represented scenes (views of whole figures in the former study, and views of the Piazza del Duomo from particular perspectives in the latter). By describing effects of neglect in terms of represented scenes, we accommodate the fact that a neglected region may not be definable in stimulus terms (because the represented scene need not correspond in any simple way to a stimulus); at the same time we avoid the confusion between representations and what they represent (because the represented scene is distinguished from the representation itself).

Two Senses of 'Spatial Representation'

With this discussion as a foundation, we can begin to sort out the senses in which a spatial representation could be spatial. In this section I consider two senses, one involving represented scenes, and the other concerning the representations themselves.

Spatial$_1$ Representation

The most obvious sense in which a representation can be spatial is by representing spatial information. Representations that are spatial in this sense I will refer to as spatial$_1$ representations. More specifically, I will say that a representation is spatial$_1$ if it is used within a computational system to stand for spatial information.

The representations affected by neglect in the studies I have described were apparently spatial$_1$ representations. For example, participants in the Bisiach et al. (1979) study presumably had to represent spatial information—the shapes of the cloudlike figures—in making same-different judgments for pairs of figures.

Claims about spatial$_1$ representation have to do with what information is represented, and therefore can be thought of as claims about the nature of the represented scenes. Some of the interesting conclusions suggested by the neglect studies are of this sort (e.g., Bisiach et al.'s conclusion that even in the dynamic condition participants represented the figures as they would have appeared if presented as wholes).

Spatial$_2$ Representation

A second sense of 'spatial representation' concerns the representations themselves. To introduce this sense I need to examine some additional implications of the illustrative neglect studies. In all of the studies, damage to spatially-defined regions of the brain affected spatially-defined regions of represented scenes. For example, in the Bisiach et al. (1979) study the participants' right-hemisphere lesions led to neglect for the left sides of the represented figures.

This pattern could be taken as evidence about the spatial layout of representations in the brain (see, e.g., Bisiach, 1993, 1996; Bisiach & Berti, 1987; Bisiach et al., 1979; Bisiach et al., 1981; Bisiach & Luzzatti, 1978). Assume first that representations of spatial information may extend over portions of both cerebral hemispheres, such that each representation is partially in the left hemisphere and partially in the right. A unilateral brain lesion could then affect a spatially-defined part of a representation (i.e., the left-hemisphere part, or the right-hemisphere part). For instance, in the Bisiach et al. (1979) study the participants' right-hemisphere lesions may have affected right-hemisphere parts of representations while leaving left-hemisphere parts intact.

In this way we can explain how damage to a spatially-defined brain region could affect a spatially-defined part of a representation. However, it remains to be explained how damage affecting a spatially-defined part of a representation (e.g., the right-hemisphere part) could lead to neglect for a spatially-defined part of a *represented scene* (e.g., the left side). For this purpose we need the additional assumption that spatially-defined parts of the representations were systematically related to spatially-defined parts of the represented scenes. In particular, we need to assume that the right-hemisphere parts of representations specified the left sides of the represented scenes, and vice versa. Damage affecting a representation-part in one hemisphere would then lead to impairment affecting the contralateral side of the represented scene. Thus, in the Bisiach et al. (1979) study the participants' right-hemisphere lesions may have affected the left sides of the represented shapes, leading to poor performance in detecting left-side differences between figures. Analogous interpretations can be offered for the Bisiach and Luzzatti (1978) and Caramazza and Hillis (1990a, 1990b) results.[3]

Given these assumptions, brain damage could affect representations in two ways (which are not mutually exclusive). First, neural tissue required for instantiating representations could be damaged, so that the parts of representations that should reside in the damaged hemisphere could not be created or maintained normally. For example, NG's left-hemisphere lesion might have damaged neural tissue needed for instantiating the parts of canonical word representations that specified the ends of words.

Second, if we assume that each hemisphere contains mechanisms for attending to or otherwise operating upon the parts of representations residing within that hemisphere, then damage to the mechanisms in one hemisphere could selectively impair processing of the representation-parts in that hemisphere. For instance, in the Bisiach and Luzzatti (1978) study NV's right-hemisphere lesion may have impaired his ability to direct attention to parts of representations in that hemisphere, even if the representation-parts themselves were intact.[4]

Could the neglect phenomena be accounted for solely in terms of separate left- and right-hemisphere processing mechanisms, without assuming any partitioning of the representations? To develop such an interpretation, one would have to assume that even though representational elements specifying the left side of the represented scene were not separated from elements specifying the right side, right-hemisphere processing mechanisms nevertheless dealt only with the former elements, and left-hemisphere mechanisms only with the latter. This assumption lacks motivation and seems (at least to me) rather implausible. Hence, I will continue to assume that the representations underlying the illustrative neglect phenomena were partitioned into left- and right-hemisphere parts, with the left-hemisphere part specifying the right side of the represented scene, and vice versa. However, the possibility that only the

---

[3]It may not be necessary to assume that each half of the represented scene is represented *solely* in the contralateral hemisphere; it may suffice to assume that for all parts of the represented scene the representation is at least *predominantly* contralateral. For example, Pouget and Sejnowski (1997a, 1997b) proposed a computational model of spatial representation in parietal cortex, and argued that the model can account for neglect phenomena. Their model assumes, on the basis of neurophysiological evidence, that each parietal lobe represents all parts of visual space, but that more cells are dedicated to the contralateral side of the space than to the ipsilateral side.

[4]The representational assumptions I have described are therefore compatible with both representational and attentional theories of neglect. (See, e.g., Humphreys & Riddoch, 1993, for an overview of these theories.)

processing mechanisms were partitioned cannot be ruled out definitively; therefore my representational assumptions should be taken not as established facts, but rather as working hypotheses.

We are now in a position to consider the second sense in which a representation could be spatial. This sense, spatial$_2$, may be defined as follows: A representation is spatial$_2$ if (a) spatially-defined parts of the representation correspond to spatially-defined parts of the represented scene, and (b) at least one spatial property defined over the parts of the representation (e.g., distance between parts) is isomorphic to a spatial property defined over the corresponding parts of the represented scene. The retinotopic map in primary visual cortex (V1) is a clear example (Figure 5.4). Each location in V1 corresponds to a location in the (two-dimensional)

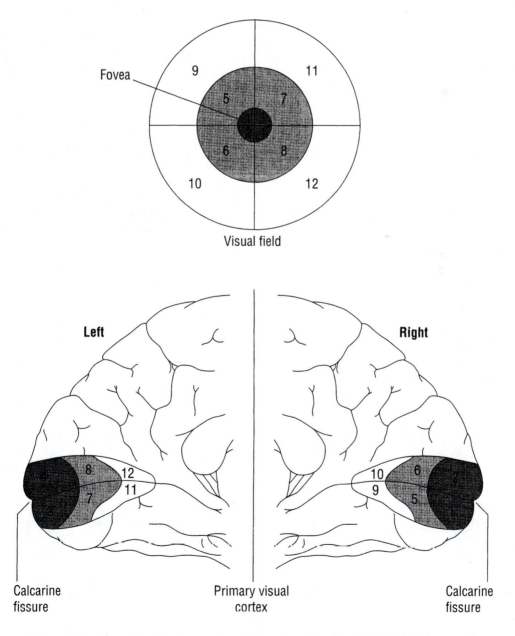

Figure 5.4: The retinotopic map in primary visual cortex (V1). After Mason and Kandel (1991), Figure 29-7, p. 426. Adapted with permission of The McGraw-Hall Companies.

visual field. Furthermore, several spatial properties defined over locations in V1 are isomorphic to spatial properties defined over locations in the visual field. For instance, distance in V1 mirrors distance in the visual field: locations that are close to one another in V1 correspond to locations that are close to one another in the visual field (although this relationship is modulated by so-called cortical magnification of central visual-field regions relative to peripheral regions). Also, spatial dimensions in V1 are isomorphic to spatial dimensions in the visual field; for example, the ventral-dorsal dimension in V1 is isomorphic to the up-down dimension in the visual field (the more ventral a location is in V1, the higher the corresponding location is in the visual field). In effect, the visual field is spread out topographically (or, to be more precise, topologically) on the cortical surface.

Do the representations revealed by the neglect studies meet the criteria for spatial$_2$ representations? The answer appears to be a qualified yes. The metaphor of an internal representational space—especially if we think of this space as something like a display screen—encourages us to think of the representations as similar to those in V1, with the represented scenes laid out point-by-point across left- and right-hemisphere parietal regions. However, the neglect phenomena I have described do not necessarily imply such a fine-grained correspondence between spatially-defined parts of the representations and spatially-defined parts of the represented scenes, or such a rich isomorphism between spatial properties of the representations and spatial properties of the represented scenes. To account for results showing neglect of the left or right side of a represented scene one need only assume a correspondence between two spatially-defined parts of the representation (a left-hemisphere part and a right-hemisphere part) and two spatially-defined parts of the represented scene (the right and left sides, respectively). No finer-grained correspondence is required; within each hemisphere there need be no correspondence between spatially-defined parts of the representation and spatially-defined parts of the represented scene.

A representation of this sort meets the criteria for spatial$_2$ representation, in that (a) two spatially-defined parts of the representation (the left- and right-hemisphere parts) correspond to two spatially defined parts of the represented scene (the right and left sides, respectively), and (b) a spatial property of the representation (the left-right relation between the left- and right-hemisphere parts) corresponds to a spatial property of the represented scene (the left-right relation between the right and left sides of the scene). However, such a representation is spatial$_2$ only in the weakest sense.

Of course, the neglect phenomena I have discussed do not rule out the possibility of a richer spatial$_2$ organization, and various other forms of evidence might be brought to bear. For example, some neglect studies have found a gradient in the severity of neglect within the affected half of the represented scene (e.g., Arguin & Bub, 1993; Baxter & Warrington, 1983; Caramazza & Hillis, 1990a; Ellis, Flude, & Young, 1987; Hillis & Caramazza, 1991). Thus, a person exhibiting left neglect may be more likely to neglect an item the farther left of center it is in the represented scene. Such results may seem to imply that the affected half of the represented scene was laid out systematically over some cortical region within the damaged hemisphere, allowing the brain lesion to affect some parts of the half-scene more than others. However, this interpretation is not compelling. For one thing, it doesn't explain why horizontal gradients of neglect are always—as far as I am aware—in the direction of increasing severity from more medial (e.g., slightly left of center) to more lateral (e.g., far left of center) regions in the affected half of the represented scene. (Why doesn't neglect sometimes *decrease* from medial to lateral regions, or reach a peak somewhere in the middle? Why don't we occasionally observe circumscribed regions of neglect analogous to the scotomas frequently produced by damage to V1?) It is also worth mentioning that neglect gradients—including their consistent direction—can be interpreted without positing any within-hemisphere spatial organization (see, e.g., Pouget & Sejnowski, 1997a, 1997b).

Other types of evidence that might be adduced are similarly equivocal in their implications,

(a)   (b)

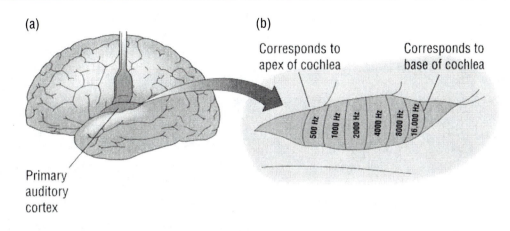

Figure 5.5: The tonotopic map in primary auditory cortex. After Purves et al. (1997), Figure 12.14, p. 242. Adapted with permission of Sinauer Associates, Inc.

and at present the extent of spatial$_2$ organization at levels of representation affected by neglect would appear to be an open question. (Note that many different types of representations can be affected by neglect, and these may differ in the extent to which they have a spatial$_2$ organization in the brain.)

Spatial$_1$ versus Spatial$_2$ Representations

I have defined the concept of a spatial$_2$ representation as if it applied only to spatial$_1$ representations (i.e., representations of spatial information). However, the concept is also applicable to representations of nonspatial information if the definition is stated in a slightly more general form. In particular, let us say that a representation is spatial$_2$ if (a) spatially-defined parts of the representation correspond to spatial *or non-spatial* parts of the represented material, and (b) at least one spatial property defined over the parts of the representation is isomorphic to a spatial *or nonspatial* property defined over the corresponding parts of the represented material.

Consider the tonotopic map in primary auditory cortex (Figure 5.5). Sounds of different frequencies are represented in different parts of auditory cortex; thus, parts of the representation correspond to parts (i.e., particular frequencies) of the represented material. In addition a spatial dimension in auditory cortex (roughly anterior–posterior) is isomorphic to the frequency dimension in the domain of sounds, such that low frequencies project to more anterior locations, and high frequencies to more posterior sites. Thus, although the representation of frequency in primary auditory cortex is not a spatial$_1$ representation, it is a spatial$_2$ representation.[5]

A Third Sense of 'Spatial Representation'

I have distinguished representation of spatial information (spatial$_1$) from spatial organization of representations (spatial$_2$), and have noted that some brain representations have a spatial$_2$ organization. On the basis of phenomena from the study of neglect, I have suggested that

---

[5]Both neurophysiological and behavioral evidence suggest that primary auditory cortex represents information about locations as well as frequencies of sounds (see, e.g., Zigmond, Bloom, Landis, Roberts, & Squire, 1999). Nevertheless, the representation *of frequency* in auditory cortex is a spatial$_2$ representation of non-spatial information.

spatial$_2$ organization may be present not only at relatively peripheral sensory and motor levels in the brain, but also at some "higher" levels (although the organization may be less rich at some levels than at others). What, though is the significance of spatial$_2$ organization in the brain? What does it tell us about how the brain works as a computational system?

Representational and Non-Representational Properties of Representations

To answer these questions we need to distinguish between representational and non-representational properties of a representation. This distinction may be illustrated through the examples in Figure 5.6, which involve not internal representations in the brain, but instead external representations on paper. Figure 5.6 panel A is a highly schematic map showing the locations of some major landmarks on the Mall in Washington, D.C. Certain spatial properties of the map stand for spatial properties of the Mall: Distances between dots represent distances between landmarks; the relative positions of dots on the right-left dimension of the map represents the relative position of landmarks on the east-west dimension of the Mall, and so forth.

Figure 5.6 panel B also represents spatial information about landmarks on the Mall. However, in this verbal representation the spatial information is carried by the words and numerals. Spatial properties of the representation—aside from the spatial arrangements of letters and digits—do not play a representational role; these properties do not represent spatial (or other) properties of the Mall. For example, spatial relations among the boxes in the representation do not represent spatial relations among the corresponding landmarks. Whereas the spatial relations among dots in the map are *representational*, the spatial relations among boxes in the verbal representation are *nonrepresentational*. (See Palmer, 1978, for related discussion.)

A property of a representation is representational (or nonrepresentational) only within a system that uses the property in accordance with its posited representational role (e.g., Gallistel, 1990; Van Gulick, 1980). Thus, the spatial relations among dots in the map would be representational within a system that used them to stand for spatial relations among landmarks on the

Figure 5.6: Two external representations of the locations of some landmarks on the Mall in Washington, D.C., illustrating the distinction between representational and non-representational properties. Panel A. A map. Panel B. A verbal representation.

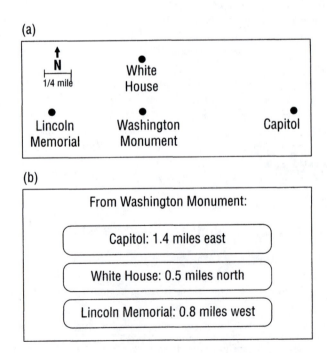

Mall. Among such systems might be a person reading the map, and a computer program that takes the map as input (via a scanner) and produces as output possible routes for walking tours of the Mall.

The example of the computer program illustrates an important point: To say that a property is representational in a system is not to say that the system knows, or is aware of, what the property stands for. Any property of a representation that appropriately affects the outcome of the system's computations is a representational property, whether or not the system has knowledge or awareness of the property's meaning. (See, e.g., Dennett, 1981; Fodor, 1980; Haugeland, 1985; Pylyshyn, 1980.)

Spatial₃ Representation

The distinction between representational and non-representational properties provides the basis for defining a third sense in which a representation could be spatial. Although this third sense, spatial₃, is similar to the second (spatial₂), I will argue that the difference between the two is important for understanding spatial representation in the brain.

The third sense of 'spatial representation' may be defined as follows: A representation is spatial₃ within a system if (a) spatially-defined parts of the representation correspond to (spatial or nonspatial) parts of the represented material, (b) at least one spatial property defined over the parts of the representation is isomorphic to *and is used to represent* a (spatial or nonspatial) property defined over the corresponding parts of the represented material. Consider once again the map in Figure 5.6 panel A. Within a system including either the map reader or computer program mentioned above, the map is a spatial₃ representation, because spatially-defined parts of the representation (e.g., the dots) correspond to spatially-defined parts of the Mall (e.g., the landmarks), and spatial properties defined over parts of the representation (e.g., distances between dots) are isomorphic to, and are used to represent, properties defined over parts of the Mall (e.g., distances between landmarks).

Table 5.1 summarizes the criteria for spatial₁, spatial₂, and spatial₃ representations. The spatial₃ criteria include those for a spatial₂ representation, but require in addition that at least one spatial property of the representation be representational. As a consequence, any spatial₃ representation is also spatial₂, but not all spatial₂ representations are spatial₃.

Consider the representation in Figure 5.7, which combines the spatial isomorphisms from the map in Figure 5.6 panel A with the verbal information in Figure 5.6 panel B. This hybrid

Table 5.1
Senses in which a Representation Can be Spatial

Sense	Criteria
spatial₁	the represented information is spatial information
spatial₂	(a) spatially-defined parts of the representation correspond to (spatial or non-spatial) parts of the represented material, and
	(b) at least one spatial property defined over the parts of the representation is isomorphic to a (spatial or non-spatial) property defined over the corresponding parts of the represented material
spatial₃	(a) spatially-defined parts of the representation correspond to (spatial or non-spatial) parts of the represented material, and
	(b) at least one spatial property defined over the parts of the representation is isomorphic to, and is used to represent, a (spatial or non-spatial) property defined over the corresponding parts of the represented material

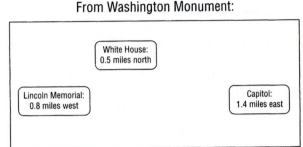

Figure 5.7: A hybrid representation, illustrating that spatial$_2$ representations may or may not be spatial$_3$.

representation clearly qualifies as spatial$_2$: Spatially-defined parts of the representation (the boxed areas) correspond to spatially-defined parts of the Mall (the landmarks), and spatial properties defined over parts of the representation (directional and distance relationships among boxes) are isomorphic to properties defined over parts of the Mall (directional and distance relationships among landmarks).

However, the representation may or may not be spatial$_3$, depending upon how it is used in a representational system. Suppose on the one hand that the representation were used by a person who ignored the positions of the boxes on the page, and relied solely on the words and numerals. Within a system consisting of this individual and the representation, the representation would not qualify as spatial$_3$, because the spatial relations among boxes are non-representational. Even though the directional and distance relationships among boxes are isomorphic to the directional and distance relationships among the corresponding landmarks, the former are not used to represent the latter. On the other hand, in a system involving a person who used the spatial relations among boxes to navigate the mall, the representation would meet the spatial$_3$ criteria.

Like the spatial$_2$ notion, the spatial$_3$ concept can be applied to representations of non-spatial as well as spatial information. For example, most graphs (e.g., a plot of the Dow-Jones Industrial Average over time) are spatial$_3$ representations of non-spatial information.

Spatial$_2$ versus Spatial$_3$ Representation in the Brain

The distinction between spatial$_2$ and spatial$_3$ representations raises an obvious question: In brain representations with a spatial$_2$ organization, are spatial properties of the representations *used to represent* the corresponding properties of the represented material? In other words, are spatial$_2$ representations in the brain also spatial$_3$ representations?

The answer appears to be no. Everything we know about the brain implies that the spatial properties of spatial$_2$ representations in the brain are non-representational. Consider once again the retinotopic map in V1. As we have seen, V1 exhibits a rich and fine-grained spatial$_2$ organization, in which spatial properties defined over locations on the cortical surface are isomorphic to spatial properties defined over the corresponding locations in the visual field (see Figure 5.4). Nevertheless, to the best of our knowledge these spatial properties of the representation do not play representational roles (e.g., Bisiach & Berti, 1987). For example, distances between points in visual cortex are presumably not used in the brain's information processing to represent distances among the corresponding locations in the visual field; as far as we know, there is no brain process that determines the distance between cortical locations and uses this distance in performing computations.

Spatial properties of the cortical representation are probably *correlated with* the properties that play representational roles. For example, neurons that are close together may be connected in different ways and to different extents than neurons that are farther apart, and these variations in patterns of connectivity presumably have representational significance. However, distances between neurons are not representational in and of themselves.[6]

These arguments apply not only to V1, but also to other brain representations with $spatial_2$ organization, such as the tonotopic map in primary auditory cortex, the somatotopic maps in somatosensory and motor areas of the brain, and the representations underlying the neglect phenomena I have described. Brain representations, although they may be $spatial_2$, are not $spatial_3$.

It is important to distinguish the spatial properties of a cortical representation from the receptive field characteristics of the cells making up the representation. The shapes and sizes of receptive fields, and the stimulus properties to which the cells respond (e.g., oriented edges), are certainly relevant for understanding what information is represented, and how it is represented for purposes of computation. However, the spatial relations among cells with particular response characteristics—for example, the fact that cells with receptive fields in the periphery of the visual field are anterior in V1 to those with more central receptive fields—do not speak directly to these representational issues. The inferences we could draw about what information was represented, and how it was represented, would be the same if neurons were scattered apparently at random in V1, such that the location of a neuron in the cortex had no relation to the location of its receptive field in visual space.

Why, then, does the brain exhibit $spatial_2$ organization? One possibility is that this organization is a by-product of processes that establish connections among neurons during brain development (e.g., axonal guidance mechanisms). That is, connection-making processes may, for their own reasons, work in such a way as to produce $spatial_2$ organization in some brain areas, even though this organization plays no functional role in representing information. Perhaps, for example, the most effective process devised by evolution for connecting sensory receptors to cortical receiving areas is one that preserves the topology of the sensory surface throughout the pathway. Such a process could account for a number of $spatial_2$ representations in the brain, including the retinotopic map in primary visual cortex and the tonotopic map (which preserves the topology of the cochlea) in primary auditory cortex.

Implications

I have distinguished three senses in which a representation could be spatial, arguing that whereas representations in the brain may be spatial in the first sense and/or in the second sense, they are not spatial in the third sense. In particular, I have asserted that even when internal representations of spatial (or nonspatial) information are organized in the brain such that spatial properties of the representation mirror properties of the represented material, the former are not used by the brain to represent the latter. These conclusions have a number of implications, a few of which I explore briefly.

Questions about Spatial Representation

One implication is that there are several distinct questions we can ask about the internal representation of spatial (or other) information, including the following:

---

[6]In some instances the lengths of connections between neurons may have representational significance. For example, in certain brainstem circuits concerned with localization of sound sources the lengths of axons are critical to the functioning of the circuits, and could be considered representational. (For an overview of auditory localization mechanisms see Zigmond et al., 1999, pp. 808–811). In such cases the connection lengths may be correlated with metric distance between locations in the brain, but it is still the lengths of the connections and not the distances between brain locations that are representational.

- What information is represented for purposes of computation?
- How is the information represented for purposes of computation?
- How are the representations arranged spatially in the brain?

It is especially important to distinguish the second and third questions; answering one of these questions does not answer the other. For instance, the question of how spatial relations among locations in the visual field (e.g., above–below) are represented in V1 for purposes of computation cannot be answered by describing the spatial$_2$ organization of V1 (e.g., the isomorphism between the ventral–dorsal dimension in V1 and the above–below dimension in the visual field). In fact the spatial$_2$ organization of V1 does not even tell us *whether* spatial relations among visual-field locations are represented in a way that is accessible to computations. Of course, we know from behavioral evidence that the visual system does represent spatial relations in computationally-relevant ways; for example, people can respond differentially to visual stimuli differing only in the spatial relations among parts (e.g., *29* vs. *92*). However, in the absence of such behavioral evidence the spatial$_2$ organization alone would not provide sufficient basis for assuming that spatial relations were represented for purposes of computation.

The neglect studies I presented as examples speak to what was represented (e.g., cloudlike figures as they would appear if presented as wholes), and how the representations were spatially organized in the brain (e.g., left halves of figures represented in the right hemisphere, and vice versa). The studies have less to say, however, about how information was represented for purposes of computation. For instance, it is not clear the anatomical separation between left- and right-hemisphere parts of representations has any significant implications for how the represented information is processed. I develop this point more fully when I discuss frames of reference in the second part of this chapter.

Quasi-Pictorial Spatial Representations?

Theorists addressing many aspects of spatial cognition (e.g., mental imagery, memory for visuo-spatial information, navigation) have assumed that the underlying representations are picture- or map-like in ways that are relevant to processing, such that processes carried out on the internal representations are somehow analogous to operations performed on pictures or maps (e.g., rotation, visual scanning). The arguments I have developed suggest, however, that this assumption is problematic.

Proponents of quasi-pictorial representations have been careful to emphasize that they are not endorsing naïve conceptions in which inner homunculi look at pictures projected on internal screens. Less clear, however, is what substantive theoretical proposals *are* being advanced. The most characteristic feature of external spatial representations like pictures and maps—the feature that most clearly distinguishes them from non-pictorial representations like words—is that spatial properties of the representation are used to represent spatial properties of the represented material. For example, a photograph of a cat represents the cat because certain spatial properties of the photograph are isomorphic to, and are used to represent, spatial properties of the cat. The external spatial representations are, in other words, spatial$_3$ representations. Yet this is exactly what internal representations of spatial information are *not*. What, then, does it mean to say that internal spatial$_1$ representations are quasi-pictorial?[7]

The Internal Representational Space Metaphor

The arguments I have developed also have implications for the internal representational space metaphor frequently invoked in discussions of unilateral spatial neglect (as well as in other

---

[7]Note that I use the pictorial expression 'represented scene' to refer to what is represented, and not to the representations themselves.

contexts). Although intuitively appealing, this metaphor has substantial potential to confuse and mislead. I have already noted that interpretations stated in terms of internal representational spaces are ambiguous unless elaborated with more explicit assumptions (see p. 107), and that the metaphor may lead us to over-interpret evidence of spatial$_2$ organization by suggesting a finer-grained organization than the evidence may imply (p. 110).

A more serious problem is that the representational space metaphor may lead us to slip from evidence about spatial$_2$ organization of representations to the conclusion that the representations are picture-like in ways relevant to processing. For example, if we conceive of NV's representations of the Piazza del Duomo (Bisiach & Luzzatti, 1978) as maps spread across internal representational spaces, we are likely to take for granted that processing the representations was somehow akin to scanning actual maps, even though the data provide no basis for this conclusion (and even though it is unclear what the conclusion might mean).

FRAMES OF REFERENCE AND COORDINATE SYSTEMS

The concept of a reference frame plays a central role in research on almost every facet of spatial cognition, including object recognition (e.g., Marr, 1982), spatial language (e.g., Levelt, 1996; Levinson, 1996; Tversky, 1996), attention (e.g., Nicoletti & Umiltá, 1989, 1994; Umiltá & Nicoletti, 1992), motor control (e.g., Soechting & Flanders, 1989, 1992), and navigation (e.g., O'Keefe & Nadel, 1978). In research on these topics and others, much effort has been expended to identify the frames of reference used by the brain in representing spatial information.

The Frame of Reference Concept

Spatial$_1$ representations specify the locations of the represented entities (be they objects, object parts, environmental surfaces, sounds, or so forth). For example, a spatial$_1$ representation of a visually-presented word might indicate that particular letters are in particular locations. The concept of a frame of reference has to do with the representation of location in spatial$_1$ representations.

In the following discussion I examine the reference-frame concept, and how reference frames have been studied in research on spatial representation. I argue that two distinct questions arise regarding the representation of location in a frame of reference:

1. What kind of location is represented?
2. How are locations specified?

I further argue that these questions are routinely conflated in reference-frame research, and that once the questions are distinguished it becomes clear that the dominant strategy for probing reference frames speaks only to the first. Finally, I suggest that the second question can and should be addressed.

In developing these arguments I begin with an extremely hypothetical example. By abstracting away from the complications and limitations of actual studies, I can lay out clearly the questions about reference frames, and the ways in which data speak (or fail to speak) to these questions.

An Extremely Hypothetical Example

Suppose that we had an almost magical device—the represento-scope, or r-scope for short—that could non-invasively monitor the computationally-relevant properties of representations in the brain. The r-scope, let us imagine, is placed on the head of a research participant, and set for a particular brain area (e.g., V1, or the ventral intraparietal area). Then, stimuli are presented one at a time, and the device inspects the resulting representations in the designated brain area. For each stimulus, the r-scope assesses all of the computationally-relevant properties of the representation, and on this basis assigns a numerical label (*1, 2, 3, . . .*) to the representation.

The representation of the first stimulus is assigned the label *1*. For each succeeding stimulus the internal representation is assigned a new label if it differs in computationally-relevant respects from all of the previously-labeled representations. However, if the representation of a stimulus is the same as some previous representation, it is assigned the same label as that representation. For example, a representation that matched (in computationally-relevant respects) a representation previously labeled *3* would also be assigned this label. For each stimulus, the only output generated by the r-scope is the label.

Consider a hypothetical participant seated in front of a display screen with head and body aligned with the screen's vertical midline, and eyes fixating a central point (Figure 5.8). Imagine that on each trial a small black square is presented at one of four screen locations. The first stimulus is presented at location A, and the r-scope's readout displays the label *1*. The next stimulus is at location B, and the r-scope displays the label *2*, indicating that the second representation was different from the first. The third stimulus is again at A, and the r-scope again produces the label *1*. Over many trials we find that a stimulus at a particular location (e.g., A) always elicits the same label from the r-scope (e.g., *1*), and that each different location yields a different label:

Stimulus Location	R-Scope Output
A	*1*
B	*2*
C	*3*
D	*4*

This pattern of results would suggest that the brain area under investigation represents the location of each stimulus (and conceivably other stimulus attributes as well).

What Kind of Location is Represented?

Given this initial pattern, we could proceed to consider the first reference-frame question: What kind of location is represented (in the brain area being studied)? The represented locations could be locations relative to the retina (retinocentric frame of reference), locations relative to the head (head-centered frame), locations relative to the trunk of the body (trunk-centered frame), locations relative to the screen (screen-centered frame), or so forth for an indefinite number of other possibilities. The retinocentric and head-centered frames of reference are *egocentric* frames, because they represent location relative to some part of the individual's own body. The screen-centered reference frame could be described as *allocentric* ('other-centered') or *environment-centered*, because location relative to some environmental feature(s) is represented.

Additional r-scope testing could tease apart at least some of the alternatives. Figure 5.9 illustrates a hypothetical experiment in which stimuli are presented at 6 locations (A–E). The participant, again sitting with head and trunk midlines aligned with the center of the screen, is tested under two conditions: Fixate Center (Figure 5.9 panel A), in which her eyes fixate the same central screen location as in the initial testing; and Fixate Right (Figure 5.9 panel B), in which she fixates a location farther to the right.

Changing the fixation point alters the retinocentric locations of the stimuli; each stimulus projects to a different retinal location in the Fixate Right condition than in the Fixate Center condition. Therefore, if the brain area under investigation represents location in a retinocentric

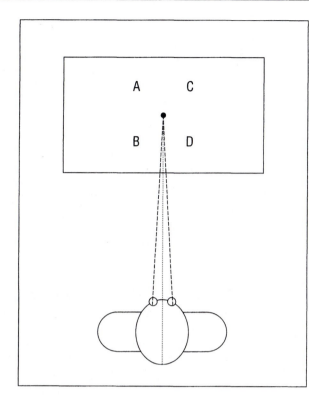

Figure 5.8: The research participant and the four stimulus locations in the hypothetical task. For convenience the schematic shows a top view of the participant and a frontal view of the screen. The dashed lines from the eyes indicate that the participant is fixating a central screen location, and the dotted line indicates that her head and body midlines are aligned with this location.

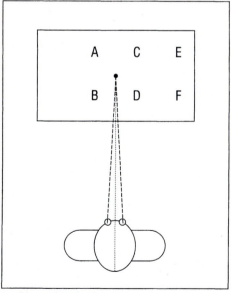

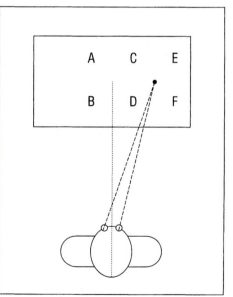

(a) Fixate Center Condition   (b) Fixate Right Condition

Figure 5.9: Panel A. Stimulus locations and placement of the research participant in the Fixate Center condition of a hypothetical experiment. Panel B. The Fixate Right condition of the experiment. The participant's head and trunk midlines are aligned with the center of the screen, but her eyes fixate a location on the right side of the screen.

frame of reference, each stimulus should have a different representation in the two conditions. More specifically, stimuli C, D, E, and F in the Fixate Right condition have the same retinocentric locations as stimuli A, B, C, and D, respectively, in the Fixate Center condition. Therefore, if location is represented in a retinocentric frame of reference, stimulus C in the Fixate Right condition should have the same representation as stimulus A in the Fixate Center condition; stimulus D in the Fixate Right condition should have the same representation as stimulus B in the Fixate Center condition; and so forth:

Stimulus Location	Condition	
	Fixate Center	Fixate Right
A	1	7
B	2	8
C	3	1
D	4	2
E	5	3
F	6	4

This pattern would tell us that the location representation for a stimulus was determined by where it was on the retina, and not where it was relative to the head, trunk, or screen.

Unlike retinocentric locations, head-centered, trunk-centered, and screen-centered locations are not affected by the change in fixation point; each stimulus has the same location relative to the head, trunk, and screen in the Fixate Right condition as in the Fixate Center condition. Therefore, if the brain area represents location in one of these reference frames, the representation for each stimulus should be the same in both conditions. Hence, the r-scope results in both conditions should be A: *1*, B: *2*, C: *3*, and so forth. This pattern would imply that what mattered in determining the representation of a stimulus was not its position on the retina, but instead its position relative to the head, the trunk, the screen, or something else that did not change between conditions.

If we obtained this result we could perform additional experiments to distinguish among head-, trunk-, and screen-centered reference frames. Figure 5.10 illustrates a hypothetical experiment that isolates the head-centered frame. In the Head Straight condition (Figure 5.10 panel A) the participant faces the center of the screen, whereas in the Head Right condition (Figure 5.10 panel B) her head is turned to face a position midway between the center (C and E) and right (D and F) stimulus locations. In both conditions her eyes fixate the center of the screen.

Retinocentric, trunk-centered, and screen-centered locations of stimuli remain constant across conditions. However, head-centered location varies, with stimuli C–F in the Head Right condition having the same head-centered locations as stimuli A–D, respectively, in the Head Straight condition. Thus, the following pattern of results would point to a head-centered frame of reference:

Stimulus Location	Condition	
	Head Straight	Head Right
A	1	7
B	2	8
C	3	1
D	4	2
E	5	3
F	6	4

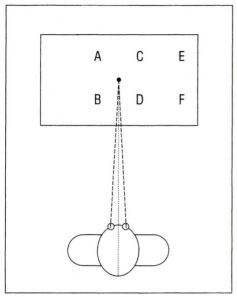

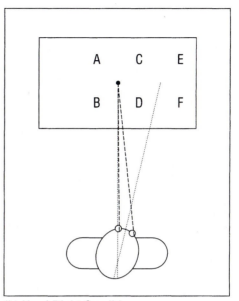

(a) Head Straight Condition   (b) Head Right Condition

Figure 5.10: Panel A. The Head Straight condition of a hypothetical experiment. Panel B. The Head Right condition, in which the participant's head is turned toward the right while her eyes and trunk remain in alignment with the center of the screen.

If we obtained this pattern, we would have strong evidence speaking to the first question about reference frames: What kind of location is represented?

How are Locations Specified?

The hypothetical data would not, however, answer the second reference-frame question: How are locations specified for purposes of computation? That is, the data would not reveal how the internal representations specified the head-centered locations of stimuli.

To clarify this point I need to say more about the distinction between the two reference-frame questions, and especially about what would constitute an answer to the second question. To do so, I turn for a moment from internal representations in the brain to consider some external representations on paper: the letters (e.g., A, B) I used to designate hypothetical stimulus locations in describing the hypothetical experiments.

In deciding how to designate the locations I had to address both of the reference-frame questions. First, I had to decide what kind of location to represent. I chose screen-centered location: The letter I assigned to a location was determined by where on the hypothetical screen the location was, regardless of where the hypothetical participant's eyes were fixated, or how her head was turned. Thus, A was the same place on the screen in the Fixate Right condition as in the Fixate Center condition. I could have chosen instead to represent retinocentric location, in which case each letter would have had the same relation to the fixation point in both conditions. For example, the location given the screen-centered designation C in the Fixate Right condition (see Figure 5.9 panel B) would have been designated A instead.

In addition to deciding what kind of location to represent, I also had to decide how to specify each location. I chose to adopt a *nominal* form of representation (Gallistel, 1990): I simply named each location with a letter of the alphabet (e.g., A, B). I could instead have chosen a coordinate system representation, in which case I might have designated the locations labeled A–F in Figure 5.9 panel A [–1, +1], [–1, _1], [+1, +1], [+1, –1], [+3, +1], and [+3, –1], respectively.

In a coordinate system the representation for a location has multiple parts, each representing some aspect of the location. For example, in a two-dimensional Cartesian coordinate system each location representation (e.g., [+3, –1]) can be analyzed into two parts, one representing displacement from the origin along the first dimension (+3), and the second representing displacement along the second dimension (–1). Each of these parts might be further analyzed into direction (+ or –) and distance (e.g., 3) components. Nominal representations, in contrast, do not separately specify different aspects of a location; the representation for a location designates that location as a whole.

Decisions about whether to adopt a nominal, coordinate, or other form of representation are independent of decisions about what kind of location to represent (e.g., retinocentric, screen-centered). Thus, Cartesian coordinates could have been used to represent retinocentric as well as screen-centered locations of the hypothetical stimuli. For example, in a retinocentric coordinate system the same coordinates (e.g., [–1, +1]) would have been assigned to the location labeled A in Figure 5.9 panel A (Fixate Center condition) and to the location labeled C in Figure 5.9 panel B (Fixate Right condition).

The hypothetical experiments bear on the kind of location represented (the first reference-frame question); however, these experiments have nothing to say about how the internal representations specify locations (the second question). For example, results showing that the representation for a stimulus was determined by its location relative to the head would tell us only that head-centered location was represented, and not whether the head-centered locations were specified nominally, as coordinates, or in some other form.

This point applies not just to the specific hypothetical experiments I have discussed, but more generally to the research strategy exemplified by these experiments. This strategy—manipulate variables that affect location representations in some reference frames but not in others, and assess whether the representations vary as a consequence—is appropriate for asking what kind of location is represented. At least in its basic form, however, the strategy does not shed light on how locations are specified by the internal representations.

The significance of this conclusion lies in the fact that the vast majority of psychological, neuropsychological, and neurophysiological studies of reference frames implement—in various forms and to varying extents—the research strategy I have described. As a consequence, most studies bear on the first frame-of-reference question (What kind of location is represented?), but have little to say about the second (How are locations specified?). This point has not been readily apparent, however, because the two questions are virtually never distinguished in reference-frame research. In the next section I describe three actual studies to illustrate how the strategy for identifying reference frames has been implemented, and how the results have been interpreted.

Three Actual Studies

Frames of Reference in Macaque Ventral Intraparietal Cortex

Duhamel, Bremmer, BenHamed, and Graf (1997) recorded from neurons in the ventral intraparietal area (VIP) of macaque monkeys, with the aim of identifying the reference frame(s) used in this brain area to represent the locations of visual stimuli. The logic of the study was the same as that of the hypothetical experiment in which the point of fixation was varied (see Figure 5.9).

Single-cell recording was carried out while the monkey, with head immobilized, viewed visual stimuli presented on a screen. For each neuron the visual receptive field—the region of the screen to which the neuron responded when appropriate stimuli were presented—was mapped while the monkey fixated various screen locations. Although more fixation and stimulus locations were tested in the Duhamel et al. (1997) study than in our hypothetical experiment, the essential features of the actual study can be explained by reference to the hypothetical example.

Suppose that recording from a neuron reveals that when the monkey is fixating the center of the screen (as in Figure 5.9 panel A), the neuron's receptive field is restricted to location C, such that the neuron responds to stimuli presented at C, but not to stimuli at other locations. Suppose now that the fixation point is moved to the right while the monkey's head and body remain in their original positions (as in Figure 5.9 panel B). The question of interest is, To what stimulus locations will the neuron now respond?; that is, Where on the screen will the receptive field be?

If the neuron is involved in representing retinocentric locations of stimuli, we might expect to see its receptive field shift to a new location on the screen when the point of fixation is changed, such that the neuron no longer responds to stimuli at location C, but instead responds to stimuli at E. On the other hand, if the neuron is implicated in representing head-, trunk-, or screen-centered location, its receptive field should not change when the fixation point is moved. The neuron should continue to respond to stimuli at location C, and only to these stimuli.

Duhamel et al. (1997) observed both of these response patterns (among others) in VIP neurons. For some neurons the receptive field moved with the eyes, whereas for other cells the receptive field remained at the same place on the screen regardless of where the monkey was fixating. These results suggest that VIP may represent visual information both in a retinocentric frame of reference and also in one or more non-retinocentric frames. (Although Duhamel et al. prefer to call the non-retinocentric representations head-centered, they acknowledge that additional experiments would be required to distinguish this interpretation from accounts positing other body-centered, or environment-centered, representations.)

The Duhamel et al. (1997) results clearly speak to the kinds of location represented in macaque VIP. However, the results have little to say about how the represented locations are specified for purposes of computation. We cannot tell for either the retinocentric or non-retinocentric reference frames whether the representations take a nominal, coordinate system, or other form.

Duhamel et al., like many other researchers, described their methods and results in the language of coordinate systems. For example, they presented their procedure as a means of dissociating "a retinal, or eye-centered coordinate system from a head-centered coordinate system" (Duhamel et al., 1997, p. 845), and described individual neurons as representing location in retinal coordinates or head-centered coordinates (e.g., pp. 846 and 847). This use of coordinate system vocabulary reflects a failure to distinguish the two reference-frame questions: Whereas the Duhamel et al. results speak to what kinds of locations were represented, claims about coordinate systems have to do with how location is specified.

However, Duhamel et al. (1997) may not have intended to posit location representations in the form of coordinates. The rather vague concept of a reference frame that pervades research on spatial representation does not distinguish between the kind of location represented (e.g., retinocentric, head-centered) and the form in which locations are specified (e.g., nominal, coordinate-system). It is perhaps for this reason that in most discussions of reference frames, coordinate-system vocabulary is apparently not intended to have any special significance; for example, *retinocentric coordinate system* and *retinocentric frame of reference* are apparently considered synonymous. Therefore, Duhamel et al.'s (1997) statements about coordinates and coordinate systems probably should not be regarded as specific claims about how locations are specified; and the same is true of most other reference-frame discussions couched in coordinate-system terms (e.g., Andersen, Snyder, Bradley, & Xing, 1997; Arguin & Bub, 1993; Behrmann

& Moscovitch, 1994; Chatterjee, 1994; Colby & Goldberg, 1999; Driver & Halligan, 1991; Farah, Brunn, Wong, Wallace, & Carpenter, 1990; Graziano, Yap, & Gross, 1994; Karnath, Schenkel, & Fischer, 1991; Ladavas, 1987; Tipper & Behrmann, 1996).

Casual use of coordinate-system language is not, however, a good idea. When results speak only to the kind of location represented, stating conclusions in terms of coordinates and coordinate systems may create the misleading impression that the data also bear on how locations are specified. Haphazard use of coordinate-system terminology also makes it difficult to recognize the difference between statements that carry no intended implications about how locations are specified, and assertions that are put forth as explicit claims about internal coordinate-system representations (e.g., Lacquaniti, Guigon, Bianchi, Ferraina, & Caminiti, 1995; McCloskey & Rapp, 2000a; Soechting & Flanders, 1989).

Neglect and Egocentric Frames of Reference

In a substantial number of studies unilateral spatial neglect has been used as a tool for distinguishing among different egocentric frames of reference, or for distinguishing egocentric from environment-centered frames (e.g., Beschin, Cubelli, Della Sala, & Spinazzola, 1997; Bisiach, Capitani, & Porta, 1985; Calvanio, Petrone, & Levine, 1987; Farah et al., 1990; Karnath, Fetter, & Niemeier, 1998; Karnath et al., 1991; Ladavas, 1987). For example, Beschin et al. (1997) tested a 65-year-old man who showed left neglect following a right-hemisphere stroke. The participant's task was to search for a marble in a tactile maze (which was covered so that vision could not be used). Across five conditions Beschin et al. independently manipulated where the participant fixated his eyes, the position of his head, and the position of his trunk (relative to the maze). The dependent variable of interest was the time required to find a marble placed in the left half of the maze.

Beschin et al. (1997) found that the participant's search time was affected only by the position of his trunk relative to the maze: Search times were longer when the trunk midline was aligned with the center of the maze (so that the left side of the maze was to the left of the trunk midline), than when the trunk was turned 30° to the left (so that the entire maze was to the right of the trunk midline). Eye and head position had no effect on performance.[8] Beschin et al. concluded that the participant relied upon a trunk-centered representation in searching the maze.

Like the Duhamel et al. (1997) single-cell recording results, the Beschin et al. (1997) behavioral data speak to the first question about frames of reference: What kind of location is represented? The findings suggest that the represented locations were locations relative to the trunk, and more specifically that the region of space to the left of the trunk midline corresponded to the left side of the represented scene, whereas the region to the right of the trunk midline corresponded to the right side of the represented scene.

Do the results have anything to say about how the represented locations were specified by the internal representations? The prominent role of the trunk midline in defining the represented scene may seem to imply a coordinate-system representation. Given that the trunk midline corresponded to the division between left and right halves of the represented scene, it may appear that the internal representation took the form of a coordinate system with a vertical axis defined by the trunk midline (or, to be more precise, by the projection of the trunk midline onto the maze).

However, as far as I can see there is nothing in the Beschin et al. (1997) results to imply that

---

[8]It may seem odd to consider the point of eye fixation in a task that does not involve vision. Note, however, that the represented locations could conceivably have been locations relative to the eye (retinocentric locations) even though the represented information was non-visual; there is nothing incoherent in the notion of a retinocentric representation of non-visual information (e.g., Stricanne, Andersen, & Mazzoni, 1996).

locations in the represented scene were designated *by specifying their distance and direction of displacement from the trunk midline* (as well as their relation to some other axis or axes). As discussed in an earlier section, neglect for the left half of a represented scene following right-hemisphere damage suggests that the representation was partitioned into left- and right-hemisphere parts, with the left half of the scene represented in the right hemisphere, and vice versa. However, this conclusion places few if any constraints on how the representation specifies the represented locations. For example, the conclusion seems equally consistent with nominal and coordinate-system representations.

This argument applies not only to the Beschin et al. (1997) study, but also to other neglect studies in which some body, environmental, or object axis partitions the represented scene into left and right halves. The fact that an axis plays a role in defining a represented scene does not imply that the axis forms part of a coordinate system that is used to specify locations in the scene.

Object-Centered Frames of Reference

In addition to evidence concerning egocentric frames of reference, recent studies of neglect have also yielded a variety of fascinating results regarding object-centered representations (e.g., Behrmann & Moscovitch, 1994; Behrmann & Tipper, 1999; Buxbaum & Coslett, 1994; Caramazza & Hillis, 1990a, 1990b; Driver, Baylis, Goodrich, & Rafal, 1994; Driver, Baylis & Rafal, 1992; Driver & Halligan, 1991; Halligan & Marshall, 1993; Marshall & Halligan, 1994; Tipper & Behrmann, 1996; Young, Hellawell, & Welch, 1992; see Walker, 1995, for a review). In an object-centered representation the locations of an object's parts are specified within a frame of reference defined by the object itself.

The previously-described Caramazza and Hillis study (1990a, 1990b) provides a convenient example. As we have seen, Caramazza and Hillis asked participant NG to read normally-oriented, vertical, and mirror-reversed words, and found that regardless of how the stimulus words were presented, NG's neglect errors involved the ends of the words (see Figure 5.3). These results were taken as evidence for abstract word representations in which letters are arranged in their canonical positions (initial letters on the left, final letters on the right), regardless of how the letters were arrayed in the visual stimulus. At this level of representation the location of a letter in the represented scene is apparently determined solely by its position in the canonically-oriented word (regardless of its actual retinocentric, head-centered, or environment-centered location, or even its location relative to the other letters in the stimulus as presented). Hence, the represented locations are apparently locations relative to the (canonical) word itself.

If words can be considered objects, the canonical word representations can be considered object-centered representations. Indeed, Caramazza and Hillis (1990a, 1990b) explicitly likened these representations (which they called word-centered representations) to the object-centered representations posited in Marr's (1982) theory of visual object recognition.

The results from NG obviously speak to the first reference-frame question, suggesting that at the level affected by NG's neglect the represented locations are locations relative to the (canonical) word. However, for the reasons I discussed in the context of the Beschin et al. (1997) study, the results do not have obvious implications for the question of how the locations of letters are specified for purposes of computation. The Caramazza and Hillis findings suggest that at the word-centered level the initial half of a word (e.g., the letters *s*, *t*, and *r* for the word *stripe*) is represented predominantly in the right hemisphere (intact in NG), whereas the final half of the word (e.g., *i*, *p*, and *e*) is represented predominantly in the left hemisphere (impaired in NG). However, as far as I can see this conclusion does not imply that the locations of letters are represented for purposes of computation by specifying their distance and direction of displacement from the center of the word.

Addressing the Second Reference-Frame Question

I have argued that most frame-of-reference studies, including those described in the preceding section, have little to say about the second reference-frame question: How is location specified for purposes of computation? This contention might lead one to wonder what kinds of evidence could be brought to bear on the question, or even whether any conceivable evidence would be germane. To illustrate that the question is accessible to empirical inquiry I briefly describe two recent studies that yielded evidence of coordinate-system representations in the brain.

Neurophysiological Evidence

Lacquaniti et al. (1995) recorded from spatially-tuned neurons in macaque area 5 (superior parietal lobule) while the monkey reached to targets in three-dimensional space. The activity of most neurons was related not to the target location taken as a whole, but rather to one of the location's three spatial coordinates. Some neurons responded according to the target's horizontal position (i.e., left–right position), independent of its vertical position (high vs. low) or depth (near vs. far). Other neurons responded selectively to vertical position, and still others to depth. For example, one neuron that responded selectively to horizontal position showed a monotonic increase in firing rate from the rightmost to the leftmost of six horizontal target positions; however, for any given horizontal position the neuron's rate of firing was the same regardless of the target's position on the vertical or depth dimensions.

These findings suggest that in the superior parietal lobule target location was specified in the form of three spatial coordinates, with different sets of neurons representing each coordinate. Lacquaniti et al. argued in particular that the neurally-represented coordinates corresponded to the azimuth, elevation, and distance coordinates of a spherical coordinate system.

Neuropsychological Evidence

Brenda Rapp and I obtained evidence of coordinate system representations in studying AH, a young woman with a developmental deficit in perceiving the location of visual stimuli (McCloskey & Rapp, 2000a; see also McCloskey et al., 1995; McCloskey & Rapp, 2000b). AH had no history of neurological injury or disease, and no abnormalities were evident on neurological exam or structural magnetic resonance imaging. Her visual acuity and visual fields were normal, as was her performance on visual object recognition tasks (e.g., picture naming).

On tasks requiring localization of visual stimuli, however, AH was severely impaired. In one experiment an X was presented on a computer screen for 250 ms at a position left, right, up, or down from the center of the screen, and AH indicated where the X had appeared by moving a mouse (e.g., move left for a stimulus at the left location). Whereas control subjects performed the task virtually without error, AH erred on about half of the left and right stimuli, and about one-third of the up and down stimuli. All of her errors were left-right or up-down confusions (e.g., moving the mouse left for a stimulus at the right location, moving down for a stimulus at the up location). Systematic left-right and up-down errors were also observed in many other tasks requiring localization of visual stimuli (e.g., reaching for objects on a table, copying visual patterns, arranging objects to match stimulus configurations).

Further testing revealed that AH's impairment was a selective deficit of visual perception. She showed normal performance in localizing non-visual stimuli (e.g., sounds), and in tasks requiring visual localization she was impaired not only when required to make spatially-directed movements, but also when responding verbally, and even when making same-different judgments.

Samples of AH's elementary through secondary schoolwork indicated that the visual localization deficit was present throughout her school years. Especially given the absence of obvious post-natal neurological insult, this evidence suggests that her impairment is probably congenital.

For present purposes the most interesting aspect of AH's performance is the nature of her localization errors: The left-right and up-down errors were highly systematic, taking the form of reflections across a central horizontal or vertical axis. For example, in one task an X was presented at one of four locations on a computer screen (see Figure 5.11 panel A), and AH touched the screen to indicate where the X had appeared. As shown in Figure 5.11 panel B all of her errors were left-right reflections across a central vertical axis (e.g., touching the far left position for a target presented at the far right position, touching the near right position for a target on the near left).

This error pattern suggests that at the level(s) of the visual system where AH's errors arise, locations of objects are represented in the form of coordinates specifying distance and direction of displacement from an origin along reference axes (McCloskey & Rapp, in press a; see also McCloskey et al., 1995). For example, given a visual display involving a fixation point and a target stimulus (Figure 5.12 panel A), a coordinate system might be defined by horizontal and vertical axes through the fixation point (Figure 5.12 panel B). Assuming for convenience that right and up are the positive directions, whereas left and down are negative, the location of the target might be represented as follows (with distance in arbitrary units):

(a) Stimulus Locations

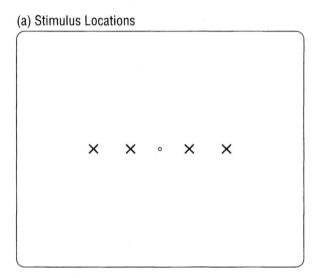

(b) AH's Localization Errors

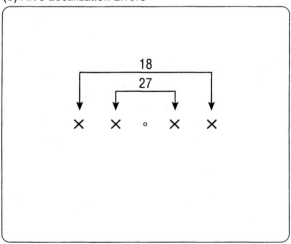

Figure 5.11: Panel A. The four screen locations at which target Xs were presented one at a time. B. AH's pattern of localization errors. The number above each arrow indicates the number of errors in which a stimulus presented at one of the connected positions was localized to the other position. For example, AH made 18 errors in which a target presented at the far left position was localized to the far right position, or vice versa. From "Attention-Referenced Visual Representations: Evidence from Impaired Visual Localization," by M. McCloskey and B. Rapp, 2000, *Journal of Experimental Psychology: Human Perception and Performance*, 26, 917–933, Figure 1. Copyright 2000 by the American Psychological Association. Reprinted with permission.

Displacement from Origin on Horizontal Axis
  Direction   –
  Distance   80

Displacement from Origin on Vertical Axis
  Direction   +
  Distance   35

Given these representational assumptions, AH's errors may be interpreted by positing a selective visual deficit in which distance along reference axes is represented accurately, but direction of displacement is frequently misrepresented. For example, if direction of displacement along the horizontal axis were mistakenly specified as '+' for the X in Figure 5.12 the result would be a left-right reflection across the vertical axis (see Figure 5.12 panel C). Similarly, if direction of displacement along the vertical axis were specified as '–' an up–down reflection across the horizontal axis would result (Figure 5.12 panel D).

The postulation of a coordinate-system form of representation plays a direct and crucial role

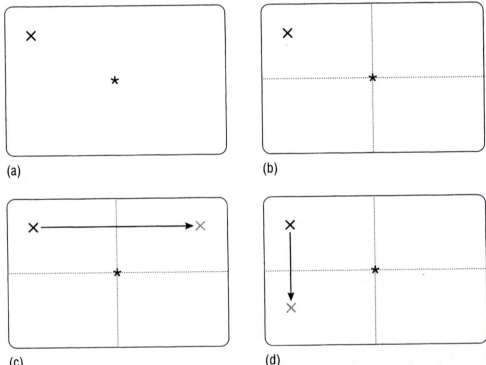

(a)   (b)

(c)   (d)

Figure 5.12: Panel A. A fixation point and an X displayed on a computer monitor. Panel B. Horizontal and vertical axes through the fixation point. Panel C. Localization error that would result from specifying + rather than – as the direction of displacement along the horizontal axis. Panel D. Localization error that would result from specifying – rather than + as the direction of displacement along the vertical axis. From "Attention-Referenced Visual Representations: Evidence from Impaired Visual Localization," by M. McCloskey and B. Rapp, 2000, *Journal of Experimental Psychology: Human Perception and Performance*, 26, 917–933, Figure 2. Copyright 2000 by the American Psychological Association. Reprinted with permission.

in interpreting AH's error pattern. The assumption that location representations consisted of separate horizontal and vertical coordinates is critical for explaining the fact that AH frequently mis-localized targets on only one dimension: horizontal in the case of the left–right errors, and vertical for the up–down errors. Further, the assumption that distance and direction of displacement were represented separately within each coordinate is essential for explaining why the errors took the form of reflections across a central axis. For these reasons, AH's error pattern constitutes evidence of coordinate-system representations in the visual system.

Rapp and I also probed the kind(s) of location represented at the level(s) giving rise to the localization errors (McCloskey & Rapp, 2000a). We found that AH's error pattern varied systematically as a function of where her attention was focused, independent of how her eyes, head, or trunk were oriented, or what environmental reference points were present. We concluded that AH's errors arise at an attention-centered level of representation (and more specifically that the focus of attention defines the origin of the coordinate system used for representing location).

Additional Questions about Spatial$_1$ Representations

In discussing reference frames I have focused on two questions concerning the representation of location in spatial$_1$ representations: What kind of location is represented? and, How are locations represented for purposes of computation? Analogous questions can be asked about the entities (e.g., objects, object parts) whose locations are represented: What information about these entities (in addition to their locations) is represented? and, How is this information specified for purposes of computation? Although not directly concerned with location, these questions may nevertheless have relevance for understanding reference frames, because particular types of (non-locational) information may be associated with particular frames of reference.

For example, Marr (1982) proposed that in visual object recognition a stimulus is represented first in terms of features extracted from the retinal image (e.g., edges), then by indicating the depth and orientation of each surface region in the visual scene, and finally by describing the three-dimensional shapes of objects. Referring to these representations as the primal sketch, the 2½-D sketch, and the 3-D model representation, respectively, Marr proposed that each involves a different frame of reference: retinocentric for the primal sketch, "viewer-centered" for the 2½-D sketch, and object-centered for the 3-D model. Similarly, in the realm of visual word recognition Caramazza and Hillis (1990a, 1990b) posited a retinocentric representation of visual features, a "stimulus-centered" representation of letter shapes, and a word-centered representation of abstract letter identities.

Relationships between reference frames and kinds of represented information have not received much attention in research on spatial representation, and exploring these relationships is a worthwhile goal for future research. The issue is clearly an empirical one, because a particular kind of represented information does not logically entail a particular frame of reference, or vice versa.

CONCLUDING REMARKS

Spatial representation is a broad and complex topic. As a consequence, there are many important issues I have not been able to explore in this chapter, and many important studies I have not been able to mention. The points I have developed may, however, prove helpful in thinking about some of these issues and studies.

Fortunately, many other chapters of this volume touch upon spatial deficits and their implications in the course of discussing specific cognitive functions (e.g., reading, attention). Of particular relevance are the chapters by Buxbaum and Coslett; Hillis; Rapp, Folk, and Tainturier; Riddoch & Humphreys; and Umiltà.

Recent surveys of several topics I could not discuss in detail (or, in some cases, at all) can be found in Aguirre and D'Esposito (1999); Farah and Ratcliff (1994); Riddoch (1991); and Robertson and Marshall (1993). Finally, for recent overviews of psychological and/or neurophysiological research on aspects of spatial representation, see Andersen et al. (1997); Bloom, Peterson, Nadel, & Garrett (1996); Colby & Goldberg (1999); Eilan, McCarthy, & Brewer (1993); and Paillard (1991).

Acknowledgements

Partial support for the preparation of this chapter was provided by grant HD34061 from the National Institutes of Health. I am grateful to Karen Neander for helpful comments on the arguments in this chapter, as well as for several years of discussions about representation. I am similarly grateful to Brenda Rapp for her comments on the chapter, and for many discussions about spatial representation. Finally, I thank Brian Glucroft for his comments, and for assistance with several neuroscience issues.

REFERENCES

Aguirre, G. K., & D'Esposito, M. (1999). Topographical disorientation: A synthesis and taxonomy. *Brain, 122,* 1613–1628.

Andersen, R. A., Snyder, L. H., Bradley, D. C., & Xing, J. (1997). Multimodal representation of space in the posterior parietal cortex and its use in planning movements. *Annual Review of Neuroscience, 20,* 303–330.

Arguin, M., & Bub, D. N. (1993). Evidence for an independent stimulus-centered spatial reference frame from a case of visual hemineglect. *Cortex, 29,* 349–357.

Baxter, D. M., & Warrington, E. K. (1983). Neglect dysgraphia. *Journal of Neurology, Neurosurgery, and Psychiatry, 46,* 1073–1078.

Behrmann, M., & Moscovitch, M. (1994). Object-centered neglect in patients with unilateral neglect: Effects of left-right coordinates of objects. *Journal of Cognitive Neuroscience, 6,* 1–16.

Behrmann, M., & Tipper, S. P. (1999). Attention accesses multiple reference frames: Evidence from visual neglect. *Journal of Experimental Psychology: Human Perception & Performance, 25,* 83–101.

Beschin, N., Cubelli, R., Della Sala, S., & Spinazzola, L. (1997). Left of what? The role of egocentric coordinates in neglect. *Journal of Neurology, Neurosurgery, and Psychiatry, 63,* 483–489.

Bisiach, E. (1993). Mental representation in unilateral neglect and related disorders: The Twentieth Bartlett Memorial Lecture. *Quarterly Journal of Experimental Psychology, 46A,* 435–461.

Bisiach, E. (1996). Unilateral neglect and the structure of space representation. *Current Directions in Psychological Science, 5,* 62–65.

Bisiach, E., & Berti, A. (1987). Dyschiria. An attempt at its systematic explanation. In M. Jeannerod (Ed.), *Neurophysiological and neuropsychological aspects of spatial neglect* (pp. 183–201). Amsterdam: North-Holland.

Bisiach, E., Capitani, E., Luzzatti, C., & Perani, D. (1981). Brain and conscious representation of outside reality. *Neuropsychologia, 19,* 543–551.

Bisiach, E., Capitani, E., & Porta, E. (1985). Two basic properties of space representation in the brain: evidence from unilateral neglect. *Journal of Neurology, Neurosurgery, and Psychiatry, 48,* 141–144.

Bisiach, E., & Luzzatti, C. (1978). Unilateral neglect of representational space. *Cortex, 14,* 129–133.

Bisiach, E., Luzzatti, C., & Perani, D. (1979). Unilateral neglect, representational schema, and consciousness. *Brain, 102,* 609–618.

Bloom, P., Peterson, M. A., Nadel, L., & Garrett, M. F. (Eds.). (1991). *Language and space.* Cambridge, MA: MIT Press.

Buxbaum, L. J., & Coslett, H. B. (1994). Neglect of chimeric figures: Two halves are better than a whole. *Neuropsychologia, 32,* 275–288.

Calvanio, R., Petrone, P. N., & Levine, D. N. (1987). Left visual neglect is both environment-centered and body-centered. *Neurology, 37,* 1179–1183.

Caramazza, A., & Hillis, A. E. (1990a). Levels of representation, co-ordinate frames, and unilateral neglect. *Cognitive Neuropsychology, 7,* 391–445.

Caramazza, A., & Hillis, A. E. (1990b). Spatial representation of words in the brain implied by studies of a unilateral neglect patient. *Nature, 346,* 267–269.

Chatterjee, A. (1994). Picturing unilateral spatial neglect: viewer versus object centered reference frames. *Journal of Neurology, Neurosurgery, and Psychiatry, 57,* 1236–1240.

Colby, C. L., & Goldberg, M. E. (1999). Space and attention in parietal cortex. *Annual Review of Neuroscience, 22,* 319–349.

Dennett, D. C. (1981). *Brainstorms.* Cambridge, MA: MIT Press.

Driver, J., Baylis, G. C., Goodrich, S. J., & Rafal, R. D. (1994). Axis-based neglect of visual shapes. *Neuropsychologia, 32,* 1353–1365.

Driver, J., Baylis, G. C., & Rafal, R. D. (1992). Preserved figure-ground segregation and symmetry perception in visual neglect. *Nature, 360,* 73–75.

Driver, J., & Halligan, P. W. (1991). Can visual neglect operate in object-centered co-ordinates? An affirmative single-case study. *Cognitive Neuropsychology, 8,* 475–496.

Duhamel, J-R., Bremmer, F., BenHamed, S., & Graf, W. (1997). Spatial invariance of visual receptive fields in parietal cortex neurons. *Nature, 389,* 845–848.

Eilan, N., McCarthy, R., & Brewer, B. (Eds.). (1993). *Spatial representation: Problems in philosophy and psychology.* Oxford, UK: Blackwell.

Ellis, A. W., Flude, B. M., & Young, A. W. (1987). "Neglect dyslexia" and the early visual processing of letters in words and nonwords. *Cognitive Neuropsychology, 4,* 439–464.

Farah, M. J., Brunn, J. L., Wong, A. B., Wallace, M. A., & Carpenter, P. A. (1990). Frames of reference for allocating attention to space: Evidence from the neglect syndrome. *Neuropsychologia, 28,* 335–347.

Farah, M. J., & Ratcliff, G. (Eds.) (1994). *The neuropsychology of high-level vision.* Hillsdale, NJ: Lawrence Erlbaum.

Fodor, J. A. (1980). Methodological solipsism considered as a research strategy in cognitive psychology. *The Behavioral and Brain Sciences, 3,* 63–109.

Gallistel, C. R. (1990). *The organization of learning.* Cambridge, MA: MIT Press.

Graziano, M. S. A., Yap, G. S., & Gross, C. G. (1994). Coding of visual space by premotor neurons. *Science, 266,* 1054–1057.

Halligan, P. W., & Marshall, J. C. (1993). The history and clinical presentation of neglect. In I. H. Robertson, & J. C. Marshall (Eds.), *Unilateral neglect: Clinical and experimental studies* (pp. 3–25). Hove, UK: Lawrence Erlbaum.

Haugeland, J. (1985). *Artificial intelligence: The very idea.* Cambridge, MA: MIT Press.

Hillis, A. E., & Caramazza, A. (1991). Deficit to stimulus-centered, letter shape representations in a case of 'unilateral neglect.' *Neuropsychologia, 29,* 1223–1240.

Hillis, A. E., & Caramazza, A. (1995). A framework for interpreting distinct patterns of hemispatial neglect. *Neurocase, 1,* 189–207.

Humphreys, G. W., & Riddoch, M. J. (1993). Interactive attentional systems and unilateral visual neglect. In I. H. Robertson, & J. C. Marshall (Eds.), *Unilateral neglect: Clinical and experimental studies* (pp. 139–167). Hove, UK: Lawrence Erlbaum.

Karnath, H. O., Fetter, M., & Niemeier, M. (1998). Disentangling gravitational, environmental, and egocentric reference frames in spatial neglect. *Journal of Cognitive Neuroscience, 10,* 680–690.

Karnath, H. O., Schenkel, P., & Fischer, B. (1991). Trunk orientation as the determining factor of the 'contralateral' deficit in the neglect syndrome and as the physical anchor of the internal representation of body orientation in space. *Brain, 114,* 1997–2014.

Kosslyn, S. M. (1995). Mental Imagery. In S. M. Kosslyn & D. N. Osherson (Eds.), *Visual cognition: An invitation to cognitive science, Volume 2* (pp. 267–296). Cambridge, MA: MIT Press.

Ladavas, E. (1987). Is the hemispatial deficit produced by right parietal lobe damage associated with retinal or gravitational coordinates? *Brain, 110,* 167–180.

Lacquaniti, F., Guigon, E., Bianchi, L., Ferraina, S., & Caminiti, R. (1995). Representing spatial information for limb movement: Role of area 5 in the monkey. *Cerebral Cortex, 5,* 391–409.

Levelt, W. J. M. (1996). Perspective taking and ellipsis in spatial descriptions. In P. Bloom, M. A. Peterson, L. Nadel, & M. F. Garrett (Eds.), *Language and space* (pp. 77–107). Cambridge, MA: MIT Press.

Levinson, S. C. (1996). Frames of reference and Molyneux's question: Crosslinguistic evidence. In P. Bloom, M. A. Peterson, L. Nadel, & M. F. Garrett (Eds.), *Language and space* (pp. 109–169). Cambridge, MA: MIT Press.

Marshall, J. C., & Halligan, P. W. (1994). The yin and yang of visuo-spatial neglect: A case study. *Neuropsychologia, 32,* 1037–1057.

Marr, D. (1982). *Vision.* San Francisco: Freeman.

Mason, C., & Kandel, E. R. (1991). Central visual pathways. In E. R. Kandel, J. H. Schwartz, & T. M. Jessell (Eds.), *Principles of neural science* (pp. 420–439). Norwalk, CT: Appleton & Lange.

McCloskey, M., Rapp, B., Yantis, S., Rubin, G., Bacon, W. F., Dagnelie, G., Gordon, B., Aliminosa, D., Boatman, D. F., Badecker, W., Johnson, D. N., Tusa, R. J., & Palmer, E. (1995). A developmental deficit in localizing objects from vision. *Psychological Science, 6,* 112–117.

McCloskey, M., & Rapp, B. (2000a). Attention-referenced visual representations: Evidence from impaired visual localization. *Journal of Experimental Psychology: Human Perception and Performance, 26,* 917–933.

McCloskey, M., & Rapp, B. (2000b). A visually-based developmental reading deficit. *Journal of Memory and Language, 43,* 157–181.

Nicoletti, R., & Umiltá, C. (1989). Splitting visual space with attention. *Journal of Experimental Psychology: Human Perception and Performance, 15,* 164–169.

Nicoletti, R., & Umiltá, C. (1994). Attention shifts produce spatial stimulus codes. *Psychological Research, 56,* 144–150.

Ogden, J. A. (1985). Contralesional neglect of constructed visual images in right and left brain-damaged patients. *Neuropsychologia, 23,* 273–277.

O'Keefe, J., & Nadel, L. (1978). *The hippocampus as a cognitive map.* Oxford: Clarendon Press.

Paillard, J. (Ed.) (1991). *Brain and space.* Oxford, UK: Oxford University Press.

Palmer, S. E. (1978). Fundamental aspects of cognitive representation. In E. Rosch & B. Lloyd (Eds.), *Cognition and categorization* (pp. 261–304). Hillsdale, NJ: Lawrence Erlbaum.

Pouget, A., & Sejnowksi, T. J. (1997a). A new view of hemineglect based on the response properties of parietal neurones. *Philosophical Transactions of the Royal Society London B, 352,* 1449–1459.

Pouget, A., & Sejnowksi, T. J. (1997b). Spatial transformations in the parietal cortex using basis functions. *Journal of Cognitive Neuroscience, 9,* 222–237.

Purves, D., Augustine, G. J., Fitzpatrick, D., Katz, L. C., LaMantia, A.-S., & McNamara, J. O. (1997). *Neuroscience.* Sunderland, MA: Sinauer Associates.

Pylyshyn, Z. (1980). Computation and cognition: Issues in the foundations of cognitive science. *The Behavioral and Brain Sciences, 3,* 111–169.

Riddoch, M. J. (Ed.) (1991). *Neglect and the peripheral dyslexias.* Hove, UK: Lawrence Erlbaum.

Robertson, I. H., & Marshall, J. C. (Eds.) (1993). *Unilateral neglect: Clinical and experimental studies.* Hove, UK: Erlbaum.

Soechting, J. F., & Flanders, M. (1989). Errors in pointing are due to approximations in sensorimotor transformations. *Journal of Neurophysiology, 62,* 595–608.

Soechting, J. F., & Flanders, M. (1992). Moving in three-dimensional space: Frames of references, vectors, and coordinate systems. *Annual Review of Neuroscience, 15,* 167–191.

Stricanne, B., Andersen, R. A., & Mazzoni, P. (1996). Eye-centered, head-centered, and intermediate coding of remembered sound locations in area LIP. *Journal of Neurophysiology, 76,* 2071–2076.

Tipper, S. P., & Behrmann, M. (1996). Object-centered not scene-based visual neglect. *Journal of Experimental Psychology: Human Perception & Performance, 22,* 1261–1278.

Tversky, B. (1996). Spatial perspective in descriptions.

In P. Bloom, M. A. Peterson, L. Nadel, & M. F. Garrett (Eds.), *Language and space* (pp. 463–491). Cambridge, MA: MIT Press.

Umiltà, C., & Nicoletti, R. (1992). An integrated model of the Simon effect. In J. Alegria, D. Holender, J. J. Morais, & M. Radeau (Eds.), *Analytic approaches to human cognition* (pp. 331–350). Amsterdam: North-Holland.

Vallar, G. (1993). The anatomical basis of spatial hemineglect in humans. In I. H. Robertson, & J. C. Marshall (Eds.), *Unilateral neglect: Clinical and experimental studies* (pp. 27–59). Hove, UK: Lawrence Erlbaum.

Van Gulick, R. (1980). Functionalism, information, and content. *Nature and system, 2*, 139–162.

Walker, R. (1995). Spatial and object-based neglect. *Neurocase, 1*, 371–383.

Young, A. W., Hellawell, D. J., & Welch, J. (1992). Neglect and visual recognition. *Brain, 115*, 51–71.

Zigmond, M. J., Bloom, F. E., Landis, S. C., Roberts, J. L., & Squire, L. R. (1999). *Fundamental neuroscience.* San Diego, CA: Academic Press.

Attention and Consciousness

...a music, strident or sweet, made by the friction
of existence.

–George Santayana

6

Mechanisms of Attention

Carlo Umiltà

INTRODUCTION

This chapter provides an overview of findings from neuropsychological and neurophysiological research that have contributed to elucidating several aspects of attention. To define the issues and introduce the key experimental paradigms each section begins with a brief review of the literature on normal participants. The organization of the chapter follows a plan that is typical in present-day psychology (and neuropsychology) of attention. The first issue to be discussed is where, in the sequence of processing stages, attention begins to exert its influence. The second issue is whether attention selects regions of space or objects for enhanced processing. The third issue is how attention moves in space. The last issue is whether attentional selection is achieved by enhancing relevant information or inhibiting irrelevant information.

Most of the studies concern patients with neglect or extinction. This is because it is assumed that in the side of space affected by the deficit there is no attention, or attention is severely impaired. Therefore, results from these patients can reveal the type of processing that occurs without attention or with very little attention. A brief discussion of neglect and extinction is provided here. Reviews can be found in Bisiach and Vallar (in press), Rafal (1998), and chapters in I. H. Robertson and J. C. Marshall (1993).

Neglect can occur after a unilateral lesion to a wide range of neural structures (Desimone & Duncan, 1995), although its cognitive consequences have most often been investigated in individuals who have suffered a unilateral lesion of the parietal lobe (more often the right parietal lobe). Neglect patients fail to report or respond to events in the contralesional side of space (more often the left side of space). In extinction, such a deficit manifests itself only if competing events are present on the intact side. Both neglect and extinction are considered to be deficits of spatial attention.

The presence of a disorder of spatial attention in neglect is apparent in the overt everyday behavior of patients, as well as in their performance on a range of tests. Neglect patients may have their eyes, head, and body turned to the right. They may ignore people who approach or address them from the left side of space. They may fail to eat food from the left side of their plate, tend to bump into objects located on their left side when walking, and their walking trajectory can deviate to the right. A typical test of neglect in the visual modality is a task in which the patient is given a page that contains various items and is asked to mark them all with a pen. A failure to mark items located on the left side of the page indicates neglect. Other common tests for spatial neglect include the bisection task and the drawing task. In the former, the patient is given a horizontal line and is asked to mark its center. The patient typically places the mark well to the right side. In the drawing task, the patient tends to omit elements on the left side when asked to draw an object either from memory or from a model. In neglect dyslexia, the patient omits letters on the left side when reading a word and/or omits the words on the left side of the page when reading a text.

It must be pointed out that Bisiach (1993; also see Bisiach & Vallar, in press; Rizzolatti, Berti, & Gallese, in press) has for many years advocated a representational account of neglect, mainly on the basis of studies that demonstrated that neglect affects also internally generated mental representations. In Bisiach's view, neglect is a deficit of space representation and the deficits of spatial attention would be caused by the representational deficit or co-occur with it.

WHEN DOES ATTENTION HAPPEN?

Two issues concerning the processing stage at which attention begins to exert its influence have been debated. The first is whether elementary features are combined to form objects preattentively or attentively. The second is whether attentional selection operates early or late in the sequence of processing stages.

Attentive versus Preattentive Processing

Some authors (e.g. Kahneman, 1973; Neisser, 1967) postulate the existence of an initial preattentive stage in which, based on Gestalt principles of organization, the visual field is parsed into objects against a background. The alternative view (e.g., Treisman, 1988; Treisman & Gelade, 1980) is that, at the preattentive stage, simple features present in the visual display are registered in parallel. Then, at a subsequent (focal) attentional stage, objects are formed by combining these simple features.

A prediction of Treisman's (1988) theory is that attention deficits, such as those of neglect and extinction, should affect search for conjunctions of features leaving search for simple features unaffected. A weaker prediction is that attention deficits should affect both feature and conjunction tasks, disrupting, however, the latter more than the former.

In a typical feature search task, normal participants detect a target defined by a salient unique feature (e.g., a red target among green distracters, or a vertical target among horizontal distracters) as rapidly when many distracters are present as when few distracters are present. In contrast, when the target is defined by a conjunction of features (e.g., a red vertical target among green vertical and red horizontal distracters) reaction time (RT) for detecting the target increases as a function of number of distracters.

Several studies tested extinction and neglect patients with versions of the search task (e.g., Arguin, Joannette, & Cavanagh, 1993; Cohen & Rafal, 1991; Eglin, Robertson, & Knight, 1989; Humphreys & Riddoch, 1993; Riddoch & Humphreys, 1987; see review in L. C. Robertson, 1998). Some found evidence in favor of the stronger prediction, showing that in the affected field search rate was slower than in the intact field for the conjunction task but not for the feature task. It would seem thus that feature integration (and, by implication, object segmentation) requires attention and cannot take place normally at a preattentive stage. Other studies, instead, showed that patients were impaired in both conjunction and feature tasks, but the deficit was greater for the conjunction task. This finding is no doubt problematic for the notion of a qualitative difference between the two types of search. In fact, it would seem that also coding simple feature requires attention and cannot take place at a preattentive stage (e.g., Joseph, Chun, & Nakayama, 1997).

However, a different picture emerges from still other studies. The process of partitioning a visual display into coherent components that can be perceived as independent objects is referred to as segmentation, segregation, grouping, or parsing. The available neuropsychological evidence suggests that this process occurs also in the field affected by neglect or extinction.

(a) Contour lines in the left hemifield
but on the right side of the figure

(b) Contour lines in the right hemifield
but on the left side of the figure

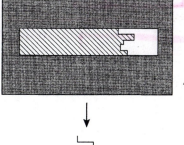

95% accuracy at judging
whether line matches

50% accuracy at judging
whether line matches

Figure 6.1: The displays used by Driver et al. (1992), adapted from Rafal's (1998) Figure 22.10. The large area with diagonal shading was red, whereas the small area was green. The task was to compare the jagged dividing line to the isolated jagged line on the bottom of the display. From: Rafal, RD: Neglect. In Parasuraman, R. (Ed.), *The Attentive Brain*. MIT Press. Adapted with permission.

That is, it occurs in the absence of attention (i.e., preattentively; Driver, Baylis, & Rafal, 1992; Driver, Baylis, Goodrich, & Rafal, 1994; see review in Driver & Baylis, 1998).

Normally, regions delimited by symmetrical contours are perceived as objects lying in front of the background. Driver et al. (1992) showed that a patient with neglect could use, in his impaired field, symmetry for parsing the visual display into objects. The patient was presented with red symmetrical figures against a green background. When he was asked to report which color was in front of the background, he, like normal individuals do, perceived the symmetrical red shapes as objects in front of the green background. However, when he was asked to judge whether the red shapes were symmetrical or not, performance was at chance. That is, even though neglect prevented the patient from perceiving symmetry, symmetry nonetheless acted in the impaired field producing visual objects that were segregated from the background.

The same patient showed that segmentation in the impaired field could be produced on the basis of other factors (also see Marshall & Halligan, 1994). Normally, a small, bright region is perceived as a figure against a large, dim background. The dividing line is perceived as the contour, belonging only to the figure. Driver et al. (1992) presented the patient with displays of this type (see Figure 6.1) and asked him to remember the shape of the dividing line between the figure and the background, and to match it with a probe line that appeared half a second later in the center of the screen. Thus, the task was only to attend to the shape of the line bordering the two areas. The patient was able to segregate the figure from the background in either the intact or the impaired visual field, demonstrating that segmentation can operate in the absence of attention.

Further evidence of preattentive object segmentation comes from extinction patients. Driver, Mattingley, Rorden, and Davis (1997) found that extinction caused by two circles that were simultaneously presented in the opposite visual fields was eliminated when the circles were linked by a horizontal line to form a single barbell. Other grouping factors, like good continuation (Ward, Goodrich, & Driver, 1994) and three-dimensionality (Mattingley, Davis, & Driver, 1997) can reduce or eliminate extinction by linking the stimulus presented in the impaired field with the stimulus presented in the intact field to form a global object. Similarly, extinction between two letter strings is reduced when they form a compound word (Behrmann, Moscovitch, Black, & Mozer, 1990).

Early Versus Late Selection

The *early-selection* view maintains that unattended information is discarded just after simple features are coded and prior to stimulus identification. The *late-selection* view maintains that unattended information undergoes semantic analysis and selective attention operates after stimulus identification.

The first studies of selective attention typically used the dichotic listening paradigm and favored the early-selection view, showing that only the physical properties of unattended stimuli are processed, and then these stimuli are filtered out before they can be processed further (e.g., Broadbent, 1958). However, very soon, results began to accumulate that showed semantic effects of non-attended stimuli (e.g., Corteen & Wood, 1972; Lewis, 1970), thus challenging Broadbent's early-selection theory and supporting Deutsch and Deutsch's (1963) late-selection theory.

The findings with visual stimuli closely replicated those with auditory stimuli. It was found that, as with dichotic listening, attending to one object resulted in negligible memory for unattended objects (e.g. Rock & Guttman, 1981; Neisser & Becklen, 1975). As in dichotic listening, however, indirect measures revealed that unattended stimuli were semantically processed and identified (see review in Kahneman & Treisman, 1984).

The Stroop effect (Stroop, 1935) and "flanker" effects (Eriksen & Eriksen, 1974), for example, implicated response competition at the (late) stage at which interference between attended and unattended information occurs. In fact, the effect of unattended information on RT could not be explained, unless unattended information had been analyzed to the point where it activated a response. In contrast, other results showed that early selection is, at least to a certain extent, possible (e.g., Kahneman & Treisman, 1984): When the experimental conditions were such as to allow the participant to focus attention narrowly on relevant information, Stroop and flanker effects virtually disappeared (e.g., Francolini & Egeth, 1980; Yantis & Johnston, 1990).

Neuropsychological Evidence

Studies of neglect and extinction patients made an important contribution toward elucidating the extent of processing that unattended stimuli undergo (see review in Driver, 1996).

Berti and Rizzolatti (1992) provided evidence of semantic processing for stimuli presented in the contralesional visual field of neglect patients. Their patients were required to make a speeded animal/vegetable decision for a line drawing presented in the intact right field. Simultaneously, a line drawing was presented in the impaired left field. The drawing in the left field could be identical to the one in the right field, could be different but from the same category, or could be different and from the opposite category. Average RTs were 777, 795, and 890 ms, respectively. Clearly, categorization of the drawing in the right field was affected by the drawing in the left field.

Làdavas, Paldini, and Cubelli (1993; also see McGlinchey-Berroth, Milberg, Verfaellie, Alexander, & Kilduff, 1993) reported a patient who could not read aloud words presented in the left field, nor judge their lexical status or semantic content. He could not even detect the presence of a string of letters. However, a lexical decision to a word in the right field was faster when it was preceded by a related than an unrelated word in the left field (883 vs. 967 ms). That is, the patient showed semantic priming caused by unattended words in the affected field.

Berti, Allport, et al. (1992) studied a patient with extinction and investigated to what stage information is processed in the impaired field. They presented two pictures of objects simultaneously, one to each field, and asked the patient to name the two objects and to judge whether they had the same name. When the objects had the same name, the pictures were identical, or depicted different views of the same object, or depicted different exemplars of the same category seen from different view points. The patient was severely impaired in naming objects presented to the left field (her average performance was 17.8 correct names out of 36) but was very accurate on the matching task (63.2 correct out of 72 pairs). In particular, she was above chance even when the objects were different exemplars of the same category (e.g., two different cameras; 8.9 correct out of 12 pairs). That is evidence that the matching task was not performed on low-level, visual information, but rather categorical information became available through the impaired field.

The picture that emerges from the studies of neglect and extinction patients is broadly consistent with the late selection view: Processing of stimuli presented in the impaired visual field, which are unattended by definition, reaches the semantic stage and leads to identification. However, neurophysiological studies are in accord with the early selection view.

Neurophysiological Evidence *early selection*

Event related potential (ERP) studies are unequivocal in showing that attention can modulate early sensory processing (see reviews in Luck, 1998; Luck & Girelli, 1998). In the auditory modality, the prototypical experiment is the one conducted by Hillyard, Hink, Schwent, and Picton (1973). In it, a rapid sequence of tones was presented to the two ears and participants were instructed to attend to one ear in some trial blocks and to the other ear in other blocks. Also, participants were instructed to attend to the stimuli delivered to one ear only (i.e., the attended ear) and press a button whenever the target (a slightly higher-pitched tone) was detected. Targets, which occurred infrequently and unpredictably, were presented occasionally in the unattended ear, but participants were instructed not to respond to them. Results showed that tones delivered to the attended ear elicited a larger negative wave (N1) than tones delivered to the unattended ear. This effect began about 60–70 ms after stimulus onset and peaked at approximately 100 ms postimulus. In addition, there was some indication that even an earlier positive wave (P1), which manifests itself 20–50 ms postimulus, was larger for the attended ear. Considering these time courses, and the generator sources of P1 and N1, it can be concluded that attention operates at an early stage of processing, probably as early as in the primary auditory cortex. This is no doubt in accord with the early selection hypothesis.

The locus-of-selection issue was addressed in the visual modality by using variants of the ERP paradigm (e.g., Heinze et al., 1994; Mangun & Hillyard, 1988; Mangun, Hillyard, & Luck, 1993; Rugg, Milner, Lines, & Phalp, 1987). Results were clear in showing that attention exerts its influence during early stages of processing. However, results were also clear in showing that attention influenced processing in the extrastriate visual cortex, but not in the primary visual cortex (V1). Therefore, it would seem that attention begins to operate later in the visual than in the auditory modality, in which attentional modulation affects the primary auditory cortex.

A single-unit study of visual attention adopted a similar paradigm (Luck, Chelazzi, Hillyard, & Desimone, 1997). In it, recordings were obtained from areas responsible for the early (V1) and intermediate (V2 and V4) stages of processing. Consistent with the ERP studies, no attentional effects were found in area V1, whereas many V2 and V4 neurons showed attentional effects.

The issue of whether attentional modulation occurs in the primary visual cortex was investigated in a functional magnetic resonance imaging (fMRI) study, in which ERPs were also recorded, by Martinez et al. (1999; also see Brefczynski & DeYoe, 1999). Displays of crosses were randomly flashed to either the left or the right visual field, and participants were instructed to maintain fixation on a central arrow and to direct attention, without moving their eyes, to the visual field indicated by the arrow. On most trials, the central element in the lateralized displays of crosses was an upright T, but in a few trials it was an upside-down T. The latter was the target, whose presence had to be signaled by a key-press. Attention-related activation was observed in all visual areas, from V1 to V4. However, ERP data cast doubt on the possible attentional modulation of V1. In fact, the attended displays elicited an enlarged P1 component 70–75 ms poststimulus and an enlarged N1 component 130–140 poststimulus, whereas no enlarged component was observed 50–55 ms after the stimulus, which would have implicated area V1. The authors proposed that the attentional modulation of V1 activation observed with fMRI could be attributable to a delayed, re-entrant feedback from higher visual areas.

WHAT IS THE OBJECT OF ATTENTION?

Whether visuospatial attention operates on the basis of locations or of objects is a matter of debate (see reviews in Egeth & Yantis, 1997; Shapiro, Hillstrom, & Husain, in press; Umiltà, in press). The object-based view holds that attention is not assigned to a specific region of visual space, but, rather, to the objects that occupy those regions (e.g., Duncan, 1984; Kahneman & Henik, 1981). The space-based view (e.g., Eriksen & Eriksen, 1974; Posner, 1980) holds, instead, that attention is directed to regions of visual space, which may be empty or occupied by objects.

A related issue concerns whether attention can be allocated in viewer-centered coordinates as opposed to object-centered coordinates. In viewer-centered coordinates, the spatial codes of the object's component parts are computed in relation to one of the observer's reference axes (e.g., his body or head midline; see, e.g., Farah, Brunn, Wong, Wallace, & Carpenter, 1990; Làdavas, 1993). In object-centered coordinates, the spatial codes of the object's component parts are computed in relation to the structural description of the object (e.g., Gibson & Egeth, 1994; Umiltà, Castiello, Fontana, & Vestri, 1995).

Space

The space-based view of attention derives support from experiments that show that focal attention shifts from one location to another, selecting particular regions in visual space. Stimuli within these selected regions are processed more efficiently than stimuli that fall into non-selected regions (see section on orienting of attention, and review in Umiltà, in press). In further support of space-based allocation of attention, several studies reported that the spatial separation among the elements in the display modulated attentional benefits and costs (e.g. Downing, 1988; Eriksen & Eriksen, 1974; Hoffman & Nelson, 1981).

The abnormalities in neglect patients' performance (see introduction) clearly suggest a deficit in directing spatial attention to the contralesional side of space. The notion of a deficit of spatial attention is corroborated by the fact that neglect improves (only temporarily, though) if the patient is trained to attend toward the left side of space (e.g., Làdavas, Menghini, & Umiltà, 1994). Also, manipulations, like vestibular caloric stimulation (e.g., Rode & Perenin, 1994), neck vibration (e.g., Karnath, 1994), and optokinetic stimulation (e.g., Pizzamiglio, Frasca, Guariglia, Incoccia, & Antonucci, 1990), which can indirectly produce a shift of attention to the left, temporarily improve neglect.

As discussed above, neglect patients ignore stimuli located on the left side of space. However, space can be defined in either egocentric or allocentric coordinates (see section on object-centered neglect). Even if one considers only egocentric coordinates, there is more than one definition of "left" (e.g., Bhermann & Moscovitch, 1994; Walker, 1995). Left can be defined in retinal coordinates (i.e., the patient's left visual field), with respect to the body trunk (i.e., left of the patient's body midline), or with respect to the head (i.e., left to the patient's head midline). It has been demonstrated that neglect can manifest itself in one or more of these frames of reference, which are dissociated when the patient's viewing position changes or the stimulus rotates (e.g., Làdavas, 1993; Behrmann & Moscovitch, 1994). That happens, for example, when the head is tilted about 90° to the left or right, so that the right visual field is above and the left visual is below, or vice versa. It appears, therefore, that spatial attention can independently operate in several frames of reference.

Another important distinction concerns the sectors of space. Rizzolatti, Matelli, and Pavesi (1983; see review in Rizzolatti et al., in press) suggested that areas of the primate brain are specialized for orienting attention in the near, peripersonal space (i.e., within grasping distance), whereas others are specialized for orienting attention in the far, extrapersonal space (i.e., within pointing or throwing distance). Another sector of space is personal space, which is occupied by the animal's own body.

Although in humans neglect in personal space, peripersonal space, and extrapersonal space very often co-occur, there is evidence for double dissociations between the three sectors of space (see Rizzolatti et al., in press). That is, a patient can show severe neglect in one sector of space, but not in the other two. Halligan and Marshall (1991) documented one of these dissociations. Their patient showed severe neglect in peripersonal space on conventional tests, including the horizontal line bisection task. However, when line bisection was performed in extrapersonal space, by pointing a light or by throwing a dart, neglect was abolished or attenuated. The patient did not show neglect in personal space either. In fact, he did not show any deficits concerning left-side parts of his own body, as often happens with neglect patients. Berti and Frassinetti (in press) have confirmed this dissociation, whereas others have documented opposite dissociations, that is neglect for extrapersonal space only (Cowey, Small, & Ellis, 1994; Vuillemieur, Valenza, Mayer, Reverdin, & Landis, 1998), and neglect for personal space only (Guariglia & Antonucci, 1992).

It appears that spatial attention is impaired in one sector of space, but continues to function more or less normally in the other sectors. That suggests that there may be independent mechanisms for orienting attention within specific representations of space (Rizzolatti et al., in press; Umiltà, 1995).

Objects

As already mentioned, the object-based view holds that attention is assigned to objects rather than to regions of space. There is also the possibility that attention is assigned to an object's component parts, whose locations are coded with reference to the object's structure (see also McCloskey, this volume, for further discussion of issues of spatial frame of reference raised in this section).

Object-Based Attention

Because objects occupy spatial locations, to support the object-based view one has to decouple objects from locations. Duncan (1984) achieved that by briefly presenting normal participants with two superimposed visual objects, an outline box and a diagonal line, which occupied (roughly) the same spatial position (see Figure 6.2). Participants had to make judgments about one or two attributes: the size of the box, the location of a gap in the box, the orientation of the line, and the texture of the line. They were able to make judgments concerning the same object (i.e., the orientation and texture for the line or the size and gap side for the box) simultaneously without loss of accuracy, compared to when only a single feature was relevant. In contrast, they showed a cost (i.e., loss of accuracy) in making two judgments rather than one for features from different objects (e.g., the orientation of the line and the size of the box). Duncan's interpretation was that attention selects one object at a time, even when objects occupy the same location in space.

Many subsequent studies replicated Duncan's (1984) findings (see reviews in Driver & Baylis, 1998; Shapiro et al., in press; Umiltà, in press). An ERP study by Czigler and Balàzs (1998) used a version of Duncan's paradigm and found a shorter P3 latency in the single-object

Figure 6.2: Examples of the displays used by Duncan (1984), adapted from his Figure 1. Left: small box with gap on right, dotted line with tilt clockwise. Right: large box with gap on left, dashed line with tilt counterclockwise.

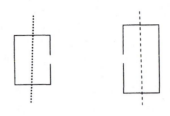

condition than in the two-object condition. This single-object advantage was present from 200 ms up to 800 ms after stimulus presentation and was most evident in lateral occipital sites. Also, Roelfsema, Lamme, snf Spekreijse (1997) found evidence of a single-object advantage in primary visual cortex with a single-cell recording study. However, the most convincing evidence of object-based attention originates from the demonstration of so-called object-based neglect (see reviews in Driver, 1998; Rafal, 1998; Walker, 1995).

Gainotti, Messerli, and Tissot (1972) provided what is perhaps the first example of object-based neglect. Their patients were asked to copy several objects drawn horizontally on a sheet of paper. The patients copied only the right side of objects, regardless of whether the objects were located on the affected or the intact side of space.

Two very elegant demonstrations of object-based neglect were provided by Driver et al. (1992) and Halligan and Marshall (1993). As already mentioned (see section on attentive vs. preattentive processing and Figure 6.1), Driver et al. presented their patient with a display containing small figures against a large background, in which a jagged dividing line was perceived as the contour of the figure. The task was to remember the shape of the dividing line and to match it with a probe line that appeared in the center of the screen. What is significant about the displays was that when the dividing line fell into the impaired field it was on the right side of the figure, whereas when it fell into the intact visual field it was on the left side of the figure. If neglect were space based, more errors would have been expected when the line was in the left than the right field. The results showed the opposite pattern: The patient was much more accurate when the line was in the left field but on the right side of the figure than when it was in the right field but on the left side of the figure.

Halligan and Marshall (1993) required their neglect patient to copy a drawing of a plant in a pot. The plant had two branches with a flower each, which departed from a stem. Thus, the drawing was unified into a single object by the presence of the common stem and pot. The patient copied the right branch only, omitting the left branch. This is in accord with either space-based or object-based neglect. Then, the drawing was changed by eliminating the common stem and pot, leaving just the two unconnected branches with the two flowers. Now the patient copied both branches and flowers, but both objects (i.e., branches with flowers) had features missing on their left side. This outcome can be explained only by assuming that neglect was object based.

Egly, Driver, and Rafal (1994; also see Egly, Rafal, Driver, & Starrveveld, 1994; Humphreys & Riddoch, 1994, 1995; Kramer, Weber, & Watson, 1997) demonstrated that both space-based and object-based mechanisms coexist. They tested normal participants and brain-damaged patients and investigated speed of target detection when attention was directed by a cue to a particular location and the target appeared in the same or a different location. On invalid trials, the target could appear either in the same object as the cue or in a different object (see Figure 6.3). Not surprisingly, both types of invalid trials were slower than valid trials (364 vs. 324 ms). More interestingly, there was an additional cost (13 ms) for between-objects invalid trials as compared to within-objects invalid trials, even though the distance between locations of cue and target was smaller on between-objects invalid trials than on within-objects invalid trials.

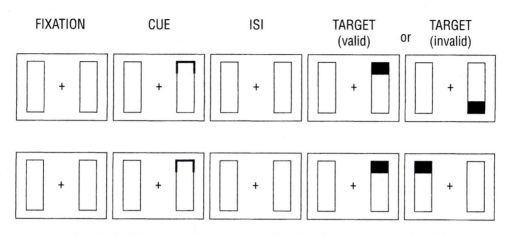

FIXATION   CUE   ISI   TARGET   TARGET
                                           (valid)   or   (invalid)

Figure 6.3: Examples of the displays used by Egly et al. (1994), adapted from their Figure 1. The heavy black lines in the panels of the second column represent the cue. The filled squares in the panels of the fourth and fifth columns represent the target. The panels in the fourth column represent a valid trial. The fifth panel of the upper row represents a within-object invalid trial, whereas the fifth panel of the bottom row represent a between-object invalid trial.

Egly, Driver, and Rafal (1994) provided evidence that the neural substrate mediating the two mechanisms differed, with the left hemisphere subserving the object-based mechanism and the right hemisphere subserving the space-based mechanism (also see Buck, Black, Behrmann, Caldwell, & Bronskill, 1997). Both right- and left-parietal patients were impaired for a contralesional target stimulus after presentation of an ipsilesional cue, but the right-parietal patients were particularly impaired (an additional cost of 22 ms). This was the space-based component of the attentional deficit. However, only the left-parietal patients showed a further abnormality concerning the object-based component: Their difficulty with contralesional targets after an ipsilesional cue was exacerbated when between-object shifts of attention were required (an additional cost of 76 ms). Also, Egly, Rafal, et al. (1994) found that the between-object cost was present only in the right visual field (left hemisphere) of a split-brain patient.

Object-Centered Attention

Objects have an intrinsic structure that depends on the spatial relations of their component parts relative to one another. Therefore, in an object-centered frame of reference, the spatial codes of the object's parts are computed in relation to the structural description of the object, and, if the object moves, the relative spatial codes of its component parts are stable with respect to the object's structure. Umiltà et al. (1995) showed that attention is allocated also in an object-centered frame of reference. In their study, a cue was presented on a vertex of a two-dimensional drawing that was perceived as a three-dimensional cube. In the critical condition, following the cue, the cube rotated and a target then appeared either in the originally cued location or in the cued vertex, which now occupied a different spatial location. Facilitation in target detection was not only observed when spatial location was the same for cue and target (i.e., space-*based* attention), but also when the target appeared in the cued vertex defined in purely object-centered coordinates (i.e., object-*centered* attention).

It important to stress that in an object-based frame of reference "left" and "right" sides of an object are defined with respect to the viewer, that is in egocentric coordinates. That is what happens in object-*based* neglect. In contrast, object-*centered* neglect should be viewer-independent, that is it should affect one side of the object, regardless of the object's location or orientation with respect to the viewer (see Walker, 1995).

The best known case of object-centered neglect is a patient (NG) studied by Caramazza and Hillis (1990a, 1990b; also see Rapp & Caramazza, 1991), who was left-handed and showed right neglect following a left-hemisphere lesion. She made reading errors only on the right, end part of words, irrespective of whether the words were presented horizontally, vertically, or mirror-reversed (see Table 6.1). That is, she continued to make errors for the word endings, which, when the words were mirror-reversed, were actually located on the left, intact side. By following Marr (1982), Caramazza and his colleagues proposed a three-level model of word representation. The level that would be impaired in their patient is a word-centered (i.e., object-cen-

Table 6.1
Examples of NG's Errors Across Orientations of the Stimulus.

Examples of NG's Errors in Normal (Horizontal) Reading (Stimulus → Response)

Word Stmuli

humid → human	hound → house	stripe → strip
sprinter → sprinkle	dumb → dump	study → stud
though → thoughts	emotionally → emotional	hazardous → hazard

Nonword Stimuli

petch → petcher	dring → drill	stould → stoutly

Examples of Reading Topographically Nonstandard Text

Errors in Vertical Reading

blending → blemish	vivid → vivian	rang → ran
motionless → motel	discovery → discover	habitual → habit
strist → strip	neithem → neither	sipter → sip

Errors in Mirror-reversed Reading

common → comet	joint → joint	regulated → regular
greenish → greenery	discovery → disco	dashes → dash
cring → crime	vigid → vigor	dring → drink

Errors in Recognition of Aural Spelling

earns → earring	sparrow → space	village → villa
basis → bass	requirement → require	planet → plane
dring → drink	fing → fine	womar → woman

Examples of Errors in Various Spelling Tasks

Errors in Written Spelling

floor → floore	sneeze → sneed	cloud → clou
unit → untie	jury → jurd	faith → fait
skart → skarr	remmun → remmey	chench → chen

Errors in Oral Spelling

career → carred	sneeze → sneed	ground → grou
poodle → poodler	afraid → afrain	period → perio
achieme → achiemd	emplain → emplained	spond → spone

Errors in Backward Spelling

absorb → absown	sky → skik	church → chur
garbage → garbsi	oyster → oyste	sample → sampl

Errors in Delayed Copying

square → squard	afraid → afrain	method → meth
turkey → turket	fabric → fabrict	starve → starv

Adapted with permission from Tables 1, 3, and 8 of "Levels of Representation, Co-oridinate Frames, and Unilateral Neglect," by A Caramazza and A. E. Hillis, 1990b, *Cognitive Neuropsychology, 7,* pp. 404. 408. and 415.

tered) grapheme description. Other patients with a similar deficit were reported by Hillis and Caramazza (1995) and Barbut and Gazzaniga (1987).

Further evidence that an object-centered mechanism can be impaired in neglect comes from a study by Behrmann and Tipper (1994; also see Tipper & Behrmann, 1996). They had patients with neglect perform a target-detection task in two conditions. In the static condition, the target appeared on either the left or the right part of a centrally presented object (a barbell). In the rotating condition, the patient watched the barbell undergo a 180° rotation. After the rotation, the left and right parts of the object, which were depicted in different colors, fell into the right and left space, respectively. In the static condition, performance was worse for targets on the left part of the object for all patients. Relative to the static condition, in the rotating condition, all patients showed poorer performance on the right part of the object, and some even showed better performance on the left part. The clearest result was that of patient P5, for whom error rate was about 75% on the left and about 25% on the right in the static condition, whereas, in the rotating condition, error rate was about 10% on the left and about 65% on the right.

HOW DOES ATTENTION MOVE?

When attention moves in visual space, one has to distinguish between overt and covert orienting. Overt orienting is accompanied by eye movements, whereas covert orienting occurs while the eye remain still. Evidence that attention can be oriented covertly was obtained through the work of Posner (e.g., 1980). Posner's spatial cueing paradigm makes use of differences in RT to a stimulus at expected and unexpected locations as a measure of the efficiency of detection attributable to the orienting of attention to the expected location. Before the imperative stimulus, a cue is presented. If the cue does not signal a specific location in space, the trial is neutral. If the cue signals a location, the trial can be either valid (the stimulus appears in the cued location) or invalid (the stimulus appears in an uncued location). The effects of spatial attention manifest themselves as attentional benefits (the difference in RT between neutral and valid trials; about 10-15 ms) and attentional costs (the difference in RT between invalid and neutral trials; about 20-30 ms).

Orienting of Attention

In Posner's (1980) paradigm, on invalid trials the orienting process may be subdivided into three more elementary operations: disengage, move, and engage. Attention is first engaged at the cued location, then, when the stimulus appears elsewhere, attention must be disengaged from the cued location, moved to the stimulated location, and engaged at the new location.

On the basis of double dissociations observed in brain-damaged patients, Posner and his colleagues (e.g., Posner, Inhoff, Friedrich, & Cohen, 1987; Posner, Walker, Friedrich, & Rafal, 1984) suggested the existence of separate neural systems that subserve these operations. Patients with extinction after unilateral parietal lesions were able to shift attention in response to the cue, and thus had normal benefits on valid trials. However, they had exceptionally great costs on invalid trials after a cue that had directed attention to the intact side. Posner and his colleagues argued that this shows a selective deficit for disengaging attention from the intact side toward the impaired side. Patients with progressive supranuclear palsy, in which the primary lesion involves the superior colliculus, had benefits and costs only when the interval between the cue and the stimulus was very long. That shows that they were very slow at moving attention. Also, there was some evidence that patients with a lesion of the pulvinar, a nucleus of the thalamus, had very small benefits on valid trials, suggesting a selective impairment of the engage operation.

The role of the parietal lobe in the disengage operation is supported by those studies that showed that neglect improves if objects, which presumably engage attention, are removed from the intact side. Mark, Kooistra, and Heilman (1988; also see Làdavas, Umiltà, Ziani, Brogi, & Minarini, 1993) used two versions of the task in which patients are required to mark with a pen lines on a sheet of paper. In the standard version, the patients failed to mark most of the lines on the left side. In the other version, they were given an eraser and were asked to actually erase the lines. Omissions on the left side were for fewer in the erasing condition than in the marking condition. The patients performed the task by first erasing the rightmost lines, which were removed from the display, gradually proceeding toward the left. That demonstrates that the disengage operation from the impaired side became easier after the objects were physically removed from the intact side. In support of the idea that attention is captured by the most ipsilesional objects, one can cite also the observation that neglect patients are faster and more accurate than controls in discriminating stimuli that occupy the right relative position in the intact visual field (Làdavas, Petronio, & Umiltà, 1990).

James (1890/1950) distinguished between active and passive attention. Modern terms for denoting the two modes of orienting are endogenous or voluntary and exogenous or automatic. In Posner's (1980) paradigm, one can use central or peripheral cues to direct attention to the peripheral position of impending targets. Central cues, like arrowheads, are cognitive in nature because they must be interpreted to extract the locational information they convey. Peripheral cues, which are shown near the location of the impending target, are not cognitive in nature because they automatically capture attention.

Central and peripheral cues are thought to give rise to different modes of orienting, endogenous and exogenous, respectively (see reviews in Umiltà, in press; Egeth & Yantis, 1997). However, the neuropsychological evidence does not provide unequivocal support for the notion that exogenous and endogenous orienting are mediated by different neural mechanisms.

The extinction-like pattern in patients with parietal lesions reported by Posner and colleagues (Posner, Walker, & Friedrich, 1984; Posner, Inhoff, & Friedrich, 1987) was observed with both peripheral and central cues, that is a flash in the intact field or an arrow pointing to the intact field. That suggests that the parietal lobe is involved in the disengage operation for both types of orienting. In contrast, a rehabilitation study of neglect (Làdavas et al., 1994; also see Riddoch & Humphreys, 1983) showed that central cues that induce the patient to endogenously orient attention to the impaired side can bring about an improvement, whereas peripheral cues do not. That suggests that in neglect the endogenous mechanism is, at least in part, still operational, whereas the exogenous mechanism is severely damaged.

The notion that endogenous and exogenous orienting are subserved by different mechanisms is only apparently contradicted by a positron emission tomography (PET) study of Nobre et al. (1997). The study used two versions of Posner's (1980) paradigm. In both conditions there were two boxes, at 7° from fixation, within which the target to be discriminated (x vs. +; a go/no-go task) appeared. In one condition, the location where attention had to be directed was signaled by the brightening of one of the peripheral boxes. The cue was valid on 80% of the trials. In the other condition, the brightening of one of the peripheral boxes signaled that the target would appear with 80% probability in the opposite box, and thus participants had to shift attention, without moving the eyes, contralateral to the cue. The idea was that the condition in which attention was directed to the cued side would produce exogenous orienting, whereas the condition in which attention was directed to the uncued side would cause endogenous orienting. In either condition, the same cortical areas were activated: the right anterior cingulate gyrus, the right posterior parietal cortex, and, bilaterally, the mesial and lateral premotor cortices. It must be pointed out, however, that the cue was always informative and had a high validity. Therefore, endogenous orienting no doubt occurred in both conditions, regardless of whether attention was directed to the cued or the uncued side.

It is interesting to note that the results of Nobre et al. (1997; also see Corbetta, Miezin, Shulman, & Petersen, 1993) were congruent with a proposal put forward by Mesulam (1981) to explain why lesions to the right hemisphere result in neglect for the left side of space, whereas lesions to the left hemisphere very seldom result in neglect for the right side of space. Mesulam proposed that the right hemisphere controls orienting to both sides of space, whereas the left hemisphere controls orienting to the right side of space only. Nobre et al. (1997) found that the right parietal cortex only was activated during attention shifts to the left field. In contrast, bilateral activation of the parietal cortex was observed during attention shifts to the right field.

A PET study by Corbetta et al. (1993) contained four conditions—that is, shifting attention (i.e., endogenous orienting), passive viewing (i.e., exogenous orienting), central detection, and central fixation. In the endogenous orienting condition, participants responded to a series of target stimuli (asterisks) that flashed in a predictable horizontal sequence in the periphery, thereby allowing voluntary orienting to the location of the impending target. In the exogenous orienting condition, participants fixated centrally while stimuli flashed randomly at the periphery. Results showed that both orienting conditions produced activation in the superior parietal region, whereas the superior prefrontal region was activated in the endogenous but not in the exogenous orienting condition. However, although the exogenous orienting condition was better controlled than in the Nobre et al. (1997) study, Corbetta et al. (1993) did not provide an optimal comparison between endogenous and exogenous orienting either. In fact, exogenous orienting was evaluated using a passive viewing condition rather than peripheral cues.

An fMRI study by Rosen et al. (1999) had carefully controlled conditions. In the endogenous orienting condition, the location of the peripheral target was predicted with 80% validity by a central arrow pointing to the left or right. In the exogenous orienting condition, two cues were used: First, a peripheral cue (a circular light) oriented attention to the periphery, then a second, identical cue re-oriented attention back to the center. Neither cue predicted the location of the forthcoming target. In the control condition, the peripheral target was preceded by a neutral central cue. Results indicated faster RTs for valid than for invalid trials for the endogenous conditions, but slower RTs for valid than for invalid trials for the exogenous condition (i.e., inhibition of return; see section on inhibition of return). Note that inhibition of return is considered to be the hallmark of exogenous orienting. Both exogenous and endogenous orienting activated the superior parietal regions bilaterally (also see Wojciulik & Kanwisher, 1999, for fMRI evidence that links the parietal lobe to various aspects of visual attention; see Rizzolatti et al., in press, for a discussion of the functional organization of parietal areas) and the dorsal premotor regions bilaterally, including the frontal eye fields (remember that premotor activation was demostrated also by Corbetta et al., 1993; Nobre et al., 1997; for a discussion of the functional organization of the frontal eye fields and other premotor areas, see Rizzolatti et al., in press). However, the right dorsolateral prefrontal region was activated by the endogenous orienting condition only.

Neuroimaging evidence points to a common network of interconnected neural structures that mediate both endogenous and exogenous orienting. However, Rosen et al. (1999) found that endogenous orienting activated a larger brain area and evoked an overall greater activation than exogenous orienting did. This is consistent with the notion that endogenous orienting is controlled and effortful, whereas exogenous orienting is automatic and reflexive. In addition, in their study the regional patterns of activation induced by the two conditions were not identical, because endogenous orienting selectively engaged the right dorsolateral prefrontal region. Finally, it is worth noting that Yamaguchi and Kobayashi (1998), in an RT and ERP study on patients with Parkinson's disease, demonstrated that the dopaminergic system contributes to endogenous orienting, but does not contribute to exogenous orienting.

Saccadic Eye Movements

A widely-held view (e.g., Posner & Dehaene, 1994; Posner & Petersen, 1990) is that there are two attentional systems—a posterior system that mediates spatial attention, and an anterior system that mediates selective attention and cognitive control. These attentional systems are thought to be separate from the systems that are in charge of processing information. That is, they would modulate the activity of perceptual and motor systems but would be independent, even anatomically, from them.

A different view (the premotor theory of spatial attention; e.g., Rizzolatti et al., in press; Rizzolatti, Riggio, & Sheliga, 1994) is that attention depends on those same systems that underlie perception and action. That is, spatial attention would originate from the activation of those cortical and subcortical neural circuits that transform spatial information into action. This activation causes an increase of motor readiness to act in the direction of the region of space that is the goal of the motor program. Also, the processing of information that originates from that same region is enhanced. Therefore, the mechanisms of spatial attention coincide with the mechanisms that generate action, and one need not invoke separate attentional mechanisms to explain spatial attention (see Craighero, Fadiga, Rizzolatti, & Umiltà, 1999, for an extension of the theory to grasping movements).

Several studies have provided evidence that, when visuospatial attention is directed to a location, an oculomotor program is prepared to perform a saccade to the target location (see review in Umiltà, in press).

Rizzolatti, Riggio, Dascola, and Umiltà (1987; also see Umiltà, Riggio, Dascola, & Rizzolatti, 1991) investigated how attention shifts in visual space by using a variant of Posner's (1980) paradigm. The main finding was that, when the stimulus was presented at non-cued locations, RT was slower on the non-cued than on the cued side, even though non-cued locations were equidistant from the cued location on either side (the so-called meridian effect). The authors proposed that, once a directional cue was presented, a motor program for a saccade was prepared, which specified the direction of the eye movement. The motor program was prepared even though the saccade was then vetoed and not executed. When the imperative stimulus appeared in the expected location, the response was immediately executed. In contrast, when the stimulus was shown on the side opposite to the cued location, the direction feature of the motor program had to be modified before execution of the response. This time-consuming change produced the meridian effect.

Sheliga, Riggio, and Rizzolatti (1994; also see Sheliga, Craighero, Riggio, & Rizzolatti, 1997) instructed participants to direct attention to a spatial location to the left or right side of fixation and to perform a vertical saccade in response to the presentation of a visual or an acoustic imperative stimulus. Results showed that, regardless of the modality in which the imperative stimulus was presented, the trajectory of the saccade deviated away (i.e., to the right or left) from the location where attention had been directed. That can be explained by assuming that, even though the eyes remained at fixation, the oculomotor program that was needed to direct attention caused the representation of space used by oculomotor centers to shift to the attended side (a "remapping" process; Sheliga et al., 1994). Therefore, when a saccade was performed, the eye trajectory veered from the side where attention had previously been directed. A different, but not necessarily alternative, explanation for why the eye trajectory veered from the side of attention is based on the circuit that modulates excitability of the superior colliculs (a "suppression" process; Rizzolatti et al., 1994; Sheliga et al., 1994).

A neurophysiological study by Kustov and Robinson (1996) provided clear evidence of the existence of links between visuospatial attention and eye movements. It showed that, in monkeys, the trajectory of a saccade evoked by electrical stimulation of the superior colliculus depended on where attention was directed. Even more interestingly, it was found that collicular excitability changed not only when the monkey was instructed to perform a saccade in response to the imperative stimulus, but also when the response was manual and the eyes did not move. That demonstrated that a shift of attention affected excitability of the oculomotor system in the absence of eye movements.

Other single unit studies reported that cortical areas, like the frontal eye fields (e.g., Kodaka, Mikami, & Kubota, 1997), the supplementary eye fields (Bon & Lucchetti, 1997), and the parietal cortex (Andersen, 1995; Snyder, Batista, & Anderson, 1997), may mediate both attention and oculomotor processes. Colby, Duhamel, and Goldberg (1996) even reported that the very same neurons in the lateral intraparietal area responded to shifts of attention and saccadic eye movements.

The studies mentioned above, as well as several others (see Hoffman, 1998, for a review of behavioral studies, and Corbetta, 1998, for a meta-analysis of brain imaging studies) demonstrated the existence of links between eye movement mechanisms and the mechanisms involved in shifts of visuospatial attention. Direct evidence of a functional anatomical overlap between attention and eye movements systems was provided by an *f*MRI study of Corbetta et al. (1998), which showed that the same anatomical regions are involved in both attention orienting and saccadic eye movements.

In the Corbetta et al. (1998) study there were three tasks. In the shifting attention task, participants had to maintain central fixation and perform sequential shifts of attention to a series of boxes, located at 1°, 3°, 5°, 7°, and 10°, to detect a visual target (an asterisk in one of the boxes). An arrow indicated the box to which attention had to be shifted. In the eye movement task, the display was identical but participants were instructed to sequentially shift their eyes, and, presumably, attention. Note that shifts of attention in the attention shifting task and saccades in the eye movement task were endogenously generated because they preceded target presentation. In the fixation control task, the display was as in the other two tasks, but neither attention nor the eyes had to be shifted, and the target was not presented.

Results showed a nearly perfect overlap in the pattern of activation for the shifting attention task and the eye movement task. The areas active in both tasks were the frontal cortex near the precentral sulcus, the posterior end of the superior frontal sulcus, the medial frontal gyrus, and the parietal cortex along the intraparietal sulcus. Importantly, no region was uniquely active in one or the other task. The only difference between shifts of covert attention and saccadic eye movements was that the former produced a lower level of activation. The functional anatomy shown by Corbetta et al. (1998) closely replicated the findings of PET studies on covert visual orienting (Corbetta et al., 1993; Nobre et al., 1997; Vandenberghe et al., 1997). Note that also the Rosen et al. (1999) *f*MRI study demonstrated that covert shifts of endogenous and exogenous attention activated the frontal eye fields.

HOW DOES ATTENTION OPERATE?

We live in cluttered environments and our senses are inundated by stimuli, only a small number of which are relevant to our goal-directed behavior. Attention allows us to pick up and process relevant stimuli while ignoring the myriad of irrelevant and potentially distracting ones.

Introspectively, it appears that selection of relevant information at the expense of irrelevant information is achieved by an enhancement of processing of the former. In effect, in most of the foregoing discussion it has been taken for granted that attention enhances (i.e., facilitates) processing of relevant information. However, the *mechanisms* of the selection process need not necessarily be *facilitatory* in nature. Selection of relevant stimuli may also be *inhibitory* in nature. That is, attentive processing of relevant information may be achieved by mechanisms that inhibit processing of irrelevant information. LaBerge (1995), among others, for example, aptly distinguished between the subjective *expression* of attention, which appears to be facilitatory, and the *mechanisms* by which that expression is achieved, which can be either facilitatory or inhibitory.

Facilitation

It is widely accepted that information to which attention is selectively allocated is processed more efficiently than non-attended information. Therefore, for sake of brevity, I will confine myself to pointing out that there are many methods that allow one to measure increases in processing efficiency caused by attention. The most frequently used are speed of response (e.g., Eriksen & Hoffman, 1972; Posner, 1980), recognition accuracy (e.g., Egly & Homa, 1984; van der Heijden & Eerland, 1973), stimulus detection (i.e., sensitivity vs. criterion shifts; see e.g., Bashinski & Bacharach, 1980; Downing, 1988), amplitude and/or latency of event related potentials (e.g., Mangun & Hillyard, 1988; Rugg et al., 1987), and brain activation (e.g., Brefczynski & DeYoe, 1999; Martinez et al., 1999). Information to which attention is allocated is operatively defined as that for which improved efficiency of processing is observed in terms of one or more of these indexes.

Inhibition

There are mechanisms that achieve attentional selection by impeding the processing of irrelevant information. Some of these inhibitory mechanisms manifest themselves through effects for which there is neuropsychological evidence: inhibition of return, negative priming, and attentional blink. For other effects, like repetition blindness and change blindness, which too are presumably attributable to inhibitory mechanisms, neuropsychological evidence is not yet available (see Shapiro et al., in press).

Inhibition of Return

This phenomenon was first described by Posner and Cohen (1984) and was termed inhibition of return (IOR) by Posner, Rafal, Choate, and Vaughan (1985). This term indicates a decreased likelihood that attention returns to a previously attended location (Klein, 1988): IOR would improve spatial selectivity by favoring the exploration of new positions at the expense of those already explored.

The characteristics of IOR and its relations with oculomotor mechanisms have been elucidated by a number of subsequent studies (see reviews in Milliken & Tipper, 1998; Umiltà, in press). Also, it was suggested that IOR can be related to either attended locations or attended objects.

Space-Based Inhibition of Return.   In variants of Posner's (1980) paradigm, appearance of the target stimulus in the cued location may cause a delay and/or a loss of accuracy in the response: When the cue is peripheral, and thus causes exogenous orienting, and is not predictive of the target position, RT is slower and accuracy is lower if cue and target locations coincide than if they do not coincide.

IOR is caused by covert shifts of attention elicited by peripheral, non-predictive cues, but it does not occur with all shifts of attention. In particular, it does not occur with endogenously activated covert shifts of attention in response to central cues that indicate where to expect the forthcoming target. However, as was shown by Posner et al. (1985), if a central arrow induces the observer to make a saccade to an eccentric location, and the eyes are then returned back to fixation, IOR does occur at the location to which the saccade had been directed. Thus, the inhibitory effect seems to be produced by a cue presented in the periphery of the visual field while the eyes do not move or by endogenous activation of a saccade. Likely, a common mechanism, related to oculomotor preparation, is involved in both circumstances (see Rafal, Calabresi, Brennan, & Sciolto, 1989).

Object-Based Inhibition of Return.   Evidence has been accumulating that IOR, besides being related to cued locations, can also be related to cued objects (Tipper, Driver, & Weaver, 1991; Tipper, Jordan, & Weaver, 1999; Tipper, Weaver, Jerreat, & Burak, 1994). In the standard experimental paradigm for IOR, attention is first oriented to, and then withdrawn from, not only a location but also an object (often an outline box). Therefore, it is unclear whether attention is inhibited from returning to recently attended locations or to recently attended objects. These two possibilities can be tested in experimental conditions in which objects move in space. The cueing of moving objects permits one to evaluate inhibition related to the object when it is in a location different from the cued one. Also, one can independently evaluate inhibition related to the location in which the cueing took place when that location is no longer occupied by the cued object.

This experimental procedure was used by Tipper et al. (1994; also see Abrams & Dobkin, 1994; Tipper et al., 1991) who showed that IOR manifests itself in both space-based and object-based frames of reference, and that both types of inhibition can coexist.

Gibson and Egeth (1994) found another type of IOR associated with objects, which too coexists with space-based IOR. In their experiments, inhibition accrued at locations that remained invariant with respect to the object's internal structure. Therefore, that would be object-centered rather than object-based IOR (see section on object-centered attention). Tipper et al. (1999) found three types of IOR: one space-based, one that follows moving objects (object-based), and one related to parts of rotating objects (object-centered).

Neural Substrate of Inhibition of Return.   That the superior colliculus mediates space-based IOR is attested by several, though indirect, lines of evidence (see review in Rafal & Henik, 1994). Patients with progressive supranuclear palsy, which, as already mentioned (see section on orienting of attention), results in damage to the superior colliculus, are the only patients who do not show IOR with a spatial cueing paradigm (Rafal, Posner, Friedman, Inhoff, & Bernstein, 1988). Space-based IOR is present in patients with hemianopia, a condition in which the geniculostriate pathway is destroyed, whereas the retinotectal pathway is preserved. When healthy participants view display monocularly, space-based IOR is greater in the temporal than in the nasal visual field, which indexes mediation by the retinotectal pathway (Rafal et al., 1989; Rafal, Henik, & Smith, 1991). Spatial cueing in newborn infants, whose visual behavior is predominantly mediated by the superior colliculus, produces IOR that is greater in the temporal than in the nasal visual field (Simion, Valenza, Umiltà, & Dalla Barba, 1995; Valenza, Simion, & Umiltà, 1994).

Direct evidence of the involvement of the superior colliculus in space-based IOR was provided by Sapir, Soroker, Berger, and Henik (1999), who tested a patient with a lesion restricted to the right superior colliculus. They used a monocular variant of Posner's (1980) paradigm. Results showed that IOR was present only in the visual field projecting to the intact left superior colliculus, and was greater in the temporal than in the nasal field. No IOR was found in the visual field projecting to the damaged right superior colliculus.

Tipper et al. (1994) speculated that different neural structures may subserve space-based and object-based IOR: The former would be mediated by the superior colliculus, whereas the latter would be mediated by the cortex. Tipper et al. (1997) found that, in two split-brain patients, object-based IOR did not transfer between hemispheres. That might be taken as supportive of the notion that object-based IOR is cortically mediated, and thus needs an intact corpus callosum to transfer from one hemisphere to the other.

Negative Priming

The phenomenon of negative priming (NP) refers to the slowing of responses to recently ignored stimuli (i.e., distracters). Even though a distracter was successfully ignored on a trial, there is a slowing of the response when that same distracter is re-presented as a target on the subsequent trial.

A study by Tipper and Cranston (1985) illustrates the NP effect. In it, participants were presented with lists of partially overlapped red and green letter pairs and were asked to read aloud the red letters and to ignore the green letters. The lists were presented under two conditions: In the ignored prime condition, the distracter (green) letter in each pair was identical to the subsequent target (red) letter. In the unrelated distracter condition, the distracter letter and the following target letter were different. NP was evidenced by slower responses in the ignored prime condition than in the unrelated distracter condition.

Negative priming has been demonstrated with many different experimental paradigms (see reviews in Milliken & Tipper, 1998; Neill, Valdes, & Terry, 1995), which suggests that the mechanism(s) that cause(s) it may play an important role in selective attention. Even though the attribution of NP to inhibitory attentional mechanisms(s) is not straightforward (e.g., Milliken & Tipper, 1998) the two more convincing explanations invoke some form of inhibition. One is that the activation of the distracter internal representation is reduced and this inhibition is still effective when the next trial is presented. The other is that the distracter representation is denied access to the response system and its isolation from the control of action must be overcome when, on the next trial, the distracter requires a response.

Diminished NP has been observed in individuals for whom it can be argued that inhibition of irrelevant information is impaired: schizophrenics (e.g., Beech, Powell, McWilliams, & Claridge, 1989), depressed patients (e.g., Benoit et al., 1992), and Alzeimer's patients (e.g., Sullivan, Faust, & Balota, 1995).

An interesting study was conducted by Fuentes and Humphreys (1996), who tested a patient with a right parietal lesion showing left visual extinction to double simultaneous stimulation. They used a version of the "flanker" task (Eriksen & Eriksen, 1974), in which the patient was required to classify two target letters at fixation, one in the prime display and one in the subsequent probe display, on the basis of whether they were same or different. The central target letters could be flanked either by two plus signs or by one plus sign and a letter (the distracter), presented to the left or right visual field. In the critical condition, the distracter in the prime display became the target in the probe display. RT was measured. Like normal participants, the patient showed NP when the distracter appeared in the intact field (1683 ms in the ignored prime condition vs. 1420 ms in the unrelated distracter condition). In contrast, he showed positive priming when the distracter appeared in the affected field (1322 ms in the ignored prime condition vs. 1607 ms in the unrelated distracter condition). Two important conclusions can be drawn from this study. First, stimuli in the neglected field activate internal representations that produce positive priming, that is faster and more accurate processing of the target (see section on early vs. late selection). Second, in the absence of attention, the inhibitory mechanism(s) that produce(s) NP cannot operate.

Stuss et al. (1999) examined three measures of inhibition, interference, NP, and IOR, in patients with frontal lesions (bilateral, left, or right) or non-frontal, predominantly parietal lesions (left or right). With regard to NP, results showed that right hemisphere lesions, either frontal or parietal, virtually eliminated it. That supports Fuentes and Humphreys's (1996) finding that areas of the right hemisphere are implicated in NP.

Attentional Blink

When a human observer has to identify two objects presented in succession, the processing of the first object interferes with the processing of the second object. This phenomenon, which lasts for several hundred milliseconds, was termed the attentional blink (AB) or dwell time, and is a measure of the observer's ability to shift attention over time (see reviews in Milliken & Tipper, 1998; Shapiro et al., in press).

The standard procedure for studying AB is based on the rapid serial visual presentation (RSVP) of stimuli. In a study by Raymond, Shapiro, and Arnell (1992), participants were presented with an RSVP stream of letters. One of the letters was white, whereas the other letters were black on a gray background. The single white letter was the target, and one of the black letters (an X) was the probe. On experimental trials, the task was to identify the white letter and to indicate whether the probe had appeared following the target. On control trials, the task was to indicate only whether the probe had appeared, without identifying the target. The RSVP streams contained between 7 and 15 pre-target items and 8 post-target items. Results showed that, on experimental trials, the participant's ability to detect the probe varied according to its temporal position in the RSVP stream: If the probe occurred within about 400 ms of the target, detection was impaired.

The term AB was used to indicate that participants experience an attentional impairment after engaging the target. The exact mechanism of this loss of attention is still a matter of debate (see Milliken & Tipper, 1998; Shapiro et al., in press). Raymond et al. (1992) originally proposed an explicit inhibitory process. Later Shapiro and Raymond (1994) proposed a competitive retrieval process. A third account is based on the notion of a bottleneck created by a capacity-limited stage of processing (Chun & Potter, 1995; Jolicoeur & Dell'Acqua, 1998).

Husain, Shapiro, Martin, and Kennard (1997) examined AB in patients with left neglect following right hemisphere stoke involving the inferior parietal lobe, the inferior frontal lobe, or the basal ganglia. These patients had an abnormally severe and protracted AB in comparison to elderly control participants (1,440 vs. 360 ms). In contrast, age-matched patients with right hemisphere stroke but without neglect showed a normal AB that lasted 360 ms. Husain et al. (1997) concluded that neglect is a disorder of directing attention in time, not only in space. In particular, it would seem that the deficit of the disengagement of attention that characterizes neglect and extinction (see section on orienting of attention) is not purely spatial in nature (also see Shapiro et al., in press). It is interesting to note, that other studies demonstrated non-spatial attentional deficits in patients with extinction by using different experimental procedures, (di Pellegrino, Basso, & Frassinetti, 1998; Humphreys, Romani, Olson, Riddoch, & Duncan, 1994; also see review in Shapiro et al., in press).

CONCLUDING REMARKS

The results reviewed here clearly show that neuropsychological and neurophysiological research has provided important contributions toward elucidating key issues concerning the mechanisms of attention. Attention selects both regions of space and objects for enhanced processing, and, likely, selection for space and selection for objects depends on different neural mechanisms. Even though attention can be shifted in space in the absence of eye movements, there can be little doubt that there is a functional neuroanatomical overlap between attention and eye movement systems. Also, it is clear that attentional selection implies both facilitation of relevant information and inhibition of irrelevant information.

A key issue in the study of attention that has yet to be fully clarified concerns the fate of unattended information. Neurophysiological evidence shows that attention modulates neural activity at very early stages along the processing pathway, perhaps even at the level of the primary sensory areas. That is clearly in favor of the early selection hypothesis. In contrast, neuropsychological evidence supports the late selection hypothesis by showing semantic interference effects produced by unattended stimuli. Perhaps, facilitation of attended information occurs at early stages, which are tapped by neurophysiological methods, whereas inhibition of unattended information occurs at later stages, which are tapped by neuropsychological tasks. However, Valdes-Sosa, Bobes, Rodriguez, and Pinilla (1998) reported suppression of P1 and N1 associated with non-attended objects, which seems to suggest that inhibition acts at early stages. Likely, as argued by Yantis and Johnston (1990), the question is not either/or: Selection is early or late depending on task demands.

Acknowledgements

The writing of this chapter was supported by grants from MURST. I thank Brenda Rapp for many helpful suggestions on an earlier version of this chapter.

REFERENCES

Abrams, R. A., & Dobkin, R. S. (1994). Inhibition of return: Effects of attentional cueing on eye movement latencies. *Journal of Experimental Psychology: Human Perception & Performance, 20,* 467-477.

Andersen, R. A. (1995). Encoding of intention and spatial location in posterior parietal cortex. *Cerebral Cortex, 5,* 457-469.

Arguin, M., Joanette, & Y. Cavanagh, P. (1993). Visual search for feature and conjunction targets with an attention deficit. *Journal of Cognitive Neuroscience, 54,* 436-452.

Bashinski, H. S., & Bacharach, V.R. (1980). Enhancement of perceptual sensitivity as the result of selective attending to spatial locations. *Perception & Psychophysics, 28,* 241-248.

Barbut, D., & Gazzaniga, M. S. (1987). Disturbances in conceptual space involving language and speech. Brain, 110, 1487-1496.

Beech, A. R., Powell, T. J., McWilliams, J., & Claridge, G. S. (1989). Evidence of reduced "cognitive inhibition" in schizophrenia. *British Journal of Clinical Psychology, 28,* 110-116.

Behrmann, M., & Moscovitch, M. (199). Object-centered neglect in patients with unilateral neglect: Effect of left-right coordinates of objects. *Journal of Cognitive Neurosciences, 6,* 1-16.

Behrmann, M., Moscovitch, M., Black, S. E., & Mozer, M. (1990). Perceptual and conceptual mechanisms in neglect: Two contrasting studies. *Brain, 113,* 1163-1183.

Behrmann, M., & Tipper, S. P. (1994), Object-based attentional mechanisms: Evidence from patients with unilateral neglect. In C. Umiltà & M. Moscovitch (Eds.), *Attention and Performance XV* (pp. 351-375). Cambridge, MA: MIT Press.

Benoit, G., Fortran, L., Lemelin, S., LaPlante, L., Thomas, J., & Everett, J. (1992). L'attention selective dans la depression majeure: Ralentissement clinique et inhibition cognitive (Selective attention in major depression: Clinical slowing and cognitive inhibition). *Canadian Journal of Psychology, 46,* 41-52.

Berti, A., Allport, A., Driver, J., Denies, Z., Oxbury, J., & Oxbury, S. (1992). Levels of processing for visual stimuli in an "extinguished" field. *Neuropsychologia, 30,* 403-415.

Berti, A., & Frassinetti, F. (in press). When far becomes near: Re-mapping of space by in a patient with visual neglect. *Journal of Cognitive Neuroscience.*

Berti, A., & Rizzolatti, G. (1992). Visual Processing without awareness: Evidence from unilateral neglect. *Journal of Cognitive Neuroscience, 4,* 345-351.

Bisiach, E. (1993). Mental representation in unilateral neglect and related disorders. *Quarterly Journal of Experimental Psychology, 46A,* 435-461.

Bisiach, E., & Vallar, G. (in press). Unilateral neglect in humans. In F. Boller & J. Grafman (Eds.), *Handbook of neuropsychology.* Amsterdam: Elsevier.

Bon, L., & Lucchetti, C. (1997). The dorsomedial frontal cortex of the macaca monkey: Fixation and saccade-related activity. *Experimental Brain Research, 89,* 571-580.

Brefczynski, J.A., & DeYoe, E. A. (1999). A physiological correlate of the 'spotlight' of visual attention. *Nature Neuroscience, 2,* 370-374.

Broadbent, D. E. (1958). *Perception and Communication.* London: Pergamon Press.

Buck, B. H., Black, S. E., Behrmann, M., Caldwell, C., & Bronskill, M. J. (1997). Spatial- and object-based attentional deficits in Alzheimer's disease. *Brain, 120,* 122-1244.

Caramazza, A., & Hillis, A.E. (1990a). Spatial representation of words in the brain implied by studies of a unilateral neglect patient. *Nature, 346,* 267-269.

Caramazza, A., & Hillis, A. E. (1990b). Levels of representation, co-ordinate frames, and unilateral neglect. *Cognitive Neuropsychology, 7,* 391-445.

Chun, M. M., Potter, M. C. (2995). A two-stage model for multiple target detection in rapid serial visual presentation. *Journal of Experimental Psychology: Human Perception & Performance, 21,* 109-127.

Cohen, A., & Rafal, R. D. (1991). Attention and feature integration: Illusory conjunctions in a patient with a parietal lobe lesion. *Psychological Science, 2,* 106-110.

Colby, C. L., Duhamel, J., & Goldberg, M. E. (1996). Visual, presaccadic, and cognitive activation of single neurons in monkey lateral intraparietal area. *Journal of Neurophysiology, 76,* 2841-2852.

Corbetta, M. (1988). Frontopoarietal cortical networks for directing attention and the eye to visual locations: Identical, independent, or overlapping neural systems. *Proceedings of the National Academy of Science, USA, 95,* 831-838.

Corbetta, M., Akbudak, E., Conturo, T. E., Snyder, A. Z., Ollinger, J. M., Drury, H. A., Linenberg, M. R., Petersen, S. E., Raichle, M. E., Van Essen, D. C., & Shulman, G. L. (1998). A common network of functional areas for attention and eye movements. *Neuron, 21,* 761-773.

Corbetta, M., Miezin, F. M., Shulman, G. L., & Petersen, Ss E. (1993). A PET study of visuospatial attention. *Journal of Neuroscience, 13,* 1202-1226.

Corteen, R. S., & Wood, B. (1992). Autonomous responses to shock associated words in an unattended channel. *Journal of Experimental Psychology, 94,* 308-313.

Cowey, A., Small, M., & Ellis, S. (1994). Left visuo-spatial neglect can be worse in far than near space. *Neuropsychologia, 32,* 1059-1066.

Craighero, L., Fadiga, L., Rizzolatti, G., & Umiltà, C. (1999). Action for perception: A motor-visual attentional effect. *Journal of Experimental Psychology: Human Perception & Performance, 25,* 1673-1692.

Czigler, I., & Balàzs, L. (1998). Object-related attention: An event-related potential study. *Brain & Cognition, 38,* 113-124.

Desimone, R., & Duncan, J. (1995). Neural mechanisms of selective visual attention. *Annual Review of Neuroscience, 18,* 193-222.

Deutsch, J. A., & Deutsch, D. (1963). Attention: Some theoretical considerations. *Psychological Review, 70,* 80-90.

Di Pellegrino, G., Basso, G., & Frassinetti, F. (1998). Visual extinction as a spatio-temporal disorder of selective attention. *Neuroreport, 9,* 835-839.

Downing, C. J. (1988). Expectancy and visual-spatial attention: Effects on perceptual quality. *Journal of Experimental Psychology, Human Perception & Performance, 14,* 188-202.

Driver, J. (1997). What can visual neglect and extinction reveal about the extent of "preattentive" processing? In A. F. Kramer, M. G. H. Coles, & G. D. Logan (Eds.), *Convergeing operations in the study of visual selective attention* (pp. 193–224). Washington, DC: American Psychological Association.

Driver, J. (1998). The neuropsychology of spatial attention. In H. Pashler (Ed.), *Attention* (pp. 297–340). Hove, UK: Psychology Press.

Driver, J., & Baylis, G. C. (1998). Attention and visual object segmentation. In R. Parasuraman (Ed.), *The Attentive Brain* (pp. 299–325). Cambridge, MA: MIT Press.

Driver, J., Baylis, G. C., Goodrich, S. J., & Rafal, R. D. (1994). Axis-based neglect of visual shapes. *Neuropsychologia, 32,* 1353–1365.

Driver, J., Baylis, G. C., & Rafal, R. D. (1992). Preserved figure-ground segregation and symmetry perception in visual neglect. *Nature, 360,* 73–75.

Driver, J., Mattingley, J. B., Rorden, C., & Davis, G. (1997). Extinction as a paradigm measure of attentional bias and restricted capacity following brain injury. In P. Thier & H. O. Karnath (Eds.), *Parietal lobe contribution to orientation in 3D Space* (pp. 233–258). Heildeberg: Springer-Verlag.

Duncan, J. (1984). Selective attention and the organization of visual information: *Journal of Experimental Psychology: General, 113,* 501–517.

Egeth, H. E., & Yantis, S. (1997). Visual attention: Control, representation, and time course. *Annual Review of Psychology, 48,* 269–297.

Eglin, M., Robertson, L. C., & Knight, R. T. (1989). Visual search performance in the neglect syndrome. *Journal of Cognitive Neuroscience, 1,* 327–385.

Egly, R., Driver, J., & Rafal, R. D. (1994). Shifting visual attention between objects and locations: Evidence from normal and parietal lesion subjects. *Journal of Experimental Psychology, General, 123,* 161–177.

Egly, R., & Homa, D. (1984). Sensitization of the visual field. *Journal of Experimental Psychology: Human Perception & Performance, 10,* 778–793.

Egly, R., Rafal, R., Driver, J., & Starrveveld, Y. (1994). Covert orienting in the split brain reveals hemispheric specialization for object-based attention. *Psychological Science, 5,* 380–383.

Eriksen, C. W., & Eriksen, B. A. (1974). Effects of noise letters upon identification of a target letter in a nonsearch task. *Perception & Psychophysics, 16,* 143–149.

Eriksen, C. W., & Hoffman, J. E. (1972). Temporal and spatial characteristics of selective encoding from visual displays. *Perception & Psychophysics, 12,* 201–204.

Farah, M. J., Brunn, J., Wong, A. B., Wallace, M. A., & Carpenter, P. (1990). Frames of reference for allocating attention to space: Evidence from the neglect syndrome. *Neuropsychologia, 28,* 335–347.

Francolini, C. M., & Egeth, H. E. (1980). On the nonautomaticity of "automatic" activation: Evidence of selective seeing. *Perception & Psychophysics, 27,* 331–342.

Fuentes, L. J., & Humphreys, G. W. (1996). On the processing of "Extinguished" stimuli in unilateral visual neglect: An approach using negative priming. *Cognitive Neuropsychology, 13,* 111–136.

Gainotti, G., Messerli, P., & Tissot, R. (1972). Qualitative analysis of unilateral and spatial neglect in relation to laterality of cerebral lesion. *Journal of Neurology, Neurosurgery and Psychiatry, 35,* 545–550.

Gibson, B. S., & Egeth, H. (1994). Inhibition of return to object-based and environment-based locations. *Perception & Psychophysics, 55,* 323–339.

Guariglia, C., & Antonucci, G. (1992). Personal and extrapersonal space: A case of neglect dissociation. *Neuropsychologia, 30,* 1001–1009.

Halligan, P. W., & Marshall, J. C. (1991). Left neglect for near but not for far space in man. *Nature, 350,* 498–500.

Halligan, P. W., & Marshall, J. C. (1993). When two is one: A case study of spatial parsing in visual neglect. *Perception, 22,* 309–312.

Heinze, H., Mangun, G. R. Burchert, W., Hinrichs, M., Scholz, M., Muente, T. F., Goes, A., Scherg, M., Johannes, S., Hundeshagen, H., Gazzaniga, M. S., & Hillyard, S. A. (1994). Combined spatial and temporal imaging of brain activity during visual selective attention in humans. *Nature, 372,* 543–546.

Hillis, A. E., & Caramazza, A. (1995). A framework for interpreting distinct patterns of hemispatial neglect. *Neurocase, 1,* 189–207.

Hillyard, S. A., Hink, R. F., Schwent, V. L., & Picton, T. W. (1973). Electrical signs of selective attention in the human brain. *Science, 182,* 177–179.

Hoffman, J. E. (1998). Visual attention and eye movements. In H. E. Pashler (Ed.), *Attention,* (pp. 120–153). Hove, UK: Psychology Press.

Hoffman, J. E., & Nelson, B. (1981). Spatial selectivity in visual search. *Perception & Psychophysics, 30,* 283–290.

Humphreys, G. W., & Riddoch, M. J. (1993), Interactions between object and space systems revealed through neuropsychology. In D. E. Meyer, S. Kornblum (Eds.), *Attention and Performance XIV* (pp. 143–162). Cambridge, MA: MIT Press.

Humphreys, G. W., & Riddoch, M. J. (1994). Attention to within-object and between-object spatial representations: Multiple sites for visual selection. *Cognitive Neuropsychology, 11,* 207–241.

Humphreys, G. W., & Riddoch, M. J. (1995). Separate coding of space within and between perceptual objects: Evidence from unilateral visual neglect. *Cognitive Neuropsychology, 12,* 283–311.

Humphreys, G. W., Romani, C., Olson, A., Riddoch, M. J., & Duncan, J. (1994). Nonspatial extinction following lesions of the parietal lobes in humans. *Nature, 372,* 357–359.

Husain, M., Shapiro, K., Martin, J., & Kennard, C. (1997). Abnormal temporal dynamics of visual attention in spatial neglect patients. *Nature, 385,* 154–156.

James, W. (1890/1950). *Principles of Psychology.* New York: Dover.

Jolicoeur, P., & Dell'Acqua, R.(1998). The demonstration of short-term consolidation. *Cognitive Psychology, 36,* 138–202.

Joseph, J. S., Chun, M. M., & Nakayama, K. (1997). Attentional requirements in a 'preattentive' feature search task. *Nature, 387,* 805–807.

Kahneman, D. (1973). *Attention and effort.* Eglewood Cliffs, NJ: Prentice Hall.

Kahneman, D., & Henik, A. (1981). Perceptual organization and attention. In M. Kubovy & J. R. Pomerantz (Eds.), *Perceptual grouping and attention* (pp. 181–211). Hillsdale, NJ: Lawrence Erlbaum.

Kahneman, D., & Treisman, A. (1984). Changing views of attention and automaticity. In R. Parasuraman & D. A. Davies (Eds.), *Varieties of attention* (pp. 29–62). New York: Academic Press.

Karnath, H. O. (1994). Subjective body orientation in neglect and the interactive contribution of neck muscles proprioception and vestibular stimulation. *Brain, 117,* 1001–1012.

Klein, R. M. (1988). Inhibitory tagging system facilitates visual search. *Nature, 334*, 430–431.

Kodaka, Y., Mikami, A., & Kubbota, K. (1997). Neuronal activity in the frontal eye fields of the monkey is modulated while attention is focused onto a stimulus in the peripheral visual field, irrespective of eye movement. *Neuroscience Research, 28*, 291–298.

Kramer, A. F., Weber, T. A., & Watson, S. E. (1997). Object-based attentional selection—Grouped arrays or spatially invariant representations? Comment on Vecera and Farah (1994). *Journal of Experimental Psychology, General, 126*, 3–13.

Kustov, A. A., & Robinson, D. L. (1996). Shared neural control of attention shifts and eye movements. *Nature, 384*, 74–77.

LaBerge, D. (1995). *Attentional processing: The brain's art of mindfulness.* Cambridge, MA: Harvard University Press.

Làdavas, E. (1994). Spatial dimensions of automatic and voluntary orienting of attention. In I. H. Robertson & J. C. Marshall (Eds.), *Unilateral neglect: Clinical and experimental Studies* (pp. 193–209). Hillsdale, NJ: Lawrence Erlbaum.

Làdavas, E., Menghini, G., & Umiltà, C. (1994). A rehabilitation study of hemispatial neglect. *Cognitive Neuropsychology, 11*, 75–95.

Làdavas, E., Paladini, R., & Cubelli, R. (1993). Implicit associative priming in a patient with left visual neglect. *Neuropsychologia, 31*, 1307–1320.

Làdavas, E., Petronio, A., & Umiltà, C. (1990). The deployement of visual attention in the intaqct field of hemineglect patients. *Cerebral Cortex, 26*, 307–317.

Làdavas, E., Umiltà, C., Ziani, P., Brogi, A., & Minarini, M. (1993). The role of right-side objects in left-side neglect: A dissociation between perceptual and directional motor neglect. *Neuropsychologia, 31*, 761–773.

Lewis, J. L. (1970). Semantic processing of unattended messages using dichotic listening. *Journal of Experimental Psychology, 85*, 225–228.

Luck, S. J. (1998). Neurophysiology of selective attention. In H. Pashler (Ed.), *Attention,* (pp. 257–295). Hove, UK: Psychology Press.

Luck, S. J., Chelazzi, L., Hillyard, S. A., & Desimone, R. (1997. Neural mechanisms of spatial selective attention in areas V1, V2, and V4 of macaque cortex. *Journal of Neurophysiology, 77*, 113–123.

Luck, S. L., & Girelli, M. (1998). In R. Parasuraman (Ed.), *The Attentive Brain* (pp. 71–94). Cambridge, MA: MIT Press.

Mangun, G. R., & Hillyard, S. A. (1988). Spatial gradients of visual attention: Behavioral and electrophysiological evidence. *Electroencephalography and Clinical Neurophysiology, 70*, 417–428.

Mangun, G. R., Hillyard, S. A., & Luck, S. J. (1993). Electrocortical substrates of visual selective attention. In D. Meyer, S. Kornblum (Eds.), *Attention and performance XIV* (pp. 219–243). Cambridge, MA: MIT Press.

Mark, V. W., Kooistra, C. A., & Heilman, K. M. (1988). Hemispatial neglect is affected by non-neglected stimuli. *Neurology, 38*, 1207–1211.

Marr, D. (1982). *Vision.* San Francisco: Freeman.

Marshall, J. C., & Halligan, P. W. (1994). The yin and yang of visuo-spatial neglect: A case study. *Neuropsychologia, 32*, 1037–1057.

Martinez, A., Anllo-Vento, L., Sereno, M. I., Frank, L. R., Buxton, R. B., Dubowitz, D. J., Wong, E. C., Hinrichs, H., Heinze, H. J., & Hillyard, S. A. (1999). Involvement of striate and extrastriate visual cortical areas in spatial attention. *Nature Neuroscience, 4*, 364–369.

Mattingley, J. B., Davis, G., & Driver, J. (1997). Preattentive filling-in of visual surfaces in parietal extinction. *Science, 275*, 671–674.

McGlinchey-Berroth, R., Milberg, W. P., Verfaellie, M., Alexander, M., & Kilduff, P. T. (1993). Semantic processing in the neglected visual field: Evidence from a lexical decision task. *Cognitive Neuropsychology, 10*, 79–108.

Mesulam, M. M. (1981). A cortical network for directed attention and unilateral neglect. *Annals of Neurology, 10*, 309–325.

Milliken, B., & Tipper, S. P. (1998). Attention and inhibition. In H. E. Pashler (Ed.), *Attention,* (pp. 191–221). Hove, UK: Psychology Press.

Neill, W. T., Valdes, L., & Terry, K. M. (1995). Selective attention and the inhibitory control of cognition. In F. N. Dempster & C. J. Brainerd (Eds.), *Interference and inhibition in cognition,* (pp. 207–261). San Diego, CA: Academic Press.

Neisser, U. (1967). *Cognitive Psychology.* New York: Appleton-Century-Crofts.

Neisser, U., & Becklen, R. (1975). Selective looking: Attending to visually specified events. *Cognitive Psychology, 7*, 480–494.

Nobre, A. C., Sebestyen, G. N., Gitelman, D. R., Mesulam, M. M., Frackowiak, R. S. J., & Frith, C. D. (1997). Functional localization of the system for visuospatial attention using positron emission tomography. *Brain, 120*, 515–533.

Pizzamiglio, L., Frasca, R., Guariglia, C., Incoccia, C., & Antonucci, G. (1990). Effects of optokinetic stimulation in patients with visual neglect. *Cerebral Cortex, 26*, 535–540.

Posner, M. I. (1980). Orienting of attention. *Quarterly Journal of Experimental Psychology, 32*, 3–25,.

Posner, M. I., & Cohen, Y. A. (1984). Components of visual orienting. In H. Bouma & D. G. Bouwhuis (Eds.), *Attention and Performance X,* (pp. 531–556). Hillsdale, NJ: Lawrence Erlbaum.

Posner, M. I., & Dehaene, S. (1994). Attentional networks. Trends in *Neuroscience, 17*, 75–79.

Posner, M. I., Inhoff, A. W., Friedrich, F. J., & Cohen, A. (1987). Isolating attentional systems: A cognitive-anatomical analysis. *Psychobiology, 15*, 107–121.

Posner, M. I., & Petersen, S. E. (1990). The attention system of the human brain. *Annual Review of Neuroscience, 13*, 25–42.

Posner, M. I., Rafal, R. D., Choate, L. S., & Vaughan, J. (1985). Inhibition of return: Neural basis and function. *Cognitive Neuropsychology, 2*, 211–228.

Posner, M. I., Walker, J. A., Friedrich, F. J., & Rafal, R. D. (1984). Effects of parietal lobe injury on covert orienting of visual attention. *Journal of Neuroscience, 4*, 1863–1874.

Rafal, R. D. (1998). Neglect. In R. Parasuraman (Ed.), *The attentive brain,* (pp. 489–525). Cambridge, MA: MIT Press.

Rafal, R. D., Calabresi, P. A., Brennan, C. W., & Sciolto, T. K. (1989). Saccade preparation inhibits reorienting to recently attended locations. *Journal of Experimental Psychology, Human Perception & Performance, 15*, 673–685.

Rafal, R. D., & Henik, A. (1994). In D. Dagenbach & T. H. Carr (Eds.), *Inhibitory processes in attention, memory, and language,* (pp. 1–51). San Diego, CA: Academic Press.

Rafal, R. D., & Henik, A., & Smith, J. (1991). Extrageniculate contribution to reflex visual orienting in normal humans: A temporal hemifield advantage. *Journal of Cognitive Neuroscience, 3, 351–358.*

Rafal, R. D., Posner, M. I., Friedman, J. H., Innhoff, A. W., & Bernstein, E. (1988). Orienting of visual attention in progressive supranuclear palsy. *Brain, 111,* 267–280.

Rapp, B. C. & Caramazza, A. (1991). Spatially determined deficits in letter and word processing. *Cognitive Neuropsychology, 8,* 275–311.

Raymond, J. E., Shapiro, K. L., & Arnell, K. M. (1992). Temporary suppression of visual processing in an RSVP task: An attentional blink? *Journal of Experimental Psychology: Human Perception & Performance, 18,* 849–860.

Riddoch, M. J., & Humphreys, G. W. (1982). The effect of cueing on unilateral neglect. *Neuropsychologia, 21,* 589–599.

Riddoch, M. J., & Humphreys, G. W. (1987). Perceptual and action systems in unilateral visual neglect. In M. Jeannerod (Ed.), *Neurophysiological and neuropsychological aspects of spatial neglect,* (pp. 151–181). Amsterdam: North-Holland.

Riggio, L., Bello, A., & Umiltà, C. (1998). Inhibitory and facilitatory effects of cue onset and offset. *Psychological Research, 61,* 107–118.

Rizzolatti, G., Berti, A., & Gallese, V. (in press). Spatial neglect: Neurophysiological bases, cortical circuits and theories. In F. Boller & J. Grafman (Eds.), *Handbook of neuropsychology.* Amsterdam: Elsevier.

Rizzolatti, G., Matelli, M., & Pavesi, G. (1983). Deficits in attention and movement following the removal of postarcuate (area 6) and prearcuate (area 8) cortex in macaque monkeys. *Brain, 106,* 655–673.

Rizzolatti, G., Riggio, L., Dascola, I., & Umiltà, C. (1987). Reorienting attention across the horizontal and vertical meridians: Evidence in favor of a premotor theory of attention. *Neuropsychologia, 25,* 31–40.

Rizzolatti, G., Riggio, L., & Sheliga, B. M. (1994). Space and selective attention. In C. Umiltà & M. Moscovitch (Eds.), *Attention and performance XV,* (pp. 231–265). Cambridge, MA: MIT Press.

Robertson, I. H., & Marshall, J. C. (Eds.) (1993). *Unilateral neglect: Clinical and experimental studies.* Hillsdale, NJ: Lawrence Erlbaum.

Robertson, L. C. (1998). Visuospatial attention and parietal function: Their role in object perception. In R. Parasuraman (Ed.), *The attentive brain,* (pp. 257–278). Cambridge, MA: MIT Press.

Rock, I., & Guttman, D. (1981). The effect of inattention on form perception. *Journal of Experimental Psychology: Human Perception & Performance, 7,* 275–285.

Rode, G., & Perenin, M. T. (1994). Temporary remission of representational hemineglect through vestibular stimulation. *Neuroreport, 5,* 869–872.

Roelfsema, P. R., Lamme, V. A. F., & Sperkreijse, H. (1997). Object-based attention in the primary visual cortex of the macaque monkey. *Nature, 395,* 376–381.

Rosen, A. C., Rao, S. M., Caffarra, P., Scaglioni, A., Bobholz, J. A., Woodley, S. J., Hammeke, T. A., Cunningham, J. M., Prieto, T. E., & Binder, J. R. (1999) Neural basis of endogenous and exogenous orienting: A functional MRI study. *Journal of Cognitive Neuroscience, 11,* 135–152.

Rugg, M. D., Milner, A. D., Lines, C. R., & Phalp, R. (1987). Modulation of visual event-related potentials by spatial and non-spatial visual selective attention. *Neuropsychologia, 25,* 85–96.

Sapir, A., Soroker, N., Berger, A., & Henik, A. (1999). Inhibition of return in spatial attention: Direct evidence for collicular generation. *Nature Neuroscience, 2,* 1053–1054.

Shapiro, K., Hillstrom, A. P., & Husain, M. (in press). Selective attention to object and time. In F. Boller, J. Grafman (Eds.), *Handbook of neuropsychology.* Amsterdam: Elsevier.

Shapiro, K. L., & Raymond, J. E. (1994). Temporal allocation of visual attention: Inhibition or interference? In D. Dagenbach & T. H. Carr (Eds.), *Inhibitory processes in attention, memory, and language,* (pp. 151–188). San Diego, CA: Academic Press.

Sheliga, B. M., Craighero, L., Riggio, L., & Rizzolatti, G. (1997). Effects of spatial attention on directional manual and ocular responses. *Experimental Brain Research, 114,* 339–351.

Sheliga, B. M., Riggio, L., & Rizzolatti, G. (1994). Orienting of attention and eye movements. *Experimental Brain Research, 98,* 507–522.

Simion, F., Valenza, E., Umiltà, C., & Dalla Barba, B. (1995). Inhibition of return in newborns is temporal-nasal asymmetrical. *Infant Behavior & Development, 18,* 189–194.

Snyder, L. H., Batista, A. P., & Andersen, R. A. (1997). Coding of intention in the posterior parietal cortex. *Nature, 386,* 167–170.

Stroop, J. R. (1935).Studies of interference in serial verbal reactions. *Journal of Experimental Psychology, 18,* 643–662.

Stuss, D. T., Toth, J. P., Franchi, D., Alexander, M. P., Tipper, S., & Criack, F. I. M. (1999). Dissociation of attentional processes in patients with focal frontal and posterior lesions. *Neuropsychologia, 37,* 1005–1027.

Sullivan, M. P., Faust, M. E., & Balota, D. (1995). Identity-negative priming in old adults and individuals with dementia of the Alzheimer's type. *Neuropsychology, 9,* 537–555.

Tipper, S. P., & Behrmann, M. (1996). Object-centered not scene-based visual neglect. *Journal of Experimental Psychology: Human Perception & Performance, 22,* 1261–1278.

Tipper, S. P., & Cranston, M. (1985). Selective attention and priming: Inhibitory and facilitatory effects of ignored primes. *Quarterly Journal of Experimental Psychology, 37A,* 591–611.

Tipper, S. P., Driver, J., & Weaver, B. (1991). Object-centred inhibition of return of visual attention. *Quarterly Journal of Experimental Psychology, 43A,* 289–298.

Tipper, S. P., Jordan, H., & Weaver, B. (1999). Scene-based and object-centered inhibition of return: Evidence for dual orienting mechanisms. *Perception & Psychophysics, 61,* 50–60.

Tipper, S. P., Reuter-Lorenz, P. A., Rafal, R., Starrveldt, Y., Ro, T., Egly, R., Danzinger, S., & Weaver, B. (1997). Object-based facilitation and inhibition from visual orienting in the human split-brain. *Journal of Experimental Psychology, Human Perception & Performance, 23,* 1522–1532.

Tipper, S. P., Weaver, B., Jerreat, L. M., & Burak, A. L. (1994). Object-based and environment-based inhibition of return. *Journal of Experimental Psychology: Human Perception & Performance, 20,* 478–499.

Treisman, A. (1988). Features and objects. *Quarterly Journal of Experimental Psychology, 40A,* 201–237.

Treisman, A., & Gelade, G. (1980). A feature integration theory of attention. *Cognitive Psychology, 12,* 97–136.

Umiltà, C. (1995). Domain specific forms of neglect. *Journal of Clinical and Experimental Neuropsychology, 17,* 209–219.

Umiltà, C. (in press). Visuospatial attention. In F. Boller & J. Grafman, *Handbook of neuropsychology.* Amsterdam: Elsevier.

Umiltà, C., Castiello, U., Fontana, M., & Vestri, A. (1995). Object-centred orienting of attention. *Visual Cognition, 2,* 165–182.

Umiltà, C., Riggio, L., Dascola, I., & Rizzolatti, G. (1991). Differential effects of central and peripheral cues on the reorienting of spatial attention. *European Journal of Cognitive Psychology, 3,* 247–267.

Valdes-Sosa, M., Bobes, M. A., Rodriguez, V., & Pinilla, T. (1998). Switching attention without shifting the spotlight: Object-based attentional modulation of brain potentials. *Journal of Cognitive Neuroscience, 10,* 137–151.

Valenza, E., Simion, F., & Umiltà, C. (1994). Inhibition of return in newborns. *Infant Behavior & Development, 17,* 293–302.

Vandenberghe, R., Duncan, J., Dupont, P., Ward, R., Poline, J. B., Bormans, G., Michiels, J., Mortelmans, L., & Orban, G. A. (1997). Attention to one or two features in left and right visual field: A positron emission tomography study. *Journal of Neuroscience, 17,* 3739–3750.

van der Heijden, A. H. C., & Eerland, E. (1973). The effects of cueing in a visual signal detection task. *Quarterly Journal of Experimental Psychology, 25,* 496–503.

Vuillemieur, P., Valenza, N., Mayer, E., Reverdin, A., & Landis, T. (198). Near and far space in unilateral neglect. *Annals of Neurology, 43,* 406–410.

Walker, R. (1995). Spatial and object-based neglect. *Neuroca, 1,* 189–207.

Ward, R., Goodrich, S., & Driver, J. (1994). Grouping reduces visual extinction: Neuropsychological evidence for weight-linkage in visual selection. *Visual Cognition, 1,* 101–129.

Wociulik, E., & Kanwisher, N. (1999). The generality of parietal involvement in visual attention. *Neuron, 23,* 747–764.

Yamaguchi, S., & Kobayashi, S. (1998). Contributions of the dopaminergic system to voluntary and automatic orienting of visuospatial attention. *Journal of Neuroscience, 18,* 1869–1878.

Yantis, S., & Johnston, J. C. (1990). On the locus of visual selection: Evidence from focused attention tasks. *Journal of Experimental Psychology: Human Perception & Performance, 16,* 135–149.

7

Consciousness

Martha J. Farah

Cognitive neuropsychology is founded on the assumption that normal and disordered cognition are each best understood in relation to each other. One of the clearest examples of how neuropsychological impairments can illuminate our understanding of normal cognition is in the area of consciousness. Much of the renewed interest in consciousness, on the part of scientifically-minded psychologists, followed from discoveries made with brain-damaged patients in the 1970s. Research with amnesic patients revealed that certain types of learning were preserved, despite the patients' unawareness of the acquired information (Warrington & Weiskrantz, 1970), and research with cortically blind patients showed residual visual abilities of which the patients were also unaware (Poppel, Held, & Frost, 1973). Soon these neuropsychological dissociations between conscious and unconscious information processing were joined by a host of others affecting visual perception, and research on consciousness developed to encompass patient-based research, behavioral methods with normal subjects, and functional neuroimaging of both patients and normal subjects.

The present chapter reviews the state of patient-based consciousness research in the area of vision, building on an earlier review (Farah, 1994) to include more recent behavioral and imaging work with patients.

NEURAL CORRELATES OF CONSCIOUS AWARENESS: TYPES OF ACCOUNTS

Neuropsychological dissociations between perception and conscious awareness of perception are of interest because of what they can tell us about the neural correlates of conscious awareness. They allow us to ask: What is different, or missing, in a patient who perceives without awareness, compared to a normal person who perceives with awareness? Various answers to this question have been proposed, and can be grouped into three broad categories (Farah, 1994), explained below. Like almost any attempt to reduce many things to a few things, this system of categorizing does not do perfect justice to all aspects of the hypotheses. Nevertheless, it does bring out some fundamental similarities and differences among them, which I believe are just as important as the details of each, though are less often discussed.

Consciousness as the Privileged Tole of Particular Brain Systems

The most straightforward account of the relation between consciousness and the brain is to conceive of particular brain systems as mediating conscious awareness. The great grandfather of this type of account is Descartes' theory of mind–body interaction through the pineal gland. Patterns of brain activity impinging on the pineal gland, unlike patterns of activity in other parts of the brain, were consciously experienced. The most direct and influential descendent of this tradition is the DICE (dissociated interactions and conscious experience) model of Schacter, McAndrews, and Moscovitch (1988, 1992), shown in Figure 7.1. Although Schacter et al. do not propose a localization for the conscious awareness system (CAS), the account does suppose that there is some brain system or systems, the CAS, separate from the brain systems concerned with perception, cognition, and action, whose activity is necessary only for conscious experience. Within this framework, the vision without awareness can be explained very simply in terms of a disconnection between visual systems and the CAS.

The brain systems that play a privileged role in mediating conscious awareness could also carry out other functions as well. For example, Gazzaniga (1988) attributes many of the differences between what one would call conscious and unconscious behavior to the involvement of left hemisphere interpretive mechanisms, closely related to speech. Thus, unconscious perception could be explained as the failure of a perceptual representation to access critical areas of the left hemisphere. For brevity, this first class of accounts will be referred to as *privileged role* accounts, because according to them, only certain systems play a role in mediating conscious awareness.

Consciousness as a State of Integration among Distinct Brain Systems

In contrast to the first type of approach, the next two types attempt to explain the relations between conscious and unconscious information processing in terms of the dynamic states of

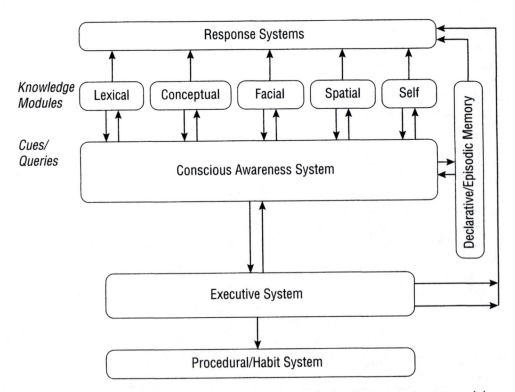

Figure 7.1: The DICE (dissociated interactions and conscious experience) model of Schacter, McAndrews, and Moscovitch (1988). Reprinted with permission of the Oxford University Press.

brain systems, rather than in terms of the enduring roles of particular brain systems them-selves. Kinsbourne's (1988) "integrated field theory" is a good example of an approach that emphasizes integration as the underlying basis of conscious awareness. According to Kinsbourne, conscious awareness is a brain state in which the various modality-specific perceptions, recol-lections, current actions, and action plans are mutually consistent. Normally, the interactions among these disparate brain systems automatically bring the ensemble into an integrated state, continually updated to reflect the current information available in all parts of the brain. However, anatomical disconnection can prevent integration, as in split-brain patients who may have two separate awarenesses, or damage to one system may weaken its influence on the global brain state, thus preventing it from updating the contents of awareness, as when neglect patients are unaware of stimuli in the neglected hemifield. Thus, vision without awareness can be explained either by disconnection of or damage to the visual system, preventing it from participating in the integrated patterns of activity over the rest of the brain.

Related accounts have been proposed by Crick and Koch (1990) and by Damasio (1989). Crick and Koch specifically focused on the issue of visual awareness, and equated the phenom-enon of visual awareness with the binding together of the different, separately represented visual properties of a stimulus (e.g., color, shape, depth, motion) into a single integrated percept. They drew heavily on the ideas of Singer and colleagues (e.g., Singer & Gray, 1995) concerning synchronized oscillations in visual cortex. According to Crick and Koch, syncronization across visual areas could enable both binding and conscious awareness of stimuli. Damasio has proposed a similar identification of binding with conscious awareness, within and beyond the visual system. The type of binding he discusses operates across different modality-specific representations of an object, as well as within each modality-specific system. In the remainder of the chapter, accounts of this second type will be referred to as *integration* accounts.

Consciousness as a Graded Property of Neural Information Processing

Information representation in neural networks is not "all or none," such that a stimulus must either be represented within the visual system or not. Rather, it may be partially represented, as a result of either impoverished input or damage to the network itself. The third view of the relation between brain mechanisms and conscious awareness is based on the observation that, in normal and in brain-damaged subjects, there is a correlation between the "quality" of the perceptual representation and the likelihood of conscious awareness. Experiments on sublimi-nal perception in normal subjects invariably dissociate perception and awareness by using very brief, masked stimulus presentations, by dividing attention, or by embedding the stimulus to be perceived in a high level of noise. In other words, to reduce the likelihood of conscious awareness in normal subjects, one must use experimental manipulations known to degrade the quality of the perceptual representation. Similarly, one could argue that in many if not all of the neuropsychological syndromes in which visual perception has been dissociated from con-scious awareness, patients' visual performance reflects a degree of impairment in visual per-ception per se, not merely the stripping away of conscious experience from a normal percept (e.g., Farah, Monheit, & Wallace, 1991; Farah, O'Reilly, & Vecera, 1993). Consciousness may be associated only with the higher-quality end of the continuum of degrees of representation. This type of account will hereafter be referred to as a *quality of representation* account.

It is worth noting that these different types of explanation are not necessarily mutually exclusive. For example, if a particular part of the brain were needed to enable the activity of widespread regions to become integrated, then there would be a sense in which the first type of explanation and the second were both correct. Alternatively, if a representation in one part of the brain were degraded, it might be less able to participate in an integrated state with other parts of the brain, in which case both the second and third types of explanation would be correct.

SPECIFIC SYNDROMES

In the next six sections of this chapter, I will offer brief reviews of what is known about perception-awareness dissociations in six different syndromes.

Blindsight

Blindsight is the term coined by Weiskrantz (1986) and colleagues for the visual abilities that are retained by some patients after lesions to primary visual cortex. By conventional testing, the regions of the visual field formerly represented by the damaged cortex are blind in these patients. For example, destruction of the right primary visual cortex leads to left hemianopia—blindness on the left half of the visual field. However, pioneering studies by Poppel, Weiskrantz, and others showed significant residual visual abilities on the hemianopic side (e.g., Poppel et al., 1973; Weiskrantz, 1986; Weiskrantz, Warrington, Sanders, & Marshall, 1974). For example, one patient was able to point to the locations of stimuli, to detect movement, to discriminate the orientation of lines and gratings, and to discriminate shapes such as X's and O's.

The pattern of preserved and impaired abilities in blindsight varies from patient to patient. Detection and localization of light, and detection of motion are invariably preserved to some degree. In addition, many patients can discriminate orientation, shape, direction of movement, and flicker. Color vision mechanisms also appear to be preserved in some cases (Brent, Kennard, & Ruddock, 1994).

Blindsight has been investigated by a variety of methods beyond the traditional psychophysical method used by its earliest investigators. One important methodological innovation has been the use of indirect tests of visual function, in which the patient does not report on the "unseen" stimulus per se, but performs a task in which the influence of that stimulus can be measured. For example, Rafal, Smith, Krantz, Cohen, and Brennan (1990) studied the effects of a second stimulus in the blind field on the speed with which hemianopic subjects could make a saccade to a stimulus in their normal field. For normal subjects and hemianopic subjects, the second stimulus was found to inhibit the saccade, showing that it was perceived. One of the most interesting aspects of Rafal et al.'s results is that the second stimulus had an inhibitory effect for the hemianopic patients only when it was presented to the temporal half of the retina, that is, to the half of the retina that projects to the superior colliculus.

Marcel (1998) used an indirect method to demonstrate the most spectacular blindsight capability of all in two patients he tested, namely word reading. Words such as *money* or *river* presented in the patients' blind hemifields were said to bias their interpretation of subsequently presented ambiguous words, such as *bank*.

Cowey and Stoerig (1997) developed an animal model of awareness in blindsight. They taught monkeys to report the number of stimuli they perceived, or the presence of a single stimulus, by different manual responses. After unilateral removal of primary visual cortex, these monkeys retained the ability to reach for stimuli in the affected hemifield, thus demonstrating preserved vision. However, the monkeys responded in the number and detection tasks as if stimuli presented in the affected hemifield were not present, in effect reporting that they did not see such stimuli. Functional neuroimaging has also been brought to bear on the phenomenon of blindsight. Previously, structural scans were used to argue against the use of residual primary visual cortex by patients with blindsight. Functional neuroimaging affords a stronger test, and has so far failed to detect activation of primary visual cortex (Barbur, Watson, Frackowiak, & Zeki, 1993; Sahraie et al., 1997; Stoerig, Kleinschmidt, & Frahm, 1998).

The mechanism of blindsight has been a controversial topic. Some researchers have argued that the phenomenon is mediated, directly or indirectly, by residual functioning of primary visual cortex, and should therefore be considered an artifact. Campion, Latto, and Smith (1983) alleged that striate cortex is involved either indirectly, by light from the affected region of the visual field reflecting off other surfaces into other regions of the visual field, or directly, by residual functioning of lesioned areas of primary visual cortex. The latter idea is an example of a quality of representation account. Fendrich, Wessinger, and Gazzaniga (1992) have also argued that preserved islands of striate cortex, which could escape detection by normal methods of measuring scotomata, enable blindsight performance. These accounts are plausible in general outline, but fail to account for psychophysical and neuroimaging data from a variety of different labs. For example, case DB (Weiskrantz, 1986) can perceive black figures on a bright background, from which scattered light would be little help. Blindsight abilities have also been documented in hemidecorticate patients, who clearly have no residual visual cortex. The neuroimaging results mentioned earlier failed to find evidence of activity in the primary visual cortex of blindsight patients. Finally, recall the results of Rafal et al. (1990) on inhibition of saccades by stimuli presented to the blind field. This result has the important property of demonstrating subcortical mediation of blindsight by a positive finding, namely nasal-temporal asymmetries, rather than by a null result concerning primary visual cortex involvement.

If blindsight is not mediated by primary visual cortex, then what neural systems are involved? Initially, the answer was thought to be the subcortical visual system, consisting of projections from the retina to the superior colliculus, and on to the pulvinar and cortical visual areas. This is an instance of a privileged role account, in that both cortical and subcortical visual systems are hypothesized to mediate various types of visual information processing, but the mediation of visual awareness is taken to be the privileged role of the cortical visual system. There is evidence in favor of the subcortical mediation hypothesis for at least some blindsight abilities. The close functional similarities between the known specializations of the subcortical visual system and many of the preserved abilities in blindsight, such as detection and localization of onsets and moving stimuli (e.g., Schiller & Koerner, 1971), constitutes one source of evidence. In addition, the nasal-temporal asymmetries found in Rafal et al.'s (1990) study are indicative of the collicular mediation.

Cowey and Stoerig (1989) have suggested that the cortical visual system, too, mediates blindsight. They marshaled evidence, from their own experiments and other research, of a population of cells in the LGN that project directly to extrastriate visual cortex, and which could therefore bring stimulus information into such areas as V4 and MT in the absence of primary visual cortex. This type of mechanism fits most naturally with the quality of representation hypotheses. According to this account, many of the same visual association areas are engaged in blindsight as in normal vision. What distinguishes normal vision and visual performance without awareness is that in the latter only a subset of the normal inputs arrive in extrastriate visual cortex. The remaining inputs are both fewer in number, and lacking whatever type of processing is normally accomplished in primary visual cortex. Consciousness awareness may only occur when these areas are operating on more complete and more fully processed visual representations.

Evidence for this hypothesis is still preliminary. In addition to the demonstration of anatomical connections between the LGN and the extrastriate visual areas, their functional significance in blindsight is hinted at by a comparison between the blindsight abilities of patients with circumscribed striate lesions and with damage to visual association areas as well. The latter group is made up of patients who have undergone hemidecortication, the removal of an entire hemisphere. Stoerig and Cowey (1997) review the findings from a number of studies that are reasonably consistent with the generalization that the ability to make explicit judgements of properties such as motion and color depends on intact visual association cortex.

In sum, blindsight is not the result of degraded normal vision, if "normal" is taken to mean relying on primary visual cortex. It is also clearly not a single homogeneous phenomenon: At the level of preserved visual abilities, subjective experience, and neural mechanisms, there is apparently much variation from subject to subject. An important research goal in this area is to establish correspondences among these three levels of individual difference, as a means of characterizing the functional and experiential roles of different components of the visual system. In the meantime, we can discern two main types of mechanisms that may account for the dissociations between visual abilities and conscious awareness in blindsight: Subcortical visual mechanisms, and direct projections from the LGN to extrastriate areas.

Preserved Vision for Action in Apperceptive Agnosia

Patients with apperceptive agnosia have a profound impairment in shape perception, failing to discriminate squares from circles or X's from O's, despite good perception of local visual qualities such as brightness and color. In one such patient, DF, researchers have documented a surprising degree of preserved vision when the response involves acting upon an object rather than making a conscious judgement about it. (See also Buxbaum & Coslett, this volume.)

The earliest clue that DF had some degree of preserved form processing came from observations of her reaching behavior. Whereas she could not accurately describe or compare the sizes, shapes, and orientations of objects, her motoric interactions with the world seemed normal, including shaping her hand to the proper grip size while reaching to grasp a door knob or a pencil. Milner, Goodale, and colleagues (Milner et al., 1991; Goodale, Milner, Jakobson, & Carey, 1991; Milner & Goodale, 1995) formalized this observation in a series of ingenious tests, for example comparing DF's hand motions when asked to put a card through a slot, with the slot at different orientations, and when asked to describe the angle of the slot or to turn a second slot to match the angle of the first. Figure 7.2 shows the difference in accuracy between the two ways of accessing her perception of orientation, by conscious judgement or matching, and by action. The former is variable and inaccurate; the latter flawless.

An interesting boundary condition on this dissociation was demonstrated by Goodale et al., 1994), who repeated the slot experiment with a T-shaped opening. DF was unable to insert T-shaped blocks into the opening, suggesting that the preserved vision for action does not extend to full-blown shape perception.

Milner and Goodale (1995) propose an anatomical disconnection in DF between early visual representations and higher level representations of object appearance in the temporal lobe. This is responsible for DF's failure on explicit judgements of shape, size and orientation, but allows the dorsal visual stream to compute at least some of these properties for purposes of action programming. Although the diffuse nature of damage from carbon monoxide makes anatomical claims inherently uncertain in cases like this, an MRI showed the greatest damage in this case to ventral visual association cortex, consistent with Milner and Goodale's claim. This explanation is an example of a privileged role account, because both dorsal and ventral streams are hypothesized to be capable of representing size and orientation, but only the ventral representations support conscious awareness of those characteristics.

Implicit Object Recognition in Associative Visual Agnosia

In associative visual agnosia, object recognition is impaired despite adequate elementary perceptual abilities and general intellectual functioning (see also Riddoch & Humphreys, this volume). Unlike apperceptive agnosia, shape perception appears to be grossly preserved. Only when the need to represent complex shapes or subtly different shapes arises do associative agnosics experience difficulty, and this difficulty is presumably what underlies their object recognition impairment. In a small number of cases of associative visual agnosia, patients have

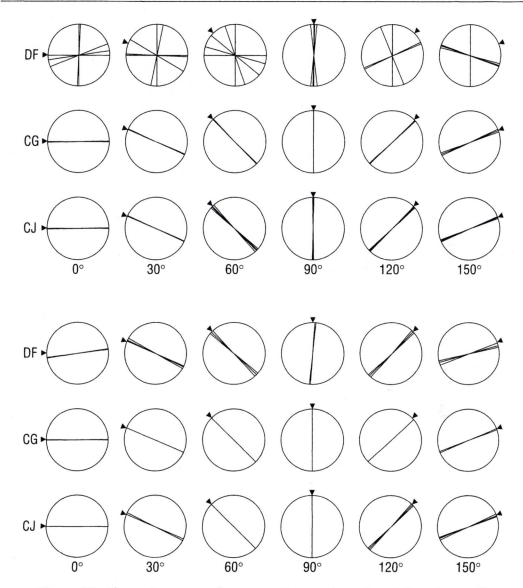

Figure 7.2: The performance of apperceptive agosic patient D.F. and control subjects at explicit judgments of slot orientation (top) and at manipulating a card to fit through slots of the same orientations (bottom), demonstrating preserved orientation perception for the guidance of action. Adapted from M.A. Goodale and D.A. Milner, "Separate visual pathways for perception and action," Trends in Neuroscience, 15(1), 1992, with permission from Elsevier Science.

been shown to retain some implicit recognition of objects which, by standard testing methods, they cannot recognize.

The earliest observation of implicit object recognition in associative agnosia was reported by Taylor and Warrington (1971), who noted that a severely agnosic patient was able to turn misoriented pictures to their upright orientation, despite being unable to recognize them, and to sort unrecognized pictures into semantic categories. Todd Feinberg and colleagues carried out a detailed examination of a similar patient (Feinberg, Dyckes-Berke, Miner, & Roane, 1995). Depite a severe impairment in naming, describing, or pantomiming the use of visually presented objects, their patient performed well above chance in multiple choice tests such as the one shown in Figure 7.3. The patient's task was to look first at the top picture, then find the picture most related to it in the bottom row. The number of choices was varied, which influenced the difficulty of the task. Feinberg and colleagues also asked the patient both to assess her knowledge of the top picture before choosing a picture from the bottom row, and to assess the accuracy of her choices after having chosen. The two judgements provide direct measures of her awareness of perception, and will therefore be discussed in the following section. Of interest here is that despite her profound agnosia, when the choice set was limited to a relatively small number of pictures the patient performed above chance, and furthermore, the smaller the choice set the better the performance.

Like all associative visual agnosics, this patient denied recognizing most stimuli; consistent with this, her assessment of her recognition, prior to performing the multiple choice task, was a poor predictor of her accuracy. In other words, she was unaware of her perception. In contrast, once she had chosen a picture in the multiple choice task, she had some basis for assessing her accuracy. Even on trials for which she had rated herself as entirely unable to recognize the picture at the outset, once she had made a choice she was able to assess its accuracy to some degree, stating she was sure of her response on almost 80 percent of the trials on which she was correct compared to only 25 percent of the trials in which she was not.

Feinberg and colleagues argue that the patient's reasonably good awareness of her accuracy is not consistent with two separate systems, one for awareness and one for recognition, as hypothesized in the DICE model (Schacter et al., 1988, 1992) for example. They point to several aspects of the case that favor the hypothesis of degraded object representations, underlying both recognition and awareness: the above-chance performance with multiple choices, the dependence of the multiple choice performance on the number of choices, and the correlation between the patient's judgements of her own knowledge and of her performance with her performance accuracy. The idea that degraded object representations can support performance and self-assessment of accuracy in sufficiently constrained tasks, but can support neither in open-ended tasks, is an example of a quality of representation account.

Figure 7.3: A picture association task on which an associative agnosic performed moderately well, despite her inability to assess her own recognition of the object to be associated. Adapted from M. J. Farah and T. E. Feinberg, "Perception and Awareness," in T. E. Feinberg and M.J. Farah (eds.), *Behavioral Neurology and Neuropschology*, New York, McGraw-Hill, 1997.

Covert Recognition of Faces in Prosopagnosia

Prosopagnosia is a form of visual agnosia in which face recognition is disproportionately impaired. In some cases of prosopagnosia there is a dramatic dissociation between the loss of face recognition ability as measured by standard tests of face recognition and patients' own introspections, and the apparent preservation of face recognition when tested by certain indirect tests. (See also De Haan, this volume.)

The literature on covert recognition in prosopagnosia is large, dating back to the early 1980s and involving researchers from a number of different labs who were quickly drawn in by this remarkable phenomenon. Only a small sample of the relevant findings will be summarized here. One of the most widely-used methods of demonstrating preserved face recognition in prosopagnosia is by the paired-associate face–name relearning task, in which patients are taught to associate the facial photographs of famous people (whom they cannot recognize) with the names of famous people. For some prosopagnosics, fewer learning trials are required when the pairing of names and faces is correct, than when incorrect (e.g., Robert Redford's face paired with the name "Harrison Ford"). De Haan, Young, and Newcombe (1987a) showed this pattern of performance held even when the stimulus faces were selected from among those that the patient had been unable to identify in a pre-experiment stimulus screening test.

Evidence of covert recognition has also come from reaction time tasks in which the familiarity or identity of faces are found to influence processing time. In a visual identity match task with simultaneously presented pairs of faces, de Haan, Young, and Newcombe (1987a) found that a prosopagnosic patient was faster at matching pairs of previously familiar faces than unfamiliar faces, as is true of normal subjects. In contrast, he was unable to name any of the previously familiar faces.

In another RT study, de Haan, Young, and Newcombe (1987b; also 1987a) found evidence that photographs of faces could evoke covert semantic knowledge of the depicted person, despite the inability of the prosopagnosic patient to report such information about the person when tested overtly. Their task was to categorize a printed name as belonging to an actor or a politician as quickly as possible. On some trials an irrelevant (i.e., to be ignored) photograph of an actor's or polician's face was simultaneously presented. Normal subjects are slower to categorize the names when the faces come from a different occupation category relative to a no-photograph baseline. Even though their prosopagnosic patient was severely impaired at categorizing the faces overtly as belonging to actors or politicians, he showed the same pattern of interference from different-category faces.

Prosopagnosic patients who manifest covert recognition appear to lack the subjective experience of recognition, at least for many of the faces for which they show covert recognition. Note that these patients may occasionally recognize a face overtly, that is, assign it the correct name and express a degree of confidence that they know who the person is. However, this happens rarely, and the dissociation between covert recognition and awareness of recognition holds for many faces that they fail to identify and for which they report no sense of familiarity.

There are several competing explanations for covert recognition in prosopagnosia. The oldest is that the face recognition system is intact in these patients, but has been prevented from conveying information to other brain mechanisms necessary for conscious awareness. An explicit statement of this view comes from de Haan, Bauer, and Greve (1992), who proposed the model shown in Figure 7.4. According to their model, the face-specific visual and mnemonic processing of a face (carried out within the "face-processing module") proceeds normally in covert recognition, but the results of this process cannot access the CAS because of a lesion at location number 1. This account clearly falls into the privileged role category, in that it entails a specific brain system needed for conscious awareness, separate from the brain systems needed to carry out perception and cognition.

Another type of explanation was put forth by Bauer (1984), who suggested that there may be

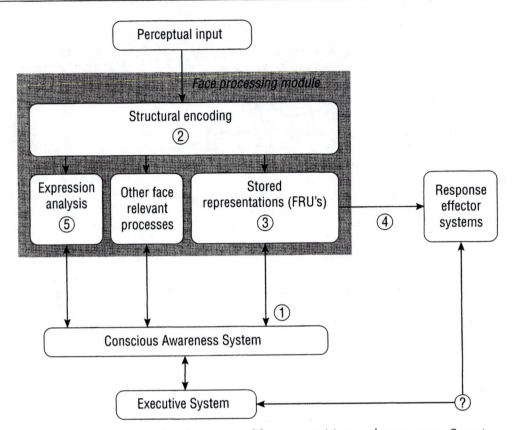

Figure 7.4: Functional architecture of face recognition and awareness. Covert face recognition is attributed to a lesion at locus 1. Adapted from De Haan, Bauer, and Greeve (1992).

two neural systems capable of face recognition, only one of which is associated with conscious awareness. According to Bauer, the ventral visual areas damaged in prosopagnosic patients are the location of normal conscious face recognition. But the dorsal visual areas are hypothesized to be capable of face recognition as well, although they do not mediate conscious recognition but, instead, affective responses to faces. Covert recognition is explained as the isolated functioning of the dorsal face system. This account also fits into the general category of consciousness as a privileged property of particular brain systems. It is analogous to theorizing about the subcortical visual system in blindsight, and the dorsal visual system in apperceptive agnosia, in that two systems are postulated, which carry out related but distinct visual functions, and only one of which is endowed with conscious awareness.

Tranel and Damasio (1988) interpret covert recognition as the normal activation of visual face representations, which is prevented by the patients' lesions from activating representations in other areas of the brain, such as representations of the people's voices in auditory areas, affective valences in limbic areas, names in language areas, and so on. This interpretation is therefore of the second type described earlier, in that it requires an integration of active representations across different brain areas in order for conscious awareness to occur; we cannot be consciously aware of an isolated, modality-specific representation. This idea was recently embodied in a computer simulation of semantic priming effects, in which covert recognition was modelled as a partial disconnection separating intact visual recognition units from the rest of the system, as shown in Figure 7.5 (Burton, Young, Bruce, Johnston, & Ellis, 1991).

The last account of the mechanism by which overt and covert recognition are dissociated is that covert recognition reflects the residual processing capabilities of a damaged, but not obliterated, visual face-recognition system. Randy O'Reilly, Shaun Vecera, and I have argued that lower quality visual information processing is needed to support performance in tests of covert recognition (e.g., to show savings in relearning, and the various RT facilitation and interference effects) relative to the quality of information processing needed to support normal overt recognition performance (e.g., naming a face, sorting faces into those of actors and politicians; Farah et al., 1993; see also O'Reilly & Farah, 1999). This account falls into the third category reviewed earlier, in that the difference between face recognition with and without conscious awareness is the quality of representations activated by the face.

All but the last explanation of covert recognition assume both normal face perception and normal covert recognition in prosopagnosics. However, neither assumption is empirically supported at present. When tested rigorously, face perception in prosopagnosia is not normal (Farah, 1990). As to the question of whether covert recognition is truly normal, appropriate tests have not yet been carried out. When and if they are, a finding of impaired covert recognition would be immediately interpretable, but a finding of normal covert recognition would require further scaling studies with normal subjects to determine whether the normalcy is due to a ceiling effect.

Is there any independent evidence in favor of the quality-of-representation account? In one study, Wallace and Farah (1992) showed that savings in face-name relearning can be obtained with normal subjects who are trained on a set of face-name associations and then allowed to forget these associations over a six-month interval. Presumably normal forgetting does not involve the diverting of intact information from conscious awareness, but rather the degradation of representations (albeit in a different way from prosopagnosia).

Probably the strongest evidence for this view, however, is computational. Farah et al. (1993) trained a neural network, shown in Figure 7.6, to associate "face" patterns with "semantic"

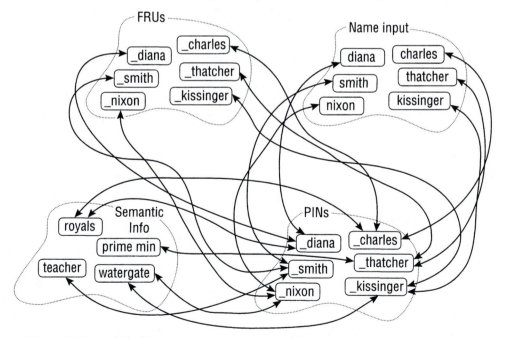

Figure 7.5: Model of face recognition proposed by Burton et al. (1991), in which covert recognition is simulated by attenuating connections between FRUs (face recognition units) and PINs (personal identity nodes). Reproduced with permission from the British Journal of Developmental Psychology, © The British Psychological Society.

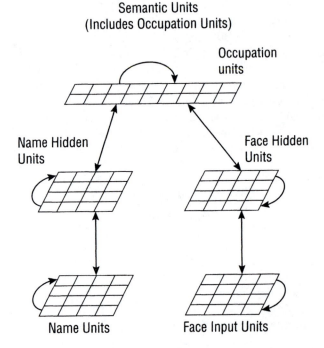

Figure 7.6: Model of face recognition proposed by Farah, O'Reilly, and Vecera (1993), in which covert recognition is simulated by damaging either face input or face hidden units. Copyright © 1993 by the American Psychological Association. Reprinted with permission.

patterns, and to associate these, in turn, with "name" patterns. We found that, at levels of damage to the face representations that led to poor or even chance performance in overt tasks such as naming and occupation categorization, the network showed all of the behavioral covert recognition effects reviewed above: It relearned correct associations faster than novel ones, it completed the visual analysis of familiar faces faster than unfamiliar, and it showed priming and interference from the faces on judgements about names. Figure 7.7a-b shows representative results. More recently, O'Reilly and Farah (1999) simulated several more covert recognition tasks with the same basic model.

Why should a damaged neural network support performance in this range of covert tasks when overt recognition is poor or even at chance? The answer lies in the nature of information representation and processing in distributed, interactive networks. Representations in such networks consist of patterns of activation over a set of units or neurons. These units are highly interconnected, and the extent to which the activation of one unit causes an increase or decrease in the activation of a neighboring unit depends on the "weight" of the connection between them. For the network to learn that a certain face representation goes with a certain name representation, the weights among units in the network are adjusted so that presentation of either the face pattern in the face units or the name pattern in the name units causes the corresponding other pattern to become activated. Upon presentation of the input pattern, all of the units connected with the input units will begin to change their activation in accordance with the activation value of the units to which they are connected and the weights on the connections. As activation propagates though the network, a stable pattern of activation eventually results, determined jointly by the input activation and the pattern of weights among the units of the network.

Our account of covert face recognition is based on the following key idea: The set of the weights in a network that cannot correctly associate patterns because it has never been trained (or has been trained on a different set of patterns) is different in an important way from the set of weights in a network that cannot correctly associate patterns because it has been trained on those patterns and then damaged. The first set of weights is random with respect to the

(a)

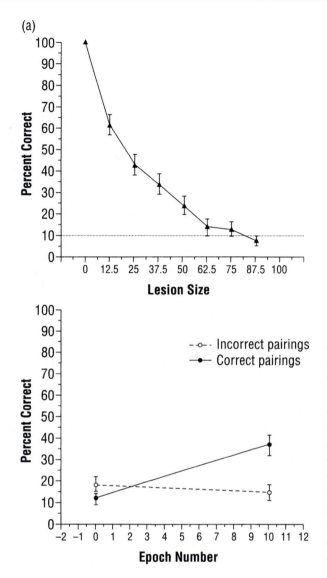

Figure 7.7a: Selected results from the model of Farah, O'Reilly, and Vecera (1993). (a) Performance of model in 10-alternative forced-choice naming task after different amounts of damage to face hidden units (top). Relearning correct and incorrect face-name associations after removal of 75 percent of face-hidden units (bottom). Copyright © 1993 by the American Psychological Association. Reprinted with permission.

associations in question, whereas the second is a subset of the necessary weights. Even if it is an inadequate subset for performing the association, it is not random; it has, "embedded" in it, some degree of knowledge of the associations. Hinton and colleagues (Hinton & Plaut, 1989; Hinton & Sejnowski, 1986) have shown that such embedded knowledge can be demonstrated when the network relearns, suggesting the findings of savings in relearning face-name associations may be explained in this way. In general, consideration of the kinds of tests used to measure covert recognition suggest that the covert measures would be sensitive to this embedded knowledge. The most obvious example is that a damaged network would be expected to relearn associations that it originally knew faster than novel associations because of the nonrandom starting weights. Less obvious, but confirmed by our simulations, the network would settle faster when given previously learned inputs than novel inputs, even though the pattern into which it settles is not correct, because the residual weights come from a set designed to create a stable pattern from that input. Finally, to the extent that the weights continue to activate partial and subthreshold patterns over the nondamaged units in association with the input, then these resultant patterns could prime (i.e., contribute activation towards) the activation of patterns by intact routes.

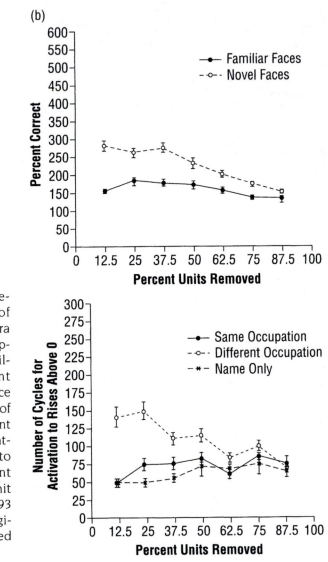

Figure 7.7b: Selected results from the model of Farah, O'Reilly, and Vecera (1993). (b) Speed of perception of familiar and unfamiliar faces after different amounts of damage to face hidden units (top). Effect of faces with same or different occupation on time to categorize a name according to occupation, after different amounts of face-hidden unit damage. Copyright © 1993 by the American Psychological Association. Reprinted with permission.

    The general implication of these ideas is that as a neural network is increasingly damaged, there will be a window of damage in which overt associations between patterns (e.g., faces and names) would be extremely poor while the kinds of performance measures tapped by the covert tasks might remain at high levels.

    In conclusion, all three types of explanation outlined earlier have been advanced to account for covert recognition in prosopagnosia. Many of the explanations would appear to run aground on evidence of perceptual impairment in prosopagnosia, as they maintain that the locus of impairment is post-perceptual. However, the perceptual impairments could conceivably be distinct but associated impairments. The quality of representation explanation has the advantage of accounting for these perceptual impairments, and of accounting for performance in the range of covert recognition tasks. However, not everyone agrees with this (see Young & Burton, 1999, for a dissenting opinion).

Unconscious Perception in Neglect and Extinction

The behavior of patients with neglect and extinction suggests that they do not perceive neglected and extinguished stimuli (see also Umiltà, this volume). However, there is some evidence that, here too, considerable information about neglected and extinguished stimuli may be perceived by some patients. As with covert recognition in prosopagnosia, this information is generally only detectable using indirect tests.

The first suggestion that patients with extinction may see more of the extinguished stimulus than is apparent from their conscious verbal report came from Volpe, LeDoux, and Gazzaniga (1979). They presented four right parietal-damaged extinction patients with pairs of visual stimuli, including drawings of common objects and three-letter words, one in each hemifield. On each trial, subjects were required to perform two types of task: First, to state whether the two stimuli shown were the same or different and second, to name the stimuli. Figure 7.8 shows the stimuli and results from a typical trial. As would be expected, the subjects did poorly at overtly identifying the stimuli on the left. Two subjects failed to name any of the left stimuli correctly, and the other two named less than 50%. In view of this, their performance on the same/different matching task was surprising: Even though this task also requires perception of the left stimulus, subjects achieved between 88% and 100% correct. The same dissociation between identification of the left stimulus and cross-field same/different matching has also been obtained with parietal-damaged neglect patients, whose attentional impairment is so severe that contralesional stimuli may fail to be identified even in the absence of a simultaneously occurring ipsilesional stimulus (Karnath, 1988; Karnath & Hartje, 1987).

Unfortunately, it seems possible that the dissociation between naming and same/different matching could be explained by the differing demands these tasks make on the patient's damaged visual system. Consider the example of the comb and apple, shown in Figure 7.8. If only partial stimulus information were picked up on the left, for example, the perception that

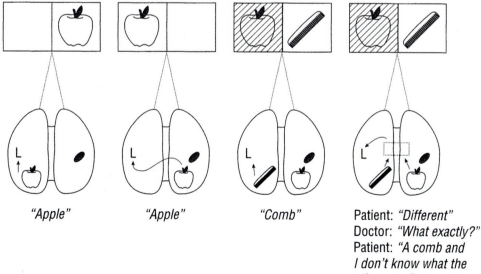

"Apple"   "Apple"   "Comb"   Patient: *"Different"*
Doctor: *"What exactly?"*
Patient: *"A comb and I don't know what the other was."*

Figure 7.8: Typical trials from the experiment of Volpe, LeDoux, and Gazzaniga (1979), showing extinction of the left stimulus with preserved same/different matching. Reprinted by permission of Nature Vol. 282, pp. 722–724. Copyright © 1979 Macmillan Magazines Ltd.

there is something roundish and light-colored, this would be sufficient to enable fairly accurate same/different judgements. However, there are so many roundish, light-colored objects in the world, this partial perception would be of no help in naming the stimulus on the left. My colleagues and I performed two experiments to test the hypothesis that the differential amounts of stimulus information required for same/different matching and overt identification is what causes the dissociation between them (Farah et al., 1991). First, we degraded the left side of the display with a translucent mask and repeated the Volpe et al. experiment with normal subjects. This manipulation was not intended as a simulation of extinction, but rather as a test of our hypothesis concerning the quality of visual information needed in the two kinds of task. Merely depriving normal subjects of some information from the left stimulus produced the same dissociation in normal subjects observed by Volpe et al. in patients with extinction.

Second, we repeated the Volpe et al. (1979) paradigm with extinction patients in its original form, and replicated the original finding, and also in an altered form, in which the overt identification task was administered in a forced-choice format. The purpose of this alteration was to enable us to equate the same/different trials and identification trials for the amount of information needed from the left stimulus. We did this by yoking trials from the two conditions, such that if there was a same/different trial with a triangle and a square, there was an identification trial in which one of these stimuli was presented on the left and the subject was asked "Did you see a triangle or a square?" When same/different matching and identification were equated for their demands on the quality of the subjects' representations of the left stimuli, the dissociation vanished. We concluded that the task of same/different matching and identification differ significantly in their demands on the quality of visual representation. This implies that the results of Volpe et al. are consistent with extinction affecting perception per se, and do not require us to conclude that perception is normal and only post-perceptual access to conscious awareness is impaired by extinction. Specifically, our results suggest that extinction results in low-quality representations of stimuli, which support performance in matching tasks more adequately than in naming tasks.

This neat conclusion was challenged recently by Verfaellie, Milberg, McGlinchy-Berroth, and Grand (1995), who equated the same/different matching and the identification tasks in the same way we had, and found evidence of two subtypes of patient. One type performed above chance on the identification of the contralesional stimulus, and equivalently with the ostensibly implicit same/different matching task, thus replicating our findings. The other type had more severe neglect and performed at chance in identifying the contralesional stimulus. These patients did show a bona fide dissociation, performing significantly better on the same/different matching task.

Verfaellie's study was also designed to address a question originally raised by Berti et al. (1991), namely whether the representation of the extinguished contralesional stimulus is limited to partial visual information or also includes semantic information. Berti and colleagues had varied the similarity relations among the left and right stimuli, including pictures that were visually similar but semantically distinct or semantically similar but visually distinct. The Verfaellie group adopted this design as well, and although they critiqued Berti's methods of data analysis, their conclusions were compatible: It took patients longer to respond "different" when the two pictures bore either a visual or a semantic similarity to each other, implying that both types of information had been at least partly extracted from the contralesional stimulus.

Further evidence of semantic encoding of neglected stimuli comes from studies of semantic priming. When a semantically related word or picture accompanies a target word, that word is recognized more quickly. Ladavas, Paladini, and Cubelli (1993) presented a neglect patient with priming words on the neglected side of fixation and letter strings for a lexical-decision task on the right. They also assessed the patient's ability to perform various tasks with the left-sided priming words, such as reading them aloud and classifying them by semantic category. Despite chance performance in a number of these tasks testing explicit perception of the contralesional words, the patient's lexical decision latencies to words on the right were significantly primed as a function of the semantic content of the words on the left. Similar findings have been reported by McGlinchy-Berroth, Milberg, Verfaellie, Alexander, and Kilduff (1993).

The earliest and most straightforward interpretation of the dissociation between perception and awareness in patients with neglect and/or extinction was offered by Volpe et al. (1979). They suggested that extinction in their subjects consisted of "a breakdown in the flow of information between conscious and non-conscious mental systems. The stimulus comparison task in our study appears to have been carried out at a post-perceptual, pre-verbal level, with only the resultant comparison entering consciousness" (pp. 723). This account clearly falls into the privileged property category. Although the authors are not very explicit on the point, it appears from the quote just excerpted and from another reference to "some level of neuronal processing which allows for verbal description, if not conscious awareness," that the system required for consciousness is the language system (cf. Gazzaniga, 1988).

An alternative interpretation of the kinds of dissociations reviewed here has been offered by Kinsbourne (1988). Rather than viewing consciousness as a property of some neural systems and not others, he considers it a state of integration among different neural systems. According to this view, neglect does not divert percepts from conscious awareness by somehow preventing their transmission to another system that is required for consciousness. Rather, it weakens or degrades the representation of the stimulus, such that the representation does not have sufficient influence over the other, concurrent, patterns of activity in the brain to create a new global brain state into which the stimulus representation is integrated.

The dissociations reviewed above can also be explained by a quality of representation account. According to this type of account, extinction and neglect result in poor quality perceptual representations, which supply input, albeit degraded input, to higher levels of semantic processing. This account and Kinsbourne's differ mainly in emphasis, in that the latter stresses the lessening of influence on the rest of the system, whereas the quality of representation account stresses the existence of the residual influence.

One might ask how a degraded perceptual representation, postulated by both the integration and quality of representation accounts, could support semantic priming and produce other evidence of semantic processing of neglected stimuli. The answer is that the visual system need not have completed its processing of a stimulus and have derived a high quality representation in order for it to pass some information on to semantic levels of processing. One source of evidence for this is the literature on subthreshold semantic priming with normal subjects. Marcel (1983) and others have shown that subliminal tachistoscopic presentations of words can prime judgements about subsequent supraliminal words. Limiting the exposure duration of a word and following it with a mask clearly interferes with the perceptual processing of the word. Therefore, we should not infer that if a word or picture can semantically prime subsequent stimulus processing, that it must have been perceived normally.

A recent functional neuroimaging study by Rees et al. (2000) lends further support to the idea that neglect and extinction result in the correct but degraded representation of the neglected stimulus. Building on earlier work showing distinct loci for the processing of faces and houses in inferior temporal cortex, these investigators presented pairs of stimuli, bilaterally, to a right parietal-damaged patient. When a face was shown contralesionally, and was extinguished, there was nevertheless activation of the face area, albeit reduced in magnitude relative to nonextinguished face trials, and the same pattern was obtained for houses. Consistent with preserved vision, face and house areas were activated in a selective manner. Consistent with the quality of representation account of preserved vision, these areas were less activated than during normal perception.

A mechanistic explanation of how poor-quality perceptual representations could produce priming at semantic levels is suggested by the covert face recognition model of Farah et al. (1993), already discussed. In our model the locus of damage was visual, and the quality of the visual representations was such that multiple choice naming was poor or at chance. However, the model showed semantic priming. This was because the patterns of activation reaching semantic levels of representation contained partial, noisy, and subthreshold information about the semantic identity of the stimulus. The resultant pattern in semantics would, on average, be more consistent with the semantics of that stimulus, or a semantically related stimulus, than with an unrelated stimulus, and hence tended to have a net facilatory effect on the semantic representation of identical or related stimuli, relative to unrelated stimuli. However, because much of this priming effect was caused by subthresold activation in the semantics units, the semantic representations engendered by the poor-quality visual input were not, themselves, able to activate response representations such as names. This suggests a reason why indirect tests may be more sensitive to the residual capabilities of damaged systems: Such tests generally require that residual knowledge affect the processing of a probe stimulus within the perceptual and semantic layers, as opposed to requiring that knowledge to be propagated through additional levels of representation for an overt response. The model of Farah et al. (1993) is sufficiently simple and generic that it is equally relevant to priming in neglect as in prosopagnosia.

Verfaellie and colleagues' (1995) finding of a true dissociation in the severest cases of neglect between overt forced choice identification performance and same/different matching provides more of a challenge to accounts based on degraded perceptual processing. As these authors point out, this would seem to implicate a qualitative rather than quantitative difference between the modes of perception needed for the two kinds of tasks. However, the difference need not be in conscious awareness per se. These same authors point out that the overt identification task that they used required the maintenance of a memory trace while patients awaited and then interpreted the multiple choice alternatives, whereas the same/different matching task could be performed on the stimuli the instant they appeared. In fact, the possibility that severe neglect impairs memory for stimuli disproportionately to the perceptual impairment finds some independent support in the literature (Heilman, Watson, & Shulman, 1974; Samuels, Butters, & Goodglass, 1971).

IMPLICIT READING IN PURE ALEXIA

Patients with pure alexia are impaired at reading, despite being able to write normally and understand spoken words. When they do succeed at recognizing a written word, it is usually by reading it letter by letter. The everyday behavior and clinical test performance of pure alexics suggests that they cannot understand words that they fail to decipher by letter-by-letter reading, but in at least some cases these two measures of reading success dissociate.

This was first noted by Landis, Regard, and Serrat (1980), in a case study of a patient recovering from surgery for a left occipital tumor. The patient was a pure alexic, and when tested with a week of the surgery, was unable to read words that were flashed for only 30 ms in a tachistoscope. However, he was able to point to objects in the room whose names had been presented in this manner. Unfortunately, he was tested with relatively few words on that day, and when re-tested a week later, had lost his ability to point to the words' referents, even though his explicit reading performance had improved.

Subsequent studies have examined the implicit reading of pure alexics more thoroughly. Patterson and Kay (1982) reported several unsuccessful attempts to elicit evidence of comprehension of briefly presented unread words in their pure alexic subjects. Shortly thereafter, Grossi, Fragassi, Orsini, De Falco, and Sepe (1984) presented evidence of disproportionately preserved picture-word matching in one case of pure alexia, and Shallice and Saffran (1986) carried out a comprehensive investigation of implicit word recognition and comprehension in another pure alexic. Shallice and Saffran's subject was able to perform lexical decision with relatively high accuracy on letter strings that were presented for two seconds, which was too quickly for him to reliably identify the words explicitly. The subject was best at recognizing high frequency words, and the closer the resemblance between nonwords and words, the harder it was for him to reject the nonwords. For high frequency words, he was able to classify 90% as words, and false alarmed to only 38% of the pseudowords derived from the high frequency words by changing one or two letters. An interesting exception to his generally good lexical decision ability was that he was unable to discriminate appropriately and inappropriately affixed words, for example calling *applaudly* a word. Shallice and Saffran also demonstrated that their subject was able to make reasonably accurate semantic categorizations of words presented too briefly to be read. For example, he correctly classified 94% of unread place names as in or out of Europe, 93% of unread people's names as authors or politicians, and 87% of unread concrete nouns as living or nonliving.

Coslett and Saffran (1989) replicated and extended these findings with four new cases of pure alexia. Like Shallice and Saffran (1986), they found effects of word frequency on lexical decision, and an insensitivity to affixes. They also found better lexical decison performance for concrete and imageable words, and for content words, in general, relative to functors. In a subsequent study, Coslett and Saffran (1992) report that they tested one of their subjects on rhyme/nonrhyme judgements with written words, and found that he performed at chance. Perhaps their most striking finding is that their subjects performed the implicit reading tasks more accurately with brief exposures of the words, such as 250 msec, than with exposures of 2 seconds. They interpret this in terms of the different strategies needed for implicit and explicit reading. Explicit letter-by-letter reading is incompatible with the strategy needed for implicit reading. Coslett and Saffran were able to foil subjects' attempts at letter-by-letter reading by using extremely short exposure durations, and thereby enabled the alternative strategy to be expressed. This is consistent with Landis et al.'s (1980) original case study, in which implicit reading was lost as explicit reading improved. It also suggests a reason why Patterson and Kay (1982) may not have detected any preserved implicit reading in their subjects: In attempting to maximize the chances of eliciting implicit reading in their subjects, they used words that were most likely to be recognized explicitly, that is, very short words and words that had been successfully read explicitly.

The striking dissociation in these cases is between knowing the specific word presented and knowing its lexical status and semantic category. However, this dissociation does not have any direct implications for the neural correlates of awareness. Or, to the extent that it does, so do dissociations between recognition and awareness in normal subjects viewing tachistoscopic displays. Only when exposure durations are extremely short, for subjects who would otherwise persist in letter-by-letter reading, do subjects manifest knowledge in their implicit reading performance that they, themselves, are not aware of possessing. Under these circumstances, however, the dissociation between performance and awareness may be attributable to the same mechanisms as subthreshold perception in normal subjects, with thresholds being higher for brain-damaged subjects.

Because it is not clear whether implicit reading necessarily involves a dissociation between subjects' experience of reading and their performance, it is equally unclear whether the types of explanations discussed above are really relevant. Nevertheless, for the sake of completeness, I will review the proposals that have been put forth by researchers studying implicit reading.

The DICE model has been applied to implicit reading, and suggests that implicit reading is simply normal reading, drawing as usual upon the critical left hemisphere-mediated processing, deprived of access to other systems necessary for conscious awareness (Schacter et al., 1988). This is an example of a privileged role account. Unfortunately, it does not provide an explanation of the peculiarities of implicit reading with regard to part of speech, morphology, and concreteness, and so on, and is therefore not a very satisfactory account of the phenomenon.

Implicit reading has also been explained by a quality of representation account. Shallice and Saffran (1986) suggested that "lexical decision above chance but well below normal levels; recognition of morphemes but insensitivity to the appropriateness of their combination; limited access to semantic information [and] the failure to identify the stimulus explicitly, could conceivably be explained in terms of decreased levels of activation within the system that normally subserves explicit identification" (p. 452). This hypothesis fits well with some aspects of the data, and poorly with others. For example, the representations of high frequency words and concrete words might well be more robust, and these words are in fact more likely to be read. In contrast, the more regular mapping between orthography and phonology, relative to the mapping between orthography and semantics, would seem to predict the relative preservation of phonological judgements relative to semantic ones, just the opposite of what is observed. This would be because, with distributed representations at least, to the extent that sets of similar looking words have similar sounding pronounciations, the learning accomplished for each one will also generalize towards the others (e.g., one's knowledge that *cap* is pronounced ____ would partially support the pronounciation of *cat* as ____). The lack of regularity in the orthography to semantics mapping eliminates this source of robustness (e.g., you should not try to put a cat on your head). Finally, the finding that shorter exposure durations lead to better implicit reading in at least some patients is awkward for a quality of representation account.

Finally, Shallice and Saffran also discuss the possibility that implicit reading reflects the operation of right hemisphere reading mechanisms, a view that Coslett and Saffran (1989) have also endorsed. This constitutes a different type of privileged role account, according to which the normal left hemisphere component of the reading system is uniquely endowed with the ability to mediate conscious awareness of reading (if the account is to be applied to awareness) and with the more fine-grained semantic distinctions and syntactic and morphological capabilities found to be lacking in implicit reading. This is consistent with independent findings that the right hemisphere is better at reading high frequency and concrete words, and is ignorant of morphology (see, e.g., Baynes, 1990, for a review). The right hemisphere is also believed to be deficient at deriving phonology from print, consistent with the inability of one of Coslett and Saffran's subjects to make rhyme judgements on pairs of printed words, which Klein and I also observed with our implicit reader. Finally, Coslett and Monsul (1994) used transcranial magnetic stimulation (TMS) with one alexic patient to find out which hemisphere was mediating his residual reading ability. Only right hemisphere TMS interfered with the patient's reading, providing a very direct demonstration of that hemisphere's role.

In sum, there is a good deal of relatively fine-grained information about implicit reading, concerning the effects of different stimulus properties, instructions, and tasks, and these enable us to evaluate the different explanations of the phenomenon that have been put forward. Most of the available evidence supports right hemisphere mediation of implicit reading.

GENERAL CONCLUSIONS

What generalizations can be drawn about the six syndromes reviewed here? And, more importantly, what general conclusions follow from them for the neural correlates of conscious awareness?

In six neuropsychological syndromes, visual awareness and visual perception appear to be dissociable. It is tempting to consider the six dissociations as replications, at different levels of processing, of the same basic phenomenon. On closer examination, however, both the sense in which visual awareness can be said to be impaired, and the criteria by which visual perception can be said to be preserved, differ across the syndromes. This heterogeneity is not, in my view, reason to discount some or all of the the syndromes as irrelevant. With the possible exception of implicit reading, all seem to be showing us something about the way perception and awareness can come unglued. We must simply be aware of the differences among these dissociations at a descriptive, empirical level if we are eventually to make sense of them in terms of the likely underlying neural mechanisms.

Visual awareness has been operationalized in different ways. The literature on blindsight contains the richest information about patients' introspective self-reports, and includes a number of ways in which visual awareness can be said to be absent or impaired (Weiskrantz, 1986). In some instances, patients claim that they are guessing on the basis of no subjective experience whatsoever, with resulting very low confidence. In other instances, they say that they are answering based on an experience, but not one that they would classify as "visual." Very occasionally a specifically visual experience is reported.

The agnosic patients studied differ in their degree of confidence in their perceptions, which is presumably a measure of their subjective awareness of having perceived. The apperceptive agnosic patient reports no awareness of the sizes and orientations that her visuomotor system deals with so accurately (e.g., Milner & Goodale, 1995), whereas the associative agnosic does retain some feeling of knowing, and this feeling is strongest, crucially, for items on which her implicit recognition performance is better (Feinberg, Dyckes-Berke, Miner, & Roaane, 1995). Prosopagnosics typically report no sense of familiarity when they view a face and have low confidence in their identifications, and some demonstrations of covert face recognition have used only faces for which the patient earlier demonstrated no overt recognition (DeHaan, Young, & Newcombe, 1987a,b).

In neglect and extinction, the perception-awareness dissociation is sometimes framed in terms of the patients' unawareness of having seen anything at all. However, the only systematically collected data concerns their ability to make various explicit judgements about the stimuli. Finally, in implicit reading, the dissociation that holds for all patients is between the ability to report a specific word and the ability to make judgements about the lexicality and semantic category of the word, not the dissociation between word perception and awareness of that perception. For two cases, at least, subjects report being aware of the information they are using to make these judgements, and confident of their answers. In sum, the six syndromes comprise a heterogeneous group from the point of view of awareness.

The six syndromes also appear to be heterogeneous in terms of the way in which preserved vision is operationalized and the scope and degree of preservation. Consider the way in which the aware-unaware distinction is operationalized. Matching tasks were used with an apperceptive agnosic patient to operationalize aware vision, and with extinction patients to operationalize preserved vision without awareness. There appears to be no principled basis for deciding when a task requires visual awareness, and thus no uniformity across syndromes in the way vision without awareness is measured.

Consider also the scope of preserved vision in the syndromes. In apperceptive agnosia, it comprises only a small fraction of the abilities impaired in conscious vision (size and orientation, but not shape). In implicit reading, many but not all properties of words are recognized. Specifically, implicit readers appear to be blind just to the morphological and phonological properties of words. The limits of implicit or covert recognition in the associative object agnosia and prosopagnosia are less clearly delineated, but they appear to comprise a much fuller range of recognition abilities (implicit access to semantic information from objects and faces, and even name information from faces).

The degree of preservation of vision without awareness also varies and, surprisingly, not in a way correlated with the scope. For example, although the apperceptive agnosic shows preservation of only a narrow range of the abilities compromised at the level of aware vision in her syndrome, her performance within that range is normal. In contrast, the associative object agnosic was merely above chance in her ability to pair semantically related objects, but nowhere near normal. At this point we do not know whether the priming and other implicit perception effects in neglect and prosopagnosia are truely normal or merely present to some degree.

If the phenomena themselves are heterogeneous, then it is unlikely that a single mechanism will be responsible for the vision-awareness dissociation in each case. In fact, all three of the general types of hypotheses concerning the neural correlates of awareness seem to have their place in explaining one syndrome or another. There is evidence from blindsight for a priviledged role for the cortical visual system, as opposed to the subcortical, in visual awareness. Similarly, observations in one case of apperceptive agnosia implicate the ventral pathway of the cortical visual system as playing a privileged role. Other aspects of blindsight, as well as associative object agnosia, prosopagnosia, extinction, and neglect are generally consistent with an explanation in terms of either degraded quality of representation or disrupted integration caused by that degradation. Although the phenomenon of implicit reading per se is probably not directly relevant to awareness, as some implicit readers are aware, a quality of representation account probably explains the lack of awareness for patients whose implicit reading can only be demonstrated with tachistoscopically presented words.

What general conclusions emerge from this heterogeneous set of phenomena concerning the neural correlates of awareness? The six syndromes together support both a type of privileged role account, which is nevertheless quite different from the best-known privileged role accounts in which there is a dedicated consciousness module (e.g., the CAS of Schacter et al., 1988, or DeHaan et al., 1992). According to this conclusion, some but not all visual-system representations which are necessary for some perceptual functions are also necessary for awareness. However, versions of a quality of representation and integration account also seem correct. This is because even those representations that normally play a privileged role in awareness will not if they are degraded and, hence, unable to integrate their content into the global state of the cognitive system as a whole.

Acknowledgment

This chapter is a revised version of Farah, M. (1997). Visual Perception and Visual Awareness after Brain Damage: A Tutorial Oberview. In N. Block, O. Flanagan, & G. Güzeldere (Eds.), *The Nature of Consciousness: Philosophical Debates.* Cambridge, MA: The MIT Press.

REFERENCES

Bauer, R. M. (1984). Autonomic recognition of names and faces in prosopagnosia: A neuropsychological application of the guilty knowledge test. *Neuropsychologia* , 22, 457–469.

Barbur, J. L., Watson, J. D., Frackowiak, R. S., & Zeki, S. (1993). Conscious visual perception without V1. *Brain, 116,* 1293–1302.

Baynes, K. (1990). Language and reading in the right hemisphere: Highways or byways of the brain? *Journal of Cognitive Neuroscience, 2,* 159–79.

Berti, A., Allport, A., Driver, J., Deneis, Z., Oxbury, J., & Oxbury, S. (1992). Levels of processing for visual stimuli in an "extinguished" field. *Neuropsychologica, 30,* 403–415.

Brent, P. J., Kennard, C., & Ruddock, K. H. (1994). Residual colour vision in a human hemianope: spectral responses and colour discrimination. *Proceedings of the Royal Society of London. Series B: Biological Sciences, 256,* 219–225.

Burton, A. M., Young, A. W., Bruce, V., Johnston, R. A., & Ellis, A. W. (1991). Understanding covert recognition. *Cognition, 39,* 129–166.

Campion, J., Latto, R., & Smith, Y. M. (1983). Is blindsight an effect of scattered light, spared cortex, and near-threshold vision? *The Behavioral and Brain Sciences, 3,* 423–447.

Coslett, H. B., & Monsul, N. (1994). Reading with the right hemisphere: Evidence from transcranial magnetic stimulation. *Brain and Language, 46,* 198–211.

Coslett, H. B., & Saffran, E. M. (1989). Evidence for preserved reading in "pure alexia". *Brain, 112,* 327–359.

Coslett, H. B., & Saffran, E. M. (1992). Optic Aphasia and the Right Hemisphere: A Replication and Extension. *Brain and Language, 43,* 148–161.

Cowey, A., & Stoerig, P. (1989). Projection patterns of surviving neurons in the dorsal lateral geniculate nucleus following discrete lesions of striate cortex: Implications for residual vision. *Experimental Brain Research, 75,* 631–638.

Cowey, A., & Stoerig, P. (1997). Visual detection in monkeys with blindsight. *Neuropsychologia, 35,* 929–939.

Crick, F., & Koch, S. (1990). Some reflections on visual awareness. *Cold Spring Harbor Symposia on Quanititative Biology, 55,* 953–962.

Damasio, A. R. (1989). Time-locked multiregional retroactivations: A systems-level proposal for the neural substrates of recall and recognition. *Cognition, 33,* 25–62.

De Haan, E. H., Bauer, R. M., & Greve, K. W. (1992). Behavioral and physiological evidence for covert face recognition in a prosopagnosic patient. *Cortex, 28,* 77–95.

De Haan, E. H., Young, A. W., & Newcombe, F. (1987a). Face recognition without awareness. *Cognitive Neuropsychology, 4,* 385–415.

De Haan, E. H., Young, A., & Newcombe, F. (1987b). Faces interfere with name classification in a prosopagnosic patient. *Cortex, 23,* 309–316.

Farah, M. J. (1990). *Visual agnosia: Disorders of object recognition and what they tell us about normal vision.* Cambridge, MA: MIT Press/Bradford Books.

Farah, M. J. (1994). Visual perception and visual awareness after brain damage: A tutorial review. In M. Moscovitch & C. Umilta (Eds.), *Conscious and unconscious information processing: Attention and performance XV* (pp. 37–76). Cambridge, MA: MIT Press.

Farah, M. J., & Feinberg, T. E. (1997). Perception and awareness. In T. E. Feinberg & M. J. Farah (Eds.), *Behavioral Neurology and Neuropsychology.* New York: McGraw-Hill.

Farah, M. J., Monheit, M. A., & Wallace, M. A. (1991). Unconscious perception of "extinguished" visual stimuli: Reassessing the evidence. *Neuropsychologia, 29,* 949–958.

Farah, M. J., O'Reilly, R. C., & Vecera, S. P. (1993). Dissociated overt and covert recognition as an emergent property of a lesioned neural network. *Psychological Review, 100,* 571–588.

Feinberg, T. E., Dyckes-Berke, D., Miner, C. R., & Roane, D. M. (1995). Knowledge, implicit knowledge and metaknowledge in visual agnosia and pure alexia. *Brain, 118,* 789–800.

Fendrich, R., Wessinger, C. M., & Gazzaniga, M. S. (1992). Residual vision in a scotoma: Implications for blindsight. *Science, 258,* 1489–91.

Gazzaniga, M. S. (1988). Brain modularity: Towards a philosphy of conscious experience. In A. J. Marcel & E. Bisiach (Eds.), *Consciousness in contemporary science.* Oxford, UK: Clarendon Press.

Goodale, M. A., & Milner, D. A. (1992). Separate visual pathways for perception and action. *Trends in Neuroscience, 15.*

Goodale, M. A., Milner, A. D., Jakobson, L. S., & Carey, D. P. (1991). A neurological dissociation between perceiving objects and grasping them. *Nature, 349,* 154–156.

Goodale, M. A., Jakobson, L. S., Milner, A. D., Perre, H. D. I., Benson, P. J., & Hietanen, J. K. (1994). The nature and limits of orientation and pattern processing supporting visuomotor control in a visual form agnosic. *Journal of Cognitive Neuroscience, 6,* 46–56.

Grossi, D., Fragassi, N. A., Orsini, A., De Falco, F. A., & Sepe, O. (1984). Residual reading capability in a patient with alexia without agraphia. *Brain and Language, 23,* 337–348.

Heilman, K. M., Watson, R. T., & Schulman, H. (1974). A unilateral memory defect. *Journal of Neurology, Neurosurgery, and Psychiatry, 37,* 790–793.

Hinton, G., & Plaut, D. C. (1987). *Using fast weights to deblur old memories.* Paper presented at the Proceedings of the 9th Annual Meeting of the Cognitive Science Society.

Hinton, G. E., & Sejnowski, T. J. (1986). Learning and relearning in Boltzmann machines. In D. E. Rumelhart & J. L. McClelland (Eds.), *Parallel distributed processing: Explorations in the microstructure of cognition.* Cambridge, MA: The MIT Press.

Karnath, H. O. (1988). Deficits of attention in acute and recovered visual hemi-neglect. *Neuropsychologia, 26,* 27–43.

Karnath, H. O., & Hartje, W. (1987). Residual information processing in the neglected visual half-field. *Journal of Neurology, 234,* 180–184.

Kinsbourne, M. (1988). Integrated field theory of consciousness. In A. J. Marcel & E. Bisiach (Eds.), *Consciousness in contemporary science.* Oxford, UK: Clarendon Press.

Ladavas, E., Paladini, R., & Cubelli, R. (1993). Implicit associative priming in a patient with left visual neglect. *Neuropsychologia, 31,* 1307–1320.

Landis, T., Regard, M., & Serrat, A. (1980). Iconic reading in a case of alexia without agraphia caused by brain tumor: A tachistoscopic study. *Brain and Language, 11,* 45–53.

Marcel, A. J. (1983). Conscious and unconscious perception: Experiments on visual masking and word recognition. *Cognitive Psychology, 15,* 197–237.

Marcel, A. J. (1998). Blindsight and shape perception: Deficit of visual consciousness or of visual function? *Brain, 121,* 1565–1588.

McGlinchey-Berroth, R., Milberg, W. P., Verfaellie, M., Alexander, M., & Kilduff, P. T. (1993). Semantic processing in the neglected visual field: Evidence from a lexical decision task. *Cognitive Neuropsychology, 10,* 79–108.

Milner, A. D., & Goodale, M. A. (1995). *The visual brain in action.* Oxford, UK: Oxford Science Publications.

Milner, A. D., Perrett, D. I., Johnston, R. S., Benson, P. J., Jordan, T. R., Heeley, D. W., Bettucci, D., Mortara, F., Mutani, R., Terrazzi, E., & Davidson, D. L. W. (1991). Perception and action in "visual form agnosia". *Brain, 114,* 405–428.

O'Reilly, R. C., & Farah, M. J. (1999). Simulation and explanation in neuropsychology and beyond. *Cognitive Neuropsychology, 16,* 1–48.

Patterson, K. E., & Kay, J. (1982). Letter-by-letter reading: Psychological descriptions of a neurological syndrome. *Quarterly Journal of Experimental Psychology: Human Experimental Psychology, 34A,* 411–441.

Poppel, E., Held, R., & Frost, D. (1973). Letter: Residual visual function after brain wounds involving the central visual pathways in man. *Nature, 243,* 295–296.

Rafal, R., Smith, J., Krantz, J., Cohen, A., & Brennan, C. (1990). Extrageniculate vision in hemianopic humans: Saccade inhibition by signals in the blind field. *Science, 250,* 118–121.

Rees, G., Wojcivlik, E., Clarke, K., Husain, M., Frith, C., & Driver, J. (2000). Unconscious activation of visual cortex in the damaged right hemisphere of a parietal patient with extinction. *Brain, 123,* 1624–1633.

Saharie, A., Weiskrantz, L., Barbur, J. L., Simmons, A., Williams S. C., & Brammer, M. J. (1997). Pattern of neural activity associated with conscious and unconscious processing of visual signals. *National Academy of Sciences, 94,* 9406–9411.

Samuels, I., Butters, N., & Goodglass, H. (1971). Visual memory deficits following cortical-limib lesions: Effect of field of presentation. *Physiological Behavior, 6,* 447–452.

Schacter, D. L., McAndrews, M. P., & Moscovitch, M. (1988). Access to consciousness: Dissociations between implicit and explicit knowledge in neuropsychological syndromes. In L. Weiskrantz (Ed.), *Thought without language.* Oxford, UK: Oxford University Press.

Schiller, P. H., & Koerner, F. (1971). Discharge characteristics of single units in superior colliculus of the alert rhesus monkey. *Journal of Neurophysiology, 34,* 920–936.

Shallice, T., & Saffran, E. (1986). Lexical processing in the absence of explicit word identification: Evidence from a letter-by-letter reader. *Cognitive Neuropsychology, 3,* 429-58.

Singer, W., & Gray, C. M. (1995). Visual feature integration and the temporal correlation hypothesis. *Annual Review of Neuroscience, 18,* 555-586.

Stoerig, P., & Cowey, A. (1997). Blindsight in man and monkey. *Brain, 120,* 535-559.

Stoerig, P., Kleinschmidt, A., & Frahm, J. (1998). No visual responses in denervated V1: High-resolution functional magnetic resonance imaging of a blindsight patient. *Neuroreport, 9,* 21-25.

Taylor, A. M., & Warrington, E. K. (1971). Visual agnosia: A single case report. *Cortex, 7,* 152-161.

Tranel, D., & Damasio, A. R. (1988). Non-conscious face recognition in patients with face agnosia. *Behavioral Brain Research, 30,* 235-249.

Verfaellie, M., Milberg, W. P., McGlinchey-Berroth, R., & Grande, L. (1995). Comparison of cross-field matching and forced-choice identification in hemispatial neglect. *Neuropsychology, 9,* 427-434.

Volpe, B. T., LeDoux, J. E., & Gazzangia, M. S. (1979). Information processing of visual stimuli in an "extinguished" visual field. *Nature, 282,* 722-724.

Wallace, M. A., & Farah, M. J. (1992). Savings in relearning face-name associations as evidence for covert recognition in prosopagnosia. *Journal of Cognitive Neuroscience, 4,* 150-154.

Warrington, E. K., & Weiskrantz, L. (1970). Amnesic syndrome: Consolidation or retrieval? *Nature, 228,* 628-630.

Weiskrantz, L. (1986). *Blindsight: A Case Study and Implications.* Oxford, UK: Oxford University Press.

Weiskrantz, L., Warrington, E. K., Sanders, M. D., & Marshall, J. (1974). Visual capacity in the hemianopic visual field following a restricted occipital ablation. *Brain, 97,* 709-728.

Young, A. W., & Burton, A. M. (1999). Simulating face recognition: Implications for modelling cognition. *Cognitive Neuropsychology, 16,* 49-72.

Young, A. W., & DeHaan, E. H. F. (1988). Boundaries of covert recognition in prosopagnosia. *Cognitive Neuropsychology, 5,* 317-336.

Words

Words are things, and a small drop of ink, falling like dew upon a thought, produces that which makes thousands, perhaps millions think.

—Lord Byron

8

The Organization
of the Lexical System

Argye E. Hillis

The topic of the types of representations that comprise our knowledge of words, and how these representations are accessed and interact, has been the most investigated topic in all of cognitive neuropsychology. In this chapter I will make no attempt to review all of the excellent papers that have enhanced our understanding of the lexical system. Rather, I will focus on selective studies that have helped to answer basic questions about the architecture of the system and the internal structure of each processing component. More detailed questions about the nature of the representations and how they are processed are addressed in other chapters. The evidence I will present that bears on each question will come from neurologically-impaired patients. Although investigations of normal subjects have clearly had an important impact in understanding the lexical system, the focus here will be on how data from brain-damaged patients have led to specific proposals about how lexical representations and processes are organized.

The chapter is organized into two parts. Part I deals with the basic architecture of the lexical system—identifying the major component processes and how they relate to each other. Part II deals with the types of errors and lexical effects that arise from damage to various components of the architecture. In this section I attempt to dispel some simple interpretive heuristics for identifying a given patient's level of impairment within the system. I also summarize reports that show how a given patient's pattern of performance can lead to a better understanding of the internal mechanisms of each component. This organization reflects a general "two-step" approach to cognitive neuropsychological research. The first step is to identify, for an individual case, the level of breakdown in processing that can account for the pattern of performance. The second step involves learning more about the representations and mechanisms of processing at the affected level of the system. The goal of this chapter is to show how this general approach has allowed researchers in this field to articulate, in increasing detail, the representations and processes that underlie lexical processing.

PART I: THE BASIC ARCHITECTURE OF THE LEXICAL SYSTEM

In this section I begin with the most fundamental questions, and gradually narrow the focus of questions. The evidence reviewed will serve as the basis for "building" a widely (but not universally) accepted architecture of the lexical system.

Are There Functionally Independent Semantic (Meaning) and Lexical (Form) Representations?

Dissociations between Semantic and Lexical Impairments

Goodglass and Baker in 1976 identified one group of patients who had naming deficits with comprehension deficits and another group of patients who had naming deficits without comprehension deficits. They concluded that the groups had lesions to two separate components of lexical processing—the semantic system (representations of word meanings) in patients with comprehension deficits, and the lexicon (representations of word forms) in patients without comprehension deficits. This distinction has received abundant support and has found wide acceptance in recent decades, and patients whose impaired naming is not associated with impaired comprehension have come to be known as "anomic." Despite the widely-accepted notion of independent semantic and lexical (both phonological and orthographic word form) representations, there has been some evidence that the distinction may not always be clear cut. For example, Caramazza, Berndt, and Brownell, 1982, studied a group of anomic patients on a nonverbal task of distinguishing cups versus glasses. They found that anomic patients seemed to differ from normal subjects in making nonverbal semantic distinctions (for example, categorizing drawings of cups versus glasses). This study prompted a series of further investigations of the degree of independence between semantics and word form representations. The strongest evidence in favor of a distinction between these two components of naming comes from patients who have damage to only one or the other component.

First consider patient PW, a right-handed man who had anomic aphasia due to a left fronto-parietal stroke at the age of 51 (Rapp & Caramazza, 1997). PW made frequent errors in written and oral naming, but showed normal performance on various comprehension tasks, such as spoken word/picture verification tasks and drawing in response to object names. He often made different errors in written and oral naming of the same item, on the same occasion (see Table 8.1). The fact that PW accurately repeated words without articulatory errors and accurately copied words without orthographic errors constitutes evidence against motor-output deficits as the cause of his errors. And, the fact the he understood words well rules out damage to the semantic system. His errors in written and oral naming seemed to arise at the level of accessing the phonological and orthographic representations of the words. In other words, PW seems to have intact processing through the level of accessing a semantic representation, but subsequently encounters problems in accessing phonological and orthographic output word forms.

Table 8.1
PW's Errors in Written and Oral Naming on the Same Occasion

Picture Stimulus	Written Name	Spoken Name
brush	brush	comb
onion	onion	banana
owl	owl	turtle
thread	thread	needle
racoon	racoona	sheep
knife	spoon	fork
thread	iron	thread
lips	nail	lips
table	den	table
tongue	teeth	tongue
pillow	bed	pillow

Adapted from "The Modality Specific Organinzations of Lexical Categories" by B. C. Rapp and A. Caramazza, 1997, *Brain and Language*, *56*, 246–286.

However, another interpretation of these data is that PW has a mild semantic impairment that does not affect his performance on the semantic tasks that were selected, but affects performance on the more difficult tasks of oral and written naming. This explanation is unlikely to be correct, because for many items, his naming was consistently accurate in one of the modalities of output. But the best way to rule outo the possibility that the dissociation between semantics and accessing lexical form representations for output is merely due to the higher level of difficulty on the semantic tasks is to demonstrate the reverse dissociation (Shallice, 1988a). In this case, we would need to demonstrate impaired semantics in the face of intact access to the lexical form representations, preferably using the same tasks and stimuli. However, since access to the lexical form representations in production tasks may well depend on first accessing the semantic representation, it would be difficult to find patients with intact naming but poor comprehension. Another way of showing that access to semantic representations is impaired in the face of intact access to lexical representations, is to show that the errors in naming tasks can be fully explained by damage to the semantic system, without postulating additional impairments to any output system

Consider a patient with a frontoparietal infarct, KE (Hillis, Rapp, Romani, & Caramazza, 1990), who also made semantically related word errors in oral and written naming (to pictures and tactually presented objects), oral and written word/picture verification, oral reading, and writing to dictation. He made nearly the identical rate of total errors and semantic errors in all lexical tasks, across all input and output modalities, using the same set of 144 items, in counterbalanced, blocked order (Figure 8.1). KE's comparable rates and types of semantic errors across lexical tasks indicate that there is a single locus of damage that gives rise to all of these errors. The only cognitive mechanism that should be shared by reading, writing to dictation, printed word/picture matching, spoken word/picture matching, visual object naming, and tactile object naming is the semantic system. Another patient with a similar profile is WMA (Miceli, Benvengnu, Capasso, & Caramazza, 1997). We can be confident that WMA and KE did not have additional impairment in accessing representations in the phonological output lexicon or the orthographic output lexicon, because they each made identical rates and types of errors in all output modalities (in written and oral naming, as well as in word/picture matching). We can also be confident that they did not have additional input deficits, since they each made identical errors in tasks with different input modalities (e.g., naming objects from tactile exploration or pictures; writing the names of objects in response to pictures or dictated words).

A final bit of evidence that KE's errors resulted from a unitary source of damage[1] is that his performance on any one of the 6 lexical tasks could predict which items would be missed on a different lexical task just as well as it could predict which items would be missed on repetition of the same task. For example, the item-to-item consistency between oral reading and the other lexical tasks was 72%; the test–retest item consistency for oral reading was 66%. Similar consistency results were reported for WMA. These results provide additional support for the proposal that WMA's and KE's errors in each case arise from damage to a single source—the semantic system. Together with PW, they show a double dissociation between semantics (damaged in WMA and KE, intact in PW) and output lexicons (damaged in PW, intact in KE and WMA).

Together, patients like PW on the one hand and WMA and KE on the other, provide evidence that there are functionally independent stores of semantic representations (that

---

[1]Although his semantic errors all can be said to have "come from" the damaged semantic system, we also have to assume that KE had an additional impairment in using sublexical mechanisms for converting print to sounds and sound to print. If these sublexical mechanisms had been intact, we would have expected them to have "blocked" production of phonologically unrelated errors (see Hillis & Caramazza, 1995d). Furthermore, we would have expected him to produce plausible spellings and pronunctiation of pseudowords in spelling to dictation and oral reading. However, he could not spell or write any pseudowords plausibly).

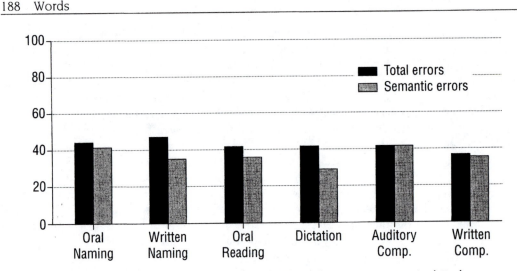

Figure 8.1: Rate of KE's Semantic and Total Errors Across Lexical Tasks.

encode meaning) and lexical representations (that encode word forms), which can be independently damaged by focal brain injury. Now we turn to the questions of whether the semantic and lexical form stores of knowledge are further subdivided.

Are There Multiple Semantic Systems?

Several authors in the 1970s reported cases of what appeared to be semantic impairments that were specific to a particular input modality. In modality-specific aphasias, naming errors could be restricted to the visual modality (so-called "optic aphasia"; Lhermitte & Beauvois, 1973), the tactile modality (Beauvois, Saillant, Meininger, & Lhermitte, 1978), or the auditory modality (Denes & Semenza, 1975). These cases were not ascribed to impairments in recognition in one modality or impairments in accessing amodal semantic information, because patients were able to produce gestures to indicate the use of objects that they could not name. For example, patient Jules F, described by Lhermitte and Beauvois (1973) named a picture of a comb as "toothbrush," but correctly gestured combing the hair. Thus, these cases were taken as evidence that there are separate semantic systems, distinguished by the input modality from which they are accessed. For example, Beauvois (1982) proposed that optic-aphasic patients access an intact visual semantic system that supports the production of gestures in response to pictures, and have access to an intact verbal semantic system that supports naming to definition and other purely lexical semantic tasks, but there is a loss of the connection between the two semantic systems which is necessary for naming visual stimuli. This and other evidence given in support of the hypothesis of modality-specific semantic systems is subject to methodogical problems or other weaknesses; for critical evaluations and responses to these critiques, see Riddoch, Humphreys, Coltheart, and Funnell (1988), Humphreys and Riddoch (1988), Caramazza, Hillis, Rapp, and Romani (1990), Hillis et al. (1990), Shallice (1988b, 1993), McCarthy and Warrington (1989), Rapp, Hillis, and Caramazza (1993), Chertkow, Bub, and Caplan (1992), and Hillis, Rapp, and Caramazza (1995). An extensive review is beyond the scope of this chapter. Here, I will merely provide an alternative account of the pattern of performance that has been taken as the strongest evidence in favor of the hypothesis of multiple, modality-specific semantic systems (Figure 8.2, panel A) over the hypothesis of a unitary semantic system (Figure 8.2, panel B).

Patient DHY sustained strokes in the left occipital lobe and splenium of the corpus collosum that resulted in severely impaired naming of objects presented visually, despite intact naming

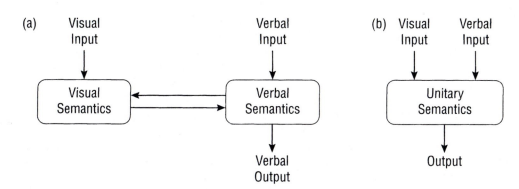

Figure 8.2: Multiple Semantic Systems versus Unitary Semantic System Accounts. Panel A: Hypothesis of multiple semantic systems distinguished by input modality (Beauvois, 1982); Panel B: Hypothesis of a unitary (modality-independent) semantic system (Caramazza et al., 1990; Hillis et al., 1990).

of the same items when presented for tactile exploration or described verbally (Hillis & Caramazza, 1995a). Her errors in naming pictures were very similar to those of PW and KE (Table 8.2). And, like KE, she made frequent semantic errors in matching pictures to names. Unlike KE, however, DHY made no errors in comprehending words, or in naming nonvisually-presented stimuli (e.g., naming to definition or to tactile exploration). Importantly, the problem was shown not to be due to failure of low level visual processing, or even failure to recognize pictures, since DHY could copy, produce gestures in response to pictures, and make certain types of semantic judgments about pictures. Critically, however, we demonstrated that DHY was impaired in accessing detailed semantic information from vision, even when no verbal responses were required. For example, like other so-called optic aphasic patients (Coslett & Saffran, 1989), DHY was unimpaired in choosing which two out of three pictures were semantically related, even when the semantically unrelated pictures were structurally similar to each other. For example, when shown pictures of a light bulb, a light switch, and a pear (structurally similar to the light bulb), DHY correctly identified the light switch and the light bulb as being semantically related. However, in a similar task that required more detailed semantic knowledge, she made errors. For instance, when shown a picture of a light switch, followed by pictures of a light bulb or a traffic light, she could not correctly identify which of the latter two pictures was more related to the first. Therefore, we argued that DHY accessed only partial semantic information from vision, whether or not the task involved any verbal input or output. We further claimed that this partial semantic information, along with structural information derived directly from pictures, was adequate to support her gestures in response to pictures.

Table 8.2

Semantic Errors in Picture Naming by DHY, PW, and KE
(Picture Stimulus → Spoken Name)

PW	DHY	KE
zebra → horse	bear → hippopotamus	bear → fox
cigar → cigarette	nose → finger	nose → ear
brush → comb	dress → scarf	sock → gloves
onion → banana	celery → lettuce	onion → carrot
owl → turtle	frog → cricket	frog → turtle
thread → needle	iron → sewing machine	sofa → chair
racoon → sheep	giraffe → racoon	tiger → lion
knife → fork	frying pan → cup	fork → knife

Therefore, her pattern of performance could be accounted for by assuming a single, modality-independent semantic system, which could not be adequately accessed from vision. Thus, the type of performance that has been presented as the best evidence for the existence of multiple, modality-specific semantic systems, can also be interpreted within a framework that assumes only a single semantic system (see also Riddoch et al., 1988; DeRenzi & Saetti, 1997).

Another variant of the multiple semantic systems hypothesis is that there are separate "stores" of perceptual information versus functional information that can be accessed by any modality of input. For example, it has been proposed that the visual features of objects (e.g., that an apple is red, green, or yellow) are stored independently of the functional features (e.g., that an apple is edible and palatable). Sartori and Job (1988) described a patient, Michelangelo, who was very poor in reporting visual features of objects, but was able to report functional features. Thus, he said that an oyster has four legs, but correctly reported how oysters are eaten. The authors conclude that Michelangelo had selective impairment in "visual semantics" (see also Hart & Gordon, 1993). The shortcomings of this hypothesis are extensively discussed by Shelton and Caramazza (this volume) and thus will not be further discussed here.

It is worth pointing out, however, that additional evidence that a common semantic system is activated by both pictures and words comes from PET studies of normal subjects engaged in semantic decisions. Vandenberghe, Price, Wise, Josephs, and Frackowiak (1996) reported that semantic decisions about both picture and word stimuli activated a region extending from the left superior occipital gyrus, through the middle and inferior temporal gyrus, to the inferior frontal gyrus. Their tasks involved triplets of pictures or words, about which subjects made judgments (on separate trials) about their meanings (semantic associations), the real life size of their referents (requiring access to structural representations), or the physical size of the objects/words (baseline). There were regions of the brain that were activated only in response to one or the other stimulus type, in the baseline and structural conditions, which were thought to be independent of semantic processing, as well as a common region activated during the semantic association judgments, with both pictures and words. The latter region was interpreted to be a distributed semantic network shared by verbal and nonverbal pictorial stimuli.

Are There Independent Phonological and Orthographic Output Lexicons?

An important question concerns whether or not access to the orthographic representation of a word requires first accessing the phonological representation of the word—these two possibilities are depicted in Figure 8.3. Current evidence, in fact, supports the organization depicted in Figure 8.3, Panel A. Here I summarize that evidence (also see Tainturier & Rapp, this volume).

Patient AF (Hier & Mohr, 1977) had fluent, well-articulated "empty" speech and was completely unable to name objects aloud. However, he could write the names of many objects. Although AF may have had some semantic impairment, he at least seemed to access a complete semantic representation of items for which he could write the names. His access to the correct orthographic lexical representation without access to the corresponding phonologic representation provides some evidence for the independence of the two output lexicons. The evidence would be stronger if it could be demonstrated that the semantic system was entirely preserved, and that the problem in spoken output was restricted to accessing information in the phonological output lexicon. Such was the case for RGB (Caramazza & Hillis, 1990) who, after a left temporoparietal stroke, had fluent, well-articulated speech, but made frequent semantic errors and circumlocutions in oral naming and oral reading. He had no impairment in comprehending spoken or printed words, sentences, or narrative, as documented by numerous standardized tests. Furthermore, he could provide full and accurate definitions of words that elicited semantic errors in oral reading, or of pictures that elicited semantic errors in oral naming, as shown in Table 8.3 (for a somewhat similar case, see Bub & Kertesz, 1982). RGB produced accurate

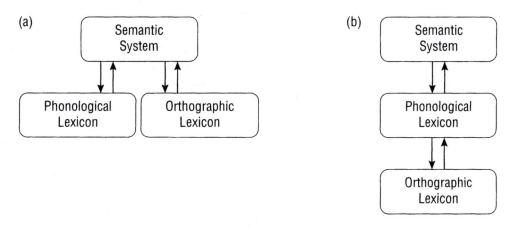

Figure 8.3: Access to Orthographic Word Forms: Competing Accounts. Panel A: Independent access to separate output lexicons hypothesis; Panel B: Phonologic mediation hypothesis.

(or misspelled but recognizable) written names for virtually all pictures, although he made more than 30% errors (all semantically related to the picture) in producing spoken names of the same pictures. For example, in response to a picture of a clam, he produced the oral name "octopus" but correctly wrote, *clam*.

Importantly, there have also been reported cases of the opposite dissociation shown by AF and RGB. RCM was an 82-year-old woman who sustained a left frontal stroke (Hillis, Rapp, & Caramazza, 1999). We reporteded that RCM was 100% accurate in oral picture naming, oral reading, written word/picture verification, and spoken word/picture verification, *using the same items* that elicited predominantly semantic errors in written picture naming and spelling to dictation. For example, in naming a picture of a turtle, RCM wrote, *snake*, but said, "turtle." Yet, she rejected both the spoken and the written word, "snake" as the name of a pictured turtle in word/picture verification tasks. In spelling to dictation, she repeated the stimulus, "eagle," correctly, but wrote *owl*. She rejected both the spoken and the written word, *owl*, as the name of a pictured eagle. RCM was unable to spell pseudowords at all. We proposed that RCM had selective damage to the orthographic output lexicon, sparing the phonological lexicon, as well as damage to mechanisms for converting sound to print (spelling phonetically). A similar case is that of GOS, described in Baxter and Warrington (1985).

This set of cases clearly supports the notion of independent lexical orthographic and phonological output lexicons.

Table 8.3

Examples of Semantic Errors in Oral Reading with Preserved Definitions
of Written Words by RGB

Written Word Stimulus →	Oral Reading Response →	Definition
records	radio	You play 'em on a phonograph . . . can also mean notes you take and keep.
vehicle	motor	You get from one place to another in it, like a car.
grey	blue	The color of hair when you get old.
dollar	money	A bill, a hundred cents.
volcano	lava	Fire comes out of it, a big thing, a mountain.
pharmacist	drugs	He gives you your prescriptions.
quill	feather	They're long and have a point. Animals, porcupines have them.

How is Lexical Syntax Represented?

So far, we have distinguished between modality-specific structural representations (visual, tactile), modality-independent lexical-semantic representations, and modality-specific (orthographic and phonologic) lexical representations. About these distinctions there is very little controversy. But the issue of whether or not there are additional levels of representation in lexical processing is far more controversial.[2]

One proposal regarding the representation of lexical syntactic information is that there is a lemma, a modality-independent lexical representation that specifies the semantic and syntactic features of a word, and mediates between the modality-independent lexical-semantic representation and modality-specific lexical representations or lexemes (Garrett, 1992; Bock, 1982; Butterworth, 1989; Levelt, 1989; Roelofs, 1992). As argued by these authors, the rationale for postulating such an intermediate lexical representation is that there is evidence that syntactic information about a word is accessed independently of semantic information and phonological information. For a review of this evidence see Nickels (this volume). However, it is also possible to account for the evidence cited in support of the lemma without postulating a syntactically based representation that mediates between lexical semantic representations and modality-specific lexical representations (Figure 8.4). Caramazza (1997; see also Caramazza & Miozzo, 1997) has proposed that syntactic features of a word, orthographic lexemes, and phonological lexemes are each accessed independently, and directly, from lexical-semantic representations. Since Nickels (this volume) discusses the relative merits of the Caramazza and Levelt proposals, here I will summarize a line of evidences that Nickels does not discuss.

Evidence against the hypothesis that a modality-independent lexical representation mediates between a lexical-semantic representation and modality-specific lexical representations can be found in the data we have reported earlier, concerning patients who make semantic errors that are restricted to a single output modality. Recall that patient RGB made semantic errors only in spoken production tasks, and RCM made semantic errors virtually only in written production tasks. If these patients had accessed the lemma level of representation, but failed to access the lexeme, they should not have made semantic errors. That is, the lemma (in all extant models of lexical processing that include this level) specifies the complete semantic features of the word, and activates only one lexeme corresponding to those semantics. The lemma would not activate a set of semantically related representations in the output lexicons. If, instead, the impairment of these patients was not at the level of the lexeme, but at the level of the lemma itself (which would account for semantic errors), their errors should not be restricted to a single output modality. That is, because the lemma is modality-independent, access to orthographic and phonologic lexemes should be equally affected by damage to the lemma. One could argue that the lemma does activate numerous semantically related lexemes, either because several lemmas are activated weakly at the same time, and each activate their corresponding lexemes (as in "cascading" or parallel processing models) or because each lemma has "connections" to a number of semantically related representations. However, it is not clear how this hypothesis differs from the hypothesis that the lexical-semantic representations activate (in parallel) a number of semantically related lexical representations. That is, a lemma in this case would be precisely analogous to our proposed "lexical semantic representation" except that the latter does not specify arbitrary syntactic features (i.e., syntactic features like gender that are, in some cases, unrelated to the meaning).

---

[2]One postulated level of representation discussed in greater detail by Nickels (this volume) is a "conceptual representation"—a level that is distinguished from lexical semantics because it includes idiosyncratic knowledge about an object. In contrast, lexical semantics is limited to shared knowledge about what defines the word and distinguishes it from other words. For example, the lexical-semantic representation of "dog" would include only those features that make a dog a dog, and distinguish dog from related concepts like cat and horse. The conceptual representation of dog, in contrast, would include one's personal knowledge and encounters with that concept, such as the fact that one once owned a brown dog, that one loves (or hates) dogs, that the dog next door is friendly, and so on.

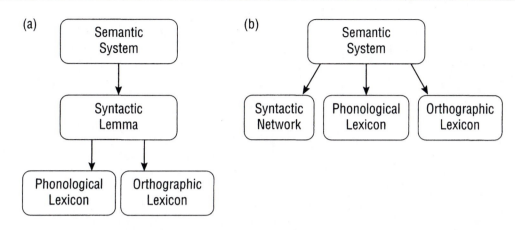

Figure 8.4: Access to Word Forms: Competing Models. Panel A: Syntactic (lemma) mediation (Garrett, 1992; Levelt, 1989); Panel B: Independent access to syntactic information and word forms (Caramazza, 1997; Caramazza & Miozzo, 1997).

Are There Functionally Independent Input and Output Lexicons?

One Phonologic Lexicon or Two?

In 1874, Wernicke, based on the work of his contemporaries and predecessors such as Dax and Broca, put forth the notion that there are separate stores of word representations: one for auditory input (a phonologic input lexicon in recent terminology) and one for articulation (a phonologic output lexicon). The former store was thought to be found in the posterior superior temporal lobe, or Wernicke's area; and the latter in the inferior third frontal convolution, or Broca's area (see De Bleser, 1997, for review). Freund (1891) was among the first to challenge this view. He proposed the existence of a single, central store of auditory representations that subserves both input and output. Broca's area was considered to be involved only in the motor programming of the sounds represented in Wernicke's area.

There have been a number of well-documented cases of "pure word deafness," in which patients can understand written words, but are unable to understand spoken words, despite intact auditory acuity (e.g., pure tone audiometry and brainstem auditory evoked potentials). To illustrate, Auerbach, Allard, Naeser, Alexander, and Albert (1982) described a patient with bilateral temporal strokes who presented with sudden onset of difficulty understanding speech. He said that it was as though people were "speaking in a foreign language," but he could often understand them by lipreading. Despite severe trouble understanding spoken input and repeating, he had no trouble speaking, writing, or understanding printed input. In this case and several other cases, spoken naming was intact (Kussmaul, 1877; Benson, 1979; Gazzaniga, Glass, Sarno, & Posner, 1973; Geschwind, 1965). These cases have often been interpreted as impaired access to phonological representations for input but intact access to phonological representations for output, indicating the possibility of distinct phonological lexicons for input and output (Figure 8.5). However, in all cases in which prelexical auditory processing has been investigated carefully, the patient has been found to have impairment in either prephonemic processing, such as temporal auditory acuity and cortical auditory evoked potentials (Auerbach, et al., 1982) or phonemic discrimination (Denes & Semenza, 1975; Saffran, Marin, & Yeni-Komshan, 1976). Therefore, these patients may have trouble accessing a single phonological lexicon from auditory input due to this lower-level processing deficit (Figure 8.5, panel A).

On the other hand, some patients with severely impaired auditory word recognition in the

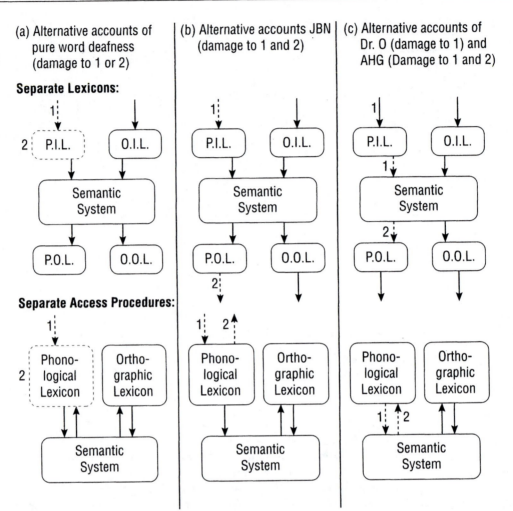

(a) Alternative accounts of pure word deafness (damage to 1 or 2)

(b) Alternative accounts JBN (damage to 1 and 2)

(c) Alternative accounts of Dr. O (damage to 1) and AHG (Damage to 1 and 2)

Separate Lexicons:

Separate Access Procedures:

Figure 8.5: Alternative Accounts of Functionally Distinct Input and Output Lexicons.

face of spared written-word recognition have been found to have intact phonemic discrimination. The reported cases all had concomitant difficulty in spoken, but not written, output. For example, patient JBN (Hillis, Boatman, Hart, & Gordon, 1999) made many errors in spoken word/picture verification but no errors in written word/picture verification (92% vs. 0% errors; χ^2 40; df 1; $p <$ .0001), indicating selective difficulty understanding spoken words. JBN's flawless performance on printed word/picture verification, written naming and a variety of semantic tasks provided evidence of intact lexical semantics. Yet, her trouble with spoken word input was not due to a peripheral hearing impairment, since she made no errors in spoken word discrimination (deciding if 2 spoken words, such as *bun* and *bus* were the same or different) using the same 34 word pairs and foils presented for spoken word/picture verification, which elicited 91% errors in that task. Her performance was also normal in repeating CV syllables, indicating spared phoneme discrimination. JBN made frequent errors in spoken lexical decision, but no errors in written lexical decision (χ^2 59; df 1; $p <$ .0001). Her difficulty with spoken input was also reflected in writing words to dictation (26% errors) compared to writing words to pictures (0% errors). Together, these results indicate a marked deficit in accessing phonological representations from spoken input, despite adequate hearing and word and phoneme discrimination.

In spoken output, JBN made many errors in oral naming to definition (64% errors), oral picture naming (62%), oral naming to tactile identification of objects (76%), and oral reading (35%) on lists matched for frequency, word length, concreteness, and word class. In contrast, she made very few errors in written output using the same stimuli (e.g., 0% errors in written naming to tactile identification). The difference between spoken and written output was highly significant in all tasks, with various input modalities (χ^2 14–56; df 1; p < .0001).

JBN's errors in both spoken input and spoken output were phonological errors, initially raising the possibility that she had a single deficit, at the level of the phonological lexicon, responsible for her errors in speech comprehension and production. However, JBN's output impairment seemed to be more severe than her input impairment, and she did not systematically err on the same items in input and output. Furthermore, she was able to match rhyming pictures, providing some evidence that JBN accessed the phonological representation for output, but had trouble selecting the sequence of phonemes corresponding to that representation. Also, her error rate (85%) in repetition, which involved both phonological input and output, approximated the arithmetic sum of her deficit in phonological input (26% errors in writing to dictation) and phonological output (62% oral picture naming), using the same stimuli. This pattern of performance was interpreted as an impairment in accessing phonological lexical representations from sublexical phonologic units during input, and trouble accessing sublexical phonological units from phonological lexical representations for output. The additive impairment in repetition most likely reflected damage to two functionally distinct lexicons or access procedures (Figure 8.5, panel B).

Still other patients with a form of "pure word deafness" may have impaired connections from the phonological lexicon to semantics (in tasks with spoken word input), with or without impaired connections from semantics to the phonological lexicon (for spoken output). For example, after a left hemisphere stroke, Dr. O (Franklin, Turner, & Morris, 1994) was severely impaired in understanding spoken words, although he very often understood written forms of the same words, and had no impairment of spoken output. Franklin et al. argued that Dr. O's trouble comprehending spoken words arose after preserved auditory processing, since he could repeat well, and after accessing the phonological input lexicon, since he was able to discriminate spoken words and pseudowords well. An illustration of Dr. O's intact repetition without comprehension of spoken words is his response to the word *slow*: "Slow, slow, slow; I know what it is, but I can't get it. You'll have to write it down for me. [word is written down] Oh, slow, well slow is the opposite of fast" (p. 1161). His performance in various lexical tasks can be explained by postulating selective impairment in connections between the phonological lexicon and semantics during input but not output. These results again indicate that either there are separate phonological lexicons for input and output, or functionally separate access to phonological representations for comprehending versus speaking (Figure 8.5, panel C).

The dissociations reported above provide evidence for either separate lexicons or separate access procedures (Figure 8.5). The striking associations between phonologic input and output deficits in other cases indicate that the separate procedures/representations are likely to be anatomically close to one another (e.g., Hillis & Selnes, 1999).

One Orthographic Lexicon or Two?

One line of evidence supporting the view of a single orthographic lexicon concerns the consistency in items that give rise to errors in both reading and spelling (Behrmann & Bub, 1992; Coltheart & Funnell, 1987; Friedman & Hadley, 1992). This evidence is discussed in Tainturier and Rapp (this volume), therefore here I will summarize an additional line of evidence that is relevant to this question.

This source of evidence comes from treatment studies. To illustrate, patient PS (Hillis, 1993), showed: (a) excellent reading and spelling of nonwords like *gand* and *thell*; (b) relatively good reading and spelling of regular words and high frequency irregular words, (c) severely impaired reading and spelling of low frequency irregular words; and (d) "regularization" errors and other phonologically plausible errors in reading (e.g., *sweat* → *sweet*) and spelling (e.g., *laugh* → *laff*). This pattern was identical to that reported by Behrmann and Bub (1992), except that PS also had preserved lexical-semantics (excluding lexical-semantic representations of animals, which were mildly impaired at the time of the study). Like other patients who have so-called "surface dyslexia," PS made homophone confusions in reading. For example, he read the word *stake* correctly, but understood it to refer to a type of meat. When PS was trained to match a set of printed homophone pairs to their definitions (e.g., matching *stake* to *pole,* and *steak* to *a cut of beef*), he improved not only in reading and understanding the trained printed homophones, but also in spelling the same homophones to definition. Untrained homophone reading, comprehension, and spelling, did not improve during the treatment, indicating that PS improved in accessing specific orthographic representations (e.g., of *stake* and *steak*) for the tasks of reading and spelling.

These results provide support for the proposal that there is a single lexicon of orthographic representations. Despite this evidence that there is a single store of orthographic word forms for input and output, this orthographic lexicon must have independent access procedures for input and output, to account for patients who have selectively impaired written word *recognition* (and intact written word production) and those who have selectively impaired written word *production* (and intact written word recognition). For example, we have described patient RCM who failed to access orthographic word forms for output (and made semantic errors or omissions in written naming), although they had no trouble reading any types of words. There have also been a wealth of cases of selectively impaired written word recognition, in the face of intact written word production (patients with "alexia without agraphia" or "letter-by-letter reading"; see papers in Coltheart, 1998). These cases indicate that the orthographic lexicon, if it is a single lexicon subserving input and output, must at least have independent access procedures for reading and writing. Thus, in building our model, we will assume *functionally* distinct input and output lexicons (and depict them as separate), recognizing that there may be a single store of orthographic representations that are independently accessed for input (reading) and output (spelling).

Is There a Distinction Between Sublexical and Lexical Representations?

Lexical and Sublexical (Orthography-to-Phonology Conversion) Processes in Reading

Marshall and Newcombe (1973) described patients who were able to read pseudowords and regular words (e.g., *mint*) well, but made "regularization" errors in reading irregular words (e.g., *pint* → [pInt] rhyming with mint; *sweat* → *sweet*). In addition, they described two patients, GR and KU, who could not read pseudowords at all, and showed no difference in reading regular versus irregular words. GR and KU made a variety of errors in reading words, but none of them were regularization errors. Rather, they made semantic errors, such as *duel* being read as *sword,* or they read words as visually similar words. These two contrasting patterns are most easily explained by assuming that there are (at least) two different ways to read words: (a) via sublexical print-to-sound conversion mechanisms or "rules" (also referred to as grapheme-to-phoneme conversion, or orthography-to-phonology conversion; hereafter, OPC, mechanisms); and (b) by activating a semantic representation, then a lexical phonological representation. Normally, one would need to read pseudowords through the OPC mechanisms, since there are no semantic or lexical representations for pseudowords. Irregular words would be most accurately read through semantic and lexical representations, since reliance on OPC mechanisms to read irregular words would yield "regularization" errors. Thus, reading of patients like PS would reflect pathologic use of OPC mechanisms for irregular words as well as regular words and pseudowords (presumably due to damage to the semantic/lexical "route"), whereas reading of patients GR and KU would reflect sole use of the "route" via semantic and lexical representations, due to damage to OPC mechanisms. Of course, an additional, partial impairment of the semantic/lexical route must be proposed to account for the numerous errors in reading words by GR and KU (Coltheart, 1980). That is, if the only damage were to OPC mechanisms, words like "duel" should be read correctly, not as semantically related words. In fact, patients who have intact reading of words, but severely impaired reading of pseudowords, attributed to selective damage to OPC mechanisms have been reported (Beauvois & Derousne, 1979). For example, Funnell (1983) reported that patient WB was able to read more than 90% of words accurately (including low frequency, abstract words like satirical), but was unable to read even monosyllabic pseudowords.

It is important to note here that patients might rely on sublexical OPC mechanisms for reading as a consequence of damage to any one of several components of the lexical system. Most of the reported patients with this pattern have had deficits at the level of the orthographic input lexicon or in accessing semantics from the orthographic input lexicon, indicated by failure to understand written words that they are unable to pronounce (Patterson, Coltheart, & Marshall, 1985). For example, patient PS (Hillis, 1993) understood bear as "what you drink at a bar" and pronounced bear as beer (see also Parkin, 1983; McCarthy & Warrington, 1986). However, other patients rely on OPC mechanisms for reading as a result of damage to the semantic system and/or the phonological output lexicon (Kremin, 1985). For example, patient HG (Hillis, 1991) had fluent, grammatical speech with almost no content, due to a profound deficit at the level of the phonological output lexicon. She was unable to name, read, or repeat even high frequency, concrete words correctly. In naming a picture of a pear or repeating the word pear, for example, she merely produced fluent jargon ("it is that which you do"). But in reading the word pear, she produced "pier," indicating use of OPC mechanisms. Nevertheless, HG showed comprehension of the word pear, by matching the word to a picture of the fruit, and not to a picture of a pier. Interestingly, after many tests of oral reading (which provided practice), HG began to use OPC mechanisms in repetition, naming, and spontaneous speech as well. That is, when given a picture of a bear or the word bear to repeat, she said "beer" [bir]. When she wanted sugar for her coffee she asked for "sooger" [sugɚ]. Such responses can be understood by assuming that HG accessed a semantic representation that in turn accessed an orthographic representation (due to severe damage in accessing phonological representations) for output, which she then converted to spoken output via OPC mechanisms. Perhaps the strongest evidence from HG that there are independent "routes" to reading came from her pattern of recovery of a limited number of lexical phonological representations. HG relearned the accurate pronunciation of a set of words, through presentation of the "phonetic" spelling of each item. For example, she learned pizza is pronounced like "peetsa" rather than [pɪzə] and that shoe is pronounced like "shu" rather than like "show." Once she correctly produced "shoe" in naming and reading, she also began to access the lexical representation of shoe in response to semantically related words like sock and boot. So, she read the sentence, He wears cowboy boots as "He weers [wirz] co-boy shoes." Whereas most words in the sentence were read via OPC mechanisms, the word boot was clearly read via the semantic/lexical route. The word boot was not read correctly via this route, because she was unable to access a lexical phonological representation of "boot." This pattern of recovery can only be easily explained by assuming that HG relied on OPC mechanisms exclusively until she developed some stored lexical representations.

The proposal of separate lexical and sublexical means of reading is not universally accepted, however. For example, Seidenberg and McClelland (1989) and Plaut and Shallice (1993) have described connectionist models of reading that can simulate some, but not all, patterns of normal and impaired reading performance without independent lexical representations (see chapter on reading, this volume). None of these simulations can reproduce the pattern of patients who make only semantic errors in oral reading (such as RGB described earlier) or the pattern of HG, who made only phonologically plausible errors in reading until she learned the pronunciation of a few words. For further discussion see Rapp and Folk (this volume). In sum, the weight of evidence therefore favors the hypothesis that there are distinct lexical representations and sublexical OPC mechanisms, although there is almost certainly some interaction between lexical and sublexical mechanisms.

Lexical and Sublexical (Phonology-to-Orthography Conversion) Processes in Writing

Just as described for reading, there are contrasting patterns of impaired performance in writing, with selectively impaired spelling of pseudowords (Shallice, 1981; Baxter & Warrington, 1985; Roeltgen, Rothi, & Heilman, 1986) or irregular words (Beauvois & Derousne, 1981; Hatfield & Patterson, 1983). These reported double dissociations in spelling irregular words and pseudowords provide evidence that there are separate sublexical and lexical mechanisms for spelling. These studies and their implications for models of spelling are further discussed in Tainturier and Rapp (this volume).

Lexical and Sublexical (Acoustic-to-Phonological Conversion) Mechanisms in Repetition

Word repetition is often considered the "easiest" lexical task, because it is often the most resistant to brain damage. That is, many patients are able to repeat words even when reading, writing, comprehension, and naming are profoundly impaired. For example, KE (Hillis et al., 1990), who we described above as a case of impaired lexical semantics, with impaired OPC and POC procedures, made frequent semantic errors in all lexical tasks except repetition. He was unable to read or write pseudowords at all, and his impaired OPC and POC mechanisms thus forced him to rely on his partially impaired lexical semantic system for reading and writing. Yet, he could repeat both words and pseudowords well, indicating selectively spared repetition. How was this accomplished? Clearly, KE was not relying on his impaired lexical-semantic system to repeat words, or he would have made semantic errors of the type he made in reading, writing, naming, and comprehension of words. Are sublexical mechanisms used for repeating words as well as pseudowords? An answer to this question can be derived from patients who can repeat words but not pseudowords and from patients who show the opposite pattern. For instance, patient JL (Beauvois, Derousne, & Bastard, 1980) could repeat familiar words quite well, but was unable to repeat pseudowords. A low-level auditory discrimination problem cannot adequately explain his problem repeating pseudowords, because such a deficit should lead to phonologically similar word errors in repeating short words, such as fat/sat or sip/sit. Instead, his excellent repetition of words was likely accomplished via the intact lexical system; and his poor repetition of pseudowords likely reflects selectively impaired sublexical mechanisms for repetition, sometimes referred to as "acoustic to phonologic conversion" (Parkin, 1996). Earlier, we discussed patient JBN, who showed the opposite pattern in repetition. JBN was markedly impaired in understanding spoken words (with > 90% errors in spoken word/ picture verification with phonologically similar foils) and in repeating spoken words (> 70% errors). Yet, she could flawlessly repeat nonword CV syllables, as long as she was informed that they were nonwords. This result indicates that JBN has spared sublexical mechanisms for repetition, in the face of impaired lexical mechanisms. When she was not informed of the lexical status of stimuli consisting of both words and nonwords, she incorrectly accepted nonwords as words (in lexical decision), and made phonological errors in repeating them. In this case, she seemed to be utilizing damaged connections from sublexical phonological units to lexical representations to repeat both words and nonwords. Together, JBN and JL show a double dissociation between lexical and sublexical mechanisms for repetition, comparable to the double dissociations between lexical and sublexical procedures for reading and spelling.

How many Lexical Routes Exist for Reading, Writing, and Repetition?

We have just discussed a number of patients who are unable to use sublexical mechanisms to accomplish tasks of reading aloud, spelling to dictation, or repetition. We have concluded that in each case the patient relies on a lexical route to accomplish the task. In many cases, it is clear that the "lexical route" entails accessing a semantic representation, as well as lexical representations for input and output, because the patient's errors (in reading, spelling, or repetition, depending on the case) are semantically related to the stimulus (Katz & Goodglass, 1990; Martin & Saffran, 1992; see also material on HG, described above and in Hillis, 1993). Nevertheless, it has been argued that when sublexical mechanisms are impaired, oral reading, spelling to dictation, and repetition of words can also be accomplished via a "direct route" from input lexicon to output lexicon that bypasses semantics. This claim is based on the observation that patients with severely impaired word comprehension, and often with severely impaired sublexical mechanisms, may nonetheless be able to read irregular words (Funnell, 1983; Coslett, 1991; Cipolotti & Warrington, 1995) or spell irregular words (Patterson, 1986) despite severely impaired comprehension of the same words. It is argued that irregular words cannot be read or spelled correctly by these patients via the semantic system, since the semantic system is damaged, and cannot be read or spelled correctly via sublexical mechanisms because OPC and POC mechanisms should not support production of irregular words, and so they must be read or spelled via direct connections between the phonological and orthographic lexicons. An alternative account of most of these cases is that partial information from the semantic system and partial information from damaged OPC or POC mechanisms can together activate lexical representations for output, as argued in Hillis and Caramazza (1991, 1995d; see also Patterson & Hodges, 1992, and chapters by Rapp and Folk, this volume). Although it is difficult to obtain such evidence for a similar direct route in repetition, since orthophonologically regular and irregular words would be repeated equally well by sublexical mechanisms, such a third, direct route for repetition has been proposed by analogy to reading and writing (Parkin, 1996).

Dissociations between Sublexical Mechanisms in Reading, Writing, and Repetition

Having made a distinction between lexical and sublexical mechanisms, it is reasonable to ask whether the sublexical mechanisms for reading are the same as those used for writing (but operating in "reverse"). A basis for this hypothesis is found in the observation that most patients who are impaired in reading pseudowords are also impaired in writing pseudowords to dictation. Likewise, most patients who rely on sublexical mechanisms for reading (patients with "surface dyslexia") indicated by "regularization errors" and other phonologically plausible errors in reading irregular words, also rely on sublexical mechanisms for writing. Of course, this finding may merely reflect anatomical proximity of the neural mechanisms underlying two independent mechanisms for OPC and POC, such that a single lesion might affect both. Support for the alternative hypothesis, that there are functionally independent OPC and POC mechanisms comes the dissociation between damage to OPC and POC mechanisms. That is, there are several reported cases of selectively impaired POC with intact OPC (e.g., HG; Hillis, 1991, and described below).

Finally, there are patients like KE (Hillis et al., 1990; see above), who make frequent semantic errors in oral reading, spelling to dictation, naming, and comprehension and mostly omissions in reading and spelling pseudowords, but make no errors in repetition of words or pseudowords. This pattern shows that sublexical mechanisms for repetition can be spared in the face of profoundly impaired OPC and POC mechanisms. But this pattern does not merely suggest that repetition is "easier" than reading or spelling. There are also patients like HG (Hillis, 1991) who are unable to repeat or spell pseudowords and make frequent semantic errors in repetition and spelling to dictation, but make no errors in reading pseudowords.

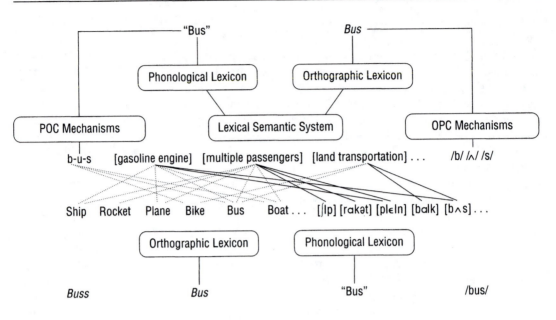

Figure 8.6: A Schematic Representation of the Organization of the Lexical System

About 30% of HG's responses in spelling to dictation, written naming, oral naming, spoken word/picture matching, written word/picture matching and repetition were semantic errors. For instance, she wrote the dictated word "bureau" as *chair*. However, as noted earlier, her responses in oral reading were quite different. She sounded out each letter in reading pseudowords and real words (yielding phonologically plausible errors), indicating OPC mechanisms can be spared even when sublexical mechanisms for both spelling and repetition are impaired.

Summary

In this section I have reviewed evidence for proposing the functional independence of each of the components of the lexical system depicted in Figure 8.6, and for their general arrangement. In the next section I address the patterns of performance (error types and effects of various lexical parameters, such as grammatical word class and frequency) that have implications for how representations *within* each level of the lexical system are organized and accessed.

PART II: UNDERSTANDING ASPECTS OF LEXICAL PROCESSING

What are the Origins of Specific Types of Errors in Lexical Tasks?

Semantic Errors

In Part I, I discussed a number of patients (PW, WMA, KE, DHY, AF, RGB, and RCM) who made semantic errors in naming—specifically misnaming with semantically related words. Traditionally, these types of errors have been taken to imply semantic underspecification (Goodglass & Wingfield, 1997, p.10). Indeed, a plausible hypothesis about WMA's and KE's semantic errors across all tasks is that they each access incomplete, or underspecified, semantic representations. Here we will assume that semantic representations consist of the set of semantic (including both visual and functional) features that define the meaning of the word and serve to distinguish it from all other related objects. For example, the semantic representation of "toothbrush" might include features like <for brushing>, <plastic>, <hand held>, <for teeth>. Suppose WMA accesses a semantic representation of toothbrush that consists only of the features <hand held> and <for teeth>. This representation would activate lexical representations of "dental floss" and "toothpaste" just as well as "toothbrush". Therefore, he might name a toothbrush as dental floss or match a picture of dental floss to the word toothbrush. Thus, the hypothesis of underspecified semantic representations would explain WMA's and KE's errors in naming and comprehension tasks. It would also explain the fact that each of these patients made different semantic errors in different modalities at the same time, and in the same modality at different times, since the underspecified semantic representations would activate several lexical form representations in each modality. For instance, accordian named as *zampogna* (pipes) in writing and simultaneously as "grammofono" (gramophone) in speaking by WMA; and a picture of a lion named once as "tiger" and at a different time as "leopard" by KE. The specific lexical form representation selected for output would depend on its current "availability" (e.g., "threshold" or "resting state" of activation), which might be different in separate modalities or at different times. For example, its availability might depend on how frequently it is produced, or how recently it was produced, in a particular modality.

A similar account has been given to explain semantic errors arising from impaired access to the semantic system from vision, in DHY, the patient with "optic aphasia" described earlier (Hillis & Caramazza, 1995a). Her semantic errors, in naming pictures and word/picture verification, can be accounted for by the following hypotheses. When DHY encounters a picture of a familiar object, her intact low level visual processing mechanisms culminate in computation of 3-D representation of the object, which then accesses a stored, structural description of the object shape. This stored, structural description supports "recognition" of the object as familiar, accurate judgments about the color of the object (even if the picture is black and white) and so on. However, because of a partial "disconnection" between stored, structural description and the semantic system, she only activates a subset of semantic features that define that object. Thus, like WMA or KE, she might activate only features <for teeth> and <hand held> in response to a picture of a toothbrush. This would account for her semantic errors in naming, of the type toothbrush → "toothpaste," and her acceptance of semantically related names for pictures, such as "dental floss" for toothbrush. But, when she is given a real toothbrush to explore tactually, or a verbal definition of toothbrush, she accesses the complete semantic representation, and is able to name it correctly. This would account for her accurate naming to definition and tactile naming. Finally, we can explain DHY's ability to produce gestures in response to visual stimuli, by assuming that gestures can be supported by a combination of a stored structural description (e.g., recognition of bristles would support a brushing action) and partial semantic information (access to the feature <for teeth> would direct the brushing action to the teeth rather than the hair or clothes).

So far it has been argued that WMA, KE, and DHY each made semantic errors in naming when they failed to activate the full set of semantic features that comprise the semantic representation of the object, noting that this failure may result from damage to different levels of the lexical system. However, we argued that other patients with good comprehension, like PW, made the same type of semantic errors in spite of accessing completely intact semantic representations. So where do PW's semantic errors in naming come from? One possibility is that PW makes semantic errors in naming whenever the representation in the output lexicon is inaccessible. In this situation a *semantic* error is produced because the semantic representation has activated a number of semantically related representations in the output lexicon. This proposal depends on some additional assumptions about how lexical representations are activated. First, we will assume that the semantic features that comprise the semantic representation each activate, to some degree, all of the lexical representations to which they correspond. So, for example, the feature <for brushing> activates the lexical form representations of "hair brush," "toothbrush," "paint brush," etc. The feature <for teeth> activates lexical form representations for "toothbrush," "dental floss," "toothpaste," "dentist," etc. The lexical representation of "toothbrush" will be the only representation in the output lexicon that will receive activation from all of the semantic features, and so it will be the most active. Therefore, it will normally be the one selected for output. However, in the face of damage to the phonologic output lexicon, the representation of "toothbrush" might be unavailable. In this case, one of the other, partially activated representations could be selected instead. This would explain PW's variable semantic errors, such as tweezers named as "pliers" in oral naming and as *needle* in written naming. The word pliers might be the most accessible of these related representations in the phonological output lexicon (e.g., because it is spoken most frequently by PW), while needle might be the most accessible in his orthographic output lexicon.

In summary, the four patients described above, WMA, KE, DHY, and PW all made semantic errors in naming objects and pictures. Although their errors were seemingly indistinguishable, they arose as a consequence of different levels of damage in the lexical system: impairment at the level of the semantic system for WMA and KE; impaired access to the semantic system from vision for DHY; and impairment at the level of the output lexicon(s) for PW (see Hillis, 1998, for other cases of semantic paraphasias arising from each of these three levels of processing). These cases point out that determining point of disruption in the lexical system that results from brain damage requires not only consideration of the types of errors made, but also examination of performance across lexical tasks that share some processing components but not others.

Phonological Errors

Semantic errors are not the only types of errors that might result from damage to the output lexicon. The preceding account of semantic errors resulting from lexical deficits assumes that the target lexical representation is wholly unavailable, and so another lexical representation, partially activated by the intact semantic features, is selected instead for output. But in some cases, a lexical representation may be partially available. To illustrate, suppose only part of the lexical representation of "toothbrush" were available. In this case, the patient might either make no response (e.g., say, "I don't know"), or might describe the semantic information he or she has accessed normally (e.g., "It's the thing you use to clean your teeth . . . you put toothpaste on it."), or might articulate the partial phonological information that is available (e.g., [tu]). Alternatively, the partial phonological information might be used to access post lexical phonological units (phonemes or syllables) or articulatory programs. Suppose the partial lexical information [t–b–] were available. The [t] might activate postlexical units for [tu], [ti], [ta], etc. and [b] would also activate corresponding units and the patient might articulate nonwords like, "tibu." Alternatively, by chance, he or she might produce a word like, "tabu," "T.B.," "tuber," etc. Still another possibility is that partial phonological information s might "feedback" to lexical representations, and activate one or more of them to some threshold that will result in selection of the word for output. In this case, the patient might select "table," "tail brush," or other phonologically similar words. There have been many reported cases of patients who make these types of errors (phonologically similar words or nonwords, circumlocutions, or omissions) as a result of post-semantic impairments (Assal, Buttet, & Jolivet, 1981; Ellis, Miller, & Sin, 1983; Patterson & Shewell, 1987). For example, the patient reported by Assal and Buttet named allumettes (matches) as "amettes, bumettes, vumettes, dumettes, adumettes, amulettes." These patients have all had fluent, well-articulated speech with no detectable motor speech deficits. Nevertheless, it is often difficult to determine whether these errors are a result of damage at the lexical level or a post-lexical, pre-articulatory level (see Rapp, Benzing, & Caramazza, 1997; Butterworth, 1992; Buckingham & Kertesz, 1976, for discussion). Post-lexical levels might include a level at which phonological units are represented (Dell, 1986) and/or a level at which the phonological units that constitute the lexical representation are held in a "buffer" while segmental and prosodic information is assigned and the word is being articulated (for further discussion see also Nickels, this volume). One test that has been used to distinguish lexical from post-lexical deficits is rhyming judgments. The ability to judge whether or not the names of two pictures rhyme, whether or not the names of the pictures can be produced, is taken as evidence that the lexical phonological representations have been accessed (Hier & Mohr, 1977; Bub & Kertesz, 1982). For example, MH (Bub & Kertesz, 1982) and JBN (Hillis, Boatman, Hart, & Gordon, 1999) both had intact processing through the level of the semantic system, as indicated by intact performance on comprehension tasks, and accurate (or recognizable) written naming, but severely impaired spoken naming, despite the absence of articulatory difficulties. MH made mostly omissions in oral naming, and JBN made mostly phonologically related word and nonword errors, such as dollar → "dolly," and envelope → "nevelope" [nɛvəlop]. MH could not make rhyming judgments, and so his impaired oral naming was attributed to disruption at the level of the phonological output lexicon. JBN was 100% correct in a rhyming pictures task, and her impaired oral naming was attributed to a post-lexical, pre-articulatory level of processing.

In short, like semantic errors, phonologically similar word errors (formal errors) or nonword errors (neologisms) might arise from damage to different parts of the lexical system.

What are the Factors that Influence Processing at Each Level?

Frequency and Familiarity

It was noted above that damage at the level of one of the output lexicons often results in a significant advantage for high frequency words for spoken or written output. This observation can be explained by assuming that high frequency words have lexical representations that are more "available" (have a higher "resting state of activation" or a lower "threshold for selection") compared to low frequency words. Therefore, when the target representation is unavailable due to damage at this level, another representation that is partially activated by the intact semantic representation above its threshold level might be selected instead. Consistent with this hypothesis, all of the patients we have described with orthographic or phonologic lexical deficits (PW, RGB, EBA, and RCM) have shown a significant effect of word frequency. But KE and other patients with semantic impairments also show an effect of word frequency. The assumption that high frequency words have lexical representations that are more "available" (e.g., have a lower "threshold for selection") compared to low frequency words can also account for an advantage for high frequency words in the face of semantic impairments. Consider the proposal that KE accessed underspecified representations (e.g., just the features <for teeth> + <hand held> for the concept [toothbrush]). These few features would equally activate lexical representations for toothbrush, toothpaste, and dental floss. It is plausible that in a case like this, when several lexical representations are partially activated by the (underspecified) semantic representation, the one with the highest word frequency should have the highest likelihood of being selected.

The familiarity of an object is often confounded with its frequency, since highly familiar objects are likely to be named more frequently and a common processing mechanism is likely to form the basis of both frequency and familiarity effects. However, the two variables can also be shown to be independent, particularly in the process of visual recognition. Funnell and Sheridan (1992) showed that apparent category effects, which were seen in a brain damaged patient even when items were matched for word frequency, disappeared when items were matched for familiarity. In the case they described, the effect of familiarity reflected impairment at the level of semantics. Significant effects of familiarity are also observed in the presence of recognition impairments, which are beyond the scope of this chapter (see Humphreys & Riddoch, 1987).

Semantic Category

Since the seminal papers by Goodglass (Goodglass, Klein, Carey, & Jones, 1966) and by Warrington and colleagues (Warrington & McCarthy, 1983, 1987; Warrington & Shallice, 1984) describing patients who were selectively impaired in naming either living things or nonliving things, there have been an explosion of reports of naming deficits (with or without comprehension deficits) that are restricted to certain semantic categories. Various accounts of these category-specific deficits, and the implications for hypotheses about organization of stored knowledge, are considered in a separate chapter (Shelton & Caramazza, this volume). Here we focus on the multiple possible loci of these category effects, within the lexical system. In most carefully studied cases, the category effects have been shown to result from damage to either the level of semantic representations or the level of pre-semantic, structural representations. For example, KE, who was shown earlier to have selective damage, within the lexical system, to the semantic system, had the most trouble naming body parts and furniture and the least trouble naming vegetables and other foods. Importantly, these category differences were nearly identical across tasks of oral naming, written naming, oral reading, spelling to dictation, printed word/picture verification, and spoken word/picture verification. The homogeneity of his category effects across all lexical tasks that engage the semantic system provided further evidence that his errors originated from this one component shared by all of these tasks. The similarity across tasks also confirms that these category effects arose at the level of the semantic system. If they arose at a lexical form or presemantic level, the effects should vary across input or output modality. In other cases, the category effects are specific to single input modality (usually vision), and are thought to arise from a pre-semantic level of stored, structural descriptions (Riddoch & Humphreys, 1987; Gaffan & Haywood, 1993).

Can category-specific effects be observed as a consequence of damage to one of the output lexicons? Unless one makes the *ad hoc* assumption that the representations in each of the form lexicons are arbitrarily organized into semantic categories, one category of words should not be more easily accessed than another. Nevertheless, category differences restricted to one modality have been reported. For example, many cases of selective difficulty naming, but not comprehending, proper names have been reported (Damasio, 1990; Lucchelli & DeRenzi, 1992; McKenna & Warrington, 1978; Semenza & Zettin, 1989). Similarly, we (Caramazza & Hillis, 1990) reported that RGB, who had intact comprehension and written naming in all categories, was much more accurate in oral naming of foods and clothing than other categories of words. In RGB's case, although the category effect cannot be attributed to a word frequency effect (because categories were matched in word frequency), they are likely due to varying degrees of personal familiarty with the items. According to his caregivers, RGB spoke about almost nothing other than food and clothes. He was quite obese, and his main past-time was eating. Consequently, he frequently needed new clothes, and needed to be helped into his clothes. Nearly all of his requests to those around him concerned either foods or items of clothing. Therefore, his apparent "category effect" with relative preservation of foods and clothing was likely to reflect a familiarity effect, or more accurately, an effect of personal frequency of production.

Concreteness

The degree of concreteness versus abstractness of a word has often been reported to affect performance on naming and comprehension tasks. This effect is generally thought to reflect a semantic impairment (Shallice, 1988a). For example, Warrington (1975, 1981; see also Warrington & Shallice, 1984) reported patients who were more impaired in processing concrete words relative to abstract words, counter to the intuition that concrete words are "easier." Indeed, the opposite dissociation, with more trouble naming and comprehending abstract words, is more common. Generally, it has been assumed that errors on abstract words come from a damaged semantic system; and often that they are manifestations of a type of category-specific semantic impairment, in which the semantic representations of abstract (or concrete) words are more vulnerable to damage.

Recently, however, Franklin, Howard, and Patterson (1995), described a patient whose difficulty with abstract words was limited to spoken production tasks. Even when abstract words and concrete words were matched for frequency, familiarity, word class, and length, their patient continued to have selective difficulty "retrieving" the abstract words, without difficulty understanding abstract words. The absence of a comprehension deficit rules out damage to the semantic system. A similar difficulty with abstract words, but limited to *written* production, was observed in the two patients described above, GOS (Baxter & Warrington, 1985) and RCM (Hillis et al., 1999). Since neither GOS nor RCM had any comprehension problem, it is unlikely that the effect of concreteness was a consequence of damage to the semantic system. We argued instead that RCM had a selective impairment, within the lexical system, at the level of the orthographic output lexicon. We further hypothesized that her significant concreteness effect emerged as a consequence of the way in which lexical representations are activated by the semantic system. That is, it was hypothesized that concrete words have semantic features that correspond to fewer lexical representations, such that there are fewer competing form representations activated for concrete versus abstract words. For example, the semantic representation of a concrete concept like "bus" shares a majority of its semantic features with only a few items (train, subway/underground, trolley, van), whereas the semantic features of an abstract word, such as "faith," shares a majority of its semantic features with many other abstract concepts (belief, credence, creed, confidence, certainty, conviction, doctrine, dogma, denomination, hope, reliance, religion, trust, tenet, persuasion, sect), at least in some contexts. Therefore, impaired access to the target orthographic representation of the word "faith" might result in selection of any one of a large number of competing lexical representations that are partially activated by the semantic representation of <faith>. The probability of selecting the correct representation by chance would be lower with the greater number of competitors for abstract, compared to concrete, words. On this account, we would not expect the opposite pattern—better performance for abstract words—in the case of a lexical form deficits, but one might see such a dissociation as a result of a semantic impairment affecting only concrete words.

Grammatical Word Class

Just as for concreteness effects, a significant effect of grammatical word class is often taken as evidence of a semantic deficit (particularly in "deep dyslexic" patients) or syntactic deficit. As first described in patient GR (Marshall & Newcombe, 1966, 1973), the characteristic word class effects observed in reading performance by patients with "deep dyslexia" is that nouns are produced most accurately, followed by verbs, then adjectives, and then function words, which are produced least accurately. A syntactic source of a noun/verb dissociation is certainly plausible, since nonfluent, agrammatic patients, usually with anterior lesions, tend to have more trouble with verbs, whereas fluent, paragrammatic patients, typically with posterior lesions, tend to have more trouble with nouns (Miceli, Silveri, Villa, & Caramazza, 1984; Miceli, Silveri, Nocentini, & Caramazza, 1988; Zingeser & Berndt, 1990).

However, other cases of of striking noun/verb dissociations demand a different sort of explanation. We have described a series of left hemisphere stroke patients with modality-specific lexical output deficits that were relatively specific to either nouns or verbs. All of the patients had fluent, grammatical speech and excellent comprehension of both nouns and verbs, but made frequent semantic errors, mostly on one grammatical word class, either in writing or in speech (but no semantic errors in the other output modality). SJD (Hillis & Caramazza, 1995b) and HW (Caramazza & Hillis, 1991) both made many more errors on verbs than nouns (matched for frequency and length). SJD's difficulty with verbs was confined to writing (for a similar case see Rapp, Benzing, & Caramazza, 1994), whereas HW's difficulty with verbs was confined to speech production. In contrast, using the same stimuli, EBA (Hillis & Caramazza, 1995c) had more difficulty on the verbs than the nouns, in the spoken modality only. Table 8.7 shows performance of the three patients on the same sets of stimuli. It is also of note that the dissociation between nouns and verbs was observed in all three of these patients, even when the orthographic and phonological forms were identical for the nouns and verbs, such as, when homonyms were tested, once in verb contexts and once in noun contexts. That is, HW could say the word, "crack" in the sentence "There's a crack in the mirror," but not in the sentence, "Don't crack the nuts here." EBA showed the opposite pattern in oral production. SJD had trouble on the verb forms, but not with the nouns forms, in written production. These striking dissociations between nouns and verbs are not readily explained by proposing that one class is "more difficult" to access for output than the other, particularly since patients HW and SJD showed a grammatical word class effect (selective difficulty with verbs) opposite to that of EBA (selective difficulty with nouns). Therefore, these results have been taken to imply that the output lexicons are organized by grammatical word class, such that separate neural mechanisms subserve nouns and verbs (see also Damasio & Tranel, 1993, for additional evidence from lesion studies and PET, and Warburton et al., 1996, for additional evidence from PET studies).

Other patients have had a marked dissociation between nouns and verbs in both output modalities, despite unimpaired comprehension of either class of words. For example, Kremin (in press) described a patient, GI, whose written and oral naming of nouns was at least 95% accurate, but whose written naming and oral naming of verbs were each only 45% accurate. Patient HY (Zingeser & Berndt, 1988) showed the opposite dissociation: more accurate verbs than nouns in both written and oral naming. One account of this pattern of performance is that the effect arises in access to the output lexicons from the semantic system (Zingeser & Berndt, 1988). In the same vein, Rapp and Caramazza (1997) described a patient, PBS, who was severely impaired in producing nouns and function words in oral production of sentences, but showed selective *sparing* of nouns in writing sentences (see Assal, Buttet, & Jolivet, 1981, and Bub & Kertesz, 1982, for similar cases). They proposed that PBS was impaired in the retrieval of orthographic representations of verbs to satisfy the syntactic/semantic constraints

Figure 8.7: Performance on Nouns versus Verbs in a single output modality by HW, SJD, and EBA.

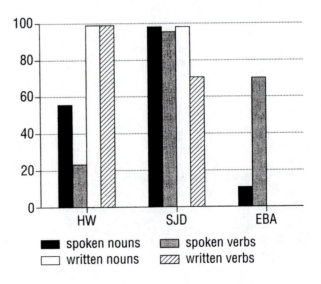

of the sentence plan. This case provides strong evidence that these processes and/or representations are both: (a) independent of comparable processes for retrieving phonological representations for sentence production, and (b) sensitive to grammatical word class distinctions. The data from all of these cases converge in support of the proposal that the output lexicons are organized by grammatical word class.

Summary

In this chapter, evidence for proposing each of the components of the lexical system, schematically represented in Figure 8.6, has been reviewed. As noted, the existence of a number of these components has been questioned. For example, the possibility that there is only one phonological lexicon, with separate access procedures for input and output, has been raised. In addition, evidence for and against proposing additional components, such as a lemma level of representation mediating between semantics and the output lexicons, or a separate "visual semantic system" have been considered. Other controversial aspects of the proposed lexical system, such as the degree of interaction between various components, and whether or not there is feedback from "later" components to earlier components are addressed in other chapters. Finally, the character of representations and the organization of information within each of these components of the lexical system has been addressed in only a cursory fashion, but is the focus of much of the current focus of investigations in this field. It is hoped that future work will make extensive progress, not only toward characterizing the representations and their interactions in this system, but also toward identifying the neural basis of these representations and processes.

Acknowledgments

The author's research in this area is supported by a K23 award from NIDCD, DC00174-01, and by the National Stroke Association.

REFERENCES

Assal, G., Buttet, J., & Jolivet, R. (1981). Dissociations in aphasia: A case report. *Brain and Language, 13*, 223-240.

Auerbach, S.H., Allard, T., Naeser, M., Alexander, M., & Albert, M. (1982). Pure word deafness: analysis of a case with bilateral lesions and a defect at the prephonemic level. *Brain, 105*, 271-300.

Baxter, D. M., & Warrington, E. K. (1985). Category-specific phonological dysgraphia. *Neuropsychologia, 23*, 653-666.

Beauvois, M. F. (1982). Optic aphasia: A process of interaction between vision and language. *Philosophical Transactions of the Royal Society of London, B 289*, 35-47.

Beauvois, M. F., & Derousne, J. (1981). Lexical or orthographic agraphia. *Brain, 104*, 21-49.

Beauvois, M. F., & Derousne, J. (1979). Phonological alexia: Three dissociations. *Journal of Neurology, Neurosurgery, and Psychiatry. 42*, 115-1124.

Beauvois, M. F., Derousne, J., & Bastard, V. (1980). Auditory parallel to phonologic alexia. Paper presented to the third European Conference of the International Neuropsychological Society, Chianciano, Italy.

Beauvois, M. F., Saillant, B., Meininger, V., & Lhermitte, F. (1978). Bilateral tactile aphasia: A tacto-verbal dysfunction. *Brain, 101*, 381-401.

Behrmann, M., & Bub, D. (1992). Surface dyslexia and dysgraphia: dual routes, single lexicon. *Cognitive Neuropsychology, 9*, 209-251.

Benson, D. F. (1979). *Aphasia, alexia, and agraphia.* New York: Churchill Livingstone.

Bock, J. K. (1982). Toward of cognitive psychology of syntax: Information processing contributions to sentence processing. *Psychological Review, 89*, 1-47.

Bub, D., & Kertesz, A. (1982). Evidence for lexico-graphic processing in a patient with preserved written over oral single word naming. *Brain, 105*, 697-717.

Buckingham, H. W., & Kertesz, A. (1976). *Neologistic jargon aphasia.* Amsterdam: Swets and Zeitlinger.

Butterworth, B. (1992). Disorders of phonological encoding. *Cognition, 42*, 261-286.

Butterworth, B. (1989). Lexical access in speech production. In W. Marslen-Wilson (Ed.), *Lexical representation and process.* Cambridge, MA: MIT Press.

Caramazza, A. (1997). How many levels of processing are there in lexical access? *Cognitive Neuropsychology, 14*, 177-208.

Caramazza, A., Berndt, R. S., & Brownell, H. H. (1982). The semantic deficit hypothesis: Perceptual parsing and object classification by aphasic patients. *Brain and Language, 15*, 161-189.

Caramazza, A., & Hillis, A. E. (1990). Where do semantic errors come from? *Cortex, 26,* 95–122.

Caramazza, A., & Hillis, A. E. (1991). Lexical organization of nouns and verbs in the brain. *Nature, 349,* 788–790.

Caramazza, A., Hillis, A. E., Rapp, B. C., & Romani, C. (1990). Multiple semantic or multiple confusions? *Cognitive Neuropsychology, 7,* 161–168.

Caramazza, A., & Miozzo, M. (1997). The relation between syntactic and phonological knowledge in lexical access: Evidence from the "tip-of-the-tongue" phenomenon. *Cognition, 64,* 309–343.

Caramazza, A., & Shelton, J. (1998). Domain specific knowledge systems in the brain: The animate-inanimate distinction. *Journal of Cognitive Neuropsychology, 10,* 1–34.

Chertkow, H., Bub, D., & Caplan, D. (1992). Constraining theories of semantic memory processing: Evidence from dementia. *Cognitive Neuropsychology, 9,* 327–365.

Cipolotti, L., & Warrington, E. K. (1995). Semantic memory and reading abilities: a case report. *Journal of the International Neuropsychological Society, 1,* 704–710.

Coltheart, M. (1980). Reading, phonological recoding and deep dyslexia. In M. Coltheart, K. E. Patterson, & J. C. Marshall (Eds.), *Deep dyslexia.* London: Routledge and Kegan Paul.

Coltheart, M. (1998). Pure alexia (letter-by-letter reading). Special issue of *Cognitive Neuropsychology,* 15(12).

Coltheart, M., & Funnell, E. (1987). Reading and writing: One lexicon or two? In D. A. Allport, D. G. Mackay, W. Prinz, & E. Scheerer (Eds.), *Language perception and production: Shared mechanisms in listening, reading, and qriting.* London: Academic Publishers.

Coltheart, M., Patterson, K., & Marshall, J. C. (1980). (Eds.). *Deep dyslexia.* London: Routeledge & Kegan Paul.

Coslett, H. B. (1991). Read but not write 'idea': Evidence for a third reading mechanism. *Brain and Language, 40,* 425–443.

Coslett, H. B., & Saffran, E. M. (1989). Preserved object recognition and reading comprehension in optic aphasia. *Brain, 112,* 1091–1110.

Damasio, A. R. (1990) Category-related recognition defects as a clue to the neural substrates of knowledge. *Trends in Neuroscience, 13,* 95–98.

Damasio, A. R., & Tranel, D. (1993). Nouns and verbs are retrieved with differently distributed neural systems. *Proceedings of the National Academy of Sciences, 90,* 4957–4960.

De Bleser, R. (1997). Modality-specific lexical dissociations. In H. Goodglass (Ed.), *Anomia* (pp. 93–114). London: Academic Press.

Dell, G. S. (1986). A spreading activation theory of retrieval in sentence production. *Psychological Review, 93,* 283–321.

Denes, G., & Semenza, C. (1975). Auditory modality-specific anomia: Evidence from a case of pure word deafness. *Cortex, 11,* 401–411.

DeRenzi, E., & Saetti, M. C. (1997). Associative agnosia and optic aphasia: Qualitative or quantitative difference? *Cortex, 33,* 115–130.

Ellis, A. W., Miller, D., & Sin, G. (1983). Wernicke's aphasia and normal language processing: A case study in cognitive neuropsychology. *Cognition, 15,* 111–114.

Franklin, S., Howard, D., & Patterson, K. (1995). Abstract word anomia. *Cognitive Neuropsychology, 12,* 549–566.

Franklin, S., Turner, J., & Morris, J. (1994). *Word meaning deafness: Effects of word type.* Paper presented at the Internation Congress on Spoken Word Processing.

Freund, C. S. (1889). Uber optische aphasia and seelenblindheit (About optical aphasia and agnosia). *Archiv Psychiatrie und Nervenkrankheiten, 20,* 276–297.

Friedman, R. B., & Hadley, J. A. (1992). Letter-by-letter surface alexia. *Cognitive Neuropsychology, 9,* 185–208.

Funnell, E. (1983). Phonological processes in reading: New evidence from acquired dyslexia. *British Journal of Psychology, 74,* 159–180.

Funnell, E., & Sheridan, J. (1992). Categories of knowedge? Unfamiliar aspects of living and nonliving things. *Cognitive Neuropsychology, 9,* 135–153.

Gaffan, D., & Haywood, C. A. (1993). A spurious category specific visual agnosia for living things in normal human and nonhuman primates. *Journal of Cognitive Neuroscience, 5,* 118–28.

Garrett, M. F (1992). Disorders of lexical selection. *Cognition, 42,* 143–180.

Gazzaniga, M. S., Glass, A. A., Sarno, M. T., & Posner, J. B. (1973). Pure word deafness and hemispheric dynamics: A case history. *Cortex, 9,* 136–143.

Geschwind, N. (1965). Disconnexion syndromes in animals and man. *Brain, 88,* 237–294, 585–644.

Goodglass, H., & Baker, E. (1976). Semantic field, naming, and auditory comprehension in aphasia. *Brain and Language, 3,* 359–374.

Goodglass, H., Klein, B., Carey, P., & Jones, K. J. (1966). Specific semantic word categories in aphasia. *Cortex, 2,* 74–89.

Goodglass, H., & Wingfield, A. (1997). Word-finding deficits in aphasia: Brain-behavior relations and symptomatology. In H. Goodglass (Ed.), *Anemia.* London: Academic Press.

Hart, J., Berndt, R., & Caramazza, A. (1985). Category-specific naming deficit following cerebral infarction. *Nature, 316,* 338.

Hart, J., & Gordon, B. (1993). Neural subsystems for object knowledge. *Nature. 359,* 60–64.

Hatfield, F. M., & Patterson, K. (1983). Phonological spelling. *Quarterly Journal of Experiemental Psychology, Section A, 35( ),* 451–468.

Hier, D. B., & Mohr, J. P. (1977). Incongruous oral and written naming. *Brain and Language, 4,* 115–126.

Hillis, A. E. (1991). Effects of a separate treatments for distinct impairments within the naming process. In T. Prescott (Ed.), *Clinical Aphasiology, Vol. 19* (pp. 255–265). Austin, TX: Pro-Ed.

Hillis, A. E. (1993). The role of models of language processing in rehabilitation of language impairments. *Aphasiology, 7,* 5–26.

Hillis, A. E. (1998). What's in an Name? A Model of the Cognitive Processes Underlying Object Naming. In E. Vischbrink & R. Baastiaanse (Eds.), *Linguistic Levels in Aphasia* (pp. 35–48). New York: Singular.

Hillis, A. E., Boatman, D., Hart, J., & Gordon, B. (1999). Making sense out of jargon: A neurolinguistic and computational account of jargon aphasia. *Neurology, 53,* 1813–1824.

Hillis, A. E., & Caramazza, A. (1991). Mechanisms for accessing lexical representations for output: Evidence from a category-specific semantic deficit. *Brain and Language, 40,* 106–144.

Hillis, A. E., & Caramazza, A. (1994). Category- and modality specific deficits in lexical processing. In M. Sugishita (Ed.), *New horizons in neuropsychology* (pp. 209–224). Amsterdam: Elsevier.

Hillis, A. E., & Caramazza, A. (1995a). Cognitive and neural mechanisms underlying visual and semantic processing. *Journal of Cognitive Neuroscience, 7,* 457–478.

Hillis, A. E., & Caramazza, A. (1995b). "I know it but I can't write it": Selective deficits in long and short-term memory. In R. Campbell (Ed.), *Broken memories: Neuropsychological case studies* (pp. 344–365). London: Blackwell.

Hillis, A. E., & Caramazza, A. (1995c). The representation of grammatical categories of words in the brain. *Journal of Cognitive Neuroscience, 7,* 396–407.

Hillis, A. E., & Caramazza, A. (1995d). Converging evidence for the interaction of semantic and phonological information in accessing lexical information for spoken output. *Cognitive Neuropsychology, 12,* 187–227.

Hillis, A. E., Rapp, B. C., & Caramazza, A. (1999). When a rose is a rose in speaking but a tulip in writing. *Cortex, 35,* 337–356.

Hillis, A. E., Rapp, B., Romani, C., & Caramazza, A. (1990). Selective impairments of semantics in lexical processing. *Cognitive Neuropsychology, 7,* 191–243.

Hillis, A. E., Rapp, B. C., & Caramazza, A. (1995). Constraining claims about theories of semantic memory: More on unitary vs. multiple semantics. *Cognitive Neuropsychology, 12,* 175–186.

Hillis, A. E., & Selnes, O. (1999). Cases of aphasia or neglect due to Creutzfeldt-Jakob Disease. *Aphasiology, 13,* 743–754.

Humphreys, G. W., & Riddoch, M. J. (1988). On the case for multiple semantic systems: A reply to Shallice. *Cognitive Neuropsychology, 5,* 143–150.

Humphreys, G., & Riddoch, M. J. (1987). *Visual object processing: A cognitive neuropsychological approach.* London: LEA.

Katz, R., & Goodglass, H. (1990). Deep dysphasia: An analysis of a rare form of repetition disorder. *Brain and Language, 39,* 153–185.

Kussmaul, A. (1877). Die storungen der sprache (The disorders of language). *Ziemssens Handbuch der SpeciellenPathologie und therapie, 12,* 1–300.

Levelt, W. J. M. (1989). *Speaking: From intention to articulation.* Cambridge, MA: MIT Press.

Lhermitte, E., & Beauvois, M. F. (1973). A visual-speech disconnexion syndrome: Report of a case with optic aphasia, agnosic alexia and colour agnosia. *Brain, 96,* 695–714.

Lucchelli, F., & DeRenzi, E. (1992). Proper name anomia. *Cortex, 28,* 221–30.

Kremin, H. (1985). Routes and strategies in surface dyslexia. In K. E. Patterson, M. Coltheart, & M. Marshall (Eds), *Surface dyslexia.* London: LEA.

Kremin, H. (In press). Apropos the mental lexicon: the naming of nouns and verbs. In F. J. Stachowiak et al. (Eds), *Developments in the assessment and rehabilitation of brain damaged patients—Perspectives from a European concerted action.* Tubingen, Germany: Narr Verlag.

Marshall, J. C., & Newcombe, F. (1966). Syntactic and semantic errors in paralexia. *Neuropsychologia, 4,* 169–176.

Marshall, J. C., & Newcombe, F. (1973). Patterns of paralexia: A psycholinguistic approach. *Journal of Psycholinguistic Research, 2,* 175199.

Martin, N., & Saffran, E. M. (1992). A computational account of deep dysphasia: Evidence from a single case study. *Brain and Language, 43,* 240–274.

McCarthy, R. A., & Warrington, E. K. (1986). Phono-

logical reading: Phenomena and paradoxes. *Cortex, 22,* 359–380.

McCarthy, R. A., & Warrington, E. K. (1989) Evidence for modality-specific meaning systems in the brain. *Nature, 334,* 428–430.

McKenna, P., & Warrington, E. K. (1978). Category-specific naming preservation: A single case study. *Journal of Neurology, Neurosurgery and Psychiatry, 41,* 571–574.

Miceli, G., Benvegnu, B., Capasso, R., & Caramazza, A. (1997). The independence of phonological and orthographic lexical forms: Evidence from aphasia. *Cognitive Neuropsychology, 14,* 35–69.

Miceli, G., Silveri, M. C., Nocetini, U., & Caramazza, A. (1988). Patterns of dissociation in comprehension and production of nouns and verbs. *Aphasiology, 2,* 351–358.

Miceli, G., Silveri, M. C., Villa, G., & Caramazza, A. (1984). On the basis of agrammatic's difficulty in producing main verbs. *Cortex, 20,* 217–220.

Parkin, A. J. (1996). *Explorations in cognitive neuropsychology.* Oxford, UK: Blackwell.

Patterson, K. E. (1986). Lexical but nonsemantic spelling? *Cognitive Neuropsychology, 3,* 341–367.

Patterson, K. E., Coltheart, M., & Marshall, J. C. (1985). *Surface dyslexia.* London: LEA.

Patterson, K., & Hodges, J. (1992) Deterioration of word meaning: implications for reading. *Neuropsychologia, 30,* 125–40.

Patterson, K. E., & Shewell, C. (1987). Speak and spell: Dissociations and word-class effects. In M. Coltheart, G. Sartori, & R. Job (Eds.), *The cognitive neuropsychology of language.* London: Lawrence Erlbaum.

Plaut, D., & Shallice, T. (1993). Deep dyslexia: A case study of connectionist neuropsychology. *Cognitive Neuropsychology, 10,* 377–500.

Rapp, B. C., Benzing, L., & Caramazza, A. (1994). *Evidence regarding the independence of orthographic and phonological representations.* Paper presented at TENNET, Montreal.

Rapp, B. C., Benzing, L., & Caramazza, A. (1997) The autonomy of lexical orthographic representations. *Cognitive Neuropsychology, 14,* 71–104.

Rapp, B. C., & Caramazza, A. (1997). The modality specific organization of lexical categories: Evidence from impaired spoken and written sentence production. *Brain and Language, 56,* 248–286.

Rapp, B. C., Hillis, A. E., & Caramazza, A. (1993). The role of representations in cognitive theory: more on multiple semantics and the agnosias. *Cognitive Neuropsychology, 10,* 235–249.

Riddoch, M. J., & Humphreys, G. W. (1987). Visual optic processing in optic aphasia: A case of semantic access agnosia. *Cognitive Neuropsychology, 4,* 131–185.

Riddoch, M. J., Humphreys, G. W., Coltheart, M., & Funnell, E. (1988). Semantic systems or system? Neuropsychological evidence re-examined. *Cognitive Neuropsychology, 5,* 1, 3–25.

Roelofs, A. (1992). A spreading activation theory of lemma retrieval in speaking. *Cognition, 42,* 107–142.

Roeltgen, D. P., Rothi, L., & Heilman, K. M. (1986). Linguistic semantic agraphia: A disscoiation of the lexical spelling system from semantics. *Brain and Language, 27,* 257–280.

Sachett, C., & Humphreys, G. W. (1992). Calling a squirrel a squirrel but a canoe a wigwam: A category-specific deficit for artefactual objects and body parts. *Cognitive Neuropsychology, 9,* 73–86.

Saffran, E. M., Marin, O. S. M., & Yeni-Komshan, G. (1976). An analysis of speech perception in word deafness. *Brain and Language, 3,* 209–228.

Sartori, G., & Job, R. (1988). The oyster with four legs: A neuropsychological study on the interaction of visual and semantic information. *Cognitive Neuropsychology, 5,* 105–132.

Schwartz, M. F., Marin, O. S. M., & Saffran, E. M. (1979). Dissociations of language function in dementia: A case study. *Brain and Language, 7,* 277–306.

Schwartz, M. F., Saffran, E. M., & Marin, O. S. M. (1980). Fractionating the reading process in dementia: Evidence for word-specific print-to-sound associations. In M. Coltheart, K. Patterson, & J.C. Marshall (Eds.), *Deep dyslexia.* London: Routledge & Kegan Paul.

Seidenberg, M., & McClelland, J. L. (1989). A distributed, developmental model of visual word recognition and naming. *Psychological Review, 96*(4), 523–568.

Semenza, C., & Zettin, M. (1989). Evidence from aphasia for the role of proper names as pure referring expressions. *Nature, 342,* 678–9.

Shallice, T. (1981). Neurological impairment of cognitive processes. *British Medical Bulletin, 37,* 187–192.

Shallice, T. (1988a). *From neuropsychology to mental structure.* Cambridge, UK: Cambridge University Press.

Shallice, T. (1988b). Specialisation within the semantic system. *Cognitive Neuropsychology, 5,* 133–142.

Shallice, T. (1993). Multiple semantics: whose confusions? *Cognitive Neuropsychology, 10,* 251–261.

Vandenberghe, R., Price, C., Wise, R., Josephs, O., & Frackowiak, R. S. J. (1996). Functional anatomy of a common semantic system for words and pictures. *Nature, 383,* 254–256.

Warburton, E., Wise, R. J. S., Price, C.J ., Weiller, C., Hadar, U., Ramsay, S., & Frackowiak, R. J. S. (1996). Noun and verb retrieval by normal subjects: Studies with PET. *Brain, 119,* 159–179.

Warrington, E. K. (1975). The selective impairment of semantic memory. *Quarterly Journal of Experimental Psychology, 27,* 635–657.

Warrington, E. K. (1981). Concrete word dyslexia. *British Journal of Psychology, 72,* 175–196.

Warrington, E. K., & McCarthy, R. A. (1987). Categories of knowledge: further fractionations and an attempted explanation *Brain, 110,* 1273–1296.

Warrington, E. K., & McCarthy, R. A. (1983). Category-specific access dysphasia. *Brain, 106,* 859–878.

Warrington, E. K., & Shallice, T. (1984). Category specific semantic impairments. *Brain, 107,* 829–853.

Wernicke, K. (1874). *Der aphasische symptomkomplex* (The complex of aphasia symptoms). Breslau: Kohn & Neigat.

Zingeser, L. B., & Berndt, R. S. (1988). Grammatical class and context effects in a case of pure anomia: Implications for models of language production. *Cognitive Neuropsychology, 5,* 473–516.

Zingeser, L. B., & Berndt, R. S. (1990). Retrieval of nouns and verbs in agrammatism and anomia. *Brain and Language, 39,* 14–32.

9

Morphology:
The Internal Structure of Words

Mark Allen
William Badecker

In this chapter we will consider how the breakdown of word formation capacities in individuals with acquired language deficits might inform theories about the way in which the unimpaired language system represents and processes morphologically complex words. To make the issues that relate to morphological processing more concrete, consider the relationships among the words that are used in the following strings that express ideas about trucks:

(a) The trucks were stopped.
(b) The trucks were stopping.
(c) The trucks were unstoppable.
(d) truck stop.

When we say that we want to understand how people comprehend complex words, we want to know what the memory structures and processing routines are that get us from the strings (a–d) to the unique meaning (a'–d') that each string has. When we say that we want to understand how people produce complex words, we want to know what the memory structures and process-ing routines are that get us from each meaning (a'–d') to the unique strings (a–d). Clearly, part of the process of comprehending and producing these structures will involve mechanisms of phrasal syntax, but part of it must involve mechanisms that interpret or compose words with complex internal structure such as *trucks, were, stopped, stopping, unstoppable,* and *truck stop.*

Because complex words—like sentences—are often composed of recognizable sub-parts (e.g., truck-s), and because people are able to use these familiar sub-parts (morphemes) in order to produce and understand novel complex words (beer truck, modems) many of the issues in morphologically related processing research have centered around a few recurring questions relating to the role of combinatorial mechanisms. These questions include the following:

- Are the operations used in complex word processing like those used in sentence process-ing? Are the meanings of complex words derived/identified by putting together/taking apart independently stored morpheme representations (decomposition)? Or are complex words stored in long-term memory along with their associated complex meanings as whole-word units?

- How are related complex words (e.g., *stops, stopped, stopping*) represented with respect to one another? Do they ever engage the very same representations in the lexicon?
- What levels of representation (meaning, abstract word, surface form) are critically engaged in the representation and processing of complex words?
- Are the (de)compositional mechanisms used in complex word processing the very same mechanisms used in sentence processing?

Answers to these questions have been pursued through psycholinguistic investigations with neurologically intact and also brain-damaged subjects with the goal of understanding how the unimpaired lexical processing system works. The aim of this chapter is to illustrate how neuropsychological approaches to morphological processing can provide useful evidence about the normal system by exploring some of the details that have proven difficult to approach using unimpaired subject testing techniques. For us, this approach is most successful when we find patient data that constrains the types of hypotheses that we can accept about the normal system, especially when the available evidence from other approaches does not compel as many theoretical exclusions. We will mostly be concerned with understanding the combinatorial properties of morphological representation and processing. Each section is organized around a question or set of related questions where we provide brief examples of the way that theoretical linguists and psycholinguists have thought about the issue(s) and then review evidence from a sample of aphasia case studies that may bear on the issue.

SIMPLE WORDS, COMPLEX WORDS, AND LEVELS OF REPRESENTATION

When we see, hear, or produce a familiar word (simple or complex) we reveal knowledge of an assortment of information about that word. For example, we know about the word *want* that it has a phonological form (/want/) and an orthographic form ({want}). We also know how to use it and understand it in its syntactic context as being a verb with certain argument-taking requirements (*John wants a house, *John wants to his friends*)[1] and certain inflection-taking requirements (*wanted, wants, *wantest*). We also know exactly what *want* means and, of specific interest here, we know that the basic meaning and other lexical properties (subcategory requirements) remain constant when *want* occurs in its various inflectional forms (*want, wants, wanted*). Because inflectionally related words (*want-wanted*) share basic lexical information (components of form, morphosyntax, and meaning), a question arises as to how this 'sharing' is represented in the lexical processing system. Do *wanted* and *want* converge onto the very same representation in the lexical processing system? If so, at which level(s) do they converge: form, lexical-syntax, or meaning? Following the terminology of current lexical processing theories, we will refer to the level where a word's written or spoken form is encoded as the *lexeme* level, and to the level where its lexical-syntax and meaning are encoded as the *lemma* level.[2]

Notions of how shared lexical-morphological information might be encoded in the processing system can be put more concretely in terms of the role of morphological decomposition in comprehension theories. Consider the written complex word *wanted* for example. A primary concern for recognition theories is whether the semantic and lexical-syntactic properties of *wanted* (WANT, VERB, +PAST . . .) are computed algorithmically each time *wanted* is encountered—by accessing the lexical-semantic and syntactic information associated with an orthographic representation of the stem *want-* (WANT, VERB, ...) and combining it with the lexical-syntactic information associated with an independently stored orthographic representation of the affix *-ed* (+PAST, . . .)—or whether instead, a unitary orthographic representation for *wanted*

---

[1] * = ungrammatical.
[2] In some single-word production theories (e.g., Levelt, Roelofs, & Meyer, 1999) the lemma level is designated as the repository of lexical syntax information alone, with lexical semantic information encoded at its own level.

is stored in long-term memory and associated directly with a representation of its lexical-semantic/syntactic properties.

Some morphological processing models are exclusively non-decompositional in this regard. For example, according to the lexical network model of Bybee (1988), each known complex word is stored as a unitary orthographic or phonological representation and is associated with its own lexical syntactic/semantic representation. Other processing models propose that complex words are represented as whole-words at the lexeme level (orthography and phonology), but that related forms (e.g., *want, wants, wanted*) may be linked to common representations at the lemma level. This style of morphological representation and processing is present in the multi-level network models described in Fowler, Napps, and Feldman (1985), Schreuder, Grendel, Poulisse, Roelofs, and van de Voort (1990), Grainger, Colé, and Segui (1991), Schriefers, Zwitserlood, and Roelofs (1991), Schriefers, Frederici, and Graetz (1992), and Drews and Zwitserlood (1995; see McQueen & Cutler, 1998, for a recent review).

In contrast to the models presented above, other comprehension models posit morphological decomposition at the lexeme level. In the Augmented Addressed Morphology (AAM) model (Caramazza, Laudanna, & Romani, 1988; Laudanna, Badecker, & Caramazza, 1989, 1992) and in the multi-level decompositional model presented in Allen and Badecker (1999), for example, form-level decomposition is exploited as a standard recognition procedure for complex words that are transparently parsable from their surface representations into their constituent parts, even for complex words that have been encountered on many occasions. According to these models, a written complex word, like *wanted*, is represented and accessed in terms of its decomposed orthographic constituents *want-* and *-ed* at the level of orthographic form, such that the very same orthographic stem representation (*want*) is engaged in the recognition of *want, wants,* and *wanted*. Importantly, models that include form-level decomposition as the standard representational format for transparently parsable complex words may also posit decomposition at other levels for complex words that are not transparently parsable at the level of form (e.g., *gave, held*). For example, according to the decompositional models presented in Allen and Badecker (1999) and in Marslen-Wilson and Tyler (1998), the inflected word *gave*, though not parsable into its stem representation *give* (and a regular past-tense affix) at the level of form, will nonetheless map onto the same abstract representation that *give* does at the morpho-semantic level, because *gave* is parsable into the abstract components GIVE and [+past] at that level.

To summarize, we have identified at least two levels where related complex words may encode and access shared lexical information: the lexeme level and the lemma (morphosyntactic/semantic) level. According to some whole-word theories (e.g., Bybee, 1988), all lexical information is redundantly specified for each lexical entry, so there will be no shared representation for morphologically related words at any level. For some multi-level network theories (e.g., Drews & Zwitserlood, 1995) shared morphological representation is not expressed at the level of form, but may exist at form-independent lexical levels (e.g., decomposition at the lemma level). And finally, for some "fully" decompositional theories (Allen & Badecker, 1999; Laudanna et al., 1989, 1992; Marslen-Wilson & Tyler, 1998), shared representation may be expressed both at the form-level and at form-independent levels for some related complex words (e.g., *want, wants, wanted*), and shared representation may be expressed at the morpho-semantic/syntactic level, but not at the form level, for other related complex words (e.g., *write, wrote, written*).

The recognition routines that are implicated by morphological decomposition at the level of form resemble those in theoretical approaches to sentence processing, in which meaning is derived compositionally by accessing independently stored lexical representations and then integrating these meanings into a discourse representation or mental model according to algorithms of combination specified by the grammar.

A number of morphological processing studies have presented arguments in favor of form-level decomposition. One of the basic techniques is to compare average response times, error rates, or eye-fixation times for sets of complex words. For example, sets of complex words may be grouped into categories depending on how frequently they (and/or their constituent parts) occur in a large language corpus. Given that lexical responses are typically faster for high frequency than low frequency words (Forster & Chambers, 1973; Monsell, 1985; Whaley, 1978), it is assumed that each lexical representation in the processing system has some stable activation level and that representations with low resting levels take longer to access than representations with high resting levels. These resting levels are thought to vary as a function of how often a unit is engaged—activation is hypothesized to be higher if the representation is accessed frequently and lower if it is accessed infrequently. Furthermore, it is often assumed that a unit's resting level will also depend on the number and frequency of all the other units that it is linked to. So by contrasting average response behavior to different subsets of complex-word stimuli, one hopes to infer something about what kinds of units are represented in the system (e.g., words, morphemes, syllables) and to what units they are linked (Alegre & Gordon, 1999; Baayen, Dijkstra, & Schreuder, 1997; Bertram, Laine, & Karvinen, 1999; Bradley, 1980; Burani & Caramazza, 1987; Colé, Segui, & Taft, 1997; Kelliher & Henderson, 1990; Laine, Vainio, & Hyönä, 1999; Schreuder & Baayen, 1997; Sereno & Jongman, 1997; Taft, 1979).

For example, Taft (1979) found that when morphologically complex words were matched in terms of whole word frequency (e.g. *sized-raked*), but differed in cumulative stem frequencies (where *size* occurs more frequently in surface forms than *rake*), the complex forms with the more frequent stems were recognized significantly faster in a lexical decision task. These and similar results have been used to argue that because cumulative stem frequency and not just whole-word frequency has an influence on recognition times, stems must exist independently of their affixes at the level of form (i.e., that all inflectional variants of a word access the same form-level stem). However, there are a number of ways that cumulative frequency effects might be made compatible with whole-word models as well. For example, suppose, as in Bybee's network model (1995), that morphologically related words are strongly connected to one another by activation-spreading links, so that every time the word *size* is accessed, it sends activation to its past-tense form *sized*, raising its resting activation level some. By this arrangement, recognition times to whole-word past-tense forms that are linked to high-frequency stems would be expected to be shorter than response times to whole-word past-tense forms that are linked to low-frequency stems. This would account for the cumulative frequency effects that Taft cites without appealing to decomposition of affixed forms.[3]

Another potential concern with using cumulative frequency effects to motivate form-level decomposition is that cumulative frequency effects need not derive exclusively from activation registered at the level of form. This becomes evident when considering frequency effects observed by Kelliher and Henderson (1990) for irregularly inflected verbs. In this study, lexical decision response times were compared for irregular past-tense forms that were matched in terms of surface frequency (e.g., *broke* and *hung*), but not in terms of the frequency of their respective stems (*break* is more frequent than *hang*). Kelliher and Henderson found that responses to targets with more frequent stems (*broke*) were faster than those to targets with low frequency stems (*hung*). Unlike the case with *sized* and *size*, though, *bought* is not composed of a stem (*buy*) and an affix representation at the lexeme level. Nevertheless, assuming that morphologically complex words engage units at multiple levels where long-term activation is registered, *broke* may receive activation every time *break* is accessed by way of the representations they may share at other lexical levels. This finding makes cumulative stem frequency effects ambiguous as evidence for form-level morphological decomposition, because it raises the possibility that the task is also sensitive to shared and/or related representations at other levels. In this case specifically, any cumulative frequency effects that might be construed as

---

[3]Taft (1979, 1994) does not necessarily assume that inflected words are represented decompositionally in the lexicon. Rather, he argues that the recognition system employs (pre-lexical) morpheme-sized units in order to gain access to stored whole-word representations.

evidence for repeated access to a common decomposed stem for *sized* and *size*, might also be explained on a whole-word-based model where, for example, *size* and *sized*—like *buy* and *bought*—share frequency-derived activation through a common lemma representation, but share no (decomposed) representation at the lexeme level.

Priming effects have also been taken as evidence that complex word forms are represented and processed decompositionally. In a classic morphological priming study Stanners, Neiser, Hernon, and Hall (1979) found that lexical decisions were faster when target words (e.g., *cars*) were preceded by their morphological stems (e.g., *car*) than when they were preceded by unrelated words; but that facilitation was not observed when primes were merely orthographically related to their targets (*car-card*). Facilitative priming between inflectionally related words (in the absence of purely formal relatedness effects) has been replicated in several languages using visual, auditory, and auditory-visual (cross-modal) prime/target presentations (Allen & Badecker, 1997; Bentin & Feldman, 1990; Downie, Milech, & Kirsner, 1985; Emmory, 1989; Feldman, 1994; Fowler et al., 1985; Kempley & Morton, 1982; Marslen-Wilson, Hare, & Older, 1993; Napps, 1989; Orsolini & Marslen-Wilson, 1997). This result is often interpreted as reflecting repeated access to a common decomposed stem representation (*car*) in inflectional priming conditions but not in orthographic or phonological priming conditions.

While these and other studies appear to rule out phonological and orthographic interpretations of facilitative inflectional priming, they do not rule out higher level sources, such as shared representation at the lemma/meaning level. Can facilitation derived from shared morpheme representations in the input lexicon be distinguished from facilitation derived from higher levels? Some have argued that morphological priming effects can be distinguished from semantic priming effects based on the finding that facilitation from semantic priming is shorter-lived than facilitation from morphological priming (Bentin & Feldman, 1990; Henderson, Wallis, & Knight, 1984) and that sometimes semantic effects are entirely absent when morphological effects are present (Emmory, 1989; Napps, 1989; Orsolini & Marslen-Wilson, 1997), even when very closely related items are employed in semantic priming conditions (Rastle, Davis, Marslen-Wilson, & Tyler, 1999). Note however that even when semantically-based interpretations for morphological priming are weakened, morphological priming might still be interpreted as the effect of repeated access to a shared entry at an abstract word level (e.g., the lemma level of Levelt, Roelofs, & Meyer, 1999), as opposed to one at the level of lexical form. These source ambiguity issues seriously limit the role of facilitative inflectional priming results as transparent evidence for lexeme-level decomposition.

Although some of the facilitative effects cited above may be difficult to interpret, response time effects from other studies appear to motivate morphological decomposition more transparently. Caramazza et al. (1988) used non-word interference results to argue for inflectional decomposition in Italian. They found that non-words composed of verbal stems with inappropriate inflections (e.g., *cantevi*, in which the first-conjugation verb root *cant-* occurs with the second-conjugation suffix *-evi*) took longer to reject in a lexical decision task than non-words composed of either real stems and nonce suffixes (e.g., *cantovi*) or nonce stems with real suffixes (e.g., *canzevi*). In turn, these took longer to reject than non-words composed entirely of nonce constituents (e.g., *canzovi*). The relevant point for decomposition is that if inflected words were represented at the level of form as whole-word units, then neither of the three non-word types would be any more word-like than the others. Therefore, if whole-word processing were the norm, then lexical decision would be nothing more than a simple matter of checking for whole-word matches in the lexicon; so all three non-word types should have been equally easy to reject. If, however, lexical verification normally operates over a lexicon where stems and affixes are represented as independent orthographic units, then one might expect exactly the result Caramazza et al. (1988) found: The more real-word constituents encountered in a non-word, the harder that non-word will be to reject.

Further evidence in support of form-level inflectional decomposition comes from the stem-homograph priming experiments of Laudanna et al. (1989, 1992) and Allen and Badecker (1999). For example, in Spanish, *mor-ía* ('she/he/it died') and *mor-os* ('Moor,' masc. pl.) are related neither semantically nor morphologically, yet their respective stems (in both cases *mor*) are orthographically indistinguishable. Allen and Badecker (1999) showed that lexical decisions to a word like *mor-os* were slower when preceded by a stem homograph (*mor-ía*) than when preceded by either an unrelated word (e.g., *sill-a;* 'chair,' fem. sg.) or an orthographically related word (e.g., *moral;* 'moral'). Because orthographically related primes shared the same number of word-initial letters (*m-o-r*) as the stem homograph primes shared with the targets, this inhibition was interpreted as reflecting a competitive relationship between stem representations (rather than whole-word representations) in the mental lexicon; when a stem entry like *mor-* is activated in the input lexicon by a stem-ambiguous prime (e.g., *mor-ía*), it temporarily diminishes the capacity for any other word sharing that stem (*mor-os*) to access it. What makes this an argument for morphological decomposition is that the ambiguity that gives rise to inhibition between stem-homographs (*mor-ía, mor-os*), but not between orthographic relatives (*moral, mor-os*), arises only when inflectional endings are ignored.

The studies above represent a few examples of how focused questions about the morphological processing system may be addressed experimentally with neurologically unimpaired populations. One limitation of this approach is that for the most part unimpaired people (by definition) perform at or near ceiling in language processing tasks (they're really good at using language). So for the most part, 'normal' psycholinguistic techniques involve detecting subtle performance differences within participants while pushing the processing system to its limits. Due to the speed and novel circumstances of many psycholinguistic experiments, though, one usually expects some (hopefully tolerable) within- and between-participant variation in terms of the size (and sometimes direction) of the effects that the experimental manipulations have on actual performance. However, the fact that unimpaired language users are typically fast, accurate, and may use any number of cognitive processing mechanisms simultaneously makes it difficult to devise tasks and stimulus conditions that will yield sufficiently transparent outcomes. Furthermore, it is often hard to induce detectable differences within normal or stressed-normal performance without creating so much artificiality that meaningful interpretations of the differences become seriously undermined.

While psycholinguistic approaches have nonetheless proved highly useful in constraining language processing models, a complementary approach is to use converging evidence from detailed case studies of individuals with missing or compromised processing abilities. Although the data from unimpaired performance cited above provide compelling support for decomposition in complex word recognition, there are many details that remain to be explored. For example, the studies above focused exclusively on *de*composition in lexical comprehension; does composition play an analogous role in output processes? Also, are there differences in modality (written versus spoken) and among complex-word types (inflection, derivation, compounding) with respect to form-level (de)composition? What role do complex-word properties like regularity, transparency, and productivity play in (de)compositional approaches? Do (de)compositional procedures reflect a primary language processing approach, or do they instead reflect a back-up system? And finally, there are questions about what form–level (de)compositional procedures might mean for higher-level processes and how morphologically complex meanings are derived/produced when form–level (de)compositional mechanisms do not apply. In the following sections, we present brief reviews of several of the available neuropsychological studies that are directly relevant to these issues.

FORM–LEVEL DECOMPOSITION AND COMPLEX WORD TYPES

Performance errors involving grammatical morphemes (omissions and substitutions) are a prominent feature in the speech of many language impaired individuals characterized as agrammatic or paragrammatic. One problem, however, is that these errors often cannot be transparently related to morphological processing theories because patients who produce them also produce other error types (e.g., formal and/or semantic paraphasias). As many have noted (Badecker & Caramazza, 1987; Funnell, 1987; Pillon, de Partz, Raison, & Seron, 1991), what might seem like a straightforward morphological error, for example, a suffix omission error (*welds* → *weld*), might instead implicate either a disruption to the phonological system (e.g., that *weld* is produced because it is a higher frequency neighbor of *welds* and/or because it has a less complex phonological ending) or a disruption to the semantic system (e.g., that *weld* is produced because semantically less complex than *welds*). If it were true that every case of morphological paraphasia in every patient were subject to alternative (phonological/semantic) interpretations, then it is unlikely that one could derive any clear evidence for morphological decomposition from neuropsychological studies. Fortunately, there are case studies of patients who present with morphological paraphasias that unambiguously indicate a deficit to the system that handles morphological representations.

Morphological Composition in Spoken Production

SJD is an English speaking patient who presents with an acquired lexical output impairment that affects spontaneous speech as well as reading and repetition (Badecker & Caramazza, 1991). Most of SJD's reading errors are morphological but she also produced whole-word form-based substitutions and phonemic paraphasias. The fact that SJD produced relatively few non-word phonemic errors compared to morphological errors (13% versus 65%, respectively) lessens the likelihood that her morphological errors were merely phonological errors. The plausibility of such a (non-morphological) origin is further limited by a contrast in her reading performance on affixed versus unaffixed homophones (e.g., teas/tease; links/lynx). In a list of homophones matched on grammatical category and frequency, SJD produced more errors when reading affixed words like *bowled* [bold] and *links* [lɪŋks] than when reading the mono-morphemic homophones of these words, *bold* and *lynx* (50% versus 20%, respectively). Moreover, errors on affixed targets were predominantly morphological (e.g., *bowled* → *bowling*, *frays* → *frayed*), while no pseudo-morphological errors were observed for monomorphemic targets. Had errors like *bowled* → *bowling* been the product of segmental substitutions (as opposed to morpheme substitutions), one should have observed similar errors for the unaffixed items as well (e.g., *bold* → *bowling, phrase* → *frayed*), because the affixed and unaffixed targets had identical pronunciations. But since SJD did not produce morphological errors on the mono-morphemic items, it is unlikely that her affix production impairment derives from phonological confusions based on whole-word representations of morphologically complex words. There are other features of her performance that also argue against whole-word based explanations of output errors. For example, she produced illegal combinations of morphemes (e.g., *poorest* ® "**poorless*: "*the most poorless Indians have very little money*"). If her morphological paraphasias were merely the result of having mistakenly accessed an existing whole-word form related to the target, then one would not expect to see the illegal morpheme combinations that SJD commonly produced (*youthful* → **youthly*) because (presumably) no such representations exist in long term memory. These facts make it difficult to view the morphological paraphasias as deriving from either lexical or sublexical phonological paraphasias. Instead, the pattern of SJD's performance leaves little room for accounts other than those that posit morphologically based compositional mechanisms in lexical production.

Additional evidence that morphological composition plays an active role in output word-formation comes from patients who present with severe semantic, syntactic, and phonological production deficits but preserved word-formation capacities. Several studies have reported patients who commonly produce abstruse neologisms in spontaneous and elicited speech which, due to lack of phonological similarity with the intended target words they replace, cannot be explained as phonological deformations of any particular word in the language (Buckingham, 1981; Butterworth & Howard, 1987; Caplan, Keller, & Locke, 1972). Thus, some patients who regularly produce neologistic jargon often do so without revealing any evidence that a phonological form was retrieved from the output lexicon. Nevertheless, these patients often show a preserved capacity to inflect words, and this capacity extends to neologisms as well. Some examples of jargon production where neologistic word forms are appropriately inflected for syntactic context are given below:

This guy, he's really knawl*ing* over me.	progressive participle
I know that somebody here's *heffin'* my drinks.	progressive participle

(from Buckingham & Kertesz, 1976, pp. 72)

when she [wiksəz] a [zen] from me	3rd Singular
if you get [dæbd] up	past participle
with a pair of [laɪsɪz] or whatchemecallem	plural
she then [dɪfraɪdɪd] that . . .	past tense

(from Butterworth & Howard, 1987, pp. 24)

Butterworth and Howard (1987, p. 24) describe five neologistic jargon aphasics with preserved use of inflectional affixes (on neologisms and on actual stems); two of these patients never made inflectional errors on neologisms, the other three were reported to have used context-appropriate inflections (or lack of inflections) on far more instances than when they were excluded or used inappropriately. Regardless of their syntactic appropriateness, though, the very presence of inflectional affixes on non-existing bases suggests that the stem and inflectional affix representations that are exploited in normal production processes have distinct origins in the phonological output lexicon (see further discussion below for reports of suffixed neologisms that involve derivations as well as inflections).

Morphological Composition in Written Production

Evidence that affixed forms are composed in written as well as spoken output processes comes from patients with various patterns of acquired dysgraphic performance. Patient BH, reported in Badecker, Rapp, and Caramazza (1996), for example, displayed an output impairment somewhat analogous to that of the jargon aphasics reported above, in that he encountered difficulties retrieving stems, but not affixes, from the orthographic output lexicon. When BH could not spell words lexically, he resorted to a sub-lexical approach to spelling based on regular phonology-to-orthography correspondences (e.g., *census* → *sensis*, *benign* → *benine*). The likelihood that BH would fail to retrieve a lexical form (and resort to sublexical spelling) revealed a striking difference between stems and affixes; BH's spellings of stems often showed that he had resorted to sublexical strategies, but not his spellings of affixes. For example, BH would spell *surfed* as *sourphed*, but not as *sourpht*; and *cabooses* as *cabuses*, but not as *cabusiz*, which suggests that BH found it considerably more difficult to retrieve stems than affixes. This selective preservation of affixes cannot be reduced to a general tendency to produce the most likely phonology-to-orthography mappings available (which includes [t] → *ed* word-finally). BH would spell *wolfed* as *woulphed*; but he would spell *concoct* as *concauct*, not as *conkauked*. This pattern of errors would not be easily explained were the lexical system to store the affix as part of a whole word representation of an inflected form. If the complex words involved in BH's output errors were stored and retrieved as whole-word units, then there would be no reason to expect preserved spellings just on the affixes of complex words (*cabooses*), but not on the ends of (pseudo-affixed) monomorphemic words (*census*). If, on the other hand, affixed forms like *cabooses* are not normally represented in the lexicon but are composed on output, then we have a ready explanation for why affixes may still be available for output even when stems are not.

(DE)COMPOSITION AS A BACK-UP MECHANISM

It is possible to formulate an alternative whole-word explanation for the patterns of performance observed in the cases of SJD and BH, by appealing to the notion of decomposition as a back-up procedure that operates only when the compromised normal (whole-word) system fails (Butterworth, 1983). However, details about the performance of these patients present serious problems for this alternative account. As a case in point, we may consider the consequences of SJD's morphological deficit for her performance with inflected versus uninflected verbs. On several occasions, SJD was asked to read both regular and irregular past-tense verbs and their uninflected based forms (e.g., *bought-buy* and *walked-walk*). On each occasion, her performance on the irregularly inflected forms and the uninflected forms for both regular and irregular verbs was quite good (between 90% and 95% correct). However, her reading performance for regular past tense forms was substantially worse (from 50% to 60% correct), and the predominant type of error she produced for these targets was morphological (either omission or substitution). This pattern, along with other details of her performance (e.g., her performance on the *links-lynx* task; and the morphological paraphasias that she produced), indicates that SJD was impaired in composing morphologically complex forms. But if the normal means for producing regularly affixed words (e.g., regular past-tense verb forms) were based on whole-word retrieval, then we would not expect her morphological deficit to alter the error rate across these stimulus categories (regularly inflected, irregularly inflected, and uninflected control). Instead, the hypothesized deficit should only affect the type of error that SJD produces when the presumed whole-word based system fails. SJD's relatively preserved capacity to produce irregularly inflected verbs indicates that her whole-word based processes are intact (in comparison to the available mechanisms for composing regularly affixed forms); while her poor performance on regularly affixed forms indicates that the compositional procedures that are compromised in this case function normally as a front-line production mechanism.

REGULARITY, TRANSPARENCY, AND PRODUCTIVITY

While facts about SJD and other patients make it clear that decompositional procedures are used as a primary mechanism in complex-word processing, there are other dimensions of morphological complexity—regularity, formal and semantic transparency, and productivity—that might place restrictions on the capacity for (de)compositional procedures to produce and comprehend complex words. While the terms *regularity, transparency,* and *productivity* invoke variable notions in morphological theorizing,[4] their properties (or at least standard notions of them) tend to cluster together in the types of alternations that are seen in languages with complex word structure, such that there will often be a large body of familiar complex words that are irregular, formally opaque, and non-productive (e.g., *teach-taught, sane-sanity*) and also a large body of familiar words that are morphologically regular, formally transparent, and productive (e.g., *walk-walked, dark-darkness*). Likewise, word-formation processes that are productive, regular, and formally transparent, often result in a fully compositional meaning, where there is nothing more to the semantics of a complex word than the combined meanings of its parts (cf. the compositional *replace-replaceable* and the non-compositional *nature-natural*), and there are also many complex words that have intermediate status along each of these dimen-

---

[4] Regularity is often used to describe (among other things) the reliability of a particular word formation process: for example, the plural noun *kids* expresses noun-plurality in a regular (reliable) way, while the plural noun *children* does not. Formal transparency is used here to describe the degree to which the morphological constituents of a complex structure are apparent in its surface form: for example, the boundaries of morphological constituency are fairly obvious in the transparently inflected word *wanted*, compared to those of the opaquely (and irregularly) inflected word *taught*. Productivity describes the extent to which a word formation process can be used to form new words freely: for example, the suffix *-ness* may be used freely to derive novel nouns from adjectives (*hardness, black-ness, . . .*), while the ability to form novel nouns using the analogous de-adjectival suffix *-ity* is greatly limited.

sions. Most current decomposition-based theories of morphological processing propose that only those complex words that are fully regular, transparent, and productive will be processed decompositionally (see Marslen-Wilson, Tyler, Waksler, & Older, 1994, for a notable exception).

Evidence from patients who display unambiguous patterns of morphological impairment supports the notion that form-level (de)composition is limited to complex word types that are regular, transparent, and productive. Again, we may take SJD as a case in point. The morphological substitutions and insertions that she produced (e.g., *awkwardly* → **awkwarded* and *glory* → *glories*) predominantly engaged inflectional and productive derivational word-formation processes for both morphologically legal and morphologically illegal responses. An additional fact regarding productivity and SJD's error performance is that while her morphological paraphasias were constrained by productivity, they were not constrained by word frequency. This fact reinforces the interpretation of SJD's impairment as implicating morphological composition in the normal system. Productivity, it must be remembered, relates not to how frequently a particular word-formation process has applied in a language, but rather to how available that process is for forming new words (Baayen, 1994; Baayen, & Lieber, 1991). While we might anticipate that morphological paraphasias that arise in a whole-word based processing system would tend to be more frequent than the lexical targets they replace, the absence of such a frequency advantage might be taken as evidence in support of the compositional approach to lexical production. SJD's legal morphological substitutions and insertions typically were uninfluenced by relative frequency of target and response: responses that were less frequent than the target were just as common as those that were more frequent. These are just the types and properties of morphological paraphasias that one would anticipate if production relied on composition rather than whole-word retrieval.

Another argument that morphologically complex words are processed using compositional procedures, and that productivity places limits on the availability of this processing approach, derives from the case of the dysgraphic patient DH (Badecker, Hillis, & Caramazza, 1990). DH presents with an impairment that affects the amount of orthographic material that can be reliably buffered for post-lexical processing. In both written and oral spelling tasks, the probability that DH will produce a spelling error (letter substitution, omission, insertion, or transposition) is a function of the amount of orthographic material that must be buffered (i.e., roughly speaking, by the length of the lexical target); and his spelling errors for mono-morphemic targets are more likely to occur late in a word than early in a word. However, DH's performance in spelling regularly inflected words, derived words with productive affixes, and compounds indicated that morpheme constituents, rather than whole-word forms, were the relevant processing units over which these target length effects and error distribution patterns were defined. DH produced fewer errors on these morphologically complex targets than on matched mono-morphemic controls, and his spelling errors on the affix portion of targets was significantly lower than that on the corresponding portion of the control items. More specifically, the probability of producing an error increased toward the end of a morphemic unit, and then dropped to baseline levels at the beginning of the second morpheme in the word. These features of his spelling performance suggest that orthographic word forms are retrieved from the lexicon and loaded into the graphemic buffer in morpheme-sized units. However, when DH was asked to spell derived words with productive (level 2) versus non-productive (level 1) morphology, a strong contrast was observed. Whereas the errors on the productively derived words exhibited the distribution pattern that had been found with regularly inflected forms (increasing error rate from beginning to end of morphological root, and then falling off dramatically in the affix portion of the target), the distribution of errors for the non-productively derived targets was indistinguishable from that observed for mono-morphemic targets. That is, DH's performance suggests that non-productively derived words are stored in and retrieved from the lexicon as whole-word representations, while complex words with regular, transparent and productive morphology are stored and processed in terms of their morphemic components.

Table 9.1
Number of DH's Oral Spelling Errors on Productive (Level 2) Versus
Non-Productive (Level 1) Morphologically Derived Words by Within-Word Position.

Derived Type	Examples	Errors				
Level 2 (Productive)	*teacher* *darkness*	7	19	25	10	4
Level 1 (Nonproductive)	*personal* *difference*	5	15	26	33	28
Within-Word Position		1	2	3	4	5

Absolute letter positions were transformed into five relative positions according to the algorithm provided in A. Wing and A. Baddeley's "Spelling Errors in Handwritting: A Corpus and a Distributional Analysis, 1980, pp. 260. In U. Frith (Ed.), *Cognitive Processes in Spelling*. Copyright 1980 by Academic Press.

Further evidence for the role of productivity in active compositional morphology comes from patient RB, an Italian-speaking jargon aphasic described in Panzeri, Semenza, Ferreri, and Butterworth (1990). Like the English-speaking patient SJD, RB produced many neologistic derivational and inflectional morphological paraphasias (illegal morpheme combinations) as well as complex-word neologisms consisting of non-existent bases with real Italian inflectional and derivational endings. Morphophonemic accommodation phenomena in Italian provide a convenient means for distinguishing word-edge phonemic errors from affixation errors. Panzeri et al. noted that nearly all of the derivationally suffixed-neologisms that RB produced involved suffixes from the few derivational types (a dozen or so) that have been argued to be truly productive in Italian (Burani & Caramazza, 1987).

INFLECTION VERSUS DERIVATION

Evidence from patients like SJD shows that whether a complex word is processed (de)compositionally depends on whether it is regular and productive, but not on its status as an inflection or derivation—SJD produced morphological paraphasias involving both inflections (*bowled → bowling*) and productive derivations (*youthful → *youthly*). However, regularity, transparency, and productivity have shown up as causal factors in many morphological processing studies, often cutting across inflectional and derivational boundaries. In fact, some have proposed that the performance facts that have been attributed to the inflectional versus derivational distinction can be accounted for instead by regularity, transparency, productivity, or the degree to which a word-formation process alters meaning, such that the inflection-derivation distinction need not be explicitly represented in the lexical processing system (Bybee, 1995, p. 243; Schreuder & Baayen, 1995, p. 140; McQueen & Cutler, 1998, pp. 413–414, 424). According to traditional notions of inflection and derivation, these word-formation types are distinguished in terms of the morpho-syntactic roles they play (i.e., the kinds of abstract morpho-syntactic operations they signal), rather than in terms of their representational and/ or processing consequences. Derivational processes typically alter the lexical category of a word (Noun + *-ful* → Adjective: *truthful*) or its basic meaning (*un-* + Adjective → "not" Adjective: *untruthful*). Words that are related by derivational processes are generally considered to be different lexical items (*governor-government*). Inflectional processes, on the other hand, do not typically alter lexical category or basic word meanings, but rather create word variants that conform to different functional roles in a sentence (e.g., the marking of tense and agreement). Forms that are related by an inflectional process are generally considered to be variants of the same word (*governs-governed*). Is there evidence that inflections and derivations are represented differently in the processing system which can be attributed to these and other grammatical distinctions, and not to productivity, regularity, or transparency instead?

Evidence that derivations and inflections involve at least some distinct mechanisms (independently of other lexical factors) in the morphological processing system comes from an Italian speaking patient FS reported in Miceli and Caramazza (1988). FS presented with a lexical impairment that resulted in frequent inflectional morphological paraphasias in spontaneous and elicited speech. FS also produced many phonological paraphasias. However, there are a number of reasons to believe that his inflectional errors were not simply instances of phonological errors. For example, FS's inflectional substitutions tended to result in the production of "citation forms" (infinitival verbs, singular nouns, masculine singular adjectives) even when these citation forms were among the least common forms in their inflectional paradigms. Moreover, his preference for citation forms could not be reduced to a preference for particular phonological endings, because often the preferred (citation) form of some targets (e.g., *fort-e;* 'strong,' masc. sg.) had the very same phonological ending as a dis-preferred form in other targets (e.g., *car-e;* 'dear,' fem. pl.). Furthermore, the fact that FS's inflectional errors could not always be attributed to simple whole-word substitution errors is evident in the observation that his inflectional mis-selections would occasionally result in the production of illegal stem and affix combinations (Badecker & Caramazza, 1989). For the inflection versus derivation issue, the relevant point is that while many clear cases of inflectional errors were present in FS's spoken output, his capacity to produce appropriate derivations remained virtually unaffected. In a single-word repetition task, FS produced morphological errors for 96.5% of all his incorrect word responses (624 errors in all). Of these, 96.3% were inflectional errors, whereas only 3.7% were derivational errors. The fact that varying degrees of regularity, transparency, and productivity are present in both derivational and inflectional word-formation processes in Italian, but that morphological paraphasias were rarely observed for any derivational forms that FS produced, including the regular and productive ones, makes it difficult to appeal to these properties alone as the basis for the performance pattern observed in this patient.

The performance of FS (which was near categorical) and that of other patients that exhibit inflection-derivation dissociations (e.g., patients HH and JS; Laine, Niemi, Koivuselkä-Sallinen, Ahlsén, & Hyönä, 1994, 1995; and patient FM, Badecker, 1997), supports morphological processing theories of normal performance in which the derivation-inflection distinction derives from something other than graded differences in regularity, productivity, or the degree to which word-formation processes involve meaning changes. However, one should not assume that all impairments resulting in a disruption of inflection, but not derivation, are alike in their functional origins. Given that there are multiple ways in which derivation and inflection could differ in terms of language processing mechanisms, a closer look at individual patient cases might compel models of unimpaired performance that will provide a more refined framework for explaining how observed inflection/derivational dissociations arise in acquired deficits.

In this section we have presented several examples of impaired performance on morphological processing tasks that are consistent only with those normal processing theories that posit a dominant role for form-level morphological (de)composition. We have also observed, however, that this mechanism may not be available for the recognition and production of complex words that are derived by non-productive word-formation processes. As noted in the introduction, some current morphological processing theories posit morphological decomposition at modality-neutral levels of representation, in addition to decomposition at the level of form. In the following section, we present evidence from impaired performance that is consistent with compositional morphological representation and processing at abstract levels as well as at the form-level. Additionally, this evidence will support a functional distinction between compositional mechanisms at these separate levels.

LEVELS OF MORPHOLOGICAL REPRESENTATION AND PROCESSING

The differences between morphologically 'irregular' complex-words (*teach-taught, sane-sanity*) and 'regular' complex words (*want-wanted, dark-darkness*) are likely to have substantial consequences for comprehension and production mechanisms. For the 'regular' types, there is a one-to-one correspondence between phonological/orthographic markers that signal the lexical semantics of the word and its morpho-syntactic features or derivational properties; while for the 'irregular' types, combinations of semantics and morphosyntax at the lemma/meaning level are not signaled by a corresponding additive combination of phonological/orthographic markers at the lexeme level. The transparent additivity of the former types makes it possible for form-level routines to access meaning (or be accessed by meaning) in a combinatorial fashion by manipulating independently stored lexemes. But this processing approach is not possible for those inflected words that have unproductive, irregular, and/or nontransparent morphology (e.g., *give-gave-given*; *hit-hit*; *sleep-slept*; or *go-went*).

However, according to processing models in which morphological structure is encoded not only by manipulating discrete combinatorial units of orthography and phonology, but also by manipulating discrete combinatorial units of lexical syntax and meaning, relationships between irregular (non-transparent) inflected words are just as regular and compositional at the level of morpho-syntax and meaning as are regularly inflected words. For example, consider the irregular verb pair *give-gave*: while it may be difficult to conceive of decomposition and combinatorial processing of *gave* at the form-level, *gave* retains the same perfect sense of combination of the meaning of its stem and its morpho-syntactic features that *wanted* does—just as the difference between *want* and *wanted* is the feature [+past] and nothing else, so is the difference between *give* and *gave* the feature [+past] and nothing else. Because the processing system must handle regular combinations of semantics and morphosyntax (e.g., [GIVE, (+past)]) in the absence of regular or transparent concatenations of form-level markers (i.e., *gave*), the recognition and production of complex words appears to involve mechanisms of combinatorial analysis that engage abstract morpho-lexical representations as well as others that compose representations of surface form.

Evidence in support of a division between the combinatorial operations that handle (abstract) morphosyntactic structures (e.g., [WALK, (+past)]; [HOLD, (+past)]) for all inflectionally complex words—both regular and irregular—and those that compute regular combinations of surface morphemes (e.g., *walk + ed)* can be observed in the divergent patterns of morphological deficit in patients FM and SJD. SJD exhibited a morphological impairment that selectively disrupted the production of regularly inflected forms like *walked* and *wanted*, but left the production of irregularly inflected forms like *held* and *slept* intact. This pattern of impairment differs from that of patient FM, who presents with a morphological impairment that effects the recognition and production of both regularly and irregularly inflected forms (while leaving derivation comparatively intact; Badecker & Caramazza, 1987; Badecker, 1997). In FM's case, the morphological errors he produced were the consequence of a deficit that diminished his ability to differentiate past from present tense verb forms, or plural from singular nouns. This pattern has also been documented in patient PB (Badecker, Rapp, & Caramazza, 1995), whose impaired ability to interpret or produce both regular and irregular inflection in single word processing tasks (e.g., reading, repetition, and picture-naming) and sentence-level tasks (e.g., sentence-picture mapping and picture description) provides support for a modality-neutral level of lemma/semantic representation that can be dissociated from the representations and mechanisms responsible for spelling out and arranging the regular morpho-phonological strings that express grammatical inflection. While the performance of patients FM and PB is best understood in terms of a deficit affecting combinatorial aspects of lemma/semantic representations, the performance of patient SJD is best understood in terms of a preservation of such capaci-

Table 9.2

Single-Word Reading Performance on Inflectionally Irregular and
Regular Verbs in their Past Tense (e.g., *walked, bought*) and
Base Forms (*walk, buy*) by Patients SJD and FM.

	Irregular Verbs		Regular Verbs	
	Irregular Past Tense	Corresponding Base Form	Regular Past Tense	Corresponding Base Form
Patient SJD				
Correct	37	38	21	34
Errors:				
Morphological	2	2	19	5
Phon(w)	1	–	–	1
Total	40	40	40	40
Patient FM				
Correct	10	27	4	31
Errors:				
Morphological	18	4	32	5
Semantic	4	4	1	1
Visual/other	8	5	3	3
Total	40	40	40	40

ties, with a disruption instead to the mechanisms that compose surface morphological constituents in the output system.

Thus, the contrast between patients like FM and SJD highlights the fact that although the lexical processor is capable of representing and processing inflections by directly associating whole-form units at one level (e.g., *taught*) with pre-composed meaning/morpho-syntactic structures at another (e.g., TEACH, [+past])—which is the standard means for handling irregular inflections in the unimpaired system—this rote storage capacity is not normally exploited for handling regular inflections. Otherwise, any patient with a preserved capacity for handling abstract morphological structures, like SJD, could simply appeal to this whole-form processing resource when producing regular inflections.

While the evidence given above suggests that the unimpaired lexical system includes mechanisms that derive and compose complex structures at the lemma/meaning level in the absence of combinatorial operations at the lexeme level (e.g., irregular inflections), one might wonder whether it also includes mechanisms that derive and compose regular combinations at the lexeme level in the absence of composite structures at the lemma/meaning level. But under what circumstances might the processing system carryout form-level combination in the absence of meaning-level combination? Perhaps when comprehending and producing semantically opaque compounds, such as *lighthouse* and *highway*. A semantically opaque compounds like *highway* is the complement of an irregular inflection like *taught*, in some sense, in that *highway* is composed of two recognizable form-level constituents, yet its meaning cannot be derived simply by combining the meaning of *high* with the meaning of *way*.

CSS (Badecker, 1993, 1998) presents with an acquired anomia that results in semantic and form-related paraphasias in naming tasks with morphologically simple targets (e.g., FORK → *spoon*; PENGUIN → *pendulum*). In both picture naming and naming to definition, CSS's overall performance level was fair (ca. 80% correct) for monomorphemic targets. When asked to name objects with compound names, though, his performance drops significantly (to about 50% correct). It is the errors that CSS produces for these items, though, which indicates that the normal production system employs compositional mechanisms for deriving the forms of compounds like *seahorse* and *cheerleader*. He frequently produced neologisms involving the substitution and/or misordering of the compound constituents (e.g., WHEELCHAIR → *wheel pill*; WEIGHT

LIFTER → *weight loafer*; TRASH CAN → *can trash*); and of specific interest here, he produced these neologisms even for targets that are semantically opaque (e.g., BUTTERFLY → *butter flower*; SOUTH PAW → *south ball*; and SUNDIAL → *sunclock*). While CSS's compound neologisms are superficially distinct from the errors he produced when attempting to name objects with mono-morphemic names; they are, in fact, closely related in kind. Setting aside misordering errors, CSS's compound neologisms involved substitutions of compound constituents that were either related in form to one of the two target constituents, or related semantically to the target as a whole.[5] These errors indicate that compounds, whether semantically compositional or not, are produced by retrieving constituent lexical items and a structural specification of the target form into which the two constituents must be fit. However, the formation process that these errors implicate differs from the type of composition one observes with regular inflection, in that the fabrication of compound forms is lexically driven (cf. the notion of a 'minor rule' in Stemberger, 1985), rather than applying over an entire class of lexical items (e.g., the regular verbs). For present purposes, though, we must note that the compositional approach to compound production appears to depend on the productivity of the word-formation process, rather than on the semantic compositionality of the morphological product.

Libben (1998) describes a patient RS, who shows impaired performance in compound recognition that complements CSS's production impairment, in terms of implications for form-level combinatorial procedures. Patient RS presented with a considerable semantic impairment in verbal comprehension, including (among other impairments) a marked inability to inhibit contextually inappropriate homophone meanings. For example, for the word *carnation*, RS was unable to suppress its meaning as the brand name of canned milk, when it was presented in a context that made clear its meaning as a flower. This deficit extended to a difficulty in suppressing the literal meanings of the constituents of semantically opaque compounds. For example, in a word definition task, RS was presented with written compounds of three types: phonologically and semantically transparent (e.g., *birdhouse, blueberry*), phonologically transparent but semantically opaque (e.g., *butterfly, dumbbell, flashlight*), and phonologically and semantically opaque (e.g., *highland, breakfast, cupboard*). For those compounds that were phonologically transparent, RS tended to produce semantically transparent definitions, even for semantically opaque compounds. This resulted in correct performance for semantically transparent compounds, but odd definitions for semantically opaque compounds. Often these novel paraphrases were blends of the whole-word meaning and the literal meaning of one of the constituents:

dumbbell: Stupid weights . . . Arnold
butterfly: A pretty fly . . . it's yellow
flashlight: You can put it in your pocket and it flashes

It might be argued that RS was simply generating definitions for any of the words that she could recognize within compounds that she encountered, rather than actually attempting to access stored compound representations. This is unlikely, though: First, RS did not attempt transparent definitions for phonologically opaque compounds (e.g., *cupboard*) even though

---

[5]Analogous performance has also been reported for German-speaking patients (Hittmair-Delazer, Andree, Semenza, De Bleser, & Benke, 1994), and also for an Italian-speaking patient, MB (Delazer & Semenza, 1998). Of particular interest in the case of MB is the fact that his compound neologisms exhibited a clear sensitivity to the grammar of compounding in Italian: for example, verb component substitutions in VN compounds were properly marked according to their conjugation (e.g., *accendisigari* 'lighter,' literally: light [2nd conj.] cigar → *lanciafiamme* 'flamethrower,' literally: throw [1st conj.] flames); and phonologically reduced forms of constituent targets apeared in their required non-reduced form when their order is altered in the compound neologism (e.g., *motoscafo* 'motor boat' → *scafomotore* 'boat motor [neologism]'). Hence, MB's neologistic errors help to motivate a compositional approach to the production of compounds insomuch as they manifest formal constraints on lexical well-formedness that are unexpected outside the domain of this word-formation process.

these types consist of recognizable word sub-components (i.e., *cup, board*). Second, RS was able to distinguish existing compounds from novel compounds in a lexical decision task. Thus, RS appeared to have fairly preserved knowledge that certain word combinations constitute compound entries in her lexicon while others do not.

Given these facts, Libben argues that RS's 'blended' compound paraphrases are consistent with her inability to suppress contextually inappropriate meanings of homographs, and most importantly, that it implies that individual lexeme-level constituents are engaged in normal compound recognition procedures, even when the whole-word meanings of compounds turn out to be non-compositional. Specifically, Libben argues that for normal comprehension, all phonologically transparent compounds are automatically parsed and each constituent accesses its own meaning. Additionally, the whole word (structured) representation is recognized and it gains access to the non-composed meaning of the compound. When the system operates normally, the whole-word meaning will eventually inhibit any individual constituent meanings that are incompatible with it, because the whole-word meaning corresponds to more of the representation at the form level than either constituent alone. However, in the event that a neurological impairment compromises the mechanisms that normally suppress inappropriate meanings, as in the case of RS, comprehension of semantically opaque compounds will suffer, because the meanings of unsuppressed constituents will mistakenly contribute to its interpretation.

To summarize, we have identified several sources of evidence that the combinatorial procedures involved in morphological processing operate at the level of form independently from levels where abstract morpho-syntactic and morpho-semantic operations are engaged. First, where processing involves complex words that are non-compositional in form, but compositional in morphosyntax (i.e., irregular verbs such as *gave*), we have identified a contrast between a patient with spared capacities of abstract morphology, but an impaired ability to compose form-level morphemes on output (SJD), and patients with impaired capacities of abstract morphology, which affects performance at all levels of complex word processing (FM and PB). This implicates a processing component in which combinatorial operations of (abstract) morphology are engaged regardless of formal constituency (preserved in the case of SJD, and disrupted in FM and PB). Second, where processing involves complex words that are transparently compositional in form, but not in meaning (e.g., opaque compounds), we have identified patients (CSS, RS) whose impairments implicate a processing system that engages combinatorial procedures of formal constituency, even in the absence of higher-level morpho-semantic composition.

RELATIONSHIPS BETWEEN MORPHOLOGICAL AND SENTENCE PROCESSING

We have cast our discussion of (de)composition in terms of how a combinatorial style of lexical processing might resemble the combinatorial approach involved in sentence processing. Because languages such as English have limited word-formation capacity, and because most other languages with greater word-formation capacities (such as Italian, German, and Dutch) are nonetheless finite, we may ask whether all known complex words in these languages are stored in long-term memory. However, this question seldom arises in sentence processing theories, presumably because other properties of phrasal syntax in natural languages (e.g., recursion), make it impossible that every sentence that one has encountered is stored in long-term memory, or that one's capacity to produce new sentences could be based on "sentence retrieval" processes. We have presented evidence from studies of normal and language-impaired populations that regular, productive, and transparent complex-words—like sentences—are composed during production and decomposed during comprehension. Because this complex word building capacity parallels the capacities that are evident in the processing of phrasal syntax (e.g., novel structure formation), one might wonder whether the very same mechanism is implicated in both cases.

From a purely descriptive view, the differences that have been observed between word-level and sentence-level structures within many languages might lead one to believe that distinct processing mechanisms are involved. For example, Anderson (1992, p. 34) points out that in many languages with rich morphology, the ordering of agreement markers (with respect to grammatical roles) is often very different from the order of arguments at the sentence level; in Kʷakʷala, Anderson notes, the word-internal 'syntax' violates virtually every principle of the phrasal syntax. Some historical analyses suggest that the word internal constituent order is often the same as the word order that the language had before the agreement morphemes were grammaticalized (from pronouns or clitics). These and other facts have lead some linguists to posit separate components of the competence grammar for word-level and phrase-level syntax (Anderson, 1992; Beard, 1995; Jackendoff, 1997). This approach stands in contrast to those who argue that the principles of morphology are just those of the phrasal syntax applied to lexical structure (Baker 1988; Halle & Marantz, 1993; Lieber, 1992).

From a processing perspective, the issue is whether the mechanism that composes regular and productive complex words out of sub-lexical morphemic constituents is the same mechanism as the one that composes sentences out of whole-word forms; and if it's not, then how the process of putting sentences together might influence the process of putting words together and vice-versa. There is some evidence from patients with acquired language impairments that at least some of the mechanisms involved in productive word formation are not the same mechanisms involved in sentence processing.

Patient BN (Tyler, Behrens, Cobb, & Marslen-Wilson, 1990), who presented with a morphological comprehension impairment, exhibited a lack of sensitivity to inflectional and derivational ill-formedness when monitoring for words presented in sentence contexts. Tyler and colleagues have demonstrated in several studies that when unimpaired participants monitor for a target word in a sentence context (i.e., press a button as soon as they hear a pre-specified word in a spoken sentence), they will often show a disruption (longer reaction times) when the target word is preceded by some linguistically defined anomaly (Tyler, 1992). For example, reaction times to the target word *cook* are found to be slower when preceded by the ill-formed word *wastely*, as in "He was the most *wastely cook* : . . . ," than when preceded by the well-formed word *wasteful*, as in "He was the most *wasteful cook.* . . . " Tyler et al. (1990) report that BN, unlike unimpaired participants, failed to show monitoring disruptions when he encountered inappropriate inflections (e.g., detecting the word *pain* in "It *often causes/*causing pain* . . . "), inappropriate derivations (e.g., detecting the word *bumps* in " . . . *to flatten/*flatly bumps* . . . "), or illegal combinations of derivational bases and affixes (. . . *to flatten/*flatment bumps* . . .). However, in single-word presentation contexts, BN showed relatively intact performance. For example, he performed well on a lexical decision task, which included legal and illegal affixed forms like *wasteful* and *wastely* in the word and non-word stimuli respectively, and he performed well in a lexical gating task (Grosjean, 1980), in which he could recognize simple and complex spoken words as quickly as normal control participants. This suggests that BN does not have an impairment in using the morpho-lexical information encoded in stems and affixes of complex words in order to evaluate whether a particular word-level combination of morphemes at the lexeme level is acceptable. Instead, BN appears insensitive to the syntactic and semantic information encoded in morphological stems and affixes in terms of the contribution that this information makes in determining whether a particular structure is coherent at the sentence level.

Consistent with the notion of syntactic and lexical autonomy, some current theories of sentence production (e.g., Garrett, 1982, 1984; Lapointe, 1985) predict that morphological paraphasias, such as agreement errors, can result from deficits to sentence processing mechanisms while single-word processing remains unimpaired. Two such cases have been reported: patients 'Clermont' (Nespoulous et al., 1988) and ML (Caramazza & Hillis, 1989).

Patient ML exhibits an intact ability to produce lexical forms of all categories (including open and closed class vocabularies) in single-word tasks such as reading aloud, writing to dictation, and repetition. However, in all production tasks involving sentence-level processing (including spontaneous speech, oral and written story telling and picture description, sentence reading and repetition), her output was substantially impaired with respect to phrase length, word order, and closed-class vocabulary. The impairment with regard to closed-class items is most notable. ML produced more (omission) errors with free-standing grammatical morphemes than with bound morphemes, but the morphological errors that she produced were limited to inflectional morphology. These inflectional errors included the omission of obligatory agreement morphology and errors in the expression of tense and aspect. However, unlike FM and PB, who produce analogous morphological errors in single-word tasks (as well as sentence-level production tasks), ML exhibited impairments to inflectional processing in sentence-level production tasks alone.

The presence of agreement errors in ML's speech supports the hypothesis that morphological deficits can arise from damage to syntactic (non-lexical) processing components, further evidence for this position is found in other studies as well. For example, cases have been documented of patients with acquired morphological deficits that result in impaired capacities to produce inflections in some syntactic contexts but not in others (Bastiaanse & van Zonneveld, 1998; Benedet, Christiansen, & Goodglass, 1998; Miceli, Silveri, Romani, & Caramazza, 1989). For example, Bastiaanse and van Zonneveld (1998) have recently reported a study in which sentences were elicited from Dutch-speaking aphasic patients by means of a framed-response picture description task, in which patients described an event in a picture (e.g., a farmer milking a cow) using a designated sentence structure (e.g., [*I think that*] *the X verbs the Y*). In this task, sentence descriptions were elicited that required patients to produce inflected verbs in main clauses on some occasions, and inflected verbs in subordinate clauses on other occasions. An analogous task in English would require something like "The farmer <u>milks</u> the cow" in the main clause condition and "I think that the farmer <u>milks</u> the cow" in the subordinate clause condition.[6] Nine aphasic patients who were observed to produce inflectional errors in spontaneous speech completed the study. Eight of these patients exhibited a greater capacity to retrieve and inflect verbs correctly when inflection was required in a subordinate clause than when it was required in a main clause, while one patient could not retrieve any verbs in either context. Thus, there was a clear advantage for the retrieval of inflection-bearing verbs in subordinate clauses. Furthermore, when patients could retrieve subordinate clause verbs correctly, they also tended to inflect them correctly, whereas when verbs were correctly retrieved in main clauses, appropriate inflection was not as likely. Other studies that reveal contrasting patterns of inflectional impairment have documented that some patients make more production and comprehension errors in grammatical agreement for some types of syntactic relationships than for others (e.g., subject-verb, noun-adjective, determiner-noun, etc.) (Benedet et al., 1998; Miceli et al., 1989). Currently, however, it is not well understood how the normal sentence processing and lexical processing systems could be disrupted such that the production and comprehension of grammatical inflection for some aphasic patients is more difficult in some syntactic contexts than in others.

SUMMARY AND CONCLUSION

In this chapter, we have presented a case-study review that focuses on patterns of impaired morphological performance that reveal something about the combinatorial properties of the unimpaired morphological processing system. Many of the formal properties of languages involving complex words have motivated compositional-style analyses of regular, transparent,

---

[6]Note that in the corresponding Dutch sentences, the verb occurs clause-medially (in second position) in main clauses, and clause-finally in subordinate clauses.

and productive inflections and derivations in the competence grammar. These language properties have also prompted researchers to ask questions about how recurring lexical symbols are detected and analyzed by the language hearer and how they are selected and arranged by the language speaker. Many neuropsychological studies of morphological processing have focused on whether complex words are stored and processed in terms of their constituent parts or whether they are stored and processed as whole-word units. The evidence that we have discussed indicates that the lexical system exploits compositional mechanisms in normal processing contexts for the production of morphologically complex forms, as well as corresponding mechanisms for the recognition of these complex forms. Furthermore, the compositional approach to lexical production appears to be the normal option for regularly inflected forms (even familiar forms like *walked*), as well as for productively derived and compound forms. Although composition may be taken to be the norm for inflection, compounding, and productive derivation, some of the mechanisms underlying composition in these morphological categories may differ from one another in important ways. For example, the mechanisms that underlie feature-spelling 'rules' for expressing regular inflection (e.g., the mechanisms that build or analyze the form-level structure *walk+ed*) may need to be distinguished from lexically driven composition procedures, as hypothesized in the case of productive compounding (e.g., the mechanisms that build or analyze the form-level structure *butter+fly*). The evidence from acquired aphasia also indicates that, at a more abstract level of processing, 'simple' lexical representations are combined with morpho-syntactic features to form inflectionally elaborated lexical representations. The representations and mechanisms that are implicated in the construction of these inflectionally elaborated representations enjoy some degree of computational independence both from the mechanisms that must be invoked for the production of uninflected (mono-morphemic) forms, and from the mechanisms for composing productively affixed and compound representations at the level of form.

The issue of morphological compositionality relates to more than one lexical level, and to both lexical and syntactic processing domains. Many details of the lexical system as it pertains to morphological processing remain to be elaborated more fully than we have done here (a discussion of some of these open issues may be found in Badecker & Caramazza, 1998). One point that we should not fail to emphasize here, though, is that the study of acquired language deficits provides a rich and informative basis for the study of normal language representation and processing. Rather than portraying this body of evidence as standing apart from the findings of normal psycholinguistic research, though, we would reiterate that its significance lies in its ability to complement and to direct the interpretation of findings from standard chronometric studies of intact processing. Often neuropsychological data is comprised of compellingly evocative task responses—errors such as reading *fearless* as *fearing* or *fearly*, or naming a picture of a trash can a *can trash*—that bear a wealth of information about their origins. The virtue of this evidence, like any other, is that with careful analysis it may offer up to us how its properties are determined by the nature of the complex system that underlies our language faculty. The real importance of this research is simply that it provides another route that can lead, along with many potential others, to a clearer picture of how the language processing system is organized, and what its representational properties are.

REFERENCES

Alegre, M., & Gordon, P. (1999). Frequency effects and the representational status of regular inflections. *Journal of Memory and Language, 40*, 41–61.

Allen, M., & Badecker. W. (1997, November). *Recoding and cross-modal priming of inflected verbs in English.* Poster presented at the 38th Annual Meeting of the Psychonomic Society, Philadelphia, PA.

Allen, M., & Badecker. W. (1999). Stem homograph inhi-

bition and stem allomorphy: Representing and processing inflected forms in a multilevel lexical system. *Journal of Memory and Language, 41*, 105–123.

Anderson, S. (1992). *A-morphous morphology.* Cambridge, UK: Cambridge University Press.

Baayen, H. (1994). Productivity in language production. *Language and Cognitive Processes, 9*, 447–469.

Baayen, H., & Lieber, R. (1991). Productivity and English derivation: A corpus-based study. *Linguistics, 29,* 801–843.

Baayen, H., Dijkstra, T., & Schreuder, R. (1997). Singulars and plurals in Dutch: Evidence for a parallel dual-route model. *Journal of Memory and Language, 37,* 94–117.

Badecker, W. (1993, October). *Compound neologisms and their meaning.* Presented to the 31st Annual Meeting of the Academy of Aphasia, Tucson, AZ.

Badecker, W. (1997). Levels of morphological deficit: Indications from inflectional regularity. *Brain and Language, 60,* 360–380.

Badecker, W. (1998). *Lexical composition and the production of compounds: Evidence from errors in naming.* Unpublished manuscript, Johns Hopkins University.

Badecker, W., & Caramazza, A. (1987). The analysis of morphological errors in a case of acquired dyslexia. *Brain and Language, 32,* 278–305.

Badecker, W., & Caramazza, A. (1989). A lexical distinction between inflection and derivation. *Linguistic Inquiry, 20,* 108–116.

Badecker, W., & Caramazza, A. (1991). Morphological composition in the lexical output system. *Cognitive Neuropsychology, 8,* 335–367.

Badecker, W., & Caramazza, A. (1998). Morphology and aphasia. In A. Zwickey & A. Spencer (Eds.), *Handbook of morphology* (pp. 390–405). Oxford, UK: Blackwell.

Badecker, W., Hillis, A., & Caramazza, A. (1990). Lexical morphology and its role in the writing process: Evidence from a case of acquired dysgraphia. *Cognition, 35,* 205–243.

Badecker, W., Rapp, B., & Caramazza, A. (1995, November). *A modality-neutral lexical deficit affecting morpho-syntactic representations.* Paper presented at the 33rd Annual Meeting of the Academy of Aphasia, San Diego, CA. (Abstract in *Brain and Language, 51,* 83–84).

Badecker, W., Rapp, B., & Caramazza, A. (1996). Lexical morphology and the two orthographic routes. *Cognitive Neuropsychology, 13,* 161–175.

Baker, M. (1988). *Incorporation: A theory of grammatical function changing.* Chicago: University of Chicago Press.

Bastiaanse, R., & van Zonneveld, R. (1998). On the relation between verb inflection and verb position in Dutch agrammatic aphasiacs. *Brain and Language, 64,* 165–181.

Beard, R. (1995). *Lexeme-morpheme base morphology.* Albany, NY: State University of New York Press.

Benedet, M., Christiansen, J., & Goodglass, H. (1998). A cross-linguistic study of grammatical morphology in Spanish- and English-speaking agrammatic patients. *Cortex, 34,* 309–336.

Bentin, S., & Feldman, L. (1990). The contribution of morphological and semantic relatedness to repetition priming at short and long lags: Evidence from Hebrew. *Quarterly Journal of Experimental Psychology, 42A,* 693–711.

Bertram, R., Laine, M., & Karvinen, K. (1999). The interplay of word formation type, affixal homonymy, and productivity in lexical processing: Evidence from a morphologically rich language. *Journal of Psycholinguistic Research, 28,* 213–226.

Bradely, D. (1980). Lexical representation of derivational relation. In M. Aronoff & M.-L. Kean (Eds.), *Juncture* (pp. 37–55). Saratoga, CA: Academic Press.

Buckingham, H. (1981). Where do neologisms come from? In J. Brown (Ed.), *Jargonaphasia* (pp. 39–62). New York: Academic Press.

Buckingham, H., & Kertesz, A. (1976). *Neologistic jargon aphasia.* Amsterdam: Swets & Zeitlinger.

Burani, C., & Caramazza, A. (1987). Representation and processing of derived words. *Language and Cognitive Processes, 2,* 217–227.

Butterworth , B. (1983). Lexical representation. In B. Butterworth (Ed.), *Language production, Vol. 2* (pp. 257–294). San Diego, CA: Academic Press.

Butterworth, B., & Howard, D. (1987). Paragrammatisms. *Cognition, 26,* 1–37.

Bybee , J. L. (1988). Morphology as lexical organization. In M. Hammond & M. Noonan (Eds.), *Theoretical morphology: Approaches in modern linguistics* (pp. 119–141). San Diego, CA: Academic Press.

Bybee , J. L. (1995). Diachrony and typology. In L. Feldman (Eds.), *Morphological aspects of language processing* (pp. 225–246). Hillsdale, NJ: Lawrence Erlbaum.

Caplan, D., Keller, L., & Locke, S. (1972). Inflection of neologisms in aphasia. *Brain, 95,* 169–172.

Caramazza, A., & Hillis, A. (1989). The disruption of sentence production: Some dissociations. *Brain and Language, 36,* 625–650.

Caramazza, A., Laudanna, A., & Romani, C. (1988). Lexical access and inflectional morphology. *Cognition, 28,* 297–332.

Colé, P., Segui, J., & Taft, M. (1997). Words and morphemes as units for lexical access. *Journal of Memory and Language, 37,* 312–330.

Delazer, M., & Semenza, C. (1998). The processing of compound words: A study in aphasia. *Brain and Language, 61,* 54–62.

Downie, R., Milech, D., & Kirsner, K. (1985). Unit definition in the mental lexicon. *Australian Journal of Psychology, 37,* 141–55.

Drews, E., & Zwitserlood, P. (1995). Morphological and orthographic similarity in visual word recognition. *Journal of Experimental Psychology: Human Perception and Performance, 21,* 1098–1116.

Emmory, K. (1989). Auditory morphological priming in the lexicon. *Language and Cognitive Processes, 4,* 73–92.

Feldman, L. (1994). Beyond orthography and phonology: Differences between inflections and derivations. *Journal of Memory and Language, 33,* 442–470.

Forster, K., & Chambers, S. (1973). Lexical access and naming time. *Journal of Verbal Learning and Verbal Behavior, 12,* 627–635.

Fowler, C., Napps, S., & Feldman, L. (1985). Relations among regular and irregular morphologically related words in the lexicon as revealed by repetition priming. *Memory and Cognition,13,* 241–255.

Funnell, E. (1987). Morphological errors in acquired dyslexia: A case of mistaken identity. *The Quarterly Journal of Experimental Psychology, 39A,* 497–539.

Garrett, M. (1982). Production of speech: Observations from normal and pathological langauge use. In A. Ellis (Ed.), *Normality and pathology in cognitive functions* (pp. 19–76). New York: Academic Press.

Garrett, M. (1984). The organization of processing structure for language production: Applications to aphasic speech. In D. Caplan, A. Lecours, & A. Smith (Eds.), *Biological perspectives on language* (pp. 172–193). Cambridge, MA: MIT Press.

Grainger, J., Colé, P., & Segui, J. (1991). Masked morphological priming in visual word recognition. *Journal of Memory and Language, 30,* 370–384.

Grosjean, F. (1980). Spoken word recognition processes and the gating paradigm. *Perception and Psychophysics, 28*, 267–283.

Halle, M., & Marantz, A. (1993). Distributed morphology. In K. Hale & S. Keyser (Eds.), *The view from building 20: Essays in linguistics in honor of Sylvain Bromberger* (pp. 111–176). Cambridge, MA: MIT Press

Henderson, L., Wallis, J., & Knight, K., (1984). Morphemic structure and lexical access. In H. Bouma & D. Bouwhuis (Eds.), *Attention and Performance X: Control of language processes* (pp. 211–226). Hillsdale, NJ: Lawrence Erlbaum.

Hittmair-Delazer, M., Andree, B., Semenza, C., and Benke, C. (1994). Naming by German compounds. *Journal of Neurolinguistics, 8*, 27–41.

Jackendoff, R. (1997). *The architecture of the language faculty*. Cambridge, MA: MIT Press.

Kelliher, S., & Henderson, L. (1990). Morphology based frequency effects in the recognition of irregularly inflected verbs. *British Journal of Psychology, 81*, 527–539.

Kempley, S., & Morton, J. (1982). The effects of priming with regularly and irregularly related words in auditory word recognition. *British Journal of Psychology, 73*, 441–454

Laine, M., Niemi, J., Koivuselkä-Sallinen, P. Ahlsén, E., & Hyönä, J. (1994). A neurolinguistic analysis of morphological deficits in a Fininsh-Swedish bilingual aphasic. *Clinical Linguistics and Phonetics, 8*, 177–200.

Laine, M., Niemi, J., Koivuselkä-Sallinen, P., & Hyönä, J. (1995). Morphological processing of polymorphemic nouns in a highly inflected language. *Cognitive Neuropsychology, 12*, 457–502.

Laine, M., Vainio, S., & Hyönä, J. (1999). Lexical access routes to nouns in a morphologically rich language. *Journal of Memory and Language, 40*, 109–135.

Lapointe, S. (1985). A theory of verb form use in the speech of agrammatic aphasia. *Brain and Language, 24*, 100–155.

Laudanna, A., Badecker, W., & Caramazza, A. (1989). Priming homographic stems. *Journal of Memory and Language, 28*, 531–546.

Laudanna, A., Badecker, W., & Caramazza, A. (1992). Processing inflectional and derivational morphology. *Journal of Memory and Language, 31*, 333–348.

Levelt, W. Roelofs, A., and Meyer, A. S. (1999). A theory of lexical access in speech production. *Behavioral and Brain Research, 22*, 1–38.

Libben, G. (1998). Semantic transparency in the processing of compounds: Consequences for representation, processing, and impairment. *Brain and Language, 61*, 30–44.

Lieber, R. (1992). *Deconstructing morphology: Word formation in syntactic theory*. Chicago: University of Chicago Press.

Marlsen-Wilson, W. D., & Tyler, L. (1998). Rules, representations, and the English past tense. *Trends in Cognitive Science, 2*, 428–435.

Marslen-Wilson, W. D., Hare, M., & Older, L. (1993). Inflectional morphology and phonological regularity in the Enlgish mental lexicon. *Proceedings of the 15th Annual Conference of the Cognitive Science Society* (pp. 693–698). Hillsdale, NJ: Lawrence Erlbaum.

Marslen-Wilson, W.D., Tyler, L., Waksler, R. & Older, L. (1994). Morphology and meaning in the English mental lexicon. *Psychological Review, 101*, 3–33.

McQueen, J., & Cutler, A. (1998). Morphology in word recognition. In A. Zwicky & A. Spencer (Eds.), *Hand-book of morphology*. (pp. 406–427). Oxford, UK: Blackwell.

Miceli, G., & Caramazza, A. (1988). Dissociation of inflection and derivational morphology. *Brain and Language, 35*, 24–65.

Miceli, G., Silveri, M., Romani, C., & Caramazza, A. (1989). Variation in the pattern of omission and substitutions of grammatical morphemes in the spontaneous speech of so-called agrammatic patients. *Brain and Language, 36*, 447–492.

Monsell, S. (1985). Repetition and the lexicon. In A. Ellis (Ed.), *Progress in the Psychology of Language, Vol. 2* (pp. 147–195). London: Lawrence Erlbaum.

Napps, S. E. (1989). Morphemic relationships in the lexicon: Are they distinct from semantic and formal relationships? *Memory and Cognition, 17*, 729–739.

Nespoulous, J.-L., Dordain, M., Perron, C., Ska, B., Bub, D., Caplan, D., Mehler, J., & Lecours, A. (1988) Agrammatism in sentence production without comprehension deficits: Reduced availability of syntactic structures and/or grammatical morphemes? A case study. *Brain and Langauge, 33*, 273–295.

Orsolini, M., & Marslen-Wilson, W. (1997). Universals in morphological representation: Evidence from Italian. *Language and Cognitive Processes, 12*, 1–47.

Panzeri, M., Semenza, C., Ferreri, T., & Butterworth, B. (1990). Free use of derivational morphology and Italian jargon aphasic. In J.-L. Nespoulous & P. Viliard (Eds.), *Morphology, Phonology, and Aphasia* (pp. 72–94). Berlin: Springer Verlag.

Pillon, A., de Partz, M.-P., Raison, A.-M., & Seron, X. (1991). L'orange, c'est le frutier de l'orangine: A case of morphological impairment? *Language and Cognitive Processes, 6*, 137–167.

Rastle, K., Davis, M., Marslen-Wilson, W., & Tyler, L. (1999) *Morphological and semantic effects in visual word recognition: A time-course study*. Manuscript submitted for publication.

Schreuder, R., & Baayen, H. (1995). Modeling morphological processing. In L. Feldman (Ed.), *Morphological aspects of language processing* (pp. 131–154). Hillsdale, NJ: Lawrence Erlbaum.

Schreuder, R., & Baayen, H. (1997). How complex simplex words can be. *Journal of Memory and Language, 37*, 118–139.

Schreuder, R. Grendel, M., Poulisse, N., Roelofs, A., & van de Voort, M. (1990). Lexical processing, morphological complexity, and reading. In D. A. Balota, G. B. Flores d'arcais, & K. Rayner (Eds.), *Comprehension processes in reading* (pp. 125–141). Hillsdale, NJ: Lawrence Erlbaum.

Schriefers, H., Zwitserlood, P., & Roelofs, A. (1991). The identification of morphologically complex words: Continuous processing or decomposition? *Journal of Memory and Language, 30*, 26–47.

Schriefers, H., Friederici, A., & Graetz, P. (1992). Inflectional and derivational morphology in the mental lexicon: Symmetries and asymmetries in repetition priming. *Quarterly Journal of Experimental Psychology, 44A*, 373–390.

Sereno, J., & Jongman, A. (1997). Processing of English inflectional morphology. *Memory & Cognition, 25*, 425–437.

Stanners, R., Neiser, J., Hernon, W., & Hall, R. (1979). Memory representations for morphologically related words. *Journal of Verbal Learning and Verbal Behavior, 18*, 399–412.

Stemberger, J. (1985). *The lexicon in a model of language*

production. (Doctoral dissertation, University of California at San Diego, 1982). New York: Garland.

Taft, M. (1979). Recognition of affixed words and the word frequency effect. *Memory and Cognition, 7,* 263–272.

Taft, M. (1994). Interactive-activation as a framework for understanding morphological processing. *Language and Cognitive Processes, 9,* 271–294.

Tyler, L. (1992). *Spoken language comprehension: An experimental approach to disordered and normal processing.* Cambridge, MA: MIT Press.

Tyler, L., Behrens, S., Cobb, H., & Marslen-Wilson, W. (1990). Processing distinctions between stems and affixes: Evidence from a non-fluent aphasic patient. *Cognition, 36,* 129–153.

Whaley, C. (1978). Word-nonword classification time. *Journal of Verbal Learning and Verbal Behavior, 17,* 143–154.

Wing, A., & Baddeley, A. (1980). Spelling errors in handwriting: A corpus and a distributional analysis. In U. Frith (Ed.), *Cognitive processes in spelling* (pp. 251–285). London: Academic Press.

10

Word Reading

Brenda Rapp
Jocelyn R. Folk
Marie-Josèphe Tainturier

The development of written language ranks among humankind's great cognitive and cultural achievements. Written language allows us to communicate meanings to others across vast distances of time and space. Unlike spoken language, written language is acquired only with instruction and effort, and thus cannot be said to reflect the natural unfolding of a genetic program. Written language represents a true achievement of human cognition, and apparently an achievement not easily come by: successful written languages have developed independently at only a few places and times in human history (for a history of written-language development see DeFrancis, 1989). Therefore, a better understanding of the reading process is important not only for its own sake, but also because it promises to reveal some of the basic principles of human cognitive representation, computation, and problem-solving. Furthermore, an understanding of the reading process provides a basis for understanding the difficulties that many individuals experience when initially learning to read, or subsequent to neural injury.

The problem in reading is that of extracting meaning from the written stimulus. The stimulus may correspond to a word, phrase, or sentence. However, this chapter will consider only the reading of single words and we focus on the following three basic questions: (1) How is the written stimulus represented? 2) Is phonology required to extract meaning from print? and 3) How do we go from print to sound?

REPRESENTING THE STIMULUS: A QUESTION OF WHAT AND WHERE

Reading requires, at a minimum, that the reader determine *what* letters are in the stimulus (letter identity) and *where* they are (letter position). Our discussion of stimulus representation, therefore, will be organized around these two questions.

What?

Most theories of reading assume that information is extracted from the stimulus and mentally represented and that this representation is used to search memory for stored information about the stimulus. Access to this stored information then forms the basis for retrieving the meaning and pronunciation corresponding to the stimulus. Given this, the stimulus should be represented in a manner that corresponds to or is compatible with the form of the information

233

stored in memory. Two issues have dominated the question of stimulus representation in reading. One is whether the visual attributes of letters or abstract letter identities form the basis of word identification. The second issue concerns the "size" of the units represented— single letters, spelling units, syllables, morphemes, etc.

Visual Features and Abstract Letter Identities

It is clear that the visual features of a written stimulus must be processed and represented. At issue is whether word identification is based on a featural representation or on a subsequent representation of abstract letter identities. Abstract letter identities, or ALIs (Polk & Farah, 1997), are representations of letters that lack name or physical form; for example R, r, *R*, *r* all correspond to the same ALI.

A number of a priori, computational reasons make it unlikely that reading is based directly on visual features or shape information. Such a view would require that we store the spellings of all the words we've previously encountered in multiple fonts and cases (and what about sizes?). Furthermore, it leaves unexplained how we recognize a word in a form or font we have never EnCouNtEReD *bEfORE* (see Polk & Farah, 1997, for a discussion of how ALIs might be acquired).

Nonetheless, a number of observations have led researchers to suggest that visual features may play an important role in word identification in reading. This work has examined font-specific effects and the role of the "word envelope." The word envelope is the pattern of ascending and descending letters that correspond to a word's lower-case form (e.g., "apple" has a very different word envelope than "hotel").

Evidence comes from studies such as that of Posnansky and Rayner (1977), who asked subjects to quickly name an object containing a written word or nonword. They found facilitation in naming times if, for example, the picture was of an apple and the written stimulus was either 'apple' or another letter string with the same envelope (oqqtc). In another study, McClelland (1977) found that subjects who were taught to associate meanings with nonwords performed better when both trained and tested with stimuli in the same font (see Henderson, 1982, for a review).

These effects, and many others that have been used as evidence for the role of visual features in written word identification, can be explained as occurring at the level of letter identification rather than in word identification per se (see Mayall, Humphreys, & Olson, 1997). Furthermore, numerous studies have failed to find support for predictions derived from the feature-based hypothesis. For example, Paap, Newsome, and Noel (1984) hypothesized that if word-shape information is used in recognition it would be useful to the extent that a word's shape was rare or unique. They found, however, that response times to words with rare versus common shapes did not differ in a lexical decision task. Additionally, various studies found evidence that supports the prediction of an ALI-based account. Rayner, McConkie, and Zola (1980) reported that switching the case of letters in mid-saccade did not disrupt naming performance (see also, Adams, 1979; Baron & Strawson, 1976; Besner, 1983; Besner, Coltheart, & Davelaar, 1984; Coltheart & Freeman, 1974; Evett & Humphreys, 1981; Monk & Hulme, 1983; Mozer, 1989; Underwood & Bargh, 1982).

Thus the preponderance of evidence from unimpaired subjects favors the position that word recognition requires the computation of ALIs. Data from neurologically impaired subjects converges on the same conclusion.

Evidence from Deficits

Strong support for the crucial role of ALIs is provided by a performance pattern indicating a reading impairment that cannot be attributed either to a loss of knowledge of word spellings (lexical orthographic knowledge) or to difficulties in processing letter shapes.

The cases of JGE (Rapp, Link, & Caramazza, 1993) and GV (Miozzo & Caramazza, 1998) constitute clear examples (see also Rapp & Caramazza, 1989; but see Howard, 1987). As indicated in Table 10.1, both subjects exhibited severe impairments in oral reading (JGE: 45% correct, GV: 0% correct). JGE and GV's difficulties were not, however, attributable to loss of knowledge of word spellings since both subjects were able to name words correctly when the letter names were spoken by the examiner.

An impairment in some aspect of letter identification was signaled by relatively low accuracy in naming single letters. They were, however, able to correctly produce letter names in tasks, such as oral spelling that didn't involve visual input, indicating that the letter identification difficulty was not attributable to an output problem. Nor could these difficulties be attributed to visual misperception, as both subjects performed very well in physical letter matches, and JGE was very accurate in copying letters. Furthermore, the difficulty was not one of recognizing letter shapes, as both subjects performed with 100% accuracy in letter decision tasks where they were asked to make yes/no judgements to letters and letter-like shapes. Additionally, GV showed normal performance in discriminating normally oriented from reflected letters. Critically, the letter-processing task on which both subjects were impaired (JGE: 78%, GV: 62%) was one that required the computation of ALIs from visual input—a cross-case letter identification task (e.g., Are *E* and *e* the same letter?).

To account for this full pattern of performance, the authors argued that one must assume a level of abstract letter identity representation that forms the basis for the recognition of written words. With this assumption the subjects' performance can be understood by positing a deficit affecting their ability to go from letter shapes to ALIs.

Higher-Order Units?

Assuming that reading involves representing the ALIs in the written stimulus, many researchers have asked whether ALI's are organized into higher order units—sometimes referred to as the question of sublexical orthographic structure. A number of such units have been proposed, they include: morphemes (Caramazza, Laudanna, & Romani, 1988; Fowler, Napps, & Feldman, 1985; Murrel & Morton, 1974; Stanners, Neisser, Hernon, & Hall, 1979; Taft & Forster, 1975,

Table 10.1
Performance on Tasks Assessing the Integrity of Abstract Letter Identities
for JGE and GV.

	Percent Correct	
	JGE	GV
Oral reading	45	0
Rec. of orally spelled words	91	100
Letter naming	80	37
Oral word spelling	100	97
Cross-case letter identification	78	62
Physical letter matching	99	93
Copying	97	–
Letter decision	100	100
Letter orientation	–	normal

Data on JGE adapted from "The Role of Graphemic Representations in Reading: Evidence from a Deficit to the Recognition System," by B. Rapp, K. Link, and A. Caramazza, 1993. Paper presented at the annual meeting of the Academy of Aphasia, Tucson, Arizona. Data on GV adapted from "Varieties of Pure Alexia: The Case of Failure to Access Graphemic Representations," by M. Miozzo and A. Caramazza, 1998. *Cognitive Neuropsychology, 15*, pp. 203–238.

1976), syllables (Prinzmetal & Millis-Wright, 1984), syllable-like units such as Basic Ortho-graphic Syllable Structure (BOSS; Taft, 1979), as well as subsyllabic units such as onset and rime (Treiman & Chafetz, 1987; Treiman & Zukowski, 1988), word body (Kay & Bishop, 1987; Patterson & Morton, 1985), spelling units (Gibson, Pick, Osser, & Hammond, 1962; Pring, 1981), and consonant and vowel clusters (Warrington & Shallice, 1980).

What purpose would be served by organizing a letter string into one or more of these unit types? Presumably it would be to facilitate the further processing required to extract meaning and/or pronunciation. The argument for the morphological organization of the stimulus is that stored forms of words are represented in a morphologically decomposed manner. Arguably this is necessary to explain the combinatorial properties of morphemes—the fact that they can be productively combined, and recombined (WALK+ ING, ED, ER, S) and that we can easily recognize novel combinations (PRECINCT+ING).

An argument for submorphemic orthographic organization into syllable and subsyllabic units might be that this too reflects the organization of the stored material. However, the motivation for this is less obvious than in the case of morphemes. A stronger argument is that subsyllabic units play an important role in the procedures we use to process unfamiliar strings (FLOPE, YASHMANT). We easily derive plausible pronunciations for such strings although we may never have previously encountered them. Thus the pronunciations are not based on long-term memory representations of the whole strings. Presumably the stimulus is organized into sub-morphemic units that access stored information derived from our experiences with the pronunciations of these smaller units. These types of units may be useful in representing important aspects of pronunciation. For example, the pronunciation of UI varies if it is a part of a spelling unit or not (as in FRUIT vs. FLUID) or the pronunciation of Y varies depending on whether it occurs at the beginning or the end of a syllable (YOUNG vs. STUDY), etc.

Evidence for syllabic orthographic organization was provided by Prinzmetal and colleagues (e.g., Prinzmetal, Treiman, & Rho, 1986) who found that perceptual errors referred to as "illusory conjunctions" are constrained by the syllabic structure of a written stimulus. When subjects are briefly presented words consisting of colored letters, occasional misperceptions occur whereby a letter is perceived as having the color of another letter in the string. These misconjunctions of color and form were more likely to occur among letters within the same syllable than among letters from different syllables (see also Rapp, 1992). On this basis, Prinzmetal et al. (1986) argued for the notion of the orthographic syllable.

Much of the evidence for subsyllabic elements such as onset and body comes from the work of Treiman and colleagues (Treiman & Chafetz, 1987; Treiman & Zakowski, 1988). The onset of a syllable is the initial consonant or consonant cluster of the syllable and the body is the remainder of syllable (e.g., CR//ISP is divided into onset and body (or rime). In one study, Treiman and Chaftez (1987) found faster lexical decision times to words divided into onset-rime segments (CR//ISP) than to words divided otherwise (CRI//SP; for other evidence of higher order units also see Bowey, 1990; Joubert & Lecours, 2000; Mewhort & Beal, 1977; Rey, Jacobs, Schmidt-Weigand, & Zeigler, 1998; Santa & Santa, 1979; Treiman & Zukowski, 1988).

Evidence from Deficits

Evidence from deficits supporting the notion of morphological decomposition in reading is well reviewed in Allen and Badecker (this volume). We focus here on findings concerning sub-morphemic units.

Lesch and Martin (1998) described ML who exhibited good word reading (100% with nouns), but severely impaired nonword reading (38% correct). Investigation of his sublexical processing abilities revealed normal performance with syllable units and severe difficulties with subsyllabic units. In segmentation tasks, ML divided visually presented words into syllables with normal accuracy (FU-TURE) but scored far below control subjects in dividing words into onset and body units (C-AST) and into spelling units (or graphemes[1]) (CH-UR-CH). In nonword reading, ML was extremely impaired in pronouncing individually presented onsets (e.g., BL-) or bodies (e.g., -ACK; 14% and 20% correct, respectively) but was far more accurate in pronouncing syllables. Specifically, ML was better able to read syllables that are contained in actual words (e.g, FLUT from FLUTTER; 71% correct) than possible syllables that do not appear in any words (FURB; 28%). These difficulties could not be attributed to a spoken production problem because ML's repetition performance, although far from perfect, did not exhibit the pattern shown in nonword reading.

The authors argued that ML's knowledge of units below the word and syllable level was disrupted, producing selective difficulties in nonword reading (see also Berndt, Haendiges, Mitchum, & Wayland, 1996). They further argued that the results support the proposal that we normally store in memory the pronunciation of units of many sizes to be used for nonword spelling—single letters, letter clusters, syllables, onsets, bodies (see Shallice & McCarthy, 1985; Shallice & Warrington, 1980; Shallice, Warrington, & McCarthy, 1983; and for computer simulation see Norris, 1994).

Additional evidence for this proposal comes from reports of other "dissociations" across different sublexical unit types. For example, FL (Funnell, 1983) could read nonwords with reasonable accuracy (74%), although she accurately produced the 'sound' of only 33% of single written letters. The difficulty with single letter "reading" was not one of oral production because nonwords whose pronunciations corresponded to the "pronunciations" of letters (BUH, FUH, etc.) were read correctly (see also, Dickerson, 1999). In contrast, a number of individuals have been described as having difficulty reading units larger than the single letter or grapheme. MS's (Newcombe & Marshall, 1985) oral reading errors indicated intact knowledge of the pronunciation of single letters (e.g., TOUCH read as /t ɒ kə hə /) but a lack of ability with larger units (see also, Derouesne & Beauvois, 1979; Holmes, 1978; Marshall & Newcombe, 1973).

Summary

These results from normal and impaired performance indicate that, at least for the purposes of generating a pronunciation for an unfamiliar word, letter strings may be organized into higher order units. These results have prompted questions regarding whether higher level units such as syllables, onsets, bodies, and even morphemes are explicitly represented or if, instead, the observed results can be explained by patterns of frequent and infrequent letter co-occurrence correlated with higher order units (e.g., bigram frequency, among others) (Seidenberg, 1987; Seidenberg & McClelland, 1989). This possibility has been directly addressed in a number of studies that have failed to find support for it (for a review see Rapp, 1992). Nonetheless, it continues to play a role in the broader debate regarding the statistical versus symbolic character of mental representation and computation.

Where?

Given that written language is replete with words that share letters but differ only in terms of the positions of letters (e.g., BREAD/BEARD/BARED), it is obvious that letter-position information must both be extracted from the stimulus and also form a part of stored representations. Given this it is somewhat surprising that the topic has received so little attention. We review two proposals regarding the representation of positional information originating from

---

[1]The term "grapheme" is used in the literature to mean either an ALI or the letter or letters that correspond to a single phoneme. On the first definition SHOE has four graphemes, on the second it as two (SH/OE). In this chapter we adopt the second definition.

the study of deficits: Caramazza and Hillis' (1990, 1991) spatial encoding proposal, and Greenwald and Berndt's (1999) work on ordinal encoding.

Caramazza and Hillis (1990, 1991) described NG, who exhibited difficulties in processing/representing the right-side of stimuli across a number of tasks: reading, line bisection, copying, etc.[2] For example, NG read HUMID as "human," HOUND as "house," SPRINTER as "sprinkle." What was striking was that she made precisely the same types of errors regardless of the topographical presentation of the stimulus. That is, errors at the "end" of the word were produced for stimuli presented horizontally, vertically, or mirror-reversed (i.e., in mirror reversed presentation COMMON was read as "comet" although the "end" was presented to the left). Furthermore, this pattern was observed regardless of the modality of input: visually or when NG heard the names of letters and had to say the word. Additionally, the same pattern was seen in written and oral spelling and even backward spelling. The authors concluded that the similar pattern across all modalities of input and output indicates that the deficit affected a representation of letters that is insensitive to form and modality—ALIs.

In addition, the distribution of errors across letter positions was consistent across these various tasks. NG didn't simply produce more errors on the ends versus beginnings of words; her rate of errors was distributed across letter positions in a very specific manner. Table 10.2 compares the her error rate displayed by ordinal letter position (1st, 2nd, 3rd, etc.) for different lengths with a word-centered display. It is apparent that the word-centered display captures the similarity across word lengths better than does the ordinal one. This is because the point in a word at which NG made spelling errors moved rightward as words increased in length. Thus it is apparent from the word-centered display that errors largely affected the right half of a word, regardless of its length.

The authors claimed that NG's performance argues for a spatial rather than an ordinal encoding of letter position. An ordinal encoding does not readily capture the fact that accuracy is determined by whether a letter is on the right versus left side of the word and by its distance from the center of the word. They specifically proposed that letter positions are represented in a word-centered, spatially defined co-ordinate system such that HOUSE is represented as: H/-2, O/-1, U/ 0, S/+1, E/+2 (but see McCloskey, this volume, Chapter 5).

Greenwald and Berndt (1999) described the performance of DES who, like NG, exhibited comparable difficulties in reading and oral and written spelling, suggesting a deficit at the level of ALIs. Also like NG, her performance was better at the beginning than the ends of words. However, her performance differed from NG's in that she showed no signs of visuo-spatial neglect in other spatial tasks and, furthermore, her error rate across letter positions did not show the rightward shift that NG's did (see Figure 10.1). Whereas NG's proportion of errors on the fourth position of four letter words was 25% and on the fourth position of seven letter words it was only 5%, DES's error rates were approximately 35% and 40% on these positions.

On this basis the authors argued that DES's pattern of errors was better captured by assuming an ordinal rather than a word-centered representation of letter position (e.g., H/1st, O/2nd, U/3rd, S/4th, E/5th). As a further test of this hypothesis DES was shown a printed word and asked to choose a matching word from two auditorily presented words. The distractor words were spatial or ordinal distractors. Spatial distractors shared initial letters with the target (e.g., MEMBER/memory) and ordinal distractors contained all of the target word letters but in a different order (e.g., COTTON/control). DES made significantly more errors with ordinal versus spatial distractors. This led the authors to argue that DES had a deficit affecting her ability to encode the ordinal position of letters.

As stated above, very little is known about the representation of letter position information.

---

[2]This general pattern of performance, referred to as visuo-spatial neglect, as well as this particular case, are described elsewhere in this volume in chapters by Umiltà and McCloskey (Chapter 5).

Table 10.2
Rate of Spelling Errors at Each Position of Words of Lengths 4–7. Left-Aligned Display and Word-Centered Display.

Length in letters	Position in the Word						
	1	2	3	4	5	6	7
Left-Aligned:							
4	0	2	13	25			
5	0	0	6	20	29		
6	0	0	5	15	26	39	
7	0	0	3	5	15	28	51
				Word Center — x			
Word-Centered:							
4			0	2	13	25	
5		0	0	6	20	29	
6		0	0	5	15	26	39
7	0	0	3	5	15	28	51

Adapted from "Levels of Representation, Co-ordinate Frames, and Unilateral Neglect," by A. Caramazza and A. E. Hillis, 1991, *Cognitive Neuropsychology, 7*, pp. 391–445.

Clearly more research is required to determine how seemingly disparate findings like those of NG and DES can be understood.

SUMMARY

This section has dealt with basic issues regarding the manner in which the relevant information contained in the written stimulus is mentally represented. The evidence for abstract letter identities seems fairly strong. However, numerous questions remain regarding higher order units and the representation of letter position. One possibility to explore is that the use of

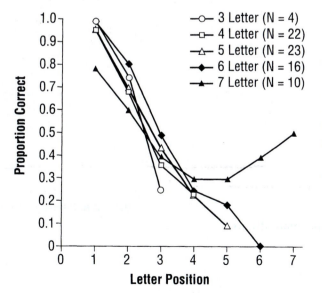

Legend:
—○— 3 Letter (N = 4)
—□— 4 Letter (N = 22)
—△— 5 Letter (N = 23)
—◆— 6 Letter (N = 16)
—▲— 7 Letter (N = 10)

Figure 10.1: Error Rate by Letter Position for Words 3–7 Letters in Length, Exhibited by DES In Oral Reading. Adapted from "Impaired Encoding of Abstract Letter Order: Severe Alexia in a Mildly Aphasic Patient by M. L. Greenwald & R. S. Berndt, 1999, *Cognitive Neuropsychology, 16*, 512–536.

higher order units may play a crucial role in representing letter position. Higher order units may form the scaffolding to which ALIs are assigned and, in this way, contribute to encoding position (see Dell, 1986 in the context of phonology).

IS PHONOLOGY REQUIRED TO EXTRACT WORD MEANING FROM PRINT?

The Positions

The acquisition of written language skills (reading and spelling) clearly builds upon spoken language skills and knowledge. Less clear, however, is the relationship between written and spoken language in the competent written-language user. The relationship between written and spoken language has consequently been the topic of considerable controversy (also see Tainturier & Rapp, this volume). The debate has centered around two competing positions: *direct access* to meaning from print, and *mandatory phonologically-mediated access*. The direct access hypothesis holds that the meaning of a written word can be recovered without any involvement of phonology (see Coltheart, 1980; see Coltheart & Coltheart, 1997). In contrast, the hypothesis of mandatory phonological mediation assumes that meaning can be recovered from print only if the written stimulus is first recoded in phonological form (Frost, 1998; Lukatela & Turvey, 1991, 1993, 1994a, 1994b; Van Orden, 1987, 1991; Van Orden, Johnston, & Hale, 1988; Van Orden, Pennington, & Stone, 1990).

Direct Access

The direct access proposal is represented schematically in Figure 10.2A. According to this view, a written stimulus is recognized as a familiar letter sequence if it makes contact with a stored representation in orthographic memory (the *orthographic lexicon*). The activation of the stored representation constitutes the basis for accessing the word's meaning in the *lexical semantic system*. This is the core part of the direct access proposal.

Figure 10.2: Different hypotheses concerning the relationship between phonology and orthography in reading. (a) corresponds to a direct access architecture; (b) and (c) correspond to different instantiations of the mandatory phonological mediation hypothesis.

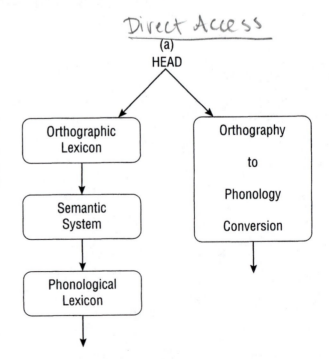

Mandatory Phonological Mediation

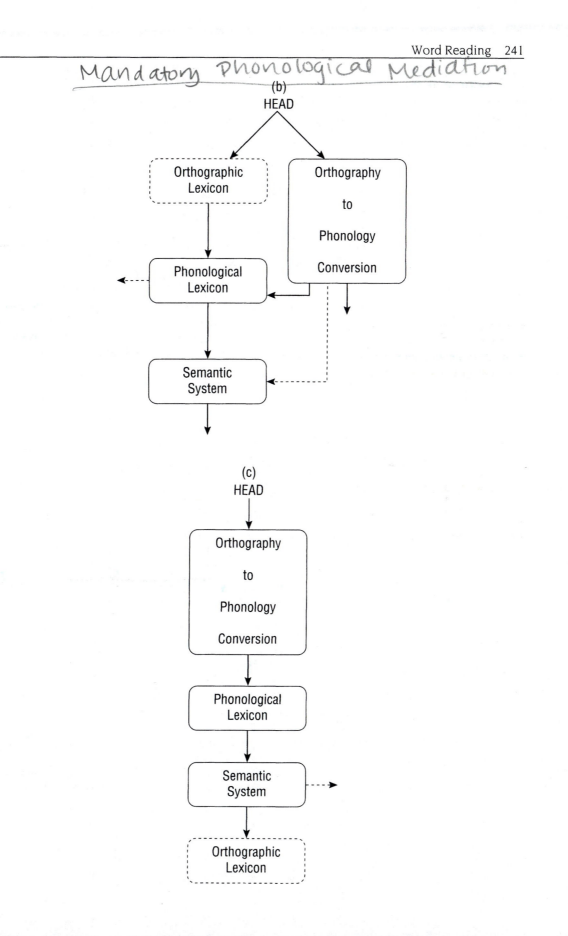

Figure 10.2A also depicts how phonological recoding may take place within a direct access architecture. One option is that after semantic access, a stored memory of the word's phonological form is retrieved from a long-term memory store (the *phonological lexicon*). A second option is that phonological recoding takes place based on the reader's knowledge of the regularities in the sublexical relationships between the letters and sounds of the language; these are represented in the *orthography-to-phonology conversion system* (OPC system). This system will be discussed in the following section; for present purposes it suffices to say that the OPC system is generally assumed to represent common or highly regular relationships (e.g., EA -> /i/) more strongly than less common relationships (e.g., /EA -> /ε/). For example, the written stimulus HEAD could be phonologically recoded by the GPC system as either /h i d/ or /h ε d/ but /h i d/ is more likely because the /i/ pronunciation of EA is more common in English than /ε /.

It is important to note that proponents of direct access do not claim that direct access is the only means of contacting meaning, they typically accept that phonologically based access can also take place. For example, phonologically based access can occur when a phonological representation computed by the OPC system serves as input to the phonological comprehension system, and engages the spoken language recognition system (not depicted in Figure 10. 2A). Some investigators assume that direct access, although not the only means of contacting meaning, is the predominant one, others are neutral with regard to the relative importance of direct access and phonological recoding.

Mandatory Phonological Recoding

Two versions of the mandatory phonological mediation position are represented in Figures 10.2B and 10.2C. Both proposals assume that phonological recoding necessarily precedes access to meaning; they differ only in whether the recoding is lexical or sub-lexical (also referred to as "non-lexical"). According to the position depicted in Figure 10.2b, the written stimulus makes contact with a stored lexical phonological representation (this process may or may not involve the orthographic lexicon) and this representation then provides access to word meaning. This view also allows for sublexical phonological recoding through OPC.

According to the position depicted in Figure 10.2C, a written stimulus is submitted to the OPC system and a phonological representation is generated that then accesses a stored representation in the phonological lexicon. This phonological representation, in turn, serves as the basis for accessing meaning in the semantic system. Only later (and only according to some authors) is contact made with the orthographic lexicon.

A large number of studies with normal subjects have examined the role of phonology in reading. However, relatively few of them have been specifically concerned with the role of phonology in deriving meaning from printed words. Most have considered simply whether or not phonological recoding occurs across a range of tasks involving written stimuli, whether or not comprehension is required. For this reason it is important to make a distinction between evidence indicating that phonological recoding is mandatory for deriving meaning from print, and evidence that phonology is automatically (obligatorily) generated, even if not required for accessing meaning. Thus, there are various hypotheses to be considered: (a) direct access is possible and phonology is not automatically generated in processing written text; (b) direct access is possible and phonology is automatically generated; and (c) direct access is not possible and phonological recoding is both automatic and mandatory for accessing meaning.

Evidence for Obligatory Phonological Recoding in Written Word Processing.

A number of studies have shown that phonology is generated in the course of processing written words in tasks where it is not required and may even hinder performance. For example, Perfetti, Bell, and Delaney (1988) reported that in the backward masking paradigm subjects can better identify a briefly presented target (e.g., RAKE) if it is followed by a briefly presented pseudoword that is phonologically similar (e.g., RAIK) rather than graphemically similar to the target (e.g., RALK), even when subjects have no conscious recollection of having perceived the masking pseudoword. This suggests that the pseudoword prime is phonologically recoded and that this phonological code contributes to the processing of the target. Phonological effects have also been reported in letter search tasks (Ziegler & Jacobs, 1995), Stroop tasks (Dennis & Newstead, 1981), and in lexical decision tasks (Lukatela, Savíc, Gligorijevíc, Ogjennovic, & Turvey, 1978).

These findings, while they don't speak directly to the role of phonology in accessing meaning, suggest that phonological recoding is automatic, even when it is not required for the task. Problematic for this conclusion, however, are findings that phonological effects may be present or absent depending on specific experimental manipulations. For example, Verstaen, Humphreys, Olson, and d'Ydewalle (1995) showed that the phonological effects described above in the backward masking paradigm disappear if all of the target words are homophones (in which case the use of phonological information in identifying targets would be particularly misleading). Phonological recoding effects have also been shown to depend on the proportion of homophones or pseudohomophones in a stimulus list in lexical decision (Waters & Seidenberg, 1985; Davelaar, Coltheart, Besner, & Jonasson, 1978; Hawkins, Reicher, Rogers, & Peterson, 1976; Pugh, Rexer, & Katz, 1994; see also, Davis, Castles, & Iakovidis, 1998). If phonological effects can be eliminated under certain conditions then it is hard to argue that phonological recoding occurs obligatorily and automatically in the course of processing written stimuli.

Phonological Recoding in Accessing Meaning from Print

Much of the evidence favoring a role for phonology in retrieving meaning from print has involved homophones, words in which the spoken form is associated with multiple meanings (e.g., /s ɛi l/ -> bargain or boat?); whereas their written form is not (e.g., SALE–bargain; SAIL–boat). If phonology is involved in accessing meaning from print, multiple meanings may be activated when a written homophone is encountered.

In a semantic categorization task (e.g., Flower–is X a flower?), Van Orden (1987) found that incorrect yes responses were more common for homophones of a category exemplar (ROWS) than for control words (ROBS). This was interpreted as evidence that phonological recoding of ROWS (/r ou z/) led to activation of both meanings (flower and lines) even though the spelling (ROWS) was consistent with only one meaning. Van Orden et al. (1988) found a similar pattern of false positive errors with homophonic nonwords (e.g., responding yes to the question: Is CROE a BIRD)? Van Orden and colleagues concluded that "word identification in reading proceeds from spelling to sound to meaning" (Van Orden et al., 1988, p. 371). However, Jared and Seidenberg (1991) found that if broader semantic categories were used (e.g., LIVING THINGS), then the homophone effects obtained only for low frequency words, suggesting that the results reported by Van Orden et al. (1988) were, at least in part, strategic[3] (see also Taft & van Graan, 1998).

In a priming study, Lukatela and Turvey (1994 a, 1994b) reported that oral reading (e.g., FROG) was equally facilitated by the prior presentation of a semantic associate (TOAD), a word homophonic with the associate (TOWED), or a nonword homophonic with the associate (TODE). This was interpreted to mean that a phonological form is automatically activated by the written prime. It then serves to activate all meanings consistent with the phonological form,

---

[3]Specifically, Jared and Seidenberg (1991) suggested that the results observed by van Orden might have resulted from subjects generating predictions of possible exemplars when presented with a category label because, in fact, a number of very narrow category labels were used (e.g., a member of a convent–NONE).

such that when the target is presented, its meaning has already been preactivated and processing is facilitated.

Folk (1999) embedded homophones in sentences and measured eye-fixation times while subjects read silently for comprehension. She found that readers' initial fixation times were longer on homophones (e.g., BALE) relative to control words, indicating that multiple meanings associated with the common phonological code of the homophone were active initially, even though the spelling clearly indicated which meaning was intended.

All of these studies reveal that when the task requires reading for comprehension, the meanings of words that are only phonologically related to the target may be activated. Thus, these results support the view that phonological recoding very often occurs in circumstances when it is not required or helpful. They are not, however, incompatible with a direct access view. Within the architecture in Figure 10.2A one explanation is simply that these findings stem from trials on which, indeed, access to the meaning of the target does take place via the phonological code generated by the OPC. Another explanation, however, is that there is direct access to the meaning of the target and also concomittant access to its phonology (either via the OPC or lexically). The phonological code then activates all corresponding meanings (including the target's again). For this explanation to account for the data, it must be assumed that this happens with sufficient speed that the meanings of the target and its competitors are active within the same time frame.[4] Until more is known about the speed of these processes it won't be possible to determine if this assumption is unreasonable.

Finally, not only are homophone-based findings compatible with a direct access view, our ability to understand the meaning of homophones is considerably more straightforward under direct access than under mandatory phonological mediation. Under direct access, ROWS contacts its meaning directly from the Orthographic Lexicon. However, if ROWS is phonologically recoded to /r ou z/, how do we reliably access the correct meaning? Mandatory phonological mediation would require a rather convoluted account such that after accessing multiple meanings from the phonology the orthographic lexicon is accessed and generates two candidate spellings ROWS and ROSE which are then checked with the representation of the input stimulus and the inappropriate meaning is suppressed.

Given, therefore, that findings such as those reviewed here are compatible with both hypotheses, it is especially important to find paradigms and results that distinguish between them; evidence from deficits does just that.

Evidence from Deficits

Deficits allow us to examine reading comprehension in cases where access to phonology is impaired. The phonological mediation hypothesis predicts that such deficits should necessarily affect written word comprehension, whereas direct access allows for intact comprehension in such cases.

Shelton and Weinrich (1997) reported the case of EA, who exhibited excellent repetition but severely impaired spoken picture naming and oral reading (23–40% correct). His errors consisted primarily of semantically-related responses (e.g., STRAWBERRIES read as "grapes"). In contrast, reading comprehension of concrete words was quite good. This was evidenced by 90% accuracy in a written word/picture verification task in which half of the distractors were semantically related words and also in written lexical decision (98% correct).

Clearly, what is to be explained is the large discrepancy between EA's inability to derive phonology from print and his ability to derive meaning from print. This pattern is readily

---

[4]In tasks that require potentially "time consuming" decision-making such as Van Orden et al.'s (1988) this is not especially problematic. However, for simple reading tasks such as Lukatela, Cavello, & Turveys (1999) and Folk's (1999), some researchers find it implausible that there should be overlapping time frames.

understood under a direct access architecture since access to meaning precedes access to phonology and, therefore, a deficit in going from meaning to phonology should leave written word comprehension intact (Figure 10.2A). The similarity in EA's oral reading and spoken naming difficulties is explained by this deficit locus, as is his good repetition which indicates intact post-lexical processing.

In contrast, it is not obvious how mandatory phonological recoding can explain good reading comprehension of STRAWBERRIES based on a spoken response "grapes." If phonological recoding yielded "grapes," then this representation should form the basis of access to meaning.[5] One possibility to consider is that recoding is occurring sublexically; that is, that a phonological representation internally generated by the OPC system forms the basis for semantic access (Figure 10.2B) and that the erroneous spoken responses somehow result from disruption to subsequent processes. On this view nonword reading should be relatively intact. However, EA's ability to read pseudowords was extremely limited: 0–4% of nonwords were read correctly.

In sum, EA's pattern of performance and that of many other similar individuals (see cases in Coltheart, Patterson, & Marshall, 1980) is easily accounted for within a direct access architecture but is extremely problematic for either of the mandatory phonological mediation positions depicted in Figure 10.2.

Another relevant case is that of PS (Hanley & McDonnell, 1997). PS was only 43% correct in oral reading. In contrast, his comprehension of those same words—as evaluated by having him define written words—was 100%. Excellent comprehension of written words was also demonstrated (90–99% accuracy) across a range of written comprehension tasks such as lexical decision, written synonym matching, the Pyramids and Palm Trees Test (Howard & Patterson, 1992), and sentence-picture matching. Like EA, PS was also severely impaired in nonword reading: 17–34% correct. However, in contrast with EA, PS's errors were almost entirely phonologically related to the target, including both phonologically similar word (e.g., WEEKS → "wheat") and nonword errors (e.g., CONCEPT → /kamsεps/). The errors seemed to be phonological rather than visual since targets and responses often shared more phonology than orthography (e.g., BUILD → bill, KNIFE → night; GREAT → grave). Also unlike EA, PS made similar errors in repetition as well as in oral reading and picture naming (auditory comprehension was intact).

The fact that the errors were phonological leaves open the possibility that written stimuli were correctly recoded, that this phonological recoding served as the basis for access to meaning, and that the phonological errors arose only later at a *post*lexical level of processing required for actual production of spoken forms. Such a scenario would be consistent with a mandatory phonological recoding account. This hypothesis predicts that PS should be able to use these correct, internally generated phonological forms as the basis for making certain phonological judgements (see Caplan & Waters, 1995). Hanley and McDonnell (1997) specifically tested this by asking PS to discriminate pseudohomophones (e.g., BRANE) from nonhomophonic nonwords and to discriminate homophone word pairs (e.g., SAIL/SALE) from nonhomophones (e.g., CLOWN/CLONE). Performance on both of these tasks was no better than chance. He was also asked to decide whether pairs of written words rhymed. His accuracy of 73% on this task was well outside the normal range.

---

[5]One might try to argue as does Frost (1998) that the oral reading responses don't actually reflect the phonological form that served as the basis for meaning retrieval. Frost (1998) suggests that such patients correctly phonologically recode the written word internally, then derive from this the word's meaning, but subsequently forget the phonological code and have to generate another one based on the activated meaning. Presumably the deficit, then, resides in rapid forgetting of the internally generated phonological code. Besides being rather contrived, this seems unlikely because it assumes that semantics is normally imprecise—so much so that not only does it not distinguish close synonyms (which might be understandable) but it also allows for confusion between distinct concepts such as strawberries/grapes or foot/sock. This leaves unexplained why we don't normally make semantic errors in speaking, a situation where phonology is derived strictly from meaning.

These findings, therefore, provide no evidence of correct internal phonological recoding of the written stimuli and, therefore, constitute further support for the hypothesis of direct access.

Summary

The cognitive neuropsychological literature reveals performance patterns that can readily be accounted for and are predicted by a direct access view but which are incompatible with mandatory phonological recoding. We have also seen that research with intact subjects, although not directly addressing this issue, reveals that phonological recoding of written words occurs frequently and quickly. Thus, at least for English, the balance of the evidence favors a direct access architecture that allows for optional phonological recoding.

Nonetheless, many investigators have been struck by the fact that phonological effects are so pervasive. For these investigators, this indicates that, phonological recoding, if not the only means for accessing meaning, is the primary means for doing so. Others interpret these same findings as indicating that phonological effects occur largely automatically during written text processing and do not necessarily affect access to meaning per se. Clearly, an important goal for further investigation is to examine the specific circumstances (with regard to stimuli, tasks, languages) under which direct and/or phonologically based access to meaning take place.

HOW DO WE GO FROM PRINT TO SOUND?

The Dual-Process Hypothesis

Thus far we have assumed at least two procedures for deriving sound from print. One, generally referred to as a *lexical process* (or route), involves relating word, or morpheme-sized units in the orthography to similar units in the phonology. In this case phonology is said to be "addressed" since the phonology is retrieved from long term memory (the phonological lexicon). According to the direct access view, the lexical procedure involves first retrieving meaning from orthography and then using the word's semantics to address its phonology.

The second procedure is assumed to use knowledge of the regularities in the relationships between orthography and phonology to convert the representation of the stimulus into a phonologically plausible sequence of phonemes and is referred to as the *nonlexical* or *sublexical process* (the OPC system). Since the phonological representation is not retrieved as a whole word or morpheme from long-term memory it is often referred to as a procedure for "assembling" phonology. Before considering the exact content of these two procedures, we review evidence supporting the general claim that there are two distinct routes for deriving sound from print (Figure 10.2A).

Evidence from Intact Subjects

The clearest evidence from intact subjects for "separable" procedures for deriving sound from print comes from Paap and colleagues (Paap & Noel, 1991; Paap, Noel, & Johnsen, 1992) and Baluch and Besner (1991). These studies are based on the well-established *frequency and regularity effects* and the *frequency by regularity interaction*. The frequency effect refers to the fact that high frequency words are named more quickly than low frequency words (Forster & Chambers, 1973; Frederiksen & Kroll, 1976). Presumably this occurs because low-frequency words are more "weakly" represented in the lexical route and, therefore, are processed more slowly. The regularity effect refers to the observation that "irregular" words, those words containing at least one uncommon or low probability grapheme-phoneme (GP) mapping (Y A CHT → /y a t/) are read more slowly than "regular" words, words containing only high probability mappings (S EE D → /s i d/; Baron & Strawson, 1976; Stanovoich & Bauer, 1978).

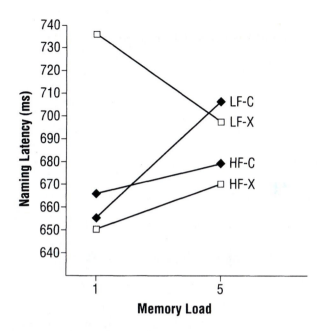

Figure l0.3: Naming time as a function of memory load for four types of words: high-frequency exception (HF-X), high-frequency control (HF-C), low-frequency exception (LF-X), and low-frequency control (LF-C). Adapted from "Dual-Route Models of Print to Sound: Still a Good Horse Race," by K. R. Paap and R. W. Noel, 1991, *Psychological Research/Psychologische Forschung*, 53, pp. 13–24.

To account for the regularity effect it is often assumed that both lexical and sublexical routes process a written stimulus in parallel. If the word contains only regular correspondences, then both procedures generate the same response. If, however, the word contains a low probability GP mapping, the lexical system generates the "correct" phonological response, while the sublexical system may generate a phonologically plausible, albeit lexically incorrect response (YACHT → /y a tʃ t/). The time required to resolve this conflict accounts for the regularity effect. The regularity by frequency interaction refers primarily to the fact that a strong regularity effect is observed only for low-frequency words (Seidenberg, Waters, Barnes, & Tanenhaus, 1984; Taraban & McClelland, 1987). This can be understood by adopting the additional assumption that the lexical route is faster than the sublexical one. High-frequency words, regardless of their regularity, are processed by the lexical route relatively quickly and often before the sublexical route generates any conflicting outputs. Thus with high-frequency words, a regularity effect is either weak or absent. With low-frequency words, because the lexical route operates more slowly, there is time for the sublexical route to generate a conflicting response for irregular versus regular words and, as a result, a strong regularity effect is generated.

Paap and Noel (1991) attempted to selectively interfere with the sublexical route. They assumed that the OPC was more resource demanding than the lexical route and thus more likely to be disrupted under dual-task conditions. Subjects had to retain either 5 digits (high load) or 1 (low load) while concurrently performing an oral reading task. Paap and Noel predicted that if the sublexical route was especially disrupted by the high load, then this condition should reveal the lexical route operating in relative isolation. In that case, regularity effects for low-frequency words should be largely eliminated. This is just what they found (see Figure 10.3) (see also Baluch & Besner, 1991; Bernstein and Carr, 1996; Herdman, 1992; Paap et al., 1992).

In a complementary manner, Baluch and Besner (1991), working in Persian, created experimental conditions that produced what they considered to be a selective deactivation of the lexical route (see also Paap et al., 1992). This constitutes further support for the notion that the routes are sufficiently independent that they can be selectively engaged or disengaged[6].

---

[6]Additional evidence for multiple reading processes is the observation of length effects for nonwords but not for words (Ans, Carbonnel, & Valdois, 1998; Weekes, 1997).

Evidence from Brain Damage

A number of cases of deficits provide strong support for the separability of the two procedures for translating print to sound by demonstrating that they can be selectively damaged.

Funnell (1983) described the case of WB who, despite severely impaired nonword reading (0% correct), largely retained his ability to read words (overall accuracy 90%), even irregular words (80% correct). Derouesné and Beauvois (1985) presented a somewhat similar case of the French-speaking subject LB. LB's nonword reading was only 30% correct while word reading was 74–98% correct. Furthermore, the nonword difficulty was unlikely to be a production problem given that nonword repetition was intact as was performance on a range of other phonological tasks. These cases represent selective damage to the non-lexical route—a pattern often referred to as "phonological dyslexia" (see also Beauvois & Derouesné, 1979, and papers in Coltheart, 1996).

The case of KT (McCarthy & Warrington, 1986) forms a striking contrast: KT's nonword reading was preserved (96% correct) while reading of low-frequency irregular words was severely affected (26% correct). In KT's case, severe damage to the lexical procedure was hypothesized. It is generally assumed that the representations of low frequency words are more vulnerable to damage than those of high frequency words. Given KT's lexical impairment, these are the words most likely to be read by the relatively intact OPC. Furthermore, since the OPC is more likely to produce common rather than infrequent pronunciations, KT would be expected to produce incorrect responses especially for low frequency, irregular words—a regularity by frequency interaction in the accuracy domain (see also Bub, Cancelliere, & Keryesz, 1985; Shallice et al., 1983; and cases in Patterson, Marshall, & Coltheart, 1985). This was indeed the case, and Table 10.3 exemplifies a pattern often referred to as "surface dyslexia."

The dual process hypothesis also makes predictions regarding error types expected subsequent to selective damage to one of the routes. In KT's case, the intact OPC should produce phonologically plausible errors (regularizations) for words unsuccessfully processed by the lexical route. Indeed, 85% of KT's errors were regularizations such as /h ei v/ for HAVE. In contrast, WB, as expected from a severe deficit to the OPC, often attempted to process nonwords as words, producing what are often referred to as lexicalization errors: PLOON read as "spoon," HEAN as "hen."

In summary, the findings from normal and impaired performance provide strong evidence for at least two distinct and dissociable procedures for translating from print to sound (for reviews see Coltheart, Curtis, Atkins, & Haller, 1993; Humphreys & Evett, 1985).

Table 10.3

KT's Reading Accuracy for High-and Low-Frequency (HF and LF) Words and Regular and Exception (reg and exc) Words, as well as Accuracy with Nonwords and Rate of Regularization Errors (Reg's).

	HF reg	LF reg	HF exc	LF exc	Reg's	Nonwords
KT	100%	89%	47%	26%	85%	100%
PMSP-1	49%	43%	38%	28%	26%	45%

Adapted from "Phonological Reading: Phenomena and Paradoxes," by R. A. McCarthy and E. K. Warrington, 1986, *Cortex*, 22, pp. 359–380. One set of the results obtained from lesioning Plaut et al.'s (1996) attractor network between the grapheme layer and the hidden layer. Similar results are obtained regardless of damage locus.

A Third Route

Various researchers have posited three routes to pronunciation of written stimuli. Some evidence for this proposal comes from unimpaired processing (see Buchanan & Besner, 1993; Strain, Patterson, & Seidenberg, 1995), but the bulk of the evidence comes from patterns of impaired performance. According to a three route position, in addition to an assembled nonlexical route to phonology (OPC), there are two lexical routes: the semantically mediated route assumed in direct access and a *nonsemantic lexical route* based on connections from a word's orthography to its phonology that bypasses semantics. We refer to this as the nonsemantic lexical route, it is also often called the "direct" lexical route (see Figure 10.4).

The evidence from deficits for a non-semantic lexical route has typically been the pattern of good reading of irregular words in the face of apparent lack of comprehension of the same words. This poses a problem for dual route accounts that assume only a semantically mediated lexical process because poor comprehension suggests that reading is not accomplished by the lexical route and irregular words cannot be reliably read through the remaining OPC route.

Examples of this pattern include the case of WLP (Schwartz, Saffran, & Mari, 1980) who read correctly 95% of words, including high and low frequency words and regular and irregular words. Yet her written comprehension of these words was severely impaired, as indicated by only 55% accuracy in matching written words to one of four category labels or 15% accuracy in matching written words to one of four pictures (see also Bub et al., 1985; Cipolotti & Warrington, 1995; Coltheart, Masterson, Byng, Prior, & Riddoch, 1983; Funnell, 1983; Lambon, Ralph, Ellis, & Franklin, 1995; Lambon, Ralph, Ellis, & Sage, 1998; McCarthy & Warrington, 1986; Raymer & Berndt, 1996; Sartori, Masterson, & Job, 1987; Shallice et al., 1983).

In sum, these cases all point to a nonsemantic lexical route from print to sound in addition to a semantically mediated route and an OPC route (see also Goodall & Phillips, 1995, for evidence from recovery of function; also see Coslett, 1991, for another pattern, but see Hillis & Caramazza, 1995, for a response to Coslett, 1991). In a later section we discuss the claim that positing a third route may be premature and that results such as those just presented can be accommodated within a dual route hypothesis.

From Print to Sound in Other Languages

Does reading in other languages also involve multiple routes? Or are multiple routes characteristic only of languages, such as English, with substantial numbers of both very regular and irregular orthography/phonology relations? Here we highlight relevant evidence.

For highly regular or transparent languages such as Spanish, Italian, Serbo-Croatian, and Korean it has been suggested that readers develop only an OPC procedure since such a procedure will be very likely to yield correct pronunciations (e.g., Ardila, 1991). By a similar logic, it has been suggested that highly opaque languages (e.g., Chinese) may have only a lexical procedure. While there is some evidence regarding this question from normal performance (Job, Perssotti, & Cusinato, 1998; Saito, Masuda, & Hawakami, 1999; Tan & Perfetti, 1997), there is also neuropsychological evidence indicating both lexical and nonlexical procedures in all of these languages.

Opaque Languages

Although Chinese might be expected to have only a lexical route, Yin and Butterworth (1992) described Chinese subjects whose reading provides evidence of a nonlexical route. These subjects had particular difficulty in correctly reading aloud "irregular" Chinese characters. Most

Chinese characters are complex and consist of two or more components (called radicals), one of which (the phonetic radical) sometimes provides information regarding the pronunciation of the character. For "regular" characters the pronunciation of the character as a whole is the same as the pronunciation of the phonetic radical; for "irregular" characters (the majority of Chinese characters) the pronunciation of the character ranges from being somewhat to very different from that of the phonetic radical. Consistent with a lexical locus of impairment, Yin's subjects had particular difficulty reading low-frequency irregular characters. Importantly, and as would be predicted if there were a sublexical reading procedure in Chinese, many of their errors consisted of assigning a pronunciation that corresponded to that of the phonetic radical, rather than that of the character itself (see also Patterson, Suzuki, Wydell, & Sasanuma, 1995 for a similar pattern in Japanese; but see Weekes & Chen, 1999, for an alternative account). Given that Chinese is a nonalphabetic language, pronunciations would not be "assembled" by the nonlexical route, raising interesting questions regarding the content and functioning of a nonlexical route in Chinese.

Transparent Languages

In Spanish, evidence of a lexical procedure comes from Cuetos, Valle-Arroyo, and Suarez (1996; see also Iribarren, Jarema, & Lecours, 1999) who described an individual, AD, who had good oral reading (89% correct) and excellent reading comprehension (100% correct), but who demonstrated severe difficulties in reading nonwords (35% correct). The nonword reading difficulty could not be attributed entirely to an output impairment as nonword repetition was 83% correct, indicating, instead, damage to a sublexical reading process. AD's excellent oral reading was, therefore, presumably mediated by some lexical process. Whether the lexical process was semantically based cannot be determined from the evidence presented. Evidence of direct access for reading in Spanish is provided by Ferreres and Miravalles (1995). Their subject's oral reading accuracy was low (29% correct) and nonword reading abolished (0% correct). Importantly, he produced significant numbers of semantic errors in word reading (40% correct), indicating that the reading responses were semantically mediated (see also Ruiz, Ansaldo, & Lecours, 1994).

Italian is transparent at the segmental level but not at the suprasegmental level of stress assignment. Although stress can be correctly assigned to many Italian words using a syllabically-based rule, there are sequences that are syllabically identical yet differing in stress (SPIRITO → /'spirito/ but SPARITO → /spa 'rito/). For these words, stress must presumably be lexically marked and therefore these words could not be read correctly by a rule-based nonlexical route. This argument finds support from the case of CLB (Miceli & Caramazza, 1993) who had no difficulty reading nonwords (99% correct) and few difficulties with words with syllabically-defined stress (91% correct), but whose accuracy dropped for words with lexically-defined stress (70% correct). Furthermore, CLB produced stress errors for only 1% of the words with syllabically-defined stress but for 26% of the words with lexically-defined stress. This is evidence of a lexically-based reading process that was damaged in CLB's case. Evidence specifically supporting a semantically-based route comes from WMA who had severe difficulties in nonword reading (13% correct; Miceli, Benvegnu, Capasso, & Caramazza, 1997). His word reading was also impaired (78% correct) but, critically for the claim of semantically mediated reading, the vast majority of his errors (73% correct) were semantic.

In sum, the available evidence indicates that languages that vary widely in terms of the transparency of their orthography/phonology relations, nonetheless, have multiple procedures for translating from print to sound.

A Closer Look at Non-Semantic, Orthography-to-Phonology Conversion (OPC)

For a long time, the default assumption was that the OPC process consists of rules that map letters and/or digraphs (graphemes) onto sounds (e.g., if P then /p/; Besner & Smith, 1992; Coltheart, 1978; Marshall & Newcombe, 1973; Meyer, Schvaneveldt, & Ruddy, 1974; Morton & Patterson, 1980; Paap & Noel, 1991). A number of reasons prompted a reconsideration of this view (Plaut, McClelland, Seidenberg, & Patterson, 1996; Reggia, Marsland, & Berndt, 1988; Seidenberg & McClelland, 1989; Sejnowski & Rosenberg, 1987).

One major impetus was the finding by Glushko (1979) that oral reading times for nonwords are influenced by the degree to which a nonword's pronunciation is consistent with the pronunciation of the "body" of other similarly-spelled words. Recall that the body of a syllable is defined as the vowel and any following consonants. Glushko found that an "inconsistent" nonword—one whose body is shared by words which vary in their pronunciations (e.g., ZAID; with RAID and SAID as body neighbors)—is read more slowly than a "consistent" nonword that shares a body with words that all have the same pronunciation (e.g., PRINK, with body neighbors such as PINK, CLINK, etc.). Glushko also reported similar results for words. He found that a word that under a traditional OPC account is considered to be regular (RAID) but whose body is shared by words that differ in their pronunciation (SAID and PAID), takes longer to read aloud than another regular word (PINK) whose body doesn't vary in its pronunciation (see also Jared, 1997; Jared, McRae, & Seidenberg, 1990; Taraban & McClelland, 1987; for "feedback consistency" effects see Stone, Vanhoy, & Van Orden, 1977; Ziegler, Montant, & Jacobs, 1997). These findings were considered to be problematic for the traditional rule-based dual-route approach because they suggested that print-to-sound translation involves more than the mapping of single graphemes onto phonemes.

One response was to propose that rules were defined over a larger unit (or units) instead of, or in addition to, individual graphemes (Paap et al., 1992; Patterson & Morton, 1985; Shallice et al., 1983). Another response was to do away with the idea of rules altogether and propose that the orthography-phonology mappings of a great number of words enter into the oral reading of any given word or nonword. For example, Glushko (1979) introduced the notion of "reading by analogy" which, although it captured the intuition that the pronunciations of many words contribute to every oral reading response, remained rather underspecified and vague (see also Kay & Marcel, 1981; Marcel, 1980).

The reading-by-analogy proposal was, however, consistent with another motivation for taking a closer look at the nonsemantic translation of print to sound. The categorical distinctions between regular/irregular, assembled/addressed, rule/look-up based processing were put in question in a number of language domains including reading (e.g., Rumelhart & McClelland, 1986). For reading, it was argued that consistency effects are a manifestation of the fact that orthography-phonology relationships in English cannot be neatly categorized as regular or irregular. Instead, they span a continuum of regularity based on the frequency of letter patterns and their phonological correspondences: some are highly frequent (INK → /Ink/), others less so (CH → /k/ as in CHORUS), and still others are unique (COLO → /k / as in COLONEL). Given this, it was suggested that it would be more coherent to assume a single process or mode of computation that captures the full range of orthography–phonology relationships and that can read all words and nonwords.

A debate ensued between two views of nonsemantic processing, with the primary contenders being the Dual Route Cascaded (DRC) proposal of Coltheart and colleagues (1993) and the PDP-based proposals of Seidenberg and McClelland (1989) that built upon Sejnowski and Rosenberg (1987) and were followed up and further developed by Plaut et al. (1996). Both positions assume at least two processes: a semantically mediated lexical process and at least

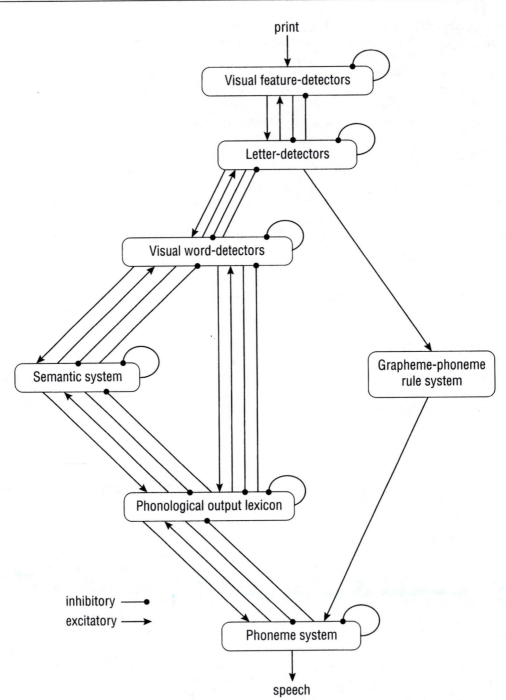

Figure 10.4: The DRC Architecture of the Reading Process. Adapted from "Models of Reading Aloud: Dual-Route and Parallel-Distributed Processing Approaches," by M. Coltheart, B. Curtis, P. Atkins, and M. Haller, 1993, *Psychological Review*, 100, 589–608.

one nonsemantic process. They differ primarily, however, regarding the nature of nonsemantic processing in that DRC assumes two nonsemantic routes whereas Seidenberg and McClelland and Plaut et al. assume only one (for other detailed theories of reading see also Ans, Carbonnel, & Valdois, 1998; Reggia et al., 1988; and Zorzi, Houghton, & Butterworth, 1998).

According to DRC (Coltheart et al., 1993) the nonsemantic mapping of print to sound is implemented in two routes: one that encodes with explicit rules the most frequent mappings between graphemes and phonemes, and another which consists of direct connections from orthographic word representations to their phonological counterparts. Thus, although the theory is called a "dual route" theory, it actually assumes three routes (see Figure 10.4). The DRC theory has been implemented in a computer simulation and Coltheart and colleagues have argued that it can account for all of the relevant empirical observations from intact performance, including the consistency effects reported by Glushko. *DRC theory*

Seidenberg and McClelland (1989) proposed that a single nonsemantic route can correctly pronounce regular and irregular words as well as nonwords without using rules, if it makes use of distributed representations and connectionist learning and processing principles. They assumed that all of our knowledge of grapheme–phoneme relationships is embedded in one network that, in the course of learning, acquires a connectivity structure that is highly sensitive to the frequency with which letter strings and their pronunciations are encountered. This connectivity structure allows for the mapping of letters onto sounds without any representations of specific words or rules (see Figure 10.5). It can encode the pronunciations of specific words that have been previously encountered, whether these are regular or irregular. *S&M theory*

Seidenberg and McClelland (1989) were not entirely successful in their defense of this proposal because their computer simulation implementing the theory (which we will refer to as SM) could not generate plausible pronunciations for many nonwords and thus also could not match patterns of impaired performance (Besner, Twilley, McCann, & Seergobin, 1990; Patterson, Seidenberg, & McClelland, 1989). Plaut et al. (1996), however, improved upon SM by changing the input and output representations. Rather than assuming widely distributed orthographic and phonological representations on input and output respectively, Plaut et al. adopted localist input and output representations of graphemes and phonemes that were syllabically organized. This modification allowed their computer simulation of a single network to accurately generate pronunciations for all previously encountered words, regardless of regularity, and also for novel letter strings. Frequency, consistency, and interaction effects were also all readily matched. *PMSP-1* We will refer to this theory as PMSP-1.

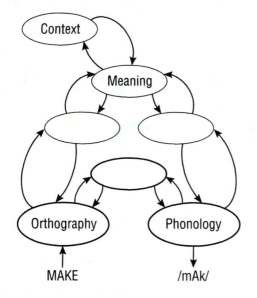

Figure 10.5: The Reading Architecture Proposed by Seidenberg and McClelland, 1989. Adapted from "A Distributed Developmental Model of Word Recognition and Naming," by M. Seidenberg and J. L. McClelland, 1989, *Psychological Review, 96,* 523–568.

Evidence from Deficits

With PMSP-1, Plaut et al. (1996) demonstrated that it is computationally possible for a single nonsemantic process to correctly read regular and irregular words as well as nonwords. The question remained, however, as to whether this was an appropriate characterization of the human nonsemantic reading process. Data from deficits played a pivotal role in answering this question.

Both DRC and S&M-2 can account for patterns (such as WB's described above) where nonword reading is severely impaired and word reading relatively spared. They do so by assuming severe damage to the nonsemantic process/es and an intact semantically mediated route. More of a challenge is the pattern exhibited by KT (Table 10.3) where nonword reading is unaffected in the face of severely impaired reading of low frequency irregular words, with reading errors for these words consisting largely of regularizations.

DRC explains KT's pattern by assuming severe damage to both lexical routes.[7] The crippled lexical routes would be operating in the context of an intact OPC system that can correctly read all nonwords and regular words. When irregular words are encountered and are unsuccessfully processed through the lexical procedures, regularizations are generated by the OPC.

Under PMSP-1 even severe damage to the semantically-mediated process would not generate KT's pattern because (as Plaut et al., 1996, had shown) a nonsemantic process operating alone should be able to read all words and nonwords. Thus, Plaut et al. (1996) examined the hypothesis that KT's performance could be understood within PMSP-1 as the result of severe damage to the semantic route in combination with additional damage to the nonsemantic process. However, after extensive simulation work they found that if the nonsemantic network was damaged sufficiently to match KT's level of exception word performance, the network's ability to correctly read nonwords and produce regularization errors was invariably reduced (see Table 10.3). This is not entirely surprising since the knowledge supporting the reading of irregular words and nonwords is embedded in an indistinguishable manner within a single network. Therefore, as knowledge supporting irregular word reading is affected so is all other knowledge.

This led Plaut et al. to the conclusion that although it is indeed computationally possible for a single network to successfully match the facts of unimpaired performance, certain characteristics of the reading process revealed by brain damage are problematic. On this basis, Plaut et al. (1996) modified their position and suggested that the nonsemantic process does not encode word-specific orthography–phonology mappings for all low frequency irregular words.[8] We will refer to this modified view as PMSP-2. Under this revised view of the nonsemantic process, Plaut and colleagues accounted for KT's pattern by assuming, as did DRC, that KT suffered from severe damage to the semantically mediated process and that his reading reflected the characteristics of the undamaged nonsemantic process.

DRC and PMSP-2 are similar in that they both assume a semantically-mediated process for reading and also in that they both assume that the OPC system cannot accurately pronounce all words and nonwords. They differ in that DRC assumes an additional nonsemantic lexical route. Furthermore they differ in terms of the content of the OPC system. DRC assumes that rules are used to encode the most frequent orthography–phonology relationships defined over phoneme–grapheme units. As a result, this process accurately pronounces only novel words

---

[7]This doesn't necessarily imply two deficits, however, as a single deficit to either the orthographic input lexicon or the phonological output lexicon will affect both processes. Evidence of damage to the semantic system requires an additional locus of damage to account for the inoperability of the third route.

[8]Specifically they argue that the nonsemantic system doesn't acquire the knowledge to pronounce low-frequency exceptions because this knowledge is not easily acquired and, in the course of learning, the semantically-mediated system (which can produce correct pronunciations for these words) reduces the pressure on the nonsemantically-mediated system to learn this information.

and regular words. PMSP-2 assumes that distributed representations (rather than rules) allow for the correct pronunciation of a range of orthography–phonology mappings including the pronunciation of irregular words that are of reasonably high frequency.

The two accounts make different predictions regarding patterns that should or should not be observed subsequent to damage. The most salient of these is that PMSP-2 predicts that low frequency irregular words cannot be read correctly without the contribution of the semantic route, whereas DRC predicts that the semantic route will be unnecessary for pronouncing these words, as long the nonsemantic lexical process is intact (later we take up qualifications offered in Plaut et al., 1996, and Plaut, 1997). Clearly, therefore, evidence reviewed above regarding the third route is highly relevant for distinguishing between DRC and PMSP-2.

Interaction between the Routes

The pattern of intact reading of low-frequency irregular words in the face of severely impaired comprehension was described earlier in support of the third nonsemantic lexical route. As indicated just above, this pattern is seemingly problematic for PMSP-2 but not for DRC. Here we review arguments that the specific patterns of performance that have been reported may not be problematic. These arguments hinge on the notion of interaction among the various reading routes.

Both DRC and PMSP-2 assume that the reading routes interact at least in that they integrate activation at the level of a phonological output layer (see Figures 10.4 and 10.5). This integration can be thought of as the routes "voting" for candidate phonemes with a pooling of the votes (albeit weighted towards the semantic route) determining the output. The extent to which the votes converge on a common set of phonemes determines the time the system takes to "settle" into a stable response.

Integration is crucial for both theories. For DRC it is needed to account for consistency effects in nonword reading (e.g., PRINK read faster than ZAID). In DRC integration provides a means by which the pronunciations of words orthographically related to a nonword stimulus can contribute to its pronunciation (see also Monsell, Patterson, Graham, Hughes, & Milroy, 1992). For PMSP-2, integration is essential to the learning process because it provides a mechanism by which the semantic route can contribute to the training of the nonsemantic process.

Hillis and Caramazza (1991b, 1995) described a number of individuals who seemingly exhibited the critical pattern and then went on to show how their performance might be accounted for without positing a third route. One case they presented was that of JJ (Hillis & Caramazza, 1991a, 1991b) who had a semantic level impairment that manifested itself in severe difficulties in spoken picture naming and comprehension (for all categories except for animals, which were selectively spared). JJ primarily made semantic errors in these tasks. However, his oral reading of the same words was correct, even for irregular words such as STOMACH, PEAR, GLOVE, SUIT. Additionally, JJ's nonword reading was reasonably intact (90% correct).

Hillis and Caramazza (1991b, 1995) argued that this pattern can be understood without a third route if we consider the possibilities provided by integration across reading routes (for similar proposals see Plaut et al., 1996; Shallice & McCarthy, 1985; Saffran, 1985; Zorzi et al., 1998). In cases such as JJ's, a damaged semantic system may yield an impoverished semantic representation. For example, BANANA may yield: <yellow>, <edible>, <fruit>. In turn, this impoverished representation may activate a set of compatible responses in the phonological lexicon: "banana," "lemon," "grapefruit," "pear." In picture naming, the most active of these would be produced, sometimes generating a semantic error such as banana → lemon. In contrast with picture naming, oral reading allows for integration of semantically-based and OPC-based information. In this example, the OPC will provide phonological information consistent with "banana" but not "lemon" and this information may prevent a semantic error. In the

Table 10.4
JJ's Reading Accuracy According to Comprehension Accuracy.

	Comprehension		
	Correct	Partially Correct	Incorrect
Reading accuracy			
Regular, consistent	100%	100%	92%
Regular, inconsistent	100%	100%	60%
Exception words	100%	100%	0%
Orthographically strange	100%	100%	0%

Adapted from "Mechanisms for Accessing Lexical Representations for Output,"
by A. E. Hillis & A. Caramazza, 1991b, *Brain & Language, 40,* pp. 106–144.

case of an irregular word such as PEAR, the semantic system will yield a similar response set—"banana," "lemon," "grapefruit," "pear"—and the OPC may generate a regularization such as /p i r/. The integration of these two sources of information, albeit both inaccurate, is likely to yield the correct response (for evidence for integration in Italian see Miceli, Capasso, & Caramazza, 1994; Miceli, Giustolisi, & Caramazza, 1991). Any integration-based explanation of the pattern requires that there must be at least some contribution from the semantic route. Hillis and Caramazza tested this in JJ's case by asking him to read aloud and define a set of 290 words that varied in regularity (see Table 10.4). They found that his oral reading accuracy was strictly tied to his comprehension such that all words that were at least partially comprehended were read correctly; words for which he showed no evidence of comprehension were often read correctly if they were regular, but never if they were irregular (see also Funnell, 1996; Graham, Hodges, & Patterson, 1994).

Hillis & Caramazza (1991b, 1995) argued that the cases they had reviewed presented no compelling evidence of good reading of low-frequency irregular words in the complete absence of comprehension. They claimed that all subjects in the literature who had been described as lacking comprehension made errors in comprehension tasks that indicated that they had at least some accurate semantic information. For example, errors in word picture matching tasks often involved selecting a semantically related distractor rather than an unrelated one. Thus, good reading of irregular words in these cases could be explained by assuming, as in JJ's case, a summation of information from semantic and OPC routes. They argued that, given the existing evidence, positing a third route was unnecessary and, therefore, less parsimonious.

A mechanism for integration across the routes is important apart from debate between DRC and PMSP-2 because it plays an important role in accounting for various other performance patterns (e.g., the fact that many of these individuals produce high rates of semantic errors in picture naming but not in oral reading). In terms of distinguishing between PMSP-2 and DRC, however, the challenge still lies in demonstrating complete lack of comprehension of low frequency irregular words that are pronounced correctly. A number of more recent cases purport to do so (Cipolotti & Warrington, 1995, and Lambon Ralph et al., 1995, among them). One response to such cases is to point to difficulties involved in convincingly establishing a "lack" of comprehension. There are also difficulties that have not been mentioned thus far that concern establishing the number of low-frequency irregular words that an OPC operating in isolation can be expected to read correctly. Under some accounts the OPC should, at least occasionally, produce correct pronunciations for some low-frequency irregular words. Establishing how often this can be expected to occur and then determining whether a subject reliably exceeds this estimate, is far from straightforward.

Another response to these cases was that of Plaut (1997; Plaut et al., 1996) who ascribed the differences among the observed patterns to premorbid individual variability in the OPC's capacity to correctly read irregular, low frequency words. Individuals with a more "competent" OPC should be able to read these words despite complete damage to the semantic routes, while those with less competent systems (such as KT, presumably) should not. Plaut et al. (1996) suggested that degree of competence may be determined by educational level. However, Plaut (1997) suggested that it may also be determined by a neural "metabolic factor." The unfortunate aspect of this latter proposal is that there is no independent means of evaluating the metabolic factor, it is simply inferred ad hoc from the pattern of reading errors. Adopting this "free parameter" renders PMSP-2 essentially unfalsifiable, at least as concerns this class of predictions.

CONCLUSIONS

This chapter has attempted to review several of the major issues in reading research and illustrate the contributions from observations of behavior subsequent to neural damage. Although due to space limitations a number of important issues were not reviewed, it is apparent even from this brief report that data from deficits has often played a critical role in answering fundamental questions.

A number of studies have indicated that abstract and structured orthographic representations are derived from written stimuli. Others have revealed that despite the pervasive presence of phonology during reading, direct access to meaning from print is possible in the competent reader. Nonetheless, questions remain concerning the specific circumstances under which direct access and phonologically mediated access to meaning occur.

The fact that various properties of the orthography/phonology relationship are continuous and graded rather than discrete and categorical has provoked questions regarding the basic computations and representations that support reading: Must we assume that they are similarly graded and continuous, as connectionist approaches suggest? Or can these continuous properties be derived from a system with discrete, symbolic structures such as rules and lexical representations, as DRC proposes? Work continues on these questions and on the specific implications they have for reading architectures.

In many of the debates we have reviewed, issues regarding the number, content, speed, and computational mode of reading processes have often been conflated, rather than independently evaluated. In examining reading theories, the primary question should be whether or not a theory can account for the principal empirical findings from impaired and unimpaired performance. When a theory falls short it is essential to determine to what aspects of the theory the failures are specifically attributable—the number of routes, their content, their computational bases, etc. This careful "credit/blame" assignment (McCloskey, 1991) has not always been done (see Paap et al., 1992, for a discussion of number of the "red herrings"). Certainly, however, progress in understanding the reading process can only benefit from proceeding in this manner.

Acknowledgements

We would like to acknowledge the support of NIMH Grant R29MH55758 to the first author. We are also grateful to Max Coltheart and Mike McCloskey for their many helpful comments on earlier drafts.

REFERENCES

Adams, M. J. (1979). Models of word recognition. *Cognitive Psychology, 11*, 133–176.

Ans, B., Carbonnel, S., & Valdois, S. (1998). A connectionist multiple-trace memory model for polysyllabic word reading. *Psychological Review, 105*, 678–723.

Ardila, A. (1991). Errors resembling semantic paralexias in Spanish-speaking aphasics. *Brain and Language, 41*, 437–445.

Baluch, B., & Besner, D. (1991). Visual word recognition: Evidence for strategic control of lexical and nonlexical routines in oral reading. *Journal of Experimental Psychology: Learning, Memory, and Cognition, 17,* 644–652.

Baron, J., & Strawson, C. (1976). Use of orthographic and word-specific knowledge in reading words aloud. *Journal of Experimental Psychology: Human Perception and Performance, 2,* 386–393.

Beauvois, M. F., & Derouesné, J. (1979). Phonological alexia: Three dissociations. *Journal of Neurology, Neurosurgery and Psychiatry, 42,* 1115–1124.

Berndt, R. S., Haendiges, A. N., Mitchum, C. C., & Wayland, S. C. (1996). An investigation of nonlexical reading impairments. *Cognitive Neuropsychology, 13,* 763–801.

Bernstein, S. E., & Carr, T. H. (1996). Dual-route theories of pronouncing printed words: What can be learned from concurrent task performance? *Journal of Experimental Psychology: Learning, Memory, & Cognition, 22,* 86–116.

Besner, D. (1983). Basic decoding components in reading: Two dissociable feature extraction processes. *Canadian Journal of Psychology, 37,* 429–438.

Besner, D., Coltheart, M., & Davelaar, E. (1984). Basic process in reading: Computation of abstract letter identities. *Canadian Journal of Psychology, 38,* 126–134.

Besner, D., & Smith, M. C. (1992). Basic processes in reading: Is the orthographic depth hypothesis sinking? In R. Frost & L. Katz (Eds.), *Orthography, phonology, morphology, and meaning* (pp. 45–66). Amsterdam: North-Holland.

Besner, D., Twilley, L., McCann, R. S., & Seergobin, K. (1990). On the association between connectionism and data: Are a few words necessary? *Psychological Review, 97,* 432–446.

Bowey, J. A. (1990). Orthographic onsets and rimes as functional units of reading. *Memory and Cognition, 18,* 419–427.

Bub, D., Cancelliere, A., & Kertesz, A. (1985). Whole-word and analytic translation of spelling to sound in a nonsemantic reader. In K. E. Patterson, J. C. Marshall, & M. Coltheart (Eds.), *Surface dyslexia.* London: LEA.

Buchanan, L., & Besner, D. (1993). Reading aloud: Evidence for the use of a whole word nonsemantic pathway. *Canadian Journal of Experimental Psychology, 47,* 133–152.

Caplan, D., & Waters, G. S. (1995). On the nature of phonological output planning processes involved in verbal rehearsal: Evidence from aphasia. *Brain and Language, 48,* 191–220.

Caramazza, A., & Hillis, A. E. (1990). Internal spatial representation of written words: Evidence from unilateral neglect. *Nature, 346,* 267–269.

Caramazza, A., & Hillis, A. E. (1991). Levels of representation, co-ordinate frames, and unilateral neglect. *Cognitive Neuropsychology, 7,* 391–445.

Caramazza, A., Laudanna, A., & Romani, C. (1988). Lexical access and inflectional morphology. Lexical access and inflectional morphology. *Cognition, 28,* 297–332.

Cipolotti, L., & Warrington, E. K. (1995). Semantic memory and reading abilities: A case report. *Journal of the International Neuropsychological Society, 1,* 104–110.

Coltheart, M. (1978). Lexical access in simple reading tasks. In G. Underwood (Ed.), *Strategies of information processing,* London: Academic Press.

Coltheart, M. (1980). Reading, phonological recoding and deep dyslexia. In M. Coltheart, K. Patterson, & J. C. Marshall (Eds.), *Deep dyslexia.* London: Routledge & Kegan Paul.

Coltheart, M. (1996). Phonological dyslexia: Past and future issues. *Cognitive Neuropsychology, 13,* 749–762.

Coltheart, M., & Coltheart, V. (1997). Reading comprehension is not exclusively reliant upon phonological representation. *Cognitive Neuropsychology, 14,* 167–175.

Coltheart, M., Curtis, B., Atkins, P., & Haller, M. (1993). Models of reading aloud: Dual-route and parallel-distributed processing approaches. *Psychological Review, 100,* 589–608.

Coltheart, M., & Freeman, R. (1974). Case alteration impairs word recognition. *Bulletin of the Psychonomic Society, 3,* 102–104.

Coltheart, M., Masterson, J., Byng, S., Prior, M., & Riddoch, J. (1983). Surface dyslexia. *Quarterly Journal of Experimental Psychology, 35A,* 469–495.

Coltheart, M., Patterson, K. E., & Marshall, J. C. (Eds.). (1980). *Deep dyslexia.* London: Routledge & Kegan Paul.

Coslett, H. B. (1991). Read but not write "idea": Evidence for a third reading mechanism. *Brain and Language, 40,* 425–443.

Cuetos, F., Valle-Arroyo, F., & Suarez, M. P. (1996). A case of phonological dyslexia in Spanish. *Cognitive Neuropsychology, 13,* 1–24.

Davelaar, E., Coltheart, M., Besner, D., & Jonasson, J. T. (1978). Phonological recoding and lexical access. *Memory and Cognition, 6,* 391–402.

Davis, C., Castles, A., & Iakovidis, E. (1998). Masked homophone and pseudohomophone priming in adults and children. *Language and Cognitive Processes, 13,* 625–651.

DeFrancis, J. (1989). *Visible speech: The diverse oneness of writing systems.* Honolulu, HI: University of Hawaii Press.

Dell, G. (1986). A spreading-activation theory of retrieval in sentence production. *Psychological Review, 93,* 283–321.

Dennis, I., & Newstead, S. E. (1981). Is phonological recoding under strategic control? *Memory and Cognition, 9,* 472–477.

Derouesné, J., & Beauvois, M. F. (1976). Phonological processing in reading: Data from alexia. *Journal of Neurology, Neurosurgery, & Psychiatry, 42,* 1125–1132.

Derouesné, J., & Beauvois, M. F. (1985). The "phonemic" stage in the non-lexical reading process: Evidence from a case of phonological alexia. In K. E. Patterson, M. Coltheart, & J. C. Marshall (Eds.), *Surface dyslexia* (pp. 399–457). London: Lawrence Erlbaum.

Dickerson, J. (1999). Format distortion and word reading: The role of multiletter units. *Neurocase: Case Studies in Neuropsychology, Neuropsychiatry, and Behavioural Neurology, 5,* 31–36.

Evett, L. J., & Humphreys, G. W. (1981). The use of abstract graphemic information in lexical access. *Quarterly Journal of Experimental Psychology, 33A,* 325–350.

Ferreres, A. R., & Miravalles, G. (1995). The production of semantic paralexias in a Spanish-speaking aphasic. *Brain and Language, 49,* 153–172.

Folk, J. R. (1999). Phonological codes are used to access the lexicon during silent reading. *Journal of Experimental Psychology: Learning, Memory, & Cognition, 25,* 892–906.

Forster, K. I., & Chambers, S. M. (1973). Lexical access and naming time. *Journal of Verbal Learning and Verbal Behavior, 12*, 627–635.

Fowler, C. A., Napps, S. E., & Feldman, L. (1985). Relations among regular and irregular morphologically related words in the lexicon as revealed by repetition priming. *Memory and Cognition, 13*, 241–255.

Frederiksen, J. R., & Kroll, J. F. (1976). Spelling and sound: Approaches to the internal lexicon. *Journal of Experimental Psychology: Human Perception and Performance, 2*, 361–379.

Frost, R. (1998). Toward a strong phonological theory of visual word recognition: True issues and false trails. *Psychological Bulletin, 123*, 71–99.

Funnell, E. (1983). Phonological processes in reading: New evidence from acquired dyslexia. *British Journal of Psychology, 74*, 159–180.

Funnell, E. (1996). W. L. P.: A case for the modularity of language function and dementia. In C. Code, W. W. Wallesch, Y. Joanette, & A. R. Lecours (Eds.), *Classic cases in neuropsychology* (pp. 203–216). Hove, UK: Psychology Press.

Gibson, E. J., Pick, A. D., Osser, H., & Hammond, M. (1962). The role of grapheme–phoneme correspondence in the perception of words. *American Journal of Psychology, 75*, 554–570.

Glushko, R. J. (1979). The organization and activation of orthographic knowledge in reading aloud. *Journal of Experimental Psychology: Human Perception and Performance, 5*, 674–691.

Goodall, W. C., & Phillips, W. A. (1995). Three routes from print to sound: Evidence from a case of acquired dyslexia. *Cognitive Neuropsychology, 12*, 113–147.

Graham, K. S., Hodges, J. R., & Patterson, K. E. (1994). The relationship between comprehension and oral reading in progressive fluent aphasia. *Neuropsychologia, 32*, 299–316.

Greenwald, M. L., & Berndt, R. S. (1999). Impaired encoding of abstract letter order: Severe alexia in a mildly aphasic patient. *Cognitive Neuropsychology, 16*, 512–556.

Hanley, J. R., & McDonell, V. (1997). Are reading and spelling phonologically mediated? Evidence from a patient with a speech production impairment. *Cognitive Neuropsychology, 14*, 3–33.

Hawkins, H. L., Reicher, G. M., Rogers, M., & Peterson, L. (1976). Flexible coding in word recognition. *Journal of Experimental Psychology: Human Perception and Performance, 2*, 380–385.

Henderson, L. (1982). *Orthography and word recognition in reading*. New York: Academic Press.

Herdman, C. M. (1992). Attentional resource demands of visual word recognition in naming and lexical decisions. *Journal of Experimental Psychology: Human Perception and Performance, 18*, 460–470.

Hillis, A. E., & Caramazza, A. (1991a). Category specific naming and comprehension impairment: A double dissociation. *Brain, 114*, 2081–2094.

Hillis, A. E., & Caramazza, A. (1991b). Mechanisms for accessing lexical representations for output: Evidence from a category-specific semantic deficit. *Brain and Language, 40*, 106–144.

Hillis, A. E., & Caramazza, A. (1995). Converging evidence for the interaction of semantic and sublexical phonological information in accessing lexical representations for spoken output. *Cognitive Neuropsychology, 12*, 187–227.

Holmes, J. M. (1978). Regression and reading breakdown.

In A. Caramazza & E. Zurif (Eds.), *Language acquisition and reading breakdown*. Baltimore: Johns Hopkins University Press.

Howard, D. (1987). Reading without letters? In M. Coltheart, G. Sartori, & R. Job (Eds.), *The cognitive neuropsychology of language*. London: Lawrence Erlbuam.

Howard, D., & Patterson, K. (1992). *The Pyramids and Palm Trees Test*. Bury, St. Edmunds, UK: Thames Valley Test Company.

Humphreys, G. W., & Evett, L. J. (1985). Are there independent lexical and nonlexical routes in word processing? An evaluation of the dual-route theory of reading. *Behavioral and Brain Sciences, 8*, 689–740.

Iribarren, I. C., Jarema, G., & Lecours, A. R. (1999). Lexical reading in Spanish: Two cases of phonological dyslexia. *Applied Psycholinguistics, 20*, 407–428.

Jared, D. (1997). Spelling-sound consistency affects the naming of high frequency words. *Journal of Memory and Language, 36*, 505–529.

Jared, D., McRae, K., & Seidenberg, M. S. (1990). The basis of consistency effects in word naming. *Journal of Memory and Language, 29*, 687–715.

Jared, D., & Seidenberg, M. S. (1991). Does word identification proceed from spelling to sound to meaning? *Journal of Experimental Psychology: General, 120 (4)*, 358–394.

Joubert, S. A., & Lecours, A. R. (2000). The role of sublexical graphemic processing in reading. *Brain and Language, 72*, 1–13.

Kay, J., & Marcel, A. (1981). One process, not two, in reading aloud: Lexical analogies do the work of nonlexical rules. *Quarterly Journal of Experimental Psychology: Human Experimental Psychology, 33A*, 397–413.

Lambon Ralph, M. A., Ellis, A. W., & Franklin, S. (1995). Semantic loss without surface dyslexia. *Neurocase: Case Studies in Neuropsychology, Neuropsychiatry, and Behavioural Neurology, 1*, 363–369.

Lambon Ralph, M. A., Ellis, A. W., & Sage, K. (1998). Word meaning blindness revisited. *Cognitive Neuropsychology, 15*, 389–400.

Lesch, M. F., & Martin, R. C. (1998). The representation of sublexical orthographic-phonologic correspondences: Evidence from phonological dyslexia. *Quarterly Journal of Experimental Psychology: Human Experimental Psychology, 51A*, 905–938.

Lukatela, G., Lukatela, K., Carello, C., & Turvey, M. T. (1999). Effects of frequency & phonological ambiguity in naming Serbo-Croatian words. *European Journal of Cognitive Psychology, 11*, 1–6.

Lukatela, G, Savíc, M, Gligorjecíc, B. Ognjenovic, P., & Tirvey, M. T. (1978). Bi-alphabetic lexical descision. *Language and Speech, 21(2)*, 142–165.

Lukatela, G., & Turvey, M. T. (1991). Phonological access of the lexicon: Evidence from associative priming with pseudohomophones. *Journal of Experimental Psychology: Human Perception and Performance, 17*, 951–966.

Lukatela, G., & Turvey, M. T. (1993). Similar attentional, frequency, and associative effects for pseudohomophones and words. *Journal of Experimental Psychology: Human Perception and Performance, 19*, 166–178.

Lukatela, G., & Turvey, M. T. (1994a). Visual lexical access is initially phonological: I. Evidence from associative priming by words, homophones, and pseudohomophones. *Journal of Experimental Psychology: General, 123*, 107–128.

Lukatela, G., & Turvey, M. T. (1994b). Visual lexical access is initially phonological: 2. Evidence from phonological priming by homophones and pseudohomophones. *Journal of Experimental Psychology: General, 123,* 331–353.

Marcel, A. J. (1980). Surface dyslexia and beginning reading: A revised hypothesis of the pronunciation of print and its impairments. In M. Coltheart, K. E. Patterson, & J. C. Marshall (Eds.), *Deep dyslexia.* London: Routledge & Kegan Paul.

Marshall, J. C., & Newcombe, F. (1973). Patterns of paralexia: A psycholinguistic approach. *Journal of Psycholinguistic Research, 2,* 175–200.

Mayall, K., Humphreys, G. W., & Olson, A. (1997). Disruption to word or letter processing? The origins of case-mixing effects. *Journal of Experimental Psychology: Learning, Memory, and Cognition, 23,* 1275–1286.

McCarthy, R. A., & Warrington, E. K. (1986). Phonological reading: Phenomena and paradoxes. *Cortex, 22,* 359–380.

McClelland, J. L. (1977). Leter and configurational information in word identification. *Journal of Verbal Learning & Verbal Behavior, 16,* 137–150.

McCloskey, M. (1991). Networks and theories: The place of connectionism in cognitive science. *Psychological Science, 2,* 387–395.

Mewhort, D. J., & Beal, A. L. (1977). Mechanisms of word identification. *Journal of Experimental Psychology: Human Perception and Performance, 3,* 629–640.

Meyer, D. E., Schvaneveldt, R. W., & Ruddy, M. G. (1974). Functions of graphemic and phonemic codes in visual word-recognition. *Memory and Cognition, 2,* 309–321.

Miceli, G., Benvegnu, B., Capasso, R., & Caramazza, A. (1997). The independence of phonological and orthographic lexical forms. *Cognitive Neuropsychology, 14,* 35–69.

Miceli, G., Capasso, R., & Caramazza, A. (1994). The interaction of lexical and sublexical processes in reading, writing and repetition. *Neuropsychologia, 32,* 317–333.

Miceli, G., & Caramazza, A. (1993). The assignment of word stress in oral reading: Evidence from a case of acquired dyslexia. *Cognitive Neuropsychology, 10,* 273–295.

Miceli, G., Giustolisi, L., & Caramazza, A. (1991). The interaction of lexical and non-lexical processing mechanisms: Evidence from anomia. *Cortex, 27,* 57–80.

Miozzo, M., & Caramazza, A. (1998). Varieties of pure alexia: The case of failure to access graphemic representations. *Cognitive Neuropsychology, 15,* 203–238.

Monk, A. F., & Hulme, C. (1983). Errors in proofreading: Evidence for the use of word shape in word recognition. *Memory and Cognition, 11,* 16–23.

Monsell, S., Patterson, K. E., Graham, A., & Hughes, C. H., & Milroy, R. (1992). Lexical and sublexical translation of spelling to sound: Strategic anticipation of lexical status. *Journal of Experimental Psychology: Learning, Memory, and Cognition, 18,* 452–467.

Morton, J., & Patterson, K. E. (1980). A new attempt at an interpretation, or, and attempt at a new interpretation. In M. Coltheart, K. E. Patterson, & J. C. Marshall (Eds.), *Deep dyslexia.* London: Routledge & Kegan Paul.

Mozer, M. C. (1989). Types and tokens in visual letter perception. *Journal of Experimental Psychology: Human Perception and Performance, 15,* 287–303.

Murrell, G. A., & Morton, J. (1974). Word recognition

and morphemic structure. *Journal of Experimental Psychology, 102,* 963–968.

Newcombe, F., & Marshall, J. C. (1985). Reading and writing by letter sounds. In K. E. Patterson, M. Coltheart, & J. C. Marshall (Eds.), *Surface dyslexia* (pp. 35–49). London: Lawrence Erlbaum.

Norris, D. (1994). A quantitative multiple-levels model of reading aloud. *Journal of Experimental Psychology: Human Perception and Performance, 20,* 1212–1232.

Paap, K. R., Newsome, S. L., & Noel, R. W. (1984). Word shape's in poor shape for the race to the lexicon. *Journal of Experimental Psychology: Human Perception and Performance, 10,* 413–428.

Paap, K. R., & Noel, R. W. (1991). Dual-route models of print to sound: Still a good horse race. *Psychological Research/Psychologische Forschung, 53,* 13–24.

Paap, K. R., Noel, R. W., & Johansen, L. S. (1992). Dual-route models of print to sound: Red herrings and real horses. In R. Frost & L. Katz (Eds.), *Orthography, phonology, morphology, and meaning* (pp. 293–318). Amsterdam: North-Holland.

Patterson, K. E., Marshall, J. C., & Coltheart, M. (1985). *Surface dyslexia.* London: Lawrence Erlbaum.

Patterson, K. E. & Morton, J. (1985). From orthography to phonology: An attempt at an old interpretation. In K. E. Patterson, M. Coltheart, & J.C. Marshall (Eds.), *Surface dyslexia.* London: Lawrence Erlbaum.

Patterson, K., Seidenberg, M. S., & McClelland, J. L. (1989). Connections and disconnections: Acquired dyslexia in a computational model of reading processes. In R. G. M. Morris (Ed.), *Parallel distributed processing: Implications for psychology and neurobiology* (pp. 131–181). Oxford, UK: Oxford University Press.

Patterson, K., Suzuki, T., Wydell, T., Sasanuma, S. (1995). Progressive aphasia and surface alexia in Japanese. *Neurocase: Case Studies in Neuropsychology, Neuropsychiatry, and Behavioural Neurology, 1,* 155–165.

Perfetti, C. A., Bell, L. C., & Delaney, S. M. (1988). Automatic (prelexical) phonetic activation in silent word reading: Evidence from backward masking. *Journal of Memory and Language, 27,* 59–70.

Plaut, D. C. (1997). Structure and function in the lexical system: Insights from distributed models of word reading and lexical decision. *Language and Cognitive Processes 12(5–6),* 765–805.

Plaut, D. C., McClelland, J. L., Seidenberg, M. S., & Patterson, K. (1996). Understanding normal and impaired word reading: Computational principles in quasi-regular domains. *Psychological Review, 103,* 56–115.

Polk, T. A., & Farah, M. J. (1997). A simple common contexts explanation for the development of abstract letter identities. *Neural Computation, 9,* 1277–1289.

Posnansky, C. J., & Rayner, K. (1977). Visual-feature and response components in a picture-word interference task with beginning and skilled readers. *Journal of Experimental Child Psychology, 24,* 440–460.

Pring, L. (1981). Phonological codes and functional spelling units: Reality and implications. *Perception and Psychophysics, 30,* 573–578.

Prinzmetal, W. & Millis-Wright, M. (1984). Cognitive and linguistic factors affect visual feature integration. *Cognitive Psychology, 16,* 305–340.

Prinzmetal, W., Treiman, R., & Rho, S. H. (1986). How to see a reading unit. *Journal of Memory and Language, 25,* 461–475.

Pugh, K. R., Rexer, K., & Katz, L. (1994). Evidence of flexible coding in visual word recognition. *Journal of*

Experimental Psychology: Human Perception and Performance, 20, 807–825.

Rapp, B. (1992). The nature of sublexical orthographic organization: The bigram trough hypothesis examined. *Journal of Memory and Language, 31*, 33–53.

Rapp, B., & Caramazza, A. (1989). Letter processing in reading and spelling: Some dissociations. *Reading and Writing, 1*, 3–23.

Rapp, B., Link, K., & Caramazza, A. (1993, October). *The role of graphemic representations in reading: Evidence from a deficit to the recognition system.* Annual meeting of the Academy of Aphasia, Tucson, Arizona.

Raymer, A. M., & Berndt, R. S. (1996). Reading lexically without semantics: Evidence from patients with probable Alzheimer's disease. *Journal of the International Neuropsychological Society, 2*, 340–349.

Rayner, K., McConkie, G. W., & Zola, D. (1980). Integrating information across eye movements. *Cognitive Psychology, 12*, 206–226.

Reggia, J., Marsland, P., & Berndt, R.S. (1988). Competitive dynamics in a dual-route connectionist model of print-to-sound transformation. *Complex Systems, 2*, 509–547.

Rey, A., Jacobs, A. M., Schmidt-Weigand, F., & Zeigler, J. C. (1998). A phoneme effect in visual word recognition. *Cognition, 68*, B71–B80.

Ruiz, A., Ansaldo, A. I., & Lecours, A. R. (1994). Two cases of deep dyslexia in unilingual hispano-phone aphasics. *Brain and Language, 46*, 245–256.

Rumelhart, D. E., & McClelland, J. L. (1986). On learning the past tenses of English verbs. In J. L. McClelland, D. E. Rumelhart, & The PDP Research Group (Eds.), *Parallel distributed process: Explorations in the microstructure of cognition: Vol. 2. Psychological and biological models* (pp. 216–271). Cambridge, MA: MIT Press.

Saffran, E. M. (1985). Lexicalisation and reading performance in surface dyslexia. In K. E. Patterson, J.C. Marshall, & M. Coltheart (Eds.), *Surface dyslexia* (pp. 53-70). London: Lawrence Erlbaum.

Santa, J. L., & Santa, C. (1979). Vowel and consonant clusters in word recognition. *Perception and Motor Skills, 48*, 951–954.

Schwartz, M. F., Saffran, E. M., & Marin, O. S. M. (1980). Fractionating the reading process in dementia: Evidence for word-specific print-to-sound associations. In M. Coltheart, K. E. Patterson, & J. C. Marshall (Eds.), *Deep dyslexia.* London: Routledge & Kegan Paul.

Seidenberg, M. (1987). Sublexical structures in visual word recognition: Access units or orthographic redundancy? In M. Coltheart (Ed.), *Attention and performance XII: The psychology of reading.* Hillsdale, NJ: Lawrence Erlbaum.

Seidenberg, M., & McClelland, J. L. (1989). A distributed developmental model of word recognition and naming. *Psychological Review, 96*, 523–568.

Seidenberg, M. S., Waters, G. S., Barnes, M. A., & Tanenhaus, M. K. (1984). When does irregular spelling or pronunciation influence word recognition? *Journal of Verbal Learning and Verbal Behavior, 23*, 383–404.

Sejnowski, T. J., & Rosenberg, C. R. (1987). Parallel networks that learn to pronounce English text. *Complex Systems, 1*, 145–168.

Shelton, J. R., & Weinrich, M. (1997). Further evidence of a dissociation between output phonological and orthographic lexicons: A case study. *Cognitive Neuropsychology, 14*, 105–129.

Shallice, T., & McCarthy, R. (1985). Phonological reading: from patterns of impairment to possible procedures. In K. E. Patterson, J.C. Marshall, & M. Coltheart (Eds.), *Surface Dyslexia.* London: Lawrence Erlbaum.

Shallice, T., & Warrington, E. K. (1980). Single and multiple component ventral dyslexic syndromes. In M. Coltheart, K. E. Patterson, and J.C. Marshall (Eds.), *Deep dyslexia.* London: Routledge & Kegan Paul.

Shallice, T., Warrington, E. K., & McCarthy, R. (1983). Reading without semantics. *Quarterly Journal of Experimental Psychology, 35A*, 111–138.

Stanners, R. F., Neiser, J. J., Hernon, W. P., & Hall, R. (1979). Memory representation for morphologically related words. *Journal of Verbal Learning and Verbal Behavior, 18*, 399–412.

Stanovich, K. E., & Bauer, D. W. (1978). Experiments on the spelling-to-sound regularity effect in word recognition. *Memory and Cognition, 6*, 410–415.

Stone, G. O., Vanhoy, M., & Van Orden, G. C. (1997). Perception is a two-way street: feedforward and feedback phonology in visual word recognition. *Journal of Memory and Language, 36*, 337–359.

Strain, E., Patterson, K., & Seidenberg, M. S. (1995). Semantic effects in single word naming. *Journal of Experimental Psychology: Learning, Memory, and Cognition, 21*, 1140–1154.

Taft, M. (1979). Lexical access via an orthographic code: The basic orthographic syllabic structure (BOSS). *Journal of Verbal Learning and Verbal Behavior, 18*, 21–39.

Taft, M., & Forster, K. I. (1975). Lexical storage and retrieval of prefixed words. *Journal of Verbal Learning and Verbal Behavior, 14*, 638–647.

Taft, M., & Forster, K. I. (1976). Lexical storage and retrieval of polymorphemic and polysyllabic words. *Journal of Verbal Learning and Verbal Behavior, 15*, 607–620.

Taft, M., & van Graan, F. (1998). Lack of phonological mediation in a semantic categorization task. *Journal of Memory and Language, 38*, 203–224.

Tan, L. H., & Perfetti, C. A. (1997). Visual Chinese character recognition: Does phonological information mediate access to meaning? *Journal of Memory and Language, 37*, 41–57.

Taraban, R., & McClelland, J. L. (1987). Conspiracy effects in word recognition. *Journal of Memory and Language, 26*, 608–631.

Treiman, R., & Chaftez, J. (1987). Are there onset- and rime-like units in written words? In M. Coltheart (Ed.), *Attention and performance XII.* London: Lawrence Erlbaum.

Treiman, R., & Zukowski, A. (1988). Units in reading and spelling. *Journal of Memory and Language, 27*, 466–477.

Underwood, G., & Bargh, K. (1982). Word shape, orthographic regularity, and contextual interactions in a reading task. *Cognition, 12*, 197–209.

Van Orden, G. C. (1987). A ROWS is a ROSE: Spelling, sound, and reading. *Memory & Cognition, 15*, 181–198.

Van Orden, G. C. (1991). Phonologic mediation is fundamental to reading. In D. Besner and G. W. Humphreys (Eds.), *Basic processes in reading: Visual word recognition* (pp. 77–103). Hillsdale, NJ: Lawrence Earlbaum.

Van Orden, G. C., Johnston, J. C., & Hale, B. L. (1988). Word identification in reading proceeds from spelling to sound to meaning. *Journal of Experimental Psychology: Learning, Memory, and Cognition, 14*, 371–386.

Van Orden, G. C., Pennington, B. F., & Stone, G. O. (1990). Word identification in reading and the promise of subsymbolic psycholinguistics. *Psychological Review, 97,* 488–522.

Verstaen, A., Humphreys, G. W., Olson, A., & d'Ydewalle, G. (1995). Are phonemic effects in backward masking evidence for automatic prelexical phonemic activation in visual word recognition? *Journal of Memory and Language, 34,* 335–356.

Warrington, E. K., & Shallice, T. (1980). Word-form dyslexia. *Brain, 30,* 99–112.

Waters, G. S., & Seidenberg, M. S. (1985). Spelling-sound effects in reading: Time course and decision criteria. *Memory and Cognition, 13,* 557–572.

Weekes, B. (1997). Differential effects of number of letters on word and nonword naming latency. *Quarterly Journal of Experimental psychology: Human Experimental Psychology, 50A,* 439–456.

Weekes, B., & Chen, H. Q. (1999). Surface dyslexia in Chinese. *Neurocase: Case Studies in Neuropsychology, Neuropsychiatry, and Behavioural Neurology, 5,* 161–172.

Yin, W., & Butterworth, B. (1992). Deep and surface dyslexia in Chinese. In H. C. Chen, & O. J. L. Tzeng (Eds.), *Language processing in Chinese* (pp. 349–366). North-Holland: Amsterdam.

Ziegler, J. C., & Jacobs, A. M. (1995). Phonological information provides early sources of constraint in the processing of letter strings. *Journal of Memory and Language, 34,* 567–593.

Zeigler, J. C., Montant, M. & Jacobs, A.M. (1977). The feedback consistency effect in lexical decision and naming. *Journal of Memory and Language, 37,* 533–554.

Zorzi, M., Houghton, G., & Butterworth, B. (1998). Two routes or one in reading aloud? A connectionist dual-process model. *Journal of Experimental Psychology: Human Perception and Performance, 24,* 1131–1161.

11

The Spelling Process

Marie-Josèphe Tainturier
Brenda Rapp

INTRODUCTION

In comparison with other research areas, such as reading, there have been relatively few studies of spelling. Furthermore, spelling is an area where most of the available evidence comes from studies of brain damaged individuals. The majority of these studies have been conducted within the theoretical framework that is schematized in Figure 11.1. According to this framework (see, e.g., Caramazza, 1988; Ellis, 1989), spelling involves a variety of functionally distinct processing components that can be selectively impaired by brain damage. Some of these components are specific to spelling while others are not.

Skilled spellers can produce correct spellings in a variety of contexts and in a variety of formats. In other words, the input can vary (e.g., spoken input in spelling to dictation tasks, visual input in written picture naming tasks), as can the output (e.g., writing, typing, spelling aloud). However, it is assumed that all of these tasks involve abstract orthographic representations that are not tied to a specific modality of input or output. Therefore, we use the term "spelling" to refer in a general sense to the expression of orthographic knowledge regardless of the modality of output.

Another central assumption of the theory depicted in Figure 11.1 is that spelling can be achieved by means of two sets of processes sometimes referred to as lexical and sublexical (or semantic and asemantic). This "dual route" system has been proposed to explain how we can both spell words with which we are familiar and generate plausible spellings for novel words. Consider the situation where you are taking a telephone message from a caller identified as "Colonel Rapp": If you are unfamiliar with this particular individual you will recognize the spoken form "colonel" and retrieve its spelling. Since, however, you are unfamiliar with the caller you will not have a stored spelling for "Rapp." Nevertheless, you will still be able to produce a spelling and although it is likely to be "wrong," it will be phonologically plausible (e.g., "you have a message from Colonel Rap/Rapp/Wrap"). This ability to produce a plausible spelling for a word that has never been seen or heard before relies on the *phonology to orthography conversion system* (POC), also known as the sublexical or nonlexical route to spelling. This process is assumed to involve the following steps:

1. the acoustic/phonological analysis of the spoken input, and its segmentation into smaller units (i.e., phonemes, syllables, or other functional units);

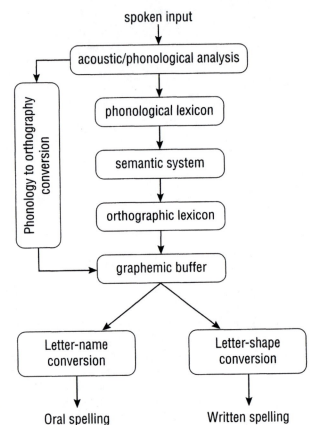

spoken input

acoustic/phonological analysis

phonological lexicon

semantic system

orthographic lexicon

graphemic buffer

Phonology to orthography conversion

Letter-name conversion

Letter-shape conversion

Oral spelling

Written spelling

Figure 11.1: A functional architecture of the spelling system.

2. the conversion of each phonological unit into a corresponding orthographic unit;
3. the assembling of these orthographic units into a correctly sequenced abstract letter string.

The POC process calls upon stored knowledge about the possible phoneme–grapheme (PG) correspondences in a given language (e.g., /s/ -> SS, /s/ -> C, etc.), their relative frequency of use (e.g., /s/ is spelled more often with SS than with C) and the context in which they can be applied (e.g., a word initial /s/ cannot be spelled SS). It is often assumed that the POC process applies PG correspondences according to their frequency; high-frequency (high-probability) correspondences are selected more often than low-frequency (low-probability) ones. The functioning of the sublexical route is usually evaluated with the task of spelling to dictation of made-up words ("nonwords") such as "flope" to ensure that all stimuli will be unfamiliar.

Many familiar words such as *cat, dog* or *cup* are composed of very common or high-probability PG correspondences. These words are likely to be spelled correctly using the sublexical procedure. However, other familiar words like "phone," "two," or "coat" have less frequent or predictable spellings, and using the sublexical route in such cases might lead to the production of incorrect, yet phonologically plausible responses (e.g., *fone, too, cote*). We will refer to phonologically plausible errors produced in response to word stimuli as PPEs. Actually, the proportion of words containing ambiguous, or low-probability, spellings is quite large in languages such as English or French. For this reason, it has been proposed that the spelling of familiar words is learned and stored in an *orthographic lexicon* (at least in such languages). The integrity of the lexical procedure can be assessed by using words with low-probability spellings in a variety of tasks, such a spelling to dictation, written picture naming, or spelling from definitions. In real life situations, the orthographic lexicon would be involved in spontaneous writing. Depending on the task, other components that are not specific to spelling may also be involved. For example, the *phonological lexicon*, in which the spoken form of familiar words are stored, would be involved in spelling to dictation, as well as in speech comprehension. Similarly the *semantic system* (the repository of word meanings) would also be involved in all modalities of word comprehension and production. According to Figure 11.1, the orthographic lexicon is activated by the semantic system. It has also been proposed that direct connections between the phonological and orthographic lexicons are involved in spelling to dictation (for a discussion of the lexical nonsemantic "route" in reading, see Rapp, Folk, & Tainturier, this volume).

In summary, spelling can be achieved by retrieving stored spellings in the orthographic lexicon, or by converting phonological representations into orthographic representations sublexically. It is assumed that up to that point the spelling representations consist of abstract letters that do not yet have a specific format. These will then need to be expressed in a specific modality and format of output: cursive writing, typing, oral spelling, etc. This will involve translating the abstract letter representations into specific letter shapes or letter names via *letter-name conversion* or *letter-shape conversion* processes. The role of the *graphemic buffer* (e.g., Caramazza & Miceli, 1990; Houghton, Glasspool, & Shallice, 1994) is to maintain the activation levels of the abstract letter sequences made available by the lexical or the sublexical spelling processes during the time it takes for the sequential assignment of format-specific information.

The theory of spelling that we have summarized has guided most of the empirical investigations of spelling. Alternative theories have recently been proposed (e.g., Brown & Loosemore, 1994; Campbell, 1983; Van Orden, Jansen op de Haar, & Bosman, 1997). The main differences among theories concern the format of orthographic representations, and the specific nature of the processing components and of their interconnections. However, all models postulate at least two different "routes" to spelling, and seem to agree on the existence of relatively abstract orthographic representations that are independent of input or output format.

In this chapter, we will discuss the following fundamental questions regarding the spelling process: (a) Is spelling contingent upon the prior retrieval of a word's phonology or can word spellings be retrieved directly from semantics, as suggested in Figure 11.1? (b) Are lexical and sublexical spelling processes strictly independent from one another or do they interact in some way? (c) To what extent do reading and spelling rely on distinct versus shared processing components? (d) What do we know about the internal structure of orthographic representations? (e) Are the different representations employed in the course of spelling format-independent or format-specific?

For each question, we will highlight the specific contribution of cognitive neuropsychological studies. We will also present related evidence from unimpaired adults when available. Due to space limitations, studies of normal or delayed written language acquisition will not be reviewed, although they often include data which are relevant to the theoretical questions that we will address (for recent reviews, see Harris & Hatano, 1999; Hulme & Joshi, 1998; Perfetti & Rieben, 1997; Treiman, 1997).

THE AUTONOMY OF ORTHOGRAPHY AND PHONOLOGY

Although spelling is often studied in dictation tasks that necessarily involve phonology, but need not involve semantics, a theory of spelling must also specify how orthographic information is accessed from meaning in order to account for our capacity to spell words in written naming as well as in spontaneous writing.

According to *the orthographic autonomy hypothesis*, the spellings of words can be retrieved from the orthographic lexicon through direct links with semantics, without any necessary involvement of phonology.

An alternative classical view is that spelling from meaning necessarily involves phonological mediation (e.g., Geshwind, 1969; Luria, 1970; and more recently Perfetti, 1997; Van Orden et al., 1997) (see Figure 11.2). There are two main forms of the *obligatory phonological mediation hypothesis*. According to one of them phonological words are translated into spellings by a sublexical phonology-to-orthography conversion procedure. Because this process in notoriously unreliable in languages with "deep" orthographies (such as English and French) for words with low probability spellings (e.g., YACHT or CHEF), it has been proposed that sublexical conversion should be followed by a checking procedure involving the orthographic lexicon (Perfetti, 1997). According to the second form of the obligatory phonological mediation hypothesis, word spellings are retrieved from the orthographic lexicon via direct links with the corresponding representations in the phonological lexicon. Under this particular form of the hypothesis, there is no need for an orthographic check, except perhaps in the case of homophones like NUN-NONE (but only if one assumes that homophones only have one stored phonological representation).

The obligatory phonological mediation and orthographic autonomy hypotheses make very different predictions as to the possible effects of brain damage on written naming. According to the phonological mediation hypothesis, a deficit at the level of the phonological lexicon should necessarily affect both spoken and written naming. On the other hand, if the orthographic lexicon can be accessed directly from semantics it should be possible to observe cases with impaired spoken naming due to damage to the phonological lexicon with no corresponding written naming deficit.

Although patients with spoken-naming deficits usually show comparable deficits in written naming, a number of dissociations have been reported (for reviews see Basso, Taborelli, & Vignolo, 1978; Rapp, Benzing, & Caramazza, 1997). However, some of these cases do not speak directly to the issue of orthographic autonomy because the locus of the deficit responsible for the spoken naming impairment is unclear. To test the orthographic autonomy hypothesis, the deficit must be at the level of the phonological lexicon, since this is the component that would be involved in phonologically-mediated written naming. The mere presence of a spoken naming disorder is not sufficient to establish a lexical deficit, because damage at the level of postlexical phonological or articulatory processes would also affect spoken naming. Under either hypothesis, damage to these more peripheral components should not interfere with spelling performance. Although distinguishing between lexical and postlexical damage is not always straightforward, superior written naming has been documented in several cases where spoken naming disorders were likely due to a lexical impairment. Such cases are problematic for the hypothesis of obligatory phonological mediation and provide strong support for the orthographic autonomy hypothesis.

For example, MH (Bub & Kertesz, 1982b) could write the names of 15 out of 20 pictures, although she could only name one orally, producing no response at all in the remaining cases. Crucially, her spoken deficit could be traced to an impairment at the level of the phonological

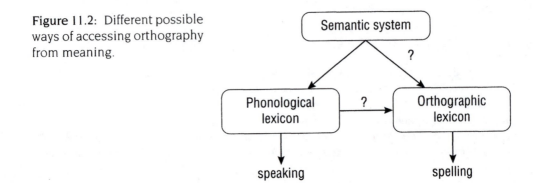

Figure 11.2: Different possible ways of accessing orthography from meaning.

Semantic system

Phonological lexicon   ?   Orthographic lexicon

?

speaking   spelling

lexicon rather than to a more peripheral level. First, her oral expression was very reduced but well articulated and without phonemic errors. Furthermore, MH performed very poorly in tasks designed to assess "inner speech"—that is in tasks that do not involve overt production but nonetheless require internal access to lexical phonology, such as judging whether two pictures correspond to rhyming words or not (for other cases see Hier & Mohr, 1977; Levine, Calvanio, & Popovics, 1982; Tainturier, Moreaud, David, Leek, Pelat, in press).

Another pattern of impaired performance supporting the orthographic autonomy hypothesis was reported by Caramazza and Hillis (1990). The patient they described, RGB, produced many semantic errors in oral naming of pictures (e.g., naming a picture of a tiger as a lion) but none in written naming. It seems unlikely that semantic errors could arise as a result of a postlexical phonological deficit, phonemic errors or neologisms being generally considered as the characteristic error types at this level. Rather, spoken semantic errors are usually considered to have a lexical origin, resulting from impairments to either the semantic system itself or, as was argued in the case of RGB, to the phonological lexicon. Under the phonological mediation hypothesis, one would therefore expect that a patient producing semantic errors in his spoken output would also produce them in his spelling. However, RGB produced no such errors in spelling (other similar cases include Beaton, Guest, & Ved, 1997; Hillis & Caramazza, 1995a; Miceli, Benvegnú, Capasso, & Caramazza, 1997; Miceli, Capasso, & Caramazza, 1999; Nickels, 1992; Rapp et al., 1997; Shelton & Weinrich, 1997).

Finally, cases of modality and grammatical category-specific deficits have been reported. These cases also support the orthographic autonomy hypothesis, as grammatical category-specific impairments are likely to have a lexical origin. For example, PBS (Rapp & Caramazza, 1997a) had a spoken-output deficit which predominantly affected open-class words (i.e., nouns, verbs, and adjectives). In striking contrast, he showed the opposite dissociation in spelling, with content words being relatively well preserved and function words and affixes very impaired. For instance, when asked to describe a picture of a boy washing a car, PBS wrote "BOY WASHED CAR" but said "the /wʌd/ are /rʌzd/ the /rʌdʒi/ with /lʌd/ and /tʌv/ in a /rədid/ ." Similarly, HW's spoken-naming deficit was much more severe for verbs than for nouns but his spelling of both categories of words was preserved (Caramazza & Hillis, 1991). Note that this dissociation between nouns and verbs in spoken naming was observed even when the stimuli were homonyms (e.g., the cut/a cut) which makes it even more unlikely that the deficit had a postlexical origin (see also Rapp & Caramazza, 1998).

In summary, evidence from cognitive neuropsychology suggests that there are direct connections between semantics and orthography and that these connections are sufficient to support accurate spelling performance. It could perhaps be argued that due to persistent deficits in accessing phonology, those patients have developed alternative pathways to spelling that are not normally available. However, a cortical stimulation study of two individuals with normal language abilities (Rapp, Boatman, & Gordon, 1999) recently showed that written naming can be preserved in the context of a temporary and reversible incapacity to access lexical phonology. For example, when stimulated in the left inferoposterior frontal area, subject STS scored 100% correct in written naming but only 29% in spoken naming. This dissociation was not due to a post-lexical articulatory/phonological deficit, as STS remained perfectly capable of reading words aloud.

Of course, the fact that spelling can be produced on the basis of semantics to orthography links alone does not mean that spelling does not involve phonology when phonological information is available, as it might be for unimpaired subjects. One possibility is that phonological mediation may be optional, another is that it may even be obligatory under specific circumstances—such as writing sentences rather than single words.

One source of relevant evidence comes from slips of the pen. The fact that normal subjects occasionally produce homophone substitution errors (e.g., there → their) as well as phonologically plausible nonword errors (e.g., error → errer) suggests that phonology is somehow involved in spelling (Ellis, 1979; Hotopf, 1980). Note, however, that *non*phonologically-related slips of the pen (e.g., error → orror) are also very common, so that it is difficult to establish how many "true" phonological errors there really are. In addition, slips of the pen are usually obtained from text samples. As a matter of fact, homophone substitutions are often characterized by some blending of adjacent words " . . . if the lie is not too greater (great a)[1] one to tell" (Hotopf, 1980, page 179).[2] Some recent studies have attempted to show an influence of phonology on reaction times in single-word spelling tasks (that is, in experimental conditions that are closer to those used in testing patients), but these have failed to show reliable effects (Bonin, Fayol, & Gombert, 1997; Bonin, Fayol, & Peereman, 1998). This raises the interesting possibility that phonology is more heavily involved in writing sentences than in writing single words. In line with this suggestion, it seems noteworthy that patients with preserved written naming despite poor access to phonology usually produce "agrammatic" written sentences. That is, they tend to produce short sentences with omissions and/or substitutions of function words and affixes (see, e.g., Bub & Kertesz, 1982b; Rapp & Caramazza, 1996). The apparently greater involvement of phonology in sentence/text writing might be related to the demand on short-term memory being greater for sentences than for single words, since rehearsal in STM is generally believed to involve phonological codes.

In conclusion, there are indications that phonology may be involved (or even obligatory) in writing sentences. However, current evidence does not support the view that phonological mediation is obligatory in writing single words. As a matter of fact, there is no real evidence of phonological effects in single-word spelling in normal adult spellers, although several recent lexical processing models clearly predict that such effects should occur (e.g., Van Orden et al., 1997).

THE INDEPENDENCE OF LEXICAL AND SUBLEXICAL PROCESSES

As mentioned earlier, virtually all accounts of spelling abilities assume the existence of two major processes or routes for translating between phonology and orthography—the lexical and sublexical or nonlexical processes. Although the existence of two processes with these general characteristics has been assumed in most written language research, there is little consensus concerning the specific nature of these processes and the relationships between them. In this section, we will specifically address the following questions: What is the evidence for distinct procedures for spelling familiar versus unfamiliar words? Is there evidence that the two processes interact or integrate information in the course of spelling?

Evidence in Favor of Distinct Lexical and Sublexical Routes to Spelling

The strongest evidence in support of the view that spelling involves at least two distinct sets of processes comes from the observation of brain-damaged individuals who seem to have selectively lost their ability to use one process or the other. Several patients have been reported with spelling impairments indicative of a lexical deficit. Given the framework depicted in Figure 11.1, a breakdown somewhere in the lexical process should: (a) result in greater difficulties spelling words versus nonwords, and (b) manifest itself by the production of phonologically plausible errors (PPEs), since spellings that can not be accessed lexically would have to be generated sublexically. As a consequence, under conditions of lexical damage, words with common (or high-probability) phoneme–grapheme mappings (e.g., *cat*) should be more likely to

---

[1]British speakers will appreciate the homophony.
[2]Homophone confusion errors do occur in single-word spelling tasks in patients (e.g., Goodman & Caramazza, 1986). However, this does not inform the debate of the normal involvement of phonology in spelling because these patients clearly have impaired access to orthographic information and, as a result, they may resort to some form of phonological mediation that they would not have used before their disease.

be spelled correctly than words with uncommon (or low probability) mappings (e.g., *yacht*). Furthermore, *yacht* is likely to be spelled in an incorrect though phonologically-plausible manner (e.g., YAT, YATT, or YAGHT).[3]

Beauvois and Derouesné (1981) published the first detailed description of a selective impairment of lexical spelling in a French patient with acquired dysgraphia. Although RG had no difficulty in providing plausible spellings for nonword stimuli, his spelling of words was clearly abnormal and spelling accuracy was a function of the degree of orthographic ambiguity of the words. That is, words that included only high probability mappings were spelled more accurately (93% correct) than words with low–probability mappings (38% correct). Furthermore, most of the errors were phonologically plausible (e.g., *cyprès* (cypress) → sipré; *rideau* (curtain) → ridot). This pattern was clearly indicative of a lesion somewhere along the lexical spelling route. Note however that it could have resulted from a deficit to one or more components along this pathway. More specifically, deficits disrupting access to either the phonological lexicon, the orthographic lexicon or even the semantic system may all lead to selective difficulties in spelling words with low probability mappings. In the case of RG, it was argued that the locus of damage was the orthographic lexicon because (a) spoken and written comprehension were normal (making phonological or semantic deficits unlikely), and (b) he showed a similar pattern of performance in all word spelling tasks, independently of the modality of input (e.g., spontaneous writing, written picture naming, spelling to dictation). Several other cases of dysgraphia reflecting a selective (or predominant) disruption of lexical spelling have been reported since (Baxter & Warrington, 1987; Behrmann & Bub, 1992; De Partz, Seron, & Van der Linden, 1992; Goodman & Caramazza, 1986; Goodman-Shulman & Caramazza, 1987; Hatfield & Patterson, 1983; Parkin, 1993; Sanders & Caramazza, 1990; Weekes & Coltheart, 1996). These cases are often referred to with the label of "surface dysgraphia," or "lexical agraphia." Note that in most cases the deficit is only partial and that the probability that a word will be spelled correctly is usually a function of its regularity and of its lexical frequency.

In contrast to a lexical deficit, a selective deficit to sublexical POC processes should manifest itself when spelling unfamiliar words or nonwords, that is with stimuli for which no stored spelling is normally available. Shallice (1981) reported the first case of a brain-damaged patient whose spelling errors were consistent with such a deficit. PR was only 18% correct in spelling nonwords to dictation whereas he was within normal limits (94% correct) in spelling both regular and irregular words. Furthermore, the author noted that when correct production of nonwords occurred, it often seemed to result from the application of some lexically based strategy: for example, when asked to write down the nonword /sIm/, PR produced "SYM," described as the first syllable of "symbol." In addition, PR was also poor at spelling individual phonemes (56% correct), suggesting that he had lost knowledge of individual phoneme–grapheme mappings. Several other cases of selective or predominant deficit to sublexical processes have been reported since (e.g., Bub & Kertesz, 1982b; Goodman-Shulman & Caramazza, 1987; Roeltgen, 1985; Roeltgen, Sevush, & Heilman, 1983). These cases are often referred to under the label of "phonological dysgraphia."

In summary, there is strong evidence from cognitive neuropsychology in support of the existence of distinct lexical and sublexical spelling processes. In addition, an interesting outcome of these studies is that they reveal that the lexical system stores the spellings of all familiar words, whether irregular or regular. As argued earlier, the spelling of irregular words must be stored in some way since applying phoneme–grapheme conversion would lead, with some probability, to phonologically plausible errors. It is less obvious whether or not the spelling of regular words are stored as well. An interesting aspect of cases like PR is that they tend to spell all words correctly, regardless of their degree of orthographic ambiguity. Therefore, these cases indicate that all word spellings are stored in the lexical system, provided they

---

[3]American speakers will appreciate the homophony.

are familiar enough. Were this not the case, a deficit to the nonlexical procedure should affect not only the production of nonwords but also the production of regular words such as "cat." The observation of selective deficits to nonword spelling in languages with shallow orthographies, like Spanish, would strengthen this point, because there is a less obvious need for a lexical spelling process in such languages. However, we are not aware that any such cases have been reported yet, although a selective deficit in nonword *reading* has been described in a Spanish patient (Cuetos, Valle-Arroyo, & Suarez, 1996).

Evidence Suggesting that Lexical and Sublexical Processes are Not Fully Independent

The studies that we have just reviewed clearly support the notion that there are distinct procedures for spelling familiar and unfamiliar stimuli (i.e., words vs. nonwords). It is commonly assumed that, although the two processes may run in parallel, the output of one of these "routes" will ultimately be selected (and the other one suppressed if needed) and then "transferred" to the graphemic buffer in preparation for more peripheral production processes. However, recent evidence from both normal and impaired performance suggests that lexical and sublexical processes are not fully independent (for a review of similar evidence regarding reading, see Rapp, et al. this volume).

Evidence from Dysgraphia

Hillis and Caramazza (1991, 1995a) presented results from four brain-damaged subjects who showed better oral reading and/or spelling to dictation performance than would have been expected based on the level of functioning of either their lexical or sublexical processes alone. For example, JJ (Hillis & Caramazza, 1991) presented with a severe deficit in spoken and written picture naming tasks which primarily resulted in semantically related responses (e.g., a picture of grapes named "banana"). In addition, he often chose the semantic distracter in spoken and written word/picture verification tasks (tasks that do not require producing a word). This pattern points to a deficit at the level of the semantic system, as all input and output modalities were affected in a comparable way (he produced 30–40% semantic errors across tasks). Yet, JJ's ability to read words aloud and to spell them to dictation was largely preserved; crucially, this was true even for words with low-probability spellings (e.g., sweater, stomach, moustache, etc.). JJ's naming and comprehension performance suggested that when he had to rely on the lexical process alone he could no longer select the appropriate response out of a set of semantically related concepts activated by the stimulus (e.g., a picture of a pear or the word PEAR may have yielded a semantic representation equally consistent with bananas, grapes, or pears). However, spelling to dictation differs from naming and comprehension in that sublexical processes can be engaged in addition to lexical ones. If, in spelling to dictation, JJ relied only on the lexical process, he should have produced as many semantic errors as in written picture naming. Alternatively if he relied only on the sublexical process, he should have produced many phonologically plausible errors (PPEs) in response to words with ambiguous spellings (e.g., *pears* → PARES). Hillis and Caramazza (1991) accounted for the absence of semantic errors and the low rate of PPEs in JJ's writing to dictation by suggesting that the outputs of lexical and sublexical processes were combined to avoid such errors. More specifically, they proposed that the relatively imprecise information provided by the damaged lexical process "summated" with preserved sublexical information to allow correct responses. For example, for the stimulus *pear*, a sublexically generated output (e.g., PARE) could serve to select the most compatible item among a set of lexically-generated candidates (e.g., banana, grapes, *pear*, etc.) (See also, Miceli, Capasso, & Caramazza, 1994; Miceli, Giustolisi, & Caramazza, 1991; Miceli et al., 1999).

Further support for the summation hypothesis was provided by case RCM whose semantic errors in spelling tasks seemed attributable to a deficit in accessing the orthographic lexicon (Hillis, Rapp, & Caramazza, 1999). Consistent with this postsemantic (rather than semantic) locus of impairment, RCM made no semantic errors in spoken picture naming or in reading and her comprehension was well preserved. RCM's word and nonword spelling abilities were evaluated at two times. At Time 1, she produced many semantic errors in both writing to dictation and written picture naming. According to the summation hypothesis, semantic errors in spelling to dictation should have been eliminated (or nearly eliminated) by input from the sublexical system. However, RCM's sublexical abilities were extremely poor at Time 1: She could not spell any nonwords completely correctly and only 42% of the individual target letters were present in her responses. As further evidence of the severity of the sublexical damage, RCM never produced PPEs when spelling words. Therefore at Time 1 there was little opportunity for sublexical information to reduce semantic error rates. However, by Time 2, RCM's sublexical processing had significantly improved. Not only did she start producing PPEs (e.g., *leopard* → LEPORD), but her nonword spelling also significantly improved (67% of target segments were spelled correctly). Crucially, as predicted by the summation account, the improvement in sublexical spelling was accompanied by a substantial reduction in the rate of semantic errors, which dropped from 56% at Time 1 to only 10% at Time 2.

A second line of evidence against strict lexical/sublexical independence comes from the analysis of PPEs. As indicated earlier, studies concentrating on this type of errors (e.g., Baxter & Warrington, 1987; Beauvois & Derouesné, 1981; Goodman & Caramazza, 1986; Sanders & Caramazza, 1990) have revealed that PPEs generally consist in replacing low probability mappings with the most frequent phoneme/grapheme mappings in the language. However, these studies also show that PPEs sometimes include lower probability mappings (e.g., *cake* → CAIK). This has been interpreted as an indication that that the sublexical conversion process encodes multiple correspondences for each phoneme (e.g., /f/ → F or FF or GH or PH) rather than only the most common one. If correspondences are selected on the basis of their frequency in the language, then frequent mappings should be produced with a high probability but low–frequency mapping should also be observed occasionally.

In addition to these basic observations which are consistent with an independent dual process framework, there have been some indications that PPEs reflect an influence of residual lexical knowledge. This would be more problematic for independent dual process account. For example, Hatfield and Patterson (1983) reported that patient TP, who made primarily PPEs in spelling, also made some errors that suggested partial lexical knowledge (e.g., *cough* → C**OU**FE and *sword* → S**W**ARD; see also Ellis, Miller, & Sin, 1983; Miller & Ellis, 1987; Hughes, Graham, Patterson, & Hodges, 1997). The bolded elements in these responses are unlikely to have been generated by the sublexical system and thus these errors suggest a combination of information from lexical and sublexical sources.

This possibility was directly examined in the case of LAT, a patient with probable Alzeimer's disease whose dysgraphia was characterized by the production of PPEs (Rapp, Epstein, & Tainturier, in press). As we have seen, such errors point to a failure of the lexical process with an increased reliance on sublexical processes when spelling words. However, LAT's errors often contained lexically correct elements that were of such low PG probability that it was very unlikely that they could have been generated by the sublexical process alone (e.g., *bouquet* → BO**U**KET; *certain* → SER**TAIN**, *knowledge* → **KN**OLIGE). In order to confirm that these low frequency elements corresponded to partial lexical knowledge, LAT was asked to spell words containing low-probability mappings as well as highly similar nonwords that were derived from the word stimuli by substituting a single phoneme (e.g., /l u k eI/ derived from *bouquet* and /fɜt ən/ from *certain*). Rapp, Epstein, and Tainturier (in press) found that LAT produced significantly more low frequency target mappings (e.g., /eI / → ET, / ə n/ → AIN) in his phonologically plausible yet erroneous responses to words than in his spelling of nonwords (e.g., BOUKET vs. LOKAY; SERTAIN vs. FERTIN). This can be understood if we assume that many of LAT's phonologically plausible errors resulted from the integration of partial lexical knowledge with sublexical information, a conclusion that provides strong support for the hypothesis that lexical and sublexical processes share information during the course of spelling.

Converging Evidence from Studies of Normal Spelling

In summary, an increasing body of evidence from the neuropsychological literature indicates that there is not a strict independence between lexical and sublexical processes. Rather, the results indicate some form of interaction/integration between the routes that goes beyond a mere competition for output. This conclusion is also supported by evidence from nonword spelling in unimpaired adults. Here again, under the hypothesis of a strict independence between the two routes, one would expect that nonword spellings should seldom include very low probability phoneme–grapheme mappings. However, some results suggest otherwise.

Of particular relevance are a series of experiments showing that the orthographic choices that subjects make when spelling nonwords are influenced by the similarity between the nonword target and a neighboring word. It has been demonstrated that nonword spellings can be influenced by the prior presentation of a rhyming "prime" word (Barry & Seymour, 1988, Burden, 1989; Campbell, 1983). In the Campbell study, for example, the spoken nonword /priːt/ was more likely to be spelled PREET if it followed the spoken word "sweet" and to be spelled PREAT if it followed "meat." Similar results have been obtained in languages with almost entirely transparent orthographies, such as Spanish (Cuetos, 1993) and Italian (Barry & de Bastiani, 1997).

Although these studies all point to some degree of lexical influence on nonword spelling, it could be that the results do not reflect processes that are normally engaged when people process unfamiliar stimuli. That is, the tasks may have triggered atypical spelling-by-analogy strategies. However, a lexical influence on nonword spelling has been observed even under more indirect priming conditions which seem less susceptible to strategy-based responding (Dixon & Kaminska, 1994; Seymour & Dargie, 1990). That is, significant (though smaller) priming effects were obtained when nonwords were preceded by a semantic associate of a word that rhymed with the nonword target. For example, /bop/ is more likely to be spelled BOPE when it is preceded by *Vatican* (a semantic associate of POPE) and as BOAP when preceded by *detergent* (a semantic associate of SOAP). In addition, Tainturier, Bosse, Valdois, and Rapp (in preparation; see also Bosse, Voldois, & Tainturier, submitted for publication) obtained converging results in French using a task that was designed to minimize lexical activation. In all prior experiments subjects heard a list composed of both words and nonwords and had to make a lexical decision before writing down the nonwords. In the Tainturier et al. study, only nonwords were presented and participants were simply requested to write down each nonword using the first spelling that came to mind. Nonwords varied according to whether they did or did not have a close phonologically similar word neighbor. Results revealed that low-probability mappings (e.g., /i/ → il, /o/→ aud) were used more often in spelling nonwords with a close phonological neighbor with that spelling (e.g., /ʒuti/ derived from *gentil*, /ʒãti/; /krepo/ derived from crapaud, /krapo/) than in spelling nonwords with no close neighbors (e.g., /myti/; /frøpo/). The effect of lexical neighborhood was relatively small. That is, even though subjects produced more low-probability spellings when nonwords had a word neighbor including that spelling, they did overall use high-probability mappings much more often than low-probability ones.

Mechanisms of Lexical-Sublexical Interaction

Several strands of evidence undermine the view that lexical and sublexical processes are strictly independent from one another and that a single output originating from only one of these processes is held in the graphemic buffer. First, some patients with lexical deficits produce fewer errors on ambiguous words than would be expected on a strict independence account. Second, PPEs sometimes indicate the integration of residual lexical information with sublexical information. Third, the orthographic choices of unimpaired adults when spelling nonwords to dictation are not a mere function of phoneme/grapheme probabilities but also show a lexical influence.

In attempting to account for such findings, some authors (e.g., Campbell, 1983) have argued against the notion of lexical and sublexical processes altogether and have proposed that nonword spelling occurs entirely via lexical analogy. However, it is not clear how such processes would work and how this proposal can account for the striking dissociations in word versus nonword spelling reported in dysgraphia studies. Similarly, Hillis and Caramazza (1991; 1995a) did not propose a specific mechanism for lexical/sublexical interaction. They simply made the general claim that the sublexical process somehow contributes to the selection of a correct unit in the orthographic lexicon among multiple candidates generated by the lexical process. Although this hypothesis does account for the patterns of performance that these authors have reported (see above), it is not clear how it applies to other findings such as the partial lexical responses of patient LAT and the lexical influence on nonword spelling in normal adults.

Several authors (e.g., Barry, 1988; Kreiner, 1992, 1996; Kreiner & Gough, 1990) have made the general suggestion that lexical and sublexical processes, although not directly influencing each other, may interact at an output level. A more specific proposal for a mechanism of lexical/sublexical integration has been put forward by Rapp, Epstein, & Tainturier (in press; see also Boss et al., submitted; Houghton & Zorzi, submitted; Tainturier, 1996a; Tainturier et al., in preparation). This proposal is based on the notion that the graphemic buffer may be more than a mere short term repository of outputs independently generated by the lexical or sublexical processes (see Introduction). Instead, the graphemic buffer may be viewed as a level at which graphemic units (i.e., letters, graphemes, orthographic syllables) are represented. Such units would be activated either by the orthographic lexicon, by sublexical POC processes, or both (Figure 11.3). The selection of a letter string for output would result from the integration of these two different sources of activation. This proposal reduces the degree of autonomy of lexical and sublexical processes, in the sense that both processes activate a common level of representation. That is, the spelling of either words or nonwords would be under the combined influence of lexical and sublexical processes (for a similar proposal applied to reading aloud see Coltheart, Curtis, Atkins, & Haller, 1993; Zorzi, Houghton, & Butterworth, 1998). Although various details of the integration process remain to be specified, this general proposal does account for the reviewed findings.

THE AUTONOMY OF READING AND SPELLING

The relationship between reading and spelling processes is one of the most debated and most difficult questions in written language research. One common view (e.g., Caramazza, 1988; Ellis, 1982) is that reading and spelling rely on distinct processing components, with the exception of an amodal semantic system (see Figure 11.4a). An alternative view (e.g., Allport & Funnell, 1981; Behrmann & Bub, 1992; Coltheart & Funnell, 1987), is that reading and spelling depend on shared processing components, with the exception of more peripheral processes (see Figure 11.4b). One issue that has been particularly debated concerns the status of lexical representations. According to the *shared-components position*, a single orthographic lexicon would be used both in reading and spelling, although the access procedures would probably be task (or modality) specific. In contrast, the *distinct-components position* distinguishes between an *input* orthographic lexicon necessary to recognize written words (reading) and an *output* orthographic lexicon necessary to produce them (spelling). One can similarly ask whether other components such as sublexical conversion or the graphemic buffer are shared in reading and spelling.

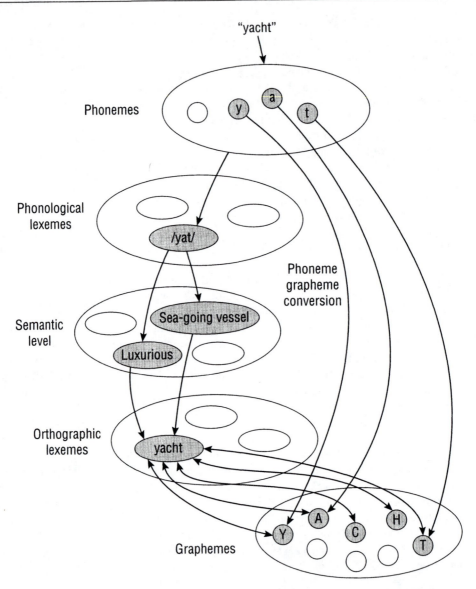

Figure 11.3: A proposal for the integration of lexical and sublexical information at the level of the graphemic buffer. (Rapp et al., in press). Adapted from "The Integration of Information Across Lexical and Sublexical Processes in Spelling," by B. Rapp, C. Epstein, & M. J. Tainturier, in press, *Cognitive Neuropsychology*. Adapted with permission.

Associations between Reading and Spelling

If one excludes cases of peripheral reading disorders (e.g. neglect, visual analysis disorder) that should be "modality" specific and only affect reading under either account, most acquired dyslexic patients also show some form of spelling impairment (although the reverse is less true, see below). This could be taken as prima facie evidence in favor of the view that reading and spelling share some processing components. However, this high rate of associated deficits could merely reflect the fact that the neural substrates of reading and spelling are located in

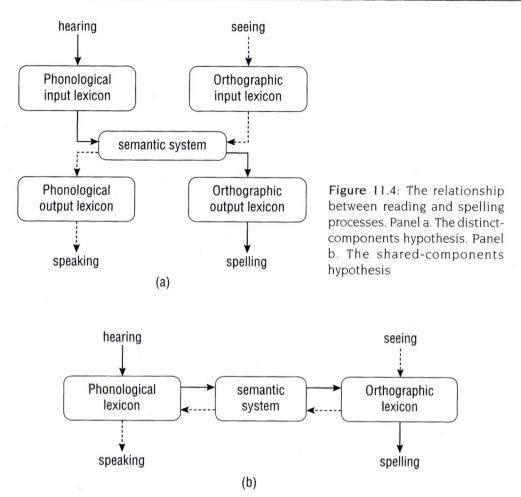

Figure 11.4: The relationship between reading and spelling processes. Panel a. The distinct-components hypothesis. Panel b. The shared-components hypothesis

adjacent or even overlapping brain areas, making it very likely for brain damage to affect both functions to some extent (e.g., Bub & Kertesz, 1982a). This is certainly a plausible hypothesis, although it is difficult to assess at the present time as relatively little is known about the neural bases of reading and especially of spelling.

Nonetheless, it is also true that not only does dysgraphia usually accompany dyslexia but that *specific* types of dyslexia often co-occur with the very same types of dysgraphia. For example, selective nonword reading disorders are often associated with nonword spelling disorders (e.g., Roeltgen, 1985). Similarly, selective deficits in reading irregular words are usually coupled with similar deficits in spelling irregular words (Baxter & Warrington, 1987; Behrmann & Bub, 1992; De Partz et al., 1992; Kremin, 1985; Hatfield & Patterson, 1983; Newcombe & Marshall, 1985; Parkin, 1993; Saffran, 1985). A similar association between deep dyslexia and deep dysgraphia has also been noted (for a review, see Coltheart, Patterson, & Marshall, 1987; and for more recent cases, Ferreres & Miravalles, 1995; Nickels, 1992; Tainturier, & Caramazza, 1996). These specific patterns of associations place further constraints on the hypothesis that anatomical proximity is responsible for the association of deficits, since this hypothesis must explain why brain damage is more likely to affect independent subcomponents of reading and spelling that perform similar functions (e.g., input and output orthographic lexicons), rather than affecting entirely unrelated reading or spelling components.

Certain studies have reported similarities that go even further. For example, some surface dyslexia/dysgraphia patients show a very high degree of consistency between the specific

Table 11.1

The case of MLB: Rate and Distribution of Errors in Nonword Reading and Spelling.

	Reading Aloud	Spelling to Dictation
Number of misspelled nonwords (n = 165)	99/165	98/165
Number of misspelled segments (n = 759)	127/759	155/759
Voicing errors (e.g., *taple* → DAPLE)	60/127	79/127
Vowel substitutions (*nefo* → NEFA)	46/127	38/127
Context errors (e.g., *guibar* → GIBAR)	10/127	23/127
Others	11/127	15/127

words that they can read and the specific words that they can spell, even when factors such as word length and frequency are partialed out (Coltheart & Funnell, 1987; Behrmann & Bub, 1992). The case of MLB, a French woman who presented with a severe dysgraphia following head trauma, provides another good example because she showed a striking parallelism in her pattern of errors in reading and spelling nonword stimuli (see Tainturier, 1996b, for a report of the spelling data). MLB seemed to rely almost exclusively on the sublexical process in spelling, such that virtually all lower probability spellings were replaced by more regular ones (e.g., *bateau* (boat) → BATO). In addition, she produced very specific and unusual substitution errors, indicative of an additional deficit to the sublexical process. In particular, most errors involving consonants consisted in the substitution of a voiced consonant for an unvoiced one and vice-versa (e.g., f → v, d → t, p → b), irrespective of visual similarity and despite the fact that MLB never produced such errors in nonorthographic tasks (e.g., nonword repetition). The results in Table 11.1 show the remarkable degree of similarity in terms of error rate and error types in reading and spelling nonwords to dictation.

The highly detailed way in which impairments in reading and spelling are similar makes it difficult to believe that these associations are purely fortuitous. Nevertheless, striking dissociations between reading and spelling disorders occur in a nonnegligible number of cases, and such dissociations are often taken as evidence of the independence of reading and spelling processes. Accordingly, the next issue we will consider is whether the dissociation cases are clearly incompatible with a shared-components position.

Dissociations of Reading and Spelling

Dissociations between reading and spelling are not uncommon following brain damage and they can take different forms. Broadly speaking, either only one of the two skills is noticeably altered, or else they are differentially impaired, either quantitatively or qualitatively. However, these dissociations do not necessarilly speak to the issue of the autonomy of reading and spelling for several reasons.

First, as we have seen, peripheral processing components are viewed as modality-specific in all theories. For example, graphic motor deficits should not correlate with reading difficulties. Similarly, a visual deficit may affect reading but not spelling. Second, dissociations between reading and spelling sometimes result from deficits that do not actually involve orthographic components per se. For example, some reading deficits occur as a result of impaired access to *phonological* rather than orthographic representations. Caramazza and Hillis (1990) described cases HW and RGB, who presented with the characteristic features of deep dyslexia but only had a slight spelling deficit, mostly consisting of letter selection errors. On the surface, this pattern supports the notion of distinct reading/spelling components. However, the authors established that the orthographic lexicon was intact (both subjects had very good written comprehension) and that the semantic errors produced in reading originated from a deficit at the level of phonological lexicon (semantic errors were also produced in spoken picture nam-ing). Given the locus of the deficit, there is actually no reason to expect a relationship between reading and spelling performance.

Thus, the crucial question is: Do dissociations between reading and spelling occur following damage to components that could be assumed to be shared by both tasks—such as the ortho-graphic lexicon? The answer is that they do (e.g., Beauvois & Derouesné, 1979, 1981; Bub & Kertesz, 1982a; Goodman & Caramazza, 1986; Sanders & Caramazza, 1990; Shallice, 1981). Although it would be beyond the scope of this chapter to review each of theses cases in detail, we will discuss a few points to bear in mind when evaluating such dissociations.

As first pointed out by Allport and Funnell (1981), dissociations between reading and spell-ing are perfectly compatible with a shared components position if it is the modality specific access procedures rather than the shared representations themselves that are impaired (as can be seen in Figure 11.4b, the orthographic lexicon has two sets of arrows corresponding to modality-specific access processes). Unfortunately, it is far from straightforward to establish whether a given pattern of impairment is better accounted for by postulating an access deficit rather than a storage deficit (Rapp & Caramazza, 1993). In other words, at the present time it is very difficult to determine which patients suffer from deficits to the components themselves and, therefore, it is difficult to determine which cases are truly problematic for the shared-components view.

Furthermore, it is possible to reconcile many patterns of dissociations with shared-compo-nents models without having to establish whether the deficit is one of access or one of storage. Our main point in the reminder of this section will be that, whatever the exact nature of the deficit, it does not always follow from the shared-components view that reading and spelling disorders should be quantitatively or even qualitatively similar.

With respect to quantitative differences, several facts need to be considered. First, cases of isolated dysgraphia are more common than cases of isolated dyslexia (still excluding peripheral deficits). Second, when both deficits co-occur, the dysgraphia is typically more severe. Third, spelling deficits tend to be less severe when isolated than when associated with reading deficits. For example, case MS (Sanders & Caramazza, 1990) only made errors 9% of the time when spelling low-probability words and he read most words correctly. In contrast, case MP (Behrmann & Bub, 1992) produced a much higher rate of phonologically plausible spelling errors and frequently regularized words in reading. These asymmetries can easily be recon-ciled with shared representations models if one considers that reading and spelling do not present the same degree of difficulty. For example, damage to a single orthographic lexicon could affect reading less than spelling because in reading an incomplete lexical representation of the spelling of table (e.g., T_BL_) may be sufficient to support identification of the written stimulus. Problems will only arise if the partial information is compatible with more than one answer, that is when a word has close neighbors (e.g., c-t → *cat* or *cot*). In spelling, however, the full letter string must be produced and for this a complete lexical representation is re-quired.

The case of MLB (Tainturier, 1996b), discussed earlier, provides a good example of how deceptive quantitative differences between reading and spelling can be. In spelling to dictation, she replaced virtually all low-probability spellings with higher-probability ones (e.g., *crapaud*/ Krapo/(toad) → CRAPO), indicating a severe deficit to the (output) orthographic lexicon. In reading, she produced similar errors but her performance was far superior (see Table 11.2). Furthermore, when tested in a standard visual lexical decision task in which she had to discriminate between real words (e.g., *yacht*) and visually related nonwords (e.g., *yicht*), she was only moderately impaired. Based on these data alone, one might postulate the existence of two distinct deficits, a severe deficit to the orthographic output lexicon, and a milder one to the orthographic input lexicon. However, we administered another lexical decision task in which we prevented the efficient use of partial lexical orthographic information by using homophonic

Table 11.2
The case of MLB: Percent Errors in Spelling, Reading and Word Recognition Tasks.

Task	Percent of Errors
Spelling to dictation of irregular words	92
Reading aloud of irregular words	31
Visual lexical decision with non-homophonic legal nonwords	12
Visual lexical decision with homophonic nonwords	49 (chance)

nonwords. If her superior performance in reading aloud were really due to better preserved input orthographic representations, then she should be able to distinguish words and nonwords based on their spelling alone, at least in a majority of cases. However, she proved entirely incapable of distinguishing correct from incorrect spellings, suggesting that her capacity to access lexical orthographic representations from print for reading was actually just as impaired as her capacity to access them from sound or meaning for spelling.

Qualitatively different patterns of performance in reading and spelling might also be expected following damage at a common level. For example, we have seen that damage to the orthographic (output) lexicon can give rise to semantic errors in written output tasks because access to the orthographic lexicon for production is semantically driven. However, damage to the orthographic lexicon should not result in semantic errors in reading since the search, in this case, is driven by the letter string. Thus, one might expect confusion among visually-orthographically-related words in reading (e.g., *cable* → *table*).

In addition, damage to a common level of processing may not affect word and nonword stimuli to a similar extent. A good illustration of this point comes from recent studies of reading in individuals with damage to the graphemic buffer. Although the graphemic buffer was originally conceived as a component dedicated to spelling (Caramazza, Miceli, Villa, & Romani, 1987), more recently, it has been proposed that it might also be involved in maintaining the level of activation of input representations of a letter string for reading (Caramazza, Capasso, & Miceli, 1996; Hillis & Caramazza, 1995b; Tainturier & Caramazza, 1994). The main empirical motivation for this proposal comes from observations of nonword reading disorders in patients with hypothesized graphemic buffer impairments.

For example, MC (Tainturier & Caramazza, 1994) presented with a characteristic graphemic buffer deficit following surgery to remove a left parietal tumour. That is, he produced spelling errors that reflected a loss of information about the identity and/or order of the letters to be produced (e.g., *congress* → CONGROSS, *giraffe* → GRAFFIE). In addition, his performance was comparable for words and nonwords and was not affected by the modality of input (pictures vs. spoken words) or output (written vs. oral spelling). Finally, his spelling showed a marked length effect and accuracy across letter positions within words was a U-shape function, both being typical of graphemic buffer deficits. In contrast to his spelling, MC's reading of words was well within normal limits; he remained an avid reader and only complained about his spelling difficulties. However, he was only about 50% correct in reading nonwords. At first glance, this suggested an additional deficit to sublexical OPC processes. Interestingly though, his nonword reading presented many similarities with his spelling. The errors he made in nonword reading and in spelling were of the same type (letter substitutions, deletions, insertions, and transpositions) and were produced in comparable proportions. MC also showed a length effect and a letter-position effect in nonword reading. Given these similarities, it might be that both the reading and spelling disorders stem from a single deficit to the graphemic buffer. This hypothesis is supported by the fact that other graphemic buffer cases also show poor nonword reading (Annoni, Lemay, de Mattos Pimenta, & Lecours, 1998; Caramazza et al., 1996; Jónsdóttir, Shallice, & Wise, 1996; Katz, 1991), the only clear exception being the case of SE (Posteraro, Zinelli, & Mazzuchi, 1988).

It is commonly assumed (e.g., Ans, Carbonnel, & Valdois, 1998) that in reading access to the orthographic lexicon is based on parallel processing of the letter sequence, whereas sublexical conversion of unfamiliar letter strings involves sequential processing of sublexical units. In contrast, the spelling of both words and nonwords is thought to be a sequential process beyond the level of the graphemic buffer. Poorer performance in reading nonwords versus words may be due to the fact that sequential processing requires that the activation of the letter string representation be maintained over a longer period of time than does parallel processing. If this were the case, one might expect reading performance to deteriorate if familiar words were presented in a format likely to interfere with parallel processing of the input. Consistent with this hypothesis, we observed that MC's word reading accuracy dropped from 99% in standard format to 78% in mirror-reversed format and 68% in recognition of aurally spelled words.[4] In contrast, performance with nonwords was not significantly affected by mode of presentation, as would be expected.

We have considered several examples of differences between reading and spelling that are nonetheless compatible with a shared-components view. However, there are some more problematic cases. Perhaps most striking is the case of RG (Beauvois & Derouesné, 1979, 1981) who presented with opposite patterns of deficits in reading and spelling. That is, RG had selective difficulties reading nonwords (phonological dyslexia) while at the same time he was good at spelling nonwords but poor with irregular words (surface dysgraphia). In this case, a deficit to the orthographic output lexicon and to POC processes was proposed. However, such cases are still subject to alternative interpretations within the shared-components view (i.e., by postulating multiple access deficits).

Converging Evidence from Skilled Readers

The question of whether reading and spelling rely on shared or distinct lexical representations has been addressed in several experiments involving skilled adult readers. One approach has been to look for cross-modal priming effects under the hypothesis that reading a word might facilitate later spelling of the same word and vice versa. Monsell (1987) had subjects write words to dictation without visual feedback. Significant repetition priming was later obtained in a word recognition task. This is consistent with the view that the same lexical entries were activated in both tasks.

Another approach has been to investigate the degree of consistency between reading and spelling errors. In short, the rationale for these studies is that if there is a single lexicon mediating reading and spelling, there should be a systematic relationship between the errors made in both modalities. Holmes and Carruthers (1998) expanded on previous work by Campbell (1987) and Funnell (1992) to investigate this question. They reasoned that the well known superiority of reading over spelling might reflect the fact that partial cues (e.g., incomplete lexical representations) may often provide sufficient information for reading but not for spelling (see above for a similar argument applied to neurological cases). Consequently, item by item consistency might also appear lower than it really is. Holmes and Carruthers (1998) observed that subjects could easily read words that they could not spell. Importantly, however, they could not discriminate between correct spellings and their own misspellings. That is, they failed on an input task that required more precise information than simply reading aloud.

Conclusions

Although the issue of the autonomy of reading and spelling is far from settled, the preponderance of evidence favors a shared-components view or is at least compatible with it. Neverthe-

---

[4]In this task a subject hears sequences of letter names and is asked to say the word to which they correspond (e.g., /di/,ou/,ʤi/ → "dog").

less, future studies may provide cases of dissociations that are clearly incompatible with a shared-components view, especially if more detailed hypotheses about reading and spelling processing are developed. Furthermore, it will be important to consider that while certain components (such as the orthographic lexicon) may be shared, others (such as sublexical conversion processes) may not.

In addition, studies of the effects of remediation on reading and spelling should contribute to the debate, as different predictions can be made with respect to the generalization of treatment effects across modality. In particular, shared-components proposals predict that certain techniques should improve both reading and spelling even if the training itself is limited to one modality. For example, Phillips and Goodall (1995) trained a patient with dyslexia and dysgraphia to read a set of nonwords. Once he had learned to pronounce these printed nonwords accurately, he was then asked to spell them to dictation. He had no problem doing so, using the very same spellings that had been used during the reading training phase. This suggests that the patient had stored the spelling of these nonwords in a lexicon accessible for the purpose of reading or spelling (but see Weekes and Coltheart, 1996).

THE STRUCTURE OF ORTHOGRAPHIC REPRESENTATIONS

What is it that we know when we know the spelling of a word? The original assumption regarding the structure of output orthographic representations was that they merely consisted of linear sequences of abstract letter identities—[R+A+B+B+I+T] (e.g., Caramazza et al., 1987; Wing & Baddeley, 1980). However, several lines of evidence now support the idea that orthographic representations encode more than just letter identity and order.

Evidence from Dysgraphia

Most of the evidence pertaining to the structure of orthographic representations comes from the analysis of the errors patterns of dysgraphic patients. Studies of graphemic buffer deficits have proved particularly revealing. Recall that the role of the graphemic buffer is to maintain the level of activation of orthographic strings generated by the lexical and/or sublexical spelling processes while more peripheral, sequential processes are taking place. Deficits at this level lead to letter substitutions, omissions, additions, and transpositions that are taken to reflect a loss of information about letter identity, order or both. If orthographic output representations were merely linear sequences of letter identities, one would not expect that the nature and position of errors should be affected in any way by the internal organization of the letter strings. Yet, several results suggest the contrary.

First, there is evidence that morphemic structure is encoded in orthographic representations. A first demonstration was provided by the analysis of serial positions effects in the misspellings of case DH (Badecker, Hillis, & Caramazza, 1990). In addition to the characteristic features of a graphemic buffer deficit, DH's spelling also showed a serial position effect such that the probability of an error on a given letter increased quasi linearly as a function of the position of that letter in the word. Strikingly, however, this pattern only held for monomorphemic words such as "table." In the case of bimorphemic words such as "darkness," error rates increased up to the end of the word stem (*dark*) but then dropped on the first letter of the suffix to increase again on subsequent letters. Badecker et al. (1990) interpreted this finding as an indication that the units retrieved from the orthographic lexicon and later held in the graphemic buffer consist of productive morphemes rather than whole words (see Allen & Badecker, this volume, for a discussion of morphological effects in spelling and other domains).

Caramazza and Miceli (1990) have proposed that orthographic representations also encode information about syllabic structure (see Figure 11.5). They reached this conclusion on the basis of a detailed analysis of the factors that constrained the misspellings of case LB, an

Italian patient with a graphemic buffer deficit. Among other things, LB showed a marked tendency to simplify the structure of words with complex syllables. For example, letter omissions were frequent in the context of letter clusters, which usually lead to the production of a simpler syllabic structure (e.g., *strada* → STADA). However, omissions virtually never occurred in simple CV sequences, where an omission would create a more complex syllable (that is LB did *not* produce errors like *creatura* → CREATRA). Caramazza and Miceli (1990) have interpreted this to mean that the graphosyllabic structure of a letter string forms a distinct dimension of orthographic representations (but see Jónsdóttir et al., 1996).

In addition, there is strong empirical support for distinct and dissociable representations of letter identity and of letter doubling information (Caramazza & Miceli, 1990; McCloskey, Badecker, Goodman-Shulman, & Aliminosa, 1994; Miceli, Benvegnú, Capasso, & Caramazza, 1995; Tainturier & Caramazza, 1996). For example, the case of SFI (Miceli et al, 1995) had a selective deficit in the production of double letters leading to errors like *leggo* → LEGO. The case of FM (Tainturier & Caramazza, 1996) showed the reverse pattern, with doubling information being much better preserved than letter identity and order (e.g., *umbrella* → UMMOUCAN, *ribbon* → BROLLOW). This relative preservation was specific to double letters and did not apply to other superficially similar groups of letters such as nonadjacent repeated letters (e.g., CaCtus) or digraphs (e.g., roCKet).

Finally, several studies of graphemic buffer deficits have shown that information about specific letter identities can be lost while knowledge of the consonant/vowel status of these letters is preserved, suggesting that letter identity and consonant/vowel status may be represented separately. In several cases (Caramazza & Miceli, 1990; Jónsdóttir et al., 1996; Miceli, Silveri, & Caramazza, 1985; McCloskey et al., 1994) substitution errors virtually always occurred within class, with consonants being substituted for consonants and vowels for vowels. That is, errors like *table* → TACLE were common, but errors like *table* → TAILE were very rare. In addition, Cubelli (1991) described two Italian patients who were disproportionally impaired in their production of vowels. CW, a graphemic buffer case, mostly produced substitution errors involving vowels (e.g., *davanti* → DEVUNTA; *perduto* → PARDETA). Case CF dropped vowels altogether, yet leaving a blank space between correctly written single consonants or clusters (e.g., *bologna* → B L GN).

Converging Evidence from Normal Spelling

Few empirical investigations of the structure of orthographic representations have been carried out in nonbrain-damaged adults. However, what little evidence is available is generally consistent with neuropsychological research and suggests that orthographic representations

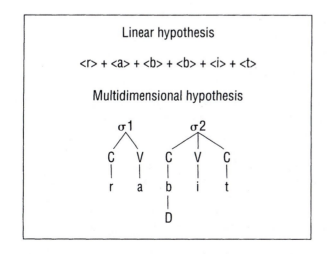

Figure 11.5: The structure of orthographic representations.

encode more than just letter identities and order. Some of these results come from the analysis of the temporal time-course of spelling in tasks like handwriting or typing. Using a digitizing tablet to record handwriting movements, Orliaguet and Boë (1993) have studied the production times of French homonyms presented auditorially in a disambiguating context. The context could either point to a monomorphemic use of the word or to an inflected use [e.g., je vais *vers* (I go 'toward') versus j'aime les *vers* (I like 'worms'; plural of *ver*). Reaction times and total production times were longer for inflected words, which the authors interpreted as evidence of a cost associated to the application of grammatical rules in the course of spelling (but note that the items were not matched for frequency). In a typing study, Zesiger, Orliaguet, Boë, & Mounoud (1994) also demonstrated an influence of syllabic structure on the temporal course of spelling. More specifically, they showed that the interval between two strokes was shorter if the two corresponding letters belonged to the same syllable (for example, the interval between "a" and "l" was shorter when subjects typed 'pal-mier' as opposed to 'pa-lette').

Discussion

In summary, there is considerable evidence that orthographic representations are more than simple linear sequences of abstract letter identities. In particular, various factors such as morphological and syllabic structure, letter doubling and CV status can affect the patterns of errors of dysgraphic subjects or the temporal properties of normal spelling. To account for these various findings, it has been proposed that the relevant processing units may be morphemes rather than words. Furthermore, as indicated in Figure 11.5, the orthographic representations of morphemes may be viewed as having a multidimensional rather than purely linear structure (Caramazza & Miceli, 1990; McCloskey et al., 1994), a proposal inspired from autosegmental phonology (e.g., Clements & Keyser, 1983). The fundamental assumption is that different features of a word's orthography are encoded at functionally distinct levels. An important implication is that each dimension can be selectively damaged, leading to a characteristic pattern of errors. In the case of letter doubling, information about letter quantity is distinct from information about letter identity. This explains how it could be that some patients suffer from a selective loss of doubling information (Miceli et al., 1995) while others present a selective preservation of this feature (e.g., Tainturier & Caramazza, 1996). Multidimensional proposals also explain why some patients retain good knowledge of the consonant/vowel status of letters without being able to access their specific identity.

Although the multidimensional view of orthographic representations has been developed to account for the performance of dysgraphic subjects, it could in principle also guide research on the influence of orthographic structure in normal spelling. For example, this framework makes specific predictions as to which types of errors are more or less likely to occur in slips of the pen.

THE DISTINCTION BETWEEN FORMAT-INDEPENDENT AND FORMAT-SPECIFIC REPRESENTATIONS IN THE SPELLING SYSTEM

A fundamental assumption of most theories of spelling is that the representations manipulated by the more central components of the spelling process—the orthographic lexicon, the POC system and the graphemic buffer—are distinct from those manipulated by the more peripheral letter shape and letter name conversion mechanisms (see Figure 11.1). Furthermore, it is specifically assumed that this difference corresponds to a distinction between abstract, format-independent representations of letter identity and format-specific ones. In this framework, orthographic information represented in a format-independent manner serves as the basis for a subsequent translation into specific formats, that is into letter shapes for written spelling and letter names for oral spelling. Although this is certainly computationally sensible, it is by no means the only logical possibility (for example, see Lesser, 1990). An alternative hypothesis is that the central processes represent letter identities in a format-specific code, as either letter names or letter shapes. This format-specific code could then be translated into other format-specific codes depending on task demands. The question we will consider in this section is: What is the empirical evidence for the format-independent/format specific representational distinction?

The claim that central spelling mechanisms represent letter identity in an abstract, format-independent manner gains some support from individuals whose performance with both words and nonwords is strikingly similar in written and oral spelling, both in terms of error rates and error type distribution (Caramazza & Miceli, 1990; Caramazza, et al., 1987; Hillis & Caramazza, 1989; Jónsdóttir et al., 1996; Katz, 1991; McCloskey et al., 1994; Piccirilli, Petrillo, & Poli, 1992; Posteraro et al., 1988). This evidence suggests a common format for the oral and written spelling of words and nonwords, but does not specifically indicate if the representations are format independent or specific, and if the latter, whether they consist of letter names or letter shapes. More informative in this regard is the finding that damage that affects spelling in one format (e.g., letter names) need not affect spelling production in the other format (letter shapes). For example, Kinsbourne and Warrington (1965) described a subject whose accuracy in oral spelling was only 7% while written spelling accuracy was 93% (see also Bub & Kertesz, 1982). In a complementary manner, individuals have been described whose oral spelling was relatively intact but who, although they exhibited no generalized motor deficits, had difficulty with written spelling (Anderson, Damasio, & Damasio, 1990; Baxter & Warrington, 1986; Black, Behrmann, Bass, & Hacker, 1989; De Bastiani, & Barry, 1989; Friedman & Alexander, 1989; Goodman & Caramazza, 1986; Kinsbourne & Rosenfield, 1974; Patterson & Wing, 1989; Rapp & Caramazza, 1989, 1997; Rothi & Heilman, 1981; Zangwill, 1954).

Rapp and Caramazza (1997b) provided strong support for the distinction between format-independent and format-specific representations by comparing the characteristics of errors arising from failures of the letter-shape conversion mechanism and those arising from graphemic buffer deficits. Rapp and Caramazza (1997b) first examined the written letter substitution errors of two subjects, HL and JGE, who produced substitutions errors almost entirely in written and not oral spelling (e.g., when asked to spell *eye*, JGE said "/i, waɪ, i/" but wrote F-Y-E). The largely intact oral spelling indicates that the orthographic lexicon and graphemic buffer are relatively intact and, thus, the written spelling errors indicate a deficit in letter-shape conversion. Their errors were analyzed to determine if targets and responses (e.g., E → F in the example above) shared visuo-spatial and/or motoric characteristics. For example, A and R are visuo-spatially similar, but not motorically; in contrast, L and T are motorically similar but not visuo-spatially. The results indicated that for both subjects the proportion of letter substitutions that shared motoric characteristics far exceeded what might be expected by a random pairing of letters, whereas rates of visuo-spatially similar substitutions occurred at chance level rates (panels A & B of Figure 11.6). Therefore, these findings specifically argue for an abstract motoric encoding of shape information by the letter-shape conversion mechanism. This conclusion is consistent with the observations by other investigators that targets and errors in the written letter substitutions of impaired (and unimpaired) subjects share what could loosely be described as a physical resemblance. Previous work did not, however, specifically distinguish between visuo-spatial and motoric resemblance (Black et al., 1989; De Bastiani & Barry, 1989; Hatfield & Patterson, 1983; Lambert, Viader, Eustache, & Morin, 1994; Weekes, 1994; Zangwill, 1954). The Rapp and Caramazza (1997) results do not, of course, preclude the possibility of there being multiple levels of letter shape representation. Thus, some researchers have suggested that letter shape information is represented in both visuo-spatial and abstract motor codes (e.g., Ellis, 1979, 1988; Margolin, 1984). The Rapp and Caramazza findings do, however, reveal that letter shape is, at a minimum, represented in an abstract motoric format.

Rapp and Caramazza then reanalyzed the written substitution errors produced by two previ-

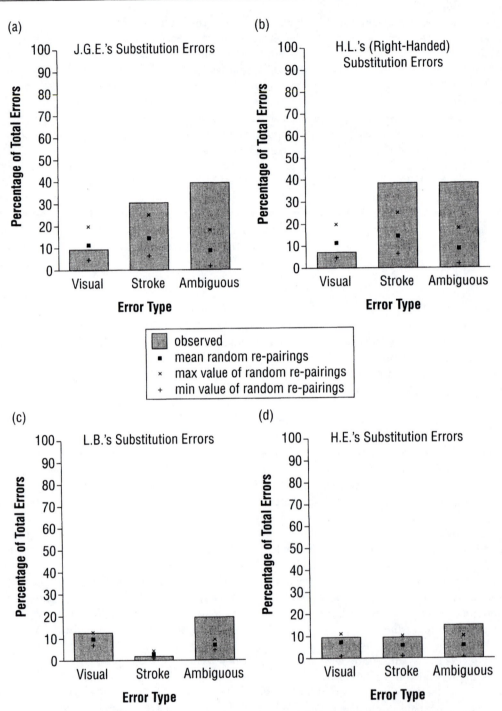

Figure 11.6: Comparison of observed levels of different errors with rates expected by chance for JGE (panel A), HL (panel B), LB (panel C), and HE (panel D). Adapted with permission from, "From Graphemes to Abstract Letter Shapes: Levels of Representation in Written Spelling," by B. Rapp and A. Caramazza, 1997, *Journal of Experimental Psychology: Human Perception and Performance*, 3(4), 1130–1152. Copyright © 1997 by the American Psychological Association.

ously reported individuals, LB (Caramaza & Miceli, 1990) and HE (McCloskey et al., 1994). In contrast with JGE and HL, LB and HE exhibited a highly similar pattern of response in written and oral spelling and their deficits were localized to the graphemic buffer. If the representations at this level are indeed format-independent, then neither motoric nor visuo-spatial similarity between targets and responses would be expected. Indeed, it was found that neither LB nor HE produced visuo-spatially similar or motorically similar substitutions at a rate higher than chance (panels C & D, of Figure 11.6).

Finally, Rapp and Caramazza (1997) considered the rates of consonant/vowel status preservation in the substitution errors of these four subjects. As indicated above, the substitution of consonants for consonants and vowels for vowels has been observed in a number of cases with graphemic buffer damage, supporting the hypothesis that abstract, format-independent letter representations encode abstract features such as consonant/vowel status. Consistent with this, LB and HE's errors exhibited extremely high rates of preservation of C/V status (99% and 90%, respectively). There is, however, no reason to assume that C/V information should be included in letter-shape representations and thus high C/V preservation rates would not be expected for JGE and HL's written substitution errors. This is, in fact, what Rapp and Caramazza found: JGE and HL's consonant/vowel preservation rates were 59% and 73%, respectively (well below the rates observed for LB and HE and well within chance rates for JGE, and only just slightly above chance levels for HL).

In sum, cognitive neuropsychological evidence provides strong support for the distinction between format-independent and format-specific representational types that is a fundamental assumption of most current theories of spelling. Although there is considerable work in the normal literature concerned with investigating the nature of the motoric codes used in hand-writing (e.g., Ellis, 1982; Teulings, Thomasen, & van Galen, 1986; Viviani & Terzuolo, 1980), this literature has not been specifically concerned with distinguishing format-specific from format-independent codes. Presumably, however, questions concerning representational format and when in the course of spelling different representational types are deployed can also be investigated with unimpaired subjects.

CONCLUSION

As indicated at the beginning of the chapter, spelling is perhaps the cognitive domain where the study of deficits most clearly constitutes the predominant source of evidence. In this chapter, we have shown how this research has revealed a highly structured system with a rich representational structure. It is our hope that work with impaired and unimpaired subjects will build upon these developments to investigate the very large number of yet unanswered questions regarding our ability to retrieve and produce the spellings of words.

Acknowledgements

We would like to acknowledge our appreciation of the support of the Région Rhône-Alpes and Ministère de la Culture of France to both authors and also of NIMH grant R29MH55758 for support to the second author.

REFERENCES

Allen, M., & Badecker, W. (2000). Morphology: The internal structure of words. In B. Rapp (Ed.), *A handbook of cognitive neuropsychology: What deficits reveal about the human mind* (pp. 211–232). Philadelphia: Psychology Press (this volume).

Allport, D. A., & Funnel, E. (1981). Components of the mental lexicon. *Philosophical Transactions of the Royal Society of London, B295*, 397–410.

Anderson, S. W., Damasio, A. R., & Damasio, H. (1990). Troubled letters but not numbers: Domain specific cognitive impairments following focal damage in frontal cortex. *Brain, 113,* 749–766

Annoni, J. M., Lemay, M. A., de Mattos Pimenta, M. A., & Lecours, A. R. (1998). The contribution of attentional mechanisms to an irregularity effect at the graphemic buffer level. *Brain and Language, 63,* 64–78.

Ans, B., Carbonnel, S., & Valdois, S. (1998). Naming polysyllabic printed words: A single-route dual-process connectionist model. *Psychological Review, 105,* 678–723.

Badecker, W., Hillis, A., & Caramazza, A. (1990). Lexical morphology and its role in the writing process: Evidence from a case of acquired dysgraphia. *Cognition, 35,* 205–243.

Barry, C. (1988). Modelling assembled spelling: Convergence of data from normal subjects and «surface» dysgraphia. *Cortex, 24,* 339–346.

Barry, C., & Seymour, P. H. K. (1988). Lexical priming and sound-to-spelling contingency effects in nonword spelling. *The Quarterly Journal of Experimental Psychology, 40A,* 5–40.

Barry, C., & de Bastiani, P. (1997). Lexical priming of nonword spelling in the regular orthography of Italian. *Reading & Writing, 9,* 499–517.

Basso, A., Taborelli, A., & Vignolo, L.A. (1978). Dissociated disorders of speaking and writing in aphasia. *Journal of Neurology, Neurosurgery and Psychiatry, 41,* 556–563.

Baxter, D. M., & Warrington, E. K. (1986). Ideational apraxia: A single case study. *Journal of Neurology, Neurosurgery and Psychiatry, 49,* 369–374.

Baxter, D. M., & Warrington, E. K. (1987). Transcoding sound to spelling: Single or multiple sound unit correspondence? *Cortex, 23,* 11–28.

Beaton A., Guest J., & Ved R. (1997). Semantic errors of naming, reading, writing, and drawing following left-hemisphere infarction. *Cognitive Neuropsychology, 14,* 459–478.

Beauvois, M. F., & Derousné, J. (1979).Phonological alexia: Three dissociations. *Journal of Neurology, Neurosurgery and Psychiatry, 42,* 1115–1124.

Beauvois, M. F., & Derousné, J. (1981). Lexical or orthographic agraphia. *Brain, 104,* 21–49.

Behrmann, M., & Bub, D. (1992). Surface dyslexia and dysgraphia: Dual routes, single lexicon. *Cognitive Neuropsychology, 9,* 209–251.

Black, S. E., Behrmann, M., Bass, K., & Hacker, P. (1989). Selective writing impairment: Beyond the allographic code. *Aphasiology, 3,* 265–277.

Bonin, P., Fayol, M., & Gombert, J. E. (1997). Role of phonological and orthographic codes in picture naming and writing: An interference paradigm study. *Current Psychology of Cognition, 16,* 299–320.

Bonin, P., Fayol, M., & Peereman, R. (1998). Masked form priming in writing words from pictures: Evidence for a direct retrieval of orthograhic codes. *Acta Psychologica, 99,* 311328.

Bosse, M. L., Valdois, J., & Tainturier, M. J. (submitted for publication). *Analogy without priming in early spelling development.*

Brown, D. A., & Loosemore, R. P. (1994). Computanional approaches to normal and impaired spelling. In D. A. Brown & N. C. Ellis (Eds.), *Handbook of spelling: Theory, process and intervention.* Chichester, UK: John Wiley.

Bub, D., & Kertesz, A. (1982a). Deep agraphia. *Brain and Language, 17,* 146–165.

Bub, D., & Kertesz, A. (1982-b). Evidence for lexico-

graphic processing in a patient with preserved written over oral single word naming. *Brain, 105,* 697–717.

Burden, V. (1989). A comparison of priming effects on the nonword spelling performance of good and poor spellers. *Cognitive Neuropsychology, 6,* 43–65.

Campbell, R. (1983). Writing nonwords to dictation. *Brain and Language, 19,* 153–178.

Campbell, R. (1987). One or two lexicons for reading and writing words: Can misspellings shed any light ? *Cognitive Neuropsychology, 4,* 487–499.

Caramazza, A. (1988). Some aspects of language processing revealed through the analysis of acquired dysgraphia: The lexical system. *Annual Review of Neuroscience, 11,* 395–421.

Caramazza, A., & Hillis, A. E. (1990). Where do semantic errors come from? *Cortex, 26,* 95–122.

Caramazza, A., & Hillis, A. (1991). Lexical organization of nouns and verbs in the brain. *Nature, 349,* 788–790.

Caramazza, A., & Miceli, G. (1990). The structure of graphemic representations. *Cognition, 37,* 243–297.

Caramazza, A., Capasso, R., & Miceli, G. (1996). The role of the graphemic buffer in reading. *Cognitive Neuropsychology, 13,* 673–698.

Caramazza, A., Miceli, G., Villa, G., & Romani, C. (1987). The role of the graphemic buffer in spelling: Evidence from a case of acquired dysgraphia. *Cognition, 26,* 5985.

Coltheart, M., & Funnel, E. (1987). Reading and writing: One lexicon or two? In D. A. Allport, D. McKay, W. Prinz, & E. Scheerer (Eds.), *Language perception and production: Common processes in listening, speaking, reading, and writing.* London: Academic Press.

Coltheart, M., Patterson, K., & Marshall, J. C. (1987). Deep dyslexia since 1980. In M. Coltheart, K. Patterson, & J. C. Marshall (Eds.), *Deep dyslexia* (2nd ed.). London, Routledge & Kegan Paul.

Coltheart, M., Curtis, B., Atkins, P., & Haller, M. (1993). Models of reading aloud: Dual-route and parallel-distributed-processing approaches. *Psychological Review, 100,* 589–608.

Cubelli, R. (1991). A selective deficit for writing vowels in acquired dysgraphia. *Nature, 353,* 258–260.

Clements, G. N., & Keyser, S. J. (1983). *CV phonology: A generative theory of the syllable.* Cambridge, MA: MIT Press.

Cuetos, F. (1993). Writing processes in a shallow orthography. *Reading & Writing, 5,* 17–28.

Cuetos, F., Valle-Arroyo, F., & Suarez, M. P. (1996). A case of phonological dyslexia in Spanish. *Cognitive Neuropsychology, 13,* 1–24.

De Bastiani, P., & Barry, C. (1989). A cognitive analysis of an acquired dysgraphic patient with an «allographic» writing disorder. *Cognitive Neuropsychology, 6,* 25–41.

De Partz, M. P., Seron, X., & Van der Linden, M. (1992). Re-education of a surface dysgraphic with a visual imagery strategy. *Cognitive Neuropsychology, 9,* 369–401.

Dixon, M., & Kaminska, Z. (1994). Casting a spell with witches and broomsticks: Direct and associative influences on nonword orthography. *European Journal of Cognitive Psychology, 6,* 383–398.

Ellis, A. W. (1979). Slips of the pen. *Visible language, 13,* 265–282.

Ellis, A. W. (1982). Spelling and writing (and reading and speaking). In A. W. Ellis (Ed.), *Normality and pathology in cognitive functions.* New York: Academic Press.

Ellis, A.W. (1988). Normal writing processes and peripheral acquired dysgraphias. *Language and Cognitive Processes, 3,* 99-127.

Ellis, A. W. (1989). *Reading, writing and dyslexia.* Hove, UK: LEA Publishers.

Ellis, A., Miller, D., & Sin, G. (1983). Wernicke's aphasia and normal language processing: A case study in cognitive neuropsychology. *Cognition, 15,* 111-144.

Ferreres, A. R., & Miravalles, G. (1995). The production of semantic paralexias in a Spanish-speaking aphasic. *Brain and Language, 49,* 153-172.

Friedman, R. B., & Alexander, M. (1989). Written spelling agraphia. *Brain and Language, 36,* 503-517.

Funnell, E. (1992). On recognising misspelled words. In C. M. Sterling & C. Robson (Eds.), *Psychology, spelling and education* (pp. 87-99). Clevedon, UK : Multilingual Matters.

Geschwind, N. (1969). Problems in the anatomical understanding of the aphasias. In A. L. Benton (Ed.), *Contributions to clinical neuropsychology.* Chicago: Aldine.

Goodman , R. A., & Caramazza, A. (1986). Aspects of the spelling process: Evidence from a case of acquired dysgraphia. *Language and Cognitive Processes, 1,* 263-296.

Goodman-Shulman, R. A., & Caramazza, A. (1987). Patterns of dysgraphia and the nonlexical spelling process. *Cortex, 23,* 143-148.

Harris, M., & Hatano, G, (Eds.). (1999). *Learning to read and write: A cross-linguistic perspective.* New York: Cambridge University Press.

Hatfield, F. M., & Patterson, K. E. (1983). Phonological spelling. *Quaterly Journal of Experimental Psychology, 35A,* 451-458.

Hier, D. B., & Mohr, J. P. (1977). Incongruous oral and written naming. *Brain and Language, 4,* 115-126.

Hillis, A. E., & Caramazza, A. (1989). The graphemic buffer and mechanisms of unilateral spatial neglect. *Brain and Language, 36,* 208-235.

Hillis, A., & Caramazza, A. (1991). Mechanisms for accessing lexical representations for output: Evidence from a category-specific semantic deficit. *Brain and Language, 40,* 106-144.

Hillis, A. E., & Caramazza, A. (1995a). Converging evidence for the interaction of semantic and sublexical phonological information in accessing lexical representations for spoken output. *Cognitive Neuropsychology, 12,* 187-227.

Hillis, A. E., & Caramazza, A. (1995b). Spatially specific deficits in processing graphemic representations in reading and writing. *Brain and Language, 48,* 263-308

Hillis, A. E., Rapp, B. C., & Caramazza, A. (1999). When a rose is a rose in speech but a tulip in writing. *Cortex, 35,* 337-356.

Holmes, V. M., & Carruthers, J. (1998). The relation between reading and spelling in skilled adult readers. *Journal of Memory and Language, 39,* 264-289.

Hotopf, W. H. N. (1980). Slips of the pen. In U. Frith (Ed.), *Cognitive processes in spelling.* New York: Academic Press.

Houghton, G., & Zorzi, M. (submitted). *A connectionist dual-route model of normal and impaired spelling.*

Houghton, G., Glasspool, D. W., & Shallice, T. (1994). Spelling and serial recall: Insights from a competitive queueing model. In G. D. A. Brown & N. C. Ellis

(Eds.), *Handbook of spelling: Theory, process and intervention.* Chichester, UK: John Wiley.

Hughes, J. C., Graham, N., Patterson, K., & Hodges, J. R. (1997). Dysgraphia in mild dementia of Alzheimer's type. *Neuropsychologia, 35,* 533-545.

Hulme, C., & Joshi, R. M. (Eds.). (1998). *Reading and spelling: Development and disorders.* Mahwah, NJ: Lawrence Erlbaum.

Jónsdóttir, M. K., Shallice, T., & Wise, R. (1996). Phonological mediation and the graphemic buffer disorder in spelling: cross-language differences? *Cognition, 59,* 169-197.

Katz, R. B. (1991). Limited retention of information in the graphemic buffer. *Cortex, 27,* 111-119.

Kinsbourne, M., & Warrington, E. K. (1965). A case showing selectively impaired oral spelling. *Journal of Neurology, Neurosurgery and Psychiatry, 28,* 563-566.

Kinsbourne, M., & Rosenfield, D. B. (1974). Agraphia selective for written spelling. *Brain and Language, 1,* 215-225.

Kreiner, D. S. (1992). Reaction time measures of spelling: Testing a two-strategy model of skilled spelling. *Journal of Experimental Psychology: Learning, Memory and Cognition, 18,* 765-776.

Kreiner, D. S. (1996). Effects of word familiarity and phoneme-grapheme polygraphy on oral spelling times and accuracy. *The Psychological Records, 46,* 49-70.

Kreiner, D. S., & Gough, P. B. (1990). Two ideas about spelling rules and word specific memory. *Journal of Memory and Language, 29,* 103-118.

Kremin, H. (1985). Routes and strategies in surface dyslexia and dysgraphia. In K. E. Patterson, J. C. Marshall & M. Coltheart (Eds.), *Surface dyslexia: Neuropsychological and cognitive studies of phonological reading.* London: LEA Publishers.

Lambert, J., Viader, F., Eustache, F. & Morin, P. (1994). Contribution to peripheral agraphia: A case of postallographic impairment? *Cognitive Neuropsychology, 11,* 35-55.

Lesser, R. (1990). Superior oral to written spellings: Evidence for separate buffers? *Cognitive Neuropsychology, 7,* 347-366.

Levine, D. N., Calvanio, R., & Popovics, A. (1982). Language in the absence of inner speech. *Neuropsychologia, 20,* 391-409.

Luria, A. R. (1970). *Traumatic aphasia.* La Haye, The Netherlands: Mouton de Gruyter.

McCloskey, M., Badecker, W., Goodman-Shulman, R. A., & Aliminosa, D. (1994). The structure of graphemic representations in spelling: Evidence from a case of acquired dysgraphia. *Cognitive Neuropsychology, 2,* 341-392.

Margolin, D. I. (1984). The neuropsychology of writing and spelling: Semantic, phonological, motor and perceptual processes. *The Quarterly Journal of Experimental Psychology, 36A,* 459-489

Miceli, G., Benvegnú, B., Capasso, R., & Caramazza, A. (1995). Selective deficit in processing double letters. *Cortex, 31,* 161-171.

Miceli, G., Benvegnù, B., Capasso, R., & Caramazza, A. (1997). The independence of phonological and orthographic lexical forms: Evidence from aphasia. *Cognitive Neuropsychology, 14,* 35-69.

Miceli, G., Capasso, R., & Caramazza, A. (1994). The interaction of lexical and sublexical processes in reading, writing and repetition. *Neuropsychologia, 32,* 317-333.

Miceli, G., Capasso, R., & Caramazza, A. (1999). Sublexical

conversion procedures and the interaction of phonological and orthographic lexical form. *Cognitive Neuropsychology, 16,* 557-572

Miceli, G., Giustolisi, L., & Caramazza, A. (1991). The interaction of lexical and non-lexical processing mechanisms: Evidence from pure anomia. *Cortex, 27,* 57-80.

Miceli, G., Silveri, C., & Caramazza, A. (1985). Cognitive analysis of a case of pure dysgraphia. *Brain and Language, 25,* 187-221.

Miller, D., & Ellis, A. W. (1987). Speech and writing errors in "neologistic jargonaphasia": A lexical activation hypothesis. In M. Coltheart & G. Sartori (Eds.), *The cognitive neuropsychology of language* (pp. 253-271). London: Lawrence Erlbaum.

Monsell, S. (1987). Nonvisual orthographic processing and the orthographic input lexicon. In M. Coltheart (Ed.), *Attention and performance XII : Reading* (pp. 299-323). Hillsdale, NJ: Erlbaum.

Newcombe, F., & Marshall, J. C. (1985). Reading and writing by letter sounds. In K. E. Patterson, J. C. Marshallm & M. Coltheart (Eds.), *Surface dyslexia: Neuropsychological and cognitive studies of phonological reading.* London: LEA Publishers.

Nickels, L. (1992). The autocue? Self-generated phonemic cues in the treatment of a disorder of reading and naming. *Cognitive Neuropsychology, 9,* 155-182.

Orliaguet, J. P., & Boë, L. J. (1993). The role of linguistics in the speed of handwriting movements: Effects of spelling uncertainty. *Acta Psychologica, 82,* 103-113.

Parkin, A. J. (1993). Progressive aphasia without dementia: A clinical and cognitive neuropsychological analysis. *Brain and Language, 44,* 201-220.

Patterson, K., & Wing, A. M. (1989). Processes in handwriting: A case for case. *Cognitive Neuropsychology, 6,* 1-23.

Perfetti, C. A. (1997). The psycholinguistics of spelling and reading. In C. A. Perfetti & L. Rieben (Eds.), *Learning to spell: Research, theory and practice across languages.* Mahwah, NJ: Lawrence Erlbaum Associates.

Perfetti, C. A., & Rieben, L. (1997). *Learning to spell: Research, theory and practice across languages.* Mahwah, NJ: Lawrence Erlbaum Associates.

Phillips, W. A., & Goodall, W. C. (1995). Lexical writing can be non-semantic and it can be fluent without practice. *Cognitive Neuropsychology, 12,* 149-174.

Piccirilli, M., Petrillo, S., & Poli, R. (1992). Dysgraphia and selective impairment of the graphemic buffer. *Italian Journal of Neurological Science, 3,* 113-117.

Posteraro, L., Zinelli, P., & Mazzuchi, A. (1988). Selective impairment of the graphemic buffer in acquired dysgraphia: A case study. *Brain and Language, 35,* 274-286.

Rapp, B. C., & Caramazza, A. (1989). Letter processing in reading and spelling: Some dissociations. *Reading and Writing, 1,* 3-23.

Rapp, B., & Caramazza, A. (1993). On the distinction between deficits of access and deficits of storage: A question of theory. *Cognitive Neuropsychology, 10,* 113-141.

Rapp, B., & Caramazza, A. (1997a). The modality specific organization of grammatical categories: Evidence from impaired spoken and written sentence production. *Brain and Language, 56,* 248-286.

Rapp, B., & Caramazza, A. (1997b). From graphemes to abstract letter shapes: Levels of representation in written spelling. *Journal of Experimental Psychology: Human Perception and Performance, 23,* 1130-1152.

Rapp, B., & Caramazza, A. (1998). A case of selective difficulty in writing verbs. *Neuro case, 4,* 127-140.

Rapp, B., Benzing L, & Caramazza A. (1997). The autonomy of lexical orthography. *Cognitive Neuropsychology, 14,* 71-104.

Rapp, B., Boatman, D., & Gordon, B. (1999). The autonomy of lexical orthography: Evidence from cortical stimulation. *Brain and Language, 69,* 392-395.

Rapp, B., Epstein, C., Tainturier, M. J. (accepted pending revisions). The integration of information across lexical and sublexical processes in spelling. *Cognitive Neuropsychology.*

Rapp, B., Folk, J. & Tainturier, M. J. (2000). Word Reading. In B. Rapp (Ed.), *A handbook of cognitive neuropsychology: What deficits reveal about the human mind/brain* (pp. 233-263). Philadelphia: Psychology Press (this volume).

Roeltgen, D. P., (1985). Agraphia. In K. M. Heilman & E. Valenstein (Eds.), *Clinical Neuropsychology* (2nd ed.). New York: Oxford University Press.

Roeltgen, D. P., Sevush, S., & Heilman, K. M. (1983). Phonological agraphia: Writing by the lexical-semantic route. *Neurology, 33,* 755-765.

Rothi, L. J., & Heilman, K. M. (1981). Alexia and agraphia with spared spelling and letter recognition abilities. *Brain and Language, 12,* 1-13.

Saffran, E. M. (1985). Lexicalisation and reading performance in surface dyslexia. In K. E. Patterson, J. C. Marshall, & M. Coltheart (Eds.), *Surface dyslexia: Neuropsychological and cognitive studies of phonological reading.* London: LEA Publishers.

Sanders, R. J., & Caramazza, A. (1990). Operation of the phoneme-to-grapheme conversion mechanism in a brain injured patient. *Reading and Writing, 2,* 61-82.

Seymour, P. H., & Dargie, A. (1990). Associative priming and orthographic choice in nonword spelling. *European Journal of Cognitive Psychology, 2,* 395-410.

Shallice, T. (1981). Phonological agraphia and the lexical route in writing. *Brain, 104,* 413-429.

Shelton, J. R., & Weinrich, M. (1997). Further evidence of a dissociation between output phonological and orthographic lexicons: A case study. *Cognitive Neuropsychology, 14,* 105-129.

Tainturier, M. J. (1996). Les dysgraphies centrales: Etat de la recherche et nouvelles perspectives (Central dysgraphias: Current state of the research and new directions). In S. Carbonnel, P. Gillet, M. D. Martory, & S. Valdois (Eds.), *Approche cognitive des troubles de la lecture et de l'écriture chez l'adulte et chez l'enfant* (Cognitive approach to the study of reading and spelling deficits in adults and children). Marseille, France: Solal.

Tainturier, M. J. (1996). Phonologically-based errors and their implications in the specification of phonology to orthography conversion processes. *Brain and Cognition, 32,* 148-151.

Tainturier, M. J., Bosse, M. L., Valdois, S., & Rapp, B. (in preparation). *Lexical neighbourhood effects in nonword spelling.*

Tainturier, M. J., & Caramazza, A. (1994). A case study of a graphemic buffer impairment affecting nonword reading. *Brain and Language, 47,* 433-435.

Tainturier, M. J., & Caramazza, A. (1996). The status of double letters in graphemic representations. *Journal of Memory and Language, 35,* 53-73.

Tainturier, M. J., Moreaud, O., David, D., Leek, E. C. &

Pellat, J. (in press). Superior written over spoken picture naming in a case of fronto-temporal dementia. *Neurocase.*

Teulings, H. L., Thomassen, A. J. W. M., & van Galen, G. P. (1986). Invariants in handwriting: The information contained in a motor program. In H. S. R. Kao, G. O. van Galen, & R. Hoosain (Eds.), *Graphonomics: Contemporary research in handwriting.* Amsterdam: North-Holland

Treiman, R. (1997). Spelling in normal children and dyslexics. In B. A. Blachman (Ed.), *Foundations of reading acquisition and dyslexia: Implications for early intervention.* Mahwah, NJ: Lawrence Erlbaum.

Van Orden, G. C., Jansen op de Haar, M. A., & Bosman, A. (1997). Complex dynamic systems also predict dissociations, but they do not reduce to autonomous components. *Cognitive Neuropsychology, 14,* 131–165.

Viviani, P., & Terzuolo, C. (1980). Space-time invariance in learned motor skills. In G. E. Stelmach & J. Requin (Eds.), *Tutorials in motor behavior.* Amsterdam: North-Holland.

Weekes, B. S. (1994). A cognitive-neuropsychological analysis of allograph errors from a patient with acquired dysgraphia. *Aphasiology, 8,* 409–425.

Weekes, B., & Coltheart, M. (1996). Surface dyslexia and surface dysgraphia: Treatment studies and their theoretical implications. *Cognitive Neuropsychology, 13,* 277–315.

Wing, A. M., & Baddeley, A. D. (1980). Spelling errors in handwriting: A corpus and a distributional analysis. In U. Frith (Ed.), *Cognitive processes in spelling.* London: Academic Press.

Zangwill, O. L. (1954). Agraphia due to a left parietal glioma in a left-handed man. *Brain, 77,* 510–520.

Zesiger, P., Orliaguet, J. P., Boë, L. J., & Mounoud, P. (1994). The role of syllabic structure in handwriting and typing production. In C. Faure, P. Keuss, G. Lurette, & A. Vinter (Eds.), *Advances in handwriting: A multidisciplinary approach.* Paris: Europia.

Zorzi, M., Houghton, G., & Butterworth, B. (1998). Two routes or one in reading aloud? A connectionist dual-process model. *Journal of Experimental Psychology: Human Perception & Performance, 24,* 1131–1161.

12

Spoken Word Production

Lyndsey Nickels

INTRODUCTION

The production of fluent speech is one of the most complex skills humans acquire. In order to be able to sustain fluency, words must be retrieved and produced at a rate of two or three per second. The aim of research in this field (across many different disciplines) is to determine HOW this occurs—there are three key questions:

- What are the levels of processing in retrieving words for speech production (lexical access)?
- What is the time course of activation of levels of processing for speech production?
- How are the retrieved lexical items prepared for articulation?

In other words, what are the different types of knowledge we have regarding words and how is this information represented in the language processing system? How is the stored information retrieved: in one unit or are different types of lexical information retrieved successively? Having retrieved the stored representations of words how are these translated into motor plans for the articulatory muscles so that we can say the words? This chapter will discuss these issues. Two of the most developed theories of spoken word production are those of Dell and Levelt and their colleagues (Dell, Schwartz, Martin, Saffran, & Gagnon, 1997; Levelt, Roelofs, & Meyer, 1999a).[1] We will primarily focus our discussion around these theories while referring to others as necessary.

Unlike other areas of cognition where the focus of research has been on experimental work, until recently in speech production the emphasis has been on analysis of the speech errors produced by unimpaired individuals (for examples see Table 12.1). Fromkin (1973) brought together a collection of papers all of which are "concerned with the ways in which spontaneously produced speech errors (i.e., utterances which in some way deviate from intended or target utterances) provide insights into the nature of language and language behaviour, and serve to test putative hypotheses" (Fromkin, 1973, p. 13). Since then many more authors have used speech errors to support theoretical positions (e.g., Dell, 1986, 1989; Fay & Cutler, 1977; Garrett, 1975, 1980; Shattuck-Hufnagel, 1979, 1987; Stemberger; 1985). Thus, speech error

---

[1]The theory described by Levelt et al. (1999a), differs in a number of important ways from that described by Levelt (1989), we will concentrate on the former as the most recent formulation of the theory, while discussing some of the more pertinent differences as appropriate. Similarly, the computational model of Dell et al. (1997) is a simplified version of Dell (1986, 1989).

data are viewed as providing "a 'window' into linguistic and mental processes" (Fromkin, 1973, p. 44). For example, as the speech signal is of a semi-continuous nature—it is usually not possible to identify where one sound ends and the next begins. Yet, speech errors frequently occur where single sounds (phonemes) are anticipated, perseverated, transposed, added, or deleted (see Table 12.1). These errors are consequently used to support the argument that discrete phonemes must exist within the language system (Fromkin, 1973, p. 15).

However, there are problems with the use of speech error data (Cutler, 1981; Stemberger, 1992). In her paper "The reliability of speech error data" Cutler (1981) discussed these difficulties focusing on the problem of 'detectability.' Speech error corpora are often collections from observations of everyday language use—the experimenter records any errors that occur. However, no experimenter can (or does) claim to record all the errors occurring in a given period of time. As Fromkin (1973) notes, listening to the content of a message may lead to errors being glossed over, and even when directing attention to errors we may miss those errors related to meaning. However, Cutler (1981) argues that selective attention is not the only problem but asserts "some kinds of errors are simply harder to hear than others" (p. 561). So even if corpora are tape-recorded and multiply checked, some errors will be detected less often. (e.g., Tent & Clark (1980; cited in Cutler, 1981) found that subjects detected only 28% of speech sound compared to over 97% of syllable and word anticipations). Thus, any claims based on the relative occurrence of different types of speech errors could be flawed if based on data of this sort.

Some of the problems inherent in collection of spontaneously occurring speech errors can be overcome by using elicited errors. For example, tongue twister tasks involving repetition of sequences of confusable words (e.g., leap note nap lute) have been used to promote the occurrence of errors (e.g., Shattuck-Hufnagel, 1983, 1987; Wilshire, 1998). However, it is possible that perceptual biases could still occur; for example, non-word errors may be less easily detected than word errors.

Table 12.1

Examples of Speech Errors Affecting Single Words. (The First Utterance is always the target, followed by the actual utterance (containing the error).

Semantically related words
the worst years for wine → the worst years for beer —I mean wine.
blond hair → blond eyes
Semantically and phonologically related words
when were you last on the east coast → on the west—east.
some semantic facts → syntactic facts
Phonologically related words
white anglo-saxon protestant → prostitute
the native values → native vowels
Phoneme anticipation
a reading list → a leading list
Phoneme perseveration
escorting → escorking
cortical → corkical
Phoneme exchange
caterpiller → patterkiller
Phoneme deletion
squib → quib
stretch → retch
Phoneme substitution
fixed → sixed
sort → hort

Adapted from Speech Errors as Linguistic Evidence, by V. Fromkin (Ed.), 1973, Appendix, pp. 243–269. Copyright Mouton de Gruyter.

While many theories of speech production have developed using data from speech errors (as discussed above), relatively recently experiments using reaction time techniques have become more widely used to develop and test theories of word production. Indeed Levelt et al. (1999a) state that their theory has been "developed and tested ... almost exclusively by means of reaction time (RT) research" (p. 2). They argue that the ultimate test of theories "cannot lie in how they account for infrequent derailments of the process (p. 2)" but should be in how well they can deal with the normal process (although they do acknowledge that the theory should be able to account for both). As Levelt et al. note, reaction time studies of word production have been around for some time (see Glaser, 1992, for a review). For example, Oldfield and Wingfield (1965) examined the effects of word frequency on speed of picture naming, finding that pictures with more frequent names were responded to quicker than those with less frequent names. They attribute this effect to a frequency sensitive mechanism during the process of word retrieval. However, in order to determine which aspect of word retrieval is affected by frequency more complex experimental manipulations are needed (for example, word-picture interference paradigms, see below). Unfortunately, the more complex the task, the more difficult and controversial the interpretation of the results becomes.

Finally, because of the difficulties with both speech error and experimental research on speech production, neuropsychological data can be of particular value in this field. Individuals with acquired language disorders (aphasias) show a wide variety of different patterns of impairment in word production, reflected in the production of errors of different types, different stimulus properties affecting performance (e.g., word frequency, word length) and dissociations between modalities (writing vs. speech; input vs. output). Thus, as will be illustrated below, cognitive neuropsychology has enabled both evaluation and development of theories of spoken word production over and above the contributions from cognitive psychology and psycholinguistics.

IDENTIFICATION OF LEVELS OF PROCESSING IN LEXICAL ACCESS FOR WORD PRODUCTION

We reach the first point of debate almost before we start our discussion—what should the starting point, or scope, of this theory be? We wish to determine what happens when someone produces a word—this word is produced in response to some thought or external object (thing, picture, or even written or spoken word). We will, for the time being, ignore any perceptual analysts that may be involved, but think about the process from the time the particular 'to-be-expressed' thing is determined. For example, you wish to identify, or to convey a message regarding, a thing that has four legs, a tail, fur, and barks. We will call this the pre-verbal concept.

Levels of Semantic Representation: Conceptual and Lexical?

One of the areas which has received the most attention recently is the nature and levels of representation of semantic (meaning) information for word production. Briefly put, the central question is whether there is a distinct lexical-semantic level of representation over and above non-verbal/pre-verbal conceptual representations.

To my mind one of the problems with this debate is a real terminological confusion— different terms being used to mean the same thing, and the same terms being used to mean different things (a point also made by Bierwisch & Schreuder, 1992, p. 31, footnote 4). Table 12.2 lists some of the terms used and it is clear that 'semantics' and 'concepts' are both used to refer to either lexically-specific aspects of meaning, or more general pre-verbal aspects of knowledge. Thus, in an attempt to avoid further confusion, whenever I refer to lexically specific aspects of meaning I shall call this 'lexical semantics' and only use 'conceptual semantics' (or pre-verbal concepts) to refer to pre-linguistic meaning.

Table 12.2

Examples of Differing Use of Terminology when Referring to the Representation of Meaning.

Term	Author	Rererent
Cognitive system	Morton (1985) Morton & Patterson (1980)	Comprises 'semantic' information, but also a parser and more general 'linguistic processor.'
Conceptual structure	Bierwisch & Schreuder (1992)	Representational system of the pre-verbal message structure; language independent (mostly); pre-verbal; based on principles and information that account for all sorts of factual knowledge or belief that are clearly not part of linguistic knowledge.
Conceptual network/level; (lexical) concepts	Levelt et al. (1999a)	". . . concepts for which there exist words in the target language" p. 8
Conceptual representation/ Semantic layer	Dell et al. (1997)	"LEXICAL knowledge is embedded in a network of three layers. . . . The semantic layer contains units that represent the concept of the pictured object" p. 805 (i.e.. refers to LEXICAL-semantics).
Semantic system	Ellis & Young (1988)	". . . some form of conceptual representation which is presumably similar to that built up by intelligent non-verbal animals like chimpanzees."
Semantic system (amodal)	Hillis et al. (1990)	". . . a modality-independent semantic representation (a list of predicates) consisting of a set of functional, perceptual, and other abstract properties that jointly constitute the meaning of the term" p. xx (i.e., *Probably* LEXICAL-semantic).
Semantic form	Bierwisch & Schreuder (1992)	part of the knowledge of a given language — ". . . lexical meaning determining the range of conceptual configurations to which lexical items and their combinations might correspond" p. xx
Semantic memory	Kintsch (1980)	". . . is our whole-world knowledge—including what we know about robins, $7 \times 4 = 28$, what to do in a restaurant, and the history of the civil war" (p. 596). ". . . word meanings are an important part of this general knowledge store, but I shall argue that attempts to equate semantic memory with word meanings only . . . are doomed to failure" (p. 596).
Semantic lexicon	Butterworth (1989)	". . . a transcoding device that takes as input a semantic code and delivers as output a phonological address" p. 110.
Lemma	Levelt (1989)	". . . a lexical item's lemma information consists of the conceptual specifications for its use (including pragmatic and stylistic conditions) and various kinds of (morpho-) syntactic properties" (p. 233).
Lemma	Dell et al. (1997)	". . . associated with semantic and grammatical information" p. 804.
Lemma	Levelt et al. (1999)	"represents the item's syntax" p. 66.

Why distinguish between lexical and conceptual semantics? Bierwisch and Schreuder (1992) argue that a systematic distinction between linguistic and extralinguistic determinants of meaning must be made. Conceptual semantics is language independent, and prelinguistic. (Lexical-)semantic form is determined by linguistic knowledge. They suggest that conceptual structure combines the conditions specified by lexical-semantics with information from different domains of encyclopedic background knowledge, contextual information and situational conditions. One could also conceive of perceptual attributes also being aspects of conceptual structure. The conceptual representations for a message are richer than their eventual linguistic expression (as evidenced by the fact that many utterances are ambiguous out of context). Moreover, Bierwisch and Schreuder argue that conceptual representations do not usually exhibit the partitioning required to map on to individual lexical items. That is to say, not all concepts have a single word to express them (and what can be expressed by a single word in one language need not be in another). For example, if I want to talk about a male duck or male swan, I can find single words to express those concepts (drake, cob); if, however, the topic of conversation is a male crow then there is no single lexical item and this (equivalent) concept has to be expressed using two words.

How do Current Theories of Spoken Word Production Deal with the Distinction Between Lexical and Conceptual Semantics?

The theories described by Dell (1986, 1989; Dell et al., 1997) and Levelt (Levelt et al., 1999a) take a similar approach—the starting point of 'serious' modelling is at the lexical-semantic level. In other words, they have nothing to say about nonlinguistic or preverbal meaning. This may be a sensible restriction on the scope of these theories—it moves 'outside' the theory problems to do with how a speaker decides to describe an event (or even an object). In other words, what determines whether someone calls a dog—"a dog," "Fido," "an animal," "you ugly beast," "sweetie," or "he," all of which might be appropriate in differing contexts. Restricting semantics in this way also avoids many of the decisions regarding which aspects of our knowledge about items are included in our conceptual knowledge, and how they might be represented (e.g., perceptual information, encyclopedic knowledge, episodic memories regarding items). Clearly, there are also issues regarding duplication of information across the two levels—how much of what must be available as preverbal concepts is also represented at the lexical-semantic level? A further possibility is that lexical-semantic information is simply a part of what is available to the conceptual system and no dissociation between the two is necessary (see Hillis, this volume, for further discussion of some of these issues).

Figures 12.1 panels a and b are representations of the two competing possibilities—one where conceptual semantics maps directly onto phonological form for output and the other where conceptual semantics addresses lexical semantics which then maps onto phonological form. The speech-production element of Morton's (1970, 1985) logogen model is of the type shown in Figure 12.1a. Preverbal conceptual–semantic representations directly address the stored phonological form of lexical items with no intervening stages. This theory has been particularly influential in cognitive neuropsychology with many case descriptions localizing deficits in word production using variants of this theory (e.g., Franklin, Howard, & Patterson, 1995; Kay & Ellis, 1987). Figure 12.1b represents the general structure of the theory described by Butterworth (1989, 1992).[2] Figure 12.1c represents a variant of 12.1b where an additional level intervenes between the lexical semantic level and phonological levels.[3] Theories of the type represented by Figure 12.1b and 12.1c frequently assume, but do not implement (or specify in any detail), a preverbal conceptual level. Indeed, it is not always easy to match Figures 12.1b and c to particular theories as often researchers do not make their assumptions explicit, despite the importance of this issue.

[2]This is also the architecture that Butterworth and many other authors (myself included) have attributed to Levelt (1989).

[3]Levelt et al. (1999a) and Dell et al. (1997) both refer to this level as a lemma level. However, in the model of Dell et al. (1997) the pre-phonological level directly addresses phoneme nodes, in contrast, the corresponding level of Levelt et al.'s model addresses phonological form nodes which, in turn, address phonemes. Thus, it is possible that a sketch of the architecture of Levelt et al.'s model could include two levels of phonology.

[handwritten: assume a preverbal conceptual level]

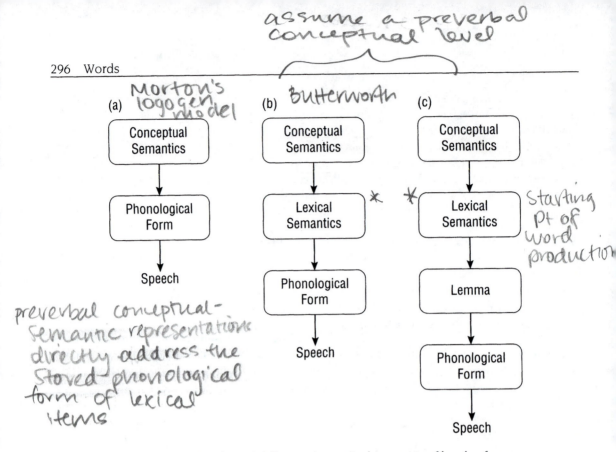

[handwritten annotations on figure: "Morton's logogen model" over (a); "Butterworth" over (b); "Starting Pt of word production" to the right of (c); "preverbal conceptual-semantic representations directly address the stored phonological form of lexical items" at lower left]

Figure 12.1: Sketches of different theoretical accounts of levels of processing in word production.

Cognitive Neuropsychology and the Lexical-Semantic Debate

What can neuropsychological data contribute to the debate regarding the distinction between lexical and conceptual semantics? Most case reports within the cognitive neuropsychological framework initially used a 'two-step' model such as that in Figure 12.1a.[4] The limitations of this model are clear in at least two ways:

First, aphasic individuals frequently have severe semantic deficits. These semantic impairments are manifested in difficulties in comprehending and producing words in all modalities. For example, errors will be made when given a word-to-picture matching task where one word has to be matched to an appropriate picture with semantically-related items as distractors. Thus, given the spoken word "finger" and pictures of a finger (the target), an ear (a semantically-related distractor), and a house (an unrelated distractor), an individual with a semantic impairment might point to the picture of an ear (but only if the semantic impairment is very severe are they likely to point to the semantically-unrelated distractor, the picture of the house). Moreover, they will also make similar errors when given a written word to match to a choice of pictures, or judge the meaning of two written or spoken words. For example, Nickels (1992) describes a man with a marked aphasia, TC, who made semantic errors in all language modalities, including in comprehension. For example, when asked to judge whether two words had similar meanings (e.g., boat ship; scheme plan; vs. boat marriage; pardon plan),[5] TC scored 80% correct when the words were written down and 60% when they were spoken (both scores are well below the level achieved by nonaphasic subjects).

---

[4]The level of preverbal concepts was usually described as the 'semantic system'. However, it has subsequently become clear that some authors were using this to refer to 'lexical-semantics' rather than more general conceptual representations, this leads to some confusion in the literature.

[5]The version of this test used with TC was an early version by Coltheart (unpublished) of the synonym judgements test incorporated into PALPA (Kay, Lesser, & Coltheart, 1992).

A semantic impairment will also lead to semantically-related errors in picture naming and spontaneous speech and writing. For example, TC correctly named only 8% of 140 pictures of common objects with 37% of his responses semantically related to the targets. For instance, he named a picture of bread as 'butter,' and said 'hammer' for a picture of a saw. Although written picture naming was far superior to spoken naming (49% correct) he still produced many semantic errors (11% of responses) such as 'otter' for a picture of a seal, and 'hair' for a picture of a brush.

However, despite often profound semantic impairments, these individuals will continue to use objects appropriately (i.e., show no symptoms of agnosia). Thus, even if they make errors such as confusing 'knife' and 'fork' in comprehension and naming, semantically-impaired aphasics will still cut with the knife and not with the fork. In addition they often continue to function well in situations where language is not involved. TC, for example, successfully returned to managing his wholesale and retail fishmonger business, organize his busy social life, and navigate around Britain driving to these functions. A clinical psychologist's assessment was that his perceptual, visuo-spatial, nonverbal reasoning skills and memory (when assessed non-verbally) were intact. These data suggest that nonlinguistic reasoning and conceptual knowledge can remain intact despite profound difficulties with linguistic tasks involving semantic access.

The fact that TC makes errors in spoken and written word comprehension and production would appear to suggest that he has a deficit at the level of semantics. However, in a theory such as that shown in Figure 1a, a semantic deficit affects both linguistic and nonlinguistic knowledge. Thus, this would predict that TC should be equally impaired on semantic tests that do not involve language. TC was therefore given a test of picture comprehension—the Pyramids and Palm Trees test (Howard & Patterson, 1992). This assessment involves the presentation of a stimulus item which has to be related to one of two pictures which are coordinates. For example, the stimulus PYRAMID has to be associated with a picture of a palm tree, rather than the distractor picture—a pine tree, and the stimulus STETHOSCOPE has to be associated with a heart rather than a tongue. It is argued that in order to perform accurately on this task, relatively complete semantic information must be retrieved about the stimuli. TC performed within normal limits on the version of this task where the stimulus was a picture (98% correct). However, when the stimulus picture is replaced with a word he did significantly worse (1 spoken word–2 pictures, 75%; 1 written word–2 pictures, 90%). Thus it appears that TC has a semantic impairment confined to linguistic material (see also Chertkow, Bub, Deaudon, & Whitehead, 1997).

In order to explain this pattern of performance on a model with just a single semantic level, like that shown in Figure 12.1a, separate impairments are necessary to all modalities of linguistic input and output from the conceptual level (see Figure 12.2a). While this pattern is possible, on the grounds of parsimony a single impairment to a level of processing that mediates all forms of language comprehension and production would seem preferable (see Figure 12.2b; i.e., a lexical-semantic impairment). Thus, neuropsychological and linguistic and psycholinguistic data from nonimpaired subjects converge on the need for some kind of lexical-semantic level of processing, with the rejection of the type of model sketched in Figure 12.1a.

From Lexical Semantics to Phonological Form

For Dell and Levelt and their colleagues (Dell et all, 1997; Levelt et al, 1999a), the starting point of word production is the activation (by a preverbal concept) of the lexical-semantic level. Following activation at this level, there is activation of a lexical level node associated with that meaning. Once again, there are differences between theories in the nature of this lexical level representation and the terminology associated with it. In some theories lexical-semantics directly addresses phonological form (Figure 12.1b; e.g., Butterworth, 1989, 1992), while in

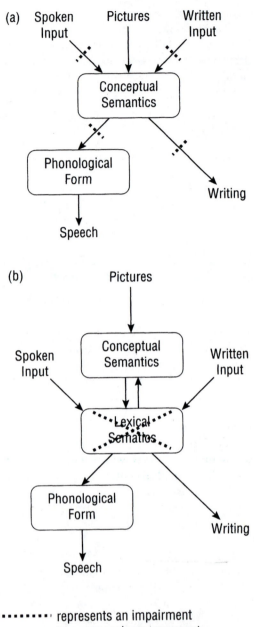

Figure 12.2: Loci of impairment necessary to account for selective preservation on non-linguistic semantic tasks within two different theories of semantic processing.

········· represents an impairment to a processing component

others there is an intervening lexical level (Figure 12.1c). This level is referred to as the lemma level by Levelt et al. (1999a). The lemma then addresses the phonological form, which is represented directly as activation of a sequence of phonemes by Dell et al. (1997) and as a single activated node for Levelt et al. (1999a).

A demonstration of the limitations of a theory where lexical-semantics directly accesses phonology (Figure 12.1b) becomes clear in the analysis of levels of breakdown in aphasic word production. Many aphasics have now been described who are argued to have no impairments to either semantic or phonological representations (and no difficulty in processes subsequent to the retrieval of phonological forms). Thus, the source of their naming deficit has necessarily been attributed to a deficit 'between semantics and phonology.' While there is no problem with this per se, what is more troubling is the wide variety of symptomatology that has been associated with this level of deficit. Thus, for example, RGB and HW (Caramazza & Hillis, 1990) produce semantic errors; EST (Kay & Ellis, 1987) produces phonological, semantic, and circumlocutory errors; RD (Ellis, Miller, & Sin, 1983) produces phonologically-related nonword errors; RB (Blanken, 1990) produces phonologically-related real word errors (formal paraphasias). All of these patients have been argued to have deficits in accessing (intact) phonological representations from an intact semantic representation (see Nickels, 1997, for further discussion). It is not at all clear that any current theory could produce all of these patterns of deficit from a single level of breakdown. One solution is that more than a single level of processing is involved in the access of phonological representations from conceptual semantic representations. Of course the question we are addressing is quite how many levels and what are their properties?

The Representation of Lexical Syntax: What are Lemmas?

There has recently been much debate regarding the need for a lemma level of representation and what the properties of such a level might be (see, e.g., Caramazza, 1997). Although introduced by Kempen and Huijbers (1983), Levelt (1989) was instrumental in bringing the term lemma into wider use. At this point Levelt defined the lemma as the meaning and syntax of a lexical entry, specifically "a lexical item's lemma information contains the lexical item's meaning or sense, i.e. the concept that goes with the word" (p. 11) and "a lemma's syntactic information specifies the item's syntactic category, its assignment of grammatical functions and a set of diacritic feature variables or parameters" (p. 190). Levelt specifies that "a lemma will be activated when its meaning matches part of the preverbal message" (p. 11).

However, since then, the defining characteristics of the lemma have changed, and in his most recent work (Levelt, 1999; Levelt et al., 1999a), Levelt equates the lemma with the syntactic word and no longer gives it a semantic function. This change has unfortunately confused still further the already complex terminology.

The 'new lemma' is a node which 'points' to syntactic properties (e.g., grammatical class, grammatical gender) and diacritics (for tense, number etc.) which can be set according to the message to be expressed. Each lemma receives activation directly from the lexical-concept which it expresses (i.e., there is a one-to-one relationship between lexical concept nodes and lemma nodes).[6] It is the 'new lemma' that we are concerned with here: that is, how does the representation and retrieval of lexical syntax relate to other aspects of word production? The issue is the relationship between the access of syntactic and phonological information. It is widely argued that syntactic information becomes available early in the lexical retrieval process to allow planning of the grammatical structure of an utterance (e.g., Garrett, 1984; Levelt, 1989), however, it is of much debate whether syntactic information must obligatorily be retrieved before word form retrieval can take place.

There are three basic accounts we will be considering (sketched in Figures 12.3 panel a and b and Figure 12.4). The first two accounts (12.3a and 12.3b) are derived from theories that have the same basic structure that was shown in Figure 12.1c. That is, a lemma-mediation architecture where a lemma level intervenes between lexical semantics and phonological form.

The lemma-mediation account (Figure 12.1c) can vary in two ways. First, it can differ in terms of whether there is one modality neutral lemma, or modality specific lemmas one for each modality of input or output. The modality neutral lemma account necessitates only one

---

[6]Levelt et al. (1999b) make explicit the relationship between the "old lemma" (Levelt, 1989) and the new lemma (Levelt et al., 1999a). In the new architecture "one node (plus its connectivity in the conceptual stratum of the network), now called the "lexical concept," represents the item's semantics. The other node (plus its connectivity in the syntactic stratum), now called "lemma," represents the item's syntax. Together, they precisely cover the "old" lemma" (Levelt et al., 1999b, p. 66).

Lemma-mediation architecture

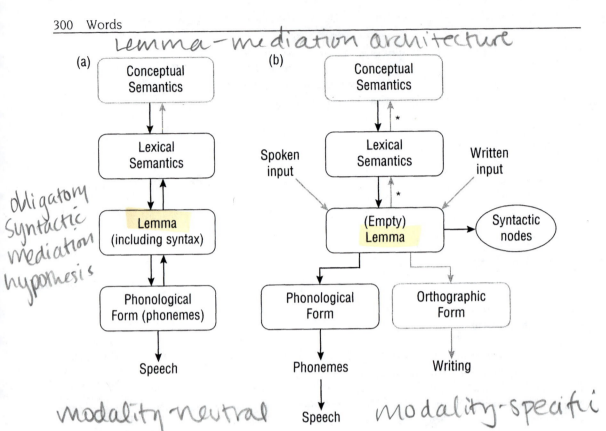

obligatory syntactic mediation hypothesis

modality neutral   *modality-specific*

Figure 12.3: Two different 'Lemma mediation' accounts of word production: (a) based on Dell et al. (1997). Note that components in gray are not implemented by Dell et al. (b) based on Levelt et al. (1999a). Note that components in gray are not implemented in Levelt et al. The links marked with * are also not implemented in the theory but would be required for comprehension. They are not intended to represent interaction within the model.

lemma that is accessed by spoken or written input (for comprehension) and accesses phonological and orthographic forms for output. The modality-specific account requires separate lemma systems, thus there will be an auditory input lemma system which accesses lexical semantics for comprehension given auditory stimuli, a phonological output lemma system which accesses phonological form for speech production; an orthographic input lemma system and an orthographic output lemma system. Levelt et al. (1999) assume that "all production lemmas are perceptual lemmas; the perceptual and production networks coincide from the lemma level upwards" (p. 7). Thus, they are advocating the modality-neutral lemma account, at least for speech comprehension and production. Although they do not address the issue of whether there are independent orthographic and phonological lemmas, we will assume that these too are shared. We will not consider the modality-specific lemma account further but instead further detail the modality neutral lemma mediation account (Figures 12.3a and 12.3b).

The second distinction within this lemma-mediation account is whether access of lexical syntax is obligatorily required before access of phonological form can take place. Dell et al.'s (1997) theory incorporates lemma level nodes which specify syntactic information (Figure 12.3a). These nodes mediate between lexical semantics and phonological form and therefore syntactic activation must occur prior to activation of the phonological form. This is the obligatory syntactic mediation hypothesis. Levelt et al.'s (1999) theory is sketched in Figure 12.3b.

This theory has 'empty' lemma nodes which point to both syntactic and phonological (and presumably orthographic) information. Roelofs, Meyer, and Levelt (1998) make the distinction

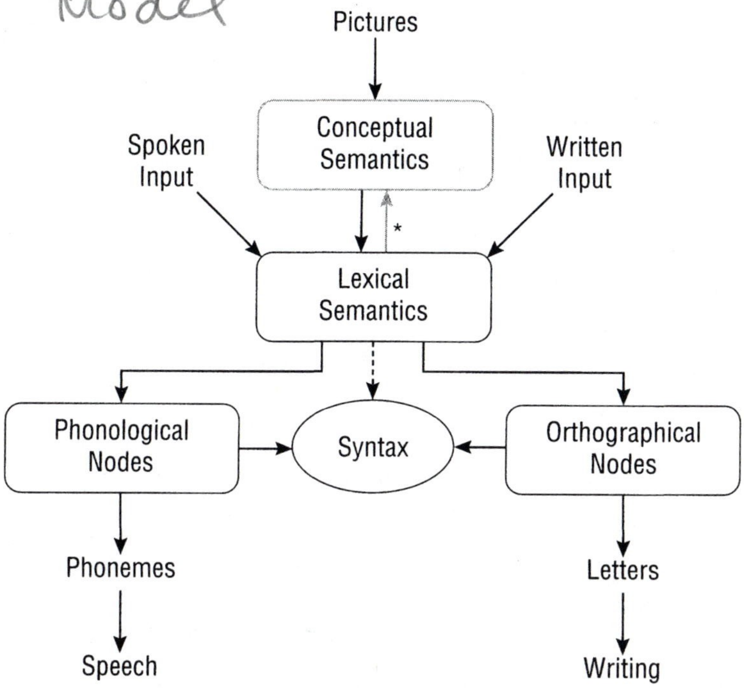

Independent Network
Model

Figure 12.4: The 'Independent network' account of word production, adapted from Caramazza (1997). Note that components in gray are not implemented by Caramazza. The links marked with * are also not implemented in the theory but would be required for comprehension. They are not intended to represent interaction within the model.

between activation and selection of nodes explicit; while selection of the lemma node is a prerequisite for the selection of gender (and other syntactic information) and phonological form, activated gender information is only selected if required.[7] Thus in this account phonological form may be retrieved without access of lexical-syntax.

The final account, shown in Figure 12.4, is derived from Figure 12.1b has no mediating lemma level. This approach where lexical semantic nodes directly address modality specific orthographic and phonological nodes has been used by many authors in their description of aphasic data (e.g., Caramazza & Hillis, 1990; Howard & Franklin, 1988; Nickels, 1997).[8] The specific architecture depicted in Figure 12.4 is that proposed by Caramazza (1997). In this "independent network model," Caramazza suggests that syntactic information is accessed via modality-specific nodes (orthographic nodes and phonological nodes). Priming of syntactic nodes can occur direct from lexical-semantics, but activation from semantics is insufficient for access of these nodes. This model therefore predicts that syntactic information can only be accessed subsequent to the activation of phonological or orthographic nodes (which in turn activate the phonemes or letters). Caramazza's paper is an excellent example of how data from

---

[7]To quote "our model does *not* assume that selection of form information depends on the selection of gender. Rather, the selection of a lemma node is a prerequisite for the selection of gender as well as form information" (Roelofs et al., 1998, p. 224). This is contrary to the claim made by Caramazza and colleagues regarding the assumptions of Levelt et al.'s theory.

[8]Although what these orthographic and phonological nodes comprise varies from representations of the orthographic and phonological form of the word (e.g., Nickels, 1997) to something more akin to modality-specific lemmas (e.g., Caramazza, 1997).

aphasic and nonaphasic subjects can converge in the development of theoretical models. Not only does he cite studies involving problems in accessing the phonological form of a word in anomia but also in the tip-of-the-tongue (TOT) state in normal subjects, as detailed below.

Dissociating these Accounts: What is the Relationship Between the Retrieval of Lexical–Syntax and Phonological (or Orthographic) Form?

Picture Word Interference Studies.   Levelt et al. (1999a) discuss a series of gender priming experiments by Schriefers (1993). Dutch participants were required to describe pictures of colored objects using phrases (e.g., 'de groene tafel,' the green table; 'het groene huis,' the green house). In Dutch which determiner is appropriate (de or het) is established by the grammatical gender of the noun (neuter 'het' with neuter 'huis'; non-neuter 'de' with non-neuter 'tafel'). The object pictures are presented with superimposed written distractor words. These are either words that share the grammatical gender of the object or words that have a conflicting gender. For example, the picture of a green house, for the neuter target 'huis,' would be superimposed either with a congruent neuter distractor such as 'hemd' (shirt, neuter) or a conflicting distractor such as muis (mouse; non-neuter). Schriefers (1993) found that when the gender of target and distractor were the same, participants were faster to name the pictures, than when the genders conflicted. This is the gender priming effect, which can be explained by assuming (within Levelt et al.'s theory) that the gender-congruent distractor boosts the level of activation of the gender node, speeding the selection process. However, crucial for the discussion here is a follow-up study by Jescheniak (1994; cited in Levelt et al., 1999a). In this study participants only had to produce a bare noun, and not a determiner (e.g. given a picture of a green house they only had to say 'huis'). Under these conditions there was no effect of whether the distractor word was gender congruent or not. In other words, there was *no* gender priming effect. Levelt et al suggest that when subjects are required to produce "bare" nouns (without articles or adjectives requiring agreement) that the gender nodes (although activated) are not necessarily selected. Thus, the boost of activation to the gender node gives no advantage when naming unless the utterance marks gender (as is the case when a determiner is produced). Of course, phonological form is retrieved under both conditions. This suggests that retrieval of phonological form can be to some extent independent of retrieval of lexical-syntax.

TOT States in Non-Impaired Subjects.   The tip-of-the-tongue (TOT) state refers to that experience of knowing that we 'know' the word we are failing to retrieve. We know what the word means and may even have some general idea regarding how it sounds (e.g., how long it is, what the first sound might be, other words that sound like it) but yet are unable to say it. A widely accepted account of the TOT state is that it reflects a failure to retrieve phonological information having achieved lexical-semantic or lemma access (Butterworth, 1989; Garrett, 1984; Levelt, 1989). In the TOT state, subjects can sometimes report partial information regarding the sounds of the word, and metrical structure (number of syllables and position of stress). More recently the availability of syntactic information (usually grammatical gender) has been investigated in TOT (e.g., Caramazza & Miozzo, 1997; Miozzo & Caramazza, 1997; Vigliocco, Antonini, & Garrett, 1997; Vigliocco et al, 1999). A TOT state is induced in subjects by providing a definition (and/or a picture) of an uncommon word (e.g., "ancient Egyptian writing system"–hieroglyphic; from Vigliocco et al, 1999). If participants are unable to name the word, they are required to give information regarding (usually) the number of syllables, initial sound/letter, final sound/letter, and grammatical gender (the studies cited were performed in Italian). They are then provided with the target and asked to verify if this was the word they were searching for (to establish if they were in a true TOT state or not). These studies have established that participants in TOT states can retrieve both grammatical (gender) and phonological (e.g., initial phoneme) information at better than chance rates (Caramazza & Miozzo, 1997; Miozzo & Caramazza, 1997; Vigliocco et al., 1997). However, retrieval of one type of information is not dependent on successful retrieval of the other. Caramazza and Miozzo (1997) found no significant correlation between correct retrieval of the gender of the target and of the initial phoneme. These results suggest that the obligatory syntactic mediation model (Figure 12.3a) is not viable but they are compatible with either of the models suggested by Caramazza or Levelt and colleagues (Figure 12.3b and Figure 12.4).

Evidence from Aphasia.   Badecker, Miozzo, and Zanuttini (1995) provide evidence suggesting the independence of grammatical and phonological access from a man with aphasia, Dante (for a similar report see Henaff Gonon, Bruckert, & Michel, 1989). Dante had good comprehension of both written and spoken words but poor naming. When unable to name a picture, Dante could give no phonological or orthographic information regarding the target. Even in a forced-choice task where he had to select the correct length of the word, the first letter, last letter, or a rhyming word, he performed at chance. However, he was extremely good at selecting the correct gender of the target (97.7% correct). Vigliocco et al. (1999) examined retrieval of a different kind of grammatical information in an aphasic individual (MS)—whether nouns are 'mass nouns' (e.g., sugar, broccoli, money) or 'count nouns' (e.g., pencil, carrot, brush). This distinction affects the choice of of phrasal frames for the noun phrase. This includes the selection of the correct quantifier (e.g., less vs. fewer) or determiner (some vs. a). They found that MS was correctly able to report whether a word he could not retrieve was a count or a mass noun. However, like the nonimpaired subjects in a TOT state, there was no relationship between the retrieval of syntactic (mass/count) and phonological information. MS was equally likely to retrieve some phonological information when he had failed to retrieve the grammatical information as when he had successfully retrieved it.

In conclusion, at present there is good data (neuropsychological data; and experimental and speech error data from nonimpaired subjects) to suggest that retrieval of syntactic and form information are retrieved independently, and therefore that there is a distinct (unimodality) lexical-semantic level and a (phonological and orthographic) form level. What, to my mind at least, remains to be determined is whether an additional modality neutral lemma level is required, and the precise 'locus' of grammatical information within the theoretical architecture. It seems that more evidence is required to clearly discriminate between the theories suggested by Levelt and colleagues and Caramazza (see Roelofs et al., 1998 and a reply by Caramazza & Miozzo, 1998, for a direct discussion of the two approaches).

THE TIME COURSE OF LEXICAL ACCESS

So far we have concentrated on the levels of processing in lexical access, however, authors who agree on the levels of processing may have divergent views on the nature of the connections and the way activation spreads between these levels (compare for example, Dell et al., 1997 and Levelt et al., 1999a). Two distinctions should be made:

1. Direction of flow of activation: Theories may allow activation to only spread in one direction (i.e., 'feed-forward' activation) or they may allow feedback from a 'later' to an 'earlier' level (i.e., 'interactive activation').
2. Continuity of flow of activation: Theories may allow activation to flow continuously ("cascade") from one level of processing to another or they may require processing at one level to be completed before activation at a subsequent level can occur (noncascaded, strictly discontinuous, and serial).

Proposals and Predictions

Although the flow of activation can be differentiated in the two ways described above, the two major speech production theories differ in both direction and continuity.

Dell

Dell et al. (1997) describe a computational model where activation cascades between levels and is interactive (see Figure 12.5). When the semantic features corresponding to a stimulus are activated at the lexical semantic level, each semantic feature then, in turn, activates every lexical (lemma) node to which it is connected. Thus for example, in one of the simulations reported, the lexical level contains the lemmas for CAT, DOG, RAT, MAT, LOG, and FOG. At the lexical-semantic level, CAT, DOG, and RAT share three of their ten features. Thus, when the semantic features corresponding to CAT are activated, CAT will become activated at the lexical level but so will DOG and RAT (to a lesser extent). On the next time step, the active nodes at the lexical level will activate all the nodes to which they are connected, this includes both 'forward' connections to phoneme nodes and 'backward' connections (interaction) to semantic feature nodes. Thus, CAT will 'refresh' the activation of its semantic features (activation gradually decays away with time), along with RAT and DOG also (partially) activating the complete set of their semantic features. Additionally, CAT activates /k/ /æ/ /t/ at the phoneme level, and dog and rat activate /d/ /ɒ/ /g/ and /r/ and /æ/ /t/ (but to a lesser extent as the lexical nodes for *dog* and *rat* were less active than for *cat*). On the next time step, each active node once again sends activation to those which it is connected. Thus, phoneme nodes will feed back to all those to which they connect—leading to the partial activation of both items phonologically related to the target (MAT) and those unrelated to the target but phonologically related to a semantic neighbor of the target (LOG and FOG). After a set number of time steps, the most active node at the lexical level is 'selected' for production. This will usually be the target. The key feature of this simulation is that many nontarget items that are semantically and/or phonologically related to the target will also be activated, because of the feedback and the spread of activation between levels.

Levelt

In contrast the theory of Levelt et al. (1999a) proposes strict seriality with no interaction or

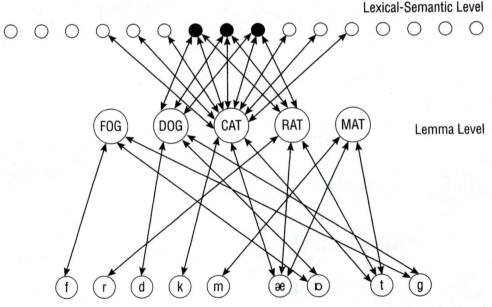

Figure 12.5: Interactive activation model of word production, adapted from Dell et al. (1997).

cascading of activation. This is implemented in a computational model WEAVER++. In this feed-forward model, an active lexical-semantic node activates its corresponding lemma node. As the lexical-semantic node will also have partially activated all those related nodes (such as nodes for superordinates, for example, DOG will activate the nodes ANIMAL and BARK), these will also activate their lemma nodes. The most active node at the lemma level is selected and it is only then that any activation occurs at the phonological level. Only the phonological form corresponding to the selected lemma becomes active, there is no activation of the phonological forms of semantically related items. The nodes of the form level are linked to the nodes for individual phonemes.

In summary, the nature of the spread of activation through a computatonal model is reflected in differences in the timing of activation of nodes at the various levels of processing. Thus, a strictly serial model like that of Levelt et al. (1999a) predicts no activation of phonology until selection has taken place at a lemma level (i.e., only the selected item becomes active at a phonological level). In contrast a model with cascading activation predicts early phonological activation of both the target and its semantic distractors (immediately semantic activation has occurred this activation cascades to the lexical and then phonological level) and, with interaction, semantic activation will persist due to feedback from the phonological level.

Dissociating the Accounts

Evidence from Unimpaired Subjects

Word-Picture Interference.   A direct discussion of the time course of the spread of activation can be found in a series of papers which use a picture-word interference paradigm (e.g., Levelt et al., 1991a; Peterson & Savoy, 1998; Schriefers, Meyer, & Levelt, 1990). As described above, this task requires participants to name pictured objects in order to examine the effects on reaction time of interfering stimuli of different types. These interfering stimuli can be words that are either semantically related or phonologically/orthographically related to the targets (e.g., for the target BED either CHAIR or BET could be presented). These words may be written superimposed on the stimulus picture or presented auditorily. They can be presented at different times relative to the presentation of the target picture (stimulus–onset asynchronies; SOAs). Schriefers et al. (1990) found that when the interfering word was presented before the picture, only semantically-related words had any effect. In other words participants were slower to name the pictures when they had already heard a semantically related word, than they were if they heard a phonologically related word or no interfering word was presented. However, when the interfering word was presented after the picture, there was no effect of semantically related words but phonologically related words speeded picture naming (relative to an unrelated word or no word). These experiments suggest that there is an early period of semantic activation when the activation of a semantically related neighbour slows selection of the target. In addition, there is a late period of purely phonological activation, when activation of shared phonemes from a phonologically related word will speed phonological processing. However, there is no evidence for any late semantic activation (for further discussion see Levelt et al., 1999a, section 5.2; & Nickels, 1997).

Levelt et al (1991a) pursue these experiments further and investigate whether items phonologically-related to semantic neighbors of the target affect reaction time (using a slightly different task—lexical decision to the interfering stimulus). For example, for a target word GOAT, does SHEET (which is phonologically-related to the semantically-related distractor SHEEP) differ from an unrelated item in terms of its effect on speed of response. Levelt et al. (1991a) found no difference. Thus they argue that there is no evidence for phonological activation of items semantically related to the target (but see Peterson & Savoy, 1998, and the response of Levelt et al., 1999a).

Levelt et al (1991a) suggest that the results of these experiments are incompatible with the interactive activation model of Dell (1989) but consistent with a discrete feedforward model. However, Dell and O'Seaghda demonstrated that their interactive activation model could also simulate the results (see also Harley, 1993, and Levelt et al., 1991b, for a response). They argue that by employing an active selection process at each level (addition of further activation to the most highly activated unit), the interactive model exhibits stage-like properties. Furthermore, they suggest that this simulation is globally modular with interaction largely occurring between adjacent levels (because of the relative levels of the decay and spreading rate parameters). Thus, while a highly interactive model may have difficulty accounting for these data, simulation of these results can be achieved by restricting the effects of the interaction.

Lexicality Bias and Mixed Error Effects.   In discussion of speech errors, two factors have been raised in support of interaction in lexical access for speech production: (a) the lexicality bias and (b) the occurrence of errors which are both semantically and phonologically related to their targets (mixed errors).

Lexicality Bias. When an error is made on one or more sounds in a word, the resulting sequence of sounds can be either a word or a nonword. For example: If the initial sound of the word *paper* is substituted with another sound, the outcome could be a word such as *caper*, or a nonword like *faper*. It is clear that random substitution of phonemes results in words simply by chance. A word is more likely to occur if a phoneme is substituted in a short word (e.g., *cat*) than a long one (e.g., *caterpillar*). However, some authors claim that speech sound errors result in words more often than would be expected by chance alone—that there is a lexicality bias. Within a model such as that of Dell et al. (1997) this lexicality bias is a natural consequence of the interaction between the phoneme and lexical levels. While patterns of phonemes that correspond to nonwords can become active, those patterns that correspond to nodes at the lexical level (words) will receive more 'support' in terms of continuing activation from the lexical level. That is, phonemes that comprise words will be more highly activated than phonemes that do not. However, Levelt et al. (1999a) argued that this account of lexical bias fails to account for some of the experimental data. For example, Baars, Motley, and Mackay (1975) demonstrated that when all the targets and fillers in an error elicitation experiment are nonwords, lexical bias does not occur. This 'context' effect cannot be reproduced in the model of Dell et al. (1997) as it stands.

Mixed Errors. Some semantically-related words are also phonologically-related (e.g., *shirt, skirt; snake, snail*). It follows that by chance some semantically related errors will also be phonologically related. However, as with lexical bias, some authors argue that these mixed (semantically and phonologically related) errors are found at greater-than-chance rates. Once again, these effects occur as a natural consequence of interaction within a model of word production such as that of Dell et al. (1997). We have already discussed how within this theory the cascading of interaction from lexical-semantics to lemmas to phonemes leads to activation of the phonology of semantically related words. Under normal circumstances it is the target lemma/lexical node that is the most highly active. However, items semantically related to the target will also be active. If any of these semantically-related items are also phonologically related to the target (e.g., for the target CAT, RAT) then these will receive more feedback of activation from the phoneme level (because of the phonemes shared with the target), than those nodes for words that do not share phonemes. If an error occurs then the most likely node to be selected will be the next most highly active node after the target—which will be the node of a phonologically and semantically related item. Hence a mixed error will result.

Neither of these effects is beyond dispute because, for instance, of potential listener bias or difficulty determining the appropriate calculation of chance. However, most authors do now accept that errors tend to be both words and to bear a mixed semantic and phonological relationship to their targets at rates greater than chance. While interactive models account naturally for these effects, they do not 'fall out' of discrete feedforward accounts. Rather, in these models they are usually explained as reflecting the action of an editor that detects errors but is more likely to 'miss' those that are words or are both semantically and phonologically related to their targets (see for example, Baars et al., 1975; Butterworth, 1981). This editor is often equated with the speech comprehension system. As these editors have yet to be implemented computationally we shall not be considering them in detail, this is not to say that they might not play an important role in speech production (see, for example, Wheeldon & Levelt, 1995).

Evidence from Aphasic Subjects

Lexicality Bias: Formal Paraphasias.   Although some studies have failed to find evidence for a lexicality bias in the phonological errors of aphasic individuals (e.g., Nickels & Howard, 1995a), there are now single case studies of aphasics who produce relatively large numbers of real word errors that are phonologically related to their targets (Best, 1996; Blanken, 1990, 1998; Martin, Dell, Saffran, & Schwartz, 1994; N. Martin & Saffran, 1992; see also Gagnon, Schwartz, Martin, Dell, & Saffron, 1997). For example, when attempting to name a picture of a parrot MF (Best, 1996) said 'carrot,' and for a picture of a coffin he said "colin." (However, only Best, 1996, performs an appropriate analysis to demonstrate that more of these errors occur than would be expected by chance[9]).

N. Martin et al. (1994) interpreted the deficit leading to the production of these formal paraphasias as a pathologically increased rate of decay of activation within Dell's interactive activation model. As the activation level of nodes decays much faster than normal, a greater reliance on feedback occurs to refresh this activation. Hence, the 'interactive' effects of the model, such as lexicality bias and mixed errors are exaggerated. However, there are some difficulties with this account. First, Dell et al. (1997, Figure 8) clearly demonstrated that absolute rates of formal paraphasias remain below rates of (phonologically related) nonword errors (even if above chance rates of occurrence) however the model is 'lesioned' (whether by increasing decay or decreasing connection strength, and whatever the severity level). Yet, several of the published patients produce more formal paraphasias than nonwords. For example, MF (Best, 1996) produces 11% formal paraphasias compared to 7% nonwords, and RB (Blanken, 1990) produces 23% and 4% respectively. Indeed, some of the patients studied by Gagnon et al. (1997) also produce higher proportions of formal paraphasias (e.g., VP; 83% of phonological errors were formal paraphasias). Thus, despite the claimed ability of the interactive activation model to be able to account easily for lexical bias, it can be demonstrated to be lacking when evaluated using aphasic data.

The discrete processing model of Levelt et al. (1999a) and related theories that rely on editing accounts of lexical bias are more difficult to evaluate. The editing account would seem to predict that all aphasics should show a lexical bias in their phonological errors provided they had intact editors. Thus, accounting for the data presented by Blanken (1990, 1998), Martin and colleagues (N. Martin et al., 1994; N. Martin & Saffran, 1992) and Best (1996) appears straightforward. However, more problematic is data from analyses performed by Nickels and Howard (1995a). None of the 15 aphasics they studied showed lexical bias in their phonological errors, despite at least some individuals having available (intact) all of the component processes for a comprehension-based monitor (and the 'output-to-input' links needed to access this).

---

[9]An argument made by Martin and Saffran (amongst others) for these errors being the result of a lexical process is that they tend to share grammatical category with their targets. However, Kelly (1999) developed a connectionist model that learned to classify nouns and verbs solely on their phonological similarity—the model achieved 75% success in classifying novel cases. Thus, Kelly argues that targets and errors (in formal paraphasias or malapropisms) will be grammatically similar by virtue of their phonological similarity.

Mixed Errors.   Martin et al. (1996) examine the prevalence of mixed (phonologically and semantically related) errors in picture naming using responses from both nonaphasic elderly subjects and aphasics. They argued that mixed (semantic and phonologically related) errors occur at rates greater than expected by chance for both groups of speakers. Dell et al. (1997) also suggested that every one of their aphasics produced more mixed errors than would be expected by chance (Dell et al.'s, Table 8, p. 820). Yet, Best (1996) demonstrated that MF did not differ from chance in his rate of production of mixed errors even though he produces formal paraphasias at greater than chance rates. Thus, although MF showed one effect, the lexicality bias, that is consistent with increased emphasis on interaction (that occurs, for example, with a decay lesion), he failed to show the mixed errors that should also occur (Dell et al. 1997, Figure 10).[10]

Simulating Aphasic Performance: Comparing Different Processing Assumptions.   The ability of discrete and interactive accounts of word production to account for patterns of breakdown in aphasic naming is examined in greater detail by Rapp and Goldrick (2000). They analyzed the semantic and mixed errors made by aphasic individuals with different patterns of language breakdown. PW and KE only produced semantic errors, they did not make phonological errors. KE produced semantic errors in all modalities of comprehension and production. However, PW produced semantic errors only in spoken naming; he had good comprehension and written naming. An analysis of the semantic errors made by each patient also showed dissociations between them: KE showed no tendency to produce mixed errors at rates greater than chance, whereas PW showed a robust mixed error effect.[11]

Rapp and Goldrick argued that in order to account for their data, a word-production model must incorporate (at least) two different mechanisms. First, one that allows activation of the phonemes associated with a semantic neighbor of the target (e.g., cascading activation), in order that mixed errors can arise at greater than chance rates. Second, a mechanism is required that provides a means by which lexical outcomes can be favored and phonological information can influence semantic errors arising from postsemantic impairments (e.g., feedback connections from a phonological level to a preceding lexical level).

Rapp and Goldrick evaluated the ability of several simulations of word production to account for the dissociations between the naming performance of KE and PW. Each simulation varied the nature of the spread of activation from a discrete feedforward model through to an interactive model with cascade and feedback between each level. The simulations clearly demonstrated that any system that allows for strong interaction across domains will have difficulty accounting for patients who produce only semantic errors, such as KE and PW. Indeed Dell et al. (1997, p. 832) acknowledge that this pattern is problematic for their model. Furthermore, the fact that KE produces semantic errors that are uninfluenced by phonology (no mixed error effect) was shown to be incompatible with a model where phonological processes influence semantic level processing, such as that of Dell et al. (1997). (As discussed above, mixed errors are a prominent feature of the lesioned versions of Dell et al.'s model.) Rapp and Goldrick note that models which incorporate feedback from a lexical to a semantic level can simulate KE's pattern if their parameters are set such that this feedback is restricted to low levels (by reducing connection strength in these links alone). However, they argue that unless there is

---

[10]Of course, if both of these error biases are the consequence of the action of an editor, one might also expect a necessary co-occurrence of the two.

[11]This mixed error effect was maintained, even when corrections were made for the fact that words within a category tend to be more phonologically similar than words across categories (sharing 17.5% vs. 14.8% of their phonology). These data contrast with those of Martin et al, (1996) who use a different method of analysis to claim that "the relationship between form and meaning of a word is largely arbitrary" (p. 272; i.e., there was no inherent tendency for semantically related words to be phonologically similar). As Rapp and Goldrick (2000) point out, the finding that phonological similarity is greater within categories than across categories is of significance for interpretations of mixed error effects in normal subjects (e.g., Martin, Gagnon, Schwartz, Dell, & Saffran, 1996).

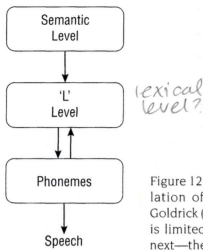

Figure 12.6: A 'Restricted Interactive Activation' simulation of word production, adapted from Rapp & Goldrick (2000). NOTE: Phoneme to L-level interaction is limited; Activation cascades from one level to the next—there is not discontinuity in processing.

independent motivation for this (limited) lexical to semantic feedback, a model with purely feedforward (cascading) semantic to lexical activation is to be preferred.[12]

Figure 12.6 sketches the architecture of the simulation that Rapp and Goldrick suggested best accounts for the data (see also Blanken, 1998). Within this simulation, KE's pattern reflects 'damage' (addition of noise) at the semantic level and PW's pattern results from lexical-level damage. With the relatively high levels of accuracy shown by PW, a lexical-level lesion produces mostly semantic errors (and mixed errors). However, as accuracy falls, more phonological errors occur, this pattern fits well with two other patients who produce modality-specific semantic errors—RGB and HW (Caramazza & Hillis, 1990). RGB, like PW, is accurate and produces purely semantic errors. In contrast, HW is less accurate at picture naming (around 40% correct) and, as Rapp and Goldrick's account predicted, produces phonological as well as semantic errors. The 'restricted interaction' theory seems to have much to commend it. However, the current parameter settings would appear to suffer from the same difficulty as Dell et al. (1997) in accounting for patients who produce formal paraphasias in greater numbers than nonword phonological errors.

Effects of Stimulus Properties on Word Production.   There are many properties of a stimulus that can affect its processing speed and accuracy. These include the frequency that a word is used, how many letters, phonemes or syllables it contains, how easily it evokes a visual or auditory image (imageability), its stress pattern and the age at which it is acquired. These variables have been demonstrated to affect word production for both aphasic and nonaphasic individuals (see Nickels, 1997, for a review). While for nonaphasics it is primarily speed of response that is affected, for aphasics naming accuracy is usually affected by at least one of these variables. For example, Nickels and Howard (1995b) investigated the effects of up to eight variables on the picture naming of 27 aphasic individuals, every aphasic showed a significant effect of at least one variable. Furthermore, only two did not show an effect of at least one of the three most commonly investigated types of variables: imageability/concreteness, word length and frequency (either objective or rated).[13] Despite the prevalence of these effects, none

---

[12]Rapp and Goldrick label the level that intervenes between semantics and phonology the 'L-level', this can be taken to correspond to either the lemma level in models such as those of Dell et al. (1997) and Levelt et al. (1999a) or the phonological form level in that of Caramazza (1997).

[13]The two aphasic individuals who did not show significant effects of any of these variables both showed effects of age of acquisition on naming.

of the current major models of spoken word production incorporate and/or investigate more than one of these variables.[14]

In Nickels (1995), I attempted to predict how discrete feedforward models and interactive activation models would perform under conditions of damage, with respect to whether imageability, frequency, and number of phonemes might be expected to affect proportions of errors of different types (if these were implemented). In line with most current thinking, I assumed that imageability was a property of the semantic level of processing, frequency reflected lexical processing, and word length was obviously to do with the number of phonemes and/or syllables in a word. I suggested that, in a discrete model, the probability of semantic errors occurring would be affected by imageability, and the probability of phonological errors would be affected by word length. This was the pattern found when the variables affecting error production were examined in a case series of 15 aphasic patients. At the time, I proposed (with many caveats regarding how difficult any predictions were!) that interactive models were likely to predict effects of both imageability and word length on each of semantic and phonological errors, and hence were inconsistent with the data. Harley (1995) demonstrated that, in an unlesioned computational model, effects of variables on other levels of processing need not be as great as I had suggested.[15] However, what needs to be shown is that a simulation with limited interaction (through, for example, low connection strength in feedback) similar to that proposed by Harley (1995; and Rapp & Goldrick, 2000) can also produce the 'desirable' effects of interaction (e.g., mixed errors in nonaphasic speech errors), and reproduce these effects on errors when lesioned.

PHONOLOGICAL ENCODING

The discussion, so far, has focused on the retrieval of stored lexical representations. However, in many ways this is only the starting point in the attempt to say a word. Having retrieved stored representations, there are several more processes that need to occur before a word can be articulated. Although no proponent of a theory lexical access would suggest that one could directly articulate the retrieved phonological representation, until recently theories of lexical access have often gone no further than this (e.g., Ellis & Young, 1988; Morton, 1970; but, for an exception, see Garrett, 1984). The most common approach to phonological encoding was that of a 'slot-and-filler' mechanism (Shattuck-Hufnagel, 1979) used by, for example, Levelt (1989) and Dell (1986). Stored metrical information (regarding number of syllables, their internal structure and stress pattern) is used to derive a series of segmental (phoneme) slots, and phonemes are inserted sequentially into these slots. Errors in this insertion process are the source of phoneme errors (exchanges, substitutions, omissions, etc.) in the nonaphasic speaker (see Nickels, 1997, for a review of this area). Thus, for example, the word 'rabbit' would have stored information comprising the phonemes /r / /æ/ /b/ /ɪ/ /t/, and the fact that it comprised two syllables with the structure CV and CVC with the first syllable being stressed. From the metrical information, a series of five slots would be derived corresponding to C'VCVC. Each phoneme would then be copied in turn to its corresponding slot. Thus, /r/ will be copied into the first consonant slot, /æ/ into the first vowel slot, /b/ into the second consonant slot and so on. This seemingly superfluous process is necessary so that in connected speech

---

[14]Levelt et al. incorporate word frequency, and although Dell's 1986 model incorporated frequency, this is not implemented computationally by Dell et al. (1997). Neither theory attempts to simulate imageability/abstractness effects (see Plaut & Shallice, 1993, for a [reading] model which does). Dell et al.'s (1997) simulations only contain single syllable 3 phoneme words and hence cannot simulate effects of word length. While Levelt et al.'s (1999) model does include polysyllabic words and syllables containing different numbers of phonemes, no discussion is made of the effects of length (in either syllables or phonemes) on performance.

[15]Making predictions from theoretical accounts is fraught with difficulty. For example, Laine and Martin (1996) derive predictions from Levelt's theory regarding form priming. However, Levelt et al. (1999b) argue that the predictions were not accurate.

adjoining words can be resyllabified as necessary. For example, the three lexical items in the utterance "I want it" are retrieved from the lexicon as the three syllables /aɪ/ /wɒnt/ and /ɪt /. However, this is not how they are produced—in connected speech /wɒnt/ and /ɪt / are resyllabified to produce an utterance /aɪ wɒn tɪt /.

Levelt et al. (1999a) made some changes to the theory outlined above. As this is the most explicit theory of phonological encoding that is incorporated into a full theory of spoken word production, we will concentrate on this. Thus, in this theory, as before, retrieval of a word's phonological representation makes available the segments of that word (with labelled links indicating their correct ordering). Although Levelt et al. argue that the unit of representation is the phoneme, they suggest that the 'internal composition' of the segments, their phonological features (e.g., +/– voicing; +/– nasal), must be visible to the processor (for applying linguistic rules successfully). Levelt et al. also suggest that the phoneme representations may be 'abstract'—specified for some phonological features, but not others (see for example, Stemberger & Stoel-Gammon, 1991).

Levelt et al. (1999a), in contrast to Levelt (1989), suggest that no metrical structure is stored for lexical items with regular default stress (at least for stress assigning languages like English and Dutch). Thus, for English and Dutch, the only words that have stored metrical structure are those that fail to stress the first syllable of the word that has a full vowel. Thus, hotel (/həʊ'tel/) and escort (/es'kɔːt/) will have stored metrical structure as they fail to stress the first syllable despite containing full vowels. In contrast, canoe /kə'nuː/ and butter /'bʌtə/ both stress the first syllable with a full vowel and so will not have a stored metrical structure. For these 'regular' words, metrical structure (number of syllables, main stress position, and syllable-internal structure) is generated on-line on the basis of universal and language specific rules. These syllabification rules include those of maximization of onset and sonority gradation (which serve to make syllables maximally pronounceable). Maximization of onset refers to the fact that when syllabifying a series of segments, as many consonants as possible are incorporated into the onset of a second syllable rather than the coda (final consonant sequence) of the preceding syllable (while ensuring the onset remains phonotactically legal. For example, when syllabifying 'hotel' the /t/ is assigned to the beginning of the second syllable rather than the end of the first, giving the two syllables /həʊ/ and /tel/ (NOT /həʊt/ and /el/). When syllabifying a stored series of segments, each vowel is assigned to the nucleus position of a different syllable node. Consonants are then inserted, and treated as onsets unless a phonotactically illegal onset cluster arises, in which case they will be assigned to the coda. For example, in the word "contract" the syllables are /'kɒn/ and /trækt/—if the syllable final /n/ was assigned to the onset of /trækt/ it would form the illegal cluster */ntr-/. Similarly, for this example, stress will be assigned by default to the first syllable as this has a full (stressable) vowel. The result of this process is a set of syllable specifications. These syllables that result from phonological assembly are then used as addresses for stored phonetic syllable templates. Levelt (1989) suggests that these are motor plans for complex articulatory gestures ('gestural scores' in Browman and Goldstein's (1992) terminology). Frequently-used syllables will be stored but rare or novel syllables may still be computed on-line. Thus, the stored motor plans for /'kɒn/ and /trækt/ or /həʊ/ and /'tel/ are retrieved. Finally, the motor plans are executed by the articulatory system.

Evidence from Nonimpaired Subjects

Experimental Evidence from Priming Studies

Form Priming. There have been a number of studies which support the proposal that phonological encoding occurs from left to right. For example, in an implicit priming task, Meyer (1990, 1991) found a facilitatory effect of having a target word preceded by a series of phonologically similar words, but only when these words shared word-initial phonemes onwards. Greater facilitation was produced the greater the number of shared phonemes provided they were continuous from left to right. Thus, LONER would not be primed by TONER but would be by LOCAL, and primed more by LONESOME (but primed no more by LINER). However, more recent studies have complicated this picture. Wheeldon (1999) notes that in a different paradigm (picture naming), the prior production of a phonologically related word slowed picture naming latency compared to the prior production of an unrelated word. However, this inhibitory effect occurred only when word initial phonemes were shared. Shared rimes produced facilitation. Levelt, Relofs, and Meyer (1999b) admit that at present their theory cannot account for Wheeldon's results.

Metrical Structure Priming.   For those words with stored metrical representations (i.e., metrically irregular words), Levelt et al. (1999a) argue that metrical and segmental spell out occur in parallel and take about the same time. They suggest that this predicts that pure metrical priming should not be found for these words. In other words, no facilitation should be found from priming the stress pattern and number of syllables of a word unless you also have priming of initial segments (and vice versa). In contrast, for words that have a regular stress assignment, Levelt et al. (1999a) argue that development of the syllable templates can occur without knowledge of the metrical structure (as this is derived by rule). This predicts that segmental priming can occur in the absence of metrical priming for words with regular metrical structure. They report experiments that produced the predicted effects and argue this provides experimental support for the distinction between words with regular and irregular metrical structure—only the latter requires stored metrical information.

Speech Errors

Levelt et al. (1999) argue that a theory should primarily be able to account for the normal speech production process and not the "infrequent derailments of the process" (p. 2) reflected by speech errors. Although they agree that, ultimately, the theory should be able to account for error patterns as well, they provide little more than a promissory note in that regard. The computational implementation of their theory (WEAVER++) does not make errors. However, Levelt et al. (1999a) suggest that a failure in its 'binding by checking' mechanism, provides a natural way to allow for errors. This mechanism involves each node having a procedure that checks whether the node, when active, links to the appropriate node one level up. They suggest that many speech sound errors can be accounted for by a failure of this mechanism when accessing the syllable nodes, leading to the wrong syllable node being selected (if two syllables are active). They presented results from a simulation arguing that WEAVER++ can successfully reproduce relative frequencies of anticipatory and perseverative errors (from Nooteboom, 1969). However, it produces far fewer exchange errors than occur in the real error corpus. It is important to note, that in this account what might appear to be substitutions of individual phonemes are in fact substitutions of syllables. For example, when 'caterpillar' is said as /pætəpɪlə/, it is not because the /k/ has been substituted by /p/ but that the first syllable /kæ/ has been substituted by another syllable /pæ/.

Evidence From Aphasia

Speech sound errors are a common feature of aphasia, and as such should be a potentially rich source of information regarding the processes of phonological encoding. Unfortunately the development of the two literatures (psycholinguistic modelling and investigations of aphasic deficits) has mostly been relatively independent. Despite the increasing specificity of Levelt et al.'s (1999a) theory, it remains difficult to predict exactly how the model might perform under conditions of damage; certainly, phonological errors will result from impairments to any process subsequent to retrieval of the stored phonological form. However, how the precise characteristics of these errors may vary as a result of impairments at different levels remains difficult to predict. The failure of binding-by-checking may not be the only possible source of errors. Nevertheless, there are important ways that data from aphasia should constrain the theory—when artificially 'lesioned,' Levelt et al.'s theory must be able to reproduce the main features of aphasic errors.

Sonority and Syllable Complexity

Like the errors made by nonimpaired individuals, most aphasic errors are phonotactically legal, that is they do not contain sequences of phonemes that are 'illegal' for the language being spoken (for example: for the target BREAK, the error "treak" might occur but "sreak" is unlikely to occur). It has been argued that theories of speech production should incorporate universal and language-specific rules in order to account for these data. One of the most widely studied linguistic properties implemented in linguistic rules is sonority.

Sonority refers to the perceptual prominence of one phoneme relative to another (Ladefoged, 1982). Although an objective measure of sonority is difficult, there is nevertheless minimal disagreement in the ranking of sounds according to this property. For example, vowels are the most sonorous, followed by liquids and glides (/r l w/), nasals (/m n ŋ/) and obstruents (fricatives (e.g., /f v s z/), stops (e.g., /p b t d/), and affricates (/tʃ dʒ/) being the least sonorant. According to the Sonority Sequencing Principle, a syllable is a string of sounds that is organized such that sonority rises from the beginning to a peak (the vowel) and then falls (Clements, 1990). In other words, /snæp/ is a legal syllable, as sonority rises from /s/ to /n/, is at a peak with the vowel and then drops with the final consonant /p/. In contrast /nsæp/ violates the Sonority sequencing principle as /s/ is less sonorant than the preceding /n/.

There have been many studies that have argued that aphasic speech sound errors are constrained by sonority (e.g., Bastiaanse, Gilbers, & Van der Linde, 1994; Béland, Caplan, & Nespoulous, 1990; Blumstein, 1973; Buckingham, 1990). Christman (1994) studied the phonological errors of three aphasics and argued that sonority played a role in their (non-contextual/no source) substitution errors. She suggested that when processing errors occur, replacement segments are generated by default constrained by sonority and phonotactics. This pattern is entirely consistent with Levelt et al. (1999), as sonority is represented in their theory to allow the detection of illegal sequences of phonemes in the application of the principle of maximization of onset during syllabification. (If a sequence of phonemes in a potential syllable onset violates the sonority gradient then the first of these will be assigned to the coda of the preceding syllable.)

The sonority sequencing principle governs the ordering of phonemes within a syllable, however, sonority has also been used to explain a hierarchy of syllable structures. Clements (1990) stated that "the preferred syllable shows a sharp rise in sonority followed by a gradual fall" (p. 323). Thus, syllables have been ranked in complexity both according to the nature of the syllable template (i.e., CV as the most simple, followed by CCV, CVC, VC, etc.) but also by the nature of the segments within the syllables (Romani & Calabrese, 1998). Thus, the most simple syllables are those with the maximum contrast in sonority (e.g., /ta/) and the most complex those with smaller sonority contrasts (e.g., /la/).

Romani and Calabrese (1998) report a thorough investigation of the effects of sonority on phonological errors produced by DB, an Italian aphasic man with articulatory difficulties. They argue that DB's errors are influenced by sonority contrasts between adjacent phonemes, and that they conformed to the ranking of syllable complexity predicted by preferred sonority gradients. Thus, DB's errors tended to reduce complexity of syllables, with three times more errors resulting in simplifications than complications. For example, when attempting /tye.pido/ he produced /te.pido/, simplifying the first syllable by deleting a consonant (see also Beland et al., 1990).

At first sight, it would seem difficult for the theory of Levelt et al. (1999a) to account for effects of sonority. Sonority is "known" to the processor, and is used for correctly syllabifying sequences of segments. Nevertheless, as Levelt et al. do not deal in any systematic way with error processes, there is no mechanism by which sonority might influence errors. However, Romani and Calabrese (1998) suggested that DB's errors might also be accurately described using a different level of explanation—that of a syllable frequency effect. They suggested that the more simple syllables are also often the more frequent in a language. This level of explanation is more easily reconciled with Levelt et al.'s model—the syllabary incorporates syllable frequency; it is possible that when a syllable cannot be retrieved, a higher-frequency (and hence more simple) syllabic neighbor will be retrieved in its place. As Romani and Calabrese point out, what is required is a study that attempts to deconfound these two levels of explanation.[16]

Nickels and Howard (in preparation, described in Nickels, 1997) discuss another possible level of explanation for these effects of syllable structure on aphasic word production. They found two patients that showed clear effects of syllable complexity on performance (words containing consonant clusters were more error prone than words with single consonants, even when confounding effects of number of phonemes had been accounted for). However, these patients showed different patterns of errors: one, EMM, tended to reduce the consonant cluster to a single consonant (the same kind of pattern as shown by Romani and Calabrese's patient), but the other, LAC, tended to make more errors elsewhere in the word when there was a cluster present. Nickels and Howard suggest that two different processes must underlie EMM and LAC's errors to account for the different error patterns. In Levelt (1989) clusters necessitate an extra processing step during segmental spell-out. Levelt et al. (1999b) suggest this is a possibility when discussing Santiago and MacKay's (1999) finding that words beginning with consonant clusters are initiated more slowly. Levelt et al. (1999b) also suggested an alternative account whereby an extra processing step might be required for clusters during the assembly of the addresses to the syllable program nodes. Thus it seems that we have (at least) three different plausible accounts for effects of syllable complexity on phonological errors in aphasia: sonority, syllable frequency, and additional processes in segmental spell-out for clusters.

Effects of Word Length

Effects of word length on accuracy are common in aphasia, and predict the rate of production of phonological errors (Nickels, 1995). As described above, Levelt et al. (1999a) suggested that the source of presumed segmental errors in nonaphasic speakers are in fact the result of selecting the wrong syllable from the syllabary rather than a segmental error per se. They argued that indexing failures occur in the device that maps syllabified phonological representations onto the mental syllabary—a failure of "binding-by-checking." This would appear to predict effects of numbers of syllables on performance (the more syllables in a word the more likely it would be that one of these errors might occur). Whether the same kind of verification error might occur between the stored phonological form and phoneme nodes (as a possible source of a phoneme length effect), is unclear. Can we find dissociations between effects of number of phonemes and number of syllables in aphasic naming errors? Unfortunately, despite the prevalence of length effects, it is rare for authors to attempt to dissociate effects of numbers of syllables and numbers of phonemes on performance.

Caplan (1987) found that one aphasic's accuracy (RL) was affected by number of syllables but not by number of phonemes. Similarly, A. D. Martin, Wasserman, Gilden, Gerstman, and

---

[16]Although Levelt and Wheeldon (1994) argue that syllable frequency affects normal subjects, effects of syllable frequency have been examined relatively little in aphasia. One recent study (Wilshire & Nespoulous, 1997) failed to find significant effects of syllable frequency for RCC, a phonologically-impaired aphasic man (despite the fact he showed effects of word frequency).

West (1975) found that for ten aphasics there was no significant differences in the frequency of errors for two versus five phoneme monosyllabic words. In contrast, Nickels and Howard (in preparation) found that 7 of their 12 aphasics showed effects of number of phonemes independent of number of syllables. However, none of the 12 showed more difficulty with words containing more syllables.[17] It seems apparent that the effects of both number of syllables and number of phonemes can affect errors for aphasic individuals, and hence any adequate model of speech production needs to incorporate both.

Effects of word length have frequently been attributed to deficits in a phonological output buffer (e.g., Ellis, Miller, & Sin, 1983; Kay, Lesser, & Coltheart, 1992). The role of the buffer is to 'hold' words in memory until they are required by the articulators. It is argued that an impaired buffer may lead to more rapid decay of the segmental structure of a word (possibly with 'later' phonemes being more prone to error than 'earlier' phonemes). In theories such as that of Dell et al. (1997), decay of information is no longer a property of a buffer per se, but rather a feature of the whole system. Levelt et al. (1999a) do not discuss the possibility of buffers playing a role in their theory.

Metrical Structure

As described above, Levelt et al. (1999a) argued that only "irregularly" stressed words will have stored metrical structures, all other words will have their metrical structure generated by the processor. Despite the fact that Levelt et al. do not discuss error production within the damaged system, the distinction would appear to make strong predictions that words with "regular" and "irregular" stress could be differentially affected. For example, damage to the stored metrical representations would predict that irregularly stressed words would then have to have their metrical structure generated on-line. This would result in stress assignment errors. For example, most bisyllabic words in English have stress on the first syllable (SW words; e.g., 'habit, 'cover), some are "irregular" with an unstressed first syllable (WS words; e.g., ro'mance, ho'tel). If the stored metrical structure was unavailable for the irregular words, and this was generated by the default rule, they would be produced with stress on the first syllable instead— a stress assignment error (e.g., * 'romance; * 'hotel). In contrast, a deficit involving the on-line generation of syllable structure (such as a general reduction of processing capacity) might be more likely to affect the regular words—the processing demands of computing the metrical structure may result in more errors on those words (in our example, those with stress on the first syllable may be more susceptible to error).

Nickels and Howard (1999) examined the effect of metrical structure (lexical stress) on aphasic word production. They found that half of a group of aphasics showed effects of lexical stress, such that they were worse at producing bisyllabic words with primary stress on the second syllable (WS words; e.g., ro'mance, ca'noe) than words with primary stress on the initial syllable (SW words; e.g., 'habit, 'cover). The remainder of the subjects showed no effects of stress on performance.

Interestingly, none of Nickels and Howard's sample made stress-assignment errors as is predicted by Levelt et al. (1999a). However, a recent replication (Smith, 1999) found a high proportion of these errors (see also Cappa, Nespor, Ielasi, & Miozzo, 1997). In both Nickels and Howard (1999) and Smith (1999) there were individual differences in the nature of the effects of metrical structure on errors. For example, some aphasic individuals were more likely to produce errors on unstressed syllables, regardless of the stress pattern of the words, whereas others showed an interaction with position of stress. Omissions of initial syllables in WS were

---

[17]In fact, three patients showed just the reverse—they were better at repeating two syllable than one syllable words matched for number of phonemes. Nickels and Howard (in preparation) suggest that this effect arises because of the inevitable confound with complexity of syllable structure that occurs with the matching of number of phonemes.

common (as would be expected from child language acquisition; e.g., Gerken, 1994) but not universal, as were 'reduplicative errors' (e.g., *romance* → *momance*). Thus, while Levelt et al.'s (1999a) theory can account for one error pattern (stress assignment errors), there are many that remain to be explained.

Perseverative Effects

A further group of phenomena that are prevalent in aphasia and must be accounted for within theories of speech production are perseverative effects in sequences of responses. Aphasic individuals frequently make more than one attempt at a target. In the case of errors phonologically related to their targets, these may progress towards the target, so that the final attempt is more accurate than the initial attempt. This is often known as 'conduite d'approche' (e.g., Gandour, Akamanon, Dechongkit, Kunadorn, & Boonklam, 1994; Joanette, Keller, & Lecours, 1980; Kohn, 1984; Valdois, Joanette, & Nespoulous, 1989). For example, when attempting to name a picture of a fork, CM (Kohn, 1989) said /flɪ fʌ fʌ fɪl fɪr fɪrk f fɔk/. Even sequences of neologisms (nonwords unrelated to the target) are often phonologically related to each other (and to earlier neologisms; e.g., Butterworth, 1979). For example, KC (Butterworth, 1979) said " the /nɔks/—the the the /mɔk mɒk/ the /ɪnvɔk wɔkʌf/ " (as part of a response to the question "What is your favorite food?").

Both of these phenomena require some means whereby previous responses can influence later productions. One possibility is by activation persisting (from one response to another) at the phoneme level (within a model such as that of Dell et al., 1997). On the first attempt, some of the target phonemes are successfully activated and some nontarget phonemes. The activation of these phonemes will persist to a subsequent attempt at producing the target. On this subsequent attempt, the damaged system will tend, once again, to activate erroneous phonemes in addition to the target phonemes. However, the target phonemes that were present in the previous response will have higher levels of activation (as a result of persisting activation) than erroneous phonemes which may vary randomly. Thus, each successive attempt is likely to contain more correct phonemes, as more and more target phonemes have become active. Does this mean that for this model the reverse pattern is a problem—when successive errors do not become closer to their targets? Possibly not—if activation decays away fast then the degree of persisting activation could be too small to have an effect on subsequent responses.

While theories such as those of Dell et al. (1997), would appear to be able to naturally explain conduite d'approche using an account of this type, even they will have difficulty accounting for perseveration of neologisms when intervening responses occur (Butterworth, 1979), as the intervening words will 'wipe out' any persisting activation. For example, KC said "I've had my piece of green and my [zʌp] stuff, my bit of ['zʌplən] . . . But he liked it. He's so ['zɪplən] to a yards . . . and yet after about two [lɪklən] I had from that man . . ." (Butterworth, 1985, p. 88). In this example, each neologism is clearly phonologically related to the next, but is separated by a number of intervening words. Thus, any persisting activation from the phonemes of one neologism will have dissipated while the phonemes of the intervening words have been activated. Butterworth (1979, 1985, 1992) provided an account of these data in terms of a "neologism generating device," which Nickels (1997) suggested can be thought of as a mechanism which generates a default when no stored lexical information is available. As this mechanism is only "called upon" to fill lexical/segmental gaps, phonemes may be perseverated by persisting activation within the device (which will be unaffected by intervening, accurate pronunciations). While this account is not part of Levelt et al.'s (1999a) theory, it is not incompatible with the spirit of their model where 'defaults' are used in the generation of metrical structure.

Summary

In sum, aphasic speech sound errors provide a wealth of information regarding the functioning of the phonological encoding system under conditions of damage. We have but skimmed the surface here. Clearly, simulations of phonological encoding should, when artificially lesioned, be able to reproduce these effects. Any model of phonological encoding must, minimally, be able to account for effects of syllable structure (or possibly syllable frequency), independent effects of number of syllables and number of phonemes on phonological errors, effects of lexical stress, and the occurrence of sequences of multiple attempts at a target that may or not become more accurate.

CONCLUSIONS

The last few years have seen greater collaboration and convergence between those scientists developing theories of speech production using data gathered from 'normal' subjects (e.g., Levelt, Roelofs, Meyer, and colleagues) and those studying individuals with aphasia (e.g., Dell, Martin, and colleagues). It is now more common for the former to include neuropsychological data to support their arguments (see for example, Levelt et al., 1999a, p. 17) and for cognitive neuropsychologists to refer to established theories in their analyses (rather than developing their own). Nevertheless, there is still a long way to go—some 'model builders' are yet to be convinced of the value (and indeed the necessity) of neuropsychological data in the evaluation of these theories[18] and cognitive neuropsychologists struggle to interpret theories that are insufficiently specified to derive predictions regarding the effects of damage on their behavior.

The fact remains that cognitive neuropsychology provides data for rigorous testing of cognitive theories which is all too frequently neglected. The most effective means of advancing our knowledge regarding word production is for all those involved in this field, be they cognitive psychologists, linguists, or cognitive neuropsychologists, to go forward together into the new millennium—a failure to do so will simply result in wasted effort and missed opportunities.

Acknowledgements

While writing this chapter the author was supported by a Wellcome Trust Fellowship and an Australian Research Council QEII Fellowship. Thanks to Brenda Rapp for her careful comments on an earlier version. Correspondence should be addressed to Dr L.A. Nickels, Macquarie Centre for Cognitive Science, Macquarie University, Sydney NSW 2109, Australia. Fax:+61-2-9850-6059. E-mail: lyndsey@maccs.mq.edu.au

---

[18]For example, Levelt et al. (1999b, p. 68) suggest "it as (sic) a bridge too far to expect a patient's behaviour to conform to our theory." Yet they commend those who "use theoretical distinctions from our theory to interpret the functioning of the damaged system in various types of aphasic patients" (Levelt et al., 1999b, p. 68). This would seem perilously close to accepting as valid, data which supports their account, but rejecting the possibility that neuropsychological data could falsify or constrain their theory.

REFERENCES

Baars, B. J., Motley, M. T., & MacKay, D. (1975). Output editing for lexical status from artificially elicited slips of the tongue. *Journal of Verbal Learning and Verbal Behaviour, 14,* 382–391.

Badecker, W., Miozzo, M., & Zanuttini, R. (1995). The two stage model of lexical retrieval: evidence from a case of anomia with selective preservation of grammatical gender. *Cognition, 57,* 193–216.

Bastiaanse, R., Gilbers, D., & van der Linde, K. (1994).

Sonority substitutions in Broca's and Conduction aphasia. *Journal of Neurolinguistics, 8,* 247–255.

Béland, R., Caplan, D., & Nespoulous, J.-L. (1990). The role of abstract phonological representations in word production: Evidence from phonemic paraphasias. *Journal of Neurolinguistics, 5,* 125–164.

Best, W. M. (1996). When racquets are baskets but baskets are biscuits, where do the words come from? A single-case study of formal paraphasic errors in aphasia. *Cognitive Neuropsychology, 13*, 443–480.

Bierwisch, M., & Schreuder, R. (1992) From concepts to lexical items. *Cognition, 42*, 23–60.

Blanken, G. (1990) Formal paraphasias: a single case study. *Brain and Language, 38*, 534–554.

Blanken, G. (1998). Lexicalisation in speech production: evidence from form-related word substitutions in aphasia. *Cognitive Neuropsychology, 15*, 321–360.

Blumstein, S. E. (1973). *A phonological investigation of aphasic speech*. The Hague: Mouton de Gruyter.

Browman, C., & Goldstein, L. (1992). Articulatory phonology: An overview. *Phonetica, 49*, 155–180.

Buckingham, H. W. (1990). Principle of sonority, doublet creation and the checkoff monitor. In J.-L. Nespoulous & P. Villiard (Eds.), *Morphology, phonology and aphasia*. New York: Springer-Verlag.

Butterworth, B. (1979). Hesitation and the production of verbal paraphasias and neologisms in jargon aphasia. *Brain and Language, 8*, 133-161.

Butterworth, B. (1981). Speech errors: old data in search of new theories. *Linguistics, 19*, 627–662.

Butterworth, B. (1985). Jargon aphasia: processes and strategies. In S. K. Newman & R. Epstein (Eds.), *Current perspectives in dysphasia*. Edinburgh: Churchill Livingstone.

Butterworth, B. (1989). Lexical access in speech production. In W. Marslen-Wilson (Ed.), *Lexical representation and process*. Cambridge, MA: MIT.

Butterworth, B. (1992). Disorders of phonological encoding. *Cognition, 42*, 261–286.

Caplan, D. (1987). Phonological representations in word production. In E. Keller & M. Gopnik (Eds.), *Tutorials in Motor Behaviour*. Hillsdale, NJ: Lawrence Erlbaum.

Cappa, S. F., Nespor, M., Ielasi, W., & Miozzo, A. (1997). The representation of stress: evidence from an aphasic patient. *Cognition, 65*, 1–13.

Caramazza, A. (1997). How many levels of processing are there in lexical access? *Cognitive Neuropsychology, 14*, 177–208.

Caramazza, A., & Hillis, A. E. (1990). Where do semantic errors come from? *Cortex, 26*, 95–122.

Caramazza, A., & Miozzo, M. (1997) The relation between syntactic and phonological knowledge in lexical access: evidence from the 'tip-of-the-tongue' phenomenon. *Cognition, 64*, 309–343.

Caramazza, A., & Miozzo, M. (1998). More is not always better: A response to Roelofs, Meyer and Levelt. *Cognition, 69*, 231–241.

Chertkow, H., Bub, D., Deaudon, C., & Whitehead, V. (1997). On the status of object concepts in aphasia. *Brain and Language, 58*, 203-232.

Christman, S. S. (1994). Target-related neologism formation in jargonaphasia. *Brain and Language, 46*, 109–128.

Clements, G. N. (1990). The role of the sonority cycle in core syllabification. In J. Kingston & M. Beckmann (Eds.), *Papers in laboratory phonology 1*. Cambridge, UK: Cambridge University Press.

Cutler, A. (1981). The reliability of speech error data. *Linguistics, 19*, 561–582.

Dell, G. S. (1986). A spreading activation theory of retrieval in sentence production. *Psychological Review, 93*, 283–321.

Dell, G. S. (1989). The retrieval of phonological forms in production: Tests of predictions from a connectionist model. In W. Marslen-Wilson (Ed.), *Lexical representation and process*. Cambridge, MA: MIT.

Dell, G. S., & O'Seaghdha, P. G. (1992). Stages of lexical access in language production. *Cognition, 42*, 287–314.

Dell, G. S., Schwartz, M. F., Martin, N., Saffran, E. M., & Gagnon, D. A. (1997) Lexical access in normal and aphasic speech. *Psychological Review, 104*, 801–838.

Ellis, A. W., Miller, D., & Sin, G. (1983). Wernicke's aphasia and normal language processing: A case study in cognitive neuropsychology. *Cognition, 15*, 111-144

Ellis, A. W., & Young, A.W. (1988). *Human cognitive neuropsychology*. London: Lawrence Erlbaum.

Fay, D., & Cutler, A. (1977). Malapropisms and the structure of the mental lexicon. *Linguistic Inquiry, 8*, 505–520.

Franklin, S., Howard, D., & Patterson, K. E. (1995). Abstract Word Anomia. *Cognitive Neuropsychology, 12*, 549–566

Fromkin, V. (Ed.). (1973). *Speech errors as linguistic evidence*. The Hague: Mouton de Gruyter.

Gagnon, D. A., Schwartz, M. F., Martin, N., Dell, G. S., & Saffran, E. M. (1997). The origins of formal paraphasias in aphasics picture naming. *Brain and Language, 59*, 450–472.

Gandour, J., Akamanon, C., Dechongkit, S., Khunadorn, F., & Boonklam, R. (1994). Sequencesof phonemic approximations in a thai conduction aphasic. *Brain and Language, 46*, 69–95.

Garrett, M. F. (1975). The analysis of sentence production. In G. H. Bower (Ed.), *The psychology of learning and motivation* (pp. 133-178). New York: Academic Press.

Garrett, M. F. (1980). Levels of processing in sentence production. In B. L. Butterworth (Ed.), *Language production, Volume 1: Speech and talk*. London: Academic Press.

Garrett, M.. F. (1984). The organisation of processing structure for language production: Applications to aphasic speech. In D. Caplan, A. R. Lecours, & A. Smith (Eds.), *Biological perspectives on language*. Cambridge, MA: MIT Press.

Gerken, L. A. (1994) A metrical template account of children's weak syllable omissions from multisyllabic words. *Journal of Child Language, 21*, 565–584.

Glaser, W. R. (1992) Picture naming. *Cognition, 42*, 61–105.

Harley, T. A. (1993). Phonological activation of semantic competitors during lexical access in speech production. *Language and Cognitive Processes, 8*, 291–309.

Harley, T. A. (1995). Connectionist models of anomia: a comment on Nickels. *Language and Cognitive Processes, 10*, 47–58.

Henaff Gonon, M. A., Bruckert, R., & Michel, F. (1989). Lexicalization in an anomic patient. *Neuropsychologia, 27*, 391–407.

Hillis, A.E., Rapp, B. C., Romani, C., & Caramazza, A. (1990). Selective impairment of semantics in lexical processing. *Cognitive Neuropsychology, 7*, 191–243.

Howard, D., & Franklin, S. (1988). *Missing the meaning?* Cambridge, MA: MIT Press

Howard, D., & Patterson, K. E. (1992). *Pyramids and palm trees*. Bury St. Edmunds, UK: Thames Valley Test Company.

Jescheniak, J.-D. (1994). *Word frequency effects in speech production*. Unpublished doctoral dissertation. Nijmegen University, Nijmegen, Holland.

Joanette, Y., Keller, E., & Lecours, A. R. (1980). Sequences of phonemic approximations in aphasia. *Brain and Language, 11*, 30–44.

Kay, J., & Ellis, A. W. (1987). A cognitive neuropsychological case study of anomia: Implications for psychological models of word retrieval. *Brain, 110,* 613–629

Kay, J., Lesser, R., & Coltheart, M. (1992). *Psycholinguistic assessment of language Processing in aphasia.* London: Lawrence Erlbaum.

Kelly, M. H. (1999) Indirect representation of grammatical class at the lexeme level. *Behavioural and Brain Sciences, 22,* 49–50.

Kempen, G., & Huijbers, P. (1983). The lexicalisation process in sentence production and naming: Indirect election of words. *Cognition, 14,* 185–209.

Kintsch, W. (1980). Semantic memory: a tutorial. In R.S. . Nickerson (Ed.), *Attention and performance VIII.* Hillsdale, NJ: Lawrence Erlbaum.

Kohn, S. E. (1984). The nature of the phonological disorder in conduction aphasia. *Brain and Language, 23,* 97–115.

Kohn, S. E. (1989). The nature of the phonemic string deficit in conduction aphasia. *Aphasiology, 3,* 209–239.

Ladefoged, P. (1982). *A course in phonetics.* New York: Harcourt Brace Jovanovich.

Laine, M., & Martin, N. (1996). Lexical Retrieval deficit in picture naming: Implications for word production models. *Brain and Language, 53,* 283–314.

Levelt, W. J. M. (1989). *Speaking: From intention to articulation.* Cambridge, MA: MIT.

Levelt, W. J. M. (1999). Models of word production. *Trends in Cognitive Sciences, 3,* 223–232.

Levelt, W. J. M., Roelofs, A., & Meyer, A. S. (1999a). A theory of lexical access in speech production. *Behavioural and Brain Sciences, 22,* 1–37.

Levelt, W. J. M., Roelofs, A., & Meyer, A. S. (1999b).Multiple perspectives on word production. *Behavioural and Brain Sciences, 22,* 61–75.

Levelt, W. J. M., Schriefers, H., Vorberg, D., Meyer, A. S., Pechmann, T., & Havinga, J. (1991a). The time course of lexical access in speech production: A study of picture naming. *Psychological Review, 98,* 122–142.

Levelt, W. J. M., Schriefers, H., Vorberg, D., Meyer, A. S., Pechmann, T., & Havinga, J. (1991b). Normal and deviant lexical processing: Reply to Dell and O'Seaghdha (1991). *Psychological Review, 98,* 615–618.

Levelt, W. J. M., & Wheeldon, L. (1994). Do speakers have access to a mental syllabary? *Cognition, 50,* 239–269.

Martin, A. D., Wasserman, N. H., Gilden, L., Gerstman, L., & West, J. A. (1975). A process model of repetition in aphasia: an investigation of phonological and morphological interactions in aphasic error performance. *Brain and Language, 2,* 434–450.

Martin, N., Dell, G. S., Saffran, E. M., & Schwartz, M. F. (1994). Origins of paraphasias in deep dysphasia: Testing the consequences of a decay impairment to an interactive spreading activation model of lexical retrieval. *Brain and Language, 47,* 609–660.

Martin, N., Gagnon, D. A., Schwartz, M. F., Dell, G. S., & Saffran., E. M. (1996). Phonological facilitation of semantic errors in normal and aphasic speakers. *Language and Cognitive Processes 11,* 257–282.

Martin, N., & Saffran, E. M. (1992). A computational account of deep dysphasia: Evidence from a single case study. *Brain and Language, 43,* 240–274.

Meyer, A. S. (1990). The time course of phonological encoding in language production: The encoding of successive syllables of a word. *Journal of Memory and Language, 29,* 524–545.

Meyer, A. S. (1991). The time course of phonological encoding in language production: phonological encoding inside a syllable. *Journal of Memory and Language, 30,* 69–89.

Miozzo, M., & Caramazza, A. (1997). Retrieval of lexical-syntactic features in tip-of-the-tongue state. *Journal of Experimental Psychology: Learning, Memory and Cognition, 23,* 1–14.

Morton, J. (1970). A functional model for memory. In D.A. Norman (Ed.), *Models of human memory.* New York: Academic Press.

Morton, J. (1985). Naming. In S.K. Newman and R. Epstein (eds.), *Current perspectives in dysphasia.* Edinburgh: Churchill Livingstone.

Morton, J., & Patterson, K. (1980). A new attempt at an interpretation, or, an attempt at a new interpretation. In M. Coltheart, K. Patterson, & J. Marshall (Eds.), *Deep dyslexia.* London: Routledge & Kegan Paul.

Nickels, L. A. (1992). The autocue? Self-generated phonemic cues in the treatment of a disorder of reading and naming. *Cognitive Neuropsychology, 9,* 155–182.

Nickels, L. A. (1995). Getting it right? Using naming errors to evaluate theoretical models of spoken word production. *Language and Cognitive Processes, 10,* 13–45.

Nickels, L. A. (1997). *Spoken word production and its breakdown in aphasia.* Hove, UK: Psychology Press.

Nickels, L. A., & Howard, D. (1995a). Phonological errors in aphasic naming: comprehension, monitoring and lexicality. *Cortex, 31,* 209–237

Nickels, L. A., & Howard, D. (1995b). Aphasic naming: what matters? *Neuropsychologia, 33,* 1281–1303.

Nickels, L. A., & Howard, D. (1999). Effects of lexical stress on aphasic word production. *Clinical Linguistics and Phonetics, 13,* 269–294.

Nickels, L. A., & Howard, D. (in preparation). *Effects of phonemes, syllables and syllabic complexity on aphasic word production.*

Nooteboom, S. G. (1969). The tongue slips into patterns. In A. G. Sciarone, A. J. van Essen, & A. A. van Rood. *Nomen: Leyden studies in linguistics and phonetics.* The Hague: Mouton de Gruyter.

Oldfield, R. C., & Wingfield, A. (1965). Response latencies in naming objects. *Quarterly Journal of Experimental Psychology, 17,* 273–281.

Peterson, R. R., & Savoy, P. (1998) Lexical selection and phonological encoding during language production: Evidence for cascaded processing. *Journal of Experimental Psychology: Learning, Memory, and Cognition, 24,* 539–557.

Plaut, D., & Shallice, T. (1993). Deep Dyslexia: A case study of connectionist neuropsychology. *Cognitive Neuropsychology, 10,* 377–500.

Rapp, B., & Goldrick, M. (2000). Discreteness and interactivity in spoken word production. *Psychological Review, 107,* 460–499.

Roelofs, A., Meyer, A. S., & Levelt, W. J.,M. (1998). A case for the lemma-lexeme distinction in models of speaking: Comment on Miozzo and Caramazza (1997). *Cognition, 69,* 219–230.

Romani, C., & Calabrese, A. (1998). Syllabic constraints in the phonological errors of an aphasic patient. *Brain and Language, 64,* 83–121.

Santiago, J., & Mackay, D. G. (1999). Constraining production theories: Principled motivation, consistency, homunculi, underspecification, failed predictions and contrary data. *Behavioural and Brain Sciences, 22,* 55–56.

Schriefers, H. (1993) Syntactic processes in the production of noun phrases. *Journal of Experimental Psychology: Learning, Memory and Cognition, 19,* 841–850.

Schriefers, H., Meyer, A. S., & Levelt, W. J. M. (1990). Exploring the time course of lexical access in language production: Picture-word interference studies. *Journal of Memory and Language, 29,* 86–102.

Shattuck-Hufnagel, S. (1979). Speech errors as evidence for a serial order mechanism in sentence production. In W. E. Cooper & E. C. T. Walker (Eds.), *Sentence processing: Psycholinguistic studies presented to Merrill Garrett.* Hillsdale, NJ: Lawrence Erlbaum.

Shattuck-Hufnagel, S. (1983) Sublexical units and suprasegmental structure in speech production planning. In P. F. MacNeilage (Ed.), *The production of speech.* New York: Springer.

Shattuck-Hufnagel, S. (1987). The role of word-onset consonants in speech production planning: New evidence from speech error patterns. In E.Keller & M. Gopnik (Eds.), *Motor and sensory processes of language.* Hillsdale, NJ: Lawrence Erlbaum.

Smith, K. E. (1999). *Effects of lexical stress on the spoken word production of patients with aphasia.* Unpublished undergraduate dissertation: University of Newcastle-upon-Tyne.

Stemberger, J. P. (1985). An interactive activation model of language production. In A. W. Ellis (Ed.), *Progress in the psychology of language: Volume 1.* London: Lawrence Erlbaum.

Stemberger, J. P. (1992). The reliability and replicability of naturalistic speech error data: A comparison with experimentally induced errors. In B. J. Baars (Ed.), *Experimental slips and human error: Exploring the architecture of volition.* New York: Plenum Press.

Stemberger, J. P., & Stoel-Gammon, C. (1991). The underspecification of coronals: Evidence from language acquisition and performance errors. *Phonetics and Phonology, 2,* 181–199.

Tent, J., & Clark, J. E. (1980). An experimental investigation into the perception of slips of the tongue. *Journal of Phonetics, 8,* 317–325.

Valdois, S., Joanette, Y., & Nespoulous, J.-L. (1989). Intrinsic organization of sequences of phonemic approximations: a preliminary study. *Aphasiology, 3,* 55–73.

Vigliocco, G., Antonini, T., & Garrett, M. F. (1997). Grammatical gender is on the tip of Italian tongues. *Psychological Science, 8,* 314–317.

Vigliocco, G., Vinson, D. P., Martin, R. C., & Garrett, M. F. (1999). Is 'count' and 'mass' information available when the noun is not? An investigation of tip-of-the-tongue states and anomia. *Journal of Memory and Language, 40,* 534–558.

Wheeldon, L. R. (1999). Competitive processes during word-form encoding. *Behavioural and Brain Sciences,* 59–60.

Wheeldon, L. R., & Levelt, W. J. M. (1995) Monitoring the time course of phonological encoding. *Journal of Memory and Language, 34,* 311–334.

Wilshire, C. E. (1998). Serial order in phonological encoding: an exploration of the 'word onset effect' using laboratory induced errors. *Cognition, 68,* 143–166.

Wilshire, C. E., & Nespoulous, J.-L. (1997). The role of syllabic frequency in aphasic phonological errors. *Brain and Language, 59,* 147–150.

13

Bilingual Lexical Access

Tamar H. Gollan
Judith F. Kroll

Although bilingualism is common it has received relatively little attention in cognitive neuropsychological research. Perhaps this has been in part because a body of research on cognitive processing in normal bilinguals has only recently begun to accumulate, and also because research on both bilingual aphasia and cognitive processing has, until recently, been dominated by a question with a narrow focus. For bilingual aphasia, the question has been differential localization (see below), and for cognitive processing, the question has been whether the two languages are stored in a single or in separate representations. These questions focus on a narrow set of issues that restrict the scope of the emerging models. In this chapter we review the evidence in each of these areas and then examine how recent research on normal bilingualism can be productively applied to the study of bilingual aphasia. Concomitantly, we attempt to demonstrate how research on bilingual aphasia can contribute to the development of better-articulated models of normal bilingual cognitive processing. We will also attempt to show that the presence of more than one language in a single cognitive system raises some questions that could not otherwise be posed, and that the answers to these questions will provide important constraints in the search for the neural substrates of cognitive performance. Finally, to demonstrate these points we will end with a *Case Illustration* to provide an example of how our suggestions could be implemented in future investigations of bilingual aphasia.

Cognitive neuropsychologists make use of the brain's unfortunate vulnerability to damage by treating each case as an "experiment of *nature*," and by asking, "What must the cognitive architecture be like such that it can fail in this particular way?" With this approach they have demonstrated quite convincingly that detailed analysis of the performance of brain damaged subjects can lead to unique and useful ways to constrain models of normal cognitive performance. Similarly, by studying bilinguals, cognitive psychologists have made use of "experiments of *nurture*" that offer the opportunity to ask, "How does the cognitive system cope with the need to develop efficient processing mechanisms for two (or more) different languages?" By merging these two questions together (i.e., by combining experiments of nature and nurture, or brain damage and bilingualism) interpretations of bilingual aphasia are likely to advance in directions that will effectively constrain normal models of both monolingual and bilingual language processing. For these reasons it is important to study bilinguals, and bilingual aphasia, not only because most people in the world are bilingual (Grosjean, 1982; Harris & McGhee Nelson, 1992; Paradis, 1998), but also because the fields of neuropsychology, cognitive neuropsychology, and cognitive psychology stand to gain by doing so.

In addition to all of the processing issues faced by monolingual speakers, bilinguals must also manage the activation of two languages, and select only words and constructions that are appropriate given the intended language of output. This simple observation raises important questions about language processing in normal bilinguals, and as a consequence, about bilingual aphasia. First, how does the cognitive system maintain separate access and representational mechanisms for each language while simultaneously connecting the concepts to each of these same languages? Any answer to this question must further explain how bilinguals are also readily able to code-switch in the presence of other bilinguals (who know the same languages). Finally, what kinds of deficits are expected to arise in bilingual aphasia given the type of mechanism proposed to solve processing problems that are unique to bilinguals? In the interest of pursuing these issues with some degree of depth we will limit our discussion to the level of single word processing and the bilingual lexicon.[1] However, we note that many of the same questions arise in studying bilinguals at the sentence level.

NEURAL BASES OF BILINGUALISM

Knowledge of the neural bases of bilingualism has come from studies of bilingual aphasia, studies of differential hemispheric lateralization in cognitively intact bilinguals, and more recently from a variety of imaging techniques. Much of this research has focused on determining whether language processing in the first language (L1) and the second language (L2) utilize the same or distinct brain regions. Research on bilingual aphasia and the localization of L1 and L2 in the brain have been reviewed by a number of investigators (Fabbro, 1999; Paradis, 1987, 1989, 1990; Vaid, in press; Vaid & Genesee, 1980). In this section we summarize these findings briefly focusing on evidence concerning the bilingual lexicon. The reader should note that in the literature on bilingualism the abbreviations L1 and L2 typically refer to 1st and 2nd languages respectively, and often (but not always) also refer to the dominant and nondominant languages respectively. Unless otherwise indicated, in this paper we assume that L1 refers to both the dominant language and the language that was acquired first, and that L2 is less dominant and was acquired second.

Early research on bilingual aphasia attempted to correlate lesion location with performance in each language, and to predict recovery patterns on the basis of language acquisition history. This work assumed that L1 and L2 may be represented and processed in distinct brain regions and that language acquisition history may determine the localization of L1 and L2 in the brain. The latter notion has received little support (with few exceptions but see section below on contemporary approaches); most cases of bilingual aphasia show similar patterns of deficits in both languages. Moreover, Paradis (1989) has argued that no combination of different environmental variables can predict patterns of recovery in aphasia. Similarly, attempts to localize L1 and L2 in distinct regions have also been largely unsuccessful. For example, one hypothesis, henceforth called *differential lateralization*, was that L2, perhaps because of the way it is acquired, involves increased reliance on the right hemisphere (Albert & Obler, 1978; Lebrun, 1981). This idea seemed to be supported by the abundance of case reports of crossed aphasia (a situation in which damage to the nonlanguage-dominant hemisphere nevertheless produces aphasia) in bilinguals. However, subsequent research generated little support for this hypothesis. Specifically, a number of researchers (Solin, 1989; Vaid & Genesee, 1980; Zatorre, 1989) showed that crossed aphasia is no more common in bilingual aphasia than it is in monolingual aphasia.

The differential lateralization hypothesis has also been explored in the context of research

---

[1]There is some confusion arising concerning distinctions between lexical and semantic representations and between semantic and conceptual representations. For present purposes, we use will use semantic and conceptual interchangeably but assume that the level at which lexical forms are represented does not include meaning. See Francis (1999b) for a recent discussion of the way in which these terms have been used in the literature.

on the intact bilingual brain; however, this endeavor has also produced inconclusive findings (Vaid & Genesee, 1980; Zatorre, 1989). Most recently this proposal reemerged as a framework for motivating imaging research with intact bilinguals. The majority of these studies also suggest that L1 and L2 are represented primarily in the same brain regions, i.e., within the language system and *primarily* in the left hemisphere (Zatorre, 1989). Although much of the research in this domain converges on this same conclusion, it does not allow the differential localization alternative to be rejected. The word "primarily" leaves room for interpreting this view as a kind of compromise between the extreme versions of the differential localization hypothesis rather than a flat rejection of the hypothesis.

A recent development regarding differential localization of L1 and L2 suggests that this hypothesis may best apply to bilinguals who acquire L2 late in life, and particularly with respect to grammatical processing. Evidence for the latter claim has emerged in research on bilingual ERPs (Weber-Fox & Neville, 1996, 1999) showing that early and late acquirers of L2 processed semantic anomaly similarly, whereas robust group differences were observed when they were asked to process grammatical anomaly. Other researchers have also suggested that late-acquirers process L2 in different brain regions on the basis of an fMRI study in which early and late bilinguals were asked to silently describe previously occurring events using their native and second languages (Kim, Relkin, Lee, & Hirsch, 1997). Ullman (1999) argued that the proposal regarding grammatical processing in L2 bears resemblance to findings in research on monolinguals suggesting that procedural memory is more sensitive to the critical period. He suggested that acquisition of a second language late in life often involves explicit learning of L2 grammar and that this leads to (at least partially) distinct neural substrates for grammatical processing in L1 and L2. More specifically, this proposal stipulates that, regardless of age of acquisition, lexical processing in both L1 and L2 takes place in brain regions that are associated with declarative memory (facts and events). In contrast, grammatical processing takes place in brain regions associated with procedural memory (cognitive and motor skills), but only if both languages are learned early. If L2 is learned late in life, then grammatical processing in L2 also relies on brain regions that typically process declarative memory alone.

Other research consistent with this notion suggests that processing in L2 is less consistently lateralized (across studies and across subjects within studies) to the left hemisphere which is more heavily linked to procedural memory skills (Dehaene et al., 1997; Paradis, 1998). It must be noted however, that some researchers (including some of the same investigators who endorsed this view) have since questioned these findings. For example, Perani et al. (1998) obtained imaging evidence suggesting that language proficiency (which may be correlated with age of acquisition) rather than differential lateralization can account for the previously obtained findings. Moreover, other researchers have reported evidence from PET scans and fMRI that indicates that L1 and L2 involves the same neural substrates, and that only pronunciation in L2 produces distinct activation patterns relative to those observed for L1 (Klein, Zatorre, Milner, Meyer, & Evans, 1994; Hernandez, Martinez, & Kohnert, in press).

Another approach is to set aside issues of differential localization of L1 and L2 and instead to return to case studies of bilingual aphasia with an emphasis on detailed psycholinguistic analyses of error patterns (e.g., Dronkers, Yamasaki, Ross, & White, 1995; Nilipour & Paradis, 1995). This approach introduces different constraints to the interpretation of deficits and possibly avoids some of the disadvantages inherent in the localization approach. Such studies have demonstrated that the relative preservation of L1 and L2 cannot be interpreted without considering the combination of languages tested. For example, Nilipour and Paradis (1995) demonstrated that Farsi-English bilingual aphasics were more likely to make errors of a certain type (i.e., omission or substitution of compound verb elements) in L1 (Farsi) relative to L2 (English), simply because Farsi (L1) offered many more opportunities for making this kind of error. In contrast, in L2 (English) these patients made a larger number of errors of another type (i.e., the omission of free grammatical morphemes in obligatory contexts) because English requires this type of construction more often than Farsi (L1). To account for these findings, the authors concluded that a single deficit might have different surface manifestations in two different languages depending on the degree to which each language provides opportunities for the deficit to influence processing. Similar arguments regarding aphasic syndromes and the variation in their phenotypic presentation cross-linguistically have also been discussed in the literature on monolingual aphasia (Bates, Wulfeck, & MacWhinney, 1991; Miceli, Silveri, Romani, & Caramazza, 1989). These studies suggest paradoxical recovery patterns, in which L2 is better preserved relative to L1, may sometimes merely reflect cross-linguistic differences rather than differential localization. Moreover, it is not sufficient to merely report respective recovery patterns in each language, but that the particular language spoken must be taken into account as a part of the interpretation of the impairment. Finally, as we will see in the final section of this chapter, this kind of analysis goes beyond global descriptions of bilingual aphasia (e.g., L1 is more impaired than L2) and thus lends itself more easily to interpretation within recently developed models of cognitive processing in bilinguals.

ONE LEXICON OR TWO?

Cognitive psychologists studying normal bilingual processing have asked whether L1 and L2 share common or independent systems. The history of cognitive research on whether words in the bilingual's two languages reside in integrated or segregated systems has been reviewed extensively (e.g., Brysbaert, 1998; Chen, 1992; De Groot, 1992b, 1993, 1995; Francis, 1999b; Keatley, 1992; Kroll, 1993; Kroll & De Groot, 1997). To illustrate the way in which claims about bilingual lexical representation have been tested, consider the evidence on cross-language repetition priming. When individuals are asked to make a lexical decision in their L1 (i.e., to decide whether a letter string forms a real word or not), the speed of their responses is typically facilitated if a given stimulus was presented earlier in the experiment (e.g., Scarborough, Cortese, & Scarborough, 1977). In the bilingual version of the paradigm, cross-language trans-lations are substituted; instead of repeating the same word form twice, a word is presented initially and later its translation equivalent appears. For example a Spanish-English bilingual might first see the letter string HOUSE and then the Spanish equivalent CASA in a second phase of the experiment. If words in a bilingual's two languages are represented in a common lexical representation, then priming should be observed across as well as within languages. The results of many cross-language repetition studies failed to obtain evidence for priming (e.g., Brown, Sharma, & Kirsner, 1984; Gerard & Scarborough, 1989; Kirsner, Smith, Lockhart, King, & Jain, 1984; Scarborough, Gerard, & Cortese, 1984). Given the logic of the empirical test, this failure was interpreted as evidence for separate lexicons for each language.

The results of other studies provided converging support for the separate lexicon model. For example, Scarborough et al. (1984) showed that bilinguals could effectively filter words from the nontarget language when required to reject them as nonwords in a language-exclusive lexical decision task, with no apparent effects of word frequency for the nontarget words. Furthermore, Gerard and Scarborough (1989) demonstrated that interlingual homographs, words with the same form but different meaning in the bilingual's two languages (e.g., the word *fin* in English which means *end* in Spanish), produced no observable differences relative to nonhomographs when lexical decision was performed in one language alone.

An initial challenge to the separate lexicon model came from a series of cross-language semantic priming experiments. Unlike the repetition-priming paradigm, in which prime and target words are separated by a long delay and many intervening trials, the semantic priming task involves only a brief delay with no intervening trials. If words in the bilingual's two languages activate the same underlying meaning representation, then priming would be ex-pected across as well as within languages. Thus, DOG should prime CAT but it should also prime GATO (the Spanish word for *cat*) if the bilingual is fluent in English and Spanish. The results of a large number of experiments demonstrated that it was indeed possible to obtain semantic priming across the bilingual's two languages (Altarriba, 1990; Chen & Ng, 1989; Keatley, Spinks, & De Gelder, 1994; Meyer & Ruddy, 1974; Schwanenflugel & Rey, 1986; Tzelgov & Henik, 1989), although the magnitude of priming is typically larger from L1 to L2 than the reverse. (See Francis, 1999b, and Kroll, 1993, for reviews of this evidence.) Subsequent experiments (see below) also showed that noncognate translation priming (e.g., GATO primes CAT) can also be obtained at very short lags.

The fact that cross-language semantic priming is observed even with very brief duration between prime and target make translation strategies unlikely, and suggests not only that the two languages access the same concepts, but that the process is direct. Some recent evidence that is even more compelling in this regard is that under some circumstances priming for noncognate translations is obtained even when prime words are masked beyond the participant's ability to detect them, and hence participants do not report knowing that words from two languages were presented. Interestingly, masked cross-language priming effects are more consistently obtained when languages do not share the same orthography (Gollan, Forster, & Frost, 1997; Jiang, 1998); when the languages employ the same alphabet sometimes priming is obtained (De Groot & Nas, 1991) and sometimes it is not (Grainger & Frenck-Mestre, 1998; Sánchez-Casas, Davis, & García-Albea, 1992).

The response to the apparently conflicting evidence regarding the separation or integration of lexical information across languages was to assume that both alternatives were correct, but that they characterized different aspects of the bilingual's memory system. Thus, the failure to obtain cross-language repetition priming (at long lags) was interpreted as evidence for language-specific representations at the level of lexical form, whereas the observation of cross-language semantic priming was taken as evidence for a shared semantic system. This resolution led in part to a focus on hierarchical models with independent form lexicons for L1 and L2, shared semantic representations, and research examining the nature of the connections between lexical and conceptual representations (e.g., Kroll & Stewart, 1994; Potter, So, von Eckardt, & Feldman, 1984). This way of conceptualizing the connections between L1 and L2 in bilingual memory has been especially influential in understanding the development of proficiency in two languages. This issue is addressed in a later section and is becoming increasingly important for integrating the results obtained across multiple studies on bilingualism.

Recent studies on the one-or-two-lexicons question distinguish between the structure of the lexicon itself and the question of whether access to words in the two languages is selective or not. This increased level of detail in the conceptualization of bilingual lexical access has reduced the amount of disagreement regarding the interpretation of the evidence. As Van Heuven, Dijkstra, and Grainger (1998) noted, the question of whether words in the two languages are represented separately, or as part of an integrated system, is independent of the question of whether access itself is selective or not. For example, it is logically possible to conceptualize separate lexicons for each language at the level of form, but with interactive access mechanisms to each of these lexicons. Similarly, it is possible to conceive of integration in the sense that words across languages are linked associatively, but with noninteractive access mechanisms for L1 and L2. Finally, functional separation between lexicons could also be achieved after the activation of lexical forms in L1 and L2 if each language were to have its own selection mechanism that could only recognize lexical candidates tagged as belonging to one language (as suggested by Costa, Miozzo, & Caramazza, 1999).

Because the issue of access and representation in bilingual memory is not necessarily dependent on the issue of anatomical localization of L1 and L2 it is not limited by the constraints particular to that question. Hence, this way of approaching bilingualism may offer an alternative to mainstream research on bilingual aphasia that thus far, has largely been dominated by the localization question. The assumption that lexical and semantic information may also be organized at different levels within the language processing system is an idea that is now widely accepted in models of the bilingual lexicon (see Smith, 1997 for a review). This notion is also assumed more generally within models of monolingual language production (e.g., Bock & Levelt, 1994; Levelt, Roelofs, & Meyer, 1999) and language comprehension (Balota, 1994; Frauenfelder & Tyler, 1987).

CROSS-LANGUAGE ACTIVITY IN BILINGUAL COMPREHENSION

The focus in contemporary research on bilingualism has shifted from the question of whether there are one or two lexicons in L1 and L2 to the question of when words in each language are active, and what types of information must be active during different kinds of tasks. The research we have reviewed (e.g., on masked cross-language priming effects, and see below discussion of neighborhood effects) rules out an extreme version of language selective models in which it is assumed that the lexical forms of the inactive language are effectively "turned off" when the active language is being utilized. Many of these findings, however, can also be explained by models that assume L1 and L2 have independent form-lexicons, access mechanisms, or both, but that also assume that access is always launched in parallel to both lexicons. The current evidence provides overwhelming support for the claim that information about words in both languages is active even when a task requires explicit processing in one language alone.

But if this claim is correct, then what prevents bilinguals from mixing words from both languages involuntarily? A particular focus in recent work, therefore, has been to understand the mechanisms that modulate cross-language activity. These proposed mechanisms have significant consequences for interpreting bilingual aphasic performance. For example, some cases of bilingual aphasia may be explained by appealing to these mechanisms of control rather than to differential localization of L1 and L2 (e.g., Paradis, 1995; Price, Green, & von Studnitz, 1999).

The development of interactive models of the bilingual lexicon show that it is possible to simulate performance that appears consistent with the notion of independent lexica but in a model that adopts highly interactive access mechanisms to L1 and L2 (e.g., Dijkstra, Van Jaarsveld, & Ten Brinke, 1998; Thomas, 1997). The most compelling evidence for nonselective access was reported by Van Heuven et al. (1998). These authors used the presence of neighborhood effects in word recognition as a tool to examine potential interactions within versus across languages. Word recognition in monolinguals is influenced by the presence and frequency of form-related words (see Andrews, 1997, for a review of within-language neighborhood effects). Thus, Van Heuven et al. hypothesized that if access mechanisms are shared across languages, then neighbors in both languages should affect word recognition in either language, and this is the result that they obtained. For example, when a Dutch-English bilingual is asked to recognize the English word WORD the time to perform the task will be affected by the presence of words in both English (e.g., WORE, WORK, WORM) and in Dutch (e.g., BORD, WOND, WORP).

Van Heuven et al. (1998) also demonstrated that it was possible to simulate cross-language neighborhood effects with the Bilingual Interactive Activation (BIA) model, a computational model of word recognition that extends the basic architecture of McClelland and Rumelhart's (1981) Interactive Activation model to the bilingual case (see also Dijkstra, Grainger, & Van Heuven, 1999; Dijkstra & Van Heuven, 1998; Dijkstra, Van Heuven, & Grainger, 1998; Grainger & Dijkstra, 1992). The model is shown in Figure 13.1. The essential claim of the BIA model is that when a letter string is presented, there is nonselective, bottom-up activation of words in any language that contain the presented letter features. However, by also including a layer of language nodes, the model is able to selectively control, in a top-down manner, the relative activation of one language to the other effectively converting the model into a language-selective model when one language is strongly inhibited. This top-down language node, and the

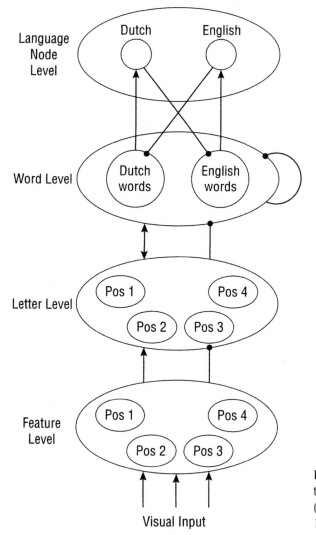

Figure 13.1: Bilingual interactive activation (BIA) model (adapted from Dijkstra et al., 1998).

manner in which it simulates segregated and integrated lexicons in the bilingual system will become very important for interpreting cases of bilingual aphasia (e.g., see section concluding *Case Illustration*).

A number of other recent results provide additional support for nonselective access to the bilingual lexicon. Dijkstra et al. (1998) found that lexical decisions for interlingual homographs (e.g., the Spanish word *red* means *net*) were no different than controls when the task was performed exclusively in L2, replicating Gerard and Scarborough (1989). As argued above, this result appears to support the selective or separate lexica hypothesis because it suggests that the alternative L1 reading of the homograph was not available. However, Dijkstra et al. (1998) also manipulated the list and task conditions and found that the null effect for homographs could be turned into interference when L1 words were included among the nonwords to be rejected in L2 lexical decision, and facilitation when the task became inclusive lexical decision, with the judgment dependent only on the recognition that the letter string was a word in either language. The latter findings suggest that when the task is overtly bilingual (i.e., words from both languages are presented) the bilingual accesses information about lexical representations in both languages very rapidly, and that this information cannot be suppressed strategically. Moreover, they require a model of the bilingual lexicon in which the presence of interlingual effects will depend on the nature of the task and list composition (See also De Groot, Delmaar, and Lupker, 2000).

Dijkstra et al. (1998) and Gerard and Scarborough (1989) also reported that cognates, words that share the same form and meaning across the bilingual's two languages (e.g., the Dutch word for *wheel* is *wiel*), were facilitated relative to controls in the less-dominant language. The presence of cognate facilitation effects in bilingual lexical processing has long been recognized (see Francis, 1999b for a review) and recently demonstrated in a masked priming paradigm even when languages do not share the same orthography (Gollan et al., 1997). The exact mechanism of cognate priming, however, has not yet been identified. Evidence from bilingual aphasia may turn out to be particularly useful in this regard. For example, if cognate effects are produced solely by simultaneous activity in both lexicons, then bilinguals with selective aphasia, i.e., bilinguals who appear not to have access to one of their languages, should not show cognate effects. On the other hand, if cognate representations (in both languages although presumably L2 representations would be more strongly affected) are permanently influenced by repetition in either language then cognate effects should still be obtained in the intact language in selective aphasia. The mechanism of cross-language homograph effects (e.g., the Spanish word *red* means *net* in English) is also not clear. However, the lack of overlap in meaning may make permanent effects (that do not require both languages to be intact) of repeated simultaneous activation in each language over time less likely. Hence, homograph effects may be less likely to remain intact in cases of selective aphasia (unless the language assumed to be "erased" is still active to some degree).

CROSS-LANGUAGE ACTIVITY IN BILINGUAL LANGUAGE PRODUCTION

The evidence regarding the activation of words in both languages in bilingual comprehension also extends to studies on language production. The topic of language production has been an especially active area of research in psycholinguistics for the past ten years. It is beyond the scope of the present chapter to do more than give a very brief account of the hypothesized mechanisms that underlie production, but a number of recent papers and chapters provide an overview of this work (e.g., Bock & Levelt, 1994; Levelt et al., 1999; Nickels, this volume). Past studies of language production within a single language have debated the issue of when in the course of production there is competition among alternative names for a given object. For example, when a picture is named the picture must first be recognized, its meaning identified, and only then can a single lexical candidate be selected for phonological specification. Most accounts of this process agree that meaning activation must occur prior to phonological specification. A great deal of evidence from picture naming experiments shows that there are generally effects of semantics early in processing and effects of phonology late in processing. However, beyond this general constraint, there is disagreement about the extent to which the fine-tuning of the process proceeds interactively or discreetly. According to strictly serial models (e.g., Levelt, 1989; Levelt et al., 1999; Schriefers, Meyer, & Levelt, 1990), a single lexical competitor is chosen and only then is the form of the word activated. According to interactive models (e.g., Dell, 1986; Dell & O'Seaghdha, 1991; Starreveld & La Heij, 1995), the process of specifying word forms is initiated soon after meaning is activated (i.e., activation "cascades" across levels) so that lexical competitors and their respective phonological representations may be available in parallel (especially for very close semantic competitors).

A series of studies provides support for an interactive, cascaded view of language production, and also has important implications for language production in bilinguals. Peterson and Savoy (1998) and Jescheniak and Schriefers (1998) demonstrated phonological activation of lexical competitors when the competitors were close synonyms (e.g., *sofa* and *couch*). The implications of these findings for bilinguals may be crucial. Close synonyms are relatively few in number. But if almost every concept has at least two lexical alternatives (i.e., the word in L1 and its translation equivalent in L2), then (because most words have translation equivalents) for bilinguals virtually every word may have a close competitor that could potentially interfere with language production. However, analyses of bilingual speech errors (e.g., Poulisse, 1997) suggest that cross-language blends (e.g., producing "cato" instead of "cat" or "gato"), and involuntary code-switch errors, occur rarely perhaps indicating that competition between translations is resolved in a relatively early stage of lexical activation (i.e., prior to phonological specification). A number of recent studies have examined the on-line consequences of cross-language competition and seem to corroborate this suggestion.

Hermans, Bongaerts, De Bot, and Schreuder (1998) investigated the activity of L1 during L2 picture naming in a picture-word interference paradigm. Relatively fluent Dutch-English bilinguals named pictures in English, their L2. In different experiments, distractors were words in L1 or in L2 that were semantically or phonologically related to the name of the picture. In the critical condition of each experiment, a word that sounded like the L1 name of the picture was presented. For example, when the target was the English word MOUNTAIN the Dutch word BERM was used as a distractor because it resembles the Dutch word *berg* which is the translation equivalent of MOUNTAIN. The results for these "phono-Dutch" words were robust at the same SOAs as semantic, but not phonological distractors (i.e., they followed a similar time course), suggesting that the translation equivalent is active through the stage of semantic (sometimes called lemma) selection but that competition is resolved prior to phonological specification. A study by Costa et al., (1998) reported similar cross-language effects in the picture-word interference task and demonstrated that even L2 distractors can influence L1 picture naming performance. However, unlike the Hermans et al. study, Costa et al. failed to obtain evidence of competition at the level of lexical-semantic representation (in fact they observed facilitation) and therefore argued that bilingual production is fundamentally language selective in that only target language lexical candidates are considered for selection.

Other recent results provide converging evidence for the claim that words in the nontarget language are active during production even when the bilingual speaks in one language alone. Kroll and Peck (1998) developed the cued picture-naming task to obtain a more direct measure of L1 activity during L2 picture naming (for a similar approach see Kohnert, Bates, & Hernandez, 1999). Participants are presented with a pictured object and told that they are to produce the object's name as soon as they hear an auditory cue. The cue is presented with the picture or following a variable SOA. In blocked language conditions, participants are instructed to name the picture in their L1 or L2 when they hear the cue. In mixed language conditions, participants are instructed to name the picture in L1 if the cue is a high tone and in L2 if the cue is a low tone (or vice versa). The mixed conditions require that both language alternatives be active because the language of naming is uncertain, whereas in the blocked conditions it is, at least theoretically, possible to prepare one language alternative only. The logic of the task is to use the comparison of the mixed and blocked conditions as a way of determining whether the translation equivalent in the nontarget language is normally active. If performance under the mixed conditions, which forces the activity of words in both languages, resembles performance under blocked conditions, which permits selective preparation, then the result would suggest that lexical candidates in the other language are normally active during production.

In a series of experiments with relatively fluent English-Spanish bilinguals, Kroll and Peck (1998) found that the mixed conditions had more serious consequences for production in L1. The data from this study are shown in Table 13.1, where mean reaction times (in milliseconds) are given for mixed and blocked picture naming in L1 and L2 as a function of the SOA at which the cue was presented. These data show that under blocked conditions L1 is not necessarily influenced by the activation of an L2 alternative, whereas L2 is always affected by L1, whether the activation of L1 is an optional or required feature of the task. L1 picture naming latencies were much longer in the mixed than in the blocked task, whereas the same difference for L2 was much smaller. The differential cost of mixing for L1 suggests that L2 alternatives do not

Table 13.1

Time to Name Pictures (in ms) in the Cued Picture Naming Task
Under Blocked and Mixed Language Conditions at Three SOAs.

| SOA (ms) | Language of Picture Naming | | | |
| | English (L1) | | Spanish (L2) | |
Condition:	Blocked	Mixed	Blocked	Mixed
0	776	1075	1172	1292
250	658	945	1088	1179
750	590	855	778	1026

Data from "Competing Activation Across a Bilingual's Two Languages:
Evidence from Picture Naming," by J. F. Kroll & A. Peck, April, 1998.
Paper presented at the 43rd Annual Meeting of the International Lin-
guistic Association.

normally interfere with L1 performance. Forcing them to be active has serious consequences
for L1 performance. However, naming in L2 is less affected by the same manipulation suggesting that at least up to some point, there is competition from the more dominant L1 alternative
that needs to be resolved. In the blocked language conditions, there was a sharp decline in
picture naming latencies for L2 at the long SOAs, consistent with hypothesis that competition
from alternative L1 lexical candidates is eventually resolved. The cued picture naming results
also closely resemble the results of language switching experiments where there are typically
greater switch costs to switch into L1 than L2 (e.g., Meuter & Allport, 1999).

CONTROL MECHANISMS: COORDINATING MULTIPLE LANGUAGES

Models of Control Processes

If words in both languages are always, or often, active simultaneously, then how is this competition ultimately resolved? In language comprehension this fact may simply require a delay in
lexical access. However, during language production there must be a mechanism that allows for
language-specific selection; that is how does a bilingual prevent herself from producing words
in the unintended language? Two recent proposals have addressed the manner in which the
bilingual modulates the activity of one language relative to the other. One alternative, described by Green (1986, 1993, 1998a) is that this control of the two languages is achieved via
an externally driven inhibitory mechanism (this mechanism is similar to the language node in
the BIA model). The level of resources that need to be allocated to these inhibitory processes
will then influence the ease or difficulty of the task. The resulting pattern of performance will
be determined at least in part by the nature of the schemas required for a particular task as
well as by the activation produced within the bilingual lexicon.

Evidence for an inhibitory control mechanism has been provided by experiments on language switching which show that the cost to switch from L2 to L1 is greater than the cost to
switch from L1 to L2 (e.g., Loasby, 1998; Meuter & Allport, 1999). Although it might seem
counterintuitive that the more dominant L1 would suffer the greater switch cost, according to
the inhibitory control account, greater inhibition of L1 is required to allow L2 processing to
take place than the reverse. Thus, if L1 must be produced shortly after it has been inhibited (to
allow access to L2), then processing costs will be observed. Because production in L1 is
hypothesized to require only minimal inhibition of the less active L2, comparable costs will not
occur. Of particular interest is that these differential switch costs occur even when the switching trials are predictable and even when there is no particular relation between sequential
items, suggesting global rather than local inhibition.

An alternative account that attributes responsibility for the relative activation of the two languages to a combination of factors within and outside the language processing system is the language mode hypothesis proposed by Grosjean (1997, 1998, in press). Grosjean's claim is that bilinguals place themselves along a continuum whereby the two languages are engaged more or less equally depending on the circumstances in which they are used. A large number of factors are hypothesized to control this engagement, including the knowledge that the bilingual has about his or her intended audience and their bilingualism, the bilingual's relative proficiency in each language, and momentary changes in the nature of the linguistic input.

Presently there is insufficient empirical evidence, and models of bilingual control are not detailed enough, to allow estimation of the relative contribution of lexical activation versus control processes to lexical selection in bilingual cognitive systems. However, there are a number of general implications that can be drawn from these recent proposals that will be important for future research. One is that they provide an alternative means for understanding both the development and the breakdown of performance in L2. If performance is determined by a unique interaction between representation and control, then there may be changes in either or both that will affect an individual's bilingualism (see concluding *Case Illustration*). Another is that we can expect to obtain results that appear superficially to be contradictory but that are only a reflection of the differential influence of these factors. Some support for this view comes from the experiments on the recognition of interlingual homographs described earlier (Dijkstra et al., 1998). Whether the very same interlingual homographs produced interference, facilitation, or no effect, depended on subtle aspects of the task and composition of the stimulus list. It seems likely that similar interactions with task will be observed across many of the research topics that we have reviewed. To understand the neural substrates of bilingualism, it will be important to distinguish which effects may be attributed to task demand characteristics, and which neural mechanisms are involved in processing at different levels.

Price et al. (1999) recently reported a PET study in which translation and language switching performance were examined. Translation can be considered a special case of language switching, and may require additional control processing, because translation necessarily involves a language switch and also because translation of equivalent word pairs may maximize cross-language interference. They found that only the translation task increased the activity of areas believed to control action (anterior cingulate and subcortical areas) but that switching produced activity in areas associated with sublexical processing (e.g., the supramarginal gyri). Although this approach is at an early stage of development, it promises to provide an important source of complementary evidence to constrain models of lexical representation and control because it emphasizes the need to compare performance across tasks as well as languages.

Control Mechanisms and Bilingual Deficits

There has been some disagreement about the degree of control and language mixing that may be considered as "normal." Perecman (1984, 1985) argued that a pattern of language mixing that was observed in a case of bilingual aphasia reflected a linguistic deficit. However, Grosjean (1985) argued that this same patient's performance was within the range of mixing patterns observed in normal bilinguals, and that the mixing was part of a deliberate intention to improve communication. Improved models of control may serve to settle such debates in the future. Similarly, relatively little is known about the development of bilingual control across the life span. One study suggested that older (neurologically intact) bilinguals were far more subject to interference in picture naming when the task demanded switching from one language to another (Hernandez & Kohnert, 1999). Further studies such as these are necessary to determine whether this age-related change is always correlated with change in tasks that require mental control, or whether there is a component of mental control that becomes specialized for bilingual switching in particular.

Perhaps the single most impressive pattern of recovery in bilingual aphasia has been called "alternate antagonism," henceforth AA (Paradis, 1989). This refers to cases in which first only one language recovers, and then there is a switch; the other language comes back while the language that recovered first disappears, and then they switch back again. A number of cases of AA have been reported subsequent to focal brain lesions. Thus, the AA pattern cannot be explained by assuming that the locus of brain damage moves (like a cyst in a blob of jelly) from one location (where one language might be stored) back to another (where the other language might be stored). Instead, it suggests that representations in both languages themselves are relatively intact, and that the locus of impairment must be within a mechanism that controls access to representations in each language (otherwise it would be difficult to explain how a language could spontaneously recover).

This same mechanism has been suggested as an account of the involuntary language mixing in bilingual aphasia which may reflect deficits, or temporary deficits, in the ability to reduce activation in one language relative to the other (Paradis, 1989). It also seems that all cases of selective aphasia (i.e., one language is impaired and the other is intact) could be explained as a consequence of damage to the control mechanism by assuming that the mechanism becomes permanently set in one language. At a superficial level of analysis, virtually all of the global recovery patterns that are described by Paradis (1987) could be explained by appealing to a control mechanism rather than by damage to language specific brain regions. For example, differential recovery (i.e., one language is impaired more than the other relative to estimated levels of premorbid functioning) seems like strong evidence for (at least partially) differential localization. However, if it is assumed that the control mechanism can become permanently lodged in one state of activation, then this same mechanism could also be used to explain differential recovery patterns. Until models of the control mechanism are better developed, with further research on normal bilingual's ability to switch languages and inhibit activation in each language, it will be very difficult to distinguish whether a patient's performance can be attributed to control mechanism or representational damage.

This discussion also highlights the importance of identifying ways to test lexical representation and access separately when interpreting patterns of bilingual performance. This issue has been discussed extensively in the literature on monolingual cognitive neuropsychology (e.g., McCarthy & Warrington, 1990). The appearance of the same topic in these two domains seems to suggest that a solution that would link the two lines of research may be possible. However, as noted by Caramazza, Hillis, Rapp, and Romani (1990), addressing this distinction meaningfully will likely require a considerable increase in the specificity of models of lexical representation.

One way to begin increasing the level of detail in models of the control mechanism may be to focus on the coordination of activation across modalities. By modality we refer to any mode of language processing; thus, written language, spoken language, reading, and auditory comprehension are four different modalities. At the moment no model specifies the extent to which the control mechanism may or may not be altered strategically, or solely on the basis of bottom-up activation. Similarly, there is little to no empirical evidence that indicates how the different modalities are related to this mechanism, and current models of the control mechanism appear to be modality independent but little (if any) discussion of this point can be found in papers on the issue of bilingual control. These assumptions will have implications for interpretations of bilingual aphasic performance. For example, if an amodal control mechanism is to be used to account for the AA performance, then the same pattern of language dominance should be observed in each modality. If not, then alternative possibilities must be considered (e.g., separate control mechanisms for each modality, or at least partially distinct mechanisms for connecting each modality with the control mechanism).

This discussion of AA also raises an interesting and unexplored direction for future research in bilingual aphasia. The AA recovery pattern seems to have two components and models of bilingual control may provide the same or different accounts for each component. The control mechanisms described above can explain how (without any direct intervention) a language may spontaneously recover after apparently being virtually "erased" from memory. However, the switching pattern itself also requires an explanation; what causes the switch? Do the same factors that seem to influence language switching in normal bilingual processing also influence cases of alternate antagonism? Recent evidence from research with intact bilinguals (Van Heuven et al., 1998) suggests that top-down processing (e.g., whether the task explicitly includes one or two languages) can increase the magnitude of implicit cross-language effects observed (i.e., cross-language neighborhood density effects). Similar explorations with cases of AA may begin to provide some answers to this question.

Another direction for future research is to explore more extensively the depth of actual language loss in cases of AA as well as in cases of selective aphasia (damage to one language only). To our knowledge no researcher has attempted to determine if access to the language that is presumed to be temporarily "erased" is so damaged as to prevent even the most subtle of manipulations from revealing some evidence of preserved knowledge. For example, would an English–Hebrew bilingual diagnosed with AA (alternate antagonism) be unable to distinguish English words from Spanish words when she is "stuck" in the Hebrew language? This kind of question would lead to a more precise identification of the degree or level of processing at which access to English was blocked.

THE REPRESENTATION AND PROCESSING OF MEANING

The contemporary research we have reviewed has focused primarily on aspects of word form similarity across a bilingual's two languages. We address ourselves now to the issue of meaning. Two questions have been central in considering the nature of semantic representation for bilinguals. One is the issue of whether the same meanings are accessed for translation equivalents in each language. The other is the issue of whether bilinguals and second language learners are capable of accessing meaning independently for L2 words without mediation through L1.

Common or Distinct Semantic Representations?

The notion that words in different languages correspond to distinct lexical concepts and that the resulting differences in meaning may have consequences for the relation between language and thought is an idea that has been discussed in a number of different contexts, including the debate over the Whorfian hypothesis (e.g., Green, 1998b; Paradis, 1997). But very little empirical research on bilinguals has examined precisely the level at which differences in meaning arise (See Kroll & Tokowicz, in press, for a discussion of the consequences of operationalizing conceptual variables in different ways).

At a high level of cognitive processing, of the sort required to perform complex reasoning and decision making, it seems clear that the bilinguals utilize conceptual resources that are common to both of their languages (Francis, 1999a, and see Francis, 1999b, for a review). However, accessing common meaning representations does not necessarily imply that knowledge about which language was actually used to communicate that information is lost; recent autobiographical memory studies suggest that language is a potentially powerful cue for memory retrieval (e.g., Schrauf & Rubin, 1998).

At the level of the early processes that are responsible for semantic priming, the general result is that cross-language priming is observed, but not under all circumstances. L1 words are more likely to prime L2 than the reverse (e.g., Keatley et al., 1994). However, many of the factors that have been identified as limiting full semantic exchange between the two languages have been associated with the nature of the bilingual's proficiency in his or her two languages, rather than the way in which concepts are represented. If a bilingual is less proficient in L2 than L1, which is the case for most bilinguals, even those who are relatively fluent in their second language, then L2 may not always engage semantics as fully or as quickly as L1.

Another limit to the generality of the claim that semantic representation is shared across the bilingual's two languages is that a great deal of the research on this topic has been based on tasks such as picture naming which necessarily restrict materials to concrete objects and their names. De Groot and her colleagues (De Groot, 1992a, 1992b; De Groot, Dannenburg, & Van Hell, 1994; Van Hell, 1998, Van Hell & De Groot, 1998) have argued that concrete concepts may indeed share the same meaning representation for words in two languages but that this result does not necessarily generalize to other types of concepts. They have shown that bilingual performance on tasks such word translation, lexical decision, and word association is consistently faster and more accurate for words that name concrete concepts than for words that are more abstract. They argue that translation equivalents for concrete words are more likely to activate the same subset of semantic features than the corresponding translation equivalents for abstract words. If so, then concrete words, and particularly the concrete nouns that are the names of pictured objects, may be unique in the extent to which they activate shared semantics across the bilingual's two languages.

There is a long history of research on concreteness effects in which processing advantages for concrete words have been interpreted as effects of image availability (e.g., Paivio, 1971, 1986). More recent research suggests a conceptual locus for the concreteness effects (e.g., Schwanenflugel, Harnishfeger, & Stowe, 1988; Schwanenflugel & Shoben, 1983). The results of De Groot and her colleagues thus challenge a unitary view of the bilingual semantic system. However, it important to note that they don't necessarily imply that stored meanings differ across the two languages. Rather, the words in the two languages may activate a distinct pattern of semantic features or primitives and the product of that computation may have the consequence of creating slightly different or quite distinct senses of meaning (this particular distinction is important when predicting the co-occurrence of semantic errors in L1 and L2 in bilingual aphasia). When a bilingual is asked to translate, activation of the meaning of a target in one language may only partially activate the meaning of the closest translation "equivalent" in the other language.

In addition to word concreteness, a number of recent studies suggest that there is an effect of the number of translation equivalents a word has on the time it takes to translate it (Schönpflug, 1997; Tokowicz, 1997). Because the number of translation equivalents is related to ambiguity, with more ambiguous words within a language being more likely to have multiple translations across languages, the result suggests that one-to-one correspondences in word meaning may be restricted to only those concepts that are unambiguous in either of the bilingual's languages.

Developing Second Language Proficiency

Potter et al. (1984) proposed a hierarchical framework to understand the ways in which lexical and conceptual information might be interconnected for the bilingual. In one arrangement, the word association model, words in the bilingual's L2 are directly associated to their translation equivalents in L1, but all access to meaning is mediated via L1. In contrast, the concept mediation model assumes that words in each of the bilingual's two languages have direct access to meaning and that these meaning relations are the basis of interlanguage connection. These alternatives are shown in Figure 13.2. Hierarchical models of bilingual representation assume that words in the bilingual's two languages access a common semantic representation. Similar assumptions are made in studies of monolingual processing regarding access to the same semantic representations via different modalities (Caramazza et al., 1990). This notion is also consistent with a number of results that have been reported on word translation (from L1 to

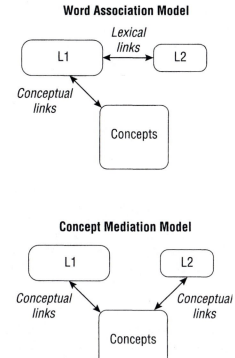

Word Association Model

Lexical links

L1 ⟷ L2

Conceptual links

Concepts

Concept Mediation Model

L1   L2

Conceptual links   *Conceptual links*

Concepts

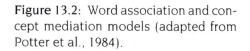

Figure 13.2: Word association and concept mediation models (adapted from Potter et al., 1984).

L2 and the reverse), and picture naming in bilinguals (Potter et al., 1984; for a more recent review see Kroll & De Groot, 1997), suggesting that this way of describing bilingual lexical representation can be applied to both language comprehension and production.

Potter et al. (1984) used a comparison of picture naming and translation performance to test the predictions of the two models. They reasoned that the word association model predicts that during translation (where the goal is to retrieve the equivalent word in the other language) there should be direct access to the correct response without need to access semantics. However, in picture naming, the concept must necessarily be accessed first and only then can the L1 name of the picture mediate the connection to the L2 lexicon (via word association). By this view, translation from L1 into L2 should be faster than picture naming in L2, because translation, but not picture naming, would benefit from the direct lexical connections. In contrast, if the concept mediation model is correct, then there is no basis on which to predict differences in performance on the two tasks. In two experiments, one with fluent Chinese-English bilinguals, and the other with native English speakers learning French, they found evidence for the concept mediation prediction. For each of the bilingual groups, there was no significant difference in the time to translate words and name pictures in L2. The remarkable aspect of Potter et al.'s results was that even though the second-language learners were slower than the fluent bilinguals to perform translation and picture naming in L2, the pattern of data was the same for both groups, suggesting that even relatively novice learners were able to access concepts for L2 words without lexical mediation.

Subsequent research challenged the general conclusion that all bilinguals, regardless of their proficiency, are able to directly access concepts for L2 words. A series of studies replicated the Potter et al. (1984) experiments with second language learners at earlier stages of L2 acquisition (Chen & Leung, 1989; Kroll & Curley, 1988). They found that there was indeed evidence for the word association model (i.e., faster translation from L1 to L2 than picture naming in L2) among L2 learners who were less proficient relative to those that Potter et al. had tested. This result was taken to suggest that both the word association and concept mediation models were correct, but that they described different phases of the development of L2 proficiency. These results highlight the importance of assessing the level of language proficiency in every experiment with bilingual participants, and that it is especially important for all studies on bilingualism to adopt a uniform way of assessing proficiency so that comparisons across studies will be possible (Grosjean, 1998).

What is the consequence of a developmental process whereby there is initial reliance on lexical-level connections? Kroll and Stewart (1994) suggested that there was not a simple shift from words to concepts with increasing expertise in L2. Instead, they argued that the early reliance on L1 to mediate access to meaning for L2 words created an asymmetry in the form of interlanguage connections. Although direct conceptual processing becomes increasingly possible for L2 words, L2 is less effective than L1 in directly engaging semantics. However, the lexical form connections that were hypothesized to mediate access early on, are proposed to remain as an alternative form of interlanguage connection once the individual does acquire greater L2 proficiency. Kroll and Stewart provided evidence for this view in an experiment in which the translation performance of highly fluent Dutch-English bilinguals was compared in the context of semantically categorized and randomly mixed lists. They demonstrated that translation from L1 to L2 was affected by the semantic manipulation (in this case the categorized lists produced interference) but that translation from L2 to L1 was not. If L2 to L1 translation can be accomplished without access to semantics, then it seemed likely that lexical mediation provided the means.

Kroll and Stewart (1994) proposed the revised hierarchical model to incorporate both lexical and conceptual connections for the two languages and also to reflect the asymmetry in their strength. The model is shown in Figure 13.3. Lexical and conceptual connections are assumed to exist for both languages. However, L1 is assumed to hold some privilege in its ability to access meaning, and L2 is assumed to have stronger lexical links to L1 as a consequence of the lexical transfer hypothesized to occur during early stages of second language learning.

A number of experimental findings provide support for the predictions of the revised hierarchical model. The asymmetrical pattern of semantic priming mentioned earlier, with more priming from L1 to L2 than the reverse, is consistent with the notion that L1 is more likely to engage semantic processes than L2. Comparisons of translation performance have also shown that the two directions of translation differentially engage semantics, with larger effects from L1 to L2 than L2 to L1 (e.g., De Groot et al., 1994; Sholl, Sankaranarayanan, & Kroll, 1995). Translation from L1 to L2 is also typically slower and more error prone than translation from L2 to L1, a result hypothesized to reflect the necessity for semantic processing in one direction but not in the other (e.g., Cheung & Chen, 1998; Kroll & Stewart, 1994; Sánchez-Casas et al., 1992; Sholl et al., 1995). However, some studies have failed to support the predictions of the revised hierarchical model in that semantic effects are obtained in both directions of translation and/or translation latencies are not longer for the forward direction of translation (e.g., De Groot & Poot , 1997; La Heij, Kerling, & Van der Velden, 1996). (See Kroll & De Groot, 1997, and Kroll & Tokowicz, in press, for a discussion of the evidence regarding the revised hierarchical model.)

Figure 13.3: Revised hierarchical model (adapted from Kroll & Stewart, 1994).

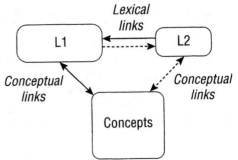

Semantic Deficits and Proficiency Levels in Bilingual Aphasia

The assumption of overlapping semantic representations in bilingual memory is important when considering the expected patterns of performance in bilingual aphasia. To the extent that access to L1 and L2 is mediated by the same semantic representations, patients who demonstrate evidence of deficits to the semantic level should show similar deficits in both L1 and L2. Recent fMRI evidence (Illes et al., 1999) shows that at least for comprehension in fluent bilinguals, the same neural system appears to be activated for both languages. As noted above, the research of De Groot (1992a, 1995) and colleagues regarding increased semantic overlap for semantic representations of cognate and concrete words, suggests that this prediction may hold to a greater extent for these types of words.

However, one reason that semantic deficits may not be expected to overlap across L1 and L2, even if there are overlapping semantic representations, would be if there were reason to predict that subtle damage to the semantic level should have differential effects on access to lexical forms in L1 and L2. For example, if selection for language production in L2 occurs later in the time-course of semantic activation, then L2 may be more vulnerable to the disruptive influences of a variety of factors and different kinds of deficits, thus producing differential consequences of semantic damage for lexical access in each language. Similarly, semantic representations may not be as complete or inclusive in L2 as in L1 (e.g., Dufour & Kroll, 1995). By this view, the loss of access to only part of semantic memory could seriously impact L2 but may only have subtle influences on L1. Obtaining evidence to support this hypothesis would entail specifying the nature of semantic representations in L2, and on that basis predicting the kinds of subtle changes that should be observed in L1 given this claim. Finally, given that in the course of L2 acquisition semantic access in language comprehension seems to appear before it appears in language production (e.g., Frenck-Mestre & Prince, 1997), semantic errors in L1 and L2 may tend to overlap to a greater extent in comprehension than they do in language production.

CASE ILLUSTRATION: THE CASE OF E. M.

To illustrate how interpretations of bilingual aphasia may be altered by recent evidence on cognitive processing in normal bilinguals we conclude by considering the case of patient E.M. (Aglioti & Fabbro, 1993; Aglioti, Beltramello, Girardi, & Fabbro, 1996) who presented with selective paradoxical bilingual aphasia. In this recovery pattern, performance in L2 is (paradoxically) spared relative to performance in L1.[2] E.M.'s L1 was Venetian (Veronese dialect), and her L2 was standard Italian. According to Aglioti et al., Venetian is " . . . so different from standard Italian that a person speaking in a given dialect cannot be understood by another Italian who has never been exposed to it." It is worth noting that most people who live in Italy today learn standard Italian at a very young age. E.M., however, was born in 1922 and therefore grew up before the widespread use of modern technology which now makes it more difficult to avoid being exposed to, and to using, standard Italian. At the time of injury E.M. and her family reported that she watched TV and read Italian magazines, but she hardly ever spoke Italian (aproximately 2–3 times/year).

We will begin by examining the case, and attempting to use the data that were collected to identify the locus of impairment within a model of normal bilingual processing. We will attempt to demonstrate how conclusions about the patient's performance might have been different had models of cognitive processing in normal bilinguals motivated the analysis. Formal

---

[2]In such cases it is essential to discern whether L1 corresponds to both the first learned, and the dominant languages at the time of brain injury. Sometimes what appears to be a paradoxical recovery pattern merely reflects the fact that the language that was acquired first was no longer dominant at the time of brain-injury (Kohnert, Hernandez, & Bates, 1998).

measures administered to assess E.M.'s language and other cognitive abilities included the Token Test, the Aachener Aphasie Test in Italian and an ad hoc translation of this test into Venetian, the Wisconsin Card Sorting Test, Corsi's Block Tapping test, and the WAIS (administered in standard Italian). Interpretation of these tests (and relative levels of accuracy in each language) is limited because they were not designed for use with Venetian-Italian bilinguals, however E.M.'s performance on these tests was consistent with informal observations of her behavior in natural settings. E.M. presented with relatively intact general knowledge and memory.

E.M.'s accuracy on confrontation naming was better in L2 (105 out of 120) than in L1 (63 out of 120), however, overall the pattern of errors she made in spontaneous speech was similar in L1 and L2 with just one exception. Spontaneous production in L1 was interrupted by 51.7% intrusions from L2, whereas the reverse occurred on only 4.4% of the time. Otherwise her errors included the following types of errors in L1 and L2 respectively: word-finding difficulty 3.7 and 2.9%, agrammaticisms (omission of free-standing grammatical morphemes) 5.8 and 8%, paragrammaticisms (substitution or addition of grammatical morphemes) 1.2 and 2.6%, neologisms (producing a nonword) 0.9 and 0.7%, phonemic errors 2.3 and 2%, semantic errors 0.3 and 0.1%, verbal paraphasias (word-substitution errors) 0.2 and 0.5%, echolalia (repeating the examiner without specific instructions to do so) 1.4 and 1.1%, and perseverations (inappropriate, immediate, successive repetition of words) 5.8 and 3.7%. Formal testing also showed that E.M.'s forward translation (i.e., translating from L1 into L2) was worse than her backward translation (i.e., from L2 to L1). These data are shown in Table 13.2. There were no significant differences between comprehension in L1 (35 out of 50) and L2 (36 out of 50).

We will assume that as indicated above, E.M.'s L1 (Venetian) was also her dominant language in all modalities at the time of brain injury (although it could be argued that she should be characterized as L2-dominant in reading and writing simply because Venetian is primarily a spoken dialect). Based on estimated functioning prior to E.M.'s stroke, her performance in L1 should have been dominant on all the tasks that were tested. Hence the obtained pattern of performance was interpreted as a selective impairment of L1 (so-called "paradoxical aphasia"). Further, the locus of brain damage was considered to be consistent with the observed pattern of performance because the stroke affected areas that are often implicated in tasks that require intact "implicit memory," and the authors hypothesized that L1 may rely more heavily on implicit memory relative to L2.

We will consider at least two types of functional impairments that could account for paradoxical aphasia, and will evaluate whether E.M.'s performance is equally well explained by each of these in turn. First, there may have been damage to a control mechanism such that L1 was permanently inhibited at a global level. Aglioti et al., (1996) briefly considered this possibility but only with respect to its plausibility given E.M.'s lesion location, and not with respect to cognitive processing models of the bilingual control mechanism. Second, lexical representations specific to L1 may have been damaged more extensively than those specific to L2. It is also possible, of course, that both explanations were correct but in the interest of simplicity we will not discuss this possibility here.

E.M.'s translation performance can be explained by assuming that her brain damage affected a control mechanism only if another assumption is also adopted, that is that the control mechanism can be *partially* damaged. E.M.'s translation performance was as paradoxical as her naming performance. The typical pattern for intact bilinguals has been well documented and reviewed (e.g., Kroll & De Groot, 1997) and normally involves better performance translating backwards (i.e., L2 to L1) relative to forwards (i.e., L1 to L2). However, E.M.'s performance was better when she translated from L1 to L2. Because translation in any direction requires that access to L1 is at least partially intact, the control mechanism account requires the assumption that damage to the control mechanism was only partial (i.e., access to representations in L1 was only partially inhibited). This is reasonable given that E.M. was able to produce

Table 13.2
Patient's (E.M.) and Control's (A.B.) Results in Word-Translation Tasks.

Stimuli	from → to	Correct Responses	x^2 df = 1	p	MEAN RT (s)	S.D.
E.M. (patient)						
Words	L1 → L2	52/75	11.89	<0.0001	7.47	6.64
Words	L2 → L1	31/75			10.91	11.05
A.B. (control)						
Words	L1 → L2	68/75	2.95	0.08	2.08	2.2
Words	L2 → L1	73/75			1.88	2.1

Errors in translation into L1 were non-responses, whereas 13 out of 23 errors in translation into L2 were either pertinent circumlocutions or semantic paraphasias (e.g., 'rápola' [wrinkle in L1] translated into L2 as 'vecchiaia' [old age]). Reaction times (RTs), reported on the right side of the table, were recorded for each item by means of a manually activated stop-watch. E.M.'s RTs were significantly longer in translation tasks from L2 into L1 than from L1 into L2, whereas no significant difference in translation direction was found in the control subject. Analysis of variance (ANOVA) on RTs with completely randomized design evinced $F(3,220) = 29.39$; $p < 0.001$. Multiple comparisons (Newman-Keuls) also showed significantly slower performances of E.M. as opposed to A.B.

Adapted from "Paradoxical Selective Recovery in a Bilingual Aphasic Following Subcortical Lesions," by S. Aglioti & F. Fabbro, 1993, *Neuroreport, 4*, pp. 1359–1362.

and comprehend at least some words in L1. Moreover, because a similar pattern of performance was observed in E.M.'s written performance which would also be expected given damage to an amodal control mechanism. However, given that Venetan is predominantly a spoken dialect it is difficult to assess how compelling this particular bit of evidence is.

One may wonder why, given the hypothesis that L1 has been suppressed, E.M. was able to translate from L1 to L2. To make sense of this we must take into account the widely held assumption that language comprehension is "easier" than language production. The amodal control mechanism account remains possible because backward translation (L2 to L1) requires production in L1 whereas forward translation (L1 to L2) only requires comprehension in L1. Given the nature of damage to the control mechanism (i.e., the activation of L1 was partially inhibited), translation from L2-L1 should have been relatively more affected than translation from L1-L2, thus producing the paradoxical translation pattern. Thus, the possibility of partial damage to the control mechanism, along with the inherent difference in task difficulty between language comprehension and production, makes it possible to observe some variation in impairment across comprehension and production without stipulating different control mechanisms for each. On the assumption that language production requires more lexical activation relative to language comprehension, damage that was sufficiently strong to cause a dominance switch in language production, may or may not be expected to produce the same switch in language comprehension.

One concern regarding the use of control mechanisms to explain patterns of performance in bilingual aphasics is that the currently rather unconstrained nature of bilingual control models seem to leave open the possibility of explaining virtually any pattern of performance, perhaps even patterns that have never been observed at all. We have argued that E.M.'s data seem compatible with the notion of an amodal control mechanism. However, at least in theory, modality specific impairments paradoxical aphasias (e.g., in which performance in L2 is better than in L1 but only in written language) could also be explained as bilingual control deficits if it were also stipulated that there are separate pathways that connect each modality to the amodal control mechanism. Finally, and perhaps most importantly, is that other than predicting cross-language intrusions and blends, no current model of bilingual control can make clear predictions regarding the nature of other types of errors that should be observed. Hence, the control mechanism account cannot explain E.M.'s other errors (as listed above), and it is interesting to note that the author's explanation of E.M's performance (i.e., damage to brain structures responsible for implicit processing) is also incomplete for this reason.

Having considered the possibility of explaining E.M.'s performance by appealing to an amodal control mechanism we now consider how representational explanations of E.M.'s performance can be explored. In this type of explanation, we could begin by assuming (as the authors did) that the brain damage that occurred differentially affected neural substrates responsible for L1 and L2 (note that this explanation assumes that the differential localization hypothesis is at least partially correct). By attempting to explain the data at levels that encompass more than just a very general description (e.g., "performance in L1 was worse than it was in L2"), additional constraints in interpretations of the data arise.

For example, one important aspect of E.M.'s performance, that is unexplained on the basis of the assumption of damage to neural mechanisms specific to L1, is the co-occurrence of her paradoxical aphasia with the production of neologisms (i.e., nonwords) and phonemic errors. These kinds of errors occur very rarely in normal speech production, and could suggest the presence of damage to phonological representations (Rapp & Goldrick, in press). If damage at this level happened to affect phonemes that are used more frequently in L1, then the expected pattern of performance would include paradoxical aphasia in language production, and these types of errors in L1. This explanation assumes that E.M.'s L1 lexicon was intact at the levels of semantics and form representations, and that lexical selection was intact up to the point of phonological assembly, assumptions that would be testable. The absence of paradoxical performance in language comprehension, a task that requires access to semantics via lexical representations in L1, but does not require the production of words in L1, also seems consistent with this notion.

One way to explore this question would be to use cognates, or words with similar "lexical stems" across languages. Perhaps in the interest of emphasizing the differences between L1 and L2, the authors specifically avoided using such words (Aglioti et al., 1996), thus making it difficult to test this hypothesis on the basis of the data reported. For example, if E.M.'s deficit were at a stage of lexical access that is earlier than phonological specification, then she might have been able to produce cross-language homographs (same form but different meaning across languages) when she was asked to name them in L2 but not in L1. On the other hand, if the deficit was phonological in nature, then a similar error rates would be expected across languages (particularly if the test items were limited to homographs that are very close in phonological form across languages). Similarly, if the deficit were phonological in nature then E.M. should have produced more similar error rates in L1 and L2 when tested on cognates relative to noncognates. Two facts that make the hypothesized deficit to phonological representations seem unlikely was the relatively low rate of phonemic errors, and the fact that they were not more prevalent in L1 (as the argument should predict).[3]

The latter point raises another important factor to consider. First, the items in all the experimental tests used to examine E.M.'s performance were restricted to very high frequency words. This approach may have been adopted because of the apparently profound damage to E.M.'s knowledge of L1, and also to guarantee that the items tested only included words that were known to E.M. in both L1 and L2 prior to her brain damage. However, a limitation of this approach is that it may favor the conclusion that knowledge of L2 was relatively preserved. For example, because E.M. was a housewife, it seems likely that, prior to brain-damage, she might have easily produced words in L1 (Venetian) referring to relatively obscure items related to

---

[3]One potential problem with this account is that E.M. performed equally well in comprehending L1 and L2. If damage to L1 were restricted solely to the level of phonological representations, then comprehension in L1 should have remained superior to that in L2. This is assuming that the comprehension tests used in both languages were sufficiently sensitive to detect a difference, and that L1 was better than L2 prior to her brain damage. However, the latter assumption may not be warranted especially given that members of E.M.'s family reported being very surprised to learn of E.M.'s unexpectedly degree of proficiency in L2 production.

cooking (e.g., *food mill*), whereas her knowledge of these words in L2 (Italian) may not have been as good. Thus, extensive testing of low-frequency words may have revealed a preserved pattern of L1 dominance, or at least may have attenuated the paradoxical nature of her deficits in formal testing. It is important to note in this context, that the increased ability to produce low-frequency words in L1 would be another way to rule out the possibility of explaining E.M.'s performance with an amodal control mechanism that globally reduces activation in L1.

To end our illustration we will briefly consider the implications of one recent finding in research with intact bilingual cognitive systems for interpreting E.M.'s brain damage. Above we noted that, relative to language comprehension, language production seems to be especially vulnerable to the effects of cross-language competition; and that production of words in L2 in particular, requires the active suppression of L1 competitors. Because language production is more vulnerable during intact bilingual processing, it may also be especially vulnerable to the effects of brain damage. By this view, damage specific to L1 may not only have compromised the ability to produce words in L1, but it may actually have improved some aspects of L2 production by reducing the resources needed to suppress L1. This point is consistent with the fact E.M. herself, and her family members were surprised at how much Italian (L2) E.M. was able to speak. An additional aspect of E.M.'s performance comes to mind in this context; her productions in L1 were frequently interrupted by cross-language intrusions. This aspect of her performance suggests that the brain damage she sustained converted L2 into a strong competitor and suggests that another important issue to explore is to what extent the bilingual mechanism of control may depend on, or interact with, the relative levels of resting activation in each lexicon.

CONCLUSIONS

We have attempted to demonstrate how recent developments in research on cognitive processing in neurologically intact bilinguals can provide a framework for research on bilingual aphasia that will increase our understanding of bilingual processing deficits as well as of normal cognitive processing in bilinguals. This approach to research on bilingual aphasia takes advantage of recent developments in cognitive research by introducing an increasing the level of detail to the interpretations of bilingual processing deficits. By considering possible cognitive accounts of bilingual aphasia, new, testable, and we believe interesting, predictions arise that are often not dependent on having knowledge that is often unavailable (e.g., how the patient would have performed prior to brain damage). Similarly, we have also argued that because the cognitive models are not necessarily tied to the issue of localization of function, this approach is also less dependent on the limitations of current imaging techniques, and is less compromised by the lack of experimental control often inherent in studying brain damage.

Finally, we also suggest that an increased level of detail in explanations of bilingual deficits and normal processing will ultimately be necessary to make sense of the rapidly accumulating imaging data which has become (and will likely continue to become) increasingly complex. As imaging techniques advance the level of detail offered by descriptions of bilingual aphasia in terms of global recovery patterns (e.g., alternate antagonism) will likely fall short of the concomitantly possible increase in the degree of detail in localization theories. It is impossible to find something in the brain without first having an adequate description of what it is that one is looking for and this is what cognitive models can provide.

Acknowledgements

The research reported in this chapter was supported in part by Training Grant DC00041-06 from the National Institute on Deafness and Other Communication disorders to the Center for

Research on Language at the University of California, San Diego, by NSF Grant BCS-9905850 to Judith F. Kroll at The Pennsylvania State University, and by a sabbatical grant to Judith F. Kroll from the Nijmegen Institute for Cognition and Information. We thank David Green for helpful comments on an earlier version of the manuscript. Correspondence should be addressed to Tamar Gollan, Center for Research in Language, 9500 Gilman Drive, 0526, La Jolla, CA 92093-0526. E-mail: tgollan@ucsd.edu

REFERENCES

Aglioti, S., Beltramello, A., Girardi, F., & Fabbro, F. (1996). Neurolinguistic and follow-up study of an unusual pattern of recovery from bilingual subcortical aphasia. *Brain, 119,* 1551–1564.

Aglioti, S., & Fabbro, F. (1993). Paradoxical selective recovery in a bilingual aphasic following subcortical lesions. *Neuroreport, 4,* 1359–1362.

Albert, M. L., & Obler, L. K. (1978). *The bilingual brain: Neuropsychological and neurolinguistic aspects of bilingualism.* New York: Academic Press.

Altarriba, J. (1990). *Constraints on interlingual facilitation effects in priming in Spanish-English bilinguals.* Unpublished dissertation, Vanderbilt University.

Andrews, S. (1997). The effect of orthographic similarity on lexical retrieval: Resolving neighborhood conflicts. *Psychonomic Bulletin & Review, 4,* 439–461.

Balota, D. (1994). Visual word recognition: The journey from feature to meaning. In M. Gernsbacher (ed.), *Handbook of psycholinguistics* (pp. 303–357). New York: Academic Press.

Bates, E., Wulfeck, B., & MacWhinney, B., (1991). Cross-linguistic studies in aphasia: An overview. *Brain & Language, 41,* 123–148.

Bock, K., & Levelt, W. J. M. (1994). Language production: Grammatical encoding. In M. A. Gernsbacher (Ed.), *Handbook of psycholinguistics* (pp. 945–984). San Diego, CA: Academic Press.

Brown, H., Sharma, N. K., & Kirsner, K. (1984). The role of script and phonology in lexical representation. *Quarterly Journal of Experimental Psychology, 36A,* 491–505.

Brysbaert, M. (1998). Word recognition in bilinguals: Evidence against the existence of two separate lexicons. *Psychologica Belgica, 38,* 163–175.

Caramazza, A., Hillis, A. E., Rapp, B. C., & Romani, C. (1990). The multiple semantics hypothesis: Multiple confusions? *Cognitive Neuropsychology, 7,* 161–189.

Chen, H.-C. (1992). Lexical processing in bilingual or multilingual speakers. In R. J. Harris (Ed.), *Cognitive processing in bilinguals* (pp. 253–264). Amsterdam: Elsevier.

Chen, H.-C., & Leung, Y.-S. (1989). Patterns of lexical processing in a nonnative language. *Journal of Experimental Psychology: Learning, Memory, and Cognition, 15,* 316–325.

Chen, H.-C., & Ng, M-L. (1989). Semantic facilitation and translation priming effects in Chinese-English bilinguals. *Memory & Cognition, 17,* 454–462.

Cheung, H., & Chen, H-C. (1998). Lexical and conceptual processing in Chinese-English bilinguals: Further evidence for asymmetry. *Memory & Cognition, 26,* 1002–1013.

Costa, A., Miozzo, M., & Caramazza, A. (1998). Lexical selection in bilinguals: Do words in the bilingual's two lexicons compete for selection? *Journal of Memory and Language, 41,* 365–397.

De Groot, A. M. B. (1992a). Determinants of word translation. *Journal of Experimental Psychology: Learning, Memory, and Cognition, 18,* 1001–1018.

De Groot, A. M. B. (1992b). Bilingual lexical representation: A closer look at conceptual representations. In R. Frost & L. Katz (Eds.), *Orthography, phonology, morphology, and meaning* (pp. 389–412). Amsterdam: Elsevier.

De Groot, A. M. B. (1993). Word-type effects in bilingual processing tasks: Support for a mixed representational system. In R. Schreuder & B. Weltens (Eds.), *The bilingual lexicon* (pp. 27–51). Amsterdam: John Benjamins.

De Groot, A. M. B. (1995). Determinants of bilingual lexicosemantic organization. *Computer Assisted Language Learning, 8,* 151–180.

De Groot, A. M. B., & Nas, G. L. (1991). Lexical representation of cognates and noncognates in compound bilinguals. *Journal of Memory and Language, 30,* 90–123.

De Groot, A. M. B. Dannenburg, L., & Van Hell, J. G. (1994). Forward and backward word translation by bilinguals. *Journal of Memory and Language, 33,* 600–629.

De Groot, A. M. B., Delmaar, P., & Lupker, S. (2000). The processing of interlexical homographs in translation recognition and lexical decision: Support for nonselective access to bilingual memory. *Quarterly Journal of Experimental Psychology, 53A,* 397–428.

De Groot, A. M. B., & Poot, R. (1997). Word translation at three levels of proficiency in a second language: The ubiquitous involvement of conceptual memory. *Language Learning, 47,* 215–264.

Dehaene, S., Dupoux, E., Mehler, J., Cohen, L., Paulesu, E., Perani, D., Van de Moortele, P. F., Lehericy, S., & Le Bihan, D. (1997). Anatomical variability in the cortical representation of first and second language. *Neuroreport, 8,* 3809–3815.

Dell, G. S. (1986). A spreading-activation model of retrieval in sentence production. *Psychological Review, 93,* 283–321.

Dell, G. S., & O'Seaghdha, P. G. (1991). Mediated and convergent lexical priming in language production: A comment on Levelt et al. (1991). *Psychological Review, 98,* 604–614.

Dijkstra, A., Grainger, J., & Van Heuven, W. J. B. (1999). Recognition of cognates and interlingual homographs: The neglected role of phonology. *Journal of Memory and Language, 41,* 496–518.

Dijkstra, T., & Van Heuven, W. J. B. (1998). The BIA-model and bilingual word recognition. In J. Grainger & A. Jacobs (Eds.), *Localist connectionist approaches to human cognition* (pp. 189–225). Mahwah, NJ: Lawrence Erlbaum.

Dijkstra, T., Van Heuven, W. J. B., & Grainger, J. (1998). Simulating cross-language competition with the bilingual interactive activation model. *Psychologica Belgica*, *38*, 177–196.

Dijkstra, A., Van Jaarsveld, H., & Ten Brinke, S. (1998). Interlingual homograph recognition: Effects of task demands and language intermixing. *Bilingualism: Language and Cognition, 1*, 51–66.

Dronkers, N., Yamasaki, Y., Ross, G. W., & White, L. (1995). Assessment of bilinguality in aphasia: Issues and examples from multicultural Hawaii. In M. Paradis (Ed.), *Aspects of bilingual aphasia* (pp. 123–138). Tarrytown, NY: Elsevier.

Dufour, R., & Kroll, J. F. (1995). Matching words to concepts in two languages: A test of the concept mediation model of bilingual representation. *Memory & Cognition, 23*, 166–180.

Fabbro, F. (1999). *The neurolinguistics of bilingualism: An introduction.* Hove, England UK: Psychology Press/Taylor & Francis.

Francis, W. (1999a). Analogical transfer of problem solutions within and between languages in Spanish-English bilinguals. *Journal of Memory and Language, 40*, 301–329.

Francis, W. (1999b). Cognitive integration of language and memory in bilinguals: Semantic representation. *Psychological Bulletin, 125*, 193–222.

Frauenfelder, U., & Tyler, L. (1987). *Spoken word recognition.* Cambridge, MA: MIT Press/Bradford Books.

Frenck-Mestre, C., & Prince, P. (1997). Second language autonomy. *Journal of Memory and Language, 37*, 481–501.

Gerard, L. D., & Scarborough, D. L. (1989). Language-specific access of homographs by bilinguals. *Journal of Experimental Psychology: Learning, Memory, and Cognition, 15*, 305–315.

Gollan, T., Forster, K. I., & Frost, R. (2997). Translation priming with different scripts: Masked priming with cognates and noncognates in Hebrew-English bilinguals. *Journal of Experimental Psychology: Learning, Memory, and Cognition, 23*, 1122–1139.

Grainger, J., & Dijkstra, T. (1992). On the representation and use of language information in bilinguals. In R. J. Harris (Ed.), *Cognitive Processing in Bilinguals* (pp. 207–220). Amsterdam: Elsevier.

Grainger, J., & Frenck-Mestre (1998). Masked priming by translation equivalents in proficient bilinguals. *Language & Cognitive Processes, 13*, 601–623.

Green, D. W. (1986). Control, activation, and resource: A framework and a model for the control of speech in bilinguals. *Brain and Language, 27*, 210–223.

Green, D. W. (1993). Towards a model of L2 comprehension and production. In R. Schreuder & B. Weltens (Eds.), *The bilingual lexicon* (pp. 249–277). Amsterdam: John Benjamins.

Green, D. W. (1998a). Mental control of the bilingual lexico-semantic system. *Bilingualism: Language and Cognition, 1*, 67–81.

Green, D. W. (1998b). Bilingualism and thought. *Psychologica Belgica, 38*, 251–276.

Grosjean, F. (1982). *Life with two languages: An introduction to bilingualism.* Cambridge, MA: Harvard University Press.

Grosjean, F. (1985). Polyglot aphasics and language mixing: A comment on Perecman (1984). *Brain & Language, 26*, 349–355.

Grosjean, F. (1997). Processing Mixed Language: Issues, Findings, and Models. In A. M. B. De Groot & J. F. Kroll (Eds.), *Tutorials in bilingualism: Psycholinguistic perspectives* (pp. 225–254). Mahwah, NJ: Lawrence Erlbaum.

Grosjean, F. (1998). Studying bilinguals: Methodological and conceptual issues. *Bilingualism: Language and Cognition, 1*, 131–149.

Grosjean, F. (in press). The bilingual's language modes. In J. L. Nicol & T. D. Langendoen (Eds.), *Language processing in the bilingual.* Oxford: Blackwell.

Harris R. J. & McGhee Nelson, E. M. (1992). Bilingualism: Not the exception any more. In R. J. Harris (Ed.), *Cognitive processing in Bbilinguals* (pp. 3–14). North-Holland, The Netherlands: Elsevier.

Hermans, D. , Bongaerts, T., De Bot, K., & Schreuder, R. (1998). Producing words in a foreign language: Can speakers prevent interference from their first language? *Bilingualism: Language and Cognition, 1*, 213–229.

Hernandez, A. E., & Kohnert, K. J. (1999). Aging and language switching in bilinguals. *Aging, Neuropsychology, & Cognition, 6*, 69–83.

Illes, J., Francis, W. S., Desmond, J. E., Gabrieli, J. D. E., Glover, G. H., Poldrack, R., Lee, C. J., & Wagner, A. D. (1999). Convergent cortical representation of semantic processing in bilinguals. *Brain and Language, 70*, 347–363.

Jescheniak, J. D., & Schriefers, K. I. (1998). Discrete serial versus cascading processing in lexical access in speech production: Further evidence from the coactivation of near-synonyms. *Journal of Experimental Psychology: Learning, Memory, and Cognition, 24*, 1256–1274.

Jiang, N. (1998). Testing processing explanations for the asymmetry in masked cross-language priming. *Bilingualism: Language and Cognition, 2*, 59–75.

Keatley, C. W. (1992). History of bilingualism research in cognitive psychology. In R. J. Harris (Ed.), *Cognitive processing in bilinguals* (pp. 15–49). Amsterdam: Elsevier.

Keatley, C., Spinks, J., & De Gelder, B. (1994). Asymmetrical semantic facilitation between languages. *Memory & Cognition, 22*, 70–84.

Kim, K. H. S., Relkin, N. R., Lee, K. M., & Hirsch, J. (1997). Distinct cortical areas associated with native and second languages. *Nature, 388*, 171–174.

Kirsner, K., Smith, M. C., Lockhart, R. S., King, M. L., & Jain, M. (1984). The bilingual lexicon: Language-specific units in an integrated network. *Journal of Verbal Learning and Verbal Behavior, 23*, 519–539.

Klein, D., Zatorre, R. J., Milner, B., Meyer, E., & EVans, E. H. (1994). Left putaminal activation when speaking a second language: Evidence from PET. *Neuroreport, 5*, 2295–2297.

Kohnert, K. J., Bates, E., & Hernandez, A. E. (1999). Balancing bilinguals: Lexical-semantic production and cognitive processing in children learning Spanish and English. *Journal of Speech, Language, and Hearing Research, 42*, 1400–1413.

Kohnert, K. J, Hernandez, A. E., & Bates, E. (1998). Bilingual performance on the Boston Naming Test: Preliminary norms in Spanish and English. *Brain and Language, 65*, 422–440.

Kroll, J. F. (1993). Accessing conceptual representation for words in a second language. In R. Schreuder & B. Weltens (Eds.), *The bilingual lexicon* (pp. 53–81). Amsterdam: John Benjamins.

Kroll, J. F., & Curley, J. (1988). Lexical memory in novice bilinguals: The role of concepts in retrieving second language words. In M. Gruneberg, P. Morris, & R. Sykes (Eds.), *Practical aspects of memory* (Vol. 2, pp. 389–395). London: John Wiley.

Kroll, J. F., & De Groot, A. M. B. (1997). Lexical and conceptual memory in the bilingual: Mapping form to meaning in two languages. In A. M. B. De Groot & J. F. Kroll (Eds.), *Tutorials in bilingualism: Psycholinguistic perspectives* (pp. 169–199). Mahwah, NJ: Lawrence Erlbaum.

Kroll, J. F., & Peck, A. (1998, April). *Competing activation across a bilingual's two languages: Evidence from picture naming.* Paper presented at the 43rd Annual Meeting of the International Linguistic Association, New York University, New York.

Kroll, J. F., & Stewart, E. (1994). Category interference in translation and picture naming: Evidence for asymmetric connections between bilingual memory representations. *Journal of Memory and Language, 33,* 149–174.

Kroll, J. F., & Tokowicz, N. (in press). The development of conceptual representation for words in a second language. In J. L. Nicol & T. Langendoen (Eds.), *Language processing in bilinguals.* Cambridge, MA: Blackwell.

La Heij, W., Kerling, R., & Van der Velden, E. (1996). Nonverbal context effects in forward and backward translation: Evidence for concept mediation. *Journal of Memory and Language, 35,* 648-665.

Lebrun, Y. (1981). Bilingual and the brain: A brief appraisal of Penfield's views. In H. Baetens Beardsmore (Ed.), *Elements of bilingual theory* (pp. 66-75). Brussels, Vrije Universiteit Brussel.

Levelt, W. J. M. (1989). *Speaking. From intention to articulation.* Cambridge, MA: MIT Press.

Levelt, W. J. M., Roelofs, A., & Meyer, A. S. (1999). A theory of lexical access in speech production. *Behavioral and Brain Sciences, 22,* 1-75.

Loasby, H. A. (1998). *A study of the effects of language switching and priming in a picture naming task.* Unpublished manuscript, University of Oxford, U.K.

Luzzatti, C., Willmes, K., & DeBleser, R. (1991). *Aachener Aphasia Test (AAT) Versione Italiana.* Firenze: Organizzazioni Speciali.

McCarthy, R. A., & Warrington, E. K. (1990), *Cognitive neuropsychology: A clinical introduction.* San Diego, CA: Academic Press.

McClelland, J. L., & Rumelhart, D. E. (1981). An interactive activation model of context effects in letter perception, Part 1: An account of basic findings. *Psychological Review, 88,* 375-405.

Meuter, R. F .I., & Allport, A. (1999). Bilingual language switching in naming: Asymmetrical costs of language selection. *Journal of Memory and Language, 40,* 25-40.

Meyer, D. E., & Ruddy, M. G. (1974, April). *Bilingual word recognition: Organization and retrieval of alternative lexical codes.* Paper presented at the Eastern Psychological Association Meeting, Philadelphia, PA.

Miceli. G., Silveri, M. C., Romani, C., & Caramazza, A. (1989). Variation in the pattern of omissions and substitutions of grammatical morphemes in the spontaneous speech of so-called agrammatic patients. *Brain and Language, 36,* 447-492.

Nilipour, R., & Paradis, M. (1995). Breakdown of functional categories in three Farsi-English bilingual aphasic patients. In M. Paradis (Ed.), *Aspects of bilingual aphasia* (pp. 123-138). Tarrytown, New York: Elsevier.

Paivio, A. (1971). *Imagery and verbal processes.* Toronto,

CAN: Holt, Rinehart, and Winston.

Paivio, A. (1986). *Mental representations: A dual coding approach.* New York: Oxford University Press.

Paradis, M. (1987). Neurolinguistic perspectives on bilingualism. In M. Paradis & G. Libben (Eds.), *The assessment of bilingual aphasia* (pp. 1–17). Hillsdale, NJ: Lawrence Erlbaum.

Paradis, M. (1989). Bilingual and polyglot aphasia. In F. Boller & J. Graffman (Eds.), *Handbook of Neuropsychology* (Vol. 2, pp. 117–140) Amsterdam: Elsevier.

Paradis, M. (1990). Language lateralization in bilinguals: Enough already! *Brain and Language, 39,* 576-586.

Paradis, M. (1995). *Aspects of bilingual aphasia.* Oxford, UK: Elsevier.

Paradis, M. (1997). The cognitive neuropsychology of bilingualism. In A. M. B. De Groot & J. F. Kroll (Eds.), *Tutorials in bilingualism: Psycholinguistic perspectives* (pp. 331-354). Mahwah, NJ: Lawrence Erlbaum.

Paradis, M. (1998) Aphasia in bilinguals: How atypical is it? In P. Coppens & Y. Lebrun (Eds.), *Aphasia in atypical populations* (pp. 35-66) Mahwah, NJ: Lawrence Erlbaum.

Perani, D., Paulesu, E., Galles, N. S., Dupoux, E., Dahaene, S., Bettinardi, V., Cappa, S. F., Fazio, F., & Mehler, J. (1998). The bilingual brain: Proficiency and age of acquisition of the second language. *Brain, 121,* 1841-1852.

Perecman, E. (1984). Spontaneous translation and language mixing in a polyglot aphasic. *Brain and Language, 23,* 43-63.

Perecman, E. (1985). Language mixing in polyglot aphasia: Conscious strategy or preconscious necessity? A reply to Grosjean. *Brain and Language, 26,* 356-359.

Peterson, R. R., & Savoy, P. (1998). Lexical selection and phonological encoding during language production: Evidence for cascaded processing. *Journal of Experimental Psychology: Learning, Memory, and Cognition, 24,* 539-557.

Potter, M. C., So, K.-F., Von Eckardt, B., & Feldman, L. B. (1984). Lexical and conceptual representation in beginning and more proficient bilinguals. *Journal of Verbal Learning and Verbal Behavior, 23,* 23-38.

Poulisse, N. (1997). Language production in bilinguals. In A. M. B. De Groot & J. F. Kroll (Eds.), *Tutorials in bilingualism: Psycholinguistic perspectives* (pp. 201-224). Mahwah, NJ: Lawrence Erlbaum.

Price, C. J., Green, D. W., & von Studnitz, R. (1999). A functional imaging study of translation and language switching. *Brain, 122,* 2221-2235.

Rapp, B., & Goldrick, M. (2000). Discreteness and interactivity in spoken word production. *Psychological Review, 107,* 460-499.

Sánchez-Casas, R. M., Davis, C. W., & García-Albea, J. E. (1992). Bilingual lexical processing: Exploring the cognate-noncognate distinction. *European Journal of Cognitive Psychology, 4,* 293-310.

Scarborough, D. L., Cortese, C., & Scarborough, H. S. (1977). Frequency and repetition effects in lexical memory. *Journal of Experimental Psychology: Human Perception and Performance, 3,* 1-17.

Scarborough, D. L., Gerard, L., & Cortese, C. (1984). Independence of lexical access in bilingual word recognition. *Journal of Verbal Learning and Verbal Behavior, 23,* 84-99.

Schönpflug, U. (1997, April). *Bilingualism and memory.* Paper presented at the International Symposium on Bilingualism, Newcastle-upon-Tyne, U.K.

Schrauf, R., & Rubin, D. (1998). Bilingual autobiographical memory in older adult immigrants: A test of cognitive explanations of the reminiscence bump and the linguistic encoding of memories. *Journal of Memory and Language, 39*, 437-457.

Schriefers, H., Myers, A. S., & Levelt, W. J. M. (1990). Exploring the time course of lexical access in production: Picture-word interference studies. *Journal of Memory & Language, 29*, 86-102.

Schwanenflugel, P. J., Harnishfeger, K. K., & Stowe, R. W. (1988). Context availability and lexical decisions for abstract and concrete words. *Journal of Memory and Language, 27*, 499-520.

Schwanenflugel, P. J., & Rey, M. (1986). Interlingual semantic facilitation: Evidence for a common representational system in the bilingual. *Journal of Memory and Language, 25*, 605-618.

Schwanenflugel, P. J., & Shoben, E. J. (1983). Differential context effects in the comprehension of abstract and concrete verbal materials. *Journal of Experimental Psychology: Learning, Memory, and Cognition, 9*, 82-102.

Sholl, A., Sankaranarayanan, A., & Kroll, J. F. (1995). Transfer between picture naming and translation: A test of asymmetries in bilingual memory. *Psychological Science, 6*, 45-49.

Smith, M. C. (1997). How do bilinguals access lexical information? In A. M. B. De Groot & J. F. Kroll (Eds.), *Tutorials in bilingualism: Psycholinguistic perspectives* (pp. 145-168). Mahwah, NJ: Lawrence Erlbaum Publishers.

Solin, D. (1989). The systematic misrepresentation of bilingual-crossed aphasia data and its consequences. *Brain and Language, 36*, 92-116.

Starreveld, P., & La Heij, W. (1995). Semantic interference, orthographic facilitation, and their interaction in naming tasks. *Journal of Experimental Psychology: Learning, Memory, and Cognition, 21*, 686-698.

Thomas, M. (1998). Distributed representations and the bilingual lexicon: One store or two? In J. Bullinaria, D. Glasspool, & G. Houghton (Eds.), *Proceedings of the 4th Annual Neural Computation and Psychology Workshop*, London, April 9-11, 1997 (pp. 240-253). London: Springer-Verlag.

Tokowicz, N. (1997). *Reevaluating concreteness effects in bilingual translation*. Unpublished Master's Thesis, The Pennsylvania State University, University Park, PA.

Tzelgov, J., & Henik, A. (1989, July). *The insensitivity of the semantic relatedness effect to surface differences and it implications*. Paper presented at the First European Congress of Psychology, Amsterdam, The Netherlands.

Ullman, M. T. (1999, March). *The functional neuroanatomy of end-state language*. Paper presented at the Annual Conference of the American Association for Applied Linguistics. Stamford, Connecticut.

Vaid, J. (in press). Bilingualism. V. S. Ramachandran (Ed.), In *Encyclopedia of the human brain*. San Diego, CA: Academic Press,

Vaid, J., & Genesee, F. (1980). Neuropsychological approaches to bilingualism: A critical review. *Canadian Journal of Psychology, 34*, 417-445.

Van Hell, J. G. (1998). *Cross-language processing and bilingual memory organization*. Unpublished Doctoral Dissertation, University of Amsterdam, Amsterdam, The Netherlands.

Van Hell, J. G., & De Groot, A. M. B. (1998). Conceptual representation in bilingual memory: Effects of concreteness and cognate status in word association. *Bilingualism: Language and Cognition, 3*, 193-211.

Van Heuven, W. J. B., Dijkstra, T., & Grainger, J. (1998). Orthographic neighborhood effects in bilingual word recognition. *Journal of Memory and Language, 39*, 458-483.

Weber-Fox, C., & Neville, H. J., (1996). Maturational constraints on functional specializations for language processing: ERP and behavioral evidence in bilingual speakers. *Journal of Cognitive Neuroscience, 8*, 231-256.

Weber-Fox, C. M., & Neville, H. J., (1999). Functional neural subsystems are differentially affected by delays in second language immersion: ERP and behavioral evidence in bilinguals. In D. Birdsong (Ed.), *Second language acquisition and the critical period hypothesis*, (pp. 23-38). Mahwah, NJ: Lawrence Erlbaum.

Zatorre, R. J. (1989). On the representation of multiple languages in the brain: Old problems and new directions. *Brain and Language, 36*, 127-147.

Part 5

—

Sentences

—

The apparel in which your thoughts parade
before the public.

—*George W. Crane*

14

Sentence Comprehension

Randi Martin

Studies in the 1970s demonstrated impaired sentence comprehension in patients with good single word comprehension (e.g., Caramazza & Zurif, 1976; von Stockert & Bader, 1976). These findings generated a good deal of excitement among researchers in and outside the field of aphasia because they seemed to provide strong evidence for an independent syntactic processing module (e.g., see Caramazza & Berndt, 1978; Jackendoff, 1993, chapter 11). That is, the results appeared to provide support for linguistic theories that hypothesized a system of rules for specifying grammatical well-formedness that was independent of semantics. Despite this initial enthusiasm, a survey of current theorizing on sentence processing published in mainstream cognitive journals (e.g., Boland & Cutler, 1996; MacDonald, Pearlmutter, & Seidenberg, 1994; Trueswell & Tanenhaus, 1994) indicates little or no reliance on findings from aphasia in supporting or refuting current models. This lack of connection between neuropsychological findings and theories of normal processing differentiates the domain of sentence comprehension from other areas of language processing such as single word reading, spoken word production, and short-term memory. In these domains, there is a much more lively interaction between researchers who study normal populations and those who study impaired populations (e.g., Coltheart, Curtis, Atkins, & Heller, 1993; Dell, Schwartz, Martin, Saffran, & Gagnon, 1997; Martin, Lesch, & Bartha, 1999; Plaut, McClelland, Seidenberg, & Patterson, 1996).

One reason for this lack of influence of neuropsychological findings on sentence processing may be that the topics of interest have diverged for researchers studying normal sentence processing and researchers studying sentence processing deficits. Among those focusing on normal sentence processing, interest switched from an early concern with the analysis of the relative comprehension difficulty of different sentence types (Fodor & Garrett, 1967; Kimball, 1973; Miller & McKean, 1964) to investigations of the timing of the influence of syntactic and lexical or semantic factors in comprehension (e.g., Frazier & Rayner, 1982; Trueswell, Tanenhaus, & Kello, 1993).[1] In contrast, researchers in aphasia have continued to be concerned with explaining the basis for the relative difficulty of different sentence types because of striking variations in comprehension accuracy for different syntactic constructions (e.g., see Caplan & Hildebrandt, 1988; Schwartz, Saffran, Linebarger, & Pate, 1987).

---

[1]One reason for the switch in interests may have been the downfall of the Derivational Theory of Complexity (see Slobin, 1971) which had provided a theoretical basis for predicting sentence complexity. See discussion under Sentence Processing Theories.

A second reason for the lack of influence may be the many contradictory findings and claims that have been generated from the syndrome-based approach which has dominated research on sentence processing deficits (see Ellis & Young, 1988, pp. 241-251, for discussion). Much of the research has focused on the clinical group of Broca's aphasics, and has attempted to contrast them with other clinical groups such as Wernicke's aphasics or conduction aphasics. Broca's aphasics tend to produce speech that is "agrammatic"—that is, marked by simplified grammatical structure and the omission of function words and inflectional markers (Goodglass & Kaplan, 1972). These patients have also been shown to have difficulty with sentence comprehension when they have to use the syntactic structure of the sentence for correct interpretation (e.g., Caramazza & Zurif, 1976; Schwartz, Saffran & Marin, 1980). For instance, for reversible sentences like "The boy was pushed by the girl," in which either noun can plausibly be either agent or patient, the passive structure of the sentence has to be processed in order to realize that it is the girl that is doing the pushing. Broca's aphasics have difficulty with the reversible sentence types on tasks such as sentence-picture matching in which a choice has to be made between the correct picture and one that reverses the role of agent and theme (i.e., the thing or person acted upon). They do not have difficulty if the incorrect picture depicts a lexical substitution (i.e., substituting a different noun for agent or theme, or a different action; see Berndt & Caramazza, 1980, for an overview). This comprehension pattern has been termed "asyntactic comprehension."

The co-occurrence of agrammatic speech and asyntactic comprehension led Berndt and Caramazza (1980) to hypothesize the syntactic deficit hypothesis, that is, that Broca's aphasics have a selective disruption of syntactic processes that affects both language production and comprehension. This hypothesis had a great deal of appeal to some researchers in psychology and linguistics because, if true, it would support the existence of an autonomous syntactic module. However, soon after its original formulation, several papers were published that called this syntactic deficit hypothesis into question. An excellent review of this literature and subsequent revisions of the hypothesis and challenges to the revisions has been provided by Berndt (1991, 1998). Only a brief summary of some of the more salient problems for this hypothesis will be presented here.

One major challenge for the syntactic deficit hypothesis is that dissociations between these comprehension and production patterns have been demonstrated: some patients who produce agrammatic speech do not show asyntactic comprehension (e.g., Kolk, van Grunsven, & Keyser, 1985; Miceli, Mazzucchi, Menn, & Goodglass, 1983) and other patients who demonstrate asyntactic comprehension do not produce agrammatic speech (e.g., Caramazza & Miceli, 1991; Martin & Blossom-Stach, 1986; see Bates & Goodman, 1997, for discussion). Within a group of Broca's aphasics, great variation has been documented in their performance on syntactic comprehension tests (Kolk & van Grunsven, 1985), with little relation between the degree of agrammatism and the degree of comprehension deficit (Martin, Wetzel, Blossom-Stach, & Feher, 1989). As is evident in the data presented by Berndt, Mitchum, and Haendiges (1996), it is far from rare for patients to have agrammatic speech and yet show normal comprehension for reversible sentences. Even the term "agrammatic" is misleading since patients with agrammatic speech may show qualitatively different patterns, not just variations in severity—with some showing only morphological deficits and not structural deficits and others showing the reverse pattern (see Howard, 1985, for discussion). Similarly, among patients showing comprehension deficits on reversible sentences, the relative difficulty that patients have with active versus passive sentences versus relative clause sentences varies considerably (Berndt et al., 1996). Thus, lumping together all patients classed as Broca's aphasics in order to look at group average performance is a highly questionable practice given the heterogeneity of production and comprehension deficits within this group (see Badecker & Caramazza, 1985, for discussion).

Another major challenge for the syntactic deficit hypothesis came from a study by Linebarger,

Schwartz, and Saffran (1983) which demonstrated remarkably well preserved ability to judge sentence grammaticality among patients showing the combination of agrammatic speech and asyntactic comprehension thought to signify a syntactic deficit. These patients performed well on a variety of complex grammatical constructions, even though the detection of ungrammaticality often hinged on the correct interpretation of function words and grammatical markers—the lexical items that were the most impaired in their speech production. A number of subsequent studies have replicated the findings of good performance on grammaticality judgments together with impaired performance on comprehension (see Berndt, 1991, and Linebarger, 1990, for discussion). To explain this dissociation, Linebarger, Saffran, and colleagues have proposed the "mapping deficit" hypothesis (Linebarger, 1990; Saffran & Schwartz, 1988). According to this hypothesis, these patients are able to parse a sentence (i.e., analyze its syntactic structure) but are unable to carry out the mapping between grammatical roles and thematic roles that is implied by this structural information.

Some researchers have called into question the data from grammaticality judgments on the grounds that these judgements require unnatural "off-line" syntactic processing procedures unlike those involved during normal comprehension (Zurif & Grodzinsky, 1983). (Off-line procedures, such as grammaticality judgments, require conscious reflection on the outcomes of comprehension processes and typically require judgments at the end of the sentence. On-line procedures tap comprehension as it occurs on a word-by-word basis, and use indirect measures, such as reaction time on a secondary task, to reveal unconscious processes.) As discussed by Linebarger (1990), this criticism seems unfounded on several grounds. First, one would have to assume that there is another set of syntactic processing mechanisms used in off-line tasks (but not everyday comprehension) that can handle all of the sentence structures they employed. The reason for the existence of this second set of syntactic processing mechanisms is hard to fathom. Second, typical comprehension tests such as sentence-picture matching and enactment (acting out the action in a sentence with dolls or other figures) are also "off-line" in that subjects use the end product of comprehension to perform the task. Comprehension in these tasks is not tapped on a moment-by-moment basis. Third, subsequent studies of grammaticality judgments that have used on-line processing techniques have also demonstrated preserved performance (Shankweiler, Crain, Gorrell, & Tuller, 1989; Wulfeck, 1988).

Some researchers have defended a revised version of the syntactic deficit hypothesis, postulating that only some aspects of syntactic knowledge or syntactic processing have been disrupted in Broca's aphasics, and these disruptions have not been picked up in most studies using grammaticality judgments. For instance, it has been suggested that Broca's aphasics have difficulty in comprehension only for sentences which, according to linguistic theory, have "moved elements" (Grodzinsky, 1995). That is, according to some linguistic accounts, there is a deep structure representation of a sentence in which the arguments of a verb are in their canonical position (e.g., "The girl liked the boy"). Other syntactic structures that express the same meaning can be generated by moving some of these arguments to other positions (see Radford, 1988). For instance, in a sentence such as "That's the boy that the girl liked," it is assumed that "boy" plays the role of object with respect to the verb "liked" in the relative clause, but has been moved out of this deep structure position to its surface structure position in the main clause. This movement is hypothesized to leave behind a trace that links it from its position in the main clause to this empty position (termed a "gap") in the relative clause. (The "boy" fills this gap, and consequently is referred to as a "filler." The process of linking "boy" to the object gap is termed the processing of filler-gap dependencies.) A deficit specific to moved elements should only cause difficulty in a grammaticality test for sentences where the ungrammaticality depended on illegal movement. Again, several problems can be noted with this hypothesis. First is the heterogeneity of comprehension patterns among Broca's aphasics. Second, even if only a subset are hypothesized to have this deficit specific to moved elements, there appears to be no report of even a single patient who had difficulty with all structures involving movement and only those structures (see Badecker, Nathan, & Caramazza, 1991). Third, some of the sentence types that were used in the Linebarger et al. (1983) study did involve the processing of moved elements, and patients performed well on these sentence types (see Linebarger, 1990, for discussion). Finally, it is evident that patients who are not Broca's aphasics (and do not have agrammatic speech) have difficulty with sentences with moved elements (e.g., see Caplan & Hildebrandt, 1988). Even though a recent study demonstrated difficulties on grammaticality judgments for sentences with moved elements for Broca's aphasics, Wernicke's aphasics showed the same difficulties, but the Wernicke's simply performed worse overall (Grodzinsky & Finkel, 1998). Moreover, this study did not report comprehension data for the same patients, so one cannot determine if there was any correspondence between grammaticality judgment performance and performance on comprehension of sentences with moved elements.

Another type of hypothesis about a selective syntactic processing deficit suggests that Broca's aphasics, while not having a disruption of all syntactic knowledge, have a disorder related to the time course of the activation of syntactic information. Haarmann and Kolk (1991) reported that Broca's aphasics were insensitive to grammatical violations with short time intervals between the two words signaling a grammatical error (e.g., noun-verb number agreement) but did show such sensitivity with a longer time interval—suggesting that the activation of syntactic information was slowed for these patients. In contrast, Friederici and Kilborn (1989) and Haarmann and Kolk (1994) reported evidence suggesting these patients showed rapid access to, but overly rapid decay of, syntactic information. These contradictory findings led Haarmann and Kolk (1994) to hypothesize that Broca's may show one or the other temporal processing disorder, but not both. Exactly why brain damage in the same area should give rise to opposite outcomes is far from clear.

Some of the studies purporting to show temporal processing disorders have used difficult cross-modal priming paradigms, that is, where the subject has to respond to a written word that appears at some point during the presentation of a spoken sentence (Friederici & Kilborn, 1989; Haarmann & Kolk, 1994). Tyler, Ostrin, Cooke, and Moss (1995) found that many of the patients they tested were unable to perform a cross-modal task at a high enough level of accuracy to give reliable reaction time results. Instead, they used a word monitoring paradigm (in which subjects had to defect the presence of a target word in a sentence) which was easier for the patients to perform accurately. They showed that some Broca's aphasics showed rapid processing of grammatical information whereas others did not; however, the Broca's aphasics could not be distinguished from other patients (anomic, fluent), some of whom also showed impaired processing of grammatical information.

As can be seen in this brief review, the approach of trying to tie some type of syntactic processing deficit to the clinical category of Broca's aphasic has not proved to be a fruitful enterprise. A variety of mutually contradictory hypotheses have been entertained about what may underlie the comprehension deficits seen in some of these patients, with evidence claimed to support each hypothesis. No consensus has emerged and, no doubt, never will, given the heterogeneity of deficits among patients that fall within this clinical category.

The remainder of the chapter will focus not on what might be causing the comprehension deficits of certain clinical categories, but rather on case studies that demonstrate striking dissociations or associations between aspects of sentence processing and the implications of these findings for current theories. Before going into the case study literature, however, current models of sentence processing will be discussed in order to provide a framework for considering the patient results.

SENTENCE PROCESSING THEORIES

An early application of linguistic theory to the study of psycholinguistic processes resulted in a model termed the derivational theory of complexity (Fodor & Garrett, 1967). This theory, based on Chomsky's (1965) generative theory of grammar, assumed that prior to semantic analysis, comprehenders had to recover the deep structure of a sentence by taking the surface form and undoing any transformations. The more transformations (e.g., question, passive) that had to be undone, the more difficult comprehension would be. As discussed by Slobin (1971), this approach failed on several grounds. One problematic aspect of this theory was that it implied that semantic analysis would be delayed until the end of a clause. However, a large body of evidence has accumulated that supports "immediacy of processing"—that is, that listeners (or readers) determine sentence interpretation to the extent possible as each word is perceived, using a variety of sources of information (i.e., semantic, syntactic, pragmatic; e.g., see Just & Carpenter, 1980; Marslen-Wilson & Tyler, 1980).

Although all current models assume a rapid interplay of different types of information in determining sentence interpretation, they differ in whether any special status should be assigned to syntactic information and in whether different types of information are represented independently or are all intertwined. One influential model of sentence comprehension, termed the garden-path model, does make a "syntax first" assumption. According to this model, heuristics that depend solely on syntactic criteria guide the initial assignment of syntactic structure (Frazier, 1987). A "garden path" effect occurs when these heuristics lead to an incorrect assignment of an ambiguous syntactic structure. For example, in a sentence beginning "The defendant examined by . . . ," these heuristics would lead the comprehender to take "examined" as a main verb rather than a past participle that is part of a reduced relative clause construction. On encountering "by," this interpretation would have to be revised. In the garden path model, semantic information affects parsing (i.e., the assignment of syntactic structure) only by aiding in the revision of incorrect structural interpretations.

A number of studies carried out in the 1980s by Frazier and colleagues supported the predictions of the garden path model (Ferreira & Clifton, 1986; Frazier & Rayner, 1982; Rayner, Carlson, & Frazier, 1983). However, there has been a growing number of results that challenge the assumptions of the model, in particular the assumption that syntactic information (and, specifically, only word-class information) is used first and other sources of information only come in later to aid in reanalysis. One challenge has come from studies showing that information specific to particular lexical items influences parsing decisions (e.g., Boland & Boehm-Jernigan, 1998; MacDonald, 1994; Spivey-Knowlton & Sedivy, 1995). For example, Spivey-Knowlton and Sedivy (1995) showed that preferences for attachment of a prepositional phrase to a verb or to a noun (as in the ambiguous "He saw the girl with the binoculars") depended on whether the verb was a perception verb (*saw*) or an action verb (e.g., *hit*). Other recent findings indicate that lexical-semantic and even discourse level semantics can influence initial parsing decisions (Spivey & Tanenhaus, 1998; Trueswell, Tanenhaus, & Garnsey, 1994; van Berkum, Hagoort, & Brown, in press). For example, Trueswell et al. (1994) found that both the likelihood of the initial noun as an agent and its likelihood as a theme of the verb influenced initial parsing decisions in sentences with main verb/reduced relative ambiguities.

While these studies indicate immediate influences of a variety of sources of information during sentence parsing, most theorizing maintains a distinction between a syntactic parsing system and a semantic system. That is, syntactic and semantic systems generate constraints independently, and it is the products of processing in these different domains that are integrated into an interpretation (Boland & Cutler, 1996; Trueswell & Tanenhaus, 1994). However, some researchers have gone a step further and suggested that syntactic knowledge and parsing procedures are not represented independently of other kinds of information (Bates & Goodman,

1997; MacDonald et al., 1994; McClelland, St. John, & Taraban, 1989). In the position advocated by MacDonald et al. (1994), syntactic structure is represented as part of the lexical representation of each word in terms of the phrase structures in which a particular lexical item can participate. Assignment of sentence structure involves linking the phrase structures from the different lexical representations making up the sentence.[2]

To summarize, the emerging consensus is that many constraints (syntactic, lexical, semantic, and discourse) act simultaneously to determine initial sentence interpretation. These findings do not rule out the possibility that *knowledge* of syntactic constraints is represented autonomously from lexical and semantic information. However, they do indicate that during sentence *processing*, syntactically-based heuristics do not play some over-riding role that is unaffected by other sources of information. The results also suggest that at points of ambiguity, different possible structures may be activated in parallel with different strengths, with the strength being determined by several factors. While some models do away with the assumption that syntactic information is represented separately from other types of linguistic information, most models maintain this distinction. One example of a model assuming representational independence but processing interaction is Boland's (1997) concurrent model. This model assumes that all of the syntactic structures consistent with the input are generated in parallel as each word is processed, with the strength of the different structures varying based on frequencies associated with lexically specific information. Semantic interpretations are constructed concurrently assigning noun constituents to likely roles based on lexical and pragmatic information. The output of the syntactic system also feeds into the semantic system. When more than one syntactic structure is possible, semantic information is used immediately to select the most likely syntactic structure. Thus, in this model, syntactic and semantic information is represented independently, but the products of these different analyses are integrated as each word is processed.

SENTENCE PROCESSING DEFICITS AND IMPLICATIONS FOR THEORY

As discussed earlier, initial interpretations of sentence processing deficits in aphasic patients hypothesized a loss of syntactic knowledge. In terms of early syntactic parsing theories, the hypothesis of a complete disruption of knowledge or a total inability to assign syntactic structure seemed a plausible outcome of brain damage. However, according to more recent theorizing, partial damage or a general reduction in the strength of syntactic influences might seem more likely. Even if one maintains that syntactic knowledge (such as that encompassed by phrase structure rules) is represented autonomously, one might hypothesize that such knowledge is represented in an interactive activation framework where different syntactic configurations vary in strength depending on frequency of occurrence (Boland, 1997; Spivey & Tanenhaus, 1998). Brain damage could generally affect this knowledge system such that all of the outputs from the system were weakened and thus played a lesser (but not nonexistent) role in sentence interpretation compared to other constraints such as semantic or discourse constraints. According to the hypothesis that syntactic structures are embedded in each lexical entry, it is somewhat difficult to see how brain damage could selectively affect syntax but not semantics or the reverse.[3]

Thus, we can return to the issue of whether there is evidence from the study of brain-damaged patients that reveals selective deficits to grammatical versus semantic information

---

[2]As MacDonald et al. (1994) concede, it is not transparent how this approach can be used to account for the processing of long distance dependencies, that is dependencies between words occurring earlier in a sentence and overt or implied grammatical positions later in the sentence. (See Caplan & Hildebrandt, 1988; McElree & Griffith, 1998, for discussion)

[3]One possibility would be to assume that there are general lexical syntactic structures and that semantic representations for individual words are linked to these syntactic structures in much the way that semantic representations might be linked to general phonological forms like syllable structures in specifying the phonological form of a word.

and, within grammatical information, selective deficits to phrase structure versus subcategorization or thematic role information. As discussed earlier, research on the question of the disruption of syntax coexisting with preserved semantics has focused on patients termed agrammatic; however, the evidence from agrammatism is problematic on a number of grounds. Before returning to evidence for the selective disruption of syntax, let us consider evidence for the opposite side of the dissociation, that is, the preservation of syntax in the face of severely disrupted semantics.

Independence of Syntax and Semantics?

Preserved Syntax with Disrupted Semantics

A number of studies have shown that patients with Alzheimer's dementia or progressive aphasia may show severe disruptions of semantic knowledge but better preserved syntactic abilities (Breedin & Saffran, 1999; Hodges, Patterson, & Tyler, 1994; Kempler, Curtiss, & Jackson, 1987; Schwartz & Chawluk, 1990; Schwartz, Marin, & Saffran, 1979).

One example of this dissociation comes from a study by Hodges et al. (1994). They tested a semantic dementia case, patient PP, in both "off-line" and "on-line" language processing tasks. PP was impaired on a variety of off-line semantic tasks including naming, picture-word matching, and attribute judgments, with performance approaching chance levels as the dementia progressed. In order to assess her ability to process syntactic and semantic information in sentences in an "on-line" fashion, PP was tested in a word monitoring paradigm. In this paradigm, which has been used extensively by Lorraine Tyler and colleagues in studies of normal and aphasic sentence processing, subjects listen to spoken sentences and press a button when they detect a target word (for an overview of methods, see Tyler, 1992). A number of studies have demonstrated that word monitoring time is sensitive to the semantic and grammatical well-formedness of the sentence up to the target. In the Hodges et al. study there where three conditions: normal prose, anomalous prose (grammatically well-formed but semantically anomalous), and scrambled prose (neither grammatically well-formed nor semantically interpretable). The target word could occur at an early, middle, or late position in the sentence. (See Table 14.1 for examples of the early and late sentences.) Normal subjects' word monitoring times (shown in Figure 14.1a) are fastest for normal prose, slower for anomalous prose and slowest for the scrambled prose. In addition, times to detect target words decrease as the

Table 14.1

Examples of Word Monitoring Materials Used by Tyler and Colleagues (from Hodges et al., 1994 and Tyler, 1992) with target Word is in Capitals.

Early Target Position
> *Normal Prose.* He said the BUS always left on time and he didn't want to miss it.
> *Anomalous Prose.* It said the BUS always tells in space, and he didn't hope to guess it.
> *Scrambled Prose.* The said he BUS and want left always he on didn't it time miss to.

Late Target Position
> *Normal Prose.* Apparently in the middle of the night some thieves broke into the CHURCH and stole a golden crucifix.
> *Anomalous Prose.* Apparently at the distance of the wind some ants pushed around the CHURCH and forced a new item.
> *Scrambled Prose.* Of middle apparently the some the into the broke night in thieves CHURCH and crucifix stole a golden.

Note. From "Loss of Semantic Memory: Implications for the Modularity of Mind," by J. Hodges, K. Patterson, and L. Tyler, 1994, *Cognitive Neuropsychology, 11,* p. 518; and *Spoken Language Comprehension: An Experimental Approach to Disordered and Normal Procession* by L. Tyler, 1992, pp. 128–129. Copyright MIT Press.

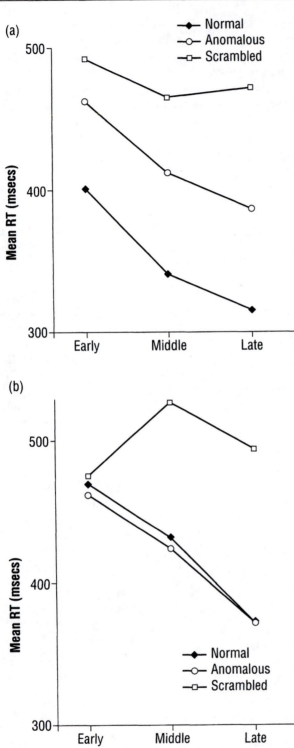

Figure 14.1: Word monitoring times for (a) control subjects (b) patient PP (from Hodges et al., 1994) for normal prose, anomalous prose, and scrambled prose for early, middle, and late target positions. Adapted with permission.

target word occurs later in the normal and anomalous prose, but not in the scrambled prose. These findings are interpreted as indicating that syntactic structure in the normal and anomalous prose conditions aids word detection, and semantic meaningfulness in the normal prose condition provides an additional benefit. The decreasing reaction times with distance into the sentence indicate that these benefits accumulate as the listener develops more elaborate syntactic and semantic interpretations as more of the sentence is processed.

As shown in Figure 14.1b, patient PP showed a reaction time advantage for detecting targets in the anomalous prose and normal prose conditions relative to the scrambled prose condition; however, unlike normal subjects, she showed no difference in reaction times for the anomalous prose and normal prose conditions. For both the normal prose and anomalous prose conditions reaction times decreased with distance into the sentence. Thus, PP showed evidence of on-line processing of syntactic structure. The absence of any benefit for the normal prose condition relative to the anomalous prose condition indicates a failure to process semantic information on-line.

In their recent study of another semantic dementia case (DM), Breedin and Saffran (1999) showed that this patient's performance on a grammaticality test tapping a wide range of grammatical structures remained at the same high level (95%—within normal range) during a time period in which performance on semantic tasks declined dramatically. Using a task involving the writing of homophones to dictation, Schwartz et al. (1979) and Kempler et al. (1987) demonstrated that Alzheimer's patients were better able to use syntactic cues (e.g., "I see" vs. "the sea") than semantic cues (e.g., "look-see" vs. "lake-sea") in producing the appropriate spelling of the homophone.

The evidence discussed so far indicates that patients with severe semantic deficits may be able to access the syntactic properties of individual words (e.g., word class) and be able to process phrase structure. One could further ask whether such patients could carry out thematic role assignments based on sentence structures and verb argument structure. Of course, one would not expect patients with severe semantic deficits to be able to perform well on a standard test of sentence-picture matching using semantically reversible sentences (e.g., "The lion was chased by the tiger") and two picture choices (e.g., a lion chasing a tiger and a tiger chasing a lion) since the patient might be unable to discriminate between lion and tiger. However, Schwartz et al. (1979) and Breedin and Saffran (1999) carried out a modified version of this task which revealed preserved abilities to assign thematic roles based on sentence structure. In the Schwartz et al. task, the patient heard a sentence and saw only one picture depicting two animals involved in some action and was asked to point to one of the animals in the sentence. On some trials the sentence correctly described the picture whereas on others the sentence reversed the roles in the picture. So, for example, the picture might show a tiger chasing a lion, and on a matching trial the patient would hear "The lion was chased by the tiger. Show me tiger." On a non-matching trial the patient would hear "The tiger was chased by the lion. Show me lion." Both patients in these studies showed a preserved ability to indicate the correct animal on the matching trials. Breedin and Saffran used a similar task, but instead of using pictures, the experimenter acted out the action with toy animals. Their sentences included subject (e.g., "That's the lion that chased the tiger") and object cleft (e.g., "That's the lion that the tiger chased") constructions in addition to active and passive sentences, and the patient performed flawlessly on these complex structures. On the nonmatching trials, both patients routinely chose the wrong animal, indicating that they were making their choice on the basis of the syntactic information in the sentence rather than on lexical-semantics. Although the Breedin and Saffran case did show better preserved semantic knowledge of verbs than nouns, knowledge of the argument structure of verbs would not, on most accounts, be sufficient to assign nouns to thematic roles for the noncanonical word orders that occur in passives and object-clefts. Thus, these results indicate that some patients with severe semantic deficits can process grammatical structure, including the long-distance dependencies in cleft object sentences, and map grammatical structure onto thematic roles even though the semantics of single words may be severely disrupted.

Preserved Semantics with Disrupted Processing of Syntax

We can now turn back to the issue of whether dissociations are seen in the opposite direction—that is, with patients showing preserved semantic processing but impaired syntactic processing. Ostrin and Tyler (1995) reported the case of JG, who showed a marked disruption of all syntactic abilities together with relatively preserved lexical-semantic abilities. In a standard sentence-picture matching paradigm, he showed an asyntactic comprehension pattern with poor performance when the distracter picture depicted a reversal of agent and object, but good performance when the distracter picture included a lexical substitution. Unlike the patients reported in Linebarger et al. (1983), he performed poorly on a grammaticality judgment task. In on-line word and sentence processing tasks he also showed a dissociation between disrupted syntactic but preserved semantic processing. In a series of word monitoring tasks involving the processing of words in sentence contexts, he showed an insensitivity to a variety of grammatical violations—violations of subcategorization frame, violations of inflectional and derivational morphology, and, in a previous study, violations of word order (Tyler, 1992). However, like normal subjects he showed semantic priming in a lexical decision task. This case thus showed the reverse pattern as the case of Hodges et al. (1994; described above) on a similar set of tasks.

Interactions between Syntax and Semantics

The data from brain-damaged patients suggest that at least some aspects of semantic and syntactic information are represented independently as they can be selectively affected by brain damage. However, as discussed earlier, such a conclusion does not imply that semantic and syntactic constraints would not interact during sentence processing. Several recent models of sentence processing derived from the study of normal subjects are consistent with representational autonomy but processing interaction (Boland, 1997; Spivey & Tanenhaus, 1998).

As discussed earlier with regard to the mapping deficit hypothesis, one might surmise that for some patients syntactic knowledge is weakened though not completely disrupted. Within Boland's (1997) model, one might hypothesize that the strengths of all syntactic structures are lessened, with the result that the least frequent structures are most affected. If one assumes that the processes involved in assigning thematic roles based on semantic and pragmatic information are preserved in these patients, then one might see that semantic factors override syntactic information in role assignment, particularly for less frequent syntactic structures. When semantic information provides less strong constraints, then the influence of syntactic structure may appear.

Results consistent with this theoretical framework were reported recently by Saffran, Schwartz, and Linebarger (1998). They tested aphasic patients who showed an asyntactic comprehension pattern on sentence-picture matching tasks and normal control subjects. Their patients were classified as Broca's aphasics (5), conduction aphasic (1), and transcortical motor aphasic (1). A sentence anomaly task was used in which syntactic and semantic constraints were varied. All of the sentences had two nouns—one playing the role of agent or experiencer and one playing the role of patient. Two types of sentences were used—(a) verb-constrained and (b) proposition-based. (see Table 14.2). In the verb constrained sentences, one of the nouns was implausible as a filler of one thematic role of the verb but the other noun was plausible in either role. For example, in the implausible sentence "The cat barked at the puppy," a puppy can bark or be barked at, but a cat can only be barked at. In the proposition-based sentences, both nouns could fill either role; however, for the implausible versions, the overall proposition was implausible.

Table 14.2
Examples of Sentence Types From Saffran, Schwartz, and Linebarger (1998)

	Plausible	Implausible
Verb–constrained		
Active	The audience was watching the performance.	The cat barked at the puppy.
Passive	My car was demolished by the tornado.	The movie was frightened by the child.
Cleft Subject	It was the artist that disliked the painting.	It was the cheese that ate the mouse.
Cleft Object	It was the children that the crash frightened.	It was the idea that the professor surprised.
Proposition-based		
Active	The robin ate the insect.	The insect ate the robin.
Passive	The rat was squashed by the truck.	The frog was swallowed by the fly.
Cleft Subject	It was the boys who caught the turtle.	It was the worm that swallowed the bird.
Cleft Object	It was the boy whom the doctor lifted up.	It is the cat that the mouse is carrying.

Note. From "Semantic Influences on Thematic Role Assignments: Evidence from Normals and Aphasics," by E. Saffran, M. Schwartz, and M. Linebarger, 1998, *Brain and Language, 62*, pp. 292–294.

For example, in the implausible sentence "The insect ate the robin," both robins and insects can eat and be eaten, but it is implausible for something as small as an insect to eat a robin. For both the verb-constrained and proposition-based sentences, active, passive, cleft subject, and cleft object versions of each of the sentences were presented.

The results are shown in Table 14.3. For the control subjects, reaction times for the plausible sentences were faster for the verb constrained sentences than for the proposition based sentences.[4] The authors argued that the processing time differences could be attributed to the relative degree of competition between the two nouns for roles with respect to the verb. That is, when both nouns could fill either role, as in the proposition based sentences, resolution of thematic roles took longer than when one of the nouns could fill only one role, as in the verb constrained sentences. Supporting this contention were negative correlations between reaction times and a "polarization index" which reflected ratings of fit of the nouns to the inappropriate roles versus fit to their appropriate roles. The error data on the implausible sentences were also consistent with the role competition notion as more errors were made on the verb constrained sentences (4.7%) than on the proposition based sentences (1.3%). The control subjects apparently had some degree of difficulty suppressing the tendency to interpret the implausible verb constrained sentences by assigning nouns to their most semantically plausible slot, even though the syntax indicated otherwise.

For the aphasic patients, only error data were analyzed. The patients showed an exaggeration of the error effect demonstrated by the control subjects, performing much worse on the implausible verb constrained sentences than on the implausible proposition based sentences. This pattern indicates that there was a large effect of thematic role plausibility on patients' assignments of nouns to roles. Thus, for even a simple active sentence such as "The deer shot the hunter," the patients often said that the sentence was plausible, presumably because role assignments had been made on the basis of semantic constraints rather than on the basis of

---

[4]Reaction times for the implausible sentences were not analyzed as the position at which a sentence became implausible varied across syntactic type and was not matched across the proposition based and verb constrained sentences.

Table 14.3

Results for (a) Control Subjects and (b) Aphasic Patients on Sentence Plausibility Judgments From Saffran, Schwartz, and Linebarger, 1998.

Control Subjects	Active	Passive	Subject Cleft	Object Cleft	Mean
Reaction Time					
(Plausible only)					
Verb-constrained	675	739	611	868	723
Proposition -based	901	961	896	877	909
Percent Error					
Verb-constrained					
Plausible	2.5	8.8	1.3	1.3	3.4
Implausible	2.5	3.8	5.0	7.5	4.7
Mean	2.5	6.3	3.1	4.4	4.1
Proposition-based					
Plausible	1.3	1.3	2.5	1.3	1.6
Implausible	1.3	1.3	0.0	1.3	0.9
Mean	1.3	1.3	1.3	1.3	1.3
Aphasic Patients	Active	Passive	Subject Cleft	Object Cleft	Mean
Percent Error					
Verb-constrained					
Plausible	7.1	14.3	7.1	15.7	11.1
Implausible	42.9	55.7	34.3	50.0	45.7
Mean	25.0	35.0	20.7	32.9	28.4
Proposition-based					
Plausible	12.9	12.9	15.7	27.1	17.2
Implausible	11.4	21.4	12.9	45.7	22.9
Mean	12.2	17.2	14.3	36.4	20.0

Note. From "Semantic Influences on Thematic Role Assignments: Evidence from Normals and Aphasics," by E. Saffran, M. Schwartz, and M. Linebarger, 1998, *Brain and Language, 62*, pp. 268–282.

syntactic structure of the sentence. However, their performance on the proposition based sentences indicates that these patients were not insensitive to syntactic structure. For these sentences with weak semantic constraints on role filling, they made only 12–17% errors on the active, passive, and cleft subject sentences. Even on the cleft object sentences, performance was above chance when considering the plausible and implausible sentences together (36% errors overall).

The results imply a weakened, though not totally disrupted, influence of syntactic structure and a stronger role of semantic influences on sentence comprehension. As the authors indicate, the results are supportive of a mapping deficit explanation for these patients as they reveal difficulties in mapping between grammatical roles and thematic roles, even for sentences with simple structures and/or canonical word orders (i.e., actives and subject clefts). The results of the study are not consistent with proposals that hypothesize that Broca's aphasics have difficulty in comprehending only those sentences with moved arguments, given the patients' poor performance on all sentence types on the implausible verb constrained sentences. Also, it should be noted that the results for the conduction aphasic and transcortical motor aphasic were similar to those obtained for the Broca's aphasics.

Other evidence of an interaction between semantic and syntactic influences comes from Tyler's (1989) word monitoring studies of an agrammatic aphasic patient DE, who had shown evidence in a previous study of difficulty in structuring prose materials syntactically (Tyler, 1985). Tyler's (1989) study showed that DE was sensitive to local syntactic violations (e.g., "slow very kitchen") in sentences which were otherwise well formed syntactically, but semantically anomalous. However, for meaningful prose sentences, the patient's sensitivity to the local syntactic violations disappeared. Tyler concluded that for meaningful materials, the patient's analysis focused on the use of word meaning and pragmatic inference to construct an interpretation of the sentence, and made little use of at least some aspects of syntactic structure.

Aspects of Syntactic Processing

Mapping between Grammatical and Thematic Roles

As discussed earlier, some patients demonstrating asyntactic comprehension on sentence-picture matching and enactment tasks have performed well on grammaticality judgment tasks. This dissociation has been attributed to a deficit in mapping between grammatical roles and thematic roles (Linebarger, 1990; Saffran & Schwartz, 1988). However, if patients were completely unable to carry out this mapping process, they should perform poorly on all sentence types whether or not the sentence had a canonical S-V-O structure. In fact, although aphasic patients often do show some impairment in the comprehension of sentences with canonical word orders they typically show a greater impairment for noncanonical word orders—as in passive sentences and in cleft object and subject-object relative clause sentences (Berndt et al., 1996; Schwartz et al., 1980).

Schwartz et al. (1987) hypothesized that mapping becomes more difficult for noncanonical word orders because of the nonstandard mappings between thematic roles and grammatical roles (e.g., subject as theme in a passive sentence). They also argue that these patients' ability to determine grammatical roles in complex sentence types is unimpaired. However, if this is true, then it becomes a bit difficult to see how the mapping deficit is exacerbated by unusual grammatical structures. For example, for a subject–object relative sentence such as "The boy that the girl pushed had red hair," their logic would imply that patients can determine that the boy plays the role of the subject in the main clause and the role of the (moved) object in the embedded clause. (See Linebarger, 1990, for discussion.) Thus, it is unclear why the patients should have particular difficulty with this structure in determining that "girl" is the agent and "boy" the theme of "pushed." That is, once "boy" has been linked to the object position in the embedded clause, the mapping between grammatical roles and thematic roles is the standard one for "pushed." Only in the case of the passive would there appear to be a nonstandard linkage.

Perhaps some notion of "strength" of a syntactic analysis can be introduced here to help explain this pattern of results. As discussed earlier, recent models of sentence comprehension assume that multiple syntactic interpretations of an ambiguous string may be generated in parallel with different strengths assigned to each which depend on the frequency with which each is encountered (Boland, 1997). To use this approach to explain the patient data, one would have to suppose that for even unambiguous sequences such as "The boy that the girl pushed" the assignment of "boy" to object position in the embedded clause has a relatively weak strength because of the overall infrequency of this type of object relative construction. (Note that this relatively weak strength is assumed to exist for normal subjects as well as patients.) One could further surmise that although syntactic analysis is being carried out by the patients, the strengths throughout the system have been weakened due to brain damage. Such a hypothesis is consistent with the fact that although some patients with asyntactic comprehension do remarkably well on grammaticality judgments, their performance is typically below that (and outside the range) of control subjects. Thus, this difficulty with syntactic analysis in combination with a mapping deficit, gives rise to particular difficulties in mapping for infrequently encountered structures.

This explanation thus assumes that these patients have two deficits rather than one. If, however, syntactic analysis and mapping are independent processes, then one might expect to find *some* patients who show a deficit only in the mapping process. A case demonstrating this pattern was reported by Breedin and Martin (1996) in their study of verb comprehension deficits. However, this patient's deficit was hypothesized to be due to a disruption in verb-specific information concerning the mapping between grammatical and thematic roles, rather than in an abstract mapping process. Thus, this patient is discussed in the next section concerned with lexical deficits.

The Role of the Verb.

Breedin and Martin (1996) reported on the single word and sentence processing abilities of four patients who were worse at producing verbs than nouns in single picture naming. Of particular relevance to the issue of thematic role mapping in comprehension was patient LK. LK performed at chance (54% correct) in choosing between two pictures to match a verb when the distracter picture depicted a "reverse-role" verb. Reverse-role pairs included verbs like "buy-sell," "chase-flee," and "borrow-lend," where the thematic roles of the participants were the same but their mapping to grammatical roles with respect to the verb differed for the words within the pair. (See example of borrow-lend stimuli in Figures 14.2a and 14.2b.) In order that subjects could choose between two pictures depicting similar events (e.g., buying or selling), the same individual ("Elizabeth") was depicted as the subject of each verb. Thus for the verb *buy*, Elizabeth was purchasing something, whereas for *sell*, Elizabeth was doing the selling. LK's poor performance on the reverse role pairs could not be attributed to difficulty with semantically complex verbs as he performed significantly better (92% correct) when asked to discriminate one of the reverse role verbs from a semantically related verb that was equally complex (e.g., lend vs. distribute—see Figure 14.2b and 14.2c). Thus, LK's difficulty seemed to be specifically in discriminating between verbs that had very similar semantic representations but where the mapping between grammatical and thematic roles differed. Despite this difficulty with the mapping of thematic roles, LK performed within the range of control subjects

(a)

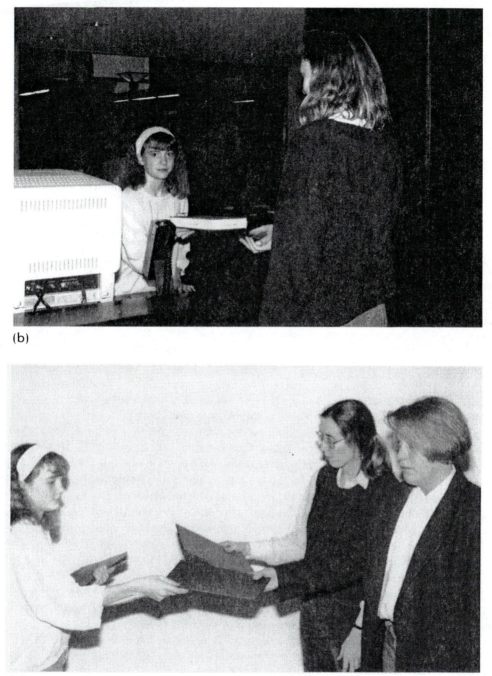

(b)

(c)

Figure 14.2: Examples of picture stimuli from Breedin and Martin, 1996. LK was told that Elizabeth was the girl in the white sweatshirt and headband, and all verbs referred to what Elizabeth was doing. On a reverse-role trial, LK might see photos a and b, and have to choose the one that shows "lend." On a semantically-relted-to-reverse-role trial, LK might see photos b and c, and have to choose the one that shows "distribute."

(LK: 96% correct, controls: 95–100% correct) on a grammaticality judgment task that assessed knowledge of subcategorization frames for verbs. He scored at the mean for controls (96%) for the sentences that used the reverse role verbs.

To account for these findings, Breedin and Martin (1996) postulated that LK's representation of particular verbs was disrupted. For example, they assumed that for the verbs "lend" and "borrow," LK knows that these verbs imply that someone owns some object and that this owner allows someone else to temporarily take possession. What seems to be impaired is his knowledge that in the case of "lend" the agent role is assigned to the permanent owner, whereas in "borrow" the agent is the person temporarily taking possession. (See also Byng, 1988; Jones, 1984.) It is possible that, because of the similarity in semantics of the verb, including a high overlap in the thematic roles that are involved, auditory input of one of these verbs serves to activate not only the correct verb representation but also that of the highly related reverse role verb. LK's difficulty would thus be in inhibiting the activation of the meaning of the reverse role verb, making it difficult to select between pictures depicting these two verbs.

Berndt, Haendiges, Mitchum, and Sandson (1997) have provided evidence that difficulties with verb representation may underlie some patients' difficulty in comprehending reversible sentences. In their study, patients who showed worse verb than noun retrieval in single word and sentence production (a group which included both Broca's aphasics and some fluent aphasics) also showed comprehension deficits for reversible relative to nonreversible sentences. Patients who showed better verb than noun retrieval or equivalent noun and verb retrieval performed well on comprehension of both reversible and nonreversible sentences.

Disruptions of Specific Aspects of Syntactic Parsing

Few case studies in aphasia have been carried out which have begun with linguistic theory and a specific processing model to determine whether dissociations between knowledge of different types of linguistic rules or categories could be documented.[5] An exception in this regard are the cases reported by Caplan and Hildebrandt (1988) and Caplan et al. (1987). These researchers examined sentence processing deficits from the point of view of Chomsky's (1982) government and binding theory, comparing patients' comprehension of sentences with and without referential dependencies. In their studies, referential dependencies refer to noun phrases that depend on the linkage with another noun phrase for their interpretation—such as the linkage between a reflexive and its referent or between a trace and the noun phrase that was moved from that position.[6] As in these examples, the referential dependencies could involve overt noun phrases (as in the case of reflexives) or empty noun phrases (as in the case of a trace).

In the Caplan et al. study (1987), patient KG was tested on a wide range of sentence types in order to assess his ability to process sentences with moved elements (and traces) and sentences with other types of referential dependencies. The other referential dependencies included pronouns and reflexives, and sentences hypothesized to have a missing subject (termed PRO[7]) of an embedded infinitival verb such as "Tom persuaded Bill to shave," and "Tom promised Bill to shave." As can be seen in these examples, the determination of which noun is the subject of the infinitival verb depends on the main verb, that is, whether it is an object control verb like "persuaded" or a subject control verb like "promised." KG showed a striking deficit on an enactment task for many of the structures involving moved elements. However, as

---

[5]It has been more often the case that group studies on agrammatism have used linguistic theory to generate hypotheses about the locus of deficits (e.g., Grodzinsky, 1995; Kean, 1977).
[6]As discussed earlier, some linguistic theorizing hypothesizes that when a noun phrase is moved from its deep structure position, it leaves behind a trace (see Radford, 1988). Traces and filler-gap dependencies are highly related notions. A trace differs from a gap in that it is presumed to be a hypothetical (empty) entity that appears in a gap.
[7]PRO, like trace, is a hypothetical empty element. It differs from a trace in that no movement from a deep structure position is presumed to be involved with PRO. The term PRO is used because the empty element acts like a pronoun referring back to an entity earlier in the sentence.

Table 14.4

Proportion Correct for Patient KG on Enactment Task from Caplan and Hildebrandt, 1988.

Sentences with Moved Elements	Proportion Correct
Simple Sentences	
Cleft object sentences with 2 nouns. It was the monkey that the elephant (trace) kicked.	11/12
More Complex Sentences	
Cleft object Sentences (dative verbs and 3 nouns): It was the monkey that the elephant gave (trace) to the goat.	6/12
Subject object relative clauses; The monkey that the elephant kicked (trace) kissed the goat.	3/12
Sentences Involving PRO and Reflexives	
Simple Sentences with PRO	
Object control: Tom persuaded Bill (PRO) to shave.	24/24
Subject control: Tom promised Bill (PRO) to shave.	19/24
Simple Sentences with Reflexives	
Bill shaved himself.	22/24
Sentences Combining Subject Control and Reflexives	
Bill promised Tom (PRO) to shave himself.	4/12

Note. From *Disorders of Syntactic Comprehension* by D. Caplan and N. Hildebrandt, 1988, pp. 180–193. Copyright by MIT Press. Reprinted with permission of the authors.

demonstrated in Table 14.4, his performance was affected by the complexity of the sentence involving moved elements—with good performance for cleft object sentences with transitive verbs and two nouns and poorer performance for cleft object sentences with dative verbs and three nouns and subject-object relative clauses. As also shown in the table, he performed well on simple sentences involving either PRO or reflexives, but he performed poorly on sentences combining both.

Given the effect of complexity on performance, one could not conclude that KG had a complete disruption of knowledge of, for instance, the processing of empty noun phrases. Caplan et al. (1987) thus interpreted this pattern of results as indicating a capacity limitation specific to syntactic parsing. They hypothesized that several factors contribute to capacity demands during parsing including: (a) having to postulate empty noun phrases (relative to the processing of overt noun phrases), (b) having to hold a noun phrase without a thematic roles assignment while assigning thematic roles to other noun phrases, and (c) searching over a long distance in the syntactic structure to determine the mapping of referential dependencies. Although KG could handle one of these capacity demands, when two or more combined, his performance broke down. It should be noted that KG's capacity constraint for syntactic parsing could not be attributed to a general verbal memory span deficit, as his performance on a variety of span tasks was within normal range.

Caplan and Hildebrandt (1988) reported several other case studies of patients with mild or more severe deficits on their syntactic comprehension battery. The mildly impaired patients demonstrated difficulty only on sentences with empty noun phrases whereas the patients with more severe deficits had difficulties on sentences with referential dependencies involving both overt and empty noun phrases. Among the mildly impaired patients, the pattern of deficits across sentence types differed. For instance, patient GS had difficulty with a variety of relative clause constructions involving object movement, but not with sentences termed NP-raising constructions (e.g., "Joe seems to Patrick to be praying") where the subject of the main verb

(Joe) must be interpreted as the subject of the embedded verb phrase (to be praying). Patient JV showed the opposite dissociation.

The highly specific deficits demonstrated in these patients suggest that there are different parsing operations associated with comprehending these various linguistic constructions that may be selectively affected by brain damage. Caplan and Hildebrandt (1988) make suggestions regarding what these operations might be (see pp. 198-199 for a summary), but they imply that parsing theories are not well-specified enough to accommodate all of their findings. Even though these papers appeared over a decade ago, it is still the case that parsing models have not been elaborated enough to handle all of the constructions tapped in these studies. Much of the psycholinguistic literature has focused on an analysis of a few sentence types with ambiguous structures in order to determine the role of lexical and semantic information in resolving these ambiguities. However, findings like those of Caplan and Hildebrandt (1988) would be very useful in helping to delineate different aspects of parsing. It should be noted, though, that all of their data summarized here came from a single task (enactment). For some of the sentence types (e.g., "Patrick promised Joe to pray"), patients were instructed to act out only the action at the end of the sentence. As discussed by Berndt (1991), some patients may have had difficulty interpreting this instruction since the agent of the final verb in the subject control and "seems" constructions occurred at the beginning of the sentence—as in "Joe promised Bill to shave." Also, the action in the final verb in the subject control sentences did not actually occur—but was only promised to occur some time in the future. Although these potential difficulties in interpreting the instructions could not account for the pattern of performance demonstrated by KG (Caplan et al., 1987), given his good performance on simple subject control and "seems" constructions, they might underlie the data from some of the patients. Also, given the different patterns of performance that have been demonstrated in other studies across grammaticality judgments, sentence anomaly judgments, and sentence-picture matching tasks (Cupples & Inglis, 1993; Linebarger et al., 1983), it would be important to verify that patients who demonstrated problems on particular constructions in the enactment task would do so across all tasks.

The Role of Working Memory in Sentence Comprehension

Models of sentence processing sometimes assume that inputs to sentence processing procedures or outputs from these procedures are stored in buffers awaiting the completion of other processes that make use of these representations. According to these models, deficits in sentence comprehension might arise not because of disruptions to the procedures themselves, but because of diminished buffer capacity. Brain damaged patients with language deficits very often have reduced short-term memory capacities as measured by standard digit and word span tasks. Thus, to the extent that these span tasks tap the buffer storage capacity involved in sentence processing, one would predict consequences for sentence comprehension specifically for those sentences that draw on these buffer capacities.

The ability to retain phonological information appears to be one major component of standard span measures. As phonological forms serve as input to sentence processing mechanisms, capacity constraints in phonological retention should have an impact whenever several words had to be maintained in a phonological form prior to the application of syntactic or semantic procedures. Findings in the memory span literature suggest that the retention of phonological information might be particularly critical for maintaining order information and for maintaining units with weak semantic representation such as function words and inflectional morphemes. These considerations led researchers to hypothesize that phonological information might be particularly important in syntactic analysis (e.g., Caramazza, Basili, Koller, & Berndt, 1981; Saffran & Marin, 1975). However, as reviewed by Martin and colleagues (Martin, 1993; Martin & Romani, 1994; see also, Baddeley, Gathercole, & Papagno, 1998), there is considerable evidence against the notion that phonological retention plays an important role in syntactic analysis. Several patients have been reported in the literature who have very reduced spans yet who show a good or even normal ability to comprehend syntactically complex sentences (e.g., Butterworth, Campbell, & Howard, 1986; Martin, Blossom-Stach, Yaffee, & Wetzel, 1995; Waters, Caplan, & Hildebrandt, 1991). Martin and Romani (Martin, 1993; Martin & Romani, 1994) have argued that these results are consistent with the notion that syntactic and semantic analyses are applied to each word in a sentence as it is perceived, and it is the output of these analyses which must be retained during comprehension. Whatever the capacity demands for retaining these outputs, they appear to be distinct from those tapped by span tasks.

It is the case, however, that some patients have been reported who have memory span deficits and who show better comprehension of syntactic information with written than spoken sentences (e.g., Baddeley & Wilson, 1988; Hillis & Caramazza, 1995; Romani, 1994). These results have often been interpreted as showing the dependence of auditory comprehension on phonological retention in short-term memory. Visual presentation is assumed to make fewer demands on this short-term memory buffer since the patient is free to reread all or portions of the sentence, and can read it at his or her own rate. However, given that some patients with similar span deficits do not have difficulties with spoken sentence comprehension, the most likely hypothesis is that these patients have some additional deficit that affects spoken input more than written. For instance, the patient's syntactic processing procedures may be slowed such that, with auditory input, the patient cannot keep up with the input (see Romani, 1994, for discussion). With written input, the patient can take as much time as needed in processing each word. Another possibility is that the patients have some specific difficulty with auditory word recognition that is particularly relevant to syntactic analysis, such as difficulty in processing inflectional morphemes with spoken input. This latter hypothesis may apply to the case of Hillis and Caramazza (1995) as this patient made errors in repeating single words when they were morphologically complex.

Martin and colleagues (Martin & Romani, 1994; Martin, Shelton & Yaffee, 1994) hypothesized that some aspects of word retention that are tapped by span tasks do play a role in sentence comprehension. They argued that some patients' reduced spans appear to be due to a deficit in the retention of lexical-semantic information rather than phonological information. Patients with difficulty retaining lexical-semantic information have difficulty comprehending sentences in which the integration of individual word meanings into propositional representations is delayed. For instance, in a sentence with several prenominal adjectives such as "the rusty old red pail," the integration of the first adjective with the noun ("rusty" with "pail") is delayed in comparison to a sentence in which the adjectives appear postnominally (e.g., "The pail was old, red, and rusty . . . "). Thus, the meaning of the adjectives in the "before" condition must be maintained in a lexical-semantic form for some time prior to integration compared to the "after" condition in which integration is immediate. Similar arguments can be made for sentences in which several nouns come before (e.g., "The vase, mirror, and platter cracked) or after a verb (e.g., "the movers cracked the platter, the mirror, and the vase"). When the nouns come before the verb, their assignment to thematic roles with respect to the verb is delayed in comparison to when the nouns appear after the verb. Martin and Romani (1994; Martin, 1995a) tested two patients (AB and ML) with lexical-semantic retention deficits and one patient (EA) with a phonological retention deficit on a sentence anomaly task with one, two or three adjectives preceding or following a noun and one, two or three nouns preceding or following a verb. (See Table 15.5 for example sentences with one or three adjectives or nouns.) As shown in Figure 14.3, both patients with a semantic retention deficit showed a large effect of the number of adjectives or nouns in the before condition but not in the after condition. In contrast, the patient with a phonological retention deficit performed like control subjects in showing a small effect of number of adjectives or nouns in both the before and after conditions. Thus, a short-term memory capacity specific to semantic retention appears critical for maintaining lexical-semantic information prior to integration with other word meanings.

Table 14.5

Examples of Distance 1 and Distance 3 Sentences From Anomaly Judgment Task of Martin & Romani (1994).

	Sensible	Anomalous
Distance 1		
<u>Adj-N</u>		
Before	The rusty pail was lying on the beach.	The rusty swimsuit was lying on the beach.
After	The pail was rusty but she took it to the beach anyway.	The swimsuit was rusty by she took it to the beach anyway.
<u>N-V</u>		
Before	The platter cracked during the move.	The cloth cracked during the move.
After	The movers cracked the platter.	The movers cracked the cloth.
Distance 3		
<u>Adj-N</u>		
Before	The rusty, old, red pail was lying on the beach.	The rusty, old, red swimsuit was lying on the beach.
After	The pail was old, red, and rusty but she took it to the beach anyway.	The swimsuit was old, red, and rusty by she took it to the beach anyway.
<u>N-V</u>		
Before	The platter, the vase and the mirror cracked during the move.	The cloth, the vase, and the mirror cracked during the move.
After	The movers cracked the vase, the mirror, and the platter.	The movers cracked the vase, the mirror, and the cloth.

Note. From "Verbal Working Memory and Sentence Processing: A Multiple Components View"

Caplan and Waters (1999), while agreeing that phonological retention has little do with syntactic processing, have made somewhat different claims about the relation between memory span measures and sentence comprehension. They divide sentence processing procedures into interpretive and postinterpretive processes. Interpretive processes include syntactic analysis and "the assignment of thematic roles, focus, and other aspects of propositional and discourse-level semantics" (p. 78). Postinterpretive processes involve using the products of interpretive

Figure 14.3: Difference in percent errors for (mean of Distance 2 and 3 – Distance 1) on sentence anomaly judgments. "After" condition allows for immediate integration whereas "before" condition involves delayed integration. Patients AB and ML show a semantic STM deficit whereas patient EA shows a phonological STM deficit.

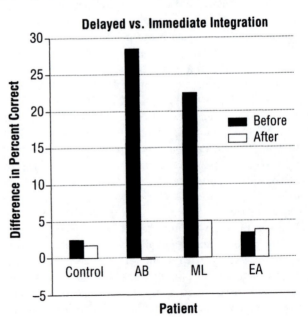

processing to carry out some task such as enactment or picture matching. Based on a large number of findings from normal and brain damage subjects examining the effects of working memory capacity and extraneous memory load on comprehension, Caplan and Waters claim that postinterpretive processes, but not interpretive processes, draw on the working memory capacity tapped by various span tasks. One problematic finding for this conclusion is that working memory capacity and an extraneous load interact with number of propositions in a sentence in determining comprehension performance. It is unclear why an influence of number of propositions should be relegated to "postinterpretive" processing. Also, it is unclear how they would account for Martin and Romani's (1994) findings concerning immediate versus delayed integration of semantic information, as the effects of this manipulation did relate to particular aspects of memory span performance of aphasic patients.

Another approach to working memory and sentence processing deficits has been proposed by Miyake, Just, & Carpenter (1994). This approach is based on Just and Carpenter's (1992) theory that there is one working memory capacity for all aspects of sentence comprehension (including lexical, semantic, syntactic, and discourse processes) and normal individuals differ in this capacity. According to Miyake et al. (1994), aphasic patients are just farther down on the capacity scale than the lowest of normal subjects. Consequently, the pattern of comprehension difficulty across sentence types for aphasic patients differs only quantitatively, and not qualitatively, from what is found with normal subjects. However, as argued by Martin (1995b), and, as should be evident from the literature reviewed here, double dissociations have been reported for semantic versus syntactic processing, and, even within syntactic processing, double dissociations have been found for the comprehension of different sentence types (e.g., see case studies in Caplan & Hildebrandt, 1988). Consequently, sentence comprehension deficits cannot all be attributed to a general reduction in capacity.

The question remains, however, whether some patients' deficits should be considered as capacity deficits. As discussed earlier, Caplan et al. (1988) proposed a deficit to a capacity specific to syntactic processing to account for the patient KC's comprehension pattern. One general difficulty with the capacity approach is that it is hard to separate "capacity" from the efficiency or strength of the processing mechanisms themselves (see Martin, 1995b, for discussion). In the previous section, results were discussed indicating interactions between syntactic and semantic processing with weakened input from syntactic processing in some patients. In some cases, a capacity argument might be put forward to account for the findings. For instance, one might hypothesize that Tyler's (1989) patient DE had reduced capacity for sentence processing and thus when semantic analysis used up this capacity there was little left for syntactic processing. However, for sentence with little semantic content the capacity could be devoted to local syntactic analysis. For the patients reported in Saffran et al. (1998), one might hypothesize that more capacity is needed to block the assignment of nouns to highly plausible roles with respect to a verb, leaving less capacity for syntactic analyses in the verb-constrained than proposition based sentences. However, one could as easily attribute these patterns to weakened syntactic processing per se. That is, given that current theories of normal sentence processing assume that different syntactic structures or lexical information related to syntactic structure (e.g., verb subcategorization frames) differ in strength, one might hypothesize that brain damage has served to generally lower these strengths.

One difficulty with a general capacity approach is the lack of a strong theoretical basis for predicting a priori what sentence types will make greater demands on this capacity. That is, for almost any pattern of results, a capacity explanation can be invented post hoc. For example, with regard to Tyler's (1989) study, one might have hypothesized that in the semantically anomalous sentences, a great deal of capacity would be needed in making thematic role assignments because none of them were plausible—which should have left less, rather than more, capacity for syntactic analysis. In the case of the Saffran et al. (1998) study, one might have predicted a priori that implausible verb constrained sentences would demand less capacity to reject than implausible proposition based sentences since one of the nouns would strongly violate semantic restrictions on verb role fillers.

SUMMARY AND CONCLUSIONS

As discussed in the introduction, findings on sentence comprehension deficits in Broca's aphasia in the 1970s aroused a good deal of interest among psycholinguistics and linguists as they seemed to provide strong support for the existence of an independent syntactic processing module. Basing this conclusion on the findings from the clinical category of Broca's aphasia proved to be a mistake, however, as subsequent findings revealed that many of these patients had remarkably well preserved syntactic abilities when tested on grammaticality judgments. Nonetheless, if one moves away from arguments about what characterizes the comprehension deficits of clinical categories to the consideration of findings from individual cases, evidence for a separation between syntax and semantics can be seen. Dementia cases have been reported with severe semantic deficits who yet show an ability to process complex grammatical constructions (e.g., Breedin & Saffran, 1999). Contrasting cases from aphasia have been reported who show preserved semantic processing and a disruption of syntactic processing (Ostrin & Tyler, 1995). These dissociations have been demonstrated in both off-line and on-line processing tasks. These findings are thus consistent with sentence processing theories that assume some separation between the representation of syntactic and semantic knowledge (e.g., Boland, 1997), and cause difficulties for theories in which all syntactic information is assumed to be represented lexically, along with semantic information (e.g., MacDonald et al., 1994).

In addition to this broad distinction between semantic and syntactic processes, the evidence from brain damaged patients also supports more fine-grained distinctions about components of sentence processing. As argued by Linebarger (1990) the ability of some patients to make grammaticality judgments about a range of syntactic structures while performing near chance on sentence-picture matching tasks for simple passive sentences supports a distinction between the processes involved in determining the hierarchical structure of a sentence and those involved in mapping grammatical roles to thematic roles. There is also evidence for the fractionation of aspects of lexical representation involved in syntactic processing, as Breedin and Martin (1996) reported a case who showed a preservation of knowledge of verb subcategorization frames but a disruption of the mapping of thematic roles for verbs with highly similar role relations.

With regard to the disruption of specific aspects of syntactic parsing, there appears to be much less evidence. However, relatively few case studies have have addressed this issue. Caplan et. al (1987) and Caplan and Hildebrandt (1988) presented interesting data along these lines. As noted earlier, their data all came from a single task, and it would be important to follow up on their findings to determine if the double dissociations they reported could be replicated in other patients when tested on a variety of tasks. Even for the cases that Caplan and Hildebrandt reported, the deficit was typically not in the processing of all sentences involving a specific aspect of syntactic processing, such as all sentences with empty elements, but appeared when the sentences involved some other complicating factor. Perhaps such findings are to be expected, however. That is, it may be very unlikely that brain damage would totally disrupt a particular process while leaving all others intact. Instead, it may be much more likely that brain damage diminishes the strength of the output of a particular process such that its influence can be observed in some conditions, but not in others where other constraints may override the weak output of the damaged process.

Along these lines, interesting data has been reported from patients that is consistent with current sentence processing theories in showing an interaction between semantic and syntactic influences. In these studies, patients have been shown to have a sensitivity to grammatical structure when semantic influences are weak, but a relative insensitivity to grammatical structure when semantic influences are strong (Saffran et al., 1998). Some might take these findings to be cautionary, as evidence of syntactic processing deficits might be undermined if patients were tested on materials with fewer semantic or other constraints. However, if one abandons the notion that syntactic deficits have to be all or none, but can be a matter of degree, such findings are entirely consistent with a syntactic disruption.

It is clear that although some progress has been made in understanding sentence processing deficits and their implications for theories of normal sentence comprehension, much work remains to be done. The topic is obviously very complex and the researcher is faced with a daunting task of choosing an appropriate battery of tasks to narrow down the source of deficits in a given patient. Despite the abundant research on sentence processing in normal subjects, much of it has focused on a narrow range of topics. Although there is evidence for the involvement of many different processes in sentence comprehension, there is a great deal of under-specification with regard to any number of issues: the means by which hierarchical structure is computed, the processing of empty elements in different constructions, the means by which thematic role mapping is carried out, the nature of lexical constraints on the generation of syntactic structure. Clearly, theoretical developments along any of these lines would be an aid in guiding research on neuropsychological cases. Conversely, findings from neuropsychology could play an important role in the future in helping to address these issues.

Acknowledgements

Preparation of this manuscript was supported in part by NIH grant DC-00218 to Rice University.

REFERENCES

Baddeley, A., Gathercole, S., & Papagno, C. (1998). The phonological loop as a language learning device. *Psychological Review, 105*, 158–173.

Baddeley, A. D., & Wilson, B. (1988). Comprehension and working memory: A single case neuropsychological study. *Journal of Memory and Language, 27*, 479–498.

Badecker, W., & Caramazza, A. (1985). On consideration of method and theory governing the use of clinical categories in neurolinguistics and cognitive neuropsychology: The case against agrammatism. *Cognition, 20*, 97–126.

Badecker, W., Nathan, P., & Caramazza, A. (1991). Varieties of sentence comprehension deficits: A case study. *Cortex, 27*, 311–321

Bates, E., & Goodman, J. (1997). On the inseparability of grammar and the lexicon: Evidence from acquisition, aphasia and real-time processing. *Language and Cognitive Processes, 5*(6), 507–584.

Berndt, R. S. (1991). Sentence processing in aphasia. In M. Sarno (Ed.), *Acquired aphasia* (2nd ed., pp. 223–270). San Diego, CA: Academic Press.

Berndt, R. S. (1998). Sentence processing in aphasia. In M. Sarno (Ed.), *Acquired aphasia* (3rd ed.) pp. 229–267. San Diego, CA: Academic Press.

Berndt, R. S., & Caramazza, A. (1980). A redefinition of the syndrome of Broca's aphasia: Implications for a neuropsychological model of language. *Applied Psycholinguistics, 1*, 225–278.

Berndt, R. A., Haendiges, A., Mitchum, C., & Sandson, J. (1997). Verb retrieval in aphasia. 2: Relationship to sentence processing. *Brain and Language, 56*, 107–137.

Berndt, R. S., Mitchum, C., & Haendiges, A. (1996). Comprehension of reversible sentences in "agrammatism": A meta-analysis. *Cognition, 58*, 289–308.

Boland, J. (1997). The relationship between syntactic and semantic processes in sentence comprehension. *Language and Cognitive Processes, 12*, 423–484.

Boland, J., & Boehm-Jernigan, H. (1998). Lexical constraints and prepositional phrase attachment. *Journal of Memory and Language, 39*, 684–719.

Boland, J., & Cutler, A. (1996). Interaction with autonomy: Multiple output models and the inadequacy of the Great Divide. *Cognition, 58*, 309–320.

Breedin, S., & Martin, R. (1996). Patterns of verb deficits in aphasia: An analysis of four cases. *Cognitive Neuropsychology, 13*, 51–91.

Breedin, S., & Saffran, E. (1999). Sentence processing in the face of semantic loss: A case study. *Journal of Experimental Psychology: General, 128*, 547–562.

Butterworth, B., Campbell, R., & Howard, D. (1986). The uses of short-term memory: A case study. *The Quarterly Journal of Experimental Psychology, 38A*, 705–737.

Byng, S. (1988). Sentence processing deficits: Theory and therapy. *Cognitive Neuropsychology, 5*, 629–676.

Caplan, D., & Hildebrandt, N. (1988). *Disorders of syntactic comprehension*. Cambridge, MA: MIT Press.

Caplan, D., Hildebrandt, N., & Evans, K. (1987). The man$_i$ left t$_i$ without a trace: A case study of aphasic processing of empty categories. *Cognitive Neuropsychology, 4*, 257–302.

Caplan, D., & Waters, G. (1999). Verbal working memory and sentence comprehension. *Behavioral & Brain Sciences, 22*, 77–126.

Caramazza, A., Basili, A.G., Koller, J., & Berndt, R.S. (1981). An investigation of repetition and language processing in a case of conduction aphasia. *Brain and Language, 14*, 235–271.

Caramazza, A., & Berndt, R. S. (1978). Semantic and

syntactic processes in aphasia: A review of the literature. *Psychological Bulletin, 85,* 898918.

Caramazza, A., & Miceli, G. (1991). Selective impairment of thematic role assignment in sentence processing. *Brain and Language, 41,* 402–436.

Caramazza, A., & Zurif, E. (1976). Dissociation of algorithmic and heuristic processes in language comprehension: Evidence from aphasia. *Brain and Language, 3,* 572–582.

Chomsky, N. (1965). *Aspects of the theory of syntax.* Cambridge, MA: MIT Press.

Chomsky, N. (1982). *Some concepts and consequences of the theory of government and binding.* Cambridge, MA: MIT Press.

Coltheart, M., Curtis, B., Atkins, P., & Haller, M. (1993). Models of reading aloud: Dual-route and parallel-distributed-processing approaches. *Psychological Review, 100,* 589–608.

Cupples, L., & Inglis, A. L. (1993). When task demands induce "asyntactic" comprehension: A study of sentence interpretation in aphasia. *Cognitive Neuropsychology, 10,* 201–234.

Dell, G., Schwartz, M., Martin, N., Saffran, E., & Gagnon, D. (1997). Lexical access in aphasic and nonaphasic speakers. *Psychological Review, 104,* 801–838.

Ellis, A., & Young, A. (1988). *Human cognitive neuropsychology.* Hove, UK: Lawrence Erlbaum.

Ferreira, F., & Clifton, C. (1986). The independence of syntactic processing. *Journal of Memory and Language, 25,* 348–368.

Fodor, J., & Garrett, M. (1967). Some syntactic determinants of sentential complexity. *Perception and Psychophysics, 2,* 289–296.

Frazier, L. (1987). Sentence processing: A tutorial review. In M. Coltheart (Ed.), *Attention and performance: Vol. XII. The psychology of reading* (pp. 559–586). Hove, UK: Lawrence Erlbaum.

Frazier, L., & Rayner, K. (1982). Making and correcting errors during sentence comprehension: Eye movements in the analysis of structurally ambiguous sentence. *Cognitive Psychology, 13,* 178–210.

Friederici, A., & Kilborn, K. (1989). Temporal constraints on language processing: Syntactic priming in Broca's aphasia. *Journal of Cognitive Neuroscience, 1,* 262–272.

Goodglass, H., & Kaplan, E. (1972). *The assessment of aphasia and related disorders.* Philadelphia: Lea and Febiger.

Grodzinsky, Y. (1995). A restrictive theory of agrammatic comprehension. *Brain and Language, 50,* 27–51.

Grodzinsky, Y., & Finkel, L. (1998). The neurology of empty categories: aphasics' failure to detect ungrammaticality. *Journal of Cognitive Neuroscience, 10,* 281–292.

Haarmann, H., & Kolk, H. (1991). Syntactic priming in Broca's aphasia: Evidence for slow activation. *Aphasiology, 5,* 247–263.

Haarmann, H., & Kolk, H. (1994). On-line sensitivity to subject-verb agreement violations in Broca's aphasics: The role of syntactic complexity and time. *Brain and Language, 46,* 493–516.

Hillis, A., & Caramazza, A. (1995). "I know it, but I can't write it": Selective deficits in long- and short-term memory. In R. Campbell & M. Conway (Eds.), *Broken memories: Case studies in memory impairment.* (pp. 344–365). Oxford, UK: Blackwell.

Hodges, J., Patterson, K., & Tyler, L. (1994). Loss of semantic memory: Implications for the modularity of mind. *Cognitive Neuropsychology, 11,* 505–542.

Howard, D. (1985). Agrammatism. In S. Newman & R. Epstein (Eds.), *Current perspectives in dysphasia.* New York: Churchill Livingstone.

Jackendoff, R. (1993). *Patterns in the mind.* New York: Harvester Wheatsheaf.

Jones, E. (1984). Word order processing in aphasia. Effect of verb semantics. In F. C. Rose (Ed.), *Advances in neurology, 42; Progress in aphasiology* (pp. 159–181). New York: Raven.

Just, M., & Carpenter, P. (1980). A theory of reading: From eye fixations to comprehension. *Psychological Review, 87,* 441–480.

Just, M., & Carpenter, P. (1992). A capacity theory of comprehension: Individual differences in working memory. *Psychological Review, 99,* 122–149.

Kean, M. (1977). The linguistic interpretation of aphasia syndromes: Agrammatism in Broca's aphasia, an example. *Cognition, 5,* 9–46.

Kempler, D., Curtiss, S., & Jackson, C. (1987). Syntactic preservation in Alzheimer's disease. *Journal of Speech and Hearing Research, 30,* 343–350.

Kimball, J. (1973). Seven principles of surface structure parsing in natural language. *Cognition, 2,* 15–27.

Kolk, H., & van Grunsven, M. (1985). Agrammatism as a variable phenomenon. *Cognitive Neuropsychology, 2,* 347–384.

Kolk, H., van Grunsven, M., & Keyser, A. (1985). On parallelism between production and comprehension in agrammatism. In M. L. Kean (Ed.), *Agrammatism.* New York: Academic Press.

Linebarger, M. (1990). Neuropsychology of sentence parsing. In A. Caramazza (Ed.), *Cognitive neuropsychology and neurolinguistics. Advances in models of cognitive function and impairment.* Hillsdale, NJ: Lawrence Erlbaum.

Linebarger, M., Schwartz, M., & Saffran, E. (1983). Sensitivity to grammatical structure in so-called agrammatic aphasics. *Cognition, 13,* 361–392.

MacDonald, M. (1994). Probabilistic constraints and syntactic ambiguity resolution. *Language and Cognitive Processes, 9,* 157–201.

MacDonald, M., Pearlmutter, N., & Seidenberg, M. (1994). The lexical nature of syntactic ambiguity resolution. *Psychological Review, 101 ,* 676–703.

Marslen-Wilson, W., & Tyler, L. (1980). The temporal structure of spoken language understanding. *Cognition, 8,* 1–71.

Martin, R. C. (1993). Short-term memory and sentence processing: Evidence from neuropsychology. *Memory and Cognition, 21,* 176–183.

Martin, R. (1995a, November). *A multiple capacities view of working memory in language.* Paper presented at the Psychonomics Society Meeting, Los Angeles, CA.

Martin, R. (1995b). Working memory doesn't work: A critique of Miyake et al.'s capacity theory of aphasic comprehension deficits. *Cognitive Neuropsychology, 12,* 623–636.

Martin, R., & Blossom-Stach, C. (1986). Evidence for syntactic deficits in a fluent aphasic. *Brain and Language, 28,* 196–234.

Martin, R. C., Blossom-Stach, C., Yaffee, L., & Wetzel, F. (1995). Consequences of a central motor programming deficit for rehearsal and reading comprehension. *Quarterly Journal of Experimental Psychology, 48A,* 536–572.

Martin, R. C., Lesch, M., & Bartha, M. (1999). Independence of input and output phonology in word processing and short-term memory. *Journal of Memory and Language, 41*, 3–29.

Martin, R.C., & Romani, C. (1994). Verbal working memory and sentence processing: A multiple components view. *Neuropsychology, 8*, 506-523.

Martin, R. C., Shelton, J. R., & Yaffee, L. S. (1994). Language processing and working memory: Neuropsychological evidence for separate phonological and semantic capacities. *Journal of Memory and Language, 33*, 83–111.

Martin, R. C., Wetzel, F., Blossom-Stach, C., & Feher, E. (1989). Syntactic loss versus processing deficit: An assessment of two theories of agrammatism and syntactic comprehension deficits. *Cognition, 32*, 157–191.

McClelland, J., St. John, M., & Taraban, R. (1989). Sentence comprehension: A parallel distributed processing approach. *Language and Cognitive Processes, 4*, 287–336.

McElree, B., & Griffith, T. (1998). Structural and lexical constraints on filling gaps during sentence comprehension: A time-course analysis. *Journal of Experimental Psychology: Learning, Memory and Cognition, 24*, 432–460.

Miceli, G., Mazzucchi, A., Menn, L., & Goodglass, H. (1983). Contrasting cases of Italian agrammatic aphasia without comprehension disorder. *Brain and Language, 19*, 65–97.

Miller, G., & McKean, K. (1964). A chronometric study of some relations between sentences. *Quarterly Journal of Experimental Psychology, 16*, 297–308.

Miyake, A., Just, M., & Carpenter, P. (1994). A capacity approach to syntactic comprehension disorder: Making normal adults perform like aphasic patients. *Cognitive Neuropsychology, 11*, 671–717.

Ostrin, R., & Tyler, L. (1995). Dissociations of lexical function: Semantics, syntax, and morphology. *Cognitive Neuropsychology, 12*, 345–389.

Plaut, D., McClelland, J., Seidenberg, M., & Patterson, K. (1996). Understanding normal and impaired word reading: Computational principles in quasi-regular domains. *Psychological Review, 103*, 56–115.

Radford, A. (1988). *Transformational grammar: A first course*. New York: Cambridge University Press.

Rayner, K., Carlson, M., & Frazier, L. (1983). The interaction of syntax and semantics during sentence processing: Eye movements in the analysis of semantically biased sentences. *Journal of Verbal Learning and Verbal Behavior, 22*, 348–374.

Romani, C. (1994). The role of phonological short-term memory in syntactic parsing: A case study. *Language and Cognitive Processes, 9*, 29–67.

Saffran, E. M., & Marin, O. S. M. (1975). Immediate memory for word lists and sentences in a patient with deficient auditory short-term memory. *Brain and Language, 2*, 420–433.

Saffran, E., & Schwartz, M. (1988). "Agrammatic" comprehension it's not: Alternatives and implications. *Aphasiology, 2*, 389–394.

Schwartz, M., & Chawluk, J. (1990). Deterioration of language in progressive aphasia: A case study. In M. Schwartz (Ed.), *Modular deficits in Alzheimer-type dementia*. Cambridge, MA: MIT Press.

Schwartz, M., Marin, O. S. M., & Saffran, E. (1979). Dissociations of language function in dementia: A case study. *Brain and Language, 7*, 277–306.

Saffran, E., Schwartz, M., & Linebarger, M. (1998). Semantic influences on thematic role assignments: Evidence from normals and aphasics. *Brain and Language, 62*, 255–297.

Schwartz, M., Saffran, E., Linebarger, M., & Pate, D. (1987). Syntactic transparency and sentence interpretation in aphasia. *Language and Cognitive Processes, 2*, 85–113.

Schwartz, M., Saffran, E., & Marin, O. S. M. (1980). The word order problem in agrammatism: I. Comprehension. *Brain and Language, 10*, 249–262.

Shankweiler, D., Crain, S., Gorrell, P., & Tuller, B. (1989). Reception of language in Broca's aphasia. *Language and Cognitive Processes, 4*, 1–33.

Slobin, D. (1971). *Psycholinguistics*. Glenview, IL: Scott, Foresman.

Spivey, M., & Tanenhaus, M. (1998). Syntactic ambiguity resolution in discourse: Modeling the effects of referential context and lexical frequency. *Journal of Experimental Psychology: Learning, Memory, & Cognition, 24*, 1521–1543.

Spivey-Knowlton, M., & Sedivy, J. (1995). Resolving attachment ambiguities with multiple constraints. *Cognition, 55*, 226–267.

Trueswell, J., & Tanenhaus, M. (1994). Toward a lexicalist framework of constraint-based syntactic ambiguity resolution. In C. Clifton, L. Frazier, & K. Rayner (Eds.), *Perspectives on sentence processing*. (pp. 155–179). Hillsdale, NJ: Lawrence Erlbaum.

Trueswell, J., Tanenhaus, M., & Garnsey, S. (1994). Semantic influences on parsing: Use of thematic role information in syntactic ambiguity resolution. *Journal of Memory and Language, 33*, 285–318.

Trueswell, J., Tanenhaus, M., & Kello, C. (1993). Verb-specific constraints in sentence processing: Separating effects of lexical preference from garden-paths. *Journal of Experimental Psychology: Learning, Memory, and Cognition, 19*, 528–553.

Tyler, L. (1985). Real-time comprehension problems in agrammatism: A case study. *Brain and Language, 26*, 259–275.

Tyler, L. (1989). Syntactic deficits and the construction of local phrases in spoken language comprehension. *Cognitive Neuropsychology, 6*, 333–355.

Tyler, L. (1992). *Spoken language comprehension: An experimental approach to disordered and normal processing*. Cambridge, MA: MIT Press.

Tyler, L.. Ostrin, R., Cooke, M., & Moss, H. (1995). Automatic access of lexical information in Broca's aphasics: Against the automaticity hypothesis. *Brain and Language, 48*, 131–162.

van Berkum, J., Hagoort, P., & Brown, C. (in press). Early referential context effects in sentence processing: Evidence from event-related potentials. *Journal of Memory and Language*.

von Stockert, T. & Bader, L. (1976). Some relations of grammar and lexicon in aphasia. *Cortex, 12*, 49–60.

Waters, G., Caplan, D., & Hildebrandt, N. (1991). On the structure of verbal short-term memory and its functional role in sentence comprehension: Evidence from neuropsychology. *Cognitive Neuropsychology, 8*, 81–126.

Wulfeck, B. (1988). Grammaticality judgments and sentence comprehension in agrammatic aphasia. *Journal of Speech and Hearing Research, 31*, 72–81.

Zurif, E., & Grodzinsky, Y. (1983). Sensitivity to grammatical structure in agrammatic aphasics: A reply to Linebarger, Schwartz, and Saffran. *Cognition, 15*, 207–213.

15

Sentence Production

Rita Sloan Berndt

The fluent production of sentences in the service of communication is an ability that most normal adults think about very little. Although everyone experiences occasional difficulty finding exactly the right words to convey an intended message, and though we may misuse or stumble over a word, for the most part we turn thoughts into sentences with little apparent effort. For aphasic speakers, on the other hand, producing sentences is often a formidable task that can go awry in a number of different ways. This chapter considers what is known (and hypothesized) about the processes underlying normal sentence production, and it attempts to relate elements of production models to characteristics of aphasic deficits. We will limit discussion to the processes sometimes referred to as "grammatical encoding," in other words, to those processes that yield a syntactically and phonologically specified representation that can drive the mechanisms responsible for achieving detailed phonetic encoding.

One goal is to use the normal model to explain the functional source(s) of different patterns of aphasic production. Realization of this goal would not only provide a more coherent account of a complex array of symptoms, but could point the way to underlying processing impairments that might be successfully targeted for treatment. A second reason to consider aphasic sentence production in the context of normal models is more controversial. Patterns of aphasic production can be regarded as a source of experimental data that may motivate and/or constrain development of the normal model (Caramazza, 1986). Postulated model architectures should be able to accommodate patterns of aphasic breakdown without the necessity of creating new processing mechanisms (but see Levelt, Roelofs, & Meyer, 1999b, for an opposing view).

A MODEL OF NORMAL SENTENCE PRODUCTION

The dominant theoretical approaches to sentence production share a basic framework incorporating discrete processing stages that mediate between thoughts to be expressed and articulated speech. This framework had its genesis in the work of Fromkin (1971) and was elaborated by Garrett (1975, 1980) to account for regular patterns that appear in normal speakers' "slips of the tongue." Although sentence production models continue to exploit the distributional characteristics of normal speech errors to support distinctions among their components, evidence from a small number of experimental paradigms has become increasingly important in elaborating details about the temporal relationships among processing elements (e.g., Schriefers,

Meyer, & Levelt, 1990) and about the precise characterization of the representations that are assumed to be computed during sentence construction (e.g., Bock, Loebell, & Morey, 1992).

Framework of the Model

We will begin by considering the framework proposed by Garrett (1988), which postulates the computation of three distinct levels of representation prior to the engagement of the motor systems required to achieve spoken output. This model is schematized in Figure 1.[1] The production of a sentence is assumed to begin with the formulation of a nonlinguistic "message" representation. Messages can incorporate information from many sources, including the substantive content that the speaker intends to convey, information contributed by elements of an on-going discourse, and conditions relating to the speaker's motivations and current state-of-mind (see Levelt, 1989, Chapter 3). Messages instigate a number of processes that yield, in succession, two distinct types of mental representation: A *functional level representation* includes semantically and syntactically (but not phonologically) specified lexical items (sometimes called "lemmas") that are assigned to syntactic functions; a *positional level representation* contains phonologically-specified, ordered word forms that are retrieved from a form lexicon and assigned to slots in a hierarchically organized constituent structure.

An immediate question that one might raise about this architecture is why it is necessary to have two distinct levels mediating between the message to be conveyed and the spoken sentence. Can't the functional and positional levels be parsimoniously reduced to a single stage of grammatical encoding? In fact, the "two-stage" model of production is a feature of most contemporary models of lexical and sentence production. The need for distinct levels is motivated first by distributional properties of normal speech errors. One primary error distinction supporting the reality of two levels involves the comparison of word and segment exchanges. Word exchanges typically involve words from the same grammatical class exchanging across phrases (e.g., "forgot to add the *roof* to the *list*" → "forgot to add the *list* to the *roof*"; Garrett, 1980). Segment exchanges, in contrast, tend to involve segments of lexical elements that differ in grammatical class but fall within the same phrase (e.g., "this is the *parietal lobe*" → "this is the *larietal pobe*"; Garrett, 1982b). Word exchange errors appear to implicate a level at which words are specified for grammatical class, but not yet organized into phrases; sound exchanges appear to arise as segments are retrieved during ordered word form encoding.

As described above, the functional level is conceived as an abstract representation of phonologically-unspecified lexical entities that are linked to meanings and functional roles corresponding to elements of the message. The precise nature of the functional roles to be filled at this level is somewhat unclear, and the speech error data provide little to go on. Nonetheless, the functional level of the model has often been interpreted as linking abstract lexical structures (lemmas) to deep structure grammatical roles such as deep subject and deep object (e.g., Lapointe & Dell, 1989). Another possibility (e.g., Schwartz, 1987) is that the roles relevant at the functional level correspond to thematic roles such as "agent" and "theme," as described by Jackendoff (1987). Recent elaborations of the model have weighed in against both of these possibilities and have proposed that selected lemmas are linked to surface grammatical roles as in a lexical functional grammar (Bresnan, 1982). Thus, surface grammatical functions such as subject, direct object, etc. are linked to lemmas selected to match "event roles" (e.g., agent, theme) that are argued to be specified at the message level (Bock & Levelt, 1994; Levelt, 1989).

---

[1]This model has recently been elaborated and expanded, especially in terms of the mechanisms responsible for lexical access (K. Bock & Levelt, 1994; Levelt, 1989; Levelt et al., 1999a). The earlier model is selected for discussion here because it has been widely used to organize discussion of sentence production deficits. The more recent models differ in a number of ways that complicate consideration of aphasic patterns. The most important of these are the postulation of separate lexical representations for conceptual/semantic and syntactic information, and the separation of phonological encoding processes from the construction of a positional level representation. These modifications of the model will be considered when they are relevant to interpretation of the aphasic data.

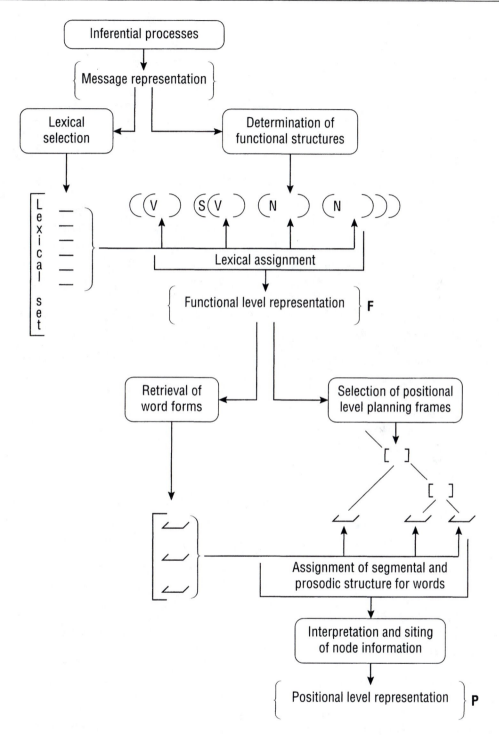

Figure 15.1: Schematic of Garrett's model of sentence production from Garrett, 1988. Adapted with the permission of Cambridge University Press.

Thus, recent modifications of the model, based largely on experimental findings with normal subjects, have moved away from a transformation-based view of meaning-to-form mapping and have adopted a more lexicalist approach.

One of the critical questions regarding the construction of the functional level representation involves the factors governing the assignment of lemmas to grammatical functions. There is some agreement that function assignment depends on information carried by the verb, specifically the verb's argument structure (Bock & Levelt, 1994). For example, the lemma representations for the verbs "give" and "receive" will assign noun lemmas corresponding to the message level event role of "goal" to different grammatical functions (indirect object and subject, respectively; see Levelt, 1989, p. 192ff). The critical role of the verb in function assignment is consistent with data suggesting that advance planning in production must include information about the verb (Lindsley, 1975).

The representation generated at the functional level thus can be viewed as an unordered set of lemmas linked to a set of syntactic functions through the argument structure of verb lemmas. The representation that will constitute the positional level must consist of ordered and phonologically-specified words linked together by grammatical morphemes in a structural frame. Grossly speaking, two types of operations are necessary to accomplish this translation: retrieval of the specific word form corresponding to each selected lemma, and creation of a structural frame. The structural frames generated during sentence production are commonly viewed as products of a hierarchical constituent structure, as schematized in Figure 1. However, the linear structure of words produced in sentences could in principle reflect a variety of different types of information, including the relative accessibility of distinct event structures generated at the message level, prosodic or metrical information (Bock, 1986; Bock & Loebell, 1990), and the persistence of structures heard in the immediate environment as part of the ongoing discourse (Levelt & Kelter, 1982).

A particularly important aspect of the generation of sentence frames (for present purposes) involves the retrieval of specific bound and free grammatical morphemes. There is some reason to believe that the production of function words and inflections (as well as of derivational suffixes) is not conditioned by the same processes that generate content words. One important difference between function words and content words is that the former do not regularly participate in speech errors. Further, inflections tend to stay put even when the stems to which they are attached are exchanged. An example of such a "stranding exchange" error is the production of "she's already trunk*ed* two packs" in lieu of "pack*ed* two trunk*s*" (Garrett, 1975). Garrett (1982) has argued that this error type constitutes evidence that grammatical morphemes are intrinsic features of the structural frame, and are in place when the phonological forms of content words are integrated into the developing frame.

Bock (1989) has marshaled evidence against the idea that grammatical morphemes are inherent in structural frames, using a structural priming paradigm in which normal subjects show a marked tendency to repeat syntactic structures across successive utterances. Bock found that structural frames could be primed even when the function words involved in prime and target were different. For example, the production of prepositional dative structures such as "the man gives the book to the woman" could be primed (relative to double object datives such as "the man gives the woman the book"), even when the prime sentence contained a prepositional phrase beginning with "for" rather than "to." This result suggests that priming is operating on a level of syntactic structure that is abstract enough to be indifferent to the specific function words employed. Thus, the status of the grammatical function words, and the question of how they are chosen and integrated into developing syntactic structures, is unclear. Speech error data suggest that they behave differently from content words in their involvement of speech errors, but the priming evidence suggests that their identity is only loosely linked to a specific syntactic structure. Another possibility, to be discussed further below, is that bound grammatical morphemes (such as the elements that retain their position in stranding exchange errors) may be intrinsic to structural frames, while free-standing function words are not.

Processing Assumptions

A number of constraints have been placed on the flow of information through the levels outlined above that have particular relevance for the interpretation of aphasic deficits. Several other processing issues that are likely to be important for understanding patient performance have received little attention in studies of normal production and will be discussed below.

One controversial processing characteristic of the production model is the strict requirement of serial information flow: processing at each of the postulated levels can be influenced only by information generated at the level above it. This means, for example, that the selection of lemmas and their assignment to grammatical functions is controlled by information at the message level and is not influenced by feedback from phonological elements as they become available at the next level. This sequential processing assumption was adopted initially because of the apparent segregation of semantically-conditioned and phonologically-conditioned speech errors; that is, errors reflecting an intersection of those processes ("mixed errors") were said to occur infrequently in speech error corpora. However, evidence from experimentally-induced speech errors has demonstrated that errors of lexical selection and of phonological specification may not be completely independent (Dell & Reich, 1981; N. Martin, Weisberg, & Saffran, 1989). The possibility that phonological factors can influence semantically-driven lexical selection has been extensively investigated using the picture/word interference paradigm (e.g., Levelt et al., 1991a), but the debate as to whether lexical selection and phonological encoding interact during production continues (Dell & O'Sheaghdha, 1991; Levelt et al., 1991b). This is an important issue in the interpretation of aphasic production impairments, where one might expect consistent failures at late stages in production to affect processing at earlier stages in models that allow such feedback.

Another processing assumption adopted in recent versions of the model somewhat moderates the requirement of discrete, serial processing. Following Kempen and Hoenkamp (1987), Levelt (1989) has argued that language production is "incremental" (p. 24). That is, information may be delivered from one level to the next in a piecemeal fashion, so that fragments of information may cascade to the next level before the entire representation that will be computed at that level is completed. This assumption thus allows limited parallel processing to occur across stages, while maintaining the requirement that all information flows forward only.

It should be evident that these two processing assumptions yield a system with dynamic information flow, where the timing relations among computed fragments are critical to a successful outcome. These timing relations and other issues have been studied (especially with regard to their lexical aspects) using implemented computational models based on spreading activation (Dell, 1986; Kempen & Hoenkamp, 1987; Rapp & Goldrick, 2000; Roelofs, 1992). These models force explicit consideration of processing details, and provide a means for evaluating perturbations in the timing of lexical activation and decay. These modeling efforts have generated some interesting insights into aphasic symptoms (Dell, Schwartz, Martin, Saffran, & Gagnon, 1997; Kolk, 1987). One particularly comprehensive theory of aphasic performance is built upon assumptions regarding the timing of information availability during sentence production (Kolk, 1995). This theory will be discussed below as we consider various attempts to explain aphasic symptoms.

Another consideration that has not been factored into normal production models, but which might well be involved in the disordered sentences of aphasic speakers, involves nonlinguistic cognitive capacities that may underlie the fluent production of sentences. Bock and Cutting

(1992) have invoked the notion of "mental energy," following Jespersen, 1924, to refer to a limited resource that might be taxed by situations in which a specific element to be produced at one point in time depends on another element produced much earlier. Such "discontinuous dependencies" occur, for example, when sentence subject and verb are separated by another clause or a prepositional phrase: "the report of the destructive forest fires were/was broadcast on the evening news"). The idea is that sentences like this might require more "mental energy" to achieve subject/verb agreement, especially when the intervening material contains a second noun that differs in number from the subject noun (as in the example). An idea akin to the notion of "mental energy" has been proposed to explain individual variation in sentence comprehension abilities, which are said to rely on a limited pool of cognitive resources (Just & Carpenter, 1992). Although the contribution of general cognitive limitations to disordered aphasic sentence production must be considered seriously, the issue is raised here simply to point out that the role of such factors in *normal* sentence production is rarely considered (see, for example, Carr's, 1999, commentary on Levelt, Roelofs, & Meyer, 1999a, with regard to attentional mechanisms).

SENTENCE PRODUCTION IN APHASIA

The framework for normal production sketched above, and variants of this general scheme, have for some years provided an organizing model against which the deficits found in aphasia have been compared. Many of these accounts have paid relatively little attention to the actual patterns of performance produced by aphasic patients, but have relied instead on idealized patterns of performance that rarely, if ever, describe the speech of individual patients (see Berndt, 1991, for a review). More recently, these general descriptions have largely given way to more detailed analyses of sentences produced by individual patients. Here we will attempt to summarize this shift toward more focused attention to specific symptoms and their co-occurrence. Before proceeding, however, there are several methodological points that should be raised.

Study of Aphasic Production: Some Caveats

The use of aphasic data to address issues of cognitive representation and processing requires that speech samples, perhaps best viewed as clinical descriptions, be turned into experimental data that are appropriate for analysis. This requires, minimally, that the patterns of performance subjected to interpretation are reliably produced by an individual patient, and reliably reconstructed by observers. Analysis of aphasic speech is a challenge; there is often very little to go on when reconstructing patients' utterances to a form that can be analyzed. Although some attempts have been made to develop reliable methods of production analysis (Goodglass, Christiansen, & Gallagher, 1994; Menn & Obler, 1990c; Saffran, Berndt, & Schwartz, 1989), many studies are carried out with little attention to issues regarding sample elicitation, transcription conventions, scoring reliability, etc. Here we will focus to the extent possible on findings from studies that have provided evidence of concern for these critical issues.

A second point that cuts across all of the interpretations of patient performance that will be discussed here is the fact that the utterances a patient produces may reflect the operation of a number of factors in addition to those issuing directly from the functional source of the impairment. The specific form that patients' sentences take may reflect the adoption of idiosyncratic patterns of responding that are influenced by the methods used to elicit speech (Hofstede & Kolk, 1994). Although the effects of individual patients' "adaptations" to task demands constitute an important part of at least one account of agrammatism (Kolk, 1987, 1995), other approaches to interpreting aphasic data appear to assume that performance is a direct reflection of a specific linguistic impairment. One important effect of idiosyncratic response patterns is to exacerbate the appearance of heterogeneity in performance patterns across patients. That is, if patients with the same underlying processing deficit alter their production in different ways (e.g., consistently omitting vs. substituting troublesome elements), the similarity of their underlying problems may be difficult to discern. This factor must be considered when interpreting differences in performance across patients, especially when those differences are to be interpreted as a symptom dissociation.

The Contrast between Broca's and Wernicke's Aphasia

As noted above, many of the earliest efforts to characterize aphasic sentence production were based on a broad characterization of general trends in performance. An important element of these accounts was the occurrence of what appeared to be contrasting patterns of performance for different patient groups. These differences suggested that distinct disturbances of speech production could occur as a result of brain lesions to different neural substrates, giving rise to the hope that the underlying disturbance for each of the types could ultimately be linked to a specific brain area. The most compelling of these contrasts is that between the classic categories of Broca's and Wernicke's aphasias. Sentence production in the "agrammatic" form of Broca's aphasia is generally characterized by omission of grammatical morphemes from simplified but interpretable sentences uttered nonfluently, with significant apparent effort. Figure 15.2 presents a speech sample from a prototypical Broca's aphasic patient, who is narrating the fairytale, "Cinderella."

In contrast to this pattern, in which the deficit appears primarily to affect structure-marking elements, patients with Wernicke's aphasia speak fluently in sentences with normal prosody and considerable evidence of structure. A sample from a chronic patient with Wernicke's aphasia is shown in Figure 15.3. Although grammatical elements are produced with apparent ease, the structures produced may be quite aberrant (e.g., "these dresses were very rags"). Content words are subject to paraphasic errors in which target words appear to be replaced by semantically related words, or by phonemically aberrant forms. An example of a semantic error can be seen in ML's substitution of "ants" for the apparent target "mice" (sharing the semantic feature "small").

Jakobson (1956) characterized the contrast apparent in these two patterns as reflecting the well-known linguistic distinction between syntagmatic and paradigmatic aspects of language. Broca's aphasics manifest difficulty with (syntagmatic) relations among elements in a string of segments, while Wernicke's aphasics have more difficulty with (paradigmatic) relationships between words and their referents. This characterization views the two patterns as essentially reflecting disturbances of form versus meaning; thus, it is quite easily associated with the positional/functional level distinction captured by the Garrett model (see Garrett, 1982a). That single fact may account for the many attempts that have been made to characterize sentence production symptoms using these two theoretical levels of representation. Such attempts have been complicated by two related problems. First, close scrutiny of the sentences produced by these patient types shows considerable overlap in both directions. Broca's aphasics manifest failures of lexical retrieval (for content words) that clearly contribute to their dysfluency; Wernicke's aphasics frequently show gross misordering and mis-selection of grammatical words ("paragrammatism") that may look very similar to the structural failures of Broca patients (Butterworth & Howard, 1987).

The second type of problem that undermines any simple attribution of symptoms to break-

---

[2]For all speech samples included here, perseverations and repaired material has been deleted in an attempt to convey core narrative structures. Material in quotes is spoken in character voice; articulatory distortions are glossed, and words in parentheses are patients' comments to the examiner; pauses < 2 sec indicated by . . .

One time long ago [4 sec] Cinderella [5 sec] mother and one two sisters [9 sec] uh one two sisters and [4 sec] pants shoes [5 sec] and uh two sisters [9 sec] "what's wrong?" "you stay home you stay home Cinderella" [2 sec] one two sisters at a ball [3 sec] a magic wand a nice lady [2 sec] fairy godmother "what's wrong?" [3 sec] at the ball no money [2 sec] so one two three four five six men magic wand [4 sec] rats now men oh [8 sec] magic wand ok nice [3 sec] glass slippers [2 sec] twelve o'clock no money now rich [3 sec] ok castle uh prince [3 sec] and too short too big [6 sec] and many girls uh [8 sec] Cinderella is [4 sec] I like you [3 sec] dance oh [2 sec] quarter to twelve [4 sec] go home go home hey come on prince come on [4 sec] twelve o'clock hurry up go home uh one she fell off [4 sec] prince is sad [2 sec] "what's wrong?" [3 sec] tomorrow I go [3 sec] prince and a shoe [3 sec] "oh good to see you" [3 sec] sit down [2 sec] then ah too small too small [2 sec] "you try it" [5 sec] fit [4 sec] prince is [3 sec] a lady [3 sec] prince and [8 sec] Cinderella [2 sec] happy after

Figure 15.2: Transcription of Speech Sample from Patient F.M., a Chronic Agrammatic Broca's Aphasic Patient.

down "at level X of the model" is that the general characterization of each of these two clinical patterns gives way to a variety of actual performance characteristics when production is analyzed in detail. That is, there are a number of symptom dissociations within the gross syndromes of Broca's and Wernicke's aphasia that can present challenges to any simple mapping of symptoms onto the model's components.

In ancient times we go through Cinderella upstairs in the attic and we have uh we have like uh uh and we have the mopping and the baking and the but all these dresses were very rags . . . and really sad . . . and the other the mother the the mother . . . girls were all mothers not all but he was like uh uh cousins I think.. old beautiful dress but real nose . . . and a really bad really dumb girls . . . and his mother-in-law got /g/ /g/ /ʌ/ /ʌ/ okay and the mother and uh their uh their . . . have two the uh the prince have uh the uh and a part ok . . . but uh Cinderella said no because she real sad in the attic and all and go two girls /gʌ/ /waɪ/ to (unintelligible) horses and carriage ok then um uh suddenly uh this the princess no the /stɛri/ godmother comes "hello how are you?" and she said no my really the dress was really /ʃ/ she real poor /kæt/ a water uh hot water um a pumpkin and all of a sudden boom was a was like a carriage and a (unintelligible) little five horses on three horses or seven horses twenty horses then uh and /hæns/ /tæns/ with the little uh [5 sec] in the uh anyway the little uh little ants (not ants, I'm sorry) uh she had an apple they have like one thing (unintelligible) it's like a little thing it's a (I can't say it) then uh the fairy godmother they had a beautiful dressing beautiful it's really something so go to the prince and to to party and all of a sudden it's twelve o'clock and oh my God and I'm gonna have to run outside running running running but it's now dirty and all... there's pumpkin and the uh little small ants (I can't say) and the real bad . . . anyway so the the prince said to please get the girls but maybe not ok (unintelligible) so anyway the uh the uh the old the old sisters old girls take on the shoes and they "oh my God" like a real cause tiny shoes ok and say so all the finally the girl said Cinderella said and they real tiny and there with the shoes so the mother uh the the the and the . . . happy forever after.

Figure 15.3: Transcription of Speech Sample from Patient M.L., a Chronic Wernicke's Aphasic Patient.

Here we are not concerned with distinguishing among these clinical types of aphasia. Instead, we will focus on specific symptoms even when they fail to respect classification boundaries. Practically speaking, however, the study of sentence production in aphasia is overwhelmingly focused on Broca's aphasia, and that bias will necessarily be reflected here.

Attempts to Interpret the Agrammatic Pattern

The defining feature of the agrammatic production pattern is the omission of grammatical morphemes. However, it has long been noted that this symptom is accompanied by structural aberrations that extend beyond the effects of these omissions (Goodglass, 1976). These additional "constructional" problems are usually described as structural simplification or failure to elaborate beyond the most basic syntactic forms, although more aberrant, fragmentary speech is often seen (Saffran et al., 1989).

Attempts to account for a production pattern that seems to reflect both morphological and constructional deficits, and that shows the "bias toward reference" in patients' residual speech, have emphasized possible ways in which all elements of the production pattern might reflect a single underlying deficit. For example, Saffran, Schwartz, and Marin (1980b) argued that agrammatic speech is generated without benefit of logical relations among lexical elements (computed on the model sketched above at the functional level). The speech that is produced thus represents a direct mapping from elements of the message to a skeletal structural form such as noun-verb-noun. Goodglass et al. (1994) have recently made a similar proposal: because Broca's aphasics have difficulty generating a syntactic frame, they rely on purely heuristic, nonsyntactic procedures to generate some elements of the message. These investigators, however, locate the primary impairment at the positional level.

These two accounts of the agrammatic pattern, though they differ in their interpretation of the locus of impairment in the model, essentially attempt to capture the same general phenomena, i.e., simplified and aberrant sentences that seem to convey an interpretable message. Many other investigators have invoked the functional-to-positional levels of the Garrett model in an attempt to account for these general findings, but it has been difficult to move beyond rather general claims. Caramazza and Hillis (1989) identified several reasons why more specific proposals about the source of these impairments have been elusive. These investigators carried out a detailed investigation of an agrammatic patient's spoken and written sentence production, and they gathered data on a number of other tasks. Although they concluded that the patient's symptoms could be interpreted as a manifestation of an impairment at the positional level of the model (or to some aspect of the processes that generate this representation), they pointed out a number of limitations of this account. A disruption at this level would be expected to cause difficulty in the generation of structural frames, including the realization of grammatical morphemes, accounting for the general pattern of symptoms observed. However, the patient's performance manifested several characteristics that are not predictable from the model as described. For example, she produced many more omissions of free-standing than of bound grammatical morphemes, and she produced apparent word order errors. Without more detailed specification of the processes that result in a positional level representation, it is difficult to claim that these symptoms result from an impairment at that level. Caramazza and Hillis (1989) pointed out further that the model does nothing to constrain the precise form that a "disruption" might take; that is, it is unclear why a disruption at the positional level involving grammatical morphemes would take the form of omissions in one patient and substitutions in another. These comments underscore some of the difficulties that arise when patients' symptoms are considered in enough detail that important deviations from the general pattern can be discerned.

CHALLENGES TO MODELING THE SYMPTOMS OF AGRAMMATISM

We will refer to the agrammatic pattern discussed above, in which grammatical morpheme omission occurs in the context of other structural problems, as the "modal" pattern. Although it is grossly true that the symptoms tend to occur together, it has long been recognized that morphological and structural problems can occur to differing degrees in individual patients (Tissot, Mounin, & Lhermitte, 1973). If it is the case that morphological and structural symptoms can dissociate, then more than one underlying impairment may be responsible for the modal pattern. More importantly, dissociations between the two symptoms may be difficult to interpret within the constraints of the serial model discussed above.

It has also been recognized for some time that the omission of grammatical morphemes by aphasic patients does not occur across-the-board; some morphemes are much more likely to be omitted than others (DeVilliers, 1974). Since grammatical morphemes are realized during the generation of a structural frame at the positional level, some account needs to be developed for why some morphemes are spared in conditions of positional level disruption.

Morphological versus Structural Agrammatism

Detailed analyses of aphasic sentence production have provided some support for the separability of morphological impairments from other structural problems. One important consideration is whether this dissociation represents impairments to distinct components of production that can be selectively impaired, or merely indexes variation along some sort of severity continuum affecting structural frames. For this reason, it is important to consider the question of whether double dissociations of these symptoms can be supported: Are simplified or disordered sentence structures ever produced by a patient who shows normal production of grammatical morphemes? Does the classical agrammatic symptom of grammatical morpheme omission ever occur in the context of otherwise well-formed sentences?

One half of this double dissociation appears to be established: numerous patients have been described who produce grossly simplified sentence structures, and generally appear to have difficulty producing words within the context of sentences, but at the same time produce a relatively normal complement of grammatical morphemes (Berndt, 1987; Saffran, Schwartz, & Marin, 1980a). Saffran et al. (1989) studied 10 nonfluent aphasic patients using a reliable system for scoring elements of patients' narrative sentences (the Quantitative Production Analysis, or QPA). Compared to normal controls, five patients showed the typical "agrammatic" pattern of omission of grammatical morphemes, with gross simplification of sentences and other structural deficits. Another five patients also showed the abnormal simplification of sentences, but in the context of normal use of grammatical morphemes. One of these patients, CJ, although very nonfluent (speech rate = 28 words/minute), produced normal ratios of nouns to pronouns and of verb inflections and determiners in obligatory contexts. However, his sentences did not differ from the agrammatic patients on a number of measures of sentence elaboration. A speech sample from CJ is presented in Figure 15.4.

In further support of this dissociation, Bird and Franklin (1995/1996) used the QPA of Saffran et al. (1989) and found that even fluent patients with relatively normal grammatical morpheme production generated structurally simplified sentences that were indistinguishable from those of nonfluent patients. Thus, limitations on the structural elaboration of sentences do not necessarily affect the realization of grammatical morphemes.

The first attempt to interpret the impairment of structural abilities in patients with spared production of grammatical morphemes proposed that the modal pattern results from two separable deficits (Saffran et al., 1980a). These authors revised their account of the modal pattern discussed above. They proposed that a failure to lexicalize message elements into a functional structure gives rise to constructional problems of various types, but the omission of

> in (6 sec) toytown (5 sec) mother and two (2 sec) daughters lived in (2 sec) the
> house . . . and a step-daughter Cinderella (3 sec) the girls and her mother (7 sec)
> said Cinderella (3 sec) light the light uh Cinderella wash the dishes Cinderella (9
> sec) the uh woman and two daughters met uh a knight . . . he had (3 sec) uh
> invitation to the ball (8 sec) March 15th . . . uh he rode away (4 sec) merrily . . . hey
> tried to find a better dress (3 sec) Cinderella worked (3 sec) uh worked at spinning
> yarn or rat poisoning . . . they went away for the ball and (5 sec) Cinderella stayed
> home . . . suddenly he heard a noise . . . she turned and the fairy godmother
> arrived . . . she said "godmother said I will dress you up uh a pumpkin is magically
> a carriage . . . the mice has (4 sec) the horses . . . she hurried (8 sec) hurried to fill
> the clothes and she uh godmother said remember (3 sec) you're (3 sec) going to
> the ball . . .

Figure 15.4: Transcription of a Speech Sample from Patient C.J., a Non-fluent
Patient without Significant Morphological Agrammatism.

grammatical morphemes requires an additional later breakdown—when the disordered structural frame is phonologically specified and readied for articulation. The latter disorder was associated with late stage processes that drive articulation, thus leading to the proposal that morphological agrammatism will occur only in patients with articulation disturbance. The proposal was that modal agrammatism requires both deficits: Articulation impairment affects the realization of grammatical morphemes *only* when functional structures are also disordered. When articulation alone is impaired, the patient will not omit grammatical morphemes. When the function assignment impairment occurs without an articulation disorder, structural impairments (simplification, etc.) will occur despite normal production of grammatical morphemes.

This explanation predicts that the dissociation of morphological and structural impairments will occur in only one direction; that is, morphological omissions (because they require both articulation disorder *and* a functional assignment problem) should not be found to occur in the context of otherwise normal sentence structures. A functional assignment problem, even occurring alone, will cause structural problems of some description. Thus, it should not be possible to find grammatical morpheme omissions occurring in otherwise normal sentences. At first blush, this statement appears to be a tautology: If grammatical morphemes are omitted, the sentences produced certainly will not have normal structure. Yet, several cases have been described in which grammatical morphemes were omitted, but the utterances produced were longer and/or more complex than is typical of modal agrammatic speech. These cases have been interpreted as constituting the second half of the double dissociation between structural and morphological symptoms discussed above, and thus deserve some further scrutiny.

Four patients—speakers of four different languages—have been described as omitting grammatical morphemes in the context of fluent, relatively long utterances. In contrast to the prediction made above, three of the four were described as having no (or very mild) articulation disorder, suggesting that problems of phonetic realization did not contribute to their omission of function words and inflections. The case that most closely approximates a dissociation of morphology and structure was an Italian-speaking patient described by Miceli, Mazzucchi, Menn, and Goodglass (1983), Case 2. The pattern of interest was manifested within the first month post onset, after which time the patient's speech was normal. During this acute period, he omitted and substituted many bound and free grammatical morphemes, while producing utterances that approached normal length when not penalized for the grammatical morpheme omissions. Inspection of the translations of the patient's speech reveals utterances that may be somewhat simpler than normal, but that do not manifest the fragmented and grossly simplified speech of modal agrammatism.[3]

The other three patients, whose omissions of grammatical morphemes persisted beyond the acute period, produced utterances that were somewhat longer than usually found in agrammatism. In all cases, however, other aspects of their speech were clearly aberrant (Kolk, VanGrunsven, & Keyser, 1985; Nadeau & Rothi, 1992; Nespoulous et al., 1988). Of interest is the possibility that the structural problems exhibited by two of these patients reflected a different source than is typical in agrammatism; competition between two separate sentence structures that leads to a paragrammatic type of sentence blend (Nadeau and Gonzalez-Rothi, 1992; Nespoulous, Dordain, Perron, Jarema, & Chazal, 1990, p. 642). We will discuss this pattern of production below.

These four cases do not constitute strong evidence that grammatical morpheme omissions can occur outside the context of other structural symptoms. Although the transient case of Miceli et al. is intriguing, the complexity and well-formedness of the structures he produced during this acute period is difficult to ascertain. In addition, the possibility that the acute impairment reflected some strategic response on the patient's part cannot be entirely ruled out.[4] The other patients were unusual in some ways, but their speech was clearly fraught with structural problems that appeared to go beyond the effects of their morphological omissions. Therefore, the postulation of a double dissociation between structural and morphological impairments does not appear tenable without additional supporting cases.[5] This is an important point, since many accounts of grammatical morpheme omission locate the disruption at the level of construction of the structural frame (Caramazza & Hillis, 1989; Schwartz, 1987). It is not clear how omissions arising at that level (or earlier in the serial model) could *fail* to result in structural deficiencies in addition to grammatical morpheme omissions. For the present, therefore, we will assume that results to date generally support the model's requirements: omission of grammatical morphemes occurs in the context of disruption to other aspects of sentence construction.

A comprehensive account of the relationship between grammatical morpheme omissions and other constructional problems, such as utterance simplification, is offered by Kolk (1987, 1995), who views the relative prominence of these two symptoms as a complex function of the patient's impairment and adaptation to the impairment. In Kolk's model, sentence production symptoms in aphasia are caused by disturbances of temporal coordination during the generation of a syntactic structure. Kolk (1995) proposes a modification of the standard interpretation of the positional level in which lexical items are thought to be inserted into slots in a structural frame already containing grammatical morphemes. Instead, Kolk proposes that both content words and grammatical morphemes must be integrated with specific syntactic slots in an emerging phrase structure. An asynchrony in this insertion process arises either when information takes too long to become activated, or decays too quickly, to be integrated properly with other information. Critically, the complexity of the message to be generated determines

---

[3]We have not included a speech sample from this patient, following the caution given by Miceli et al. (1983): "The reader will, of course, understand the limitations of the procedures we have had to follow in reconstructing the patient's apparent intended utterance and in constructing the English paraphrase. . . . The latter, at two removes from the original utterance, should be viewed only as a "crib" for the Italian and not as a text for serious comparison with transcripts of English-speaking aphasics" (p. 83).

[4]A very similar case involving a Finnish-speaking patient was described by Niemi, Laine, and Koivuselka-Sallinne, 1990). This patient also demonstrated a transient pattern of acute symptoms largely limited to omission of bound morphemes (a very prominent symptom in Finnish). However, the etiology of this disorder was unclear, and there was some possibility that the symptoms were psychogenic rather than neurogenic in origin.

[5]There are some reasons to be cautious about this conclusion, however. One possible reason that so few such cases have been reported is that isolated morphological agrammatism may occur in the context of speech that approaches normal in terms of phrase length and articulation. This factor might result in selection bias: the studies that have generated the most substantial data on agrammatic production have used nonfluency as a patient selection criterion (Menn & Obler, 1990c; Saffran et al., 1989). On the other hand, the omission of grammatical morphemes in speech is a symptom that has engendered much interest over a period of many years; it is difficult to believe that it would fail to be noticed simply because the patient was relatively fluent.

the extent of the effect that these temporal limitations will have on production. More complex messages, for example, those with more elements per constituent, place greater burdens on the patient's residual capacity for temporal integration.

The second important component of the theory is that patients have some options for dealing with this deficit. They can simplify their messages, and thereby produce a better-formed sentence (with fewer omissions), or they can try to convey something more complex, and omit some elements of the target structure. The most controversial aspect of this account (cf. Tesak & Niemi, 1997) is that when patients omit elements to adapt to their impairment they are relying on speech registers that are part of the normal repertoire—elliptical speech used in situations such as composing a telegram or trying to make oneself understood by a speaker of a foreign language. This "adaptation" feature of the model clearly leaves room for considerable intrasubject variability. Kolk and colleagues have demonstrated that the same patients perform quite differently under different task demands (Hofstede & Kolk, 1994), and that agrammatic speakers begin to look like paragrammatic speakers (substituting rather than omitting grammatical morphemes) in some types of tasks (Kolk & Heeschen, 1992).

This account seems to predict that grammatical morpheme omissions and structural simplifications will occur together, although the relative prevalence of each symptom may shift across speaking situations. In support of this proposal, Bastiaanse (1995) described a Dutch-speaking patient who demonstrated a complete change of production pattern in the middle of a testing session. In the early part of the session, sentences were complete but contained numerous morphological and structural errors. Later in the interview, she began speaking in the classic "telegraphic" style. Exactly what governed this shift is unclear, as the patient denied making a conscious decision to alter speaking style.

A critical element of Kolk's theory is that the proposed deficit affects processing requirements rather than structural representations themselves. Thus, sentence types that never occur in free speech may be produced if processing complexity is minimized. Hartsuiker and Kolk (1998) reported data indicating that production of more complex structures may be possible if the activation levels of those structures are raised through structural priming. Priming of passive voice and dative structures was achieved in a group of 12 Broca's aphasic patients, suggesting that the syntactic knowledge required to produce such structures was available. One important finding of this study was that structural priming was very robust in the patient group (even greater than in normal control subjects), but only in a testing condition in which patients were not made aware of the prime sentences. When patients were explicitly asked to model the prime sentence when describing pictures, no priming was obtained. Hartsuiker and Kolk interpreted this difference across conditions as an indication that the priming did not result from strategic attention to the prime, but rather reflected an automatic raising of activation levels. However, it is not entirely clear how this change in activation levels affects the timing disturbance discussed in Kolk (1995); rather, priming is interpreted as overcoming a cognitive resource limitation that appears to be more general than the specific impairment of temporal integration hypothesized in the earlier work.

Dissociations among the Grammatical Morphemes

The "telegram" analogy to agrammatism implies that all inessential words, including most grammatical function words, will be omitted from agrammatic speech. Even a cursory glance at transcripts of agrammatic speech samples (such as found in Figure 15.2; see also Menn & Obler, 1990a) indicate that this is an inaccurate description. Rather, there is variability both across and within individual patients as to which grammatical morphemes are omitted, and with what frequency. Moreover, it is now widely recognized that errors involving bound grammatical morphemes, which in English appear to be omissions, are more accurately described as substitutions of a default form, such as the infinitive (which in English carries no inflection).

Many attempts have been made to characterize the distribution of grammatical markers in agrammatic speech in terms of some principled hierarchy.

Within the framework discussed above, Kolk (1995) predicted a hierarchy of difficulty for the grammatical morphemes based on how much information speakers must have in order to specify a particular morpheme. That is, the extent to which the hypothesized timing impairment (desynchronization) will affect the production of a specific morpheme depends on the complexity of the syntactic hierarchy that must be generated for a particular structure to be realized. For example, a plural inflection on a noun requires that the minimal NP be generated, while the production of an adjective inflection requires a complex NP with head noun modified by an adjective. Based on this reasoning, it is predicted that plural inflections will be easier than adjective inflections, which will be easier than verb inflections. Similarly, determiners are predicted to be easier than lexical prepositions, which are in turn predicted to be easier than auxiliary verbs. These predictions were tested in a study in which Broca's and Wernicke's aphasics produced these elements in a cloze task (Haarmann & Kolk, 1992). Patients produced a single word spoken response to complete a sentence with a target free-standing grammatical morpheme or a word with an appropriate inflection. For example, a preposition is needed to complete "Grandmother writes _____a pen," and a verb with third person singular inflection to complete "I write; he _____." Both patient groups produced errors on this task that supported the predicted hierarchy, suggesting that the same basic underlying structural impairment contributes to both types of aphasia.

Another approach to variability in grammatical morpheme omissions has been to consider the degree to which free standing function words carry some meaning (Goodglass & Menn, 1985). Many pronouns and prepositions, for example, encode important semantic information regarding (respectively) conceptual gender and number, or a locative relationship. Levelt (1989) has suggested that these more meaningful types of function words may differ from morphemes with purely syntactic function in that they are generated by the same conceptually-driven processes of lemma selection as are content words. In contrast, words that function only syntactically may be "indirectly" elected through their association with other lemmas (e.g., verb particles), or generated directly by syntactic mechanisms operating at the positional level. There is some indication that semantic content versus syntactic function may indeed affect patient performance. Friederici (1982) found that the same (German) preposition was omitted much more frequently in a cloze task when it appeared in a purely syntactic context than when it carried more content. The implication is that if a patient's impairment is located at the level of construction of the positional level, prepositions with semantic content may be spared because they are selected earlier through message-driven lexical selection.

Although this type of explanation may accommodate some of the heterogeneity in function word production, it is limited in its scope. One important type of variability across patients that does not appear to be a function of variation in semantic load is the finding that bound and free standing grammatical morphemes may be differentially subject to omission across patients. Miceli, Silveri, Romani, and Caramazza (1989) analyzed samples from 20 patients classified as agrammatic, and concluded that difficulty producing free-standing and bound grammatical morphemes appeared to be independent. Similarly, Saffran and colleagues (1989) identified clear examples of double dissociations between determiner production and verb inflection production using the QPA. Table 15.1 presents the results of several measures from the QPA for two agrammatic Broca's aphasics, FM (whose speech sample is shown in Figure 15.2), and another chronic agrammatic patient, ME. These two patients were very similar in showing clear deficits of the agrammatic type; they performed at the low end of the agrammatic group on measures of production of words in sentences and of production of closed class words in general. Nonetheless, they differed markedly on measures of determiner use (with FM performing the best of the agrammatic group and ME the worst), and of verb inflection use

Table 15.1

Comparison of Two Agrammatic Broca's Aphasics' Scores
on Morphological Indices from the Quantitative Production
Analysis (Saffran et al., 1989).

Index	Control (N = 5) range	Agrammatic (N = 5) range	F.M.	M.E.
Proportion words/ Sentences	1.0	.25–.60	.25	.35
Proportion sentences well-formed	.9–1.0	.00–.58	.45	.42
Closed class words/ total words	.5–.6	.20–.42	.30	.20
Proportion nouns with determiner	1.0	.02–.70	**.70**	**.02**
Proportion verbs with affixes	.9–1.0	.09–.80	**.09**	**.80**

(with ME performing the best of the group and FM the worst). A fragment of ME's sample is reproduced in Figure 15.5, showing her tendency to inflect verbs with "-ed."

This type of dissociation appears to pose some difficulties for the Garrett model as described, since the grammatical frame produced at the positional level is argued to consist of both bound and free morphemes. It is difficult to account for the disruption of one and sparing of the other in a patient if both are computed at the same level of the model.

Lapointe (1985) proposed an elaboration of the creation of the positional level elements of verb form use, based largely on data from Italian-speaking agrammatic patients that showed this general pattern of dissociation. In Lapointe's account, verb inflections (which are always required in Italian) and auxiliary verbs are retrieved in separate operations. The positional level is made up of structural fragments, consisting of minimal syntactic phrases containing grammatical markers and slots to be filled by main verb and auxiliary. The latter are retrieved from a specialized "function word store" (see also Lapointe & Dell, 1989). The postulation of separate operations for realizing verb affixes and their auxiliaries allows for the possibility that the operations could be selectively impaired. Saffran et al. (1989) have suggested that such a division would need to be generalized to forms other than those involved with the verb phrase in order to account for the bound/free dissociations that have been described.

This modification of the Garrett model, although it may provide an account of the dissociation between bound and free morphemes, may conflict with recent findings from the structural priming paradigm. As noted above, Bock (1989) found that structural priming occurred across sentences sharing constituent structures, even when they did not share identical grammatical

Cinderella poor . . . um 'dopted her .. they took um I no we . . . Cinderella in 'dopted . . . um scrubbed floor . . . um tidy . . . poor . . . 'dopted.. sisters and mother . . . ball . . . it's a dumpty and dumpty (laughs) ball . . . prince um shoe um . . . (it's uh terrible) scrubbed and uh washed and tidy . . . sisters mother prince no prince yes . . . Cinderella hooked prince (laughs) um shoes . . . twelve o'clock ball finished . . . Jack Beanstalk Dumpty Dumpty

Figure 15.5: Transcription of Speech Sample from Chronic Agrammatic Broca's Aphasic Patient M.E. (pause times not available).

morphemes. Although this point was made most clearly with regard to the free-standing morphemes involved in dative structures, it also applies to the verb morphological elements of passive voice (see also Saffran & Martin, 1997). This suggests that the representation of the structural frame is more abstract than the traditional positional level representation, in which grammatical morphemes are intrinsic to the frame itself. Such an account is consistent with Kolk's (1995) proposal, reviewed above, that grammatical morphemes as well as content words must be inserted into appropriate slots in phrase structures. However, this modification also removes the clear representational distinction between content words and grammatical morphemes that was paramount in the functional/positional level contrast and so attractive to aphasia researchers.

VARIETIES OF CONSTRUCTIONAL DEFICITS

To this point, the "constructional" deficit that we have considered has been limited to a form of structural simplification in which the variety of structures produced is small and limited to single clauses with canonical word order. A number of other types of structural aberrations have been described in aphasia, and these disorders seem less clearly linked than those described above to breakdown in the generation of a positional level representation.

Absence of Elaboration within Phrases

In addition to simplification to canonical sentence forms in agrammatism discussed above, there is another type of simplification that has received somewhat less attention but appears to be pervasive in the utterances of a wide range of patients. This is the finding that individual noun phrases receive little internal elaboration with adjectives, prepositional phrases, or other descriptors (Goodglass et al., 1994; Menn & Obler, 1990b; Saffran et al., 1989). For example, agrammatic patients rarely produce prenominal adjectives to elaborate subject or object noun phrases (Menn & Obler, 1990b; Saffran et al., 1989), a symptom that is unlikely to arise because of problems producing grammatical morphemes. In fact, this type of simplification characterizes the sentences produced by patients without agrammatism, both nonfluent (Saffran et al., 1989) and fluent (Bird & Franklin, 1995). Furthermore, data from the Cross-Language Agrammatism Study (Ahlsen et al., 1996; Menn & Obler, 1990b) indicate that agrammatic patients are more likely to integrate adjectives into noun phrases in languages (such as French) in which the modifier appears *after* the noun. Thus, this type of simplification seems to constitute a structural impairment rather than a deficit linked to lexical retrieval within a particular grammatical class.

How might we account for this symptom on the model? One possibility is that the events to be described (i.e., information at the message level) have been simplified to the core propositional content that needs to be conveyed (Goodglass et al., 1994; Kolk, 1995). This account falters, however, on data from tasks eliciting adjective + noun constructions in contrastive picture naming, where the adjective is critical to the message to be conveyed. Ahlsen et al. (1996) found clear difficulty producing prenominal adjectives among agrammatic speakers of six different languages. Many errors resulted in production of the correct adjective in postnominal position, suggesting that the patient was well aware of the important content of the adjective within this context but could not produce the adjective + noun structure.

Another possible contributor to this symptom is suggested by recent work on the relationship between language and short-term memory. Martin, Katz, and Freedman (1998) proposed that planning at the lexical semantic level (here, functional level) requires retrieval and retention of the lexical head of each phrase and all words that will occur prior to it. For example, planning a noun phrase with a prenominal adjective requires retrieval and maintenance of an adjective and a noun before phonological planning can proceed. Patients who have difficulty maintaining lexical/semantic information in memory (and who therefore rely on phonological retention) may have particular difficulty producing elaborated noun phrases of this type. Preliminary data support this proposal, as two patients with lexical semantic retention deficits had difficulty using adjective + noun constructions in a contrastive naming task, but a patient with primarily phonological retention difficulties had no trouble producing adjective + noun structures. These results suggest that the discrete levels of planning required for sentence production may have very specific cognitive support systems, rather than a general purpose "computational resource" that supports all of sentence production.

Fragmented Utterances and Failed Sentences

One characteristic of agrammatic patients' attempts to communicate is that many if not most of the words they produce occur outside the context of even the most rudimentary of sentences. Saffran et al. (1989) found that only 25% to 60% of the words produced by five agrammatic patients occurred within a minimal sentence (noun + verb), even when the word count was undertaken *after* the sample had been culled of false starts, perseverations, and repairs. One reason for the scarcity of sentence structures is clearly related to a concomitant scarcity of verbs: many agrammatic patients have difficulty producing verbs across a range of tasks including picture naming (Goodglass et al., 1994; Miceli, Silveri, Villa, & Caramazza, 1984; Zingeser & Berndt, 1990).

It has been proposed that an inability to lexicalize verbs contributes to the fragmentary utterances and other structural anomalies found in agrammatism (Saffran et al., 1980a). However, the effect of verb retrieval difficulties on other aspects of sentence production is clearly dependent on the point within the production process at which retrieval fails. As noted above, selection of the verb lemma during construction of a functional level representation provides the argument structure that links selected noun lemmas to syntactic functions. Thus if lexical selection fails for the verb at this level, it would be impossible for the patient to generate a structural frame. In contrast, if verb retrieval fails at the positional level, the patient should be able to produce a structure with some elements (such as the required noun arguments) in place.

The model as described above suggests that retrieval failures reflecting grammatical class distinctions should occur during lemma selection, since that is the level at which grammatical class information is said to be represented. However, this interpretation has been challenged by modality-specific grammatical class effects (Caramazza & Hillis, 1991). If verb retrieval fails only in speech (but not in writing), or vice versa, the locus of the impairment would seem to be at the positional level, where phonological (and separate orthographic) forms are specified. Since written sentence production is not often tested in agrammatism, the modality specificity of the verb deficit cannot be used to delimit the locus of verb retrieval failure. We have attempted to find other means to identify the level at which verb production falters, and have accrued evidence to support the claim that some but not all failures of verb retrieval lead to widespread breakdown of sentence structures, including the omission of noun arguments (Berndt, Haendiges, Mitchum, & Sandson, 1997). For example, the fragmented constructions of some agrammatic patients may be improved by providing the patient with a (spoken) verb around which to construct a sentence. This type of evidence suggests that difficulty producing verbs, to the extent that it emanates from problems in construction of a functional level representation, contributes to fragmented and incomplete attempts to produce sentences.

It is important to note that particular difficulty retrieving verbs is not found only among patients with agrammatism, and therefore is not causally linked to grammatical morpheme omissions. However, it appears that problems with verb retrieval contribute importantly to a number of types of structural problems experienced by a wide range of patients. For example, a common failed utterance among fluent patients with paragrammatic speech appears to result when two planning frames are active simultaneously, resulting in sentence "blends." Butterworth and Howard (1987) list several interesting examples: the paragrammatic utterance: "isn't look very dear, is it?" is interpreted as a blend of "isn't very dear, is it?" and "doesn't look very dear, does it?"

In this and many other cases, there seem to be two verbs active simultaneously during sentence planning. Garrett (1982b) has proposed that separate clause groups, dominated by different verbs, are frequently active simultaneously during functional level processing, based on hesitation and speech error data from normal subjects. Sentence blends such as the one above, which have been reported in the speech of patients with symptoms of both paragrammatism and agrammatism (Nadeau & Gonzalez-Rothi, 1992; Nespoulous et al., 1990) are likely to occur because neither verb (and its related clause) becomes active enough to suppress elements of its competitor. These types of aberrant utterances are particularly difficult to interpret. However, more detailed study of these types of planning breakdowns could be useful in elaborating the requirements of functional level processing.

Word-Order Problems

One of the most important structure-marking devices in English is the order in which words are produced, so it may be surprising that a disorder of word order processing has not yet been discussed here. Word order errors are not typically found in the free speech of aphasic patients (Menn & Obler, 1990b), but they may become evident in structured elicitation tasks (Caramazza & Hillis, 1989). Saffran et al. (1980b) found that agrammatic speakers could not reliably produce noun-verb-noun or noun-preposition-noun orderings to describe pictures when the nouns involved were alike in animacy. Other studies have found word order difficulties in agrammatic as well as other types of patients when the task constrains production to active or passive voice structures by dictating which noun should begin the sentence used to describe a picture (Berndt, 1991; Caramazza & Berndt, 1985). One problem with the interpretation of word order errors in such tasks for agrammatic patients is that their morphological impairment makes it difficult to interpret sentences such as "boy kiss girl" to describe a picture of a girl kissing a boy as an order error. Although this utterance may reflect a misordering of the nouns, it might also reflect a morphologically failed attempt at a passive voice sentence (Caramazza & Berndt, 1985; Caramazza & Hillis, 1989).

This concern is considerably less apparent when patients can produce the grammatical morphology required to distinguish active from passive voice, but it remains difficult to interpret errors. For example, fluent patient ML (see Figure 15.3) produced numerous word order errors when constrained to begin his sentence using the nonagent noun, even when he was describing pictures in which the nouns differed in animacy (e.g., he produced sentences such as "the bike is riding the girl"). However, he also produced other aberrant sentences that suggested lack of control over the grammatical morphemes ("the girl was hitting from the boy"; "the woman is stab with a boy") Although it is possible that this symptom reflects an inability to link logical roles (e.g., agent of the action) to grammatical roles (e.g., subject of the sentence), it could also reflect confusion about the verb inflection and preposition required for passive voice. ML also had great difficulty producing verbs across a wide range of tasks, and we hypothesized that the word order problem may have been related to the inaccessibility of verb-specific mapping rules (see also Berndt, 1991; Berndt et al., 1997; Mitchum & Berndt, 1994).

The relative scarcity of word order errors in aphasic speech may reflect the fact that a number of factors, in addition to verb argument structures, influence the order in which words are produced (Hartsuiker, Kolk, & Huiskamp, 1999). In a series of structural priming studies, Bock and colleagues have shown that the order in which nouns are mentioned in the sentences of normal subjects can be influenced by the accessibility of both the concepts to be conveyed

(Bock & Warren, 1985; McDonald, Bock, & Kelly, 1993) and the word forms needed to convey them (Bock, 1987). Conceptual accessibility involved factors such as noun animacy (McDonald et al., 1993), prototypicality (Kelly, Bock, & Keil, 1986) and imageability (Bock & Warren, 1985), all of which were shown to affect the order in which nouns were produced. Such factors might be expected to play a greater role in aphasic sentence production when other (syntactic) influences on order are weakened. Reliance on such factors may result in utterances that do not violate word order. Although it is clear that agrammatic patients may use animacy as an ordering principle (Saffran et al., 1980b), the effects of these other variables on order production have yet to be investigated. Because of the importance of word order in languages such as English, this is a topic in need of much more study.

FUTURE DIRECTIONS

This review demonstrates that substantial research effort has been directed at the issue of sentence production in aphasia. What have we learned about the source of aphasic symptoms from these efforts? Attempts to use the normal production models as a guide in interpreting aphasic performance have had one obvious effect, that is, to demonstrate that no simple distinction of symptoms as relating to meaning versus form will suffice. Rather, aphasic symptoms appear to reflect a complex interaction of the effects of one or more language impairments, compounded perhaps by other cognitive limitations. Recent elaborations of the model that specify timing details, or that demonstrate systematic effects of nonlinguistic factors on utterance form, offer some hope that more detailed links can be forged between the symptoms and their precursors in the normal system.

Further progress in this area seems to require focused study of specific aspects of aphasic performance in individual patients. As noted above, for example, it is not clear how to interpret production patterns that seem to indicate problems with word order, due to the possible contribution of morphological deficits to the utterances produced. It is possible that new experimental paradigms, or focused treatment studies, could address this confound. For example, if morphological problems could be alleviated, or subverted, the relationship between noun order and sentence structure could more easily be investigated.

Has consideration of the aphasia data contributed to the evolution of the normal model? The answer to this question is less clearly affirmative than in other areas of cognitive neuropsychology, such as memory research, where data from patients has played an important role in model development. In fact, the contribution of recent, detailed study of aphasic sentence production might be viewed as largely negative because it fails to support a clear-cut dichotomy between "closed class" and "open class" vocabularies. However, the complicated symptom patterns leading to this view have also forced more careful consideration of the roles played by specific function words within their grammatical contexts. In fact, data from patients have been used to work out detailed modifications of components of the model (e.g., Lapointe, 1985; Lapointe & Dell, 1989). These linguistically sophisticated analyses of aphasic performance present clear evidence of the potentially rich source of data supplied by aphasic speech, and there is a particular need for extension of this approach beyond elements of the verb phrase. Other contributions to thinking about normal sentence production can be identified from the commonalities found in the Cross Language Agrammatism Study (Menn & Obler, 1990a), which support the processing equivalence across languages of a number of hypothesized structure-marking devices.

The aberrant sentences produced by aphasic subjects cannot be viewed as simple extensions of normal speech errors. Rather, they may reflect a number of cognitive limitations, timing perturbations, and strategic responses superimposed upon one or more disruptions to the processes outlined in models of sentence production. Thus, the identification of selective interpretable deficits to sentence production may be difficult. Nonetheless, the models provide a critical organizing framework for the systematic analysis of sentence production deficits, and the aphasic data present formidable challenges to be solved through development and modification of the model.

Acknowledgements

The preparation of this paper was supported by grant R01-DC00262 from the National Institute on Deafness and Other Communication Disorders to the University of Maryland Medical School.

REFERENCES

Ahlsen, E., Nespoulous, J.-L., Dordain, M., Stark, J., Jarema, G., Kadzielawa, D., Obler, L. K., & Fitzpatrick, P. M. (1996). Noun phrase production by agrammatic patients: A cross-linguistic approach. *Aphasiology, 10,* 543–559.

Bastiaanse, R. (1995). Broca's aphasia: A syntactic and/or a morphological disorder? A case study. *Brain and Language, 48,* 1–32.

Berndt, R. S. (1987). Symptom co-occurrence and dissociation in the interpretation of agrammatism. In M. Coltheart, G. Sartori, & R. Job (Eds.), *The cognitive neuropsychology of language.* Hillsdale, NJ: Lawrence Erlbaum.

Berndt, R. S. (1991). Sentence processing in aphasia. In M. T. Sarno (Ed.), *Acquired aphasia* (2nd ed.). New York: Academic Press.

Berndt, R. S., Haendiges, A. N., Mitchum, C., & Sandson, J. (1997). Verb retrieval in aphasia. 2. Relationship to sentence processing. *Brain and Language, 56,* 107–137.

Bird, H., & Franklin, S. (1995/1996). Cinderella revisited: A comparison of fluent and non-fluent aphasic speech. *Journal of Neurodiagnostics, 9,* 187–206.

Bock, J. K. (1986). Syntactic persistence in language production. *Cognitive Psychology 18,* 355-387.

Bock, J. K., & Warren, R. K. (1985). Conceptual accessibility and syntactic structure in sentence formulation. *Cognition, 21,* 47–67.

Bock, K. (1987). An effect of the accessibility of word forms on sentence structures. *Journal of Memory and Language, 26,* 119–137.

Bock, K. (1989). Closed-class immanence in sentence production. *Cognition, 31,* 163–186.

Bock, K., & Cutting, C. (1992). Regulating mental energy: Performance units in language production. *Journal of Memory and Language, 31,* 99–127.

Bock, K., & Levelt, W. (1994). Language production. Grammatical encoding. In M. A. Gernsbacher (Ed.), *Handbook of psycholinguistics.* San Diego, CA: Academic Press.

Bock, K., & Loebell, H. (1990). Framing sentences. *Cognition, 35,* 1–39.

Bock, K., Loebell, H., & Morey, R. (1992). From conceptual roles to structural relations: Bridging the syntactic cleft. *Psychological Review, 99,* 150–171.

Bresnan, J. (Ed.). (1982). *The mental representation of grammatical relations.* Cambridge, MA: MIT Press.

Butterworth, B., & Howard, D. (1987). Paragrammatisms. *Cognition, 26,* 1–37.

Caramazza, A. (1986). On drawing inferences about the structure of normal cognitive systems from the analysis of impaired performance: The case for single-patient studies. *Brain and Cognition, 5,* 41–66.

Caramazza, A., & Berndt, R .S. (1985). A multicomponent deficit view of agrammatic Broca's aphasia. In M. L. Kean (Ed.), *Agrammatism.* New York: Academic Press.

Caramazza, A., & Hillis, A. E. (1989). The disruption of sentence production: Some dissociations. *Brain and Language, 36,* 625–650.

Caramazza A., & Hillis, A. (1991). Lexical organization of nouns and verbs in the brain. *Nature, 349,* 788-790.

Carr, T. H. (1999). How does WEAVER pay attention? *Behavioral and Brain Sciences, 22,* 39–40.

Dell, G. S. (1986). A spreading activation theory of retrieval in sentence production. *Psychological Review, 93,* 283–321.

Dell, G. S., & O'Seaghdha, P. G. (1991). Mediated and convergent lexical priming in language production: A comment on Levelt et al. *Psychological Review, 98,* 604–614.

Dell, G. S., & Reich, P. A. (1981). Stages in sentence production: An analysis of speech error data. *Journal of Verbal Learning and Verbal Behavior, 2,* 611-629.

Dell, G. S., Schwartz, M. F., Martin, N., Saffran, E. M., & Gagnon D. A. (1997). Lexical access in aphasic and nonaphasic speakers. *Psychological Review, 104,* 801–838.

DeVilliers, J. (1974). Quantitative aspects of agrammatism in aphasia. *Cortex, 10,* 36–54.

Friederici, A. D. (1982). Syntactic and semantic processes in aphasic deficits: The availability of prepositions. *Brain and Language, 15,* 249–258.

Fromkin, V. A. (1971). The non-anomalous nature of anomalous utterances. *Language, 47,* 27–52.

Garrett, M. F. (1975). The analysis of sentence production. In G. H. Bower (Ed.), *The psychology of learning and motivation* (pp. 133–177). London: Academic Press.

Garrett, M. F. (1980). Levels of processing in sentence production. In B. Butterworth (Ed.), *Language production* (Vol. 1, pp. 170–220), London: Academic Press.

Garrett, M. F. (1982a). The organization of processing structure for language production: Applications to aphasic speech. In D. Caplan, R. Lecours, & A. Smith (Eds.), *Biological perspectives on language.* Cambridge, MA: MIT Press.

Garrett, M. F. (1982b). Production of speech: Observations from normal and pathological language use. In A. Ellis (Ed.), *Normality and pathology in cognitive functions* (pp. 19–76). London: Academic Press.

Garrett, M. F. (1988). Processes in language production.

In F. J. Newmeyer (Ed.), *Linguistics: The Cambridge survey: III. Language: Psychological and biological aspects* (pp. 69-96). Cambridge, UK: Cambridge University Press.

Goodglass, H. (1976). Agrammatism. In H. Whitaker & H. A. Whitaker (Eds.), *Studies in neurolinguistics* (Vol. 1), New York: Academic Press.

Goodglass, H., Christiansen, J. A., & Gallagher, R. E. (1994). Syntactic constructions used by agrammatic speakers: Comparison with conduction aphasics and normals. *Neuropsychology, 8*, 598-613.

Goodglass, H., & Menn, L. (1985). Is agrammatism a unitary phenomenon? In M.-L. Kean (Ed.), *Agrammatism*. New York: Academic Press.

Haarmann, H. J., & Kolk, H. H. J. (1992). The production of grammatical morphology in Broca's and Wernicke's aphasics: Speed and accuracy factors. *Cortex, 28*, 97-102.

Hartsuiker, R. J., & Kolk, H. H. J. (1998). Syntactic facilitation in agrammatic sentence production. *Brain and Language, 62*, 221-254.

Hartsuiker, R. J., Kolk, H. H. J., & Huiskamp, P. (1999). Priming word order in sentence production. *The Quarterly Journal of Experimental Psychology, 52A*(1), 129-147.

Hofstede, B. T. M., & Kolk, H. H. J. (1994). The effects of task variation on the production of grammatical morphology in Broca's aphasia: A multiple case study. *Brain and Language, 46*, 278-328.

Jackendoff, R. (1987). The semantic organization of some simple nouns and verbs. *Journal of Verbal Learning and Verbal Behavior, 18*, 141-162.

Jakobson, R. (1956). Two aspects of language and two types of aphasic disturbances. In R. Jakobson & M. Halle (Eds.), *Fundamentals of language*, The Hague: Mouton de Gruyter.

Jespersen, O. (1924). *The philosophy of grammar*. London: Allen & Unwin.

Just, M. A., & Carpenter, P. A. (1992). A capacity theory of comprehension: Individual differences in working memory. *Psychological Review, 99*, 122-149.

Kelly, M. H., Bock, J. K., & Keil, F. C. (1986). Prototypicality in a linguistic context: Effects on sentence structure. *Journal of Memory and Language, 25*, 59-74.

Kempen, G., & Hoenkamp, J. (1987). An incremental procedural grammar for sentence formulation. *Cognitive Science, 11*, 201-258.

Kolk, H. (1987). A theory of grammatical impairment in aphasia. In G. Kempen (Ed.), *Natural language generation*. Dordrecht, The Netherlands: Martinus Nijhoff Publishers.

Kolk, H. (1995). A time-based approach to agrammatic production. *Brain and Language, 50*, 282-303.

Kolk, H., & Heeschen, C. (1992). Agrammatism, paragrammatism and the management of language. *Language and Cognitive Processes, 7*, 89-129.

Kolk, H. H.., Van Grunsven, M. J. F., & Keyser, A. (1985). On parallelism between production and comprehension in agrammatism. In M. L. Kean (Ed.), *Agrammatism*. New York: Academic Press.

Lapointe, S. G. (1985). A theory of verb form use in the speech of agrammatic aphasics. *Brain and Language, 24*, 100-155.

Lapointe, S. G., & Dell, G. S. (1989). A synthesis of some recent work in sentence production. In G. N. Carlson & M. K. Tanenhaus (Eds.), *Linguistic structure in language processing*. Dordrecht, The Netherlands: Kluwer Academic Press.

Levelt, W. J. M. (1989). *Speaking: From intention to articulation*. Cambridge, MA: MIT Press.

Levelt, W. J. M., & Kelter, S. (1982). Surface form and memory in question answering. *Cognitive Psychology, 14*, 78-106.

Levelt, W. J. M., Roelofs, A., & Meyer, A. S. (1999a). A theory of lexical access in speech production. *Behavioral and Brain Sciences, 22*(1), 1-75.

Levelt, W. J. M., Roelofs, A., & Meyer, A.S. (1999b). Multiple perspectives on word production. *Behavioral and Brain Sciences, 22*(1), 61-75.

Levelt, W. J. M., Schriefers, H., Vorberg, D., Meyer, A. S., Pechmann, T., & Havinga, J. (1991a). The time course of lexical access in speech production: A study of picture naming. *Psychological Review, 98*, 122-142.

Levelt, W. J. M., Schriefers, H., Vorberg, D., Meyer, A. S., Pechmann, T., & Havinga, J. (1991b). Normal and deviant lexical processing: Reply to Dell and O'Seaghdha. (1991). *Psychological Review, 98*, 615-618.

Lindsley, J. R. (1975). Producing simple utterances: How far ahead do we plan? *Cognitive Psychology, 7*, 1-19.

Martin, N., Weisberg, R. W., & Saffran, E.M. (1989). Variables influencing the occurrence of naming errors: Implications for models of lexical retrieval. *Journal of Memory and Language, 28*, 462-485.

Martin, R.C., Katz, M., & Freedman, M. (1998). Lexical-semantic retention and language production. *Brain and Language, 65*, 99-101.

McDonald, J. L., Bock, J. K., & Kelly, M. H. (1993). Word and world order: Semantic, phonological, and metrical determinants of serial position. *Cognitive Psychology, 25*, 188-230.

Menn, L., & Obler, L. K. (1990a). *Agrammatic aphasia*. Amsterdam: John Benjamins.

Menn, L., & Obler, L. K. (1990b). Cross-language data and theories of agrammatism. In L. Menn & L. K. Obler (Eds.), *Agrammatic aphasia* (Vol. 2). Amsterdam: John Benjamins.

Menn, L., & Obler, L. K. (1990c). Methodology: Data collection, presentation and guide to interpretation. In L. Menn & L. K. Obler (Eds.), *Agrammatic aphasia* (Vol. 1). Amsterdam: John Benjamins.

Miceli, G., Mazzucchi, A., Menn, L., & Goodglass, H. (1983). Contrasting cases of Italian agrammatic aphasia without comprehension disorder. *Brain and Language, 19*, 65-97.

Miceli, G., Silveri, M. C., Romani, C., & Caramazza, A. (1989). Variation in the pattern of omissions and substitutions of grammatical morphemes in the spontaneous speech of so-called agrammatic patients. *Brain and Language, 36*, 447-492.

Miceli, G., Silveri, M. C., Villa, G., & Caramazza, A. (1984). On the basis for the agrammatics' difficulty in producing main verbs. *Cortex, 20*, 207-220.

Mitchum, C. C., & Berndt, R. S. (1994). Verb retrieval and sentence construction: Effects of targeted intervention. In G. Humphreys & J. Riddoch (Eds.), *Cognitive neuropsychology and cognitive rehabilitation*. London: Lawrence Erlbaum.

Nadeau, S. E., & Rothi, L. J. (1992). Morphologic agrammatism following a right hemisphere stroke in a dextral patient. *Brain and Language, 43*, 642-667.

Nespoulous, J.-L., Dordain, M., Perron, C., Jarema, G., & Chazal, M. (1990). Agrammatism in French: Two case studies. In L. Menn & L. K. Obler (Eds.), *Agrammatic aphasia* (Vol. 1). Amsterdam: John Benjamins.

Nespoulous, J.-L., Dordain, M., Perron, C., Ska, B., Bub, D., Caplan, D., Mehler, J., & Lecours, A. R. (1988). Agrammatism in sentence production without comprehension deficits: Reduced availability of syntactic structures and/or of grammatical morphemes? A case study. *Brain and Language, 33,* 273–295.

Niemi, J., Laine, M., & Koivuselka-Sallinen, P. (1990). A fluent morphological agrammatic in an inflectional language? In J.-L. Nespoulous & P. Villiard (Eds.), *Morphology, phonology and aphasia.* New York: Springer-Verlag.

Rapp, B., & Goldrick, M. (2000). Discreteness and interactivity in spoken word production. *Psychological Review, 107,* 460–499.

Roelofs, Å. (1992). A spreading activation theory of lemma retrieval in speaking. *Cognition, 42,* 107-142.

Saffran, E. M., Berndt, R. S., & Schwartz, M. F. (1989). The quantitative analysis of agrammatic production: Procedure and data. *Brain and Language, 37,* 440-479.

Saffran, E. M., & Martin, N. (1997). Effects of structural priming on sentence production in aphasics. *Language and Cognitive Processes, 12,* 877–882.

Saffran, E. M., Schwartz, M. F., & Marin, O. S. M. (1980a). Evidence from aphasia: Isolating the components of a production model. In B. Butterworth (Ed.), *Language production* (Vol. 1). London: Academic Press.

Saffran, E. M., Schwartz, M. F., & Marin, O. S. M. (1980b). The word order problem in agrammatism. II. Production. *Brain and Language, 10,* 263–280.

Schriefers, H., Meyer, A. S., & Levelt, W. J. M. (1990). Exploring the time course of lexical access in language production: Picture-word interference studies. *Journal of Memory and Language, 29,* 86–102.

Schwartz, M. F. (1987). Patterns of speech production deficit within and across aphasia syndromes: Application of a psycholinguistic model. In M. Coltheart, G. Sartori, & R. Job (Eds.), *The cognitive neuropsychology of language.* Hillsdale, NJ: Lawrence Erlbaum.

Tesak, J., & Niemi, J. (1997). Telegraphese and agrammatism: A cross-linguistic study. *Aphasiology, 11,* 145–155.

Tissot, R. J., Mounin, G., & Lhermitte, F. (1973). *L'agrammatisme.* Brussels: Dessart.

Zingeser, L., & Berndt, R. S. (1990). Retrieval of nouns and verbs by agrammatic and anomic aphasics. *Brain and Language, 39,* 14-32.

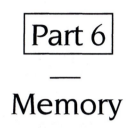

Part 6

—

Memory

—

The charm, one might say the genius, of memory is that it
is choosy, chancy and temperamental;
it rejects the edifying cathedral and indelibly
photographs the small boy outside,
chewing a hunk of melon in the dust.

—*Elizabeth Bowen*

16

The Structure and Mechanisms of Memory

Alan J. Parkin

Memory, of all the powers of the mind, is the most delicate and the most frail.

Ben Johnson

The study of human memory disorder has a long history, making it, perhaps, the oldest topic within neuropsychology. As with most areas of psychology, longevity is no guarantee of theoretical development and, in many ways, amnesia remains as much a challenge now as it did 50 years ago. In this chapter I will discuss the contribution that research into human amnesia has made to our understanding of normal memory and will conclude by considering the direction of future research into human memory disorder.

WHAT IS AMNESIA?

The term amnesia is so general as to be largely meaningless except as an indication that someone has a faulty memory. As we shall see, memory can go wrong in many different ways and this has major implications at both theoretical and clinical levels. The first distinction we must make is between psychogenic disorders (also known as functional disorders) and those whose origin is organic.

Psychogenic disorders are losses of memory which arise following psychological trauma. They can be classified into a number of subtypes. Most common is *dissociative* or *hysterical amnesia* in which there is a partial loss of memory for events surrounding a traumatic event. Other types include *post-traumatic stress disorder* (PTSD), *fugue,* and *multiple personality disorder.* Their existence has proved valuable as a device in fiction but their frequency of occurence in this context betrays a scant knowledge of how memory impairment can arise as a consequence of psychological trauma.

Organic disorders are by far the most important from the point of view of cognitive neuropsychology. They exist in two essential subtypes: (a) *transient,* where memory function is impaired for a limited period, following which normal functioning returns; and (b) *chronic,* where the impairment is permanent.

The most well-known transient organic disorder is *transient global amnesia* (TGA) in which the person experiences a severe loss of memory which can range from a few hours to several days. There is a degree of systematicity in the pattern of recovery (Kapur, Millar, Abbott, & Carter, 1998) and usually only events during the TGA period itself are permanently lost

(Hodges, 1998). TGA has been associated with epilepsy and electroconvulsive therapy (ECT). Because of its duration and systematic availability, post-ECT amnesia is the only transient state which has received extensive investigation at a cognitive level, but there is continuing controversy about the possible long-term effects of ECT (Parkin, 1997c).

The cognitive neuropsychology of memory has focused mostly on patients with chronic disorders of memory. These include the *dementias,* in which there is a gradual loss of memory, *focal retrograde amnesia,* where the primary deficit is a loss of memory for the past, and the *amnesic syndrome,* which is dominated by a severe and permanent anterograde amnesia.[1]

Most of the research discussed in this chapter involves the amnesic syndrome and so it would be useful to review the syndrome's characteristic features at this point (in Parkin, 1997c. pp. 87–88). They are as follows:

1. Unimpaired short-term storage as measured by tasks such as digit span.
2. A severe and permanent anterograde amnesia, with exceptionally poor performance on tests of recall such WMS-R hard-paired associate learning. WMS-R logical memory and visual reproduction scores are very low. Recognition is also poor, with chance performance often observed on tests such as RMT.
3. Semantic memory, and other intellectual functions, as measured by tests such as WAIS-R, are generally intact. Thus, to be classified as amnesic a patient would have an average IQ but scores on the WMS-R indices (especially the delayed memory index) would be well below normal levels.
4. Skill learning, conditioning, perceptual learning, and priming are relatively intact.
5. Retrograde amnesia will inevitably be present but its extent can be extremely variable with some patients having extensive deficits and others lacking memory only for very recent parts of the premorbid period.

THE NEURAL BASES OF MEMORY AND AMNESIA

Figure 16.1 illustrates the various brain structures which, when damaged, can give rise to the amnesic syndrome. These structures occur in two distinct areas of the brain, the *midline diencephalon* and the *medial temporal lobes.*

Much of what we know about the amnesic syndrome has stemmed from investigations of patients with Korsakoff's Syndrome. These patients have suffered damage to a variety of diencephalic structures, most notably the dorso-medial thalamic nucleus, the mamillary bodies, the mamillo-thalamic tract, and certain areas adjacent to the third ventricle. However, there is also a degree of cortical involvement, especially in the frontal cortex, and more recently it has been pointed out that Korsakoff patients may have additional damage in the medial temporal lobe.

Although Korsakoff's Syndrome is the primary cause of amnesia arising through damage to the diencephalon, there are other causes. The thalamic region is prone to vascular disorders which can give rise to amnesia (Parkin, Rees, Hunkin, & Rose, 1994; see Figure 16.2). Diencephalic amnesia can also arise from the presence of tumours (Parkin & Hunkin, 1993b). The floor of the third ventricle is adjacent to diencephalic structures and tumors here can exert local pressure on those structures, causing memory loss. Tumors can also damage the mamillary bodies, as can paranasal penetrating head injuries (Dusoir, Kapur, Byrnes, McKinstry, & Hoare, 1990). A case of paranasal penetrating head injury involving more extensive damage is NA. When he was first scanned it was claimed that he had a lesion restricted to the dorso-medial nucleus of the thalamus. More detailed neuroimaging has since shown much more extensive damage, including complete destruction of the mamillary bodies. Significantly, however, there is no damage to the hippocampal formation (Parkin, 2000b).

---

[1]Retrograde amnesia refers to an inability to remember things known prior to the precipitating trauma or illness. Anterograde amnesia refers to difficulty in acquiring new information following the trauma or illness.

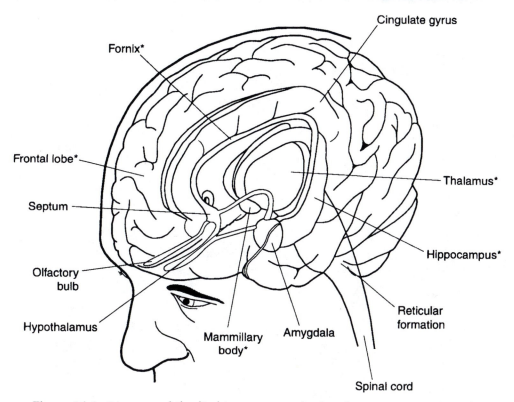

Figure 16.1: Diagram of the limbic system and related structures. Areas indicated with an asterisk are known to be associated with memory function.

Involvement of the temporal lobes in memory was only firmly established in the 1950s, although it had long been suspected from isolated clinical reports. The evidence came from temporal lobectomy in which areas of the temporal lobe responsible for epileptic seizures were selectively removed. The most famous of these patients is HM, whose dense amnesia I have discussed in detail elsewhere (Parkin, 1996b). Notes taken during his operation and others led to the view that the critical structure involved in amnesia was the hippocampus. However, conclusions about HM's underlying pathology must now be qualified by the discovery that he also has significant atrophy of the mamillary bodies, at least in the present day (Corkin, Amaral, Gonzalez, Johnson, & Hyman, 1997).

A patient with selective damage to the CA1 field of the hippocampus resulting from a small ischaemic lesion has been described by Zola-Morgan, Squire, and Amaral (1986). RB exhibits anterograde amnesia with little evidence of retrograde amnesia. In a follow-up study it has been argued that lesions restricted to CA1 essentially produce anterograde amnesia alone, whereas more extensive damage, although still restricted to the hippocampal formation, gives rise to anterograde amnesia and an extensive retrograde amnesia (Rempel-Clower, Zola, Squire, & Amaral, 1996).

Selective ischaemic lesions of the hippocampal formation are rare and attempts to examine amnesia following hippocampal pathology have largely relied on survivors of herpes simplex encephalitis. This is a viral infection of the brain that rapidly causes extensive brain damage centred on the temporal lobes. MRI scans of patients who survive this illness invariably show hippocampal lesions but the damage is always more extensive than this, extending most commonly into the temporal cortex and the prefrontal cortex (especially orbito-frontal). There is

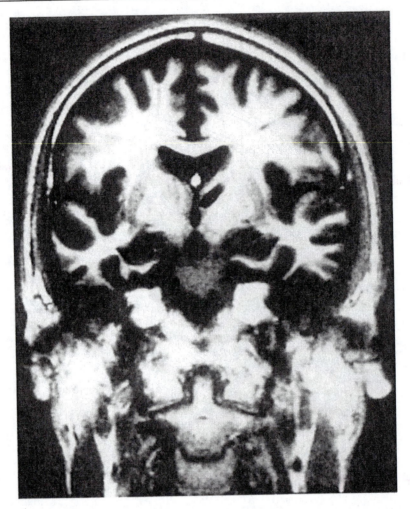

Figure 16.2: MRI scan of patient JR. Note the dark region in the centre. A small lesion in the region of the dorsomedial nucleus of the thalamus.

little indication that herpes simplex encephalitis leads to any significant damage to the diencephalic structures identified with amnesia (Parkin & Leng, 1993).

The question of whether there are two forms of amnesia arising from damage to two different areas of the brain (the midline diencephalon and the medial temporal lobes) is not easily answered because the data are not as "clean" as one would like. Firstly, as we have seen, the major sources of "diencephalic" and "temporal lobe" amnesia stem from aetiologies which produce large lesions extending beyond those structures assumed to be crucial to the memory impairment. Secondly, we may be restricted by the accuracy of the neuropathological information available as, for example, in the case of HM who has now been shown to have additional diencephalic damage. There are, therefore, relatively few cases of the amnesic syndrome in which we can be confident there is no overlapping lesion.

Another important fact to bear in mind when considering the various lesion sites which contribute to amnesia is that they are all part of the *limbic system.* The hippocampus projects to the anterior thalamus both directly, via the fornix, and indirectly, via the mamillary bodies and mamillothalamic tract. There are further projections from the anterior thalamic nucleus to cingulate and frontal cortex as well as projections back to the hippocampus and adjacent cortical areas via the cingulum. If memory relied on a "circuit" then damage anywhere along that circuit could disrupt memory functioning.

THE STRUCTURE OF MEMORY

The Dichotomy between Short and Long Term Storage (STS and LTS)

William James' seminal distinction between primary and secondary memory (James, 1890) had, by the end of the 1960s, transformed into the dichotomy between *short-* and *long-term store* (STS and LTS) (Atkinson & Shiffrin, 1968). Various lines of evidence from normal subjects were put forward in support of this dichotomy. Further evidence came from patients who had suffered lesions to the hippocampus as a result of temporal lobectomy, the most well-known of these patients being HM. Atkinson & Shiffrin considered this line of evidence provided "perhaps the single most convincing demonstration of a dichotomy in the memory system" (p. 97).

Milner (1966) reported that patients with bilateral surgical lesions in the hippocampal region shows a severe and persstent disorder of memory. Although material known prior to the operation remained intact, patients were unable to acquire further information. Immediate registration of new information seemed to take place normally and material which could be rehearsed verbally was retained for many minutes without loss. However, material which could not be verbalized decayed in a matter of seconds, and interruption of rehearsal led to immediate loss.

The pattern of impairment is the most consistent feature of all patients presenting the amnesic syndrome, regardless of etiology. They invariably show normal range performance on tests of immediate apprehension such as digit span alongside marked impairments of longer-term retention (Parkin & Leng, 1993). Indeed, without the evidence from amnesia the STS/LTS distinction would be rather shaky. Functional double dissociation of the serial position curve in unimpaired subjects, so long considered as incontrovertible evidence for the STS/LTS distinction, is now thought to reflect differences in strategic influences on memory. Otherwise, only a few drug studies provide support for the STS/LTS distinction (Parkin, 2000a).

The Nature of LTS: Distinctions between Episodic, Semantic, and Procedural Memory

By the early 1980s the pattern of deficits in amnesic patients was also forming an important foundation for theories concerning the organization of LTS. Anecdotal observations had, across many years, documented residual learning by amnesic patients in a variety of situations. In a detailed summary of these findings (Parkin, 1982) it was noted that amnesic patients retained skills acquired in the premorbid period and, at a more limited level, acquired new skills in the postmorbid period. There was also evidence of perceptual learning, classical and operant conditioning, alteration of verbal preferences, and even concept formation. Despite their wide variation, one factor links all these instances of residual learning: in no case did patients have any significant recollection of the events that gave rise to this learning. Thus descriptions of residual learning were consistently accompanied by comments such as:

> When shown the [closure] pictures again, one hour later, H.M.'s performance improved by 48%, although he did not remember having taken the test before." (Milner, Corkin, & Teuber, 1968, p. 230)

Observations of this kind quickly became an essential component for theories proposing that LTS was best regarded as a tripartite structure comprising *episodic, semantic,* and *procedural memory* (Tulving, 1985). This proposal drew distinctions between memory which is consciously accessible and that which is not (episodic/semantic versus procedural), and between memory which involves recollecting a specific past event and that which does not (episodic versus semantic). The nature of LTS in amnesic patients had a direct bearing on both distinctions.

Little controversy surrounds the view that data from amnesics supports the distinction between episodic/semantic memory on the one hand and procedural memory on the other. As well as the evidence documented in Parkin (1982) there has been a wealth of new evidence supporting preserved procedural memory in amnesic patients (Parkin & Leng, 1993). Nonetheless it should be pointed out that this evidence does not support the existence of a "procedural memory system"; it supports the idea that there are a variety of learning systems within the cognitive system that operate outside the sphere of cognitive awareness/penetrability. Furthermore, it can be speculated that these procedural abilities show the closest affinity with the learning capabilities of other animals.

In contrast, the idea that amnesia supports the distinction between episodic and semantic memory is a matter of some considerable argument. At a clinical level it is quite easy to be convinced that amnesia results in a selective failure of episodic memory. Thus an amnesic patient will typically converse normally and show relatively unimpaired performance on tests of intelligence and language. In contrast, memory for ongoing events, such as a previously presented word list or the lunch time menu, will be severely disrupted. This relative imbalance in performance was held to support the relative sparing of semantic memory (the system underlying language and general knowledge) from episodic memory (the system needed for recollecting specific events; Tulving, 1985).

Unfortunately this seemingly straightforward conclusion is marred by one major problem—the tests used in the original formulations of this argument were not equally sensitive. Put simply, the tasks used to test preserved semantic memory were easier than those used to test episodic memory. A key line of evidence for the claim that amnesic patients have normal semantic memory is their normal performance on intelligence tests like the WAIS-R. However, it has been pointed out that these tests deal primarily with information already acquired by early adult life. This creates a major problem because retrograde amnesia exhibits a temporal gradient—the earlier that information is acquired in life, the less vulnerable it is to the effects of a brain lesion (see later section). As a result, normal performance on WAIS-R is not a sensitive test of spared semantic memory (Squire, 1987).

The point is illustrated by the case of PZ, a university professor who became amnesic shortly after writing his autobiography (Butters, 1984). As one would expect, his ability to recall episodes portrayed in his autobiography showed a marked temporal gradient, with only those from the 1920s intact. However, when his semantic memory for scientific terms was assessed he showed a similar retrograde amnesia and was only able to define those terms acquired earlier in his career. This parallel loss of event memory and general knowledge has also been demonstrated elsewhere. For example, Verfaellie, Reiss, and Roth (1995) have shown that Korsakoff patients are poor at defining words that came into use during the decades for which they have a dense amnesia for events.

Doubts about the episodic/semantic distinction have led the majority of researchers to use the umbrella term *declarative memory*—referring to any memory that is consciously accessible. This solves some of the problems raised above for the episodic/semantic distinction but there is the odd case which it does not easily handle. RFR became densely amnesic as a result of herpes simplex encephalitis (Warrington & McCarthy, 1988). He could retain little information on standard memory tests and could not even identify close friends and family. It was thus surprising to discover that he had nonetheless learned the meaning of new words and abbreviations (e.g., AIDS) that had come into use during the period for which he was now amnesic. In addition he retained a remarkable ability to describe his friends in a general sense, even though he could not remember any event involving a particular person. There are now other instances of remote memory breaking up in selective ways. For example, Kapur, Young, Bateman, and Kennedy (1989) described a dense amnesia for public events with intact personal event memory, and the converse was described by O'Connor, Butters, Miliotis, Eslinger, and Cermak (1992).

The episodic/semantic debate has received new impetus from the study of children who have suffered brain lesions that disrupt memory. Vargha-Khadem et al. (1997) described three patients (aged 14–22 yrs) with brain injuries that occurred at birth, age 4, or age 9. MRI revealed bilateral hippocampal pathology in all three cases. Despite their pronounced amnesia for everyday events, all three patients attended normal schools and attained levels of language competence, literacy, and factual knowledge within the low average to average range. On the basis of these findings it was suggested that the episodic and semantic components of memory are partly dissociable, with only the episodic component being fully reliant on the hippocampus. (See also Mishkin, Vargha-Khadem, & Gadian, 1998.)

Ahern, Wood, and McBrien (1998) described a 9-year-old male whose amnesia resulted from congenital brain damage. Memory, attention, vocabulary, and reading skills were measured prior to, and following, a reading intervention. Despite severe impairment for day-to-day events, reading and vocabulary acquisition were shown to be within normal limits at age 9. Along with observational data, these results are interpreted as evidence of a dissociation between semantic and episodic memory systems. These types of finding, which echo a much earlier study (Wood, Brown, & Felton, 1989), have been highlighted by Tulving and Markowitsch (1998). They propose that episodic memory is distinguishable from other forms of conscious memory because only episodic memory relies exclusively on the hippocampus.

Whereas, with a few exceptions, the data from adult studies argue for a single declarative memory system, the child data appear to support the episodic/semantic distinction. My own view is that the child data must be treated carefully. First, it is notable in the study by Vargha-Khadem et al. (1997) that learning achievement was "low average to average," suggesting that it was not entirely normal. In addition, educational achievement may not be a measure of semantic memory alone—grammar learning is widely conceived to be procedural and the development of reading depends a lot on processes which become automatized. These are forms of learning known not to be impaired in amnesia. Moreover, normal development of arithmetic skills must be considered in light of the fact that arithmetical priming occurs in amnesic patients (Delazer, Ewen, & Benke, 1997). Finally there is the simple problem of degree of learning. By definition an episode happens only once, whereas the types of knowledge tapped by attainment tests are the result of many hours of tuition (and in the case of a child known to have a brain injury, probably an above average number of hours).

The Nature of LTS: The Distinction between Implicit and Explicit Memory

During the 1980s human memory research became dominated by a new Zeitgeist, the distinction between implicit and explicit memory (Schacter, 1992b). Unlike the procedural versus declarative (episodic/semantic) approach in which the emphasis is on defining the nature of different stores, this approach attempts to understand LTS by examining how it responds to different forms of memory test, known as explicit and implicit tests. Implicit memory tests (also known as indirect tests) can be defined as those in which memory for past experience can be demonstrated without requiring conscious access to the past. In contrast explicit memory tests (or direct tests) tests do require conscious recollection of a previous experience. Once again research on human amnesia has figured heavily, and some would say crucially, in the ensuing debate.

Modern experimental evidence for implicit memory has been drawn from a variety of different tasks but here we will concentrate on the fragment completion task (Tulving, Schacter, & Stark, 1982). In this task subjects first study a list of unusual multisyllabic words such as

VENDETTA. After a retention interval, which may be anything from a few minutes to a week, the subjects are presented with what is ostensibly a word puzzle test comprising a series of word fragments from which some letters are missing (e.g., _EN_ _TT_). It is not explained to the subjects that half of the solutions to the fragments are words presented previously, and they are simply asked to complete as many of the fragments as possible. The usual result of this type of experiment is that people produce more completed fragments for words in the previously exposed list than for words not in the list—a phenomenon known as repetition priming.

The interpretation of repetition priming effects has been extremely controversial. Proponents of an implicit memory interpretation have laid great emphasis on the supposed stochastic independence between priming and explicit recollection of solution words. However, others have viewed this statistical argument with more than a little scepticism (Parkin, 1999). Nor has the alternative solution of the test awareness criterion been received with universal enthusiasm. In this procedure priming effects are assessed separately in people who realize, or do not realize, that there is a link between the fragment test and the previous list. Interpretative difficulties arise because the direction of awareness cannot be accurately specified—is the link noted when the subject solves a fragment and recognizes the solution word or does the fragment itself cue explicit recollection of the solution? It is impossible to tell.

The alternative approach is to look for implicit memory effects when we know that explicit memory is impaired or absent. If priming effects are observed under these conditions it cannot be because explicit recollection has helped out. By far the best situation for observing this is to carry out implicit memory experiments on amnesic subjects, where one can assume, a priori, that explicit recollection is essentially inoperative in task performance. Implicit memory has been extensively investigated in amnesic patients and there have been several studies concerned specifically with fragment completion. These have shown intact performance on the fragment completion task despite impairment on parallel explicit tests. Similar results have been obtained with the closely related stem completion task and also the picture completion task. These findings support the argument that implicit test performance can be normal in the absence of explicit memory, and undermine the view that implicit performance may always be contaminated by explicit influences (Jenkins, Russo, & Parkin, 1998; Vaidya, Gabrieli, Verfaellie, Fleischman, & Askari, 1998).

Beyond the basic definition of implicit memory as performance under a set of task demands in which memory is accessed without recollection of specific previous events, there have been recent attempts to specify the *type* of memory underlying priming effects. Schacter (1992a) proposed that certain implicit memory effects are caused by a perceptual representation system which comprises a series of subsystems each dealing with a particular domain of information. Each of these subsystems contains information about the form and structure of a particular stimulus category (e.g., a word or object) but does not store information about meaning; it is therefore termed presemantic.

For reasons that are too detailed to go into here, it can be shown that the mechanisms involved in fragment completion can be considered as presemantic, as in many of the other tasks which demonstrate implicit memory in amnesic subjects. An additional issue is whether implicit memory effects can also be obtained at a semantic level. McAndrews, Glisky, and Schacter (1987) presented amnesic subjects with puzzle sentences such as THE HAYSTACK WAS IMPORTANT BECAUSE THE CLOTH RIPPED and asked them to think of the concept that made sense of the sentence (e.g., "parachute"). This task was then presented again at intervals of up to a week and the solution time was compared with that for similar novel sentences. At all intervals a semantic or conceptual priming effect was obtained, with previously exposed sentences being understood quicker than novel sentences. The study compared severely amnesic subjects with moderately amnesic subjects. Despite far better recognition memory for the sentences in the moderately impaired group, the extent of conceptual priming for the two patient groups was indistinguishable, demonstrating that the priming effect could not be attributed to some of the amnesics having explicit memory available.

Evidence for more remarkable semantically-based implicit memory comes from the study of KC, a man who became densely amnesic following a closed head injury. He was shown pictures accompanied by a vaguely related sentence (e.g., a picture of a man in a hospital with the sentence "MEDICINE cured HICCUP"). Even after an interval of a year, KC could reliably produce the final word of many of these sentences despite having no explicit recollection of having seen them before (Tulving, Hayman, & MacDonald, 1991).

A particular issue of interest has been whether amnesic patients can show priming for novel associations, as again this would indicate that implicit memory was operating at a semantic level. Graf and Schacter (1985) exposed amnesics to pairs of unrelated words (e.g., WINDOW - REASON) and then gave a stem completion test for the second member of each pair. During the stem completion test the second word was either paired with its original partner (e.g., WINDOW - REA___) or a different one (e.g., OFFICER - REA___). In this way priming could be compared as a function of same or different semantic context. The logic of this experiment is that a higher level of priming in the same context versus different context indicates that new semantic associations have been established between the previously unrelated words in the pairs, and are contributing to the priming effect. Graf and Schacter's finding was ambiguous in that only the less memory-impaired patients showed better priming in the same context condition, suggesting the effect may have been explicitly mediated. Shimamura and Squire (1989) followed up the Graf and Schacter study by presenting amnesic subjects with sentences in which two words were highlighted (e.g., A BELL WAS HANGING OVER THE BABY'S CRADLE). The same manipulation of context was then undertaken but no evidence of enhanced priming in the same context was found. Musen and Squire (1993) obtained inconclusive results with regard to novel association priming in amnesia. Using reading speed as a measure, they compared pre-exposed pairs of unrelated words with re-pairings of the same words. Implicit memory would be demonstrated by faster reading of the unchanged word pairs. Two experiments which used a single exposure trial did not show any evidence of novel association learning but, when multiple exposures were used, evidence for novel association learning was obtained.

Failure to demonstrate implicit memory for associations in amnesia is consistent with recent work reported by Cohen, Poldrack, and Eichenbaum (1997). Control and amnesic subjects viewed a series of 40 scenes twice. A third presentation followed in which half the scenes were presented in their "old" form (i.e., unchanged) and half were manipulated (each scene contained a set of objects, such as a chair and an orange, in which the spatial arrangement was arbitrary so allowing changes in position). Memory was measured in two ways: reaction time to questions about the pictures, and amount of time subjects spent viewing the region of the scenes that had been manipulated. The results are shown in Figure 16.3. Both groups of subjects took longest to answer questions about scenes that were only presented at test. Control subjects also took longer to answer questions about manipulated "old" scenes than unchanged scenes but this did not occur for amnesics. This suggests that the amnesics were not sensitive to the change of relational information in the "old" stimuli. This was confirmed by eye movement patterns (again see Figure 16.3) which showed that controls spent more time viewing the critical region of manipulated scenes. These data show that the implicit memory underlying faster processing of old stimuli is based on individual item representation.

Deficits in amnesics' encoding of relational information is also shown by recent data from Reinitz, Verfaellie, and Milberg (1996). Twelve amnesics and age-matched controls were presented with compound words (e.g., cowboy) and performed either a deep or a shallow encoding task. Later they received an incidental old /new recognition test or perceptual identification test that contained old, recombined, partially new, and completely new words. Controls were better than amnesics at discriminating old from recombined stimuli, but there was no differ-

(a) RT

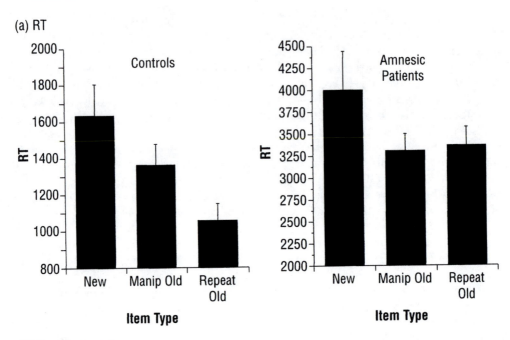

(b) Eye Movements

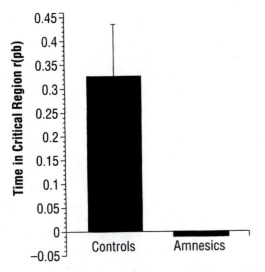

Figure 16.3: (a) Reaction times to answer questions about new scenes, manipulated scenes, and repeated old scenes in the relational manipulation test for controls (left) and amnesic patients (right). Both control subjects and amnesic patients showed a repetition effect (repeated old vs. new scenes), but only the control subjects showed a relational manipulation effect (repeated old vs. manipulated scenes). (b) Point biserial correlations indicating the amount of viewing time during which eye movements were directed to the critical regions of the scenes in which relational manipulations occurred, comparing the manipulated items versus the repeated old items. The positive value on this measure for control subjects indicates that they spent more time in the critical regions for the manipulated items than for the repeated old times; the near-zero value for amnesic patients indicates that they failed to show this relational manipulation effect.

ence between the patients and controls in discriminating old from new stimuli. This indicates that the amnesics experienced specific difficulties learning the inter-relation between the elements of the compound words.

MECHANISMS OF MEMORY

Now we turn to the issue of what has gone wrong in amnesia and what this reveals about the psychological mechanisms of memory.

Within memory research it is still the accepted view that memory involves *encoding, storage,* and *retrieval* stages. Encoding refers to those aspects of the stimulus that are extracted to form the basis of a memory trace for that stimulus. With word stimuli, for example, three encoding dimensions—orthography, phonology, and semantics—are identified. Storage refers to those processes that may lead to the alteration or loss of information while it is held in long-term memory. At a physiological level storage can be linked to the process of *consolidation*—those biological processes that ultimately underlie trace formation. Retrieval refers to those processes that are responsible for bringing information out of storage.

Research into the stages of memory has largely focused on encoding and retrieval rather than storage. The reason for this is principally a pragmatic one. An encoding deficit can be identified if it is shown that a memory disordered patient benefits disproportionately from a manipulation designed to enhance encoding. Similarly retrieval deficits can be inferred if situations are devised which make the same information differentially available. In contrast, storage impairments tend to be identified by default—they are only assumed if neither encoding or retrieval impairments can be demonstrated.

Encoding

The first theoretical account of amnesia in the postcognitive period was put forward by Milner (1966). Based essentially on case HM, it was proposed that amnesia arose from a deficit in consolidation. This theory was motivated solely by observational data—HM had normal STS function but, even with a few seconds distraction, information was lost. It seemed a straightforward and completely intuitive idea that he simply did not form permanent memories. There were complications to this interpretation however. HM was known to be capable of new learning in a number of situations, and this necessitated an explanation which separated motor skill and perceptual skill memory from whatever other form of memory was impaired in HM. The theoretical plot was further complicated by two seminal studies.

Warrington and Weiskrantz (1970) carried out an investigation in which single words were pre-exposed followed, at a later stage, by a fragmented word test. In this test words were presented through a filter which enabled successively larger amounts of information about the target word to be revealed (see Figure 16.4). It was found that amnesic subjects could identify previously exposed words in a more fragmented form than new words.

In retrospect we can see this experiment as a striking demonstration of implicit memory, but this was not the authors' interpretation at the time. They considered their finding to provide evidence against the consolidation theory and argued instead that it showed a retrieval deficit. Essentially they postulated that amnesic patients suffer from massive proactive interference at the time of retrieval—many targets come to mind but none seem correct. Ingeniously they suggested that the word fragments served as surrogate retrieval cues in that only the target word "fitted." Evidence quickly accrued to rule out the retrieval deficit theory however, one argument being that if retrieval was affected one would not see variable retrograde amnesia in the presence of comparable levels of anterograde amnesia. A retrieval deficit should affect anterograde and retrograde memories equally.

In a second seminal experiment, Craik and Lockhart (1972) brought the notion of "encoding

Figure 16.4: Degraded words of the type used by Warrington and Weiskrantz (1970). Adapted from: "Disorders of Memory" in *Clinical Neuropsychology*: *Behavior and Brain Science* by J. Bradshaw and J. B. Mattingly, copyright © 1995 by Academic Press, reproduced by permission of the publisher.

levels" to the fore with a central finding that "shallow" levels of encoding gave rise to poorer memory than "deeper" levels, so launching the levels of processing movement. They demonstrated this with verbal stimuli, showing that orthographic processing produced far inferior memory to semantic processing. The very poor levels of retention associated with shallow processing quickly promoted the view that amnesia could arise from an encoding deficit. A central piece of evidence concerned the performance of amnesics on the "release from proactive interference" paradigm. Here triads of words from the same category are presented with distracting activity interpolated before recall. As learning progresses, the use of successive triads from the same category leads to a diminution of recall and an increase in intrusions from previous triads. At some point a "release" trial occurs in which a triad from a different category is presented. In normal subjects recall is enhanced at this point and this occurs for both semantic (e.g., taxonomic) and nonsemantic (e.g., alpha-numeric) switches. Butters and Cermak (1980) found that amnesics only showed "release" when nonsemantic categories were used and this supported the view that amnesic patients did not differentiate words on the basis of their semantic features and, thus, suffered from an encoding deficit. However, this effect has been questioned by failures to replicate, suggestions that it is really an effect of super-imposed frontal lesions, and the fact that the interpretation of "release" as an encoding phenomenon may itself be suspect (Gardiner, Craik, & Birtwhistle, 1972; Mayes & Downes, 1997). An alternative attempt to demonstrate an encoding deficit in amnesia involved the introduction of a semantic orienting task at acquisition, with the prediction that amnesics would gain a disproportionate benefit from this. Results from this manipulation also produced equivocal results (Mayes & Downes, 1997).

Recent research into frontal lobe memory disorders has again focused attention on encoding, and the role it plays in judgements of veridicality. Interest in this area has been revived by the discovery of frontal patients whose memory disorder is characterized by a tendency to make high levels of false alarms in the presence of a normal hit rate. Delbecq-Derousne, Beauvois, and Shallice (1990) reported RW who made large numbers of false alarms on forced-choice recognition. This was mirrored by an abnormally high intrusion rate on recall. (For discussion see Dodson & Schacter, this volume.)

Another frontal patient who produces large numbers of false alarms on most tests of recognition memory is JB (Parkin, 1997b; Parkin, Ward, Bindschaedler, Squires, & Powell, 1999). His hit rate is within the normal range (around 80%) but his false alarm rate is extremely high (around 40%). In one experiment he was asked to judge whether he was "sure" or "not sure" about whether he had correctly recognized a stimulus. For both hits and false alarms he gave predominantly "sure" responses. Like RW he produces large numbers of recall intrusions in amongst correct information (see also Schacter, Curran, Galluccio, Milberg, & Bates, 1996).

Retrieval based and encoding based explanations for JB's deficit have recently been explored (Parkin et al., 1999). Attempts to enhance retrieval by the use of monetary incentive, accuracy instructions, or response restrictions (only allowing JB to make a total response equal to the original number of targets) were found to have no effect. In contrast, the imposition of semantic encoding tasks, including imagery during acquisition, greatly reduced false alarms without affecting hit rates. Other evidence favouring an encoding deficit was that JB exhibited no deficit on yes–no recognition tests tapping premorbid general knowledge and, on a test of autobiographical cueing, the quality of his premorbid memories was normal. A recent study of another frontal patient, MR, has shown similar findings with, if anything, the patient showing greater responsiveness to the encoding manipulation than JB (Ward & Parkin, in press).

Another recent study involving JB explored the nature of his memory traces when he is exhibiting high levels of false alarms. JB has a normal hit rate so he must be storing away sufficient information for target identification; the question is what is this information? A clue is provided by the only experiment in which JB has shown a normal pattern of recognition. This involved a recognition test for abstract designs in which one set of distracters were devised from a completely different set of features (nonoverlapping) and another where, for each target, there was a distracter that differed by only one feature (overlapping) (See Figure 16.5).

JB's performance was massively impaired on the overlapping condition but he made no false alarms on the nonoverlapping condition. This result suggested that JB's memory deficit might arise because he learned items at a "subtarget" level, meaning as collections of features rather than an integrated whole. To test this idea further we constructed an experiment in which the nonoverlapping condition involved a target list constructed using one half of the alphabet, and a recognition test constructed from the other half. Thus, although all items were words, they differed entirely in their letter constituents. This condition was contrasted with an overlapping condition in which targets and distracters were constructed from the whole alphabet. The results showed that both controls and JB performed better on the nonoverlapping condition, even though neither JB nor the controls had conscious knowledge of the manipulation used (indicating that the manipulation is tapping into data-driven aspects of recognition). This effect and its unconscious characteristics have recently been replicated and it has also been shown that older subjects are more susceptible to the effects of overlap, suggesting greater data driven recognition with age (Parkin, Ward, Squires, & Townshend; accepted subject to revision).

Our interpretation of JB's deficit, therefore, is that his high false alarm rates reflect an

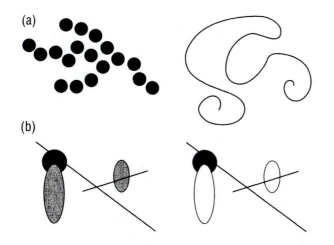

(a)

(b)

Figure 16.5: Stimuli from (a) non-overlapping and (b) overlapping figures test.

impaired encoding process that operates at the level of features and does not effectively encode the whole stimulus. For words, this "sublexical" representation means that on a standard overlapping test distracters resemble targets because they share common letter elements. Discrimination is eased for JB when there is no overlap. This also explains the interesting finding that JB is prepared to make high levels of recognition responses when there are in fact no words from the target list in the supposed test. Since the lists nonetheless overlap at the sub-lexical level, this effect is entirely predictable (Parkin et al., 1999)

Storage, Consolidation, and Temporal Gradients

Since the early writings of Ribot (1882) it has been known that the extent of retrograde amnesia shows a lawful pattern: the vulnerability of a given memory is inversely related to its time of initial formation—the so-called *Ribot's Law* or *temporal gradient* (see Figure 16.6). Psychologists are not that accustomed to "laws" and when one is found it usually generates a lot of theoretical and empirical interest. This is not the case with Ribot's law, however, and its explanation still largely remains a mystery.

One idea, the continuity hypothesis, came from the frequent association of temporal gradients with Korsakoff's Syndrome. Because of this syndrome's frequent alcoholic aetiology, it was proposed that the gradient actually arose from increasingly poor encoding stemming from the cumulative effects of constant intoxication. However, this theory can be discounted on the grounds that temporally graded retrograde amnesia can be found in amnesic patients without a history of alcoholism, including rare examples of Korsakoff's Syndrome of non-alcoholic aetiology (Parkin, Blunden, Rees, & Hunkin, 1991).

An alternative approach is that temporal gradients stem from *redundancy* inherent in the long-term storage of information. Briefly, it can be argued that every time a memory is retrieved, the record of that retrieval constitutes another memory. As each retrieval will be carried out in a different context, the information associated with a given memory will become richer. If one assumes that, on average, older memories will have been retrieved more, then they will be associated with a higher degree of redundancy (over-representation) and will be able to withstand partial degradation of storage sites (Parkin, Montaldi, Leng, & Hunkin, 1990).

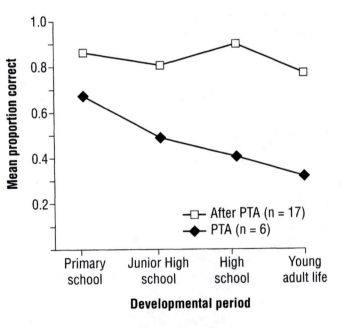

Figure 16.6: Mean proportion of correct recall of autobiographical events plotted across developmental periods for head-injured patients in PTA (n = 6) and after PTA (n = 17). From: Levin, H. S., et al. *Journal of Neurology, Neurosurgery, and Psychiatry*, 48, p. 561, with permission from the BMJ Publishing Group.

A different theory, which one could term the *long-term consolidation hypothesis*, suggests that temporal gradients arise because the process of consolidation is extremely prolonged. In a study referred to earlier, Rempel-Clower et al. (1996) described three patients with lesions restricted to the hippocampal formation. One had a lesion only within CA1 field whereas the other two had CA1 damage plus more extensive lesions into the dentate gyrus and entorhinal cortex. Only the latter two showed extensive retrograde amnesia (in one case 25 years). On the grounds that it was implausible to suggest that the hippocampal formation was a storage site, these authors argued that the hippocampal formation may serve to modulate an extremely long-term consolidation process disruption of which can cause a long-term temporally-graded retrograde amnesia. Although this seems implausible from an adaptive point of view, the theory does help to account for certain puzzling case histories (e.g., Kapur et al., 1997; O'Connor, Sieggreen, Ahern, Schomer, & Mesulam, 1997). In both these instances epilepsy was associated with normal initial retention but with subsequent forgetting over longer time periods—something that might be expected if a long-term consolidation process was interupted.

Retrieval

Kapur (1992) has identified what he has termed *focal retrograde amnesia* (FRA). This refers to a memory impairment in which the primary deficit is a loss of remote memory, with performance on anterograde tests only mildly impaired. These patients are interesting because the selective impairment of retrieval may shed light on the way the process operates normally. A problem with this type of disorder, however, is that some of the patients may be suffering from psychogenic disorders resulting from psychological trauma, or they may be malingering—in some way faking or dissimulating memory impairment. However, once these possibilities have been discounted, there remains a range of cases where focal retrograde amnesia occurs in the context of known brain injury (Kapur, 1992; Kapur, Ellison, Parkin, Hunkin, & Burrows, 1994).

There are essentially two types of patient showing this unusual deficit: those with identifiable brain lesions and those who appear to have developed the disorder from extremely minor injuries (Parkin, 1996a). Examining the former group, two important points emerge: they almost all have lesions to the temporal lobes but with sparing of the hippocampus (see Figure 16.7); and performance on tests of anterograde memory is not normal although it is far better than that found in amnesics.

With these two points in mind it is relatively easy to explain what is going on. As we have seen, the hippocampus is crucial for memory function and the general view is that it in some way moderates the process of consolidation in some way. However, because the hippocampus is small it cannot be the actual storage site of memory. For storage to occur the hippocampus must in some way recruit sites in the temporal cortex. It would appear that FRA patients have an intact consolidation mechanism but lack the normal availability of storage sites because of temporal lobe damage. As a result of damage to the storage areas, remote memory is disrupted and patients do not learn new information normally. It should also be borne in mind that the assessment of anterograde amnesia made in these cases usually involves relatively short retention intervals which maximizes the possibility that patients will perform normally.[2]

A rather different case of FRA is DH (Hunkin, 1997; Hunkin, Parkin, Bradley, Jansari, &

---

[2] Cases where FRA has been reported following minor brain injury (often not even involving unconsciousness) are more problematic. For example De Renzi, Luchelli, Muggia, and Spinnler (1995) report a man who presented with a dense retrograde memory loss following a road accident, even though there was no evidence of head trauma. In addition he reported loss of procedural memory such as how to shave. This case is rather similar to others that have been reported (see Parkin, 1996a) and there is some disagreement as to how these cases should be interpreted. Some, such as Luchelli, Muggia, and Spinnler (1995), have suggested that these impairments have an organic basis (see Kapur, 1996, for a critique of this study). However, it also the case that these disorders might be of psychogenic origin. Loss of procedural memory, for example, is frequently considered as a sign of psychogenic or malingered amnesia. In connection with this it is notable that most of these cases recover their lost memories.

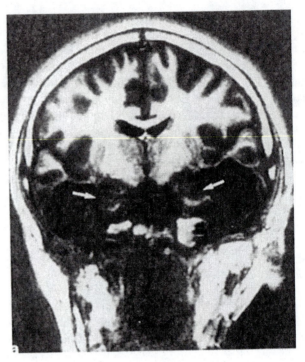

Figure 16.7: Cross-section of patient TJ's brain. Arrows indicate intact hippocampal regions. Large dark areas adjacent to arrows correspond to temporal lobe lesions. Reprinted from *Neuropsychologia*, 32, Kapur, N., Ellison, D., Parkin, A. J., Hunkin, N. M., et al. (1994), Bilateral temporal lobe pathology with sparing of medial lobe temporal lobe structures: lesion profile and pattern of a memory disorder, with permission of Elsevier Science.

Aldrich, 1995), who suffered a closed head injury at the age of 21. Assessment of anterograde memory function indicated near-normal performance. However, autobiographical memory was severely impaired in that he could not recollect a single personal event from the premorbid period. Interestingly he had good memory for public events occurring in the premorbid period. DH's focal retrograde amnesia also had a surprising neuropathology, with two lesions in the occipital lobes plus a small lesion in the right parietal lobe. Notably there were no lesions in the temporal cortex or hippocampal formation. Recent functional neuroimaging has consistently identified a parietal lobe structure known as the *precuneus* as being active in retrieval situations (Fletcher, Frith, Grasby, & Shallice, 1995). Although detailed comparison is not possible, the location of DH's lesion appears to be in the region of the precuneus.

If DH's memory impairment stems from a lesion to the right precuneus, what are the implications of this for a psychological explanation of his deficit? Damasio and Damasio (1993) have suggested that memory retrieval involves a reconstructive process in which various features of entity (e.g., colors, shapes, emotions) are retrieved from different locations in the cortex and combined to give a unified representation. Areas of the brain responsible for this combinatorial function are known as *convergence zones* (CZ's) and these will vary in their scope depending on the type of information being represented. Thus, for an object, a CZ might only be visual. At the highest level of this hierarchy are CZ's which deal with events. Here an event will be characterised as the time-locked co-occurrence of various entities which together constitute a particular event. It is conceivable the precuneus may be involved in this hypothetical combinatorial process regarding events. Accordingly premorbid event retrieval cannot occur because the various entities that need to be retrieved concurrently to reproduce the event are no longer bound together by a CZ. For a related idea concerning the retrosplenial cortex see Gainotti, Almonti, Di Betta, and Silveri (1998).

More recently Incisa Della Rocchetta and Milner (1993) have demonstrated that frontal lesions too can cause problems in retrieval. A well known phenomenon in normal memory is the part list cueing effect. If subjects are asked to learn a word list and, at test, presented with part of the list as a cue, their recall of the other items will be poorer than if no cues are given at all. This deficit presumably arises because the cue words come to dominate the retrieval process at the expense of the uncued items. The authors found that, compared with controls and other brain damaged subjects, patients with left frontal lesions showed a much greater part-list cueing effect. This suggested that the left frontal lobe was specifically involved in strategic aspects of retrieval.

The exaggerated part list cueing effect shown by patients with left frontal lesions is also relevant to a much more recent debate relating to the Hemispheric Encoding Retrieval Asymmetry (HERA) theory. On the basis of functional neuroimaging of normal adults, this theory proposed that the left frontal cortex was dominant for all encoding operations and the right frontal cortex was involved with retrieval (Tulving, Kapur, Craik, Moscovitch, & Houle, 1994). Subsequent neuroimaging has cast serious doubt on the HERA hypothesis and suggested instead that the nature of materials, rather than the type of memory operation, may determine frontal hemispheric asymmetry (Kelley et. al., 1998; Nolde, Johnson, & D'Esposito, 1998; Nolde, Johnson, & Raye, in press).

Finally, it is worth mentioning that at least some of the memory difficulties associated with what is considered to be a psychogenic disorder—dissociative states—may be related to retrieval difficulties. Dissociative states are commonly reported after witnessing or committing violent crimes, or experiencing other negative life events such as bereavement. Parkin and Stampfer (1995) described the case of "Elizabeth," who had a long history of adverse life events including alcoholic parents, a violent husband, and the death of her baby. She presented with "atypical psychosis" which was characterized by a "memory block" in that she could not recall any of these adverse events. Neuropsychological testing at the time of this impairment produced a marked "frontal profile" (e.g., inability to perform the Wisconsin Card Sort; highly abnormal copying of the Rey Figure). However, over the weeks of the investigation the memory block "lifted" and, in parallel, the frontal signs disappeared. These concomitant changes suggest that the memory block was associated with frontal lobe dysfunction in this case.

The Role of Context in Memory

Context can be defined as information associated with a specific memory that allows differentiation of that memory from other memories. In modern research it is usual to distinguish between two forms of context—intrinsic and extrinsic. *Intrinsic context* refers to features that are an integral part of the stimulus itself. In a face, for example, intrinsic contextual features would be eye color, hair length, size of nose and so on. In the case of words, intrinsic context would relate to the particular meaning extracted from the word at the time of learning. *Extrinsic context* corresponds to those features that are merely incidentally associated with the stimulus itself. These extrinsic features include time of encounter and surroundings (often referred to as temporo-spatial attributes). Studies of amnesia have concentrated on memory for extrinsic context.

The most widely supported account of amnesia is the context deficit theory (CDT) which was first suggested 20 years ago. (The fact that it survives today is witness both to the lack of theoretical development in the field and the growing preoccupation with functional neuroimaging as a means of addressing the cognitive neuroscience of memory.) Before we can examine the theory, however, a more detailed consideration of the term "recognition" is required. Mandler (1980) emphasized that recognition memory comprises two separable components, *familiarity* and *recollection*. Familiarity is the awareness that a stimulus has been encountered before, without requiring recall of when or where. Recollection refers to the additional ability to retrieve the specific context within which a familiar stimulus has been encountered.

CDT has its origins in two studies reported in the late 1970s. Winocur and Kinsbourne (1978) looked at the performance of Korsakoff amnesics on the A → B; A → C learning paradigm. (This is a procedure where subjects learn two sets of word pairs, but the sets share the same initial word for each pair, so learning of the first set impedes learning of the second.) They found that the degree of cross-list interference shown by Korsakoff amnesics was disproportionately reduced if learning of the two lists occurred in physically distinct environments. More widely cited, however, is the study of Huppert and Piercy (1978) who investigated the performance of Korsakoff amnesics and normal people on a task involving temporal discrimination. Subjects saw 80 pictures on one day followed by a different set of 80 pictures on the following day. Within each set half the pictures were shown once and the remainder were shown three times. Ten minutes after the presentation on day 2 ended subjects were shown a sample of pictures from days 1 and 2. Subjects were asked to decide whether or not each picture had been seen "today" (i.e., on day 2 as opposed to day 1). As one would expect, both groups placed pictures seen three times on day 2 in the "today" category most often, and pictures shown once on day 1 least often. However, the groups differed in that amnesics were just as likely to categorize as "today" pictures seen three times on day 1 as those seen once on day 2. In contrast, control subjects placed very few of the repeated day 1 pictures in the "today" category and correctly categorized over two thirds of the pictures seen only once on day 2. The performance of amnesics indicates that their decisions about context were based on the overall familiarity of each picture. Thus, pictures presented three times on day 1 seemed as recent to amnesics as those presented once on day 2, both being associated with similar amounts of familiarity. In contrast, the performance of normal subjects seems determined both by familiarity and recollection. The more accurate identification of pictures presented three times on day 2 compared with those presented once suggests that familiarity does play a role in normal subjects' judgements. However, the fact that normal subjects could accurately distinguish pictures presented three times on day 1 from those presented once on day 2 indicates that they were not just responding on the basis of familiarity. Their responses involved an additional search stage in which each picture was linked to its specific temporal context (i.e., "day 1" or "day 2"). The fact that the amnesics could not do this implies they have no record of temporal context.

Recently Jacoby and colleagues (Jacoby, 1991; Jacoby, Toth, & Yonelinas, 1993) have proposed the *process dissociation framework* as an experimental method of measuring the extent to which a subject's recognition response is determined by familiarity or contextual retrieval. In a typical experiment using the process dissociation framework, subjects are presented with two successive lists of words, one spoken and the other written. Two types of recognition test follow. In the exclusion condition, subjects are required to demonstrate contextual recollection by identifying only words from list 2. In the inclusion condition, no contextual demands are imposed and subjects are just told to indicate which words were presented earlier. The assumption of this methodology is that recognition of a list 1 word in the exclusion condition indicates that the subject has forgotten the context of that word's presentation and that the recognition response is based on familiarity. The extent to which familiarity based responding is occurring is based on comparing incorrect recognition of list 1 words in the exclusion condition with the recognition rate for those words in the inclusion condition.

Using the process dissociation framework, Verfaellie and Treadwell (1993) demonstrated that amnesic recognition memory was largely based on estimates of familiarity, suggesting that the amnesic deficit lies primarily in failure to remember context. However, a critique of this study has argued that the Jacoby procedure is difficult to interpret with amnesics because their recognition memory is so defective (Roediger & McDermott, 1994). A subsequent reply (Verfaellie, 1994) addresses these concerns and upholds the original conclusion. However, more recent studies have produced further objections to the logic of the process dissociation procedure (e.g., Russo, Cullis, & Parkin, 1998).

In conclusion, there is good evidence to suppose that the amnesic syndrome can be associated with a failure to make use of context in memory but the issue of whether this is an encoding or storage failure remains to be determined.

It is worth noting here that the role of context in memory may contribute to understanding *post-traumatic stress disorder* (PTSD). The effects of PTSD on memory are somewhat complex. Typically the sufferer is amnesic for the traumatic experiences but, from time to time, flashbacks occur in which the traumatic experience is vividly recreated in the individual's mind. There is now abundant evidence that PTSD victims also have impaired ability to remember new information. Importantly, flashbacks are known to be sensitive to *state dependency* in that they are more likely to occur if the individual's mood state matches that experienced at the time of the traumatic experience. Also, consistent with the state dependency view of PTSD, victims of PTSD show greater recall of trauma related words but poorer recall of neutral and positive affect words (Bremner & Marmar, 1998).

The role played by context in memory and amnesia has also been noted in one of the few well documented case studies of fugue. Fugue is a rare dissociative disorder in which patients lose their identity and may assume a new one. In this case a young man was deeply disturbed by the death of his grandfather and remained in a fugue state for some time, exhibiting only fragments of memory about his own past (Schacter, Wang, Tulving, & Freedman, 1982). However, while watching the funeral scene in the film *Shogun* his memory of himself came back, demonstrating the important role that state dependency may play in the mediation of psychogenic memory dysfunction.

Executive Aspects of Memory

The predominant view of memory impairments which originate from frontal damage is that they reflect an *executive disorder*. This view arises from early ideas about frontal function such as those proposed by Luria (1966) and, more recently, the framework put forward by Norman and Shallice (1986). Norman and Shallice proposed that an individual's responses can be controlled in two fundamentally different ways. The majority of responses are under fairly automatic control and are triggered by environmental cues which engage specific schema, each of which has many subcomponents. To deal with clashes between routine activities the authors proposed a *contention scheduling* process in which the relative importance of different actions is assessed and routine behavior adjusted accordingly. As we all know, however, our behavior is not simply a set of routine automatic operations and there are many occasions when we deliberately and consciously imposed a specific strategy to achieve our goal. To explain these "willed" actions the authors propose an additional *Supervisory Activating System* (SAS) which is activated whenever the routine selection of operations is inappropriate (for a review see Humphreys & Riddoch, this volume).

The "executive theory" of frontal memory impairments views retrieval as a problem-solving act (in the words of Neisser [1967, p. 285], " . . . out of a few stored bone chips, we remember a dinosaur"). The success of retrieval depends on the use of appropriate strategies. This idea has been formalized by suggesting that retrieval has two components—a description stage and a verification stage (Norman & Bobrow, 1979)—an idea which has much in common with the older idea of generation-recognition. According to the theory, "description" involves forming a hypothesis about the contents of memory and "verification" involves establishing "the truth" of memory. (It is notable that this theory gets no further in establishing the information source used to establish truth.)

Evidence to support this distinction comes from ROB, a woman who sustained damage to the caudate nucleus, a basal ganglia structure interrelated with the frontal lobes (Hanley, Davies, Downes, & Mayes, 1994; see also Hanley & Davies, 1997). On a recall and recognition test matched for difficulty (Calev, 1984), she showed very poor performance on recall but normal performance on recognition. Hanley, et al. suggest that this deficit would arise if there had been disruption to the system specifying descriptions. Thus ROB's recall is impaired because targets cannot be specified accurately but recognition is normal because a recognition test bypasses the need for specifying any description. Hanley et al. go on to suggest that high false alarm/intrusion rates arise from defective verification–a deficit that, more generally, could be used to account for exaggerated part list cueing effects and confabulation.

It is interesting to note that frontal lobe theories of memory have placed a heavy emphasis on retrieval. Milner (1964) proposed the deficits observed were essentially retrieval based, and more recently Schacter et al. (1996) proposed a "focused retrieval deficit" to explain high false alarm rates in their patient BG. Their view was that BG's retrieval description amounted to little more than "a bunch of words" (p. 806), with the result that recognition only operated effectively when there was a strong taxonomic distinction between targets and distracters. One could equally argue, however, that BG's deficit is one of encoding–perhaps he has efficient retrieval processes but lays down very superficial traces.

In the case of JB referred to earlier (Parkin et al., 1999), we have argued that the explanation of his high false alarm rate rests squarely in the domain of encoding efficiency. This is still consistent with an executive explanation because, presumably, the choice of an appropriate strategy depends on intact decision making. In JB's case it is plausible to argue that this deficit in encoding stems from inappropriate allocation of attention. Informal observations of JB indicate that his recollection of events is certainly unusual (Parkin, 1997b). At a more fundamental level it has been shown that JB lacks fundamental inhibitory processes–he does not, for example, exhibit negative priming (Metzler & Parkin, 2000).

There is, however, evidence that deficits in frontally-mediated retrieval strategies do underlie pathological false recognition. Recently it was shown that high false alarm rates by frontal patients in a test involving the identification of famous people could be markedly reduced if a stringent response criterion was introduced–only say "yes" if you can recollect the occupation of the person (Rapcsak, Reminger, Glisky, Kaszniak, & Comer, 1999). Another study showed that MR, a patient with a left frontal demyelinating lesion, produced high levels of false alarms in a task involving recognizing famous faces and names amongst nonfamous distractors (Ward et al., 1999). In a number of instances these false alarms were associated with the false recollection of additional biographical knowledge as well. An interesting feature of these findings was that MR exhibited high false-alarm rates only for people. For instance, in one experiment he was asked to recognize famous names from fiction (e.g., Oliver Twist) from amongst distractors (e.g., Agnes Blyth). Subsequently, using the same list of names, he was asked to recognize which were book titles. When recognizing the names of people he produced false alarms but when recognizing the names of books he did not, even though the stimuli were identical. MR's deficit was attributed to a lax retrieval criterion which allowed the triggering of partial biographical knowledge by unfamiliar faces. (This can be likened to the first-day-on-holiday effect, where one mistakenly thinks that a number of the fellow guests are colleagues from work. This presumably arises because recognition thresholds for frequently encountered people are lower.) In addition Ward argues that MR's propensity to produce false alarms in a person-identification task is also detrimentally influenced by distorted meta-memorial knowledge concerning the potential rate of encountering famous people.

THE FUTURE OF AMNESIA RESEARCH

What should be clear from this chapter is that the study of human amnesia has branched off from the original question: Why do amnesics forget? We have seen the development of many different but interconnected research themes. Most of these themes still have some degree of currency–even the issue of STS/LTS and amnesia has been revived recently (Carlesimo, Marfia, Loasses, & Caltagirone, 1996).

An important development in the future is likely to be the increasing interest in neuropsychiatric disorders of memory from a clinico-legal, as well as a cognitive, point of view. Accounts of "recovered memories" of sexual abuse have provoked wide interest and legal proceedings.

Cognitive neuropsychology has entered the fray with various lines of research connected with false memory and the veridicality aspect of memory function (Schacter, 1999). However, the broader relevance of this research depends on developing paradigms which more closely reflect the circumstances in which false recollections infiltrate real life.

The enterprise of explaining amnesia itself has been rather in the doldrums since the late 1980s. Partly this stems from the gradual tide of support for single case methodology which brings with it the ever increasing fractionation of issues. Theories of amnesia emerged mainly from group studies, particularly of Korsakoff patients, and the single case design seems to have done little for general theories. Thus we have increasingly seen the study of amnesia as a kaleidoscope of disorders with no obvious link to one another (Parkin, 1997a). In addition, with interest in the implicit/explicit distinction on the wane, another major motivation for amnesia studies is decreasing.

Another factor working against amnesia as a front line topic of theoretical research is that so much research effort is being invested in functional neuroimaging. It is curious to think that, at the birth of cognitive neuropsychology, neuroanatomical correlates of cognitive dysfunction were regarded as largely irrelevant—model building was seen as the essential occupation. Such high-minded concerns now seem to have deserted us and functional neuroimaging has offered us a neo-localizationist framework which has been embraced in a largely uncritical fashion. Yet one step back shows us that this large (and extremely expensive) science has done very little to enhance theorizing. It has been concerned principally with identifying neuroanatomical correlates of basic memory functions (many of which we already knew about). Amnesia research has always depended on a healthy theoretical sector and functional neuroimaging has not driven theory to any significant extent. When the Memory Disorders Research Society was formed in the late 1980s, Laird Cermak proposed, in only semi-joking fashion, that there should be a moratorium on MRI scanning. I would only partly agree with him, because good scanning has enabled better differentiation of patients, but I agree with the underlying tone. A little less emphasis on neuroanatomical correlation and more thought about theory would be no bad thing, both for amnesia research and cognitive neuropsychology more generally. The tangibility of neuroimaging data should not lead us to overestimate its explanatory value.

Acknowledgement

Preparation of this chapter was supported by grant RG 126/97 from the Human Frontiers Research Program.

REFERENCES

Ahern, C. A., Wood, F. B., & McBrien, C. M. (1998). Preserved vocabulary and reading acquisition in an amnesic child. In K. H. Pribram (Ed.), *Brain and values: Is a biological science of values possible?* (pp. 277–297). Mahwah, NJ: Lawrence Erlbaum.

Atkinson, R. C., & Shiffrin, R. M. (1968). Human memory: A proposed system and its control processes. In K. W. Spence & J. T. Spence (Eds.), *Psychology of learning and motivation,* (Vol. 2). New York: Academic Press.

Bremner, J. D., & Marmar, C. R. (1998). *Trauma, memory, and dissociation. Progress in psychiatry, No. 54.* Washington, DC: American Psychiatric Association.

Butters, N. (1984). Alcoholic Korsakoff's Syndrome: An Update. *Seminars in Neurology, 4,* 226–244.

Butters, N., & Cermak, L. S. (1980). *Alcoholic Korsakoff's syndrome. An information processing approach to amnesia.* New York: Academic Press.

Calev, A. (1984). Recall and recognition in mildly dis-turbed schizophrenics: The use of matched tasks. *Journal of Abnormal Psychology, 93,* 172–177.

Carlesimo, G. A., Marfia, G. A., Loasses, A., & Caltagirone, C. (1996). Recency effect in anterograde amnesia: Evidence for distinct memory stores underlying enhanced retrieval of terminal items in immediate and delayed recall paradigms. *Neuropsychologia, 34,* 177–184.

Cohen, N. J., Poldrack, R. A., & Eichenbaum, H. (1997). Memory for items and memory for relations in the procedural/declarative memory framework. *Memory, 5,* 131–177.

Corkin, S., Amaral, D. G., Gonzalez, R. G., Johnson, K. A., & Hyman, B. T. (1997). H. M.'s medial temporal lobe lesion: Findings from magnetic resonance imaging. *Journal of Neuroscience, 17,* 3964–3979.

Craik, F. I. M., & Lockhart, R. S. (1972). Levels of processing: A framework for memory research. *Journal of Verbal Learning and Verbal Behavior, 11,* 671–684.

Damasio, A. R., & Damasio, H. (1993). Cortical systems for retrieval of concrete knowledge: The convergence zone framework. In C. Koch & J. L. Davis (Eds.), *Large scale neural theories of the brain.* Cambridge, MA: MIT Press.

De Renzi, E., Luchelli, F., Muggia, S., & Spinnler, H. (1995). Persistent retrograde amnesia following a minor trauma. *Cortex, 31,* 531–542.

Delazer, M., Ewen, P., & Benke, T. (1997). Priming arithmetic facts in amnesic patients. *Neuropsychologia, 35*(5), 623–634.

Delbecq-Derousne, J., Beauvois, M. F., & Shallice, T. (1990). Preserved recall versus impaired recognition. *Brain, 113,* 1045–1074.

Dusoir, H., Kapur, N., Byrnes, D. P., McKinstry, S., & Hoare, R. D. (1990). The role of diencephalic pathology in human memory disorder: Evidence from a penetrating paranasal brain injury. *Brain, 113,* 1695–1706.

Eich, E., Macaulay, D., Loewenstein, R. J., & Dihle, P. H. (1997). Memory, amnesia, and dissociative identity disorder. *Psychological Science, 8,* 417–422.

Fletcher, P. C., Frith, C. D., Grasby, P. M., & Shallice, T. (1995). Brain systems for the encoding and retrieval of auditory-verbal memory: An in vivo study in humans. *Brain, 118,* 401–416.

Gainotti, G., Almonti, S., Di Betta, A. M., & Silveri, M. C. (1998). Retrograde amnesia in a patient with retrosplenial tumour. *Neurocase: Case Studies in Neuropsychology, Neuropsychiatry, and Behavioural Neurology, 4,* 519–526.

Gardiner, J. M., Craik, F. I. M., & Birtwhistle. J. (1972) Retrieval cues and release from proactive inhibition. *Journal of Verbal Learning and Verbal Behavior, 11,* 71–78.

Graf, P., & Schacter, D. L. (1985). Implicit and explicit memory for novel associations in normal and amnesic subjects. *Journal of Experimental Psychology: Learning, Memory and Cognition, 11,* 501–518.

Hanley, J. R., & Davies, A. D. M. (1997). Impaired recall and preserved recognition. In A. J. Parkin (Ed.), *Case studies in the neuropsychology of memory.* Hove, UK: Psychology Press.

Hanley, J. R., Davies, A. D. M., Downes, J. J., & Mayes, A. R. (1994). Impaired recall of verbal material following rupture and repair of an anterior communicating artery aneurysm. *Cognitive Neuropsychology, 11,* 543–578.

Hodges, J. R. (1998). Unravelling the enigma of transient global amnesia. *Annals of Neurology, 42,* 151–153.

Hunkin, N. M. (1997). Focal retrograde amnesia: Implications for the organisation of memory. In A.J. Parkin (Ed.), *Case Ssudies in the neuropsychology of memory.* Hove, UK: Psychology Press.

Hunkin, N. M., Parkin, A. J., Bradley, V. A., Jansari, A., & Aldrich, F. K. (1995). Focal retrograde amnesia following closed head injury: A case study and theoretical account. *Neuropsychologia, 33,* 509–523.

Huppert, F. A., & Piercy, M. (1978). The role of trace strength in recency and frequency judgements by amnesic and control subjects. *Quarterly Journal of Experimental Psychology, 30,* 346–354.

Incisa Della Rocchetta, A., & Milner, B. (1993). Strategic search and retrieval inhibition: The role of the frontal lobes. *Neuropsychologia, 31,* 503–541.

Jacoby, L. L. (1991). A process dissociation framework: Separating automatic from intentional uses of memory. *Journal of Memory and Language, 30,* 513–541.

Jacoby, L. L., Toth, J. P., & Yonelinas, A. P. (1993). Separating conscious and unconscious influences of memory: Measuring recollection. *Journal of Experimental Psychology: General, 122,* 139–154.

James, W. (1890). *Principles of psychology.* New York: Henry Holt.

Jenkins, V., Russo, R., & Parkin, A. J. (1998). Levels of processing and single word priming in amnesic and control subjects. *Cortex, 34,* 577–588.

Kapur, N. (1992). Focal retrograde amnesia in neurological disease: A critical review. *Cortex, 29,* 217–234.

Kapur, N. (1996). Paradoxical functional facilitation in brain-behaviour research: A critical review. *Brain, 119,* 1175–1790.

Kapur, N., Ellison, D., Parkin, A. J., Hunkin, N. M., & Burrows, E, (1994). Bilateral temporal lobe pathology with sparing of medial temporal lobe structures: Lesion profile and pattern of memory disorder. *Neuropsychologia, 32,* 23–38.

Kapur, N., Millar, J., Abbott, P., & Carter, M. (1998). Recovery of function processes in human amnesia: Evidence from transient global amnesia. *Neuropsychologia, 36,* 99–107.

Kapur, N., Millar, J., Colbourn, C., Abbott, P., Kennedy, P., & Docherty, T. (1997). Very long-term amnesia in association with temporal lobe epilepsy: Evidence for multiple-stage consolidation processes. *Brain and Cognition, 35,* 58–70.

Kapur, N., Young, A. W., Bateman, D., & Kennedy, P. (1989). Long-term clinical and neuropsychological follow-up of focal retrograde amnesia. *Cortex, 25,* 387–402.

Kelley, W. M., Miezin, F. M., McDermott, K. B., Buckner, R. L., Raichle, M. E., Cohen, N. J., Ollinger, J. M., Akbudak, E., Conturo, T. E., Snyder, A. Z., & Petersen, S. E. (1998). Hemispheric Specialisation in Human Dorsal Frontal Cortex and Medial Temporal Lobe for Verbal and Nonverbal Memory Encoding. *Neuron, 20,* 927–936.

Levin, H. S., High, W. M., Jr., Myers, C. A., Von Laufen, A., Hyde, M. E., & Eisenberg, H. M. (1985). Impairment of remote memory after closed head injury. *Journal of Neurology, Neurosurgery, and Psychiatry, 48,* 556–563.

Lucchelli, F., Muggia, S., & Spinnler, H. (1995). The "Petites Madeleines" phenomenon in two amnesic patients: Sudden recovery of forgotten memories. *Brain, 118,* 167–183.

Luria, A. R. (1966). *The higher cortical functions in man.* New York: Basic Books.

Mandler, G. (1980). Recognising: The judgement of a previous occurrence. *Psychological Review, 27,* 252–271.

Mayes, A. R., & Downes, J. J. (1997). What do theories of the functional deficit(s) underlying amnesia have to explain? *Memory, 5,* 3–36.

McAndrews, M. P., Glisky, E. L., & Schacter, D. L. (1987). When priming persists: Long-lasting implicit memory for a single episode in amnesic patients. *Neuropsychologia, 25,* 497–506.

Metzler, C., & Parkin, A. J. (2000). Reversed neagtive priming following frontal lobe lesions. *Neuropsychologia, 38,* 363–379.

Meudell, P. R., Mayes, A. R., Ostergaard, A., & Pickering, A. (1985). Recency and frequency judgements in alcoholic amnesias and normal people with poor memory. *Cortex, 21,* 487–511.

Milner, B. (1964). Some effects of frontal lobectomy in man. In J. Warren & K. Akert (Eds.), *The frontal granular cortex and behavior*, (pp. 31–334). New York: McGraw-Hill.

Milner, B. (1966). Amnesia following operation on the temporal lobes. In C. W. M. Whitty & O. L. Zangwill (Eds.), *Amnesia*. London: Butterworths.

Milner, B., Corkin, S., & Teuber, H.-L. (1968). Further analysis of the hippocampal amnesic syndrome: 14-year follow-up study of HM. *Neuropsychologia, 6*, 215–234.

Mishkin, M., Vargha Khadem, F., & Gadian, D. G. (1998). Amnesia and the organisation of the hippocampal system. *Hippocampus, 8*, 212–216.

Musen, G., & Squire, L. R. (1993). On the implicit learning of novel associations by amnesic subjects. *Neuropsychology, 7*, 119–135.

Neisser, U., (1967). *Cognitive Psychology*. New York: Appleton-Century-Crofts.

Nolde, S. F., Johnson, M. K., & D'Esposito, M. D. (1998). Left prefrontal activation during episodic remembering: An event-related fMRI study. *NeuroReport, 9*, 3509–3514.

Nolde, S. F., Johnson, M. K., & Raye, C. L. (in press). The role of prefrontal cortex during tests of episodic memory. *Trends in Cognitive Sciences*.

Norman, D. A., & Bobrow, D. G. (1979). Descriptions: An intermediate stage in memory retrieval. *Cognitive Psychology, 11*, 107–123.

Norman, D. A., & Shallice, T. (1986). Attention to action: Willed and automatic control of behaviour. In R. J. Davidson, G. E. Schwartz, & D. E. Shapiro (Eds.), *Consciousness and self-regulation* (Vol. 4). New York: Plenum Press.

O'Connor, M., Butters, N., Miliotis, P., Eslinger, P., & Cermak, L. S. (1992). The dissociation of anterograde and retrograde amnesia in a patient with Herpes encephalitis. *Journal of Clinical and Experimental Neuropsychology, 14*, 159–178.

O'Connor, M., Sieggreen, M. A., Ahern, G., Schomer, D., & Mesulam, M. (1997). Accelerated forgetting in association with temporal lobe epilepsy and paraneoplastic encephalitis. *Brain and Cognition, 35*, 71–84.

Parkin, A. J. (1982). Residual learning capability in organic amnesia. *Cortex, 18*, 417–440.

Parkin, A. J. (1996a). Focal retrograde amnesia: A multifaceted disorder? *Acta Neuropathologica Belgica, 96*, 43–50.

Parkin, A. J. (1996b). H.M.: The medial temporal lobes and memory. In C. Code, C.-W. Wallesch, Y. Joanette, & A. Roch (Eds.), *Classic cases in neuropsychology*. Hove, UK: Psychology Press.

Parkin, A. J. (1997a). *Case studies in the neuropsychology of memory*. Hove, UK: Psychology Press.

Parkin, A. J. (1997b). The long and winding road: Twelve years of frontal amnesia. In A. J. Parkin (Ed.), *Case studies in the neuropsychology of memory*. Hove, UK: Psychology Press.

Parkin, A. J. (1997c). *Memory and amnesia: An introduction* (2nd ed.). Hove, UK: Psychology Press.

Parkin, A. J. (1999). Component processes versus systems: Is there really a difference? In J. K. Foster & M. Jelcic (Eds.), *Memory: Systems, Process, or Function?* Oxford, UK: Oxford University Press.

Parkin, A. J. (2000a). *Essential Cognitive Psychology*. Hove, UK: Psychology Press.

Parkin, A. J. (2000b). Low velocity intra-nasal penetrating head injury: Case NA. In C. Code, C.-W. Wallesch,

Y. Joanette, & A. Roch (Eds.), *Classic cases in neuropsychology* (Vol. 2,). Hove, UK: Psychology Press.

Parkin, A. J., Blunden, J., Rees, J. E., & Hunkin, N. M. (1991). Wernicke-Korsakoff Syndrome of non-alcoholic origin. *Brain and Cognition, 21*, 1–19.

Parkin, A. J., & Hunkin, N. M. (1993b). Impaired temporal context memory on anterograde but not retrograde tests in the absence of frontal pathology. *Cerebral Cortex, 29*, 267–280.

Parkin, A. J., & Leng, N. R. C. (1993). *Neuropsychology of the Amnesic Syndrome*. Hove, UK: Lawrence Erlbaum.

Parkin, A. J., Montaldi, D., Leng, N. R. C., & Hunkin, N. (1990). Contextual cueing effects in the remote memory of alcoholic Korsakoff patients. *Quarterly Journal of Experimental Psychology, 42A*, 585–596.

Parkin, A. J., Rees, J. E., Hunkin, N. M., & Rose, P. E. (1994). Impairment of memory following discrete thalamic infarction. *Neuropsychologia, 32*, 39–51.

Parkin, A. J., & Stampfer, H. G. (1995). Keeping out the past. In R. Campbell & M. A. Conway (Eds.), *Broken Memories*. Hove, UK: Lawrence Erlbaum.

Parkin, A. J., Ward, J., Bindschaedler, C., Squires, E. J., & Powell, G. (1999). False recognition following frontal lobe damage: The role of encoding factors. *Cognitive Neuropsychology, 16*, 243–265.

Parkin, A. J., Ward, J., Squires, E., & Townshend, J. (accepted subject to revision). *Data-driven recognition memory: A new technique and some data on age differences*. Manuscript submitted for publication.

Rapcsak, S. Z., Reminger, S. L., Glisky, E. L., Kaszniak, A. W., & Comer, J. F. (1999). Neuropsychological mechanisms of false recognition following frontal lobe damage. *Cognitive Neuropsychology, 16*, 267–292.

Reinitz, M. T., Verfaellie, M., & Milberg, W. P. (1996). Memory conjunction errors in normal and amnesic subjects. *Journal of Memory and Language, 35*, 286–299.

Rempel-Clower, N. L., Zola, S. M., Squire, L. R., & Amaral, D. G. (1996). Three cases of enduring memory impairment after bilateral damage limited to the hippocampal formation. *Journal of Neuroscience, 16*, 5233–5255.

Ribot, T. (1882). *Diseases of Memory*. New York: Appleton.

Robertson, L. C., Knight, R. T., Rafal, R., & Shimamura, A. P. (1993). Cognitive neuropsychology is more than single case studies. *Journal of Experimental Psychology: Learning, Memory and Cognition, 19*, 710–717.

Roediger, H. L., & McDermott, K. B. (1994). The problem of differing false alarm rates for the process dissociation procedure: Comment on Verfaellie and Treadwell (1993). *Neuropsychology, 8*, 284–288.

Russo, R., Cullis, A. M., & Parkin, A. J. (1998). Consequences of violating the assumption of independence in the process dissociation procedure: A word fragment completion study. *Memory & Cognition, 26*, 617–632.

Sagar, H. J., Gabrieli, J. D. E., Sullivan, E. V., & Corkin, S. (1990). Recency and frequency judgement in the amnesic patient HM. *Brain, 113*, 581–602.

Schacter, D. L. (1992a). Priming and multiple memory systems: Perceptual mechanisms of implicit memory. *Journal of Cognitive Neuroscience, 4*, 244–256.

Schacter, D. L. (1992b). Understanding implicit memory. *American Psychologist, 47*, 559–569.

Schacter, D. L. (1999). *Cognitive neuropsychology of false memory*. Hove, UK: Psychology Press.

Schacter, D. L., Curran, T., Galluccio, L., Milberg, W. P., & Bates, J. F. (1996). False recognition and the right frontal lobe: A case study. *Neuropsychologia, 34,* 793–808.

Schacter, D. L., Wang, P. L., Tulving, E., & Freedman, M. (1982). Functional retrograde amnesia: A quantitative case study. *Neuropsychologia, 20,* 523–532.

Shimamura, A. P., & Squire, L. R. (1989). Impaired priming of new associations in amnesia. *Journal of Experimental Psychology: Learning, Memory and Cognition, 15,* 721–728.

Squire, L. R. (1987). *Memory and brain.* New York: Oxford University Press.

Tulving, E. (1985). How many memory systems are there? *American Psychologist, 40,* 385–398.

Tulving, E., Hayman, C. G., & MacDonald, A. (1991). Long-lasting perceptual priming and semantic learning in amnesia: A case experiment. *Journal of Experimental Psychology: Learning, Memory and Cognition, 17,* 595–617.

Tulving, E., Kapur, S., Craik, F. I. M., Moscovitch, M., & Houle, S. (1994). Hemispheric encoding/retrieval asymmetry in episodic memory: Positron emission tomography findings. *Proceeding of the National Academy of Sciences, USA, 91,* 2016–2020.

Tulving, E., & Markowitsch, H. J. (1998). Episodic and declarative memory: Role of the hippocampus. *Hippocampus, 8*(3), 198–204.

Tulving, E., Schacter, D. L., & Stark, H. (1982). Priming effects in word-fragment completion are independent of recognition memory. *Journal of Experimental Psychology: Human Learning and Memory, 8,* 336–342.

Vaidya, C. J., Gabrieli, J. D. E., Verfaellie, M., Fleischman, D., & Askari, N. (1998). Font-specific priming following global amnesia and occipital lobe damage. *Neuropsychology, 12*(2), 183–192.

Vargha-Khadem, F., Gadian, D. G., Watkins, K. E., Connelly, A., Van Paesschen, W., & Mishkin, M.. (1997). Differential effects of early hippocampal pathology on episodic and semantic memory. *Science, 277,* 376–380.

Verfaellie, M. (1994). A re-examination of recognition memory in amnesia: A reply to Roediger and McDermott. *Neuropsychology, 8,* 289–292.

Verfaellie, M., & Treadwell, J. R. (1993). Status of recognition memory in amnesia. *Neuropsychology, 7,* 5–13.

Verfaellie, M., Reiss, L., & Roth, H. L. (1995). Knowledge of English vocabulary in amnesia: An examination of premorbidly acquired semantic memory. *Journal of the International Neuropsychological Society, 1,* 443–453.

Ward, J., & Parkin, A. J. (in press). Pathological false recognition and source memory deficits following frontal lobe damage. *Neurocase.*

Ward, J., Parkin, A. J., Powell, G., Squires, E. J., Townshend, J., & Bradley, V. (1999). False recognition of familiar people: "Seeing film stars everywhere." *Cognitive Neuropsychology, 16,* 293–315.

Warrington, E. K., & McCarthy, R. A. (1988). The fractionation of retrograde amnesia. *Brain and Cognition, 7,* 184–200.

Warrington, E. K., & Weiskrantz, L. (1970). Amnesic syndrome: Consolidation or retrieval? *Nature, 228,* 628–630.

Winocur, G., & Kinsbourne, M. (1978). Contextual cueing as an aid to Korsakoff amnesics. *Neuropsychologia, 16,* 671–682.

Wood, F. B., Brown, I. S., & Felton, R. H. (1989). Long-term follow-up of a childhood amnesic syndrome. *Brain and Cognition, 10,* 76–86.

Zola-Morgan, S., Squire, L. R., & Amaral, D. G. (1986). Human amnesia and the medial temporal region: Enduring memory impairment following a bilateral lesion limited to field CA1 of the hippocampus. *Journal of Neuroscience, 6*(10), 2950–2967.

17

The Organization
of Semantic Memory

Jennifer R. Shelton
Alfonso Caramazza

A central question in psychology concerns how knowledge is represented and organized in the brain. Researchers examine the contents and representation of information "in" semantic memory and distinguish this type of knowledge from other types of knowledge, such as autobiographical memory (e.g., Tulving, 1985). Semantic memory consists of knowledge about the world, such as what we know about animals, negotiating, tools, clothing, cooking, furniture, etc. Several avenues of research bear directly on the issues of representation and organization of semantic knowledge, including results with nonbrain-damaged individuals, children, and brain-damaged populations. Our intent in this chapter is to provide an overview of the issues currently being addressed and to relate relevant results to our understanding of the neural organization of knowledge.

Perhaps the most intriguing results come from the neuropsychological literature. As the result of brain damage, some patients show specific problems with certain types of semantic categories, such as selective impairment to knowledge about animals, or plant life, or artefacts (Warrington & McCarthy, 1987; Warrington & Shallice, 1984).[1] Patients JJ and PS, reported by Hillis and Caramazza (1991), illustrate this type of deficit. JJ suffered a stroke when he was in his late sixties, resulting in damage to the left temporal lobe and basal ganglia. PS sustained a severe blow to the head when he was in his middle forties, resulting in damage to a large area of the left temporal lobe, and smaller areas of the right temporal and frontal lobes. Both patients showed disproportionate difficulties naming and understanding certain categories of items relative to other categories of items. For example, JJ named line-drawings of animals very well (42 out of 46 = 91% correct) but performed quite poorly on all other categories (20 out of 98 = 20% correct). In contrast, PS had significant problems naming line-drawings of animals (18 out of 46 = 39% correct) and vegetables (3 out of 12 = 25% correct) but performed quite well on all other categories (82 out of 86 = 95% correct). A comparison of their ability to provide definitions for items within the animal and the nonanimal categories further demonstrates their selective difficulties in naming and understanding living (PS) or nonliving (JJ) concepts:

---

[1]We refer to all living things (i.e., animals and plants, including fruits and vegetables) as living items and the animal subset as animate items.

JJ: *lion*: a large animal, about 4 feet tall, maybe taller at the shoulders, it has a long body and very large paws and stands on all four legs. It has a monstrous head with which it growls; and it has a mane—a large body of hair. It lives in Africa.

melon: I'm not sure. It's a fruit, a soft material. I don't remember if it is yellow or green or orange. I've forgotten too many things.

PS: *heron*: a fish

apricot: like a peach, only smaller. You can buy them canned or dried or fresh.

As these cases illustrate, brain injured patients may show selective problems with certain categories of items but not others, and this observation has now been established in a large number of patients (see Forde & Humphreys, 1999; Gainotti, Silveri, Daniele, & Guistolisi, 1995; Shelton & Caramazza, 1999, for reviews). The fact that damage to certain areas of the brain can result in problems restricted to some domains of knowledge but not others could lead to the remarkable conclusion that different domains of knowledge are organized in different areas of the brain. While it has long been known that different areas of the brain are responsible for different functions (e.g., motor, vision, audition, etc.), the idea that brain areas might be dedicated to specific knowledge domains remains controversial.

We begin this chapter by discussing whether true category-specific knowledge effects exist in brain-damaged populations or whether the effects emerge merely because of processing difficulty as measured by variables such as familiarity and visual complexity. The "processing difficulty" hypothesis was proposed to explain the disproportionate number of cases reported who have deficits with living things, since living things tend to be less familiar and more visually complex (e.g., Funnell & Sheridan, 1992; Gaffan & Heywood, 1993). We will show that although it is likely that at least *some* of the reported cases may not be true category-specific deficits, but rather reflect greater processing difficulty with living things, not all reported cases of category-specific deficits can be explained by processing difficulty. We will argue that a category-specific deficit is a true effect for many of the reported cases.

We then present three types of theories of semantic memory: modality-specific theories, feature-intercorrelation theories, and domain-specific theories. The first two theories do not allow for semantic organization according to categorical knowledge and explain category-specific effects as emerging from the properties by which semantic knowledge is organized. By contrast, the domain-specific theory suggests that knowledge is broadly organized into specific knowledge domains, i.e., that certain brain areas are dedicated to the processing of specific domains of knowledge.

Modality-specific theories suggest that semantic knowledge is organized into perceptual and nonperceptual information that is differentially important for certain categories of knowledge such that damage to a specific type of knowledge (e.g., perceptual knowledge) will necessarily result in deficits to those categories of items for which that knowledge is critical (e.g., some have hypothesized that perceptual knowledge is crucial for the understanding of living things). For example, damage to the brain areas in which perceptual knowledge is represented will result in disproportionate difficulty with living things (and any other category for which perceptual information is important). Although various results in patient studies, computer modeling, and normal studies, were initially interpreted to provide support for the sensory/functional theory, recent work reveals weaknesses in the data cited in support of the theory as well as limitations of the theory in explaining a number of empirical facts.

Feature intercorrelation theories provide an alternative framework for the organization of semantic memory. Although specific theories differ in detail, the general idea is that certain properties of items are shared (are intercorrelated) among members of a given category and that members of the living things category tend to share more common properties than members of artefact categories. Properties that are highly correlated are hypothesized to be clustered together in the brain, and therefore, damage to a certain brain area can result in damage to categories for which these properties are important. Because living things tend to share more common properties, items from the living things category are more likely to be damaged together. Different variations of this general idea will be discussed, along with computational models that have been developed to account for the patient data from lesion studies and also from studies of category-specific effects in dementia. Although these types of theories can account for a range of reported results, they too fail to capture certain aspects of the data.

A final class of theory proposes that specific areas of the brain are dedicated to the processing of evolutionarily important domains of knowledge (e.g., animals and plant life). According to this hypothesis, category-specific effects arise from damage to those brain areas which are important for the processing of certain domains of knowledge. This theory offers a broad organizational scheme that can accomodate the relevant data reported thus far. However, the theory is silent as to the way in which knowledge is organized within domains.

We hasten to point out that although these three classes of theories are distinct in the ways in which knowledge is thought to be organized, they need not be mutually exclusive. There are likely to be many levels of organization of semantic knowledge in the brain such that a broad distinction such as biological versus nonbiological domains does not preclude a more fine-grained organization at a specific level of knowledge. For example, we can ask whether or not there is further structure within the category of biological concepts (and we will later show that we must distinguish between animate and inanimate biological objetcs). We can then ask whether there is further structure within the category of animate items and if so, what might be its organizational principles (e.g., perhaps intercorrelations between properties play an important role in organizing knowledge at a more detailed level). Therefore, the hypothesis of domain-specific knowledge organization provides a general scheme of organization but does not imply necessarily a categorical structure at more detailed levels of organization.

In the final section of the chapter we will discuss findings from lesion and neuroimaging studies in an attempt to outline what brain areas might be important in processing semantic memory, in general, and certain types or categories of information, more specifically. Results from these studies can provide additional information regarding the organization of semantic categories in the brain.

ARE THERE TRUE CATEGORY-SPECIFIC DEFICITS?

In the early 1990s, researchers questioned whether deficits to specific categories of knowledge were true category effects or whether they emerged merely from the influence of familiarity, frequency, visual complexity, or a combination of these factors (e.g., Funnell & Sheridan, 1992; Gaffan & Heywood, 1993: Stewart, Parkin, & Hunkin, 1992). Most patients reported to show category-specific effects have had deficits to knowledge of animals and living things (e.g., see Forde & Humphreys, 1999, for review). Funnell and Sheridan (1992) demonstrated that item familiarity (as determined by familiarity ratings provided by normal subjects from the Snodgrass & Vanderwart, 1980, picture set) had a strong influence on naming performance in their patient, SL. In fact, when items in living and nonliving categories were matched on familiarity, the previously demonstrated "category-specific" effect found with SL was no longer statistically reliable (see Table 17.1).

Stewart et al. (1992) reported similar results: Their patient, HO, demonstrated a strong effect of category in picture naming, with living things being named at a much lower rate than nonliving things (see Table 17.1). However, when items were matched on familiarity, word frequency, and the visual complexity of the picture, the category effect was no longer obtained (see Table 17.1).

In general, living things tend to be more difficult to process for nonbrain-damaged subjects. Capitani, Laiacona, Barbarotto, and Trivelli (1994) demonstrated that both normal elderly subjects and normal young subjects had greater difficulty answering questions about living things than nonliving things, even when the items on which knowledge was assessed were

Table 17.1
Effects of Processing Difficulty on Performance (Proportion Correct)

Funnell & Sheridan, 1992: Patient SL
Experiment 1: Naming of Low-Frequency Items

	Living	Nonliving
	2/16 (.13)	14/26 (.54)

Experiment 2: Naming of Items Matched on Frequency and Familiarity

	Living	Nonliving
	16/34 (.47)	12/34 (.35)

Stewart, Parking & Hunkin, 1992: Patient HO
Experiment 1: Naming of Items Matched on Frequency

	Living	Nonliving
	18/43 (.42)	40/50 (.80)

Experiment 2: Naming of Items Matched on Frequency, Familiarity, and Complexity

	Living	Nonliving
	15/36 (.42)	13/36 (.36)

matched for prototypicality, familiarity, and frequency.[2] Gaffan and Heywood (1993) also demonstrated a difference between processing of living and nonliving things, with living things being harder to visually discriminate than nonliving things. These results all suggest that the so-called category-specific impairment for animals or living things may actually be the result of a greater overall difficulty with these items, due to their greater visual complexity and lower familiarity.

Not all cases of category-specific effects can be explained in this manner, however. For example, there are patients who demonstrate greater difficulty with nonliving things, the "easier," "more familiar" category. As discussed in the introduction, two cases, PS and JJ, showed similar overall levels of performance but contrasting effects of category (Hillis & Caramazza, 1991; also see Table 17.6 for further comparison of performance). PS had the greatest difficulty naming and defining living things, whereas JJ had the greatest difficulty naming and defining nonliving things. If the effect were just one of difficulty due to factors such as familiarity and visual complexity, we would not expect patients to show a greater difficulty with nonliving things (see also, Cappa, Frugoni, Pasquali, Perani, & Zorat, 1998; Sacchett & Humphreys, 1992; Warrington & McCarthy, 1983, 1987).

Moreover, recent results demonstrate that some patients show category-specific effects even after items have been matched in terms of processing difficulty. For example, our patient EW demonstrated a significant naming and comprehension problem for animals but normal naming and comprehension of nonanimals (Caramazza & Shelton, 1998), even after items were matched for frequency and familiarity (see Table 2)[3]: naming animals: 33%–55%, naming nonanimals: 67%–94%. For comprehension, we matched *knowledge* of items (and the items

[2]In this study, items were matched for familiarity but the probed knowledge was not.
[3]For picture naming, items were taken from the set used by Funnell & Sheridan (1992) which were not matched on visual complexity. However, visual complexity is not important when testing comprehension using sentence verification, since pictures are not used as stimuli. In these tasks, EW (and several other patients) demonstrate category-specific effects for items matched on familiarity and frequency.

themselves) on familiarity by having elderly control subjects rate how familiar they were with each question asked about an item. For example, questions such as "does a giraffe live on land?" and "does a robin have 4 legs" were given to the elderly subjects and they had to answer the question and then rate how familiar this information was to them. After gathering this information, we matched items in the animal and nonanimal categories and examined EW's performance (see Table 17.2). She still performed poorly with animals and normally with nonanimals. Many other reports have recently demonstrated that after controlling for processing difficulty, patients still show category-specific deficits (e.g., Farah, Meyer, & McMullen, 1996; Gainotti & Silveri, 1996; Hart & Gordon, 1992; Kurbat, 1997; Laiacona, Barbarotto & Capitanti, 1993; Laiacona, Capitani, & Barbaratto, 1997; Moss, Tyler, Durrant-Peatfield, & Bunn, 1998; Sheridan & Humphreys, 1993).

However, a recent finding reported by Capitani, Laiacona, and Barbarotto (1999) raises questions concerning the appropriateness of using only familiarity ratings as a means for equating different semantic categories. They found that gender influenced semantic fluency, with males outperforming females on tools and females outperforming males on fruits. No other significant gender differences between categories emerged. Also, Capitani, Albanese, Barbarotto, and Laiacona (1999) found that females rate living categories as more familiar than males, and there was no difference between nonliving categories (see also Laiacona, Barbarotto, & Capitani, 1998). However, when reanalyzing two previously-reported cases of category-specific effects, one female who performed best with living things and one male who performed best with nonliving things, Capitani et al. (1999) found that category-specific effects were still present after controlling for gender-specific familiarity ratings. Thus, gender differences do not necessarily invalidate category-specific effects.

Although Capitani et al. (in press) demonstrated that gender can have an influence on performance with specific categories, there is still an abundance of evidence to suggest that once processing difficulty is matched between categories, patients may still demonstrate category-specific effects. And, there is the contrasting effect of worse performance for inanimate items as compared to animate items, which cannot be explained by processing difficulty.

We conclude then that at least *some* patients do show true category-specific effects, although we will argue below that this is especially difficult to establish in some of the early published cases in which processing difficulty was not controlled. We will also argue that processing difficulty (i.e., familiarity) very likely influenced certain results regarding performance on different types of information (sensory vs. nonsensory information) within categories.

Table 17.2

Categorical Effects for Items Matched on Processing Difficulty
(Proportion Correct)

Caramazza & Shelton, 1998: Patient EW

Naming

	Animate	Inanimate
High-familiarity	6/11 (.54)	170/181 (.94)
Low Familiarity	10/36 (.28)	18/22 (.81)

Comprehension (items and attributes matched on familiarity)

	Animate	Inanimate
	425/601 (.71)	434/445 (.98)

IS SEMANTIC INFORMATION REPRESENTED AND ORGANIZED ACCORDING TO SENSORY MODALITIES OF KNOWLEDGE?

In this section we discuss results from three areas of work that are taken as support for the modality-specific knowledge theories: patient studies, computational modeling, and studies of priming effects in normal subjects. We then present criticisms and challenges to the data and raise questions regarding theoretical issues, concluding there is little support from these data for modality-specific knowledge organization.

A prevalent idea concerning the representation of knowledge is that information is distinguished according to modality of information—that is, the brain segregates information according to the *type* of information (e.g., perceptual or nonperceptual) represented. This type of scheme has been proposed by a number of authors (e.g., Allport, 1985; Farah & McClelland, 1991; Warrington & McCarthy, 1983, 1987; Warrington & Shallice, 1984). In fact, Allport (1985) outlined a model of semantic memory in which each type of sensory information was represented in separately organized but connected "nodes." In his model, information belongs to a certain node depending on the content of that information: action-oriented elements, kinesthetic elements, visual elements, tactile elements, auditory elements. Thus, information about an object is represented in a distributed fashion throughout the brain depending on the modality of information.

Warrington and Shallice (1984) provided the first well documented evidence of category-specific processing deficits in four patients suffering from brain-damage. The two patients studied most in depth, JBR and SBY, showed dramatic differences in naming, defining, and comprehending concepts associated with different natural categories. Examples of their definitions include:

JBR: *tent:* temporary outhouse, living home
     briefcase: small case used by students to carry papers
     daffodil: plant
     snail: insect animal
SBY: *towel:* material used to dry people
     submarine: ship that goes underneath sea
     wasp: bird that flies
     holly: what you drink

The difference in performance for living and nonliving items was quite striking: SBY identified or defined 75% (36 out of 48) of nonliving things but no living things and JBR identified or defined 94% (45 out of 48) of nonliving things but only 4% (2 out of 48) of living things. However, these category-specific effects did not honor strict category boundaries (i.e., a living/nonliving dichotomy). JBR was impaired not only on living things but also on items in categories such as musical instruments, gemstones, metals, fabrics, and foods (see Table 17.3). Other patients have also been reported to have problems with categories falling outside the natural boundaries of the living/nonliving distinction and include associations between deficits to animals and foods (e.g., De Renzi & Lucchelli, 1994; Sheridan & Humphreys, 1993; Silveri & Gainotti, 1988) and living things and musical instruments (e.g., Silveri & Gainotti, 1988).

The co-occurrence of damage to multiple categories that do not respect category boundaries was taken to support the view that semantic knowledge is organized according to modality (or type) of information. Warrington and colleagues (Warrington & McCarthy, 1983; 1987; Warrington & Shallice, 1984) argued that category-specific effects result from damage to a particular type of knowledge—either perceptual or nonperceptual knowledge.[4] They argued that

---

[4] We refer to the distinction as perceptual and nonperceptual, which was the initial hypothesis. However, the terms "visual" versus "functional" came to be short-hand terms for this distinction, and Warrington and colleagues tend to support the notion that the distinction between visual and functional information is the most important.

Table 17.3
JBR's Definition Performance for Specific Categories
in Warrington and Shallice, 1984.

Category	Obtained Score	Expected Score
Insect	3	8.5
Metal	4	9.6
Drink	2	6.1
Cloth	2	8.5
Musical Instruments	2	8.1
Disease	1	6.7
Fish	1	7.7
Precious Stone	1	6.1
Flower	0	5.9
Fruit	0	7.7
Trees	0	7.5
Vegetables	0	6.9

Note: These are categories on which JBR's obtained score was significantly worse than the expected score (see "Category-specific Semantic Impairments," E. K. Warrington & T. Shallice, 1984, *Brain, 107,* pp. 843 for determination of expected score and for performance on all categories examined).

perceptual attributes are especially important for identification and understanding of living things whereas nonperceptual attributes are especially important for identification and understanding of nonliving things. There is an association of deficits to categories outside the living/nonliving distinction, then, because those categories also have a strong emphasis on perceptual information. So, for example, perceptual properties are hypothesized to be important chiefly for understanding living things, foods, and musical instruments, and when damage occurs to those brain areas that important for processing perceptual information, category-specific effects can emerge.

This interpretation of category-specific effects makes the prediction that damage to perceptual properties should result in damage to *any* category that is strongly defined by these properties. A second prediction is that patients should have disproportionate difficulty with questions regarding the damaged information; that is, a co-occurrence of category-specific and modality-specific deficits. A third predication is based on an additional, common assumption of the modality specific semantics hypothesis. The assumption is that perceptual and nonperceptual semantic subsysems are interdependent (see Farah & McClelland, 1991). This interdependence is such that for concepts composed largely of perceptual features, nonperceptual information is negatively affected by damage to the perceptual semantic system. Additionally, in a complementary manner, for concepts composed largely of nonperceptual features, the nonperceptual features provide support to the damaged perceptual features. On this basis, we should expect that (a) although there should be some detriment in performance with perceptual information across all categories, those categories that are defined primarily by nonperceptual information should show less difficulties with perceptual information and (b) there should be an additional detriment in performance with nonperceptual information for those categories that depend strongly on perceptual information. Thus the third prediction of the modality specific semantics hypothesis is that we should observe a modality by category interaction when all appropriate conditions are tested.

As mentioned earlier, cases were reported to show deficits to associated categories for which perceptual information is hypothesized to be most important (and conversely, for associated categories for which nonperceptual information is most important, e.g., Warrington & McCarthy, 1983, 1987). Moreover, patients were reported to show the expected impairment in performance with the critical information associated with the damaged categories, (i.e., a co-occurrence of category and modality-specific deficits; e.g., Basso, Capitani, & Laiacona, 1988; Farah, Hammond, Mehta, & Ratcliff, 1989; Hart & Gordon, 1992; Sartori & Job, 1988; Silveri & Gainotti, 1988). For example, Silveri and Gainotti demonstrated that their patient, LA, was impaired in regard to living things as compared to nonliving things (e.g., 20% vs. 79%, respectively) and was more impaired with visual than nonvisual information associated with living things (9% vs. 58%, respectively), the predicted co-occurrence of category and modality-specific deficits. Thus, initially there appeared to be independent support for the idea that category-specific effects emerged from damage to a type of information that is disproportionately important for some categories than others.

Category-Specific Knowledge deficits Fail to Support the Modality-Specific Theory

A careful examination of patient performance and careful balancing between processing difficulty of information probed within catgories reveals little support for the modality-specific interpretation of category-specific knowledge deficits. The first prediction of the theory—that damage to perceptual or nonperceptual properties should result in damage to those categories most reliant on these properties—has been disconfirmed. Patients have been reported who show deficits to a subset of the living items category—animals only—and the effects are not due to influences of familiarity and frequency (e.g., Caramazza & Shelton, 1998; Hart & Gordon, 1992; Hillis & Caramazza, 1991). Moreover, these patients do not show problems with the expected associated categories such as musical instruments or foods. For example, our patient described above, EW, had a selective deficit affecting animals only and performed normally on items in the fruits and vegetables category, other food stuff, and musical instruments. Other patients have been reported to have difficulties with only fruits and vegetables (e.g., Farah & Wallace, 1992; Hart, Berndt, & Caramazza, 1985) or only body parts (e.g. Goodglass, Klein, Carey, & Jones, 1966; Semenza & Goodglass, 1985, see also Shelton, Fouch, & Caramazza, 1998; for selective sparing of body parts).

Also, several patients have been reported to have difficulty processing visual information *without* having any category-specific processing deficits (e.g., Coltheart et al., 1998; Lambon-Ralph, Howard, Nightengale, & Ellis, 1998). For example, Lambon-Ralph et al. presented the case of IW, who showed significant problems processing visual information but no associated category-specific deficit in name comprehension. As shown in Table 17.4, IW performed significantly worse when asked to select the name (from 5 choices) when given perceptual information as compared to selecting the name when given nonperceptual information, but no associated category effect was observed. IW was also much better with nonperceptual information when asked questions about items and provided much more nonperceptual information when asked to define items. On none of these tasks did she show category-specific effects; that is, she performed equally with living and nonliving items.

Table 17.4
Deficit to Visual Knowledge without a Corresponding Living Things Deficit
(Proportion Correct)

Lambon-Ralph et al., 1998: pt. IW
Definition to Word Matching

	Perceptual Definition	Nonperceptual Definition	Total
Animals	8/16 (.50)	13/16 (.81)	21/32 (.66)
Artefacts	5/12 (.42)	9/12 (.75)	14/24 (.58)
Total	13/28 (.46)	22/28 (.79)	

These cases pose a strong challenge to the first prediction from the sensory/nonsensory hypothesis of semantic knowledge organization. We argued previously (Caramazza & Shelton, 1998) that the associated patterns of category impairments (e.g., living things and musical instruments) reported in the early studies may have reflected influences of familiarity (either instead of or in addition to deficits to a specific category). Thus, when familiarity and other factors are controlled, deficits to associated categories disappear (see Bunn, Tyler, & Moss, 1998 for a demonstration of this with the classic patient JBR).

The Influence of Familiarity on Processing Visual Information about Animals

The second prediction of the modality-specific theory, that category and modality-specific deficits should co-occur and, ultimately, that there should be a category X modality interaction, has not been found when the familiarity of the stimuli was controlled. Stewart et al. (1992) demonstrated that normal subjects were significantly slower in verifying visual/perceptual attributes than nonperceptual attributes of living things. They argued this demonstrates that perceptual attributes of living things are less familiar than their nonperceptual attributes (Experiment 5). As shown in Table 17.5, their patient, HO, performed much worse on a naming-to-definition task with perceptual than nonperceptual information; however, when visual and nonvisual judgments were matched for familiarity, the difference in performance disappeared (Experiment 6). Stewart et al. clearly demonstrated that their patient's putative category-specific deficit and expected patterns of performance predicted by the modality-specific semantics hypothesis emerged solely because of the influence of familiarity on HO's performance. This result raises questions regarding the findings reported for cases in which the stimuli used were not controlled for familiarity, a problem associated with many of the early reports of category-specific effects.

In recent years, researchers have controlled for familiarity in their stimuli and have assessed

Table 17.5
Performance on Perceptual and Nonperceptual Attributes

Stewart et al., 1992 Patient HO		
Experiment 5 (items NOT matched on familiarity)		
Naming to definition (proportion correct)		
	Perceptual	Nonperceptual
HO	45%	79%
Control	76%	99%

Reaction times for control subjects verifying perceptual and nonperceptual statements

Perceptual	Nonperceptual
1769 ms	1699 ms

Experiment 6 (items matched on familiarity; proportion correct)

Perceptual	Nonperceptual
27/32 (.84)	26/32 (.81)

Caramazza & Shelton, 1998: Patient EW		
Performance on perceptual and nonperceptual attribute questions		
	Perceptual	Nonperceptual
Animate	202/301 (.67)	223/300 (.74)
Inanimate	217/226 (.96)	217/219 (.99)

Note. Error rates for reaction time data were very low (< 1%)

the expectation of a co-occurrence of category and modality-specific deficits and a category by modality interaction (e.g., Caramazza & Shelton, 1998; Laiacona et al., 1997; Lambon-Ralph et al., 1998; Sheridan & Humphreys, 1992). For example, our patient EW was tested on a very large number of items and attributes matched on familiarity. Questions about perceptual and nonperceptual attributes were matched on familiarity by having elderly control subjects rate how familiar they were with the information being asked in each question. EW showed no difference in performance with perceptual and nonperceptual attributes of animals, and no difficulty in performance with perceptual attributes of nonanimals (see Table 17.5). That is, contrary to the predictions derived from the modality-specific semantic hypothesis, EW showed only a main effect of category and no interaction between category and modality.

The recent results from patients with category-specific effects cast strong doubt on the original interpretations of the co-occurrence of modality- and category-specific deficits. reported in the early studies of patients with category-specific deficits. Thus, there now appears to be little support from the neurological literature to suggest that semantic knowledge is organized according to modality of information—specifically, along a perceptual/nonperceptual dichotomy. However, there are other areas of research cited in support of modality-specific semantic organization of knowledge, which we now evaluate to determine the support these data provide for modality-specific theories of semantic knowledge organization.

Computational Models of Modality-Specific Semantics and Problems with the Underlying Assumptions of the Models

Farah and McClelland (1991) developed a computer model of semantic memory in which perceptual ("visual") and nonperceptual ("functional") information is represented in separate but interconnected networks. An item was represented by the sum of its features, and to accomodate the assumption that is necessary for a modality-specific theory to account for category-specific effects, living items had a large number of perceptual features and nonliving items had a large number of functional features. The ratio of visual and functional features for living and nonliving items was determined empirically by having subjects classify information in the dictionary definition of each item as either visual ("what it looks like") or functional ("what it is used for"). Based on these data, the ratio of visual to functional features was set to 16.1:2.1 for living things and 9.4:6.7 for nonliving things. Because the model is interactive, when visual information is activated, functional features related to that item are activated as well and vice versa.[5] Farah and McClelland (1991) damaged the perceptual network and found that damage to visual features resulted in worse performance on living things. Thus, if visual features are more numerous for living things, damage to these features will result in difficulties with living things.

However, Caramazza and Shelton (1998) argued that there was little empirical support for the notion that certain categories of items rely more heavily on perceptual attributes for identification, and questioned the results obtained by Farah and McClelland (1991) regarding the ratios of perceptual and nonperceptual knowledge for living and nonliving things. In Farah and McClelland's study, subjects were instructed to identify nonsensory properties on only one dimension, their function ("what it is for"), which omits such important nonsensory information concerning what an animal might eat, where it lives, how it reproduces, how it moves, etc. However, this is the exact information that is termed "functional" information in studies examining category-specific deficits. Using the exact stimuli and definitions as Farah and McClelland, we asked subjects to identify either sensory properties or nonsensory properties (i.e., not limiting nonsensory properties to only functional information). When we changed the

---

[5]This dimension of the model makes the prediction that there should be a category-by-modality interaction, which we have already argued is *not* found in patients with category-specific deficits.

instructions to include all nonsensory information, the resulting sensory to nonsensory attribute ratios were 2.9:2.5 for living things and 2.2:2.3 for nonliving things. Thus, there is little evidence of a strong bias of sensory attributes for living things if we include *all* nonsensory information from the definitions. Given these ratios, a model of the structure proposed by Farah and McClelland cannot produce category-specific effects if damage were restricted either to sensory or nonsensory attribute knowledge.

Similar results have been found by McRae, de Sar, & Seidenberg et al. (1997). In their study, 300 subjects listed features of items that referred to physical properties, functional properties and encyclopedic facts. The results demonstrated that the frequency of functional features was much greater for nonliving things but that the overall number of physical properties was quite similar between the two categories. And, encyclopedic information was equally frequent for living and nonliving things. Taken together, the results from these two studies suggest that the intuition first proposed by Warrington and colleagues regarding the importance of physical properties for our understanding of certain categories, especially living things, has little empirical support. Without this assumption, it is unclear exactly how a modality-specific theory of semantics could account for category-specific deficits.

Normal Studies of Semantic Priming: Tests of the Modality-Specific Hypothesis

With regard to studies of normal populations, proponents of modality-specific semantics have argued that support for this theory comes from semantic priming studies reported by Flores d'Arcais, Schreuder, and Glazenborg (1985) and Schreuder, Flores d'Arcais, and Glazenborg (1984). In these studies, priming effects were examined for word pairs that shared a perceptual dimension but were not conceptually related. For example, PAINTBRUSH and CARROT are visually similar in shape and contour but do not share any meaning with regard to function or natural category. The authors hypothesized that if information is organized/represented only by modality (i.e., is distributed according to type of information), priming should obtain for word pairs that are perceptually similar but are not conceptually related. In fact, this is what they found and they proposed a model of semantic memory in which information is organized into perceptual and nonperceptual subsystems.

However, a recent study suggests that methodological problems with the experiments by Schreuder et al. (1984) and Flores d'Arcais et al. (1985) may have been responsible for the effects reported by those authors. When the experiments are conducted properly, there is no evidence of priming for perceptually related, conceptually unrelated word pairs (e.g., *paint-brush-carrot*). Pecher, Zeelenberg, and Raaijimakers (1998) re-examined priming for perceptually related (e.g., *pizza-coin*) and conceptually related (e.g., *pizza-hotdog*) items. In the earlier studies by Flores d' Arcais and colleagues, target items were presented four times, once in each condition, to a single subject and the prime remained on the screen while the target was presented for either lexical decision or naming. Pecher et al. (1988) argue that under these conditions subjects are made overly aware of the perceptual relationships between the prime and target and may use this information to perform the task. Pecher et al. corrected these methodological problems and found no evidence of priming for perceptually-related word pairs and only found priming for conceptually related word pairs.

Conclusion: Little Support for Modality-Specific Theories and Problems Defining Perceptual and Nonperceptual Knowledge

It appears then that there is little support from any sector for the division of semantic knowledge on the basis of modality. Early support for this distinction, which came from several areas of research, has been shown to suffer from methodological problems. Moreover, the specific predictions made by theories which suggest that knowledge is organized according to sensory/nonsensory information have not been upheld. Reports of patients who show selective deficits to narrow categories of knowledge and show the same pattern of performance for types of knowledge within the spared and impaired categories pose great challenges to modality-specific theories of semantic memory.

Moreover, the theory is vague as to how semantic memory is organized and how properties of items become differentiated between perceptual and nonperceptual information. How do we determine if something is a perceptual or a nonperceptual feature? Why are the features of a horse such as "four legs," "mane," or "tail" considered perceptual features but "runs fast," or "is ridden" considered nonperceptual features? What is it about each of those features that makes them one type of feature and not the other, especially since they can both be experienced only perceptually, only through nonperceptual input, or both ways? For example, if we have never seen a certain type of animal (e.g., wombat) we may still know many things about it that are perceptual (e.g., color, shape, size) and nonperceptual (e.g., where it lives, what it eats, how it reproduces). How does each of these specific types of information get encoded properly? The same questions can be asked about learning the functionality of objects. We often learn to use items by watching someone else use them (e.g., fork) yet this information is not coded with perceptual information but rather with nonperceptual information. The idea of a perceptual/nonperceptual knowledge distinction can only be useful if we establish exactly what is meant by these terms and how knowledge is acquired and organized based on this distinction.

Having shown that modality-specific semantic theories suffer from a number of problems that limit their usefulness, we turn now to consider another type of feature-based theory of semantic memory.

IS SEMANTIC KNOWLEDGE ORGANIZED BY INTERCORRELATIONS AMONG FEATURES?

In this section, we discuss studies of category-specific effects in dementia, a disease that often results in diffuse brain damage, as well as studies of category-specific effects in stroke and other instances of trauma. We also discuss attempts at developing feature-based computer models of semantic memory, their usefulness in explaining category-specific effects, and the problems with these approaches. We conclude that feature-based theories provide a better means of capturing some aspects of the neuropsychological data but there are still limitations.

The Development of Computerized Models and Initial Support from Patients with Dementia

Studies have shown that there are systematic relationships among properties of members of a category (a "natural" category such as animals, furniture, vehicles, flowers). For example, Malt and Smith (1984) had subjects rate properties as belonging to a certain category (e.g., if beak was related to bird) and found that within categories, properties tended to correlate. Within the category "bird," for example, the properties "large," "beak," "large wings," and "eats fish" were correlated to one another. Within the category "furniture," for example, the properties "springs," "cushions," "sit on," "comfortable," and "soft" were correlated to one another. The results suggest that the properties of members of a certain category tend to be related to one another such that the likelihood of a member having a certain property, A, increases if they also have property B.

Building on this idea, Mc Rae et al. (1997) developed a computer model of semantic memory that captures the correlational aspect among semantic features. In their model, correlated features were more prominent for living things than for artefacts, and the larger number of correlations among features of living things was responsible for a dissociation in processing between living and nonliving items. This is the basic assumption of other models of semantic memory that rely on correlated features to explain category-specific semantic deficits in Alzheimer's disease (e.g., Devlin, Gonnerman, Andersen, & Seidenberg, 1998). In Devlin et al.'s model, living things have a high number of intercorrelated properties (i.e., few distinctive features) and the degree of correlation between these properties is higher for living things and nonliving things. The authors demonstrated that with mild damage, nonliving things were impaired but as damage became more severe, living things were more impaired. These computational results were supported by behavioral data from Gonnerman, Andersen, Devlin, Kempler, and Seidenberg (1997). They showed that patients with probable Alzheimer's disease who were mildly impaired showed more difficulty with nonliving things and as the severity increased, the impairment shifted to a deficit with living things.

Moss, Tyler, Durrant-Peatfield, and Bunn (1998) propose a slightly different account of semantic memory and make several basic assumptions in developing their computer model (see also Durrant-Peatfield, Moss, & Tyler, 1998). The first assumption is that the distribution of distinctive versus shared properties differs between living and nonliving things such that living things have many more shared properties and these shared properties tend to be correlated with one another (similar to Devlin et al.'s, 1998, proposal). For example, animals fall into well-defined categories such as mammals, birds, or reptiles but man-made things do not, and the boundaries between artefact categories are less clear, e.g., vehicles, toys, household objects. The second assumption, which differentiates this model from the Devlin et al. model, is that "functional" properties are important for both living and nonliving things, but "function" for living things involves biological motion rather than a specific use. And, function for living things tends to be shared among many members of the category whereas function for artefacts tends to be specific to a particular item. Moss et al.'s (1988) model stresses the importance of functional semantic properties, resulting in great overlap between both perceptual and functional properties for living things. This results in many features being intercorrelated for living things across different types of semantic properties. Moreover, semantic properties of nonliving things have few intercorrelated properties but strong correlations between specific perceptual and functional features associated for individual items (e.g., has a blade—used for cutting).

Although the models have slight differences in their basic assumptions, the structure of all these models makes very clear predictions regarding when category-specific deficits should emerge. Because of the strong sharing of properties among living things (regardless of the type of property), the Devlin et al. (1998) model predicts only severe damage would result in specific deficits to the living things category. However, when the damage is mild, deficits should arise for artefacts. The reasoning is that mild damage should impair distinctive features (which are more prevalent for nonliving things) since damage to a shared feature of an item can be compensated by the undamaged features. The Moss et al. (1998) model predicts that living things will be affected at any level of damage, except severe, since the individual features of animals are more unique and therefore more likely to be damaged. However, artefacts are impaired only at more severe levels of damage since the distinctive relationship between form and function is strongly correlated and therefore robust to brain damage.[6] Thus, these computer models demonstrate that using the basic structure of correlated features, category-specific deficits can emerge based on the severity level of the damage to the system. These models also account for the fact that when familiarity is controlled, patients do *not* show any specific problems with a certain type of knowledge within a category (i.e., co-occurrence of category and modality-specific deficits and/or a category-by-modality interaction).

---

[6] However, Moss et al. (1988) also allow that artefacts may also be impaired at mild levels of damage if the specific form-function features are damaged. It is unclear how this prediction is instantiated in their model and what it implies about the organization of distinctive features for artefactual concepts.

Challenges to the Theories

One important problem is that the original results of Gonnerman et al. (1997) with dementia patients have not been replicated. Garrard, Patterson, Watson, and Hodges (1998) examined naming and comprehension performance in a group of patients with probable Alzheimer's disease and investigated whether or not severity of the disease related to performance with different categories of knowledge. Garrard et al. (1998) failed to find a relationship between disease stage and the direction of the category-specific dissociation. In general, their patients as a whole showed a deficit to living things, regardless of the degree of the severity of the disease.

Equally important, the models have difficulty accounting for two well-established patterns of performance. First, the model(s) cannot account for selective deficits to narrowly defined categories; for example, how would diffuse damage result in a deficit only to animals (e.g., Caramazza & Shelton, 1998; Hart & Gordon, 1992; Hillis & Caramazza, 1991) or only to fruits and vegetables (e.g., Farah & Wallace, 1992; Hart, Bendt, & Caramazza, 1985) or only to body parts (e.g., Goodglass et al., 1966; Semenza & Goodglass, 1985; see also Shelton et al., 1998). The assumptions about the number and degree of intercorrelated properties is relevant to all *living things*, which includes animals, plant life, fruits, and vegetables. Second, a potentially more serious problem concerns the idea of severity level and how it relates to the type of category-specific deficit that will emerge. The two patients reported by Hillis and Caramazza (1991) described earlier have similar levels of performance and yet show complementary deficits to living and nonliving categories (see Table 17.6). For example, at 13 months post-onset, JJ was impaired in naming nonliving objects (69% correct) as compared to animals (100% correct) whereas PS was impaired in naming animals (62% correct) as compared to nonliving objects (92% correct). Note the comparable levels of performance for the impaired category. These patients demonstrate quite clearly that severity level is not related to the nature of the category-specific deficit, as would be predicted by the Devlin et al. and Moss et al. models of semantic memory.

The Organized Unitary Content Hypothesis

Another model of semantic memory that relies on intercorrelated features (but has not been simulated) is the Organized Unitary Content Hypothesis (OUCH; Caramazza, Hillis, Rapp, & Romani, 1990; Caramazza, Hillis, Leek, & Miozzo, 1994). This model makes two assumptions: 1) members of a semantic category tend to share attributes (e.g., animals breathe; they are

Table 17.6

Similar Accuracy Levels in Patients with Contrasting Category-Specific Deficits
(Percentage Correct)

Hillis & Caramazza, 1991: Patients JJ and PS

	n	Oral Naming	Written Naming	Auditory Comp.	Visual Comp.
JJ					
animals	46	91.3	70.0	91.3	97.8
inanimate	98	20.4	15.3	60.2	42.9
PS					
animals	46	39.1	34.8	93.5	89.1
vegetables	12	25.0	33.3	91.7	83.3
inanimate	86	89.5	76.7	100.0	83.7

Note. Levels of performance at 6 months post-onset.

made of certain kinds of substances, etc.), and 2) core semantic properties of an object tend to be highly intercorrelated (e.g., objects that breathe also tend to be made of certain kinds of stuff). An implication of these assumptions is that semantic space will be "lumpy" in the sense that members of semantic categories will cluster closely together in feature space. For example, a horse has a mouth, which is related to its ability to eat, move, and breathe, or a chair has a flat surface for sitting, which is related to it's material (e.g., wood), inertness, and inability for self-initiated motion. Category-specific deficits result from brain damage to a lumpy region of semantic space. Thus, for example, damage to a region of the brain that represents the highly intercorrelated features shared by living things would result in a category-specific deficit for living things.[7]

Unlike the models reviewed above, OUCH naturally accounts for the finer-grained distinctions within the categories of living things (e.g., impairment only to animals). This is because the model assumes that the "lumpiness" in semantic space directly reflects the shared properties of category members and therefore we expect that animals will cluster closely together and separately from fruits and vegetables, say. However, a weakness of the model is that it is too unconstrained—any tightly correlated set of features is a candidate for a category-specific deficit. Furthermore, as it stands, it is not clear which semantic categories are sufficiently compactly represented to allow for selective damage (see Caramazza & Shelton, 1998, for further discussion).

Conclusions

The intercorrelated features models of Devlin et al. (1998) and Moss et al. (1998) are based on the established empirical fact that many more features are correlated to a stronger degree within the categories of living things. These models can capture the distinction between the broad categories of living and nonliving things and thus, explain reports of patients who demonstrate better performance with nonliving things as compared to living things (and the opposite dissociation). However, neither model can readily capture the finer-grained dissociations which have been demonstrated, nor can they explain the fact that types of semantic category-specific deficits do not depend on severity level. The OUCH model can in principle account for fine-grained categorical distinctions at all levels of severity, but is currently too unconstrained.

IS SEMANTIC KNOWLEDGE ORGANIZED BY NATURAL DOMAINS?

The idea that the organization of knowledge in the brain honors some natural categorical distinctions has been rejected outright (but see Laiacona, Barbarotto, & Capitani, 1993; Warrington, 1981). Instead, as reviewed above, most researchers have sought alternative explanations for category-specific knowledge deficits that reduce the distinctions among categories to the differences in underlying representations or the type of knowledge important for each category.

The Domain-Specific Knowledge Hypothesis

Recently, we have reviewed the literature and presented 2 case studies that motivated us to propose a "categorical" organization of evolutionarily important knowledge—the domain-specific knowledge hypothesis (Caramazza, 1998; Caramazza & Shelton, 1998; Shelton & Caramazza, 1999; Shelton et al., 1998). According to this hypothesis, knowledge is organized into broad

---

[7]The difference between this model and the Moss et al. (1998) and Devlin et al. (1998) models is that OUCH does not make assumptions regarding the nature of the features important for living or nonliving categories. That is, the other models assume that the categorical deficits (at the broad level of living-nonliving) emerge due to the featural properties important to the items within those categories.

domains (categories) reflecting evolutionarily salient distinctions in semantic knowledge; thus, we propose that there are specialized neural mechanisms for recognizing and understanding certain categories of knowledge. The assumption is that the categories of animals, plant life, and conspecifics are important for survival. Animals are predators and prey, plant life provides food and medicine, and the recognition of conspecifics is important for physical and social needs.

This proposal was made as a way to account for the highly selective categorical deficits that have been reported. As mentioned earlier, patients have been reported to have selective deficits/sparing to just animals (e.g., Caramazza & Shelton, 1998; Hillis & Caramazza, 1991), to just fruits and vegetables (Farah & Wallace, 1992; Hart et al., 1983) or a selective deficit to vegetables in comparison to animals (Hillis & Caramazza, 1991). Many patients show deficits to body parts (e.g., Goodglass et al., 1966; Semenza & Goodglass, 1985) and there is recent evidence for the selective sparing of body part processing (Shelton et al., 1998). Our patient, IOC, was severely impaired at naming and showed mild-to-moderate comprehension problems, but what was striking about her performance was her preserved ability to process body parts (see Table 17.7). This result complements the previously reported cases of impairment to body parts (e.g., Semenza & Goodglass, 1985) and suggests that body parts can be a selectively impaired category of semantic knowledge.

Data from developmental studies also converge with the findings from neurological studies to suggest that the brain respects categorical knowledge distinctions. Infants make fundamental distinctions very early on between biological and nonbiological entities (e.g., Carey, 1995). For example, infants as young as three months old can distinguish between biological and nonbiological motion (Berenthal, 1993; Berenthal, Proffitt & Cutting, 1984). And, nine month old infants can correctly categorize animals and nonanimals even when items from different categories are more perceptually similar than items from the same categories (Mandler, 1994; Mandler, Bauer, & McDonough, 1991; Mandler & McDonough, 1993). Other evidence suggests that within the biological domain further distinctions should be made between animate and

Table 17.7

Naming and Comprehension of Body Parts in Shelton et al., 1998: Patient IOC

Picture Naming (from Snodgrass & Vanderwart set)

Category	Proportion Correct	Category	Proportion Correct
Body Parts	11/12 (.92)	Musical Instruments	0/9 (.0)
Animals	6/48 (.13)	Tools	1/12 (.08)
Appliances	5/14 (.36)	Vegetables	0/13 (.0)
Clothing	14/19 (.74)	Vehicles	1/10 (.10)
Fruit	4/11 (.36)	Other	22/98 (.22)
Furniture	3/14 (.21)		

Picture-Word Verification

Category	Proportion Correct	Category	Proportion Correct
Body Parts	11/12 (.92)	Musical Instruments	6/9 (.67)
Animals	30/48 (.63)	Tools	8/12 (.67)
Appliances	9/14 (.64)	Vegetables	10/13 (.77)
Clothing	15/19 (.79)	Vehicles	8/10 (.80)
Fruit	8/11 (.73)	Other	79/98 (.81)
Furniture	8/14 (.57)		

Note: Familiarity had a strong effect on IOC's performance but, for naming, category effects still emerged even after familiarity was controlled. For comprehension, category effects emerged on some tasks but not others after familiarity was controlled. Since comprehension was fairly good, these tasks may not have been sufficiently demanding to uncover a deficit to specific categories. Data from "The Selective Sparing of Body Part Knowledge: A Case Study," by J. R. Shelton, E. Fouch, & A. Caramazza, 1998, Neurocase, 4, pp. 343–345.

inanimate concepts. For example, research has demonstrated that the notion of self-propelled motion is important for the infant's concept of "human" (e.g., Mandler, 1992; Spelke, Phillips, & Woodward, 1995). That is, infants appreciate the distinction between self-initiated movement and movement caused by another object (e.g., Spelke et al., 1995).

The domain-specific hypothesis readily accounts for the established patterns of observed deficits and can accommodate the data from the developmental literature. The problem with this hypothesis is the lack of specificity regarding how knowledge within categories is represented. Although the hypothesis speaks to broad distinctions of domains in the brain, the representation and organization of that knowledge within the domains is unspecified. Thus, we can ask whether or not further structure exists within, for example, the biological domain. Since it has been established that plant life and animals can be damaged independently of each other, we know there must be further differentiation within the biological domain.

We make the distinction between animals and plant life and artefacts as a means of accounting for the highly selective deficits shown by some patients, deficits that do not respect the broad distinction living/nonliving things. We have hypothesized that there may have been important survival reasons in the evolution of humans for the brain to honor distinctions among these categories, specifically respecting distinctions between the animal and plant life categories. Although items in both categories are living, there are few other shared features between the two. The ability to recognize and identify those things that are capable of attacking and killing (animals) versus those things that are not (plants) would be important for survival. Further, identifying a dangerous (poisonous) plant would rely on highly specific features that are quite different from those features involved in identifying a dangerous animal. Although these two categories both represent living items, there is little other similarity between the two. Thus, there is no reason to suppose that brain damage would necessarily affect both categories of living things.

When we initially proposed the domain-specific knowledge hypothesis, we treated the artefacts category as the default category for nonbiological concepts. But, there may be certain domains of nonbiological knowledge that have crucial dimensions that may have led to the development of neural areas dedicated to processing these domains. For example, in several papers we have suggested that "tools" may form an evolutionarily important category (Caramazza & Shelton, 1998; Shelton & Caramazza, 1999), a position that has recently been discussed by Hauser (1997) in relation to nonhuman primate data. It is not inconceivable that the ability to use tools may have conferred a distinct survival advantage that could have led to specialized mechanisms for the recognition and use of such objects. Thus, some artefactual categories may have evolved into separate domains, implying that these categories of items could dissociate from other categories following brain damage.

But other than outlining the reasons for the broad distinctions between animals, plants, and artefacts (and perhaps tools), the domain-specific knowledge hypothesis provides little detail about the nature of the representation of information within categories. That is, why do the objects in each of these categories cluster together? What is the nature of the knowledge representation such that animals, for example, form a category that differs from plants? We hypothesize that a featural hypothesis, such as OUCH, could provide the framework for understanding how information is represented within categories. This hypothesis states that items within categories share many properties and that core properties tend to be intercorrelated. So, animals tend to share many properties (e.g., related to movement, digestion, number of legs, eyes, mouth, ferocity, etc.) that are intercorrelated (e.g., mouth implies ingestion) and these properties are not likely to be shared with plants (e.g., plants have few of the above properties which are central to our understanding of animals).[8] Therefore, the featural proper-

---

[8]Note that the lack of similarity between the features shared between animals and plants is a different assumption than that made by the Moss et al. (1998) and Devlin et al. (1998) theories, which assume all living things have many shared, intercorrelated features.

ties for defining animals and plants are quite different, a difference that is captured at a broad level by assuming domain-specificity and at a more specific level by assuming that members of a given domain share certain properties important for defining most members of that category.

In light of the above considerations it could be assumed that same category items are represented in close neural areas dedicated to processing items within a specific category, represented by features important for the definition of those items (and perhaps the category itself). This does not imply, however, that specific features are represented redundantly between categories. For example, the feature "move" could be represented in the animal category but could also be represented in other categories such as plants or vehicles. However, the meaning of "move" is very different for each category and would not be expected to be represented by a single feature "move." There might be exceptions to this, but we suggest that there is very little redundancy in the features represented between categories.

Conclusions

The domain-specific knowledge hypothesis provides a natural way of accounting for the dissociations in processing observed in patients demonstrating category-specific semantic deficits. Data from developmental studies also provide support for the notion that there may be neural mechanisms dedicated to processing specific classes of objects corresponding to the broad domains of biological and nonbiological concepts. Further distinctions may be found within these categories, such as plants, animals, body parts, and perhaps tools. There are likely to be multiple levels of organization of semantic knowledge and this hypothesis is one way in which to conceptualize the organization of semantic knowledge at a broad level.

NEUROANATOMICAL CONSIDERATIONS: ARE CERTAIN BRAIN AREAS DEDICATED TO PROCESSING SPECIFIC CATEGORIES OF KNOWLEDGE?

When examining lesion sites reported for cases with category-specific knowledge deficits, the clearest picture comes from those patients showing selective deficits to living things (see Gainotti et al., 1995, and Saffran & Schwartz, 1994, for reviews). Most patients with deficits to living things have sustained damage to the left temporal lobe and in some cases to the right temporal lobe as well although some have been reported to have only right temporal lobe damage (Barbarotto et al., 1995; Laws et al., 1995). Furthermore, some cases with a deficit to living things have sustained damage to the frontal and inferior parietal areas (Caramazza & Shelton, 1998; Hillis & Caramazza, 1991; Laicona et al., 1993) while other cases have sustained widespread damage due to traumatic brain injuries (e.g., Farah et al., 1989; Laiacona et al., 1993; Samson, Pillon, & De Wilde, 1998).

There is even less agreement when we examine lesion sites reported for cases with selective deficits to artefacts. Some cases have sustained damage to the left temporal lobe and basal ganglia (Hillis & Caramazza, 1991) or just the left temporal lobe (Cappa et al., 1998). Other cases have sustained damage to left frontal and parietal areas (Sacchett & Humphreys, 1992; Warrington & McCarthy, 1983; 1987).

Several neuroimaging studies (using PET) have examined normal understanding of living and nonliving things (Damasio, Grabowski, Tranel, Hichwa, & Damasio, 1996; Martin, Wiggs, Underleider, & Harvey, 1996; Perani et al., 1995) and shown different brain areas involved in processing the two categories. All the studies found activation in the inferior temporal lobe for processing living things/animals, either bilaterally (Perani et al., 1995) or in the left hemisphere only (Damasio et al., 1996; Martin et al., 1996). Both Martin et al. and Perani et al. also found activation bilaterally in the occipital lobes for processing of living things. There was little agreement among the studies in the activation of the brain areas involved in normal understanding of nonliving things. Damasio et al. found activation in the posterior middle and inferior temporal gyri; Martin et al. found activation in the fusiform gyri of the temporal lobes and left inferior frontal region; Perani et al. found activation in the lingual, parahippocampal gyri, middle occipital gyrus, and dorsolateral frontal regions.

Thus, some evidence suggests that there may be nonoverlapping areas of the brain that are important for processing different categories of items. The inferior areas of the temporal lobe appear to be especially important for processing living things and the posterior area of the temporal lobe and fronto-parietal areas appear more important for processing nonliving things.

CONCLUSIONS

We have examined three hypotheses regarding semantic knowledge organization: 1) the modality-specific semantic hypothesis, 2) the feature-intercorrelation hypothesis, and 3) the domain-specific knowledge hypothesis. At least as currently formulated, there is little support for the hypothesis of modality-specific semantics. Well-controlled studies of normal processing and patient performance have provided little support for a theory of semantics that divides knowledge into two broad categories of perceptual and nonperceptual knowledge. We have proposed that one aspect of the overall organization of semantic memory is the domain-specific knowledge hypothesis and that other principles of organization can exist within each of the domains. Further structure within each of the domains may be provided by other theories of knowledge organization, such as OUCH.

Acknowledgements

Preparation of this chapter was supported in part by NIH grant NS22201. We thank Brenda Rapp for her very helpful comments.

REFERENCES

Allport, D. A. (1985). Distributed memory, modular subsystems and dysphasia. In S. K. Newman & R. Epstein (Eds.), *Current perspectives in dysphasia* (pp. 207–244). Edinburgh: Churchill Livingstone.

Barbarotto, R., Capitani, E., Spinnler, H., & Trivelli, C. (1995). Slowly progressive semantic impairment with category specificity. *Neurocase, 1*, 107–119.

Basso, A., Capitani, E., & Laiacona, M. (1988). Progressive language impairment without dementia: A case with isolated category specific semantic defect. *Journal of Neurology, Neurosurgery, and Psychiatry, 51*, 1201–1207.

Berenthal, B. I. (1993). Infants' perception of biomechanical motions: Intrinsic image and knowledge-based constraints. In C. Granrud (Ed.), *Visual perception and cognition in infancy. Carnegie Mellow symposia on cognition,* (pp. 175–214. Hillsdale, NJ: Lawrence Erlbaum.

Berenthal, B. I., Proffitt, D. R., & Cutting, J. E. (1984). Infant sensitivity to figural coherence in biomechanical motions. *Journal of Experimental Child Psychology, 37,* 213–230.

Bunn, E. M., Tyler, L. K., & Moss, H. E. (1998). Categoryspecific semantic deficits: The role of familiarity and property type re-examined. *Neuropsychology, 12,* 367–379.

Capitani, E., Albanese, E., Barbarotto, R., & Laiacona, M. (1999). *Semantic category dissociation, familiarity, and gender.* Seventeenth European Workshop on Cognitive Neuropsychology, Bressenone, Italy.

Capitani, E., Laiacona, M., & Barbarotto, R. (1999). Gen-

der affects word retrieval of certain categories in semantic fluency tasks. *Cortex, 35,* 273–278.

Capitani, E., Laiacona, M., Barbarotto, R., & Trivelli, C. (1994). Living and nonliving categories: Is there a "normal" asymmetry? *Neuropsychologia, 32,* 1453–1463.

Cappa, S. F., Frugoni, M., Pasquali, P., Perani, D., & Zorat, F. (1985). Semantic activiation during recognition of referential words. *Neurocase, 4,* 391–397.

Caramazza, A. (1998). The interpretation of semantic category-specific deficits: What do they reveal about the organization of conceptual knowledge in the brain? *Neurocase, 4,* 265–272.

Caramazza, A., Hillis, A. E., Leek, E. C., & Miozzo, M. (1994). The organization of lexical knowledge in the brain: Evidence from category- and modality-specific deficits. In L. A. Hirschfeld & S. A. Gelman (Eds.), *Mapping the Mind: Domain specificity in cognition and culture* (pp. 68–84). New York: Cambridge University Press.

Caramazza, A., Hillis, A. E., Rapp, B., & Romani, C. (1990). Multiple semantics or multiple confusions? *Cognitive Neuropsychology, 7,* 161–190.

Caramazza, A., & Shelton, J.R. (1998). Domain specific knowledge systems in the brain: The animate-inanimate distinction. *Journal of Cognitive Neuroscience, 10,* 1–34.

Carey, S. (1995). On the origin of causal understanding. In D. Sperber, D. Premack, & A. J. Premack (Eds.), *Causal cognition: A multidisciplinary debate* (pp. 268–

302). New York: Oxford University Press.

Coltheart, M., Inglis, L., Cupples, L., Michie, P., Bates, A., & Budd, B. (1998). A semantic subsystem of visual attributes. *Neurocase, 4*, 353–370.

Damasio, H., Grabowski, T. J., Tranel, D., Hichwa, R. D., & Damasio, A. R. (1996). A neural basis for lexical retrieval. *Nature, 380*, 499–505.

De Renzi, E., & Lucchelli, F. (1994). Are semantic systems separately represented in the brain? The case of living category impairment. *Cortex, 30*, 3–25.

Devlin, J. T, Gonnerman, L. M., Andersen, E. S., & Seidenberg, M. S. (1998). Category-specific semantic deficits in focal and widespread brain damage: A computational account. *Journal of Cognitive Neuroscience, 10*, 77–94.

Durrant-Peatfield, M .R., Moss, H. E., & Tyler, L. K. (1998). *The distinctiveness of form and function in category structure: A connectionist model.* Meeting of the Cognitive Neuroscience Society, April, 1998.

Farah, M. J., & McClelland, J. L. (1991). A computational model of semantic memory impairment: Modality specificity and emergent category specificity. *Journal of Experimental Psychology: General, 120*, 339–357.

Farah, M. J., Hammond, K. M., Mehta, Z., & Ratcliff, G. (1989). Category-specificity and modality-specificity in semantic memory. *Neuropsychologia, 27*, 193–200.

Farah, M. J., Meyer, M. M., & McMullen, P. A. (1996). The living/nonliving dissociation is not an artefact: Giving an a priori implausible hypothesis a strong test. *Cognitive Neuropsychology, 13*, 137–154.

Farah, M. J., & Wallace, M. A. (1992). Semantically-bounded anomia: Implications for the neural implementation of naming. *Neuropsychologia, 30*, 609–621.

Flores d'Arcais, G. B., Schreuder, R., & Glazenborg, G. (1985). Semantic avtivation during recognition of referential words. *Psychological Research, 47*, 39–49.

Forde, E. M., & Humphreys, G. W. (1999). Category-specific recognition impairments: A review of important case studies and influential theories. *Aphasiology, 13*, 169–193.

Funnell, E., & Sheridan, J. S. (1992). Categories of knowledge? Unfamiliar aspects of living and nonliving things. *Cognitive Neuropsychology, 9*, 135–153.

Gaffan, D., & Heywood, C. A. (1993). A spurious category-specific visual agnosia for living things in normal humans and nonhuman primates. *Journal of Cognitive Neurosciences, 5*, 118–128.

Gainotti, G., & Silveri, M.C. (1996). Cognitive and anatomical locus of lesion in a patient with a category-specific semantic impairment for living beings. *Cognitive Neuropsychology, 13*, 357–389.

Gainotti, G., Silveri, M. C., Daniele, A., & Giustolisi, L. (1995). Neuroanatomical correlates of category-specific semantic disorders: A critical survey. In R. A. McCarthy (Ed.), *Semantic Knowledge and Semantic Representations. Memory, Vol. 3, Issues 3 & 4* (pp. 247–264). Hove, UK: Lawrence Erlbaum/Taylor & Francis.

Garrard, P., Patterson, K., Watson, P. C., & Hodges, J. R. (1998). Category specific semantic loss in dementia of Alzheimer's type: Functional-anatomical correlations from cross-sectional analyses. *Brain, 121*, 633–646.

Gonnerman, L. M., Andersen, E. S., Devlin, J. T., Kempler, D., & Seidenberg, M. S. (1997). Double dissociation of semantic categories in Alzheimer's disease. *Brain and Language, 57*, 254–279.

Goodglass, H., Klein, B., Carey, P., & Jones, K. (1966). Specific semantic word categories in aphasia. *Cortex, 2*, 74–89.

Hart, J., Berndt, R. S., & Caramazza, A. (1985). Category-specific naming deficit following cerebral infarction. *Nature, 316*, 439–440.

Hart, J., & Gordon, B. (1992). Neural subsystems for object knowledge. *Nature, 359*, 60–64.

Hauser, M. (1997). Artefactual kinds and functional design features: What a primate understands without language. *Cognition, 64*, 285–308.

Hillis, A. E., & Caramazza, A. (1991). Category-specific naming and comprehension impairment: A double dissociation. *Brain, 114*, 2081–2094.

Kurbat, M. A. (1997). Can the recognition of living things really be selectively impaired? *Neuropsychologia, 35*, 813–827.

Laiacona, M., Barbarotto, R., & Capitani, E. (1993). Perceptual and associative knowledge in category specific impairment of semantic memory: A study of two cases. *Cortex, 29*, 727–740.

Laiacona, M., Barbarotto, R., & Capitani, E. (1998). Semantic category dissociations in naming: Is there a gender effect in Alzheimer's disease? *Neuropsychologia, 36*, 407–419.

Laiacona, M., Capitani, E., & Barbarotto, R. (1997). Semantic category dissociations: A longitudinal study of two cases. *Cortex, 33*, 441–461.

Lambon-Ralph, M. A., Howard, D., Nightingale, G., & Ellis, A. (1998). Are living and nonliving category-specific deficits causally linked to impaired perceptual or associative knowledge? Evidence from a category-specific double dissociation. *Neurocase, 4*, 311–338.

Laws, K. R., Evans, J. J., Hodges, J. R., & McCarthy, R. A. (1995). Naming without knowing and appearance without awareness. Evidence for constructive processes in semantic memory? *Memory, 3*, 409–433.

Mandler, J. M. (1992). How to build a baby: II. Conceptual primitives. *Psychological Review, 99*(4), 587–604.

Mandler, J. M. (1994). Precursors of linguistic knowledge. *Philosophical transactions of the royal society of London, 346*, 63–69.

Mandler, J. M., Bauer, P. J., & McDonough, L. (1991). Separating the sheep from the goats. Differentiating global categories. *Cognitive Psychology, 23*, 263–298.

Mandler, J. M., & McDonough, L. (1993). Concept formation in infancy. *Cognitive Development, 8*, 291–318.

Malt, B. C., & Smith, E. E. (1984). Correlated features in natural categories. *Journal of Verbal Learning and Verbal Behavior, 23*, 250–269.

Martin, A., Wiggs, C. L., Ungerleider, L. G., & Haxby, J. V. (1996). Neural correlates of category-specific knowledge. *Nature, 379*, 649–652.

McRae, K., de Sa, V. R., & Seidenberg, M. S. (1997). On the nature and scope of featural representations for word meaning. *Journal of Experimental Psychology: General, 126*, 99–130

Moss, H. E., Tyler, L. K., Durrant-Peatfield, M., & Bunn, E. M. (1998). Two eyes of a see-through: Impaired and intact semantic knowledge in a case of selective deficit for living things. *Neurocase, 4*, 291–310.

Pecher, D., Zeelenberg, R., & Raajmakers, J. G. W. (1998). Does pizza prime coin? Perceptual priming in lexcal decision and pronunciation. *Journal of Memory and Language, 38*, 401–418.

Perani, D., Cappa, S. F., Bettinardi, V., Bressi, S., Gorno-Tempini, M., Matarrese, M., & Fazio, F. (1995). Different neural systems for the recognition of animals and man-made tools. *NeuroReport, 6,* 1637-1641.

Sacchett, C., & Humphreys, G. W. (1992). Calling a squirrel a squirrel but a canoe a wigwam: A category-specific deficit for artefactual objects and body parts. *Cognitive Neuropsychology, 9,* 73-86.

Saffran, E. M., & Schwartz, M. F. (1994). Of cabbages and things: Semantic memory from a neuropsychological perspective—A tutorial review. In C. Umilta & M. Moscovitch (Eds.), *Attention and performance 15: Conscious and nonconscious information processing* (pp. 507-536). Cambridge, MA: MIT Press.

Samson, D., Pillon, A., & De Wilde, V. (1998). Impaired knowledge of visual and nonvisual attributes in a patient with a semantic impairment for living entities: A case of a true category-specific deficit. *Neurocase, 4,* 273-290.

Sartori, S., & Job, R. (1988). The oyster with four legs: A neuropsychological study on the Interaction of visual and semantic information. *Cognitive Neuropsychology, 5,* 105-132.

Schreuder, R., Flores d'Arcais, G. B., & Glazenburg, G. (1984). Effects of perceptual and conceptual similarity in semantic priming. *Psychological Research, 45,* 339-354.

Semenza, C., & Goodglass, H. (1985). Localization of body parts in brain injured subjects. *Neuropsychologia, 23,* 161-175.

Sheridan, J., & Humphreys, G. W. (1993). A verbal-semantic category-specific recognition impairment. *Cognitive Neuropsychology, 10,* 143-184.

Shelton, J. R., & Caramazza, A. (1999). Deficits in lexical and semantic processing: Implications for models of normal language processing. *Psychonomic Bulletin & Review, 6,* 5-27.

Shelton, J .R., Fouch, E., & Caramazza, A. (1998). The selective sparing of body part knowledge: A case study. *Neurocase, 4,* 339-351.

Silveri, M. C., & Gainotti, G. (1988). Interaction between vision and language in category-specific impairment. *Cognitive Neuropsychology, 5,* 677-709.

Snodgrass, J. G., & Vanderwart, M. (1980). A standardized set of 260 pictures: Norms for name agreement, familiarity, and visual complexity. *Journal of Experimental Psychology: Human Learning and Memory, 6,* 174-215.

Stewart, F., Parkin, A. J., & Hunkin, N. M. (1992). Naming impairments following recovery from Herpes Simplex Encephalitis: Category-specific? *Quarterly Journal of Experimental Psychology, 44A,* 261-284.

Tulving, E. (1985). How many memory systems are there? *American Psychologist, 40,* 385-398.

Warrington, E. K. (1981). Concrete word dyslexia. *British Journal of Psychology, 72,* 175-196.

Warrington, E. K., & McCarthy, R. (1983). Category specific access dysphasia. *Brain, 106,* 859-878.

Warrington, E. K., & McCarthy, R. (1987). Categories of knowledge: Further fractionation and an attempted integration. *Brain, 100,* 1273-1296.

Warrington E. K. & Shallice, T. (1984). Category-specific semantic impairments. *Brain, 107,* 829-853.

18

Memory Distortion

Chad S. Dodson
Daniel L. Schacter

INTRODUCTION

In a 1992 op-ed piece for the New York Times, Garry Trudeau recollected some of his experiences related to the draft for the Vietnam War. Trudeau remembered receiving calls of concern from friends and family on the night of the draft lottery, after they had heard about his low number. He then recalled a series of events involving his attempts to gain a draft deferment: requesting a national security deferment from the draft board for his work with a magazine; deciding not to apply for conscientious objector status because he could imagine circumstances in which he would take another's life; preparing for his interview with the draft board by receiving a "memorable haircut"; and finally, gaining a medical deferment from the board after sending them, upon his physician father's advice, X-rays revealing a past ulcer. This recollection, he reported, remained unchanged for 20 years.

However, after talking to others and examining the records of his draft correspondence, Trudeau uncovered some notable discrepancies between his recollection and what actually happened. No family member or friend remembers making a call of concern. Trudeau now believes he imagined their concerns, because the act of examining this recollection led him to remember that he was in fact out having a few beers that night. He discovered that he actually applied for an occupational deferment and, upon reflection, wonders how he could have believed that working for a "glorified travel magazine" was justification for a national security deferment. He also never received a "memorable haircut," and the actual reason he did not apply for conscientious objector status, was, in part because of the prohibitive paperwork.

Trudeau's misrecollection of his past is unsettling, but far from uncommon. As Marcia Johnson has asked: "To what extent is the life we remember, the knowledge and expectations we have, and the self we seem to ourselves to be, a product of experience and to what extent a product of our imagination?" (Johnson, 1985, p. 2). The answer to this question depends on understanding the properties of our memory systems that contribute to both distorted and veridical memories.

Cognitive psychologists have long focused on memory distortion, and have produced numerous findings and ideas that have increased our understanding of why memory is sometimes inaccurate (for reviews, see Johnson, Hashtroudi, & Lindsay, 1993; Roediger, 1996; Schacter, 1995, 1999b). Cognitive neuropsychologists, by contrast, have traditionally shown less interest in questions concerning accuracy and distortion in memory, focusing instead on such issues as multiple forms of memory (e.g., Gabrieli, 1998; Schacter & Tulving, 1994; Squire, 1992) and the nature of encoding and retrieval deficits in amnesic patients (e.g., Mayes & Downes, 1997). Although studies of such striking clinical phenomena as confabulation have long been of interest to cognitive neuropsychologists (for review and discussion, see Burgess & Shallice, 1996; Johnson, 1991; Moscovitch, 1995), there have been relatively few systematic experimental or theoretical attempts to apply a cognitive neuropsychological approach to phenomena of memory distortion.

During the past few years, however, the situation has begun to change: a new line of research concerning the cognitive neuropsychology of memory accuracy and distortion has emerged (for a collection of relevant papers, see Schacter, 1999a). These newer studies have attempted to examine memory distortion in brain-damaged patients with a view toward obtaining insights into basic mechanisms of accuracy and distortion in memory.

In this chapter we consider research that has explored various aspects of the cognitive neuropsychology of memory distortion. To provide a conceptual context for this discussion, we first outline a general framework for understanding the processes that contribute to constructive memory phenomena. We then focus on a particular type of memory distortion, referred to as *false recognition*, and consider how this phenomenon is influenced by factors operating primarily at the encoding or retrieval stages of memory. This approach allows us to integrate findings from both cognitive studies and neuropsychological investigations of patients with brain damage.

A CONSTRUCTIVE MEMORY FRAMEWORK

Constructive memory phenomena are generally characterized by the acceptance of something occurring that did not occur, such as misrecollecting that John said something when in fact it was Tom (i.e., source confusion), or recognizing something as previously studied that is actually a new item (i.e., false recognition). Our view of constructive memory, which we refer to as the constructive memory framework (CMF; Schacter, Norman, & Koutstaal, 1998), draws on the ideas of several investigators, including Johnson et al. (1993), McClelland, McNaughton, and O'Reilly (1995), Moscovitch (1994), Norman and Schacter (1996), Reyna and Brainerd (1995), and Squire (1992), among others. This framework focuses on the important encoding and retrieval processes that contribute to both accurate and inaccurate memories.

When we encode an experience, such as talking with a friend in a café, the resulting memory representation will consist of a pattern of features constituting a record of the processes that were active during the experience. Some features, for instance, would represent the output of different sensory processes, such as the various sights, sounds, and smells in the café. Other features would reflect the output of conceptual processes, such as what we were thinking and feeling. This pattern of features is widely distributed across different parts of the brain, such that no single location contains a complete record of the trace or engram of a specific experience (Damasio, 1989; Squire, 1992). In short, the memory representation is this distributed pattern of features. Remembering this experience involves a process of reactivating the features making up the desired memory representation. Specifically, retrieval is a process of *pattern completion* (McClelland et al., 1995) in which a retrieval cue activates a subset of the features comprising a particular past experience, and activation spreads to the rest of the constituent features of that experience.

To produce largely accurate representations of past experiences, a memory system that operates in such a manner must solve several problems. At encoding, the features comprising an episode must be linked together to form a bound or "coherent" representation (i.e., *feature binding* process; see Johnson & Chalfonte, 1994; Moscovitch, 1994; Schacter, 1989). When the features of a memory are inadequately bound together because of factors like stress, distractibility, intoxication, and so forth, the individual may subsequently retrieve fragments of the memory without remembering how or when the fragments were acquired, a phenomenon known as *source memory failure* (Johnson et al, 1993; Schacter, Harbluk, & McLachlan, 1984, Squire, 1995). For instance, after inadequate feature binding a person might remember sitting in a café and not remember which friend she was talking to. Or conversely, she might remember the friend and not remember where she was talking. The binding process is the "glue" that holds the different features of the pattern or memory together. A closely related encoding process, sometimes referred to as *pattern separation* (McClelland et al., 1995), is required to keep bound episodes separate from one another. For instance, if an individual regularly meets a friend in a particular café then the memory representations for these different episodes will share many characteristics. The patterns comprising the separate memories of these episodes will overlap. If the patterns overlap extensively with one another, then the person may subsequently only recall the general similarities (Hintzman & Curran, 1994) or gist (Reyna & Brainerd, 1995) common to the many episodes. She may fail to recollect distinctive, item-specific information that distinguishes one episode from another, such as remembering what she was talking about with the friend on a particular day.

Similar kinds of problems arise when retrieving information from memory. Retrieval cues can potentially match stored representations other than the sought-after one (Nystrom & McClelland, 1992). For instance, if given the retrieval cue "having coffee with a friend" there could be countless memories that contain this characteristic and that would potentially be remembered. Thus, retrieval often involves a preliminary stage in which the rememberer forms a more refined description of the characteristics of the episode to be retrieved (Burgess & Shallice, 1996; Norman & Bobrow, 1979), referred to as a process of *focusing* (Norman & Schacter, 1996). Poor retrieval focus can lead to recollection of information that does not pertain to the target episode. It can also produce impaired recall of an episode's details when activated information from nontarget episodes interferes with recall of target information.

When we remember we complete a pattern that was initiated by the retrieval cue. What is remembered, however, is not simply an activated engram. The retrieved pattern of information is a product of the contributions of the retrieval cue and the stored memory representation. Once memorial information is successfully retrieved, a decision must be made about whether the activated information constitutes a veridical recollection of a previously experienced event, or whether it is a generic image, fantasy, or thought (Johnson & Raye, 1981). This phase of retrieval involves a *criterion setting* process: the rememberer needs to consider the diagnostic value of perceptual vividness, semantic detail, and other kinds of information for determining the origin of the retrieved pattern (Johnson et al., 1993). For instance, as Johnson and colleagues have emphasized lax criteria can contribute to source confusions, such as mistaking imagined ideas for actually perceived events. Occasionally, as in Gary Trudeau's recollection, exceptionally vivid false memories sail through this criterion phase.

Numerous brain regions are likely implicated in these and other aspects of memory. Two brain regions are especially relevant to constructive memory: the medial temporal area, including the hippocampal formation, and the prefrontal cortex. A widely shared view has begun to emerge regarding how the hippocampus implements feature binding and pattern separation (recently expressed by McClelland et al., 1995; see also Squire & Alvarez, 1995; Treves & Rolls, 1994). According to this view, distributed patterns of activity in the neocortex, constituting the memory representations for different episodes, are linked to sparse neuronal representations in region CA3 of the hippocampus, such that each episode is assigned its own hippocampal "index." To the extent that the hippocampus is able to assign nonoverlapping CA3 representations to different episodes, pattern separation is achieved and this will facilitate remembering distinctive characteristics about particular episodes. The medial temporal region also contributes to pattern completion at retrieval (cf. Moscovitch, 1994). According to McClelland et al. (1995), for instance, during retrieval of recent episodes (for which there is still a hippocampal index corresponding to the episode), cues activate the episode's index in region CA3 of the hippocampus, and activation spreads from the index to all the features comprising that episode. Once an episode has been consolidated in the neocortex, however, activation can spread directly between the episode's features, and the hippocampus no longer plays an important role in pattern completion.

Prefrontal cortex also plays a role in the retrieval of memories. Perhaps the strongest evidence comes from studies using neuroimaging techniques, which have consistently shown prefrontal activity during episodic retrieval, often in a right anterior frontal region (for reviews, see Buckner, 1996; Nyberg, Cabeza, & Tulving, 1996; Tulving, Markowitsch, Kapur, Habib, & Houle, 1994). Although the exact nature of the functions indexed by these activations remains open to debate, they appear to tap effortful aspects of retrieval (Schacter, Alpert, Savage, Rauch, & Albert, 1996a) related to focusing or entering the "retrieval mode" (Nyberg et al., 1995), postretrieval monitoring and criterion setting (Rugg, Fletcher, Frith, Frackowiak, & Dolan et al., 1996; Schacter, Buckner, Koutstaal, Dale, & Rosen, 1997), or both (Norman & Schacter, 1996).

In summary, CMF emphasizes encoding processes of feature binding and pattern separation, and retrieval processes of focusing, pattern completion, and criterion setting. Although problems with any of these processes can result in memory distortion, in this chapter we will mainly emphasize the encoding process of pattern separation and the retrieval processes of focusing and criterion setting. In addition, throughout this chapter we will refer to two broad categories of memorial information. The first is typically characterized as a *feeling of familiarity* that is based on some unidimensional variable resulting from the similarity of the familiar item to memory for other items (e.g., Gillund & Shiffrin, 1984; Hintzman, 1988; Humphreys, Bain, & Pike, 1989; Murdock, 1982), the frequency of prior exposure of the familiar item (e.g., Atkinson & Juola, 1974; Underwood, 1972), or the fluency of processing the recognized item (e.g. Jacoby & Dallas, 1981). The second, often referred to as *recollection*, is described as involving memory for more specific item information, such as multiple attributes of an event, a remembered event and the context in which it occurred, or an event and associated, elaborative information (e.g., Anderson & Bower, 1972, 1974; Gillund & Shiffrin, 1984; Humphreys, Bain & Pike, 1989; Mandler, 1980). As we will discuss, there is sometimes an opposition relationship between familiarity and memory for more specific item information (Jacoby, 1991), as when seemingly familiar items can be rejected when more specific information is remembered. However, as Trudeau's example illustrates, having a vivid recollection that is full of specific information, such as receiving a "memorable haircut," does not guarantee that the memory is accurate. Both recollection of specific information and more general familiarity can contribute to constructive memory phenomena (see Johnson et al., 1993).

MEMORY DISTORTION AND FALSE RECOGNITION

One of the most frequently studied types of memory distortion is known as false recognition, which occurs when people claim incorrectly to have previously encountered a novel word, object, face, or event (e.g., Underwood, 1965). False recognition can occur because preexisting knowledge influences memory for new information (e.g., Alba & Hasher, 1983). For example, Arkes and Freedman (1984) examined the memory of individuals who were either experts or novices with respect to their knowledge of baseball. After reading a story about a baseball game both groups completed a recognition test about what they had read. Although the experts showed more accurate memory for neutral sentences (e.g., "Bench moved up to second base.") than did the novices, there was a cost to their knowledge. The experts were more likely than novices to falsely recognize statements that were synonymous with sentences in the story. For instance, if the story contained the sentence, "The Cubs' first and third basemen crept in close expecting a sacrifice," the expert would be more likely than the novice to falsely recognize a distractor sentence in which "sacrifice" was replaced with the synonymous word "bunt" for this situation. Apparently, in the act of comprehension (i.e., encoding) people go beyond the information that is provided and use their background knowledge to build a representation of the situation. Because this representation is not just a reflection of the external world, there is the danger of including information that was not part of the actual event. In terms of the CMF, the "bound" representation of the story includes both features that were present in the text as well as features that were imported from the person's background knowledge. As we will discuss in a later section, the features that are retrieved depend, in part, on both the cues used to query memory and the criteria used to assess the remembered information.

Extremely high levels of false recognition have been demonstrated recently in experiments using a paradigm initially developed by Deese (1959), and revived and modified by Roediger and McDermott (1995; see also Read, 1996). In the Deese/Roediger-McDermott (DRM) paradigm, people study lists of words (e.g., one list might consist of the words TIRED, BED, AWAKE, REST, DREAM, NIGHT, BLANKET, DOZE, SLUMBER, SNORE, PILLOW, PEACE, YAWN, and DROWSY) that are related to a nonpresented lure word (e.g., SLEEP). On a subsequent old–new recognition test containing studied words (e.g., TIRED, DREAM), new unrelated words (e.g., BUTTER) and new related lure words (e.g., SLEEP), participants frequently judge that they previously studied the related lure words. In fact, the false recognition rate of the related lure words is so high that it is typically equivalent to the correct recognition rate of studied words (Dodson & Schacter, in press; Mather, Henkel, & Johnson, 1997; Norman & Schacter, 1997; Payne, Elie, Backwell, & Neuschatz, 1996; Roediger & McDermott, 1995; Schacter, Verfaellie, & Pradere, 1996).

The CMF offers some potential explanations of this false recognition effect. First, false recognition of the lure words is a product of pattern separation failure. Studying many related words may produce unacceptably high levels of overlap among the corresponding memory representations. This failure to keep representations separate will result in good memory for what the items have in common but poor memory for the unique aspects of each item. Because subjects will have difficulty recollecting the characteristics of the specific studied items they will be forced to respond on the basis of overall familiarity or similarity of the lure item to memory for the studied items. Therefore, subjects will be likely to respond that a lure item was studied before since it matches so many of the representations. Second, the high false recognition rates of the lure items may be a result of the process of "implicit associative responses" (Underwood, 1965). That is, when people study the related words (e.g., BED, TIRED, etc.) they may generate on their own the new lure word (i.e., SLEEP). On the subsequent memory test people may experience source confusion with the lure words and mistakenly believe that they saw this word when in fact it was one that they had generated (e.g., Johnson et al., 1993). Although these two accounts are difficult to distinguish with the DRM paradigm, Koutstaal and Schacter (1997) have provided data that are consistent with the pattern separation failure account. After studying large numbers of pictures from various categories (e.g., cars, shoes, and so forth), participants often falsely recognized new pictures from the same categories as studied pictures. Koutstaal and Schacter reasoned that it is highly improbable that participants had generated the new related pictures in the same way that they might generate the word "sleep" when studying associated words in the DRM procedure. Instead, falsely recognizing new pictures seems to be a result of the high similarity among target items, producing robust memory for what the related items have in common but poor memory for specific items.

FALSE RECOGNITION AND AMNESIA

As noted earlier, neuropsychological studies have only recently begun to examine systematically false recognition and related aspects of constructive memory (for a review see Schacter et al., 1998). In this section we focus on how studies of amnesic patients have contributed to our understanding of constructive memory. Patients with damage to the inner or medial regions of the temporal lobes and related structures in the diencephalon typically have difficulty remembering recent experiences, but they have normal perceptual and linguistic abilities along with IQ scores within the normal range (e.g., Parkin & Leng, 1993; Squire, 1992). Although much is known about amnesics' poor memory for events that actually occurred, little is known about amnesics' tendencies to experience false memories of events that did not occur.

To examine false recognition in amnesic patients, Schacter et al. (1996) used the DRM paradigm. Amnesics and control subjects studied lists of semantically related words (e.g., BED, TIRED, DREAM) and then completed a recognition test containing studied words (e.g., BED), new related words (e.g., SLEEP), and new unrelated words (e.g., POINT). Schacter et al. found that, as expected, amnesics recognized fewer studied items than did the matched controls. But amnesics also exhibited a lower false recognition rate of the related lure words than did the controls (see Melo, Winocur, and Moscovitch, 1999, for replication and extension). A follow-up experiment by Schacter, Verfaellie, and Anes (1997) demonstrated that amnesics' reduced false recognition of related lure items extends to perceptual materials. After studying perceptually related words (e.g., FADE, FAME, FACE, FAKE, MATE, HATE, LATE, DATE, and RATE) amnesics were less likely than controls both to correctly recognize studied words and falsely recognize perceptually related lure words (e.g., FATE). Apparently, for amnesics the same processes that support accurate recognition of studied words also contribute to the false recognition of critical lures.

In contrast to the preceding findings of reduced false recognition by amnesics in the DRM paradigm, an earlier study by Cermak, Butters, and Gerrein (1973) showed that amnesics produced *increased* levels of false recognition as compared to control subjects. In the Cermak et al. study, Korsakoff amnesics and alcoholic controls were presented a series of words and were instructed to indicate for each word whether or not they had seen it before in the list (i.e., a continuous recognition task). The key manipulation was that some of the new words were semantically or acoustically related to earlier words, such as initially seeing BEAR and then later seeing in the list the new lure word BARE. Cermak et al. found that amnesics were more likely than controls to falsely recognize the lure words (See Kroll, Knight, Metcalfe, Wolf, & Tulving, 1996, who also found that amnesics with either left or right hippocampal damage had higher than normal false recognition rates).

Why would amnesics have higher than normal false recognition rates in the Cermak et al. (1973) paradigm, but lower than normal false recognition in the DRM paradigm? In the Cermak et al. study, the number of items separating a word from its lure (i.e., the lag) may have been sufficiently small that control subjects recollected the initial study word when seeing the lure. For instance, when confronted with the new lure word BARE the control subjects may have recollected that they had earlier seen BEAR and, thus, concluded that although BARE is familiar it does not match the initially studied word. Amnesics, by contrast, are particularly deficient in reactivating earlier studied words (e.g., Johnson & Chalfonte, 1994). This deficiency may have prevented them from using recollection to counter the familiarity of the new lure word, and consequently, contributed to their higher than normal false recognition rate in the Cermak et al. paradigm.

By contrast, the amnesics' lower than normal false recognition rate in the DRM paradigm may have had less to do with recollective deficiencies and more to do with the processes that contribute to a related lure item's feeling of familiarity. Whereas in the Cermak et al. paradigm the new word (e.g., BARE) is related to a single studied word (e.g., BEAR), in the DRM paradigm the critical new word (e.g., SLEEP) is related to many studied words (e.g., BED, TIRED, etc.). A growing number of studies have shown that individuals with intact memory are more likely to falsely recognize a new item when they have earlier studied many rather than few items related to this new item (i.e., false recognition is directly related to category size) (e.g., Arndt & Hirshman, 1998; Koutstaal & Schacter, 1997; Robinson & Roediger, 1997; Shiffrin, Huber, & Marinelli, 1995). Thus, one contributor to the likelihood of falsely recognizing related lure items is the degree to which the lure item activates memory representations similar to it.

When normal controls are presented with a new lure word they may experience a strong sense of familiarity (or even feel that they can recollect earlier studying it) because this theme word activates the representations of so many earlier studied words. Amnesic patients, by contrast, encode or retain less information about the individual items on the list. In comparison to control subjects, amnesics are less likely to falsely recognize the theme word because it activates the representations of fewer associated words and/or they are activated less strongly.

In sum, different processes may contribute to the occurrence of false recognition in the continuous recognition task of the Cermak et al. (1973) study and in the DRM paradigm. The inability to recollect previously studied items likely contributed to amnesics' increased false recognition rate (relative to the control subjects) in the Cermak et al. study. But in the DRM paradigm, the amnesics' low false recognition rate is likely attributable to the reduced amount of activation (and therefore, familiarity) that is generated by the lure item. In this paradigm, since people are instructed to remember the studied words, the amnesics' inability to associate the related studied items, and construct an organized representation of the list may have diminished the activation generated by the lure items and therefore, produced the low false recognition rate. Subsequent experiments have further examined these processes in amnesics and controls by manipulating (a) the number of study/test repetitions in the DRM paradigm and (b) the number of studied items related to the lure item in a similar paradigm.

Schacter, Verfaellie, Anes, and Racine (1998) examined false recognition in the DRM paradigm by presenting amnesic patients (both Korsakoff and amnesics of mixed etiology) and matched controls with lists of associated words, testing their memory for the lists, and then repeating this study and test cycle with the same lists five times (i.e., five different trials). As seen in panels A and C of Figure 18.1, with repeated study and testing both amnesics and controls correctly recognized increasingly more studied words. False recognition rates to the related lure words are presented in panels B and D of Figure 18.1. As shown in these panels, control subjects falsely recognized fewer related lure words across the five study-test trials (see also McDermott, 1996). By contrast, the Korsakoff amnesic patients falsely recognized increasingly more related lure words with repeated study and testing (see panel B), whereas the mixed amnesic patients showed fluctuating levels of false recognition across trials (see panel D). With repeated study and testing, the controls presumably encoded more distinct features of the individual words on the lists. Put in terms of the CMF, the representations of the words overlapped less and less with repeated study and testing; there was more pattern separation. Greater pattern separation heightened the probability that the control subjects recollected the studied words, and thus increased the recognition rate for these words. In addition, with better pattern separation for the studied words these subjects were more likely to notice a difference between the studied words and the related lure word, resulting in a diminished false recognition rate across trials. For instance, after repeated study and testing control subjects may reject the related lure word SLEEP because they remember studying TIRED, DREAM, and PILLOW and so forth and they do not remember studying SLEEP. In short, with repetition of the study and test lists the healthy controls used their increasingly better memory for the studied words to reject the related lure words.

By contrast, the higher levels of false recognition across trials by the Korsakoff amnesics indicate that they were not able to use memory for the studied items to suppress false recognition responses of the lure words. Instead, repeated study and testing likely allowed the Korsakoff amnesics to form additional memory representations of the studied items (and enrich existing ones). But repetition did not increase the pattern separation amongst the memory representations; apparently, they still overlapped considerably. Consequently, the Korsakoff amnesics falsely recognized increasingly more lures with repeated study and testing because of the activation of increasingly more memory representations. And, importantly, these amnesics were not able to counteract the occurrence of false recognition by remembering specific item information since the memory representations of the studied items overlapped

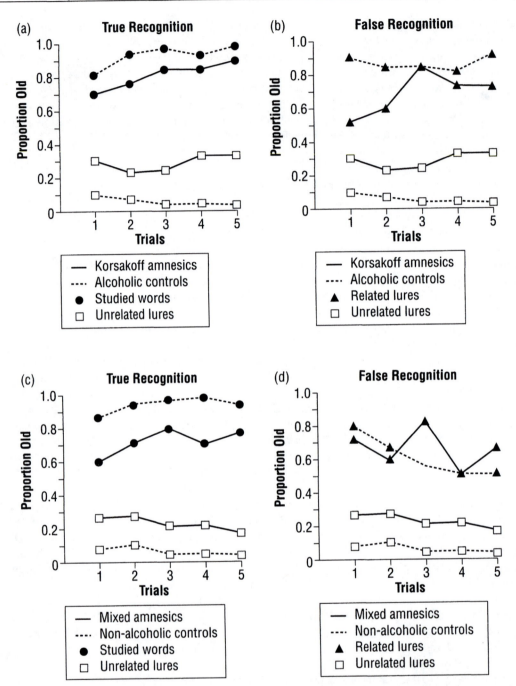

Figure 18.1: Proportions of old responses to studied words (panels A and C), related lures (panels B and D), and unrelated lures (panels A–D) in the two subgroups of amnesics (Korsakoff and mixed) and their respective control groups (alcoholic and nonalcoholic) as a function of study-test trial. Korsakoff and mixed amnesics showed similarly impaired true recognition. However, Korsakoff patients showed increasing false recognition across trials, whereas mixed amnesics showed a fluctuating pattern across trials.

too much (poor pattern separation) and they were too impoverished. In sum, these data highlight the importance in healthy individuals of recollecting detailed information for resisting the tendency to falsely recognize similar items.

In addition to recollecting item-specific information, occurrences of false recognition are affected by factors that influence the "false familiarity" of the related lure item. For instance, Koutstaal, Schacter, Verfaellie, Brenner, and Jackson (1999) examined the effect of varying the number of studied items (i.e., category size) on the false recognition rate of related lure items. In their experiment, control subjects and amnesics (both Korsakoff and mixed etiology) studied pictures of abstract objects. Each of the pictures belonged to a particular perceptual category and was similar to a prototype that defined the category. The categories varied in size and included either 1, 3, 6, or 9 pictures. All participants then completed a recognition test containing studied pictures and new pictures that were either related or unrelated to studied items. In line with previous studies using words, Koutstaal et al. found that for control subjects both true and false recognition of the abstract pictures increased with category size. In other words, healthy individuals were more likely both to correctly recognize previously studied pictures and to falsely recognize new pictures that were related to studied pictures from large categories (e.g., 6 or 9 pictures) than from small categories (e.g., 1 or 3 pictures). By contrast, the amnesics' true and false recognition rates were only slightly affected by the number of related pictures that were studied; category size had a minimal effect on true and false recognition.

One explanation of the above results involves processes that contribute to the activation of memory representations corresponding to studied items. For the control subjects, the false recognition rate of the related abstract pictures was proportional to the number of related studied pictures (as has been found for verbal materials by Arndt & Hirshman, 1998, and Shiffrin et al., 1995). This pattern indicates that when control subjects are presented with a related new item it will engender "false familiarity" to the degree that it activates the representations of earlier studied items. Amnesics, however, are likely to have formed degraded representations of the studied pictures so that a related new item will less strongly match and activate features of studied items. Thus, as Koutstaal et al. (1999) note, the differential build-up of familiarity in amnesics and controls appears to be a consequence of their differing abilities to encode or retain information about the studied items.

The foregoing studies illustrate two processes that affect the false recognition of related lure items. First, recollecting specific information about past events can counteract false recognition responses. As suggested by the Cermak et al. (1973) study, the amnesics' deficiency in remembering item-specific information contributed to their higher than normal false recognition rate. Thus, healthy individuals may become more vulnerable to distorted memories as they fail to recollect the discriminative features of past events (e.g., Riccio, Rabinowitz, & Axelrod, 1994). Second, occurrences of false recognition are influenced by variables, such as how many related items have been studied, that contribute to the "false familiarity" of related lure items. In short, memory distortion depends upon a dynamic interaction between processes contributing to familiarity and memory for item-specific information.

RETRIEVAL ORIENTATION, THE DISTINCTIVENESS HEURISTIC, AND FALSE RECOGNITION

Remembering is not simply a process of passively activating stored information. Instead, people's expectations, metamemorial beliefs, even how they are instructed to examine their memory, influence the kind and amount of information that is remembered (e.g., Dodson & Johnson, 1993, 1996; Dodson & Schacter, in press; Johnson et al., 1993; Lindsay & Johnson, 1989; Marsh & Hicks, 1998; Multhaup, 1995; Schacter, Israel, & Racine, 1999; Strack & Bless, 1994). Consider, for example, the effects of misleading postevent suggestions, studied extensively by Loftus and her colleagues (for a recent review, see Loftus, Feldman, & Dashiell, 1995).

In this paradigm, subjects view a sequence of slides depicting an event and then receive an ostensibly accurate written description of the previously seen material. However, the description contains misleading information, such as inaccurately characterizing an object presented earlier (e.g., a stop sign is referred to as a yield sign). On a final recognition test, subjects often respond on the basis of the misleading information, claiming to have seen items that were only read about. In essence, subjects confuse the origin of their memories, mistakenly reporting that the misinformation was seen in the slides. However, subjects are better able to distinguish between which objects were seen in the slides and which were only suggested when they are given a memory test that requires them to identify the source of each test item (i.e., was it seen, read, both seen and read, or new; Lindsay & Johnson, 1989; Zaragoza & Lane, 1994). Apparently, people may not always recognize the need to consider the source of their memory, and instead respond on the basis of overall familiarity. This bias to rely on familiarity unless oriented otherwise may stem from the fact that familiarity information seems to be retrieved faster and more automatically than is source information (e.g., Johnson, Kounios, & Reeder, 1994). In short, false recognition is partly attributable to the retrieval strategies that people use to query their memories of past events.

Retrieval strategies can be affected not only by the type of test but also by the metamemorial beliefs that people possess about what they feel they ought to remember about past events (Johnson & Raye, 1981). That is, according to the source monitoring framework of Johnson and colleagues people can flexibly weight different characteristics of a memory depending on the conditions of the test and/or their metamemorial beliefs. Consistent with this notion, we have shown that people can use a "distinctiveness heuristic" to suppress the large false recognition rate of lure words in the DRM false memory paradigm (Dodson & Schacter, in press; Israel & Schacter, 1997; Schacter et al., 1999). Recall that in the DRM paradigm participants initially study lists of words that are related to a nonpresented lure word. On a subsequent old-new recognition test, participants frequently judge the related lure words as having been studied before. However, as seen in Figure 18.2, Dodson and Schacter showed that saying the words aloud at study, as opposed to hearing them, reduces the false recognition rate of the related lure words. Notice that the correct recognition rate of studied words and the false recognition rate of unrelated new words are comparable between the Hear Words group and the Say Words group. This suggests that the reduced false recognition rate of the related words in the Say Words group is not a byproduct of better memory (e.g., better pattern separation) for the said words.

Figure 18.2: Proportions of old responses to studied words, related lures, and unrelated lures in the two groups of participants who encoded the words by either hearing them or saying them aloud.

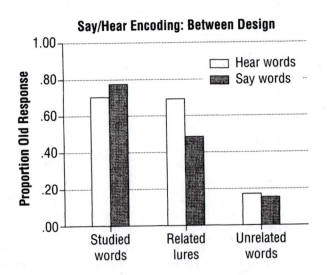

Building on earlier studies by Israel and Schacter (1997) and Schacter et al. (1999; see also, Rotello, 1999; Strack & Bless, 1994), Dodson and Schacter (in press) argued that rejecting related lure words after say-aloud encoding, as opposed to hear-encoding, stems from participants' metamemorial belief that they ought to remember this distinctive "say" information. These participants used a distinctiveness heuristic whereby they demanded access to say information as a basis for judging items as previously studied. In addition, when participants failed to recall this distinctive information they inferred that the test item is new. By contrast, participants who heard words at study would not expect to have detailed recollections about studied items and, thus, would not base recognition decisions on the presence or absence of memory for distinctive information. These results are consistent with earlier studies indicating that people exhibit a bias during the memory test that appears to be based on the expectation that said information is especially memorable (e.g., Conway & Gathercole, 1987; Foley, Johnson, & Raye, 1983; Johnson, Raye, Foley, & Foley, 1981; Hashtroudi, Johnson, & Chrosniak, 1989).

Dodson and Schacter confirmed the role of a distinctiveness heuristic in a follow-up experiment by constructing a situation in which it was difficult to use it. Following the logic of Schacter et al. (1999), they used a within-groups design in which everyone heard some lists of related words and said other lists of words during the study phase, instead of the between-groups design used in the previous experiment. As seen in Figure 18.3, there was no difference in the false recognition rate of lure words that were related to words that had been earlier said or heard. In this within-groups design, the distinctiveness heuristic is rendered ineffective because there is no longer a particular kind of information that is solely diagnostic of a test item's oldness or newness. Whereas in the prior experiment the absence of information about having said an item suggested that the item was new, this is not the case in the present experiment. Because some items were said and others were heard, failing to remember "say" information does not mean a test item is new; it may only mean the item was one that was heard.

It is important to ask whether a similarity account, instead of the distinctiveness heuristic, can explain the preceding results in Figures 18.2 and 18.3. A similarity account explains recognition decisions in terms of the overall similarity between a test item and memory for studied items (e.g., Gillund & Shiffrin, 1984; Hintzman, 1988). Test items that are sufficiently similar to studied items are judged "old" and those that are not are judged "new." By this view, the typically large false recognition rates of related lures in the DRM paradigm occurs because of their high similarity to studied items (Arndt & Hirshman, 1998). To explain the suppression

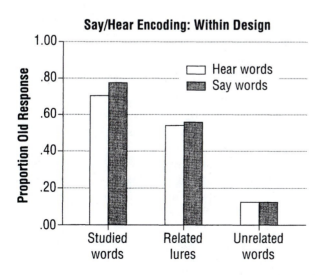

Figure 18.3: Proportions of old responses to studied words, related lures, and unrelated lures after participants heard some words and said other words during the encoding phase.

of the related lures in Figure 18.2, this similarity account would contend that say encoding is sufficiently different from hear encoding that the related lures are in some sense less similar to previously said words than to previously heard words. This dissimilarity between the related lures and memory leads to the successful rejection of the related lures after saying words aloud than after hearing words.

There are problems, however, with this explanation of our results. First, if say and hear encoding produce sufficiently different representations to account for the suppression of false memories in Figure 18.2, then this similarity explanation would predict differences in the recognition rates of spoken and heard words. This prediction was not supported by the data: in Figure 18.2, the said and heard words yielded nearly identical recognition rates for the studied words. Second, Figure 18.3 presents the data from the experiment using the within-groups design and provides further evidence against the similarity account. In this experiment, participants showed slightly higher recognition scores for spoken than for heard words. Nonetheless, there was no difference in the false recognition rate of false targets that were related to spoken and heard lists. Thus, the similarity account offers no ready explanation of these results. According to the distinctiveness heuristic account, in contrast, the absence of expected say information is diagnostic of a test item's nonoccurrence in the experiment depicted in Figure 18.2 but it is not diagnostic in the experiment depicted in Figure 18.3.

In summary, we have reviewed research that point to two different retrieval mechanisms for minimizing false memories. One mechanism involves the manner in which individuals are oriented to query their memory, with source tests generally leading to better performance than old–new recognition tests. The second mechanism involves strategies, such as the distinctiveness heuristic, for evaluating the retrieved information. The focusing mechanism of the CMF can account for the reductions in false recognition when subjects are given a source test instead of an old–new recognition test. This mechanism refers to the process by which subjects establish a description or characterization of the study episode which they then use to cue memory, such as searching memory for information that indicates that the test item was earlier seen or read. By this account, the source test is effective because it orients subjects to use retrieval cues, such as the query "is there memorial evidence that I saw this object earlier?" that are sufficiently detailed that they are likely to match some aspect of the sought-for trace, and importantly, not match aspects of competing traces. This increases the probability that the pattern completion process will retrieve the target memory. The distinctiveness heuristic, by contrast, operates on how the retrieved information is evaluated. This heuristic depends on the metamemorial knowledge about the kind of events that are likely to be remembered, such as having said something earlier. Based on this knowledge, people can make inferences that the absence of memory for this expected characteristic is diagnostic that this event did not actually occur, despite how familiar it may feel.

THE FRONTAL LOBES AND FALSE RECOGNITION

The frontal lobes comprise roughly one-third of the cerebral cortex and are associated with a wide range of behaviors (Fuster, 1989; Goldman-Rakic, 1987). Patients with frontal lobe damage are characterized by disorders involving motor control, personality, language, problem solving, or memory (e.g., Luria, 1966; Schacter, 1987; Shimamura, 1995). Patients with frontal lobe damage have shown difficulty remembering (a) the source of previously learned facts (Janowsky, Shimamura, & Squire, 1989a), (b) reconstructing the order of a recently studied list of words (Shimamura, Janowsky, & Squire, 1990), (c) determining the relative recency of items (e.g., Milner, Corsi, & Leonard, 1991), and (d) recollecting whether a word was earlier spoken by a male or a female (Johnson, O'Connor, & Cantor, 1997). A number of recent studies have described patients with frontal lobe damage who have abnormally high false recognition rates (e.g., Curran, Schacter, Norman, & Galluccio, 1997; Delbecq-Derouesné, Beauvois, & Shallice,

1990; Rapscak, Reminger, Glisky, Kasniak, & Comer, 1999; Schacter, Curran, Galluccio, Milberg, & Bates, 1996a; Ward et al., 1999).

Schacter, Curran, and colleagues described a patient, BG, with right frontal damage who shows no signs of amnesia, does not spontaneously confabulate, and is generally alert, attentive and cooperative (Curran et al., 1997; Schacter, Curran, et al., 1996). BG, however, is prone to extremely high rates of false recognition. For example, on a memory test of earlier studied unrelated words, BG recognized studied words at a comparable rate to normal control subjects. But BG was much more likely than controls to respond that new test words had also been studied; BG falsely recognized 50% of the new words whereas the controls incorrectly claimed that 17% of the new words were studied (Schacter, Curran, et al., 1996). BG exhibits abnormal false recognition to a wide variety of stimuli, including words, sounds, and pictures, although he tends to have greater difficulty with nonverbal stimuli, such as faces, than with verbal stimuli (Schacter, Curran, et al., 1996). BG is especially likely to falsely recognize new items that are related to studied items, such as claiming to remember seeing the new word "cellar" on the study list when he had studied "basement." Building on this observation, in a follow-up experiment BG and control subjects studied pictures of inanimate objects and then completed a memory test in which the distractors were either related or unrelated to studied items. Some distractors were similar to the studied pictures in that both were from the same semantic category, such as pictures of tools or toys. Other distractors were taken from a semantic category that had not been studied, such as a picture of an animal (Schacter, Curran, 1996b). As in the prior studies, BG recognized the studied items at a comparable rate to controls and showed an abnormally high false recognition rate for related distractors. By contrast, BG almost never falsely recognized distractors that were from a different semantic category.

Schacter, Curran, et al. (1996) proposed that BG uses inappropriate decision criteria during the test. In terms of the CMF, his pathological false recognition rate stems from an excessive reliance on information about the general correspondence between a test item and earlier studied words. Responding on the basis of overall similarity led BG to exhibit very high false recognition rates to similar distractors, but not to dissimilar distractors. Alternatively, it is possible that BG fails to encode specific features of items at study so that he is forced to rely on overall similarity. That is, the memory representations of the items do not include enough item-specific information so that at test they can be identified on the basis of this specific information. Moreover, encoding items in a vague manner would result in feelings of familiarity for features that are common to many items, including both studied and new lure items that contain these features (see Curran et al., 1997).

Rapcsak et al. (1999) discussed two patients with frontal lobe damage who are also prone to falsely recognizing items. JS sustained bilateral damage to the basal forebrain/septal area and the ventromedial frontal region; BW is characterized by widespread damage to the right frontal lobe. Like BG, both patients exhibit pathologically high false recognition rates and are able to sharply attenuate their false recognition rates when presented with new items that are substantially different from studied items. For example, after studying a series of unfamiliar faces of white males both frontal patients and control subjects completed a recognition test containing the studied faces as well as similar distractor faces (i.e., other white males) and dissimilar distractor faces (i.e., white females and nonwhite males). The frontal patients showed comparable recognition rates of the studied faces as the control subjects (94% vs. 81%, respectively), and overall, the frontal patients showed much higher false recognition rates to the distractors (averaged across both kinds) than did the controls (42% vs. 11%). Both frontal patients and controls, however, made many more false alarms to the similar distractors than to the dissimilar distractors. Rapcsak et al. suggest that the frontal patients rely on the overall familiarity of the test item as a basis for judging items "old" whereas the control subjects may rely on memory for additional item-specific information.

Subsequent experiments by Rapcsak et al. (1991) further examined the retrieval processes in patients JS and BW. Healthy controls and these two patients were given a famous faces test in which a series of famous faces (e.g., politicians, entertainers, etc.) were intermingled with nonfamous faces and subjects were instructed to respond "yes" when the face was that of a famous person, and "no" when it was not. This test probes memory for information that was learned long before the patient had brain damage and, thus, specifically taps processes operating during retrieval. The frontal patients and control subjects identified comparable numbers of faces that were actually famous (94% vs. 85%, respectively). However, JS and BW showed a much greater tendency to respond that the nonfamous faces were also famous (52%) than did the controls (6%). In a follow-up experiment the same famous faces were intermixed with a new set of unfamiliar faces and all subjects were instructed to base fame judgments solely on whether or not they could remember the name and occupation of the person. With these instructions, the false recognition rates of the nonfamous faces dropped down to normal levels for the frontal patients (i.e., 6% false alarm rate for frontal patients and 1% for controls). Hit rates to the famous faces were also no different for the frontal patients and control subjects. The finding that instructions greatly improved the frontal patients' performance is in line with the results of group studies of patients with prefrontal cortex damage (Gershberg & Shimamura, 1995; Hirst & Volpe, 1988). For instance, Hirst and Volpe found that when studying categorized lists of words, frontal patients seemed unaware of the strategy of learning words by grouping them together according to category; subsequently, they recalled fewer of these words than did control subjects. However, when this mnemonic strategy was pointed out to them the frontal patients recalled just as many words as the control subjects did.

The foregoing studies indicate that frontal damage can result in a bias to rely on overall familiarity or similarity as a basis for a response unless patients are directly instructed to make judgments contingent on retrieving more specific information. In terms of the CMF, problems generating a focused description of the study episode can account for the pattern of false recognition of BG and of the frontal patients of Rapcsak et al. (1991; see Curran et al., 1997, Norman & Schacter, 1996, and Schacter, Curran, et al., 1996 for further discussion of BG's memory deficit). That is, one basis for judging an item as "old" is noting a match between the search description and the retrieved information. In the previous studies, the frontal patients may generate a search description that is extremely vague, such as whether or not the test item is a member of one of the studied categories of items. This vague description is sufficient for correctly rejecting distractors that are from nonstudied categories, but it does not exclude similar distractors from studied categories. In the Rapcsak et al. study, the instructions to base fame judgments on the retrieval of specific information about the person has the effect of focusing or refining the search description. Apparently, when they are instructed to do so these frontal patients are capable of focusing their search description and relying on more specific information since they performed as well as the control subjects in this condition.

Whereas the performance of BW and JS indicate that their faulty focusing is due to processes at retrieval, Parkin, Ward, Bindschaedler, Squires, and Powell (1999) suggest that processes at encoding can also result in an unfocused retrieval description. They present a patient, JB, who suffered a ruptured anterior communication artery (ACoA) aneurysm that damaged his left frontal cortex and left caudate. JB, like the previous case studies, has an abnormally high false-recognition rate. But, in contrast to these other patients, JB's false-recognition rate is unaffected when he is presented with new items that are either similar to or substantially different from studied items. However, JB does benefit from encoding manipulations. His false recognition rate drops dramatically after he has encoded items in a manner that focuses on the meaning of the item than after receiving no encoding orientation. Parkin et al. (1999) suggest that JB spontaneously encodes events in such a superficial and impoverished manner that during the test he does not have the appropriate specific information available that would allow for a more focused description. For instance, if JB does not register at encoding that the studied items were from particular taxonomic categories then this information will be of little help during the test. In short, whereas BW and JS fail to construct focused retrieval descriptions unless they are instructed to do so, JB is incapable of constructing a focused description because he does not spontaneously encode the necessary item-specific information.

Finally, an additional characteristic of patients with high false recognition rates is that their problems are sometimes specific to particular materials. For instance, Rapcsak et al. (1999) discovered that BW's pathological false recognition rate does not occur with verbal materials but rather appears to be specific to visual information. BW, JS, and normal controls were given various kinds of verbal materials to study, such as animal names, unrelated nouns, and pronounceable nonwords (e.g., FRONGE). On a later recognition test, everyone correctly recognized studied items at nearly identical rates. False recognition rates, however, were dramatically different among these individuals: JS incorrectly claimed that 50% of the new words had been studied, whereas BW and the control subjects falsely recognized only 2% and 9% of the new words, respectively.

Although material-specific deficits tend to involve differences between memory for verbal and visual information (e.g., Hanley, Davies, Downes, & Mayes, 1994; Milner et al., 1991), Ward et al. (1999) described a patient, MR, with left frontal lobe damage (related to multiple sclerosis) who exhibits an unusual kind of material-specific memory deficit. Like the previous case studies, he is prone to high rates of false recognition, but his false recognitions are restricted to faces and people's names. For example, on a famous faces test MR recognized 98% of the famous faces and incorrectly judged 77% of the nonfamous faces as famous. By comparison, the control subjects attained true and false recognition rates of 85% and 14%, respectively. MR's pathological false recognition is not limited to visual materials. When presented with names of historical figures (e.g., Duke of Wellington) intermixed with distractor names that could pass as historical figures (e.g., Horatio Felles) MR correctly recognized all of the historical figures and falsely recognized 70% of the distractors (as compared to 88% correct recognition and 6.5% false recognition for the control subjects).

There are some interesting constraints on MR's excessive false recognition rate. When either the famous and nonfamous faces or names are presented together and he is instructed to choose the famous face (or name) in the pair (i.e., a forced-choice recognition task), MR's performance was similar to controls (77% recognition of the faces for MR and 86% for the controls). In addition, MR has no problem distinguishing between real and fictional place names and does not have abnormally high false recognition rates of low frequency words or nonwords. Lastly, MR's high false recognition rate of personal names is dramatically decreased to normal levels when he receives search instructions that emphasize a nonpersonal name characteristic. For example, MR was given a list consisting of four different kinds of names: 1) books with names as titles (e.g., Oliver Twist); 2) fictitious names (e.g., Agnes Blythe); 3) books without a personal name as a title (e.g., Little Women), and 4) fictitious nonpersonal titles (e.g., Love and Hope). MR was much less likely to falsely recognize the fictitious names when given instructions to circle names of book titles than to circle literary characters' names.

The pattern of relatively normal performance on forced-choice recognition tests and impaired performance on single-probe tests supports Ward et al.'s (1999) hypothesis that MR has a problem using the appropriate criteria to make a response. On single-probe recognition tests it is necessary to set a criterion above which one judges items as "old" or "famous" and below which one judges items as "new" or "nonfamous." MR may use a pathologically liberal criterion for judging whether a name is famous or deciding that he has studied something before. This liberal criterion would inflate his false recognition rate in single probe tests. But the forced choice recognition test attenuates the effects of criteria on recognition because subjects must compare the relative familiarity of the two items in the pair and choose the more familiar one. Moreover, the fact that MR's performance improves when he is instructed to search for book titles as compared to characters' names suggests that the criteria MR use to identify items depends on how he is oriented to assess them. His pathologically liberal criteria emerge when he is attempting to identify faces and names but not when he is identifying book titles. In terms of the CMF, identifying book titles may orient MR to establish a more focused description of the information that is necessary to make a response, such as only choosing book titles for which he can remember associated information, such as the plot or the author's name. For an unknown reason, MR appears to use especially lax criteria for searching and assessing memory for faces and personal names.

In sum, the foregoing studies indicate that frontal lobe damage is associated with abnormally high false recognition rates. We have suggested that this pattern reflects a malfunctioning focusing mechanism. That is, the patients in the previous case studies tend to base recognition decisions on the presence of memorial information that is inappropriately vague or underspecified. Melo, Winocur, and Moscovitch (1999) have proposed a similar account to explain the performance of a group of patients with frontal lobe damage in the DRM paradigm. After studying lists of related words their frontal patients were more likely (but not significantly) to falsely recognize the related lure words than were the control subjects. Melo et al. argued that the frontal patients' defective monitoring mechanism led them to accept as "old" test items, such as the critical lure words, that matched the gist or general features of the studied words.

One clue as to why patients with frontal lobe damage assess memory in a nonoptimal manner comes from a study by Janowsky, Shimamura, and Squire (1989b). Janowsky et al. observed that frontal patients were less able than healthy controls to predict that they could recognize information that they were not able to recall. After learning a series of sentences, such as "Mary's garden was full of marigolds," frontal patients and healthy control subjects were given a cued recall test for a target word in the sentence (e.g., "Mary's garden was full of _____"). When subjects could not recall the target word they indicated their "feeling of knowing" for this target word by rating the likelihood of correctly recognizing this word on a subsequent multiple choice test. While recall and recognition performance was comparable between the two groups, the frontal lobe patients were at chance levels in their feeling of knowing judgments and the control subjects had high scores. Interestingly, the frontal patients had poor feeling of knowing scores because they tended to overestimate their knowledge. The frontal patients only recognized 27% of the items that they had judged as being moderately or highly confident of subsequently recognizing, whereas the control subjects recognized 42% of these items. This tendency on the part of frontal patients to overestimate their knowledge would contribute to abnormally high false recognition rates in the following way. Their apparent overconfidence that an item's familiarity means that it must have been studied earlier may have lead them to *not* use a more focused search description (e.g., search memory for more specific item information) and rely on a test item's familiarity.

CONCLUSION

An important strategy in cognitive neuroscience research is examining how processes malfunction in order to understand how they work. We have examined memory distortion in patients with brain damage from the perspective of the CMF. The reviewed studies indicate that healthy individuals are susceptible to falsely recognizing items when they fail to recollect detailed item information. This may occur when there is a pattern separation failure and the representations of similar studied items overlap, such as in the DRM paradigm. The medial temporal lobes and related structures appear important for storing and/or retaining both familiarity information and more specific information about an item. False recognition also can be a byproduct of the retrieval process when, for instance, people use lax criteria to search memory, such as accepting memories as true that are vaguely familiar. The frontal lobes are implicated in the criteria people use to search and evaluate their memories. In short, a variety of brain mechanisms underlie the occurrence of true and false memories.

REFERENCES

Alba, J. W., & Hasher, L. (1983). Is memory schematic? *Psychological Bulletin, 93,* 203-231.

Anderson, J. R., & Bower, G. H. (1972). Recognition and retrieval processes in free recall. *Psychological Review, 79,* 97-123.

Anderson, J. R., & Bower, G. H. (1974). A propositional theory of recognition memory. *Memory & Cognition, 2,* 406-412.

Arkes, H. R., & Freedman, M. R. (1984). A demonstration of the costs and benefits of expertise in recognition memory. *Memory & Cognition, 12,* 84-89.

Arndt, J., & Hirshman, E. (1998). True and false recognition in MINERVA2: Explanations from a global matching perspective. *Journal of Memory and Language, 39,* 371-391.

Atkinson, R. C., & Juola, J. F. (1974). Search and decision processes in recognition memory. In D. H. Krantz, R. C. Atkinson, R. C. Luce, & P. Suppes (Eds.), *Contemporary developments in mathematical psychology* (Vol. 1). San Francisco: W. H. Freeman.

Burgess, P. W., & Shallice, T. (1996). Confabulation and the control of recollection. *Memory, 4,* 359-411.

Buckner, R. L. (1996). Beyond HERA: Contributions of specific prefrontal brain areas to long-term memory retrieval. *Psychonomic Bulletin and Review, 3,* 149-158.

Cermak, L. S., Butters, N., & Gerrein, J. (1973). The extent of the verbal encoding ability of Korsakoff patients. *Neuropsychologia, 11,* 85-94.

Conway, M. A., & Gathercole, S. E. (1987). Modality and long-term memory. *Journal of Memory and Language, 26,* 341-361.

Curran, T., Schacter, D. L., Norman, K. A., & Galluccio, L. (1997). False recognition after a right frontal lobe infarction: Memory for general and specific information. *Neuropsychologia, 35,* 1035-1049.

Damasio, A. R. (1989). Time-locked multiregional retroactivation: A systems-level proposal for the neural substrates of recall and recognition. *Cognition, 33,* 25-62.

Deese, J. (1959). On the prediction of occurrence of particular verbal intrusions in immediate recall. *Journal of Experimental Psychology, 58,* 17-22.

Delbecq-Derouesné, J., Beauvois, M. F., & Shallice, T. (1990). Preserved recall versus impaired recognition. *Brain, 113,* 1045-1074.

Dodson, C. S., & Johnson, M. K. (1993). Rate of false source attributions depends on how questions are asked. *American Journal of Psychology, 106,* 541-557.

Dodson, C. S., & Johnson, M. K. (1996). Some problems with the process dissociation approach to memory. *Journal of Experimental Psychology: General, 125,* 181-194.

Dodson, C. S., & Schacter, D. L. (in press). "If I had said it I would have remembered it": Reducing false memories with a distinctiveness heuristic. *Psychological Bulletin and Review.*

Foley, M. A., Johnson, M. K., & Raye, C. L. (1983). Age-related changes in confusion between memories for thoughts and memories for speech. *Child Development, 54,* 51-60.

Fuster, J. M. (1989). *The prefrontal cortex: Anatomy, physiology, and neuropsychology of the frontal lobe* (2nd ed.). New York: Raven.

Gabrieli, J.D.E. (1998). Cognitive neuroscience of human memory. *Annual Review of Psychology, 49,* 87-115.

Gershberg, F. B., & Shimamura, A. P. (1996). The role of the frontal lobes in the use of organizational strategies in free recall. *Neuropsychologia, 13,* 1305-1333.

Gillund, G., & Shiffrin, R. M. (1984). A retrieval model for both recognition and recall. *Psychological Review, 91,* 1-67.

Goldman-Rakic, P. S. (1987). Circuitry of primate prefrontal cortex and regulation of behavior by representational memory. In F. Plum (Ed.), *Handbook of Physiology: The Nervous System* (pp. 373-417), Vol. 5. Bethesda, MD: American Physiological Society.

Hanley, J. R., Davies, A. D. M., Downes, J. J., & Mayes, A. R. (1994). Impaired recall of verbal material following rupture and repair of an anterior communicating artery aneurysm. *Cognitive Neuropsychology, 11,* 543-578.

Hashtroudi, S., Johnson, M. K., & Chrosniak, L. D. (1989). Aging and source monitoring. *Psychology and Aging, 4,* 106-112.

Hintzman, D. L. (1988). Judgments of frequency and recognition memory in a multiple-trace memory model. *Psychological Review, 95,* 528-551.

Hintzman, D. L., & Curran, T. (1994). Retrieval dynamics of recognition and frequency judgments: Evidence for separate processes of familiarity and recall. *Journal of Memory and Language, 33,* 1-18.

Hirst, W., & Volpe, B. T. (1988). Memory strategies and brain damage. *Brain and Cognition, 8,* 379-408.

Humphreys, M. S., Bain, J. D., & Pike, R. (1989). Different ways to cue a coherent memory system: A theory for episodic, semantic, and procedural tasks. *Psychological Review, 96,* 208-233.

Israel, L., & Schacter, D. L. (1997). Pictorial encoding reduces false recognition of semantic associates. *Psychological Bulletin and Review, 4,* 577-581.

Jacoby, L. L. (1991). A process dissociation framework: Separating automatic from intentional uses of memory. *Journal of Memory and Language, 30,* 513-541.

Jacoby, L. L., & Dallas, M. (1981). On the relationship between autobiographical memory and perceptual learning. *Journal of Experimental Psychology: General, 3,* 306-340.

Janowsky, J. S., Shimamura, A. P., & Squire, L. R. (1989a). Source memory impairment in patients with frontal lobe lesions. *Neuropsychologia, 27,* 1043-1056.

Janowsky, J. S., Shimamura, A. P., & Squire, L. R. (1989b). Memory and metamemory: Comparisons between patients with frontal lobe lesions and amnesic patients. *Psychobiology, 17,* 3-11.

Johnson, M. K. (1985). The origin of memories. In P. C. Kendall (Ed.), *Advances in cognitive behavioral research and therapy* (Vol 4). New York: Academic Press.

Johnson, M. K. (1991). Reality monitoring: Evidence from confabulation in organic brain disease patients. In G. P. Prigatano & D. L. Schacter (Eds.), *Awareness of deficit after brain injury: Clinical and theoretical issues* (pp. 176-197). New York: Oxford University Press.

Johnson, M. K., & Chalfonte, B. L. (1994). Binding complex memories: The role of reactivation and the hippocampus. In D. L. Schacter & E. Tulving (Eds.), *Memory Systems 1994* (pp. 311-350). Cambridge, MA: MIT Press.

Johnson, M. K., Hashtroudi, S., & Lindsay, D. S. (1993). Source monitoring. *Psychological Bulletin, 114,* 3-28.

Johnson, M. K., Kounios, J., & Reeder, J. A. (1994). Time-course studies of reality monitoring and recognition.

Journal of Experimental Psychology: Learning, Memory, and Cognition, 20, 1409-1419.

Johnson, M. K., O'Connor, M., & Cantor, J. (1997). Confabulation, memory deficits, and frontal dysfunction. *Brain & Cognition, 34,* 189-206.

Johnson, M. K., & Raye, C. L. (1981). Reality monitoring. *Psycholigical Review, 88,* 67-85

Johnson, M. K., Raye, C. L., Foley, H. J., & Foley, M. A. (1981). Cognitive operations and decision bias in reality monitoring. *American Journal of Psychology, 94,* 37-64.

Koutstaal, W., & Schacter, D. L. (1997). Gist-based false recognition of pictures in older and younger adults. *Journal of Memory and Language, 37,* 555-583.

Koutstaal, W., Schacter, D. L., Verfaellie, M., Brenner, C., & Jackson, E. M. (1999). Perceptually-based false recognition of novel objects in amnesia: Effects of category size and similarity to category prototypes. *Cognitive Neuropsychology, 16,* 317-341.

Kroll, N. E. A., Knight, R. T., Metcalfe, J., Wolf, E. S., & Tulving, E. (1996). Cohesion failure as a source of memory illusions. *Journal of Memory and Language, 35,* 176-196.

Lindsay, D. S., & Johnson, M. K. (1989). The eyewitness suggestibility effect and memory for source. *Memory & Cognition, 17,* 349-358.

Loftus, E. F., Feldman, J., & Dashiell, R. (1995). The reality of illusory memories. In D. L. Schacter, J. T. Coyle, G. D. Fischbach, M. M. Mesulam, & L. E. Sullivan (Eds.), *Memory distortion: How minds, brains and societies reconstruct the past* (pp. 47-68). Cambridge, MA: Harvard University Press.

Luria, A. R. (1966). *Higher cortical functions in man.* New York: Basic Books.

Mandler, G. (1980). Recognizing: The judgement of previous occurrence. *Psychological Review, 87,* 252-271.

Marsh, R. L., & Hicks, J. L. (1998). Test formats change source-monitoring decision processes. *Journal of Experimental Psychology: Learning, Memory, and Cognition, 24,* 1137-1151.

Mather, M., Henkel, L. A., & Johnson, M. K. (1997). Evaluating the characteristics of false memories: Remember/know judgments and memory characteristics questionnaire compared. *Memory and Cognition, 25,* 826-837.

Mayes, A. R., & Downes, J. J. (1997). What do theories of the functional deficit(s) underlying amnesia have to explain? *Memory, 5,* 3-36.

McClelland, J. L., McNaughton, B. L., & O'Reilly, R. C. (1995). Why there are complementary learning systems in the hippocampus and neocortex: Insights from the successes and failures of connectionist models of learning and memory. *Psychological Review, 102,* 419-457.

McDermott, K. B. (1996). The persistence of false memories in list recall. *Journal of Memory and Language, 35,* 212-230.

Melo, B., Winocur, G., & Moscovitch, M. (1999). False recall and false recognition: An examination of the effects of selective and combined lesions to the medial temporal lobe/diencephalon and frontal lobe structures. *Cognitive Neuropsychology, 16,* 343-359.

Milner, B., Corsi, P., & Leonard, G. (1991). Frontal-lobe contribution to recency judgments. *Neuropsychologia, 29,* 601-618.

Moscovitch, M. (1994). Memory and working-with-memory: Evaluation of a component process model and comparisons with other models. In D. L. Schacter & E.

Tulving (Eds.), *Memory Systems 1994* (pp. 269-310). Cambridge, MA: MIT Press.

Moscovitch, M. (1995). Confabulation. In D. L. Schacter, J. T. Coyle, G. D. Fischbach, M. M. Mesulam, & L. E. Sullivan (Eds.), *Memory distortions: How minds, brains and societies reconstruct the past* (pp. 226-251). Cambridge, MA: Harvard University Press.

Multhaup, K. S. (1995). Aging, source, and decision criteria: When false fame errors do and do not occur. *Psychology and Aging, 10,* 492-497.

Murdock, B. B., Jr. (1982). A theory for the storage and retrieval of item and associative information. *Psychological Review, 89,* 609-626.

Norman, D. A., & Bobrow, D. G. (1979). Descriptions: An intermediate stage in memory retrieval. *Cognitive Psychology, 11,* 107-123.

Norman, K. A., & Schacter, D. L. (1996). Implicit memory, explicit memory, and false recollection: A cognitive neuroscience perspective. In L. M. Reder (Ed.), *Implicit Memory and Metacognition* (pp. 229-259). Hillsdale, NJ: Lawrence Erlbaum.

Norman, K. A., & Schacter, D. L. (1997). False recognition in young and older adults: Exploring the characteristics of illusory memories. *Memory and Cognition, 25,* 838-848.

Nyberg, L., Cabeza, R., & Tulving, E. (1996). PET studies of encoding and retrieval: The HERA model. *Psychonomic Bulletin and Review, 3,* 135-148.

Nyberg, L., Tulving, E., Habib, R., Nilsson, L.-G., Kapur, S., Houle, S., Cabeza, R., & McIntosh, A. R. (1995). Functional brain maps of retrieval mode and recovery of episodic information. *NeuroReport, 6,* 249-252.

Nystrom, L. E., & McClelland, J. L. (1992). Trace synthesis in cued recall. *Journal of Memory and Language, 31,* 591-614.

Parkin, A. J., Ward, J., Bindschaedler, C., Squires, E. J., & Powell G. (1999). False recognition following frontal lobe damage: The role of encoding factors. *Cognitive Neuropsychology, 16.*

Parkin, A. J., & Leng, N. R. C. (1993). *Neuropsychology of the Amnesic Syndrome.* Hillsdale, NJ: Lawrence Erlbaum.

Payne, D. G., Elie, C. J., Blackwell, J. M., & Neuschatz, J. S. (1996). Memory illusions: Recalling, recognizing, and recollecting events that never occurred. *Journal of Memory and Language, 35,* 261-285.

Rapcsak, S. Z., Reminger, S. L., Glisky, E. L., Kaszniak, A., & Comer, J. F. (1999). Neuropsychological mechanisms of false facial recognition following frontal lobe damage. *Cognitive Neuropsychology, 16,* 267-292.

Read, J. D. (1996). From a passing thought to a false memory in 2 minutes: confusing real and illusory events. *Psychonomic Bulletin and Review, 3,* 105-111.

Reyna, V. F., & Brainerd, C. J. (1995). Fuzzy-trace theory: An interim synthesis. *Learning and Individual Differences, 7,* 1-75.

Riccio, D. C., Rabinowitz, V. C., & Axelrod, S. (1994). Memory: When less is more. *American Psychologist, 49,* 917-926.

Roediger, H. L., III. (1996). Memory illusions. *Journal of Memory and Language, 35,* 76-100.

Roediger, H. L., III., & McDermott, K. B. (1995). Creating false memories: Remembering words not presented in lists. *Journal of Experimental Psychology: Learning, Memory, and Cognition, 21,* 803-814.

Robinson, K. J., & Roediger, H. L., III. (1997). Associative processes in false recall and false recognition. *Psychological Science, 8,* 231-237.

Rotello, C. M. (1999). Metacognition and memory for nonoccurrence. *Memory, 7*, 43-63.

Rugg, M. D., Fletcher, P. C., Frith, C. D., Frackowiak, R. S. J., & Dolan, R. J. (1996). Differential response of the prefrontal cortex in successful and unsuccessful memory retrieval. *Brain, 119*, 2073-2083.

Schacter, D. L. (1987). Memory, amnesia and frontal lobe dysfunction. *Psychobiology, 15*, 21-36.

Schacter, D. L. (1989). Memory. In M. I. Posner (Ed.), *Foundations of cognitive Science* (pp. 683-725). Cambridge, MA: MIT Press.

Schacter, D. L. (1995). Memory distortion: History and current status. In D. L. Schacter, J. T. Coyle, G. D. Fischbach, M. M. Mesulam, & L. E. Sullivan (Eds.), *Memory distortion: How minds, brains and societies reconstruct the past* (pp. 1-43). Cambridge, MA: Harvard University Press.

Schacter, D. L. (Ed.) (1999a). *The cognitive neuropsychology of false memories*: East Sussex, UK: Psychology Press.

Schacter, D. L. (1999b). The seven sins of memory: Insights from psychology and cognitive neuroscience. *American Psychologist, 54*, 182-203.

Schacter, D. L., Alpert, N. M., Savage, C. R., Rauch, S. L., & Albert, M. S. (1996). Conscious recollection and the human hippocampal formation: Evidence from positron emission tomography. *Proceedings of the National Academy of Sciences of the USA, 93*, 321-325.

Schacter, D. L., Buckner, R. L., Koutstaal, W., Dale, A. M., & Rosen, B. R. (1997). Late onset of anterior prefrontal activity during true and false recognition: An event-related FMRI study. *NeuroImage, 6*, 259-269.

Schacter, D. L., Curran, T., Galluccio, L., Milberg, W. P., & Bates, J. F. (1996). False recognition and the right frontal lobe: A case study. *Neuropsychologia, 34*, 793-808.

Schacter, D. L., Harbluk, J. L., & McLachlan, D. R. (1984). Retrieval without recollection: An experimental analysis of source amnesia. *Journal of Verbal Learning and Verbal Behavior, 23*, 593-611.

Schacter, D. L., Israel, L., & Racine, C. A. (1999). Suppressing false recognition in younger and older adults: The distinctiveness heuristic. *Journal of Memory and Language, 40*, 1-24.

Schacter, D. L., Norman, K. A., & Koutstaal, W. (1998). The cognitive neurosciences of constructive memory. *Annual Review of Psychology, 49*, 289-318.

Schacter, D. L., & Tulving, E. (1994). Memory systems 1994. In D. L. Schacter & E. Tulving (Eds.), *Memory Systems 1994* (pp. 1-38). Cambridge, MA: MIT Press.

Schacter, D. L., Verfaellie, M., & Anes, M. D. (1997). Illusory memories in amnesic patients: Conceptual and perceptual false recognition. *Neuropsychology, 11*, 331-342.

Schacter, D. L., Verfaellie, M., Anes, M. D., & Racine, C. (1998). When true recognition suppresses false recognition: Evidence from amnesic patients. *Journal of Cognitive Neuroscience, 10*, 668-679.

Schacter, D. L., Verfaellie, M., & Pradere, D. (1996). The neuropsychology of memory illusions: False recall and recognition in amnesic patients. *Journal of Memory and Language, 35*, 319-334.

Shiffrin, R. M., Huber, D.E., & Marinelli, K. (1995). Effects of category length and strength on familiarity in recognition. *Journal of Experimental Psychology: Learning, Memory and Cognition, 21*, 267-287.

Shimamura, A. P. (1995). Memory and frontal lobe function. In M. S. Gazzaniga (Ed.), *The cognitive neurosciences* (pp. 803-813). Cambridge, MA: MIT Press:

Shimamura, A. P., Janowsky, J. S., & Squire, L. R. (1990). Memory for the temporal order of events in patients with frontal lobe lesions and amnesic patients. *Neuropsychologia, 28*, 803-813.

Squire, L. R. (1992). Memory and the hippocampus: A synthesis from findings with rats, monkeys, and humans. *Psychological Review, 99*, 195-231.

Squire, L. R. (1995). Biological foundations of accuracy and inaccuracy in memory. In Schacter, D. L., Coyle, J. T., Fischback, G. D., Mesulam, M. M., & Sullivan, L. E. (Eds.), *Memory distortion: How minds, brains and societies reconstruct the past*. Cambridge, MA: Harvard University Press.

Squire, L. R., & Alvarez, P. (1995). Retrograde amnesia and memory consolidation: A neurobiological perspective. *Current Opinions in Neurobiology, 5*, 169-177.

Strack, F., & Bless, H. (1994). Memory for nonoccurrences: Metacognitive and presuppositional strategies. *Journal of Memory and Language, 33*, 203-217.

Treves, A., & Rolls, E. T. (1994). Computational analysis of the role of the hippocampus in memory. *Hippocampus, 4*, 374-391.

Tulving, E., Markowitsch, H. J., Kapur, S., Habib, R., & Houle, S. (1994). Novelty encoding networks in the human brain: Positron emission tomography data. *NeuroReport, 5*, 2525-2528.

Underwood, B. J. (1972). Word recognition memory and frequency information. *Journal of Experimental Psychology, 94*, 276-283.

Underwood, B. J. (1965). False recognition produced by implicit verbal responses. *Journal of Experimental Psychology, 70*, 122-129.

Ward, J., Parkin, A. J., Powell, G., Squires, E., Townshend, J., & Bradley, V. (1999). False recognition of unfamiliar people: "Seeing film stars everywhere." *Cognitive Neuropsychology, 16*, 293-315.

Zaragoza, M. S., & Lane, S. M. (1994). Source misattributions and the suggestibility of eyewitness memory. *Journal of Experimental Psychology: Learning, Memory, and Cognition, 20*, 934-945.

Part 7

—

Music, Numbers, and Time

—

Music is . . . geometry in time.

—Arthur Honeggar

19

Time Perception

Jennifer A. Mangels
Richard B. Ivry

Temporal processing is an integral component of many everyday goal-oriented behaviors. One need look no further than the processes involved in cooking an evening meal to see the importance of accurate timing. Efficient planning of task sequence is determined to a large degree by how long each task will take, such as the time required for butter to melt or water to boil. To increase efficiency, one might schedule a series of shorter, timed tasks to take place while waiting for a longer task to come to completion. Thus, one often must keep track of multiple intervals simultaneously. If distracted by a telephone call at a critical juncture, we may "lose track of time," and have to estimate how much time has elapsed and act accordingly. In such situations, we often turn to external timekeeping devices, such as timers and watches. However, we are not wholly dependent on them. People are capable of measuring time with a degree of accuracy that implies the presence of specific cognitive components for temporal processing. In this chapter, we outline the cognitive models that have been used to understand temporal cognition in humans. We then discuss how these theories have shaped the investigation of temporal processing disorders in neurology patients with neurological disorders, as well as how the resulting neurological data have constrained and modified our cognitive theories.

Despite the fact that we might talk about having a "time sense" or a "sense of time," the subjective experience of time does not appear to arise from a dedicated sensory system. Investigations have uncovered no specialized receptor for time. Yet, it is unlikely that the perception of time is merely an epiphenomenon of neural activity *within* other sensory systems. Although judging whether two stimuli are presented simultaneously or not (i.e., the fusion threshold) varies as a function of sensory modality, the interstimulus interval necessary to accurately determine the order in which two nonsimultaneous stimuli are presented does not (i.e., the temporal order threshold); (for review see Wittman, 1999). Moreover, our ability to represent temporal intervals is minimally affected by whether or not the stimulus is present: We can measure both the duration that a stimulus is present or the duration that one is absent. The representation of an interval can also be marked by one modality at the onset and a different modality at the offset. Together, these phenomena indicate that certain components of temporal processing must be centralized with respect to sensory input. In addition, internal timing mechanisms must be designed to perceive change, rather than simply capture and process information from one particular instance. Timing is dynamic by definition. It requires processing of not only of individual events, but also of the relationship between them.

The particular cognitive processes involved in time estimation may depend, however, on the direction in which this relationship is evaluated. Specifically, time can be measured either *prospectively* from some well-demarcated event to some point in the future, or *retrospectively* from some point backward into the past. Prospective and retrospective tasks yield different behavioral results (reviewed in Block, 1992; Block & Zakay, 1997). Briefly stated, the same interval will generally produce shorter and more variable subjective estimates when measured retrospectively than when measured prospectively. These two types of estimates are also affected differently by the demands of a concurrent task in which time is not explicitly measured, such as proofreading, mental arithmetic, word categorization, and intensity or frequency discrimination. When time is measured prospectively, there is a negative relationship between demands of a concurrent non-temporal task and estimated duration; the more difficult the non-temporal task, the shorter the perceived duration (Brown, 1997). In contrast, absolute processing difficulty has little effect on retrospective estimates. Instead, these types of estimates are more sensitive to the number of salient changes in environment, mood, or task that take place during an interval. The relationship of between contextual change and estimated duration is typically positive; the greater the number of contextual changes that can be retrieved at the time the estimate is made, the longer the perceived duration of the interval. Contextual change has little effect on prospective estimates of time.

The behavioral differences between prospective and retrospective timing can be easily understood if one assumes that the explicit monitoring of time is an active process that requires attention. The degree to which temporal and non-temporal tasks compete for attention will depend on whether time is measured prospectively or retrospectively. In prospective tasks, subjects are aware that they must actively monitor passing time, and therefore are intentionally engaged in temporal processing. Time is explicitly experienced and a hypothetical internal clock in engaged. In retrospective tasks, subjects are engaged in a non-temporal task and are unaware that they will have to estimate duration until the moment at which the experimenter asks the subject for an estimate of elapsed time. Thus, in retrospective tasks, any temporal processing that takes place while the subject is engaged in the non-temporal task could be viewed as "incidental." Because less explicit temporal processing takes place, the subject is left to infer duration from the contents of memory. Passage of time must be reconstructed based on memory for events, the number of transitions between events, and expectations of how long these events should take (e.g., Ornstein, 1969; Zakay & Block, 1997).

The present chapter will focus on models of prospective timing, given that the majority of the extent neuropsychological evidence examines this aspect of timing behavior. However, later in the chapter we will consider the possibility that as the length of the target duration extends beyond the limits of working memory, both prospective and retrospective estimation may converge on long-term memory processes.

MEASURING TIME PROSPECTIVELY

Unlike the circadian clock, which has an endogenous, though entrainable periodicity, the ideal measurement tool for timing in a prospective task would be an internal mechanism analogous to a stopwatch. With this type of interval timing mechanism, arbitrary start and stop points could be triggered by internal or external stimuli, providing the high degree of flexibility necessary for adaptive temporal processing. The cognitive processes underlying interval timing have been investigated in the context of both perception and production tasks. In the next section, we briefly describe the procedures and dependent measures of the most common of these tasks. A more detailed description of the methods of time measurement can be found in Allan (1979; see also Nichelli, 1996).

Perception Tasks

In perception tasks, subjects generally make comparisons between a test stimulus of variable duration and one or more reference durations. For example, in a *time discrimination* task, subjects hear two successive intervals and determine whether the second interval is shorter or longer than the first (see Figure 19.1 panel A). The set of test durations can either be fixed or it can be determined via an adaptive psychophysical procedure. It is also not essential, however, that the standard be unitary or presented on each trial. Participants can also be presented with two standards to indicate the upper and lower limits of the stimulus range. The standard(s) also can be presented either at the start of a block or in a prior test session.

Two dependent variables are generally reported in such experiments, obtained from the psychometric function (Figure 19.1 panel B). First, the point of subjective equality (PSE) corresponds to the duration at which the person is equally likely to classify the stimulus as short or long. In Figure 19.1B, the person tends to classify the test stimuli as long and thus the PSE is shown at a duration shorter than the 500 ms standard. A change in PSE may indicate that a particular experimental manipulation has produced a change in the speed of an internal clock or it may indicate a change in criterion. Second, the difference threshold can be calcu-

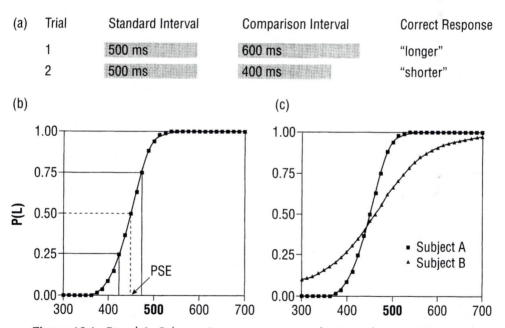

Figure 19.1: Panel A: Schematic representation of a time discrimination task. Subjects are presented with two durations separated by a brief inter-stimulus interval and must judge whether the second interval (comparison) is shorter or longer than the first interval (standard = 500 ms). Panel B: Hypothetical (idealized) data from the time discrimination task in Panel A. The ordinate represents the probability of making a response of "longer." The abscissa represents the duration of the comparison interval. Lower threshold: P(L) = 0.25; upper threshold: P(L) = 0.75; Point of subjective equality (PSE): P(L) = 0.50. The PSE for this subject is 450 ms. See text for further explanation. Panel C Hypothetical data from two subjects. Both subjects demonstrated a left-ward shift in PSE (relative to the standard). In addition, the slope of the psychometric function of Subject A is shallower than that of Subject B, indicating a larger difference threshold and poorer discrimination ability.

lated as the point at which the person's performance achieves some arbitrarily defined criterion. For example, if the criterion is set at 75% accuracy, lower and upper thresholds would correspond to the points at which the psychometric function crosses the 25% and 75% probabilities. The difference threshold is generally reported as this value divided by two. In the example given in Figure 19.1 panel B, subjects are expected to be correct on 75% of the trials when the test duration differs from the reference duration by 25 ms. The difference threshold provides an estimate of variability in the discrimination process. The worse the discrimination ability, the larger the difference threshold, as reflected by a more shallow psychometric function (Figure 19.1 panel C, Subject B).

Temporal acuity is not absolute, but rather is scaled to the reference duration. It is frequently expressed in terms of a coefficient of variation (COV), taken as the difference threshold divided by the point of subjective equality. The COV is sometimes referred to as the Weber fraction, and when this value remains constant, then temporal acuity is said to obey Weber's law, similar to that observed on discrimination tasks for many other perceptual dimensions, including numerosity (e.g., Krueger, 1989, p. 268). The fact that variability scales with duration indicates that the underlying noise is associated with the operation of an internal clock. Nonscalar sources of variability are attributed to other processes such as those associated with starting and stopping the timing process or various decision sources.

Time estimation tasks constitute another class of commonly used perception tasks. In verbal estimation tasks, subjects are presented with a stimulus of a particular duration and have to estimate its length using conventional time units as a reference (e.g., "that was about 2 s"). Although easy to administer, subjects' bias to report durations in round numbers may limit the sensitivity of this measure. Estimation by analogical comparison, in which subjects draw a line of similar "length" to the perceived duration, may get around this particular bias, but introduces additional ones and is rarely used in neuropsychological studies. In both estimation tasks, the primary measures are the accuracy of the estimate relative to the target duration (i.e., does the subject over- or underestimate the duration), and the consistency (i.e., the variability) of these estimates over multiple trials.

Production Tasks

Production tasks require subjects to make timed movements. In *time reproduction* tasks, subjects reproduce an interval of a specific duration by making a single movement (i.e., pressing a button for 2 s) or a set of movements (i.e., to signal start and stop times). One particular type of production task that is common to both animal and human studies of timing is the *peak-interval [PI] procedure*. As shown in Figure 19.2 panel A, subjects first receive fixed-interval [FI] trials in which they either receive reinforcement (animal studies) or perceive a stimulus change (human studies) after a criterion period. Once they have learned the duration of the criterion period, fixed-interval [FI] trials are randomly intermixed with peak-interval [PI] trials. For the former, the subject is rewarded for the first response after the target interval has elapsed. For the latter, responding does not produce reward (i.e., there is no end signal) and eventually, the subject ceases to respond. As with perceptual tasks, the response function yields multiple dependent variables. The peak of the response function corresponds to the point of maximal expectation and can indicate temporal accuracy; the spread of the function provides a window on temporal variability. Again, variability increases with duration (see Figure 19.2 panel B), but when normalized the functions will generally superimpose, consistent with Weber's law.

Other production tasks measure repetitive tapping performance. In these tasks, subjects produce a continuous series of timed responses, either designed to match a pacing rhythm (*synchronization*) or to maintain the target interval when unassisted (*continuation*). Measures of accuracy and variability can be obtained by looking at the mean and standard deviation of

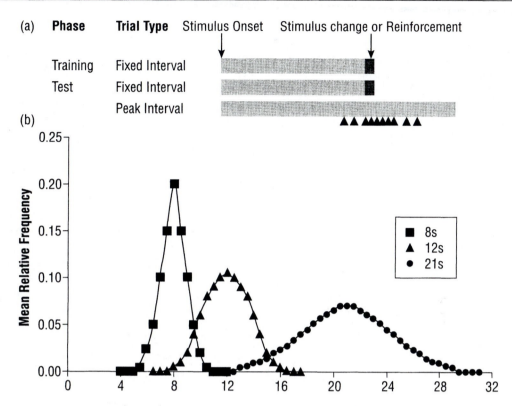

Figure 19.2: Panel A: Schematic representation of the peak interval procedure. During training, subjects are exposed to multiple trials of a fixed interval. The start of this interval is indicated by stimulus onset and the end is indicated by reinforcement (i.e., food reward in animal studies) or a change in the stimulus (i.e., human studies). This termination is illustrated by the dark gray rectangle. Once the target (criterion) time has been acquired, subjects are tested with peak intervals, in which a change or reinforcement does not occur to signal the end of the interval, intermixed with some fixed intervals. In normal subjects, responding, as illustrated by the black triangles, typically starts before the criterion time is reached, peaks around the criterion time and then falls off after the criterion time has passed. Panel B: Hypothetical data illustrating mean relative frequency distributions of responding when target times were 8, 12, and 21 s. Note that as target durations increase, variability in responding also increases. However, the peak of these distributions remains close to the target duration. Adapted from "Coupled temporal memories in Parkinson's disease: A dopamine-related dysfunction," by C. Malapani et al., 1998, *Journal of Cognitive Neuroscience*, 10(3), pp. 316–331.

the inter-tap intervals. Quantitative models have been developed to partition the total variability observed on these tasks into component sources such as that associated with an timing, motor implementation, and error correction processes (Wing & Kristofferson, 1973; Pressing, 1999).

Evidence for a Common Clock

Although each of these perception and production methods involve task-specific components, evidence accruing from studies with both normal and neurologically impaired individuals suggests that both perception and production tasks tap into a unitary internal timing system. Ivry and Hazeltine (1995) measured the temporal variability of normal adults on duration discrimination and repetitive tapping tasks across four durations ranging from 325 ms to 550 ms. For both tasks, the standard deviation was linearly related to the target duration, thus conforming to Weber's law. This similar manifestation of this scalar property across both perception and production tasks suggests that they utilize a common clock (see also Keele, Pokorny, Corcos, & Ivry, 1985). Furthermore, the Weber fraction (or slope of the variability function) also was similar for the two tasks. When the participants were presented with a single interval on each trial, either for categorization on the perception task (long or short) or reproduction on the motor task, the Weber fraction was 4.6% in both conditions. Support for a central timekeeper also comes from studies of timing deficits in patients with focal lesions. Patients with cerebellar damage (Ivry & Keele, 1989) or Parkinson's disease (Harrington & Haaland, 1998; Pastor, Artieda, Jahanshahi, & Obeso, 1992) demonstrate similar deficits in both temporal discrimination and repetitive tapping tasks.

Assuming the existence of a central timekeeping mechanism, studies of time perception may have some advantage over production tasks because performance on temporal processing tasks can be examined while minimizing motor requirements. In particular, perception tasks may be particularly advantageous for testing individuals with deficits in motor control, such as those suffering from cerebellar degeneration or Parkinson's disease. Yet, tests of explicit time perception also require cognitive components including attention, memory, and decision making processes. These cognitive processes are hypothesized to be necessary for conscious access to temporal information for the purpose of guiding behavior (e.g., when one must judge how long a pot has been boiling on the stove). In the following section, we present a current model of temporal processing that includes both an internal clock and this additional set of non-temporal components that serve to bridge the output of the endogenous clock with behavior.

INFORMATION PROCESSING MODELS OF INTERVAL TIMING

A neuropsychological approach to understanding temporal processing requires a theoretical model of the cognitive components involved and the flow of information between them. Thus far, the dominant theoretical model of interval timing has been the scalar expectancy theory, or SET (see Figure 19.3). Originally developed to account for the performance of rats in the peak interval procedure (see Gibbon, Church, & Meck, 1984; Roberts, 1981), this model has been successfully adapted to the wide variety of temporal behaviors expressed by both animals and humans (Gibbon, Malapani, Dale, & Gallistel, 1997; Wearden, 1991). This information-processing model has served as a framework for many recent neuropsychological studies of interval timing.

The Scalar Expectancy Theory (SET)

According to the SET model, tasks requiring prospective timing involve three distinct stages: a clock stage, a memory stage, and a decision stage. The clock stage is composed of a pacemaker and accumulator, separated by a gate. The pacemaker forms the core of the clock stage and produces the temporal values that bear an orderly relationship to objective time. When the gate is switched open by an appropriate stimulus trigger, the outputs from the pacemaker are directed into an accumulator. This latter process continually sums these values to produce a dynamic representation of current time. When a stimulus occurs that signals the end of the interval, the gate closes and accumulation terminates. When the task requires a response based on this temporal information, the individual decodes (retrieves) the reference interval from memory and compares it with the current temporal representation. The ratio of the current time to these retrieved representations determines how the individual will respond. If the decision the subject makes is reinforced, this reinforced interval is subsequently encoded into reference memory.

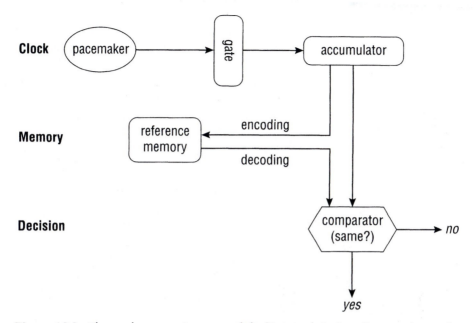

Figure 19.3: The scalar-expectancy model of interval timing. See text for explanation. Adapted from "Coupled temporal memories in Parkinson's disease: A dopamine-related dysfunction," by C. Malapani et al., 1998, *Journal of Cognitive Neuroscience*, 10(3), pp. 316–331.

Each of these stages can contribute variance to temporal behavior, resulting in temporal estimates that are relatively imprecise compared to external time-keeping mechanisms. Indeed, most of us prefer to use watches or other external clocks when temporal precision is critical. Nonetheless, durations in the millisecond to seconds range adhere to the scalar property or Weber's law described above (Allan & Gibbon, 1991). Beyond this range, our estimates still remain closely related to objective time. However, there is a consistent foreshortening of perceived duration as objective duration increases.

The SET model is appealing to neuropsychological researchers because of the well-specified component processes. A priori predictions can be made concerning how damage to the different components should effect measures of temporal accuracy and variability. For example, consider performance on a peak-interval (PI) task. If the internal clock were damaged, three different patterns of performance could occur, depending on how such damage changed the operation of this component. First, a clock that is consistently running faster or slower during *both* training and test phases would not appreciably affect accuracy because both current and reference intervals would be distorted by a similar amount. If damage affecting clock speed took place *between* training and test, however, a shift in peak response time would be observed during the first few test trials. This shift would eventually disappear, however, as new intervals made with the altered clock were encoded into reference memory. A third possibility is that damage could impair the precision of the clock, causing an overall increase in variability without any systematic shift in peak interval.

All three patterns can be contrasted with the effects of damage to the memory stage, which would result in nonscalar increases in variability (Gibbon, 1992). Damage to the memory stage would also result in a relatively permanent shift in accuracy because temporal representations that are improperly encoded, stored, or retrieved cannot be corrected simply through feedback (Malapani et al., 1998). Finally, a bias in the decision phase might cause temporary over- or under-estimation, but these errors should be corrected after subjects are given feedback regarding the correct interval.

The Attentional-Gate Model

Although the SET model is rooted in the animal timing literature, it has been adapted by researchers seeking a more cognitive model for timing in humans. The attentional-gate model proposed by Zakay and Block (e.g., Block, 1990; Zakay & Block, 1996, 1997) is just such a model and extends SET by including three additional cognitive components that are invoked when time must be monitored explicitly and represented in conscious awareness (see Figure 19.4). First, general *arousal* level is proposed to mediate the speed of the internal pacemaker. Greater-than-normal systemic arousal will increase the speed of the pacemaker, whereas lower-than-normal arousal will decrease its speed. Second, *selective attention* is assumed to operate on the gating mechanism and allow output of the clock system to become available to conscious awareness. Essentially, when attention is directed toward the temporal aspects of current processing demands, temporal pulses are gated from the pacemaker into an accumulator. The accumulator acts as a working memory buffer that actively updates the representation of current (elapsed) time. Third, in some versions of this model, an additional *"switch"* is placed between the attentional gate and the accumulator to signal when a task-relevant stimulus has occurred and set the accumulator to zero for a new count. These three components together form the "clock-counter" unit, in which the accumulator counts off intervals of the pacemaker—similar to the way a minute hand counts off revolutions of the second hand on an analog clock. Values in this accumulator are transferred to working memory for comparison with a stored target interval. When the gate is "closed," however, sensory and motor systems can still access the internal clock for behaviors that do not require explicit representation of time. For example, the millisecond timing underlying voluntary and involuntary movements can be automatically triggered by stimuli and occur outside the scope of conscious awareness.

This attentional-gate model makes additional predictions about the explicit processing of temporal information not specifically made by SET. First, it predicts that when intervals exceed the range relevant for typical sensory and motor events (e.g., 1 s), greater demands are placed on sustained attention and the capacity of working memory. These non-temporal components then will begin to make disproportionate contributions to the overall variance. Second, the model predicts that a concurrent non-temporal task should divert resources away from the gating of temporal information, resulting in a slower and more variable accumulation of time. Because this relationship results from the mutual competition between temporal and non-temporal tasks for attentional resources, the converse will also be true. When attention is directed toward gating temporal information, resources are correspondingly diverted from processing non-temporal information and performance on these non-temporal dimensions will suffer. Finally, cognitive models of time perception allow for the possibility that top-down processes, such as strategy can modulate timing components. For example, the presence of a cognitive counter suggests that verbal counting strategies (i.e., one-one-thousand, two-one-thousand, etc.) could lead to more precise estimates of time by reducing variability in the counter component.

NEUROPSYCHOLOGICAL EVIDENCE FOR COMPONENT PROCESSES IN INTERVAL TIMING

Disturbances in time perception are not a generic problem associated with neurological damage. Dissociations between tasks requiring temporal and non-temporal analysis of similar perceptual events indicate that modular clock components can be selectively impaired. Thus far, these types of dissociations have been found in patients with damage in subcortical regions, primarily the basal ganglia and lateral cerebellum (Casini & Ivry, 1999; Harrington & Haaland, 1998; Ivry & Keele, 1989; Ivry, Keele, & Diener, 1988; Malapani, Khati, Dubois, & Gibbon, 1997; Nichelli, Alway, & Grafman, 1996), as well as cortical regions, including dorsolateral

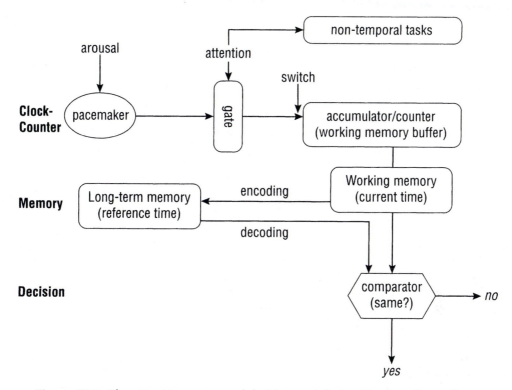

Figure 19.4: The attention-gate model of interval timing. See text for explanation. Adapted from "Temporal cognition," by D. Zakey and R. A. Block, 1996, *Current Directions in Psychological Science*, 6(1), pp. 12–16.

prefrontal cortex and inferior parietal cortex (Harrington & Haaland, 1998; Harrington, Haaland, & Knight, 1998; Nichelli, Clark, Hollnagel, & Grafman, 1995). Although converging evidence from neuroimaging studies supports the involvement of these subcortical and cortical regions in a network for temporal processing (e.g., Jueptner et al., 1995; Lejeune et al., 1997; Rao et al., 1997), determining the specific functions of particular areas has proven more difficult. Relatively few neuropsychological studies have systematically manipulated variables such as temporal range, memory, attention, or strategy that could serve to dissociate different processing modules and determine how they interact. Therefore, for the purpose of this review, we will focus on those studies that shed the greatest light on these issues, and where necessary, include supporting evidence from neurophysiological studies with animals.

The Internal Clock and Its Underlying Mechanism

The Pacemaker Hypothesis

Fundamental to many theories of temporal processing, including the SET model, is the construct of the pacemaker, an endogenous process that provides a basic temporal unit. This process is most often conceptualized as a recurrent or oscillatory process that emits pulses at a mean rate, but with variability that is multiplicative and consistent with Weber's Law (e.g., Gibbon, Church, & Meck, 1984; Treisman, Faulkner, & Naish, 1992). Evidence in support of the pacemaker hypothesis has primarily come from pharmacological studies, with the focus of this work centered on the nigrostriatal dopamine system. Numerous studies have shown that dopaminergic manipulations can distort the perception of time in a manner consistent with a change in the operating speed of an endogenous pacemaker (reviewed in Meck, 1996). For example, when rats that are trained on the peak interval procedure in a drug-free state are given dopamine D2 agonists at test, they respond earlier than expected, consistent with an increase in clock speed. When these animals are given dopamine antagonists, they respond later than expected, consistent with a decrease in clock speed.

Comparable findings have been shown in humans. Schizophrenics, who typically have increased levels of endogenous dopamine, appear to subjectively experience time as passing more quickly than objective time (Wahl & Sieg, 1980). Conversely, some studies have shown that patients with Parkinson's disease (PD), a degenerative disease of the nigrostriatal pathway which produces dopamine depletion in the neostriatum, subjectively experience time as passing more slowly than objective time when their dopamine levels are at their nadir (Malapani et al., 1998; Pastor et al., 1992). A direct relationship between these deficits and level of dopamine is supported by the finding that pharmacological restoration of normal dopamine levels can significantly ameliorate timing dysfunction in both schizophrenics (Angel, 1973) and PD patients (Pastor et al., 1992). Dopamine-dependent manipulations in timing performance have also been found in neurologically healthy adults. Administration of haloperidol, a D2 antagonist, resulted in significant deficits in time perception of both 50 ms and 1000 ms intervals relative to placebo controls (Rammsayer, 1993, 1999). In contrast, individuals given scopolamine, a muscarinic cholinergic antagonist, were unimpaired on duration perception of either interval (Rammsayer, 1999).

Nonetheless, dopamine is not the only psychoactive substance capable of producing distortions in perceived time on prospective tasks. Central stimulants such as caffeine and nicotine, which work on non-catecholaminergic neurotransmitter systems, also lead to verbal overestimates of time that are consistent with an increase in clock speed (Ague, 1974; Frankenhaeuser, 1959). Central depressants, such as alcohol, have the opposite effect (Lindman & Taxell, 1975). Variations in clock speed also can result from psychological manipulation. When subjects are stressed by the threat of electric shock (Curton & Lordahl, 1974), failure on a cognitive task (Lindman & Taxell, 1975), or annoying environmental stimuli (e.g., arrhythmic honking of a loud car horn for 5 minutes; Boltz, 1994), their perception of elapsed time is distorted in a manner consistent with a faster internal clock. The induction of relaxation through calming environmental sounds (e.g., gently lapping waves) leads to underestimation of elapsed time as if the rate of the internal clock has been slowed (Boltz, 1994). Taken together, these results suggest that any modulation of general arousal can influence the rate of an endogenous clock. Moreover, this arousal effect does not appear to be associated solely with the nigrostriatal dopaminergic system. Indeed, the ability of dopamine to regulate clock speed may relate fundamentally to its role in producing and maintaining states of high arousal in response to salient stimuli (e.g., Horvitz, 2000).

The Interval Timer Hypothesis

An alternative form of temporal representation is the interval timer. Similar to the way an egg timer or hour glass represents a specific duration, an interval timing model posits that a population of timing units exist, each tuned to a particular interval (Ivry, 1996). The contrast between this type of model and pacemaker models can be demonstrated by the following example. Consider a production task, such as periodic finger tapping, in which the target interval is either 400 or 600 ms. For the pacemaker model, a common periodic process is engaged for either duration, with the latter condition requiring a larger value in the accumulator prior to each response. In contrast, an interval model would posit that distinct elements would be activated for the two conditions. The activation of one element would result in responses every 400 ms while a different element would result in responses every 600 ms (see

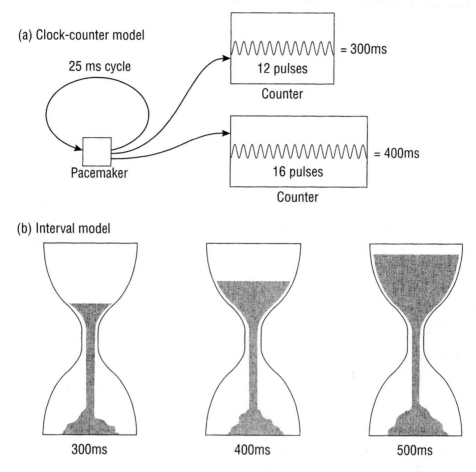

Figure 19.5: Two mechanisms for representing temporal information. (a) Clock-counter models postulate a pacemaker that produces output to a counter. Longer intervals are represented by increases in the number of pacemaker outputs that accumulate in the counter. (b) Interval-based models assume that different intervals are represented by distinct elements, each corresponding to a specific duration. Adapted from Current Opinion in Neurobiology, Vol 6, Ivry, R. B. The representation of temporal information in perception and motor control, 851-857, Copyright (1996), with permission from Elsevier Science.

also Figure 19.5). The elements here can be considered psychologically as functional units and may correspond physiologically to populations of neural signals that vary in their activation properties (Buonomano & Mauk, 1994). As such, at a functional level, a population of interval timing elements might form a chronotopic map in the brain, similar to the tonotopic organization of the auditory cortex (Ivry, 1996).

Early models of interval-based timing mechanisms focused on structural properties of neural connectivity, such as delay lines, which that might serve as the neural "hardware" for timing (e.g., Braitenberg, 1967). More recent theories, however, have favored "software" mechanisms that exploit relatively slow physiological processes to create a time-varying pattern of neural activity that can be modified through learning (Buonomano & Mauk, 1994). Much of this work is based on the findings that the cerebellum is the essential neural structure for eye blink conditioning in which a neutral stimulus such as a tone comes to predict an aversive unconditioned stimulus (e.g., an airpuff). For this form of learning to be adaptive, the animal must not only learn the association between the two stimuli, but it must also represent the precise interval between these events. Various computational models have been proposed, all of which explicitly postulate how the learning mechanisms associated with the cerebellar cortex might operate on time-varying physiological processes to create representations of arbitrary intervals (Buonomano & Mauk, 1994; Fiala, Grossberg, & Bullock, 1996). Such models are in accord with evidence showing that lesions of the cerebellar cortex disrupt the adaptive timing of the conditioned responses without abolishing the conditioned response itself (Perret, Ruiz, & Mauk, 1993).

Humans with cerebellar lesions are also impaired on this form of learning, although here the problem tends to be a failure to acquire the conditioned response (Daum et al., 1993; Topka, Valls Sole, Massaquoi, & Hallett, 1993; Woodruff-Pak, Papka, & Ivry, 1996). In such studies, of course, the damage is present prior to training and failure to acquire the conditioned response could result from an inability to accurately represent the critical interval. Interestingly, these same individuals exhibit normal autonomic conditioning under the same conditions, showing an increase in the galvanic skin response (GSR) over the conditioning period (Daum et al., 1993). Unlike the eyeblink response, the GSR does not require a temporal representation of the relationship between the conditioned and unconditioned stimuli. Thus, the eyeblink studies indicate that the cerebellum is not essential for all forms of aversive classical conditioning, but rather is specifically involved in those forms of learning that require precise timing (Ivry, 1993).

Interval models offer a flexible form of temporal coding. By combining broadly tuned temporal elements, a continuous representation of duration can be created. Pacemaker models, on the other hand, generally predict that performance will reflect the operation of a periodic process. These two models have been compared in time perception studies in which a standard interval is established through the repeated presentation of a periodic tone. This series presumably would entrain a pacemaker, and the output from this pacemaker should provide a reference that could facilitate perceptual judgments. Thus, the essential manipulation in these studies is to present the test interval either on or off the induced beat (see Figure 19.6). For example, if the first tone of the test interval falls on the beat, the interval will be judged as "short" if the second tone comes before the next beat. Performance here should be superior compared to a condition in which the test interval does not fall on the beats. In contrast,

Figure 19.6: S is the standard interval and t is the test interval. In the top row, the test interval is continuous with the last standard interval and can utilize a beat induced by the series of standard intervals. In the second row, the test interval is separated by a gap, but the first tone of the test interval occurs at a time aligned with the beats induced by the standard intervals (i.e., if they had continued). In the third row, the first tone of the test interval does not fall on a beat induced by the standard intervals. While pacemaker models predict superior performance for conditions depicted in the second row compared to the third row, the results have failed to demonstrated such an advantage. Adapted from "Mechanisms of perceptual timing: Beat-based or interval-based judgements?" by S. W. Keele et al., 1989, *Psychological Research*, 50, 251–256.

|s|s|s|s|s|s|s|s|t|

|s|s|s|s|s|s|s|s| |t|

|s|s|s|s|s|s|s|s| |t|

interval models do not require reference to the beats. Thus, these models do not predict a difference in performance between "on" and "off" beat conditions since the representation of the target interval can be arbitrarily triggered, much as one can start an egg timer in a flexible manner. The results of several studies of this type have favored the interval model (e.g., Keele, Nicoletti, Ivry, & Pokorny, 1989; Pashler, in press).

The proposed neural architecture of the interval timing system has functional limitations, however. Unlike pacemakers that could sum indefinitely, interval timers should be limited in terms of the range of intervals they can represent. It is unlikely that a neural system that provides real-time representations via differences in physiological events such as temporal summation, local inhibition, or variation in synaptic efficacy would be able to extend beyond a second or so. Eye blink conditioning, in both rabbits and humans is optimal when the interval between the conditioned and unconditioned stimuli is in the range of 200 to 500 ms (Smith, 1968). Thus, it can be hypothesized that the cerebellum provides interval-based representations, but must work in tandem with additional neural systems when the task requires temporal processing over a longer duration. Another problem for interval-based models is that they fail to provide a simple account of studies showing an inverse relationship between arousal and perceived duration (see previous section). Indeed, interval models have been developed to account for effects on the *variability* in temporal representations rather than effects indicative of a change in rate at which these representations are acquired.

One way of accommodating both cerebellar-based interval models and nigrostratial-based pacemaker models is to hypothesize that a pacemaker process comes into play when the temporal extent of an interval timing system is exceeded. In general, the effects of dopamine, as well as other substances/stimuli that produce increased arousal, have been assessed on tasks using longer intervals than those thought to be supported by interval timing mechanisms. Yet, as previously mentioned, distortions of relatively short intervals (<1 s) have been observed in patients with Parkinson's disease (Artieda, Pastor, Lacruz, & Obeso, 1992; Rammsayer & Classen, 1997) and following dopaminergic manipulations with normal individuals (Rammsayer, 1999). An alternative means of integrating the data from nigrostriatal and cerebellar models of timing would be to propose that interval timers alone provide basic temporal information, and manipulations of dopamine and/or arousal change the threshold associated with the gating of this temporal information into an accumulator. In support of this model, evidence suggests that dopamine levels influence the threshold at which sensory events trigger motor responses (Horvitz & Eyny, in press; White, 1986). If increased levels of dopamine decreased the threshold at which the gate to the accumulator was raised, accumulation of temporal events might occur earlier and at a faster rate. The resultant behavioral change would be similar to what one would expect if the speed of pacemaker were increased. Correspondingly, if lowered levels of dopamine and/or arousal increased the gate threshold then the behavioral consequences would be similar to what one would expect if the speed of a pacemaker was slowed.

Attention as a Gate to Working Memory for Current Time

Selective Attention to Time: the "Gate"

Even if general arousal modulates the threshold required to gate information from an endogenous clock into an accumulator, selective attention to time is necessary to trigger the flow of temporal information into working memory. This gating role of attention is evident in the familiar idioms "time flies when you're having fun," and "the watched pot never boils." Such sayings colorfully illustrate the interactions that can occur between temporal and non-temporal processing requirements, a relationship that has been the focus of many cognitive studies of time perception (e.g., Brown, 1997; Fortin & Breton, 1995; Macar, Grondin, & Casini, 1994; Zakay & Block, 1996). To the extent that a non-temporal task requires our attention, less attention will be paid to time. When attention is distracted by a non-temporal task, the amount of temporal information gated into working memory is reduced, resulting in a lower subjective estimate of elapsed time. Behaviorally, the individual will make errors of underestimation and overproduction that are typically proportional to the difficulty of the non-temporal task (Brown, 1997). In addition to a bias toward underestimation, variability may also increase because the trade-off of attention between the temporal and non-temporal task is not always consistent. On the other hand, a boring non-temporal task (e.g., waiting for water to boil) will allow attention to be overly focused on the gating of temporal information. If during this boring task the amount of attention focused on processing of temporal information is greater than the "baseline" level for that individual, he or she will sense that time is "dragging on" and produce greater estimates of elapsed time.

The role of attention in gating temporal information into working memory is evident in patients with compromised attentional resources, such as those with frontal lobe damage, even when attention is not distracted by a non-temporal secondary task. Mangels, Ivry, & Shimizu (1998) compared patients with frontal lesions and control participants on a time discrimination of 400 and 4000 ms intervals. In this task, subjects first listened to a tone of constant duration (i.e., the "standard"), then maintained that standard in working memory while a second tone was played for comparison. Compared with controls, the second tone had to be played longer for the patients in order for it to be judged as equal in duration to the standard. This increase suggests that the attention allocated to maintaining the standard diverted attention away from perception of the comparison. When the comparison tone was played, the gate had to left open longer in order to achieve an equal number of counts to the standard, which had been encoded without any additional working memory load.

Trade-offs in attention between temporal and non-temporal tasks appear to occur even for extremely short durations (<100) as long as the task demands explicit representation of time. Both normal (Witherspoon & Allan, 1985) and amnesic subjects (Paller, Mayes, McDermott, Pickering, & Meudell, 1991) judge briefly presented words (40–200 ms) as lasting for shorter durations when the word was primed by prior exposure than when shown for the first time (i.e., unprimed). The relatively greater perceptual fluency of the primed words may have made more attention available for simultaneously processing duration, or alternatively, allowed an earlier switch of attention from word identification to duration perception. Yet, although selective attention is necessary to gain conscious access to temporal information regardless of duration to be timed, this does not mean that it is uninfluenced by the length of the interval. The longer that attention must be sustained on temporal processing, the greater the likelihood that attentional focus will wander, gating will become erratic and temporal representations will become more variable (Mangels et al., 1998).

In order for these types of attentional trade-off effects to occur, the gating process must be under the control of a central processor that has access to both temporal and non-temporal representations, and can prioritize the allocation of attention across these representations in response to exogenous or endogenous cues. Baddeley's (1986) model of working memory provides a framework for such a central processor, as well as domain-specific components for maintaining the representations themselves. In this model, working memory is conceptualized as consisting of *multiple "slave" systems* that are primarily responsible for temporary storage and rehearsal of internal representations and a *central executive* that, among other things, determines how attention will be allocated across these slave systems. Damage to these different components would result in different patterns of impairment. Whereas damage to a single slave system would selectively impair on-line maintenance and manipulation of information in that particular domain, damage to the central executive would primarily impair performance when information had to be managed simultaneously across multiple domains. Thus, investigations of central and domain-specific temporal processing deficits have involved comparisons of single- and dual-task performance in which a temporal processing task is performed alone or in combination with a non-temporal task.

Casini and Ivry (1999) tested patients with frontal or cerebellar lesions on auditory duration discrimination and pitch discrimination tasks (standard interval = 400 ms, 600 Hz), performed either as independent, single-tasks, or as a dual-task requiring simultaneous duration and pitch judgments. Although both patient groups were impaired relative to controls on the single-task discriminations, only the frontal patients were impaired disproportionately in the dual-task condition on both duration and pitch judgments. In contrast, the dual task condition led to an added deficit only on the duration task for the cerebellar patients. Thus, deficits following frontal damage were nonspecific with regard to domain, but particularly apparent under dual-task demands, consistent with the proposed role of the central executive (see also Baddeley & Della Salla, 1996; Baddeley, Della Salla, Papagno, & Spinnler, 1997). The specificity of cerebellar patient's dual-task deficits is consistent with the hypothesis that the cerebellum is essential for maintaining temporal representations. Alternatively, temporal processing may simply demand more attention than pitch processing and thus may be more sensitive to reduced resources. To demonstrate that the dual-task deficit in cerebellar patients is truly selective for temporal information it will be necessary to demonstrate a double-dissociation between dual-task deficits in temporal and non-temporal tasks.

Although evidence of competition for resources between temporal and non-temporal tasks is one of the most robust findings in the cognitive literature on temporal processing, interference between temporal and non-temporal processes does not occur in all situations. Boltz (1998) has shown that when temporal and non-temporal information are well integrated and interdependent, one can be processed without cost to the other. This level of integration is achieved in music where melodic and rhythmic accent structures co-occur in predictable places, thereby giving it "structural coherence" (e.g., the Star Spangled Banner). Specifically, Boltz demonstrated that the duration of structurally coherent music was remembered accurately regardless of whether subjects attended to pitch, duration, both, or neither. On the other hand, when temporal and pitch accent structures were dissociated (e.g., matching the rhythm of the Star Spangled Banner with the pitches of America the Beautiful), subjects were only able to estimate the duration of incoherent melodies, when they attended to duration. When asked to attend to pitch, the subjects overestimated the duration of the song. If told to attend to both, they underestimated its duration in a manner consistent with the interference effects described earlier.

Thus far, neuropsychological studies of time perception have primarily used paradigms in which intervals are arbitrarily determined by the experimenter and linked to neutral stimuli such as a light or tone. Thus, the relationship between temporal and non-temporal information is either unstructured or at least unlearned and not readily apparent. These well-controlled paradigms have been critical in isolating timing components. Yet, they lack the coherent structure present in music, language, and many everyday temporally-guided behaviors (Boltz, 1992). Neuropsychological studies using structural coherence as a dependent variable would not only provide ecological validity, but might help distinguish between those processes associated with attention to time from those fundamental to generating the representations of time themselves.

Working Memory for Time

In the cognitive models of time perception described earlier, the gate that allows clock pulses (or subintervals) to flow into working memory is modeled as separate from the working memory buffer that serves to accumulate and maintain this temporal information over a brief delay. Specifically, the working memory buffer serves a dynamic updating system that keeps a running tally of the accumulated output from the pacemaker, as well as serving to keep the target interval temporarily available for comparison. Both functions come into play in time discrimination tasks, in which a target interval or standard is presented on each trial and followed, after a short delay (˜1–4 s), by an interval that is shorter or longer than the standard. While encoding the second interval, the working memory buffer must keep an active representation of the recently encoded standard interval for comparison.

Could the working memory buffer that is involved in the acquisition and maintenance of temporal information represent a distinct slave system? Baddeley's original model included only two slave systems: an articulatory loop for verbal information and a sketchpad for visuo-spatial information. These systems were differentiated by the way in which information was coded for rehearsal, as well as their hemispheric lateralization in the brain. Whereas the articulatory loop used phonological codes in left frontal region, the visuospatial sketchpad used imaginal codes in the right frontal region (Baddeley, 1986; Baddeley & Della Salla, 1996). Since then, however, models of working memory have undergone additional fractionation. Data from neurophysiological and neuroimaging studies strongly suggest that visuo-spatial working memory may actually be composed of separate neural systems for maintaining object and spatial information (e.g., Goldman-Rakic 1996; Smith and Jonides 1998). Furthermore, Baddeley has recently postulated an additional, "episodic" working memory buffer that sustains multi-dimensional codes (Baddeley, 2000). Consistent with this idea, (Prabhakaran, Narayanan, Zhao, & Gabrieli, 2000) identified a region in the right frontal cortex (BA10) that was differentially active when subjects had to temporarily maintain spatial and object information in an integrated format compared to when the two attributes were maintained separately.

Despite the fact that the current trend toward fractionation may make existence of a separate working memory for time more agreeable, cognitive and neurophysiological evidence for an independent system is currently inconclusive. Presence of an independent temporal working memory buffer would gain support from studies demonstrating greater interference when multiple durations must be maintained in working memory than when a single duration must be maintained along with information of a non-temporal nature (i.e., within-domain interference > between-domain interference). At least one cognitive study has used this type of selective interference task to demonstrate that temporal and spatial working memory systems do not necessarily interfere with each other. Halbig and colleagues (Halbig, Mecklinger, Schriefers, & Friederici, 1998) measured performance on working memory tasks in which subjects held either temporal information (400, 700, or 1000 ms durations) or spatial information (position of a dot) over a brief (< 10 s) delay. During this delay, subjects simply waited until the test phase or were engaged in one of two tasks: a spatial classification task in which they compared

Figure 19.7: Mean accuracy for temporal and spatial memory tasks as a function of three interference tasks. Crosses represent performance during the non-interference baseline condition, triangles during the temporal classification task and dots during the spatial classification task. Adapted from *Neuropsychologia*, 36, Halbig et al., Double dissociation of processing temporal and spatial information in working memory, 305–311, Copyright 1998, with permission of Elsevier Science.

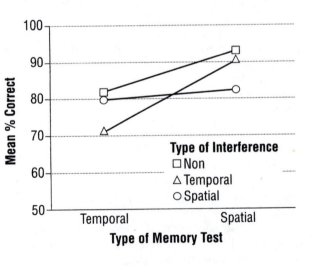

the position of two successive stimuli, or a temporal classification task in which they compared the duration of two successive stimuli. Halbig et al. (1998) found that the spatial classification task interfered with working memory for spatial, but not temporal information, whereas a temporal classification task interfered with working memory for temporal, but not spatial information (see Figure 19.7). This double dissociation is particularly interesting given that both spatial and temporal information have been shown to involve similar parietal and frontal regions (Cabeza & Nyberg, 1997), and both require dynamic, relational processing (Petrides, 1994). At present, however, the majority of data addressing this issue comes from cognitive rather than neuropsychological studies. Neuropsychological studies have primarily focused on the role of selective attention in governing the gating of information into working memory, rather the working memory functions themselves. Thus, further research is necessary to determine the degree of cognitive and neural overlap between the "slave" systems for temporal and non-temporal information.

Encoding and Decoding of Reference Intervals for Comparison with Current Time

Thus far, we have discussed the cognitive and neural mechanisms that support internal representations of objective time and how this information may be subject to attention and working memory constraints. For tasks that require the comparison of two closely presented intervals of arbitrary duration, working memory may be sufficient for acquisition, storage and comparison. Other situations, however, require that stored intervals be retrieved from long-term reference memory for comparison with a current estimate of time past. For example, suppose that you stop at the traffic light right in front of your house—one which you have encountered enough times to have encoded the time it takes to turn green. On this particular day, the "waiting time" seems to have greatly exceeded this stored value and you suspect that the light is broken. Having waited what you feel is "long enough," you might look around for on-coming cars (and a lurking policeman) and proceed through the red light. In this example, an interval that was encoded into long-term memory must be decoded or retrieved for comparison with the contents of working memory.

It is well-established that patients with anterograde amnesia due to damage in medial temporal lobe/hippocampal or diencephalic regions have deficits in encoding information in long-term declarative memory (Milner, Squire, & Kandel, 1998). Thus, we would expect these patients also would have difficulty in encoding target intervals into long-term memory. Yet, to our knowledge, long-term memory for duration has not been assessed in amnesics. Studies of temporal estimation in amnesic patients have systematically varied the duration of the interval, but not the duration between interval training and test (Kinsbourne & Hicks, 1990; Richards, 1973; Shaw & Aggleton, 1994; Williams, Medwedeff, & Haban, 1989). Temporal estimations were made immediately following presentation of stimulus and, therefore, were based on the contents of working memory, which is intact in these patients. In addition to assessing short-term memory for long durations however, it would also be of interest to assess long-term memory for short durations. For example, one would predict that amnesics would demonstrate the same explicit/implicit dissociations in long-term memory for short durations—those that can be acquired accurately using working memory—that they do for non-temporal information. Repeated exposure to stimulus-duration pairings might allow for acquisition of target intervals via spared neural structures, such as the cerebellum or basal ganglia, which are implicated in both clock timing and procedural learning (e.g., Knowlton, Mangels, & Squire, 1996).

Although the medial temporal/hippocampal regions are likely necessary for successful encoding of temporal representations, recent evidence suggests that the dopamine-dependent circuits affected by Parkinson's disease are necessary for the subsequent "decoding," or retrieval of that information. Parkinson's patients tested "off" medication demonstrated an un-

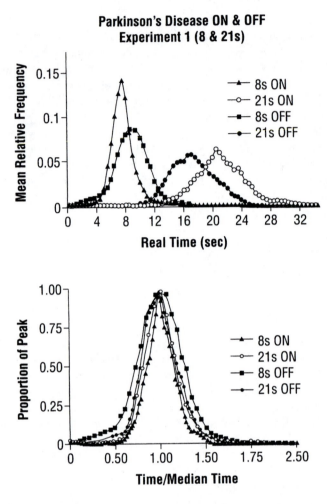

Figure 19.8: Relative frequency distributions for the two target durations (8 and 21 sec) showing accuracy and variability of estimation in PD patients ON (white) and OFF (black) medication (upper panel). The two functions of the same subjects when plotted in time relative to the median time and normalized as proportions of the maximum relative frequency superpose in the ON state but not in the OFF state (lower panel) (Malapani et al., 1998). Adapted with permission of MIT Press.

usual effect on the peak interval task following training with two intervals (dual-interval peak procedure), one short (8 s) and one long (21 s) (Malapani et al., 1998). As shown in Figure 19.8, the shorter signal was overestimated and the longer signal was underestimated as if the two intervals in reference memory had been integrated—what the authors called a "migration effect." This effect is not consistent with what one would expect if dopamine reduction only led to a slowing of an endogenous pacemaker or difficulty in gating of representations to an accumulator. Nor could a clock deficit account for the persistence of the migration effect over a test session with intermittent feedback. Rather it appears that the reference memory component of the timing system was impaired.

In an interesting follow-up study, Malapani, Deweer, and Gibbon (2000) tested a new group of Parkinson patients on a similar dual-interval peak procedure over two sessions, a training session and a test session. In the training session, the participants were provided with feedback to learn the intervals of 6 s and 17 s. In the test session, retrieval processes were assessed by eliminating the feedback. Four groups of subjects were tested by the factorial combination of "on" and "off" medication states during training or test. Patients in the "off" state during the testing phase replicated the migration effect regardless of whether they had been trained in the "off" or "on" state. However, when trained in an "off" state and tested in an "on" state, the migration effect was absent, even though it had been present during training. The authors suggest that dopamine depletion may impair the ability to suppress interference from other intervals learned in that context and results in a coupling between different temporal representations at retrieval. Not only would deficits in suppressing interference from prior reinforcement be consistent with difficulties in task switching evidenced by PD patients on non-temporal tasks (e.g., Hayes, Davidson, Keele, & Rafal, 1998), but they would also suggest that dopamine-related gating deficits can affect both the on-line acquisition and long-term memory retrieval of temporal representations.

Counting the Seconds

An appealing aspect of the SET model is that it is designed to account for temporal phenomena over a wide range of intervals. Yet, people generally choose to alter their strategy for temporal processing when the target duration extends into the seconds to minutes range. In particular, we quickly resort to a verbal strategy of counting out longer durations in order to maintain precision. Counting effectively decomposes these longer intervals into smaller temporal units that subjectively may be more "manageable" because they are within the optimal range of an internal timing system. Given that timing of these shorter intervals produces less clock variance (noise) than timing a longer interval, counting should reduce overall variance in timing performance as long as the counter itself does not add substantial noise (Kileen, 1992; Kileen & Weiss, 1987). Thus, one would expect that the COV would be smaller when the subjects are counting explicitly. This expected decrease in COV has been shown in both time perception (Mangels et al., 1998; Wearden, 1991), and time production (Fetterman & Killeen, 1990; Grondin, 1992).

What is the minimum duration at which we begin to count? And what is an optimal subinterval for counting? Answers to these questions might reveal fundamental principles regarding functional attributes of the internal clock, such as its upper limit and optimal rate. Grondin, Meilleur-Wells and Lachance (1999) attempted to measure the minimum interval at which counting became beneficial in a time perception task. Subjects were tested on a series of discrimination tasks with the reference duration ranging from 700 to 1900 ms. Using a variety of analytic procedures, estimates were made of the point at which counting facilitated performance in terms of the temporal acuity. Counting was found to confer a benefit for durations longer than about 1.2 s. Time production tasks also suggest a breakpoint somewhere between 1 and 2 s (Mates, Mueller, Radil, & Poeppel, 1994). When asked to synchronize tapping with a series of isosynchronous tones (tones with a constant ISI), people tap in anticipation of the tone for intervals below 2 s, but respond reactively for intervals above this range. Finally, rhythmic events fail to appear temporally grouped if the interval between successive events spans is much more than 1500 ms (Fraisse, 1978). Similarly, eyeblink conditioning becomes poorer when the interval between the conditioned and unconditioned stimuli is lengthened (e.g., >600 ms), and appears to require the recruitment of neural circuits outside the cerebellum (McGlinchey-Berroth, 2000). Together, these results suggest that timing below the breakpoint may rely primarily on real-time representations, whereas above this point, the influence of attention, memory and strategy become more apparent.

As for the optimal subdivision for counting, intervals between 250 and 500 ms have been shown to provide optimal timing performance for durations in the range of 1 to 5 s (Grondin, 1992; Kileen & Weiss, 1987). Although the duration of this optimal subinterval varies by 250 ms, that variation is due mainly to individual differences between subjects. Within-subjects, the preferred rate of counting is relatively consistent across different durations (Fetterman & Killeen, 1990). Nonetheless, a counting tempo of 2–4 Hz would likely prove tedious for durations much above 5 s. For intervals of 5–30 s we often resort to subdivisions in the 1-s range, which we regulate by "filling" with words that take approximately 1 s to say when articulated at a prototypical rate (i.e., one-one-thousand, two-one-thousand, three-one-thousand, etc.).

Despite the fact that counting may be a relatively ubiquitous component of duration processing above 1 s, it is rarely studied in patient groups (for exceptions see Pastor et al., 1992;

Rubia, Schuri, von Cramon, & Poeppel, 1997). Indeed, many neuropsychological studies of temporal processing in the seconds range have considered counting an undesirable strategy that could interfere with direct evaluation of clock function. For example, to prevent counting, Malapani and colleagues (Malapani et al., 2000; Malapani et al., 1997; Malapani et al., 1998) interposed a digit-reading distracter task while patients with Parkinson's disease (PD) or cerebellar damage timed 8 and 21 s intervals. The purpose of the secondary task was to eliminate potential strategy differences that might exist between the groups. Yet, it also reduces the amount of attentional resources available for tracking time. Patients with PD may have secondary deficits in frontal-lobe functions, including the regulation of attention (e.g., Brown & Marsden, 1986; Taylor, Saint-Cyr, & Lang, 1986) and patients with cerebellar damage show differential interference from a secondary task on time perception (Casini & Ivry, 1999). Thus, active prevention of a counting strategy may not only have prevented optimal timing performance in these subjects, but may have introduced additional variance in attentional gating and/or working memory.

Mangels et al. (1998) evaluated the use of counting strategies in a study involving patients with lesions of the cerebellum or lateral prefrontal cortex. In an initial experiment, the cerebellar patients were impaired on time discrimination tasks involving standard intervals of either 400 ms or 4 s. Patients with frontal lesions were found to exhibit larger deficits in time discrimination of a 4 s interval, relative to a 400 ms interval. Additionally, only the frontal group failed to exhibit a decrease in COV between the 400 ms and 4 s conditions, suggesting that the frontal patients failed to use a variance-reducing counting strategy in the 4 s task.

To test this hypothesis directly, various types of strategic support were introduced in a second experiment. In one condition, tones were presented to subdivide the 4 s standard interval into 10 equal subintervals of 400 msec each. Although these pacing tones could be used to guide a counting strategy, no explicit instruction about how to use these markers was given. In a subsequent session, the subjects were given a subdivided standard interval, plus explicit instruction to use the subdivision as a rhythm for regulating a counting strategy. As can be seen in Figure 19.9, the control participants demonstrated immediate improvement when provided with the subdividing markers even when a counting strategy was not explicitly given. In contrast, the patients did not demonstrate significant improvement unless these subdivisions were paired with explicit counting instructions. Thus, long-duration timing deficits in prefrontal patients appear to be attributable, in part, to the same type of deficit in self-initiated strategy use that is responsible for their poor performance on other cognitive tasks (Gershberg & Shimamura, 1995; Levine et al., 1998; Mangels, 1997). In contrast, the timing deficits of a group of patients with cerebellar damage were not as strongly influenced the markers and/or counting instruction, suggesting that their deficit lies outside the influence of strategy.

How Many Clocks?

Our tools for measuring time are designed to approximate the duration in question. It would be impossible to measure seconds using a calendar, and foolish to measure months or years with a stopwatch. Throughout this chapter, we have hinted at the possibility that multiple cognitive and neural mechanisms are necessary to accommodate measurement of all possible temporal durations. Yet, an implicit implication of many models is that the same pacemaker provides the pulses for all temporal intervals with different temporal representations being a function of an accumulation process. It does not seem plausible that a single pacemaker would underlie all of the temporal phenomena and regularities that are manifest in an organism's ecology. We should not expect that the representation of a 24-hour day requires the accumulation of the number of pulses required for 1 s × 86,400. Rather, it is more likely that multiple endogenous clocks are used across various ranges. Clocks that are optimal for representing the short

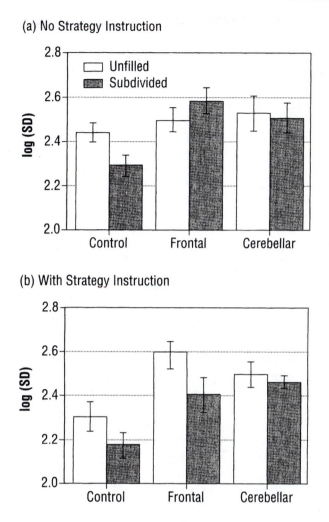

(a) No Strategy Instruction

(b) With Strategy Instruction

Figure 19.9: Mean difference threshold (log transform of the standard deviation [SD] of the psychophysical discrimination function) of frontal patients, cerebellar patients and control subjects on a 4s time discrimination task. The standard was either an unfilled interval or subdivided into ten 400 ms intervals with brief (50 ms) marker tones. Panel A: The effect of subdivision when no explicit strategy on how to use these markers was provided. Only control subjects benefited from the markers. Panel B: The effect of the subdivision when subjects were explicitly instructed to use the markers to count out the duration of the standard and comparison intervals. Both frontal patients and control subjects benefited from the markers when this additional instructional support was provided. Adapted from Mangels, Ivry and Shimizu (1998).

intervals that are used for regulating our immediate actions are likely distinct from those required for representing longer intervals. For example, Aschoff (1985) found that estimations in the range of hours, but not minutes, were influenced by wakefulness and circadian rhythms. Even within the milliseconds to seconds range that characterizes most of the research on time psychophysics, temporal acuity may require a population of timing elements. As described previously, these could take form a population of interval timers, or they may consist of a set of pacemakers that span a range of frequencies (e.g., Church & Broadbent, 1990).

A recent review of animal and human studies of temporal processing supports the view that there may be different processing mechanisms for different intervals (Gibbon et al., 1997). Comparisons across studies measuring intervals ranging from milliseconds to hours indicate that the coefficient of variation (COV) is not constant across all time ranges. For short durations from a few milliseconds up to 100 ms, the COV decreases. It is likely that processing in this region is constrained by sensory limitations such as masking effects and other non-temporal factors. The COV becomes roughly constant between 100-1500 ms, the range over which we have hypothesized that real-time representations are available. When counting-type strategies are prevented, another increase in the COV becomes apparent after 1500 ms, and remains constant at this new value up to about 500 s (8.3 min). A final increase is found for tasks spanning longer intervals up to hours. The break points suggest that the relative involvement of temporal and/or non-temporal processing components varies as one shifts from timing in the subsecond, seconds-to-minutes and minutes-to-hours range. However, as Gibbon et al. (1997) point out, the nature of the temporal task can have a large effect on the absolute COV, making between-study comparisons of interval range problematic. Unfortunately, as of yet, the complete range of milliseconds to minutes has not been examined systematically within a single study.

One way to address this issue of multiple clocks is to see if dissociations arise in the performance of neurological groups when tested over various temporal ranges. Such dissociations, either within or between patient groups, could point to range-specific timing components. Although there are few studies that address this issue, the data thus far suggest that the cerebellum and basal ganglia both contribute to timing in the millisecond and seconds ranges. Patients with cerebellar damage consistently demonstrate impaired timing of intervals from 400 ms to at least 21 s (Ivry & Keele, 1989; Malapani et al., 1997; Mangels et al., 1998; Nichelli et al., 1996), although one study found that cerebellar patients performed normally when intervals were less than 300 ms (Nichelli et al., 1996). Timing deficits in the millisecond and second range also have been found in patients with Parkinson's disease (PD) tested "off" medication (Malapani et al., 1998; Pastor et al., 1992). Although some studies have also found impaired timing in patients tested "on" medication (Harrington & Haaland, 1998), the results are more mixed (Duchek, Balota, & Ferraro, 1994; Hellstrom, Lang, Portin, & Rinne, 1997; Ivry & Keele, 1989).

The frontal cortex, on the other hand, appears to become more critical as the target interval becomes longer. Patients with frontal lobe lesions are consistently impaired on tasks in which the intervals span the seconds range, but are either unimpaired (Mangels et al., 1998) or less impaired (Nichelli et al., 1995) on durations in the millisecond range. The potentially systematic relationship between frontal lobe function and duration length further supports the role of this region in the sustained attention and working memory components of time perception. Consistent with this hypothesis, people that were given midazolam, a benzodiazepine with known effects on memory, were impaired on temporal processing of 1 s, but not 100 ms durations (Rammsayer, 1999). In addition, normal aging, which is associated with declines in attention and working memory function presumably due to frontal dysfunction (e.g., West, 1996), has been shown to impair duration estimation in the seconds-to-minutes range (Craik & Hay, 1999), without affecting discrimination of intervals less than 100 ms (Rammsayer, Lima, & Vogel, 1993).

If working memory serves as a buffer for accumulating temporal information, we should expect some upper limit on the range that this system could effectively subserve. Although optimal for use within the seconds range, it would most likely be of limited usefulness for durations in the minutes to hours range. At these longer ranges, it would become extremely challenging to maintain constant and focused attention to time. Use of an internal clock may be inefficient and attention and long-term memory process, such as those involved in retrospective time estimation, may become more dominant.

To determine the duration at which timing exceeds the limits of working memory and begins to require long-term memory processes, Kinsbourne and colleagues have examined time estimation performance in patients with frontal lobe damage and patients with anterograde amnesia. Frontal patients overestimated intervals ranging around 10 s (Mimura, Kinsbourne, & O'Conner, in press), and the degree of overestimation was associated with perseveration on standard neuropsychological tests of frontal function. At longer durations (20 s), the extent of the overestimation decreased and eventually reversed to a mild underestimation by 30 s. In contrast, patients with anterograde amnesia showed no systematic bias toward over- or underestimation for durations in the 10–30 s range, but severely underestimated durations in the minutes range (Kinsbourne & Hicks, 1990; Richards, 1973; Shaw & Aggelton, 1994; Williams et al., 1989). Intervals longer than 30 s were perceived by amnesics to last about 15–30 s, regardless of their actual length. These results suggest that 15–30 s is the upper limit of the working memory span for time. Durations of more than 30 s appear to rely on storage of events or event transitions in long-term memory, similar to retrospective estimation. Indeed, greater reliance of longer durations on long-term memory provides a possible explanation for why they are underestimated even in normal individuals. In the normal transition from short-term to long-term memory, there will be some measure of information loss. If decision processes do not compensate for that loss, long durations will be evaluated as having fewer event transitions than actually occurred.

CONCLUSIONS

We have chosen to structure this review around the two related temporal processing models, scalar expectancy theory (SET) and the attentional-gating model. Both models specify a series of distinct cognitive modules underlying temporal cognition, and therefore provide a framework for neuropsychological studies that seek to establish the cognitive and neural mechanisms for temporal processing tasks. Specifically, they make predictions concerning patterns of spared and impaired performance following damage to clock, memory and decision making operations. As such, they separate those processes that are specific to temporal processing, such as an internal clock, from those that may provide less domain-specific operations, such as attention, memory, and decision making. For even if they may are not specific to temporal processing, these latter operations are still essential to temporally-constrained behaviors, perhaps permitting conscious access to temporal information and supporting declarative memory systems that are required for representing temporal contingencies.

The usefulness of applying these cognitive frameworks to neuropsychological data has been borne out over the past 20 years. In particular, they have informed our understanding of the neural basis of time perception. For example, demonstration of impaired temporal discrimination tasks in patients with basal ganglia or cerebellar damage challenged traditional views that linked these two subcortical regions exclusively with motor control. Even though simply correlating these subcortical regions with specific timing deficits has not revealed the underlying neural mechanism of the endogenous clock directly, they have provided a neuroanatomical starting point from which to investigate clock physiology. Indeed, the present debate between pacemaker and interval timer mechanisms of clock function will probably be resolved at the neurophysiological level, rather than the neuropsychological level. Neuropsychological studies have been instrumental, however, in demonstrating that the clock stage can be decomposed into processes that generate, gate and accumulate temporal representations. This approach is currently being extended to examine issues related to how temporal representations are encoded and decoded into long-term memory. These results provide some examples of areas in which neuropsychological findings have not only specified the brain regions involved in time perception, but also have served the complementary purpose of furthering our understanding of the cognitive operations that underlie timing behaviors.

Many issues in this arena remain to be clarified, however. For example, we suggested that both arousal and selective attention could act upon the gating mechanism separating the clock from conscious awareness, but in slightly different ways. Selective attention most likely controls whether output from the neural clock will have access to working memory, whereas variation in arousal may influence the threshold of this gating operation. Although prior theorizing has tended to assume that arousal has a direct effect on the clock itself, postulating that arousal influences temporal processing at the gating operation is also consistent with the extant data. Future experiments are required to evaluate the merits of these two views. In addition, we argue that this gate serves as a point of interface between a central executive with access to both temporal and non-temporal processes and a working memory buffer that may be domain-specific. Current behavioral evidence suggests that temporal information may be maintained in a working memory buffer that is dissociable from that which maintains spatial information. A separate neural system for temporal working memory could also be argued on the basis that frontal regions interact with subcortical regions for the purpose of maintaining active representations of time, where as they interact with posterior cortical regions for the purpose of representing words, objects, and space. Nonetheless, even if working memory for time involves some neural and cognitive components that are separate from other domains of working memory, there is likely to be considerable overlap. Counting involves the use of verbal codes, and our metaphors for time are frequently spatial in nature (i.e., time moving forwards, flying by, etc.; Traugott, 1978). An understanding of how we code temporal information will be essential as we seek to specify the operations that utilize these representations.

REFERENCES

Ague, C. (1974). Cardiovascular variables, skin conductance and time estimation: Changes after the administration of small does of nicotine. *Psychopharmacologia, 37,* 109–125.

Allan, L. G. (1979). The perception of time. *Perception & Psychophysics, 26,* 340–354.

Allan, L. G., & Gibbon, J. (1991). Human bisection at the geometric mean. *Learning and Motivation, 22,* 39–46.

Angel, H. V. (1973). Role of chlorpromazine in maintaining timing behavior in schizophrenics. *Psychopharmacologia, 28,* 185–194.

Artieda, J., Pastor, M. A., Lacruz, F., & Obeso, J. A. (1992). Temporal discrimination is abnormal in Parkinson's disease. *Brain, 115,* 199–210.

Aschoff, J. (1985). On the perception of time during prolonged temporal isolation. *Human Neurobiology, 4,* 41–52.

Baddeley, A. (1986). *Working memory.* Oxford, UK: Oxford University Press.

Baddeley, A. (2000). *The episodic buffer: A new component of working memory?* Manuscript submitted for publication.

Baddeley, A., & Della Salla, S. (1996). Working memory and executive control. *Philosophical Transactions of the Royal Society of London: Series B, Biological Sciences, 351*(1346), 1397–1403.

Baddeley, A., Della Salla, S., Papagno, C., & Spinnler, H. (1997). Dual-task performance in dysexecutive and nondysexecutive patients with a frontal lesion. *Neuropsychology, 11*(2), 187–194.

Block, R. A. (1990). Models of psychological time. In R. A. Block (Ed.), *Cognitive models of psychological time* (pp. 1–35). Hillsdale, NJ: Lawrence Erlbaum.

Block, R. A. (1992). Prospective and retrospective duration judgment: The role of information processing and memory. In F. Macar & V. Pouthas (Eds.), *Time, action and cognition: Towards bridging the gap* (pp. 141–152). Dordrecht, Netherlands: Kluwer Academic.

Block, R. A., & Zakay, D. (1997). Prospective and retrospective duration judgments: A meta-analytic review. *Psychonomic Bulletin & Review, 4*(2), 184–197.

Boltz, M. G. (1992). The remembering of auditory event durations. *Journal of Experimental Psychology: Learning, Memory and Cognition, 18,* 938-956.

Boltz, M. G. (1994). Changes in internal tempo and effects on the learning and remembering of event durations. *Journal of Experimental Psychology: Learning, Memory and Cognition, 20*(5), 1154–1171.

Boltz, M. G. (1998). The processing of temporal and nontemporal information in the remembering of event durations and musical structure. *Journal of Experimental Psychology: Human Perception and Performance, 24*(4), 1087–1104.

Braitenberg, V. (1967). Is the cerebellar cortex a biological clock in the millisecond range? *Progress in Brain Research, 25,* 334–346.

Brown, R. G., & Marsden, C. D. (1986). Visuospatial function in Parkinson's disease. *Brain, 109,* 987–1002.

Brown, S. W. (1997). Attentional resources in timing: Interference effects in concurrent temporal and nontemporal working memory tasks. *Perception & Psychophysics, 59*(7), 1118–1140.

Buonomano, D., & Mauk, M. (1994). Neural network model of the cerebellum: Temporal discrimination and the timing of motor responses. *Neural Computation, 6,* 38–55.

Cabeza, R., & Nyberg, L. (1997). Imaging cognition: An empirical review of PET studies with normal subjects. *Journal of Cognitive Neuroscience, 9*(1), 1–26.

Casini, L., & Ivry, R. (1999). Effects of divided attention on time perception in patients with lesions of the cerebellum or frontal lobe. *Neuropsychology, 13*(1), 10–21.

Church, R., & Broadbent, H. A. (1990). Alternative representations of time, number and rate. *Cognition, 37,* 55–81.

Craik, F. I. M., & Hay, J. F. (1999). Aging and judgments of duration: Effects of task complexity and method of estimation. *Perception & Psychophysics, 61*(3), 549–560.

Curton, E. D., & Lordahl, D. S. (1974). Effects of attentional focus and arousal on time estimation. *Journal of Experimental Psychology, 103,* 861–867.

Daum, I., Schugens, M. M., Ackermann, H., Lutzenberger, W., Dichgans, J., & Birbaumer, N. (1993). Classical conditioning after cerebellar lesions in humans. *Behavioral Neuroscience, 107*(5), 748–756.

Duchek, J. M., Balota, D. A., & Ferraro, F. R. (1994). Component analysis of a rhythmic finger tapping task in individuals with senile dementia of the Alzheimer's type and in individuals with Parkinson's disease. *Neuropsychology, 8*(2), 218–226.

Fetterman, J. G., & Killeen, P. R. (1990). A componential analysis of pacemaker-counting timing systems. *Journal of Experimental Psychology: Human Perception and Performance, 16,* 766–780.

Fiala, J. C., Grossberg, S., & Bullock, D. (1996). Metabotropic glutamate receptor activation in cerebellar Purkinje cells as substrate for adaptive timing of the classically conditioned eye-blink response. *Journal of Neuroscience, 16,* 3760–3774.

Fortin, C., & Breton, R. (1995). Temporal interval production and processing in working memory. *Perception and Psychophysics, 57*(2), 203-215.

Fraisse, P. (1978). Time and rhythm perception. In E. C. Carterette & M. P. Friedman (Eds.), *Handbook of perception* (Vol. 8, pp. 203-254). New York: Academic Press.

Frankenhaeuser, M. (1959). *Estimation of time: An experimental study.* Stockholm: Almquist & Wiksell.

Gershberg, F. B., & Shimamura, A. P. (1995). The role of the frontal lobes in the use of organizational strategies in free recall. *Neuropsychologia, 13,* 1305-1333.

Gibbon, J. (1992). Ubiquity of scalar timing with a Poisson clock. *Journal of Mathematical Psychology, 36,* 283-293.

Gibbon, J., & Church, R. M. (1984). Sources of variance in an information processing theory of timing. In H. L. Roitblat, T. G. Bever, & H. S. Terrace (Eds.), *Animal cognition* (pp. 465-488). Hillsdale, NJ: Lawrence Erlbaum.

Gibbon, J., Church, R. M., & Meck, W. (Eds.). (1984). *Scalar timing in memory* (Vol. 423).

Gibbon, J., Malapani, C., Dale, C. L., & Gallistel, C. R. (1997). Toward a neurobiology of temporal cognition: Advances and challenges. *Current Opinion in Neurobiology, 7,* 170-184.

Goldman-Rakic, P. S. (1996). The prefrontal landscape: implications of functional architecture for understanding human mentation and the central executive. *Philosophical Transactions of the Royal Society of London: Series B, Biological Sciences, 351*(1346), 1445-1453.

Grondin, S. (1992). Production of time intervals from segmented and nonsegmented inputs. *Perception and Psychophysics, 52*(3), 345-350.

Grondin, S., Meilleur-Wells, G., & Lachance, R. (1999). When to start explicit counting in a time-intervals discrimination task: A critical point in the timing process of humans. *Journal of Experimental Psychology: Human Perception and Performance, 25*(4), 993-1004.

Halbig, T. D., Mecklinger, A., Schriefers, H., & Friederici, A. D. (1998). Double dissociation of processing temporal and spatial information in working memory. *Neuropsychologia, 36*(4), 305-311.

Harrington, D. L., & Haaland, K. Y. (1998). Temporal processing in the basal ganglia. *Neuropsychology, 12*(1), 3-12.

Harrington, D. L., Haaland, K. Y., & Knight, R. T. (1998). Cortical networks underlying mechanisms of time perception. *Journal of Neuroscience, 18*(3), 1085-1095.

Hayes, A. E., Davidson, M. C., Keele, S. W., & Rafal, R. D. (1998). Toward a functional analysis of the basal ganglia. *Journal of Cognitive Neuroscience, 10*(2), 178-198.

Hellstrom, A., Lang, H., Portin, R., & Rinne, J. (1997). Tone duration discrimination in Parkinson's disease. *Neuropsychologia, 35*(5), 737-740.

Horvitz, J. C. (2000). Mesolimbic and nigrostriatal dopamine responses to salient non-reward events. *Neuroscience, 96*(4), 652-656.

Horvitz, J. C., & Eyny, Y. (in press). Dopamine D2 receptor blockade reduces response likelihood but does not affect latency to emit a learned sensory-motor response: Implications for Parkinson's disease. *Behavioral Neuroscience.*

Ivry, R. (1993). Cerebellar involvement in the explicit representation of temporal information. *Annals of the New York Academy of Sciences, 682,* 214-230.

Ivry, R. (1996). The representation of temporal information in perception and motor control. *Current Opinion in Neurobiology, 6,* 851-857.

Ivry, R., & Hazeltine, R. E. (1995). Perception and production of temporal intervals across a range of durations: evidence for a common timing mechanism. *Journal of Experimental Psychology: Human Perception and Performance, 21*(1), 3-18.

Ivry, R., & Keele, S. (1989). Timing functions of the cerebellum. *Journal of Cognitive Neuroscience, 1,* 136-152.

Ivry, R., Keele, S. W., & Diener, H. C. (1988). Dissociation of the lateral and medial cerebellum in movement timing and movement execution. *Experimental Brain Research, 73,* 167-180.

Jueptner, M., Rijntjes, M., Faiss, J. H., Timmann, D., Mueller, S. P., & Diener, H. C. (1995). Localization of a cerebellar timing process using PET. *Neurology, 45,* 1540-1545.

Keele, S. W., Nicoletti, R., Ivry, R. I., & Pokorny, R. A. (1989). Mechanisms of perceptual timing: Beat-based or interval-based judgments? *Psychological Research, 50,* 251-256.

Keele, S. W., Pokorny, R. A., Corcos, D. M., & Ivry, R. (1985). Do perception and motor production share common timing mechanisms: A correlational analysis. *Acta Psychologica, 60,* 173-191.

Kileen, P. R. (1992). Counting the minutes. In F. Macar, V. Pouthas, & W. J. Friedman (Eds.), *Time, action and cognition: Towards bridging the gap* (pp. 203-214). Netherlands: Kluwer Academic.

Kileen, P. R., & Weiss, N. A. (1987). Optimal timing and the Weber function. *Psychological Review, 94*(4), 455-468.

Kinsbourne, M., & Hicks, R. E. (1990). The extended present: Evidence from time estimation by amnesics and normals. In G. Vallar & T. Shallice (Eds.), *Neuropsychological impairments of short-term memory* (pp. 319-330). London: Cambridge University Press.

Knowlton, B. J., Mangels, J. A., & Squire, L. R. (1996). A neostriatal habit learning system in humans. *Science, 273,* 1399-1402.

Krueger, L. E. (1989). Reciling Fechner and Stevnens. Toward a unified psychophysical law. *Behavioral Brain Sciences, 12,* 251-267.

Lejeune, H., Maquet, P., Bonnet , M., Casini, L., Ferrara, A., Macar, F., Pouthas, V., Timsit-Berthier, M., & Vidal, F. (1997). The basic pattern of activation in motor and sensory temporal tasks: Positron emission tomography data. *Neuroscience Letters, 235,* 21-24.

Levine, B., Stuss, D. T., Milberg, W. P., Alexander, M., Schwartz, M., & Macdonald, R. (1998). The effects of focal and diffuse brain damage on strategy application: Evidence from focal lesions, traumatic brain injury and normal aging. *Journal of the International Neuropsychological Society, 4,* 247-264

Lindman, R., & Taxell, H. (1975). The effects of alcohol and variable amount of cognitive stress on the estimation of time. *Scandinavian Journal of Psychology, 16,* 65-71.

Macar, F., Grondin, S., & Casini, L. (1994). Controlled attention sharing influences time estimation. *Memory & Cognition, 22*(6), 673-686.

Malapani, C., Deweer, B., & Gibbon, J. (2000). *Separating storage from retrieval dysfunction of temporal memory in Parkinson's disease.* Manuscript submitted for publication.

Malapani, C., Khati, C., Dubois, B., & Gibbon, J. (1997).

Damage to cerebellar cortex impairs precision of time estimation in the seconds range. Paper presented at the 4th Annual Meeting of the Cognitive Neuroscience Society, Boston, MA.

Malapani, C., Rakitin, B., Levy, R., Meck, W. H., Deweer, B., Dubois, B., & Gibbon, J. (1998). Coupled temporal memories in Parkinson's disease: A dopamine-related dysfunction. *Journal of Cognitive Neuroscience, 10*(3), 316–331.

Mangels, J. A. (1997). Strategic processing and memory for temporal order in patients with frontal lobe lesions. *Neuropsychology, 11*(2), 207–221.

Mangels, J. A., Ivry, R. B., & Shimizu, N. (1998). Dissociable contributions of the prefrontal and neo-cerebellar cortex to time perception. *Cognitive Brain Research, 7*, 15–39.

Mates, J., Mueller, U., Radil, T., & Poeppel, E. (1994). Temporal integration in sensorimotor synchronization. *Journal of Cognitive Neuroscience, 6*, 332–340.

McGlinchey-Berroth, G. (2000). Eyeblink classical conditioning in amnesia. In D. Woodruff-Pak & J. E. Steinmetz (Eds.), *Eyeblink classical conditioning, Vol. 1: Applications in Humans* (pp. 205–227). Boston: Kluwer Academic.

Meck, W. H. (1996). Neuropharmacology of timing and time perception. *Cognitive Brain Research, 3*, 227–242.

Milner, B., Squire, L. R., & Kandel, E. R. (1998). Cognitive neuroscience and the study of memory. *Neuron, 20*(3), 445–468.

Nichelli, P. (1996). Time perception measurements in neuropsychology. In M. A. Pastor & J. Artieda (Eds.), *Time, internal clocks and movement* (Vol. 115, pp. 187–204). Amsterdam: Elsevier.

Nichelli, P., Alway, D., & Grafman, J. (1996). Perceptual timing in cerebellar degeneration. *Neuropsychologia, 34*(9), 863–871.

Nichelli, P., Clark, K., Hollnagel, C., & Grafman, J. (1995). Duration processing after frontal lobe lesions. In J. Grafman, K. J. Holyoak, & F. Boller (Eds.), *Annals of the New York Academy of Sciences* (Vol. 769, pp. 183–190). New York: New York Academy of Sciences.

Ornstein, R. E. (1969). *On the experience of time.* Harmondsworth, England: Penguin Books.

Paller, K. A., Mayes, A. R., McDermott, M., Pickering, A. D., & Meudell, P. R. (1991). Indirect measures of memory in a duration-judgement task are normal in amnesic patients. *Neuropsychologia, 29*(10), 1007–1018.

Pashler, H. (in press). Perception and the production of brief durations: Beat-based versus interval-based timing. *Journal of Experimental Psychology: Human Perception and Performance.*

Pastor, M. A., Artieda, J., Jahanshahi, M., & Obeso, J. A. (1992). Time estimation and reproduction is abnormal in Parkinson's Disease. *Brain, 115*, 211–225.

Perret, S., Ruiz, B., & Mauk, M. (1993). Cerebellar cortex lesions disrupt learning dependent timing of conditioned eyelid responses. *Journal of Neuroscience, 13*, 1708–1718.

Petrides, M. (1994). Frontal lobes and working memory: Evidence from investigations of the effects of cortical excisions in nonhuman primates. In F. Boller & J. Grafman (Eds.), *Handbook of Neuropsychology* (Vol. 9, pp. 59–82): Elsevier.

Prabhakaran, V., Narayanan, K., Zhao, Z., & Gabrieli, J. D. E. (2000). Integration of diverse information in working memory within the frontal lobe. *Nature Neuroscience, 3*(1), 85–89.

Pressing, J. (1999). The referential dynamics of cognition and action. *Psychological Review, 106*(4), 714–747.

Rammsayer, T. (1993). On dopaminergic modulation of temporal information processing. *Biological Psychology, 36*, 209–222.

Rammsayer, T., & Classen, W. (1997). Impaired temporal discrimination in Parkinson's disease: Temporal processing of brief durations as an indicator of degeneration of dopaminergic neurons in the basal ganglia. *International Journal of Neuroscience, 91*(1–2), 45–55.

Rammsayer, T. H. (1999). Neuropharmacological evidence for different timing mechanisms in humans. *Quarterly Journal of Experimental Psychology B, 52*(3), 273–286.

Rammsayer, T. H., Lima, S. D., & Vogel, W. H. (1993). Aging and temporal discrimination of brief auditory intervals. *Psychological Research, 55*, 15–19.

Rao, S. M., Harrington, D. L., Haaland, K. Y., Bobholz, J. A., Cox, R. W., & Binder, J. R. (1997). Distributed neural systems underlying the timing of movements. *Journal of Neuroscience, 17*(14), 5528–5535.

Richards, W. (1973). Time reproductions by H.M. *Acta Psychologica, 37*, 279–282.

Roberts, S. (1981). Isolation of an internal clock. *Journal of Experimental Psychology: Animal Behavior Processes, 7*, 242–268.

Rubia, K., Schuri, U., von Cramon, D. Y., & Poeppel, E. (1997). Time estimation as a neuronal network property: A lesion study. *NeuroReport, 8*, 1273-1276.

Shaw, C., & Aggelton, J. P. (1994). The ability of amnesic subjects to estimate time intervals. *Neuropsychologia, 32*(7), 857–873.

Smith, M. C. (1968). CS-US interval and US intensity in classical conditioning of the rabbit's nictitating membrane response. *Journal of Comparative and Physiological Psychology, 66*, 679–687.

Topka, H., Valls Sole, J., Massaquoi, S. G., & Hallett, M. (1993). Deficit in classical conditioning in patients with cerebellar degeneration. *Brain, 116*, 961–969.

Traugott, E. (1978). On the expression of spatiotemporal relations in language. In J. H. Greenberg (Ed.), *Universals of human language: Word structure* (Vol. 3, pp. 369–400). Stanford, CA: Stanford University Press.

Treisman, M., Faulkner, A., & Naish, P. L. (1992). On the relation between time perception and the timing of motor action: Evidence for a temporal oscillator controlling the timing of movement. *Quarterly Journal of Experimental Psychology: Human Experimental Psychology, 45*, 235–263.

Wahl, O. F., & Sieg, D. (1980). Time estimation among schizophrenics. *Perceptual and Motor Skills, 50*, 535–541.

Wearden, J. H. (1991). Do humans possess an internal clock with scalar timing properties? *Learning and Motivation, 22*, 59-83.

West, R. L. (1996). An application of prefrontal cortex function theory to cognitive aging. *Psychological Bulletin, 120*(2), 272–292.

White, N. M. (1986). Control of sensorimotor function by dopaminergic nigrostriatal neurons: Influence on eating and drinking. *Neuroscience & Biobehavioral Reviews, 10*(1), 15–36.

Williams, J. M., Medwedeff, C. H., & Haban, G. (1989). Memory disorder and subjective time estimation. *Journal of Clinical and Experimental Psychology, 11*(5), 713-723.

Wing, A. M., & Kristofferson, A. B. (1973). Response delays and the timing of discrete motor responses. *Perception & Psychophysics, 14,* 5–12.

Witherspoon, D., & Allan, L. G. (1985). The effect of a prior presentation on temporal judgments in a perceptual identification task. *Memory and Cognition, 13,* 101–111.

Wittman, M. (1999). Time perception and temporal processing levels of the brain. *Chronobiology International, 16*(1), 17–32.

Woodruff-Pak, D., Papka, M., & Ivry, R. (1996). Cerebellar involvement in eyeblink classical conditioning in humans. *Neuropsychology, 10,* 443–458.

Zakay, D., & Block, R. A. (1996). The role of attention in time estimation processes. In M. A. Pastor & J. Artieda (Eds.), *Time, internal clocks and movement* (Vol. 115, pp. 143–163). Amsterdam: Elsevier Science.

Zakay, D., & Block, R. A. (1996). Temporal Cognition. *Current Directions in Psychological Science, 6*(1), 12–16.

20

Numerical Cognition

Marie-Pascale Noël

INTRODUCTION

The numerical domain is unique in at least three ways. First, numbers represent a particular aspect of reality (i.e., numerosity). Second, numbers are the object of specific processing such as calculation, parity judgment, magnitude comparison, and so on. And third, numbers can be represented in different formats: Arabic numbers (i.e., digit strings, e.g., *25*), written numbers (i.e., letter strings; e.g., twenty-five) or spoken numbers (i.e., sequences of sounds; e.g., TWENTY-FIVE), Roman numerals (XXV), and so on[1].

These characteristics have raised specific questions. Four of them will be considered in this chapter. First, are there functionally independent systems to process the different formats for numbers? Second, how does the human subject translate a number presented in one format into another format? Third, what are the basic functional components for calculation? And fourth, in which internal code(s) are arithmetic facts stored in memory?

THE BASIC COMPONENTS OF THE NUMBER PROCESSING SYSTEM

Number Comprehension and Production

Any task with numbers requires understanding and/or producing numbers. In examining these basic processes in patients, interesting dissociations have emerged. In particular, Benson and Denckla (1969) reported the case of a patient who could understand the quantity expressed by a number but could no longer produce numbers. So, he could point to the Arabic number corresponding to a spoken number or choose the answer to simple arithmetic problems among numbers written on a sheet of paper but failed in tasks such as counting, writing, reading numbers, or repeating them (i.e., all tasks that required producing numbers).

This difficulty in producing numbers contrasted with the problems in comprehending numbers reported by Gardner, Strub, and Albert (1975). More specifically, their patient's deficit appeared in tasks requiring the comprehension of spoken numbers (e.g., writing numbers to dictation, matching spoken and written numbers, or solving simple arithmetic problems pre-

---

[1]Spoken numbers will be put into quotes, written Arabic digits will be italicized, and written verbal numbers will be capitalized.

sented orally) whereas tasks using written Arabic numbers were correctly executed (e.g., comparing the magnitude of two Arabic numbers).

These two case studies were more anecdotal reports than detailed single-case studies but they nevertheless point to interesting dissociations between the ability to comprehend versus produce numbers, and between the comprehension of written Arabic versus spoken numbers.

Syntactic Mechanisms

Later case studies have tried to deepen the analysis of patient performance by examining not only the number of errors produced but also their nature. For instance, Noël and Seron (1992) described the case of a demented patient (NR) who produced many more errors in tasks requiring comprehension of Arabic numbers than in those involving comprehension of spoken numbers (e.g., in positioning numbers on an analogical scale,[2] she made 82% errors for 3-digit Arabic numbers but 35% for spoken numbers; in giving the number directly following a target; e.g., if presented *230*, she had to say "two hundred and thirty-one." She made 95% errors if the target was an Arabic number but only 15% if the target was presented orally). An analysis of her difficulty showed that identification of the digits composing the number was nearly perfect but that the global size of the Arabic number was not well captured. For instance, *236* was read as "two thousand three hundred and six," *489* was judged bigger than *3000* and when required to say the number coming after *268*, she said "two thousand six hundred and nine." We concluded that NR's deficit lay in the syntactic mechanisms that allowed an understanding of the combinatorial rules of Arabic digits. Indeed, identifying the quantity to which an Arabic number refers, does not simply require an understanding of the value of each individual digit (e.g., *732* and *327* do not refer to the same quantity). Our Arabic number system is a strict positional base-10 system. The quantity expressed by each digit depends upon its position within the number (2 means two in 72, twenty in 720, two hundred in 7231, and so on). More precisely, the quantity expressed by an Arabic number corresponds to the sum of the quantity expressed by each individual digit multiplied by a power of ten corresponding to the digit's position within the number (starting from the right). For instance, $273 = [3 \times 10exp0] + [7 \times 10exp1] + [3 \times 10exp2]$. In such a positional system, it is essential to have clear indications of the power of ten associated with each basic quantity (e.g., to be able to distinguish $[3 \times 10exp0] + [7 \times 10exp1]$ from $[3 \times 10exp0] + [7 \times 10exp4]$). The digit zero has this function: it holds the positions which are not occupied by basic quantities (e.g., zeros allow us to distinguish 73 from 70,003). In this context, NR's difficulties can be seen as related to some part of this process since she generated the same representation of quantity for 236 and 2306.

NR's impairment to the syntactic mechanisms for comprehending Arabic numbers[3] can be nicely contrasted with DM's syntactic difficulties in producing Arabic numbers. DM (Cipolotti, Butterworth, & Warrington, 1994) could comprehend spoken numbers, but was incorrect in writing the corresponding Arabic forms. For instance, he transcoded FOUR THOUSAND THREE HUNDRED AND TWO as *4000 302*, thus selecting the right digits but not the correct number of zeros so that the magnitude of the number was not respected (for similar descriptions, see Singer & Low, 1933, or Noël & Seron, 1995). By contrast, DM's comprehension of Arabic numbers seemed preserved: He could read aloud or compare the magnitude of Arabic numbers. The cases NR and DM thus illustrate the fact that syntactic processes for Arabic numbers can be selectively lesioned. Furthermore, within the syntactic processing of Arabic numbers, DM (but not in NR) showed a dissociation between production and comprehension mechanisms.

---

[2]A scale with its ends marked 0 on the left and 3000 on the right was used. Three marks were drawn on the scale and the patient had to select the one corresponding to the position of the number presented (e.g., 1492 should be located near the middle of the scale).

[3]NR's difficulties with Arabic numbers were not restricted to the comprehension process. When asked to produce Arabic numbers (e.g., to dictation or from written verbal numbers), she was also error prone.

Difficulties with the syntax of the verbal system have also been described. Sokol and McCloskey's (1988) patient had difficulty when required to produce verbal numbers in both written and spoken modalities. For instance, he read 407013 as "four hundred thousand seven, thirteen" or wrote *106230* as ONE HUNDRED THOUSAND SIX TWO HUNDRED THIRTY one hundred thousand six two hundred thirty (although he was able to comprehend the Arabic numbers given as input). Most of the errors corresponded to the production of ill-formed verbal numbers. The other important observation made by McCloskey et al. (1988) was the high similarity (both in terms of nature and rate) between the written and spoken verbal responses. From that observation, the authors argued that the syntactic mechanisms for producing verbal numbers are shared by spoken and written modalities.

Lexical Mechanisms

The processing of the individual elements that make up the numbers, namely, the Arabic digits or the words, has also attracted the attention of many authors. One of the most striking observations concerning the processing of individual Arabic digits (their identification or their production) is their very strong resistance to brain damage. Indeed, all the cases reported so far show relatively spared processing of single digits in patients who are severely impaired with the reading of other written material such as words, verbal numbers, or letters (see Cohen & Dehaene, 1995, or Holender & Peereman, 1987). According to Dehaene (1992), this strong resistance to brain damage is due to the fact that Arabic digits are processed by both of the two cerebral hemispheres so that only patients with bilateral lesions should show problems with individual Arabic digits.

Difficulties in the processing of individual verbal numbers are more frequent. McCloskey, Sokol, and Goodman (1986) described the case of HY, a patient who made errors in reading aloud Arabic numbers. For instance *902* was read as "nine hundred and *six*", *5* as *seven* or *17* as *"thirteen."* These errors stemmed from a difficulty in producing spoken numbers.[4] The vast majority consisted of the subtitution of one word for another. But these word substitutions were far from random! Indeed, according to Deloche and Seron (1982a, 1982b, 1987; Seron & Deloche, 1983, 1984), the words making up the verbal numbers are organized in ordered lexical classes with the *Units* (from one to nine), the *Teens* (from eleven to nineteen), the *Tens* (from ten to ninety), and the *Multipliers* (such as hundred, thousand,), see Table 20.1. Taking this theoretical proposal, McCloskey et al. (1986) discovered that most of the time, HY substituted a units word by another units word, a tens word by another tens word and a teens word by another teens word. Following Deloche and Seron's terminology, HY was thus producing *position errors,* namely, correct selection of the lexical class (unit, teens, tens) but not of the position within this class (e.g., thirteen and fifteen are both teens words but one holds the third position and the other holds the fifth).

Another type of word substition was observed in the reading of JG (McCloskey et al., 1986). For instance, this patient read *960* as "nineteen hundred sixteen" or *620* as "six hundred and *two."* Here, the substitutions respected the position within the class but not the lexical class itself (i.e., *nine,* the expected word in 960, and *nineteen,* the produced word, both hold the ninth position in their respective lexical class but *nineteen* is a teens word whereas a unit word is expected).

The observation of these two specific type of errors (i.e., position and class errors) indicated that accessing the representation of a number word requires two pieces of information: the lexical class and the position within the class.

---

[4]Indeed, they were not observed in tasks that required comprehension of Arabic numbers without production of spoken numbers and they were much less frequent if a written, rather than a spoken, verbal number had to be produced.

Table 20.1
Lexical Structure of the Number Words.

Position	Units	Lexical Class Teens	Tens
1st	One	Eleven	Ten
2nd	Two	Twelve	Twenty
3rd	Three	Thirteen	Thirty
4th	Four	Fourteen	Forty
5th	Five	Fifteen	Fifty
6th	Six	Sixteen	Sixty
7th	Seven	Seventeen	Seventy
8th	Eight	Eighteen	Eighty
9th	Nine	Nineteen	Ninety

A Functional Architecture for Number Processing

The analysis of brain-damaged patients has shown multiple dissociations and associations. On this basis, McCloskey, Caramazza, and Basili (1985) proposed a general framework for number processing (see Figure 20.1) in which they distinguished between comprehension and production modules for Arabic and verbal formats. The comprehension modules are used to generate a semantic representation of the number, namely, a representation of the quantity to which the number refers. The production modules convert the semantic representation of the number into the appropriate output (Arabic or verbal) format. For McCloskey et al. (1985) the semantic representation is a base-10 representation: It specifies in abstract form the basic quantities and the power of ten associated with each. For instance, *5060* and "five thousand sixty" both activate the same base-10 semantic representation: {5}10EXP3, {6}10EXP1. Within both the comprehension and production components, lexical and syntactic processing mechanisms are identified. Lexical processing involves the comprehension or the production of individual elements in the number (i.e., the words, e.g., SIX, the digits, e.g., *6*). Separate lexicons are supposed to contain the representations of the digits (Arabic lexicon), the written verbal numbers (graphemic lexicon), and the spoken numbers (phonologic lexicon). The processing of the relations between these lexical elements is made through syntactic mechanisms. In these, a distinction is introduced between the number formats: the Arabic syntactic mechanisms process Arabic numbers and the verbal syntactic mechanisms process both the written and the spoken verbal numbers.

This architecture provides a general framework that allows the interpretation of most case studies of number processing disorders. However, the content of some of these components still deserves investigation. In particular, the lexicon might contain more units than just the lexical primitives. For instance, Cohen, Dehaene, and Verstichel (1994) have argued that very familiar numbers such as famous dates, brands of cars, and so on might also be represented in the lexicon of the comprehension system. Others, such as Noël, Fias, and Brysbaert (1997) have suggested that numbers corresponding to products of simple multiplication (e.g., 36) might also be represented as wholes in the lexicon of the production system. The syntactic mechanisms also need to be described in greater detial.

Another important issue is how these different components are related to one another. For instance, how do we write the words corresponding to an Arabic number or read it out loud?

TRANSCODING PROCESSES

The Issue

Transcoding processes refer to the translation of a number from one format to another one, such as reading aloud Arabic numbers, writing a written number word to dictation, and so on.

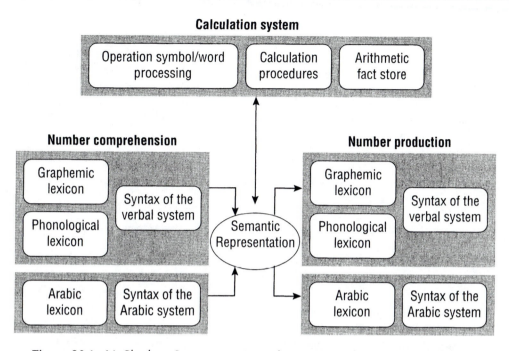

Figure 20.1: McCloskey, Caramazza, & Basili's (1985) architecture for calculation and number processing. Adapted from "Cognitive Mechanisms in Number Processing and Calculation: Evidence from Dyscalculia," by M. McCloskey, A. Caramazza, and A. Basili, 1985, *Brain and Cognition*, 4, 173, 174, & 190.

In McCloskey et al.'s (1985) model, transcoding is assumed to be realized by the successive actions of the comprehension and production modules: The former converts the input number into the corresponding base-10 semantic representation and the later translates this base-10 semantic representation into the expected production format. For instance, reading aloud *52* requires first generating the base-10 semantic representation {5}10EXP1, {2}10EXP0 through the Arabic number comprehension system and then, translating this base-10 semantic representation into the corresponding sequence of spoken words ("fifty-two") through the verbal number production system. In this framework, the base-10 semantic representation of numbers constitutes the obligatory bottle-neck between the satellite input and output systems for transcoding operations.

Some authors however, such as Deloche and Seron (1982a, 1982b; Seron & Deloche, 1983, 1984), Cipolotti and Butterworth (1995) or Dehaene (1992) have argued that other transcoding mechanisms should also be posited that would not require the generation of a semantic representation of the corresponding quantity and are therefore referred to as *asemantic transcoding algorithms*. An important debate has thus emerged between those postulating only semantic transcoding paths (the *semantic models*) and those assuming the existence of additional asemantic transcoding mechanisms (the *asemantic models*).

Neuropsychological Data[5]

At first glance, two types of dissociations should be looked for in order to demonstrate the existence of parallel semantic and asemantic transcoding algorithms: (a) patients showing

---

[5]This section has been largely inspired by Seron and Noël's (1995) review of that question.

impaired semantic processing of numbers, though being able to transcode them and (b) patients with preserved semantic transcoding route but impaired asemantic transcoding. Yet, in this latter case, if the semantic pathway were intact, it could still be used to transcode any number and so, no transcoding errors should be expected. The situation is thus more complicated than at first thought: it seems indeed that only one side of the dissociation could be encountered, i.e., the first one. Yet, as we will see, the real situation of the data collected so far is quite unexpected since none of the cases reported correspond to this first side of the dissociation.

Three types of arguments for the existence of asemantic transcoding mechanisms have been proposed: (a) traces of the characteristics of the input in the output form, (b) impaired transcoding with spared number comprehension and production, and (c) transcoding performance varying according to the task demands.[6]

TRACES OF THE INPUT'S CHARACTERISTICS ON THE OUTPUT FORM

According to McCloskey et al. (1985), number production is based on the base-10 semantic representation corresponding to a number. Since this representation is independent of the presentation format of the input number, then errors in number production should be free of the characteristics of the format of the input number.

Yet, these assumptions were put into question by Cohen and Dehaene (1991) who argued for the existence of transcoding mechanisms acting directly on a visual-spatial code, and by Noël and Seron (1995) who proposed that the transcoding process could directly operate on the verbal input.

Cohen and Dehaene's (1991) patient, YM (whose left temporal tumor extended into the left temporal lobe and the lower part of the splenium of the corpus callosum) produced a substantial rate of errors (22%) in reading aloud Arabic numbers. These were mainly substitutions (87%) which tended to be visually similar to the corresponding correct digits. Furthermore with the standard horizontal presentation of Arabic numbers, YM was more likely to err on the leftmost digit than on the others, but when Arabic numbers were presented vertically, this spatial bias disappeared. The visual and spatial characteristics of these errors suggested a deficit located at a very peripheral stage of the visual encoding of the Arabic numbers. Yet, in a magnitude comparison task with pairs of Arabic numbers, YM was perfect, which indicated a preservation of the Arabic number comprehension mechanisms. This paradoxical profile led Cohen and Dehaene (1991) to argue that the reading of Arabic numbers was using asemantic mechanisms based on a visuo-spatial code which preserved the visual and the spatial characteristics of the stimulus and which were impaired in YM, while the comparison was mediated by an unimpaired semantic system.

The strength of these data has, however, been questioned by McCloskey (1992) and Noël (1994) who, among other things, argue that perfect performance in the comparison of Arabic digits does not necessarily imply that the Arabic number comprehension component is intact.[7]

---

[6]A fourth type of argument has to do with the observation of better reading of familar Arabic numbers (e.g., 1789, the French revolution) than unfamiliar ones (e.g., 8179; see, Beauvois & Derouesné, 1979; Cohen et al., 1994; Delazer & Girelli, 1997). An effect of the familairty status of the numbers can not be explained within the semantic model of McCloskey et al. (1985). However, it is problemantic for the other models as well. To account for such a profile, Cohen et al. (1994) have proposed that the referent of the number in various domains such as dates, ages, brands of cars, etc. (what they called *encyclopedic knowledge*) should also be coded for at the semantic level. Transcoding of familiar numbers could thus be mediated by this specific semantic representation of encyclopedic knowledge; whereas non-familiar numbers could not. The question here is thus the type of semantic representation that is activated during transcoding and not whether semantic mediation is necessary for transcoding. Therefore, we will not go into this type of data in this chapter.

[7]Let us suppose that *5* is read "four" and *8* as "six." This double error in digit identification could still lead to correct comparison of the magnitude: In both the Arabic numbers presented and those incorrectly identified, the second number is the larger.

Table 20.2

Examples of LR's Arabic Production from Different Verbal Structures that Represent the Same Numerosity.

Thousand-Sum Relationships	Response
One thousand two hundred	1200
One thousand three hundred	1000300
One thousand seven hundred	1000700
One thousand seven hundred and thirty-eight	100070038
One thousand five hundred and twenty-three	100050023
Hundred-Product Relationships	Response
Twelve hundred	1200
Thirteen hundred	1300
Seventeen hundred	1700
Seventeen hundred and thirty-eight	170038
Fifteen hundred and twenty-three	150023

The case presented by Noël and Seron (1995), LR (who had a probable dementia of the Alzheimer's type) made many errors in writing Arabic numbers corresponding to written or spoken verbal numbers (respectively, 50% and 33% of errors). These errors consisted of writing too many zeros (e.g., THREE THOUSAND SEVEN HUNDRED AND ONE was transcoded 3000701). Tasks tapping the comprehension of verbal numbers gave rise to only a few errors. But up to 75% of errors were obtained in tasks requiring the production of comparable Arabic numbers (i.e., writing the Arabic number corresponding to the quantity expressed by sets of tokens of different values). Furthermore, the errors produced were of the exact same type as those obtained in transcoding. On this basis, it was concluded that LR's transcoding errors were due to a deficit in the Arabic-number production system. However, a fine-grained analysis revealed that LR's errors were actually a function of the syntactic structure of the verbal numbers to transcode. Indeed, errors appeared mainly on sum relationships with Thousand (e.g, MILLE DEUX means MILLE + DEUX, or one thousand plus two) but not on product relations (e.g., DEUX MILLE means DEUX × MILLE, or two times one thousand). This gave rise to astonishing differences when comparing the transcoding of two verbal numbers that contact the same base-10 semantic representation but that have different syntactic structure. For instance, DOUZE CENTS (twelve hundred) refers to the same quantity as MILLE DEUX CENTS (one thousand two hundred) but only the later involves a sum relation with Thousand. Errors were more frequent in the case of thousand-sum structures (such as ONE THOUSAND TWO HUNDRED) than in hundred-product structures (such as TWELVE HUNDRED). And when errors were produced for the two comparable verbal forms, the faulty production of Arabic numbers differed according to the presented item (see Table 20.2 for a few examples). Such a profile is totally unexpected in a model such as McCloskey's which assumes that the same base-10 semantic representation (e.g., {1}10exp3; {2} 10exp2 for TWELVE HUNDRED or for ONE THOUSAND TWO HUNDRED) is activated by the two types of verbal numbers[8]. Accordingly, a deficit in the Arabic production system should lead to the same type and rate of errors regardless of the syntactic structure of the verbal input which has generated this base-10 semantic representation. Noël and Seron (1995) interpreted this case by suggesting that transcoding was not operating on the basis of base-10 semantic representations but on verbal number representations.

---

[8]LR could indeed understand the verbal numbers with both structures: He could select tokens to represent the corresponding magnitude, indicate how many times one hundred was contained in the numbers, or compare the magnitude of two numbers with the same verbal structure.

Transcoding Errors without Any Comprehension or Production Deficit

According to McCloskey et al. (1985), transcoding results from the succession of comprehension and production processes so that errors in transcoding should come from either impaired comprehension or production. Yet, several case studies have been reported with impaired transcoding but no underlying functional deficit in comprehension and production mechanisms. This, of course, is very problematic for the architecture proposed by McCloskey at al. (1985).

The case of AT (Blanken, Dorn, & Sinn, 1997) illustrates this situation (but see also SF; Cipolotti, 1995) but criticized by Seron and Noël (1995) or SAM (Cipolotti & Butterworth, 1995). AT is a German patient (CVA in the territory of the left middle cerebral artery) who produced errors in reading aloud Arabic numbers which consisted in the failure to apply correctly the inversion rule of the German number system. Thus, when asked to read *28*, Germans say "eight and twenty" but AT said "two and eighty." This type of error also occurred in verifying the equivalence between spoken and Arabic numbers or in selecting among 4 Arabic numbers, the one that matched a spoken verbal number (e.g., for "six and seventy" he selected *67* instead of *76*).

According to Blanken et al., 1997 these inversion errors were not due to an early visual deficit as AT could make a same/different judgment with pairs of Arabic numbers. Neither were they due to an Arabic comprehension deficit: AT was indeed fast and flawless in comparing the magnitude of pairs of Arabic numbers and could arrange triplets of Arabic numbers according to their ascending magnitude (e.g., *43, 34, 37*). Finally, the inversion errors could not be located at the level of the verbal production system since they did not appear in repetition, reading aloud verbal numbers, or when required to speak out loud the approximate age of 30 human faces.

Blanken et al. thus concluded that these inversion errors could not find a proper explanation in the semantic transcoding model of McCloskey et al. (1985). Rather, they interpreted AT's profile by suggesting that Arabic number reading was made through asemantic transcoding processing based on visual input. The inversion errors would be motivated by the conflict between the left-to-right visual-spatial arrangement of the Arabic digits and the reverse temporal sequence of German spoken numbers. In contrast, the magnitude tasks with Arabic numbers or the reading tasks of written verbal numbers were based on a strict left-to-right parsing where the inversion rule did not interfere.

In summary, AT was not able to read aloud Arabic numbers, but could still generate the semantic representation of Arabic numbers and produce spoken numbers from semantic representations. But, if the comprehension and production systems were unimpaired, why did this patient not use the seemingly intact semantic transcoding route instead of the supposedly defective asemantic one? This question has been tentatively answered by Cipolotti (1995) who argued that the instruction to "read the Arabic numbers" would preferentially activate the "asemantic route" and that, furthermore, there is reciprocal inhibition between the semantic and the asemantic transcoding routes, so that, activation of one inhibits the other. This hypothesis concerning the role of task demand in the selection between semantic or asemantic transcoding routes was more extensively studied by Cohen and Dehaene (1995).

Effects of Task Demands

Cohen and Dehaene (1995) reported the cases of SMA and GOD, two patients who were mildly impaired in reading aloud single digits (8% and 18% errors for SMA and GOD respectively). Yet, their reading performance differed when exactly the same Arabic numbers had to be processed in the context of magnitude comparison (e.g., *read these two digits aloud and tell me which is larger*: 10–15% errors) or for subsequent addition (*read these two digits aloud and give me their sum*: 31–45% errors). For Cohen and Dehaene, this suggested that at the very first stages of digit identification, task demands already influence the use of one processing route or the other.

The authors explained these patterns by assuming the existence of two distinct visual identification processes for digits, one in each cerebral hemisphere. However, as they also assumed that each hemisphere is not equally implicated in every numerical task, the task determines whether it is the left or the right digit identification system that is used. Accordingly, if one of the digit identification systems is impaired, then different error rates in digit identification might be observed depending on task demands.

A new model for numerical cognition was proposed by Dehaene (1992), accompanied later by an anatomical implementation of this architecture (Dehaene & Cohen, 1995). This model is called the *triple-code model* (see Figure 20.2) as it assumes the existence of three types of internal representations for numbers: Two of them are format-dependent: a *visual Arabic number form* and a *verbal word frame*, and one is format-independent: an *analog magnitude representation*. The two format-dependent representations are directly interfaced by format-specific comprehension and production mechanisms. The visual Arabic number form represents numbers as strings of digits on an internal visual-spatial sketchpad. Arabic number forms can be processed or generated in each of the cerebral hemispheres in the occipital-temporal regions of the ventral visual pathway. The verbal word frames represent numbers as syntactically organised sequences of words and their processing is only present in the left hemisphere within the classic perisylvian language areas. Finally, the analog magnitude representation is supposed to be the real semantic representation of quantity. Based on data from normal subjects (e.g., Dehaene, Dupoux, & Melher, 1990), Dehaene pictured it as an oriented number line with quantities being represented by local distributions of activations. Small numbers are on the left side and large numbers on the right side. In addition, this representation obeys Weber's Law such that it becomes increasingly imprecise as numbers get larger. Both hemispheres possess an analog magnitude representation of numbers in the vicinity of the parieto-occipito-temporal junction. These representations are typically used for tasks requiring the processing of the magnitude such as selecting the bigger of two numbers or giving approximations (e.g., how much is 13% of 1567?). Yet, contrary to the model proposed by McCloskey et al. (1985), the two format-dependent representations, i.e., the visual Arabic number form and the verbal word frame, are not only used for activating the corresponding analog magnitude representation from a sequence of digits or of words. In particular, the visual Arabic number form is supposed to code for parity information (i.e., whether numbers are odd or even) and is used in multi-digit operations. Conversely, the verbal word frames are used for counting and for storing addition and multiplication tables.[9]

Finally, the model specifies how internal representations are connected with one another: there are paths linking the different representations within each of the hemispheres, and paths connecting (through the corpus callosum) the left and right analog magnitude representations and the left and right Arabic visual systems.

---

[9]Dehaene and collaborators have tested the anatomical implementation of their model with neuroimaging studies but the picture obtained is not clear. Multiplication of two numbers should activate the left language areas. However, activation in the left hemisphere but located at in the inferior parietal cortex was obtained using ERPs (Keifer & Dehaene, 1997). Furthermore, activation of the bilateral inferior parietal lobules (with a small left assymetry) was measured for multiplication (relative to a magnitude comparison task) using PET (Dehaene et al., 1996). Conversely, bilateral activation in the parieto-occipito-temporal junctions is expected in case of magnitude comparison of numbers. Yet, Dehaene et al. (1996) could not find specific cortical activation for comparison (relative to multiplication) in the PET study. Using ERPs, Dehaene (1995) measured significant activation on sites close to the parieto-occipito junction, but with a right lateralization. However, a bilateral activation in the inferior parietal lobules (with a left-sided predominance) was observed by Pinel et al. (1999) with functional magnetic resonance. A bilateral activation was also measured by Thioux, Seron, and Pesenti (1999; with PET) in the intra-parietal lobes for two semantic tasks with numbers (judging if a number was odd or even, or larger and smaller than 5). Let us note that parity judgements are supposed to rely on the visual Arabic number forms (occipito-temporal regions) and not on the analog magnitude representations (parieto-occipito-temporal junctions).

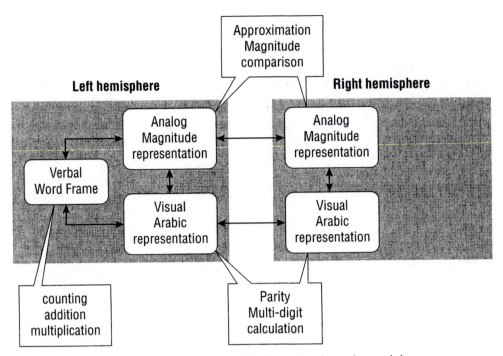

Figure 20.2: Dehaene and Cohen's triple-code model.

Accordingly, transcoding between Arabic and verbal numbers can use several paths. First, there is an asemantic transcoding route in the left hemisphere that directly connects the visual Arabic system (which generates the visual Arabic number representation) to the verbal system (which generates verbal word frames). Second, two paths link the visual Arabic system to the verbal system through the analog magnitude representation. The first of these semantic transcoding routes relates the left visual Arabic system to the verbal system through the left analog magnitude representation. The second semantic transcoding path goes from the right visual Arabic system, connects to the right analog magnitude representation which, in turn, contacts its homologue in the left hemisphere, which itself, is related to the verbal system. However, given that these analog magnitude representations follow Weber's law, these semantic routes can only be used for rounding up and are thus not suitable for precise transcoding of numbers (e.g., the analog magnitude representation of *212* would be rounded down to activate the quantity 200).

The triple-code model differs from McCloskey et al.'s (1985) in three main ways. First, the semantic representation is supposed to be an analog representation of magnitude. Second, the precision of that representation is not perfect so that semantic transcoding decreases in precision with larger numbers (following Weber's law). Third, the semantic representation is not the obligatory bottle-neck of all transcoding nor of all numerical processing (parity judgments or retrieval of arithmetic facts, for instance, do not require the activation of the analog magnitude code).

If we come back to the cases of SAM and GOD, we see that the differences in their Arabic reading according to task demands is nicely accounted for by the triple-code model. Indeed, if one considers that their lesions affect the left visual Arabic system (or a disconnection of this system), then we would predict that tasks mediated by the left hemisphere would lead to more errors than tasks mediated by the right hemisphere. As simple addition is assumed to rely on the left verbal system, reading Arabic digits for subsequent addition would preferentially acti-vate the *left* visual Arabic system, (i.e., the one that is damaged). Conversely, tasks such as magnitude comparison which can be equally handled by both hemispheres would not lead to a preferential use of the left, impaired, visual Arabic system so that reading of Arabic numbers in the context of a magnitude comparison would be better than for a subsequent addition.

The triple-code model has also been used recently by Miozzo and Caramazza (1998) to account for the performance of GV (lesion in the left occipital and posterior temporal areas, extending to the corpus callosum). This patient produced many errors in reading Arabic digits (42% incorrect) although he could access magnitude from Arabic digits (i.e., compare the magnitude of 1- or 2-digit Arabic numbers) and produce verbal numbers in other contexts (i.e., solving simple calculations presented orally, answering numerical questions such as "how many pennies are there in one dollar?"). According to Miozzo and Caramazza, the patient's profile could be interpreted as resulting from an impaired left visual Arabic system. Accordingly, Arabic number magnitude comparisons could be carried out using the intact right visual Arabic system. But reading would be error prone because the transcoding path going from the right visual Arabic system would be insufficient to drive the verbal system in the left hemisphere without error: because the information was incomplete or it was degraded through inter-hemispheric transfer (remember that the patient's lesion extended to the corpus callosum).

However, two aspects of the patient's data do not fit with Dehaene and Cohen's model (1995). First, if Arabic number reading uses the right visual Arabic system, then, it necessarily goes through the analog magnitude representation system (both on the right and then on the left). As these representations give only an approximation of the quantity, errors would be expected for large numbers but they should still tend to respect the global magnitude of the number. However, Miozzo and Caramazza did not find any numerical proximity between the targets and errors he produced.[10] Second, if the right visual Arabic system was preserved, then the patient should have been able to determine whether Arabic numbers are odd or even as Arabic number forms are supposed to code for parity information. Yet, such a task was impossible for the patient.

Data with Normal Subjects

The rapid development of the debate between proponents of semantic and asemantic transcoding models in neuropsychology has finally given rise to a few attempts to address that issue in research with unimpaired subjects. But, as we will see, the data obtained are quite controversial.

First, using a physical matching task (e.g., *3 = 3* but *3 ≠ THREE*, *3 ≠ FOUR* or *3 ≠ 4*), Dehaene and Akhavein (1995) noticed a trend for incorrectly responding *same* to physically different pairs representing the same quantity (e.g., *2- TWO*). Girelli (1998) replicated this observation: subjects were slower and less accurate when they had to reject the physical identity of an Arabic and a verbal number representing the same quantity (*2 - TWO*) than when they represented different quantities (*2 - THREE*). These observations were taken as an argument in favor of connections between the Arabic and the verbal systems. However, are these connections semantically mediated? If so, then some effects typically found in tasks activating the magnitude representation should arise. In particular, a distance effect should be observed: rejecting a pair of two numerically close numbers (e.g., *2 - THREE)* should be slower than rejecting a pair of numerically distant numbers (e.g., *2 - SIX*). Yet, Girelli could not find any evidence of such a distance effect and concluded that semantic representations of numbers were not activated during that task, that is, that the connection between verbal and Arabic numbers is not semantically mediated.

---

[10]The same prediction could also be made for SMA and GOD in the «read and compare task». However, the authors did not analyze the distance between errors and targets. Furthermore, the task only used single-digit Arabic numbers, namely, numbers that allow a precise representation in the analog magnitude system.

In contrast, Fias (1998) proposed two main arguments for the existence of a single, semantically mediated, path for Arabic number reading. First, in a phoneme monitoring task of Arabic digits (i.e., detecting an /e/ sound—which requires Arabic-to-verbal transcoding), Fias, Brysbaert, Geypens, and d'Ydewalle (1996) showed the presence of a SNARC effect (which stands for Spatial-Numerical Association of Response Codes), usually considered to be an indicator of the activation of analog magnitude representations.[11] Second, in reading aloud Arabic digits, the presence of a written verbal number exerted an influence such that there was a faster response if it corresponded to the Arabic digit than if it did not (e.g., *4 – FOUR* vs. *4 - FIVE*). By contrast, reading verbal numbers was not influenced by the accompanying digit. According to Fias et al., these results argue in favour of obligatory semantic mediation in the Arabic to verbal transcoding.

However, this conclusion does not seem to be the only possible one. Indeed, the second experiment showed that Arabic number reading was influenced by a simultaneously presented number word. This means that at some point, the target and the distractor activated representations at the same level of processing. This common level could well be the semantic representation. But the verbal number production system might also be a possible candidate: digits activate it as required by the task whereas number words automatically activate the corresponding phonemes. We think that a stronger case for Fias' conclusion would be to show that not only do words influence the reading of digits but also that this influence shows semantic properties such as a distance effect (i.e., in reading *3*, greater interference from SEVEN vs. FOUR).

An indication of the activation of the analog magnitude representation (the SNARC effect) was observed in the phoneme monitoring task. Yet, a SNARC effect was also obtained by Fias (1998) in low-level visual tasks with Arabic digits such as judging whether there is a closed shape in the visually presented digit or whether a triangle superimposed on the digit is pointing upwards or downwards. Would we conclude from these experiments that those visual processes are semantically mediated? Probably not. Rather, we would conclude that semantic activation is quite automatic from the presentation of an Arabic digit. Accordingly, the semantic activation observed in the phoneme monitoring task indicates that the semantic representation was activated but it does not imply the nonexistence of a parallel asemantic processing route.

Finally, if, as observed by Fias, Arabic digits automatically activate their corresponding semantic representations then, showing the existence of a second (or several), nonsemantic route(s), seems quite difficult in studies with normal subjects and thus points to the great importance of testing patients to clarify the debate.

Conclusion

Should asemantic transcoding algorithms be posited to supplement semantic ones? According to McCloskey (1992) there is, currently, no evidence justifying this addition. Yet, Cipolotti and Butterworth (1995) argue that asemantic transcoding should be added. Dehaene and Cohen (1995) agree with this conclusion but they differ from Cipolotti and Butterworth in that they also assume the existence of multiple semantic transcoding routes (depending on whether it is the left or right hemisphere visual Arabic system that is used and also whether the semantic system involved is the left or right analog magnitude representation). The models also differ in their conception of the semantic representations of numbers. Both McCloskey (1992) and Dehaene and Cohen (1995) assume that these should represent quantity but the former supposes that quantity is represented by a base-10 semantic representation that would be precise even for large numbers, whereas Cohen and Dehaene hypothesize that an analog magnitude representation codes for approximate quantity.

---

[11]The SNARC effect corresponds to the fact that small numbers are responded to faster with the left side and large numbers faster with the right side (i.e., usually corresponding to left and right hand, respectively), which is consistent with a left-right orientation of the representation of number magnitude.

Three types of evidence have been presented in support of the existence of asemantic transcoding routes: (a) cases in which the production of numbers is influenced by visual or verbal characteristics of the input, (b) cases presenting impaired transcoding but seemingly spared comprehension and production mechanisms, and (c) transcoding performance that is influenced by task demands.

All of these cases can be accounted for by assuming damaged asemantic transcoding mechanisms together with spared semantic pathways. However, many of the cases presented could find alternative explanations. More importantly, no one has ever reported the opposite side of the dissociation (i.e., spared asemantic transcoding in the case of impaired semantic mechanisms, as emphasized by Seron & Noël, 1995). So, no one has ever described the case of a patient who was unable to access the magnitude of numbers though being able to read or write them down. Two cases were reported with difficulties in comprehending numbers, but both also showed difficulties in transcoding! In particular, CG (Cipolotti, Butterworth, & Denes, 1991) showed a dramatic loss of all numerical knowledge for numbers beyond 4 regardless of presentation format, but she was also unable to transcode any of these numbers! Similarly, NR (Noël & Seron, 1993) showed difficulties in comprehending some Arabic numbers and showed striking similarities between the errors produced in transcoding tasks and those appearing in other tasks tapping the semantic system[12]. The description of patients constituting the second side of the double dissociation between semantic and asemantic transcoding paths, will thus be crucial.

THE BASIC COMPONENTS OF THE CALCULATION SYSTEM

Among the operations that are specific to the numerical domain, those that have been the most extensively studied are the single-digit arithmetical operations such as addition, multiplication or subtraction. Once more here, cognitive neuropsychology has proven to be very useful in specifying the different functional components.

Among the first studies of patients with calculation deficits were those of Ferro and Botelho (1980). Their patients, AL (brain trauma) and MA (CVA), produced errors in simple calculation such that the responses provided corresponded to an incorrect operation applied on the two operands presented (e.g., *3 × 5 = 8* or *9 × 3 = 6*). An analysis of the patients' responses indicated that their errors came from impaired identification of the operation symbols (+, −, ×, ...). However, the words of operations (i.e., plus, minus, times) were correctly understood, by MA at least, as he made no errors when calculation problems were presented orally. The patient's difficulty did not extend to other types of written symbols such as digits, letters, flags and playing cards. This argues for the existence of mechanisms specifically dedicated to the identification of arithmetical operation symbols.

Two years later, Warrington (1982) reported the case of DRC, who also produced errors in calculation (11% errors in addition, 8% for subtraction, and 9% for multiplication) yet was perfectly able to recognize and define the symbols of arithmetic operations. This patient's difficulty was in retrieving the answers of previously familiar single-digit problems. Consequently, he had to reconstruct solutions by using back-up counting procedures. So that, in time-unlimited tasks, he was perfect but erred when time pressure was applied. From this pattern, Warrington concluded that solutions to single-digit problems are usually retrieved from long-term memory, called *arithmetical facts*, but that DRC suffered damage affecting access to this store.

This case study contributed to the debate that was, at that time, between those who assumed that single-digit addition problems were solved by counting procedures (Groen & Parkman,

---

[12] For instance, the patient read correctly *1258* but said "two thousand three hundred and six" for *236*. Accordingly, *236* was judged bigger than *1258*!

1972) and those who hypothesized a simple retrieval of the solution from memory (Ashcraft & Battaglia, 1978). Subsequent work has largely supported the latter view, although LeFevre and her collaborators have showed that even educated adults keep using procedural strategies (e.g., counting, decomposition, transformation, etc.) to solve some single-digit problems (LeFevre, Bisanz, et al., 1996; LeFevre, Sadesky, & Bisanz, 1996).

If answers are merely retrieved from long-term memory, then the issue of how these solutions to single-digit problems are organized in long-term memory can be raised. To handle this question, McCloskey, Aliminosa, and Sokol (1991) analyzed the errors in single-digit multiplication produced by 13 patients. From that pattern, they distinguished two types of problems: the M × N and the 0's problems. The M × N problems (with M and N being any number from 2 to 9) gave rise to a very heterogeneous pattern of errors. Within the same patient, some problems led to many errors while others were perfect. For instance, MD was 95% incorrect on 9 × 3 but only 10% incorrect on 9 × 4 and perfect on 9 × 2. Such an observation creates difficulties for models assuming that arithmetic facts are stored in a table-like structure (e.g., Ashcraft & Battaglia, 1978). Within these models, the presentation of a problem activates the corresponding rows and columns in the table (i.e., the entry nodes for the first and second operand, respectively) and this activation spreads until an intersection at the location where the correct answer is stored. Accordingly, if the node of 9 × 3 is lost (e.g., links are destroyed), the multiplication problems that require activation beyond that point in the table (e.g., 9 × 4) should not be accessible anymore, which, as shown by McCloskey et al.'s patients, was not the case. Instead, these results suggest that each fact (e.g., 9 × 3 or 9 × 4) has its own separate representation in memory that can be selectively damaged (see Ashcraft, 1995, for a review of these models).

By contrast, the 0's problems (M × 0 or 0 × M) showed a uniform profile with either global loss or preservation and could dissociate from the M × N problems. For instance, HM was 100% incorrect on 0 × N problems but only 3% incorrect on M × N problems whereas CM made no error on 0 x N problems but 17% errors on M × N problems. Finally, recovery on these 0's problems can be sudden and directly generalized to all 0's problems. For instance, JG was trained on 0 × 8 and 9 × 0 problems: Prior to training, he was uniformly incorrect on all the 0's problems but after the training, he was 99.3 % correct on all of them (and not just on 0 × 8 and 9 × 0). Let us note finally, that rules are also found in other operations (e.g., 0 + N, 0 / N) or with numbers different from zero (N / 1, N - N, N / N, and so on).

Another point that has been raised concerns the relationship between arithmetical facts from different operations. Dagenbach and McCloskey (1992) hypothesized that the arithmetical fact store was segregated by operations. Their proposition was supported by observations of dissociations among arithmetical operations. For instance, their patient RG (CVA in the left posterior parietal region) was more severely impaired in multiplication and addition than in subtraction (respectively, 22%, 25% and 61% correct). Other dissociations among operations were also reported by Pesenti, Seron, and Van der Linden (1994), McCloskey et al. (1991), Hittmair-Delazer, Semenza, and Denes (1994), or Cipolotti and De Lacy Castello (1995).

Yet data from normal subjects indicate that these stores are not totally independent from one another. For instance, confusions among operations are obtained both in production (e.g., producing 20 in response to 4 + 5) and in verification (rejecting more slowly 4 + 5 = 20 than 4 + 5 = 18). These data have led Ashcraft (1982) to propose that addition and multiplication are stored in inter-related networks.

The question of the relationship between multiplication and division is also interesting. Indeed, do we solve a division problem (e.g., 68/8) by retrieving the corresponding division fact or do we rather rely on multiplication (e.g., 8 × ? = 64)? This question was studied by Campbell (1997; see also Campbell, 1999) with normal adults. He showed that RTs and error characteristics are highly correlated for corresponding division and multiplication problems. Priming between operations was also obtained but asymmetrically: multiplication errors (e.g., 7 × 9 = 56) were primed by previous division trials (*56/7 = 8*), but not the reverse. Campbell suggested that division and multiplication problems involve separate memory representations but that multiplication is often used as a check *after* direct retrieval of the quotient. This checking procedure would explain the assymetry of the priming effect.

Using a different methodology, LeFevre and Morris (1999) showed that multiplication performance benefited from prior solution of division problems more than division benefited from prior solution of multiplication problems. This priming was greater on large multiplication problems than on small ones. Furthermore, participants reported using multiplication to solve division problems (e.g., *56/7 = ?* recast as *7 x ? = 56*) on a substantial proportion of trials, and more often on large than on small division problems. The authors assumed that multiplication and division are stored in independent representations but that solution of division problems is sometimes mediated by direct access to multiplication knowledge.

These data clearly show some relationship between division and multiplication facts. However, it is still not perfectly clear whether multiplication is used to *check* or to *mediate* division. These relations between division and multiplication facts are well in line with the case study of Hittmair-Delazer, et al. (1994). Their patient was impaired for both multiplication and division in such a way that the division problems that were incorrect corresponded to the multiplication problems that could not be solved by the patient. Furthermore, the effects of rehabilitation of multiplication transferred to division which led the authors to conclude that the patient's division performance depended on the availability of the corresponding multiplication facts.

However, the case reported by Cipolotti and de Lacy Costello (1995) contradicts this. This patient (infarct in the left parietal and probably posterior frontal regions) was much better in multiplication (about 70% correct) than in division (20% correct) which suggests that he was not relying on multiplication for carrying out division (e.g., solving *48/6 = ?* by searching 6 × ?= 48). This hypothesis was further supported by the fact that "N times ?" problems (e.g., 6 × ? = 48) were as poor as division problems (48/6 = ?; respectively, 16% and 24% correct, compared with 88% correct for the corresponding multiplication problems).

One way to account for this pattern is to consider the existence of individual differences in this domain. According to Campbell (1999), individuals with a very well-developed memory for division facts presumably rely very little on multiplication. Another possible explanation would be that some patients have completely lost the links between operations. This seemed to be the case for JG (Delazer & Benke, 1997): She was correct on *59/64* multiplication problems but was completely unable to answer division problems. This dissociation was explained by the fact that she had completely forgotten the meaning of the division operation and did not realize the relation between multiplication and division, so that she never recast division problems into multiplication.

In summary, data so far argue for distinguishing, within the calculation system, a subcomponent for processing words or symbols corresponding to the operations as well as interconnected arithmetical fact stores. These components are schematically represented in McCloskey et al.'s model,[13] (see Figure 20.1). Yet, Hittmair-Delazer and colleagues (Delazer & Benke, 1997; Hittmair-Delazer, Sailer, & Benke, 1995; Hittmair-Delazer et al., 1994) pointed to the need to consider another important aspect of calculation abilities that was not part of McCloskey et al.'s (1985) model (i.e., what she calls *conceptual knowledge about arithmetic*). Her idea came from the study of BE (but see also DA in Hittmair-Delazer et al., 1995), a patient who presented with severe acalculia after a cerebral embolism (left basal ganglia). In multiplication, he was able to give an immediate and correct response to only 28 out of 64 single-digit problems. For the remaining 36 items, he developed complex strategies to generate answers, on the basis of the few multiplication facts that he had kept in memory. For instance, to solve *4 × 9* he

---

[13]The calculation component also involves a module for "calculation procedures" which contains the algorithms for multi-digit operations. However, this chapter will only consider single-digit calculation. This calculation procedures module will thus not be presented here.

computed $(9 \times 2) + (9 \times 2)$ or $(9 \times 10 / 2) - 9$. The complexity of these (correct) strategies strikingly showed the preservation, in this patient, of a deep understanding of the principles of the mathematical operations involved (e.g., commutativity, associativity, distributivity).

The opposite pattern was also reported (Delazer & Benke, 1997): JG was unable to define arithmetical operations (e.g., multiplication is: "to multiply"), complete a task of arithmetical reasoning in which the answer to a second problem should be inferred from the answer to a first one (e.g., *if 12 × 4 = 48 then 4 × 12 = ?*) or use back-up strategies for solving a calculation for which she had forgotten the answer. However, she could nevertheless realize some calculations (multiplication: 59/64 correct; addition: 28/64 correct; subtraction: 12/28 correct; but no division correct) just by resorting to stored answers. This double dissociation thus argues in favor of the functional independence of arithmetical fact stores on the one hand and conceptual knowledge about arithmetic on the other.

STORAGE FORMAT OF ARITHMETICAL FACTS

Theoretical Perspectives

One of the important issues that has been raised about arithmetical facts is the nature of the stored representations. Two broad categories of hypotheses have been proposed. First, the *multiple-format position* assumes that arithmetical facts are stored in a variety of internal codes as determined by the formats in which they have been encountered (see Campbell & Clark, 1988; Clark & Campbell, 1991). For instance, *3 × 7* gives rise to strong activation of the visual Arabic representation of *<3 × 7 = 21>* as well as to weaker activation of other representations such as the corresponding phonological representation "three times seven is twenty-one." By contrast, the spoken multiplication "three times seven" gives rise to a stronger activation of the corresponding phonological representation and weaker activation of non-verbal representations.

Instead, the *single-format position* assumes that, although problems are encountered in many different formats, arithmetical facts are stored in a unique type of representation. In particular, McCloskey et al.'s (1985, but see also McCloskey & Macaruso, 1995) assume that arithmetic facts are stored in the form of base-10 semantic representations. So that *3 × 7* or "three times seven" would both generate the same base-10 semantic representation of the problem (i.e., {3}10EXP0 [×] {7}10EXP0 which would then trigger the base-10 semantic representation of the corresponding product {2}10EXP1, {1}10EXP0).

Another single-format position has been proposed by Dehaene (1992) and Dehaene and Cohen (1997): addition and multiplication facts would be stored as *verbal representations*. According to that hypothesis, retrieving the solution to a multiplication problem presented in a nonverbal format (e.g., written in Arabic digits) would first require a translation of the presented form into the corresponding verbal representation to trigger the verbal representation of the answer.

Single or Multiple Formats for Arithmetical Facts?

The single-format and multiple-format hypotheses make different predictions regarding the effects of manipulating presentation format. According to the single-format view, effects of format manipulation could only be located at problem encoding (i.e., when generating the base-10 or verbal representation corresponding to the problem). By contrast, the multiple-format view assumes that manipulating the presentation format of a problem should give rise to differences in the retrieval stage.

A series of studies with normal subjects has reported the effects of manipulating the presentation format of calculation problems (for a review, see Noël et al., 1997). Some of them, such as LeFevre, Bisanz, and Mrkonjic (1988) or McClain and Shih Huang (1982) failed to find any effect of the manipulation. Others did obtain effects but the question is to determine their functional locus: Is it in the encoding or retrieval stages?

For instance, Gonzalez and Kolers (1982) used a verification task of addition problems presented either in Arabic digits (*4 + 5*), Roman symbols (IV + V) or in a combination of the two formats. They obtained interactions between the presentation format and parameters measuring the difficulty of the addition. Yet, Noël and Seron (1992) showed that these interactions might well be due to factors at play at the encoding level. Indeed, the encoding time of Roman numbers varies: I, II, III, V, and X are processed faster than IV, VI, VII, and VIII. Noël and Seron showed how this variability could explain the pattern of RTs obtained in calculation by Gonzalez and Kolers.

Stronger effects of presentation format were obtained by Campbell (1994; Campbell & Clark 1992). For instance, Campbell and Clark (1992) reported for single-digit multiplication, greater increase in RTs and error rates due to problem difficulty in the written verbal (SEVEN × FIVE) than in the Arabic condition (*7 × 5*). Yet, once more, the locus of these effects was criticized by McCloskey, Macaruso, and Whetstone (1992). They ran a regression analysis on the RT-differences between the word and the digit formats and found that problem difficulty disappeared as a signficant predictor if the frequency of each word and digit was controlled (for other criticism, see Noël et al., 1997).

Sokol, McCloskey, Cohen, and Aliminosa (1991) used a similar methodology, but on a brain-damaged patient (PS, left-hemispheric CVA) who showed major problems in single-digit multiplication. They varied the presentation format of the problems but found no effect on PS's multiplication performance. The type of errors were the same in all the conditions (see Table 20.3) and PS tended to err on the same problems (the error rate measured for each individual problem was highly correlated between the different presentation formats with r varying between .83 and .90). These results thus supported the single-format assumption but did not address directly the claim that these representations were base-10 semantic versus verbal representations. Yet, Sokol et al. (1991) noted that the errors made by PS reflected numerical rather than phonological similarity between problems, which is more in line with a semantic representation of quantity rather than a verbal one.

In summary, some studies have found interactions between presentation format and factors related to the retrieval stage of arithmetical facts. Yet, in most cases, a reinterpretation of the effects at an encoding or production stage is possible. Thus, as of yet, there is no strong argument in favor of the multiple-format hypothesis and we are thus left with the two single-format proposals: the base-10 semantic hypothesis of McCloskey et al. (1985) and the verbal hypothesis of Dehaene (1992).

Table 20.3
Patient PS's Error Distribution as a Function of the Presentation Format.

Format	Operand-related*	Error Type Omission	Other
Arabic numbers	37	17	6
Written words	41	15	7
Dots	41	14	8

*Operand-related errors correspond to errors belonging to the table of at least one of the operands of the problem (e.g., 3 × 5 = 10).

Verbal Representations for Addition and Multiplication Facts?

According to Dehaene (1992), addition and multiplication facts are stored as verbal representations such that a problem (regardless of format) is first transcoded into a verbal representation for retrieving the solution. This process is blind to the meaning of the numbers as no semantic processing of the numbers is needed.

Dehaene and Cohen (1997) do not assume stored verbal representations of this sort for complex addition and multiplication (e.g., *13 + 5*) problems nor for subtraction and division because these problems are not normally acquired by rote learning. Arriving at answers for these problems would require "meaningful manipulations" of analog magnitude representations. Semantic processes of this sort would also be used if the verbal representations corresponding to single-digit addition or multiplication problems were lost or inaccessible.

On this basis Dehaene and Cohen (1997) expected that more severe difficulties in addition and multiplication than in subtraction or division should be associated with a more general impairment of rote verbal memory. By contrast, greater impairment for subtraction and division than for addition and multiplication, should be accompanied by difficulties in the activation or manipulation of analog magnitude representations of numbers. Dehaene and Cohen (1997) reported two case studies that illustrate those two situations.

The first case, MAR (left-handed man, infarct in the right, supposedly dominant hemisphere, inferior parietal lobule) had greater difficulties with subtraction (25% correct) and division (46%) than with addition (68%) and multiplication (73%). Accordingly, MAR was also impaired when required to manipulate the magnitude of numbers (i.e., comparing Arabic numbers: 84% correct, selecting between two Arabic numbers the one that was closest to a third one: 80% correct) but was good in tasks tapping rote verbal memory (e.g., counting, reciting the alphabet, the days of the week, the months, the musical notes).

Dehaene and Cohen (1997) concluded that "MAR's deficit might be best described as a complete disconnection between a partially impaired quantitative system and a fully intact verbal system" (p. 241). Yet, how could a "fully intact verbal system" produce 30% errors in addition and multiplication, in other words, operations that are supposedly realized through this verbal system? Furthermore, a disconnection between the partially impaired quantitative system and the verbal system should lead to errors in tasks that rely on the analog magnitude representation of verbal numerals. Yet, the patient was perfect in two tasks of this type: positioning a verbal numeral on an analog scale (a thermometer from 0 to 100) and orally producing cognitive estimates (i.e., Shallice & Evans', 1978, test).

The second case, BOO (left-hemispheric capsulo-lenticular haemorrhage, Dehaene & Cohen, 1997) presents the opposite profile: spared performance in tasks tapping the analog magnitude representation of numbers (e.g., Arabic number comparison or calculation approximation) but impaired rote verbal memories (the patient was no longer able to recite musical notes and letters of the alphabet, or to remember nursery rhymes, prayers, and so on[14]). Accordingly, in arithmetic, BOO should show the inverse profile of MAR, namely, errors mainly in addition and multiplication. Actually, BOO showed significantly more difficulties with multiplication (72% correct) than with addition (94%) or subtraction (94%; the division data were unreliable).

The difference between the expected pattern and the observed one is interpreted as coming from the fact that back-up strategies using semantic processing can take place when verbal representations are lost or inaccessible. This idea fits quite well with the very long RTs measured in addition (mean of 2,792 ms) and multiplication (mean of 2,556 ms) but long RTs were also observed for subtraction (mean RTs of 2,854 ms when it takes usually about 1 s to carry out such calculations), an operation which should not be affected in BOO. Moreover,

---

[14]Yet, the patient scored 9/9 on automatized sequences and 2/2 on reciting subtests of the Boston Diagnostic Aphasia Examination which is not in agreement with a global loss of verbal routines.

semantic-based processing of multiplication should result in errors that are close in magnitude to the correct solution (e.g., *6 × 8 = 46, 47, 49, 50*) but the mean distance was large (*8.7 ± 6.4*) and 13 out of the 15 errors produced belonged to the multiplication table (e.g., *8 × 8 = 36, 3 × 7 = 27*) which suggests that incorrect verbal routines were used.

In summary, the two cases constitute a double dissociation which only grossly fits with the prediction of the model. But they might also be interpreted within the architecture proposed by McCloskey et al., (1985). MAR could be impaired in the comprehension of Arabic numerals[15] (see impaired performance on comparison test with Arabic digits and errors in all the arithmetical operations) as well as in the arithmetical facts store (mainly subtraction). For BOO, Dehaene and Cohen (1997) themselves proposed that: "It may never be fully excluded that her multiplication impairment and her deficits of rote verbal knowledge were due to two independent lesions" (p. 242). Thus, a simple hypothesis of a selective deficit in the multiplication fact store could explain her profile in an architecture such as that of McCloskey et al. (1985). These two cases illustrate the predictions of the triple-code model but they do not constitute strong evidence against the view proposed by McCloskey et al.

To evaluate Dehaene and Cohen's (1997) proposal, we have examined the single cases reported in the literature with deficits in arithmetical-fact retrieval. According to Dehaene and Cohen, greater impairment for addition and multiplication should be accompanied by general problems in rote verbal memories whereas greater difficulty in subtraction or division should be related to difficulties with the manipulation of analog magnitude representation for numbers. Unfortunately, many of the cases considered here were published before Dehaene and Cohen's (1997) proposal, so that the available information is not always as complete and detailed as one would like.

Nearly all the cases reviewed show lower performance in multiplication or addition than in the other operations. One should thus expect associated difficulties with more general rote verbal memories.

This is indeed the type of profile encountered in RG (Dagenbach and McCloskey, 1992: 22% correct in addition, 25% in multiplication, and 61% in subtraction). This patient was unable to recite the days of the week or the months of the year. He could only produce the first letters of the alphabet and the first 9 numbers when asked to count from 1 to 21.

The case of Rossor, Warrington, and Cipolotti (1995) also showed worse performance for multiplication (77% correct) than for addition (96%) and subtraction (100% correct). Furthermore, many of the correct products seemingly derived from back-up strategies (e.g., beside the answer *45* for *9 × 5*, he wrote "*18 + 18 + 9*," similarly, "*16+16*" was written next to *8 × 4*). As expected, this patient also had difficulties with verbal routines: he was profoundly aphasic and was unable to produce or continue automatic sequences.

By contrast, BB (Pesenti et al., 1994), who was more impaired in multiplication and addition than for subtraction (respectively, 43%, 67%, and 92% correct), showed no indication of impaired rote verbal memories: She could produce the days of the week, the letters of the alphabet, count from 1 to 21, and recite, although slowly, the months of the year.

Similarly, Cohen and Dehaene's (1994) patient was severely impaired in multiplication (58% correct) and less in addition (80% correct; no other operations were tested) but "she was fast and accurate in reciting automatic series (days of the week, months of the year, counting aurally, completing familiar proverbs)" (p. 218).

The opposite pattern of deterioration in arithmetic (i.e., better performance in multiplication compared to the other operations) has only been reported in the case of JG (Delazer & Benke, 1997: 92% correct in multiplication, 44% in addition, 32% in subtraction, and division is impossible). We have no specific information about the patient's verbal routines but the patient's verbal skills were reported to be intact, she was fluent and could count up to twenty without

---

[15]In neither of these cases was there an evaluation of number comprehension and production in the different formats.

error. We also have clinical observations suggesting that the verbal medium was of great importance in carrying out calculation. Indeed, when problems were written in Arabic digits, JG always read them out loud first, produced a spoken answer and finally wrote the corresponding digits. If verbal suppression was used in calculation task (repeating "the"), she was unable to deal with the task, even if she had only to point to the correct answer among several. She said that it was impossible for her to recognize the correct answer if she could not read the problem aloud. However, her need for verbal mediation was not specific to addition or multiplication.

A further prediction is that her poor subtraction should be related to poor manipulation of magnitude representations. In this respect, results are not clear-cut. Indeed, on the one hand, JG had no difficulty in comparing the magnitude of two Arabic numerals but on the other hand, she produced 9/14 as errors when asked to select poker chips of different values that corresponded to a given Arabic numeral and she never used back-up strategies for solving facts for which she could not retrieve an answer.

We could thus consider that this patient was impaired in operations relying on analog magnitude representations (subtraction and division) but good in those relying on verbal routines (multiplication). The poor scores with addition could be accounted for by assuming that this operation was realized through semantic processing rather than verbal routines. Accordingly, the authors wrote that, in their country, addition, subtraction, and division are not taught through verbal recitation.

Another way of testing the verbal representation hypothesis for addition and multiplication is to examine the underlying "translation" hypothesis. Indeed, according to Dehaene and Cohen (1997), a multiplication (or an addition) problem presented in Arabic digits must first be translated into the corresponding verbal representation for accessing the verbal representation of the solution. If, for example, we consider a patient with a deficit specifically affecting the translation of Arabic to verbal, one should expect more errors in addition and multiplication presented in Arabic than in verbal. By contrast, such a manipulation of the presentation format should not affect subtraction or division since they do not require verbal translation.

The case of HAR (McNeil & Warrington, 1994; glioma affecting the left occipital and parietal as well as the right occipital lobes) illustrates this point. In oral presentation, HAR was good in addition (92% correct), multiplication (100% correct), and subtraction (98% correct). Yet, if problems were written in Arabic digits, difficulties appeared in multiplication (48% correct), and addition (63% correct) but not in subtraction (96% correct). This pattern of performance can hardly be interpreted in McCloskey et al.'s (1985) model. In Dehaene's, it can be accounted for by assuming a difficulty in transcoding the Arabic problem into the corresponding verbal representation. The fact that the patient was bad in reading aloud Arabic digits (74% correct for single digits) argues in favor of that hypothesis. But how could we account for HAR's ability to match Arabic digits to spoken verbal numerals (using the same digits as those involved in arithmetical operations)?

However, all cases presenting difficulties in translating an Arabic digit problem into the corresponding verbal form do not show the expected effect of arithmetical operation.

For instance, Whalen (1994) presented the case of a patient who made many errors in reading Arabic numbers. When multiplication problems were presented in the Arabic format, he read correctly only 12% of them. If required to give an oral answer, he was 41% correct but if the answer had to be written in Arabic digits, he was 98% correct. For instance, 9 × 7 was read as "nine times six" but the correct answer 63 was written by the patient. This profile is quite unexpected under the verbal translation hypothesis. Indeed, under this hypothesis, a visually presented problem must to be translated into corresponding verbal representation and it is this verbal representation that activates the corresponding answer. Consequently, the patient's answer (spoken or written) should match the verbal representation of the problem (frequently wrong in this patient) and not the visually presented problem.

A similar pattern was observed in ZA (Delazer & Girelli, 1997). This patient was presented with calculation problems written in Arabic digits and was asked to first give his answer orally and then to write it down in Arabic digits. Here also, errors were more frequent for spoken answers (35% errors) than for written digit ones (7% errors).

These two cases are extremely problematic for Dehaene's (1992) hypothesis of an auditory verbal code for addition and multiplication facts. However, in more recent articles, Dehaene and Cohen (1995, 1997) have abandoned the assumption that facts are stored in an auditory verbal code (i.e., in the form of a phonological representation; e.g., /fIfti-tu/) and have proposed instead that facts are represented in *verbal word frames*. That is, they are stored as syntactically organized sequences of words (e.g., Tens {5}, Ones {2} for FIFTY-TWO) in which Tens {5} and Ones {2} constitute abstract word lemmas (or nodes) that are the basis for *subsequent* access to both phonological and graphemic representations of the word forms. In the context of this more recent proposal, Delazer and Girelli (1997) interpreted ZA's reading errors as a difficulty in accessing the phonological representation of spoken numbers from the verbal word frame. Accordingly, errors appear in all tasks requiring the production of spoken numbers, including oral multiplication. By contrast, translating an Arabic problem into the corresponding verbal representation (i.e., the verbal word frame) would not require the step of lexical access to the phonological word form itself. For that reason, fewer errors would be expected when multiplication problems are responded to in the Arabic modality than in the spoken modality. Unfortunately the authors did not obtain any independent evidence for this locus of impairment.

Conclusions

About half of the cases fit with the hypothesis of verbal representations for addition and multiplication. Yet, in neuropsychology, the question is not to find a majority of patients showing the expected profile but rather, to show that all patterns are consistent with a hypothesis.

Furthermore, the model assumes that addition and multiplication facts are stored as verbal representations. If some cases do indeed show similar performance with these two operations (e.g., MAR, RG), others show greater impairment for multiplication than addition (e.g., BOO, Rossor et al.'s patient, BB; Cohen and Dehaene's (1994) patient, HAR) or sometimes also the reverse (HAR). How should we account for these results? Perhaps, depending on the education system, some people have verbal representations for multiplication but not for addition whereas others have verbal representations for both?

The Dehaene and Cohen (1997) hypothesis assumes that semantic processing takes place for subtraction and division. Yet, the manipulations of analog magnitude representations required for these operations are not defined and are not easy to imagine (e.g., what types of simple manipulations of analog magnitude representations could be used for solving division problems?). These assumptions also lead to certain predictions. For instance, simple retrieval of a stored verbal representation should be faster than semantic processing. A size effect (i.e., RTs and error rate increase as the numbers of the calculation problem get bigger) should be more important for operations involving the analog magnitude representation than for those requiring the simple retrieval of a verbal representation. All these points need to be considered in evaluating the Dehaene and Cohen hypothesis.

Finally, nearly all of the cases presented (but not HAR for instance) could find an interpretation within the architecture of McCloskey et al. (1985) although one must recognize that these interpretations are often less economical and less elegant than those provided in Dehaene and Cohen's model. Furthermore, the McCloskey et al. framework does not say anything about the frequent (but not obligatory) association between deficits in multiplication and addition and difficulty with rote verbal memories: one possibility is that this association is fortuitous, another is that it is not.

GENERAL CONCLUSIONS

In the mathematical cognition domain, the neuropsychological method has been very fruitful in determining the basic components of number processing and calculation. This type of work culminated in McCloskey et al.'s (1985) proposal of a cognitive architecture for calculation and number processing. However, the content of some of the components (e.g., the different number lexicons) are still open to question, whereas others (e.g., the syntactic mechanisms) need to be specified in more detail.

Another important contribution of neuropsychology has been to raise theoretical questions regarding the way in which these basic components are connected to one another, including the role of the semantic system as an obligatory bottleneck. For most of these questions, turning to pathology seems unavoidable as in normal subjects, semantic activation appears to be quite automatic. However, in using the cognitive neuropsychological method, it is important to avoid anecdotal reports and focus insted on detailed investigations of specific hypotheses informed by the literature of published cases.

In the numerical domain, the cognitive neuropsychological approach has thus, not only brought new data into the field, but has also raised questions and generated interesting theoretical frameworks.

Acknowledgement

The author was supported by the National Research Fund of Belgium (FNRS). I would also like to warmly thank Xavier Seron and Brenda Rapp for reading a first draft of this manuscript and giving me helpful comments.

REFERENCES

Ashcraft, M. H. (1982). The development of mental arithmetic: A chronometric approach. *Developmental Review, 2*, 213–236.

Ashcraft, M. H. (1995). Cognitive psychology and simple arithmetic: A review and summary of new directions. *Mathematical Cognition, 1*(1), 3–34.

Ashcraft, M. H., & Battaglia, J. (1978). Cognitive arithmetic: Evidence for retrieval and decision processes in mental addition. *Journal of Experimental Psychology: Human Learning and Memory, 4*, 527–538.

Beauvois, M. F., & Derouesné, J. (1979). Phonological alexia: Three dissociations. *Journal of Neurology, Neurosurgery and Psychiatry, 42*, 1115–1124.

Benson, D. F., & Denkla, M. B. (1969). Verbal paraphasia as a source of calculation disturbance. *Archives of Neurology, 21*, 96–102.

Blanken, G., Dorn, M., & Sinn, H. (1997). Inversion errors in Arabic number reading: Is there a nonsemantic route? *Brain & Cognition, 4*, 404–423

Campbell, J. I .D. (1994). Architectures for numerical cognition. *Cognition, 53*, 1–44.

Campbell, J. I. D. (1997). On the relation between skilled performance of simple division and multiplication. *Journal of Experimental Psychology: Learning, Memory and Cognition, 23*, 1140–1159.

Campbell, J. I. D. (1999). Division by multiplication. *Memory and Cognition, 27*(5), 791–802.

Campbell, J. I. D., & Clark, J. M. (1988). An encoding complex view of cognitive number processing: Comment on McCloskey, Sokol and Goodman (1986). *Journal of Experimental Psychology, General, 117*, 204–214.

Campbell, J. I. D., & Clark, J. M. (1992). Cognitive number processing: An encoding-complex perspective. In J. I. D. Campbell (Ed.), *The nature and origin of mathematical skills* (pp. 457–491). Elsevier: Amsterdam.

Cipolotti, L., (1995). Multiple routes for reading words, why not numbers? Evidence from a case of Arabic numeral dyslexia. *Cognitive Neuropsychology, 12*, 313–342.

Cipolotti, L., & Butterworth, B. (1995) Towards a multiroute model of number processing: Impaired number transcoding with preserved calculation skills. *Journal of Experimental Psychology: General, 24*, 375–390.

Cipolotti, L., Butterworth, B., & Denes, F. (1991). A specific deficit for numbers in a case of dense acalculia, *Brain, 114*, 2619–2637.

Cipolotti, L., Butterworth, B., & Warrington, E. K. (1994). From "one thousand nine hundred and forty five" to 1000,945. *Neuropsychologia, 32*, 503–509.

Cipolotti, L., & De Lacy Castello, A. (1995). Selective impairment for simple division. *Cortex, 31*, 433–449.

Clark, J. M., & Campbell, J. I. D. (1991). Integrated versus modular theories of number skills and acalculia. *Brain and Cognition, 17*, 204–239.

Cohen, L., & Dehaene, S. (1991). Neglect dyslexia for numbers? A case report. *Cognitive Neuropsychology, 8*, 39–58.

Cohen, L., & Dehaene, S. (1994). Amnesia for arithmetic facts: A single-case study. *Brain and Language, 47*, 214–232.

Cohen, L., & Dehaene, S. (1995) Number processing in pure alexia: The effect of hemispheric asymmetries and tasks demands. *Neurocase, 1*, 121-137.

Cohen, L., Dehaene, S., & Verstichel, P. (1994). Verbal numbers and number non-words: A case of deep dyslexia extending to Arabic numerals. *Brain, 117*, 267-279.

Dagenbach, D., & McCloskey, M. (1992). The organization of arithmetic facts in memory: Evidence from a brain-damaged patient. *Brain and Cognition, 20*, 345-366.

Dehaene, S. (1992). Varieties of numerical abilities, *Cognition, 44*, 1-42.

Dehaene, S. (1995). Electrophysiological evidence for category-specific word processing in the normal human brain. *Neuroreport, 6*(16), 2153-2157.

Dehaene, S., & Akhavein, R. (1995). Attention, automaticity and levels of representation in number processing. *Journal of Experimental Psychology: Learning, Memory and Cognition, 21*, 314-326.

Dehaene, S., & Cohen, L. (1995). Towards an anatomical and functional model of number processing. *Mathematical Cognition, 1*(1), 83-120.

Dehaene, S., & Cohen, L. (1997). Cerebral pathways for calculation: double dissociation between rote verbal and quantitative knowledge of arithmetic. *Cortex, 33*, 219-250.

Dehaene, S., Dupoux, E., & Mehler, J. (1990). Is numerical comparison digital? Analogical and symbolic effects in two-digit number comparison. *Journal of Experimental Psychology: Human Perception and Peformance, 16*, 626-641.

Dehaene, S., Tzourio, N., Frak, V., Raynaud, L., Cohen, L., Mehler, J., & Mazoyer, B. (1996). Cerebral activations during number multiplication and comparison: A PET study. *Neuropsychologia, 34*, 1097-1106.

Delazer, M., & Benke, Th. (1997). Arithmetic facts without meaning. *Cortex, 33*, 697-710.

Delazer, M., & Girelli, L. (1997). When 'Alfa Romeo' facilitates 164: Semantic effects in verbal number production. *Neurocase, 3*, 461-475.

Deloche, G., & Seron, X. (1982a). From one to 1: An analysis of a transcoding process by means of neuropsychological data. *Cognition, 12*, 119-149.

Deloche, G., & Seron, X. (1982b). From three to 3: A differential analysis of skills in transcoding quantities between patients with Broca's and Wenicke's aphasia. *Brain, 105*, 719-733.

Deloche, G., & Seron, X. (1987). Numerical transcoding: A general production model. In G. Deloche & X. Seron (Eds), *Mathematical disabilities: A cognitive neuropsychological perspective* (pp. 137-170). Hillsdale, NJ: Lawrence Erlbaum.

Ferro, J. M., & Botelho, M. A. S. (1980). Alexia for arithmetical signs. A cause of disturbed calculation. *Cortex, 16*, 175-180.

Fias, W. (1998). *The functional locus of magnitude information in mental number processing*. Unpublished doctoral dissertation, Katholieke Universiteit Leuven, Belgium.

Fias, W., Brysbaert, M., Geypens, F., & D'Ydewalle, G. (1996). The importance of magnitude information in numerical processing: Evidence from the SNARC efect. *Mathematical Cognition, 2*(1), 95-110.

Gardner, H., Strub, R., & Albert, M. L. (1975). A unimodal deficit in operational thinking. *Brain and Language, 2*, 333-344.

Girelli, L. (1998). *Accessing number meaning in adults and children*. Unpublished doctoral dissertation. University College of London.

Goldstein, K. (1948). *Language and language disturbances*. New York: Grune & Straton.

Gonzalez, E. G., & Kolers, P. A. (1982). Mental manipulation of arithmetic symbols. *Journal of Experimental Psychology, Learning, Memory and Cognition, 4*, 308-319.

Groen, G. J., & Parkman, J. M. (1972). A chronometric analysis of simple addition. *Psychological Review, 79*, 329-343.

Hittmair-Delazer, M., Sailer, U., & Benke, Th. (1995). Impaired arithmetic facts but intact conceptual knowledge. A single case study of dyscalculia. *Cortex, 31*, 139-147.

Hittmair-Delazer, M., Semenza, C., & Denes, G. (1994). Concepts and facts in calculation. *Brain, 117*, 715-728.

Holender, D., & Peereman, R. (1987). Differential processing of phonographic and logographic single-digit by the two hemispheres. In G. Deloche & X. Seron (Eds.), *Mathematical disabilities: A cognitive neuropsychological perspective*. Hillsdale, NJ and London: Lawrence Erlbaum.

Keifer, M., & Dehaene, S. (1997). The time course of parietal activation in single-digit multiplication: Evidence from event-related potentials. *Mathematical Cognition, 3*, 1-30.

LeFevre, J., Bisanz, J., Daley, K. E., Buffone, L., Greenham, S. L., & Sadesky, G. S. (1996). Multiple routes to solution of single-digit multplication problems. *Journal of Experimental Psychology: General, 125*, 284-306.

LeFevre, J., Bisanz, J., & Mrkonjic, L. (1988). Cognitive arithmetic: Evidence for obligatory activation of arithmetical-facts. *Memory and Cognition, 16*, 45-53.

LeFevre, J., & Morris, J. (1999). More on the relation between division and multiplication in simple arithmetic: Evidence for mediation of division solutions via multiplication. *Memory and Cognition, 27*(5), 803-812.

LeFevre, J., Sadesky, G. S., & Bisanz, J. (1996). Selection of procedures in mental addition : Reassessing the problem-size effect in adults. *Journal of Experimental Psychology: Learning, Memory and Cognition, 22*, 216-230.

McClain, L., & Shih Huang, J. Y. (1982). Speed of simple arithmetic in bilinguals. *Memory and Cognition, 10*, 591-596.

McCloskey, M. (1992). Cognitive mechanisms in numerical processing: Evidence from acquired dyscalculia. *Cognition, 44*, 107-157.

McCloskey, M., Aliminosa, D., & Sokol, S. M. (1991). Facts, rules, and procedures in normal calculation: Evidence from multiple single-patient studies of impaired arithmetical fact retrieval. *Brain and Cognition, 17*, 154-203.

McCloskey, M., Caramazza, A., & Basili, A. (1985). Cognitive mechanisms in number processing and calculation: Evidence from dyscalculia. *Brain and Cognition, 4*, 171-196.

McCloskey, M., & Macaruso, P. (1995). Representing and using numerical information. *American Psychologist, 50*, 351-363.

McCloskey, M., Macaruso, P., & Whetstone, T. (1992). Defending the Modular Model. In J. I. D. Campbell (Ed.), *The nature and origin of mathematical skills* (pp. 493-537). North Holland: Elsevier.

McCloskey, M., Sokol, S. M., & Goodman, R. A. (1986) Cognitive processes in verbal-number production: Inferences from the performance of brain-damaged subjects. *Journal of Experimental Psychology: General, 115,* 307–330.

McNeil, J. E., & Warrington, E. K. (1994). A dissociation between addition and subtraction with written calculation. *Neuropsychologia, 32,* 717–728.

Miozzo, M., & Caramazza, A. (1998). Varieties of pure alexia: The case of failure to access graphemic representations. *Cognitive Neuropsychology, 15,* 203–238.

Noël, M.-P. (1994) *Transcoder et calculer: Une approche cognitive* (To transcode and calculate: A cognitive approach). Unpublished doctoral dissertation. Université Catholique de Louvain.

Noël, M.-P., Fias, W., & Brysbaert, M. (1997). About the influence of the presentation format on arithmetical-fact retrieval processes. *Cognition, 63,* 335–374.

Noël, M.-P., & Seron, X. (1992). Influence of notational system on number processing, a reappraisal of the Kolers and Gonzales hypothesis. *Quaterly Journal of Experimental Psychology, 45A(3),* 451–478.

Noël, M.-P. & Seron, X. (1993). Arabic numeral reading deficit: a single case study. Or, When 236 is read (2306) and judged superior to 1258. *Cognitive Neuropsychology, 10,* 317–339.

Noël, M.-P., & Seron, X. (1995) Lexicalization errors in writing Arabic numerals. *Brain and Cognition, 29,* 151–179.

Peritz, G. (1918). Zur Pathopsychologie des Rechens. *Deutsche Zeitschrift für Nervenheilkunde* (German Journal of Neurology), *61,* 234–340.

Pesenti, M., Seron, X., & Van der Linden, M. (1994). Selective impairment as evidence for mental organisation of arithmetical facts: BB, a case of preserved subtraction? *Cortex, 30,* 661–671.

Pinel, P., Le Vlec'H, G., van de Moortele, P. F., Naccache, L., Le Bihan, D., & Dehaene, S. (1999). Event-related fMRI analysis of the cerebral circuit for number comparison. *Neuroreport, 10(7),* 1473–1479.

Rossor, M. N., Warrington, E., & Cipolotti, L. (1995). The isolation of calculation skills. *Journal of Neurology, 242,* 78–81.

Seron, X., & Deloche, G. (1983). From 4 to four: A supplement to "From three to 3". *Brain, 106,* 735–744.

Seron, X., & Deloche, G. (1984). From 2 to two: An analysis of a transcoding process by means of neuropsychological evidence. *Journal of Psycholinguistic Research, 13,* 215–235.

Seron, X., & Noël, M.-P. (1995). Transcoding numbers from Arabic code to the verbal one or vice versa: How many routes? *Mathematical Cognition, 1(2),* 215–243.

Shallice, T., & Evans, M. E. (1978) The involvment of the frontal lobes in cognitive estimation. *Cortex, 14,* 294–303.

Singer, H. D., & Low, A. A. (1933). Acalculia (Henschen): A clinical study. *Archives of Neurology and Psychiatry, 29,* 476–498.

Sokol, S. M., & McCloskey, M. (1988). Levels of representation in verbal number production. *Applied psycholinguistics, 9,* 267–281.

Sokol, S. M., McCloskey, M., Cohen, N. J., & Aliminosa, D. (1991). Cognitive representations and processes in arithmetic: Inferences from the performance of brain-damaged subjects. *Journal of Experimental Psychology: Learning, Memory and Cognition, 17,* 355–376.

Thioux, M., Seron, X., & Pesenti, M. (1999). Functional neuroanatomy of the semantic system: The case for numerals. *Brain and Language, 69(3),* 488–490.

Warrington, E. K. (1982). The fractionnation of arithmetical skills: A single case study. *Quarterly Journal of Experimental Psychology, 34A,* 31–51.

Whalen, J. (1994, December 10–14). Presentation of a case study. From "Concepts of number and simple arithmetic—An interdisciplinary workshop," Trieste, Italy.

21

Music Perception
and Recognition

Isabelle Peretz

All human societies have music. As far as we know, they have always had. Unlike other widespread human systems such as writing, music was not invented by some groups and then spread to others. Instead, music seems to have emerged spontaneously in all forms of human societies. Moreover, this emergence is not recent in human evolution. Music apparently emerged as early as 40,000 to 80,000 years ago, as suggested by the recent discovery of a bone flute attributed to the Neanderthals (Turk, Dirjec, & Kavur, 1996). Thus, music is not only ubiquitous in human societies, it is also old in evolutionary terms. The development of music may well pertain more to human biology than human culture. As such, music may be subserved by dedicated neural networks[1] that evolved specifically for the processing of music.

Support for the existence of such neural modules can be found in the observation of remarkable sparing or selective loss in cases of brain damage. Prenatal brain anomalies allow people to be musical savants while mentally retarded (e.g. Hermelin, O'Connor, & Lee, 1987). Similarly, in cases of accidental brain damage in adulthood, music cognition can be retained despite severe disruption of other similar functions, such as language (Basso & Capitani, 1985; Luria, Tsvetkova, & Futer, 1965; Signoret, Van Eeckhout, Poncet, & Castaigne, 1987). Conversely, brain damage can selectively interfere with musical abilities while the rest of the cognitive system remains essentially intact (e.g., Steinke, Cuddy, & Holden, 1997). Therefore, at the level of the musical faculty, evidence of selective loss and of selective sparing has been documented. These neuropsychological observations indicate that music cognition is isolable both functionally and neuroanatomically from the rest of the cognitive system. That is, the musical networks do not appear to be intermingled with the networks devoted to the processing of other complex patterns, such as speech sounds. Otherwise, selective breakdowns for music should never be

---

[1]In this respect, it is noteworthy that music enjoys an interesting localization relative to other functions, such as vision. This advantage is due to its major implementation in the temporal regions on both sides of the brain. These regions are among the most vulnerable to vascular accidents. As a consequence, musical deficits should be rather frequent. Although we do not know of any large scale study aiming at measuring this incidence, our own data are supportive of such a claim (Peretz, 1990; Ayotte et al., 2000). From the 40 unilateral brain-damaged patients selected on the basis of the unilaterality of the lesion, 29 scored on one of the tests far below the lowest score of Controls. Although these depressed scores may not all reflect genuine amusic disorders, they support the idea that deficits in music processing are rather frequent. If such reports are rare, compared, for instance, to aphasic disorders, it is perhaps simply due to the low value or status that music has in our society, unless one has it as a profession. This remark should be viewed as an invitation to explore musical abilities more systematically than they have been in the past.

observed. This issue will be further examined here by focussing on the music recognition system (MRS).

The MRS is the most investigated musical function in both cognitive psychology and neuropsychology, probably because it carries out a basic musical activity that is shared by all listeners, nonmusicians and musicians alike. I assume that all listeners are equipped with common core abilities that underlie music recognition. These shared abilities are not confined to a single network. Music recognition abilities do not correspond to a monolithic system that one has or has not. Music recognition is a complex procedure that depends on the adequate functioning of multiple components. Disruption of any one component can lead to the observation of a musical recognition disorder. The goal of this chapter is to show how these disorders contribute to our understanding of the cognitive and neural organizational principles underlying music perception and music memory in the brain of the majority.

AUTONOMY AND DOMAIN-SPECIFICITY OF THE MRS

Disorders of music recognition abilities that can lead to failures to recognize familiar music, which we refer to as *music agnosia*, are a relatively common consequence of brain injury. This condition has been known for a long time. Bonvicini (1905, reported in Ombredane, 1944) describes a patient who could still process musical information adequately but could no longer recognize well-known tunes. For instance, the patient could detect wrong notes deliberately inserted in musical excerpts but could not recognize any of the excerpts themselves, even the most familiar ones. Yet, the deficit is rarely "pure" in that the patients are often also profoundly aphasic and can no longer recognize speech sounds. This was the case of Lamy's (1907) aphasic patient, who was even more spectacular in being able to write down correctly his national anthem (auditorily presented to him) in musical notation, without any feeling of knowing it.

Such cases of music agnosia are not the most common form of auditory disorders, though. Usually, the auditory disorder is general or global, in the sense that it applies to all types of auditory events. The typical patient complains of hearing all sounds as unintelligible noises. The patients behave like deaf people who can still read, speak, and write; they are not completely deaf, however, since they can usually perceive changes in frequency, intensity, and duration of the sounds. By way of example, an agnosic patient studied by Klein and Harper (1956, p. 114) made the following remarks: "I know exactly what I want to say but I don't know whether it is right or wrong. . . . I know I am speaking but I can't hear the words right, not the actual words, I can hear the voice." Such a disorder involves a problem of recognition and identification that cannot be explained by deafness as such, nor by a difficulty in verbal expression. This condition is referred to as *auditory agnosia*.

Most early descriptions of auditory agnosia are limited to this general characterization. Since the 1970s, however, further subdivisions have been drawn (see Polster & Rose, 1998, for a recent historical review). A major line of division lies between verbal agnosia (involving comprehension of speech) and nonverbal agnosia (involving recognition of sounds other than speech). This differentiation echoes the claim of Liberman and his colleagues that speech perception involves special mechanisms (Liberman, Cooper, Shankweiler, & Studdert-Kennedy, 1967). They (see, in particular, Mann & Liberman, 1983) argue that there are essentially two modes of auditory perception. One is dedicated to speech—the phonetic or speech mode, and the other—the auditory mode—is a general-purpose system handling all the nonspeech sounds. Thus, there would be essentially two types of dissociable systems depending on whether the information to be processed is speech or not.

The available evidence is largely supportive of this claim. As can be seen in Table 21.1, there are several reports of agnosia for speech, sparing either music or environmental sounds. Conversely, there are cases of impaired processing for both musical patterns and environmental sounds (e.g., animal cries, traffic noises, etc.), with no impairment of speech. This set of

Table 21.1

Case Reports of Selective Impairment in the Recognition of Speech Sounds, Music, and Environmental Sounds.

Reports	Domain		
	Speech	Music	Environmental sounds
Metz-Lutz & Dahl (1984)	–	+	+
Yaqub et al. (1988)	–	+	+
Takahashi et al. (1992)	–	+	+
Spreen et al. (1965)	+	–	–
Habib et al. (1995)	+	–	–
Peretz et al. (1994), CN and GL	+	–	+
Peretz et al. (1997), IR	+	–	+
Griffith et al. (1997)	+	–	+
Laignel-Lavastine and Alajouanine (1921)	–	+	–
Godefroy et al. (1995)*	–	+	–
Tanaka et al. (1987)	–	–	+
Eustache et al. (1990), Case I	–	–	+
Mendez & Geehan (1988),* Case II	–	–	+
Motomura et al. (1986)*	+	+	–

+ = normal recognition; – = impaired recognition
* during recovery

studies therefore constitutes evidence of a double dissociation between the recognition of speech and nonspeech sounds.

As suggested earlier, however, a single system does not govern all nonspeech sounds. Music agnosia, with no difficulty in recognizing environmental sounds or in understanding speech, has been documented in four cases. Conversely, there are cases of impaired processing for both speech and environmental sounds with no apparent problem for music recognition. These recent observations suggest further fractionation of nonverbal auditory agnosias. The pattern of selective disruption and of selective sparing points to the existence of a specialized system for music recognition. The MRS appears to be an autonomous system.

Cases of selective impairment involving only environmental sounds (i.e., in sparing speech and music) have never been documented, to our knowledge, except during recovery (see below). The fact that this domain can be selectively spared suggests, however, that environmental sounds may constitute a category distinct from music and speech.

Taken together, the data strongly suggest the existence of at least three distinct systems for auditory recognition. These divisions by domain seem to correspond to differences in kind, not to differences in degree. In effect, if the three domains under consideration were differentially vulnerable to brain damage, while being mediated by a single system, observations of double dissociations should never occur. Only single dissociations should be observed in a constant direction. Moreover, if a single system were involved, recovery of auditory functions should proceed in a consistent order, namely in the order of increasing difficulty. Yet, two case studies present diametrically opposed sequences of recovery. In the first (Mendez & Geehan, 1988), environmental sounds were recovered first, followed by music and finally speech; in the second (Motomura, Yamadori, Mori, & Tamaru, 1986), the order was reversed. Yet, both cases were similar since they suffered primarily from perceptual deficits. Consequently, there are probably several auditory recognition systems in the brain and these are specialized according to the nature of the sound event. The evidence is particularly strong for both speech and music.

Although speech, music, and environmental sounds are the three classes of stimuli that are traditionally compared in the auditory modality, there is another important class of recognizable sounds that is generally neglected: That of human *voices*. This is unfortunate because voice recognition appears mediated by a further specialized auditory system, as cases of phonagnosia would suggest (Van Lancker & Canter, 1982) and as recent functional imagery data show (Belin, Zatorre, Lafaille, Ahad, & Pike, 2000). Phonagnosia seems to occur without accompanying disorder in auditory speech comprehension (Van Lancker & Kreiman, 1987). However, the reverse condition, that of speech comprehension deficit with good retention of voice recognition abilities has, to our knowledge, never been reported. The recent discovery of specialized areas in the superior temporal gyri for voices, as measured by functional magnetic resonance imagery (fMRI) in neurologically intact subjects by Belin and collaborators (2000), suggests that selective cases of phonagnosia should be observed.

At any rate, the available neuropsychological evidence is largely consistent with the notion that music recognition corresponds to an autonomous specialized system. Hence, by exhibiting the potential for selective breakdown, the function of music recognition appears associated with neuroanatomical specialization. We should expect to obtain converging neuroanatomical evidence for separate localization of the MRS with respect to the recognition of speech and other sounds, using PET and fMRI procedures. Unfortunately, evaluation of this issue has not yet taken place.

Finally, the relation among these domain-specific disorders of auditory recognition remains poorly understood. The selectivity of the cases suggests that recognition of words, music and other familiar sounds differ in important ways. Understanding the nature of each type of disorder in such selective cases can help us to specify how and at what level of auditory processing music differs from the other classes of auditory patterns. What is necessary at this stage is a grid for decomposing the whole system of music recognition in order for its relevant components to be identified, and later compared with the other domains. This is the strategy pursued in the rest of this chapter.

FRACTIONATION OF THE MRS

Recognition of familiar music is immediate and easy for every human being. Despite its apparent effortlessness, music recognition is a complex procedure that presupposes the intervention of multiple processing components. At the very least, the perceptual input must be processed along the *melodic dimension* (defined by sequential variations in pitch) and the *temporal dimension* (defined by sequential variations in duration) and then mapped onto a stored long-term representation that represents some of the invariant properties of the musical selection. This outline is embedded in Figure 21.1.

Figure 21.1 represents a plausible functional architecture of the MRS. The model was first put forward in 1993 (Peretz, 1993a) and has undergone development since (see also Caroll-Phelan & Hampson, 1996, for another variation of the same model). This model reflects the sequence of recognition of a simple musical excerpt (containing a single voice). First, some aspect of the musical input causes the system to become active (We do not yet know what aspect of the musical input will trigger the system. Identification of this essential element is, I believe, empirically tractable and should be the goal of future studies.). Then, the musical input is analyzed by two parallel and largely independent subsystems whose functions are to specify, respectively, the melodic content (i.e., representing the melodic contour and the tonal functions of the successive pitches) and the temporal content (by representing the metrical organization as well as the grouping of the successive durations). To simplify, the melodic route represents the *what* and the temporal route represents the *when* events occur in the auditory musical input. Both routes, defining the musical analysis components, send their respective outputs—or perhaps a combination of the two—to the repertoire. The *repertoire* is

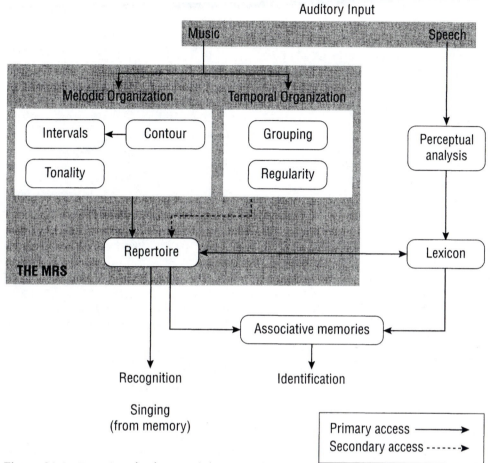

Figure 21.1: Functional schema of the music recognition recognition system (MRS).

conceived as a perceptual representation system, available to all listeners, which contains all the representations of the specific musical pieces to which one has been exposed during his/her lifetime. In turn, the repertoire output can activate stored representations in other systems, such as the lexicon for the retrieval of the accompanying lyrics, if any, or the associative memories for retrieving and pronouncing the title (i.e., identification) of the musical excerpt and for retrieval of all sorts of nonmusical information (such as an episode related to the first hearing of the music concerned). Naming a musical excerpt via associative memories is, however, not necessary for recognition. Successful activation (or selection) of one particular musical candidate in the repertoire will evoke a sense of familiarity and hence lead to recognition.

Each component depicted in Figure 21.1 will be briefly described in what follows. The neuropsychological evidence supporting the independence and position of each component in the model will be summarized as well. I will proceed from Figure 21.1 top to bottom and from left to right.

Two Routes to Recognition

As posited in Figure 21.1, the musical input is conceived as undergoing transformations along two parallel perceptual routes: the melodic and temporal route. This is a controversial issue in the literature on neurologically intact listeners. However, the neuropsychological evidence is rather consistent in showing separability of these two organization principles in music.

The current debate centers around the question of whether or not melodic and temporal dimensions are treated independently or in combination in the musical input. These two dimensions have long been treated independently, both in theory (for example, Deutsch & Feroe, 1981, and Krumhansl & Kessler, 1982, for pitch organization models; and Longuet-Higgins & Lee, 1982; Povel, 1984; for temporal organization models) and in practice (see any textbook on music cognition, such as that of Dowling & Harwood, 1986, and of Sloboda, 1985). Recently, this tradition has been seriously put into question by Jones, Boltz, and their collaborators (e.g., Boltz, 1989; Boltz & Jones, 1986; Jones, 1987; Jones, Boltz, & Kidd, 1982). They argue, quite persuasively, that melody and rhythm are not psychologically independent but rather are integrated in music perception and memory; that is, in their view, listeners treat melody and rhythm as a unified dimension (see Bigand, 1997, for additional evidence and a recent review of the literature).

Nevertheless, the neuropsychological literature is more consistent with the traditional view, by which melodic and temporal structures are processed independently from one another. Demonstrations of functional autonomy of melodic and temporal mechanisms have been repeatedly observed in different spheres of musical activities. In singing, rhythmic organization may be spared when melody is lost (Mann, 1898, and Josmann, 1926, reported in Dorgeuille, 1966), and vice versa (Brust, 1980; Mavlov, 1980). The same double dissociation has been reported in reading music (see Brust, 1980, and Dorgeuille, 1966, for a selective losses of rhythm; Assal, 1973, and Dorgeuille, 1966, for selective losses of melody). More recently, this double dissociation between melody and rhythm has been extended to perception. The first indications were provided informally. Sacks (1985) reports the case of OM who "herself complained that recently the hymns in the chapel seemed more and more alike so that she could scarcely distinguish them by tone or tune, but had to rely on the words, or the rhythm" (pp. 135–136). Similarly, Fries and Swihart (1990) describe the case of an amateur musician who was intact on rhythm discrimination and impaired on melody processing. Conversely, Mavlov (1980) reports the case of a musician who developed a severe difficulty for processing rhythms but who could still adequately process pitch sequences.

We have replicated the phenomenon several times, in different experimental settings. The task usually involves a same–different classification of successive musical sequences. In melodic conditions, the comparison stimuli are altered by changing the pitch structure while leaving the temporal structure unchanged. In rhythmic conditions, the stimuli are the same but this time the temporal structure is modified in the comparison sequence and the pitch structure remains unchanged. Comparison of the results of unilaterally brain-damaged patients with those of neurologically healthy subjects (matched in terms of age and education) reveals dissociations that are very robust. Some patients score well below the normal range (established by control subjects) in the deficient dimension, but within the normal range in the unaffected dimension. In each study, involving different populations of brain-damaged patients (Ayotte, Peretz, Rousseau, Bart, & Bojanowsk, 2000; Liégeois-Chauvel, Peretz, Babai, Laguitton, & Chauvel, 1998; Peretz, 1990) there were patients who could no longer discriminate the musical stimuli when the discrimination cue was melodic and who performed normally when the distinguishing cue was rhythmic, and vice versa. Thus, brain damage can produce a selective loss for either melody or rhythm. The evidence strongly supports the claim that these two dimensions involve the operation of separable perceptual subsystems.

In a further case, that of CN (Peretz & Kolinsky, 1993), we were able to show that a dissociation between melody and rhythm could be still observed in situations that promote integration of the melodic and rhythmic dimensions in an intact brain. To this end, we created a Stroop-like situation with sequences varying in both melody and rhythm, while maintaining the "same-different" classification requirements. Subjects were now asked to pay selective attention to rhythm in spite of any potential changes in melody, since the patient CN could only process rhythm reliably. An illustration of the musical stimuli and design is presented in Figure 21.2.

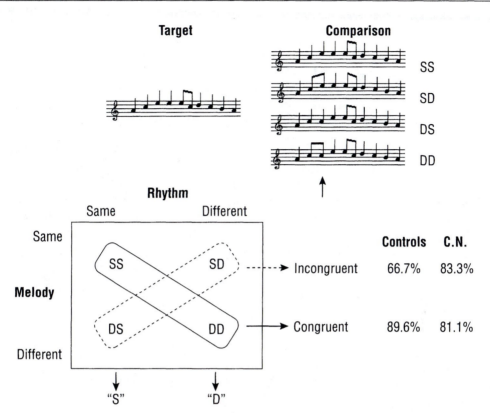

Figure 21.2: In the top part is represented the structure of the stimuli used in our Stroop-like situation with CN (See "Boundaries of Separability Between Melody and Rhythm in Music Discrimination: A Neuropsychological Perspective," by I. Peretz & Kolinsky, 1993, *Quarterly Journal of Experimental Psychology, 46A*, pp. 301–325 for details). On each trial, a target followed by a comparison melody is presented auditorily to the subject. The task is to judge whether the target and the comparison are "same" (S) or "different" (D) rhythmically and to ignore all pitch variations. There were four types of comparison melodies: half contained a rhythmic change (see SD and DD examples) and half contained a melodic change (see DS and DD). As illustrated in the left bottom part of the Figure, Stroop-like interference is expected to occur when responses (S or D) conflict between the attended dimension (rhythm) and the ignored dimension (melody). Because Stroop interference arose from the failure to ignore melodic variations, responses were more accurate when they were congruent (i.e., SS and DD) than when they were incongruent (SD and DS). This Stroop-like effect occurred for control subjects but was absent in CN's data.

As can be seen, control subjects failed to ignore the irrelevant melodic variations, thus showing Stroop interference effects. CN did not. For her, melody and rhythm were entirely separable.

Thus, the data from brain-damaged subjects favor the view that melodic structure, arising from the organization of sequential pitch variations, and rhythmic structure, arising from the organization of temporal variations, both have processing autonomy. This distinction would not only concern receptive behaviors but expressive ones as well, as suggested earlier, thus indicating central or general separation of the subsystems. Such a conclusion is controversial since, as explained previously, there is currently a large debate on this issue in the literature on neurologically intact subjects. However, the recurrent observation of a separation between these two dimensions in patients reflect the observation that functional dissociations are often easier to demonstrate in brain-damaged subjects, with selective deficits, than in intact brains where the integration of information often precludes access to early distinct codes.

In the preceding discussion, I have treated unfamiliar music (as represented in Fig. 21.2) as if it were processed similarly to familiar music. This assimilation is deliberate. I assume that up to the level of the *repertoire* represented in Figure 21.1, familiar and unfamiliar musical selections are processed by identical mechanisms. The only difference is that unfamiliar sequences do not yet have a mental representation stored in the *repertoire* when presented for the first time. With repeated exposure, however, the unfamiliar excerpt will leave a record in the same network as where highly familiar music is stored. Neuropsychological data are consistent with this view. As explained in more detail in the section entitled The Repertoire (beginning on page 532) when the *repertoire* component is damaged, the patient can no longer learn novel musical materials or relearn familiar ones. Similarly, at the perceptual level, familiar and unfamiliar musical sequences are processed along the same principles. For instance, IR was found to have depressed scores on equivalent tests in two musical batteries, while one battery involved only unfamiliar music and the other, solely familiar music (see Peretz, Belleville, & Fontaine, 1997, for the results on the unfamiliar set, and Peretz & Gagnon, 1999, for the results on the familiar set).

The Melodic Route

Recognition of a single melodic line relies on essentially three kinds of features: contour, intervals, and scale degree. Consider the well-known first notes of Beethoven's Symphony No. 5 represented in Figure 21.3. Notes are typically heard as motifs that are repeated with slight variations in pitch. The notes are heard as grouped into motifs by the application of a set of simple rules, of which pitch direction and pitch distance play a crucial role. Pitch directions contribute to the *contour* of the melody. Pitch distance between consecutive notes defines the melodic *intervals*. As can be seen in Figure 21.3, the famous motif is repeated at different pitch level without losing its identity. The exact pitch level is not important for music recognition. A familiar tune can be easily recognized whether sung by a man or a woman. Contour, however, such as the one defining the famous motif (e.g., ⎯⎯⎯⟍) plays a crucial role in melody discrimination (e.g., Dowling, 1982b). Intervals provide critical information as well. The last interval of the motif (expressed in Figure 21.3 in terms of semitones) varies in size by one or two semitones (which is the smallest musical distances that can separate two pitches in the Western musical system). Listeners show sensitivity over time for these slight changes in interval sizes which create variation and deviation from exact repetition (see Dowling & Harwood, 1986, for a tutorial). These intervals also typically evoke a particular *scale* (which is C minor in the excerpt represented in Fig. 21.3). The scale refers to a particular subset of pitch intervals. These intervals, or scale degrees, confer in turn a particular structure to the melodic line. In our Western musical system, this structure reflects a set of tonal constraints by which each tone receives a varying degree of stability (see Krumhansl, 1991). For instance, a tonal piece usually begins and ends on the most stable pitch (called the tonic or the first degree, which is C, the last tone in our illustration). The second in importance is the fifth degree and often replaces the tonic (e.g., in our illustration, the fifth degree is G and is the starting note). The contribution of contour, intervals and scale to melodic perception is relatively well-documented in both neurologically intact subjects and in brain-damaged patients.

Contour versus Intervals

Neuropsychological support for the existence of two separate codes, one best described in terms of contour and the other in terms of interval sizes, comes from the study of the

Motifs

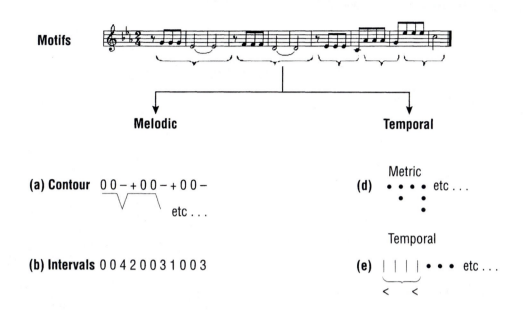

Melodic   **Temporal**

(a) Contour 0 0 − + 0 0 − + 0 0 −

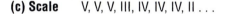

etc . . .

(b) Intervals 0 0 4 2 0 0 3 1 0 0 3

(c) Scale   V, V, V, III, IV, IV, IV, II . . .

Metric

(d) • • • • etc . . .

Temporal

(e) | | | | • • • etc . . .

Figure 21.3: Illustration of the different codes that can be assigned to the musical structure of the begining of Beethoven's Symphony No. 5. The musical line is expressed in: (a) successive pitch directions with 0 meaning a plateau, − down and + up, for the *contour*; (b) successive pitch *intervals* in semitones with 0 meaning repeating note, 1 one semitone, etc.; (c) successive pitches expressed in terms of *scale degrees* with V meaning the fifth degree, also called the dominant, etc.; (d) successive tones represented by dots which represent levels of *metrical structure*, with the first beat in a measure receiving the highest weight; (e) successive tone onsets represented by bars and tone duration or silence represented by dots, with the first and last bar/tone onset of a *temporal group* marked with an accent (represented by <).

functional differences between the cerebral hemispheres in melody processing. The original impulse for distinguishing the differential contribution of the left and right hemisphere in terms of contour versus intervals, respectively, comes from the influential study of Bever and Chiarello (1974). These authors demontrated that the recognition of melodies was subserved by two distinct components implemented in different cerebral structures. The distinction stemmed from the comparison of musicians and nonmusicians' performance. In a melody recognition task, musicians exhibited a right-ear advantage (taken to reflect a left-hemisphere superiority) whereas nonmusicians displayed a left-ear advantage (taken to reflect a right-hemisphere superiority). Support for relating the observed laterality effects to the use of distinct processing components was gathered in the same study by considering the success with which the two groups could identify a two-tone probe as part of the whole melody. Only musicians were able to perform above chance on this subsidiary task. This was taken as evidence that musicians used an interval-based route for melody recognition, which would be typical of the left-hemisphere mode of functioning, and that nonmusicians recognized melodies holistically, probably on the basis of the melodic contour, in the right hemisphere.

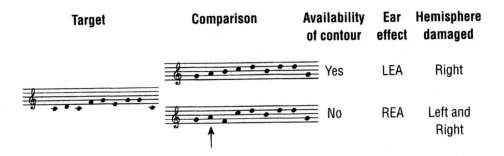

Figure 21.4: The target and comparison melodies represented here are real examples of stimuli used in a "same–different" classification task (as used in Peretz, 1987, and Mottron, Perez, & Menard, 2000) and are representative of the stimuli used in numerous studies performed with neurologically intact as well as impaired patients. As can be seen, contour change can be used as a discrimination cue in the top comparison but not in the bottom comparison. In the latter case, only exact interval sizes can serve for discrimination. Note that target and comparison are played at different pitch level to prevent subjects from using absolute pitch for discrimination. In the contour-violated condition, left-ear advantages (LEA) reflecting right-hemisphere superiority, are usually obtained (e.g., Peretz, 1987) and patients with lesions on the right side of the brain are usually impaired (e.g., Peretz, 1990). In the contour-preserved condition, right-ear advantages (REA) reflecting left-hemisphere superiority, are usually obtained (e.g., Peretz & Morais, 1987) and patients with lesions on the left and right side are typically impaired (e.g., Liégeois-Chauvel et al., 1998).

In subsequent studies, we were able to demonstrate a link between contour processing in the right hemisphere and interval processing in the left hemisphere, while testing nonmusicians (see Peretz & Morais, 1988, for a review). These conditions were assessed in nonmusicians in order to ascertain that superiority effects of the left hemisphere, which is also the speech-dominant hemisphere, were due to the encoding of melodic intervals and not to the use of a verbal code (pitch naming is a well-trained ability in musicians). A typical experiment is represented in Figure 21.4, along with recurrent findings. Taken together, the results converge to show that neurologically intact subjects tend to rely on contour representation to discriminate melodies and in doing so involve predominantly their right hemisphere. When contour cues are not available and interval information is required, neurologically intact subjects shift to the left hemisphere.

The lateralization of the underlying mechanisms that subserve the computations of contour and intervals has been verified and refined with brain-damaged patients who had sustained a vascular lesion to one of the hemispheres (Ayotte et al., 2000; Peretz, 1990) or had undergone unilateral excision of temporal lobe structures for the relief of intractable epilepsy (Liégeois-Chauvel et al., 1998). In all three studies, a lesion in the left hemisphere was found to spare the ability of representing melodies in terms of their contour but to interfere with an interval-based procedure, whereas a lesion in the right hemisphere was found to disrupt both procedures. This pattern of results suggests a hierarchical principle of cooperation between the hemispheres. According to this principle, a right-hemisphere lesion, by disrupting the procedures required for representing the melody contour, deprives the intact left-hemispheric structures of the anchorage points necessary for encoding interval information. This is expressed by an unidirectional arrow between the contour and interval processing component in Figure 21.1.

A Module for Tonal Encoding of Pitch

Although melodic features such as contour are essential characteristics of musical structure, they are not unique to music. Pitch contours are also used in speech, as we will see in a later section under the heading Relation with Prosody, beginning on page 535. In contrast, tonal encoding of pitch can be considered as the "germ around which a musical faculty could have evolved" (Jackendoff, 1987, p. 257). Central to pitch organization is the perception of pitch along musical scales. In music, pitch variations generate a determinate scale, whereas in human speech the intonation contours do not usually elicit such effects (Balzano, 1982). Moreover, perception of tonal pitch may require universal processing mechanisms. Even though the commonly used scales differ somewhat from culture to culture, most have common properties. Most musical scales make use of unequal-spaced pitches, that are organized around 5 to 7 focal pitches (Dowling, 1978, 1982a).

The tonal encoding of pitch, is presumably mediated by several cognitive operations. Since these operations have not yet been distinguished, they are grouped in a single component in Figure 21.1 under the term " tonality." This tonality component involves knowledge and procedures that reflect several constraints, the minimal ones being as follows. The set of musical tones consists of a finite ensemble of pitches, roughly corresponding to the tones of the piano keyboard. From these, only a small subset are generally used in a given piece, namely those from a particular musical scale. Scale tones are not equivalent and are organized around a central tone, called the tonic, as mentioned previously and illustrated in Figure 21.3. Usually, a piece starts and ends on the tonic. Among the other scale or diatonic tones, there is a hierarchy of importance or stability, with the fifth scale tone (G in the example) and the third scale tone (being E) being more closely related to the tonic (C) than the other scale tones. The remaining scale tones are less related to the tonic, and the nonscale tones are the least related; the latter often sound like "foreign" tones.

There is substantial empirical evidence that listeners use this tonal regularities in perception, albeit in an implicit manner. As we have argued elsewhere in detail (Peretz & Morais, 1989), translation of pitch onto tonal scales fits with the definition of a modular system in Fodor's (1983) sense. Most notably, the tonal system seems to mediate perception of musical pitch in an automatic way and without conscious awareness (Shepard & Jordan, 1984) and to operate very early in ontogenetic development (e.g., Trehub, Schellenberg, & Kamenetsky, 1999). Finally, tonal knowledge can be selectively impaired by brain damage (Peretz, 1993b).

Claiming modularity for tonal encoding of pitch is not meant to apply only to the Western tonal system. This specificity refers to some sort of abstract principles that are instantiated in the tonal system but that essentially cut across styles and time. It is analogous in essence, to the less controversial notion that there are modules devoted to the understanding of speech in general, not just of French in particular.

The pioneering neuropsychological study of tonal encoding of pitch was realized by Françès, Lhermitte, and Verdy in 1973. In their study, a large group of aphasic patients was presented with pairs of short melodies and required to judge which tone in the melody had changed on the second playing. Melodies within a pair were either both tonal or nontonal. Aphasics failed to exhibit the normal superiority effect for tonal sequences over nontonal ones. This was taken as evidence that aphasic patients had lost tonal knowledge, thus accounting for their poor melodic discrimination abilities.

Recently, in the single case study of GL, I (Peretz, 1993b) had the opportunity to replicate this finding, and furthermore I was able to demonstrate that it arises from a true disturbance in tonal interpretation of pitch, as opposed to difficulties from other sources (such as an impairment in short term memory, contour or interval processing). This impairment affected perception of pitch structure so that pitch was no longer encoded in terms of its tonal function but rather pitches were perceived into a unidimensional continuum of pitch height (i.e., intervals) and an ordinal dimension (i.e., contour). As a consequence, the patient encountered specific difficulties with melodic as opposed to temporal patterns, encountered memory difficulties for pitch material, and was relatively insensitive to tonal structure in perception (in singing, though, residual tonal knowledge was noted).

One of the tasks was drawn directly from experimental research in neurologically intact subjects and is known in this literature as the probe-tone task after the seminal work of Krumhansl (see Krumhansl, 1990, for a detailed analysis of the task). The results obtained by

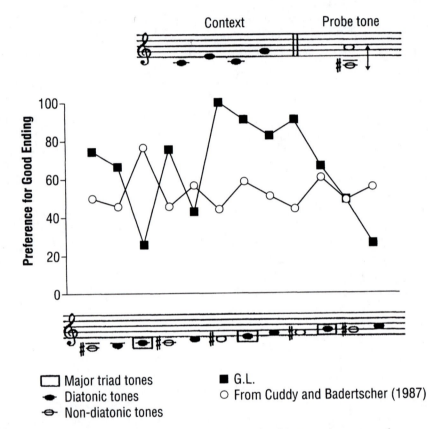

Figure 21.5: An example of stimuli and graph of GL's judgments of appropriateness of final tone as a function of the pitch of the last tone of the context sequence. The results obtained under the same conditions by six year-old children tested by Cuddy and Badertscher (1987) are included for comparison. Children's judgments preserve tonal constraints—they systematically prefer scale tones (filled notes on the musical staff), and most notably those making up the major triad (boxed notes on the same staff). GL, however, proceeded otherwise. As he himself explained, his judgments were based on his impression that singers normally conclude on a note that is close but lower in pitch. In other words, he relied on interval size and contour. This is effectively what emerges from an analysis of his responses. Apart from the most distant tones (A# and B, which in fact had an ambiguous pitch), GL felt that the last tone was appropriate when it descended (i.e., all tones preceding G) and more particularly so when it was close in pitch, and rejected those that ascended (i.e., G#, A). His judgments were thus made without regard to the tonal status of the pitches.

GL on this task illustrates his loss of tonal sense. In this task (taken from Cuddy & Bardetscher, 1987), listeners hear a context sequence followed by a tone that can take any value in the octave (see the example given in Figure 21.5). Their task is to assess the extent to which this final tone constitutes an acceptable conclusion to the melody. Judgments given by children and by adults with no musical training generally correspond to tonal constraints—subjects systematically prefer scale tones and most notably those making up the major triad (e.g., C-E-G in C major). However, GL's judgments were determined by pitch direction and pitch proximity, not the tonal status of the pitches.

In this respect, GL represents the reverse dissociation of that reported earlier by Tramo, Bharucha, and Musiek (1990). These authors describe a patient who also suffered from bilateral brain damage but who could still use tonal knowledge despite severely degraded pitch discrimination abilities. This patient with GL thus constitute together a double dissocation for the encoding of pitch intervals and of tonal pitch. This should, however, be taken cautiously, for the two patients were tested with different procedures. Nevertheless, GL's study provides neuropsychological support for the existence of a tonal module.

Despite numerous attempts that have been made to localize the tonal module in the brain, no clear picture has yet emerged. For example, the two studies, in which a laterality effect was obtained, have yielded conflicting results. Pechstedt, Kershner, and Kinsbourne (1989) found evidence for a left-hemispheric locus, and Tramo and Bharucha (1991) for a right-hemispheric one. The experimental settings were markedly different in the two studies, and thus many different factors can account for this discrepancy. Yet, even if tonal knowledge cannot be clearly lateralized, it does not imply that it is not accomplished via modular mechanisms. The critical neuropsychological property of a modular system is not so much its precise localization but rather it is its potential to exhibit selective breakdown after brain damage. Now that cases of selective loss (and sparing) of tonal knowledge have been reported in the literature, future studies, exploiting brain imaging procedures, should aim at identifying its neural underpinnings.

The Temporal Route

Two types of temporal organization appear fundamental to the perceived "rhythm" of musical sequences: The segmentation of an ongoing sequence into temporal groups of events on the basis of their durational values and the extraction of an underlying temporal regularity or beat. The first type of temporal organization corresponds to the tendency to group events according to temporal proximity, without regard to periodicity. The first two motifs illustrated for the beginning of the Beethoven's Symphony No. 5 in Figure 21.3 follow this principle (along several melodic ones described earlier): the boundaries fall after the longest note—the minim. The second type of fundamental temporal organization is regularity and refers to the tendency to perceive events that occur at regular intervals in time, in the form of an underlying beat. Beat perception leads to the perception of a metrical organization corresponding to periodic alternation between strong and weak beats (the strong beats generally correspond to the spontaneous tapping of the foot). In Western music, metrical patterns contain either binary or ternary beats, by inducing a major accent on the first beat of two or three beats (as in a waltz: one, two, three, one, two, three, ...). The most frequent structure is the binary one, as is the case of the beginning of the 5th symphony (see Figure 21.3).

Regularity and grouping are conceived by certain researchers (Benjamin, 1984; Cooper & Meyer, 1960; Povel & Essens, 1985) as hierarchically organized, while others (Drake, 1998; Lerdahl & Jackendoff, 1983) conceive regularity and grouping as the result of completely distinct mental operations. For the proponents of the interactive view, regularity or meter is basically derived from grouping which confers accentual relationships between tones. In this case, the same accent pattern characterizes both meter and grouping structure (see Figure

21.3). For the proponents of the independence view, meter is determined by a different set of rules from those determining grouping. To our knowledge, distinguishing between these two types of models has not yet been the subject of experimental work. There are, however, indications that meter cannot be viewed as the sole result of conferring accentual relationships according to the durational value of the tones, as proposed by Povel (1984; Povel & Essens, 1985). Meter is in part determined by the abstract knowledge of the regularities that are typical of the Western metrical system and thus can not be totally governed by sensory cues (Palmer & Krumhansl, 1990).

Similarly, temporal grouping and metric interpretation of music have rarely been distinguished in neuropsychological studies. The three studies that have addressed the question (not intentionally in all cases) have obtained neuropsychological dissociations, thus validating the independence view.

For example, Ibbotson and Morton (1981) were the first to show that subjects far more easily tapped a rhythmic pattern with their right hand and the beat with their left hand, than the other way around. These findings suggest that the beat is better handled by the right hemisphere whereas grouping would rely essentially on the left hemisphere. Such hemispheric separation for the two types of organization mediating temporal pattern processing is consistent with the claim that the two aspects are mediated by distinct mechanisms. Further support has been provided by the study of a patient with a right-hemispheric lesion (but in a left-hander) who could no longer tap the beat but who was still able to reproduce temporal patterns (Fries & Swihart, 1990). In both studies, however, it can be argued that the outcome is more related to the programming and coordination of fine motor skills than to temporal processing per se. Nevertheless, in our studies in which more perceptual aspects of temporal processing were assessed, convergent evidence for dissociating meter from grouping was also found (Liégeois-Chauvel et al., 1998; Peretz, 1990).

In our studies, two tasks were used: a standard same–different classification task and a "waltz–march" decision task. With respect to the former, grouping was the only cue available for discrimination. In the other task, subjects had to make a waltz–march judgment for each musical excerpt to assess its metrical organization. In our initial study (Peretz, 1990), both patient groups, that is with a lesion in either hemisphere, were found to be impaired on the temporal grouping task while performing normally on the metric test. In the second study (Liégeois-Chauvel et al., 1998), the reverse pattern was observed. Patients, having sustained an excision in either their left or right temporal lobe, performed normally on the grouping discrimination test and failed to reach control performance on the metric test. Thus, the results were not very informative with regard to the hemispheric basis of these two components. However, the double dissociation suggests that meter is not only distinct but also is not derived from grouping. Therefore, the data can be viewed as fitting Lerdahl and Jackendoff's (1983) two-component model rather than the interactive one proposed by Povel and his collaborators (Povel, 1984; Povel & Essens, 1985). This explains why regularity and rhythm have been represented separately and without an arrow relating them in Figure 21.1. This is tentative since task parameters were not equivalent for evaluating grouping and regularity.

The Repertoire

Little research has been done on how music is represented and organized in memory. A related question is the nature of the perceptual cues that will be effective in activating the appropriate stored musical representation. Knowledge of such factors should clarify both the nature of processing that must precede access to the repertoire and the internal structure of the repertoire itself. As stated previously, the melodic line and the rhythmic pattern are conceived as two relatively independent structural cues for access to the repertoire. However, as we will see, the two routes are not equally effective.

Access

Melodic cues play a prominent role in accessing the music representations within the repertoire. This hypothesis comes from our neuropsychological investigations of CN and GL (Peretz et al., 1994). Both patients were no longer able to recognize highly familiar music such as "Happy Birthday." Yet, neither CN nor GL had any impairment in discriminating and retaining rhythmic patterns. In theory, both patients could have used the rhythm as a basis to recognize music. The fact that they did not raises the possibility that the melodic route, which was disrupted in both patients, is the most diagnostic of music identity. In support of this idea is the oft-cited study of White (1960), who found that neurologically intact listeners correctly identified 88% of familiar melodic lines of which temporal variations were removed, whereas they were only 33% correct when presented with the rhythmic pattern deprived from its pitch variations. We have replicated and extended this result with unanticipated musical excerpts in university students (Hébert & Peretz, 1997). In the first experiment, we took identification (i.e., title production) as well as familiarity ratings as response measures. Participants were found to be able to name only one out of 25 excerpts from their rhythmic patterns, whereas the participants achieved identification of half of them from hearing the melodic variations alone. The same pattern of results emerged on the familiarity ratings, and in subsequent experiments. Altogether the results consistently showed that the melodic pattern is more diagnostic for music identification than the rhythmic pattern, and that this advantage is basically perceptual.

The implication of this finding is that patients, such as CN and GL, who are impaired along the melodic route, should systematically experience difficulties in recognizing familiar music. These patients would thus be music agnosic because of a perceptual defect. In contrast, patients who are selectively impaired along the temporal route should not be agnosic, unless their repertoire is damaged as well. These predictions remain to be verified.

Content

The repertoire is a perceptual representation system that mediates music recognition; it pertains to the same class of domain-specific systems that have been identified for, say, words and faces (e.g., Ellis & Young, 1988). These are conceived as representing information about the form and structure of events, and not the meaning or other associative properties.

There are several lines of evidence that suggest the existence of a perceptual representation system that is specific to music. First of all, music is by essence perceptually-driven. Unlike speech, music is not associated with a fixed semantic system. Music does not generally refer to external objects or concepts. Music is self-referenced, for the most part, in that it refers to internal events or structure. Although one can view some level of structural elaboration as the conceptual core of the music (for instance, a single chord can represent a whole movement in Schenker's (1935/1979) theory; see Serafine, Glassman, & Overbeeke, 1989), this representation is still dependent on the perceptual organization of the input. Secondly, the stored representations can preserve highly specific aspects of the input. Memory for surface features, such as absolute pitch and precise tempo, has been revealed by the singing renditions of popular songs (Levitin, 1994; Levitin & Cook, 1996) as well as by mental rehearsal (Halpern, 1988, 1989).

Along with these surface representations of popular music, listeners have access to abstract structural representations that allow recognition despite transposition to a different key (i.e., absolute pitch level; e.g., Dowling & Fujitani, 1971), change in instrumentation (i.e., in timbre; Radvansky, Fleming, & Simmons, 1995) and change in tempo (i.e., absolute speed; Warren, Gardner, Brubaker, & Bashford, 1991). This duality between surface and abstract representations is congruent with our intuitions as to the role of memory in music listening. On the one hand, most listeners will not remember every detail of a musical segment but instead will follow the piece by a process of abstraction and organization, remembering its "gist" (Dowling & Harwood, 1986; Large, Palmer, & Pollack, 1995). On the other hand, appreciation of interpretation requires the consideration of surface characteristics that are unique to a particular rendition (Raffman, 1993). Thus, both surface and structural features may be contained in the stored representations and fit with the role and definition of the perceptual representation systems that are posited in other perceptual domains.

Empirical support for a perceptually-based memory system for music derives mainly from neuropsychological studies. In effect, persistent loss of recognition abilities for music can occur despite normal or near normal perceptual processing of musical input (Eustache, Lechevvalier, Viader, & Lambert, 1990; Peretz, 1996). Above all, such memory loss can be limited to music (Peretz, 1996). For example, seven years post-onset, CN had recovered her musical perceptual abilities and yet suffered from persisting recognition failures for music. For instance, CN always recognized spoken lyrics immediately and accurately. With musical selections, she was always hesitant and on most occasions performed at chance. At best, she could name 10% of the musical excerpts when listening to them, although all selections evoked precise memories when presented by title.

Thus, CN's recognition deficit was not only modality-specific but music-specific as well. In another testing condition that is more demanding in terms of memory, by presenting CN in the auditory modality with 20 lines of text (taken from familiar songs) spoken at a normal rate and requesting her to recognize these among 40 spoken lines, all equally familiar and of which half corresponded to the target lines, CN's score was excellent. She performed equally well when tested under the same task conditions but with familiar environmental sounds. In sharp contrast with this intact performance on nonmusical sounds, when presented with 20 musical excerpts taken from a familiar repertoire (and corresponding to the text lines presented in the auditory verbal task) or with 20 unfamiliar musical selections to be recognized from 20 distractors matched in familiarity, CN performed at chance. Control subjects have no difficulty with these two musical tasks (Peretz, 1996).

Indirect effects of memorization were assessed with CN as well. They were indexed by the preference bias created by prior exposure, known as "the mere exposure effect" after Zajonc's (1968) work. CN exhibited no preference for familiar over unfamiliar music nor higher preference ratings for previously heard music over nonpresented music. Each of these latter effects was present in the responses of her matched controls as well as university students (Peretz, Gaudreau, & Bonnel, 1998). Thus, CN showed no sign of implicit memory.

The results are highly consistent with the existence of a perceptual memory system that is specialized for music and that can be selectively disturbed by brain damage so as to prevent most forms of recognition and interfere with the acquisition of new memories.

One major implication of this conclusion is that CN's deficit now appears to be most consistent with a recognition model that distinguishes between perceptual analysis and memory representations. This distinction between perceptual and memory forms of agnosia was first put forward by Lissauer (1889). He argued that patients have a problem in apperception or in association; that is, in forming a perceptual representation of an object or in using that representation to retrieve associated knowledge. In Lissauer's terms, CN has an associative agnosia that is specific to music. Hence, memory appears dissociable from perception. Accordingly, the repertoire is represented in Figure 21.1 as a distinct processing component of the MRS.

Although I have referred to the functioning of the repertoire in an all or none manner, this is obviously an oversimplification. Brain damage is not expected to respect and to be restricted to a complete processing component but rather to disturb a given function in a graded fashion. It is unquestionable that the damage sustained by CN to her music recognition system was extremely severe. The principles along which the repertoire can be impaired, when partially damaged, should be very instructive with respect to the structure of its internal organization. Such degradation remains, however, to be observed and systematically studied.

LEVELS OF AUTONOMY

In this review, I have presented evidence that the MRS is likely to correspond to a modular autonomous system, in being a domain-specific system that is isolable in the brain. We have also seen that the MRS is not monolithic. Rather it is composed of multiple separable processing components. The question that arises is to what extent we should consider each of these components as modular. One of these components—tonality—is modular in a restrictive sense, as we have briefly explained previously. What about the other components? For example, should we consider the contour component to be specific to music or to be shared with speech perception? Similarly, should we consider that songs are represented in memory with the melody represented in the repertoire and the accompanying lyrics stored in another network? These questions have recently received some empirical attention. The work is just beginning and hence will just be outlined here.

Relation with Prosody

The conceptual similarity between contour processing in music and intonation processing in speech is striking. In speech, the pattern of fundamental frequency changes over time is a basic part of the perceptual organization of spoken language. Notably, it contributes to the marking of intention and affect. It seems reasonable to expect that the processing of melodic contour and speech intonation share some cognitive and neural resources (Patel & Peretz, 1997).

To assess this prediction, we (Patel, Peretz, Tramo, & Labreque, 1998) conducted an experiment with CN and IR. Both, at some point, exhibited deficits in processing melodic contour. Yet, it was not clear whether or not this contour processing deficit was associated with a prosodic impairment. Music and speech comparisons are not straightforward, even when the pitch dimension is considered in isolation. For instance, pitch variations in speech appear much larger than those used in music. Therefore, the prosodic and musical patterns need to be tailored to one another. The strategy that we adopted was to use the intonation patterns of speech and to make them sound "musical" by removing all phonological information and pitch glides. The spoken sentences and the musical derivations were presented in separate conditions to the subjects, in a same–different discrimination task.

Using these prosodic and music-like conditions, we observed that IR experienced similar difficulties with both speech and nonspeech stimuli. CN had recovered and hence performed normally on these tasks. Yet, IR's results suggest the existence of a common processing mechanism for tracking pitch contours in both speech and music. Of course, as with any case of functional association, the possibility exists that the processes in question are in fact neurally and functionally distinct, but are disrupted by the same lesion. This issue remains to be settled.

Memory for Songs

Songs also represent a challenge to modularity. In songs, music and speech are intrinsically related. Yet, there is now substantial evidence that, in songs, melody and text are perceptually separable. Neurologically-intact listeners can monitor opera excerpts for incongruities in speech and in music independently (Bonnel, Faïta, Peretz, & Bessan, 2000) and, in doing so, elicit distinctive brain potentials (Besson, Faïta, Peretz, Bonnel, & Requin, 1998). When presented with sung digits, musicians engage opposite cerebral hemispheres for the recall of the pitch patterns and of the digits (Goodglass & Calderon, 1977). Finally, as said previously, brain-damaged patients can recognize lyrics normally while failing to recognize the melody (e.g., Peretz et al., 1994) even when lyrics and melody are sung together in their original pairing or in a false pairing (Hébert & Peretz, 2000). Melody and text that are integrated in songs appear nevertheless separable for the brain.

There is, however, a paradox. It has been repeatedly shown that, in a memory recognition task, neurologically intact listeners behave as though they cannot access the melody without having access to the text of the studied song. The task consists a forced-choice memory task in which subjects are required to recognize the tune, the lyrics, or both, of *novel songs* that they had previously heard; among the alternatives are excerpts in which the tune of one song and the lyrics of another song are combined (mismatch songs). The integration effects are revealed by the systematic superiority of recognition scores for match songs over mismatch songs. This recurrent finding, which is taken as evidence for lyrics and tune integration in song memory, has been documented in adults (Serafine, Crowder, & Rapp, 1984; Serafine, Davidson, Crowder, & Rapp, 1986; Crowder, Serafibe, & Rapp, 1990), in preschool children (Morrongiello & Roes, 1990) and in epileptic patients after unilateral temporal lobe resections (Samson & Zatorre, 1991). However, all these studies were derived from the use of the same paradigm that does not allow us to distinguish between an integrated stored representation, where the musical and the linguistic component would be represented in some combined or common code, from an associative organization, where the musical and linguistic components would be represented as distinct entities related by associative links (but see Crowder et al., 1990, Experiment 3, for providing support to the latter option). Thus, there is a particular need here for both diversity in experimental tasks and systematic neuropsychological investigations before we can draw any firm conclusions about the relation between music and language in song memory.

Similarly, singing performance should be more systematically explored. For example, it is well-known that subjects with nonfluent aphasia can sing words that they cannot pronounce when spoken (as initially reported by Broca, 1861). However, the significance of this behavior to the relation of melody and text representation is not clear. Studies of aphasic singing have been anecdotal (e.g., Yamadori, Osumi, Masuhara, & Okubo, 1977).

Therefore, in the current state of knowledge, there is good evidence that music and speech are treated independently, for the most part, up to the repertoire and the phonological input lexicon. This is why I have represented the perceptual analysis of music and of speech as subserved by totally distinct functional architectures in Figure 21.1. This position may, however, be too extreme since, as we have seen here, some processing components might be shared by music and speech.

RELATION WITH EMOTIONS

Recognition of music is an everyday activity. However, music recognition is probably not the central reason why we listen to music. We listen to music because of its emotional appeal. The question is then how the MRS is related to our emotions. In theory, there are two possibilities. Either emotional responses to music have no relation to the MRS, or emotional appreciation relies on the same system as the MRS. Presently, the evidence favors the independence view.

Recognition of the emotional tone in music can be spared by brain damage while recognition of music identity is impaired (Peretz & Gagnon, 1999). Furthermore, recognition of the emotional tone of music relies on perceptual determinants that play little role in music recognition. For example, the happy–sad distinction is conveyed by the mode (major or minor) in which the music is written and the tempo (fast or slow) at which it is played (e.g., Peretz, Gangon, & Bouchard, 1998). In contrast, music can be easily recognized despite changes in mode and tempo; mode and tempo are not perceptually discriminant for recognition (e.g., Halpern, Bartlett, & Dowling, 1998). Finally, the neural system involved in pleasantness judgments, as determined by manipulation of pitch dissonance, appears located in different structures than those usually associated with nonemotional judgments for music (Blood, Zatorre, Bermudez, & Evans, 1999).

Emotional appreciation of music is a new research avenue in both cognitive psychology and cognitive neuroscience. It is likely, however, that this new direction will flourish in the next decade. Hence, progress in that direction should not be long.

FLEXIBILITY OF THE MRS

As posited earlier in the chapter, I take as a reasonable postulate that the MRS functions in musicians and nonmusicians in a qualitatively similar manner. This postulate should, however, be assessed empirically. In effect, there is substantial evidence in both cognitive psychology and neuroscience that musicians outperform nonmusicians in quantitative terms. Musicians appear to recruit more neural tissue or to use better-wired networks than nonmusicians (as measured with magnetic electrophysiological responses in Pantev et al.'s 1998 study, for example). At present, there is little evidence that this expertise effect is associated with a qualitatively different architecture for the purpose of music recognition.

In closing, the MRS appears subserved by an autonomous organization which may be reduced to the modular properties of some of its components. For example, tonal organization of pitches may well be the central component around which the MRS develops. By examining the autonomy and the internal organization of the MRS, a number of fundamental issues related to the neurobiological study of music cognition were addressed. In doing so, I hope to have convincingly shown how contemporary neuropsychological research is instrumental for building functional models.

Acknowledgements

The present paper has been written while the author was supported by a grant from the Medical Research Council of Canada (MT-13627) and the Natural Science and Engineering Research Council of Canada. The chapter has greatly benefited from the detailed and insightful comments made by Brenda Rapp, the editor of this volume.

REFERENCES

Assal, G. (1973). Aphasie de Wernicke chez un pianiste (Wernicke aphasia in a pianist). *Revue Neurologique, 29,* 251–255.

Ayotte, J., Peretz, I., Rousseau, I., Bard, C., & Bojanowski, M. (submitted). Is the rupture of the middle artery a royal road to music agnosia? *Neuropsychologia.*

Ayotte, J., Peretz, I., Rousseau, I., Bard, C., & Bojanowski, M. (2000). Pattern of music agnosia associated with middle cerebral artery artefact. *Brain, 123,* 1926–1938.

Balzano, G. (1982). The pitch set as a level of description for studying musical pitch perception. In M. Clynes (Ed.), Music, mind and brain. New York: Plenum Press.

Basso, A., & Capitani, E. (1985). Spared musical abilities in a conductor with global aphasia and ideomotor apraxia. *Journal of Neurology, Neurosurgery and Psychiatry, 48,* 407–412.

Belin, P., Zatorre, R., Lafaille, P., Ahad, P., & Pike, B. (2000). Voice-selective areas in human auditory cortex. *Nature, 403,* 309–312.

Benjamin, W. (1984). A theory of musical meter. *Music Perception, 1,* 355–413.

Besson, M., Faïta, F., Peretz, I., Bonnel, A.-M., & Requin, J. (1998). Singing in the brain: Independence of Lyrics and Tunes. *Psychological Science, 9*(6), 494–498.

Bever, T., & Chiarello, R. (1974). Cerebral dominance in musicians and non musicians. *Science, 185,* 537–539.

Bigand, E. (1997). Perceiving musical stability : The effects of tonal structure, rhythm, and musical expertise. *Journal of Experimental Psychology: Human Perception and Performance, 23,* 808–822.

Blood, A., Zatorre, R., Bermudez, P., & Evans, A. (1999). Emotional responses to pleasant and unpleasant music correlate with activity in paralimbic brain regions. *Nature Neuroscience, 2,* 382-387.

Boltz, M. (1989). Perceiving the end: Effects of tonal relationships on melodic completion. *Journal of Experimental Psychology: Human Perception and Performance, 15,* 749–761.

Boltz, M., & Jones, M.R. (1986). Does rule recursion make melodies easier to reproduce? If not, what does? *Cognitive Psychology, 18,* 389–431.

Bonnel, A.-M., Faïta, F., Peretz, I., & Besson, M. (2000). Divided attention between lyries and tunes in Opera. Evidence for independent processing. Manuscript submitted for publication.

Broca, P. (1861). *Remarques sue le siège de la faculté du langage articulé, suivies, d'une observation d'aphémie* (Remarks on the site of the faculty of articulated speech, followed by an observation of aphemia. Bulletin et Mémoires do la Société Anatomique de Paris, 2, 330–357.

Brust, J. (1980). Music and language: Musical alexia and agraphia. *Brain, 103,* 367–392.

Carroll-Phelan, & Hampson, P. (1996). Multiple components of the perception of musical sequences: A cognitive neuroscience analysis and some implications for auditory imagery. *Music Perception, 13,* 517–561.

Cooper, G., & Meyer,L. (1960). *The rhythmic structure of music.* Chicago: Chicago University Press.

Crowder, R., Serafine, M. L., & Rapp, B. (1990). Physical interaction and association by contiguity in memory for the words and melodies of songs. *Memory & Cognition, 18,* 469–76.

Cuddy, L., & Badertscher, B. (1987). Recovery of the tonal hierarchy: Some comparisons across age and levels of musical experience. *Perception & Psychophysics, 41,* 609–620.

Darwin, C. (1871). *The descent of man and selection in relation to sex.* New York: Appleton.

Deutsch, D., & Feroe, J. (1981). The internal representation of pitch sequences in tonal music. *Psychological Review, 88,* 503–522.

Dorgeuille, C. (1966). *Introduction à l'étude des amusies* (Introduction to the study of amusias). Unpublished doctoral dissertation, Paris.

Dowling, W. (1978). Scale and contour : Two components of a theory of memory for melodies. *Psychological Review, 85,* 341–354.

Dowling, W. (1982a). Musical scales and psychological scales : Their psychological reality. In R. Falk & T. Rice (Eds.), *Cross-cultural perspectives on music.* Toronto, Canada: University of Toronto Press.

Dowling, W. (1982b). Melodic information processing and its development. In, D. Deutsch (Ed.), *The psychology of music.* New York: Academic Press.

Dowling, J., & Fujitani, D. (1971). Contour, interval, and pitch recognition in memory for melodies. *Journal of the Acoustical Society of America, 49,* 524–531.

Dowling, W., & Harwood, D. (1986). *Music cognition.* Series in cognition and perception. New York: Academic Press.

Drake, C. (1998). Psychological processes involved in the temporal organization of complex auditory sequences: Universal and acquired processes. *Music Perception, 16,* 11–26.

Ellis, A., & Young, A. (1988). *Human cognitive neuropsychology.* London: Lawrence Erlbaum.

Eustache, F., Lechevalier, B., Viader, F., & Lambert, J. (1990). Identification and dicrimination disorders in auditory perception: A report on two cases. *Neuropsychologia, 28,* 257–270.

Fodor, J. (1983). *The modularity of mind.* Cambridge, Mass.: MIT Press.

Fraisse, P. (1982). Rhythm and tempo. In D. Deutsch (Ed.), *The psychology of music* (pp. 149–181). New York: Academic Press.

Francès, R., Lhermitte, F., & Verdy, M. (1973). Le déficit musical des aphasiques (The musical deficit of aphasics). *Revue Internationale de Psychologie Appliquée, 22,* 117–135.

Fries, W., & Swihart, A. (1990). Disturbance of rhythm sense following right hemisphere damage. *Neuropsychologia, 28,* 1317–1323.

Goodglass, H., & Calderon, M. (1977). Parallel processing of verbal and musical stimuli in right and left hemisphere. *Neuropsychologia, 15,* 397–407.

Godefroy, O., Leys, D., Furby, A., De Reuck, J., Daems,

C., Rondepierre, P., Dabachy, B., Deleume, J.-F., & Desaulty, A. (1995). Psychoacoustical deficits related to bilateral subcortical hemorrhages: A case with apperceptive auditory agnosia. *Cortex, 31,* 149–159.

Griffith, T., Rees, A., Witton, C., Cross, P., Shakir, R., & Green, G. (1997). Spatial and temporal auditory processing deficits following right hemisphere infarction: A psychophysical study. *Brain, 120,* 785–794.

Habib, M., Daquin, G., Milandre, L., Royere, M. L., Rey, M., Lanteri, A., Salamon, G., & Khalil, R. (1995). Mutism and auditory agnosia due to bilateral insular damage—role of the insula in human communication. *Neuropsychologia, 33*(3), 327–339.

Halpern, A. (1988). Perceived and imagined tempos of familiar songs. *Music perception, 6,* 193–202.

Halpern, A. (1989). Memory for the absolute pitch of familiar songs. *Memory & Cognition, 17,* 572–581.

Halpern, A., Bartlett, J., & Dowling, J. (1998). Perception of mode, rhythm, and contour in unfamiliar melodies: Effects of age and experience. *Music Perception, 15,* 335–356.

Hébert, S., & Peretz, I. (1997). Recognition of music in long-term memory: Are melodic and temporal patterns equal partners? *Memory & Cognition, 25,* 518–533.

Hébert, S., & Peretz, I. (in press). Are text and tune of familiar songs separable by brain damage? *Brain and Cognition.*

Hermelin, B., O'Connor, N., & Lee, S. (1987). Musical inventiveness of five idiot-savants. *Psychological Medecine, 17,* 685–694.

Ibbotson, N., & Morton, J. (1981). Rhythm and dominance. *Cognition, 9,* 125–138.

Jackendoff, R. (1987). *Consciousness and the computational mind.* Cambridge, MA: MIT Press/Bradsfort.

Jones, M. (1987). Dynamic pattern structure in music: Recent theory and research. *Perception & Psychophysics, 41,* 621–634.

Jones, M., Boltz, M., & Kidd, G. (1982). Controlled attending as a function of melodic and temporal context. *Perception & Psychophysics, 32,* 221–218.

Klein, R., & Harper, J. (1956). The problem of agnosia in the light of a case of pure word deafness. *Journal of Mental Science, 102,* 112–120.

Krumhansl, C. (1990). *Cognitive foundations of musical pitch.* Oxford, UK: Oxford University Press.

Krumhansl, C. (1991). Music psychology: Tonal structures in perception and memory. *Annual Review of Psychology, 42,* 277–303.

Krumhansl, C., & Kessler, R. (1982). Tracing the dynamic changes in perceived tonal organization in a spatial representation of musical keys. *Psychological Review, 89,* 334–368.

Laignel-Lavastine, M., & Alajouanine, T. (1921). Un cas d'agnosie auditive (A case of auditory agnosia). *Revue Neurologique, 37,* 194–198.

Lamy, M. (1907). Amnésie musicale chez un aphasique sensoriel (Musical amnesia in a sensory aphasic). *Revue Neurologique, 15,* 688–693.

Large, E., Palmer, C., & Pollack, J. (1995). Reduced memory representations for music. *Cognitive Science, 19,* 53–96.

Lerdahl, F., & Jackendoff, R. (1983). *A generative theory of tonal music.* Cambridge, MA: MIT Press.

Levitin, D. (1994). Absolute memory for musical pitch: Evidence from the production of learned melodies. *Perception & Psychophysics, 56,* 414–423.

Levitin, D., & Cook, P. (1996). Memory for musical tempo: Additional evidence that auditory memory is absolute. *Perception & Psychophysics, 58,* 927–935.

Liberman, A. Cooper, F., Shankweiler D., & Studdert-Kennedy, M. (1967). Perception of the speech code. *Psychological Review, 74,* 431–461.

Liégeois-Chauvel, C., Peretz, I., Babaï, M., Laguitton, V., & Chauvel, P. (1998) Contribution of different cortical areas in the temporal lobes to music processing. *Brain, 121,* 1853–1867.

Lissauer, H. (1889, 1988). A case of visual agnosia with a contribution to theory. *Cognitive Neuropsychology, 5,* 157–92 (trans. from the German by M. Jackson; original published in *Archiv für Psychiatrie und Nervenkrankheiten, 21,* 222–270, 1889).

Longuet-Higgins, H., & Lee, C. (1982). The perception of musical rhythms. *Perception, 11,* 115–128.

Luria, A., Tsvetkova, L., & Futer, J. (1965). Aphasia in a composer. *Journal of Neurogical Science, 2,* 288–292.

Mann, V., & Liberman, A. (1983. Some differences between phonetic and auditory modes of perception. *Cognition, 14,* 211–235.

Marin, O. (1983). Neurological aspects of music perception and performance. In D. Deutsch (Ed.), *The psychology of music.* New York: Academic Press.

Mavlov, L. (1980). Amusia due to rhythm agnosia in a musician with left hemisphere damage: A non auditory supramodal defect. *Cortex, 16,* 321–338.

Mendez, M. F., & Geehan, G. R. (1988). Cortical auditory disorders: Clinical and psychoacoustic features. *Journal of Neurology, Neurosurgery and Psychiatry, 51,* 1–9.

Metz-Lutz, M.-N., & Dahl, E. (1984). Analysis of word comprehension in a case of pure word-deafness. *Brain and Language, 23,* 13–25.

Morrongiello, B., & Roes, C. (1990). Children's memory for new songs: Integration or independent storage of words and tunes? *Journal of Experimental Child Psychology, 50,* 25–38.

Motomura, N., Yamadori, A., Mori, E., & Tamaru, F. (1986). Auditory agnosia: Analysis of a case with bilateral subcortical lesions. *Brain, 109,* 379–391.

Mottron, L., Peretz, I., & Ménard, E. (2000). Local and global processing of music in high-functioning persons with autism: Beyond cerebral coherence? *Child Psychology and Psychiatry,* in press.

Ombredane, A. (1944). Perception and Langage. *Etudes de Psychologie Médicale.* Tome I. Rio-de-Janeiro, Brazil: Atlantica Editera.

Palmer, C., & Krumhansl, C. (1990). Mental representations for musical meter. *Journal of Experimental Psychology: Human Perception and Performance, 16,* 728–741.

Pantev, C., Oostenveld, R., Engelien, A., Ross, B., Roberts, L., & Hoke, M. (1998). Increased auditory cortical representations in musicians. *Nature, 392,* 811–814.

Patel, A., & Peretz, I. (1997). Is music autonomous from language? A neuropsychological appraisal. In I. Deliège & J. Sloboda (Eds.), *Perception and cognition of music* (pp. 191–215). Hove, UK: Psychology Press.

Patel, A. D., Peretz, I., Tramo, M., & Labrecque, R. (1998). Processing prosodic and musical patterns: A neuropsychological investigation. *Brain and Language, 61*(2), 123–144.

Pechstedt, P., Kershner, J. & Kinsbourne, M. (1989). Musical training improves processing of tonality in the left hemisphere. *Music Perception, 6,* 275–298.

Peretz, I. (1987). Shifting ear-asymmetry in melody comparison through transposition. *Cortex, 23,* 317–323.

Peretz, I. (1990). Processing of local and global musical information in unilateral brain-damaged patients. *Brain, 113,* 1185–1205.

Peretz, I. (1993a). Auditory agnosia: A functional analysis. In S. McAdams & E. Bigand (Eds.), *Thinking in sound. The cognitive psychology of human audition* (pp.199–230). NY: Oxford University Press.

Peretz, I. (1993b). Auditory Atonalia for Melodies. *Cognitive Neuropsychology, 10,* 21–56.

Peretz, I. (1996). Can we loose memories for music? The case of music agnosia in a nonmusician. *Journal of Cognitive Neurosciences, 8*(6), 481–496.

Peretz, I., & Babaï, M. (1992). The role of contour and intervals in the recognition of melody parts: Evidence from cerebral asymmetries in musicians. *Neuropsychologia, 30,* 277–292.

Peretz, I., Belleville, S., & Fontaine, F. S. (1997). Dissociations entre musique et langage après atteinte cérébrale: un nouveau cas d'amusie sans aphasie Dissociations between music and language after brain damage: A further case of amusia without aphasia. *Revue Canadienne de Psychologie Expérimentale, 51*(4), 354–367.

Peretz, I., & Gagnon, L. (1999). Dissociation between recognition and emotional judgment for melodies. *Neurocase, 5,* 21–30.

Peretz, I., Gagnon, L., & Bouchard, B. (1998). Music and emotion: Perceptual determinants, immediacy and isolation after brain damage. *Cognition, 68,* 111–141.

Peretz, I., Gaudreau, D., & Bonnel, A.-M. (1998). Exposure effects on music preference and recognition. *Memory and Cognition, 26*(5), 884–902.

Peretz, I., & Kolinsky, R. (1993). Boundaries of separability between melody and rhythm in music discrimination: A neuropsychological perspective. *Quarterly Journal of Experimental Psychology, 46A,* 301–325.

Peretz, I., Kolinsky, R., Tramo, M., Labrecque, R., Hublet, C., Demeurisse, G., & Belleville, S. (1994). Functional dissociations following bilateral lesions of auditory cortex. *Brain, 117,* 1283–1302.

Peretz, I., & Morais, J. (1987). Analytic processing in the classification of melodies as same or different. *Neuropsychologia, 25,* 645–652.

Peretz, I., & Morais, J. (1988). Determinants of laterality for music: Towards an information processing account. In K. Hugdahl (Ed.), *Handbook of dichotic listening: Theory, methods and research.* New York: Wiley.

Peretz, I., & Morais, J. (1989). Music and modularity. *Contemporary Music Review, 4,* 277–291.

Polster, M., & Rose, S. (1998). Disorders of auditory processing: Evidence for modularity in audition. *Cortex, 34,* 47–65.

Povel, D. (1984). A theoretical framework for rhythm perception. *Psychological Research, 45,* 315–337.

Povel, D., & Essens, P. (1985). Perception of temporal patterns. *Music Perception, 2,* 411–440.

Radvansky, G., Fleming, K., & Simmons, J. (1995). Timbre reliance in nonmusicians' and musicians' memory for melodies. *Music Perception, 13,* 127–140.

Raffman, D. (1993). *Language, music and mind.* Cambridge, MA: MIT Press/Bradford.

Sacks, O. (1985). *The man who mistook his wife for a hat and other clinical tales.* New York: Summit Books.

Samson, S., & Zatorre, R. (1991). Recognition for text and melody of songs after unilateral temporal lobe lesion: Evidence for dual encoding. *Journal of Experimental Psychology Learning, Memory and Cognition, 17,* 793–804.

Schenker, H. (1935/1979). *Free composition.* New York: Longman. (original work published in 1935)

Serafine, M. L., Crowder, R. G., & Rapp, B. (1984). Integration of melody and text in memory for song. *Cognition, 16,* 285-303.

Serafine, M. L., Davidson, J., Crowder, R. G., & Rapp, B. (1986). On the nature of melody-text integration in memory for songs. *Journal of Memory and Language, 25,* 123-35.

Serafine, M. L., Glassman, N., & Overbeeke, C. (1989). The cognitive reality of hierarchic structure in music. *Music Perception, 6,* 397-430.

Shepard, R., & Jordan, D. (1984) Auditory illusions demonstrating that tones are assimilated to an internalized musical scale. *Science, 226,* 1333-1334.

Signoret, J. L., Van Eeckhout, P., Poncet, M., Castaigne, P. (1987) Aphasie sans amusie chez un organiste aveugle (Aphasia without amusia in a blind organist). *Revue Neurologique, 143,* 172-181.

Sloboda, J. (1985). *The musical mind: The cognitive psychology of music.* London, UK: Oxford University Press.

Spreen, O., Benton, A., & Fincham, R. (1965). Auditory agnosia without aphasia. *Archives of Neurology, 13,* 84-92.

Steinke, W., Cuddy, L., & Holden, R. (1997). Dissociation of musical tonality and pitch memory from nonmusical cognitive abilities. *Canadian Journal of Experimental Psychology, 51,* 316-335.

Takahashi, N., Kawamura, M., Shinotou, H., Hirayaha, K. Kalia, K., & Shindo, M. (1992). Pure word deafness due to left-hemisphere damage. *Cortex, 28,* 295-303.

Tanaka, Y., Yamadori, A., & Mori, E. (1987). Pure word deafness following bilateral lesions. A psychophysical analysis. *Brain, 110,* 381-403.

Tramo, M., & Bharucha, J. (1991). Musical priming by the right hemisphere post-callosotomy. *Neuropsychologia, 29,* 313-325.

Tramo, M., Bharucha, J., & Musiek, F. (1990). Music perception and cognition following bilateral lesions of auditory cortex. *Journal of Cognitive Neuroscience, 2,* 195-212.

Trehub, S., Schellenberg, E., & Kamenetsky, S. (1999). Infants' and adults' perception of scale structure. *Journal of Experimental Psychology: Human Perception & Performance, 25,* 965-975.

Turk, I., Dirjec, J., & Kavur, B. (1996). The oldest musical instrument in Europe discovered in Slovenia? *Arheoloski Vestnik.* (English translation available: www.zrc-sazu.si/www/iza/piscal.html).

Van Lancker, D., & Canter, G. (1982). Impairments of voice and face recognition in patients with hemispheric damage. *Brain & Cognition, 1,* 185-192.

Van Lancker, D., & Kreiman, J. (1987). Voice discrimination and recognition are separate abilities. *Neuropsychologia, 25,* 829-834.

Warren, R., Gardner, D., Brubaker, B., & Bashford, J. (1991). Melodic and nonmelodic sequences: Effects of duration on perception. *Music Perception, 8,* 277-290.

White, B. (1960). Recognition of distorted melodies. *American Journal of Psychology, 73,* 100-107.

Yaqub, B. A., Gascon, G. G., Al-Nosha, M., & Whitaker, H. (1988). Pure word deafness (Acquired verbal auditory agnosia) in an arabic speaking patient. *Brain, 111,* 457-466.

Yamadori, A., Osumi, Y., Masuhara, S. & Okubo, M. (1977). Preservation of singing in Broca's aphasia. *Journal of Neurology, Neurosurgery, and Psychiatry, 40,* 221-224.

Zajonc, R. (1968). Attitudinal effects of mere exposure. *Journal of Personality and Social Psychology Monograph, 9,* part 2, 1-28.

Part 8

Actions and Plans

Never confuse movement with action.

—*Ernest Hemingway*

22

Spatiomotor Aspects
of Action

Laurel J. Buxbaum
H. Branch Coslett

INTRODUCTION

Although the history of psychological inquiry into the action system dates at least to Sherrington's studies of the reflex arc, the last two decades represent a period of rapidly growing interest in the cognitive aspects of action. There is increasing evidence that spatiomotor processing is not modular and encapsulated, but is intimately tied to and influenced by knowledge systems—cognitive processes involved in object and gesture recognition—as well as by mechanisms related to goal establishment and maintenance. Furthermore, spatiomotor processes involved in planning and programming actions are highly dynamic and integrative, incorporating information about body part position relative to objects and other body parts that is derived from multiple sources. In this chapter, we describe some recent developments in cognitive and neurophysiological studies of spatiomotor aspects of action, review relevant neuropsychological studies of brain lesioned patients, and explore the potential implications of this work for rehabilitation of patients with action system deficits. Throughout the chapter, we focus largely upon work which elucidates two major kinds of egocentric spatiomotor coding used by the action system: one used for positioning the body in space, and the other for interacting with objects.

The study of disorders of action planning and execution was initiated by Liepmann in a series of contributions from the early twentieth century (e.g., 1905). Liepmann reported patients with cerebral lesions who were unable to execute gestures of the upper extremity to command or, in some instances, to imitation. This disorder, which Liepmann termed "apraxia," could not be attributed to language deficit or elementary motor impairment (e.g., corticospinal tract deficit, tremor, etc.). Additionally, Liepmann and Maas (1907) described a patient with a lesion of the corpus callosum who was unable to produce gestures with the left hand to verbal command. On the basis of these findings, Liepmann proposed that the left hemisphere was "dominant" for gesture in the sense that the left hemisphere supported the learned "movement formulae" or "time-space-form picture of the movement" which specified the timing, trajectory, and content of learned movements.

Liepmann's ideas were resurrected and extended by Geschwind (Geschwind, 1965) who

543

proposed a specific neural circuitry for movement representations. Like Liepmann, Geschwind argued that the left hemisphere was responsible for the programming of skilled, learned movements. On his account, failure to produce a movement on command was attributable either to a disruption of Wernicke's area, with resultant failure to understand the command, or to a disconnection between the posterior language areas and motor cortices in the frontal lobe. A failure to imitate familiar movements was attributed to a lesion involving the arcuate fasciculus which was assumed to connect the visual association cortex to motor cortices.

More recently, Gonzalez Rothi, Ochipa, and Heilman (1991) have developed a model of the praxis system to accommodate numerous dissociations of gesture imitation, gesture to command, and gesture to sight of objects observed in apraxic syndromes. The model includes two routes to gesture production and imitation: an indirect or 'lexical' route which processes meaningful actions via access to stored movement representations, or 'gesture engrams,' and a direct route which bypasses gesture engrams and enables imitation of meaningless gestures. Gesture comprehension requires access to the former route.

The model of Gonzalez Rothi, Ochipa, and Heilman, (1991), like the models of Liepmann and Geschwind, represents an important contribution to the study of apraxia, but raises several questions. What are the mechanisms and procedures instantiated in gesture engrams? What are the spatiomotor processes enabling imitation of the gestures of others? How do skilled and novel movements differ? How are the biomechanical constraints of the body represented for the purpose of performing gesture, and how does this differ for the representations enabling actions on objects in space? Recent advances in the physiological literature enable us to describe a spatiomotor model of the action system which provides some tentative answers to such questions, and it is to these studies that we turn next.

A SPATIOMOTOR MODEL OF ACTION

Not Just Where, How

Relatively recently, Ungerleider and Mishkin (1982) described the now-familiar dissociation of ventral and dorsal visual processing streams. The former courses from the occipital lobe through temporal lobe structures, and is specialized largely for the identification of objects (the 'what' system), whereas the latter projects from the occipital through the parietal and frontal lobes, and is concerned with the coding of location, independent of identity (the 'where' system). On several accounts, knowledge of 'which object is where' is derived from the 'binding' of information processed by each system (e.g., Coslett & Saffran, 1991; Kahnemann & Treisman, 1984; Kahnemann, Treisman, & Gibbs, 1992).

More recently, Milner and Goodale (1992) have argued that the dorsal stream is more accurately characterized as the 'how' system, in that it represents the locations of objects *for the purpose of action*. Contemporary evidence suggests that the "action system" (which maps roughly onto the domain of the dorsal stream) possesses several properties that had not previously been associated with it in classical models. The first property is the tight linkage between spatial and motor coding. The spatial coding of target location in the dorsal stream is not absolute or fixed with respect to environmental axes,[1] but is a dynamic map that shifts constantly depending upon the locations of the effectors with respect to the target. Spatial and motor systems are thus not modular, encapsulated entities that can be 'disconnected' by brain lesions. The spatial locations of objects within the environment are likely to be specified in

---

[1]Environment-centered coding may be characteristic of the ventral stream, however. Milner and Goodale (1995), for example, provide evidence that comparison of objects in an array affects judgments regarding object size, a "ventral" function, but does not affect hand-aperture characteristics for grasping calculated by the dorsal stream. Wong and Mack (1981) also report data suggesting that the perceptual system, unlike the action system, computes environment-centered information about object location with respect to other objects.

terms of a movement vector (or motor "plan") that would be required for a given effector (e.g., eye, head, hand) to "acquire" the target. Thus, spatial information in the dorsal stream is actually *spatiomotor* in nature.

Evidence supporting this contention comes from investigations in monkeys. For example, the oculocentric coding characteristic of the lateral intraparietal cortex in monkeys (area LIP) appears to register the location of objects in terms of a vector that would be required to bring the target onto the fovea of the eye (Duhamel, Colby, & Goldberg, 1992). Thus, when the eyes are deviated left, an object at head midline would be coded in terms of a rightward movement vector. The vector, specifying direction and amplitude of movement, is the emergent product of a population of neurons, each programming movement in a slightly different direction. The neuronal population coding takes the form of a 'planar gain field' in which the amplitude of the visual response is modulated linearly by horizontal and vertical eye position (see Andersen, Snyder, Li, & Stricanne, 1993). Similarly, the hand centered coding that has been identified in premotor cortex results in a constantly updated map which takes into consideration the position of objects with respect to the hand (Graziano, Yap, & Gross, 1994). Collectively, such effector-centered coding can be termed 'egocentric' spatial coding, in that it specifies the locations of objects in the environment (and the motor plans required to acquire the objects) with respect to the body and its parts. Later, we will contrast this 'extrinsic' egocentric coding of objects vis-à-vis the body with 'intrinsic' spatial coding of body parts with respect to one another.

Spatiomotor Transformations in the Action System

Another recently recognized property of spatiomotor coding in the action system is that visuomotor information is progressively transcoded into multiple coordinate systems. Although the process is not strictly linear, as a general rule spatial information about object location progresses from a form of information relevant to the eye, to a format relevant to the limbs for the purpose of action. Figure 22.1 provides a schematic of the transformation process (for further discussion about spatial reference frames and coordinate systems see McCloskey, this volume).

Incoming visual information is initially coded in retinotopic coordinates, meaning that the axes of the reference frame used to define location are at the center of the retina. This form of coding is short-lasting, decaying after about 100–200 ms. (Irwin & Yeomans, 1986). Another representation useful for guiding action over short time intervals is oculocentric coding, in which stimuli are mapped with respect to the geometric center of the eye. Unlike retinotopic receptive fields, which are fixed to retinal coordinates and move with the eye, the excitability of oculocentric neurons is systematically modulated by gaze position (Duhamel, Colby, & Goldberg, 1992). For example, a given oculocentric neuron might fire maximally when the eyes are deviated to the left superior quadrant, moderately when the eyes are positioned in the left inferior quadrant, and not at all when the eyes are deviated to the right inferior quadrant—even in the dark, when there is no target on the retina (Bracewell, Barash, Massoni, & Andersen, 1991; Boussaoud, Bremmer, & Jouffrais, 1998). Information about the position of the eye in the orbit is combined with retinotopic target position information to achieve a more stable head-centered representation of target location. Since head-centered representations combine information about where the target is on the retina and where the eyes are in the orbits (head), this representation enables calculation of where the target is relative to the head, and thus, permits direction of gaze to the target irrespective of head position (Jeannerod, 1988). Coding of the location of the target with respect to the head is then integrated with information about the position of the head on the neck to map target location in body-centered reference frames, which include torso, shoulder, arm, and hand centered coordinates. The latter are particularly important in planning and performing reaching movements to targets (e.g., Burnod et al., 1992; Soechting et al., 1990; Caminiti, Johnson, Galli, Ferraina, & Bernod, 1991; Caminitti, Johnson, & Urbano, 1990).

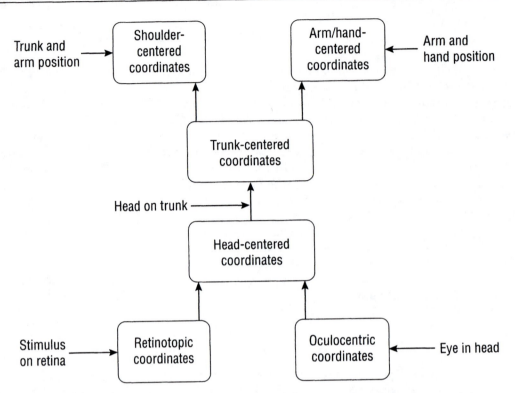

Figure 22.1: Schematic showing how spatiomotor coordinates for action might be computed. The figure should be read from bottom to top. Modified from "Coordinate transformations and motor planning in posterior parietal cortex," by R. A. Anderson, in M. S. Gazzaniga (Ed.), *The Cognitive Neurosciences*. Cambridge: MIT Press, 519–532.

Flexibility in Frames of Reference for Coding Action

An additional property of the action system not described in earlier models is its flexibility. Given that spatial information about target locations is mapped with respect to several different reference frames centered on different effectors, many of these frames are potentially available to 'stand in' for portions of the spatial transformation process should they be damaged. For example, errors in the transformation process re-mapping information from oculocentric to 'higher' coordinate frames (e.g., head-centered, torso-centered, shoulder-centered) can be partially compensated by reliance on spatial coding in the intact oculocentric frame. That is, information about target location can be coded with respect to the position of the eye in the head, and this position information used to program a reach trajectory.

Recently, we described two patients who appeared to rely upon a pathologic compensatory linkage of spatiomotor systems coding the actions of the eye and hand (Buxbaum & Coslett, 1997; Buxbaum & Coslett, 1998a). Patient DP was a 26-year-old man who suffered a gunshot wound to the bilateral superior fronto-parietal cortices. While his voluntary and reflexive eye movements were normal, DP was unable to reach to locations other than those to which he gazed; that is, he exhibited a severe optic ataxia when reaching extrafoveally. When looking in a mirror, for example, DP was unable to reach to an object on the table while looking at its reflection, but instead repeatedly reached to the reflection of his eyes in the mirror, all the while verbalizing that he recognized this to be incorrect. We termed the form of the disorder exhibited by DP *nonfoveal optic ataxia*. In milder versions, a pattern of accurate reaching to foveated targets with misreaching errors to non-foveated targets is the most common from of optic ataxia (Perenin & Vighetto, 1987).

In a detailed series of investigations (Buxbaum & Coslett, 1997, 1998a), we provided evidence that DP's retinotopic coding of target location was normal, but that he was unable to transform the retinotopic information into frames of reference appropriate for the reaching apparatus (shoulder-, arm-, and hand-centered frames). Such coding normally enables independence of gaze direction and reach direction. Instead, DP relied on a more primitive form of coding, common in vertebrate animals without visual neocortices, in which gaze direction and movement direction are linked (Wise, de Pellegrino, & Boussaoud, 1996). We suggested that this might be accomplished by referencing both the target and the hand to the same oculocentric coordinate frame. Once the eye was positioned in the orbit so that targets were centered at the midline of the eye (the 0,0 origin of the oculocentric frame), the oculomotor information about eye position could be used to program a movement vector directing the reaching apparatus to the origin of the oculocentric frame without any explicit information about target location with respect to the reaching apparatus.

We reported a second patient along with DP who also exhibited a pathologic yoking of eye and hand. AM suffered left mesial fronto-parietal and right temporal-occipital infarcts which resulted in a severe left neglect and rendered him unable to direct his gaze voluntarily to auditory or visual stimuli in either visual field. We observed that at times when attempting to attend to visual stimuli, AM's gaze appeared to be captured by his hand. Using an oral reading task, we assessed whether this phenomenon could be exploited to the benefit of AM's visual attention. When reading single words with his hands passively resting in his lap (baseline condition), AM performed correctly on only 35% of trials, and the majority of errors were visually based (e.g., *funnel* → *final*). In several studies, AM was asked to tap on or near the site of words, and we examined the effect of the location at which he tapped. In initial studies, no differences between left and right hand tapping benefits were observed, and subsequent studies were carried out using the right hand. When DP tapped 6 inches to the left of words, he read 63% of words correctly, whereas he was correct on only 17% of the same words when he tapped 6 inches to the right. The effect was extremely spatially precise: when DP tapped immediately adjacent to the left end of the words his performance was 60% correct, and only 16% of his errors involved omission of initial letters of the word. In contrast, when he tapped immediately adjacent to the words' right end, his performance dropped to 29% correct, and 53% of his errors involved initial-letter omissions (e.g., *fact* → *act*). Thus, there was a left–right gradient of accuracy as a function of whether DP tapped on the far left, left, near right, or far right of stimuli. The spatially-specific effect of hand position is critical, as it indicates that the benefit from tapping can not be attributed to a general cue to shift attention. The benefit derived from tapping at words' left ends could also not be attributed to visual cueing, as performance was as impaired as in the baseline condition when the examiner provided a visual cue by tapping at the site of the words (32% correct). Finally, there was evidence that recruitment of the action system was necessary for the beneficial effect, as when AM rested his hand passively at the left end of words, his performance was also as impaired as it had been in the baseline condition. The data suggest that AM's visual attention (and gaze) was allocated to the visual array as a function of spatiomotor coordinates of hand activity. We suggested that AM's performance represented the converse of that observed in DP; in AM, hand-centered spatiomotor coding was 'borrowed' to ameliorate deficient oculomotor procedures. Another interesting aspect of AM's performance was that objects (words, letters) to the right of the tapping hand were well-attended, whereas objects to the left of the hand were neglected. To our knowledge, this is the first demonstration that a left-right gradient of attention in neglect may be hand-centered. Later in the chapter, we will detail two additional studies of hand-centered attentional asymmetries in neglect.

MULTIPLICITY OF BODY REPRESENTATIONS

Coding Body-Part Location: Intrinsic Spatial Coding for Action

There is an additional kind of spatiomotor coding performed by the action system that is related to extrinsic 'egocentric' coding of object location, but differs from it in an important way. This form of spatial representation, which has been termed 'intrinsic' spatial coding, specifies the dynamic positions of the body parts *with respect to one another* in space over time (Soechting & Flanders, 1989a, 1989b; Vindras & Viviani, 1998). Intrinsic spatial coding is likely to be accomplished with input from proprioceptive, tactile, and vestibular systems, and provides dynamic information about complex configurations of body parts, such as where the hand is with respect to the knee (Sakata, Takaoka, Kawarasaki, & Shibutani, 1973). Recent physiological evidence indicates that normal pointing to external objects may depend upon the transformation of extrinsic egocentric hand centered coordinates of target location into intrinsic coordinates representing target location in terms of the final posture of body parts involved in the response (i.e., in terms of joint angles and/or limb orientations). This final posture, in conjunction with intrinsic information coding starting posture, may be used to generate a motor program specifying the direction and distance of the hand trajectory required for accurate pointing (Vindras & Viviani, 1998; see also Caminiti et al., 1990; Caminiti et al., 1991; Burnod et al., 1992). Soechting and Flanders (1989) provide data suggesting that errors in reaching to targets may occur as a result of faulty linear transformations between the extrinsic and intrinsic coordinate systems.

Intrinsic spatial coding is likely to be particularly critical in the planning and performance of reach trajectories to ones own body parts, as when, for instance, one touches ones own chin (Vindras & Viviani, 1998). When the target is a body part that can not be seen (such as a part of the face), extrinsic egocentric coding (which requires visual guidance) is not available, and intrinsic coding is normally necessary. Notably, intrinsic spatial coding bears resemblance to one of the types of spatial coding proposed to be represented by the *body schema* in classical accounts (Head & Holmes, 1911/1912). Below, we will further detail the concept of the body schema and describe several studies in which we have explored its integrity in brain damaged patients.

Intrinsic Spatial Coding for Recognition

An elegant body of work by Parsons (1987a, 1987b, 1994) indicates that judgements about the orientations of the body parts of others is accomplished with reference to a dynamic internal representation of the position of ones own body parts. Thus, for example, subjects are faster to make judgements about whether drawings represent left or right hands (see Figure 22.2) if their own hands are in the same positions as the stimuli.

Moreover, subjects' latencies to respond "left" or "right" is affected by the mechanical constraints of the subject's body, such that discontinuities in reaction time are observed which suggest that the mental rotation of subjects' body schema is constrained by the biomechanical properties of the human body. These data are consistent with the claim that the left-right judgements are accomplished by referring the stimulus to an internal model of the subject's body which takes into account its dynamic position in space.

Recently, Reed and Farah (1995) demonstrated that subjects who were asked to make same-different judgments about the positions of others' bodies were influenced by their own body movements. When asked to make same-different judgments about others' arm positions, subjects' responses were facilitated by movements of their own arms, but not by movements of their own legs. The reverse was true when they were asked to make judgments about the positions of others' legs. Like the data from Parsons (1987a, 1987b, 1994), these findings

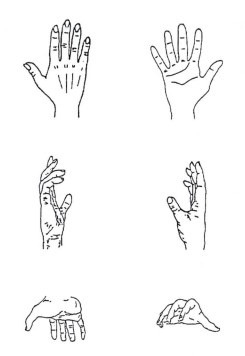

Figure 22.2: Examples of stimuli used by L. M. Parsons, 1994, in "Temporal and Kinetic Properties of Motor Behavior Reflected in Mentally Stimulated Action," *Journal of Experimental Psychology: Human Perception and Performance*, 20(4), pp. 709–730.

suggest that a representation of the dynamic position of ones own body parts with respect to one another (that is, intrinsic spatial coding) is involved in the recognition of the body positions of others. There is historical precedent for characterizing intrinsic spatial coding as one of the functions of the so-called 'body schema' or 'plastic schema,' (Head & Holmes, 1911/1912), an "on-line" map of the position of the body parts in space over time which enables measurement of postural changes and appreciation of passive movement.

One of several neuropsychological disorders which may involve deficient intrinsic spatial coding is personal neglect, a deficit in using, attending to, and, in some instances, recognizing the left side of the body. Personal neglect often co-occurs with spatial (extrinsic egocentric) neglect, but can dissociate from it (Buxbaum, unpublished data; Coslett, 1998). One possibility is that personal neglect reflects disruption of (or failure to attend to) a portion of the body schema (intrinsic spatial coding). We recently investigated this hypothesis in a series of experiments (Coslett, 1998).

The first experiment was motivated by work of Parsons described above (Parsons, 1987a, 1987b, 1994) demonstrating that identification of left and right hands is accomplished by mentally rotating an internal image of the subjects' own body. We reasoned that if left neglect is associated with a disruption of the left-sided portion of the body schema, then patients with neglect should be deficient in mentally rotating the representation of the left hand, and thus, impaired on tasks requiring discrimination between right and left hands. We showed participants with cerebral infarctions a series of photographs of right or left hands in palm up or palm down positions and asked then to indicate which hand was depicted. Subjects were 3 patients with right-hemisphere lesions who exhibited left neglect on line bisection and cancellation tasks, 3 right-hemisphere lesioned patients without neglect, and 7 left-hemisphere lesioned patients without neglect. As can be seen in Table 22.1, all three subjects with neglect were significantly more accurate with right as compared to left hands; moreover, these were the only subjects to exhibit a significant difference between hands. These data are consistent with the hypothesis that neglect may be associated with an impairment in intrinsic spatial coding for the contralesional side of the body.

Table 22.1

Accuracy of Subjects' Left–Right Judgements About Hand
Stimuli (Percent Correct)

Subjects	Left-Hand Pictures	Right-Hand Pictures
Neglect		
Cl	45*	74*
AL	58*	92*
JM	72*	85*
Right Hem. Without Neglect		
LP	100	100
AT	82	84
RL	98	94
Left Hem. Without Neglect		
AG	96	92
AW	96	98
RH	100	100
JM	80	79
WP	88	83
EP	100	100

In another recent study, we explored the possibility that tactile extinction may reflect asymmetric allocation of attention across the body schema. On this hypothesis, left-sided extinction should be ameliorated by placing a well-attended right-sided body part in contact with the poorly attended left-sided body part.

We tested this possibility with a 52-year-old right-handed man (CB) who had suffered a right parietal-occipital stroke and exhibited prominent and consistent left-sided tactile extinction with double simultaneous stimulation (Coslett & Lie; Under review). We assessed his extinction over numerous trials in which the dorsum of the right, left hand or both first fingers were touched in a random sequence while his eyes were closed. First, CB was tested in the "Standard" condition with his hands resting on a table. He responded correctly on 88% of left-sided trials, 93% of right-sided trials, and only 11% of bilateral trials. All errors with bilateral stimulation were left-sided omissions. He was next tested with his fingers interleaved in the midline. He responded correctly to 97% of unilateral stimuli with both the right and left hands and 67% of bilateral stimuli. Thus, extinction of the left hand was significantly reduced by placing the right hand in contact with his left hand.

To rule out the possibility that this improvement was attributable to extrinsic egocentric spatial factors, CB was also tested with the hands near one another (but not touching) in the midline, with the hands crossed into the opposite hemispace, and with the left and right hands placed in the left and right hemispaces, respectively. None of these conditions differed from the baseline condition. As the benefit conferred by the right hand was not obtained by placing it in close proximity to the left hand or by other spatial manipulations, these data strongly suggest that attention may be allocated selectively in intrinsic spatial coordinates as a function of the position of the body parts with respect to one another. To our knowledge, this represents the first report of hand-centered spatial coding influencing attention to other body parts rather than attention to objects in extrinsic space.

The Relationship Between Coding for Action and for Recognition

In the Introduction, we reviewed an influential model of the action system which focuses largely upon the performance of skilled actions, but also contains a 'direct route' that can be used for imitation of others' gestures. However, only recently have there been explorations of the procedures instantiated in the 'direct route' and of the relationship of memorial gesture engrams to these on-line procedures.

Patients with ideomotor apraxia make errors in pantomiming both object-related (transitive) and non-object related (intransitive) gestures (e.g., hammering, waving goodbye) to command and imitation. In some cases, performance improves when the patient is permitted to touch and use an actual object or imitate the movements of the examiner, but in other patients errors persist in these circumstances. Ideomotor apraxics do not substitute gestures appropriate to another object or symbolic movement, but instead make errors that are spatiotemporal in nature (Gonzalez, Rothi et al., 1991; Heilman, Rothi, & Valenstein, 1982). Recent studies by Poizner and colleagues (Poizner, Mack,Verfaellie, Rothi, & Heilman, 1990) using three dimensional motion analysis have demonstrated that ideomotor apraxics perform skilled movements using abnormal limb trajectories, and that they apportion arm angles differently than control subjects. In the context of evidence, discussed above, that the intrinsic spatial relationships of body parts with respect to one another are coded in terms of joint angles and the orientations of body parts, these data suggests that some ideomotor apraxics may suffer deficits in intrinsic spatial coding procedures performed normally by the 'body schema.'

We recently reported a case study supporting this hypothesis (Buxbaum, Giovannetti, & Libon, in press). Patient BG exhibited 'primary progressive apraxia' in that apraxia was by far the most severe aspect of a gradual dementing process. In a series of investigations, we demonstrated that BG made spatiotemporal errors in gesture pantomime and object use, and in imitating the gestures of the examiner, but was even more severely impaired when she performed novel, meaningless movements to imitation. We also demonstrated that BG was impaired in matching gestures across transformations in orientation; that is, she had trouble distinguishing whether two gestures viewed from different angles were the same or different. She performed severely deficiently, as well, on a variant of the 'hand rotation' task of Parsons (1987a, 1987b, 1994) described above. In contrast, she was able to position her body accurately with respect to external objects in reaching and grasping tasks, and had no trouble matching or recognizing objects across transformations in orientation. The observed dissociations between impaired body rotation and recognition, on the one hand, and intact object-oriented action and recognition, on the other, suggested that BG suffered deficits in intrinsic spatial coding procedures in the context of integrity of extrinsic egocentric coding.

It is not likely to be the case that all ideomotor apraxia is attributable to deficits in intrinsic spatial coding procedures. PET and CT scans revealed that the neuroanatomic substrate of BG's deficit was probably the left superior parietal lobe, including area 5. Thus, her lesion affected the dorsal spatiomotor action system, but left the stored gesture system relatively spared. Consistent with this, her ability to imitate meaningful gesture was superior to her ability to imitate meaningless movements. This suggests that stored gesture engrams were relatively intact, and could provide a form of 'top down' support to deficient intrinsic spatial coding procedures. Other subtypes of ideomotor apraxia due to relatively more inferior parietal lesions (the region originally identified by Liepmann as the substrate of stored movement formulae) are likely to have deficits in the gesture engram system itself. Such patients should not show the superiority for meaningful gestures observed in BG.

The fact that BG exhibited spatial deficits in gesture production and had trouble matching gestures across shifts in spatial orientation also suggested the possibility that the *same* deficits in intrinsic spatial coding might underlie her impaired performance on both production and recognition tasks. In fact, in keeping with the findings of Parsons (1987a, 1987b, 1994), it has been proposed that perception and recognition of human gestures are both mediated by implicit knowledge the central nervous system has about the movements it is capable of producing (see Jeannerod, 1999 for a review of relevant literature). This suggestion has precedent as well in accounts of ideomotor apraxia. Heilman and colleagues (Heilman, Rothi, & Valenstein, 1982) have proposed that the spatiomotor representations (gesture engrams) permitting the production of gesture also enable recognition of the gestures of others.

This notion has an interesting parallel in recent physiological studies in monkeys, although the evidence to this point indicates that the neuroanatomic loci of gesture recognition/production neurons in monkey and man may be somewhat different. Rizzolatti and colleagues (Di Pellegrino, Fadiga, Fogassi, Gallese, & Rizzolatti, 1992; Gallese, Fadiga, Fogassi, & Rizzolatti, 1996; Rizzolatti, Fadiga, Gallese, & Fogassi, 1996 have described neurons in area F5 of the premotor cortex of monkeys that respond both when the monkey performs a specific action on an object (e.g., grasping) and when it observes the same action (but not different actions) made by the experimenter or another monkey. The investigators called these neurons "mirror neurons" and proposed that they form abstract representations of specific actions. Fadiga, Fogassi, Pavesi, and Rizzolatti (1995) demonstrated that evoked potentials recorded from the motor cortex during induction by transcranial magnetic stimulation were selectively enhanced when subjects observed the experimenter grasping objects. These data, they suggested, are consistent with a neural system which is sensitive both to action observation and execution. This hypothesis was supported by a subsequent PET study (Rizzolatti et al., 1996) which showed selective activation of left posterior inferior frontal cortex when subjects viewed an experimenter grasping objects. Note that F5 forms part of a circuit that includes posterior parietal cortex, and it is possible that neurons in other regions of the circuit possess properties similar to the observation/action sensitive regions elucidated by Rizzolatti and colleagues. It is also possible that the observation and execution of complex gestures—and not just simple grasping—may be represented when one views others' actions. A recent PET study of Decety and colleagues (1997) is consistent with this possibility.

Coding the Body by Structural Descriptions

Intrinsic spatial coding of body part positions vis-à-vis each other and extrinsic coding of body part location vis-à-vis objects comprise two types of cognitive body representation processed by the dorsal stream. Both intrinsic and extrinsic spatial coding appear to be related to the classic concept of the body schema as described by Head and Holmes (1911/1912). Two other types of body representation are likely to be represented largely by the ventral processing stream, as they are concerned with 'what' information about the body. The first of these 'what' body representations is contained in the semantic system and includes propositional information of the type 'a wrist is where a watch is worn,' and 'the eyes are above the nose.' The second type of body information likely to be represented largely by the ventral stream is a system of perceptual structural descriptions of the body and its parts. These are similar to the representations involved in the recognition of objects across variations in viewing angle and orientation, and may permit viewpoint-independent recognition of the body (Buxbaum & Coslett, 1999b; Buxbaum & Coslett, in press; Sirigu, Grafman, Bressler, & Sunderland, 1991).

Autotopagnosia is a rare disorder of body part recognition. Patients with autotopagnosia are unable to identify body parts of self or others, whether cued by verbal command (e.g., "point to your knee") or instructions to model the performance of another person (e.g., "point to the same part on yourself that I am touching on myself"). The disorder has classically been attributed to a deficit in the body schema (Pick, 1908, 1922). Deficits in a 'mental image' (Ogden, 1985) and in semantic knowledge of the body have also been posited (Semenza, 1998). Most of the evidence bearing on the nature of the representation impaired in the disorder has

Table 22.2
Number of Errors Made by the Patient of Sirigu et al. (1991) in Pointing
to Command to Body Parts and to Objects Attached to the Same Body Parts.*

	I	II	III	IV	V	VI
Verbal Command						
Body parts	6	5	6	6	6	
Objects on body parts	1	1	1	0	0	
Non-Verbal Command						
Body parts	5	5	6	5	7	6
Objects on body parts	0	1	0	0	0	0

*Roman numerals refer to replications of the task.
Note. From "Multiple Representations Contribute to Body Knowledge Processing," by A. Sirigu, J. Grafman, K. Bressler, and T. Sunderland, 1991, *Brain, 114*, pp. 629–642.

been equivocal or indirect. Recently, Sirigu et al. (1991) reported a case study which speaks relatively clearly to the nature of the damaged representation. Their patient was unable to point to her own body parts or those of the examiner, but performed well in naming body parts when these were pointed to, defining body part functions, and pointing to parts of inanimate objects. Critically, she was also able to point to the locations (and remembered locations) of small objects taped to the same body parts she had been unable to localize. (See Table 22.2)

Sirigu et al. (1991) proposed that the patient's ability to define body part functions was consistent with intact semantic knowledge of body parts. Her ability to map the location of objects with respect to the body suggested integrity of the body schema. Finally, the investigators suggested that the patient's autotopagnosia was attributable to impairments in the system of structural descriptions of the body and its parts.

We recently reported a series of investigations in a patient with autotopagnosia which enabled us to support and extend this account (Buxbaum & Coslett, in press). GL, like other reported autotopagnosics, was unable to localize body parts on himself or others, whether cued by verbal or visual input. In contrast, he used body parts precisely in reaching and grasping tasks, correctly matched items of clothing to body parts, and errorlessly localized the parts of animals and man-made objects. We also demonstrated that GL was unable to match pictured or real human body parts across shifts in orientation or changes in visual appearance, but could perform analogous matching tasks with animal body parts and man-made object parts. The data extend the account of Sirigu et al. (1991) in suggesting that human body part localization depends upon a representation of human (but not animal) bodies which enables viewpoint independent body part recognition and participates in the calculation of equivalence between the body parts of self and others across transformations in orientation. One possibility is that this damaged representation is a structural description system, as Sirigu et al. (1991) suggest. Unlike 'intrinsic' spatial coding, which represents changes in body part positions relative to one another, the body structural description system would represent stable neighborhood relationships among body parts across transformations in orientation or changes in joint angles.

In the next section, we turn again to extrinsic egocentric coding procedures in action, focusing on spatiomotor coding of objects vis-à-vis the hand.

SELECTION FOR ACTION: ATTENTIONAL PROCESSING AND ACTION

Spatial Compatibility and the Premotor Theory of Attention

In choice–reaction-time tasks, the time required to respond depends upon the spatial relationship between the stimulus and the response. For example, when a target is presented to the right of fixation, subjects are faster to respond to it with the right as compared to left hand, whereas a target on the left is responded to more quickly with the left hand. Critically, stimulus–response compatibility effects are also observed with the hands crossed. For example, if the right and left hands are crossed into the opposite hemispaces, RTs for the right hand are shorter for stimuli in the left hemispace.

Such effects occur even when the location of the target is irrelevant to the response. For example, if asked to press a right button when they see a red target and a left button when they see a green target, subjects are faster to respond to red targets when these happen to appear on the right, and to green targets when they appear on the left. This is known as the Simon effect (Hedge & Marsh, 1975; Simon, Craft, & Small, 1970). Recent reports have documented stimulus-response compatibility effects in representational space. Bachtold, Baumulla, & Brugger, 1998, for example, demonstrated that subjects responded faster with the left hand to the number 8 presented at midline when instructed to conceive of the number as the location on a clock face. In contrast, subjects responded faster to the number 8 with the right hand when instructed to conceive of the location as the number on a ruler.

A number of accounts of spatial compatibility effects and the Simon effect have been proposed. The first group of accounts suggest that the Simon effect is due to an attentional bias to respond toward the source of stimulation, much like an orienting reaction (Simon et al., 1970). According to Heilman and colleagues, attentional biases affect the selection and preparation of motor responses in addition to the selection and processing of stimuli (Heilman, Watson, & Valenstein, 1985). Consistent with this possibility, Verfaellie and colleagues (Verfaellie, Bowers, & Heilman, 1990) and Bradshaw and coworkers (Bradshaw, Nettleton, Pierson, Wilson, & Nathan, 1987) have presented data suggesting that the locus of the Simon effect is in response preparation rather than in stimulus registration stages of processing. Verfaellie et al. (1990) propose that preparation of a response readies the corresponding hemisphere for action, and additionally for processing incoming information on the corresponding side of space.

A second account invokes common spatial coding of stimulus and response (e.g., Nicoletti & Umilta, 1994; Umilta & Nicoletti, 1990). On this account, the effect is attributed to a conflict between the spatial code of the stimulus and that of the response which interferes with processing at the level of response selection.

Although controversy persists regarding the interpretation of stimulus response compatibility effects (see also Kornblum, Hasbroug, & Osman, 1990), their major significance in this context lies in their suggestion that the spatial relationship between the hand and the target are automatically marked in an egocentric spatial frame of reference (Zorzi & Umilta, 1995) and that this relationship has important implications for action.

Spatial compatibility effects have relevance to the "premotor theory of attention" developed by Rizzolatti and colleagues (e.g., Rizzolatti & Carmarda, 1987; Rizzolatti, Riggio, Dascola, & Umilta, 1987). According to this theory, space is represented in numerous 'pragmatic maps' that transform spatial information into motor commands. Activity of neural circuits programming motor plans produces a shift of attention to the spatial regions where the action is to be executed. The intention to perform a movement in a certain region of space, then, serves to shift attention automatically to that region. In other words, visual attention to a particular location in space comprises the facilitation of neurons involved in preparing and directing actions to that part of space.

Action Influences Attention

Earlier in the chapter, we reviewed physiological evidence from studies with monkeys that egocentric spatial coding can take several forms, depending upon the effectors involved in the action. Recently, such evidence has begun to inform studies of attentional selection in human subjects.

Traditional studies of visual attention have explored the degree to which distractor objects in an array compete with target objects for the control of action by measuring latencies to perform a simple motor task (e.g., a button press upon target detection) when the target is presented alone as compared to when it is presented with distractors (e.g., Treisman & Gelade, 1980; see also Allport, 1993, for review). These studies have characteristically provided evidence that perceptual attributes of distractors (e.g., similarity and spatial proximity to targets) affect their salience and thus the slowing they exert upon reaction times. In recent years, there has been increasing evidence that motor factors, including the positions of the acting limbs, may affect attentional processing of objects in arrays. This evidence comes both from cognitive psychological studies with healthy subjects, as well as from studies with brain damaged populations.

One of the most seminal of the former is a study by Tipper, Lortie, and Baylis (1992), which used a selective reaching-to-target task to demonstrate that distractor interference was a function of the location of the distractor with respect to the hand and not a function of location in retinotopic or body-centered coordinates. Targets and distractors, which were red and yellow lights, respectively, were arrayed on a board angled away from the viewer so that top positions were furthest from the body and bottom positions were closest to the body. Because of the board's angle and the effect of visual foreshortening, top row distractors were retinotopically closest to center row targets. In one condition, each subject began the reaching task with his or her hand at the bottom of the board and reached to targets in the center of the board. Distractors between the hand and the target, at the bottom of the board, caused more interference than those beyond the target, at the top of the board. Distractors close to the hand at the bottom of the board also caused more interference than top row distractors, which were closer to the target in retinotopic space. In a second condition, subjects began each reach with the hand positioned at the top of the board and reached downward to center targets. Increased interference by distractors close to the hand (in this case, in the top row) was observed in this condition as well. Since bottom row distractors were closest to the subjects' bodies even in the 'hand at top' condition, the relatively large interference caused by top row distractors could not be attributed to interference effects arising within 'body centered' frames of reference.

Tipper, Howard, and Jackson (1997) also provide data demonstrating that hand path trajectories veer away from distractor objects. They argue that distractors and targets activate action plans in parallel, and that distractor interference is a measure of the cost of uncoupling the action plan associated with the distractor from the control of action. The observed deviations in hand path trajectories can be accounted for by a neuronal population model of reach-direction vector coding, in which distributed and partially overlapping populations of neurons participate in coding movement vectors for both target and distractor. Figure 22.3 provides a diagram of this model.

For example, when a distractor is located to the right of the target, and the distractor location is "de-selected" and uncoupled from action control, neurons coding movement toward it are inhibited below baseline. Since there is overlap in the neurons coding reaches to the right sided distractor and left sided target, this means that a portion of the "right-directional" neurons coding reaches to the target are also inhibited below baseline. As a result, the reach trajectory is programmed by the remaining population of neurons, which program relatively "left-directional" movement vectors. Consequently, the reach that is programmed veers away from the right-sided distractor, toward the left.

In unilateral neglect associated with right parietal damage, there is an asymmetry in the processes which select targets (and actions to target locations) and inhibit distractors and their locations. Selection processes are biased toward stimuli on the right (as "right" is usually defined by head and body hemispace) and stimuli further to the left appear to exert less influence on selection processes (see Mattingley & Driver, 1996). Some patients with neglect are also significantly slower to initiate and perform leftward as compared to rightward arm

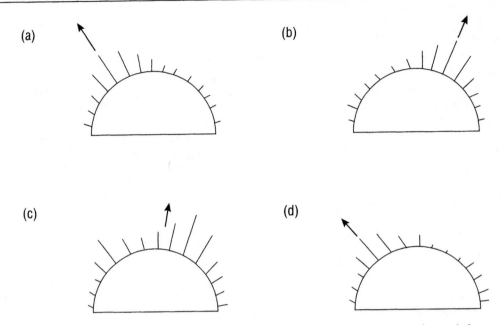

Figure 22.3: Schematic diagram of neural activity representing a reach to a left-sided target in the presence of a right-sided distractor. (a) shows (abstract) activation levels associated with a far left target. (b) shows activation levels associated with a near right distractor. (c) shows combined activity of cells involved in reaching to both locations. (d) represents reach direction after inhibition of the distractor. The activity of some cells is reduced below baseline levels, and the mean of the distribution remaining above baseline has shifted to the left, away from the right-sided distractor. "Selective Reaching to Grasp: Evidence for Distraction Interference Effects" by S. P. Tipper, L. A. Howard, and S. R. Jackson, 1997, *Visual Cognition*, 4.

movements; thus, they exhibit *directional hypokinesia* (Heilman, Bowers, Coslett, Whelan, & Watson, 1985), suggesting a deficit in selecting *responses* requiring leftward movements.

One possibility is that the selection asymmetry in neglect may be defined with respect to a number of different reference frames, depending upon the effectors involved in the action. In the context of a reaching task, the asymmetry may be hand-centered. If neglect can arise with respect to hand-centered coordinates, then distractors to the left of the hand (i.e., requiring leftward movements for contact) should compete less strongly for the control of action than stimuli to the right of the hand (i.e., requiring rightward movements for contact). We tested this possibility by asking 8 right parietal lesioned patients with neglect (and 12 age-and-education-matched controls) to reach to targets from right or left start positions (Buxbaum & Permaul, manuscript submitted). On each experimental trial, a target (a red light) could be presented alone in the central position of the board or with a distractor (a yellow light) in a surrounding top, bottom, left, or right position. As the position of stimuli with respect to the eyes, head, and body is unaffected by the start position manipulation, any observed differences in patterns of distractor interference with left versus right start positions would indicate that attention is allocated to the array as a function of where the hand is; i.e., in hand-centered coordinates. Furthermore, if selection processes in neglect are biased toward stimuli on the right (as "right" is defined by the position of the *hand)*, then stimuli to the left of the hand should exert less interference in selection processes than stimuli to the right of the hand.

As can be seen in Figure 22.4, patients, but not controls, were slower from right as compared to left start in trials in which targets were presented alone (No Distractor; ND). Thus,

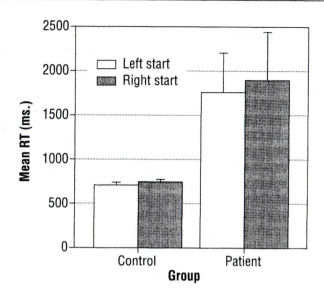

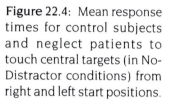

Figure 22.4: Mean response times for control subjects and neglect patients to touch central targets (in No-Distractor conditions) from right and left start positions.

the patients exhibited directional hypokinesia. We also found that on Left Start trials, patients were significantly slower with distractors compared to ND (distractor *interference*) and on Right Start trials, were significantly faster with distractors compared to ND (distractor *facilitation*). In other words, neglect patients show *interference* from distractors to the right of the hand (i.e., distractors which would require rightward movements to acquire) and *facilitation* from distractors to the left of the hand (i.e., distractors that would require leftward movements to acquire). This indicates that the gradient of attention in neglect may be hand-centered (as noted above, Buxbaum & Coslett, 1998a, provides a previous demonstration). Controls, in contrast, showed equal interference with Left Start and Right Start (see Figure 22.5). Finally, patients showed relatively greater distractor *facilitation* (as compared to controls) for distractors in bottom and left positions. Patients tended to show more *interference* than did controls from distractors in the right position (see Figure 22.6).

Figure 22.7 illustrates a possible mechanism by which the *directional hypokinesia, interference,* and *facilitation* effects may be reconciled. We consider reaching from left start positions and right start positions separately.

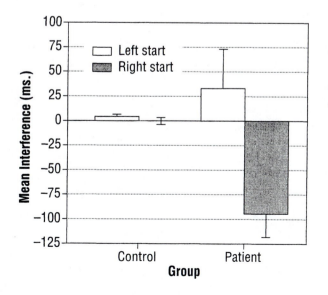

Figure 22.5: Mean total interference on response times of control subjects and neglect patients to touch central targets from right and left start positions.

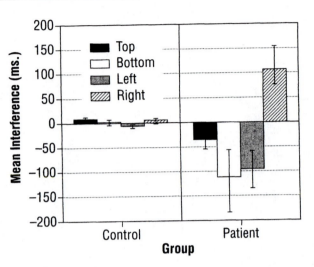

Figure 22.6: Mean total interference by distractors in different positions in the array in right and left start conditions.

When reaching from left start, neuronal populations coding rightward movement vectors are activated. The intact left hemisphere predominates in this coding. When two locations (target and distractor) are activated, initial excitation of an overlapping, broadly tuned neural population is followed by relatively precise inhibition of the distractor location. The inhibitory process exerts a cost on the time to perform reaches to the target. This is similar to the distractor interference effect seen in normals.

When reaching from right start, the lesioned right hemisphere predominates. Neuronal populations coding leftward movements are weakly excited, resulting in directional hypokinesia. Location coding is coarse and more broadly tuned than is normal; as a result, target and distractor locations are poorly registered. Two possible mechanisms account for the facilitory effect of distractor observed in this case. The first is probability summation, in which the first stimulus to be detected is sufficient to initiate a response (race model). The second is neural summation, in which facilitation results from the pooled activity of the neuronal population (see Reuter-Lorenz, Nozawa, Gazzaniga, & Hughes, 1995). Figure 22.7 illustrates the latter mechanism. The data suggest that initial placement of the hand in reaching tasks may be a significant influence on the asymmetric pattern of distractor interference and facilitation observed in neglect.

THE ROLE OF OBJECTS IN ACTION

A final property of the 'how' system in the dorsal stream is that it codes several object attributes formerly thought to be the domain of the ventral stream, including shape, size, and orientation. Neurons in posterior parietal cortex (anterior intraparietal area, AIP) and frontal premotor area (F5) in monkeys are sensitive to the visual characteristics of objects to be grasped, and respond selectively to objects which 'afford' certain types of hand movements, but not to objects affording different hand postures (see Craighero, Fadiga, Rizzolatti, & Umilta, 1998, for review). In this context, the term 'affordance' refers to the idea that the actions appropriate to an object are intrinsic to its representation and derived from its perceptual properties.[2] The object representations computed in the dorsal stream, then, are concerned not with object recognition, but with the body movements appropriate to interacting with objects.

---

[2] "Note that the Gibsonian concept of an affordance refers to the properties of an object with respect to the actor/observer. Thus, for example, a given object affords grasping because it is of a size that can readily be enclosed by the human hand. Such affordances can only be perceived through experience in interacting with objects. Although there is likely to be a certain amount of generalization from familiar to novel objects, it is not clear whether new objects presenting fundamentally novel perceptual properties have perceptible 'affordances' in the Gibsonian sense (Gibson, 1977).

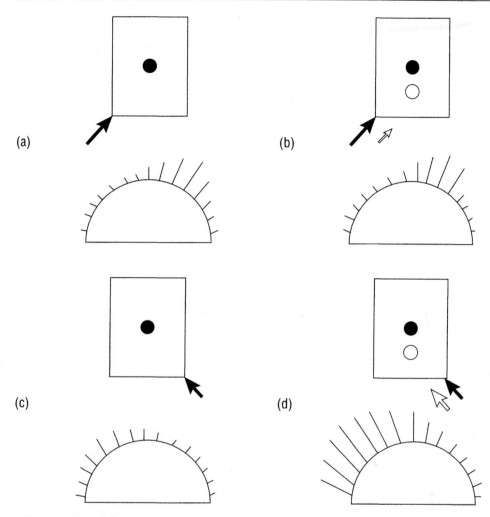

Figure 22.7: Schematic diagram of neural activity representing a reach to a central target alone and in the presence of a bottom distractor in a right-hemisphere lesioned patient with a left neglect. Panel (a) shows a reach into the non-neglected hemisphere to a target alone. Panel (b) shows a reach into the non-neglected hemisphere to a target with distractor present after inhibition of the distractor. As in the Tipper, Howard, and Jackson (1997) model, the activity of some cells is reduced below baseline levels, and the mean of the distribution remaining above baseline has shifted to the left. Panel (c) shows a reach into the neglected hemispace to a target alone. Location coding is coarse and excitation of the neural population is weak and diffuse. Panel (d) shows reaching into the neglected hemisphere to a target with a distractor. Coarseness of location coding results in spatial summation, followed by later weak inhibition of the distractor location.

The evidence that the action system is well-equipped to process the affordances of objects raises questions about the roles of affordances in determining actions. One possibility is that motor responses appropriate to objects are activated more or less automatically when objects are viewed. On the other hand, the premotor theory of attention described above suggests that the egocentric space around us is processed differently as a function of what we intend to do in that space. Perhaps such intentional effects extend to the processing of objects.

In fact, several recent studies suggest that the affordances of objects may automatically elicit their corresponding actions, even in the absence of intention. Tucker and Ellis (1998), for example, used a spatial compatibility paradigm to explore these issues. Subjects were shown pictures of objects presented upright or inverted, and the subjects' task was to press a key to indicate the objects' orientations. Subjects were faster to respond with the hand congruent with the objects' affordance for action (e.g., they were relatively faster to respond with the right hand to a pan with a right-sided handle), even though the direction of the handle was irrelevant to the orientation-discrimination task. This suggests that action corresponding to the object is automatically evoked by the sight of the object, even when there is no intention to act upon the object.

A recent neuropsychological case study of a patient with "anarchic hand"[3] behavior due to corticobasal degeneration suggests similar conclusions (Riddoch, Edwards, Humphreys, West, & Heafield, 1998). Although the subject performed adequately in tests in which she had to respond to left-sided objects with her left hand and vice versa, manual interference was observed when she used her left hand to respond to right-sided objects and right hand for left-sided objects. Interference was also influenced by the spatial relationship between the acting hand and the part of the object affording the action (e.g., the handle of a cup). Thus, for example, manual interference was observed when the patient attempted to reach for a right-handled cup with the left hand. This study, too, indicates that object affordances may automatically elicit compatible actions regardless of intent.

In an ongoing series of studies in our laboratory performed in collaboration with Antonella Pavese, Myrna Schwartz, and John Duncan, we are exploring the relationship between object affordances and task goals (Pavese & Buxbaum, submitted). In one experiment, subjects are asked to reach to a target (a blue, handled cup) while ignoring a similar distractor. In one condition, the distractor is a different color than the target, but like the target, has a handle (i.e., a purple, handled cup), and in another condition, it is handle-less but otherwise like the target in size shape, and color (i.e., a blue cylinder). Distractors are presented both close to and far from the acting hand. In a given block of trials, the subject's task is to either grasp the handle of the target cup, or alternatively, to tap it lightly with a poking gesture. Stimulus exposure is controlled by means of liquid crystal goggles that clear at the beginning of each trial, and initiation latencies and reaction times are registered by means of touch sensitive switches.

Initially, we predicted that distractors with handles would cause more interference when the subjects' task was to grasp the handle of the target, and less interference when the subjects' task was to poke the target. What we have found, instead, is that handled distractors cause more interference than no-handled distractors, provided they are close to the acting hand, regardless of the task demands. The hand-centered interference effects are not simply due to greater perceptual interference caused by the visual attributes of a handle in the distractor, as they are not present in a control condition in which subjects must press a button located at midline in lieu of reaching to the target. In other words, distractors with handles are highly interfering when the task is to perform an action—any action—upon objects in the array, but not when the task does not require interaction with the objects.

These findings suggest that the rapid programming of object oriented actions may be facilitated by automatic activation of a prehensile response associated with objects, but only when the intention of the subject is to act on the objects to begin with. Thus, it is possible that the intention to interact with objects with the hand (in any way) causes a corresponding attentional highlighting of the features of objects that are highly salient to the grasp system. A cup's handle may be just such a feature. It would appear to be a useful property of the action system

---

[3]Anarchic hand syndrome is a condition in which each hand appears to respond to its own action plan. Thus, for example, the left hand might attempt to tighten the lid of a bottle while the right hand attempts to loosen it. In some cases, this can lead to "intermanual conflict," in which the hands appear to actively compete with one another (e.g., Goldberg, Mayer, & Toglia, 1981).

that objects do not continually call forth the actions associated with them even when, for example, one is sitting quietly with hands folded. Instead, the ability of objects to evoke their corresponding actions may normally be reserved for situations in which premotor (intentional) processes are biased to the objects. These results, then, suggest a potentially different model of the role of affordances than the Tucker and Ellis (1998) study. It is possible that differences between the Tucker and Ellis findings and ours are related to the level at which affordance effects are investigated. While the Tucker and Ellis study examined the general left–right compatibility of affordance and response, our work is investigating affordance-response compatibilities for specific prehensile gestures. In subsequent studies, we are exploring whether the 'goodness of fit' of an affordance (such as a rightward vs. leftward facing handle for a right-handed grasp) affects the degree to which the affordance feature competes for the control of attention and action. Preliminary data suggest an affirmative answer to this question.

CONCLUSIONS

Historically, neuropsychological models of action have focused largely upon memorial gesture representations associated with skilled actions. In recent years, evidence from physiological animal studies, cognitive psychology, and cognitive neuropsychology have contributed to a spatiomotor model of the action system which recognizes the importance of "on-line" dynamic coding procedures in skilled action as well as in motor mental imagery, recognition of gesture, body part identification, spatial attention, and object selection. The system includes a dynamic representation of the body forming the basis for the calculation of numerous frames of reference centered upon the body parts involved in a given action. These body-centered spatial reference frames participate in spatiomotor coding of the locations of body parts with respect to one another, and with respect to external objects in the environment. Finally, the system is flexible, permitting alternative reference frames to substitute for or augment damaged spatio-motor coding processes.

Although recent work in this area has contributed immeasurably to our knowledge of spatio-motor aspects of action, there are still many remaining questions. A large question concerns the precise relationship of memorial and 'on-line' representations, for example, the manner in (and degree to) which putatively *stored* representations of the body (i.e., body structural descriptions, body semantics) and of action (i.e., gesture knowledge, gesture engrams) contribute to *dynamic* spatio-motor processes like reaching to targets, gesturing, and pointing to body parts. Conversely, we are just beginning to appreciate that *dynamic* spatio-motor procedures (i.e., extrinsic and intrinsic spatial coding) contribute to *cognitive (non-action)* tasks such as motor imagery and recognition of gestures and body positions. One possibility to be explored is that the "spatiomotor action system" is actually a distributed network of cognitive nodes in which stored, memorial representations and "on-line" dynamic procedures relevant to the body and action are proportionally activated as a function of the demands of the task at hand.

REFERENCES

Allport, D. A. (1993). Attention and control: Have we been asking the wrong questions? *Attention and Performance XIV: A Silver Jubilee,* Cambridge, MA: MIT Press.

Andersen, R. A. (1995). Coordinate transformations and motor planning in posterior parietal cortex. In M. S. Gazzaniga (Ed.), *The Cognitive Neurosciences* (pp. 519–532). Cambridge, MA: MIT Press.

Anderson, R. A., Snyder, L. H., Li, C-S, & Stricanne, B. (1993). Coordinate transformations in the representation of spatial information. *Current Opinion in Neurobiology, 3,* 171–176.

Bachtold, D., Baumulla, M., & Brugger, P. (1998). Stimulus-response compatibility in representational space. *Neuropsychologia, 36 ,* 711–715.

Bracewell, R. M., Barash, S., Massoni, P., & Andersen, R. A. (1991). Neurons in the macaque lateral intra-parietal cortex (LIP) appear to encode the next intended saccade. *Society for Neuroscience Abstracts, 17,* 1282.

Bradshaw, J. L., Nettleton, N. C., Pierson, J. M., Wilson, L. E., & Nathan, G. (1987). Coordinates of extracorporeal space. In M. Jeannerod (Ed.), *Neurophysiology and Neuropsychological Aspects of Spatial Neglect.* North

Holland: Elsevier.

Burnod, Y., Grandguillaume, P., Otto, I., Ferraina, S., Johnson, P. B., & Caminiti, R. (1992). Visuomotor transformations underlying arm movements toward visual targets: A neural network modal of cerebral cortical operations. *The Journal of Neuroscience, 12,* 1435–1453.

Boussaoud, D., Bremmer, F., & Jouffrais, C. (1998) Eye position effects on the neuronal activity of dorsal premotor cortex in monky. *Journal of Neurophysiology, 80,* 1132–1150.

Buxbaum, L. J., & Coslett, H. B. (1997). Subtypes of optic ataxia: Reframing the disconnection account. *Neurocase, 3,* 159–166.

Buxbaum, L. J., & Coslett, H. B. (1998a). Spatio-motor representations in reaching: evidence for subtypes of optic ataxia. *Cognitive Neuropsychology, 15*(3), 279–312.

Buxbaum, L. J., & Coslett, H. B. (1998b). Evidence for selective impairments of body-part structural descriptions in autotopagnosia. *Journal of the International Neuropsychological Society, 4*(1).

Buxbaum, L. J., & Coslett, H. B. (in press). Specialized structural description for human body parts: Evidence from autotopagnosia. *Cognitive Neuropsychology.*

Buxbaum, L. J., Giovannetti, T., & Libon, D. (in press). The role of the dynamic body schema in praxis: Evidence from primary progressive apraxia. *Brain and Cognition*

Buxbaum, L. J., & Permaul, P. (submitted). *Hand-centered attentional and motor asymmetrics in unilateral*

Caminiti, R., Johnson, P. B., Galli, C., Ferraina, S., & Burnod, Y. (1991). Making arm movements within different parts of space: The premotor and motor cortical representation of a coordinate system for reaching to visual targets. *Journal of Neuroscience, 11,* 1182–1197.

Caminiti, R., Johnson, P. B., & Urbano, A. (1990). Making arm movements within different parts of space: Dynamic aspects in the primate motor cortex. *Journal of Neurophysiology, 10,* 2039–2958.

Coslett, H. B. (1998). Evidence for a disturbance of the body schema in neglect. *Brain and Cognition, 37*(3), 527–544.

Coslett, H. B., & Lie, E. (2000). *Hand-centered attention: Evidence from patients with brain lesions.* Manuscript submitted for publication.

Coslett, H. B., & Saffran, E. M. (1991). Simultanagnosia: To see but not two see. *Brain, 114,* 1523–1545.

Craighero, L., Fadiga, L., Rizzolatti, G., & Umilta, C. (1998). Visuomotor priming. *Visual Cognition, 5,* 109–125.

Decety, J., Grezes, J., Costes, N., Perani, D., Jeannerod, M., Procyk, E., Grassi, F., & Fazio, F. (1997). Brain activity during observation of action. Influence of action content and subject's strategy. *Brain, 120,* 1763–1777.

Di Pellegrino, G., Fadiga, L., Fogassi, L., Gallese, V., & Rizzolatti, G. (1992). Understanding motor events: A neurophysiological study. *Experimental Brain Research, 91,* 176–180.

Duhamel, J. R., Colby, C. L., & Goldberg, M. E. (1992). The updating of the representation of visual space in parietal cortex by intended eye movements. *Science, 255,* 90–92.

Fadiga, L., Fogassi, L., Pavesi, G., & Rizzolatti, G. (1995). Motor facilitation during action observation: A magnetic stimulation study. *Journal of Neurophysiology, 73*(6), 2608–2611.

Gallese, V., Fadiga, L., Fogassi, L., & Rizzolati, G. (1996). Action recognition in the premotor cortex. *Brain, 119*(2), 593–609.

Geschwind, N. (1965). Disconnection syndromes in animals and man. *Brain, 8,* 237–294, 585–644.

Gibson, J. J. (1977). The theory of affordances. In R. Shaw & J. Bransford (Eds.). *Perceiving, acting, and knowing: Toward an ecological psychology.* Hillsdale, NJ: Lawrence Erlbaum.

Goldberg, G., Mayer, N. H., & Toglia, J. U. (1981). Medial frontal cortex infarctions and the alien hand sign. *Archives of Neurology, 38,* 683–686.

Gonzalez Rothi, L. J., Ochipa, C., & Heilman, K. M. (1991). A cognitive neuropsychological model of limb apraxia. *Cognitive Neuropsychology, 8*(6), 443–458.

Gonzalez Rothi, L. J., Raymer, A. M., Ochipa, C., Maher, L. M., Greenwald, M. L., & Heilman, K. M. (1991). *Florida Apraxia Battery: Experimental Edition.*

Graziano, M. S. A., Yap, G. S., & Gross, C. G. (1994). Coding of visual space by premotor neurons. *Science, 266,* 1054–1057.

Hanlon, R. E., Mattson, D., Demery, J., & Dromerick, A. W. (1998). Axial movements are relatively preserved with respect to limb movements in aphasic patients. *Cortex, 34,* 731–741.

Head, H., & Holmes, G. 1911/1912. Sensory disturbances from cerebral lesions. *Brain, 34,* 102–254.

Hedge, A., & Marsh, N. W. A. (1975). The effect of irrelevant spatial correspondence on two-choice response time. *Acta Psychologica, 39,* 427–439.

Heilman, K. M., Bowers, D., Coslett, H. B., Whelan, H., & Watson, R. T. (1985). Directional hypokinesia: prolonged reaction time for leftward movements in patients with right hemisphere lesions and neglect. *Neurology, 35,* 855–859.

Heilman, K. M., Gonzalez Rothi, L., Mack, L., Feinberg, T., & Watson, R. T. (1986). Apraxia after a superior parietal lesion. *Cortex, 22,* 141–150.

Heilman, K. M., Rothi, L., & Valenstein, E. (1982). Two forms of ideomotor apraxia. *Neurology, 32,* 342–346.

Heilman, K. M., Watson R. T., & Valenstein, E. (1985). Neglect and related disorders. In K. M. Heilman & E. Valenstein (Eds.), *Clinical neuropsychology* (2nd ed., pp. 243–293). New York: Oxford University Press.

Irwin, D. E., & Yeomans, J. M. (1986). Sensory registration and informational persistence. *Journal of Experimental Psychology: Human Perception and Performance, 12,* 343–360.

Jeannerod, M. (1988). The hierarchical organization of visuomotor co-ordination. In M. Jeannerod (Ed.), *The neural and behavioral organization of goal-directed movements* (pp. 41–83). London: Oxford University Press

Jeannerod, M. (1999). To act or not to act: Perspectives on the representation of actions. *Quarterly Journal of Experimental Psychology, 52A,* 1–29.

Kahneman, D., & Treisman, A. (1984). Changing views of attention and automaticity. In R. Parsuraman & D. R. Davies (Eds.), *Varieties of Attention* (pp. 29–61). Orlando, FL: Academic Press.

Kahneman, D., Treisman, A., & Gibbs, B. J. (1992). The reviewing of object files: Object-specific integration of information. *Cognitive Psychology, 24,* 175–219.

Kornblum, S., Hasbroug, T., & Osman, A. (1990). Dimensional overlap: Cognitive basis for stimulus-response compatibility. A model and a taxonomy. *Psychological Review, 97,* 253–270.

Liepmann, H. (1905). *The left hemisphere and action* (Doreen Kimura, 1980, Trans.) London, Ontario:

University of Western Ontario.

Liepmann, H., & Maas, O. (1907). Fall von linksseitiger agraphic und apraxis bei rechtsseitiger lahmung. Journal fur Psychologie und Neurologie, 10, 214–227.

Mattingley, J. B., & Driver, J. (1996). Distinguishing sensory and motor deficits after parietal damage: An evaluation of response selection biases in unilateral neglect. In P. Their & H.-O. Karnath (Eds.), Parietal Lobes Contributions to Orientation in 3D Space. Heidelberg, Germany: Springer-Verlag.

Milner, A. D., & Goodale, M. A. (1995). The visual brain in action. Oxford, UK: Oxford University Press.

Nicoletti, R., & Umilta, C. (1994). Attention shifts produce spatial stimulus codes. Psychological Resumes, 56, 144–150.

Ogden, J. (1985). Autotopagnosia. Brain, 108, 1009–1022.

Parsons, L. M. (1987a). Imagined spatial transformations of one's hands and feet. Cognitive Psychology, 19, 178–241.

Parsons, L. M. (1987b). Imagined spatial transformations of one's body. Journal of Experimental Psychology: General, 116, 172–191.

Parsons, L. M. (1994). Temporal and kinematic properties of motor behavior reflected in mentally simulated action. Journal of Experimental Psychology: Human Perception and Performance, 20(4), 709–730.

Pavese, A., & Buxbuam. L. J. (submitted). Action Matters: The role of action plans and abject affordances in selection for action.

Perenin, M. T., & Vighetto, A. (1988). Optic ataxia: A specific disruption in visuomotor mechanisms. Brain, 111, 673–674.

Pick, A. (1908). Uber storungen der orientierung am eigenen korper. Arbeiten aus der deutschen psychiatrischen Universtats-klinic in Prag. (pp. 1–19). Karger, Berlin.

Pick, A. (1922). Storrung der Orientierung am eigenen Korper. Psychologische Forschung, 2, 303–318.

Poizner, H., Mack, L., Verfaellie, M., Rothi, L. J., & Heilma, K. M. (1990). Brain, 113, 85–101

Poizner, H., Merians, A. S., Clark, M. A., Macauley, B., Rothi, L. J., & Heilman, K. M. (1998). Left hemispheric specialization for learned, skilled, and purposeful action. Neuropsychology, 12, 163–182.

Reed, C. L., & Farah, M. J. (1995). The psychological reality of the body schema: A test with normal participants. Journal of Experimental Psychology: Human Perception Performance, 21 (2), 334–343.

Reuter-Lorenz, P. A., Nozawa, G., Gazzaniga, M. S., & Hughes, H. C. (1995). The fate of neglected targets: A chronometric analysis of redundant target effects in the bisected brain., Journal of Experimental Psychology: Human Perception and Performance, 21, 211–230

Riddoch, M. J., Edwards, M. G., Humphreys, G. W., West, R., & Heafield, T. (1998). Visual affordances direct action: Neuropsychological evidence from manual interference. Cognitive Neuropsychology, 15, 645–683.

Rizzolatti, G., & Camarda, R. (1987). Neural circuits for spatial attention and unilateral neglect. In M. Jeannerod (Ed.), Neurophysiological and neuropsychological aspects of spatial neglect (pp. 289–313). North-Holland: Elsevier.

Rizzolatti, G., Fadiga, L., Gallese, V., & Fogassi, L. (1996). Premotor cortex and the recognition of motor actions. Cognitive Brain Research, 3, 131–141.

Rizzolatti, G., Fadiga, L., Matelli, M., Bettinardi, V., Paulesu, E., Perani, D., & Fazio, F. (1996). Localization of grasp representations in human by PET. 1.

Observation vs. execution. Experimental Brain Research, 111, 246–-252.

Rizzolatti, G., Riggio, L., Dascola, J., & Umilta, C. (1987). Reorientating attention across the horizontal and vertical meridians: Evidence in favor of a premotor theory of attention. Neuropsychologia, 25, 31–40.

Sakata, H., Takaoka, Y., Kawarasaki, A., & Shibutani, H. (1973). Somatosensory properties of neurons in superior parietal cortex (area 5) of the rheusus monkey. Brain Research, 64, 85–102.

Semenza, C. (1988). Impairments in localization of body parts following brain damage. Cortex, 24, 443–449.

Simon, J. R., Craft, J. L., & Small, A. M. (1970). Manipulating the strength of a stereotype: Interference effects in an auditory information processing task. Journal of Experimental Psychology, 86, 63–68.

Sirigu, A., Grafman, J., Bressler, K., & Sunderland, T. (1991). Multiple representations contribute to body knowledge processing. Brain, 114, 629–642.

Soechting, J. F., & Flanders, M. (1989a). Sensorimotor representation for pointing to targets in three-dimensional space. Journal of Neurophysiology, 62, 582–594.

Soechting, J. F., & Flanders, M. (1989b). Errors in pointing are due to approximations in sensorimotor transformation. Journal of Neurophysiology, 62, 595–608.

Soechting, J. T., Tillery, S. I. H., & Flanders M. (1990). Transformation from head- to shoulder-centered representatin of target direction in arm movements. Journal of Cognitive Neuroscience, 2, 32–43.

Tipper, S. P., Howard, L. A., & Jackson, S. R. (1997). Selective reaching to grasp: Evidence for distractor interference effects. Visual Cognition, 4, 1–38.

Tipper, S. P., Lortie, C., & Baylis, G. C. (1992). Selective reaching: evidence for action-centered attention. Journal of Experimental Psychology: Human Perception and Performance, 18, 891–905.

Treisman, A., & Gelade, G. (1980). A feature integration theory of attention. Cognitive Psychology, 12, 97–136.

Tucker, M., & Ellis, R. (1998). On the relations between seen objects and components of potential actions. Journal of Experimental Psychology, 24, 830–846.

Umilta, C., & Nicoletti, R. (1990). Spatial stimulus-response compatibility. In R. W. Proctor & T. G. Reeve (Eds.), Stimulus-response compatibility (pp. 89–116). North Holland: Elsevier

Ungerleider, L. G., & Mishkin, M. (1982). Two cortical visual systems. In J. Ingle, M. A. Goodale, & R. J. W. Mansfield (Eds.), Analysis of visual behavior (pp. 549–586). Cambridge, MA: MIT Press.

Verfaellie, M., Bowers, D., & Heilman, K. M. (1990). Attentional processes in spatial stimulus-response compatibility. In R. W. Proctor & T. G. Reeve (Eds.), Stimulus-response compatibility. North Holland: Elsevier.

Vindras, P., & Viviani, P. (1998). Frames of reference and control parameters in visuomanual pointing. Journal of Experimental Psychology: Human Perception and Performance, 24, 569–591.

Warrington, E. K., & McCarthy, R. A. (1987). Categories of knowledge: Further fractionations and an attempted integration. Brain, 110, 1273–1296.

Wise, S.P., di Pellegrino, G., & Boussaoud, D. (1996). The premotor cortex and nonstandard sensorimotor mapping. Canadian Journal of Physiological Pharmacology, 74, 469–482.

Wong, E., & Mack, A. (1981). Saccadic programming and perceived location. Acta Psychologica, 48, 123–131.

Zorzi, M., & Umilta, C. (1995). A computational model of the Simon effect. Psychological Review, 58, 193–205.

23

The Planning and Execution
of Everyday Actions

Glyn W. Humphreys
Emer M. E. Forde
M. Jane Riddoch

INTRODUCTION

Consider the tasks involved in cooking a three-course dinner. The general structure of the meal will be similar to others you have cooked before, but, while you are very familiar with some of the courses for the meal, others you may be cooking for the first time. Producing such a dinner successfully involves a number of complex procedures. First it requires that you retrieve general knowledge about the forms of such meals (a starting course, followed by a main course, followed by a dessert), along with the specific courses you will cook (either from your own long-term knowledge or from another source, such as a cookbook). These courses should be complementary, so that the knowledge retrieved for specific courses must be integrated together, with one course influencing the selection of others. You then need to retrieve the various items of food to be cooked, plus also the relevant cooking utensils. During the cooking process, the correct food stuffs for each course have to be selected and cooked at the appropriate times and in the appropriate order—a process involving the retrieval of the component actions in cooking each dish and their implementation in a correct sequence. Some of these component actions may be highly learned and relatively routine (e.g., filling a kettle with water and boiling it), some may be relatively unfamiliar (e.g., separating the albumin from the yolk of an egg). In a behavior as complex as preparing a three-course meal, the temporal ordering of the component tasks may even need to be integrated across courses, in a novel manner, so that one action is timed appropriately with regard to the others being carried out.

Clearly, cooking a successful three-course dinner is no mean feat! Most likely it involves a substantial number of cognitive processes, including: the recognition of individual objects, the retrieval of learned knowledge at different levels (from something as abstract as 'a three-course meal' to something as specific as 'boil a kettle' within the context of one's kitchen), the implementation of component actions in the correct temporal sequence, the maintenance of a record of the steps carried out and those yet to be completed, the use of this record to prevent errors such as the inappropriate repetition of action (add two, not three, tablespoons of water!), and the inter-linking of component behaviors in relatively novel ways. It is perhaps not surprising that the complexity of the enterprise defeats many of us! Nevertheless, most people are able to carry out at least the more rudimentary and routine components of the tasks, for example making coffee at the end of the meal, and so forth. Following brain damage, though, patients can have problems in carrying out even these more routine actions that presented few difficulties pre-morbidly. For example, patients categorized as having 'action disorganization syndrome' can have marked difficulties in performing the routine, multi-step tasks that characterize much of our everyday behavior. These difficulties are typically not motor in nature (due to hemiplegia or motor weakness), and, as we will discuss below, the patients may be able to recognize all the objects involved in a task, even so, when carrying out the multi-step tasks the patients may use the objects inappropriately, they may leave out component actions, incorporate other actions that are not normally conducted, carry out some actions in the wrong order, and repeat some steps multiple times. One example protocol, from a patient we have studied, is given in Figure 23.1. These deficits in carrying out multi-step tasks are interesting for the theoretician because they can help to constrain our understanding of the cognitive processes that normally mediate performance. For therapists, such deficits are of more practical importance, since they can provide some of the major hurdles to a patient returning to an independent life, more severe than motor impairments alone. In this chapter we will review attempts to understand such deficits in relation to emerging theories of how both novel and routine multi-step tasks are achieved. In the first section, we consider some of the processes normally involved in carrying out multi-step tasks, along with relevant theories. In the second section we review the neuropsychological evidence. In the third section, we consider the implications of the neuropsychological data for the theories.

THE PROCESSES INVOLVED IN CARRYING OUT MULTI-STEP TASKS

Stored Memory Representations

The routine tasks that we perform in everyday life likely depend on a number of cognitive operations. One initial operation involves retrieving a stored memory for the task, that details both the component behaviors and their temporal sequencing. For many tasks, normal subjects list highly similar, almost stereotyped protocols when asked to describe both the component steps and their order, consistent with these steps being stored as part of our long-term knowledge (see Humphreys & Forde, 1998). These memories may be described as 'schema' for

Task: Make a Cup of Tea with Sugar

Normal Basic Level Actions:	Actions by Patient:	Error Type:
Put teabag in teapot		Omission
Pour water into teapot	Pour water into teapot	
Put milk in cup	Pour milk into teapot	object substitution
Pour tea in cup	Stirs teapot	object substitution
Put sugar in tea	Pours teapot-> cup	omission
Stir tea	Stirs tea in cup	

Figure 23.1: Example of a response protocol produced by a patient showing action disorganization syndrome (ADS), relative to the basic component actions generated for the task by control subjects. "Disorder Action Schema and Action Disorganization Syndrome," by G. W. Humphreys and E. M. E. Forde, 1998, Cognitive Neuropsychology, 15, pp. 771–811.

particular tasks (cf. Grafman, 1989; Schank & Abelson, 1977). For less routine behaviors, schema may only be described in rather general terms, with the component steps not represented in detail. For instance, in order to bake a sponge cake one might remember that a mixture of flour and eggs should be mixed and then placed in an oven, but the precise details may not be known. In making the cake, then, one might need to rely on other 'problem solving' strategies—such as reasoning by logic or, by analogy, comparing this cake with other cakes one might have baked. We elaborate below on the implications of these differences in the specificity of memories for multi-step actions.

Even with routine behaviors, for which stereotyped protocols are generated, actions are typically listed at a level of specificity above that of the actual motor responses that are effected when the actual behavior takes place. For example, asked to list the actions involved in 'making a cup of tea,' normal participants generate component behaviors such as: boil the kettle, place tea bags in the teapot, pour water from kettle into teapot, pour milk into cup, pour tea from teapot into cup—they typically do not list the microstructure of the actions involved (e.g., grasp kettle, lift and place under tap, lift and plug in, grasp tea bag, reach and drop into teapot, etc.). These higher-level actions listed by subjects can be described as the *basic level* components of action (see Cooper, in press; Humphreys & Forde, 1998). An analogy can be drawn here with the idea of a 'basic level' of representation involved in object recognition, which is accessed first before we retrieve more detailed information at a subordinate level about a particular object (cf. Rosch, Mervis, Gray, Johnson, & Boyes-Braem, 1976). For example, we might recognize first that a particular animal is a dog before recognizing it as a labrador. Here 'dog' is the basic level representation and 'labrador' the subordinate representation. In action, we can suppose that a basic level component is accessed first and then used to 'direct' actions at a lower level. Note that these lower level (subordinate) components of actions will be context dependent—exactly how the kettle is grasped, lifted, and plugged-in will depend on the specific kettle and kitchen in which the action takes place. Basic level actions, however, are context-independent and can be utilized irrespective of the particular implements present or their spatial arrangement. Basic-level actions are represented at a level of abstraction that enables learning in one context to generalize to others.

The distinction between basic and subordinate levels of action, even in routine tasks, indicates that stored knowledge of actions is hierarchical in nature; high levels of representation may be accessed first and activation of these higher levels of representation may in turn enable lower level procedures to be enacted. Indeed, maintenance of activation of the higher-level representations may be important for successful completion of all the lower-level procedures, a point we return to later when we discuss how action schema may be involved in the on-line control of behavior.

Working Memory

Now, as we have noted, the basic-level actions of less routine tasks (e.g., making a sponge cake) may well not be specified in our stored representations of these behaviors. In such cases, the appropriate basic-level actions may need to be computed on-the-fly (by logic, by analogy, etc.), which in turn is likely to place greater demand on information processing structures which must keep representations active while their interrelations are computed. This could include representing possible component actions that may be incorrect and so must be rejected in order to enable to appropriate actions to be made. For example, the computations involved in representing the basic actions for making a sponge cake could include the following: retrieval of high-level knowledge from those 'cooking schema' for which flour and eggs are involved. But since the schema are coded at a high-level, other component objects may be activated in addition to flour and eggs, such as milk, which can be mixed with flour and eggs to make other items of food (e.g., pancakes). There would then need to be consideration (and rejection) of the mixture produced by adding together flour, eggs, and milk, so that only flour and eggs are represented for the 'making sponge cake' task.

Note that this temporary coding of non-relevant objects, plus their rejection, would not be involved in representing basic actions for a routine behavior, where the basic-level components are well represented within the overall action schema. Hence the resources involved in the temporary representation of information will be greater for less routine tasks. This may be described as in increase in working memory demands, though, to be clear, we need to specify what is meant by 'working memory' in this context.

Psychological theories of temporary memory storage have traditionally derived from studies of verbal short-term memory, which likely comprises of some form of phonological storage system plus also a system for maintaining activation within the phonological system via recurrent rehearsal (e.g., Baddeley, 1986). In addition, many current theories also hypothesize an analogous storage system for visual/spatial information (e.g., the visuo-spatial scratchpad), and another 'executive system,' which acts to modulate processing within the phonological and visual/spatial slave systems (Baddeley, 1986). The majority of studies of temporary memory storage have used experimental manipulations in which subjects are asked to maintain and reproduce information relating to an external stimulus (e.g., a list of letter names, a set of visual patterns and so forth). However, in the case of routine (and even to some degree non-routine) actions, the stimulus is internally generated (e.g., the schema for making a cup of tea). Nevertheless, we suggest that similar processing mechanisms may be involved, as temporary information is held about the actions, the objects for the actions, and the sequence of actions needed, while the behavior is effected. Multi-step behaviors depend on temporary maintenance of information in working memory while tasks are being completed. One source of difficulty, then, for patients following brain injury may be because there is damage to the working memory modulating task performance.

These arguments, both for a role of working memory in multi-step tasks and for its impairment leading to difficulties in performance, are close to proposals made by Kimberg and Farah (1993). We consider their account in some detail, since it provides a concrete illustration of how we might think about working memory in complex multi-step tasks, and it will enable us to review the relations between ideas of working memory in this literature relative to ideas derived from work on memory for new (external) stimulus materials (the 'classical' literature; see above). Kimberg and Farah used the ACT-R model of cognition (Anderson, 1993) to simulate neuropsychological difficulties with complex problems such as the Wisconsin Card Sort Task (WCST). In this task, the participant has to discover a rule by which to categorize cards according to one of three dimensions: color, form, number. Each card contains a pattern or patterns, varying along each dimension (e.g., a single red triangle or two blue circles). Participants start by not knowing the rule for categorization and are asked to place their cards, in series on one of cards of the experimenter distinguished by color, form, and number of items. Initially they are reinforced to categorize by color (e.g., they are told they are correct every time they place a card on the experimenter's card with the same color), but, having learned the rule, the reinforcement schedule is then shifted so that positive reward is given for categorization by shape. After this categorization is learned, the rule again shifts to categorize by number, and so forth. The task requires category learning, switching away from previously reinforced stimulus dimensions and switching into previously ignored stimulus dimensions. Patients with damage to the frontal lobes often fare particularly badly at the task.

ACT-R models human cognition in terms of production rules for action of the type: If condition X holds *then* perform action Y. These production rules are activated by the degree to which they match stimulus representations, which are connected by weighted links to the production rules. For the WCST, Kimberg and Farah had production rules for card sorting by each stimulus dimension (sort by color, form, and number) and for feedback. For example, a 'sort' production rule for color might comprise conditions such as: if the stimulus has a color and the category pile has the same color, place the stimulus in that category pile. There were links between stimulus representations and matching sort rules (e.g., from the representation of stimulus color to the rule 'sort by color'), so that the presence of a particular stimulus would trigger a particular sorting behavior. The model operated first in a 'sort' phase and then in a 'feedback' phase. When in the sort phase a particular 'card sort' production rule fired, the cards would be categorized according to the dimension involved. The model subsequently entered a feedback phase. Feedback was positive or negative. Positive feedback biased the current category production rule in favor of activation from the dimension appropriate on the last trial (color, in the above example). With negative feedback the system was biased against the incorrect category production rule, applied on the last trial, so favoring the other possible categories of response. Kimberg and Farah suggest that these production rules form part of the working memory representation used during task performance, along with representations of stimuli in the environment. They simulated the effects of frontal lobe lesions by weakening the connections between the stimulus, the sort and the feedback production systems in working memory. Under these conditions, they found that the model made errors characteristic of frontal-lobe patients, such as persisting with an incorrect response despite negative feedback (a 'perseverative error'). This occurred because, when the connections were damaged, there was reduced modulation of processing by feedback—reducing the discriminability of the different 'sort' productions. According to Kimberg and Farah, damage to the frontal lobes leads to the weakening of associations between elements in working memory, where these elements can include representations of goals (e.g., the 'sort' production rules, for the WCST), of stimuli and of response contingencies (the feedback production rules).

The idea that goal and response states may form part of the temporary memory representations guiding performance on complex tasks is different in many respects from traditional views of working memory. These traditional accounts have tended to emphasize the properties of the 'slave' systems that maintain representations of external stimuli, and the processes involved in representing goals and response contingencies have not been specified beyond general discussions of the role of executive processes in modulating memory performance (Baddeley, 1986). However, within a framework such as that suggested by Kimberg and Farah it becomes possible to study the relation between the different forms of working memory representation involved in complex, multi-step tasks, especially if brain damage can disrupt linkage across representations. For example as we will discuss below, within this framework we can begin to understand how verbal working memory representations can be maintained even when patients make errors that indicate loss of goal-based guidance of their 'on-line' behavior.

The notion that working memory can include temporary representations of internal goals is also captured to some degree in connectionist models of serial performance, which have been developed to simulate behaviors such as immediate verbal recall, typing, and spelling (e.g., Burgess & Hitch, 1992, 1999; Houghton, 1990; Houghton, Glasspool, & Shallice, 1994; Houghton, Tipper, Weaver, & Shore, 1996; Rumelhart & Norman, 1982). In such models, serial order is determined by an activation profile imposed across processing units that represent the responses to be output (e.g., letter names, for models of verbal memory). This activation profile specifies the temporal order in which the responses should be made, and it needs to be maintained over time as responses are effected. Which response is produced is governed by whichever output unit is activated most, and output units operate competitively so that only one at a time can 'win' and generate an action: Typically, for the first step in the sequence of actions, this will be the output unit excited most by the imposed activation profile. Once the first response has been effected, however, there needs to be a process to prevent the same unit entering the competition again, otherwise it will continue to 'win,' given the continued imposition of the activation profile. No other responses will be made! To prevent this, and to enable other outputs to be made in sequence, models have employed a process of 'rebound' inhibition that prevents 'winning' output units from competing for some time after they have generated a response. Due to rebound inhibition of the first winning output unit, the subsequent winner will be the unit next most excited by the imposed activation gradient, and so on—a process known as competitive queuing (see Houghton, 1990). This process of competition based on the activation profile, followed by immediate inhibition, can continue over time, to enable a sequence of behaviors to be made. Old responses can eventually be repeated too, if the immediate rebound inhibition decays.

Humphreys and Forde (1998) suggested that competitive queuing models of this type could also be used to explain our performance of multi-step everyday tasks, such as making a cup of tea. The notion here is that the output units in such a model would correspond to the basic-level actions generated when normal subjects describe routine tasks (see above). An activation profile is imposed upon these output units by adoption of the task goal ('make a cup of tea'), and the particular activation profile that is imposed comprises our stored knowledge our the temporal sequence of the basic-level actions. Successful performance of the multi-step task requires that the goal state is maintained in an active state, along with the activation profile across the basic-action units. This is the memory load that must be carried during everyday tasks, and activation in this system forms what we will term an 'action working memory.' A framework illustrating these suggestions is given in Figure 23.2.

One property of the framework presented in Figure 23.2 is that competition for action occurs at the level of basic component actions. Once one basic component 'wins' the competi-

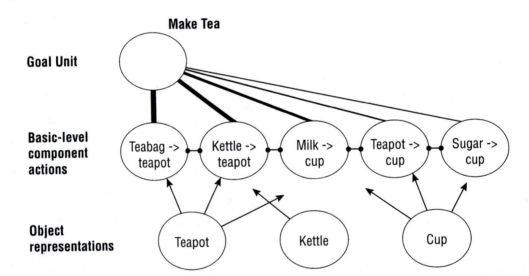

Figure 23.2: Example of a competitive queuing model applied to the production of multi-step routine actions. The upper unit corresponds to a goal for the task ('make a cup of tea'). The middle units correspond to the basic-level component actions for the task. The lower units correspond to representations of individual objects activated by the visual and semantic properties of stimuli. Activation of the units for the basic-level actions is determined by (a) the strength of the connection from the goal unit for the task to each component action unit (the top-down signal), and (b) the presence of visual and semantic cues from objects in the environment (the bottom-up signal). In the figure the width of the connections from the 'goal unit' to the representations of basic-level actions represents the strength of the top-down signal. This signal provides an 'activation gradient' that governs output order. Units at both the level of goals and the level of component actions are competitive with one another, so that, normally, only one goal and one basic-level action are triggered at a time.

tion, we presume that activation is transmitted to an output system that effects that action at a microscopic level, in terms of the precise motor responses necessary in a given context. There is not competition between components of the different motor responses (e.g., the action for 'put the teabag in the teapot' vs. that for 'pour the water'), but there is competition for which high-level action is selected first. Although not shown in Figure 23.2, our suggestion is that each basic-level action would link to specific motor responses (the grasp action for a tea bag vs. that for a teapot), that are paramaterized by the visual environment. Thus a particular grasp response would be influenced by the size of the objects, its distance from the actor and so forth, once the basic-level component action had been selected.

Let us now suppose that the task is non-routine (e.g., making a sponge cake, rather than a cup of tea). We have suggested above that less familiar tasks will have less precise links from their goal states to their component actions, and, within a competitive queuing framework, this may also mean a less well-defined activation gradient. Due to the less precise links, incorrect basic actions may sometimes be activated (e.g., a component action such as 'add milk to eggs and flour,' for the sponge cake task) and there will also be more prolonged competition in order to determine which component actions should be made first, even when the correct components are activated. Hence, as we inferred above, the working memory load will increase.

Bottom-Up Factors: Learned Associations and Affordances

We have proposed that the performance of routine actions requires the retrieval of stored knowledge about the component actions and their order, and this knowledge is then used 'on-line' to guide action as it evolves. This stresses the role of top-down guidance in action. Of course, representations activated in a top-down manner need also to be interfaced with representations activated in a bottom-up manner, from the environment, so that actions are made to the most appropriate objects present (e.g., those that are closest, most familiar, and so forth). It seems likely that objects present in the environment can activate stored routines for action. Reason (1984) assessed slips in everyday action from diaries kept by normal volunteers. These slips can include the initiation of whole action sequences cued by familiar stimuli—such as when one follows the usual route to work instead of taking a route to a meeting in a different location. Selection of the correct action in multi-step tasks will typically be based on an interaction between the stored routines generated top-down and actions cued in a bottom-up manner.

The information that leads to bottom-up cueing of actions may take a number of forms. For example, there is considerable evidence indicating that objects gain rapid access to semantic information (e.g., Potter & Faulconer, 1975), and this semantic information may activate an associated response to an object. Indeed studies of functional imaging are consistent with the idea that associated representations for action are activated even in simple naming tasks with tools, suggesting that representations for action are triggered in a bottom-up fashion even when they are not formally required for the task (e.g., Chao, Haxby, & Martin, 1999; Grabowski, Damasio, & Damasio, 1998; Grafton, Fadiga, Arbib, & Rizzolatti, 1997; Martin et al., 1995). Thus neural areas associated with motion and with action knowledge are activated in naming tasks with tools. These same areas are not activated to the same degree by other objects not associated with human action (e.g., animals). There is increasing evidence, however, that actions are not only activated by semantic information from objects, but also directly from their visual properties. Rumiati and Humphreys (1998), for example, had normal subjects make gestures under deadline conditions to objects and words. They found that, while errors to words were primarily semantic in nature (e.g., gesturing to the written word 'razor' as a shaving brush), errors to objects were frequently related to the visual properties of the stimuli (e.g., gesturing to a razor as a hammer). They proposed that there is direct activation of actions from either stored visual representations for objects or from object parts that are associated with actions (e.g., a cup handle with gripping, a blade of a knife with cutting, etc.). Tucker and Ellis (1998) similarly found that manual responses made with the left and right hands as to whether objects are upright or not are affected by the irrelevant dimension of the left–right orientation of the object (e.g., determined by the position of the handle on the object). Here it appears that a motor response (for the left or right hand) is activated by position of the handle of the object, even though it is irrelevant to the task. Craighero, Fadiga, Rizzolatti, and Umilta (1998) also report priming effects based on the relationship between the orientation of a prime and the orientation of the hand used in responding to a target. Responses were made by rotating a rectangular bar clockwise or anti-clockwise, according to a target signal. Latencies were faster when targets were preceded by a prime in the same orientation as the response bar than when it was in a different orientation.

Thus evidence from normal subjects indicates that actions can be triggered in a bottom-up fashion irrespective of their relevance for the task, and this is based on visual as well as semantic properties of the objects. In multi-step behaviors this bottom-up activation may help to moderate competition between component actions, depending on factors such as the 'rigidity' of the order information (in a competitive queuing model, this would be reflected in the gradient of the activation function). For instance, there is considerable disagreement as to whether milk should be added before or after tea is poured into a cup, suggesting that the order of these two actions is not rigidly fixed (see Humphreys & Forde, 1998). Whether milk is added before or after, then, may depend on how close the milk is to the cup, which will affect the magnitude of bottom-up activation favoring the response to the milk.

It is most natural to think of the bottom-up information, based on visual and semantic representations activated by objects, being much the same as that activated by the same objects presented in isolation. Of course, in everyday-life tasks objects will appear in contexts that can generate increased activation between related items. In addition, in complex tasks there can be top-down activation which could trigger an inappropriate action with an object in that context, even if the same object may be used appropriately when shown in isolation. In the section entitled Neuropsychological Disorders, later in the chapter, we consider further the relations between the visual and semantic information activated from single objects and that activated from objects in everyday-life contexts.

Executive Processes

When non-routine behaviors are carried out, it can be argued that qualitatively different processes are called upon, relative to when routine behaviors are effected. In the sponge cake example, it may be that new processes to do with conflict resolution are required to discriminate between appropriate and inappropriate component actions, over and above the competition between components that is involved in routine actions (see Figure 23.2). There may also be a requirement for novel inhibitory processes, for example to prevent an overlearned response being made when it is not part of the task, or to switch from a learned set of sequence of actions to enable a new component behavior to be introduced (e.g., making a cup of tea with lemon rather than milk). These additional, qualitatively different processes are often assigned the term 'executive functions,' consistent with their moderating activity in other information-processing systems (see Robbins, 1996).

Norman and Shallice (1986) suggested that non-routine behaviors make special call upon a 'supervisory attentional system' (SAS) that acts in an executive capacity, to modulate processing within a system responsible for routine actions (they term this latter system a 'contention scheduling system,' CSS). The CSS contains hierarchically-organized schema for action which are activated by stimuli in the environment (see the section entitled Bottom-Up Factors, above). Conflicting schemas compete for control, with the winning schema controlling activation of low-level routines that generate actions. In this framework, the SAS can excite or inhibit representations in the CSS that are normally activated by particular stimuli—so preventing those stimuli from generating routine actions when a novel response is required. The framework is illustrated in Figure 23.3.

The distinction between the SAS and the CSS mirrors the long-standing dichotomy in psychology between automatic and controlled processes (e.g., Schneider & Shiffrin, 1977; Shallice, 1994; Shiffrin & Schneider, 1977). Typically the distinction between automatic and controlled processes is defined in various ways based on factors such as: speed of operation (automatic processes being fast, controlled slow), whether processes are affected by voluntary control (automatic operations being difficult to control), whether they demand working memory capacity, and whether they are disrupted by secondary tasks (automatic processes being indifferent to secondary tasks). Here we might infer that routine behaviors are fast, difficult to control voluntarily, demand little working memory capacity, and are indifferent to secondary tasks. A strong argument for automaticity, though, is unlikely to hold; indeed we have suggested that the organization of even familiar sequential actions will make demands on the capacity of an action working memory, albeit that the demands are less than when a non-routine behavior is effected. Studies of patients with deficits in carrying out routine tasks also indicate that some errors arise because of a failure to maintain in working memory a goal representation for the task (see under the heading section Neuropsychological Disorders below). In addition, studies of the errors made by normal subjects in everyday action indicate effects of secondary task loads. In his diary studies Reason (1984) found that errors tended to occur under conditions in which subjects were involved in some form of secondary task—including thinking of some other event at the time. Thus errors arose under conditions in which "attention has been claimed by some internal preoccupation or by some external distraction" (Reason, 1984, p. 547). Of course, since the errors reported come from uncontrolled diary studies, it is possible that some of the actions were non-routine and so depended on attention-demanding executive processes. Humphreys, Forde, and Francis (in press), however, went on to manipulate the secondary task load when normal subjects carried out routine behaviors. They had subjects perform multi-step actions such as 'making a cup of tea,' when simultaneously conducting the 'trails test' (here subjects are given a letter and number to start and then have to recite aloud a changing letter-number sequence, as each is altered by 1 (e.g., 'C3', 'D4', 'E5', and so forth). Errors in routine

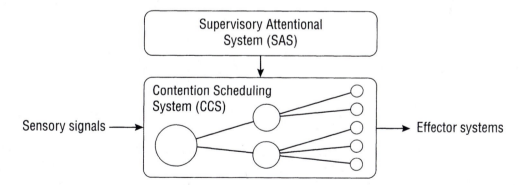

Figure 23.3: Outline of the Norman and Shallice (1986) framework which distinguishes a Contention Scheduling System (CCS) from a Supervisory Attentional System (SAS). Within this framework the CCS is thought to control routine actions, but it can be modulated by the SAS when novel actions are performed. Adapted from "Attention to Action: Willed and Automatic Control of Behavior," by D. Norman and T. Shallice, 1986. In R. Davidson, R. Schwartz, and D. Shapiro (Eds.), *Consciousness and Self-Regulation: Advances in Research and Theory,* Vol. 4., pp. 1–18. Copyright, 1986 by Plenum Press.

behaviors increased under conditions of secondary task load, with many errors co-incident with when subjects made errors on the secondary task—in particular, component actions were omitted when a subject made an error in reciting the letter-number sequence and then re-started the sequence from the point of error. This last result is consistent with Reason's contention that errors arise on routine actions when attention is diverted to another task. It is also relevant here to note that, in other studies of normal subjects performing everyday tasks, few omission errors have been found relative to other types of mistake (e.g., making actions out of sequence; see Schwartz et al., 1998). Hence secondary tasks not only generally increase errors on routine behaviors, they also induce particular types of errors that are otherwise rare. Both the diary and the secondary-task studies indicate that routine behaviors remain vulnerable to variations in attention.

Now the secondary task study of Humphreys et al. (in press) did point to one difference between controls and neuropsychological patients with problems in everyday life behaviors. This was that the controls frequently made 'hesitation' responses in which they reached towards an inappropriate object but then stopped and corrected their reach so that it was to an appropriate object. As we discuss below, many patients make similar mis-reaches but, instead of self-correcting, the patients often continue and make an overt error by picking up the wrong object. These hesitation responses indicate that normal subjects are able to monitor their behavior, in order to prevent potential errors arising. From this it might be thought that the patients have a deficit in one specific executive function: error monitoring (see also Hart, Giovannetti, Montgomery & Schwartz, 1998). However the interesting result with normal subjects was that the secondary task increased hesitations but it did not prevent error monitoring from occurring. This suggests that the secondary task did not specifically disrupt the executive process (error monitoring), though it did disrupt the ability to select only appropriate objects as targets for action (otherwise hesitation responses would not occur). In a framework such as that outlined in Figure 23.2, the ability to confine selection to appropriate objects may be contingent on the goal setting for the task, which constrains the activation of objects in a top-down manner. Secondary tasks may disrupt top-down control rather than error-monitoring per se. This could occur because secondary tasks compute with setting and maintaining the goal for everyday routine actions, perhaps because high-level goal states are themselves competitive. Competition at the goal-level is not shown in Figure 23.2.

There is thus some controversy over whether routine and non-routine tasks differ qualitatively in the nature of the processes that are brought to bear, or whether the differences are quantitative, with factors such as working memory load and competition between component actions simply being greater when non-routine behaviors are enacted. Our contention is that routine actions are not isolated from working memory or from competition for resources when multiple tasks operate.

NEUROPSYCHOLOGICAL DISORDERS

Disturbances in carrying out everyday tasks following brain damage could occur for a large number of reasons, some of which are not specific to the execution of multi-step tasks. This would be the case if impairments were due to a motor deficit, to poor object recognition, to spatial deficits in reaching, or to poor retrieval of stored actions associated with individual objects (as in cases of ideational apraxia; see De Renzi & Lucchelli, 1988; Liepmann, 1900; see also Buxbaum & Coslett, this volume). Our concern here is with deficits that arise in multi-step tasks which are not due to a motor impairment or to a deficit in recognition. Also, deficits in multi-step tasks can arise even though some patients perform well with single objects presented in isolation, though in other cases deficits in retrieving actions with single objects may be contributory.

Utilization Behavior

Problems in multi-step actions can be observed in patients exhibiting so-called 'utilization behavior' (Lhermitte, 1983), where actions to individual objects are intact but are made inappropriately in the context of a particular task. Thus patients may take a spoon and stir it in a cup if the cup and spoon are present in front of them, even if the task is to write a letter! In degenerate cases, utilization behavior may reduce to picking irrelevant objects up and putting them down without going through with the full action ('toying'; see Shallice, Burgess, Schon, & Baxter, 1989). Clearly the introduction of such irrelevant actions will disrupt performance in multi-step tasks. Utilization behavior appears to arise because there is poor task-based control of action, with actions then being triggered in an abnormally strong fashion by environmental cues.

Interestingly, in some cases there can be selective preservation of certain aspects of task-based control. Riddoch and colleagues (e.g., Humphreys & Riddoch, in press; Riddoch, Edwards, Humphreys, West, & Heafield, 1998; Riddoch, Humphreys, & Edwards, in press) have used simple laboratory tasks in which patients have to reach to objects placed on one side of their body using the hand aligned with the object (left hand to left-side object, right hand to right-side object). They used stimuli that had a strong familiar response that was either compatible or incompatible with the hand aligned with the object—cups, whose handle was either compatible with the required response (handle left for left-side object) or incompatible with the required response and compatible with the opposite-hand response (handle right for left-side object). They reported evidence from two patients, one with cortico-basal degeneration and one with bilateral frontal lobe damage, who found it difficult to follow this task instruction; both patients often responded with the hand compatible with the familiar rather than the task-based response (e.g., reaching with the right hand to a left-side cup with a handle on the right side). Hence the patients were unable to select the appropriate response when it was placed in competition with a response activated by the stimulus. The stimulus-based activation was shown to depend on both the visual properties of the object and its familiarity. For example, the incorrect responses were still triggered by a cup-like non-object made by joining two cylinders together, but they were reduced relative to when a real cup was used; they were also reduced when a real cup was turned upside down so that it was in an unfamiliar orientation (Riddoch et al., 1998).

Despite showing poor task-based response selection, the patients studied by Riddoch and colleagues were able to select the appropriate stimulus to respond to. There was appropriate selection of the stimulus even when distractors were present which should have evoked a stronger familiar response than the target object. Take the example of reaching to an upside down target cup, when an upright distractor cup was also present. The instruction might be: "reach to the red cup using the hand on the side where the cup is presented." Riddoch et al. (in press) reported that errors were not made by responding to the more familiar upright cup; rather responses were made to the target (the upside down cup), but they were sometimes made using the hand triggered by the target's handle rather than by the task instruction (e.g., using the right hand to reach to a left-side cup with its handle facing right). This shows that a process of *visual object selection*, based on task requirements, can be relatively preserved (the patient responds to the appropriate object) even when task-based *response selection* is severely impaired (the patient uses the inappropriate hand). From this we presume that the activation of component actions is contingent to some degree on earlier processes of object selection, so that actions are evoked primarily by selected objects and not by every object in the environment. This process of object selection provides one means of constraining bottom-up activation of actions. In some patients, utilization behavior can reflect impaired response selection after an object has been visually selected according to task requirements.

If object-based selection is preserved, one might wonder why patients showing utilization behavior use inappropriate objects sometimes, even when the objects fall outside the set usually employed in a task (e.g., reaching to stir a spoon in a cup when writing a letter). However it may be that object as well as action-selection is impaired in some patients. It may also be that there is visual selection of inappropriate objects sometimes by both normal subjects and patients alike; the difference is that patients with utilization behavior fail to control their response, so that they actually act to the object after it has been selected.

Action Disorganization Syndrome (ADS): Long-Term Knowledge of Actions

Not all patients who have impairments in performing routine tasks in everyday life show utilization behavior. Schwartz et al. (1995), for example, described a patient (JK) who did not show clinical signs of utilization behavior. Indeed, when presented with single tools JK was unable to show how they were used—this contrasts with patients showing utilization behavior, who may pick up and use a tool even when this is not relevant to the task! JK was able to use two tools together correctly, indicating that learned actions could be generated when strong associations were evoked by stimuli. However, he still failed on many tasks of everyday action. Thus when given the task of brushing his teeth JK placed shaving cream rather than toothpaste on the toothbrush on one occasion and on another occasion he wet a razor and went to brush his teeth with this (fortunately being stopped by the therapist before his carried out the action!). In such a case it appears that, even though a patient is not drawn to act inappropriately under all circumstances, there are aspects of multi-step tasks that can elicit inappropriate behavior. The term 'action disorganization syndrome' (ADS) was introduced by Schwartz (1995) to describe deficits in routine multi-step actions of this form, that are cognitive in nature and not due to motor incapacity. Patients are diagnosed with ADS because their problems on everyday-life tasks are beyond the level found with control subjects. The deficit should not simply be motor in nature, and it should not be consequent on impaired object recognition.

In an attempt to evaluate why patients can have specific problems on routine tasks, Schwartz and colleagues (e.g., Schwartz, Mayer, Fitzpatrick, & Montgomery, 1993; Schwartz, Reed, Montgomery, Palmer, & Mayer, 1991; Schwartz, 1995) introduced an 'action coding scheme' (ACS) in which unitary, component acts are labelled and interrelated. The component acts are called A-1s. Examples are: place a teabag in a teapot, and pour from a kettle into the teapot (see Figure 23.2). Normally, the consecutive component acts that we generate can all be linked into a group of actions: an A-2. In our example, the A-2 action could be termed 'prepare tea in the teapot.' Tasks can then be described in terms of a hierarchical relationship between A-1 and A-2 behaviors, with one essential property of organized behavior being that consecutive A-1 actions are not drawn from different A-2 behaviors unless there has been completion of an A-2 behavior. Referring to Figure 23.2, the teabag → teapot A-1 action should not be followed by the milk à cup A-1 action, since these belong to different A-2 behaviors ('prepare tea in teapot' and 'prepare cup for tea') and the first A-2 behavior ('prepare the teapot') has not been completed before the A-1 action linked with the next A-2 behavior is initiated ('prepare cup for tea'). Schwartz and colleagues reported that, unlike normal subjects, ADS patients make many errors in which they carry out consecutive A-1 behaviors which cannot be assigned to a common A-2 group. Instead, basic-level A-1 behaviors are elicited in a somewhat fragmentary manner. Scoring behavior in terms of A-1 and A-2 actions can provide a means of analysis that does not depend on a normative model of task performance, since A-2 actions can be described from the behavioral protocols of patients.

However, given that normal subjects perform routine tasks in relatively stereotyped ways, it is also possible to score performance in relation to normative schemas for tasks (e.g., Buxbaum, Schwartz, & Montgomery, 1998; Humphreys & Forde, 1998; Schwartz et al. 1998). Humphreys and Forde (1998), for example, documented 2 ADS patients who made far more errors than non brain-damaged subjects when carrying out everyday life tasks, and who were worse also than 'control' patients, chosen to have some of the ancillary deficits found in the ADS subjects. In particular, the 'control' patients were matched to the ADS patients in terms of their performance on some tests of 'executive function' (e.g., the ability to inhibit an over-learned response, as measured in the Stroop color-word naming task) and in terms of their ability to recall information in episodic information. Since the ADS patients fared worse than the 'control' patients, it would appear that neither impaired executive functions, nor impaired episodic recall, are alone able to explain the deficits in routine tasks.

There are a variety of errors typically made by ADS patients on everyday actions. These include: omissions of steps, additions, perseverations, object substitutions (e.g., using a razor as a toothbrush; Schwartz et al., 1995), and spatial/quality errors (e.g., using a tool in the wrong spatial plane; see Figure 23.1). Though some of these errors are occasionally seen in normal subjects performing free of secondary task loads, at least two are seen relatively rarely: 'flagrant' object substitutions and omissions. These two error types may reflect some qualitative shift in the behavior of the ADS patients, relative to controls, and hence we consider them in further detail.

One interesting aspect of flagrant object substitutions is that they can arise in some patients who appear to have good semantic knowledge of individual objects. Buxbaum, Schwartz, and Carew (1997) and Forde and Humphreys (in press) have both documented patients who could name visually presented objects and who could use individual objects appropriately. Forde and Humphreys showed this even when using the same objects as those incorporated into the everyday action tasks. Despite this good semantic knowledge of objects, though, both patients made object substitution errors in action use. Our patient, HG, both named and used objects such as a toothbrush and a teapot correctly when presented with them individually, but he used a toothbrush as a shaving brush and he drank directly from the teapot when engaged in multistep tasks.

To conceptualize such problems, we emphasize the distinction between representations for basic-level actions (the 'component action units' in Figure 23.2) and representations within the semantic system generated by individual objects (the 'object representations' in Figure 23.2). In the patients described above (Buxbaum et al., 1997; Forde & Humphreys, in press), activation within the semantic system appears to be intact, given their good usage of single objects. Hence we suggest that 'object representations' would be activated normally, in a bottom-up manner. The object selection errors in everyday tasks, then, may arise because connections between the component action units and object representations are damaged. This may make component actions to some objects vulnerable to competition from other objects that are semantically associated and/or visually appropriate for the action, so that the action becomes linked to the incorrect object. Normally it may be the case that linkage between object representations in semantic system and the representations of basic-level component actions help bias competition to favor actions being performed with appropriate objects. In addition, object substitution errors may be a consequence of impaired top-down activation of component actions or of impairments to the component actions themselves. If the component actions are not specified fully from stored knowledge, then actions may be generated to objects that are partially associated with the appropriate behavior even if they are not necessarily the usual objects for the task. An analogy can be drawn here with how we might behave in a non-routine task—our example being 'making a sponge cake.' This task requires that flour be 'folded' into a mixture of sugar and eggs, after the eggs and sugar have been whisked together. A fork might be used for whisking and a spoon for folding. However, when the task is non-routine an 'object substitution' error might be made by using the fork rather than the spoon to fold the flour into the mixture, perhaps because the fork 'affords' the folding action or perhaps because it is already associated with the whisking part of the routine. In this instance, there will be partial activation of the component action of 'folding' from the fork, and this might be sufficient to produce an object substitution error when there is damage to the action-selection process. Nevertheless, given the fork in isolation, we would probably use it correctly. Our point is that object substitutions could reflect poor task-specification of component actions.

For normal subjects, omission errors arise under conditions of dual-task load, but are not prevalent otherwise (Schwartz et al., 1998; though see Humphreys & Forde, 1998; Rusted & Sheppard, 2000, for evidence of some omissions). One effect of the dual task here may be to reduce top-down activation of the component actions, so that a particular component may be omitted as the sequence unfolds. Additionally secondary tasks may increase noise in the activations assigned to component actions.[1] Omissions in the production of learned sequences have been simulated in competitive queuing models when noise is added to the activation functions for the output units (e.g., Houghton et al., 1994). In patients showing aspects of ADS, we may attribute omission errors to the same cause (see also Schwartz et al., 1991, for similar suggestions).

The above argument for ADS being linked to impaired use of learned action routines is indirect. More direct evidence was reported by Humphreys and Forde (1998), who found effects on performance of the number of steps making up a task. The number of errors made by ADS patients increased in tasks with more component actions, and errors were more likely to occur on steps in the later half of a given task. This effect of the position of the action in the sequence can be found even when performance is measured contingent on the last action being correct, so that effects are not simply due to there being a mounting number of errors as patients stray further from a task (Humphreys, Forde, & Francis, in preparation; see also Rusted & Sheppard, 2000). This pattern of performance, however, is consistent with either (a) a natural tendency for errors to arise towards the end of sequential behaviors due to decreases in an activation gradient that defines output order, or (b) a decaying trace for the goal state, so that end components are less well specified.

In addition to the object substitution and omission errors found in ADS, the perseverative errors found in these patients are also of considerable interest. Humphreys and Forde (1998) reported a dissociation between the temporal characteristics of perseverations in the two patients they studied: One patient made many immediate perseverations and relatively few 'delayed' perseverations which involved the repetition of actions completed some time before; the other patient made few immediate and many delayed perseverations. An example of an immediate perseveration here would be continued cutting of wrapping paper in a task such as wrapping a present; a delayed perseveration would involve going back to add more tea to the pot after having earlier put tea in the pot and poured water onto it. Humphreys and Forde (1998) suggest that this dissociation indicates that there are separate mechanisms that prevent the repetition of immediate and delayed actions. Using the framework of a competitive queuing model (Figure 23.2), they argue that immediate perseverations are prevented by the process of 'rebound inhibition,' while delayed perseverations are prevented by an activation gradient; this gradient enables the current action to maintain a higher state of excitation than that achieved by other actions that, having been produced, have their representations re-set to baseline. It is possible that each process could be selectively damaged, to produce contrasting patterns of error in different patients.[2] Rusted and Sheppard (2000) studied everyday actions in patients with Alzheimer's Disease (AD). They noted that perseverations were more likely to be made

---

[1] Increased noise might arise if the level of noise in the system were affected in some general way by dual task loads; or increased noise may be a consequence of reduced top-down activation.

[2] It is conceivable that damage to the activation gradient alone could generate increased numbers of immediate perseveration response. However, if there is damage to a single process it is difficult to account for dissociatons between patients, with one patient showing fewer immediate and more delayed perseverations than another, across a range of tasks. For instance, if the patient showing delayed perseverations had simply sustained more damage to the activation gradient then more immediate perseverations should also be found. To generate a dissociation with a single mechanism (e.g., the activation gradient), then damage would have to produce the same non-arbitrary changes across a range of activation gradients for different tasks, which is not plausible.

when the patients had the objects in front of them and were performing the tasks relative to when they were simply describing the steps in the task. Perseverations seem particularly likely to occur when the objects present cue already-completed actions, with this bottom-up activation then competing with top-down activation imposed by an activation gradient.

Humphreys and Forde (1998) also examined the stored knowledge of ADS patients for routine actions by having patients recall the sequence of actions verbally, sort cards with a component action written on each, or sort photographs of an actor carrying out each component action. They found that the ADS patients were impaired on all of these tasks. On the other hand, the patients could sequence other learned sequences relatively well (e.g., a number series) and one could also sequence stimuli on the basis of perceptual differences (Humphreys, Forde, & Francis, in preparation). These data are consistent with these patients having impaired long-term knowledge of routine behaviors (see also Rusted & Sheppard, 2000, for a similar finding), in addition to any problems in maintaining that knowledge in action working memory while the task is being performed. It is of further interest that one of the patients studied by Humphreys and Forde had good semantic knowledge about individual objects (Forde & Humphreys, in press). This is consistent with the proposal that long-term knowledge of component actions in multi-step tasks can dissociate from semantic knowledge of individual objects. This dissociation fits with the distinction in Figure 23.2 between units for basic-level actions and units activated bottom-up by individual objects. The units for basic-level actions are sensitive to long-term knowledge about the component actions, and their order in tasks, where this knowledge is imposed by the activation gradient. This gradient is in turn generated according to the weights on connections between the action units and the goal unit for a given task. Activation in the units for object-representations, in contrast, is sensitive to stored visual and semantic knowledge about individual objects.

Resource Deficits and Other Procedures for Action, in ADS

Schwartz and colleagues (1998; Buxbaum et al., 1998) have gone on to explore behavior not just on routine tasks performed in isolation, but also when tasks must be performed in more complex situations. For example, patients may be asked to carry out the tasks when distractors are present; they may be given the objects for two separate tasks and asked to perform them in any order; they may be given the objects for two tasks with a limited amount of material (e.g., two 'wrapping' tasks with a set amount of wrapping paper), so they must plan to make sure that the material is used for both tasks. Under all of these conditions the performance of the patients can worsen, and there can also be a differential impact on some patients relative to controls. Thus some patients who present with very few errors on single tasks begin to make disproportionate numbers of errors in the more difficult task conditions. Also, some of the classes of error that characterize ADS, such as omissions, begin to be made under the more difficult task conditions (Schwartz et al., 1998).

Now, since such patients can complete routine tasks performed in isolation, it is difficult to argue that their deficit is due to loss of stored representations for the tasks. There must be some other cause of the deficit. Schwartz et al. argue that the deficits can arise because patients have reduced processing resources, which are needed to enable them to inter-relate two tasks together or to avoid actions when related distractors are present and so forth. Buxbaum et al. (1998) further point out that, in group studies, patients with right hemisphere lesions tend to perform worse than both left hemisphere lesioned patients and patients with more diffuse brain damage following closed head injury. This is consistent with right hemisphere lesions reducing the arousal levels of patients (Posner, Inhoff, & Cohen, 1987; Robertson, 1993) and consequently limiting the resources available for performance.

The exact nature of the resources involved, and how they affect routine multi-step tasks, was not defined by Schwartz and colleagues. Clearly this is a problem if we are aiming to generate explicit models of task performance. On other hand, the general pattern of the data fits with the idea that patients are unable to maintain adequate working memory representations of the tasks, when representations have to be maintained for several tasks at once, and when competition for action from distractors must be over-ruled. This would lead to an impairment in imposing stored knowledge on both component actions and their ordering, even when the basic stored knowledge itself is not impaired. A general 'resource deficit' may be re-described in terms of a limited ability to represent actions in working memory.

Forde and Humphreys (in press) also varied the conditions under which everyday life tasks were conducted, but in attempt to improve the performance of ADS patients. They examined a variety of conditions including: having the patient read through the full set of actions before the task; having the patient follow a written instruction for each component action before the action; having the patient copy the whole task as performed by the examiner; having the patient copy half the steps in each task, followed by the other half. They found that performance was little improved in the written instructions conditions, even though the patients did then not have to rely on stored knowledge to complete the tasks. However since there were extra switching costs involved in moving between the reading and the action tasks, this could have worsened performance. In contrast to performance with written instructions, the tasks were improved in the copying condition, especially when the memory load was relatively small (with the two half-task presentations). They suggest that this improvement in the copying condition may be due to patients using neural circuitary that by-passes the working memory representations normally supporting performance but which may be impaired in ADS—for instance, copying may be dependent on so-called 'mirror neurons' that directly translate seen gestures into motor actions (see Gallese, Fadiga, Fogassi, & Rizzolatti, 1996). These mirror neurons may be independent of action working memory.

Fractionating Working Memory

In addition to investigating performance on everyday tasks, Humphreys and Forde (1998) also introduced a novel procedure for examining how working memory interfaces with action. Rather than have patients recall the task from long-term memory (as when they complete routine behaviors), Humphreys and Forde had patients carry out tasks based on new instructions held in immediate memory. Patients were presented with a set of objects and instructions to act with two of the objects present. The instructions could require a 'standard' (familiar) action between the objects ('pour from the teapot into the cup') or a novel action that was at odds with the standard application of the verb to the objects present ('pour from the cup into the teapot'). Humphreys and Forde reported that (a) patients made more errors on the novel action than on the standard-action tasks; (b) the majority of errors on the novel action tasks were due to (inappropriate) production of the standard action; and (c) the standard action errors arose even on trials where the patients were able to repeat back the command. Apparently good maintenance of information in verbal working memory was not sufficient for the instructions to override the standard use of the objects, in the novel action task.

The relations between standard-action errors and working memory were examined in further detail by Humphreys et al. (in press). They varied the number of instructions given to patients on a trial (from 1 to 4). Perhaps not surprisingly, they found that performance deteriorated as the instruction set increased. More interestingly, the likelihood that a standard–action error arose on an incorrect trial increased when the patients had to remember more instructions. This occurred despite the patients again being able to verbally repeat back the instructions on many trials.

These results indicate a dissociation between verbal working memory and a system that applies the instructions to action: Verbal working memory can be relatively intact even when the system that applies the instruction to action is impaired (action working memory). Moreover the system that applies the instructions to actions tends to be overruled by familiar actions activated in a bottom-up manner from the objects present and perhaps also from some parts of the instruction set (the verb), and this is more likely to occur when there is an increased working memory load (with more instructions). We suggest that patients can lack the information in action working memory to overrule activation driven bottom-up from the stimuli, so that 'standard' action errors result.

The dissociation between good verbal report and impaired action in these novel instruction tasks mirrors dissociations that can be observed when patients perform everyday life tasks. For example, the patient documented by Forde and Humphreys (in press), HG, made many errors by perseverating with actions. In some instances, HG remarked that he was making an error, yet this was disconnected from his actions, which continued. Thus when wrapping a present HG perseverated on cutting the wrapping paper until the paper became smaller than the present. He noted that "this paper is too small," but nevertheless proceeded to cut the paper to be even smaller! In this example, verbal error monitoring takes place but still fails to interrupt the bottom cue to action (cutting the paper again, with the scissors).

Such dissociations between verbal knowledge and action can be related to the argument of Kimberg and Farah (1993) considered in the section on the multi-step tasks, above, that patients can have selective damage to the connections between elements in working memory. On our account damage to an 'action working memory,' as outlined in Figure 23.2, disrupts links to verbal working memory and even to procedures of verbal error monitoring. The consequence is that patients show impaired actions to novel verbal instructions while being concurrently able to repeat the instructions and to verbally monitor their actions. The same action working memory could also mediate the temporary representation of learned actions, required in order to effect actions over time, in the correct sequence.

In one other manipulation carried out by Humphreys et al. (in press), the patients were required to act out the novel instructions to cards with the names of objects written on them, rather than acting to the objects themselves. For example, given the instruction *pour from the teapot into the cup*, patients were supposed to pick up the card saying *teapot* and to use it in a pouring action over the card saying *cup*. The patients were able to read the words on the cards. Humphreys et al. found that the patients performed better with cards than with objects, and they were better able to abstain from making 'standard action' errors in the card condition (picking up the card saying *cup* and making a pouring action over the card saying *teapot*). This is interesting because the task is more 'abstract' when performed with cards. The fact that performance improved suggests that the novel task is not difficult because of its abstract nature but rather because the instructions must be used to overrule actions cued from the environment, and the patients find it difficult to do this. The cueing of actions is stronger from objects than from words—either because of a direct route from vision to action and/or because objects have facilitated access to semantic information relative to words (see section early in the chapter under the heading The Process Involved in Carrying Out Multi-Step Tasks).

The Effects of Semantic Impairments on Action

We have noted that patients can have marked impairments in everyday actions despite having intact semantic knowledge about individual objects (Buxbaum et al., 1997; Forde & Humphreys, in press). There is also evidence that actions can be made to objects even when patients have impaired semantic knowledge. In the syndrome of optic aphasia, patients show impaired naming of visually presented objects and they can also be impaired at making semantic judgements from vision (e.g., point to the two objects that are used together: hammer, nail, screwdriver; see Hillis & Caramazza, 1995; Riddoch & Humphreys, 1987). Despite this, such patients can produce relatively good gestures to visually presented objects. This dissociation between impaired visual recognition and relatively preserved gestures is consistent with there being a direct route to action that by-passes semantic knowledge about inter-object associations and context (see on multi-step tasks, above).

This maintenance of action in the face of impoverished semantic knowledge can also be observed in 'semantic dementia.' Semantic dementia refers to a degenerative disorder that affects the expression and reception of conceptual knowledge, although many other aspects of behavior can be preserved (e.g., Hodges, Patterson, Oxbury, & Funnell, 1992; Snowden, Goulding, & Neary, 1989). One aspect of preserved behavior can be the performance of actions, especially when objects are both seen and held. Lauro-Grotto, Piccini, and Shallice (1997) interpreted this pattern of maintained performance on everyday life tasks in terms of their patient having preservation of a specific form of semantic knowledge—visual semantic knowledge—that can be disconnected from forms of semantic knowledge accessed from verbal material. Indeed their patient performed poorly on associative matching tasks with verbal material and fared some-what better with pictorial material. However, Hodges, Spatt, and Patterson (1999) documented two semantic dementia patients who, despite showing good completion of everyday life tasks, were severely impaired at making associative match judgements from vision (see also Buxbaum & Schwartz, 1997, for a similar result). The semantic dementia patients reported by Hodges et al. (1999) were not only able to perform routine multi-step tasks but also successfully com-pleted a 'novel tool' task, which required judgements about which of three novel tools to use with a pictured object. This last result suggests that the preserved performance in these patients may not simply be because stored action knowledge is spared, but also because there are direct visuo-motor associations between parts of objects and action (see section on multi-step tasks, above). Note that such visuo-motor associations seem still to operate even when associative semantic knowledge about objects is degenerate.

Neural Substrates of Everyday Action

Buxbaum et al. (1998) and Schwartz et al. (1998) have reported group studies of patients with impairments in routine action, including patients with unilateral right or left brain damage, plus also patients with closed head injury. They found few qualitative differences between the patients, even though impairments with single object usage are typically associated with left hemisphere damage (Liepmann, 1900); indeed, as we have already pointed out, patients with right-hemisphere lesions tended to more impaired than the other groups. Since the patients with left-hemisphere damage were no worse than the other groups, we can conclude that impairments in retrieving stored actions for single objects are not the sole cause of deficits on routine multi-step tasks (see also Buxbaum et al., 1998). Though such impairments should disrupt routine tasks, other deficits linked to impoverished stored knowledge or to poor imple-mentation of stored knowledge in action are also likely to be important (see sections on ADS, resource deficits, and fractionating working memory above). These other deficits may be found after right as well as left-hemisphere damage.

At least some of the errors that can contribute to poor everyday life activity are associated with damage to the frontal lobes—utilization behaviors being the clearest examples (Lhermitte, 1983). It can also be argued that impairments to 'executive functions,' due to frontal lobe lesions, should be a necessary component of ADS. Schwartz (1995), for instance, proposed that even if stored knowledge of routine actions is impaired, patients should be able to complete many tasks using novel, problem solving strategies. Such problem solving strategies are linked to activation in frontal lobe structures in studies of functional brain imaging (Owen, Doyon, Petrides, & Evans, 1996; Owen, Evans, & Petrides, 1996). Patients with frontal-lobe lesions can have deficits in executive, problem-solving processes and still complete routine everyday life behaviors (Humphreys & Forde, 1998), though some deficits can be encountered when diffi-culty is increased by requiring multiple tasks to be completed together (Schwartz et al., 1998). From this it appears that executive impairments are not sufficient to produce the deficits found in more severe cases of ADS, though they may well be contributory. Consistent with this last point, Schwartz et al (1998) did find that clinical measures of some 'executive functions' (e.g., the ability to override overlearned responses in the Stroop task) predicted the number of errors on everyday tasks made by their head injured patients (with measures of clinical severity per se partialled out). However, a measure of neurological damage within the frontal lobes did not predict degree of deficit, so any conclusions on the necessary involvement of frontal damage need to remain tentative. At least in part this may be because ADS can be caused by a number of factors, including loss of action knowledge about individual objects (see Buxbaum et al., 1998, for evidence of this in a patient without deficits on several tests of 'executive function').

If executive deficits, associated with frontal lobe lesions contribute to but are not alone sufficient to produce severe ADS, what other factors (and lesions) may be important? We have argued above that ADS can be linked to deficient stored knowledge of routine actions and/or to impaired imposition of this knowledge on behavior (e.g., due to impoverished working memory for action). Disorders of stored knowledge for multi-step actions can also be linked to frontal lobe damage. Sirigu et al. (1995, 1996) have shown that patients can have difficulties in retrieving various forms of action-schema after frontal lobe damage. Non-brain damaged controls and patients with either frontal or more posterior lesions were asked to generate scripts for either routine, non-routine, or novel actions. These could include tasks such as 'going to work' (routine), 'going to Mexico' (non-routine), and 'opening a beauty salon' (novel). They found that patients with frontal lobe lesions tended to close the scripts too early and they made more sequence errors in the scripts. Frontal lobe patients also made more sequence errors when they were re-presented with the scripts they had generated and had to put the component actions in the appropriate sequence. Sirigu et al. (1995) interpreted their results in terms of frontal-lobe damage producing a 'syntactic' deficit in specifying the temporal relations between events. In contrast, they concluded that the basic 'semantic' knowledge of the component actions was relatively intact. In their 1996 study, however, patients had not only to arrange component actions in the correct sequence but also to exclude in each sequence related and unrelated distractor actions that were presented along with the correct actions. The frontal lobe patients now not only made more sequence errors but also more 'boundary violations' (including both related and unrelated actions from other scripts in a given sequence). This last result is consistent with knowledge of the component actions as well as 'syntactic' knowledge of action sequences being stored within the frontal lobes.

The retrieval of action schema has been studied using functional imaging techniques by Partiot, Grafman, Sadata, Flitman, & Wild. (1996). Subjects took part in 3 main conditions in which they had to verify if: (a) two actions belonged to the same action schema (e.g., do 'say hello' and 'open the door' both belong to the schema for 'talking'?); (b) two events belonged to the same schema (e.g., do 'go to church' and 'put on your swimsuit' belong to the schema 'go to a wedding'?); and (c) two events were presented in the correct order for a schema (e.g., 'pay the bill,' 'receive the menu'). They found activation in the left frontal and temporal lobes when actions and events had to be verified, and activation in the right frontal and temporal lobes (as well as the left temporal lobe) when the event orders had to be verified. Partiot et al. suggest that knowledge for events and actions in schema may be represented separately from knowledge for temporal order, in the left and right hemispheres respectively. To date, cases of ADS have not demonstrated dissociations between knowledge for component actions and knowledge for the ordering of the actions, even though patients with unilateral left or right hemisphere damage have been studied (Buxbaum et al., 1998; Humphreys & Forde, 1998). Nevertheless it may well be that finer-grained analysis may show that these two forms of knowledge can dissociate, perhaps leading to contrasting forms of ADS.

In addition to being linked to deficits in long-term knowledge about action schema, frontal lobe structures are known to mediate working memory—as evidenced by studies with primates

(Goldman-Rakic, 1992) and investigations using functional imaging (Owen, Doyon, 1996; Owen, Evans, et al., 1996). We have suggested that aspects of ADS are due to impaired top-down imposition of action schema through working memory, and we speculate that frontal lobe damage may be important in such instances. To assess this, more extensive studies need to be undertaken, linking site of damage to specific working memory deficits in ADS patients.

In contrast to patients with ADS, patients with semantic dementia show relatively preserved routine behaviors, even in the face of substantial losses of semantic knowledge about individual objects (Buxbaum et al., 1997; Hodges et al., 1999). This last group of patients typically have damage to the temporal lobes, while the frontal and parietal lobes can be relatively spared (see Hodges et al., 1999). From this it is tempting to conclude that performance in everyday actions can be supported by pathways through the dorsal cortex, based on connections between the parietal and frontal lobes. Hodges et al., for example, propose that such pathways provide a form of 'pragmatic' route for action, in which visual affordances may be linked to motor responses. Recent PET data from Phillips, Humphreys, and Price (2000) support this notion. They measured activation when subjects judged how they would act to a stimulus, relative to a baseline condition in which size judgements were made. They found significant activation in posterior parietal cortex, bilaterally, for action judgements to objects (see also Martin et al., 1995). Interestingly, this region was not activated for action judgements to words (when activations in size judgements were subtracted). Apparently this region mediates action retrieval from objects rather than words, consistent with a direct route to action from vision operating via dorsal visual pathways.

Electrophysiological studies of cells in the parietal cortex are consistent with this argument for direct visuo-motor interactions. Taira, Mine, Georgopoulos, Murata, & Sakata (1991) reported cells in the parietal cortex that fired when particular objects were associated with particular actions, suggesting that these cells mediate object-action coupling. Sakata and colleagues (e.g., Sakata et al., 1998) also report that cells in the parietal cortex code objects in particular orientations, which will generate different patterns of hand actions in the animals.

We conclude that ADS is likely to follow from damage to several sites. Damage to the frontal lobes may impair long-term knowledge for action schema, and it is possible that contrasting effects of left and right hemisphere damage may emerge on knowledge of component actions and knowledge of their order. Frontal lobe damage can also be important for at least two other reasons. First, it may disrupt the influence of stored knowledge on multi-step behaviors by impairing working memory for action. Second, it can impair 'executive' processes of problem-solving, which could otherwise support actions even when long-term object knowledge is damaged. Damage to more posterior regions, including the posterior parietal lobe, may also be important in ADS if this region modulates both stored knowledge of individual actions to objects (De Renzi & Lucchelli, 1988; Liepmann, 1900) and the direct transmission of visual information to action.

OTHER ACCOUNTS

Perhaps due to the complexity of the processes involved even in routine everyday life tasks, there is as yet no consensus view of why we can observe the full variety of behavioral disturbances apparent in patients. We have suggested that aspects of ADS can be attributed to: (a) impaired long-term knowledge of action schema; (b) impaired implementation of that knowledge, due to poor maintenance of the task in action working memory; (c) impaired knowledge of actions for individual objects (as in cases of 'ideational apraxia'; De Renzi & Lucchelli, 1988; Liepmann, 1900). Studies in which patients follow instructions to complete novel actions (see section on fractionating working memory, above) further indicate that different aspects of working memory can fractionate; patients can maintain good verbal memory representations but fail to implement these instructions within a form of representation that can be used for action (Humphreys & Forde, 1998; Humphreys et al., in press). We have noted that this last result can be linked to the proposal of Kimberg and Farah (1993) that neural damage can disrupt associations between elements in working memory. We have also discussed the results in terms of a 'competitive queuing' framework for the production of sequential actions (Figure 23.2). In this framework, stored knowledge of action is used to impose an activation gradient in an action working memory, to ensure that the appropriate component actions are produced in the correct temporal order. We suggest that some of the characteristics of ADS, such as the worsening of performance towards the end of tasks and the different types of perseverative errors that can be observed, can be understood in terms of such a framework.

There are, however, several other accounts that can be used to help explain cognitive disorders of everyday action. For instance, Cohen and colleagues (e.g., Cohen, Braver, & O'Reilly, 1996) have attempted to model frontal-lobe control over learned behavior by means of a context-processing system. This system operates in a top-down manner to modulate processing in other information processing structures concerned with pattern recognition and the activation of associated responses, when a new task demands that learned stimulus-response associations are irrelevant. Similar ideas are also incorporated into the Norman and Shallice (1986) framework (Figure 23.3), in which a system for implementing novel behaviors (the SAS) is used to modulate processing in a system determined by learned actions (the CCS). Within both the Cohen et al. and the Norman and Shallice accounts, however, it is not clear whether multi-step everyday actions would be thought to be moderated by the context sensitive system/SAS, or whether they could operate purely on the basis of learned knowledge. We suggest, however, that there would be a need for working memory maintenance of representations even when routine multi-step tasks are carried out.

Cooper and Shallice (Cooper, in press; Cooper & Shallice, 2000) have attempted to model ADS in terms of damage to the CCS, which, in their view, has the capability of performing routine behaviors. Their simulations were based around activation in 3 separate networks: a schema network (the CCS), an object representation network and a resource network. The resource network contained units for the effectors available (e.g., units for the left and right hands). The object representation network contained units that were activated by the presence of objects in the environment, with units representing the functional role of objects. In this network the same object could have several representations for its different roles, as the 'source,' 'target,' or 'implement' of an action. A coffee mug could be a source (of coffee), a target (reach for the mug) or an implement (drink with the coffee cup). These different forms of representation for particular objects would map onto different actions in the schema (CCS) network. Within this network, actions are hierarchically organized. For example the schema 'add sugar to the coffee mug' would have 4 components: pick up teaspoon; dip teaspoon into sugar bowl; empty teaspoon into coffee mug; discard teaspoon. The lowest level of schema in the CCS correspond to basic level actions, each with a corresponding motor response. Schema can be activated in a bottom-up or top-down fashion, for example from the objects present, from a resource being in a particular configuration or from instructions, and activation of the schema will in turn flow back to the object and resource networks. The basic level actions would be activated when specific arguments are upheld: the correct objects are present, the top-down schema set in place, and the required resource is free. In addition, within each network units are competitive, so limiting the output of any two actions at a time. Actions are produced in the correct sequential order because (a) a higher-order schema may activate lower-level schema sequentially, by setting specific pre-conditions, and (b) the configurations of objects in the environment will change as a task evolves, so that only certain basic level actions can be triggered (have their pre-conditions met).

There are many aspects of this model that link to the framework that we have used here to discuss everyday life tasks. For example, performance is controlled by a basic level of action, which is abstracted above that of specific motor responses. The selection of basic level actions depends upon top-down as well as bottom-up factors, and continued dominance of one basic level action over another will require that the appropriate higher-level schema remains activated. This can be linked to our argument that a goal state needs to be maintained in action working memory (though in the Norman & Shallice, 1986, framework, working memory is likely to be conceptualized in terms of the SAS). Also once an action is completed a schema will be 'deselected' (e.g., by higher-level schema inhibiting component schema that have been completed). The net effect of this deselection process may be similar to that of 'rebound inhibition' in a competitive queuing model, so that bias is set against recent actions. Whether additional processes are required to capture the dissociations between different forms of perseverations in patients is not clear (cf. Humphreys & Forde, 1998). The model can also explain how patients can have good semantic representations for individual objects and yet still make object substitution errors, if activation from schema flows back to alter activation in the object representations network (cf. Buxbaum et al., 1997; Forde & Humphreys, in press). Note, however, that effects of incorrect feedback might be expected even when actions are not required, due to activation of schema from the object network. Against this Forde and Humphreys found that their patient had intact gesturing for objects even when they were presented along with the other objects for a task. This suggests that object substitutions are only generated within the context of a task, consistent with the activation of object representations for action being disconnected from semantic representations mediating object recognition (see section on ADS earlier in the chapter).

One advantage of the Cooper and Shallice account over others currently being offered is that it does allow for there to be multiple levels of hierarchy in object representations. In contrast, the framework of competitive queuing (Figure 23.2) has been typically been explored using only two levels (e.g., the goal level and the component-actions level). These multiple levels of representation may be useful for explaining features of behavior such as the clustering of component actions together. A disadvantage is the seeming complexity of the model—for instance, its use of specific argument structures, triggered by only the appropriate preconditions, all of which has to be pre-specified since representations in the model are established by the experimenters rather than by learning. In models using a competitive queuing approach the order in which actions are produced can be learned, and new orders established between some of the same component actions (cf. Houghton, 1990). Also, clustering of actions together could also emerge even if there is no hierarchical organization between the goal unit for the whole task and the component units of the task, due to co-occurrence of particular component actions together.

Yet another approach to understanding disorders of everyday action can be formulated in terms of a framework suggested by Grafman (1995). He has argued that complex sequential behaviors are based on memories organized into 'structured event complexes' (at the lowest level) and 'managerial knowledge units' (at higher-levels of representation). Structured event complexes are said to store sequences of events or actions for particular tasks (e.g., how to use implements in cooking). Several structured event complexes can become associated together to form a managerial knowledge unit, and managerial knowledge units can themselves exist at different levels of abstraction. At the highest level of abstraction managerial knowledge units are context-free (e.g., there might be a high-level unit for eating in expensive restaurants), and at lower levels they become more context-bound (e.g., eating in a particular French restaurant), and able to direct action. The higher level units link behaviors across larger time scales and are thought to be represented in frontal cortices.

This account does not distinguish between executive and routine behaviors in a qualitative fashion; it is simply the case that less routine behaviors would tend to activate only higher-level schemas without appropriate lower-level schemas being activated to support behavior (since the specific context would not have been encountered before). Less routine behaviors should thus be performed less well and they should be more dependent on frontal-lobe structures (and more vulnerable to frontal lobe damage). However, the account is less clear on how managerial knowledge units act to determine the temporal order as well as the component actions in a task, or how disorders of routine action would emerge at a microgenetic level when the knowledge systems are damaged. For example, associated knowledge units could code temporal order implicitly, by having one representation 'chained' to the other (so activation of one is contingent on completion of the first). As pointed out by Lashley (1951), however, a chaining account alone is unlikely to be able to account for the errors that frequent human behavior in serial tasks. For example, a chaining account of routine behavior would hold that a task should cease once a component step is omitted, since the component would not then cue the next action; instead of this patients showing ADS can omit steps and still proceed with subsequent component actions. We suggest that firm conclusions concerning the best theoretical approach will await further research, in which the processes involved in routine multi-step tasks are evaluated in greater detail, in both pathology and normality.

Acknowledgements

This work was supported by grants to the first and third authors from the Medical Research Council, the Wellcome Trust, and the Stroke Association.

REFERENCES

Anderson, J. R. (1993). *Rules of the mind.* Hillsdale, NJ: Lawrence Erlbaum.

Baddeley, A. D. (1986). *Working memory.* Oxford, UK: Oxford University Press.

Burgess, N., & Hitch, G. J. (1992). Toward a network model of the articulatory loop. *Journal of Memory and Language, 31,* 313–348.

Burgess, N., & Hitch, G. J. (1999). Memory for serial order: A network model of the phonological loop and its timing. *Psychological Review, 106,* 551–581.

Buxbaum, L. J., Schwartz, M. F., & Carew, T. G. (1997). The role of semantic memory in object use. *Cognitive Neuropsychology, 14,* 219–254.

Buxbaum, L. J., Schwartz, M. F., & Montgomery, M. W. (1998). Ideational apraxia and naturalistic action. *Cognitive Neuropsychology, 15,* 617–644.

Chao, L. L., Haxby, J. V., & Martin, A. (1999). Attribute-based neural substrates in temporal cortex for perceiving and knowing about objects. *Nature Neuroscience, 2,* 913–919.

Cohen, J. D., Braver, T. S., & O'Reilly, R. C. (1996). A computational approach to prefrontal cortex, cognitive control and schizophrenia: Recent developments and current challenges. *Philosophical Transactions of the Royal Society, B351,* 1515–1527.

Cooper, R. (in press). The control of routine action: Modelling normal and impaired functioning. In G. Houghton (Ed.), *Connectionist models of cognition.* London: Psychology Press.

Cooper, R., & Shallice, T. (1999). Contention Scheduling and the control of routine activities. *Cognitive Neuropsychology, 17,* 297–338.

Craighero, L., Fadiga, L., Rizzolatti, G., & Umilta, C. (1998). Visuomotor priming. *Visual Cognition, 5,* 109–126.

De Renzi, E., & Lucchelli, F. (1988). Ideational apraxia. *Brain, 111,* 1173–1185.

Forde, E. M. E., & Humphreys, G. W. (in press). The role of semantic knowledge and working memory in everyday tasks. *Brain and Cognition.*

Gallese, V., Fadiga, L., Fogassi, L., & Rizzolatti, G. (1996). Action recognition in the premotor cortex. *Brain, 119,* 593–609.

Goldman-Rakic, P. S. (1992). Working memory and the mind. *Scientific American, 267,* 110–117.

Grabowski, T. J., Damasio, H., & Damasio, A. R. (1998). Premotor and prefrontal correlates of category-related lexical retrieval. *Neuroimage, 7,* 232–243.

Grafman, J. (1995). Similarities and distinctions among current models of prefrontal cortical functions. *Annals of the New York Academy of Sciences, 769,* 337–368.

Grafman, J. (1989). Plans, actions and mental sets: Managerial knowledge units in the frontal lobe. In E. Perecman (Ed.), *Integrating theory and practice in clinical neuropsychology* (pp. 93–138). Hillsdale, NJ: Lawrence Erlbaum.

Grafton, S. T., Fadiga, L., Arbib, M. A., & Rizzolatti, G. (1997). Premotor cortex activation during observation and naming of familiar tools. *Neuroimage, 6,* 231–236.

Hart, T., Giovannetti, M. S., Montgomery, M. W., & Schwartz, M. F. (1998). Awareness of errors in naturalistic action after traumatic brain injury. *Journal of Head trauma Rehabilitation, 13,* 16–28.

Hillis, A., & Caramazza, A. (1995). Cognitive and neural mechanisms underlying visual and semantic processing: implication from "optic aphasia". *Journal of Cognitive Neuroscience, 7,* 457–478.

Hodges, J. R., Patterson, K., Oxbury, S., & Funnell, E. (1992). Semantic dementia: Progressive fluent aphasia with temporal lobe atrophy. *Brain, 115,* 1783–1806.

Hodges, J. R., Spatt, J., & Patterson, K. (1999). "What" and "how": Evidence for the dissociation of object knowledge and mechanical problem-solving skills in the human brain. *Proceedings of the National Academy of Sciences, 96,* 9444–9448.

Houghton, G. (1990). The problem of serial order: A neural network model of sequence learning and recall. In R. Dale, C. Mellish, & M. Zock (Eds.), *Current research in natural language generation,* (pp. 287–319). London: Academic Press.

Houghton, G., Glasspool, D. W., & Shallice, T. (1994) Spelling and serial recall: Insights from a competitive queuing model. In G. D. A. Brown & N. Ellis (Eds.),

Handbook of spelling: Theory, process and intervention (pp. 365-404). Chichester: Wiley.

Houghton, G., Tipper, S. P., Weaver, B., & Shore, D. I. (1996). Inhibition and interference in selective attention: Some tests of a neural network model. *Visual Cognition, 3*, 119-164.

Humphreys, G. W., & Forde, E. M. E. (1998). Disorder action schema and action dysorganization syndrome. *Cognitive Neuropsychology, 15*, 771-811.

Humphreys, G. W., Forde, E. M. E., & Francis, D., (in press). The sequential organization of actions. In S. Monsell & J. Driver (Eds.), *Attention and Performance XVIII*. Cambridge, MA: MIT Press.

Humphreys, G. W., Forde, E. M. E., & Francis, D. (in preparation) *On the visual pragmatics of action: Dissociating action from verbal knowledge in a novel instruction task.*

Humphreys, G. W., & Riddoch, M. J. (2000). One more cup of coffee for the road: Object-action assemblies, response blocking and response capture after frontal lobe damage. *Experimental Brain Research, 133*, 81-93.

Kimberg, D. Y., & Farah, M. J. (1993). A unified account of cognitive impairments following frontal lobe damage: The role of working memory in complex, organized behavior. *Journal of Experimental Psychology: General, 122*, 411-428.

Lashley, K. (1951) The problem of serial order in behavior. In L. A. Jeffress (Ed.), *Cerebral mechanisms in behavior* (pp. 112-136). New York: Wiley.

Lauro-Grotto, R., Piccini, C., & Shallice, T. (1997). Modality-specific operations in semantic dementia. *Cortex, 33*, 593-622.

Lhermitte, F. (1983). Utilization behavior and its relation to lesions of the frontal lobes. *Brain, 106*, 237-255.

Liepmann, H. (1900). Das Krankheitsbild der Apraxia Motorische Asymbolie. *Monaschrift fur Psychiatrie und Neurologie, 8*, 15-44.

Martin, A., Haxby, J. V., Lalonde, F. M., Wiggs, C. L., & Ungerleider, L. G. (1995). Discrete cortical regions associated with knowledge of color and knowledge of action. *Science, 270*, 102-105.

Norman, D., & Shallice, T. (1986). Attention to action: Willed and automatic control of behavior. In R. Davidson, R. Schwartz & D. Shapiro (Eds.), *Consciousness and self-regulation: Advances in research and theory* (Vol. 4, pp. 1-18). New York: Plenum Press.

Owen, A. M., Doyon, J., Petrides, M., & Evans, A. C. (1996a). Planning and spatial working memory examined with positron emission tomography. *European Journal of Neuroscience, 8*, 353 -364.

Owen, A. M., Evans, A. C., & Petrides, M. P. (1996b). Evidence for a two-stage model of spatial working memory processing within the lateral frontal cortex: A positron emission tomography study. *Cortex, 6*, 31-38.

Partiot, A., Grafman, J., Sadato, N., Flitman, S., & Wild, K. (1996). Brain activation during script event processing. *Cognitive Neuroscience, 7*, 761-766.

Phillips, J., Humphreys, G. W., & Price, C. J. (2000). *The neural substrates of action retrieval from objects and words: An examination of semantic and visual routes to action.* Manuscript submitted for publication.

Posner, M. I., Inhoff, A. W., & Cohen, A. (1987). Isolating attentional systems: A cognitive-anatomical analysis. *Psychobiology, 15*, 107-121.

Potter, M,. & Faulconer, B. A. (1975). Time to understand pictures and words. *Nature, 253*, 437-438.

Reason, J. T. (1984). Lapses of attention in everyday life. In W. Parasuraman & R. Davies (Eds.), *Varieties of attention* (pp. 515-549). Orlando, FL: Academic Press.

Riddoch, M. J., Edwards, M. G., Humphreys, G. W., West, R., & Heafield, T. (1998). Visual affordances direct action: Neuropsychological evidence from manual interference. *Cognitive Neuropsychology, 15*, 645-684.

Riddoch, M. J., & Humphreys, G. W. (1987). Visual object processing in a case of optic aphasia: A case of semantic access agnosia. *Cognitive Neuropsychology, 4*, 131-185.

Riddoch, M. J., Humphreys, G. W., & Edwards, M. G. (in press). Visual affordance and object selection. In S. Monsell & J. Driver (Eds.), *Attention and performance, XVIII*. Cambridge, MA: MIT Press.

Robbins, T. W. (1996). Dissociating executive functions of the prefrontal cortex. *Philosophical Transactions of the Royal Society, B351*, 1463-1471.

Robertson, I. (1993). The relationship between lateralised and non-lateralised attentional deficits in unilateral neglect. In I. H. Roberston & J. C. Marshall (Eds.), *Unilateral neglect: Clinical and experimental studies* (pp. 257-278). London: Psychology Press.

Rosch, E., Mervis, C. B., Gray, W. D., Johnson, D. M., & Boyes-Braem, P. (1976). Basic objects in natural categories. *Cognitive Psychology, 8*, 382-439.

Rumelhart, D. E., & Norman, D. A. (1982). Simulating a skilled typist: A study of skilled cognitive-motor performance. *Cognitive Science, 6*, 1-36.

Rumiati, R. I., & Humphreys, G. W. (1998). Recognition by action: dissociating visual and semantic routes to actions in normal observers. *Journal of Experimental Psychology: Human Perception & Performance, 24*, 631-647.

Rusted, J., & Sheppard, L. (2000). *Action-based memory in Alzheimer's disease: A longitudinal look at tea-making.* Manuscript submitted for publication.

Sakata, H., Taira, M., Kusunoki, M., Murata, M., Tanaka, Y., & Tsutsui, K. (1998). Neural coding of 3D features of objects for hand action in the parietal cortex of the monkey. *Philosophical Transactions of the Royal Society, B 353*, 1363-1373.

Schneider, W., & Shiffrin, R. M. (1977). Controlled and automatic human information processing. 1: Detection, search and attention. *Psychological Review, 84*, 1-66.

Schwartz, M. F. (1995) Re-examining the role of executive functions in routine action production. *Annals of the New York Academy of Sciences, 769*, 321-335.

Schwartz, M. F., Mayer, N. H., Fitzpatrick-De Salme, E. J., & Montgomery, M. W. (1993). Cognitive theory and the study of everyday action disorders after brain damage. *Journal of Head Trauma and Rehabilitation, 8*, 59-72.

Schwartz, M. F., Montgomery, M. W., Buxbaum, L. J., Less, S .S., Carew, T. G., Coslett, H. B., Ferraro, M., Fitzpatrick-De Salme, E. J., Hart, T., & Mayer, N. H. (1998). Naturalistic action impairment in closed head injury. *Neuropsychology, 12*, 13-28.

Schwartz, M. F., Montgomery, M. W., Buxbaum, L. J., Less, S. S., Carew, T. G., Coslett, H. B., & Mayer, N. H. (1995). Analysis of a disorder of everyday action. *Cognitive Neuropsychology, 12*, 863-892.

Schwartz, M. F., Reed, E. S., Montgomery, M. W., Palmer, C., & Mayer, N. H. (1991). The quantitative description of action disorganisation after brain damage: A case study. *Cognitive Neuropsychology, 8*, 381-414.

Shallice, T. (1994). Multiple levels of control processes.

In C. Umilta & M. Moscovitch (Eds.), *Attention & performance XV* (pp. 395–420). Cambridge, MA: MIT Press.

Shallice, T., Burgess, P. W., Schon, F., & Baxter, D. M. (1989). The origins of utilization behavior. *Brain*, 112, 1587–1598.

Shank, R., & Abelson, P. (1977). *Scripts, plans, goals and understanding*. Hillsdale, NJ: Lawrence Erlbaum.

Shiffrin, R. M., & Schnieder, W. (1977). Controlled and automatic human information processing. II: Perceptual learning, automatic attending and a general theory. *Psychological Review*, 84, 127–190.

Sirigu, A., Zalla, T., Pillon, B., Grafman, J., Agid, Y., & Dubois, B. (1995). Selective impairments in managerial knowledge following pre-frontal cortex damage. *Cortex*, 31, 301–316.

Sirigu, A., Zalla, T., Pillon, B., Grafman, J., Agid, Y., & Dubois, B. (1996). Encoding of sequence and boundaries of scripts following prefrontal lesions. *Cortex*, 32, 297–310.

Snowden, J. S., Goulding, P. J., & Neary, D. (1989). Semantic dementia: A form of circumscribed cerebral atrophy. *Behavioral Neurology*, 2, 167–182.

Taira, M., Mine, G., Georgopoulos, A. P., Murata, A., & Sakata, H. (1991). Parietal cortex neurons of the monkey related to the visual guidance of hand movements. *Experimental Brain Research*, 83, 29–36.

Tucker, M., & Ellis, R. (1998). On the relations between seen objects and components of potential actions. *Journal of Experimental Psychology: Human Perception and Performance*, 24, 830–846.

Future Directions

Dans les champs de l'observation, l'hasard ne favorise
que les esprits prépáres.
In the field of observation, chance only favors
prepared minds.

—Louis Pasteur

24

The Future
of Cognitive Neuropsychology

Michael McCloskey

The cognitive deficits resulting from neurological disease, injury, or abnormal development range from the prosaic (e.g., difficulty in spelling common words) to the extraordinary (e.g., loss of ability to perceive motion while other aspects of vision remain largely intact; see Hess, Baker, & Zihl, 1989; Zihl, von Cramon, & Mai, 1983). Cognitive neuropsychologists study deficits with at least three objectives in mind: (a) to gain insights into the structure and functioning of the normal cognitive system; (b) to explore the localization of cognitive functions in the brain; and (c) to achieve a better understanding of the deficits *per se*, as a basis for diagnosis and treatment. The preceding chapters describe how these aims have been pursued, and what progress has been made, in research on a variety of cognitive functions. In this concluding chapter I consider the future of cognitive neuropsychology. For each of the field's major goals I consider two questions: 1) What potential does cognitive neuropsychology hold for significant future contributions to this goal?; and 2) What developments in theory and practice will be needed to realize the potential?

GOAL 1:
DEFICITS AS WINDOWS INTO NORMAL COGNITIVE MECHANISMS

As a basis for characterizing normal representations and processes, the study of cognitive deficits has impressed many observers—and even some practitioners—as crude, indirect, and fraught with interpretive difficulties (e.g., Shallice, 1988; Robertson, Knight, Rafal, & Shimamura, 1993; Seidenberg, 1988). Hence, in assessing the prospects of cognitive neuropsychology for significant future contributions to knowledge about normal cognition, it may be worthwhile to begin with a very basic question: Why study deficits when the aim is to understand normal cognitive functioning?

Why Study Deficits?

One part of an answer is that *all* of the available methods for studying human cognition—including the methods applied in research with normal participants—are indirect and subject to uncertainties of interpretation. Under these circumstances results from multiple methods, each with different strengths and weaknesses, provide a firmer basis for conclusions than results from any single approach. Another point, which I develop further in a later section, is that cognitive neuropsychological methods, far from being crude, provide a basis for remarkably fine-grained analyses of normal cognitive systems.

However, the fundamental insight underlying cognitive neuropsychological approaches to the study of normal cognition is that complex systems often reveal their inner workings more clearly when they are malfunctioning, than when they are running smoothly. For example, when I use my laser printer, I learn little about how it represents or processes information, as long as nothing goes wrong. Recently, however, a surprisingly informative problem arose when I attempted to print a diagram for use in a class lecture. After apparently accepting input from the computer for some time, the printer signaled an error. When I pressed a 'continue' button, the page shown in Figure 24.1 Panel A emerged. The printer then appeared to accept additional input from the computer, and finally produced the page shown in Figure 24.1 Panel B.

This phenomenon may be interpreted by assuming that the printer accepts input from the computer, and stores it in a limited-capacity memory until either an entire page has been received (in which case the page is printed) or the memory is filled (in which case the printer stops accepting input and signals an error). When the 'continue' button is pressed after an error, the printer produces a page from the information in the (filled) memory, then accepts the remaining information into the now-freed memory, and finally prints this information on a new page. Thus, the printing error provides a basis for inferring some aspects of the printer's internal structure and functioning—for example, that it has a limited-capacity memory, and stores an entire page in memory before printing.

More interesting, however, is what the abnormal output implies about the printer's representation of to-be-printed information. The graphics program with which I created the diagram requires the user to treat elements such as boxes, circles, and arrows as indivisible objects. That is, these elements can be manipulated (e.g., moved, resized) only as units; the component lines or points cannot be referenced individually. In contrast, the abnormal printer output provides compelling evidence that graphics elements are represented in the printer's memory not as objects or even as components such as line segments, but rather as to-be-printed dots. This conclusion follows from the fact that some elements (e.g., the box for orthography-phonology conversion), and even their component line segments, were split across the two output pages. This phenomenon implies that some of the dots making up these elements were stored in the printer's memory before it was filled, whereas other dots could not be stored until memory was freed.

Given that the printer functions properly in printing pages with less graphical material, the error shown in Figure 24.1 also suggests that the printer's memory stores the location of each to-be-printed dot, rather than an on or off (i.e., print or don't-print) value for every possible dot position on the page. (In the latter case the memory demand for a page would be constant regardless of how many dots were to be printed.) Further, the fact that all of the graphics elements were truncated abruptly at the same place on the page implies that information about to-be-printed dots was entered column-by-column into the printer's memory, starting at the leading edge of the page, and proceeding systematically toward the trailing edge. Finally, it is evident that text is somehow treated differently from graphics, given that all of the text was printed on the first output page, including text positioned beyond the truncation point for graphics elements.

Regrettably, space does not permit discussion of the extensive additional testing carried out to confirm and extend these conclusions. Perhaps, however, this brief sketch suffices to show that the printer's abnormal output revealed aspects of its internal representations and processes that could not readily be inferred by observing its normal functioning. Similarly, the impaired performance of people with cognitive deficits can offer insights into normal cognitive

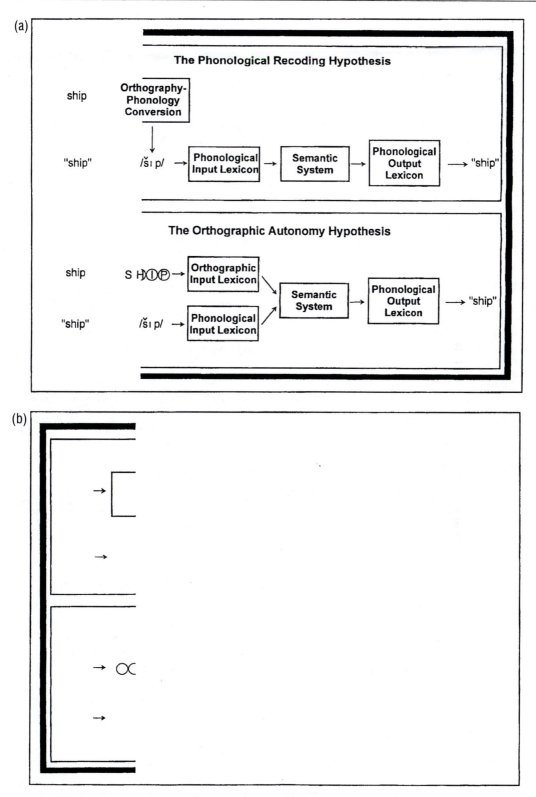

Figure 24.1: A. First page generated by laser printer. B. Second page generated by printer.

representations and processes, perhaps including insights not readily obtained through studies with normal participants.

Studying abnormalities or malfunctions to shed light on normal structures and processes is a well-established research strategy in a variety of scientific domains. For example, research on AIDS has contributed to knowledge of normal immune-system functioning; mutations are studied in part to advance our understanding of normal genetic mechanisms; and observations of damaged ecosystems offer insights into normal ecological processes. More generally, scientists of many stripes study unusual phenomena as a means of gaining insight into more typical conditions or events. For example, studies of supernovae illuminate the processes and products of nuclear fusion in stars; and research on volcanic eruptions offers insights into materials and events in the earth's interior.

Cognitive Deficits as Experiments of Nature

Potentially informative abnormalities or extraordinary phenomena can sometimes be created in the laboratory, as when brain lesions are produced surgically in neuroscience research with laboratory animals, or collisions of subatomic particles are engineered in particle accelerators. Often, however, it is beyond the researcher's power to create the preparations of interest. In such circumstances the study of naturally-occurring phenomena—experiments of nature—has proved to be a powerful tool, providing evidence not obtainable through more usual research methods. Studies of supernovae, volcanic eruptions, and human genetic abnormalities are cases in point.

Human cognitive neuropsychology also falls into this category. Obviously, it is neither possible nor desirable to make experimental brain lesions in humans. Rather, cognitive neuropsychological research takes advantage of the unfortunate natural experiments in which the brain sustains damage through accident or disease, or fails to develop normally.

Like other research with experiments of nature, cognitive neuropsychological research has its disadvantages. For example, the inability to create at will the deficits of interest is an inconvenience at best, and sometimes a serious impediment. (This point does not imply, however, that cognitive neuropsychological research is inherently observational or correlational; rigorous experimental methods can be, and are, applied in studies of cognitive deficits. The researcher's lack of control has to do with the creation of deficits, and not with the investigation of these deficits.)

Balanced against the disadvantages are some significant advantages. One I have already mentioned: Cognitive deficits often reveal in a clear and compelling fashion aspects of normal representation and processing not readily apparent from normal cognitive functioning. Another advantage stems from the inherently opportunistic nature of cognitive neuropsychological research. The cognitive neuropsychologist typically begins by screening individuals with deficits potentially relevant to issues of interest, and then explores in detail those deficits that seem to hold promise for illuminating the issues. This approach looks to nature for clues, and then follows the clues wherever they may lead. Relative to research with normal participants—which typically approaches nature with specific predetermined questions—cognitive neuropsychological research may therefore offer greater opportunity to be surprised by the unexpected. Indeed, cognitive neuropsychology has a long history of turning up remarkable phenomena (e.g., unilateral spatial neglect, blindsight, category-specific deficits, anterograde amnesias) that raise new questions, suggest novel theoretical perspectives, and give rise to productive lines of research (although not always immediately; see, e.g., Zeki, 1993, pp. 33–40). (For further discussion of the advantages and disadvantages of cognitive neuropsychological research see Caramazza, 1986, 1992; Ellis, 1987; Kosslyn & Intriligator, 1992; Kosslyn & Van Kleek, 1990; McCloskey, 1993; Robertson et al., 1993.)

Facilitating Future Progress

Science often moves forward through technological advances, such as the invention of the telescope, or the development of radiometric techniques for dating geological strata and artifacts. Cognitive neuropsychology is no exception, having benefited in recent years from advances in the computing technology available for data collection and analysis, and from the advent of structural and functional brain imaging technologies. At least in the near future, however, developments on a more abstract or conceptual level may be of greater importance for maximizing the field's contribution to knowledge about normal cognition. In this section I consider three potential developments, discussing the first two briefly and the third in greater detail.

Integrating Cognitive Neuropsychology and 'Normal' Cognitive Psychology

One pressing need is for better integration of research using deficits to study normal cognition, and research using normal performance for the same purposes. These two approaches differ only in (some aspects of) methodology, having in common not only the aim of understanding normal cognition and the conception of the mind as a representational/computational system, but also most of the specific theoretical questions under investigation. Nevertheless, studies of cognitively-impaired participants and studies of normal participants are typically conducted by different researchers, presented at different professional meetings, and published in different journals. This segregation by methodology is counterproductive, resulting not only in missed opportunities for fruitful interchange and collaboration, but also in failures of researchers adopting one approach to understand (or even know of) relevant evidence obtained through the other methodology. Some progress has been made toward increased communication between research communities, but much remains to be done.

Strengthening Cognitive Neuropsychological Research

Although much of the research in cognitive neuropsychology is of high quality, some theoretical and methodological shortcomings are relatively common. Addressing these weaknesses would almost certainly increase the rate of progress. One development that would prove beneficial is more explicit articulation of theoretical claims. In current research the theoretical concepts and hypotheses are sometimes so vague that the substance of proposals is difficult to ascertain or evaluate. (I hasten to add that this point applies not only to cognitive neuropsychology, but also, and with equal force, to research with unimpaired participants.)

Cognitive neuropsychological research could also benefit from more thorough and theoretically-grounded testing of patients. Pinning down the nature of a patient's deficit, and exploring the implications of the deficit for issues of normal cognition, often require extensive testing with a substantial number of carefully-chosen tasks. In current research the amounts and types of testing often are not sufficient to provide a firm foundation for inferences.

Finally, researchers need to ensure that the procedures they adopt are suited to the goals of their research. Caramazza and others have argued that the widespread patient-group method, in which data are averaged or otherwise aggregated over the patients in a group, is fundamentally unsound, at least for addressing issues of normal cognition (e.g., Badecker & Caramazza, 1985; Caramazza, 1984, 1986; Caramazza & Badecker, 1989, 1991; Caramazza & McCloskey, 1988, 1991; Ellis, 1987; McCloskey, 1993; McCloskey & Caramazza, 1988, 1991). I will not attempt to recount the arguments in detail. However, the central contentions are (a) that aggregating data over patients requires the assumption that the patients are homogeneous with respect to the nature of their deficits, but (b) that regardless of how patients are selected, homogeneity of deficits cannot be assumed *a priori* (and indeed is unlikely when deficits are characterized at the levels of detail required for addressing issues of current interest in the study of normal cognition). Caramazza and colleagues argue that although results from multiple patients can and should be considered when addressing issues of normal cognition, the data from each patient must be treated individually. (I will have more to say about this *multiple single-patient study* method in the next section.) These arguments, although to my mind compelling, are controversial; at the least, however, it is clear that researchers should give careful thought to the assumptions underlying their chosen methods, and whether these assumptions are warranted.

Shedding a Conceptual Straightjacket

Many cognitive neuropsychologists, as well as most other cognitive scientists, assume that cognitive deficits can be brought to bear on issues of normal cognition only by applying that I will call *task dissociation logic*. From this perspective, cognitive neuropsychology is a method for drawing inferences of the form, "Task A and Task B involve different processing mechanisms." The method is applied by testing patients on two or more tasks, and interpreting the observed dissociations and associations of deficits according to the following principles.

(1) Single Dissociations.   A finding of poor (i.e., impaired) performance on one task with good (i.e., normal, or at least reliably better) performance on the other suggests that the tasks differ in one or more of their underlying processing mechanisms. However, this pattern of results—a single dissociation—does not constitute compelling evidence for different processing mechanisms; another possible interpretation is that both tasks require the same processing mechanisms, but one task demands more from these mechanisms than the other, and consequently shows greater impairment when the mechanisms are damaged.

(2) Double Dissociations.   Because single dissociations are subject to this potential *resource artifact* interpretation (Shallice, 1988), stronger evidence is needed to warrant firm conclusions in favor of differences between tasks in underlying processing mechanisms. In particular, what is required is a double dissociation, in which one or more patients show poor performance on Task A with good performance on Task B, while one or more other patients show good performance on Task A with poor performance on Task B. A double dissociation rules out resource artifact interpretations. To interpret the A-good/B-poor dissociation in terms of resource artifacts one would have to assume that Task B places heavier demands than Task A on the required processing mechanisms; but to interpret the complementary A-poor/B-good dissociation one would have to make the contradictory assumption that Task A demands more than Task B from the mechanisms. Double dissociations are therefore the gold standard in cognitive neuropsychological research. (Note, however, that a double dissociation implies only that there is some difference in processing mechanisms between the tasks, and does not by itself say anything about the nature of the mechanisms or how they differ between tasks.)

(3) Associations.   Consider finally a pattern of results in which performance is impaired on both Task A and Task B. This pattern—an *association*—might seem to suggest that the tasks share one or more processing mechanisms, given that damage to a shared mechanism would be expected to produce impairment on both tasks. However, the association could also have resulted from two separate deficits, one affecting Task A and the other affecting Task B. As a consequence, associations are uninformative about underlying processing mechanisms.

Task dissociation logic has been widely discussed in the cognitive neuropsychology literature. Some discussions have been aimed at formulating the logic more precisely, addressing such matters as what specific forms of double dissociation are required to warrant conclusions of separate processing mechanisms (e.g., Jones, 1983; Shallice, 1988). Other commentators have criticized the logic or some of its applications (e.g., Plaut, 1995; Robertson et al., 1993), arguing for example that double dissociations do not necessarily imply a difference in processing mechanisms between tasks (e.g., Chater & Ganis, 1991; Ganis & Chater, 1991; Plaut, 1995; but see Bullinaria & Chater, 1995). Virtually all of the discussions have taken as given that task dissociation logic represents the sole method for relating cognitive deficits to theories of normal cognition. Proponents of the logic have offered their analyses as prescriptions of how to do cognitive neuropsychological research, and opponents have presented their arguments as indictments of cognitive neuropsychology in general.

Although task dissociation logic has clearly played an important role in cognitive neuropsychological research, the tacit assumption that this logic represents the only way of doing cognitive neuropsychology has imposed a conceptual and methodological straightjacket on the field. The nature and source of the self-imposed constrictions become apparent if we examine the presuppositions of the logic.

Presuppositions of Task Dissociation Logic.   Task dissociation logic rests upon two—usually implicit—assumptions. The first is that the data obtainable from studies of cognitive deficits are necessarily crude (e.g., Shallice, 1988), and in particular are limited to gross level-of-performance measures (e.g., percent correct) on a small number of tasks. The second assumption is that interpretation of evidence is a fixed mechanical process in which the logical consequences of the data are assessed in isolation from any other empirical or theoretical considerations.

Given these presuppositions, it appears self-evident that cognitive neuropsychology is limited to conclusions of the form, "Task A and Task B differ in at least one processing component," and that these conclusions can only be drawn by applying the principles of task dissociation logic. However, the presuppositions have no basis in canons of scientific method, practice in other areas of cognitive science, or intrinsic characteristics of cognitive deficits. Rather, these self-imposed strictures apparently stem primarily from a failure of imagination on the part of cognitive neuropsychologists. Fortunately, a broader conception of cognitive neuropsychology is emerging.

Cognitive Neuropsychology More Broadly Conceived

A growing body of research demonstrates that the impaired performance of individuals with cognitive deficits is often richly patterned, and that analysis of the patterning can provide a basis for specific, fine-grained inferences about cognitive representations and processes. For example, several recent studies of individual dysgraphic patients converge on conclusions about the orthographic representations underlying the ability to spell words in writing, typing, spelling aloud, and so forth. These studies provide evidence that orthographic representations are not simple linear sequences of letter tokens (e.g., C-R-O-S-S for the word *cross*), but rather are complex multidimensional structures in which (a) orthographic syllable structure is represented (Caramazza & Miceli, 1990); (b) information about the orthographic consonant/vowel status of each letter is represented independently of the letter's identity (Caramazza & Miceli, 1990; Cubelli, 1991; McCloskey, Badecker, Goodman-Schulman, & Aliminosa, 1994); and (c) information about letter doubling is specified separately from the identity of the doubled letter (Caramazza & Miceli, 1990; McCloskey et al., 1994; Tainturier & Caramazza, 1996; Venneri & Cubelli, 1993). The evidence concerning representation of letter doubling is illustrative.

Patient HE (McCloskey et al., 1994) presented with several systematic phenomena in spelling words with double letters, including errors such as the following:

Stimulus	Response
shell	sheel
needle	neddle
across	accros
confess	connfes
parrot	parott

In these *doubling shift* errors the letter that should have been doubled appeared in the response as a single letter, and another letter was doubled instead. Several analyses of HE's errors demonstrated that the occurrence of an erroneous doubling was systematically related to the presence of a double letter in the stimulus; for example, errors like *shell → sheel* were not simple letter substitutions (e.g., *l → e*) that happened by chance to replace one letter of a double-letter pair with a letter that created another double. More generally, HE's doubling shift errors, and other aspects of his performance, were inconsistent with the assumption that double letters are specified in orthographic representations simply by two tokens of the to-be-doubled letter (e.g., S-H-E-L-L). McCloskey et al. (1994) argued that the results could be interpreted only by assuming that double letters are represented by a single letter token associated with a separate specification of doubling.

Patient LB (Caramazza & Miceli, 1990) also exhibited a systematic pattern of errors in spelling words with double letters. Among the more striking aspects of this pattern were errors such as the following:

Stimulus	Response
pezzo	zeppo
cellula	leccula
blocco	bcollo
passai	sappai

These *doubling exchange* errors are extremely difficult to reconcile with representations in which double letters are specified by two tokens of the to-be-doubled letter (e.g., P-E-Z-Z-O). For example, in the *pezzo → zeppo* error how could two letter tokens (Z-Z) change places with a single letter token (P) in such a way that the single token becomes two (P-P) and the two tokens become one (Z)? On the basis of the doubling exchange errors and other phenomena— for example, *double substitution* errors such as *marrone → mazzone*—Caramazza and Miceli (1990) concluded that orthographic representations specify double letters by a single letter token plus doubling information.

Results from other patients also suggest that double-letter representations are in some sense special. Venneri and Cubelli (1993) found that patient EZ, in spelling words with double letters, omitted one of the letters in the double over 80% of the time (e.g., *Dalla Villa → Dala Vila*). Omissions were far less frequent for letters in other types of clusters, including digraphs corresponding to a single phoneme (e.g., *sc* in *pesce*). Also, Tainturier and Caramazza (1996) reported several interesting double-letter phenomena exhibited by a patient, FM, whose spelling responses were often grossly incorrect (e.g., *fate → frich*). For example, in spelling to dictation FM made no errors that "split" a double-letter sequence (e.g., *pull → plul*). In contrast, control letter sequences matched to the double-letter sequences were frequently split (e.g., *rn* in *barn → bron*). Tainturier and Caramazza (1996) interpreted this finding as further evidence that double letters are not represented by two tokens of the to-be-doubled letter (e.g., P-U-L-L).

Two specific hypotheses have been proposed concerning the form of the doubling representations (Caramazza & Miceli, 1990; McCloskey et al., 1994). For simplicity, I will describe only Caramazza and Miceli's (1990) *doubling mark* hypothesis, which assumes that double letters are represented by a single letter token associated with a doubling marker, as illustrated below for the word *shell*:

<pre>
S   H   E   L
                        |
                        𝒟
</pre>

This hypothesis about normal orthographic representations provides a basis for interpreting the various observed patterns of impairment. HE's doubling shift errors (e.g., *shell → sheel*) may be explained by assuming that his orthographic representations were sometimes disrupted (during retrieval from an orthographic lexicon or subsequent retention in a buffer memory) in such a way that the doubling mark became associated with the wrong letter token:

<pre>
S   H   E   L
                |
                𝒟
</pre>

LB's double exchanges (e.g., *pezzo → zeppo*) can also be interpreted, by assuming that the single token of the to-be-doubled letter was exchanged with the token for another letter in the word:

<pre>
P   E   Z   O   Z   E   P   O
               | → |
               𝒟   𝒟
</pre>

Similarly, LB's double substitution errors (e.g., *troppo → trocco*) can be attributed to substitution of an incorrect letter token for the single token of the to-be-doubled letter:

<pre>
T   R   O   P   O   T   R   O   C   O
               | → |
               𝒟   𝒟
</pre>

(As expected from these interpretations LB also made letter substitution and exchange errors not involving double letters.)

Patient EZ's frequent deletion of one letter in a double letter pair (e.g., *villa → vila*) may be interpreted by assuming that she was impaired in retaining the doubling mark during the spelling process:

<pre>
V   I   L   A   V   I   L   A
          | →
          𝒟
</pre>

Finally, the absence of split-double errors (e.g., *pull → plul*) in patient FM's error corpus is straightforwardly explained by the assumption that orthographic representations of double letters include only one token of the to-be-doubled letter, and not two tokens that could become separated.

Taken together, the results from these studies make a compelling case against the assumption that orthographic representations specify double letters by two tokens of the to-be-doubled letter, and argue strongly in favor of the hypothesis that double-letter representations involve a single letter token associated with a separate specification of doubling. This conclusion forms one pillar of the broader argument that orthographic representations are complex multi-dimensional structures, rather than simple linear sequences of letter tokens.

I have developed this example in some detail to illustrate several points. First, in cognitive neuropsychological research addressing issues of normal cognition the evidence need not be limited to dissociations between tasks in gross performance-level measures, and the inferences drawn from the evidence need not be limited to coarse-grained conclusions of the form, "Task A and Task B involve different processing mechanisms." The impaired performance of individuals with cognitive deficits is often richly structured, and careful analysis of the structure can provide a basis for fine-grained conclusions about cognitive processes and the representations upon which they operate.

Detailed analyses of deficits can be especially powerful when, as in the present example, results from several individual patients can be brought to bear on the theoretical issues of interest. In this multiple single-patient study method the goal is to interpret results from all of the patients in terms of the same assumptions about normal cognitive mechanisms, by specifying for each patient a form of damage that would lead to the particular pattern of impairment observed for that patient. Note that this research strategy is not aimed at finding multiple patients with exactly the same type of deficit. Cognitive deficits, when characterized at levels of detail commensurate with fine-grained conclusions about normal representations and processes, prove to be not only richly-structured but also diverse, and it is unusual to find two or more patients whose performance is the same in all potentially-relevant respects. The multiple single-patient study method acknowledges and in fact exploits this diversity, requiring that a theory be capable of accounting for each of the various forms of impairment that may result from damage to the cognitive mechanisms under investigation.

The double-letter example also illustrates the point that interpretation of evidence need not—and indeed should not—involve the mechanical application of task-dissociation logic. In the first place many forms of potentially-relevant data (e.g., the error patterns exhibited by HE and LB) do not fit neatly into any of the evidential categories defined by this logic (i.e., single dissociation, double dissociation, association). Even for results straightforwardly describable as dissociations or associations, the principles of task dissociation logic are usually not an appropriate guide to interpretation; these principles are valid only when the data are limited to gross performance-level measures, and are interpreted in a theoretical vacuum. For example, the principle that associations do not provide evidence of shared processing mechanisms may have merit in the context of results consisting solely of poorer-than-normal performance on two tasks, because such an association might plausibly have resulted from two separate deficits, each affecting one of the tasks. However, when an association involves a close correspondence across tasks in a specific and richly articulated performance pattern—such as the finding (McCloskey et al., 1994) that patient H.E.'s written spelling and oral spelling showed virtually identical accuracy, effects of variables (e.g., word frequency), and distribution of errors across error types—it strains credibility to suggest that the association reflects the accidental co-occurrence of two separate deficits. Therefore, such associations may properly be taken as evidence of shared processing mechanisms. (See Hillis, Rapp, Romani, & Caramazza, 1990, for another example.)

Similarly misconceived are the task dissociation principles for interpreting dissociations (i.e., single dissociations are weak evidence, and double dissociations are required before firm conclusions can be drawn). To be sure, a double dissociation usually constitutes stronger evidence than one of the constituent single dissociations, simply because the former represents more evidence than the latter. However, given a single dissociation, it is by no means uniformly true either that the single dissociation is weak evidence, or that the most valuable piece of additional evidence is the complementary dissociation that completes the double dissociation (Caramazza, 1986). The task-dissociation principles may apply when (a) the issue under consideration is whether two tasks involve different processing mechanisms, and (b) the single dissociation could plausibly be attributed to a resource artifact (i.e., one task demanding more than the other from the same processing mechanisms). Under such circumstances the complementary dissociation serves the important function of ruling out the resource artifact interpretation, and therefore greatly strengthens the case for separate processing mechanisms.

However, dissociations may be brought to bear on issues other than those concerning shared versus separate processing mechanisms (e.g., issues concerning the form of representations), in which case the resource artifact issue may not even arise. Furthermore, even when the focus is on shared versus separate mechanisms a resource artifact interpretation for a single disso-ciation may not be plausible, or even possible, when account is taken of the particular form of the dissociation, the particular cognitive processes under investigation, the particular hypoth-eses being entertained about these processes, and so forth (see Caramazza, 1986; Caramazza & McCloskey, 1991; McCloskey, 1993; Sokol & McCloskey, 1988). For example, Rapp, Benzing, and Caramazza (1997) reported a single dissociation in which patient PW, on some trials of a picture naming task, made semantic errors in naming the picture orally, yet wrote the name correctly. Thus, shown a picture of an owl and asked to say and then write the name several times in succession, PW responded as follows:

Spoken: "turtle"
Written: OWL
Spoken: "turtle"
Written: OWL
Spoken: "turtle"
Written: OWL

Arguing from other aspects of PW's performance that the oral-naming errors reflected an impairment in accessing phonological word representations, Rapp et al. (1997) interpreted the dissociation between written and spoken naming as evidence against the *phonological media-tion* hypothesis, which assumes that the orthographic representations underlying written word production can be accessed only via phonological representations (i.e., semantics phonology orthography). Rapp et al. instead endorsed an *orthographic autonomy* hypothesis, according to which orthographic representations may be accessed directly from semantic representations, without phonological mediation.

According to task dissociation logic, we should consider Rapp et al.'s (1997) argument questionable on grounds that their single dissociation might have resulted not from a differ-ence in processing mechanisms between spoken and written naming, but rather from a re-source artifact (i.e., spoken naming demanding more than written naming from the same processing mechanisms). Further, we should believe that the Rapp et al. conclusion would be buttressed by results providing the other half of the double dissociation (i.e., good oral but poor written naming). However, this application of task dissociation logic would be seriously mis-guided. To attribute the Rapp et al. (1997) findings to a resource artifact one would have to assume that retrieval of phonological word representations is a more demanding process in the spoken naming task than in written naming task. However, such an assumption would be not only highly unmotivated but also highly implausible, especially given that the principal alterna-tive to Rapp et al.'s interpretation—the phonological mediation hypothesis—would presumably hold that the phonological retrieval process is identical in spoken and written naming.

Furthermore, results providing the other half of the double dissociation would do very little to strengthen the Rapp et al. (1997) argument. Suppose we had results from one or more patients showing impaired written naming in the presence of intact spoken naming, and more specifically impaired access to orthographic representations in the presence of normal access to phonological representations. Although these results would certainly be consistent with Rapp et al.'s orthographic autonomy hypothesis, they would be equally consistent with the phonological mediation hypothesis, and indeed with virtually any hypothesis positing that access to orthographic representations is implicated in written naming but not in spoken naming. Hence, the findings would add little to the support for the orthographic autonomy hypothesis, and would be far less useful than additional evidence suggesting specifically that access to phonological representations is not required for access to orthographic representations (e.g., results from oral and written sentence completion similar to those reported by Rapp et al. for oral and written picture naming).[1]

This example drives home the point that contrary to the assumptions of task dissociation logic, the weight of various categories of cognitive neuropsychological evidence need not, and should not, be assessed in a vacuum. Like other forms of evidence in cognitive science (or indeed in any science) cognitive neuropsychological data can and should be evaluated in the light of such considerations as the particular theoretical issues under investigation, the tenable alternative positions on these issues, and the specific form of the evidence. Once this point is recognized it becomes clear that circumscribing *a priori* the forms of data to be considered, or the reasoning to be used in linking data with theory, is neither possible nor desirable.

GOAL 2: FUNCTIONAL LOCALIZATION

Much of our knowledge about instantiation of cognitive functions in the brain has come from research with brain-damaged patients. The study of lesion-deficit correlations has played a central role both in establishing that the brain exhibits functional specialization (e.g., Finger, 1994; Kertesz, 1994), and in linking particular cognitive functions to particular brain regions. Aphasia research, beginning with Broca and Wernicke, has taught us most of what we know about brain specialization for language; studies of organic amnesias—notably, patient HM's profound anterograde amnesia after bilateral temporal lobectomy (Scoville & Milner, 1957)— have established the importance of the hippocampus and other brain regions for memory; observations of patients with parietal lesions contributed to the recognition that this brain area is implicated in spatial processing; and so forth and so on. (For further discussion see, e.g., Banich, 1997; Farah & Aguirre, 1999; Kolb & Whishaw, 1996; McCarthy & Warrington, 1990.)

However, with the advent of functional neuroimaging comes the question of whether lesion-deficit correlation research has outlived its usefulness. Indeed, functional neuroimagers are often at pains to point out the disadvantages of the lesion-deficit correlation method relative to their newer techniques, noting that structural brain lesions are often quite large, that lesions may not respect functional boundaries in the brain, and that the possibility of functional reorganization complicates the interpretation of lesion-deficit relationships.

Functional neuroimaging methods are, without doubt, extraordinarily useful tools for probing brain localization of cognitive functions, offering improved spatial resolution and the ability to study normal participants. However, it would be a mistake to conclude that the lesion-deficit correlation method is no longer useful. The reasons are analogous to those I cited in discussing cognitive neuropsychological research that addresses issues of normal cognition. First, as long as all of the available methods are imperfect—and this is certainly true of current functional localization methods—results from multiple methods will almost always provide a firmer basis for conclusions than results from a single method.

Second, lesion-deficit correlation methods are not limited to establishing crude brain-cognition relationships (e.g., the parietal lobes are implicated in spatial cognition). Consider, for example, the multiple single-patient study of visual field defects carried out many years ago by Gordon Holmes and W. T. Lister. Holmes, a neurologist, and Lister, an ophthalmic surgeon, were officers in the British army during World War I. Stationed at a base hospital in France, they treated thousands of soldiers with head wounds. In 1916 Holmes and Lister published a study of relationships between visual field defects and brain lesion loci in 23 patients with

---

[1]It is interesting to note that in some sense PW himself provided the other half of the double dissociation. In addition to the trials in which he responded to a picture with an incorrect spoken name but a correct written name, Rapp et al. (1997) also observed trials in which PW's spoken response was correct but his written response was erroneous. These latter trials, like results from other patients showing good spoken but poor written naming, contribute little if anything to the strength of the conclusions Rapp et al. drew in favor of the orthographic autonomy hypothesis.

occipital lobe damage resulting from "penetrating and perforating wounds of the cranium by rifle bullets, shell fragments, and shrapnel, as well as local concussions and depressed fractures" (Holmes & Lister, 1916, p. 38). The x-ray techniques available at the time were of little use in delineating the location or extent of brain damage. Although in a few cases Holmes and Lister were able to observe a patient's brain during surgery, they usually had to infer the lesion locus from the location of entrance and (in some cases) exit wounds, interpreted in light of their knowledge about skull/brain relationships. Assessment of visual fields was also crude; most patients were confined to bed, and were tested with a small hand perimeter.

Despite these difficult conditions Holmes and Lister (1916) were able to establish systematic relationships between lesion loci and visual field defects; for example, patients with damage to the upper bank of the calcarine fissure consistently showed a lower quadrantanopia in the contralesional visual field. On the basis of their observations Holmes and Lister drew the following conclusions:

> The upper half of each retina is represented in the dorsal, and the lower in the ventral part of each visual area. (p. 72)

> The centre for macular or central vision lies in the posterior extremities of the visual areas, probably on the margins and the lateral surfaces of the occipital poles. (p. 72)

> The centre for vision subserved by the periphery of the retinae is probably situated in the anterior end of the visual area, and the serial concentric zones of the retina from the macula to the periphery are probably represented in this order from behind forwards in the visual area. (p. 73)

Finally, speaking to an issue that had aroused some controversy, Holmes and Lister (1916) concluded that "in common with every other part of the retina, the macula is not represented bilaterally" (p. 71). These conclusions have been confirmed many times over in subsequent studies with more sophisticated methods. Clearly, fine-grained conclusions are possible in multiple single-patient studies of lesion-deficit correlations.

A third reason for continuing to apply the lesion-deficit correlation approach is that relative to functional neuroimaging methods this approach has advantages as well as disadvantages. In particular, interpretation of lesion-deficit correlations is in some respects more straightforward than interpretation of data from functional neuroimaging methods. I refer here not to the uncertainties about relationships between brain activity and the variables assessed in functional neuroimaging (e.g., blood oxygenation), or to the complex statistical issues arising in the analysis of imaging data; rather my point has to do with differences between activation and damage as bases for inferring a brain region's involvement in a cognitive process. Results showing a consistent relationship between a particular cognitive process and activation of a particular brain area may suggest that the area is involved in carrying out the process. However, given our current state of knowledge about the brain, the possibility remains open that brain areas playing no functional role in a cognitive process may become activated when the process is executed (Farah & Aguirre, 1999). Consider, for example, results suggesting that V1 and even LGN (the lateral geniculate nucleus) are activated when subjects engage in visual imagery (e.g., Chen et al., 1998; Kosslyn et al., 1993). These results may indicate that V1 and LGN play functional roles in imagery; on the other hand it is also possible that these areas become activated during imagery (perhaps via feedback connections from higher visual areas) while playing no functional role. In contrast, results showing a consistent relationship between damage to a particular brain area and disruption of a particular cognitive process argue strongly that the area is required for execution of the process.

Also, whereas current functional neuroimaging methods typically impose significant restrictions on testing time and methods, lesion-deficit correlation studies usually allow far more extensive testing with fewer methodological restrictions. This advantage is significant. Isolating a cognitive process of interest is not trivial, and much of the functional neuroimaging research conducted to date is weak in this respect. That is, the behavioral data collected in many of the studies are not sufficient to permit clear conclusions about the cognitive processes associated with the activated brain regions.

I do not intend to suggest that lesion-deficit correlation methods are superior to functional neuroimaging methods; as mentioned above, the lesion-deficit approach has its own disadvantages. My point is simply that functional neuroimaging and lesion-deficit correlation approaches should be viewed not as competitors, but as complementary approaches to localization issues.

Facilitating Future Progress

At least two developments might contribute to progress in lesion-deficit correlation research: finer-grained characterization of lesions and deficits, and more widespread application of reversible lesion techniques.

Finer-Grained Lesion and Deficit Characterizations

Most lesion-deficit correlation studies have relied upon coarse-grained descriptions of brain lesions (e.g., left posterior, right parietal), and/or crude characterizations of cognitive deficits (e.g., dysgraphia, constructional apraxia) that refer to affected behaviors or tasks rather than underlying cognitive processes. However, current structural imaging methods allow more precise localization of brain lesions; and the theoretical and methodological tools of cognitive neuropsychology allow specific, theoretically-grounded characterizations of cognitive deficits. Exploiting these capabilities in lesion-deficit correlation studies should enhance our understanding of how and to what extent specific cognitive processes are realized by specific brain mechanisms.

Reversible Lesion Techniques

Recently-developed techniques for creating temporary local disruption of brain function also hold promise for fruitful applications of the lesion-deficit correlation approach. In one such technique grids of electrodes are surgically placed on the surface of the cortex (for clinical diagnostic purposes), and left in place for periods ranging from a few days to a few weeks. Mild electrical stimulation applied via pairs of adjacent electrodes creates a temporary disruption of cortical function in the neighborhood of the electrode pair, and cognitive testing is undertaken during stimulation to assess effects of the disruption. The cortical grid technique has produced several intriguing results showing specific relationships between stimulation sites and cognitive impairments (e.g., Boatman, Hall, Goldstein, Lesser, & Gordon,1997; Boatman, Lesser, & Gordon, 1995; Hart, Lesser, & Gordon, 1992) For obvious reasons, however, this technique is unlikely to see widespread application in research.

Transcranial magnetic stimulation (TMS) provides a less invasive alternative. In this technique a temporary local disruption of cortical function is created by applying a brief but strong magnetic field at the scalp to induce an electric current in the underlying cortex. Unlike the grid technique, TMS can be used (with appropriate safeguards; see Wasserman, 1998) in studies involving normal participants. Although relatively new, the TMS technique has already been applied in a large number of studies on perception, attention, memory, language, and motor control. Some researchers consider the method especially useful for probing the time course of cognitive processing. (See Walsh & Rushworth, 1999, for a general introduction.)

A significant advantage of reversible lesion techniques is that participants can serve as their own controls. In studies of patients with structural lesions it may be difficult to determine whether a patient's performance reflects the effects of the lesion, or whether instead the patient would have shown comparable performance even prior to brain damage. However, in a reversible lesion study participants can be tested both with and without stimulation, yielding performance measures reflecting both the normal and the disrupted functioning of the affected brain region. However, reversible lesion methods also have disadvantages, including uncertainties about the extent to which effects of stimulation are localized to the targeted brain regions, and limits on trial durations and total amounts of testing under stimulation.

GOAL 3: UNDERSTANDING DEFICITS

Thus far I have considered the study of cognitive deficits for purposes of characterizing normal cognitive mechanisms, and exploring brain localization of cognitive functions. The third major objective of cognitive neuropsychology is to achieve a better understanding of the cognitive deficits themselves, among other reasons to provide a basis for improved diagnosis and treatment.

For most purposes deficits are best characterized in terms of damage to, or abnormal development of, normal cognitive mechanisms. For example, in diagnosing reading deficits for purposes of selecting appropriate treatment strategies, one needs to determine which aspects of the normal reading process are disrupted (e.g., visual processing of stimulus words, syntactic analysis, retrieval of lexical-semantic representations, or so forth), and the nature of the disruption(s).

Traditionally, characterization of deficits has involved deficit categories and diagnostic tests not grounded in well-articulated theories of normal cognition. In some instances deficit types have been defined primarily on the basis of clinical observations suggesting that certain symptoms often co-occur (e.g., Broca's aphasia, defined by a system complex including reasonably preserved comprehension, non-fluent speech, and impaired repetition). In other instances the deficit categories have been grounded in very coarse-grained analyses of normal cognitive functions (e.g., receptive and expressive aphasia, based on the analysis of language processing into comprehension and production components). Diagnostic assessment has typically involved administering a few brief tasks chosen to reveal the critical symptoms or assess the status of the grossly-defined cognitive functions.

This approach to defining and diagnosing deficits typically yields heterogeneous deficit categories, with the individuals sorted into a category differing widely in the nature of their underlying dysfunctions (e.g., Badecker & Caramazza, 1985; Miceli & Silveri, 1989). Categories of this sort do not provide an adequate foundation for research on, or implementation of, treatment strategies. For example, research on remediation of developmental reading disorders has been hampered by reliance on the coarse, pretheoretical category of developmental dyslexia. Whereas this category is almost certainly heterogeneous, most developmental dyslexia research implicitly assumes that the underlying cognitive dysfunction is the same in all (or at least most) dyslexics (Martin, 1995; McCloskey & Rapp, 2000). As a consequence, most remediation studies have examined undifferentiated groups of dyslexic individuals, and have been aimed at formulating a single set of methods for across-the-board application. Among the results of this approach are disappointing success rates, and widespread failures to replicate. (See Martin, 1995, for more detailed discussion.)

Crude pretheoretical classifications of deficits are also a serious impediment in research aimed at uncovering genetic, neuropathological, or other bases for deficits. Here again research on developmental dyslexia is an example: Clarification of genetic and neurological bases for developmental reading deficits is unlikely to be forthcoming as long as most researchers assume that dyslexia is a unitary disorder.

Fortunately, recent years have seen a growing recognition that methods for diagnosis and treatment of cognitive deficits should be grounded in specific theoretical assumptions about normal cognitive representations and processes (e.g., Bishop & Byng, 1984; Byng, 1988; Byng & Black, 1995; Caramazza & Hillis, 1993; Castles & Coltheart, 1993; Davis & Coltheart, 1999;

Hillis, 1993, 1998; Kay, Lesser, & Coltheart, 1996; Margolin, 1992; McCloskey, Aliminosa, & Macaruso, 1991; Mitchum & Berndt, 1995; Mitchum, Haendiges, & Berndt, 1993; Nickels, 1995; Nickels, Byng, & Black, 1991). The resulting work has produced some useful diagnostic instruments (e.g., Kay et al., 1996), as well as some potentially promising treatment outcomes (e.g., Davis & Coltheart, 1999; Mitchum, Haendiges, & Berndt, 1995; Nickels, 1995).

Facilitating Future Progress

The increased emphasis on cognitive theory in research concerning diagnosis and remediation of cognitive deficits is encouraging. However, at least two additional developments will be needed if the research is to have a significant impact on clinical practice.

Balancing the Ideal and the Practical in Diagnosis

Theory-based assessment of cognitive deficits can be extremely time-consuming and labor-intensive when carried out at a sufficiently fine grain to be useful in targeting remediation efforts. At present, ascertaining which cognitive mechanisms are intact and which are impaired, and clarifying the nature of the impairment(s), often requires far more testing—perhaps even an order of magnitude more—than is feasible on a large scale in clinical settings. Accordingly, if theory-based assessment methods are to have broad application, ways will have to be found to streamline the process without major loss of detail or accuracy.

Theory of Remediation

Practical theory-based assessment methods, although probably necessary for effective treatment, are certainly not sufficient; knowing what is wrong is not the same as knowing how to fix it. At least one other element is crucial: a theory of remediation (e.g., Byng & Black, 1995; Caramazza & Hillis, 1993; Mitchum & Berndt, 1995). A remediation theory, which might have both cognitive and neurophysiological elements, would address such questions as, What sorts of changes to a cognitive system are and are not possible after the system has been damaged in various ways?; and, How can potentially-beneficial changes be brought about? Theoretical treatment of these questions would be a major step toward transforming the treatment of cognitive deficits from an art to a science.

Conclusion

Cognitive neuropsychology has made, and continues to make, major contributions to the study of normal cognition; indeed, some of the most exciting results in cognitive science are coming from studies of deficits. Furthermore, the lesion-deficit correlation method has been our major source of knowledge about localization of cognitive processes in the brain, and should continue to be valuable as a complement to the newer functional neuroimaging methods. Finally, cognitive neuropsychological research has advanced our understanding of cognitive deficits, and holds promise for contributing to the development of treatments. If theory and method continue to develop along the lines discussed in this chapter, the future of cognitive neuropsychology should be bright. The potential of the approach is just beginning to be tapped.

Acknowledgements

I thank Brenda Rapp and Karen Neander for their helpful comments.

REFERENCES

Badecker, W., & Caramazza, A. (1985). On considerations of method and theory governing the use of clinical categories in neurolinguistics and cognitive neuropsychology: The case against agrammatism. *Cognition, 20,* 97–125.

Banich, M. T. (1997). *Neuropsychology: The neural bases of mental function.* Boston, MA: Houghton-Mifflin.

Bishop, D. V., & Byng, S. (1984). Assessing semantic comprehension: Methodological considerations, and a new clinical test. *Cognitive Neuropsychology, 1,* 233–244.

Boatman, D., Hall, C., Goldstein, M. H., Lesser, R., & Gordon, B. (1997). Neuroperceptual differences in consonant and vowel discrimination: As revealed by direct cortical electrical interference. *Cortex, 33,* 83–98.

Boatman, D., Lesser, R. P., & Gordon, B. (1995). Auditory speech processing in the left temporal lobe: An electrical interference study. *Brain & Language, 51,* 269–290.

Bullinaria, J. A., & Chater, N. (1995) Connectionist modelling: Implications for cognitive neuropsychology. *Language & Cognitive Processes, 10,* 227–264.

Byng, S. (1988). Sentence processing deficits: Theory and therapy. *Cognitive Neuropsychology, 5,* 629–676.

Byng, S., & Black, M. (1995). What makes a therapy? Some parameters of therapeutic intervention in aphasia. *European Journal of Disorders of Communication, 30,* 303–316.

Caramazza, A. (1984). The logic of neuropsychological research and the problem of patient classification in aphasia. *Brain and Language, 21,* 9–20.

Caramazza, A. (1986). On drawing inferences about the structure of normal cognitive systems from the analysis of patterns of impaired performance: The case for single-patient studies. *Brain and Cognition, 5,* 41–66.

Caramazza, A. (1992). Is cognitive neuropsychology possible? *Journal of Cognitive Neuroscience, 4,* 80–95.

Caramazza, A., & Badecker, W. (1989). Patient classification in neuropsychological research. *Brain and Cognition, 10,* 256–295.

Caramazza, A., & Badecker, W. (1991). Clinical syndromes are not God's gift to cognitive neuropsychology: A reply to a rebuttal to an answer to a response to the case against syndrome-based research. *Brain and Cognition, 16,* 211–227.

Caramazza, A., & Hillis, A. (1993). For a theory of remediation of cognitive deficits. *Neuropsychological Rehabilitation, 3,* 217–234.

Caramazza, A., & McCloskey, M. (1988). The case for single-patient studies. *Cognitive Neuropsychology, 5,* 517–528.

Caramazza, A., & McCloskey, M. (1991). The poverty of methodology. *Behavioral and Brain Sciences, 14,* 444–445.

Caramazza, A., & Miceli, G. (1990). The structure of graphemic representations. *Cognition, 37,* 243–297.

Castles, A., & Coltheart, M. (1993). Varieties of developmental dyslexia. *Cognition, 47,* 149–180.

Chater, N., & Ganis, G. (1991). Double dissociation and isolable cognitive processes. In *Proceedings of the Thirteenth Annual Conference of the Cognitive Science Society* (pp. 668–672). Hillsdale, NJ: Erlbaum.

Chen, W., Kato, T., Zhu, X.-H., Ogawa, S., Tank, D. W., & Ugurbil, K. (1998). Human primary visual cortex and lateral geniculate nucleus activation during visual imagery. *NeuroReport, 9,* 3669–3674.

Cubelli, R. (1991). A selective deficit for writing vowels in acquired dysgraphia. *Nature, 353,* 258–260.

Davis, S. J. C., & Coltheart, M. (1999). Rehabilitation of topographical disorientation: An experimental single case study. *Neuropsychological Rehabilitation, 9,* 1–30.

Ellis, A. W. (1987). Intimations of modularity, or the modelarity of mind: Doing cognitive neuropsychology without syndromes. In M. Coltheart, G. Sartori, & R. Job (Eds.), *The cognitive neuropsychology of language* (pp. 397–408). Hillsdale, NJ: Lawrence Erlbaum.

Farah, M. J., & Aguirre, G. K. (1999). Imaging visual recognition: PET and fMRI studies of the functional anatomy of human visual recognition. *Trends in Cognitive Sciences, 3,* 179–186.

Finger, S. (1994). *Origins of neuroscience: A history of explorations into brain function.* Oxford, UK: Oxford University Press.

Ganis, G., & Chater, N. (1991). Can double dissociation uncover the modularity of cognitive processes? In *Proceedings of the Thirteenth Annual Meeting of the Cognitive Science Society* (pp. 714–718). Hillsdale, NJ: Lawrence Erlbaum.

Hart, J., Lesser, R. P., & Gordon, B. (1992). Selective interference with the representation of size in the human by direct cortical electrical stimulation. *Journal of Cognitive Neuroscience, 4,* 337–344.

Hess, R. H., Baker, C. L., Jr., & Zihl, J. (1989). The "motion-blind" patient: Low-level spatial and temporal filters. *The Journal of Neuroscience, 9,* 1628–1640.

Hillis, A. E. (1993). The role of models of language processing in rehabilitation of language impairments. *Aphasiology, 7,* 5–26.

Hillis, A. E. (1998). Treatment of naming disorders: New issues regarding old therapies. *Journal of the International Neuropsychological Society, 4,* 648–660.

Hillis, A. E., Rapp, B., Romani, C., & Caramazza, A. (1990). Selective impairment of semantics in lexical processing. *Cognitive Neuropsychology, 7,* 191–243.

Holmes, G., & Lister, W. T. (1916). Disturbances of vision from cerebral lesions, with special reference to the cortical representation of the macula. *Brain, 39,* 34–73.

Jones, G. V. (1983). On double dissociation of function. *Neuropsychologia, 21,* 397–400.

Kay, J., Lesser, R., & Coltheart, M. (1996). The proof of the pudding is in the eating. *Aphasiology, 10,* 202–215.

Kertesz, A. (1994). Localization and function: Old issues revisited and new developments. In A. Kertesz (Ed.), *Localization and neuroimaging in neuropsychology* (pp. 1–33). San Diego, CA: Academic Press.

Kolb, B., & Whishaw, I. Q. (1996). *Fundamentals of human neuropsychology.* New York: Freeman.

Kosslyn, S. M., Alpert, N. M., Thompson, W. L., Maljkovic, V., Weise, S. B., Chabris, C. F., Hamilton, S. E., Rauch, S. L., & Buonanno, F. S. (1993). Visual mental imagery activates topographically organized visual cortex: PET investigations. *Journal of Cognitive Neuroscience, 5,* 263–287.

Kosslyn, S. M., & Intriligator, J. M. (1992). Is cognitive neuropsychology plausible? The perils of sitting on a one-legged stool. *Journal of Cognitive Neuroscience, 4,* 96–106.

Kosslyn, S. M., & Van Kleek, M. H. (1990). Broken brains and normal minds: Why Humpty-Dumpty needs a skeleton. In E. L. Schwartz (Ed.), *Computational neuroscience* (pp. 390–402). Cambridge, MA: MIT Press.

Margolin, D. I. (Ed.). (1992). *Cognitive neuropsychology in clinical practice*. Oxford, United Kingdom: Oxford University Press.

Martin, R. (1995). Heterogeneity of deficits in developmental dyslexia and implications for methodology. *Psychonomic Bulletin & Review, 2,* 494–500.

McCarthy, R. A., & Warrington, E. K. (1990). *Cognitive neuropsychology: A clinical introduction.* San Diego, CA: Academic Press.

McCloskey, M. (1993). Theory and evidence in cognitive neuropsychology: A "radical" response to Robertson, Knight, Rafal, and Shimamura. *Journal of Experimental Psychology: Learning, Memory, and Cognition, 19,* 718–734.

McCloskey, M., Aliminosa, D., & Macaruso, P. (1991). Theory-based assessment of acquired dyscalculia. *Brain and Cognition, 17,* 285–308.

McCloskey, M., Badecker, W., Goodman-Schulman, R. A., & Aliminosa, D. (1994). The structure of graphemic representations in spelling: Evidence from a case of acquired dysgraphia. *Cognitive Neuropsychology, 11,* 341–392.

McCloskey, M., & Caramazza, A. (1988). Theory and methodology in cognitive neuropsychology: A response to our critics. *Cognitive Neuropsychology, 5,* 583–623.

McCloskey, M., & Caramazza, A. (1991). On crude data and impoverished theory. *Behavioral and Brain Sciences, 14,* 453–454.

McCloskey, M., & Rapp, B. (2000). A visually based developmental reading deficit. *Journal of Memory and Language, 43,* 157–181.

Miceli, G., & Silveri, M. C. (1989). Variation in the pattern of omissions and substitutions of grammatical morphemes in the spontaneous speech of so-called agrammatic patients. *Brain and Language, 36,* 447–492.

Mitchum, C. C., & Berndt, R. S. (1995). The cognitive neuropsychological approach to treatment of language disorders. *Neuropsychological Rehabilitation, 5,* 1–16.

Mitchum, C. C., Haendiges, A., N., & Berndt, R. S. (1993). Model-guided treatment to improve written sentence production: A case study. *Aphasiology, 7,* 71–109.

Mitchum, C. C., Haendiges, A. N., & Berndt, R. S. (1995). Treatment of thematic mapping in sentence comprehension: Implications for normal processing. *Cognitive Neuropsychology, 12,* 503–547.

Nickels, L. (1995). Reading too little into reading? Strategies in the rehabilitation of acquired dyslexia. *European Journal of Disorders of Communication, 30,* 37–50.

Nickels, L., Byng, S., & Black, M. (1991). Sentence processing deficits: A replication of therapy. *British Journal of Disorders of Communication, 26,* 175–199.

Plaut, D. C. (1995). Double dissociation without modularity: Evidence from connectionist neuropsychology. *Journal of Clinical & Experimental Neuropsychology, 17,* 291–321.

Rapp, B., Benzing, L., & Caramazza, A. (1997). The autonomy of lexical orthography. *Cognitive Neuropsychology, 14,* 71–104.

Robertson, L. C., Knight, R. T., Rafal, R., & Shimamura, A. P. (1993). Cognitive neuropsychology is more than single-case studies. *Journal of Experimental Psychology: Learning, Memory, and Cognition, 19,* 710–717.

Scoville, W. B., & Milner, B. (1957). Loss of recent memory after bilateral hippocampal lesions. *Journal of Neurology, Neurosurgery and Psychiatry, 20,* 11–21.

Seidenberg, M. (1988). Cognitive neuropsychology and language: The state of the art. *Cognitive Neuropsychology, 5,* 403–426.

Shallice, T. (1988). *From neuropsychology to mental structure.* Cambridge, UK: Cambridge University Press.

Sokol, S., & McCloskey, M. (1988). Levels of representation in verbal number production. *Applied Psycholinguistics, 9,* 267–281.

Tainturier, M.-J., & Caramazza, A. (1996). The status of double letters in graphemic representations. *Journal of Memory and Language, 35,* 53–73.

Venneri, A., & Cubelli, R. (1993). *Letter doubling is independently computed by the brain: Evidence from acquired dysgraphia.* Paper presented at TENNET IV, Montreal, Canada.

Walsh, V., & Rushworth, M. (1999). A primer of magnetic stimulation as a tool for neuropsychology. *Neuropsychologia, 37,* 125–135.

Wasserman, E. M. (1998). Risk and safety of repetitive transcranial magnetic stimulation: Report and suggested guidelines from the International Workshop on the Safety of Repetitive Transcranial Magnetic Stimulation, June 5–7, 1996. *Electroencephalography & Clinical Neurophysiology/Evoked Potentials Section 108,* 1–16.

Zeki, S. (1993). *A vision of the brain.* Oxford, UK: Blackwell.

Zihl, J., von Cramon, D., & Mai, N. (1983). Selective disturbance of movement vision after bilateral brain damage. *Brain, 106,* 313–340.

Glossary

Compiled by Jennifer R. Shelton

acalculia: a disorder of calculation and/or number processing.

achromatopsia: the inability to discriminate between different hues caused by damage to the visual association cortex.

agnosia: a failure to recognize objects, not resulting from basic sensory dysfunction.

agrammatism: difficulty in comprehending and/or producing various grammatical elements such as function words, morphological elements, and word order.

agraphia (dysgraphia): a disorder of writing or spelling.

akinetopsia: disorder of motion perception despite good perception of other visual properties.

alexia (dyslexia): a disorder of reading.

amnesia: a disorder of memory, typically expressed as difficulty in consciously remembering past events.

anarchic hand: a disorder of action in which movements of each hand may occur in response to different action plans, often resulting in conflicting actions by the two hands. It differs from "alien hand" in that in the latter, the hand is perceived as foreign and not belonging to the self, this is not the case with anarchic hand syndrome.

anarthria: a severe disorder of speech articulation due to weakness, slowness, reduced range of movement or poor coordination of the lips, tongue, jaw and palate; not an impairment of language.

anomia: a disorder of producing or thinking of the appropriate word to describe an object or action.

anosognosia: an unawareness of one's own disorders following brain damage.

anterograde amnesia: a disorder characterized by relatively normal memory for events occurring before the neurological damage but difficulty remembering events occurring after the damage.

aphasia: difficulty in comprehending and/or producing speech following brain damage, not due to deafness or a peripheral motor deficit.

apperceptive agnosia: a deficit of early perceptual processing that results in an inability to develop a correct percept of a visual stimulus.

apraxia: difficulty in carrying out skilled movements not due to paralysis or muscular weakness.

associative agnosia: an inability to understand or assign meaning to a correctly perceived three dimensional percept.

autotopagnosia: an inability to localize and name the parts of one's own body.

basal: the base of any structure.

basal ganglia: an associated set of neural structures located in the basal forebrain; includes the caudate nucleus, putamen, globus pallidus and subthalamus.

blindsight: the ability to respond to objects in the "blind" visual field at above chance rates, despite damage to primary visual cortex and typically with no conscious visual awareness of the objects.

Broca's aphasia: an expressive or nonfluent aphasia resulting in impaired speech usually characterized by telegraphic speech but typically retaining good comprehension of everyday language; grammar is restricted to the simplest forms.

caudate nucleus: part of the basal ganglia; involved in motor control.

circumlocution: a description of the meaning of a target word provided when the form of the word is unavailable.

conduction aphasia: a disorder characterized by phonetic errors in repetition and spontaneous speech, but good comprehension.

constructional apraxia: a disorder in executing a task requiring individual elements to be arranged in a given spatial order to form a whole.

contralesional: occurring on the side (left or right) opposite that of the brain lesion.

convolutions: see gyrus.

cortical stimulation: a technique for temporarily inactivating an area of cortex by applying electrical current.

CT (computed tomography): a technique for generating two-dimensional images of slices of the brain or body produced using X-rays.

declarative memory: any memory related to specific item and event (time and/or place) information that is consciously accessible.

deep dysgraphia: a spelling disorder characterized by semantic substitutions, effects of word class and poor spelling of non-words.

deep dyslexia: a reading disorder characterized by semantic substitutions, effects of word class, and poor reading on nonwords.

dentate gyrus: a neuron layer in the hippocampus.

diencephelon: a region of the brain stem that includes the thalamus and the hypothalamus.

directional hypokinesia: a decrease in movements towards the contralesional side of space; typically attributed to asymmetrical impairment to the mechanisms underlying movement planning and execution.

dorsal: a direction generally meaning toward the back; in the human brain it means in the direction of the top of the head.

double dissociation: complementary pattern of impairments across two tasks or cognitive functions such that one individual is disproportionately impaired on X relative to Y and another is disproportionately impaired on Y relative to X.

EEG (electroencephalography): electrical potentials recorded by placing electrodes on the scalp.

entorhinal cortex: a cortical area within the medial temporal lobe that provides input to the hippocampus.

episodic memory: memories for events whose time and place of occurrence form part of the remembered information.

ERP (evoked related potential): averaged electrical responses recorded at the scalp that reflect neural responses to a stimulus event.

explicit memory: memories that require conscious recollection of a previous experience to influence behavior.

extinction: an attentional deficit that is characterized by difficulty in detecting a contralesional stimulus when it is presented simultaneously with an ipsilesional stimulus, occurring in the face of relatively good detection of a contralesional stimulus when presented alone.

fluent aphasia: a disorder characterized by word finding difficulty with good articulation and good production of grammatical elements.

fMRI (functional magnetic resonance imaging): the use of MRI imaging techniques to measure levels of neural activity while subjects are performing a task; the technique is typically used to determine which brain areas are involved in the task.

formal paraphasia: word substitutions in which the substituting word is similar in phonological form to the substituted word.

fronto-parietal operculum: part of the frontal and parietal lobes that borders on the lateral sulcus and covers the insula.

geniculo-striate pathway: a visual pathway connecting the lateral geniculate nucleus of the thalamus to primary visual cortex.

Gerstmann syndrome: a collection of symptoms due to left parietal lesions including finger agnosia, right-left confusions, acalculia, and agraphia.

grapheme: an abstract letter or letter group corresponding to a phoneme.

gyrus (plural gyri): the bulges or protrusions of folded cortex.

hemianopia: a visual field defect resulting in the loss of vision for stimuli in the contralesional visual field.

hemiparesis: muscular weakness affecting the contralesional side of the body.

hemiplegia: muscular paralysis affecting one side of the body, typically contralateral to the lesion site.

ideational apraxia: a deficit in performing multiple step, naturalistic tasks (e.g., grooming, food preparation) characterized by errors in the use of objects.

ideomotor apraxia: a disorder of movement characterized by difficulty pantomiming actions to command and by imitation.

implicit memory: memories that do not require conscious recollection of a previous experience to influence behavior.

interactive activation model: a class of theories of cognitive processing in which it is typically assumed that processing at a later representational stage can begin before processing is completed at an earlier stage and also where processing at a later stage can affect processing at an earlier stage via feedback connections.

ipsilesional: occurring on the same side (right or left) as the site of brain damage.

jargon aphasia: a disorder in which spontaneous speech is characterized by a large proportion of nonword errors that may be very dissimilar to the words the individual intends to produce.

Korsakoff's syndrome: an amnesic syndrome produced by chronic alcoholism resulting from degeneration of the dorsomedial thalamic nucleus; the patient suffers from permanent long term memory loss, impaired intellectual and reasoning abilities, and loss of muscle coordination.

lateral geniculate nucleus (LGN): a group of neurons in the thalamus that relays information from the retina to the primary visual cortex.

lemma: a syntactic representation of a word that provides a link between the word's meaning and its phonological form.

lexicon (lexical): the entire set of words in a person's vocabulary, ("mental dictionary"); it may refer to particular aspects of word knowledge, for example an orthographic lexicon stores information about the spellings of the words in a person's vocabulary.

limbic system: an associated set of neural structures that includes the hippocampus, fornix, cingulate gyrus, amygdala; mamillary bodies; involved in emotion, learning and memory.

MEG (magnetoencephalography): a technique for recording the magnetic fields generated by neurons; sometimes used for investigating the time course of neural activity during task performance.

medial: a direction meaning toward the midline of a surface of structure.

modular (modularity, module): the hypothesis that different cognitive functions are instantiated in independent processing components, implying that each function can be selectively damaged.

morpheme (morphology): the smallest meaningful unit in language.

MRI (magnetic resonance imaging): a technique for generating brain images that makes use of the magnetic properties of organic tissue.

neglect: a disorder in which an individual does not respond normally to contralesional stimuli (may occur in the visual, auditory or tactile modalities); it is not due to a sensory deficit and is considered to arise from an attentional deficit.

neocortex: the most evolutionarily advanced portion of mammalian cortex; characterized by a six-layered cellular organization.

neologism: errors in speech resulting in nonwords which may or may not contain many of the phonemes of the target words.

nonfluent aphasia: a disorder characterized by effortful speech, reduced utterance length and few grammatical elements.

optic aphasia: a disorder of spoken naming that is limited to difficulty in naming of items presented visually but not in other modalities.

optic ataxia: a disorder of reaching that is limited to difficulty in reaching for items presented visually but not in other modalities.

optic nerve: the bundle of axons of retinal ganglion cells that transmits information from the eye to other neural structures, primarily to the lateral geniculate nucleus of the thalamus.

orthography: the spellings of words.

paradoxical bilingual aphasia: a special case of differential recovery where there is a different degree of impairment in each language relative to premorbid ability levels or when there is greater impairment to the language that was dominant prior to brain injury.

paragrammatism: a disorder in which an individual speaks fluently and although speech includes many grammatical and lexical items these are often substituted and misordered.

paraphasia: an error in speaking that may consist of producing a semantically related word for the target, or a response that involves the movement, omission, substitution and/or addition of phonemes; not due to a motor deficit.

perseveration: the tendency to repeat the same verbal or motor response to varied stimuli.

PET (positron emission tomography): a technique for measuring neural activity while subjects are performing a task that involves measuring the energy released during the decay of a radioactive isotope; the technique is typically used to determine which brain areas are involved in the task.

phoneme (phonology): the smallest segment of speech that distinguishes between two words.

phonological dysgraphia: a disorder of spelling in which an individual can spell words correctly but has significant difficulty in spelling nonwords; typically attributed to damage to the phoneme-to-grapheme conversion system.

phonological dyslexia: a disorder of reading in which a patient can read words correctly but cannot use grapheme-to-phoneme correspondence rules to read pseudowords.

phonology: the language system containing the knowledge of the organization and patterning of the sounds of language.

phrenology: the school of thought that assumed that the shape of the skull reflects the magnitude of the mental faculties instantiated in the immediately underlying cortical tissue.

procedural memory: memories that include actions and/or motor skills.

progressive aphasia: a progressive language disorder due to deterioration of brain tissue; not attributable to decline in general intelligence or memory.

progressive supranuclear palsy: a disorder associated with damaged nerve cells in the brain characterized by progressive speech articulation and swallowing impairments, stiffness of the neck and trunk, difficulty with eye movement, and dementia.

prosopagnosia: an inability to recognize and identify familiar faces.

psychogenic disorder: a disorder that does not have any organic pathological origin.

pure alexia (letter by letter reading): a disorder of reading characterized by an inability to recognize or read a word without identifying (often pronouncing) each letter individually; spelling abilities are typically intact.

retinotectal pathway: a visual pathway from the retina to the superior colliculus.

retinotopic map: refers to the systematic relationship between the retina and a neural structure such that neighboring areas on the retina send information to neighboring neural areas.

retrograde amnesia: a disorder characterized by relatively normal memory for events occurring after the neurological damage but difficulty remembering events occurring before the damage.

scotoma: a blind area in the visual field, caused by localized damage to the retina or in a visual pathway or brain structure.

semantic dementia: a degenerative neurological disorder that primarily affects conceptual knowledge.

simultanagnosia: a disorder in which an individual has difficulty simultaneously processing more then one item of a category; often manifests itself in letter-by-letter reading and difficulty in complex picture identification.

SPECT (single photon emission computed tomography): a technique for measuring brain activity that works on principles similar to PET; however, the spatial resolution provided by SPECT is inferior to that of PET.

stereopsis: the ability to perceive depth in a three-dimensional scene through combination of the slightly different views provided by the left and right eye.

Stroop effect: an inhibition in responding when attended and unattended information compete due to some type of conceptual relationship; for example, slowed response or errors in reading the word "blue" when it is presented in red ink.

sulcus (plural sulci): the indentations of folded cortex (See Figure G2 & G3).

supplementary motor cortex: the medial part of premotor cortex.

surface dysgraphia: a disorder of spelling in which an individual can correctly spell regular and pseudowords but has difficulty spelling irregular words.

surface dyslexia: a disorder of reading in which an individual can correctly read regular words and pseudowords but has difficulty reading irregular words.

TMS (transcranial magnetic stimulation): a technique used to produce temporary disruption in neural activity; it involves the application of a strong magnetic current field to the scalp while a subject is performing a task; it is typically used to determine which brain areas are required to perform the task.

tonotopic map: the representation of acoustic frequencies in a neural structure in a systematic way such that adjacent frequencies are represented and/or processed by adjacent neural tissue.

transcortical aphasia: a disorder characterized by good repetition but poor auditory comprehension and paraphasic speech.

transcortical motor aphasia: a disorder characterized by good repetition but poor initiation of speech and poor auditory comprehension.

vascular: pertaining to the vessels used for conveying blood within an organism.

ventral: a direction generally meaning toward the belly; in the human brain it refers to the downward direction.

ventricles: the cavities of the brain filled with cerebrospinal fluid; the two lateral ventricles are within the cerebrum and the third and fourth ventricles are in the brain stem.

vestibular caloric stimulation: a procedure to evaluate functioning of the vestibular system and associated brain areas. Electrodes are placed on either side of the eye and measure movement by picking up the displacement of charges from the cornea and retina. These are recorded as warm and cool water are placed into the external ear canal.

Weber's law: the principle that the difference threshold between two stimulus magnitudes is a certain constant fraction of the total magnitude.

Wernicke's aphasia: a fluent aphasia in which the ability to comprehend speech and produce meaningful speech is impaired.

white matter: a collection of central nervous system axons that constitute tracts connecting brain areas with one another.

NEUROANATOMICAL TERMS

amygdala: See figure G.4.

angular gyrus: See figure G.2.

anterior commissure: See figure G.3.

Broca's area: See figure G.2.

Brodmann's areas: See figure G.5.

calcarine sulcus: See figure G.2 & G.3.

central sulcus (Fissure of Rolando): See figure G.2 & G.3.

cerebellum: See figure G.3.

cingulate gyrus: See figure G.3 & G.4.

extrastriate cortex: See figure G.2.

fornix: See figure G.3 & G.4.

frontal lobe: See figure G.1 & G.4.

frontal eye fields: See figure G.2.

hippocampus: See figure G.4.

hypothalamus: See figure G.4.

inferior colliculus: See figure G.3.

lingual gyrus: See figure G.3.

mamillary body: See figure G.3 & G.4.

occipital lobe: See figure G.1.

olfactory bulb: See figure G.4.

optic chiasm: See figure G.3.

parietal lobe: See figure G.1.

pineal gland: See figure G.3.

posterior commissure: See figure G.3.

precentral gyrus: See figure G.2.

precuneus: See figure G.3.

prefrontal cortex: See figure G.2.

premotor cortex: See figure G.2.

primary auditory cortex: See figure G.2.

primary motor cortex: See figure G.2.

primary somatosensory cortex: See figure G.2.

primary visual cortex: See figure G.2.

reticular formation: See figure G.4.

septum: See figure G.4.

spinal cord: See figure G.4.

splenium: See figure G.3.

superior colliculus: See figure G.3.

supramarginal gyrus: See figure G.2.

Sylvian fissure: See figure G.2.

temporal lobe: See figure G.1.

thalamus: See figure G.3 & G.4.

Wernicke's area: See figure G.2.

BASIC NEUROANATOMY: BRAIN STRUCTURE DIAGRAMS

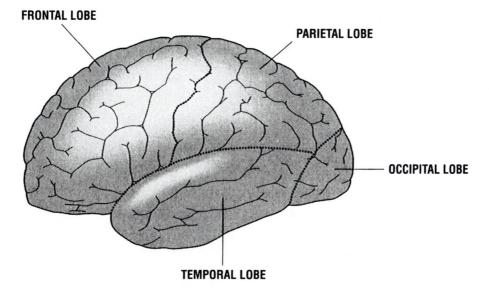

Figure G.1: The four lobes of neocortex (view of the left hemisphere).

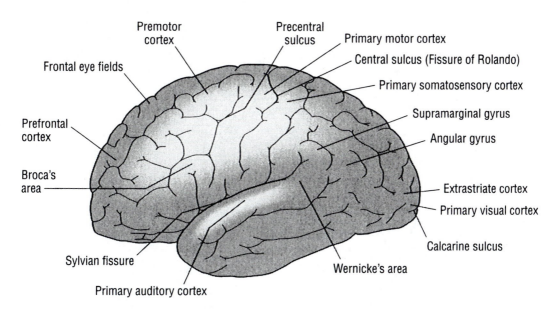

Figure G.2: Prominent functional areas and neuroanatomical landmarks of neocortex.

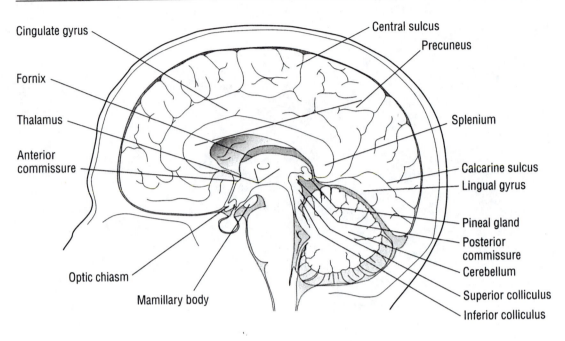

Figure G.3: Mid-sagittal view, including prominent sub-cortical structures.

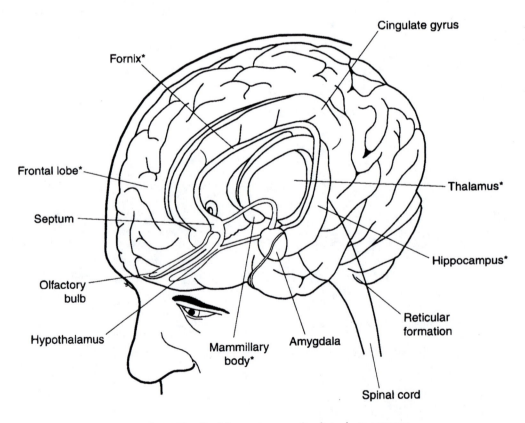

Figure G.4: The limbic system and related structures.

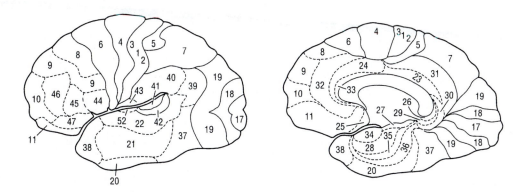

Figure G.5: Brodmann Areas.

Author Index

Subject Index

645